The Prentice Hall Anthology of

Women's Literature

Deborah H. Holdstein

Governors State University

PRENTICE HALL
Upper Saddle River, New Jersey 07458

Library of Congress Cataloging-in-Publication Data

The Prentice Hall anthology of women's literature/[selected by]
  Deborah Holdstein,
     p. cm.
    Includes index.
    ISBN 0-13-081974-3
    1. Literature—Women authors. 2. Literature, Modern—20th century.
    3. Women Literary collections. I. Holdstein, Deborah H., 1952–   .
PN6069.W65P74 1999   99–39922
808.8'99287—dc21   CIP

PN
6069
.W65
P74
2000

Editorial Director: Charlyce Jones Owen
Editor-in-Chief: Leah Jewell
Acquisitions Editor: Carrie Brandon
Editorial Assistant: Sandy Hrasdzira
AVP, Director of Production and Manufacturing: Barbara Kittle
Senior Managing Editor: Bonnie Biller
Production Editor: Randy Pettit
Manufacturing Manager: Nick Sklitsis
Prepress and Manufacturing Buyer: Mary Ann Gloriande
Marketing Director: Gina Sluss
Marketing Manager: Brandy Dawson
Interior Design: Amy Rosen
Cover Design Director: Jayne Conte
Cover Design: Kiwi Design
Portraits: Van Howell

For permission to use copyrighted material, grateful
acknowledgment is made to the copyright holders listed
on page 1072–1078, which is considered an extension of this
copyright page.

This book was set in 10.5/12.5 Minion by Progressive Information Technologies,
and printed and bound by Courier-Westford.
The cover was printed by Phoenix Color Corp.

© 2000 by Prentice-Hall, Inc.
Upper Saddle River, New Jersey 07458

Printed in the United States of America

10 9 8 7 6 5 4 3 2 1

0-13-081974-3

PRENTICE-HALL INTERNATIONAL (UK) LIMITED, *London*
PRENTICE-HALL OF AUSTRALIA PTY. LIMITED, *Sydney*
PRENTICE-HALL CANADA INC., *Toronto*
PRENTICE-HALL HISPANOAMERICA, S.A., *Mexico*
PRENTICE-HALL OF INDIA PRIVATE LIMITED, *New Delhi*
PRENTICE-HALL OF JAPAN, INC., *Tokyo*
EDITORA PRENTICE-HALL DO BRASIL, LTDA., *Rio de Janeiro*

In Memory of

Henia Freifeld Holdstein

7 July 1918, Lvov, Poland-21 March 1996,
Oak Park, Illinois

Survivor of the Shoah

A leb'n auf dayn kopf!

and for
Emily and David

Contents

Preface

*... N*ow she started out of the torpor common to us
all and asked me in a whisper (everyone whispered
there):
"Can you describe this?"
And I said: "I can."
Then something like a smile passed fleetingly over
what had once been her face.

TRANS. RICHARD MCKANE

*I*n these lines excerpted from a brief piece called "Instead of a Preface," Russian poet Anna Akhmatova suggests the power of the writer—in this instance, the certainty and strength with which she will create living testimony to pain, political upheaval, and human suffering. The writer in these lines, Akhmatova herself, demonstrates the primacy accorded a voice that can carry shared experience and give it the permanence of written language. If often for different purposes and with different means and contexts, such are powers of the myriad voices featured in the *Prentice Hall Anthology of Women's Literature.*

Yet it is with some irony that I choose Akhmatova's as the powerful voice with which to begin this anthology. In an attempt to create a useful volume of manageable length for readers of literature written by women, I have limited the scope of the anthology to the turn of the twentieth century and onward, focusing primarily on women writing in various traditions in English. As readers might be aware, debates rage about the value of writing that has been translated, reflecting the concern that much is "lost in translation." While I appreciate these issues, one must consider as well the value of disseminating work that even widely educated readers might not otherwise find accessible.

There is a formal section in this anthology devoted to Akhmatova, but her compelling, powerful work, even in translation, only marginally represents the international writers whom we could not feature. By including the words of this early twentieth-century Russian poet, we are compelled to remember several things: first, that no anthology on women writers of the twentieth century can ever pretend to be complete; and second, that writers whose work comes to us in English, however varied and deep, however representative of numerous traditions and genres, cannot and do not represent the whole of valuable writing by women.

The Prentice Hall Anthology of Women's Literature presents work by women from the very late nineteenth century and onward, from "turn-of-the-century" literature through modernism and the era before the Second World War, through post-war and contemporary literature and beyond. Perhaps fittingly and symbolically, we begin with Alice James and Emma Lazarus. Put simply, James's life represents the dark side of fine breeding: an outstanding intellect and wit imprisoned by her womanhood and stifled by her imposing, over-achieving father and brothers. While the dates of her life and death rest firmly within the nineteenth century, hers are very much twentieth-century concerns: her brother, Henry James, himself admitted that girls in their family seemed "scarcely to have a chance." Lazarus, in "The New Colossus," speaks for the out-sider, the oppressed immigrant to the United States, with a voice that we now find perhaps overly confident about the promise of a welcoming, sheltering United States. Yet, she might also seem to speak for those born here but kept on the fringes of society by elitism, racism, and prejudice—or those brought here in earlier times, for insidious purpose, and against their wills. "The New Colos-sus" also stands at the front of this anthology to represent all that Lazarus might never even have foreseen when she titled her poem: the "new," rich evolution and expansion of literary canons and of feminist and other forms of critical thought and of more penetrating, inclusive ways of looking at traditions, texts, and experiences.

From James and Lazarus, the anthology proceeds towards a vast collection of writing by women over the last one hundred years with an emphasis on con-temporary writers. Through an often agonizing, add-and-cut process, I de-signed this collection to range from frequently anthologized, celebrated writers, such as Charlotte Perkins Gilman, Alice Moore Dunbar Nelson, Edith Wharton, Tillie Olsen, and Zora Neale Hurston, to equally impressive and significant, if less-familiar, names, such as Mina Loy, Miriam Raskin, Jill Bialosky, and Allegra Goodman. Many of these authors are associated with important literary, histori-cal, and artistic movements of their respective times. For instance, Gertrude Stein, Virginia Woolf, H.D., and Mina Loy were important forces in literary modernism; Zora Neale Hurston, a folklorist-novelist, not only celebrated and preserved regional dialect, but was also an important part of the Harlem Renais-sance; Anzia Yezierska, a social documentarian, reflected the lives and the trials of hopeful immigrants to the United States in the early twentieth century. As a recent essay in the *New York Times Book Review* indicates, Allegra Goodman is one of the few writers who integrates the religious world (in the case of her new novel, the world of Orthodox Jewry) as a matter-of-fact underpinning of her narrative. What will literary history name this type of writing—or will it go un-named? How does such "naming" by the literary establishment guarantee or al-ternately deny historical importance to a work? This volume celebrates these and many other writers who might, in fact, defy categorization—even when they have been associated with literary movements or styles—or about whom literary-historical categories have yet to be named. Perhaps inclusion in anthologies such as this will assure authority to those who might otherwise go unread.

At times, I have had to choose fewer selections by a well-known author to include the work of a greater number of writers whom readers might not otherwise have occasion to know. I have also chosen to make this what is called a "clean" anthology, a collection of writings by authors interrupted only by headnotes (which have been kept fairly brief). The clean anthology allows readers with all purposes in mind—pleasure reading, learning, teaching, or all of these—to approach the various works without being steered toward particular approaches, questions for interpretation, or similar strategies for the texts. My desire to keep the anthology as unfettered as possible perhaps explains my reluctance to prescribe a particular focus other than to present a wide range of worthwhile reading by women writers, primarily from traditions in English, in roughly chronological order. The rest is up to the reader.

While I would like to suggest that anthologies are products only of intellectual and teaching interests, they are not. We could not include several of the writers we had wanted to simply because the permissions rights to acquire their works were too costly, thereby keeping some outstanding writers from a wide audience. In an attempt to make the size of this volume manageable and affordable, we decided, at least for this first edition, to include only a few works in translation. The diversity of women's writing is represented both through the major genres and, where possible, the inclusion of various works by those who wrote in several genres, as is the case of Charlotte Perkins Gilman, writer of fiction, poetry, and essays. Needless to say, *The Prentice Hall Anthology of Women's Literature* presents authors of tremendously diverse background and lifestyle, voice, tradition, and world view.

I alternate between "we" and "I" throughout this introduction, and I do so with a purpose. I do not say "we" in the royal sense. Anthologies such as this can never be the product of one person, and I have been graced by the assistance of many, some even before this project could have been foreseen. My parents, Reinhard Holdstein and Henia Freifeld Holdstein, survivors of Hitler's Holocaust, blessed me with their love of reading, of learning, of appreciating and celebrating difference while upholding and cherishing one's personal heritage and traditions. I must also acknowledge the English teachers in the New York City public schools. I especially recall Mrs. Civin, Mrs. Feinsilver, Mrs. Schutz, Mr. Phillips, and my other English teachers, people for whom the term "dedication" must certainly have been invented. It is they who made me believe that somehow the world of the "other"—as represented to me and my peer group by writers such as T.S. Eliot—could somehow become mine as well. I am grateful to them.

However, in strictly practical terms, this project would not exist at all were it not for the consummate graduate assistant, Ted Spaniak. All for the glory of literary study, a close, personal relationship with interlibrary loan and the photocopying machine, and for very little money, Spaniak's intellectual gifts and dedication have put me in awe and forever in his debt. Spaniak is already the kind of student whom one hopes to see on the class list at the start of the term; he is an outstanding writer, a reliable and able researcher, and an excellent decision-maker. He is also responsible for many of the headnotes you will read throughout this volume. I am also grateful to Nancy Spaniak and to Ted and Nancy's son, Paul, for their support and patience during what must have been Ted's long hours at the computer or photocopier. Should they so desire, I am happy to prepare for them many a home-cooked meal.

John Larrabee has certainly earned a thank-you for his thoughtful and last-minute help with biographical headnotes. And much love and appreciation go to my children, Emily Gilman and David Gilman, whose curiosity and ongoing questions about the project served as both support and necessary comic relief as they bantered with me and with their father, Roger Gilman. Thanks to Nancy Perry, formerly at Prentice Hall, for luring me to this publisher to begin with.

Thanks, too, to the fine and helpful reviewers of the list of authors — accidental collaborators, perhaps, but with whose advice I added more contemporary writers and various works to the anthology: Beth Daniell, Barbara Hackett, Roberta Rosenberg, and John Schilb. Randy Pettit, Project Manager, has helped this project overcome various logistic hurdles, with a tremendous gift for detail — and kindness. And although I spoke with her only once or twice, I share in the early, tragic loss of Bonnie Biller, who made this project one of her priorities during her last days at work. Thanks also to Cantor Julie Green for emergency assistance in Yiddish. Carrie Brandon, literature editor *extraordinare* at Prentice Hall, deserves thanks and praise for her enthusiasm, support, and practical wisdom. Carrie is a knowledgeable, fine editor, and she is always sensible and good to talk with. That she understands the value of good food as the medium for crucial business and intellectual conversations is surpassed in importance only by her abilities, her good literary tastes, and her comprehensive knowledge of the profession.

—*Deborah H. Holdstein*

Alice James 1848–1892

One might well wonder why Alice James would be included in a collection of twentieth-century women writers when the dates of her birth and death rest firmly within the nineteenth century. Indeed, she suffered from the kinds of afflictions that seem to us "very nineteeth century": for instance, attacks of nervous collapse and a final two years of life as an invalid. Her brothers and father also bore similar nervous disorders, but as men, were implicitly allowed active lives that helped them cope with what James herself called "the horrors." James's diaries were not published until the twentieth century, and the contemporary nature of her thinking stands out, as does the life journey of the only woman within a distinguished family of men—including brothers William (the philosopher-psychologist) and Henry (the writer and critic). It has been written that James dedicated her life to an "analysis of consciousness," drawing "the world outside into her . . . room"—a goal of which was to "achieve significance for myself."

From THE DIARY OF ALICE JAMES

[*May 31, 1889*]

I think that if I get into the habit of writing a bit about what happens, or rather doesn't happen, I may lose a little of the sense of loneliness and desolation which abides with me. My circumstances allowing of nothing but the ejaculation of one-syllabled reflections, a written monologue by that most interesting being, *myself,* may have its yet to be discovered consolations. I shall at least have it all my own way and it may bring relief as an outlet to that geyser of emotions, sensations, speculations and reflections which ferments perpetually within my poor old carcass for its sins; so here goes, my first Journal!

[*July 12, 1889*]

. . . .Yesterday Nurse and I had a good laugh but I must allow that decidedly she "had" me. I was thinking of something that interested me very much and my mind was suddenly flooded by one of those luminous waves that sweep out of consciousness all but the living sense and overpower one with joy in the rich, throbbing complexity of life, when suddenly I looked up at Nurse, who was dressing me, and saw her primitive, rudimentary expression (so common here) as of no inherited quarrel with her density of putting petticoats over my head;

2 Alice James 1848–1892

the poverty and deadness of it contrasted to the tide of speculation that was coursing thro' my brain made me exclaim, "Oh! Nurse, don't you wish you were inside of *me!*"— her look of dismay and vehement disclaimer—"Inside of you, Miss, when you have just had a sick head-ache for five days!"—gave a greater blow to my vanity, than that much battered article has ever received. The headache had gone off in the night and I had clean forgotten it—when the little wretch confronted me with it, at this sublime moment when I was feeling within me the potency of a Bismarck,[1] and left me powerless before the immutable law that however great we may seem to our own consciousness no human being would exchange his for ours, and before the fact that *my* glorious rôle was to stand for *Sick headache* to mankind! What a grotesque I am to be sure! Lying in this room, with the resistance of a thistle-down, having illusory moments of throbbing with the pulse of the Race, the Mystery to be solved at the next breath and the fountain of all Happiness within me—the sense of vitality, in sort, simply proportionate to the excess of weakness!—To sit by and watch these absurdities is amusing in its way and reminds me of how I used to *listen* to my "company manners" in the days when I had 'em, and how ridiculous they sounded.

Ah! Those strange people who have the courage to be unhappy! *Are* they unhappy, by-the-way?

[June 18, 1890]

I remember so distinctly the first time I was conscious of a purely intellectual process. 'Twas the summer of '56 which we spent in Boulogne and the parents of Mlle. Marie Boningue our governess had a *campagne*[2] on the outskirts and invited us to spend the day, perhaps Marie's fête-day.[3] A large and shabby calèche came for us into which we were packed, save Wm.;[4] all I can remember of the drive was a never-ending ribbon of dust stretching in front and the anguish greater even than usual of Wilky's and Bob's[5] heels grinding into my shins. Marie told us that her father had a scar upon his face caused by a bad scald in his youth and we must be sure and not look at him as he was very sensitive. How I remember the painful conflict between sympathy and the desire to look and the fear that my baseness should be discovered by the good man as he sat at the head of the table in charge of a big frosted-cake, sprinkled o'er with those pink and white worms in which lurk the caraway seed. How easy 'twould be to picture one's youth as a perpetual escape from that abhorred object!—I wonder if it is a blight upon children still?—But to arrive at the first flowering

---

[1] Otto von Bismarck (1815–1898), known as the Iron Chancellor and unifier of Germany.
[2] French: "little country house."
[3] Birthday or name day.
[4] William James (1842–1910).
[5] Wilky: Garth Wilkinson James (1845–1883); Bob: Robertson James (1846–1910).

of me Intellect! We were turned into the garden to play, a sandy or rather dusty expanse with nothing in it, as I remember, but two or three scrubby apple-trees, from one of which hung a swing. As time went on Wilky and Bob disappeared, not to my grief, and the Boningues. Harry was sitting in the swing and I came up and stood near by as the sun began to slant over the desolate expanse, as the dready h[ou]rs, with that endlessness which they have for infancy, passed, when Harry suddenly exclaimed: "This might certainly be called pleasure under difficulties!" The stir of my whole being in response to the substance and exquisite, *original* form of this remark almost makes my heart beat now with the sisterly pride which was then awakened and it came to me in a flash, the higher nature of this appeal to the mind, as compared to the rudimentary solicitations which usually produced my childish explosions of laughter; and I can also feel distinctly the sense of self-satisfaction in that I could not only perceive, but appreciate this subtlety, as if I had acquired a new sense, a sense whereby to measure intellectual things, wit as distinguished from giggling, for example.

[May 31, 1891]

To him who waits, all things come! My aspirations may have been eccentric, but I cannot complain now, that they have not been brilliantly fulfilled. Ever since I have been ill, I have longed and longed for some palpable disease, no matter how conventionally dreadful a label it might have, but I was always driven back to stagger alone under the monstrous mass of subjective sensations, which that sympathetic being "the medical man" had no higher inspiration than to assure me I was personally responsible for, washing his hands of me with a graceful complacency under my very nose. Dr. Torry[6] was the only man who ever treated me like a rational being, who did not assume, because I was victim to many pains, that I was, of necessity, an arrested mental development too.

Notwithstanding all the happiness and comfort here, I have been going downhill at a steady trot; so they sent for Sir Andrew Clark four days ago, and the blessed being has endowed me not only with cardiac complications, but says that a lump that I have had in one of my breasts for three months, which has given me a great deal of pain, is a tumour, that nothing can be done for me but to alleviate pain, that it is only a question of time, etc. This with a delicate embroidery of "the most distressing case of nervous hyperæsthesia" added to a spinal neurosis that has taken me off my legs for seven years; with attacks of rheumatic gout in my stomach for the last twenty, ought to satisfy the most inflated pathologic vanity. It is decidedly indecent to catalogue oneself in this way, but I put it down in a scientific spirit, to show that though I have no productive worth, I have a certain value as an indestructible quantity.

[6] Dr. John Cooper Torry, like Sir Andrew Clark mentioned below, was a distinguished London physician consulted by Alice James.

[March 5, 1892: Final Entry by Katharine P. Loring]

All through Saturday the 5th and even in the night, Alice was making sentences. One of the last things she said to me was to make a correction in the sentence of March 4th "moral discords and nervous horrors."

This dictation of March 4th was rushing about in her brain all day, and although she was very weak and it tired her much to dictate, she could not get her head quiet until she had had it written: then she was relieved and I finished Miss Woolson's[7] story of "Dorothy" to her.

K.P.L.

Emma Lazarus 1849–1887

Poet, novelist, playwright, essayist, and literary translator, Emma Lazarus was born the daughter of Sephardic Jewish parents in New York City. Privately educated and raised in a wealthy, cultured environment, she is best known for her sonnet, "The New Colossus," which was written to raise money for a base for the Statue of Liberty. The poem's last five lines inscribed on the pedestal are said to give the statue its "spiritual basis." Lazarus's first book, *Poems and Translations* (1867), contains translations of Hugo, Dumas, Schiller, and Heine, as well as original poems concerning romantic subjects. Her major achievement as a translator, *Poems and Translations of Heinrich Heine* (1881), still stands today in the opinion of many as the definitive English version. While in her twenties, Lazarus was mentored by Ralph Waldo Emerson, to whom she dedicated her second book, *Admetus and Other Poems* (1871). The protest rally against Jewish pogroms in Russia and the mass immigration of refugees to the United States inspired *Songs of a Semite* (1882), a translation of ancient Hebrew poems issued in an inexpensive edition so as to reach the widest audience possible. Magazine articles written in 1882 and 1883 urged the establishment of a Palestinian homeland for Jews, as well as education for America's growing population of Jewish refugees. Her prolific and tragically short life gave way to cancer at age thirty-eight.

---

[7] Woolson: Constance Fenimore Woolson (1840–1894), American author and friend of Henry James.

THE NEW COLOSSUS

ENGRAVED ON A PLAQUE ON THE STATUE OF LIBERTY

Not like the brazen giant of Greek fame,
With conquering limbs astride from land to land;
Here at our sea-washed, sunset gates shall stand
A mighty woman with a torch, whose flame
Is the imprisoned lightning, and her name   5
Mother of Exiles. From her beacon-hand
Glows world-wide welcome; her mild eyes command
The air-bridged harbor that twin cities frame.
"Keep ancient lands, your storied pomp!" cries she
With silent lips. "Give me your tired, your poor,   10
Your huddled masses yearning to breathe free,
The wretched refuse of your teeming shore.
Send these, the homeless, tempest-tost to me,
I lift my lamp beside the golden door!"

Sarah Orne Jewett 1849–1909

Willa Cather once described the publications of Sarah Orne Jewett as stories that "melt into the land and the life of the land until they are not stories at all, but life itself." Born in Berwick, Maine, Jewett was the daughter of distinguished, well-educated parents: Her mother's father was a renowned surgeon, and her father a physician descended from the first Bay Colony settlers. Jewett benefited greatly as the daughter of a country doctor, for as she accompanied her father on remote trips to the countryside, she gained a unique sensitivity for the region's landscape and a deep appreciation for the common people whom she visited. After graduating from Berwick Academy in 1865, she began publishing in *Riverside Magazine for Young People* and *Atlantic Monthly,* which at the time was edited by William Dean Howells. At the urging of Howells, Jewett published *Deephaven* (1877), a collection of "sketches" (as she called them) about her native region that had appeared in his *Atlantic.* Subsequent works include a biography of her father, *A Country Doctor* (1884), the novel *A Marsh Island* (1886), and short story collections *A White Heron* (1886) and *The Country of the Pointed Firs* (1896). Cather, who was once counseled by Jewett to give up "the masquerade" of her male narrator and, instead, assume a female point of view, compared *The Country of the Pointed Firs* with *The Scarlet Letter* and *Huckleberry Finn* as one of American literature's three enduring classics.

TOM'S HUSBAND

I shall not dwell long upon the circumstances that led to the marriage of my hero and heroine; though their courtship was to them, the only one that has ever noticeably approached the ideal, it had many aspects in which it was entirely commonplace in other people's eyes. While the world in general smiles at lovers with kindly approval and sympathy, it refuses to be aware of the unprecedented delight which is amazing to the lovers themselves.

But, as has been true in many other cases, when they were at last married, the most ideal of situations was found to have been changed to the most practical. Instead of having shared their original duties, and, as school-boys would say, going halves, they discovered that the cares of life had been doubled. This led to some distressing moments for both our friends; they understood suddenly that instead of dwelling in heaven they were still upon earth, and had made themselves slaves to new laws and limitations. Instead of being freer and happier than ever before, they had assumed new responsibilities; they had established a new household, and must fulfill in some way or another the obligations of it. They looked back with affection to their engagement; they had been longing to have each other to themselves, apart from the world, but it seemed that they never felt so keenly that they were still units in modern society. Since Adam and Eve were in Paradise, before the devil joined them, nobody has had a chance to imitate that unlucky couple. In some respects they told the truth when, twenty times a day, they said that life had never been so pleasant before; but there were mental reservations on either side which might have subjected them to the accusation of lying. Somehow, there was a little feeling of disappointment, and they caught themselves wondering—though they would have died sooner than confess it—whether they were quite so happy as they had expected. The truth was, they were much happier than people usually are, for they had an uncommon capacity for enjoyment. For a little while they were like a sail-boat that is beating and has to drift a few minutes before it can catch the wind and start off on the other tack. And they had the same feeling, too, that any one is likely to have who has been long pursuing some object of his ambition or desire. Whether it is a coin, or a picture, or a stray volume of some old edition of Shakespeare, or whether it is an office under government or a lover, when fairly in one's grasp there is a loss of the eagerness that was felt in pursuit. Satisfaction, even after one has dined well, is not so interesting and eager a feeling as hunger.

My hero and heroine were reasonably well established to begin with: they each had some money, though Mr. Wilson had most. His father had at one time been a rich man, but with the decline, a few years before, of manufacturing interests, he had become, mostly through the fault of others, somewhat involved; and at the time of his death his affairs were in such a condition that it was still a question whether a very large sum or a moderately large one would represent his estate. Mrs. Wilson, Tom's step-mother, was somewhat of an invalid; she suffered severely at times with asthma, but she was almost entirely relieved by living in another part of the country. While her husband lived, she had accepted her illness as inevitable, and rarely left home; but during the last few years she had lived in Philadelphia with her own people, making short and wheezing visits only from time to time, and had not undergone a voluntary period of suffering since the occasion of Tom's marriage, which she had entirely approved. She had a sufficient property of her own, and she and Tom were independent of each other in that way. Her only other step-child was a daughter, who had married a navy officer, and had at this time gone out to spend three years (or less) with her husband, who had been ordered to Japan.

It is not unfrequently noticed that in many marriages one of the persons who choose each other as partners for life is said to have thrown himself or herself away, and the relatives and friends look on with dismal forebodings and ill-concealed submission. In this case it was the wife who might have done so much better, according to public opinion. She did not think so herself, luckily, either before marriage or afterward, and I do not think it occurred to her to picture to herself the sort of career which would have been her alternative. She had been an only child, and had usually taken her own way. Some one once said that it was a great pity that she had not been obliged to work for her living, for she had inherited a most uncommon business talent, and, without being disreputably keen at a bargain, her insight into the practical working of affairs was very clear and far-reaching. Her father, who had also been a manufacturer, like Tom's, had often said it had been a mistake that she was a girl instead of a boy. Such executive ability as hers is often wasted in the more contracted sphere of women, and is apt to be more a disadvantage than a help. She was too independent and self-reliant for a wife; it would seem at first thought that she needed a wife herself more than she did a husband. Most men like best the women whose natures cling and appeal to theirs for protection. But Tom Wilson, while he did not wish to be protected himself, liked these very qualities in his wife which would have displeased some other men; to tell the truth, he was very much in love with his wife just as she was. He was a successful collector of almost everything but money, and during a great part of his life he had been an invalid, and he had grown, as he laughingly confessed, very old-womanish. He had been badly lamed, when a boy, by being caught in some machinery in his father's mill, near which he was idling one afternoon, and though he had almost entirely outgrown the effect of his injury, it had not been until after many years. He had been in college, but his eyes had given out there, and he had been obliged to

leave in the middle of his junior year, though he had kept up a pleasant intercourse with the members of his class, with whom he had been a great favorite.
He was a good deal of an idler in the world. I do not think his ambition, except
in the case of securing Mary Dunn for his wife, had ever been distinct; he
seemed to make the most he could of each day as it came, without making all
his days' works tend toward some grand result, and go toward the upbuilding of
some grand plan and purpose. He consequently gave no promise of being either
distinguished or great. When his eyes would allow, he was an indefatigable
reader; and although he would have said that he read only for amusement, yet
he amused himself with books that were well worth the time he spent over
them.

The house where he lived nominally belonged to his step-mother, but she
had taken for granted that Tom would bring his wife home to it, and assured
him that it should be to all intents and purposes his. Tom was deeply attached to
the old place, which was altogether the pleasantest in town. He had kept bachelor's hall there most of the time since his father's death, and he had taken great
pleasure, before his marriage, in refitting it to some extent, though it was already
comfortable and furnished in remarkably good taste. People said of him that if
it had not been for his illnesses, and if he had been a poor boy, he probably
would have made something of himself. As it was, he was not very well known
by the townspeople, being somewhat reserved, and not taking much interest in
their every-day subjects of conversation. Nobody liked him so well as they liked
his wife, yet there was no reason why he should be disliked enough to have
much said about him.

After our friends had been married for some time, and had outlived the first
strangeness of the new order of things, and had done their duty to their neighbors with so much apparent willingness and generosity that even Tom himself
was liked a great deal better than he ever had been before, they were sitting together one stormy evening in the library, before the fire. Mrs. Wilson had been
reading Tom the letters which had come to him by the night's mail. There was a
long one from his sister in Nagasaki, which had been written with a good deal of
ill-disguised reproach. She complained of the smallness of the income of her
share in her father's estate, and said that she had been assured by American
friends that the smaller mills were starting up everywhere, and beginning to do
well again. Since so much of their money was invested in the factory, she had
been surprised and sorry to find by Tom's last letters that he had seemed to have
no idea of putting in a proper person as superintendent, and going to work
again. Four per cent on her other property, which she had been told she must
soon expect instead of eight, would make a great difference to her. A navy
captain in a foreign port was obliged to entertain a great deal, and Tom
must know that it cost them much more to live than it did him, and ought
to think of their interests. She hoped he would talk over what was best to
be done with their mother (who had been made executor, with Tom, of his
father's will).

Tom laughed a little, but looked disturbed. His wife had said something to the same effect, and his mother had spoken once or twice in her letters of the prospect of starting the mill again. He was not a bit of a business man, and he did not feel certain, with the theories which he had arrived at of the state of the country, that it was safe yet to spend the money which would have to be spent in putting the mill in order. "They think that the minute it is going again we shall be making money hand over hand, just as father did when we were children," he said. "It is going to cost us no end of money before we can make anything. Before father died he meant to put in a good deal of new machinery, I remember. I don't know anything about the business myself, and I would have sold out long ago if I had had an offer that came anywhere near the value. The larger mills are the only ones that are good for anything now, and we should have to bring a crowd of French Canadians here; the day is past for the people who live in this part of the country to go into the factory again. Even the Irish all go West when they come into the country, and don't come to places like this any more."

"But there are a good many of the old work-people down in the village," said Mrs. Wilson. "Jack Towne asked me the other day if you weren't going to start up in the spring."

Tom moved uneasily in his chair, "I'll put you in for superintendent, if you like," he said, half angrily, whereupon Mary threw the newspaper at him; but by the time he had thrown it back he was in good humor again.

"Do you know, Tom," she said, with amazing seriousness, "that I believe I should like nothing in the world so much as to be the head of a large business? I hate keeping house,—I always did; and I never did so much of it in all my life put together as I have since I have been married. I suppose it isn't womanly to say so, but if I could escape from the whole thing I believe I should be perfectly happy. If you get rich when the mill is going again, I shall beg for a housekeeper, and shirk everything. I give you fair warning. I don't believe I keep this house half so well as you did before I came here."

Tom's eyes twinkled. "I am going to have that glory,—I don't think you do, Polly; but you can't say that I have not been forbearing. I certainly have not told you more than twice how we used to have things cooked. I'm not going to be your kitchen-colonel."

"Of course it seemed the proper thing to do," said his wife, meditatively; "but I think we should have been even happier than we have if I had been spared it. I have had some days of wretchedness that I shudder to think of. I never know what to have for breakfast; and I ought not to say it, but I don't mind the sight of dust. I look upon housekeeping as my life's great discipline"; and at this pathetic confession they both laughed heartily.

"I've a great mind to take it off your hands," said Tom. "I always rather liked it, to tell the truth, and I ought to be a better housekeeper,—I have been at it for five years; though housekeeping for one is different from what it is for two, and one of them a woman. You see you have brought a different element into my family. Luckily, the servants are pretty well drilled. I do think you upset them a good deal at first!"

Mary Wilson smiled as if she only half heard what he was saying. She drummed with her foot on the floor and looked intently at the fire, and presently gave it a vigorous poking. "Well?" said Tom, after he had waited patiently as long as he could.

"Tom! I'm going to propose something to you. I wish you would really do as you said, and take all the home affairs under your care, and let me start the mill. I am certain I could manage it. Of course I should get people who understood the thing to teach me. I believe I was made for it; I should like it above all things. And this is what I will do: I will bear the cost of starting it, myself,—I think I have money enough, or can get it; and if I have not put affairs in the right trim at the end of a year I will stop, and you may make some other arrangement. If I have, you and your mother and sister can pay me back."

"So I am going to be the wife, and you the husband," said Tom, a little indignantly; "at least, that is what people will say. It's a regular Darby and Joan affair, and you think you can do more work in a day than I can do in three. Do you know that you must go to town to buy cotton? And do you know there are a thousand things about it that you don't know?"

"And never will?" said Mary, with perfect good humor. "Why, Tom, I can learn as well as you, and a good deal better, for I like business, and you don't. You forget that I was always father's right-hand man after I was a dozen years old, and that you have let me invest my money and some of your own, and I haven't made a blunder yet."

Tom thought that his wife had never looked so handsome or so happy. "I don't care, I should rather like the fun of knowing what people will say. It is a new departure, at any rate. Women think they can do everything better than men in these days, but I'm the first man, apparently, who has wished he were a woman."

"Of course people will laugh," said Mary, "but they will say that it's just like me, and think I am fortunate to have married a man who will let me do as I choose. I don't see why it isn't sensible: you will be living exactly as you were before you married, as to home affairs; and since it was a good thing for you to know something about housekeeping then, I can't imagine why you shouldn't go on with it now, since it makes me miserable, and I am wasting a fine business talent while I do it. What do we care for people's talking about it?"

"It seems to me that it is something like women's smoking: it isn't wicked, but it isn't the custom of the country. And I don't like the idea of your going among business men. Of course I should be above going with you, and having people think I must be an idiot; they would say that you married a manufacturing interest, and I was thrown in. I can foresee that my pride is going to be humbled to the dust in every way," Tom declared in mournful tones, and began to shake with laughter. "It is one of your lovely castles in the air, dear Polly, but an old brick mill needs a better foundation than the clouds. No, I'll look around, and get an honest, experienced man for agent. I suppose it's the best thing we can do, for the machinery ought not to lie still any longer; but I mean to sell the factory as soon as I can. I devoutly wish it would take fire, for the insurance would be the best price we are likely to get. That is a famous letter from Alice! I am afraid the captain has been growling over his pay, or they have been giving too many little dinners on board ship. If we were rid of the mill, you and I might go out there this winter. It would be capital fun."

Mary smiled again in an absent-minded way. Tom had an uneasy feeling that he had not heard the end of it yet, but nothing more was said for a day or two. When Mrs. Tom Wilson announced, with no apparent thought of being contradicted, that she had entirely made up her mind, and she meant to see those men who had been overseers of the different departments, who still lived in the village, and have the mill put in order at once, Tom looked disturbed, but made no opposition; and soon after breakfast his wife formally presented him with a handful of keys, and told him there was some lamb in the house for dinner; and presently he heard the wheels of her little phaeton rattling off down the road. I should be untruthful if I tried to persuade any one that he was not provoked; he thought she would at least have waited for his formal permission, and at first he meant to take another horse, and chase her, and bring her back in disgrace, and put a stop to the whole thing. But something assured him that she knew what she was about, and he determined to let her have her own way. If she failed, it might do no harm, and this was the only ungallant thought he gave her. He was sure that she would do nothing unladylike, or be unmindful of his dignity; and he believed it would be looked upon as one of her odd, independent freaks, which always had won respect in the end, however much they had been laughed at in the beginning. "Susan," said he, as that estimable person went by the door with the dustpan, "you may tell Catherine to come to me for orders about the house, and you may do so yourself. I am going to take charge again, as I did before I was married. It is no trouble to me, and Mrs. Wilson dislikes it. Besides, she is going into business, and will have a great deal else to think of."

"Yes, sir; very well, sir," said Susan, who was suddenly moved to ask so many questions that she was utterly silent. But her master looked very happy; there was evidently no disapproval of his wife; and she went on up the stairs, and began to sweep them down, knocking the dust-brush about exictedly, as if she were trying to kill a descending colony of insects.

Tom went out to the stable and mounted his horse, which had been waiting for him to take his customary after-breakfast ride to the post-office, and he galloped down the road in quest of the phaeton. He saw Mary talking with Jack Towne, who had been an overseer and a valued workman of his father's. He was looking much surprised and pleased.

"I wasn't caring so much about getting work, myself," he explained; "I've got what will carry me and my wife through; but it'll be better for the young folks about here to work near home. My nephews are wanting something to do; they were going to Lynn next week. I don't say but I should like to be to work in the old place again. I've sort of missed it, since we shut down."

"I'm sorry I was so long in overtaking you," said Tom, politely, to his wife. "Well, Jack, did Mrs. Wilson tell you she's going to start the mill? You must give her all the help you can."

"'Deed I will," said Mr. Towne, gallantly, without a bit of astonishment.

"I don't know much about the business yet," said Mrs. Wilson, who had been a little overcome at Jack Towne's lingo of the different rooms and machinery, and who felt an overpowering sense of having a great deal before her in the next few weeks. "By the time the mill is ready, I will be ready, too," she said, taking heart a little; and Tom, who was quick to understand her moods, could not help laughing, as he rode alongside. "We want a new barrel of flour, Tom, dear," she said, by way of punishment for his untimely mirth.

If she lost courage in the long delay, or was disheartened at the steady call for funds, she made no sign; and after a while the mill started up, and her cares were lightened, so that she told Tom that before next pay day she would like to go to Boston for a few days, and go to the theatre, and have a frolic and a rest. She really looked pale and thin, and she said she never worked so hard in all her life; but nobody knew how happy she was, and she was so glad she had married Tom, for some men would have laughed at it.

"I laughed at it," said Tom, meekly. "All is, if I don't cry by and by, because I am a beggar, I shall be lucky." But Mary looked fearlessly serene, and said that there was no danger at present.

It would have been ridiculous to expect a dividend the first year, though the Nagasaki people were pacified with difficulty. All the business letters came to Tom's address, and everybody who was not directly concerned thought that he was the motive power of the reawakened enterprise. Sometimes business people came to the mill, and were amazed at having to confer with Mrs. Wilson, but they soon had to respect her talents and her success. She was helped by the old clerk, who had been promptly recalled and reinstated, and she certainly did capitally well. She was laughed at, as she had expected to be, and people said they should think Tom would be ashamed of himself; but it soon appeared that he was not to blame, and what reproach was offered was on the score of his wife's oddity. There was nothing about the mill that she did not understand before very long, and at the end of the second year she declared a small dividend with great pride and triumph. And she was congratulated on her success, and every one thought of her project in a different way from the way they had thought of it in the beginning. She had singularly good fortune: at the end of the third year she was making money for herself and her friends faster than most people were, and approving letters began to come from Nagasaki. The Ashtons had been ordered to stay in that region, and it was evident that they were continually being obliged to entertain more instead of less. Their children were growing fast, too, and constantly becoming more expensive. The captain and his wife had already begun to congratulate themselves secretly that their two sons would in all probability come into possession, one day, of their uncle Tom's handsome property.

For a good while Tom enjoyed life, and went on his quiet way serenely. He was anxious at first, for he thought that Mary was going to make ducks and drakes of his money and her own. And then he did not exactly like the looks of the thing, either; he feared that his wife was growing successful as a business person at the risk of losing her womanliness. But as time went on, and he found there was no fear of that, he accepted the situation philosophically. He gave up his collection of engravings, having become more interested in one of coins and medals, which took up most of his leisure time. He often went to the city in pursuit of such treasures, and gained much renown in certain quarters as a numismatologist of great skill and experience. But at last his house (which had almost kept itself, and had given him little to do beside ordering the dinners, while faithful old Catherine and her niece Susan were his aids) suddenly became a great care to him. Catherine, who had been the main-stay of the family for many years, died after a short illness, and Susan must needs choose that time, of all others, for being married to one of the second hands in the mill. There followed a long and dismal season of experimenting, and for a time there was a procession of incapable creatures going in at one kitchen door and out of the other. His wife would not have liked to say so, but it seemed to her that Tom was growing fussy about the house affairs, and took more notice of those minor details than he used. She wished more than once, when she was tired, that he would not talk so much about the housekeeping; he seemed sometimes to have no other thought.

In the early days of Mrs. Wilson's business life, she had made it a rule to consult her husband on every subject of importance; but it had speedily proved to be a formality. Tom tried manfully to show a deep interest which he did not feel, and his wife gave up, little by little, telling him much about her affairs. She said that she liked to drop business when she came home in the evening; and at last she fell into the habit of taking a nap on the library sofa, while Tom, who could not use his eyes much by lamp-light, sat smoking or in utter idleness before the fire. When they were first married his wife had made it a rule that she should always read him the evening papers, and afterward they had always gone on with some book of history or philosophy, in which they were both interested. These evenings of their early married life had been charming to both of them, and from time to time one would say to the other that they ought to take up again the habit of reading together. Mary was so unaffectedly tired in the evening that Tom never liked to propose a walk; for, though he was not a man of peculiarly social nature, he had always been accustomed to pay an occasional evening visit to his neighbors in the village. And though he had little interest in the business world, and still less knowledge of it, after a while he wished that his wife would have more to say about what she was planning and doing, or how things were getting on. He thought that her chief aid, old Mr. Jackson, was far more in her thoughts than he. She was forever quoting Jackson's opinions. He did not like to find that she took it for granted that he was not interested in the welfare of his own property; it made him feel like a sort of pensioner and dependent, though, when they had guests at the house, which was by no means seldom, there was nothing in her manner that would imply that she thought herself in any way the head of the family. It was hard work to find fault with his wife in any way, though, to give him his due, he rarely tried.

But, this being a wholly unnatural state of things, the reader must expect to hear of its change at last, and the first blow from the enemy was dealt by an old woman, who lived nearby, and who called to Tom one morning, as he was driving down to the village in a great hurry (to post a letter, which ordered his agent to secure a long-wished-for ancient copper coin, at any price), to ask him if they had made yeast that week, and if she could borrow a cupful, as her own had met with some misfortune. Tom was instantly in a rage, and he mentally condemned her to some undeserved fate, but told her aloud to go and see the cook. This slight delay, besides being killing to his dignity, caused him to lose the mail, and in the end his much-desired copper coin. It was a hard day for him, altogether; it was Wednesday, and the first days of the week having been stormy the washing was very late. And Mary came home to dinner provokingly good-natured. She had met an old schoolmate and her husband driving home from the mountains and had first taken them over her factory, to their great amusement and delight, and then had brought them home to dinner. Tom greeted them cordially, and manifested his usual graceful hospitality; but the minute he saw his wife alone he said in a plaintive tone of rebuke, "I should think you might have remembered that the servants are unusually busy to-day. I do wish you would take a little interest in things at home. The women have been washing, and I'm sure I don't know what sort of a dinner we can give your friends. I wish you had thought to bring home some steak. I have been busy myself, and couldn't go down to the village. I thought we would only have a lunch."

Mary was hungry, but she said nothing, except that it would be all right,— she didn't mind; and perhaps they could have some canned soup.

She often went to town to buy or look at cotton, or to see some improvement in machinery, and she brought home beautiful bits of furniture and new pictures for the house, and showed a touching thoughtfulness in remembering Tom's fancies; but somehow he had an uneasy suspicion that she could get along pretty well without him when it came to the deeper wishes and hopes of her life, and that her most important concerns were all matters in which he had no share. He seemed to himself to have merged his life in his wife's; he lost his interest in things outside the house and grounds; he felt himself fast growing rusty and behind the times, and to have somehow missed a good deal in life; he had a suspicion that he was a failure. One day the thought rushed over him that his had been almost exactly the experience of most women, and he wondered if it really was any more disappointing and ignominious to him than it was to women themselves. "Some of them may be contented with it," he said to himself, soberly. "People think women are designed for such careers by nature, but I don't know why I ever made such a fool of myself."

Having once seen his situation in life from such a standpoint, he felt it day by day to be more degrading, and he wondered what he should do about it; and once, drawn by a new, strange sympathy, he went to the little family burying-ground. It was one of the mild, dim days that come sometimes in early November, when the pale sunlight is like the pathetic smile of a sad face, and he sat for a long time on the limp, frost-bitten grass beside his mother's grave.

But when he went home in the twilight his step-mother, who just then was making them a little visit, mentioned that she had been looking through some boxes of hers that had been packed long before and stowed away in the garret. "Everything looks very nice up there," she said, in her wheezing voice (which, worse than usual that day, always made him nervous), and added, without any intentional slight to his feelings, "I do think you have always been a most excellent housekeeper."

"I'm tired of such nonsense!" he exclaimed, with surprising indignation. "Mary, I wish you to arrange your affairs so that you can leave them for six months at least. I am going to spend this winter in Europe."

"Why, Tom, dear!" said his wife, appealingly. "I couldn't leave my business any way in the—"

But she caught sight of a look on his usually placid countenance that was something more than decision, and refrained from saying anything more.

And three weeks from that day they sailed.

A WHITE HERON

I

The woods were already filled with shadows one June evening, just before eight o'clock, though a bright sunset still glimmered faintly among the trunks of the trees. A little girl was driving home her cow, a plodding, dilatory, provoking creature in her behavior, but a valued companion for all that. They were going away from whatever light there was, and striking deep into the woods, but their feet were familiar with the path, and it was no matter whether their eyes could see it or not.

There was hardly a night the summer through when the old cow could be found waiting at the pasture bars; on the contrary, it was her greatest pleasure to hide herself away among the huckleberry bushes, and though she wore a loud bell she had made the discovery that if one stood perfectly still it would not

ring. So Sylvia had to hunt for her until she found her, and call Co'! Co'! with
never an answering Moo, until her childish patience was quite spent. If the creature had not given good milk and plenty of it, the case would have seemed very
different to her owners. Besides, Sylvia had all the time there was, and very little
use to make of it. Sometimes in pleasant weather it was a consolation to look
upon the cow's pranks as an intelligent attempt to play hide and seek, and as the
child had no playmates she lent herself to this amusement with a good deal of
zest. Though this chase had been so long that the wary animal herself had given
an unusual signal of her whereabouts, Sylvia had only laughed when she came
upon Mistress Moolly at the swampside, and urged her affectionately homeward
with a twig of birch leaves. The old cow was not inclined to wander farther, she
even turned in the right direction for once as they left the pasture, and stepped
along the road at a good pace. She was quite ready to be milked now, and seldom stopped to browse. Sylvia wondered what her grandmother would say because they were so late. It was a great while since she had left home at half-past
five o'clock, but everybody knew the difficulty of making this errand a short
one. Mrs. Tilley had chased the hornéd torment too many summer evenings
herself to blame any one else for lingering, and was only thankful as she waited
that she had Sylvia, nowadays, to give such valuable assistance. The good
woman suspected that Sylvia loitered occasionally on her own account; there
was never such a child for straying about out-of-doors since the world was
made! Everybody said that it was a good change for a little maid who had tried
to grow for eight years in a crowded manufacturing town, but, as for Sylvia herself, it seemed as if she never had been alive at all before she came to live at the
farm. She thought often with wistful compassion of a wretched geranium that
belonged to a town neighbor.

"Afraid of folks,'" old Mrs. Tilley said to herself, with a smile, after she had
made the unlikely choice of Sylvia from her daughter's houseful of children, and
was returning to the farm. "'Afraid of folks,' they said! I guess she won't be troubled no great[1] with 'em up to the old place!" When they reached the door of the
lonely house and stopped to unlock it, and the cat came to purr loudly, and rub
against them, a deserted pussy, indeed, but fat with young robins, Sylvia whispered that this was a beautiful place to live in, and she never should wish to go
home.

The companions followed the shady wood-road, the cow taking slow steps
and the child very fast ones. The cow stopped long at the brook to drink, as if
the pasture were not half a swamp, and Sylvia stood still and waited, letting her
bare feet cool themselves in the shoal water, while the great twilight moths
struck softly against her. She waded on through the brook as the cow moved
away, and listened to the thrushes with a heart that beat fast with pleasure.
There was a stirring in the great boughs overhead. They were full of little birds

---

[1] I.e., she won't be greatly troubled.

and beasts that seemed to be wide awake, and going about their world, or else saying good-night to each other in sleepy twitters. Sylvia herself felt sleepy as she walked along. However, it was not much farther to the house, and the air was soft and sweet. She was not often in the woods so late as this, and it made her feel as if she were a part of the gray shadows and the moving leaves. She was just thinking how long it seemed since she first came to the farm a year ago, and wondering if everything went on in the noisy town just the same as when she was there, the thought of the great red-faced boy who used to chase and frighten her made her hurry along the path to escape from the shadow of the trees.

Suddenly this little woods-girl is horror-stricken to hear a clear whistle not very far away. Not a bird's-whistle, which would have a sort of friendliness, but a boy's whistle, determined, and somewhat aggressive. Sylvia left the cow to whatever sad fate might await her, and stepped discreetly aside into the bushes, but she was just too late. The enemy had discovered her, and called out in a very cheerful and persuasive tone, "Halloa, little girl, how far is it to the road?" and trembling Sylvia answered almost inaudibly, "A good ways."

She did not dare to look boldly at the tall young man, who carried a gun over his shoulder, but she came out of her bush and again followed the cow, while he walked alongside.

"I have been hunting for some birds," the stranger said kindly, "and I have lost my way, and need a friend very much. Don't be afraid," he added gallantly. "Speak up and tell me what your name is, and whether you think I can spend the night at your house, and go out gunning early in the morning."

Sylvia was more alarmed than before. Would not her grandmother consider her much to blame? But who could have foreseen such an accident as this? It did not seem to be her fault, and she hung her head as if the stem of it were broken, but managed to answer "Sylvy," with much effort when her companion again asked her name.

Mrs. Tilley was standing in the doorway when the trio came into view. The cow gave a loud moo by way of explanation.

"Yes, you'd better speak up for yourself, you old trial! Where'd she tucked herself away this time, Sylvy?" But Sylvia kept an awed silence; she knew by instinct that her grandmother did not comprehend the gravity of the situation. She must be mistaking the stranger for one of the farmer-lads of the region.

The young man stood his gun beside the door, and dropped a lumpy game-bag beside it; then he bade Mrs. Tilley good-evening, and repeated his wayfarer's story, and asked if he could have a night's lodging.

"Put me anywhere you like," he said. "I must be off early in the morning before day; but I am very hungry indeed. You can give me some milk at any rate, that's plain."

"Dear sakes, yes," responded the hostess, whose long slumbering hospitality seemed to be easily awakened. "You might fare better if you went out to the main road a mile or so, but you're welcome to what we've got. I'll milk right off, and you make yourself at home. You can sleep on husks or feathers," she proffered graciously. "I raised them all myself. There's good pasturing for geese just below here towards the ma'sh. Now step round and set a plate for the gentleman, Sylvy!" And Sylvia promptly stepped. She was glad to have something to do, and she was hungry herself.

It was a surprise to find so clean and comfortable a little dwelling in this New England wilderness. The young man had known the horrors of its most primitive housekeeping, and the dreary squalor of that level of society which does not rebel at the companionship of hens. This was the best thrift of an old-fashioned farmstead, though on such a small scale that it seemed like a hermitage.[2] He listened eagerly to the old woman's quaint talk, he watched Sylvia's pale face and shining gray eyes with ever growing enthusiasm, and insisted that this as the best supper he had eaten for a month, and afterward the new-made friends sat down in the door-way together while the moon came up.

Soon it would be berry-time, and Sylvia was a great help at picking. The cow was a good milker, though a plaguy thing to keep track of, the hostess gossiped frankly, adding presently that she had buried four children, so Sylvia's mother, and a son (who might be dead) in California were all the children she had left. "Dan, my boy was a great hand to go gunning," she explained sadly. "I never wanted for pa'tridges or gray squer'ls while he was to home. He's been a great wand'rer, I expect, and he's no hand to write letters. There, I don't blame him, I'd ha' seen the world myself if it had been so I could."

"Sylvy takes after him," the grandmother continued affectionately, after a minute's pause. "There ain't a foot o'ground she don't know her way over, and the wild creatures counts her one o' themselves. Squer'ls she'll tame to come an' feed right out o' her hands, and all sorts o' birds. Last winter she got the jay-birds to bangeing[3] here, and I believe she'd 'a' scanted herself of her own meals to have plenty to throw out amongst 'em, if I hadn't kep' watch. Anything but crows, I tell her, I'm willing to help support—though Dan he had a tamed one o' them that did seem to have reason same as folks. It was round here a good spell after he went away. Dan an' his father they didn't hitch,—but he never held up his head ag'in after Dan had dared[4] him an' gone off."

The guest did not notice this hint of family sorrows in his eager interest in something else.

"So Sylvy knows all about birds, does she?" he exclaimed, as he looked round at the little girl who sat, very demure but increasingly sleepy, in the moonlight. "I am making a collection of birds myself. I have been at it ever since I was a boy." (Mrs Tilley smiled.) "There are two or three very rare ones I have been hunting for these five years. I mean to get them on my own ground if they can be found."

---

[2] Habitation of a hermit.

[3] Idling about, visiting.

[4] Challenged, defied. "Hitch": get along well,

"Do you cage 'em up?" asked Mrs. Tilley doubtfully, in response to this enthusiastic announcement.

"Oh no, they're stuffed and preserved, dozens and dozens of them," said the ornithologist, "and I have shot or snared every one myself. I caught a glimpse of a white heron a few miles from here on Saturday, and I have followed it in this direction. They have never been found in this district at all. The little white heron, it is," and he turned again to look at Sylvia with the hope of discovering that the rare bird was one of her acquaintances.

But Sylvia was watching a hop-toad in the narrow footpath.

"You would know the heron if you saw it," the stranger continued eagerly. "A queer tall white bird with soft feathers and long thin legs. And it would have a nest perhaps in the top of a high tree, made of sticks, something like a hawk's nest."

Sylvia's heart gave a wild beat; she knew that strange white bird, and had once stolen softly near where it stood in some bright green swamp grass, away over at the other side of the woods. There was an open place where the sunshine always seemed strangely yellow and hot, where tall, nodding rushes grew, and her grandmother had warned her that she might sink in the soft black mud underneath and never be heard of more. Not far beyond were the salt marshes just this side the sea itself, which Sylvia wondered and dreamed much about, but never had seen, whose great voice could sometimes be heard above the noise of the woods on stormy nights.

"I can't think of anything I should like so much as to find that heron's nest," the handsome stranger was saying. "I would give ten dollars to anybody who could show it to me," he added desperately, "and I mean to spend my whole vacation hunting it if need be. Perhaps it was only migrating, or had been chased out of its own region by some bird of prey."

Mrs. Tilley gave amazed attention to all this, but Sylvia still watched the toad, not divining, as she might have done at some calmer time, that the creature wished to get to its hole under the door-step, and was much hindered by the unusual spectators at that hour of the evening. No amount of thought, that night, could decide how many wished-for treasures the ten dollars, so lightly spoken of, would buy.

The next day the young sportsman hovered about the woods, and Sylvia kept him company, having lost her first fear of the friendly lad, who proved to be most kind and sympathetic. He told her many things about the birds and what they knew and where they lived and what they did with themselves. And he gave her a jack-knife, which she thought as great a treasure as if she were a desert-islander. All day long he did not once make her troubled or afraid except when he brought down some unsuspecting singing creature from its bough. Sylvia would have liked him vastly better without his gun; she could not understand why he killed the very birds he seemed to like so much. But as the day waned, Sylvia still watched the young man with loving admiration. She had never seen anybody so charming and delightful; the woman's heart, asleep in the child, was vaguely thrilled by a dream of love. Some premonition of that great power stirred and swayed these young creatures who traversed the solemn woodlands with soft-footed silent care. They stopped to listen to a bird's song; they pressed forward again eagerly, parting the branches—speaking to each other rarely and in whispers; the young man going first and Sylvia following, fascinated, a few steps behind, with her gray eyes dark with excitement.

She grieved because the longed-for white heron was elusive, but she did not lead the guest, she only followed, and there was no such thing as speaking first. The sound of her own unquestioned voice would have terrified her—it was hard enough to answer yes or no when there was need of that. At last evening began to fall, and they drove the cow home together, and Sylvia smiled with pleasure when they came to the place where she heard the whistle and was afraid only the night before.

II

Half a mile from home, at the farther edge of the woods, where the land was highest, a great pine-tree stood, the last of its generation. Whether it was left for a boundary mark, or for what reason, no one could say; the woodchoppers who had felled its mates were dead and gone long ago, and a whole new forest of sturdy trees, pines and oaks and maples, had grown again. But the stately head of this old pine towered above them all and made a landmark for sea and shore miles and miles away. Sylvia knew it well. She had always believed that whoever climbed to the top of it could see the ocean; and the little girl had often laid her hand on the great rough trunk and looked up wistfully at those dark boughs that the wind always stirred, no matter how hot and still the air might be below. Now she thought of the tree with a new excitement, for why, if one climbed it at break of day could not one see all the world, and easily discover from whence the white heron flew, and mark the place, and find the hidden nest?

What a spirit of adventure, what wild ambition! What fancied triumph and delight and glory for the later morning when she could make the secret! It was almost too real and too great for the childish heart to bear.

All night the door of the little house stood open and the whippoorwills came and sang upon the very step. The young sportsman and his old hostess were sound asleep, but Sylvia's great design kept her broad awake and watching. She forgot to think of sleep. The short summer night seemed as long as the winter darkness, and at last when the whippoorwills ceased, and she was afraid the morning would after all come too soon, she stole out of the house and followed the pasture path through the woods, hastening toward the open ground beyond, listening with a sense of comfort and companionship to the drowsy twitter of a half-awakened bird, whose perch she had jarred in passing. Alas, if the great wave of human interest which flooded for the first time this dull little life should sweep away the satisfactions of an existence heart to heart with nature and the dumb life of the forest!

There was the huge tree asleep yet in the paling moonlight, and small and silly Sylvia began with utmost bravery to mount to the top of it, with tingling, eager blood coursing the channels of her whole frame, with her bare feet and fingers, that pinched and held like bird's claws to the monstrous ladder reaching up, up, almost to the sky itself. First she must mount the white oak tree that grew alongside, where she was almost lost among the dark branches and the green leaves heavy and wet with dew; a bird fluttered off its nest, and a red squirrel ran to and fro and scolded pettishly at the harmless housebreaker. Sylvia felt her way easily. She had often climbed there, and know that higher still one of the oak's upper branches chafed against the pine trunk, just where its lower boughs were set close together. There, when she made the dangerous pass from one tree to the other, the great enterprise would really begin.

She crept out along the swaying oak limb at last, and took the daring step across into the old pine-tree. The way was harder than she thought; she must reach far and hold fast, the sharp dry twigs caught and held her and scratched her like angry talons, the pitch made her thin little fingers clumsy and stiff as she went round and round the tree's great stem, higher and higher upward. The sparrows and robins in the woods below were beginning to wake and twitter to the dawn, yet it seemed much lighter there aloft in the pine-tree, and the child knew she must hurry if her project were to be of any use.

The tree seemed to lengthen itself out as she went up, and to reach farther and farther upward. It was like a great main-mast to the voyaging earth; it must truly have been amazed that morning through all its ponderous frame as it felt this determined spark of human spirit wending its way from higher branch to branch. Who knows how steadily the least twigs held themselves to advantage this light, weak creature on her way! The old pine must have loved his new dependent. More than all the hawks, and bats, and moths, and even the sweet voiced thrushes, was the brave, beating heart of the solitary gray-eyed child. And the tree stood still and frowned away the winds that June morning while the dawn grew bright in the east.

Sylvia's face was like a pale star, if one had seen it from the ground, when the last thorny bough was past, and she stood trembling and tired but wholly triumphant, high in the tree-top. Yes, there was the sea with the dawning sun making a golden dazzle over it, and toward that glorious east flew two hawks with slow-moving pinions. How low they looked in the air from that height when one had only seen them before far up, and dark against the blue sky. Their gray feathers were as soft as moths; they seemed only a little way from the tree, and Sylvia felt as if she too could go flying away among the clouds. Westward, the woodlands and farms reached miles and miles into the distance; here and there were church steeples, and white villages, truly it was a vast and awesome world!

The birds sang louder and louder. At last the sun came up bewilderingly bright. Sylvia could see the white sails of ships out at sea, and the clouds that were purple and rose-colored and yellow at first began to fade away. Where was the white heron's nest in the sea of green branches, and was this wonderful sight and pageant of the world the only reward for having climbed to such a giddy height? Now look down again, Sylvia, where the green marsh is set among the shining birches and dark hemlocks; there where you saw the white heron once you will see him again; look, look! a white spot of him like a single floating feather comes up from the dead hemlock and grows larger, and rises, and comes close at last, and goes by the landmark pine with steady sweep of wing and out-stretched slender neck and crested head. And wait! wait! do not move a foot or a finger, little girl, do not send an arrow of light and consciousness from your two eager eyes, for the heron has perched on a pine bough not far beyond yours, and cries back to his mate on the nest and plumes his feathers for the new day!

The child gives a long sigh a minute later when a company of shouting cat-birds comes also to the tree, and vexed by their fluttering and lawlessness the solemn heron goes away. She knows his secret now, the wild, light, slender bird that floats and wavers, and goes back like an arrow presently to his home in the green world beneath. Then Sylvia, well satisfied, makes her perilous way down again, not daring to look far below the branch she stands on, ready to cry some-times because her fingers ache and her lamed feet slip. Wondering over and over again what the stranger would say to her, and what he would think when she told him how to find his way straight to the heron's nest.

"Sylvy, Sylvy!" called the busy old grandmother again and again, but no-body answered, and the small husk bed was empty and Sylvia had disappeared.

The guest waked from a dream, and remembering his day's pleasure hurried to dress himself that might it sooner begin. He was sure from the way the shy little girl looked once or twice yesterday that she had at least seen the white heron, and now she must really be made to tell. Here she comes now, paler than ever, and her worn old frock is torn and tattered, and smeared with pine pitch. The grandmother and the sportsman stand in the door together and question her, and the splendid moment has come to speak of the dead hemlock-tree by the green marsh.

But Sylvia does not speak after all, though the old grandmother fretfully re-bukes her, and the young man's kind, appealing eyes are looking straight into her own. He can make them rich with money; he has promised it, and they are poor now. He is so well worth making happy, and he waits to hear the story she can tell.

No, she must keep silence! What is it that suddenly forbids her and makes her dumb? Has she been nine years growing and now, when the great world for the first time puts out a hand to her, must she thrust it aside for a bird's sake? The murmur of the pine's green branches is in her ears, she remembers how the white heron came flying through the golden air and how they watched the sea and the morning together, and Sylvia cannot speak; she cannot tell the heron's secret and give its life away.

Dear loyalty, that suffered a sharp pang as the guest went away disappointed later in the day, that could have served and followed him and loved him as a dog loves! Many a night Sylvia heard the echo of his whistle haunting the pasture path as she came home with the loitering cow. She forgot even her sorrow at the sharp report of his gun and the sight of thrushes and sparrows dropping silent to the ground, their songs hushed and their pretty feathers stained and wet with blood. Were the birds better friends than their hunter might have been, — who can tell? Whatever treasures were lost to her, woodlands and summer-time, remember! Bring your gifts and graces and tell your secrets to this lonely country child!

Kate Chopin 1850–1904

Kate Chopin, originally Katherine O'Flaherty, was born into a wealthy and well-bred St. Louis family. Descended on her mother's side from French Creole aristocrats, the controversial author-to-be received a strict Catholic education and lessons in Victorian decorum at home. After her marriage in 1870 to Creole cotton trader Oscar Chopin, Kate was regarded as a happy, dutiful wife and conscientious mother of six children. When her husband died in 1883 of swamp fever, the distraught Chopin turned to writing—an activity in which she had always casually engaged—and serious literary study. In addition to her family doctor's recommendations to renounce most of the basic tenets of Catholicism and to read forward-thinking Victorian writers such as Charles Darwin, Chopin began to study contemporary fiction. She was particularly impressed by Guy de Maupassant, defining him as "a man who had escaped from tradition and authority, who had entered into himself and looked out upon life through his own being and with his own eyes." In Chopin's fiction, she, too, pushed the boundaries of Victorian tradition and authority by exploring issues such as women's intellectual, emotional, and sexual freedom; southern culture's arbitrary race distinctions and class divisions; and the inequities of traditional marriage.

THE STORY OF AN HOUR

Knowing that Mrs. Mallard was afflicted with a heart trouble, great care was taken to break to her as gently as possible the news of her husband's death.

It was her sister Josephine who told her, in broken sentences; veiled hints that revealed in half concealing. Her husband's friend Richards was there, too, near her. It was he who had been in the newspaper office when intelligence of the railroad disaster was received, with Brently Mallard's name leading the list of "killed." He had only taken the time to assure himself of its truth by a second telegram, and had hastened to forestall any less careful, less tender friend in bearing the sad message.

She did not hear the story as many women have heard the same, with a paralyzed inability to accept its significance. She wept at once, with sudden, wild abandonment, in her sister's arms. When the storm of grief had spent itself she went away to her room alone. She would have no one follow her.

There stood, facing the open window, a comfortable, roomy armchair. Into this she sank, pressed down by a physical exhaustion that haunted her body and seemed to reach into her soul.

She could see in the open square before her house the tops of trees that were all aquiver with the new spring life. The delicious breath of rain was in the air. In the street below a peddler was crying his wares. The notes of a distant song which some one was singing reached her faintly, and countless sparrows were twittering in the eaves.

There were patches of blue sky showing here and there through the clouds that had met and piled one above the other in the west facing her window.

She sat with her head thrown back upon the cushion of the chair, quite motionless, except when a sob came up into her throat and shook her, as a child who has cried itself to sleep continues to sob in its dreams.

She was young, with a fair, calm face, whose lines bespoke repression and even a certain strength. But now there was a dull stare in her eyes, whose gaze was fixed away off yonder on one of those patches of blue sky. It was not a glance of reflection, but rather indicated a suspension of intelligent thought.

There was something coming to her and she was waiting for it, fearfully. What was it? She did not know; it was too subtle and elusive to name. But she felt it, creeping out of the sky, reaching toward her through the sounds, the scents, the color that filled the air.

Now her bosom rose and fell tumultuously. She was beginning to recognize this thing that was approaching to possess her, and she was striving to beat it back with her will—as powerless as her two white slender hands would have been.

When she abandoned herself a little whispered word escaped her slightly parted lips. She said it over and over under her breath: "free, free, free!" The vacant stare and the look of terror that had followed it went from her eyes. They stayed keen and bright. Her pulses beat fast, and the coursing blood warmed and relaxed every inch of her body.

She did not stop to ask if it were or were not a monstrous joy that held her. A clear and exalted perception enabled her to dismiss the suggestion as trivial.

She knew that she would weep again when she saw the kind, tender hands folded in death; the face that had never looked save with love upon her, fixed and gray and dead. But she saw beyond that bitter moment a long procession of years to come that would belong to her absolutely. And she opened and spread her arms out to them in welcome.

There would be no one to live for her during those coming years; she would live for herself. There would be no powerful will bending hers in that blind persistence with which men and women believe they have a right to impose a private will upon a fellow-creature. A kind intention or a cruel intention made the act seem no less a crime as she looked upon it in that brief moment of illumination.

And yet she had loved him—sometimes. Often she had not. What did it matter! What could love, the unsolved mystery, count for in face of this possession of self-assertion which she suddenly recognized as the strongest impulse of her being!

"Free! Body and soul free!" she kept whispering.

Josephine was kneeling before the closed door with her lips to the keyhole, imploring for admission. "Louise, open the door! I beg; open the door—you will make yourself ill. What are you doing, Louise? For heaven's sake open the door."

"Go away. I am not making myself ill." No; she was drinking in a very elixir of life through that open window.

Her fancy was running riot along those days ahead of her. Spring days, and summer days, and all sorts of days that would be her own. She breathed a quick prayer that life might be long. It was only yesterday she had thought with a shudder that life might be long.

She arose at length and opened the door to her sister's importunities. There was a feverish triumph in her eyes, and she carried herself unwittingly like a goddess of Victory. She clasped her sister's waist, and together they descended the stairs. Richards stood waiting for them at the bottom.

Some one was opening the front door with a latchkey. It was Brently Mallard who entered, a little travel-stained, composedly carrying his grip-sack and umbrella. He had been far from the scene of accident, and did not even know there had been one. He stood amazed at Josephine's piercing cry; at Richards' quick motion to screen him from the view of his wife.

But Richards was too late.

When the doctors came they said she had died of heart disease—of joy that kills.

THE AWAKENING

I

A green and yellow parrot, which hung in a cage outside the door, kept repeating over and over:

"*Allez vous-en! Allez vous-en! Sapristi!*[1] That's all right?"

---

[1] Go away! Go away! For God's sake!

He could speak a little Spanish, and also a language which nobody understood, unless it was the mocking-bird that hung on the other side of the door, whistling his fluty notes out upon the breeze with maddening persistence.

Mr. Pontellier, unable to read his newspaper with any degree of comfort, arose with an expression and an exclamation of disgust. He walked down the gallery and across the narrow "bridges" which connected the Lebrun cottages one with the other. He had been seated before the door of the main house. The parrot and the mocking-bird were the property of Madame Lebrun, and they had the right to make all the noise they wished. Mr. Pontellier had the privilege of quitting their society when they ceased to be entertaining.

He stopped before the door of his own cottage, which was the fourth one from the main building and next to the last. Seating himself in a wicker rocker which was there, he once more applied himself to the task of reading the newspaper. The day was Sunday; the paper was a day old. The Sunday papers had not yet reached Grand Isle.[2] He was already acquainted with the market reports, and he glanced restlessly over the editorials and bits of news which he had not had time to read before quitting New Orleans the day before.

Mr. Pontellier wore eye-glasses. He was a man of forty, of medium height and slender build; he stooped a little. His hair was brown and straight, parted on one side. His beard was neatly and closely trimmed.

Once in a while he withdrew his glance from the newspaper and looked about him. There was more noise than ever over at the house. The main building was called "the house," to distinguish it from the cottages. The chattering and whistling birds were still at it. Two young girls, the Farival twins, were playing a duet from "Zampa"[3] upon the piano. Madame Lebrun was bustling in and out, giving orders in a high key to a yard-boy whenever she got inside the house, and directions in an equally high voice to a dining-room servant whenever she got outside. She was a fresh, pretty woman, clad always in white with elbow sleeves. Her starched skirts crinkled as she came and went. Farther down, before one of the cottages, a lady in black was walking demurely up and down, telling her beads. A good many persons of the *pension* had gone over to the *Chênière Caminada* in Beaudelet's lugger[4] to hear mass. Some young people were out under the water-oaks playing croquet. Mr. Pontellier's two children were there — sturdy little fellows of four or five. A quadroon[5] nurse followed them about with a far-away, meditative air.

Mr. Pontellier finally lit a cigar and began to smoke, letting the paper drag idly from his hand. He fixed his gaze upon a white sunshade[6] that was advancing at snail's pace from the beach. He could see it plainly between the gaunt trunks of the water-oaks and across the stretch of yellow chamomile. The gulf

---

[2] Resort island, between the Gulf of Mexico and Caminada Bay, south of New Orleans.

[3] Romantic opera by Louis Hérold (1791–1833).

[4] Passenger boat. *"Pension"*: a bed-and-board hotel. *Chênière Caminada* is an island between Grande Isle and the Louisiana coast.

[5] I.e, with one-quarter ("quad") black ancestry.

[6] Parasol.

looked far away melting hazily into the blue of the horizon. The sunshade continued to approach slowly. Beneath its pink-lined shelter were his wife, Mrs. Pontellier, and young Robert Lebrun. When they reached the cottage, the two seated themselves with some appearance of fatigue upon the step of the porch, facing each other, each leaning against a supporting post.

"What folly! to bathe[7] at such an hour in such heat!" exclaimed Mr. Pontellier. He himself had taken a plunge at daylight. That was why the morning seemed long to him.

"You are burnt beyond recognition," he added, looking at his wife as one looks at a valuable piece of personal property which has suffered some damage. She held up her hands, strong, shapely hands, and surveyed them critically, drawing up her lawn[8] sleeves above the wrists. Looking at them reminded her of her rings, which she had given to her husband before leaving for the beach. She silently reached out to him, and he, understanding, took the rings from his vest pocket and dropped them into her open palm. She slipped them upon her fingers; then clasping her knees, she looked across at Robert and began to laugh. The rings sparkled upon her fingers. He sent back an answering smile.

"What is it?" asked Pontellier, looking lazily and amused from one to the other. It was some utter nonsense; some adventure out there in the water, and they both tried to relate it at once. It did not seem half so amusing when told. They realized this, and so did Mr. Pontellier. He yawned and stretched himself. Then he got up, saying he had half a mind to go over to Klein's hotel and play a game of billiards.

"Come go along, Lebrun," he proposed to Robert. But Robert admitted quite frankly that he preferred to stay where he was and talk to Mrs. Pontellier.

"Well, send him about his business when he bores you, Edna," instructed her husband as he prepared to leave.

"Here, take the umbrella," she exclaimed, holding it out to him. He accepted the sunshade, and lifting it over his head descended the steps and walked away.

"Coming back to dinner?" his wife called after him. He halted a moment and shrugged his shoulders. He felt in his vest pocket; there was a ten-dollar bill there. He did not know; perhaps he would return for the early dinner and perhaps he would not. It all depended upon the company which he found over at Klein's and the size of "the game." He did not say this, but she understood it, and laughed, nodding good-by to him.

Both children wanted to follow their father when they saw him starting out. He kissed them and promised to bring them back bonbons and peanuts.

II

Mrs. Pontellier's eyes were quick and bright; they were a yellowish brown, about the color of her hair. She had a way of turning them swiftly upon an object and holding them there as if lost in some inward maze of contemplation or thought.

---

[7] Swim.

[8] Fine, sheer muslin.

Her eyebrows were a shade darker than her hair. They were thick and almost horizontal, emphasizing the depth of her eyes. She was rather handsome than beautiful. Her face was captivating by reason of a certain frankness of expression and a contradictory subtle play of features. Her manner was engaging.

Robert rolled a cigarette. He smoked cigarettes because he could not afford cigars, he said. He had a cigar in his pocket which Mr. Pontellier had presented him with, and he was saving it for his after-dinner smoke.

This seemed quite proper and natural on his part. In coloring he was not unlike his companion. A clean-shaven face made the resemblance more pronounced than it would otherwise have been. There rested no shadow of care upon his open countenance. His eyes gathered in and reflected the light and languor of the summer day.

Mrs. Pontellier reached over for a palmleaf fan that lay on the porch and began to fan herself, while Robert sent between his lips light puffs from his cigarette. They chatted incessantly: about the things around them; their amusing adventure out in the water—it had again assumed its entertaining aspect; about the wind, the trees, the people who had gone to the *Chênière;* about the children playing croquet under the oaks, and the Farival twins, who were now performing the overture to "The Poet and Peasant."[1]

Robert talked a good deal about himself. He was very young, and did not know any better. Mrs. Pontellier talked a little about herself for the same reason. Each was interested in what the other said. Robert spoke of his intention to go to Mexico in the autumn, where fortune awaited him. He was always intending to go to Mexico, but some way never got there. Meanwhile he held on to his modest position in a mercantile house in New Orleans, where an equal familiarity with English, French and Spanish gave him no small value as a clerk and correspondent.

He was spending his summer vacation, as he always did, with his mother at Grand Isle. In former times, before Robert could remember, "the house" had been a summer luxury of the Lebruns. Now flanked by its dozen or more cottages, which were always filled with exclusive visitors from the "*Quartier Français,*"[2] it enabled Madame Lebrun to maintain the easy and comfortable existence which appeared to be her birthright.

Mrs. Pontellier talked about her father's Mississippi plantation and her girlhood home in the old Kentucky blue-grass country. She was an American woman, with a small infusion of French which seemed to have been lost in dilution. She read a letter from her sister, who was away in the East, and who had engaged herself to be married. Robert was interested, and wanted to know what manner of girls the sisters were, what the father was like, and how long the mother had been dead.

---

[1] Operetta by Franz von Suppé (1819–1895).

[2] The French Quarter of New Orleans, first settled by the French in the early 18th century and occupied at this time by wealthy, older families.

When Mrs. Pontellier folded the letter it was time for her to dress for the early dinner.

"I see Léonce isn't coming back," she said, with a glance in the direction whence her husband had disappeared. Robert supposed he was not, as there were a good many New Orleans club men over at Klein's.

When Mrs. Pontellier left him to enter her room, the young man descended the steps and strolled over toward the croquet players, where, during the half-hour before dinner, he amused himself with the little Pontellier children, who were very fond of him.

III

It was eleven o'clock that night when Mr. Pontellier returned from Klein's hotel. He was in an excellent humor, in high spirits, and very talkative. His entrance awoke his wife, who was in bed and fast asleep when he came in. He talked to her while he undressed, telling her anecdotes and bits of news and gossip that he had gathered during the day. From his trousers pockets he took a fistful of crumpled bank notes and a good deal of silver coin, which he piled on the bureau indiscriminately with keys, knife, handkerchief, and whatever else happened to be in his pockets. She was overcome with sleep, and answered him with little half utterances.

He thought it very discouraging that his wife, who was the sole object of his existence, evinced so little interest in things which concerned him and valued so little his conversation.

Mr. Pontellier had forgotten the bonbons and peanuts for the boys. Notwithstanding he loved them very much, and went into the adjoining room where they slept to take a look at them and make sure that they were resting comfortably. The result of his investigation was far from satisfactory. He turned and shifted the youngsters about in bed. One of them began to kick and talk about a basket full of crabs.

Mr. Pontellier returned to his wife with the information that Raoul had a high fever and needed looking after. Then he lit a cigar and went and sat near the open door to smoke it.

Mrs. Pontellier was quite sure Raoul had no fever. He had gone to bed perfectly well, she said, and nothing had ailed him all day. Mr. Pontellier was too well acquainted with fever symptoms to be mistaken. He assured her the child was consuming[3] at that moment in the next room.

He reproached his wife with her inattention, her habitual neglect of the children. If it was not a mother's place to look after children, whose on earth was it? He himself had his hands full with his brokerage business. He could not be in two places at once; making a living for his family on the street, and staying at home to see that no harm befell them. He talked in a monotonous, insistent way.

[3] I.e., "consumptive," feverish.

Mrs. Pontellier sprang out of bed and went into the next room. She soon came back and sat on the edge of the bed, leaning her head down on the pillow. She said nothing, and refused to answer her husband when he questioned her. When his cigar was smoked out he went to bed, and in a half a minute he was fast asleep.

Mrs. Pontellier was by that time thoroughly awake. She began to cry a little, and wiped her eyes on the sleeve of her *peignoir*. Blowing out the candle, which her husband left burning, she slipped her bare feet into a pair of satin *mules* at the foot of the bed and went out on the porch, where she sat down in the wicker chair and began to rock gently to and fro.

It was then past midnight. The cottages were all dark. A single faint light gleamed out from the hallway of the house. There was no sound abroad except the hooting of an old owl in the top of a water-oak, and the everlasting voice of the sea, that was not uplifted at that soft hour. It broke like a mournful lullaby upon the night.

The tears came so fast to Mrs. Pontellier's eyes that the damp sleeve of her *peignoir* no longer served to dry them. She was holding the back of her chair with one hand; her loose sleeve had slipped almost to the shoulder of her up-lifted arm. Turning, she thrust her face, steaming and wet, into the bend of her arm, and she went on crying there, not caring any longer to dry her face, her eyes, her arms. She could not have told why she was crying. Such experiences as the foregoing were not uncommon in her married life. They seemed never be-fore to have weighed much against the abundance of her husband's kindness and a uniform devotion which had come to be tacit and self-understood.

An indescribable oppression, which seemed to generate in some unfamiliar part of her consciousness, filled her whole being with a vague anguish. It was like a shadow, like a mist passing across her soul's summer day. It was strange and unfamiliar; it was a mood. She did not sit there inwardly upbraiding her hus-band, lamenting at Fate, which had directed her footsteps to the path which they had taken. She was just having a good cry all to herself. The mosquitoes made merry over her, biting her firm, round arms and nipping at her bare insteps.

The little stinging, buzzing imps succeeded in dispelling a mood which might have held her there in the darkness half a night longer.

The following morning Mr. Pontellier was up in good time to take the rock-away[4] which was to convey him to the steamer at the wharf. He was returning to the city to his business, and they would not see him again at the Island till the coming Saturday. He had regained his composure, which seemed to have been somewhat impaired the night before. He was eager to be gone, as he looked for-ward to a lively week in Carondelet Street.[5]

Mr. Pontellier gave his wife half the money which he had brought away from Klein's hotel the evening before. She liked money as well as most women, and accepted it with no little satisfaction.

---

[4] Four-wheeled carriage.

[5] The financial center of New Orleans.

"It will buy a handsome wedding present for Sister Janet!" she exclaimed, smoothing out the bills as she counted them one by one.

"Oh! We'll treat Sister Janet better than that, my dear," he laughed, as he prepared to kiss her good-by.

The boys were tumbling about, clinging to his legs, imploring that numerous things be brought back to them. Mr. Pontellier was a great favorite, and ladies, men, children, even nurses, were always on hand to say good-by to him. His wife stood smiling and waving, the boys shouting, as he disappeared in the old rockaway down the sandy road.

A few days later a box arrived for Mrs. Pontellier from New Orleans. It was from her husband. It was filled with *friandises,* with luscious and toothsome bits—the finest of fruits, *pâtés,* a rare bottle or two, delicious syrups, and bonbons in abundance.

Mrs. Pontellier was always very generous with the contents of such a box; she was quite used to receiving them when away from home. The *pâtés* and fruit were brought to the dining-room; the bonbons were passed around. And the ladies, selecting with dainty and discriminating fingers and a little greedily, all declared that Mr. Pontellier was the best husband in the world. Mrs. Pontellier was forced to admit that she knew of none better.

IV

It would have been a difficult matter for Mr. Pontellier to define to his own satisfaction or any one else's wherein his wife failed in her duty toward their children. It was something which he felt rather than perceived, and he never voiced the feeling without subsequent regret and ample atonement.

If one of the little Pontellier boys took a tumble whilst at play, he was not apt to rush crying to his mother's arms for comfort; he would more likely pick himself up, wipe the water out of his eyes and the sand out of his mouth, and go on playing. Tots as they were, they pulled together and stood their ground in childish battles with doubled fists and uplifted voices, which usually prevailed against the other mother-tots. The quadroon nurse was looked upon as a huge encumbrance, only good to button up waists and panties and to brush and part hair; since it seemed to be a law of society that hair must be parted and brushed.

In short, Mrs. Pontellier was not a mother-woman. The mother-women seemed to prevail that summer at Grand Isle. It was easy to know them, fluttering about with extended, protecting wings when any harm, real or imaginary, threatened their precious brood. They were women who idolized their children, worshipped their husbands, and esteemed it a holy privilege to efface themselves as individuals and grow wings as ministering angels.

Many of them were delicious in the rôle; one of them was the embodiment of every womanly grace and charm. If her husband did not adore her, he was a brute, deserving of death by slow torture. Her name was Adèle Ratignolle. There are no words to describe her save the old ones that have served so often to picture the bygone heroine of romance and the fair lady of our dreams. There was nothing subtle or hidden about her charms; her beauty was all there, flaming and apparent: the spun-gold hair that comb nor confining pin could restrain; the blue eyes that were like nothing but sapphires; two lips that pouted, that were so red one could only think of cherries or some other delicious crimson fruit in looking at them. She was growing a little stout, but it did not seem to detract an iota from the grace of every step, pose, gesture. One would not have wanted her white neck a mite less full or her beautiful arms more slender. Never were hands more exquisite than hers, and it was a joy to look at them when she threaded her needle or adjusted her gold thimble to her taper[6] middle finger as she sewed away on the little night-drawers or fashioned a bodice or a bib.

Madame Ratignolle was very fond of Mrs. Pontellier, and often she took her sewing and went over to sit with her in the afternoons. She was sitting there the afternoon of the day the boy arrived from New Orleans. She had possession of the rocker, and she was busily engaged in sewing upon a diminutive pair of night drawers.

She had brought the pattern of the drawers for Mrs. Pontellier to cut out— a marvel of construction, fashioned to enclose a baby's body so effectually that only two small eyes might look out from the garment, like an Eskimo's. They were designed for winter wear, when treacherous drafts came down chimneys and insidious currents of deadly cold found their way through keyholes.

Mrs. Pontellier's mind was quite at rest concerning the present material needs of her children, and she could not see the use of anticipating and making winter night garments the subject of her summer meditations. But she did not want to appear unamiable and uninterested, so she had brought forth newspapers which she spread upon the floor of the gallery, and under Madame Ratignolle's directions she had cut a pattern of the impervious garment.

Robert was there, seated as he had been the Sunday before, and Mrs. Pontellier also occupied her former position on the upper step, leaning listlessly against the post. Beside her was a box of bonbons, which she held out at intervals to Madame Ratignolle.

That lady seemed at a loss to make a selection, but finally settled upon a stick of nugat, wondering if it were not too rich; whether it could possibly hurt her. Madame Ratignolle had been married seven years. About every two years she had a baby. At that time she had three babies, and was beginning to think of a fourth one. She was always talking about her "condition". Her "condition" was in no way apparent, and no one would have known a thing about it but for her persistence in making it the subject of conversation.

Robert started to reassure her, asserting that he had known a lady who had subsisted upon nugat during the entire—but seeing the color mount into Mrs. Pontellier's face he checked himself and changed the subject.

---

[6] I.e., tapered.

Mrs. Pontellier, though she had married a Creole,[7] was not thoroughly at home in the society of Creoles; Never before had she been thrown so intimately among them. There were only Creoles that summer at Lebrun's. They all knew each other, and felt like one large family, amongst whom existed the most amicable relations. A characteristic which distinguished them and which impressed Mrs. Ponetellier most forcibly was their entire absence of prudery. Their freedom of expression was at first incomprehensible to her, though she had no difficulty in reconciling it with a lofty chastity which in the Creole women seems to be inborn and unmistakable.

Never would Edna Pontellier forget the shock with which she heard Madame Ratignolle relating to old Monsieur Farival the harrowing story of one of her *accouchements*,[8] withholding no intimate detail. She was growing accustomed to like shocks, but she could not keep the mounting color back from her cheeks. Oftener than once her coming had interrupted the droll story with which Robert was entertaining some amused group of married women.

A book had gone the rounds of the *pension*. When it came her turn to read it, she did so with profound astonishment. She felt moved to read the book in secret and solitude, although none of the others had done so — to hide it from view at the sound of approaching footsteps. It was openly criticized and freely discussed at table. Mrs. Pontellier gave over being astonished, and concluded that wonders would never cease.

V

They formed a congenial group sitting there that summer afternoon — Madame Ratignolle sewing away, often stopping to relate a story or incident with much expressive gesture of her perfect hands: Robert and Mrs. Pontellier sitting idle, exchanging occasional words, glances or smiles which indicated a certain advanced stage of intimacy and *camaraderie.*

He had lived in her shadow during the past month. No one thought anything of it. Many had predicted that Robert would devote himself to Mrs. Pontellier when he arrived. Since the age of fifteen, which was eleven years before, Robert each summer at Grand Isle had constituted himself the devoted attendant of some fair dame or damsel. Sometimes it was a young girl, again a widow; but as often as not it was some interesting married woman.

For two consecutive seasons he lived in the sunlight of Mademoiselle Duvigné's presence. But she died between summers; then Robert posed as an inconsolable, prostrating himself at the feet of Madame Ratignolle for whatever crumbs of sympathy and comfort she might be pleased to vouchsafe.

Mrs. Pontellier liked to sit and gaze at her fair companion as she might look upon a faultless Madonna.

---

[7] Descended from the original French and Spanish settlers of New Orleans; and thus at this time, an aristocrat.

[8] Childbirth.

"Could any one fathom the cruelty beneath that fair exterior?" murmured Robert. "She knew that I adored her once, and she let me adore her. It was 'Robert, come; go; stand up; sit down; do this; do that; see if the baby sleeps; my thimble, please, that I left God knows where. Come and read Daudet[9] to me while I sew.'"

"*Par exemple!*"[1] I never had to ask. You were always there under my feet, like a troublesome cat."

"You mean like an adoring dog. And just as soon as Ratignolle appeared on the scene, then it *was* like a dog. *'Passez! Adieu! Allez vous-en!'*"[2]

"Perhaps I feared to make Alphonse jealous," she interjoined, with excessive naïveté. That made them all laugh. The right hand jealous of the left! The heart jealous of the soul! But for that matter, the Creole husband is never jealous; with him the gangrene passion is one which has become dwarfed by disuse.

Meanwhile Robert, addressing Mrs. Pontellier, continued to tell of his one time hopeless passion for Madame Ratignolle; of sleepless nights, of consuming flames till the very sea sizzled when he took his daily plunge. While the lady at the needle kept up a little running, contemptuous comment:

"*Blagueur — farceur — gros bête, va!*"[3]

He never assumed this serio-comic tone when alone with Mrs. Pontellier. She never knew precisely what to make of it; at that moment, it was impossible for her to guess how much of it was in jest and what proportion was earnest. It was understood that he had often spoken words of love to Madame Ratignolle, without any thought of being taken seriously. Mrs. Pontellier was glad he had not assumed a similar rôle toward herself. It would have been unacceptable and annoying.

Mrs. Pontellier had brought her sketching materials, which she sometimes dabbled with in an unprofessional way. She liked the dabbling. She felt in it satisfaction of a kind which no other employment afforded her.

She had long wished to try herself on Madame Ratignolle. Never had that lady seemed a more tempting subject than at that moment, seated there like some sensuous Madonna, with the gleam of the fading day enriching her splendid color.

Robert crossed over and seated himself upon the step below Mrs. Pontellier, that he might watch her work. She handled her brushes with a certain ease and freedom which came, not from long and close acquaintance with them, but from a natural aptitude. Robert followed her work with close attention, giving forth little ejaculatory expressions of appreciation in French, which he addressed to Madame Ratignolle.

"*Mais ce n'est pas mal! Elle s'y connait, elle a de la force, oui.*"[4]

[9] Alphonse Daudet (1840–1887), French novelist.
[1] For goodness sake!
[2] Go on! Good-by! Go away!
[3] Liar — comedian — silly, go on with you.
[4] Why that's not bad at all! She knows what she's doing; yes, she has talent.

During his oblivious attention he once quietly rested his head against Mrs. Pontellier's arm. As gently she repulsed him. Once again he repeated the offense. She could not but believe it to be thoughtlessness on his part; yet that was no reason she should submit to it. She did not remonstrate, except again to repulse him quietly but firmly. He offered no apology.

The picture completed bore no resemblance to Madame Ratignolle. She was greatly disappointed to find that it did not look like her. But it was a fair enough piece of work, and in many respects satisfying.

Mrs. Pontellier evidently did not think so. After surveying the sketch critically she drew a broad smudge of paint across its surface, and crumpled the paper between her hands.

The youngsters came tumbling up the steps, the quadroon following at the respectful distance which they required her to observe. Mrs. Pontellier made them carry her paints and things into the house. She sought to detain them for a little talk and some pleasantry. But they were greatly in earnest. They had only come to investigate the contents of the bonbon box. They accepted without murmuring what she chose to give them, each holding out two chubby hands scoop-like, in the vain hope that they might be filled; and then away they went.

The sun was low in the west, and the breeze soft and languorous that came up from the south, charged with the seductive odor of the sea. Children, freshly befurbelowed,[5] were gathering for their games under the oaks. Their voices were high and penetrating.

Madame Ratignolle folded her sewing, placing thimble, scissors and thread all neatly together in the roll, which she pinned securely. She complained of faintness. Mrs. Pontellier flew for the cologne water and a fan. She bathed Madame Ratignolle's face with cologne, while Robert plied the fan with unnecessary vigor.

The spell was soon over, and Mrs. Pontellier could not help wondering if there were not a little imagination responsible for its origin, for the rose tint had never faded from her friend's face.

She stood watching the fair woman walk down the long line of galleries with the grace and majesty which queens are sometimes supposed to possess. Her little ones ran to meet her. Two of them clung about her white skirts, the third she took from its nurse and with a thousand endearments bore it along in her own fond, encircling arms. Though, as everybody well knew, the doctor had forbidden her to lift so much as a pin!

"Are you going bathing"? asked Robert of Mrs. Pontellier. It was not so much a question as a reminder.

"Oh, no," she answered, with a tone of indecision. "I'm tired; I think not." Her glance wandered from his face away toward the Gulf, whose sonorous murmur reached her like a loving but imperative entreaty.

"Oh, come!" he insisted. "You mustn't miss your bath. Come on. The water must be delicious; it will not hurt you. Come."

[5] Dressed up.

He reached up for her big, rough straw hat that hung on a peg outside the door, and put it on her head. They descended the steps, and walked away together toward the beach. The sun was low in the west and the breeze was soft and warm.

VI

Edna Pontellier could not have told why, wishing to go to the beach with Robert, she should in the first place have declined, and in the second place have followed in obedience to one of the two contradictory impulses which impelled her.

A certain light was beginning to dawn dimly within her,—the light which, showing the way, forbids it.

At that early period it served but to bewilder her. It moved her to dreams, to thoughtfulness, to the shadowy anguish which had over-come her the midnight when she had abandoned herself to tears.

In short, Mrs. Pontellier was beginning to realize her position in the universe as a human being, and to recognize her relations as an individual to the world within and about her. This may seem like a ponderous weight of wisdom to descend upon the soul of a young woman of twenty-eight—perhaps more wisdom than the Holy Ghost is usually pleased to vouchsafe to any woman.

But the beginning of things, of a world especially, is necessarily vague, tangled, chaotic, and exceedingly disturbing. How few of us ever emerge from such beginning! How many souls perish in its tumult!

The voice of the sea is seductive; never ceasing, whispering, clamoring, murmuring, inviting the soul to wander for a spell in abysses of solitude; to lose itself in mazes of inward contemplation.

The voice of the sea speaks to the soul. The touch of the sea is sensuous, enfolding the body in its soft, close embrace.

VII

Mrs. Pontellier was not a woman given to confidences, a characteristic hitherto contrary to her nature. Even as a child she had lived her own small life all within herself. At a very early period she had apprehended instinctively the dual life—that outward existence which conforms, the inward life which questions.

That summer at Grand Isle she began to loose a little of the mantle of reserve that had always enveloped her. There may have been—there must have been—influences, both subtle and apparent, working in their several ways to induce her to do this; but the most obvious was the influence of Adèle Ratignolle. The excessive physical charm of the Creole had first attracted her, for Edna had a sensuous susceptibility to beauty. Then the candor of the woman's whole existence, which everyone might read, and which formed so striking a contrast to her own habitual reserve—this might have furnished a link. Who can tell what metals the gods use in forging the subtle bond which we call sympathy, which we might as well call love.

The two women went away one morning to the beach together, arm in arm, under the huge white sunshade. Edna had prevailed upon Madame Ratignolle to leave the children behind, though she could not induce her to relinquish a diminutive roll of needlework, which Adèle begged to be allowed to slip into the depths of her pocket. In some unaccountable way they had escaped from Robert.

The walk to the beach was no inconsiderable one, consisting as it did of a long, sandy path, upon which a sporadic and tangled growth that bordered it on either side made frequent and unexpected inroads. There were acres of yellow camomile reaching out on either hand. Further away still, vegetable gardens abounded, with frequent small plantations of orange or lemon trees intervening. The dark green clusters glistened from afar in the sun.

The women were both of goodly height, Madame Ratignolle possessing the more feminine and matronly figure. The charm of Edna Pontellier's physique stole insensibly upon you. The lines of her body were long, clean and symmetrical; it was a body which occasionally fell into splendid poses; there was no suggestion of the trim, stereotyped fashion-plate about it. A casual and indiscriminating observer, in passing, might not cast a second glance upon the figure. But with more feeling and discernment he would have recognized the noble beauty of its modeling, and the graceful severity of poise and movement, which made Edna Pontellier different from the crowd.

She wore a cool muslin that morning—white, with a waving vertical line of brown running through it; also a white linen collar and the big straw hat which she had taken from the peg outside the door. The hat rested any way on her yellow-brown hair, that waved a little, was heavy, and clung close to her head.

Madame Ratignolle, more careful of her complexion, had twined a gauze veil about her head. She wore dogskin gloves, white gauntlets that protected her wrists. She was dressed in pure white, with a fluffiness of ruffles that became her. The draperies and fluttering things which she wore suited her rich, luxuriant beauty as a greater severity of line could not have done.

There were a number of bath-houses along the beach, of rough but solid construction, built with small, protecting galleries facing the water. Each house consisted of two compartments, and each family at Lebrun's possessed a compartment for itself, fitted out with all the essential paraphernalia of the bath and whatever other conveniences the owners might desire. The two women had no intention of bathing; they had just strolled down to the beach for a walk and to be alone and near the water. The Pontellier and Ratignolle compartments adjoined one another under the same roof.

Mrs. Pontellier had brought down her key through force of habit. Unlocking the door of her bath-room she went inside, and soon emerged, bringing a rug, which she spread upon the floor of the gallery, and two huge hair pillows covered with crash,[6] which she placed against the front of the building.

---

[6] Heavy linen fabric. "Rug": blanket.

The two seated themselves there in the shade of the porch, side by side, with their backs against the pillows and their feet extended. Madame Ratignolle removed her veil, wiped her face with a rather delicate handkerchief, and fanned herself with the fan which she always carried suspended somewhere about her person by a long, narrow ribbon. Edna removed her collar and opened her dress at the throat. She took the fan from Madame Ratignolle and began to fan both herself and her companion. It was very warm, and for a while they did nothing but exchange remarks about the heat, the sun, the glare. But there was a breeze blowing, a choppy stiff wind that whipped the water into froth. It fluttered the skirts of the two women and kept for a while engaged in adjusting, readjusting, tucking in, securing hair-pins and hat-pins. A few persons were sporting some distance away in the water. The beach was very still of human sound at that hour. The lady in black was reading her morning devotions on the porch of a neighboring bath-house. Two young lovers were exchanging their hearts' yearnings beneath the children's tent, which they had found unoccupied.

Edna Pontellier, casting her eyes about, had finally kept them at rest upon the sea. The day was clear and carried the gaze out as far as the blue sky went; there were a few white clouds suspended idly over the horizon. A lateen[7] sail was visible in the direction of Cat Island, and others to the south seemed almost motionless in the far distance.

"Of whom—of what are you thinking?" asked Adèle of her companion, whose countenance she had been watching with a little amused attention, arrested by the absorbed expression which seemed to have seized and fixed every feature into a statuesque repose.

"Nothing," returned Mrs. Pontellier, with a start, adding at once: "How stupid! But it seems to me it is the reply we make instinctively to such a question. Let me see," she went on, throwing back her head and narrowing her fine eyes till they shone like two vivid points of light. "Let me see. I was really not conscious of thinking of anything; but perhaps I can retrace my thoughts."

"Oh! never mind!" laughed Madame Ratignolle. "I am not quite so exacting. I will let you off this time. It is really too hot to think, especially to think about thinking."

"But for the fun of it," persisted Edna. "First of all, the sight of the water stretching so far away, those motionless sails against the blue sky, made a delicious picture that I just wanted to sit and look at. The hot wind beating in my face made me think—without any connection that I can trace—of a summer day in Kentucky, of a meadow that seemed as big as the ocean to the very little girl walking through the grass, which was higher than her waist. She threw out her arms as if swimming when she walked, beating the tall grass as one strikes out in the water. Oh, I see the connection now!"

"Where were you going that day in Kentucky, walking through the grass?"

---

[7] Triangular.

"I don't remember now. I was just walking diagonally across a big field. My sun-bonnet obstructed the view. I could see only the stretch of green before me, and I felt as if I must walk on forever, without coming to the end of it. I don't remember whether I was frightened or pleased. I must have been entertained.

"Likely as not it was Sunday," she laughed; "and I was running away from prayers, from the Presbyterian service, read in a spirit of gloom by my father that chills me yet to think of."

"And have you been running away from prayers ever since, *ma chère?*" asked Madame Ratignolle, amused.

"No! oh, no!" Edna hastened to say. "I was a little unthinking child in those days, just following a misleading impulse without question. On the contrary, during one period of my life religion took a firm hold upon me; after I was twelve and until—until—why, I suppose until now, though I never thought much about it—just driven along by habit. But do you know," she broke off, turning her quick eyes upon Madame Ratignolle and leaning forward a little so as to bring her face quite close to that of her companion, "sometimes I feel this summer as if I were walking through the green meadow again; idly, aimlessly, unthinking and unguided."

Madame Ratignolle laid her hand over that of Mrs. Pontellier, which was near her. Seeing that the hand was not withdrawn, she clasped it firmly and warmly. She even stroked it a little, fondly, with the other hand, murmuring in an undertone, *"Pauvre chérie."* [8]

The action was at first a little confusing to Edna, but she soon lent herself readily to the Creole's gentle caress. She was not accustomed to an outward and spoken expression of affection, either in herself or in others. She and her younger sister, Janet, had quarreled a good deal through force of unfortunate habit. Her older sister, Margaret, was matronly and dignified, probably from having assumed matronly and house-wifely responsibilities too early in life, their mother having died when they were quite young. Margaret was not effusive; she was practical. Edna had had an occasional girl friend, but whether accidentally or not, they seemed to have been all of one type—the self-contained. She never realized that the reserve of her own character had much, perhaps everything, to do with this. Her most intimate friend at school had been one of rather exceptional intellectual gifts, who wrote fine-sounding essays which Edna admired and strove to imitate; and with her she talked and glowed over the English classics, and sometimes held religious and political controversies.

Edna often wondered at one propensity which sometimes had inwardly disturbed her without causing any outward show or manifestation on her part. At a very early age—perhaps it was when she traversed the ocean of waving grass—she remembered that she had been passionately enamored of a dignified and sad-eyed cavalry officer who visited her father in Kentucky. She could not

---

[8] Poor dear.

leave his presence when he was there, nor remove her eyes from his face which was something like Napoleon's, with a lock of black hair falling across the forehead. But the cavalry officer melted imperceptibly out of her existence.

At another time her affections were deeply engaged by a young gentleman who visited a lady on a neighboring plantation. It was after they went to Mississippi to live. The young man was engaged to be married to the young lady, and they sometimes called upon Margaret, driving over of afternoons in a buggy. Edna was a little miss, just merging into her teens; and the realization that she herself was nothing, nothing, nothing to the engaged young man was a bitter affliction to her. But he, too, went the way of dreams.

She was a grown young woman when she was overtaken by what she supposed to be the climax of her fate. It was when the face and figure of a great tragedian began to haunt her imagination and stir her senses. The persistence of the infatuation lent it an aspect of genuineness. The hopelessness of it colored it with the lofty tones of a great passion.

The picture of the tragedian stood enframed upon her desk. Any one may possess the portrait of a tragedian without exciting suspicion or comment. (This was a sinister reflection which she cherished.) In the presence of others she expressed admiration for his exalted gifts, as she handed the photograph around and dwelt upon the fidelity of the likeness. When alone she sometimes picked it up and kissed the cold glass passionately.

Her marriage to Léonce Pontellier was purely an accident, in this respect resembling many other marriages which masquerade as the decrees of Fate. It was in the midst of her secret great passion that she met him. He fell in love, as men are in the habit of doing, and pressed his suit with an earnestness and an ardor which left nothing to be desired. He pleased her; his absolute devotion flattered her. She fancied there was a sympathy of thought and taste between them, in which fancy she was mistaken. Add to this the violent opposition of her father and her sister Margaret to her marriage with a Catholic, and we need seek no further for the motives which led her to accept Monsieur Pontellier for her husband.

The acme of bliss, which would have been a marriage with the tragedian, was not for her in this world. As the devoted wife of a man who worshiped her, she felt she would take her place with a certain dignity in the world of reality, closing the portals forever behind her upon the realm of romance and dreams.

But it was not long before the tragedian had gone to join the cavalry officer and the engaged young man and a few others; and Edna found herself face to face with the realities. She grew fond of her husband, realizing with some unaccountable satisfaction that no trace of passion or excessive and fictitious warmth colored her affection, thereby threatening its dissolution.

She was fond of her children in an uneven, impulsive way. She would sometimes gather them passionately to her heart; she would sometimes forget them. The year before they had spent part of the summer with their grandmother

Pontellier in Iberville.[9] Feeling secure regarding their happiness and welfare, she did not miss them except with an occasional intense longing. Their absence was a sort of relief, though she did not admit this, even to herself. It seemed to free her of a responsibility which she had blindly assumed and for which Fate had not fitted her.

Edna did not reveal so much as all this to Madame Ratignolle that summer day when they sat with faces turned to the sea. But a good part of it escaped her. She had put her head down on Madame Ratignolle's shoulder. She was flushed and felt intoxicated with the sound of her own voice and the unaccustomed taste of candor. It muddled her like wine, or like a first breath of freedom.

There was the sound of approaching voices. It was Robert, surrounded by a troop of children, searching for them. The two little Pontelliers were with him, and he carried Madame Ratignolle's little girl in his arms. There were other children beside, and two nursemaids followed, looking disagreeable and resigned.

The women at once rose and began to shake out their draperies and relax their muscles. Mrs. Pontellier threw the cushions and rug into the bath-house. The children all scampered off to the awning, and they stood there in a line, gazing upon the intruding lovers, still exchanging their vows and sighs. The lovers got up, with only a silent protest, and walked slowly away somewhere else.

The children possessed themselves of the tent, and Mrs. Pontellier went over to join them.

Madame Ratignolle begged Robert to accompany her to the house; she complained of cramp in her limbs and stiffness of the joints. She leaned draggingly upon his arm as they walked.

VIII

"Do me a favor, Robert," spoke the pretty woman at his side, almost as soon as she and Robert had started on their slow, homeward way. She looked up in his face, leaning on his arm beneath the encircling shadow of the umbrella which he had lifted.

"Granted; as many as you like," he returned, glancing down into her eyes that were full of thoughtfulness and some speculation.

"I only ask for one; let Mrs. Pontellier alone."

"*Tiens!*" he exclaimed, with a sudden, boyish laugh. "*Voilà que Madame Ratignolle est jealouse!*"[1]

"Nonsense! I'm in earnest; I mean what I say. Let Mrs. Pontellier alone."

"Why?" he asked; himself growing serious at his companion's solicitation.

"She is not one of us; she is not like us. She might make the unfortunate blunder of taking you seriously."

His face flushed with annoyance, and taking off his soft hat he began to beat it impatiently against his leg as he walked. "Why shouldn't she take me seri-

[9] Rural parish (county) in Louisiana, west of Baton Rouge.
[1] So, Madame Ratignolle is jealous!

ously?" he demanded sharply. "Am I a comedian, a clown, a jack-in-the-box? Why shouldn't she? You Creoles! I have no patience with you! Am I always to be regarded as a feature of an amusing programme? I hope Mrs. Pontellier does take me seriously. I hope she has discernment enough to find in me something besides the *blagueur*.[2] If I thought there was any doubt—"

"Oh, enough, Robert!" she broke into his heated outburst. "You are not thinking of what you are saying. You speak with about as little reflection as we might expect from one of those children down there playing in the sand. If your attentions to any married women here were ever offered with any intention of being convincing, you would not be the gentleman we all know you to be, and you would be unfit to associate with the wives and daughters of the people who trust you."

Madame Ratignolle had spoken what she believed to be the law and the gospel. The young man shrugged his shoulders impatiently.

"Oh! well! That isn't it," slamming his hat down vehemently upon his head. "You ought to feel that such things are not flattering to say to a fellow."

"Should our whole intercourse consist of an exchange of compliments? *Ma foi!*[3]

"It isn't pleasant to have a woman tell you—" he went on, unheedingly, but breaking off suddenly: "Now if I were like Arobin—you remember Alcée Arobin and that story of the consul's wife at Biloxi?" And he related the story of Alcée Arobin and the consul's wife; and another about the tenor of the French Opera,[4] who received letters which should never have been written; and still other stories, grave and gay, till Mrs. Pontellier and her possible propensity for taking young men seriously was apparently forgotten.

Madame Ratignolle, when they had regained her cottage, went in to take the hour's rest which she considered helpful. Before leaving her, Robert begged her pardon for the impatience—he called it rudeness—with which he had received her well-meant caution.

"You made one mistake, Adèle," he said, with a light smile; "there is no earthly possibility of Mrs. Pontellier ever taking me seriously. You should have warned me against taking myself seriously. Your advice might then have carried some weight and given me subject for some reflection. *Au revoir.* But you look tired," he added, solicitously. "Would you like a cup of bouillon? Shall I stir you a toddy? Let me mix you a toddy with a drop of Angostura."[5]

She acceded to the suggestion of bouillon, which was grateful and acceptable. He went himself to the kitchen, which was a building apart from the cottages and lying to the rear of the house. And he himself brought her the golden-

[2] Joker, liar.

[3] For heaven's sake!

[4] In New Orleans; perhaps the most distinguished American opera company of the time. Biloxi is a coastal resort town near New Orleans.

[5] Aromatic bitters.

brown bouillon, in a dainty Sèvres[6] cup, with a flaky cracker or two on the saucer.

She thrust a bare, white arm from the curtain which shielded her open door, and received the cup from his hands. She told him he was a *bon garçon*,[7] and she meant it. Robert thanked her and turned away toward "the house."

The lovers were just entering the grounds of the *pension*. They were leaning toward each other as the water-oaks bent from the sea. There was not a particle of earth beneath their feet. Their heads might have been turned upside-down, so absolutely did they tread upon blue ether. The lady in black, creeping behind them, looked a trifle paler and more jaded than usual. There was no sign of Mrs. Pontellier and the children. Robert scanned the distance for any such apparition. They would doubtless remain away till the dinner hour. The young man ascended to his mother's room. It was situated at the top of the house, made up of odd angles and a queer, sloping ceiling. Two broad dormer windows looked out toward the Gulf, and as far across it as a man's eye might reach. The furnishings of the room were light, cool, and practical.

Madame Lebrun was busily engaged at the sewing-machine. A little black girl sat on the floor, and with her hands worked the treadle of the machine. The Creole woman does not take any chances which may be avoided of imperiling her health.

Robert went over and seated himself on the broad sill of one of the dormer windows. He took a book from his pocket and began energetically to read it, judging by the precision and frequency with which he turned the leaves. The sewing-machine made a resounding clatter in the room; it was of a ponderous, by-gone make. In the lulls, Robert and his mother exchanged bits of desultory conversation.

"Where is Mrs. Pontellier?"

"Down at the beach with the children."

"I promised to lend her the Goncourt.[8] Don't forget to take it down when you go; it's there on the bookshelf over the small table." Clatter, clatter, clatter, bang! for the next five or eight minutes.

"Where is Victor going with the rockaway?"

"The rockaway? Victor?"

"Yes, down there in front. He seems to be getting ready to drive away somewhere."

"Call him." Clatter, clatter!

Robert uttered a shrill, piercing whistle which might have been heard back at the wharf.

"He won't look up."

---

[6] Fine porcelain made in Sèvres, France.

[7] Both "nice fellow" and "good waiter."

[8] A French novel by Edmond de Goncourt (1822–1896).

Madame Lebrun flew to the window. She called "Victor!" She waved a handkerchief and called again. The young fellow below got into the vehicle and started the horse off at a gallop.

Madame Lebrun went back to the machine, crimson with annoyance. Victor was the younger son and brother—a *tête montée*,[9] with a temper which invited violence and a will which no ax could break.

"Whenever you say the word I'm ready to thrash any amount of reason into him that he's able to hold."

"If your father had only lived!" Clatter, clatter, clatter, clatter, bang! It was a fixed belief with Madame Lebrun that the conduct of the universe and all things pertaining thereto would have been manifestly of a more intelligent and higher order had not Monsieur Lebrun been removed to other spheres during the early years of their married life.

"What do you hear from Montel?" Montel was a middle-aged gentleman whose vain ambition and desire for the past twenty years had been to fill the void which Monsieur Lebrun's taking off had left in the Lebrun household. Clatter, clatter, bang, clatter!

"I have a letter somewhere," looking in the machine drawer and finding the letter in the bottom of the work-basket. "He says to tell you he will be in Vera Cruz[1] the beginning of next month"—clatter, clatter!—"and if you still have the intention of joining him"—bang! clatter, clatter, bang!

"Why didn't you tell me so before, mother? You know I wanted—" Clatter, clatter, clatter!

"Do you see Mrs. Pontellier starting back with the children? She will be in late to luncheon again. She never starts to get ready for luncheon till the last minute." Clatter, clatter! "Where are you going?"

"Where did you say the Goncourt was?"

IX

Every light in the hall was ablaze; every lamp turned as high as it could be without smoking the chimney or threatening explosion. The lamps were fixed at intervals against the wall, encircling the whole room. Some one had gathered orange and lemon branches and with these fashioned graceful festoons between. The dark green of the branches stood out and glistened against the white muslin curtains which draped the windows, and which puffed, floated, and flapped at the capricious will of a stiff breeze that swept up from the Gulf.

It was Saturday night a few weeks after the intimate conversation held between Robert and Madame Ratignolle on their way from the beach. An unusual number of husbands, fathers, and friends had come down to stay over Sunday; and they were being suitably entertained by their families, with the material

[9] Impulsive character.
[1] Mexican city on the Gulf of Mexico.

help of Madame Lebrun. The dining tables had all been removed to one end of the hall, and the chairs ranged about in rows and in clusters. Each little family group had had its say and exchanged its domestic gossip earlier in the evening. There was now an apparent disposition to relax; to widen the circle of confidences and give a more general tone to the conversation.

Many of the children had been permitted to sit up beyond their usual bedtime. A small band of them were lying on their stomachs on the floor looking at the colored sheets of the comic papers which Mr. Pontellier had brought down. The little Pontellier boys were permitting them to do so, and making their authority felt.

Music, dancing, and a recitation of two were the entertainments furnished, or rather, offered. But there was nothing systematic about the programme, no appearance of prearrangement nor even premeditation.

At an early hour in the evening the Farival twins were prevailed upon to play the piano. They were girls of fourteen, always clad in the Virgin's colors, blue and white, having been dedicated to the Blessed Virgin at their baptism. They played a duet from "Zampa," and at the earnest solicitation of every one present followed it with the overture to "The Poet and the Peasant."

"*Allez vous-en! Sapristi!*" shrieked the parrot outside the door. He was the only being present who possessed sufficient candor to admit that he was not listening to these gracious performances for the first time that summer. Old Monsieur Farival, grandfather of the twins, grew indignant over the interruption, and insisted upon having the bird removed and consigned to regions of darkness. Victor Lebrun objected; and his decrees were as immutable as those of Fate. The parrot fortunately offered no further interruption to the entertainment, the whole venom of his nature apparently having been cherished up and hurled against the twins in that one impetuous outburst.

Later a young brother and sister gave recitations, which every one present had heard many times at winter evening entertainments in the city.

A little girl performed a skirt dance in the center of the floor. The mother played her accompaniments and at the same time watched her daughter with greedy admiration and nervous apprehension. She need have had no apprehension. The child was mistress of the situation. She had been properly dressed for the occasion in black tulle and black silk tights. Her little neck and arms were bare, and her hair, artificially crimped, stood out like fluffy black plumes over her head. Her poses were full of grace, and her little black-shod toes twinkled as they shot out and upward with a rapidity and a suddenness which were bewildering.

But there was no reason why every one should not dance. Madame Ratignolle could not, so it was she who gaily consented to play for the others. She played very well, keeping excellent waltz time and infusing an expression into the strains which was indeed inspiring. She was keeping up her music on account of the children she said; because she and her husband both considered it a means of brightening the home and making it attractive.

Almost every one danced but the twins, who could not be induced to separate during the brief period when one or the other should be whirling around the room in the arms of a man. They might have danced together, but they did not think of it.

The children were sent to bed. Some went submissively; others with shrieks and protests as they were dragged away. They had been permitted to sit up till after the ice-cream, which naturally marked the limit of human indulgence.

The ice-cream was passed around with cake—gold and silver cake arranged on platters in alternate slices; it had been made and frozen during the afternoon back of the kitchen by two black women, under the supervision of Victor. It was pronounced a great success—excellent if it had only contained a little less vanilla or a little more sugar, if it had been frozen a degree harder, and if the salt might have been kept out of portions of it. Victor was proud of his achievement, and went about recommending it and urging every one to partake of it to excess.

After Mrs. Pontellier had danced twice with her husband, once with Robert, and once with Monsieur Ratignolle, who was thin and tall and swayed like a reed in the wind when he danced, she went out on the gallery and seated herself on the low window-sill, where she commanded a view of all that went on in the hall and could look out toward the Gulf. There was a soft effulgence in the east. The moon was coming up, and its mystic shimmer was casting a million lights across the distant, restless water.

"Would you like to hear Mademoiselle Reisz play?" asked Robert, coming out on the porch where she was. Of course Edna would like to hear Mademoiselle Reisz play; but she feared it would be useless to entreat her.

"I'll ask her," he said. "I'll tell her that you want to hear her. She likes you. She will come." He turned and hurried away to one of the far cottages, where Mademoiselle Reisz was shuffling away. She was dragging a chair in and out of her room, and at intervals objecting to the crying of a baby, which a nurse in the adjoining cottage was endeavoring to put to sleep. She was a disagreeable little woman, no longer young, who had quarreled with almost every one, owing to a temper which was self-assertive and a disposition to trample upon the rights of others. Robert prevailed upon her without any too great difficulty.

She entered the hall with him during a lull in the dance. She made an awkward, imperious little bow as she went in. She was a homely woman, with a small weazened face and body and eyes that glowed. She had absolutely no taste in dress, and wore a batch of rusty black lace with a bunch of artificial violets pinned to the side of her hair.

"Ask Mrs. Pontellier what she would like to hear me play," she requested of Robert. She sat perfectly still before the piano, not touching the keys, while Robert carried her message to Edna at the window. A general air of surprise and genuine satisfaction fell upon every one as they saw the pianist enter. There was a settling down, and a prevailing air of expectancy everywhere. Edna was a trifle embarrassed at being thus signaled out for the imperious little woman's favor.

She would not dare to choose, and begged that Mademoiselle Reisz would please herself in selections.

Edna was what she herself called very fond of music. Musical strains, well rendered, had a way of evoking pictures in her mind. She sometimes liked to sit in the room of mornings when Madame Ratignolle played or practiced. One piece which that lady played Edna had entitled "Solitude." It was a short, plaintive, minor strain. The name of the piece was something else, but she called it "Solitude." When she heard it there came before her imagination that figure of a man standing beside a desolate rock on the seashore. He was naked. His attitude was one of hopeless resignation as he looked toward a distant bird winging its flight away from him.

Another piece called to her mind a dainty young woman clad in an Empire gown, taking mincing dancing steps as she came down a long avenue between tall hedges. Again, another reminded her of children at play, and still another of nothing on earth but a demure lady stroking a cat.

The very first chords which Mademoiselle Reisz struck upon the piano sent a keen tremor down Mrs. Pontellier's spinal column. It was not the first time she had heard an artist at the piano. Perhaps it was the first time she was ready, perhaps the first time her being was tempered to take an impress of the abiding truth.

She waited for the material pictures which she thought would gather and blaze before her imagination. She waited in vain. She saw no pictures of solitude, of hope, of longing, or of despair. But the very passions themselves were aroused within her soul, swaying it, lashing it, as the waves daily beat upon her splendid body. She trembled, she was choking, and the tears blinded her.

Mademoiselle had finished. She arose, and bowing her stiff, lofty bow, she went away, stopping for neither thanks nor applause. As she passed along the gallery she patted Edna upon the shoulder.

"Well, how did you like my music?" she asked. The young woman was unable to answer; she pressed the hand of the pianist convulsively. Mademoiselle Reisz perceived her agitation and even her tears. She patted her again upon the shoulder as she said:

"You are the only one worth playing for. Those others? Bah!" and she went shuffling and sidling on down the gallery toward her room.

But she was mistaken about "those others." Her playing had aroused a fever of enthusiasm. "What passion!" "What an artist!" "I have always said no one could play Chopin like Mademoiselle Reisz!" "That last prelude! Bon Dieu![2] It shakes a man!"

It was growing late, and there was a general disposition to disband. But someone, perhaps it was Robert, thought of a bath at that mystic hour and under that mystic moon.

---

[2] "Good Lord!" Frédéric Chopin (1810–1849), Polish composer and piano virtuoso.

X

At all events Robert proposed it, and there was not a dissenting voice. There was not one but was ready to follow when he led the way. He did not lead the way, however, he directed the way; and he himself loitered behind with the lovers, who had betrayed a disposition to linger and hold themselves apart. He walked between then, whether with malicious or mischievous intent was not wholly clear, even to himself.

The Pontelliers and Ratignolles walked ahead; the women leaning upon the arms of their husbands. Edna could hear Robert's voice behind them, and could sometimes hear what he said. She wondered why he did not join them. It was unlike him not to. Of late he had sometimes held away from her for an entire day, redoubling his devotion upon the next and the next, as though to make up for hours that had been lost. She missed him the days when some pretext served to take him away from her, just as one misses the sun on a cloudy day without having thought much about the sun when it was shining.

The people walked in little groups toward the beach. They talked and laughed; some of them sang. There was a band playing down at Klein's hotel, and the strains reached them faintly, tempered by the distance. There were strange, rare odors abroad—a tangle of the sea smell and of weeds and damp, new-plowed earth, mingled with the heavy perfume of a field of white blossoms somewhere near. But the night sat light upon the sea and the land. There was no weight of darkness; there were no shadows. The white light of the moon had fallen upon the world like the mystery and the softness of sleep.

Most of them walked into the water as though into a native element. The sea was quiet now, and swelled lazily in broad billows that melted into one another and did not break except upon the beach in little foamy crests that coiled back like slow, white serpents.

Edna had attempted all summer to learn to swim. She had received instructions from both the men and women; in some instances from the children. Robert had pursued a system of lessons almost daily; and he was nearly at the point of discouragement in realizing the futility of his efforts. A certain ungovernable dread hung about her when in the water, unless there was a hand near by that might reach out and reassure her.

But that night she was like the little tottering, stumbling, clutching child, who of a sudden realizes its powers, and walks for the first time alone, boldly and with over-confidence. She could have shouted for joy. She did shout for joy, as with a sweeping stroke or two she lifted her body to the surface of the water.

A feeling of exultation overtook her, as if some power of significant import had been given her soul. She grew daring and reckless, overestimating her strength. She wanted to swim far out, where no woman had swum before.

Her unlooked-for achievement was the subject of wonder, applause, and admiration. Each one congratulated himself that his special teachings had accomplished this desired end.

"How easy it is!" she thought. "It is nothing," she said aloud: "why did I not discover before that it was nothing. Think of the time I have lost splashing about like a baby!" She would not join the groups in their sports and bouts, but intoxicated with her newly conquered power, she swam out alone.

She turned her face seaward to gather in an impression of space and solitude, which the vast expanse of water, meeting and melting with moonlit sky, conveyed to her excited fancy. As she swam she seemed to be reaching out for the unlimited in which to lose herself.

Once she turned and looked toward the shore, toward the people she had left there. She had not gone any great distance—that is, what would have been great distance for an experienced swimmer. But to her unaccustomed vision the stretch of water behind her assumed the aspect of a barrier which her unaided strength would never be able to overcome.

A quick vision of death smote her soul, and for a second of time appalled and enfeebled her senses. But by an effort she rallied her staggering faculties and managed to regain the land.

She made no mention of her encounter with death and her flash of terror, except to say to her husband, "I thought I should have perished out there alone."

"You were not so very far, my dear; I was watching you," he told her.

Edna went at once to the bath-house, and she had put on her dry clothes and was ready to return home before the others had left the water. She started to walk away alone. They all called to her and shouted to her. She waved a dissenting hand, and went on paying no further heed to their renewed cries which sought to detain her.

"Sometimes I am tempted to think that Mrs. Pontellier is capricious," said Madame Lebrun, who was amusing herself immensely and feared that Edna's abrupt departure might put an end to the pleasure.

"I know she is," assented Mr. Pontellier; "sometimes, not often."

Edna had not traversed a quarter of the distance on her way home before she was overtaken by Robert.

"Did you think I was afraid?" she asked him, without a shade of annoyance.

"No; I knew you weren't afraid."

"Then why did you come? Why didn't you stay out there with the others?"

"I never thought of it."

"Thought of what?"

"Of anything. What difference does it make?"

"I'm very tired," she uttered, complainingly.

"I know you are."

"You don't know anything about it. Why should you know? I never was so exhausted in my life. But it isn't unpleasant. A thousand emotions have swept through me to-night. I don't comprehend half of them. Don't mind what I'm saying; I am just thinking aloud. I wonder if I shall ever be stirred again as Mademoiselle Reisz's playing moved me to-night. I wonder if any night on earth will ever again be like this one. It is like a night in a dream. The people about me are like some uncanny, half-human beings. There must be spirits abroad to-night."

"There are," whispered Robert. "Didn't you know this was the twenty-eighth of August?"

"The twenty-eighth of August?"

"Yes. On the twenty-eighth of August, at the hour of midnight, and if the moon is shining—the moon must be shining—a spirit that has haunted these shores for ages rises up from the Gulf. With its own penetrating vision the spirit seeks some one mortal worthy to hold him company, worthy of being exalted for a few hours into realms of the semi-celestials. His search has always hitherto been fruitless, and he has sunk back, disheartened, into the sea. But tonight he found Mrs. Pontellier. Perhaps he will never wholly release her from the spell. Perhaps she will never again suffer a poor, unworthy earthling to walk in the shadow of her divine presence."

"Don't banter me," she said, wounded at what appeared to be his flippancy. He did not mind the entreaty, but the tone with its delicate note of pathos was like a reproach. He could not explain; he could not tell her that he had pene-trated her mood and understood. He said nothing except to offer her his arm, for, by her own admission, she was exhausted. She had been walking alone with her arms hanging limp, letting her white skirts trail along the dewy path. She took his arm, but she did not lean upon it. She let her hand lie listlessly, as though her thoughts were elsewhere—somewhere in advance of her body, and she was striving to overtake them.

Robert assisted her into the hammock which swung from the post before her door out to the trunk of a tree.

"Will you stay out here and wait for Mr. Pontellier?" he asked.

"I'll stay out here. Good-night."

"Shall I get you a pillow?"

"There's one here," she said, feeling about, for they were in the shadow.

"It must be soiled; the children have been tumbling it about."

"No matter." And having discovered the pillow, she adjusted it beneath her head. She extended herself in the hammock with a deep breath of relief. She was not a supercilious or an over-dainty woman. She was not much given to reclin-ing in the hammock, and when she did so it was with no cat-like suggestion of voluptuous ease, but with a beneficent repose which seemed to invade her whole body.

"Shall I stay with you till Mr. Pontellier comes?" asked Robert, seating him-self on the outer edge of one of the steps and taking hold of the hammock rope which was fastened to the post.

"If you wish. Don't swing the hammock. Will you get my white shawl which I left on the window-sill over at the house?"

"Are you chilly?"

"No; but I shall be presently."

"Presently?" he laughed. "Do you know what time it is? How long are you going to stay out here?"

"I don't know. Will you get the shawl?"

"Of course I will," he said, rising. He went over to the house, walking along the grass. She watched his figure pass in and out of the strips of moonlight. It was past midnight. It was very quiet.

When he returned with the shawl she took it and kept it in her hand. She did not put it around her.

"Did you say I should stay till Mr. Pontellier came back?"

"I said you might if you wished to."

He seated himself again and rolled a cigarette, which he smoked in silence. Neither did Mrs. Pontellier speak. No multitude of words could have been more significant than those moments of silence, or more pregnant with the first-felt throbbings of desire.

When the voices of the bathers were heard approaching, Robert said good-night. She did not answer him. He thought she was asleep. Again she watched his figure pass in and out of the strips of moonlight as he walked away.

XI

"What are you doing out here, Edna? I thought I should find you in bed," said her husband, when he discovered her lying there. He had walked up with Madame Lebrun and left her at the house. His wife did not reply.

"Are you asleep?" he asked, bending down close to look at her.

"No." Her eyes gleamed bright and intense, with no sleepy shadows, as they looked into his.

"Do you know it is past one o'clock? Come on," and he mounted the steps and went into their room.

"Edna!" called Mr. Pontellier from within, after a few moments had gone by.

"Don't wait for me," she answered. He thrust his head through the door.

"You will take cold out there," he said, irritably. "What folly is this? Why don't you come in?"

"It isn't cold; I have my shawl."

"The mosquitoes will devour you."

"There are no mosquitoes."

She heard him moving about the room; every sound indicating impatience and irritation. Another time she would have gone in at his request. She would, through habit, have yielded to his desire; not with any sense of submission or obedience to his compelling wishes, but unthinkingly, as we walk, move, sit, stand, go through the daily treadmill of the life which has been portioned out to us.

"Edna, dear, are you not coming in soon?" he asked again, this time fondly, with a note of entreaty.

"No; I am going to stay out here."

"This is more than folly," he blurted out. "I can't permit you to stay out there all night. You must come in the house instantly."

With a writhing motion she settled herself more securely in the hammock. She perceived that her will had blazed up, stubborn and resistant. She could not at that moment have done other than denied and resisted. She wondered if her husband had ever spoken to her like that before, and if she had submitted to his command. Of course she had; she remembered that she had. But she could not realize why or how she should have yielded, feeling as she then did.

"Léonce, go to bed," she said. "I mean to stay out here. I don't wish to go in, and I don't intend to. Don't speak to me like that again; I shall not answer you."

Mr. Pontellier had prepared for bed, but he slipped on an extra garment. He opened a bottle of wine, of which he kept a small and select supply in a buffet of his own. He drank a glass of wine and went out on the gallery and offered a glass to his wife. She did not wish any. He drew up the rocker, hoisted his slippered feet on the rail, and proceeded to smoke a cigar. He smoked two cigars; then he went inside and drank another glass of wine. Mrs. Pontellier again declined to accept a glass when it was offered to her. Mr. Pontellier once more seated himself with elevated feet, and after a reasonable interval of time smoked some more cigars.

Edna began to feel like one who awakens gradually out of a dream, a delicious, grotesque, impossible dream, to feel again the realities pressing into her soul. The physical need for sleep began to overtake her; the exuberance which had sustained and exalted her spirit left her helpless and yielding to the conditions which crowded her in.

The stillest hour of the night had come, the hour before dawn, when the world seems to hold its breath. The moon hung low, and had turned from silver to copper in the sleeping sky. The old owl no longer hooted, and the water-oaks had ceased to moan as they bent their heads.

Edna arose, cramped from lying so long and still in the hammock. She tottered up the steps, clutching feebly at the post before passing into the house.

"Are you coming in, Léonce?" she asked, turning her face toward her husband.

"Yes, dear," he answered, with a glance following a misty puff of smoke. "Just as soon as I have finished my cigar."

XII

She slept but a few hours. They were troubled and feverish hours, disturbed with dreams that were intangible, that eluded her, leaving only an impression upon her half-awakened senses of something unattainable. She was up and dressed in the cool of the early morning. The air was invigorating and steadied somewhat her faculties. However, she was not seeking refreshment or help from any source either external or from within. She was blindly following whatever impulse moved her, as if she had placed herself in alien hands for direction, and freed her soul of responsibility.

Most of the people at that early hour were still in bed and asleep. A few, who intended to go over to the *Chênière* for mass, were moving about. The lovers, who had laid their plans the night before, were already strolling toward the wharf. The lady in black with her Sunday prayer book, velvet and gold-clasped, and her Sunday silver beads, was following them at no great distance. Old Monsieur Farival was up, and was more than half inclined to do anything that suggested itself. He put on his big straw hat, and taking his umbrella from the stand in the hall, followed the lady in black, never overtaking her.

The little negro girl who worked Madame Lebrun's sewing-machine was sweeping the galleries with long, absent-minded strokes of the broom. Edna sent her up into the house to awaken Robert.

"Tell him I am going to the Chênière. The boat is ready, tell him to hurry."

He had soon joined her. She had never sent for him before. She had never asked for him. She had never seemed to want him before. She did not appear conscious that she had done anything unusual in commanding his presence. He was apparently equally unconscious of anything extraordinary in the situation. But his face was suffused with a quiet glow when he met her.

They went together back to the kitchen to drink coffee. There was no time to wait for any nicety of service. They stood outside the window and the cook passed them their coffee and a roll, which they drank and ate from the window-sill. Edna said it tasted good. She had not thought of coffee nor of anything. He told her he had often noticed that she lacked forethought.

"Wasn't it enough to think of going to the Chênière and waking you up?" she laughed. "Do I have to think of everything? — as Léonce says when he's in a bad humor. I don't blame him; he'd never be in a bad humor if it weren't for me."

They took a short cut across the sands. At a distance they could see the curious procession moving toward the wharf — the lovers, shoulder to shoulder, creeping; the lady in black, gaining steadily upon them; old Monsieur Farival, losing ground inch by inch, and a young barefooted Spanish girl, with a red kerchief on her head and a basket on her arm, bringing up the rear.

Robert knew the girl, and he talked to her a little in the boat. No one present understood what they said. Her name was Mariequita. She had a round, sly, piquant face and pretty black eyes. Her hands were small, and she kept them folded over the handle of her basket. Her feet were broad and coarse. She did not strive to hide them. Edna looked at her feet, and noticed the sand and slime between her brown toes.

Beaudelet grumbled because Mariequita was there, taking up so much room. In reality he was annoyed at having old Monsieur Farival, who considered himself the better sailor of the two. But he would not quarrel with so old a man as Monsieur Farival, so he quarreled with Mariequita. The girl was deprecatory at one moment, appealing to Robert. She was saucy the next, moving her head up and down, making "eyes" at Robert and making "mouths" at Beaudelet.

The lovers were all alone. They saw nothing, they heard nothing. The lady in black was counting her beads[3] for the third time. Old Monsieur Farival talked

---

[3] I.e., praying.

incessantly of what he knew about handling a boat, and of what Beaudelet did not know on the same subject.

Edna liked it all. She looked Mariequita up and down, from her ugly brown toes to her pretty black eyes, and back again.

"Why does she look at me like that?" inquired the girl of Robert.

"Maybe she thinks you are pretty. Shall I ask her?"

"No. Is she your sweetheart?"

"She's a married lady, and has two children."

"Oh! well! Francisco ran away with Sylvano's wife, who had four children. They took all his money and one of the children and stole his boat."

"Shut up!"

"Does she understand?"

"Oh, hush!"

"Are those two married over there—leaning on each other?"

"Of course not," laughed Robert.

"Of course not," echoed Mariequita, with a serious, confirmatory bob of the head.

The sun was high up and beginning to bite. The swift breeze seemed to Edna to bury the sting of it into the pores of her face and hands. Robert held his umbrella over her.

As they went cutting sidewise through the water, the sails bellied taut, with the wind filling and overflowing them. Old Monsieur Farival laughed sardonically at something as he looked at the sails, and Beaudelet swore at the old man under his breath.

Sailing across the bay to the *Chênière Caminada,* Edna felt as if she were being borne away from some anchorage which had held her fast, whose chains had been loosening—had snapped the night before when the mystic spirit was abroad, leaving her free to drift whithersoever she chose to set her sails. Robert spoke to her incessantly; he no longer noticed Mariequita. The girl had shrimps in her bamboo basket. They were covered with Spanish moss. She beat the moss impatiently, and muttered to herself sullenly.

"Let us go to Grande Terre[4] to-morrow?" said Robert in a low voice.

"What shall we do there?"

"Climb up the hill to the old fort and look at the little wriggling gold snakes, and watch the lizards sun themselves."

She gazed away toward Grande Terre and thought she would like to be alone there with Robert, in the sun, listening to the ocean's roar and watching the slimy lizards writhe in and out among the ruins of the old fort.

"And the next day or the next we can sail to the Bayou Brulow,"[5] he went on.

"What shall we do there?"

[4] An island near Grande Isle.

[5] A nearby village built on stilts or platforms in a marshy area *(bayou).*

"Anything—cast bait for fish."

"No; we'll go back to Grande Terre. Let the fish alone."

"We'll go wherever you like," he said. "I'll have Tonie come over and help me patch and trim my boat. We shall not need Beaudelet nor any one. Are you afraid of the pirogue?"[6]

"Oh, no."

"Then I'll take you some night in the pirogue when the moon shines. Maybe your Gulf spirit will whisper to you in which of these islands the treasures are hidden—direct you to the very spot, perhaps."

"And in a day we should be rich!" she laughed. "I'd give it all to you, the pirate gold and every bit of treasure we could dig up. I think you would know how to spend it. Pirate gold isn't a thing to be hoarded or utilized. It is something to squander and throw to the four winds, for the fun of seeing the golden specks fly."

"We'd share it, and scatter it together," he said. His face flushed.

They all went together up to the quaint little Gothic church of Our Lady of Lourdes, gleaming all brown and yellow with paint in the sun's glare.

Only Beaudelet remained behind, tinkering at his boat, and Mariequita walked away with her basket of shrimps, casting a look of childish ill-humor and reproach at Robert from the corner of her eye.

XIII

A feeling of oppression and drowsiness overcame Edna during the service. Her head began to ache, and the lights on the altar swayed before her eyes. Another time she might have made an effort to regain her composure; but her one thought was to quit the stifling atmosphere of the church and reach the open air. She arose, climbing over Robert's feet with a muttered apology. Old Monsieur Farival, flurried, curious, stood up, but upon seeing that Robert had followed Mrs. Pontellier, he sank back into his seat. He whispered an anxious inquiry of the lady in black, who did not notice him or reply, but kept her eyes fastened upon the pages of her velvet prayer-book.

"I felt giddy and almost overcome," Edna said, lifting her hands instinctively to her head and pushing her straw hat up from her forehead. "I couldn't have stayed through the service." They were outside in the shadow of the church. Robert was full of solicitude.

"It was folly to have thought of going in the first place, let alone staying. Come over the Madame Antoine's; you can rest there." He took her arm and led her away, looking anxiously and continuously down into her face.

How still it was, with only the voice of the sea whispering through the reeds that grew in the salt-water pools! The long line of little gray, weather-beaten houses nestled peacefully among the orange trees. It must always have been

---

[6] Canoe.

God's day on that low, drowsy island, Edna thought. They stopped, leaning over a jagged fence made of sea-drift, to ask for water. A youth, a mild-faced Acadian,[7] was drawing water from the cistern, which was nothing more than a rusty buoy, with an opening on one side, sunk in the ground. The water which the youth handed to them in a tin pail was not cold to taste, but it was cool to her heated face, and it greatly revived and refreshed her.

Madame Antoine's cot[8] was at the far end of the village. She welcomed them with all the native hospitality, as she would have opened her door to let the sunlight in. She was fat, and walked heavily and clumsily across the floor. She could speak no English, but when Robert made her understand that the lady who accompanied him was ill and desired to rest, she was all eagerness to make Edna feel at home and to dispose of her comfortably.

The whole place was immaculately clean, and the big, four-posted bed, snow-white, invited one to repose. It stood in a small side room which looked out across a narrow grass plot toward the shed, where there was a disabled boat lying keel upward.

Madame Antoine had not gone to mass. Her son Tonie had, but she supposed he would soon be back, and she invited Robert to be seated and wait for him. But he went and sat outside the door and smoked. Madame Antoine busied herself in the large front room preparing dinner. She was boiling mullets[9] over a few red coals in the huge fireplace.

Edna, left alone in the little side room, loosened her clothes, removing the greater part of them. She bathed her face, her neck and arms in the basin that stood between the windows. She took off her shoes and stockings and stretched herself in the very center of the high, white bed. How luxurious it felt to rest thus in a strange, quaint bed, with its sweet country odor of laurel lingering about the sheets and mattress! She stretched her strong limbs that ached a little. She ran her fingers through her loosened hair for a while. She looked at her round arms as she held them straight up and rubbed them one after the other, observing closely, as if it were something she saw for the first time, the fine, firm quality and texture of her flesh. She clasped her hands easily above her head, and it was thus she fell asleep.

She slept lightly at first, half awake and drowsily attentive to the things about her. She could hear Madame Antoine's heavy, scraping tread as she walked back and forth on the sanded floor. Some chickens were clucking outside the windows, scratching for bits of gravel in the grass. Later she half heard the voices of Robert and Tonie talking under the shed. She did not stir. Even her eyelids rested numb and heavily over her sleepy eyes. The voices went on — Tonie's slow, Acadian drawl, Robert's quick, soft, smooth French. She under-

---

[7] A descendant of French-Canadians expelled from Nova Scotia in 1755.

[8] Cottage.

[9] Small fish.

stood French imperfectly unless directly addressed, and the voices were only part of the other drowsy, muffled sounds lulling her.

When Edna awoke it was with the conviction that she had slept long and soundly. The voices were hushed under the shed. Madame Antoine's step was no longer to be heard in the adjoining room. Even the chickens had gone elsewhere to scratch and cluck. The mosquito bar[1] was drawn over her; the old woman had come in while she slept and let down the bar. Edna arose quietly from the bed, and looking between the curtains of the window, she saw by the slanting rays of the sun that the afternoon was far advanced. Robert was out there under the shed, reclining in the shade against the sloping keel of the overturned boat. He was reading from a book. Tonie was no longer with him. She wondered what had become of the rest of the party. She peeped out at him two or three times as she stood washing herself in the little basin between the windows.

Madame Antoine had laid some coarse, clean towels upon a chair, and had placed a box of *poudre de riz*[2] within easy reach. Edna dabbed the powder upon her nose and cheeks as she looked at herself closely in the little distorted mirror which hung on the wall above the basin. Her eyes were bright and wide awake and her face glowed.

When she had completed her toilet she walked into the adjoining room. She was very hungry. No one was there. But there was a cloth spread upon the table that stood against the wall, and a cover was laid for one, with a crusty brown loaf and a bottle of wine beside the plate. Edna bit a piece from the brown loaf, tearing it with her strong, white teeth. She poured some of the wine into the glass and drank it down. Then she went softly out of doors, and plucking an orange from the low-hanging bough of a tree, threw it at Robert, who did not know she was awake and up.

And illumination broke over his whole face when he saw her and joined her under the orange tree.

"How many years have I slept?" she inquired. "The whole island seems changed. A new race of beings must have sprung up, leaving only you and me as past relics. How many ages ago did Madame Antoine and Tonie die? and when did our people from Grand Isle disappear from the earth?"

He familiarly adjusted a ruffle upon her shoulder.

"You have slept precisely one hundred years. I was left here to guard your slumbers; and for one hundred years I have been out under the shed reading a book. The only evil I couldn't prevent was to keep a broiled fowl from drying up."

"If it had turned to stone, still will I eat it," said Edna, moving with him into the house. "But really, what has become of Monsieur Farival and the others?"

"Gone hours ago. When they found out you were sleeping they thought it best not to awake you. Anyway, I wouldn't have let them. What was I here for?"

[1] Bar attached to the bedframe holding mosquito netting.
[2] Rice powder or talcum powder.

"I wonder if Lèonce will be uneasy!" she speculated, as she seated herself at table.

"Of course not; he knows you are with me," Robert replied, as he busied himself among sundry pans and covered dishes which had been left standing on the hearth.

"Where are Madame Antoine and her son?" asked Edna.

"Gone to Vespers,[3] and to visit some friends, I believe. I am to take you back in Tonie's boat whenever you are ready to go."

He stirred the smoldering ashes till the broiled fowl began to sizzle afresh. He served her with no mean repast, dripping the coffee anew and sharing it with her. Madame Antoine had cooked little else than the mullets, but while Edna slept Robert had foraged the island. He was childishly gratified to discover her appetite, and to see the relish with which she ate the food which he had procured for her.

"Shall we go right away?" she asked, after draining her glass and brushing together the crumbs of the crusty loaf.

"The sun isn't as low as it will be in two hours," he answered.

"The sun will be gone in two hours."

"Well, let it go; who cares!"

They waited a good while under the orange trees, till Madame Antoine came back, panting, waddling, with a thousand apologies to explain her absence. Tonie did not dare to return. He was shy, and would not willingly face any woman except his mother.

It was very pleasant to stay there under the orange trees, while the sun dipped lower and lower, turning the western sky to flaming copper and gold. The shadows lengthened and crept out like stealthy, grotesque monsters across the grass.

Edna and Robert both sat upon the ground — that is, he lay upon the ground beside her, occasionally picking at the hem of her muslin gown.

Madame Antoine seated her fat body, broad and squat, upon a bench beside the door. She had been talking all the afternoon, and had wound herself up to the story-telling pitch.

And what stories she told them! But twice in her life she had left the Chênière Caminada, and then for the briefest span. All her years she had squatted and waddled there upon the island, gathering legends of the Baratarians[4] and the sea. The night came on, with the moon to lighten it. Edna could hear the whispering voices of dead men and the click of muffled gold.

When she and Robert stepped into Tonie's boat, with the red lateen sail, misty spirit forms were prowling in the shadows and among the reeds, and upon the water were phantom ships, speeding to cover.

[3] Evening church service.
[4] Pirates who plundered in the area of Barataria Bay.

XIV

The youngest boy, Étienne, had been very naughty, Madame Ratignolle said, as she delivered him into the hands of his mother. He had been unwilling to go to bed and had made a scene; where upon she had taken charge of him and pacified him as well as she could. Raoul had been in bed and asleep for two hours.

The youngster was in his long white nightgown, that kept tripping him up as Madame Ratignolle led him along by the hand. With the other chubby fist he rubbed his eyes, which were heavy with sleep and ill humor. Edna took him in her arms, and seating herself in the rocker, began to coddle and caress him, calling him all manner of tender names, soothing him to sleep.

It was not more than nine o'clock. No one had yet gone to bed but the children.

Léonce had been very uneasy at first, Madame Ratignolle said, and had wanted to start at once for the *Chênière*. But Monsieur Farival had assured him that his wife was only overcome with sleep and fatigue, that Tonie would bring her safely back later in the day; and he had thus been dissuaded from crossing the bay. He had gone over to Klein's, looking up some cotton broker whom he wished to see in regard to securities, exchanges, stocks, bonds, or something of the sort, Madame Ratignolle did not remember what. He said he would not remain away late. She herself was suffering from heat and oppression, she said. She carried a bottle of salts and a large fan. She would not consent to remain with Edna, for Monsieur Ratignolle was alone, and he detested above all things to be left alone.

When Étienne had fallen asleep Edna bore him into the back room, and Robert went and lifted the mosquito bar that she might lay the child comfortably in his bed. The quadroon had vanished. When they emerged from the cottage Robert bade Edna good-night. "Do you know we have been together the whole livelong day, Robert—since early this morning?" she said at parting.

"All but the hundred years when you were sleeping. Good-night."

He pressed her hand and went away in the direction of the beach. He did not join any of the others, but walked alone toward the Gulf.

Edna stayed outside, awaiting her husband's return. She had no desire to sleep or to retire; nor did she feel like going over to sit with the Ratignolles, or to join Madame Lebrun and a group whose animated voices reached her as they sat in conversation before the house. She let her mind wander back over her stay at Grand Isle; and she tried to discover wherein this summer had been different from any and every other summer of her life. She could only realize that she herself—her present self—was in some way different from the other self. That she was seeing with different eyes and making the acquaintance of new conditions in herself that colored and changed her environment, she did not yet suspect.

She wondered why Robert had gone away and left her. It did not occur to her to think he might have grown tired of being with her the livelong day. She was not tired, and she felt that he was not. She regretted that he had gone. It was so much more natural to have him stay, when he was not absolutely required to leave her.

As Edna waited for her husband she sang low a little song that Robert had sung as they crossed the bay. It began with "Ah! *Si tu savais,*" [5] and every verse ended with "*si tu savais.*"

Robert's voice was not pretentious. It was musical and true. The voice, the notes, the whole refrain haunted her memory.

XV

When Edna entered the dining-room one evening a little late, as was her habit, an unusually animated conversation seemed to be going on. Several persons were talking at once, and Victor's voice was predominating, even over that of his mother. Edna had returned late from her bath, had dressed in some haste, and her face was flushed. Her head, set off by the dainty white gown, suggested a rich, rare blossom. She took her seat at table between old Monsieur Farival and Madame Ratignolle.

As she seated herself and was about to begin to eat her soup, which had been served when she entered the room, several persons informed her simultaneously that Robert was going to Mexico. She laid her spoon down and looked about her bewildered. He had been with her, reading to her all the morning, and had never even mentioned such a place as Mexico. She had not seen him during the afternoon; she had heard some one say he was at the house, upstairs with his mother. This she had thought nothing of, though she was surprised when he did not join her later in the afternoon, when she went down to the beach.

She looked across at him, where he sat beside Madame Lebrun, who presided. Edna's face was a blank picture of bewilderment, which she never thought of disguising. He lifted his eyebrows with the pretext of a smile as he returned her glance. He looked embarrassed and uneasy.

"When is he going?" she asked of everybody in general, as if Robert were not there to answer for himself.

"To-night!" "This very evening!" "Did you ever!" "What possesses him!" some of the replies she gathered, uttered simultaneously in French and English.

"Impossible!" she exclaimed. "How can a person start off from Grand Isle to Mexico at a moment' notice, as if he were going over to Klein's or to the wharf or down to the beach?"

"I said all along I was going to Mexico; I've been saying so for years!" cried Robert, in an excited and irritable tone, with the air of a man defending himself against a swarm of stinging insects.

Madame Lebrun knocked on the table with her knife handle.

[5] "Couldst Thou but Know," a song by Michael William Balfe (1808–1870).

"Please let Robert explain why he is going, and why he is going to-night," she called out. "Really, this table is getting to be more and more like Bedlam[6] every day, with everybody talking at once. Sometimes — I hope God will forgive me — but positively, sometimes I wish Victor would lose the power of speech."

Victor laughed sardonically as he thanked his mother for her holy wish, of which he failed to see the benefit to anybody, except that it might afford her a more ample opportunity and license to talk herself.

Monsieur Farival thought that Victor should have been taken out in mid-ocean in his earliest youth and drowned. Victor thought there would be more logic in thus disposing of old people with an established claim for making themselves universally obnoxious. Madame Lebrun grew a trifle hysterical; Robert called his brother some sharp, hard names.

"There's nothing much to explain, mother," he said; though he explained, nevertheless — looking chiefly at Edna — that he could only meet the gentleman whom he intended to join at Vera Cruz by taking such and such a steamer, which left New Orleans on such a day; that Beaudelet was going out with his lugger[7]-load of vegetables that night, which gave him an opportunity of reaching the city and making his vessel in time.

"But when did you make up your mind to all this?" demanded Monsieur Farival.

"This afternoon," returned Robert, with a shade of annoyance.

"At what time this afternoon?" persisted the old gentleman, with nagging determination, as if he were cross-questioning a criminal in a court of justice.

"At four o'clock this afternoon. Monsieur Farival," Robert replied, in a high voice and with a lofty air, which reminded Edna of some gentleman on the stage.

She had forced herself to eat most of her soup, and now she was picking the flaky bits of a *court bouillon*[8] with her fork.

The lovers were profiting by the general conversation on Mexico to speak in whispers of matters which they rightly considered were interesting to no one but themselves. The lady in black had once received a pair of prayer-beads of curious workmanship from Mexico, with very special indulgence[9] attached to them, but she had never been able to ascertain whether the indulgence extended outside the Mexican border. Father Fochel of the Cathedral had attempted to explain it; but he had not done so to her satisfaction. And she begged that Robert would interest himself, and discover, if possible, whether she was entitled to the indulgence accompanying the remarkably curious Mexican prayer-beads.

Madame Ratignolle hoped that Robert would exercise extreme caution in dealing with the Mexicans, who, she considered, were a treacherous people, un-

[6] Famous lunatic asylum in London, hence any madhouse.

[7] A small boat.

[8] Broth in which fish is poached.

[9] According to a Roman Catholic belief, some religious articles, if specifically blessed, could remit part of the punishment for sins after death.

scrupulous and revengeful. She trusted she did them no injustice in thus condemning them as a race. She had known personally but one Mexican, who made
and sold excellent tamales, and whom she would have trusted implicitly, so soft-
spoken was he. One day he was arrested for stabbing his wife. She never knew
whether he had been hanged or not.

Victor had grown hilarious, and was attempting to tell an anecdote about a
Mexican girl who served chocolate one winter in a restaurant in Dauphine
Street. No one would listen to him but old Monsieur Farival, who went into
convulsions over the droll story.

Edna wondered if they had all gone mad, to be talking and clamoring at
that rate. She herself could think of nothing to say about Mexico or the Mexicans.

"At what time do you leave?" she asked Robert.

"At ten," he told her. "Beaudelet wants to wait for the moon."

"Are you all ready to go?"

"Quite ready. I shall only take a handbag, and shall pack my trunk in the
city."

He turned to answer some question put to him by his mother and Edna,
having finished her black coffee, left the table.

She went directly to her room. The little cottage was close and stuffy after
leaving the outer air. But she did not mind; there appeared to be a hundred different things demanding her attention indoors. She began to set the toilet-stand
to rights, grumbling at the negligence of the quadroon, who was in the adjoining room putting the children to bed. She gathered together stray garments that
were hanging on the backs of chairs, and put each where it belonged in closet or
bureau drawer. She changed her gown for a more comfortable and commodious
wrapper. She rearranged her hair, combing and brushing it with unusual energy.
Then she went in and assisted the quadroon in getting the boys to bed.

They were very playful and inclined to talk—to do anything but lie quiet
and go to sleep. Edna sent the quadroon away to her supper and told her she
need not return. Then she sat and told the children a story. Instead of soothing
it excited them, and added to their wakefulness. She left them in heated argument, speculating about the conclusion of the tale which their mother promised
to finish the following night.

The little black girl came in to say that Madame Lebrun would like to have
Mrs. Pontellier go and sit with them over at the house till Mr. Robert went away.
Edna returned answer that she had already undressed, that she did not feel quite
well, but perhaps she would go over to the house later. She started to dress
again, and got as far advanced as to remove her *peignoir*. But changing her mind
once more she resumed the *peignoir,* and went outside and sat down before her
door. She was overheated and irritable, and fanned herself energetically for a
while. Madame Ratignolle came down to discover what was the matter.

"All that noise and confusion at the table must have upset me," replied
Edna, "and moreover, I hate shocks and surprises. The idea of Robert starting

off in such a ridiculously sudden and dramatic way! As if it were a matter of life and death! Never saying a word about it all morning when he was with me."

"Yes," agreed Madame Ratignolle. "I think it was showing us all—you especially—very little consideration. It wouldn't have surprised me in any of the others; those Lebruns are all given to heroics. But I must say I should never have expected such a thing from Robert. Are you not coming down? Come on, dear; it doesn't look friendly."

"No," said Edna, a little sullenly. "I can't go to the trouble of dressing again; I don't feel like it."

"You needn't dress; you look all right; fasten a belt around your waist. Just look at me!"

"No," persisted Edna; "but you go on. Madame Lebrun might be offended if we both stayed away."

Madame Ratignolle kissed Edna good-night, and went away, being in truth rather desirous of joining in the general and animated conversation which was still in progress concerning Mexico and the Mexicans.

Somewhat later Robert came up, carrying his hand-bag.

"Aren't you feeling well?" he asked.

"Oh, well enough. Are you going right away?"

He lit a match and looked at his watch. "In twenty minutes," he said. The sudden and brief flare of the match emphasized the darkness for a while. He sat down upon a stool which the children had left out on the porch.

"Get a chair," said Edna.

"This will do," he replied. He put on his soft hat and nervously took it off again, and wiping his face with his handkerchief, complained of the heat.

"Take the fan," said Edna, offering it to him.

"Oh, no! Thank you. It does no good; you have to stop fanning some time, and feel all the more uncomfortable afterward."

"That's one of the ridiculous things which men always say. I have never known one to speak otherwise of fanning. How long will you be gone?"

"Forever, perhaps. I don't know. It depends upon a good many things."

"Well, in case it shouldn't be forever, how long will it be?"

"I don't know."

"This seems to be perfectly preposterous and uncalled for. I don't like it. I don't understand your motive for silence and mystery, never saying a word to me about it this morning." He remained silent, not offering to defend himself. He only said, after a moment:

"Don't part from me in an ill-humor. I never knew you to be out of patience with me before."

"I don't want to part in any ill-humor," said she. "But can't you understand? I've grown used to seeing you, to having you with me all the time, and your action seems unfriendly, even unkind. You don't even offer an excuse for it. Why, I was planning to be together, thinking of how pleasant it would be to see you in the city next winter."

"So was I," he blurted. "Perhaps that's the— " He stood up suddenly and held out his hand. "Good-by, my dear Mrs. Pontellier; good-by. You won't— I hope you won't completely forget me." She clung to his hand, striving to detain him.

"Write to me when you get there, won't you, Robert?" she entreated.

"I will, thank you. Good-by."

How unlike Robert! The merest acquaintance would have said something more emphatic than "I will, thank you; good-by," to such a request.

He had evidently already taken leave of the people over at the house, for he descended the steps and went to join Beaudelet, who was out there with an oar across his shoulder waiting for Robert. They walked away in the darkness. She could only hear Beaudelet's voice; Robert had apparently not even spoken a word of greeting to his companion.

Edna bit her handkerchief convulsively, striving to hold back and to hide, even from herself as she would have hidden from another the emotion which was troubling—tearing—her. Her eyes were brimming with tears.

For the first time she recognized anew the symptoms of infatuation which she felt incipiently as a child, as a girl in her earliest teens, and later as a young woman. The recognition did not lessen the reality, the poignancy of the revelation by any suggestion or promise of instability. The past was nothing to her; offered no lesson which she was willing to heed. The future was a mystery which she never attempted to penetrate. The present alone was significant; was hers, to torture her as it was doing then with the biting conviction that she had lost that which she had held, that she had been denied that which her impassioned, newly awakened being demanded.

XVI

"Do you miss your friend greatly?" asked Mademoiselle Reisz one morning as she came creeping up behind Edna, who had just left her cottage on her way to the beach. She spent much of her time in the water since she had acquired finally the art of swimming. As their stay at Grand Isle drew near its close, she felt that she could not give too much time to a diversion which afforded her the only real pleasurable moments that she knew. When Mademoiselle Reisz came and touched her upon the shoulder and spoke to her, the woman seemed to echo the thought which was ever in Edna's mind; or, better, the feeling which constantly possessed her.

Robert's going had some way taken the brightness, the color, the meaning out of everything. The conditions of her life were in no way changed, but her whole existence was dulled, like a faded garment which seems to be no longer worth wearing. She sought him everywhere—in others whom she induced to talk about him. She went up in the mornings to Madame Lebrun's room, braving the clatter of the old sewing-machine. She sat there and chatted at intervals as Robert had done. She gazed around the room at the pictures and photographs hanging upon the wall, and discovered in some corner an old family album, which she examined with the keenest interest, appealing to Madame Lebrun for enlightenment concerning the many figures and faces which she discovered between its pages.

There was a picture of Madame Lebrun with Robert as a baby, seated in her lap, a round-faced infant with a fist in his mouth. The eyes alone in the baby suggested the man. And that was he also in kilts, at the age of five, wearing long curls and holding a whip in his hand. It made Edna laugh, and she laughed, too, at the portrait in his first long trousers; while another interested her, taken when he left for college, looking thin, long-faced, with eyes full of fire, ambition and great intentions. But there was no recent picture, none which suggested the Robert who had gone away five days ago, leaving a void and wilderness behind him.

"Oh, Robert stopped having his pictures taken when he had to pay for them himself! He found wiser use for his money, he says," explained Madame Lebrun. She had a letter from him, written before he left New Orleans. Edna wished to see the letter, and Madame Lebrun told her to look for it either on the table or the dresser, or perhaps it was on the mantelpiece.

The letter was on the bookshelf. It possessed the greatest interest and attraction for Edna; the envelope, its size and shape, the postmark, the handwriting. She examined every detail of the outside before opening it. There were only a few lines, setting forth that he would leave the city that afternoon, that he had packed his trunk in good shape, that he was well, and sent her his love and begged to be affectionately remembered to all. There was no special message to Edna except a postscript saying that if Mrs. Pontellier desired to finish the book which he had been reading to her, his mother would find it in his room, among other books there on the table. Edna experienced a pang of jealousy because he had written to his mother rather than to her.

Every one seemed to take for granted that she missed him. Even her husband, when he came down the Saturday following Robert's departure, expressed regret that he had gone.

"How do you get on without him, Edna?" he asked.

"It's very dull without him," she admitted. Mr. Pontellier had seen Robert in the city, and Edna asked him a dozen questions or more. Where had they met? On Carondelet Street, in the morning. They had gone "in" and had a drink and a cigar together. What had they talked about? Chiefly about his prospects in Mexico, which Mr. Pontellier thought were promising. How did he look? How did he seem—grave, or gay, or how? Quite cheerful, and wholly taken up with the idea of his trip, which Mr. Pontellier found altogether natural in a young fellow about to seek fortune and adventure in a strange, queer country.

Edna tapped her foot impatiently, and wondered why the children persisted in playing in the sun when they might be under the trees. She went down and led them out of the sun, scolding the quadroon for not being more attentive.

It did not strike her as in the least grotesque that she should be making of Robert the object of conversation and leading her husband to speak of him. The sentiment which she entertained for Robert in no way resembled that which she felt for her husband, or had ever felt, or ever expected to feel. She had all her life long been accustomed to harbor thoughts and emotions which never voiced themselves. They had never taken the form of struggles. They belonged to her and were her own, and she entertained the conviction that she had a right to them and that they concerned no one but herself. Edna had once told Madame Ratignolle that she would never sacrifice herself for her children, or for any one. Then had followed a rather heated argument; the two women did not appear to understand each other or to be talking the same language. Edna tried to appease her friend, to explain.

"I would give up the unessential; I would give my money. I would give my life for my children; but I wouldn't give myself. I can't make it more clear; it's only something which I am beginning to comprehend, which is revealing itself to me."

"I don't know what you would call the essential, or what you mean by the unessential," said Madame Ratignolle, cheerfully; "but a woman who would give her life for her children could do no more than that—your Bible tells you so. I'm sure I couldn't do more than that."

"Oh, yes you could!" laughed Edna.

She was not surprised at Mademoiselle Reisz's question the morning that lady, following her to the beach, tapped her on the shoulder and asked if she did not greatly miss her young friend.

"Oh, good morning, Mademoiselle; it is you? Why, of course I miss Robert. Are you going down to bathe?"

"Why should I go down to bathe at the very end of the season when I haven't been in the surf all summer?" replied the woman, disagreeably.

"I beg your pardon," offered Edna, in some embarrassment, for she should have remembered that Mademoiselle Reisz's avoidance of the water had furnished a theme for much pleasantry. Some among them thought it was on account of her false hair, or the dread of getting the violets wet, while others attributed it to the natural aversion for water sometimes believed to accompany the artistic temperament. Mademoiselle offered Edna some chocolates in a paper bag, which she took from her pocket, by way of showing that she bore no ill feeling. She habitually ate chocolates for their sustaining quality; they contained much nutriment in small compass, she said. They saved her from starvation, as Madame Lebrun's table was utterly impossible; and no one save so impertinent a woman as Madame Lebrun could think of offering such food to people and requiring them to pay for it.

"She must feel very lonely without her son," said Edna, desiring to change the subject. "Her favorite son, too. It must have been quite hard to let him go."

Mademoiselle laughed maliciously.

"Her favorite son! Oh dear! Who could have been imposing such a tale upon you? Aline Lebrun lives for Victor, and for Victor alone. She has spoiled him into the worthless creature he is. She worships him and the ground he walks on. Robert is very well in a way, to give up all the money he can earn to the family, and keep the barest pittance for himself. Favorite son, indeed! I miss the poor fellow myself, my dear. I liked to see him and to hear him about the place—the only Lebrun who is worth a pinch of salt. He comes to see me often in the city. I like to play to him. That Victor! hanging would be too good for him. It's a wonder Robert hasn't beaten him to death long ago."

"I thought he had great patience with his brother," offered Edna, glad to be talking about Robert, no matter what was said.

"Oh! he thrashed him well enough a year or two ago," said Mademoiselle. "It was about a Spanish girl, whom Victor considered that he had some sort of claim upon. He met Robert one day talking to the girl, or walking with her, or bathing with her, or carrying her basket—I don't remember what;—and he became so insulting and abusive that Robert gave him a thrashing on the spot that has kept him comparatively in order for a good while. It's about time he was getting another."

"Was her name Mariequita?" asked Edna.

"Mariequita—yes, that was it. Mariequita. I had forgotten. Oh, she's a sly one, and a bad one, that Mariequita!"

Edna looked down at Mademoiselle Reisz and wondered how she could have listened to her venom so long. For some reason she felt depressed, almost unhappy. She had not intended to go into the water; but she donned her bathing suit, and left Mademoiselle alone, seated under the shade of the children's tent. The water was growing cooler as the season advanced. Edna plunged and swam about with an abandon that thrilled and invigorated her. She remained a long time in the water, half hoping that Mademoiselle Reisz would not wait for her.

But Mademoiselle waited. She was very amiable during the walk back, and raved much over Edna's appearance in her bathing suit. She talked about music. She hoped that Edna would go to see her in the city, and wrote her address with the stub of a pencil on a piece of card which she found in her pocket.

"When do you leave?" asked Edna.

"Next Monday; and you?"

"The following week," answered Edna, adding, "It has been a pleasant summer, hasn't it, Mademoiselle?"

"Well," agreed Mademoiselle Reisz, with a shrug, "rather pleasant, if it hadn't been for the mosquitoes and the Farival twins."

XVII

The Pontelliers possessed a very charming home on Esplanade Street[1] in New Orleans. It was a large, double cottage, with a broad front veranda, whose round, fluted columns supported the sloping roof. The house was painted a daz-

---

[1] The most exclusive address of the Creole aristocracy.

zling white; the outside shutters, or jalousies, were green. In the yard, which was kept scrupulously neat, were flowers and plants of every description which flourishes in South Louisiana. Within doors the appointments were perfect after the conventional type. The softest carpets and rugs covered the floors; rich and tasteful draperies hung at doors and windows. There were paintings, selected with judgment and discrimination, upon the walls. The cut glass, the silver, the heavy damask which daily appeared upon the table were the envy of many women whose husbands were less generous than Mr. Pontellier.

Mr. Pontellier was very fond of walking about his house examining its various appointments and details, to see that nothing was amiss. He greatly valued his possessions, chiefly because they were his, and derived genuine pleasure from contemplating a painting, a statuette, a rare lace curtain—no matter what—after he had bought it and placed it among his household goods.

On Tuesday afternoons—Tuesday being Mrs. Pontellier's reception day[2]— there was a constant stream of callers—women who came in carriages or in the street cars, or walked when the air was soft and distance permitted. A light-colored mulatto boy, in dress coat and bearing a diminutive silver tray for the reception of cards, admitted them. A maid, in white fluted cap, offered the callers liqueur, coffee, or chocolate, as they might desire. Mrs. Pontellier, attired in a handsome reception gown, remained in the drawing-room the entire afternoon receiving her visitors. Men sometimes called in the evening with their wives.

This had been the programme which Mrs. Pontellier had religiously followed since her marriage, six years before. Certain evenings during the week she and her husband attended the opera or sometimes the play.

Mr. Pontellier left his home in the mornings between nine and ten o'clock, and rarely returned before half-past six or seven in the evening—dinner being served at half-past seven.

He and his wife seated themselves at table on Tuesday evening, a few weeks after their return from Grand Isle. They were alone together. The boys were being put to bed; the patter of their bare, escaping feet could be heard occasionally, as well as the pursuing voice of the quadroon, lifted in mild protest and entreaty. Mrs. Pontellier did not wear her usual Tuesday reception gown; she was in ordinary house dress. Mr. Pontellier who was observant about such things, noticed it, as he served the soup and handed it to the boy in waiting.

"Tired out, Edna? Whom did you have? Many callers?" he asked. He tasted his soup and began to season it with pepper, salt, vinegar, mustard—everything within reach.

"There were a good many," replied Edna, who was eating her soup with evident satisfaction. "I found their cards when I got home; I was out."

"Out!" exclaimed her husband, with something like genuine consternation in his voice as he laid down the vinegar cruet and looked at her through his glasses. "Why, what could have taken you out on Tuesday? What did you have to do?"

"Nothing. I simply felt like going out, and I went out."

"Well, I hope you left some suitable excuse," said her husband, somewhat appeased, as he added a dash of cayenne pepper to the soup.

"No, I left no excuse. I told Joe to say I was out, that was all."

"Why, my dear, I should think you'd understand by this time that people don't do such things; we've got to observe *les convenances*[3] if we ever expect to get on and keep up with procession. If you felt that you had to leave home this afternoon, you should have left some suitable explanation for your absence.

"This soup is really impossible; it's strange that woman hasn't learned yet to make a decent soup. Any free-lunch stand in town serves a better one. Was Mrs. Belthrop here?"

"Bring the tray with the cards, Joe. I don't remember who was here."

The boy retired and returned after a moment, bringing the tiny silver tray, which was covered with ladies' visiting cards. He handed it to Mrs. Pontellier.

"Give it to Mr. Pontellier," she said.

Joe offered the tray to Mr. Pontellier, and removed the soup.

Mr. Pontellier scanned the names of his wife's callers, reading some of them aloud, with comments as he read.

"'The Misses Delasidas.' I worked a big deal in futures[4] for their father this morning; nice girls; it's time they were getting married. 'Mrs. Belthrop,' I tell you what it is, Edna; you can't afford to snub Mrs. Belthrop. Why, Belthrop could buy and sell us ten times over. High business is worth a good, round sum to me. You'd better write her a note. 'Mrs. James Highcamp,' Hugh! the less you have to do with Mrs. Highcamp, the better. 'Madame LaForcé.' Came all the way from Carrolton,[5] too, poor old soul. 'Miss Wiggs,' 'Mrs. Eleanor Boltons.'" He pushed the cards aside.

"Mercy!" exclaimed Edna, who had been fuming. "Why are you taking the thing so seriously and making such a fuss over it?"

"I'm not making any fuss over it. But it's just such seeming trifles that we've got to take seriously; such things count."

The fish was scorched. Mr. Pontellier would not touch it. Edna said she did not mind a little scorched taste. The roast was in some way not to his fancy, and he did not like the manner in which the vegetables were served.

"It seems to me," he said, "we spend money enough in this house to procure at least one meal a day which a man could eat and retain his self-respect."

"You used to think the cook was a treasure," returned Edna, indifferently.

---

[3] The conventions.

[4] A form of financial speculation.

[5] Village to the west of New Orleans.

"Perhaps she was when she first came; but cooks are only human. They need looking after, like any other class of persons that you employ. Suppose I didn't look after the clerks in my office, just let them run things their own way; they'd soon make a nice mess of me and my business."

"Where are you going?" asked Edna, seeing that her husband arose from table without having eaten a morsel except a taste of the highly-seasoned soup.

"I'm going to get my dinner at the club. Good night." He went into the hall, took his hat and stick from the stand, and left the house.

She was somewhat familiar with such scenes. They had often made her very unhappy. On a few previous occasions she had been completely deprived of any desire to finish her dinner. Sometimes she had gone into the kitchen to administer a tardy rebuke to the cook. Once she went to her room and studied the cookbook during an entire evening, finally writing out a menu for the week, which left her harassed with a feeling that, after all, she had accomplished no good that was worth the name.

But that evening Edna finished her dinner alone, with forced deliberation. Her face was flushed and her eyes flamed with some inward fire that lighted them. After finishing her dinner she went to her room, having instructed the boy to tell any other callers that she was indisposed.

It was a large, beautiful room, rich and picturesque in the soft, dim light which the maid had turned low. She went and stood at an open window and looked out upon the deep tangle of the garden below. All the mystery and witchery of the night seemed to have gathered there amid the perfumes and the dusky and tortuous outlines of flowers and foliage. She was seeking herself and finding herself in just such sweet, half-darkness which met her moods. But the voices were not soothing that came to her from the darkness and the sky above and the stars. They jeered and sounded mournful notes without promise, devoid even of hope. She turned back into the room and began to walk to and fro down its whole length, without stopping, without resting. She carried in her hands a thin handkerchief, which she tore into ribbons, rolled into a ball, and flung from her. Once she stopped, and taking off her wedding ring, flung it upon the carpet. When she saw it lying there, she tamped her heel upon it, striving to crush it. But her small boot heel did not make an indenture, not a mark upon the little glittering circlet.

In a sweeping passion she seized a glass vase from the table and flung it upon the tiles of the hearth. She wanted to destroy something. The crash and clatter were what she wanted to hear.

A maid, alarmed at the din of breaking glass, entered the room to discover what was the matter.

"A vase fell upon the hearth," said Edna. "Never mind; leave it till morning."

"Oh! you might get some of the glass in your feet, ma'am," insisted the young woman, picking up bits of the broken vase that were scattered upon the carpet. "And here's your ring, ma'am, under the chair."

Edna held out her hand, and taking the ring, slipped it upon her finger.

XVIII

The following morning Mr. Pontellier, upon leaving for his office, asked Edna if she would not meet him in town in order to look at some new fixtures for the library.

"I hardly think we need new fixtures, Léonce. Don't let us get anything new; you are too extravagant. I don't believe you ever think of saving or putting by."

"The way to become rich is to make money, my dear Edna, not to save it," he said. He regretted that she did not feel inclined to go with him and select new fixtures. He kissed her good-by, and told her she was not looking well and must take care of herself. She was unusually pale and very quiet.

She stood on the front veranda as he quitted the house, and absently picked a few sprays of jessamine that grew upon a trellis near by. She inhaled the odor of the blossoms and thrust them into the bosom of her white morning gown. The boys were dragging along the banquette[6] a small "express wagon," which they had filled with block and sticks. The quadroon was following them with little quick steps, having assumed a fictitious animation and alacrity for the occasion. A fruit vender was crying his wares in the street.

Edna looked straight before her with a self-absorbed expression upon her face. She felt no interest in anything about her. The street, the children, the fruit vender, the flowers growing there under her eyes, were all part and parcel of an alien world which had suddenly become antagonistic.

She went back into the house. She had thought of speaking to the cook concerning her blunders of the previous night; but Mr. Pontellier had saved her that disagreeable mission, for which she was so poorly fitted. Mr. Pontellier's arguments were usually convincing with those whom he employed. He left home feeling quite sure that he and Edna would sit down that evening, and possibly a few subsequent evenings, to a dinner deserving of the name.

Edna spent an hour or two in looking over some of her old sketches. She could see their shortcomings and defects, which were glaring in her eyes. She tried to work a little, but found she was not in the humor. Finally she gathered together a few of the sketches—those which she considered the least discreditable; and she carried them with her when, a little later, she dressed and left the house. She looked handsome and distinguished in her street gown. The tan of the seashore had left her face, and her forehead was smooth, white, and polished beneath her heavy, yellow-brown hair. There were a few freckles on her face, and a small, dark mole near the under lip and one on the temple, half-hidden in her hair.

As Edna walked along the street she was thinking of Robert. She was still under the spell of her infatuation. She had tried to forget him, realizing the inutility of remembering. But the thought of him was like an obsession, ever pressing itself upon her. It was not that she dwelt upon details of their acquaintance,

[6] Sidewalk. "Jessamine": jasmine.

or recalled in any special or peculiar way his personality; it was his being, his existence, which dominated her thought, fading sometimes as if it would melt into the mist of the forgotten, reviving again with an intensity which filled her with an incomprehensible longing.

Edna was on her way to Madame Ratignolle's. Their intimacy, begun at Grand Isle, had not declined, and they had seen each other with some frequency since their return to the city. The Ratignolles lived at no great distance from Edna's home, on the corner of a side street, where Monsieur Ratignolle owned and conducted a drug store which enjoyed a steady and prosperous trade. His father had been in the business before him, and Monsieur Ratignolle stood well in the community and bore an enviable reputation for integrity and clear-headedness. His family lived in commodious apartments over the store, having an entrance on the side within the *porte cochère.*[7] There was something which Edna thought very French, very foreign, about their whole manner of living. In the large and pleasant salon which extended across the width of the house, the Ratignolles entertained their friends once a fortnight with a *soirée musicale,*[8] sometimes diversified by card-playing. There was a friend who played upon the 'cello. One brought his flute and another his violin, while there were some who sang and a number who performed upon the piano with various degrees of taste and agility. The Ratignolles' *soirées musicales* were widely known, and it was considered a privilege to be invited to them.

Edna found her friend engaged in assorting the clothes which had returned that morning from the laundry. She at once abandoned her occupation upon seeing Edna, who had been ushered without ceremony into her presence.

"'Cité can do it as well as I; it is really her business," she explained to Edna, who apologized for interrupting her. And she summoned a young black woman, whom she instructed, in French, to be very careful in checking off the list which she handed her. She told her to notice particularly if a fine linen handkerchief of Monsieur Ratignolle's, which was missing last week, had been returned; and to be sure to set to one side such pieces as required mending and darning.

Then placing an arm around Edna's waist, she led her to the front of the house, to the salon, where it was cool and sweet with the odor of great roses that stood upon the hearth in jars.

Madame Ratignolle looked more beautiful than ever there at home, in a negligé which left her arms almost wholly bare and exposed the rich, melting curves of her white throat.

"Perhaps I shall be able to paint your picture some day," said Edna with a smile when they were seated. She produced the roll of sketches and started to unfold them. "I believe I ought to work again. I feel as if I wanted to be doing something. What do you think of them? Do you think it worth while to take it up again and study some more? I might study for a while with Laidpore."

---

[7] Porch that protects travelers alighting from or boarding a coach.
[8] Musical evening.

She knew that Madame Ratignolle's opinion in such a matter would be next to valueless, that she herself had not alone decided, but determined; but she sought the words and praise and encouragement that would help her to put her heart into her venture.

"Your talent is immense, dear!"

"Nonsense!" protested Edna, well pleased.

"Immense, I tell you," persisted Madame Ratignolle, surveying the sketches one by one, at close range, then holding them at arm's length, narrowing her eyes, and dropping her head on one side. "Surely, this Bavarian peasant is worthy of framing; and this basket of apples! never have I seen anything more life-like. One might almost be tempted to reach out a hand and take one."

Edna could not control a feeling which bordered upon complacency at her friend's praise, even realizing, as she did, its true worth. She retained a few of the sketches, and gave all the rest to Madame Ratignolle, who appreciated the gift far beyond its value and proudly exhibited the pictures to her husband when he came up from the store a little later for his midday dinner.

Mr. Ratignolle was one of those men who are called the salt of the earth. His cheerfulness was unbounded, and it was matched by his goodness of heart, his broad charity, and common sense. He and his wife spoke English with an accent which was only discernible through its un-English emphasis and a certain carefulness and deliberation. Edna's husband spoke English with no accent whatever. The Ratignolles understood each other perfectly. If ever the fusion of two human beings into one has been accomplished on this sphere it was surely in their union.

As Edna seated herself at table with them she thought, "Better a dinner of herbs,"[9] though it did not take her long to discover that was no dinner of herbs, but a delicious repast, simple, choice, and in every way satisfying.

Monsieur Ratignolle was delighted to see her, though he found her looking not so well as at Grand Isle, and he advised a tonic. He talked a good deal on various topics, a little politics, and some city news and neighborhood gossip. He spoke with an animation and earnestness that gave an exaggerated importance to every syllable he uttered. His wife was keenly interested in everything he said, laying down her fork the better to listen, chiming in, taking the words out of his mouth.

Edna felt depressed rather than soothed after leaving them. The little glimpse of domestic harmony which had been offered her, gave her no regret, no longing. It was not a condition of life which fitted her, and she could see in it but an appalling and hopeless ennui.[1] She was moved by a kind of commiseration for Madame Ratignolle,—a pity for that colorless existence which never uplifted its possessor beyond the region of blind contentment, in which no mo-

[9] "Better is a dinner of herbs where love is, than a stalled ox and hatred therewith" (Proverbs 15:17).

[1] Boredom.

ment of anguish ever visited her soul, in which she would never have the taste of life's delirium. Edna vaguely wondered what she meant by "life's delirium." It had crossed her thought like some unsought, extraneous impression.

XIX

Edna could not help but think that it was very foolish, very childish, to have stamped upon her wedding ring and smashed the crystal vase upon the tiles. She was visited by no more outbursts, moving her to such futile expedients. She began to do as she liked and to feel as she liked. She completely abandoned her Tuesdays at home, and did not return the visits of those who had called upon her. She made no ineffectual efforts to conduct her household *en bonne ménagère*,[2] going and coming as it suited her fancy, and, so far as she was able, lending herself to any passing caprice.

Mr. Pontellier had been a rather courteous husband so long as he met a certain tacit submissiveness in his wife. But her new and unexpected line of conduct completely bewildered him. It shocked him. Then her absolute disregard for her duties as a wife angered him. When Mr. Pontellier became rude, Edna grew insolent. She had resolved never to take another step backward.

"It seems to me the utmost folly for a woman at the head of a household, and the mother of children, to spend in an atelier[3] days which would be better employed contriving for the comfort of her family."

"I feel like painting," answered Edna. "Perhaps I shan't always feel like it."

"Then in God's name paint! but don't let the family go to the devil. There's Madame Ratignolle; because she keeps up her music, she doesn't let everything go to chaos. And she's more of a musician than you are a painter."

"She isn't a musician, and I'm not a painter. It isn't on account of painting that I let things go."

"On account of what, then?"

"Oh! I don't know. Let me alone; you bother me."

It sometimes entered Mr. Pontellier's mind to wonder if his wife were not growing a little unbalanced mentally. He could plainly see that she was not herself. That is, he could not see that she was becoming herself and daily casting aside that fictitious self which we assume like a garment with which to appear before the world.

Her husband let her alone as she requested, and went away to his office. Edna went up to her atelier—a bright room in the top of the house. She was working with great energy and interest, without accomplishing anything, however, which satisfied her even in the smallest degree. For a time she had the whole household enrolled in the service of art. The boys posed for her. They thought it amusing at first, but the occupation soon lost its attractiveness when

[2] As a good housewife.
[3] Studio.

they discovered that it was not a game arranged especially for their entertainment. The quadroon sat for hours before Edna's palette, patient as a savage, while the housemaid took charge of the children, and the drawing-room went undusted. But the house-maid, too, served her term as model when Edna perceived that the young woman's back and shoulders were molded on classic lines, and that her hair, loosened from its confining cap, became an inspiration. While Edna worked she sometimes sang low the little air, *"Ah! si tu savais!"*

It moved her with recollections. She could hear again the ripple of the water, the flapping sail. She could see the glint of the moon upon the bay, and could feel the soft, gusty beating of the hot south wind. A subtle current of desire passed through her body, weakening her hold upon the brushes and making her eyes burn.

There were days when she was very happy without knowing why. She was happy to be alive and breathing, when her whole being seemed to be one with the sunlight, the color, the odors, the luxuriant warmth of some perfect Southern day. She liked then to wander alone into strange and unfamiliar places. She discovered many a sunny, sleepy corner, fashioned to dream in. And she found it good to dream and to be alone and unmolested.

There were days when she was unhappy, she did not know why,—when it did not seem worth while to be glad or sorry, to be alive or dead; when life appeared to her like a grotesque pandemonium and humanity like worms struggling blindly toward inevitable annihilation. She could not work on such a day, nor weave fancies to stir her pulses and warm her blood.

XX

It was during such a mood that Edna hunted up Mademoiselle Reisz. She had not forgotten the rather disagreeable impression left upon her by their last interview; but she nevertheless felt a desire to see her—above all, to listen while she played upon the piano. Quite early in the afternoon she started upon her quest for the pianist. Unfortunately she had mislaid or lost Mademoiselle Reisz's card, and looking up her address in the city directory, she found that the woman lived on Bienville Street, some distance away. The directory which fell into her hands was a year or more old, however, and upon reaching the number indicated, Edna discovered that the house was occupied by a respectable family of mulattoes who had *chambres garnies*[4] to let. They had been living there for six months, and knew absolutely nothing of a Mademoiselle Reisz. In fact, they knew nothing of any of their neighbors; their lodgers were all people of the highest distinction, they assured Edna. She did not linger to discuss class distinctions with Madame Pouponne, but hastened to a neighboring grocery store, feeling sure that Mademoiselle would have left her address with the proprietor.

[4] Furnished rooms.

He knew Mademoiselle Reisz a good deal better than he wanted to know her, he informed his questioner. In truth, he did not want to know her at all, anything concerning her — the most disagreeable and unpopular woman who ever lived in Bienville Street. He thanked heaven she had left the neighborhood, and was equally thankful that he did not know where she had gone.

Edna's desire to see Mademoiselle Reisz had increased tenfold since these unlooked for obstacles had arisen to thwart it. She was wondering who could give her the information she sought, when it suddenly occurred to her that Madame Lebrun would be the one most likely to do so. She knew it was useless to ask Madame Ratignolle, who was on the most distant terms with the musician, and preferred to know nothing concerning her. She had once been almost as emphatic in expressing herself upon the subject as the corner grocer.

Edna knew that Madame Lebrun had returned to the city, for it was the middle of November. And she also knew where the Lebruns lived, on Chartres Street.

Their home from the outside looked like a prison, with iron bars before the door and lower windows. The iron bars were a relic of the old *régime*,[5] and no one had ever thought of dislodging them. At the side was a high fence enclosing the garden. A gate or door opening upon he street was locked. Edna rang the bell at this side garden gate, and stood upon the banquette, waiting to be admitted.

It was Victor who opened the gate for her. A black woman, wiping her hands upon her apron, was close at his heels. Before she saw them Edna could hear them in altercation, the woman — plainly an anomaly — claiming the right to be allowed to perform her duties, one of which was to answer the bell.

Victor was surprised and delighted to see Mrs. Pontellier, and he made no attempt to conceal either his astonishment or his delight. He was a dark-browed, good-looking youngster of nineteen, greatly resembling his mother, but with ten times her impetuosity. He instructed the black woman to go at once and inform Madame Lebrun that Mrs. Pontellier desired to see her. The woman grumbled a refusal to do part of her duty when she had not been permitted to do it all, and started back to her interrupted task of weeding the garden. Whereupon Victor administered a rebuke in the form of a volley of abuse, which owing to its rapidity and incoherence, was all but incomprehensible to Edna. Whatever it was, the rebuke was convincing, for the woman dropped her hoe and went mumbling into the house.

Edna did not wish to enter. It was very pleasant there on the side porch, where there were chairs, a wicker lounge, and a small table. She seated herself, for she was tired from her long tramp; and she began to rock gently and smooth out the folds of her silk parasol. Victor drew up his chair beside her. He at once explained that the black woman's offensive conduct was all due to imperfect training, as he was not there to take her in hand. He had only come up from the

---

[5] I.e., the Spanish regime (1766–1803).

island the morning before, expected to return next day. He stayed all winter at the island; he lived there, and kept the place in order and got things ready for the summer visitors.

But a man needed occasional relaxation, he informed Mrs. Pontellier, and every now and again he drummed up a pretext to bring him to the city. My! but he had had a time of it the evening before! He wouldn't want his mother to know, and he began to talk in a whisper. He was scintillant[6] with recollections. Of course, he couldn't think of telling Mrs. Pontellier all about it, she being a woman and not comprehending such things. But it all began with a girl peeping and smiling at him through the shutters as he passed by. Oh! but she was a beauty! Certainly he smiled back, and went up and talked to her. Mrs. Pontellier did not know him if she supposed he was one to let an opportunity like that escape him. Despite herself, the youngster amused her. She must have betrayed in her look some degree of interest or entertainment. The boy grew more daring, and Mrs. Pontellier might have found herself, in a little while, listening to a highly colored story but for the timely appearance of Madame Lebrun.

That lady was still clad in white, according to her custom of the summer. Her eyes beamed an effusive welcome. Would not Mrs. Pontellier go inside? Would she partake of some refreshment? Why had she not been there before? How was that dear Mr. Pontellier and how were those sweet children? Had Mrs. Pontellier ever known such a warm November?

Victor went and reclined on the wicker lounge behind his mother's chair, where he commanded a view of Edna's face. He had taken her parasol from her hands while he spoke to her, and he now lifted it and twirled it above him as he lay on his back. When Madame Lebrun complained that it was so dull coming back to the city; that she saw so few people now; that even Victor, when he came up from the island for a day or two, had so much to occupy him and engage his time, then it was that the youth went into contortions on the lounge and winked mischievously at Edna. She somehow felt like a confederate in crime, and tried to look severe and disapproving.

There had been but two letters from Robert, with little in them they told her. Victor said it was really not worth while to go inside for the letters, when his mother entreated him to go in search of them. He remembered the contents, which in truth he rattled off very glibly when put to the test.

One letter was written from Vera Cruz and the other from the City of Mexico. He had met Montel, who was doing everything toward his advancement. So far, the financial situation was no improvement over the one he had left in New Orleans, but of course the prospects were vastly better. He wrote of the City of Mexico, the buildings, the people and their habits, the conditions of life which he found there. He sent his love to the family. He enclosed a check to his mother, and hoped she would affectionately remember him to all his friends. That was about the substance of the two letters. Edna felt that if there had been

[6] Sparkling.

a message for her, she would have received it. The despondent frame of mind in which she had left home began again to overtake her, and she remembered that she wished to find Mademoiselle Reisz.

Madame Lebrun knew where Mademoiselle Reisz lived. She gave Edna the address, regretting that she would not consent to stay and spend the remainder of the afternoon, and pay a visit to Mademoiselle Reisz some other day. The afternoon was already well advanced.

Victor escorted her out upon the banquette, lifted her parasol, and held it over her while he walked to the car with her. He entreated her to bear in mind that the disclosures of the afternoon were strictly confidential. She laughed and bantered him a little, remembering too late that she should have been dignified and reserved.

"How handsome Mrs. Pontellier looked!" said Madame Lebrun to her son.

"Ravishing!" he admitted. "The city atmosphere has improved her. Some way she doesn't seem like the same woman."

XXI

Some people contended that the reason Mademoiselle Reisz always chose apartments up under the roof was to discourage the approach of beggars, peddlars and callers. There were plenty of windows in her little front room. They were for the most part dingy, but as they were nearly always open it did not make so much difference. They often admitted into the room a good deal of smoke and soot; but at the same time all the light and air that there was came through them. From her windows could be seen the crescent of the river, the masts of ships and the big chimneys of the Mississippi steamers. A magnificent piano crowded the apartment. In the next room she slept, and in the third and last she harbored a gasoline stove on which she cooked her meals when disinclined to descend to the neighboring restaurant. It was there also that she ate, keeping her belongings in a rare old buffet, dingy and battered from a hundred years of use.

When Edna knocked at Mademoiselle Reisz's front room door and entered, she discovered that person standing beside the window, engaged in mending or patching an old prunella gaiter.[7] The little musician laughed all over when she saw Edna. Her laugh consisted of a contortion of the face and all the muscles of the body. She seemed strikingly homely, standing there in the afternoon light. She still wore the shabby lace and the artificial bunch of violets on the side of her head.

"So you remembered me at last," said Mademoiselle. "I had said to myself, 'Ah, bah! she will never come.'"

"Did you want me to come?" asked Edna with a smile.

"I had not thought much about it," answered Mademoiselle. The two had seated themselves on a little bumpy sofa which stood against the wall. "I am

---

[7] A cloth button shoe.

glad, however, that you came. I have the water boiling back there, and was just about to make some coffee. You will drink a cup with me. And how is *la belle dame?*[8] Always handsome! always healthy! always contented!" She took Edna's hand between her strong wiry fingers, holding it loosely without warmth, and executing a sort of double theme upon the back and palm.

"Yes," she went on; "I sometimes thought: 'She will never come. She promised as those women in society always do, without meaning it. She will not come.' For I really don't believe you like me, Mrs. Pontellier."

"I don't know whether I like you or not," replied Edna, gazing down at the little woman with a quizzical look.

The candor of Mrs. Pontellier's admission greatly pleased Mademoiselle Reisz. She expressed her gratification by repairing forthwith to the region of the gasoline stove and rewarding her guest with the promised cup of coffee. The coffee and the biscuit accompanying it proved very acceptable to Edna, who had declined refreshment at Madame Lebrun's and was now beginning to feel hungry. Mademoiselle set the tray which she brought in upon a small table near at hand, and seated herself once again on the lumpy sofa.

"I have had a letter from your friend," she remarked, as she poured a little cream into Edna's cup and handed it to her.

"My friend?"

"Yes, your friend Robert. He wrote to me from the City of Mexico."

"Wrote to *you?*" repeated Edna in amazement, stirring her coffee absently.

"Yes, to me. Why not? Don't stir all the warmth out of your coffee; drink it. Though the letter might as well have been sent to you; it was nothing but Mrs. Pontellier from beginning to end."

"Let me see it," requested the young woman, entreatingly.

"No; a letter concerns no one but the person who writes it and the one to whom it is written."

"Haven't you just said it concerned me from beginning to end?"

"It was written about you, not to you. 'Have you seen Mrs. Pontellier? How is she looking?' he asks. 'As Mrs. Pontellier says,' or 'as Mrs. Pontellier once said.' 'If Mrs. Pontellier should call upon you, play for her that Impromptu of Chopin's, my favorite. I heard it here a day or two ago, but not as you play it. I should like to know how it affects her,' and so on, as if he supposed we were constantly in each other's society."

"Let me see the letter."

"Oh, no."

"Have you answered it?"

"No."

"Let me see the letter."

"No, and again, no."

"Then play the Impromptu for me."

[8] The lovely lady.

"It is growing late; what time do you have to be home?"

"Time doesn't concern me. Your question seems a little rude. Play the Impromptu."

"But you have told me nothing of yourself. What are you doing?"

"Painting!" laughed Edna. "I am becoming an artist. Think of it!"

"Ah! an artist! You have pretensions, Madame."

"Why pretensions? Do you think I could not become an artist?"

"I do not know you well enough to say. I do not know your talent or your temperament. To be an artist includes much; one must possess many gifts—absolute gifts—which have not been acquired by one's own effort. And, moreover, to succeed, the artist must possess the courageous soul."

"What do you mean by the courageous soul?"

"Courageous, *ma foi!*[9] The brave soul. The soul that dares and defies."

"Show me the letter and play for me the Impromptu. You see that I have persistence. Does that quality count for anything in art?"

"It counts with a foolish old woman whom you have captivated," replied Mademoiselle, with her wriggling laugh.

The letter was right there at hand in the drawer of the little table upon which Edna had just placed her coffee cup. Mademoiselle opened the drawer and drew forth the letter, the topmost one. She placed in Edna's hands, and without further comment arose and went to the piano.

Mademoiselle played a soft interlude. It was an improvisation. She sat low at the instrument, and the lines of her body settled into ungraceful curves and angles that gave it an appearance of deformity. Gradually and imperceptibly the interlude melted into the soft opening minor chords of the Chopin Impromptu.

Edna did not know when the impromptu began or ended. She sat in the sofa corner reading Robert's letter by the fading light. Mademoiselle had glided from the Chopin into the quivering love-notes of Isolde's song,[1] and back again to the Impromptu with its soulful and poignant longing.

The shadows deepened in the little room. The music grew strange and fantastic—turbulent, insistent, plaintive and soft with entreaty. The shadows grew deeper. The music filled the room. It floated out upon the night, over the housetops, the crescent of the river, losing itself in the silence of the upper air.

Edna was sobbing, just as she had wept one midnight at Grand Isle when strange, new voices awoke in her. She arose in some agitation to take her departure. "May I come again, Mademoiselle?" she asked at the threshold.

"Come whenever you feel like it. Be careful; the stairs and landings are dark; don't stumble."

Mademoiselle reentered and lit a candle. Robert's letter was on the floor. She stooped and picked it up. It was crumpled and damp with tears. Mademoi-

[9] "My faith" (literal trans.); here, in fact.

[1] From Richard Wagner's opera *Tristan und Isolde* (1857–59); Isolde sings her *Liebstod* ("love-death") as she bids her dead lover farewell and then dies in his arms.

selle smoothed the letter out, restored it to the envelope, and replaced it in the table drawer.

XXII

One morning on his way into town Mr. Pontellier stopped at the house of his old friend and family physician, Doctor Mandelet. The Doctor was a semi-retired physician, resting, as the saying is, upon his laurels. He bore a reputation for wisdom rather than skill—leaving the active practice of medicine to his assistants and younger contemporaries—and was much sought for in matters of consultation. A few families, united to him by bonds of friendship, he still attended when they required the services of a physician. The Pontelliers were among these.

Mr. Pontellier found the Doctor reading at the open window of his study. His house stood rather far back from the street, in the center of a delightful garden, so that it was quiet and peaceful at the old gentleman's study window. He was a great reader. He stared up disapprovingly over his eyeglasses as Mr. Pontellier entered, wondering who had the temerity to disturb him at that hour of the morning.

"Ah! Pontellier! Not sick, I hope. Come and have a seat. What news do you bring this morning?" He was quite portly, with a profusion of gray hair, and small blue eyes which age had robbed of much of their brightness but none of their penetration.

"Oh! I'm never sick, Doctor. You know that I come of tough fiber—of that old Creole race of Pontelliers that dry up and finally blow away. I come to consult—no, not precisely to consult—to talk to you about Edna. I don't know what ails her."

"Madame Pontellier not well?" marveled the Doctor. "Why I saw her—I think it was a week ago—walking along Canal Street,[2] the picture of health, it seemed to me."

"Yes, yes; she seems quite well," said Mr. Pontellier, leaning forward and whirling his stick between his two hands; "but she doesn't act well. She's odd, she's not like herself. I can't make her out, and I thought perhaps you'd help me."

"How does she act?" inquired the doctor.

"Well, it isn't easy to explain," said Mr. Pontellier, throwing himself back in his chair. "She lets the housekeeping go to the dickens."

"Well, well; women are not all alike, my dear Pontellier. We've got to consider—"

"I know that; I told you I couldn't explain. Her whole attitude—toward me and everybody and everything—has changed. You know I have a quick temper, but I don't want to quarrel or be rude to a woman, especially my wife; yet I'm

[2] The main street of downtown New Orleans.

driven to it, and feel like ten thousand devils after I've made a fool of myself. She's making it devilishly uncomfortable for me," he went on nervously. "She's got some sort of notion in her head concerning the eternal rights of women; and—you understand—we meet in the morning at the breakfast table."

The old gentleman lifted his shaggy eyebrows, protruded his thick nether lip, and tapped the arms of his chair with his cushioned finger-tips.

"What have you been doing to her, Pontellier?"

"Doing! *Parbleu!*" [3]

"Has she," asked the Doctor, with a smile, "has she been associating of late with a circle of pseudo-intellectual women[4]—superspiritual superior beings? My wife has been telling me about them."

"That's the trouble," broke in Mr. Pontellier, "she hasn't been associating with any one. She has abandoned her Tuesdays at home, has thrown over all her acquaintances, and goes tramping about by herself, moping in the streetcars, getting in after dark. I tell you she's peculiar. I don't like it; I feel a little worried over it."

This was a new aspect for the Doctor. "Nothing hereditary?" he asked, seriously. "Nothing peculiar about her family antecedents, is there?"

"Oh, no, indeed! She comes of sound old Presbyterian Kentucky stock. The old gentleman, her father, I have heard, used to atone for his week-day sins with his Sunday devotions. I know for a fact, that his race horses literally ran away with the prettiest bit of Kentucky farming land I ever laid eyes upon. Margaret—you know Margaret—she has all the Presbyterianism undiluted. And the youngest is something of a vixen. By the way, she gets married in a couple of weeks from now."

"Send your wife up to the wedding," exclaimed the Doctor, foreseeing a happy solution. "Let her stay among her own people for a while; it will do her good."

"That's what I want her to do. She won't go to the marriage. She says a wedding is one of the most lamentable spectacles on earth. Nice thing for a woman to say to her husband!" exclaimed Mr. Pontellier, fuming anew at the recollection.

"Pontellier," said the Doctor, after a moment's reflection, "let your wife alone for a while. Don't bother her, and don't let her bother you. Woman, my dear friend, is a very peculiar and delicate organism—a sensitive and highly organized woman, such as I know Mrs. Pontellier to be, is especially peculiar. It would require an inspired psychologist to deal successfully with them. And when ordinary fellows like you and me attempt to cope with their idiosyncrasies the result is bungling. Most women are moody and whimsical. This is some

[3] For heaven's sake!

[4] Women's clubs flourished during the late nineteenth century in America. They were a source of education for women as well as an arena for political organization. As the Doctor's remark indicates, the club movement was met with scorn in some quarters [Culley's note].

passing whim of your wife, due to some cause or causes which you and I needn't try to fathom. But it will pass happily over, especially if you let her alone. Send her around to see me."

"Oh! I couldn't do that; there'd be no reason for it," objected Mr. Pontellier.

"Then I'll go around and see her," said the Doctor. "I'll drop in to dinner some evening *en bon ami.*"[5]

"Do! by all means," urged Mr. Pontellier, "What evening will you come? Say Thursday. Will you come Thursday?" he asked, rising to take his leave.

"Very well; Thursday. My wife may possibly have some engagement for me Thursday. In case she has, I shall let you know. Otherwise, you may expect me."

Mr. Pontellier turned before leaving to say:

"I am going to New York on business very soon. I have a big scheme on hand, and want to be on the field proper to pull the ropes and handle the ribbons.[6] We'll let you in on the inside if you say so, Doctor," he laughed.

"No, I thank you, my dear sir," returned the Doctor. "I leave such ventures to you younger men with the fever of life still in your blood."

"What I wanted to say," continued Mr. Pontellier, with his hand on the knob; "I may have to be absent a good while. Would you advise me to take Edna along?"

"By all means, if she wishes to go. If not, leave her here. Don't contradict her. The mood will pass, I assure you. It may take a month, two, three months— possibly longer, but it will pass; have patience."

"Well, good-by, *à jeudi,*"[7] said Mr. Pontellier, as he let himself out.

The Doctor would have liked during the course of conversation to ask, "Is there any man in the case?" but he knew his Creole too well to make such a blunder as that.

He did not resume his book immediately, but sat for a while meditatively looking out into the garden.

XXIII

Edna's father was in the city, and had been with them several days. She was not very warmly or deeply attached to him, but they had certain tastes in common, and when together they were companionable. His coming was in the nature of a welcome disturbance; it seemed to furnish a new direction for her emotions.

He had come to purchase a wedding gift for his daughter, Janet, and an outfit for himself in which he might make a creditable appearance at her marriage. Mr. Pontellier had selected the bridal gift, as every one immediately connected with him always deferred to this taste in such matters. And his suggestions on the question of dress—which too often assumes the nature of a problem—

[5] Like an old friend.
[6] I.e., the reins.
[7] Until Thursday.

were of inestimable value to his father-in-law. But for the past few days the old gentleman had been upon Edna's hands, and in his society she was becoming acquainted with a new set of sensations. He had been a colonel in the Confederate army, and still maintained, with the title, the military bearing which had always accompanied it. His hair and mustache were white and silky, emphasizing the rugged bronze of his face. He was tall and thin, and wore his coats padded, which gave a fictitious breadth and depth to his shoulders and chest. Edna and her father looked very distinguished together, and excited a good deal of notice during their perambulations. Upon his arrival she began by introducing him to her atelier and making a sketch of him. He took the whole matter very seriously. If her talent had been ten-fold greater than it was, it would not have surprised him, convinced as he was that he had bequeathed to all of his daughters the germs of a masterful capability, which only depended upon their own efforts to be directed toward successful achievement.

Before her pencil he sat rigid and unflinching, as he had faced the cannon's mouth in days gone by. He resented the intrusion of the children, who gaped with wondering eyes at him, sitting so stiff up there in their mother's bright atelier. When they drew near he motioned them away with an expressive action of the foot, loath to disturb the fixed lines of his countenance, his arms, or his rigid shoulders.

Edna, anxious to entertain him, invited Mademoiselle Reisz to meet him, having promised him a treat in her piano playing; but Mademoiselle declined the invitation. So together they attended a *soirée musicale* at the Ratignolles'. Monsieur and Madame Ratignolle made much of the Colonel, installing him as the guest of honor and engaging him at once to dine with them the following Sunday, or any day which he might select. Madame coquetted with him in the most captivating and naïve manner, with eyes, gestures, and a profusion of compliments, till the Colonel's old head felt thirty years younger on his padded shoulders. Edna marveled, not comprehending. She herself was almost devoid of coquetry.

There were one or two men whom she observed at the *soirée musicale;* but she would never have felt moved to any kittenish display to attract their notice—to any feline or feminine wiles to express herself toward them. Their personality attracted her in an agreeable way. Her fancy selected them, and she was glad when a lull in the music gave them an opportunity to meet her and talk with her. Often on the street the glance of strange eyes had lingered in her memory, and sometimes had disturbed her.

Mr. Pontellier did not attend these *soirées musicales.* He considered them *bourgeois,* and found more diversion at the club. To Madame Ratignolle he said the music dispensed at her *soirées* was "too heavy," too far beyond his untrained comprehension. His excuse flattered her. But she disapproved of Mr. Pontellier's club, and she was frank enough to tell Edna so.

"It's a pity Mr. Pontellier doesn't stay home more in the evenings. I think you would be more—well, if you don't mind my saying it—more united, if he did."

"Oh! dear no!" said Edna, with a blank look in her eyes. "What should I do if he stayed home? We wouldn't have anything to say to each other."

She had not much of anything to say to her father, for that matter; but he did not antagonize her. She discovered that he interested her, though she realized that he might not interest her long; and for the first time in her life she felt as if she were thoroughly acquainted with him. He kept her busy serving him and ministering to his wants. It amused her to do so. She would not permit a servant or one of the children to do anything for him which she might do herself. Her husband noticed, and thought it was the expression of a deep filial attachment which he had never suspected.

The Colonel drank numerous "toddies" during the course of the day, which left him, however, imperturbed. He was an expert at concocting strong drinks. He had even invented some, to which he had given fantastic names, and for whose manufacture he required diverse ingredients that it devolved upon Edna to procure for him.

When Doctor Mandelet dined with the Pontelliers on Thursday he could discern in Mrs. Pontellier no trace of that morbid condition which her husband had reported to him. She was excited and in a manner radiant. She and her father had been to the race course, and their thoughts when they seated themselves at table were still occupied with the events of the afternoon, and their talk was still of the track. The Doctor had not kept pace with turf affairs. He had certain recollections of racing in what he called "the good old times" when the Lecompte stables flourished,[8] and he drew upon this fund of memories so that he might not be left out and seem wholly devoid of the modern spirit. But he failed to impose upon the Colonel, and was even far from impressing him with this trumped-up knowledge of bygone days. Edna had staked her father on his last venture, with the most gratifying results to both of them. Besides, they had met some very charming people, according to the Colonel's impressions. Mrs. Mortimer Merriman and Mrs. James Highcamp, who were there with Alcée Arobin, had joined them and had enlivened the hours in a fashion that warmed him to think of.

Mr. Pontellier himself had no particular leaning toward horse-racing, and was even rather inclined to discourage it as a pastime, especially when he considered the fate of that blue-grass farm in Kentucky. He endeavored, in a general way, to express a particular disapproval, and only succeeded in arousing the ire and opposition of his father-in-law. A pretty dispute followed in which Edna warmly espoused her father's cause and the Doctor remained neutral.

He observed his hostess attentively from under his shaggy brows, and noted a subtle change which had transformed her from the listless woman he had known into a being who, for the moment, seemed palpitant with the forces of life. Her speech was warm and energetic. There was no repression in her glance or gesture. She reminded him of some beautiful, sleek animal waking up in the sun.

[8] New Orleans had been a celebrated racing center before the Civil War.

The dinner was excellent. The claret was warm and the champagne was cold, and under their beneficent influence the threatened unpleasantness melted and vanished with the fumes of the wine.

Mr. Pontellier warmed up and grew reminiscent. He told some amusing plantation experiences, recollections of old Iberville and his youth, when he hunted 'possum in company with some friendly darky; thrashed the pecan trees, shot the grosbec,[9] and roamed the woods and fields in mischievous idleness.

The Colonel, with little sense of humor and of the fitness of things, related a somber episode of those dark and bitter days, in which he had acted a conspicuous part and always formed a central figure. Nor was the Doctor happier in his selection, when he told the old, ever new and curious story of the waning of a woman's love, seeking strange, new channels, only to return to its legitimate source after days of fierce unrest. It was one of the many little human documents which had been unfolded to him during his long career as a physician. The story did not seem especially to impress Edna. She had one of her own to tell, of a woman who paddled away with her lover one night in a pirogue and never came back. They were lost amid the Baratarian Islands, and no one ever heard of them or found trace of them from that day to this. It was a pure invention. She said that Madame Antoine had related it to her. That, also, was an invention. Perhaps it was a dream she had had. But every glowing word seemed real to those who listened. They could feel the hot breath of the Southern night; they could hear the long sweep of the pirogue through the glistening moonlit water, the beating of birds' wings, rising startled from among the reeds in the salt-water pools; they could see the faces of the lovers, pale, close together, rapt in oblivious forgetfulness, drifting into the unknown.

The champagne was cold, and its subtle fumes played fantastic tricks with Edna's memory that night.

Outside, away from the glow of the fire and the soft lamplight, the night was chill and murky. The Doctor doubled his old-fashioned cloak across his breast as he strode home through the darkness. He knew his fellow-creatures better than most men; knew that inner life which so seldom unfolds itself to unanointed eyes. He was sorry he had accepted Pontellier's invitation. He was growing old, and beginning to need rest and an imperturbed spirit. He did not want the secrets of other lives thrust upon him.

"I hope it isn't Arobin," he muttered to himself as he walked, "I hope to heaven it isn't Alcée Arobin."

XXIV

Edna and her father had a warm, and almost violent dispute upon the subject of her refusal to attend her sister's wedding. Mr. Pontellier declined to interfere, to interpose either his influence or his authority. He was following Doctor Man-

---

[9] I.e., grosbeak, game birds with large (*gros*) bills.

delet's advice, and letting her do as she liked. The Colonel reproached his daughter for her lack of filial kindness and respect, her want of sisterly affection and womanly consideration. His arguments were labored and unconvincing. He doubted if Janet would accept any excuse—forgetting that Edna had offered none. He doubted if Janet would ever speak to her again, and he was sure Margaret would not.

Edna was glad to be rid of her father when he finally took himself off with his wedding garments and his bridal gifts, with his padded shoulders, his Bible reading, his "toddies" and ponderous oaths.

Mr. Pontellier followed him closely. He meant to stop at the wedding on his way to New York and endeavor by every means which money and love could devise to atone somewhat for Edna's incomprehensible action.

"You are too lenient, too lenient by far, Léonce," asserted the Colonel. "Authority, coercion are what is needed. Put your foot down good and hard; the only way to manage a wife. Take my word for it."

The Colonel was perhaps unaware that he had coerced his own wife into her grave. Mr. Pontellier had a vague suspicion of it which he thought it needless to mention at that late day.

Edna was not so consciously gratified at her husband's leaving home as she had been over the departure of her father. As the day approached when he was to leave her for a comparatively long stay, she grew melting and affectionate, remembering his many acts of consideration and his repeated expressions of an ardent attachment. She was solicitous about his health and welfare. She bustled around, looking after his clothing, thinking about heavy underwear, quite as Madame Ratignolle would have done under similar circumstances. She cried when he went away, calling him her dear, good friend, and she was quite certain she would grow lonely before very long and go to join him in New York.

But after all, a radiant peace settled upon her when she at last found herself alone. Even the children were gone. Old Madame Pontellier had come herself and carried them off to Iberville with their quadroon. The old madame did not venture to say she was afraid they would be neglected during Léonce's absence; she hardly ventured to think so. She was hungry for them—even a little fierce in her attachment. She did not want them to be wholly "children of the pavement," she always said when begging to have them for a space. She wished them to know the country, with its streams, its fields, its woods, its freedom, so delicious to the young. She wished them to taste something of the life their father had lived and known and loved when he, too, was a little child.

When Edna was at last alone, she breathed a big, genuine sigh of relief. A feeling that was unfamiliar but very delicious came over her. She walked all through the house, from one room to another, as if inspecting it for the first time. She tried the various chairs and lounges, as if she had never sat and reclined upon them before. And she perambulated around the outside of the house, investigating, looking to see if windows and shutters were secure and in order. The flowers were like new acquaintances; she approached them in a familiar spirit, and made herself at home among them. The garden walks were damp, and Edna called to the maid to bring out her rubber sandals. And there she stayed, and stooped, digging around the plants, trimming, picking dead, dry leaves. The children's little dog came out, interfering, getting in her way. She scolded him, laughing at him, played with him. The garden smelled so good and looked so pretty in the afternoon sunlight. Edna plucked all the bright flowers she could find, and went into the house with them, she and the little dog.

Even the kitchen assumed a sudden interesting character which she had ever before perceived. She went in to give directions to the cook, to say that the butcher would have to bring much less meat, that they would require only half their usual quantity of bread, of milk and groceries. She told the cook that she herself would be greatly occupied during Mr. Pontellier's absence, and she begged her to take all thought and responsibility of the larder upon her own shoulders.

That night Edna dined alone. The candelabra, with a few candles in the center of the table, gave all the light she needed. Outside the circle of light in which she sat, the large dining-room looked solemn and shadowy. The cook, placed upon her mettle, served a delicious repast—a luscious tenderloin broiled à point. The wine tasted good; the marron glacé[1] seemed to be just what she wanted. It was so pleasant, too, to dine in a comfortable *peignoir*.

She thought a little sentimentally about Léonce and the children, and wondered what they were doing. As she gave a dainty scrap or two to the doggie, she talked intimately to him about Étienne and Raoul. He was beside himself with astonishment and delight over these companionable advances, and showed his appreciation by his little quick, snappy barks and a lively agitation.

Then Edna sat in the library after dinner and read Emerson[2] until she grew sleepy. She realized that she had neglected her reading, and determined to start anew upon a course of improving studies, now that her time was completely her own to do with as she liked.

After a refreshing bath, Edna went to bed. And as she snuggled comfortably beneath the eiderdown a sense of restfulness invaded her, such as she had not known before.

XXV

When the weather was dark and cloudy Edna could not work. She needed the sun to mellow and temper her mood to the sticking point. She had reached a stage when she seemed to be no longer feeling her way, working, when in the humor, with sureness and ease. And being devoid of ambition and striving not toward accomplishment, she drew satisfaction from the work in itself.

---

[1] Glazed chestnuts. "À point": to a turn.

[2] Ralph Waldo Emerson (1803–1882), American philosopher, essayist, and poet.

On rainy or melancholy days Edna went out and sought the society of the friends she had made at Grand Isle. Or else she stayed indoors and nursed a mood with which she was becoming too familiar for her own comfort and peace of mind. It was not despair; but it seemed to her as if life were passing by, leaving its promise broken and unfulfilled. Yet there were other days when she listened, was led on and deceived by fresh promises which her youth held out to her.

She went again to the races, and again. Alcée Arobin and Mrs. Highcamp called for her one bright afternoon in Arobin's drag.[3]

Mrs. Highcamp was a worldly but unaffected, intelligent, slim, tall blonde woman in the forties, with an indifferent manner and blue eyes that stared. She had a daughter who served as a pretext for cultivating the society of young men of fashion. Alcée Arobin was one of them. He was a familiar figure at the race course, the opera, the fashionable clubs. There was a perpetual smile in his eyes, which seldom failed to awaken a corresponding cheerfulness in any one who looked into them and listened to his good-humored voice. His manner was quiet, and at times a little insolent. He possessed a good figure, a pleasing face, not overburdened with depth of thought or feeling; and his dress was that of the conventional man of fashion.

He admired Edna extravagantly, after meeting her at the races with her father. He had met her before on other occasions, but she had seemed to him unapproachable until that day. It was at his instigation that Mrs. Highcamp called to ask her to go with them to the Jockey Club[4] to witness the turf event of the season.

There were possibly a few track men out there who knew the race horse as well as Edna, but there was certainly none who knew it better. She sat between her two companions as one having authority to speak. She laughed at Arobin's pretensions, and deplored Mrs. Highcamp's ignorance. The race horse was a friend and intimate associate of her childhood. The atmosphere of the stables and the breath of the blue grass paddock revived in her memory and lingered in her nostrils. She did not perceive that she was talking like her father as the sleek geldings ambled in review before them. She played for very high stakes, and fortune favored her. The fever of the game flamed in her cheeks and eyes, and it got into her blood and into her brain like an intoxicant. People turned their heads to look at her, and more than one lent an attentive ear to her utterances, hoping thereby to secure the elusive but ever-desired "tip." Arobin caught the contagion of excitement which drew him to Edna like a magnet. Mrs. Highcamp remained, as usual, unmoved, with her indifferent stare and uplifted eyebrows.

Edna stayed and dined with Mrs. Highcamp upon being urged to do so. Arobin also remained and sent away his drag.

---

[3] Heavy coach.
[4] The exclusive New Louisiana Jockey Club.

The dinner was quiet and uninteresting, save for the cheerful efforts of Arobin to enliven things. Mrs. Highcamp deplored the absence of her daughter from the races, and tried to convey to her what she had missed by going to the "Dante reading" instead of joining them.[5] The girl held a geranium leaf up to her nose and said nothing, but looked knowing and noncommittal. Mr. Highcamp was a plain, baled-headed man, who only talked under compulsion. He was unresponsive. Mrs. Highcamp was full of delicate courtesy and consideration toward her husband. She addressed most of her conversation to him at table. They sat in the library after dinner and read the evening papers together under the drop-light;[6] while the younger people went into the drawing-room near by and talked. Miss Highcamp played some selections from Grieg[7] upon the piano. She seemed to have apprehended all of the composer's coldness and none of his poetry. While Edna listened she could not help wondering if she had lost her taste for music.

When the time came for her to go home, Mr. Highcamp grunted a lame offer to escort her, looking down at his slippered feet with tactless concern. It was Arobin who took her home. The car ride was long, and it was late when they reached Esplanade Street. Arobin asked permission to enter for a second to light his cigarette—his match safe[8] was empty. He filled his match safe, but did not light his cigarette until he left her, after she had expressed her willingness to go to the races with him again.

Edna was neither tired nor sleepy. She was hungry again, for the Highcamp dinner, though of excellent quality, had lacked abundance. She rummaged in the larder and brought forth a slice of "Gruyère"[9] and some crackers. She opened a bottle of beer which she found in the ice-box. Edna felt extremely restless and excited. She vacantly hummed a fantastic tune as she poked at the wood embers on the hearth and munched a cracker.

She wanted something to happen—something, anything; she did not know what. She regretted that she had not made Arobin stay a half hour to talk over the horses with her. She counted the money she had won. But there was nothing else to do, so she went to bed, and tossed there for hours in a sort of monotonous agitation.

In the middle of the night she remembered that she had forgotten to write her regular letter to her husband; and she decided to do so next day and tell him about her afternoon at the Jockey Club. She lay wide awake composing a letter which was nothing like the one which she wrote the next day. When the maid awoke her in the morning Edna was dreaming of Mr. Highcamp playing the

[5] I.e., her daughter preferred intellectual activities. Dante Alighiera (1265–1321), Italian poet, wrote *The Divine Comedy*.

[6] Gas lamps that could be lowered for reading.

[7] Edvard Grieg (1843–1907), Norwegian composer.

[8] I.e., matchbox.

[9] Cheese originally made in Gruyère, Switzerland.

piano at the entrance of a music store on Canal Street, while his wife was saying to Alcée Arobin, as they boarded an Esplanade Street car:

"What a pity that so much talent has been neglected! but I must go."

When a few days later, Alcée Arobin again called for Edna in his drag, Mrs. Highcamp was not with him. He said they would pick her up. But as the lady had not been apprised of his intention of picking her up, she was not at home. The daughter was just leaving the house to attend the meeting of a branch Folk Lore Society,[1] and regretted that she could not accompany them. Arobin appeared nonplused, and asked Edna if there were any one else she cared to ask.

She did not deem it worthwhile to go in search of any of the fashionable acquaintances from whom she had withdrawn herself. She thought of Madame Ratignolle, but knew that her fair friend did not leave the house, except to take a languid walk around the block with her husband after nightfall. Mademoiselle Reisz would have laughed at such a request from Edna. Madame Lebrun might have enjoyed the outing, but for some reason Edna did not want her. So they went alone, she and Arobin.

The afternoon was intensely interesting to her. The excitement came back upon her like a remittent fever. Her talk grew familiar and confidential. It was no labor to become intimate with Arobin. His manner invited easy confidence. The preliminary stage of becoming acquainted was one which he always endeavored to ignore when a pretty and engaging woman was concerned.

He stayed and dined with Edna. He stayed and sat beside the wood fire. They laughed and talked; and before it was time to go he was telling her how different life might have been if he had known her years before. With ingenuous frankness he spoke of what a wicked, ill-disciplined boy he had been, and impulsively drew up his cuff to exhibit upon his wrist the scar from a saber cut which he had received in a duel outside of Paris when he was nineteen. She touched his hand as she scanned the red cicatrice[2] on the inside of his white wrist. A quick impulse that was somewhat spasmodic impelled her fingers to close in a sort of clutch upon his hand. He felt the pressure of her pointed nails in the flesh of his palm.

She arose hastily and walked toward the mantel.

"The sight of a wound or scar always agitates and sickens me," she said. "I shouldn't have looked at it."

"I beg your pardon," he entreated, following her; "it never occurred to me that it might be repulsive."

He stood close to her, and the effrontery in his eyes repelled the old, vanishing self in her, yet drew all her awakening sensuousness. He saw enough in her face to impel him to take her hand and hold it while he said his lingering good night.

"Will you go to the races again?" he asked.

[1] The New Orleans Association of the American Folklore Society.
[2] Scar.

"No," she said. "I've had enough of the races. I don't want to lose all the money I've won, and I've got to work when the weather is bright, instead of—"

"Yes, work; to be sure. You promised to show me your work. What morning may I come up to your atelier? To-morrow?"

"No!"

"Day after?"

"No, no."

"Oh, please, don't refuse me! I know something of such things, I might help you with a stray suggestion or two."

"No. Good night. Why don't you go after you have said good night? I don't like you," she went on in a high, excited pitch, attempting to draw away her hand. She felt that her words lacked dignity and sincerity, and she knew that he felt it.

"I'm sorry you don't like me. I'm sorry I offended you. How have I offended you? What have I done? Can't you forgive me?" And he bent and pressed his lips upon her hand as if he wished never more to withdraw them.

"Mr. Arobin," she complained, "I'm greatly upset by the excitement of the afternoon; I'm not myself. My manner must have misled you in some way. I wish you to go, please." She spoke in a monotonous, dull tone. He took his hat from the table, and stood with eyes turned from her, looking into the dying fire. For a moment or two he kept an impressive silence.

"Your manner has not misled me, Mrs. Pontellier," he said finally. "My own emotions have done that. I couldn't help it. When I'm near you, how could I help it? Don't think anything of it, don't bother, please. You see, I go when you command me. If you wish me to stay away, I shall do so. If you let me come back, I—oh! you will let me come back?"

He cast one appealing glance at her, to which she made no response. Alcée Arobin's manner was so genuine that it often deceived even himself.

Edna did not care or think whether it were genuine or not. When she was alone she looked mechanically at the back of her hand which he had kissed so warmly. Then she leaned her head down on the mantelpiece. She felt somewhat like a woman who in a moment of passion is betrayed into an act of infidelity, and realizes the significance of the act without being wholly awakened from its glamour. The thought was passing vaguely through her mind, "what would he think?"

She did not mean her husband; she was thinking of Robert Lebrun. Her husband seemed to her now like a person whom she had married without love as an excuse.

She lit a candle and went up to her room. Alcée Arobin was absolutely nothing to her. Yet his presence, his manners, the warmth of his glances, and above all the touch of his lips upon her hand had acted like a narcotic upon her.

She slept a languorous sleep, interwoven with vanishing dreams.

XXVI

Alcée Arobin wrote Edna an elaborate note of apology, palpitant with sincerity. It embarrassed her; for in a cooler, quieter moment it appeared to her absurd that she should have taken his action so seriously, so dramatically. She felt sure that the significance of the whole occurrence had lain in her own self-consciousness. If she ignored his note it would give undue importance to a trivial affair. If she replied to it in a serious spirit it would still leave in his mind the impression that she had in a susceptible moment yielded to his influence. After all, it was no great matter to have one's hand kissed. She was provoked at his having written the apology. She answered in as light and bantering a spirit as she fancied it deserved, and said she would be glad to have him look in upon her at work whenever he felt the inclination and his business gave him the opportunity.

He responded at once by presenting himself at her home with all his disarming naïveté. And then there was scarcely a day which followed that she did not see him or was not reminded of him. He was prolific in pretexts. His attitude became one of good-humored subservience and tacit adoration. He was ready at all times to submit to her moods, which were as often kind as they were cold. She grew accustomed to him. They became intimate and friendly by imperceptible degrees, and then by leaps. He sometimes talked in a way that astonished her at first and brought the crimson into her face; in a way that pleased her at last, appealing to the animalism that stirred impatiently within her.

There was nothing which so quieted the turmoil of Edna's senses as a visit to Mademoiselle Reisz. It was then, in the presence of that personality which was offensive to her, that the woman, by her divine art, seemed to reach Edna's spirit and set it free.

It was misty, with heavy, lowering atmosphere, one afternoon, when Edna climbed the stairs to the pianist's apartments under the roof. Her clothes were dripping with moisture. She felt chilled and pinched as she entered the room. Mademoiselle was poking at a rusty stove that smoked a little and warmed the room indifferently. She was endeavoring to heat a pot of chocolate on the stove. The room looked cheerless and dingy to Edna as she entered. A bust of Beethoven, covered with a hood of dust, scowled at her from the mantelpiece.

"Ah! here comes the sunlight!" exclaimed Mademoiselle, rising from her knees before the stove. "Now it will be warm and bright enough; I can let the fire alone."

She closed the stove door with a bang, and approaching assisted in removing Edna's dripping mackintosh.

"You are cold; you look miserable. The chocolate will soon be hot. But would you rather have a taste of brandy? I have scarcely touched the bottle which you brought me for my cold." A piece of red flannel was wrapped around Mademoiselle's throat; a stiff neck compelled her to hold her head on one side.

"I will take some brandy," said Edna, shivering as she removed her gloves and overshoes. She drank the liquor from the glass as a man would have done. Then flinging herself upon the uncomfortable sofa she said, "Mademoiselle, I am going to move away from my house on Esplanade Street."

"Ah!" ejaculated the musician, nether surprised nor especially interested. Nothing ever seemed to astonish her very much. She was endeavoring to adjust the bunch of violets which had become loose from its fastening in her hair. Edna drew her down upon the sofa and taking a pin from her own hair, secured the shabby artificial flowers in their accustomed place.

"Aren't you astonished?"

"Passably. Where are you going? To New York? to Iberville? to your father in Mississippi? where?"

"Just two steps away," laughed Edna, "in a little four-room house around the corner. It looks so cozy, so inviting and restful, whenever I pass by; and it's for rent. I'm tired looking after that big house. It never seemed like mine, anyway— like home. It's too much trouble. I have to keep too many servants. I am tired bothering with them."

"That is not your true reason, *ma belle*.[3] There is no use in telling me lies. I don't know your reason, but you have not told me the truth." Edna did not protest or endeavor to justify herself.

"The house, the money that provides for it, are not mine. Isn't that enough reason?"

"They are your husband's," returned Mademoiselle, with a shrug and a malicious elevation of the eyebrows.

"Oh! I see there is no deceiving you. Then let me tell you; it is a caprice. I have a little money of my own from my mother's estate, which my father sends me by driblets. I won a large sum this winter on the races, and I am beginning to sell my sketches. Laidpore is more and more pleased with my work; he says it grows in force and individuality. I cannot judge of that myself, but I feel that I have gained in ease and confidence. However, as I said, I have sold a good many through Laidpore. I can live in the tiny house for little or nothing, with one servant. Old Celestine, who works occasionally for me, says she will come stay with me and do my work. I know I shall like it, like the feeling of freedom and independence."

"What does your husband say?"

"I have not told him yet. I only thought of it this morning. He will think I am demented, no doubt. Perhaps you think so."

Mademoiselle shook her head slowly. "Your reason is not yet clear to me," she said.

Neither was it quite clear to Edna herself; but it unfolded itself as she sat for a while in silence. Instinct had prompted her to put away her husband's bounty in casting off her allegiance. She did not know how it would be when he re-

[3] My pretty.

turned. There would have to be an understanding, an explanation. Conditions would some way adjust themselves, she felt, but whatever came, she had resolved never again to belong to another than herself.

"I shall give a grand dinner before I leave the old house!" Edna exclaimed. "You will have to come to it, Mademoiselle. I will give you everything that you like to eat and to drink. We shall sing and laugh and be merry for once." And she uttered a sigh that came from the very depth of her being.

If Mademoiselle happened to have received a letter from Robert during the interval of Edna's visits, she would give her the letter unsolicited. And she would seat herself at the piano and play as her humor prompted her while the young woman read the letter.

The little stove was roaring; it was red-hot, and the chocolate in the tin sizzled and sputtered. Edna went forward and opened the stove door, and Mademoiselle rising took a letter from under the bust of Beethoven and handed it to Edna.

"Another! so soon!" she exclaimed, her eyes filled with delight. "Tell me, Mademoiselle, does he know that I see his letters?"

"Never in the world! He would be angry and would never write to me again if he thought so. Does he write to you? Never a line. Does he send you a message? Never a word. It is because he loves you, poor fool, and is trying to forget you, since you are not free to listen to him or to belong to him."

"Why do you show me his letters, then?"

"Haven't you begged for them? Can I refuse you anything? Oh! you cannot deceive me," and Mademoiselle approached her beloved instrument and began to play. Edna did not at once read the letter. She sat holding it in her hand, while the music penetrated her whole being like an effulgence, warming and brightening the dark places of her soul. It prepared her for joy and exultation.

"Oh!" she exclaimed, letting the letter fall to the floor. "Why did you not tell me?" She went and grasped Mademoiselle's hands up from the keys. "Oh! unkind! malicious! Why did you not tell me?"

"That he was coming back? No great news, *ma foi*. I wonder he did not come long ago."

"But when, when?" cried Edna, impatiently. "He does not say when."

"He says 'very soon.' You know as much about it as I do, it is all in the letter."

"But why? Why is he coming? Oh, if I thought—" and she snatched the letters from the floor and turned the pages this way and that way, looking for the reason, which was left untold.

"If I were young and in love with a man," said Mademoiselle, turning on the stool and pressing her wiry hands between her knees as she looked down at Edna, who sat on the floor holding the letter, "it seems to me he would have to be some *grand esprit*,[4] a man with lofty aims and ability to reach them; one who

[4] Grand spirit (literal trans.); here, noble soul.

stood high enough to attract the notice of his fellow-men. It seems to me if I were young and in love I should never deem a man of ordinary caliber worthy of my devotion."

"Now it is you who are telling lies and seeking to deceive me, Mademoiselle; or else you have never been in love, and know nothing about it. Why," went on Edna, clasping her knees and looking up into Mademoiselle's twisted face, "do you suppose a woman knows why she loves? Does she select? Does she say to herself: 'Go to! Here is a distinguished statesman with presidential possibilities: I shall proceed to fall in love with him.' Or, 'I shall set my heart upon this musician, whose fame is on every tongue?' Or, 'This financier, who controls the world's money markets?'"

"You are purposely misunderstanding me, *ma reine*.[5] Are you in love with Robert?"

"Yes," said Edna. It was the first time she had admitted it, and a glow overspread her face, blotching it with red spots.

"Why?" asked her companion. "Why do you love him when you ought not to?"

Edna, with a motion or two, dragged herself on her knees before Mademoiselle Reisz, who took the glowing face between her two hands.

"Why? Because his hair is brown and grows away from his temples; because he opens and shuts his eyes, and his nose is a little out of drawing; because he has two lips and a square chin, and a little finger which he can't straighten from having played baseball too energetically in his youth. Because—"

"Because you do, in short," laughed Mademoiselle. "What will you do when he comes back?" she asked.

"Do? Nothing, except feel glad and happy to be alive."

She was already glad and happy to be alive at the mere thought of his return. The murky, lowering sky, which had depressed her a few hours before, seemed bracing and invigorating as she splashed through the streets on her way home.

She stopped at a confectioner's and ordered a huge box of bonbons for the children in Iberville. She slipped a card in the box, on which she scribbled a tender message and sent an abundance of kisses.

Before dinner in the evening Edna wrote a charming letter to her husband, telling him of her intention to move for a while into the little house around the block, and to give a farewell dinner before leaving, regretting that he was not there to share it, to help her out with the menu and assist her in entertaining the guests. Her letter was brilliant and brimming with cheerfulness.

XXVII

"What is the matter with you?" asked Arobin that evening. "I never found you in such a happy mood." Edna was tired by that time, and was reclining on the lounge before the fire.

---

[5] My queen.

"Don't you know the weather prophet has told us we shall see the sun pretty soon?"

"Well, that ought to be reason enough," he acquiesced. "You wouldn't give me another if I sat here all night imploring you." He sat close to her on a low tabouret,[6] and as he spoke his fingers lightly touched the hair that fell a little over her forehead. She liked the touch of his fingers through her hair, and closed her eyes sensitively.

"One of these days," she said, "I'm going to pull myself together for a while and think—try to determine what character of a woman I am; for, candidly, I don't know. By all the codes which I am acquainted with, I am a devilishly wicked specimen of the sex. But some way I can't convince myself that I am. I must think about it."

"Don't. What's the use? Why should you bother thinking about it when I can tell you what manner of woman you are?" His fingers strayed occasionally down to her warm, smooth cheeks and firm chin, which was growing a little full and double.

"Oh, yes! You will tell me that I am adorable; everything that is captivating. Spare yourself the effort."

"No; I shan't tell you anything of the sort, though I shouldn't be lying if I did."

"Do you know Mademoiselle Reisz?" she asked irrelevantly.

"The pianist? I know her by sight. I've heard her play."

"She says queer things sometimes in a bantering way that you don't notice at the time and you feel yourself thinking about afterward."

"For instance?"

"Well, for instance, when I left her today, she put her arms around me and felt my shoulder blades, to see if my wings were strong, she said. 'The bird that would soar above the level plain of tradition and prejudice must have strong wings. It is a sad spectacle to see the weaklings bruised, exhausted, fluttering back to earth.'"

"Whither would you soar?"

"I'm not thinking of any extraordinary flights. I only half comprehend her."

"I've heard she's partially demented," said Arobin.

"She seems to me wonderfully sane," Edna replied.

"I'm told she's extremely disagreeable and unpleasant. Why have you introduced her at a moment when I desired to talk of you?"

"Oh! talk of me if you like," cried Edna, clasping her hands beneath her head; "but let me think of something else while you do."

"I'm jealous of your thoughts to-night. They're making you a little kinder than usual; but some way I feel as if they were wandering, as if they were not here with me." She only looked at him and smiled. His eyes were very near. He leaned upon the lounge with an arm extended across her, while the other hand still rested upon her hair. They continued silently to look into each other's eyes.

[6] Cylindrical stool.

When he leaned forward and kissed her, she clasped his head, holding his lips to hers.

It was the first kiss of her life to which her nature had really responded. It was a flaming torch that kindled desire.

XXVIII

Edna cried a little that night after Arobin left her. It was only one phase of the multitudinous emotions which had assailed her. There was with her an overwhelming feeling of irresponsibility. There was the shock of the unexpected and the unaccustomed. There was her husband's reproach looking at her from external existence. There was Robert's reproach making itself felt by a quicker, fiercer, more overpowering love, which had awakened within her toward him. Above all, there was understanding. She felt as if a mist had been lifted from her eyes, enabling her to look upon and comprehend the significance of life, that monster made up of beauty and brutality. But among the conflicting sensations which assailed her, there was neither shame nor remorse. There was a dull pang of regret because it was not the kiss of love which had inflamed her, because it was not love which had held this cup of life to her lips.

XXIX

Without even waiting for an answer from her husband regarding his opinion or wishes in the matter, Edna hastened her preparations for quitting her home on Esplanade Street and moving into the little house around the block. A feverish anxiety attended her every action in that direction. There was no moment of deliberation, no interval of repose between the thought and its fulfillment. Early upon the morning following those hours passed in Arobin's society, Edna set about securing her new abode and hurrying her arrangements for occupying it. Within the precincts of her home she felt like one who has entered and lingered within the portals of some forbidden temple in which a thousand muffled voices bade her begone.

Whatever was her own in the house, everything which she had acquired aside from her husband's bounty, she caused to be transported to the other house, supplying simple and meager deficiencies from her own resources.

Arobin found her with rolled sleeves, working in company with the housemaid when he looked in during the afternoon. She was splendid and robust, and had never appeared handsomer than in the old blue gown, with a red silk handkerchief knotted at random around her head to protect her hair from the dust. She was mounted upon a high step-ladder, unhooking a picture from the wall when he entered. He had found the front door open, and had followed his ring by walking in unceremoniously.

"Come down!" he said. "Do you want to kill yourself?" She greeted him with affected carelessness, and appeared absorbed in her occupation.

If he had expected to find her languishing, reproachful, or indulging in sentimental tears, he must have been greatly surprised.

He was no doubt prepared for any emergency, ready for any one of the foregoing attitudes, just as he bent himself easily and naturally to the situation which confronted him.

"Please come down," he insisted, holding the ladder and looking up at her.

"No," she answered; "Ellen is afraid to mount the ladder. Joe is working at the 'pigeon house'—that's the name Ellen gives it, because it's so small and looks like a pigeon house—and some one has to do this."

Arobin pulled off his coat, and expressed himself ready and willing to tempt fate in her place. Ellen brought him one of her dustcaps, and went into contortions of mirth, which she found it impossible to control, which she saw him put it on before the mirror as grotesquely as he could. Edna herself could not refrain from smiling when she fastened it at his request. So it was he who in turn mounted the ladder, unhooking pictures and curtains, and dislodging ornaments as Edna directed. When he had finished he took off his dustcap and went out to wash his hands.

Edna was sitting on the tabouret, idly brushing the tips of a feather duster along the carpet when he came in again.

"Is there anything more you will let me do?" he asked.

"That is all," she answered. "Ellen can manage the rest." She kept the young woman occupied in the drawing-room, unwilling to be left alone with Arobin.

"What about the dinner?" he asked; "the grand event, the *coup d'état?*"

"It will be day after to-morrow. Why do you call it the '*coup d'état?*' Oh! it will be very fine; all my best of everything—crystal, silver and gold. Sèvres, flowers, music, and champagne to swim in. I'll let Léonce pay the bills. I wonder what he'll say when he sees the bills."

"And you ask me why I call it a *coup d'état?*" Arobin had put on his coat, and he stood before her and asked if his cravat was plumb. She told him it was, looking no higher than the tip of his collar.

"When do you go to the 'pigeon house?'—with all due acknowledgement to Ellen."

"Day after to-morrow, after the dinner. I shall sleep there."

"Ellen, will you very kindly get me a glass of water?" asked Arobin. "The dust in the curtains, if you will pardon me for hinting such a thing, has parched my throat to a crisp."

"While Ellen gets the water," said Edna, rising, "I will say good-by and let you go. I must get rid of this grime, and I have a million things to do and think of."

"When shall I see you?" asked Arobin, seeking to detain her, the maid having left the room.

"At the dinner, of course. You are invited."

"Not before?—not to-night or to-morrow morning or to-morrow noon or night? or the day after morning or noon? Can't you see yourself, without my telling you, what an eternity it is?"

He had followed her into the hall and to the foot of the stairway looking up at her as she mounted with her face half turned to him.

"Not an instant sooner," she said. But she laughed and looked at him with eyes that at once gave him courage to wait and made it torture to wait.

XXX

Though Edna had spoken of the dinner as a very grand affair, it was in truth a very small affair and very select, in so much as the invited were few and were se- lected with discrimination. She had counted upon an even dozen seating them- selves at her round mahogany board, forgetting for the moment that Madame Ratignolle was to the last degree *souffrante*[7] and unpresentable, and not foresee- ing that Madame Lebrun would send a thousand regrets at the last moment. So there were only ten, after all, which made a cozy, comfortable number.

There were Mr. and Mrs. Merriman, a pretty vivacious little woman in the thirties; her husband, a jovial fellow, something of a shallow-pate,[8] who laughed a good deal at other people's witticisms, and had thereby made himself ex- tremely popular. Mrs. Highcamp had accompanied them. Of course, there was Alcée Arobin; and Mademoiselle Reisz had consented to come. Edna had sent her a fresh bunch of violets with black lace trimmings for her hair. Monsieur Ratignolle brought himself and his wife's excuses. Victor Lebrun, who happened to be in the city, bent upon relaxation, had accepted with alacrity. There was a Miss Mayblunt, no longer in her teens, who looked at the world through lorgnettes and with the keenest interest. It was thought and said that she was in- tellectual; it was suspected of her that she wrote under a *nom de guerre*.[9] She had come with a gentleman by the name of Gouvernail, connected with one of the daily papers, of whom nothing special could be said, except that he was obser- vant and seemed quiet and inoffensive. Edna herself made the tenth, and at half- past eight they seated themselves at table, Arobin and Monsieur Ratignolle on either side of their hostess.

Mrs. Highcamp sat between Arobin and Victor Lebrun. Then came Mrs. Merriman, Mr. Gouvernail, Miss Mayblunt, Mr. Merriman, and Mademoiselle Reisz next to Monsieur Ratignolle.

There was something extremely gorgeous about the appearance of the table, an effect of splendor conveyed by a cover of pale yellow satin under strips of lace-work. There were wax candles in massive brass candelabra, burning softly under yellow silk shades; full, fragrant roses, yellow and red, abounded. There were silver and gold, as she had said there would be, and crystal which glittered like the gems which the women wore.

The ordinary stiff dining chairs had been discarded for the occasion and re- placed by the most commodious and luxurious which could be collected throughout the house. Mademoiselle Reisz, being exceedingly diminutive, was

[7] Ill.

[8] I.e., shallow-minded.

[9] Pseudonym.

elevated upon cushions, as small children are sometimes hoisted at table upon bulky volumes.

"Something new, Edna?" exclaimed Miss Mayblunt, with lorgnette directed toward a magnificent cluster of diamonds that sparkled, that almost sputtered, in Edna's hair, just over the center of her forehead.

"Quite new; 'brand' new, in fact; a present from my husband. It arrived this morning from New York. I may as well admit that this is my birthday, and that I am twenty-nine. In good time I expect you to drink my health. Meanwhile, I shall ask you to begin with this cocktail, composed—would you say 'composed?'" with an appeal to Miss Mayblunt—"composed by my father in honor of Sister Janet's wedding."

Before each guest stood a tiny glass that looked and sparkled like a garnet gem.

"Then, all things considered," spoke Arobin, "it might not be amiss to start out by drinking the Colonel's health in the cocktail which he composed, on the birthday of the most charming of women—the daughter whom he invented."

Mr. Merriman's laugh at this sally was such a genuine outburst and so contagious that it started the dinner with an agreeable swing that never slackened.

Miss Mayblunt begged to be allowed to keep her cocktail untouched before her, just to look at. The color was marvelous! She could compare it to nothing she had ever seen, and the garnet lights which it emitted were unspeakably rare. She pronounced the Colonel an artist, and stuck to it.

Monsieur Ratignolle was prepared to take things seriously; the *mets*, and *entre-mets*, the service, the decorations, even the people. He looked up from his pompano[1] and inquired of Arobin if he were related to the gentleman of that name who formed one of the firm of Laitner and Arobin, lawyers. The young man admitted that Laitner was a warm personal friend, who permitted Arobin's name to decorate the firm's letterheads and to appear upon a shingle that graced Perdido Street.

"There are so many inquisitive people and institutions abounding," said Arobin, "that one is really forced as a matter of convenience these days to assume the virtue of an occupation if he has it not."

Monsieur Ratignolle stared a little, and turned to ask Mademoiselle Reisz if she considered the symphony concerts up to the standard which had been set the previous winter. Mademoiselle Reisz answered Monsieur Ratignolle in French, which Edna thought a little rude, under the circumstances, but characteristic. Mademoiselle had only disagreeable things to say of the symphony concerts, and insulting remarks to make of all the musicians of New Orleans, singly and collectively. All her interest seemed to be centered upon the delicacies placed before her.

Mr. Merriman said that Mr. Arobin's remark about inquisitive people reminded him of a man from Waco[2] the other day at the St. Charles Hotel—but

---

[1] Or pompano fish, a southern delicacy. *Mets*": main course. *"Entremets"*: side dishes.
[2] Town in Texas.

as Mr. Merriman's stories were always lame and lacking point, his wife seldom permitted him to complete them. She interrupted him to ask if he remembered the name of the author whose book she had bought the week before to send to a friend in Geneva. She was talking "books" with Mr. Gouvernail and trying to draw from him his opinion upon current literary topics. Her husband told the story of the Waco man privately to Miss Mayblunt, who pretended to be greatly amused and to think it extremely clever.

Mrs. Highcamp hung with languid but unaffected interest upon the warm and impetuous volubility of her left-hand neighbor, Victor Lebrun. Her attention was never for a moment withdrawn from him after seating herself at table; and when he turned to Mrs. Merriman, who was prettier and more vivacious than Mrs. Highcamp, she waited with easy indifference for an opportunity to reclaim his attention. There was the occasional sound of music, of mandolins, sufficiently removed to be an agreeable accompaniment rather than an interruption to the conversation. Outside the soft, monotonous splash of a fountain could be heard; the sound penetrated into the room with the heavy odor of jessamine that came through the open windows.

The golden shimmer of Edna's satin gown spread in rich folds on either side of her. There was a soft fall of lace encircling her shoulders. It was the color of her skin, without the glow, the myriad living tints that one may sometimes discover in vibrant flesh. There was something in her attitude, in her whole appearance when she leaned her head against the high-backed chair and spread her arms, which suggested the regal woman, the one who rules, who looks on, who stands alone.

But as she sat there amid her guests, she felt the old ennui overtaking her; the hopelessness which so often assailed her, which came upon her like an obsession, like something extraneous, independent of volition. It was something which announced itself; a chill breath that seemed to issue from some vast cavern wherein discords wailed. There came over her the acute longing which always summoned into her spiritual vision the presence of the beloved one, overpowering her at once with a sense of the unattainable.

The moments glided on, while a feeling of good fellowship passed around the circle like a mystic cord, holding and binding these people together with jest and laughter. Monsieur Ratignolle was the first to break the pleasant charm. At ten o'clock he excused himself. Madame Ratignolle was waiting for him at home. She was *bien souffrante*,[3] and she was filled with vague dread, which only her husband's presence could allay.

Mademoiselle Reisz arose with Monsieur Ratignolle, who offered to escort her to the car. She had eaten well; she had tasted the good rich wines, and they must have turned her head, for she bowed pleasantly to all as she withdrew from table. She kissed Edna upon the shoulder, and whispered: *"Bonne nuit, ma reine;*

[3] Very ill.

soyez sage.[4] She had been a little bewildered upon rising, or rather, descending from her cushions, and Monsieur Ratignolle gallantly took her arm and led her away.

Mrs. Highcamp was weaving a garland of roses, yellow and red. She had finished the garland, she laid it lightly upon Victor's black curls. He was reclining far back in the luxurious chair, holding a glass of champagne to the light.

As if a magician's wand had touched him, the garland of roses transformed him into a vision of Oriental beauty. His cheeks were the color of crushed grapes, and his dusky eyes glowed with a languishing fire.

"*Sapristi!*" exclaimed Arobin.

But Mrs. Highcamp had one more touch to add to the picture. She took from the back of her chair a white silken scarf, with which she had covered her shoulders in the early part of the evening. She draped it across the boy in graceful folds, and in a way to conceal his black, conventional evening dress. He did not seem to mind what she did to him, only smiled, showing a faint gleam of white teeth, while he continued to gaze with narrowing eyes at the light through his glass of champagne.

"Oh! to be able to paint in color rather than in words!" exclaimed Miss Mayblunt, losing herself in a rhapsodic dream as she looked at him.

> "There was a graven image of Desire
> Painted with red blood on a ground of gold'"[5]

murmured Gouvernail, under his breath.

The effect of the wine upon Victor was, to change his accustomed volubility into silence. He seemed to have abandoned himself to a reverie, and to be seeing pleasing visions in the amber bead.

"Sing," entreated Mrs. Highcamp. "Won't you sing to us?"

"Let him alone," said Arobin.

"He's posing," offered Mr. Merriman; "let him have it out."

"I believe he's paralyzed," laughed Mrs. Merriman. And leaning over the youth's chair, she took the glass from his hand and held it to his lips. He sipped the wine slowly, and when he had drained the glass she laid it upon the table and wiped his lips with her little filmy handkerchief.

"Yes, I'll sing for you," he said, turning in his chair toward Mrs. Highcamp. He clasped his hands behind his head, and looking up at the ceiling began to hum a little, trying his voice, like a musician tuning an instrument. Then, looking at Edna, he began to sing:

> "Ah! si tu savais!"

[4] Good night, my queen; be good.
[5] From *A. Cameo,* by Algernon Charles Swinburne (1837–1909).

"Stop!" she cried, "don't sing that. I don't want you to sing it," and she laid her glass so impetuously and blindly upon the table as to shatter it against a caraffe. The wine spilled over Arobin's legs and some of it trickled down upon Mrs. Highcamp's black gauze gown. Victor had lost all idea of courtesy, or else he thought his hostess was not in earnest, for he laughed and went on:

"Ah! si tu savais
Ce que tes yeux me dissent" —

"Oh! you mustn't! you mustn't," exclaimed Edna, and pushing back her chair she got up, and going behind him placed her hand over his mouth. He kissed the soft palm that pressed upon his lips.

"No, no, I won't, Mrs. Pontellier, I didn't know you meant it," looking up at her with caressing eyes. The touch of his lips was like a pleasing sting to her hand. She listed the garland of roses from his head and flung it across the room.

"Come, Victor; you've posed long enough. Give Mrs. Highcamp her scarf."

Mrs. Highcamp undraped the scarf from about him with her own hands. Miss Mayblunt and Mr. Gouvernail suddenly conceived the notion that it was time to say good night. And Mr. and Mrs. Merriman wondered how it could be so late.

Before parting from Victor, Mrs. Highcamp invited him to call upon her daughter, who she knew would be charmed to meet him and talk French and sing French songs with him. Victor expressed his desire and intention to call upon Miss Highcamp at the first opportunity which presented itself. He asked if Arobin were going his way. Arobin was not.

The mandolin players had long since stolen away. A profound stillness had fallen upon the broad, beautiful street. The voices of Edna's disbanding guests jarred like a discordant note upon the quiet harmony of the night.

XXXI

"Well?" questioned Arobin, who had remained with Edna after the others had departed.

"Well," she reiterated, and stood up, stretching her arms, and feeling the need to relax her muscles after having been so long seated.

"What next?" he asked.

"The servants are all gone. They left when the musicians did. I have dismissed them. The house has to be closed and locked, and I shall trot around to the pigeon house, and shall send Celestine over in the morning to straighten things up."

He looked around, and began to turn out some of the lights.

"What about upstairs?" he inquired.

"I think it is all right: but there may be a window or two unlatched. We had better look; you might take a candle and see. And bring me my wrap and hat on the foot of the bed in the middle room."

He went up with the light, and Edna began closing doors and windows. She hated to shut in the smoke and the fumes of the wine. Arobin found her cape and hat, which he brought down and helped her to put on.

When everything was secured and the lights put out, they left through the front door, Arobin locking it and taking the key, which he carried for Edna. He helped her down the steps.

"Will you have a spray of jessamine?" he asked, breaking off a few blossoms as he passed.

"No; I don't want anything."

She seemed disheartened, and had nothing to say. She took his arm, which he offered her, holding up the weight of her satin train with the other hand. She looked down, noticing the black line of his leg moving in and out so close to her against the yellow shimmer of her gown. There was the whistle of a railway train somewhere in the distance, and the midnight bells were ringing. They met no one in their short walk.

The "pigeon-house" stood behind a locked gate, and a shallow *parterre*[6] that had been somewhat neglected. There was a small front porch, upon which a long window and the front door opened. The door opened directly into the parlor; there was no side entry. Back in the yard was a room for servants, in which old Celestine had been ensconced.

Edna had left a lamp burning low upon the table. She had succeeded in making the room look habitable and homelike. There were some books on the table and a lounge near at hand. On the floor was a fresh matting, covered with a rug or two; and on the walls hung a few tasteful pictures. But the room was filled with flowers. These were a surprise to her. Arobin had sent them, and had had Celestine distribute them during Edna's absence. Her bedroom was adjoining, and across a small passage were the dining-room and kitchen.

Edna seated herself with every appearance of discomfort.

"Are you tired?" he asked.

"Yes, and chilled and miserable. I feel as if I had been wound up to a certain pitch—too tight—and something inside of me had snapped." She rested her head against the table upon her bare arm.

"You want to rest," he said, "and to be quiet. I'll go; I'll leave you and let you rest."

"Yes," she replied.

He stood up beside her and smoothed her hair with his soft magnetic hand. His touch conveyed to her a certain physical comfort. She could have fallen quietly asleep there if he had continued to pass his hand over her hair. He brushed the hair upward from the nape of her neck.

"I hope you will feel better and happier in the morning," he said. "You have tried to do too much in the past few days. The dinner was the last straw; you might have dispensed with it."

---

[6] Ornamental garden.

"Yes," she admitted; "it was stupid."

"No, it was delightful; but it has worn you out." His hand had strayed to her beautiful shoulders, and he could feel the response of her flesh to his touch. He seated himself beside her and kissed her lightly upon the shoulder.

"I thought you were going away," she said, in an uneven voice.

"I am, after I have said good night."

"Good night," she murmured.

He did not answer, except to continue to caress her. He did not say good night until she had become supple to his gentle, seductive entreaties.

XXXII

When Mr. Pontellier learned of his wife's intention to abandon her home and take up her residence elsewhere, he immediately wrote her a letter of unqualified disapproval and remonstrance. She had given reasons which he was unwilling to acknowledge as adequate. He hoped she had not acted upon her rash impulse; and he begged her to consider first, foremost, and above all else, what people would say. He was not dreaming of scandal when he uttered this warning; that was a thing which would never have entered into his mind to consider in connection with his wife's name or his own. He was simply thinking of his financial integrity. It might get noised about that the Pontelliers had met with reverses, and were forced to conduct their *ménage*[7] on a humbler scale than heretofore. It might do incalculable mischief to his business prospects.

But remembering Edna's whimsical turn of mind of late, and foreseeing that she had immediately acted upon her impetuous determination, he grasped the situation with his usual promptness and handled it with his well-known business tact and cleverness.

The same mail which brought to Edna his letter of disapproval carried instructions—the most minute instructions—to a well-known architect concerning the remodeling of his home, changes which he had long contemplated, and which he desired carried forward during his temporary absence.

Expert and reliable packers and movers were engaged to convey the furniture, carpets, pictures—everything movable, in short—to places of security. And in an incredibly short time the Pontellier house was turned over to the artisans. There was to be an addition—a small snuggery;[8] there was to be frescoing, and hardwood flooring was to be put into such rooms as had not yet been subjected to this improvement.

Furthermore, in one of the daily papers appeared a brief notice to the effect that Mr. and Mrs. Pontellier were contemplating a summer sojourn abroad, and that their handsome residence on Esplanade Street was undergoing sumptuous alterations, and would not be ready for occupancy until their return. Mr. Pontellier had saved appearances!

[7] Household.

[8] Den.

Edna admired the skill of his maneuver, and avoided any occasion to balk his intentions. When the situation as set forth by Mr. Pontellier was accepted and taken for granted, she was apparently satisfied that it should be so.

The pigeon-house pleased her. It at once assumed the intimate character of a home, while she herself invested it with a charm which it reflected like a warm glow. There was with her a feeling of having descended in the social scale, with a corresponding sense of having risen in the spiritual. Every step which she took toward relieving herself from obligations added to her strength and expansion as an individual. She began to look with her own eyes; to see and to apprehend the deeper undercurrents of life. No longer was she content to "feed upon opinion" when her own soul had invited her.

After a little while, a few days, in fact, Edna went up and spent a week with her children in Iberville. They were delicious February days, with all the summer's promises hovering in the air.

How glad she was to see the children! She wept for very pleasure when she felt their little arms clasping her; their hard, ruddy cheeks pressed against her own glowing cheeks. She looked into their faces with hungry eyes that could not be satisfied with looking. And what stories they had to tell their mother! About the pigs, the cows, the mules! About riding to the mill behind Gluglu; fishing back in the lake with their Uncle Jasper; picking pecans with Lidie's little black brood, and hauling chips in their express wagon. It was a thousand times more fun to haul real chips for old lame Susie's real fire than to drag painted blocks along the banquette on Esplanade Street!

She went with them herself to see the pigs and the cows, to look at the darkies laying the cane, to thrash the pecan trees, and catch fish in the back lake. She lived with them a whole week long, giving them all of herself, and gathering and filling herself with their young existence. They listed, breathless, when she told them the house in Esplanade Street was crowded with workmen, hammering, nailing, sawing, and filling the place with clatter. They wanted to know where their bed was; what had been done with their rocking-horse; and where did Joe sleep, and where had Ellen gone, and the cook? But, above all, they were fired with a desire to see the little house around the block. Was there any place to play? Were there any boys next door? Raoul, with pessimistic foreboding, was convinced that there were only girls next door. Where would they sleep, and where would papa sleep? She told them the fairies would fix it all right.

The old Madame was charmed with Edna's visit, and showered all manner of delicate attentions upon her. She was delighted to know that the Esplanade Street house was in a dismantled condition. It gave her the promise and pretext to keep the children indefinitely.

It was with a wrench and a pang that Edna left her children. She carried away with her the sound of their voices and the touch of their cheeks. All along the journey homeward their presence lingered with her like the memory of a delicious song. But by the time she had regained the city the song no longer echoed in her soul. She was again alone.

XXXIII

It happened sometimes when Edna went to see Mademoiselle Reisz that the little musician was absent, giving a lesson or making some small necessary household purchase. The key was always left in a secret hiding-place in the entry, which Edna knew. If Mademoiselle happened to be away, Edna would usually enter and wait for her return.

When she knocked at Mademoiselle Reisz's door one afternoon there was no response; so unlocking the door, as usual, she entered and found the apartment deserted, as she had expected. Her day had been quite filled up, and it was for a rest, for a refuge, and to talk about Robert, that she sought out her friend.

She had worked at her canvas—a young Italian character study—all the morning, completing the work without the model; but there had been many interruptions, some incident to her modest housekeeping, and others of a social nature.

Madame Ratignolle had dragged herself over, avoiding the too public thoroughfares, she said. She complained that Edna had neglected her much of late. Besides, she was consumed with curiosity to see the little house and the manner in which it was conducted. She wanted to hear all about the dinner party; Monsieur Ratignolle had left so early. What had happened after he left? The champagne and grapes which Edna sent over were *too* delicious. She had so little appetite; they had refreshed and toned her stomach. Where on earth was she going to put Mr. Pontellier in that little house, and the boys? And then she made Edna promise to go to her when her hour of trial overtook her.

"At any time—any time of the day or night, dear," Edna assured her.

Before leaving Madame Ratignolle said:

"In some way you seem to me like a child, Edna. You seem to act without a certain amount of reflection which is necessary in this life. That is the reason I want to say you mustn't mind if I advise you to be a little careful while you are living here alone. Why don't you have some one come and stay with you? Wouldn't Mademoiselle Reisz come?"

"No; she wouldn't wish to come, and I shouldn't want her always with me."

"Well, the reason—you know how evil-minded the world is—some one was talking of Alcée Arobin visiting you. Of course, it wouldn't matter if Mr. Arobin had not such a dreadful reputation. Monsieur Ratignolle was telling me that his attentions alone are considered enough to ruin a woman's name."

"Does he boast of his successes?" asked Edna, indifferently, squinting at her picture.

"No, I think not. I believe he is a decent fellow as far as that goes. But his character is so well known among the men. I shan't be able to come back and see you; it was very, very imprudent today."

"Mind the step!" cried Edna.

"Don't neglect me," entreated Madame Ratignolle; "and don't mind what I said about Arobin, or having some one to stay with you."

"Of course not," Edna laughed. "You may say anything you like to me." They kissed each other good-bye. Madame Ratignolle had not far to go, and Edna stood on the porch while watching her walk down the street.

Then in the afternoon Mrs. Merriman and Mrs. Highcamp had made their "party call." Edna felt that they might have dispensed with the formality. They had also come to invite her to play *vingt-et-un*[9] one evening at Mrs. Merriman's. She was asked to go early, to dinner, and Mr. Merriman or Mr. Arobin would take her home. Edna accepted in a half-hearted way. She sometimes felt very tired of Mrs. Highcamp and Mrs. Merriman.

Late in the afternoon she sought refuge with Mademoiselle Reisz, and stayed there alone, waiting for her, feeling a kind of repose invade her with the very atmosphere of the shabby, unpretentious little room.

Edna sat at the window, which looked out over the house-tops and across the river. The window frame was filled with pots of flowers, and she sat and picked the dry leaves from a rose geranium. The day was warm, and the breeze which blow from the river was very pleasant. She removed her hat and laid it on the piano. She went on picking the leaves and digging round the plants with her hat pin. Once she thought she heard Mademoiselle Reisz approaching. But it was a young black girl, who came in, bringing a small bundle of laundry, which she deposited in the adjoining room, and went away.

Edna seated herself at the piano, and softly picked out with one hand the bars of a piece of music which lay open before her. A half-hour went by. There was the occasional sound of people going and coming in the lower hall. She was growing interested in her occupation of picking out the aria, when there was a second rap at the door. She vaguely wondered what these people did when they found Mademoiselle's door unlocked.

"Come in," she called, turning her face toward the door. And this time it was Robert Lebrun who presented himself. She attempted to rise; she could not have done so without betraying the agitation which mastered her at sight of him, so she fell back upon the stool, only exclaiming, "Why Robert!"

He came and clasped her hand, seemingly without knowing what he was saying or doing.

"Mrs. Pontellier! How do you happen—oh! how well you look! Is Mademoiselle Reisz not here? I never expected to see you."

"When did you come back?" asked Edna in an unsteady voice, wiping her face with her handkerchief. She seemed ill at ease on the piano stool, and he begged her to take the chair by the window. She did so, mechanically, while he seated himself on the stool.

"I returned day before yesterday," he answered, while he leaned his arm on the keys, bringing forth a crash of discordant sound.

"Day before yesterday!" she repeated, aloud, and went on thinking to herself, "day before yesterday," in a sort of an uncomprehending way. She had

---

[9] Twenty-one, a card game.

pictured him seeking her at the very first hour, and he had lived under the same sky since day before yesterday; while only by accident had he stumbled upon her. Mademoiselle must have lied when she said, "Poor fool, he loves you."

"Day before yesterday," she repeated, breaking off a spray of Mademoiselle's geranium; "then if you had not met me here to-day you wouldn't—when—that is, didn't you mean to come and see me?"

"Of course, I should have gone to see you. There have been so many things—" he turned the leaves of Mademoiselle's music nervously. "I started in at once yesterday with the old firm. After all there is as much chance for me here as there was there—that is, I might find it profitable some day. The Mexicans were not very congenial."

So he had come back because the Mexicans were not congenial; because business was as profitable here as there; because of any reason, and not because he cared to be near her. She remembered the day she sat on the floor, turning the pages of his letter, seeking the reason which was left untold.

She had not noticed how he looked—only feeling his presence; but she turned deliberately and observed him. After all, he had been absent but a few months, and was not changed. His hair—the color of hers—waved back from his temples in the same way as before. His skin was not more burned than it had been at Grand Isle. She found in his eyes, when he looked at her for one silent moment, the same tender caress, with an added warmth and entreaty which had not been there before—the same glance which had penetrated to the sleeping places of her soul and awakened them.

A hundred times Edna had pictured Robert's return, and imagined their first meeting. It was usually at her home, whither he had sought her out at once. She always fancied him expressing or betraying in some way his love for her. And here, the reality was that they sat ten feet apart, she at the window, crushing geranium leaves in her hand and smelling them, he twirling around on the piano stool, saying:

"I was very much surprised to hear of Mr. Pontellier's absence; it's a wonder Mademoiselle Reisz did not tell me; and your moving—mother told me yesterday. I should think you would have gone to New York with him, or to Iberville with the children, rather than be bothered here with housekeeping. And you are going abroad, too, I hear. We shan't have you at Grand Isle next summer; it won't seem—do you see much of Mademoiselle Reisz? She often spoke of you in the few letters she wrote."

"Do you remember that you promised to write to me when you went away?" A flush overspread his whole face.

"I couldn't believe that my letters would be of any interest to you."

"That is an excuse; it isn't the truth." Edna reached for her hat on the piano. She adjusted it, sticking the hat pin through the heavy coil of hair with some deliberation.

"Are you not going to wait for Mademoiselle Reisz?" asked Robert.

"No; I have found when she is absent this long, she is liable not to come back till late." She drew on her gloves, and Robert picked up his hat.

"Won't you wait for her?" asked Edna.

"Not if you think she will not be back till late," adding, as if suddenly aware of some discourtesy in his speech, "and I should miss the pleasure of walking home with you." Edna locked the door and put the key back in its hiding place.

They went together, picking their way across muddy streets and sidewalks encumbered with the cheap display of small tradesmen. Part of the distance they rode in the car, and after disembarking, passed the Pontellier mansion, which looked broken and half torn asunder. Robert had never known the house, and looked at it with interest.

"I never knew you in your home," he remarked.

"I am glad you did not."

"Why?" She did not answer. They went on around the corner, and it seemed as if her dreams were coming true after all, when he followed her into the little house.

"You must stay and dine with me, Robert. You see I am all alone, and it is so long since I have seen you. There is so much I want to ask you."

She took off her hat and gloves. He stood irresolute, making some excuse about his mother who expected him; he even muttered something about an engagement. She struck a match and lit the lamp on the table; it was growing dusk. She he saw her face in the lamplight, looking pained, with all the soft lines gone out of it, he threw his hat aside and seated himself.

"Oh! you know I want to stay if you will let me!" he exclaimed. All the softness came back. She laughed, and went and put her hand on his shoulder.

"This is the first moment you have seemed like the old Robert. I'll go tell Celestine." She hurried away to tell Celestine to set an extra place. She even sent her off in search of some added delicacy which she had not thought of for herself. And she recommended great care in dripping the coffee and having the omelet done to a proper turn.

When she returned, Robert was turning over magazines, sketches, and things that lay upon the table in great disorder. He picked up a photograph, and exclaimed:

"Alcée Arobin! What on earth is his picture doing here?"

"I tried to make a sketch of his head one day," answered Edna, "and he thought the photograph might help me. It was at the other house. I thought it had been left there. I must have picked it up with my drawing materials."

"I should think you would give it back to him if you have finished with it."

"Oh! I have a great many such photographs. I never think of returning them. They don't amount to anything." Robert kept on looking at the picture.

"It seems to me — do you think his head worth drawing? Is he a friend of Mr. Pontellier's? You never said you knew him."

"He isn't a friend of Mr. Pontellier's; he's a friend of mine. I always knew him — that is, it is only of late that I know him pretty well. But I'd rather talk about you, and know what you have been seeing and doing and feeling out there in Mexico." Robert threw aside the picture.

"I've been seeing the waves and the white beach of Grand Isle; the quiet, grassy street of the *Chênière;* the old fort at Grande Terre. I've been working like a machine, and feeling like a lost soul. There was nothing interesting."

She leaned her head upon her hand to shade her eyes from the light.

"And what have you been seeing and doing and feeling all these days?" he asked.

"I've been seeing the waves and the white beach of Grand Isle; the quiet, grassy street of the *Chênière Caminada;* the old sunny fort at Grande Terre. I've been working with little more comprehension than a machine, and still feeling like a lost soul. There was nothing interesting."

"Mrs. Pontellier, you are cruel," he said, with feeling, closing his eyes and resting his head back in his chair. They remained in silence till old Celestine announced dinner.

XXXIV

The dining-room was very small. Edna's round mahogany would have almost filled it. As it was there was but a step or two from the little table in the kitchen, to the mantel, the small buffet, and the side door that opened out on the narrow brick-paved yard.

A certain degree of ceremony settled upon them with the announcement of dinner. There was no return to personalities. Robert related incidents of his sojourn in Mexico, and Edna talked of events likely to interest him, which had occurred during his absence. The dinner was of ordinary quality, except for the few delicacies which she had sent out to purchase. Old Celestine, with a bandana *tignon* twisted about her head,[1] hobbled in and out, taking a personal interest in everything; and she lingered occasionally to talk *patois*[2] with Robert, whom she had known as a boy.

He went out to a neighboring cigar stand to purchase cigarette papers, and when he came back he found that Celestine had served the black coffee in the parlor.

"Perhaps I shouldn't have come back," he said. "When you are tired of me, tell me to go."

"You never tire me. You must have forgotten the hours and hours at Grand Isle in which we grew accustomed to each other and used to being together."

"I have forgotten nothing at Grand Isle," he said, not looking at her, but rolling a cigarette. His tobacco pouch, which he laid upon the table, was a fantastic embroidered silk affair, evidently the handiwork of a woman.

"You used to carry your tobacco in a rubber pouch," said Edna, picking up the pouch and examining the needlework.

[1] I.e., her hair is tied up with a scarf.
[2] Dialect.

"Yes; it was lost."

"Where did you buy this one? In Mexico?"

"It was given to me by a Vera Cruz girl; they are very generous," he replied, striking a match and lighting his cigarette.

"They are very handsome, I suppose, those Mexican women; very picturesque, with their black eyes and their lace scarfs."

"Some are; others are hideous. Just as you find women everywhere."

"What was she like—the one who gave you the pouch? You must have known her very well."

"She was very ordinary. She wasn't of the slightest importance. I knew her well enough."

"Did you visit at her house? Was it interesting? I should like to know and hear about the people you met, and the impressions they made on you."

"There are some people who leave impressions not so lasting as the imprint of an oar upon the water."

"Was she such a one?"

"It would be ungenerous for me to admit that she was of that order and kind." He thrust the pouch back in his pocket, as if to put away the subject with the trifle which had brought it up.

Arobin dropped in with a message from Mrs. Merriman, to say that the card party was postponed on account of the illness of one of her children.

"How do you do, Arobin?" said Robert, rising from the obscurity.

"Oh! Lebrun. To be sure! I heard yesterday you were back. How did they treat you down in Mexico?"

"Fairly well."

"But not well enough to keep you there. Stunning girls, though, in Mexico. I thought I should never get away from Vera Cruz when I was down there a couple of years ago."

"Did they embroider slippers and tobacco pouches and hat bands and things for you?" asked Edna.

"Oh! my! no! I didn't get so deep in their regard. I fear they made more impression on me than I made on them."

"You were less fortunate than Robert, then."

"I am always less fortunate than Robert. Has he been imparting tender confidences?"

"I've been imposing myself long enough," said Robert, rising, and shaking hands with Edna. "Please convey my regards to Mr. Pontellier when you write."

He shook hands with Arobin and went away.

"Fine fellow, that Lebrun," said Arobin when Robert had gone. "I never heard you speak of him."

"I knew him last summer at Grand Isle," she replied. "Here is that photograph of yours. Don't you want it?"

"What do I want with it? Throw it away." She threw it back on the table.

"I'm not going to Mrs. Merriman's," she said. "If you see her, tell her so. But perhaps I had better write. I think I shall write now, and say that I am sorry her child is sick, and tell her not to count on me."

"It would be a good scheme," acquiesced Arobin. "I don't blame you; stupid lot!"

Edna opened the blotter, and having procured paper and pen, began to write a note. Arobin lit a cigar and read the evening paper, which he had in his pocket.

"What is the date?" she asked. He told her.

"Will you mail this for me when you go out?"

"Certainly." He read to her little bits out of the newspaper, while she straightened things on the table.

"What do you want to do?" he asked, throwing aside the paper. "Do you want to go for a walk or a drive or anything? It would be a fine night to drive."

"No; I don't want to do anything but just be quiet. You go away and amuse yourself. Don't stay."

"I'll go away if I must; but I shan't amuse myself. You know that I only live when I am near you."

He stood up to bid her good night.

"Is that one of the things you always say to women?"

"I have said it before, but I don't think I ever came so near meaning it," he answered with a smile. There were no warm lights in her eyes; only a dreamy, absent look.

"Good night. I adore you. Sleep well," he said, and he kissed her hand and went away.

She stayed alone in a kind of reverie—a sort of stupor. Step by step she lived over every instant of the time she had been with Robert after he had entered Mademoiselle Reisz's door. She recalled his words, his looks. How few and meager they had been for her hungry heart! A vision—a transcendently seductive vision of a Mexican girl arose before. She writhed with a jealous pang. She wondered when he would come back. He had not said he would come back. She had been with him, had heard his voice and touched his hand. But some way he had seemed nearer to her off there in Mexico.

XXXV

The morning was full of sunlight and hope. Edna could see before her no denial—only the promise of excessive joy. She lay in bed awake, with bright eyes full of speculation. "He loves you, poor fool." If she could but get that conviction firmly fixed in her mind, what mattered about the rest? She felt she had been childish and unwise the night before in giving herself over to despondency. She recapitulated the motives which no doubt explained Robert's reserve. They were not insurmountable; they would not hold if he really loved her; they could not hold against her own passion, which he must come to realize in time. She pictured him going to his business that morning. She even saw how he was dressed; how he walked down one street, and turned the corner of another; saw him bending over his desk, talking to people who entered the office, going to his lunch, and perhaps watching for her on the street. He would come to her in the afternoon or evening, sit and roll his cigarette, talk a little, and go away as he had done the night before. But how delicious it would be to have him there with her! She would have no regrets, nor seek to penetrate his reserve if he still chose to wear it.

Edna ate her breakfast only half dressed. The maid brought her a delicious printed scrawl from Raoul, expressing his love, asking her to send him some bonbons, and telling her they had found that morning ten tiny white pigs all lying in a row beside Lidie's big white pig.

A letter also came from her husband, saying he hoped to be back early in March, and then they would get ready for that journey abroad which he had promised her so long, which he felt now fully able to afford; he felt above to travel as people should, without any thought of small economies—thanks to his recent speculations in Wall Street.

Much to her surprise she received a note from Arobin, written at midnight from the club. It was to say good morning to her, to hope that she had slept well, to assure her of his devotion, which he trusted she in some faintest manner returned.

All these letters were pleasing to her. She answered the children in a cheerful frame of mind, promising them bonbons, and congratulating them upon their happy find of the little pigs.

She answered her husband with friendly evasiveness,—not with any fixed design to mislead him, only because all sense of reality had gone out of her life, she had abandoned herself to Fate, and awaited the consequences with indifference.

To Arobin's note she made no reply. She put it under Celestine's stove-lid.

Edna worked several hours with much spirit. She saw no one but a picture dealer, who asked her if it were true that she was going abroad to study in Paris.

She said possibly she might, and he negotiated with her for some Parisian studies to reach him in time for the holiday trade in December.

Robert did not come that day. She was keenly disappointed. He did not come the following day, nor the next. Each morning she awoke with hope, and each night she was a prey to despondency. She was tempted to seek him out. But far from yielding to the impulse, she avoided any occasion which might throw her in his way. She did not go to Mademoiselle Reisz's nor pass by Madame Lebrun's, as she might have done if he had still been in Mexico.

When Arobin, one night, urged her to drive with him, she went—out to the lake, on the Shell Road.[3] His horses were full of mettle, and even a little unmanageable. She liked the rapid gait at which they spun along, and the quick, sharp

---

[3] Road by Lake Pontchartrain.

sound of the horses' hoofs on the hard road. They did not stop anywhere to eat or to drink. Arobin was not needlessly imprudent. But they ate and they drank when they regained Edna's little dining-room—which was comparatively early in the evening.

It was late when he left her. It was getting to be more than a passing whim with Arobin to see her and be with her. He had detected the latent sensuality, which unfolded under his delicate sense of her nature's requirements like a torpid, torrid, sensitive blossom.

There was no despondency when she fell asleep that night; nor was there hope when she awoke in the morning.

XXXVI

There was a garden out in the suburbs; a small, leafy corner, with a few green tables under the orange trees. An old cat slept all day on the stone step in the sun, and an old *mulatresse*[4] slept her idle hours away in her chair at the open window, till some one happened to knock on one of the green tables. She had milk and cream cheese to sell, and bread and butter. There was no one who could make such excellent coffee or fry a chicken so golden brown as she.

The place was too modest to attract the attention of people of fashion, and so quiet as to have escaped the notice of those in search of pleasure and dissipation. Edna had discovered it accidentally one day when the high-board gate stood ajar. She caught sight of a little green table, blotched with the checkered sunlight that filtered through the quivering leaves overhead. Within she had found the slumbering *mulatresse,* the drowsy cat, and a glass of milk which reminded her of the milk she had tasted in Iberville.

She often stopped there during her perambulations; sometimes taking a book with her, and sitting an hour or two under the trees when she found the place deserted. Once or twice she took a quiet dinner there alone, having instructed Celestine beforehand to prepare no dinner at home. It was the last place in the city where she would have expected to meet any one she knew.

Still she was not astonished when, as she was partaking of a modest dinner late in the afternoon, looking into an open book, stroking the cat, which had made friends with her—she was not greatly astonished to see Robert come in at the tall garden gate.

"I am destined to see you only by accident," she said, shoving the cat off the chair beside her. He was surprised, ill at ease, almost embarrassed at meeting her thus so unexpectedly.

"Do you come here often?" he asked.

"I almost live here," she said.

"I used to drop in very often for a cup of Catiche's good coffee. This is the first time since I came back."

---

[4] A mulatto woman, of mixed black and white ancestry.

"She'll bring you a plate, and you will share my dinner. There's always enough for two—even three." Edna had intended to be indifferent and as reserved as he when she met him; she had reached the determination by a laborious train of reasoning, incident to one of her despondent moods. But her resolve melted when she saw him before her, seated there beside her in the little garden, as if a designing Providence had led him into her path.

"Why have you kept away from me, Robert?" she asked, closing the book that lay open upon the table.

"Why are you so personal, Mrs. Pontellier? Why do you force me to idiotic subterfuges?" he exclaimed with sudden warmth. "I suppose there's no use telling you I've been very busy, or that I've been sick, or that I've been to see you and not found you at home. Please let me off with any one of those excuses."

"You are the embodiment of selfishness," she said. "You save yourself something—I don't know what—but there is some selfish motive, and in sparing yourself you never consider for a moment what I think, or how I feel your neglect and indifference. I suppose this is what you would call unwomanly; but I have got into a habit of expressing myself. It doesn't matter to me, and you may think me unwomanly if you like."

"No; I only think you cruel, as I said the other day. Maybe not intentionally cruel; but you seem to be forcing me into disclosures which can result in nothing; as if you would have me bare a wound for the pleasure of looking at it, without the intention or power of healing it."

"I'm spoiling your dinner, Robert; never mind what I say. You haven't eaten a morsel."

"I only came in for a cup of coffee." His sensitive face was all disfigured with excitement.

"Isn't this a delightful place?" she remarked. "I am so glad it has never actually been discovered. It is so quiet, so sweet here. Do you notice there is scarcely a sound to be heard? It's so out of the way; and a good walk from the car. However, I don't mind walking. I always feel so sorry for women who don't like to walk; they miss so much—so many rare little glimpses of life; and we women learn so little of life on the whole.

"Catiche's coffee is always hot. I don't know how she manages it, here in the open air. Celestine's coffee gets cold bringing it from the kitchen to the dining-room. Three lumps! How can you drink it so sweet? Take some of the cress with your chop; it's so biting and crisp. Then there's the advantage of being able to smoke with your coffee out here. Now, in the city—aren't you going to smoke?"

"After a while," he said, laying a cigar on the table.

"Who gave it to you?" she laughed.

"I bought it. I suppose I'm getting reckless; I bought a whole box." She was determined not to be personal again and make him uncomfortable.

The cat made friends with him, and climbed into his lap when he smoked his cigar. He stroked her silky fur, and talked a little about her. He looked at

Edna's book, which he had read; and he told her the end, to save her the trouble of wading through it, he said.

Again he accompanied her back to her home; and it was after dusk when they reached the little "pigeon-house." She did not ask him to remain, which he was grateful for, as it permitted him to stay without the discomfort of blundering through an excuse which he had no intention of considering. He helped her to light the lamp; then she went into her room to take off her hat and to bathe her face and hands.

When she came back Robert was not examining the pictures and magazines as before; he sat off in the shadow, leaning his head back on the chair as if in a reverie. Edna lingered a moment beside the table, arranging the books there. Then she went across the room to where he sat. She bent over the arm of his chair and called his name.

"Robert," she said, "are you asleep?"

"No," he answered, looking up at her.

She leaned over and kissed him—a soft, cool, delicate kiss, whose voluptuous sting penetrated his whole being—then she moved away from him. He followed, and took her in his arms, just holding her close to him. She put her hand up to his face and pressed his cheek against her own. The action was full of love and tenderness. He sought her lips again. Then he drew her down upon the sofa beside him and held her hand in both of his.

"Now you know," he said, "now you know what I have been fighting against since last summer at Grand Isle; what drove me away and drove me back again."

"Why have you been fighting against it?" she asked. Her face glowed with soft lights.

"Why? Because you were not free; you were Léonce Pontellier's wife. I couldn't help loving you if you were ten times his wife, but so long as I went away from you and kept away I could help telling you so." She put her free hand up to his shoulder, and then against his cheek, rubbing it softly. He kissed her again. His face was warm and flushed.

"There in Mexico I was thinking of you all the time, and longing for you."

"But not writing to me," she interrupted.

"Something put into my head that you cared for me; and I lost my senses. I forgot everything but a wild dream of your some way becoming my wife."

"Your wife!"

"Religion, loyalty, everything would give way if only you cared."

"Then you must have forgotten that I was Léonce Pontellier's wife."

"Oh! I was demented, dreaming of wild, impossible things, recalling men who had set their wives free, we have heard of such things."

"Yes, we have heard of such things."

"I came back full of vague, mad intentions. And when I got here—"

"When you got here you never came near me!" She was still caressing his cheek.

"I realized what a cur I was to dream of such a thing, even if you had been willing."

She took his face between her hands and looked into it as if she would never withdraw her eyes more. She kissed him on the forehead, the eyes, the cheeks, and the lips.

"You have been a very, very foolish boy, wasting your time dreaming of impossible things when you speak of Mr. Pontellier setting me free! I am no longer one of Mr. Pontellier's possessions to dispose of or not. I give myself where I choose. If he were to say, 'Here, Robert, take her and be happy; she is yours,' I should laugh at you both."

His face grew a little white. "What do you mean?" he asked.

There was a knock at the door. Old Celestine came in to say that Madame Ratignolle's servant had come around the back with a message that Madame had been taken sick and begged Mrs. Pontellier to go to her immediately.

"Yes, yes," said Edna, rising: "I promised. Tell her yes—to wait for me. I'll go back with her."

"Let me walk over with you," offered Robert.

"No," she said; "I will go with the servant." She went into her room to put on her hat, and when she came in again she sat once more upon the sofa beside him. He had not stirred. She put her arms about his neck.

"Good-by, my sweet Robert. Tell me good-by." He kissed her with a degree of passion which had not before entered into his caress, and strained her to him.

"I love you," she whispered, "only you; no one but you. It was you who awoke me last summer out of a life-long, stupid dream. Oh! you have made me so unhappy with your indifference. Oh! I have suffered, suffered! Now you are here we shall love each other, my Robert. We shall be everything to each other. Nothing else in the world is of any consequence. I must go to my friend; but you will wait for me? No matter how late; you will wait for me, Robert?"

"Don't go; don't go! Oh! Edna, stay with me," he pleaded. "Why should you go? Stay with me, stay with me."

"I shall come back as soon as I can; I shall find you here." She buried her face in his neck, and said good-by again. Her seductive voice, together with his great love for her, had enthralled his senses, had deprived him of every impulse but the longing to hold her and keep her.

XXXVII

Edna looked in at the drug store. Monsieur Ratignolle was putting up a mixture himself, very carefully, dropping a red liquid into a tiny glass. He was grateful to Edna for having come; her presence would be a comfort to his wife. Madame Ratignolle's sister, who had always been with her at such trying times, had not been able to come up from the plantation, and Adèle had been inconsolable until Mrs. Pontellier so kindly promised to come to her. The nurse had been with them at night for the past week, as she lived a great distance away. And Dr. Mandelet had been coming and going all the afternoon. They were then looking for him any moment.

Edna hastened upstairs by a private stairway that led from the rear of the store to the apartments above. The children were all sleeping in a back room.

Madame Ratignolle was in the salon, whither she had strayed in her suffering impatience. She sat on the sofa, clad in an ample white *peignoir*, holding a handkerchief tight in her hand with a nervous clutch. Her face was drawn and pinched, her sweet blue eyes haggard and unnatural. All her beautiful hair had been drawn back and plaited. It lay in a long braid on the sofa pillow, coiled like a golden serpent. The nurse, a comfortable looking '*Griffe*[5] woman in white apron and cap, was urging her to return to her bedroom.

"There is no use, there is no use," she said at once to Edna. "We must get rid of Mandelet; he is getting too old and careless. He said he would be here at half-past seven; now it must be eight. See what time it is Joséphine."

The woman was possessed of a cheerful nature, and refused to take any situation too seriously, especially a situation with which she was so familiar. She urged Madame to have courage and patience. But Madame only set her teeth hard into her under lip, and Edna saw the sweat gather in beads on her white forehead. After a moment or two she uttered a profound sigh and wiped her face with the handkerchief rolled in a ball. She appeared exhausted. The nurse gave her a fresh handkerchief, sprinkled with cologne water.

"This is too much!" she cried. "Mandelet ought to be killed! Where is Alphonse? Is it possible I am to be abandoned like this—neglected by every one?"

"Neglected, indeed!" exclaimed the nurse. Wasn't she there? And here was Mrs. Pontellier leaving, no doubt, a pleasant evening at home to devote to her? And wasn't Monsieur Ratignolle coming that very instant through the hall? And Joséphine was quite sure she had heard Doctor Mandelet's coupé.[6] Yes, there it was, down at the door.

Adèle consented to go back to her room. She sat on the edge of a little low couch next to her bed.

Doctor Mandelet paid no attention to Madame Ratignolle's upbraidings. He was accustomed to them at such times, and was too well convinced of her loyalty to doubt it.

He was glad to see Edna, and wanted her to go with him into the salon and entertain him. But Madame Ratignolle would not consent that Edna should leave her for an instant. Between agonizing moments, she chatted a little, and said it took her mind off her sufferings.

Edna began to feel uneasy. She was seized with a vague dread. Her own like experiences seemed far away, unreal, and only half remembered. She recalled faintly an ecstasy of pain, the heavy odor of chloroform, a stupor which had deadened sensation, and an awakening to find a little new life to which she had given being, added to the great unnumbered multitude of souls that come and go.

[5] I.e., the offspring of a mulatto and a black or an American Indian.
[6] Closed carriage.

She began to wish she had not come; her presence was not necessary. She might have invented a pretext for staying away; she might even invent a pretext now for going. But Edna did not go. With an inward agony, with a flaming, outspoken revolt against the ways of Nature, she witnessed the scene [of] torture.

She was still stunned and speechless with emotion when later she leaned over her friend to kiss her and softly say good-by. Adèle, pressing her cheek, whispered in an exhausted voice: "Think of the children, Edna. Oh think of the children! Remember them!"

XXXVIII

Edna still felt dazed when she got outside in the open air. The Doctor's coupé had returned for him and stood before the *porte cochère*. She did not wish to enter the coupé, and told Doctor Mandelet she would walk; she was not afraid, and would go alone. He directed his carriage to meet him at Mrs. Pontellier's, and he started to walk home with her.

Up—away up, over the narrow street between the tall houses, the stars were blazing. The air was mild and caressing, but cool with the breath of spring and the night. They walked slowly, the Doctor with a heavy, measured tread and his hands behind him; Edna, in an absent-minded way, as she had walked one night at Grand Isle, as if her thoughts had gone ahead of her and she was striving to overtake them.

"You shouldn't have been there, Mrs. Pontellier," he said. "That was no place for you. Adèle is full of whims at such times. There were a dozen women she might have had with her, unimpressionable women. I felt that it was cruel, cruel. You shouldn't have gone."

"Oh, well!" she answered, indifferently. "I don't know that it matters after all. One has to think of the children some time or other; the sooner the better."

"When is Léonce coming back?"

"Quite soon. Some time in March."

"And you are going abroad?"

"Perhaps—no, I am not going. I'm not going to be forced into doing things. I don't want to go abroad. I want to be let alone. Nobody has any right—except children, perhaps—and even then, it seems to me—or it did seem—" She felt that her speech was voicing the incoherency of her thoughts, and stopped abruptly.

"The trouble is," sighed the Doctor, grasping her meaning intuitively, "that youth is given up to illusions. It seems to be a provision of Nature; a decoy to secure mothers for the race. And Nature takes no account of moral consequences, of arbitrary conditions which we create, and which we feel obliged to maintain at any cost."

"Yes," she said. "The years that are gone seem like dreams—if one might go on sleeping and dreaming—but to wake up and find—oh! well! perhaps it is better to wake up after all, even to suffer, rather than to remain a dupe to illusions all one's life."

"It seems to me, my dear child," said the Doctor at parting, holding her hand, "you seem to me to be in trouble. I am not going to ask for your confidence. I will only say that if ever you feel moved to give it to me, perhaps I might help you. I know I would understand, and I tell you there are not many who would — not many, my dear."

"Some way I don't feel moved to speak of things that trouble me. Don't think I am ungrateful or that I don't appreciate your sympathy. There are periods of despondency and suffering which take possession of me. But I don't want anything but my own way. That is wanting a good deal, of course, when you have to trample upon the lives, the hearts, the prejudices of others — but no matter — still, I shouldn't want to trample upon the little lives. Oh! I don't know what I'm saying, Doctor. Good night. Don't blame me for anything."

"Yes, I will blame you if you don't come and see me soon. We will talk of things you never have dreamt of talking about before. It will do us both good. I don't want you to blame yourself, whatever comes. Good night, my child."

She let herself in at the gate, but instead of entering she sat upon the step of the porch. The night was quiet and soothing. All the tearing emotion of the last few hours seemed to fall away from her like a somber, uncomfortable garment, which she had but to loosen to be rid of. She went back to that hour before Adèle had sent for her; and her senses kindled afresh in thinking of Robert's words, the pressure of his arms, and the feeling of his lips upon her own. She could picture at that moment no greater bliss on earth than possession of the beloved one. His expression of love had already given him to her in part. When she thought that he was there at hand, waiting for her, she grew numb with the intoxication of expectancy. It was so late; he should be asleep perhaps. She would awaken him with a kiss. She hoped he would be asleep that she might arouse him with her caresses.

Still, she remembered Adèle's voice whispering, "Think of the children; think of them." She meant to think of them, that determination had driven into her soul like a death wound — but not to-night. To-morrow would be time to think of everything.

Robert was not waiting for her in the little parlor. He was nowhere at hand. The house was empty. But he had scrawled on a piece of paper that lay in the lamplight:

"I love you. Good-by — because I love you."

Edna grew faint when she read the words. She went and sat on the sofa. Then she stretched herself out there, never uttering a sound. She did not sleep. She did not go to bed. The lamp sputtered and went out. She was still awake in the morning, when Celestine unlocked the kitchen door and came in to light the fire.

XXXIX

Victor, with hammer and nails and scraps of scantling,[7] was patching a corner of one of the galleries. Mariequita sat near by, dangling her legs, watching him

---

[7] Small bits of wood.

work, and handing him nails from the tool-box. The sun was beating down upon them. The girl had covered her head with her apron folded into a square pad. They had been talking for an hour or more. She was never tired of hearing Victor describe the dinner at Mrs. Pontellier's. He exaggerated every detail, making it appear a veritable Lucullean[8] feast. The flowers were in tubs, he said. The champagne was quaffed from huge golden goblets. Venus rising from the foam[9] could have presented no more entrancing a spectacle than Mrs. Pontellier, blazing with beauty and diamonds at the head of the board, while the other women were all of them youthful houris[1] possessed of incomparable charms.

She got it into her head that Victor was in love with Mrs. Pontellier, and he gave her evasive answers, framed so as to confirm her belief. She grew sullen and cried a little, threatening to go off and leave him to his fine ladies. There were a dozen men crazy about her at the *Chênière;* and since it was the fashion to be in love with married people, why she could run away any time she liked to New Orleans with Célina's husband.

Célina's husband was a fool, a coward, and a pig, and to prove it to her, Victor intended to hammer his head into a jelly the next time he encountered him. This assurance was very consoling to Mariequita. She dried her eyes, and grew cheerful at the prospect.

They were still talking of the dinner and the allurements of city life when Mrs. Pontellier herself slipped around the corner of the house. The two youngsters stayed dumb with amazement before what they considered to be an apparition. But it was really she in flesh and blood, looking tired and a little travel-stained.

"I walked up from the wharf," she said, "and heard the hammering. I supposed it was you, mending the porch. It's a good thing. I was always tripping over those loose planks last summer. How dreary and deserted everything looks!"

It took Victor some little time to comprehend that she had come in Beaudelet's lugger, that she had come alone, and for no purpose but to rest.

"There's nothing fixed up yet, you see. I'll give you my room; it's the only place."

"Any corner will do," she assured him.

"And if you can stand Philomel's cooking," he went on, "though I might try to get her mother while you are here. Do you think she would come?" turning to Mariequita.

Mariequita thought that perhaps Philomel's mother might come for a few days, and money enough.

Beholding Mrs. Pontellier make her appearance, the girl had at once suspected a lovers' rendezvous. But Victor's astonishment was so genuine, and Mrs. Pontellier's indifference so apparent, that the disturbing notion did not lodge

---

[8] The first-century B.C. Roman general Lucius Licinius Lucullus was noted for his extravagant banquets.

[9] The Roman goddess of love and beauty was born out of the sea foam.

[1] Beautiful maidens in the Muslim paradise.

long in her brain. She contemplated with the greatest interest this woman who gave the most sumptuous dinners in America, and who had all the men in New Orleans at her feet.

"What time will you have dinner?" asked Edna. "I'm very hungry; but don't get anything extra."

"I'll have it ready in little or no time," he said, bustling and packing away his tools. "You may go to my room to brush up and rest yourself. Mariequita will show you."

"Thank you," said Edna. "But, do you know, I have a notion to go down to the beach and take a good wash and even a little swim, before dinner?"

"The water is too cold!" they both exclaimed. "Don't think of it."

"Well, I might go down and try—dip my toes in. Why, it seems to me the sun is hot enough to have warmed the very depths of the ocean. Could you get me a couple of towels? I'd better go right away, so as to be back in time. It would be a little too chilly if I waited till this afternoon."

Mariequita ran over to Victor's room, and returned with some towels, which she gave to Edna.

"I hope you have fish for dinner," said Edna, as she started to walk away; "but don't do anything extra if you haven't."

"Run and find Philomel's mother," Victor instructed the girl. "I'll go to the kitchen and see what I can do. By Gimminy! Women have no consideration! She might have sent me word."

Edna walked on down to the beach rather mechanically, not noticing anything special except that the sun was hot. She was not dwelling on any particular train of thought. She had done all the thinking which was necessary after Robert went away, when she lay awake upon the sofa till morning.

She had said over and over to herself: "To-day it is Arobin; tomorrow it will be some one else. It makes no difference to me, it doesn't matter about Léonce Pontellier—but Raoul and Étienne!" She understood now clearly what she had meant long ago when she said to Adèle Ratignolle that she would give up the unessential, but she would never sacrifice herself for her children.

Despondency had come upon her there in the wakeful night, and had never lifted. There was no one thing in the world that she desired. There was no human being whom she wanted near her except Robert; and she even realized that the day would come when he, too, and the thought of him would melt out of her existence, leaving her alone. The children appeared before her like antagonists who have overcome her; who had overpowered her and sought to drag her into the soul's slavery for the rest of her days. But she knew a way to elude them. She was not thinking of these things when she walked down to the beach.

The water of the Gulf stretched out before her gleaming with the million lights of the sun. The voice of the sea is seductive, never ceasing, whispering, clamoring, murmuring, inviting the soul to wander in abysses of solitude. All along the white beach, up and down, there was no living thing in sight. A bird with a broken wing was beating the air above, reeling, fluttering, circling disabled down, down to the water.

Edna had found her old bathing suit still hanging, faded, upon its accustomed peg.

She put it on, leaving her clothing in the bath-house. But when she was there beside the sea, absolutely alone, she cast the unpleasant, pricking garments from her, and for the first time in her life she stood naked in the open air, at the mercy of the sun, the breeze that beat upon her, and the waves that invited her.

How strange and awful it seemed to stand naked under the sky! how delicious! She felt like some new-born creature, opening its eyes in a familiar world that it had never known.

The foamy wavelets curled up to her white feet, and coiled like serpents about her ankles. She walked out. The water was chill, but she walked on. The water was deep, but she lifted her white body and reached out with a long, sweeping stroke. The touch of the sea is sensuous, enfolding the body in its soft, close embrace.

She went on and on. She remembered the night she swam far out, and recalled the terror that seized her at the fear of being unable to regain the shore. She did not look back now, but went on and on, thinking of the blue-grass meadow that she had traversed when a little child, believing that it had no beginning and no end.

Her arms and legs were growing tired.

She thought of Léonce and the children. They were a part of her life. But they need not have thought that they could possess her, body and soul. How Mademoiselle Reisz would have laughed, perhaps sneered, if she knew! "And you call yourself an artist! What pretensions, Madame! The artist must possess the courageous soul that dares and defies."

Exhaustion was pressing upon and over-powering her.

"Good-by—because, I love you." He did not know; he did not understand. He would never understand. Perhaps Doctor Mandelet would have understood if she had seen him—but it was too late; the shore was far behind her, and her strength was gone.

She looked into the distance, and the old terror flamed up for an instant, then sank again. Edna heard her father's voice and her sister Margaret's. She heard the barking of an old dog that was chained to the sycamore tree. The spurs of the cavalry officer clanged as he walked across the porch. There was the hum of bees, and the musky odor of pinks filled the air.

1899

Mary E. Wilkins Freeman   1852–1930

Regionalist and influential realist, Mary E. Wilkins Freeman spent the majority of her life in Randolph, Massachusetts, a town of farmers, house carpenters, and shoe industry workers. Like so many young girls brought up amidst the backdrop of the Civil War, Freeman experienced much isolation and spent this time cultivating her love of reading. She had two years of formal education, attending Mount Holyoke Female Seminary for one year and West Brattleboro Seminary in Vermont for a second year. By the age of thirty-one, with both of her parents and only sister dead, Freeman found herself impoverished and alone. She had previously earned small sums contributing poems to a local children's magazine and, in desperation, turned to writing to support herself. Her career quickly blossomed in 1882 when she won a $50 prize for adult fiction in a literary contest. She soon became widely published in *Harper's Bazaar* and a variety of influential magazines finding immediate approval in America and abroad. Wilkins's writing explored the inner lives of people who populated her region of New England, often focusing on the fortitude of defiant, destitute heroines struggling to overcome their isolation. Freeman went on to publish thirty-nine volumes of stories, novels, and plays, winning the Howell Medal for Fiction in 1926. In that same year, she and Edith Wharton became the first women elected to membership in the National Institute of Arts and Letters.

THE REVOLT OF "MOTHER"

"Father"

"What is it?"

"What are them men diggin' over there in the field for?"

There was a sudden dropping and enlarging of the lower part of the old man's face, as if some heavy weight had settled therein; he shut his mouth tight, and went on harnessing the great bay mare. He hustled the collar on to her neck with a jerk.

"Father!"

The old man slapped the saddle upon the mare's back.

"Look here, father, I want to know what them men are diggin' over in the field for, an' I'm goin' to know."

"I wish you'd go into the house, mother, an' 'tend to your own affairs," the old man said then. He ran his words together, and his speech was almost as inarticulate as a growl.

But the woman understood; it was her most native tongue. "I ain't goin' into the house till you tell me what them men are doin' over there in the field," said she.

Then she stood waiting. She was a small woman, short and straight-waisted like a child in her brown cotton gown. Her forehead was mild and benevolent between the smooth curves of gray hair; there were meek downward lines about her nose and mouth; but her eyes, fixed upon the old man, looked as if the meekness had been the result of her own will, never of the will of another.

They were in the barn, standing before the wide open doors. The spring air, full of the smell of growing grass and unseen blossoms, came in their faces. The deep yard in front was littered with farm wagons and piles of wood; on the edges, close to the fence and the house, the grass was a vivid green, and there were some dandelions.

The old man glanced doggedly at his wife as he tightened the last buckles on the harness. She looked as immovable to him as one of the rocks in his pastureland, bound to the earth with generations of blackberry vines. He slapped the reins over the horse, and started forth from the barn.

"Father!" said she.

The old man pulled up. "What is it?"

"I want to know what them men are diggin' over there in that field for."

"They're diggin' a cellar, I s'pose, if you've got to know."

"A cellar for what?"

"A barn."

"A barn? You ain't goin' to build a barn over there where we was goin' to have a house, father?"

The old man said not another word. He hurried the horse into the farm wagon, and clattered out of the yard, jouncing as sturdily on his seat as a boy.

The woman stood a moment looking after him, then she went out of the barn across a corner of the yard to the house. The house, standing at right angles with the great barn and a long reach of sheds and out-buildings, was infinitesimal compared with them. It was scarcely as commodious for people as the little boxes under the barn eaves were for doves.

A pretty girl's face, pink and delicate as a flower, was looking out of one of the house windows. She was watching three men who were digging over in the field which bounded the yard near the road line. She turned quietly when the woman entered.

"What are they digging for, mother?" said she. "Did he tell you?"

"They're diggin' for—a cellar for a new barn."

"Oh, mother, he ain't going to build another barn?"

"That's what he says."

A boy stood before the kitchen glass combing his hair. He combed slowly and painstakingly, arranging his brown hair in a smooth hillock over his forehead. He did not seem to pay any attention to the conversation.

"Sammy, did you know father was going to build a new barn?" asked the girl.

The boy combed assiduously.

"Sammy!"

He turned, and showed a face like his father's under his smooth crest of hair. "Yes, I s'pose I did," he said, reluctantly.

"How long have you known it?" asked his mother.

"'Bout three months, I guess."

"Why didn't you tell of it?"

"Didn't think 'twould do no good."

"I don't see what father wants another barn for," said the girl, in her sweet, slow voice. She turned again to the window, and stared out at the digging men in the field. Her tender, sweet face was full of a gentle distress. Her forehead was as bald and innocent as a baby's, with the light hair strained back from it in a row of curl-papers. She was quite large, but her soft curves did not look as if they covered muscles.

Her mother looked sternly at the boy. "Is he goin' to buy more cows?" said she.

The boy did not reply; he was tying his shoes.

"Sammy, I want you to tell me if he's goin' to buy more cows."

"I s'pose he is."

"How many?"

"Four, I guess."

His mother said nothing more. She went into the pantry, and there was a clatter of dishes. The boy got his cap from a nail behind the door, took an old arithmetic from the shelf, and started for school. He was lightly built, but clumsy. He went out of the yard with a curious spring in his hips, that made his loose homemade jacket tilt up in the rear.

The girl went to the sink, and began to wash the dishes that were piled up there. Her mother came promptly out of the pantry, and shoved her aside. "You wipe 'em," said she; "I'll wash. There's a good many this mornin'."

The mother plunged her hands vigorously into the water, the girl wiped the plates slowly and dreamily. "Mother," said she, "don't you think it's too bad father's going to build that new barn, much as we need a decent house to live in?"

Her mother scrubbed a dish fiercely. "You ain't found out yet we're women-folks, Nanny Penn," said she. "You ain't seen enough of men-folks yet to. One of these days you'll find it out, an' then you'll know that we know only what men-folks think we do, so far as any use of it goes, an' how we'd ought to reckon men-folks in with Providence, an' not complain of what they do any more than we do of the weather."

"I don't care; I don't believe George is anything like that, anyhow," said Nanny. Her delicate face flushed pink, her lips pouted softly, as if she were going to cry.

"You wait an' see. I guess George Eastman ain't no better than other men. You hadn't ought to judge father, though. He can't help it, 'cause he don't look at things jest the way we do. An' we've been pretty comfortable here, after all. The roof don't leak—ain't never but once—that's one thing. Father's kept it shingled right up."

"I do wish we had a parlor."

"I guess it won't hurt George Eastman any to come to see you in a nice clean kitchen. I guess a good many girls don't have as good a place as this. No-body's ever heard me complain."

"I ain't complained either, mother."

"Well, I don't think you'd better, a good father an' a good home as you've got. S'pose your father made you go out an' work for your livin'? Lots of girls have to that ain't no stronger an' better able to than you be."

Sarah Penn washed the frying pan with a conclusive air. She scrubbed the outside of it as faithfully as the inside. She was a masterly keeper of her box of a house. Her one living room never seemed to have in it any of the dust which the friction of life with inanimate matter produces. She swept, and there seemed to be no dirt to go before the broom; she cleaned, and one could see no difference. She was like an artist so perfect that he has apparently no art. To-day she got out a mixing bowl and a board, and rolled some pies, and there was no more flour upon her than upon her daughter who was doing finer work. Nanny was to be married in the fall, and she was sewing on some white cambric and embroidery. She sewed industriously while her mother cooked, her soft milk-white hands and wrists showed whiter than her delicate work.

"We must have the stove moved out in the shed before long," said Mrs. Penn. "Talk about not havin' things, it's been a real blessin' to be able to put a stove up in that shed in hot weather. Father did one good thing when he fixed that stovepipe out there."

Sarah Penn's face as she rolled her pies had that expression of meek vigor which might have characterized one of the New Testament saints. She was making mince-pies. Her husband, Adoniram Penn, liked them better than any other kind. She baked twice a week. Adoniram often liked a piece of pie between meals. She hurried this morning. It had been later than usual when she began, and she wanted to have a pie baked for dinner. However deep a resentment she might be forced to hold against her husband, she would never fail in sedulous attention to his wants.

Nobility of character manifests itself at loop-holes when it is not provided with large doors. Sarah Penn's showed itself to-day in flaky dishes of pastry. So she made the pies faithfully, while across the table she could see, when she glanced up from her work, the sight that rankled in her patient and steadfast soul—the digging of the cellar of the new barn in the place where Adoniram forty years ago had promised her their new house should stand.

The pies were done for dinner. Adoniram and Sammy were home a few minutes after twelve o'clock. The dinner was eaten with serious haste. There was never much conversation at the table in the Penn family. Adoniram asked a blessing, and they ate promptly, then rose up and went about their work.

Sammy went back to school, taking soft sly lopes out of the yard like a rabbit. He wanted a game of marbles before school, and feared his father would give him some chores to do. Adoniram hastened to the door and called after him, but he was out of sight.

"I don't see what you let him go for, mother," said he. "I wanted him to help me unload that wood."

Adoniram went to work out in the yard unloading wood from the wagon. Sarah put away the dinner dishes, while Nanny took down her curl-papers and

changed her dress. She was going down to the store to buy some more embroidery and thread.

When Nanny was gone, Mrs. Penn went to the door. "Father!" she called.

"Well, what is it!"

"I want to see you jest a minute, father."

"I can't leave this wood nohow. I've got to git it unloaded an' go for a load
of gravel afore two o'clock. Sammy had ought to helped me. You hadn't ought to
let him go to school so early."

"I want to see you jest a minute."

"I tell ye I can't, nohow, mother."

"Father, you come here." Sarah Penn stood in the door like a queen; she
held her head as if it bore a crown; there was that patience which makes authority royal in her voice. Adoniram went.

Mrs. Penn led the way into the kitchen, and pointed to a chair. "Sit down,
father," said she: "I've got somethin' I want to say to you."

He sat down heavily; his face was quite stolid, but he looked at her with
restive eyes. "Well, what is it, mother?"

"I want to know what you're buildin' that new barn for, father?"

"I ain't got nothin' to say about it."

"It can't be you think you need another barn?"

"I tell ye I ain't got nothin' to say about it, mother; an' I ain't goin' to say
nothin'."

"Be you goin' to buy more cows?"

Adoniram did not reply; he shut his mouth tight.

"I know you be, as well as I want to. Now, father, look here"—Sarah Penn
had not sat down; she stood before her husband in the humble fashion of a
Scripture woman—"I'm goin' to talk real plain to you; I never have sence I married you, but I'm goin' to now. I ain't never complained, an' I ain't goin' to complain now, but I'm goin' to talk plain. You see this room here, father; you look at
it well. You see there ain't no carpet on the floor, an' you see the paper is all
dirty, an' droppin' off the walls. We ain't had no new paper on it for ten year, an'
then I put it on myself, an' it didn't cost but ninepence a roll. You see this room,
father; it's all the one I've had to work in an' eat in an' sit in sence we was married. There ain't another woman in the whole town whose husband ain't got half
the means you have but what's got better. It's all the room Nanny's got to have
her company in; an' there ain't one of her mates but what's got better, an' their
fathers not so able as hers is. It's all the room she'll have to be married in. What
would you have thought, father, if we had our weddin' in a room no better than
this? I was married in my mother's parlor, with a carpet on the floor, an' stuffed
furniture, an' a mahogany card-table. An' this is all the room my daughter will
have to be married in. Look here, father!"

Sarah Penn went across the room as though it were a tragic stage. She flung
open a door and disclosed a tiny bedroom, only large enough for a bed and bureau, with a path between. "There, father," said she—"there's all the room I've

had to sleep in forty year. All my children were born there—the two that died, an' the two that's livin'. I was sick with a fever there."

She stepped to another door and opened it. It led into the small, ill-lighted pantry. "Here," said she, "is all the buttery I've got—every place I've got for my dishes, to set away my victuals in, an' to keep my milk-pans in. Father, I've been takin' care of the milk of six cows in this place, an' now you're goin' to build a new barn, an' keep more cows, an' give me more to do in it."

She threw open another door. A narrow crooked flight of stairs wound upward from it. "There, father," said she, "I want you to look at the stairs that go up to them two unfinished chambers that are all the places our son an' daughter have had to sleep in all their lives. There ain't a prettier girl in town nor a more ladylike one than Nanny, an' that's the place she has to sleep in. It ain't so good as your horse's stall; it ain't so warm an' tight."

Sarah Penn went back and stood before her husband. "Now, father," said she, "I want to know if you think you're doin' right an' accordin' to what you profess. Here, when we was married, forty year ago, you promised me faithful that we should have a new house built in that lot over in the field before the year was out. You said you had money enough, an' you wouldn't ask me to live in no such place as this. It is forty year now, an' you've been makin' more money, an' I've been savin' of it for you ever since, an' you ain't built no house yet. You've built sheds an' cowhouses an' one new barn, an' now you're goin' to build another. Father, I want to know if you think it's right. You're lodgin' your dumb beasts better than you are your own flesh an' blood. I want to know if you think it's right."

"I ain't got nothin' to say."

"You can't say nothin' without ownin' it ain't right, father. An' there's another thing—I ain't complained; I've got along forty year, an' I s'pose I should forty more, if it wa'n't for that—if we don't have another house. Nanny she can't live with us after she's married. She'll have to go somewheres else to live away from us, an' it don't seem as if I could have it so, noways, father. She wa'n't ever strong. She's got considerable color, but there wa'n't ever any backbone to her. I've always took the heft of everything off her, an' she ain't fit to keep house an' do everything herself. She'll be all worn out inside of a year. Think of her doin' all the washin' an' ironin' an' bakin' with them soft white hands an' arms, an' sweepin'! I can't have it so, noways, father."

Mrs. Penn's face was burning; her mild eyes gleamed. She had pleaded her little cause like a Webster; she had ranged from severity to pathos; but her opponent employed that obstinate silence which makes eloquence futile with mocking echoes. Adoniram arose clumsily.

"Father, ain't you got nothin' to say?" said Mrs. Penn.

"I've got to go off after that load of gravel. I can't stan' here talkin' all day."

"Father, won't you think it over, an' have a house built there instead of a barn?"

"I ain't got nothin' to say."

Adoniram shuffled out. Mrs. Penn went into her bedroom. When she came out, her eyes were red. She had a roll of unbleached cotton cloth. She spread it out on the kitchen table, and began cutting out some shirts for her husband. The men over in the field had a team to help them this afternoon; she could hear their halloos. She had a scanty pattern for the shirts; she had to plan and piece the sleeves.

Nanny came home with her embroidery, and sat down with her needle-work. She had taken down her curl-papers, and there was a soft roll of fair hair like an auerole over her forehead; her face was as delicately fine and clear as porcelain. Suddenly she looked up, and the tender red flamed all over her face and neck. "Mother," said she.

"What say?"

"I've been thinking—I don't see how we're goin' to have any—wedding in this room. I'd be ashamed to have his folks come if we didn't have anybody else."

"Mebbe we can have some new paper before then; I can put it on. I guess you won't have no call to be ashamed of your belongin's."

"We might have the wedding in the new barn," said Nanny, with gentle pettishness. "Why, mother, what makes you look so?"

Mrs. Penn had started, and was staring at her with a curious expression. She turned again to her work, and spread out a pattern carefully on the cloth. "Nothin'," said she.

Presently Adoniram clattered out of the yard in his two-wheeled dump cart, standing as proudly upright as a Roman charioteer. Mrs. Penn opened the door and stood there a minute looking out; the halloos of the men sounded louder.

It seemed to her all through the spring months that she heard nothing but the halloos and the noises of saws and hammers. The new barn grew fast. It was a fine edifice for this little village. Men came on pleasant Sundays, in their meeting suits and clean shirt bosoms, and stood around it admiringly. Mrs. Penn did not speak of it, and Adoniram did not mention it to her, although sometimes, upon a return from inspecting it, he bore himself with injured dignity.

"It's a strange thing how your mother feels about the new barn," he said, confidentially, to Sammy one day.

Sammy only grunted after an odd fashion for a boy; he had learned it from his father.

The barn was all completed ready for use by the third week in July. Adoniram had planned to move his stock in on Wednesday; on Tuesday he received a letter which changed his plans. He came in with it early in the morning. "Sammy's been to the post-office," said he, "an' I've got a letter from Hiram." Hiram was Mrs. Penn's brother, who lived in Vermont.

"Well," said Mrs. Penn, "what does he say about the folks?"

"I guess they're all right. He says he thinks if I come up country right off there's a chance to buy jest the kind of a horse I want." He stared reflectively out of the window at the new barn.

Mrs. Penn was making pies. She went on clapping the rolling-pin into the crust, although she was very pale, and her heart beat loudly.

"I dun' know but what I'd better go," said Adoniram. "I hate to go off just now, right in the midst of hayin', but the ten-acre lot's cut, an' I guess Rufus an' the others can git along without me three or four days. I can't get a horse round here to suit me, nohow, an' I've got to have another for all that wood-haulin' in the fall. I told Hiram to watch out, an' if he got wind of a good horse to let me know. I guess I'd better go."

"I'll get out your clean shirt an' collar," said Mrs. Penn calmly.

She laid out Adoniram's Sunday suit and his clean clothes on the bed in the little bedroom. She got his shaving-water and razor ready. At last she buttoned on his collar and fastened his black cravat.

Adoniram never wore his collar and cravat except on extra occasions. He held his head high, with a rasped dignity. When he was all ready, with his coat and hat brushed, and a lunch of pie and cheese in a paper bag, he hesitated on the threshold of the door. He looked at his wife, and his manner was defiantly apologetic. "*If* them cows come to-day, Sammy can drive 'em into the new barn," said he; "an' when they bring the hay up, they can pitch it in there."

"Well," replied Mrs. Penn.

Adoniram set his shaven face ahead and started. When he had cleared the door-step, he turned and looked back with a kind of nervous solemnity. "I shall be back by Saturday if nothin' happens," said he.

"Do be careful, father," returned his wife.

She stood in the door with Nanny at her elbow and watched him out of sight. Her eyes had a strange, doubtful expression in them; her peaceful forehead was contracted. She went in, and about her baking again. Nanny sat sewing. Her wedding-day was drawing nearer, and she was getting pale and thin with her steady sewing. Her mother kept glancing at her.

"Have you got that pain in your side this mornin'?" she asked.

"A little."

Mrs. Penn's face, as she worked, changed, her perplexed forehead smoothed, her eyes were steady, her lips firmly set. She formed a maxim for herself, although incoherently with her unlettered thoughts. "Unsolicited opportunities are the guide-posts of the Lord to the new roads of life," she repeated in effect and she made up her mind to her course of action.

"S'posin' I *had* wrote to Hiram," she muttered once, when she was in the pantry—"s'posin' I had wrote, an' asked him if he knew of any horse? But I didn't, an' father's goin' wa'n't none of my doin'. It looks like a providence." Her voice rang out quite loud at the last.

"What you talkin' about, mother?" called Nanny.

"Nothin'."

Mrs. Penn hurried her baking; at eleven o'clock it was all done. The load of hay from the west field came slowly down the cart track, and drew up at the new barn. Mrs. Penn ran out. "Stop!" she screamed—"stop!"

The men stopped and looked; Sammy upreared from the top of the load, and stared at his mother.

"Stop!" she cried out again. "Don't you put the hay in that barn; put it in the old one."

"Why, he said to put it in here," returned one of the hay-makers, wonderingly. He was a young man, a neighbor's son, whom Adoniram hired by the year to help on the farm.

"Don't you put the hay in the new barn; there's room enough in the old one, ain't there?" said Mrs. Penn.

"Room enough," returned the hired man, in his thick, rustic tones. "Didn't need the new barn, nohow, far as room's concerned. Well, I s'pose he changed his mind." He took hold of the horses' bridles.

Mrs. Penn went back to the house. Soon the kitchen windows were darkened, and a fragrance like warm honey came into the room.

Nanny laid down her work. "I thought father wanted them to put the hay into the new barn?" she said, wonderingly.

"It's all right," replied her mother.

Sammy slid down from the load of hay, and came in to see if dinner was ready.

"I ain't goin' to get a regular dinner to-day, as long as father's gone," said his mother. "I've let the fire go out. You can have some bread an' milk an' pie. I thought we could get along." She set out some bowls of milk, some bread and a pie on the kitchen table. "You'd better eat your dinner now," said she. "You might jest as well get through with it. I want you to help me afterward."

Nanny and Sammy stared at each other. There was something strange in their mother's manner. Mrs. Penn did not eat anything herself. She went into the pantry, and they heard her moving dishes while they ate. Presently she came out with a pile of plates. She got the clothes-basket out of the shed, and packed them in it. Nanny and Sammy watched. She brought out cups and saucers, and put them in with the plates.

"What you goin' to do, mother?" inquired Nanny, in a timid voice. A sense of something unusual made her tremble, as if it were a ghost. Sammy rolled his eyes over his pie.

"You'll see what I'm goin' to do," replied Mrs. Penn. "If you're through, Nanny, I want you to go up-stairs an' pack up your things; an' I want you, Sammy, to help me take down the bed in the bedroom."

"Oh, mother, what for?" gasped Nanny.

"You'll see."

During the next hours a feat was performed by this simple, pious New England mother which was equal in its way to Wolfe's[1] storming of the Heights

---

[1]Wolfe: Wolfe-James (1727–1759) English general who led an army up steep cliffs in the Battle of Quebec.

of Abraham. It took no more genius and audacity of bravery for Wolfe to cheer his wondering soldiers up those steep precipices, under the sleeping eyes of the enemy, than for Sarah Penn, at the head of her children, to move all their little household goods into the new barn while her husband was away.

Nanny and Sammy followed their mother's instructions without a murmur; indeed, they were overawed. There is a certain uncanny and superhuman quality about all such purely original undertakings as their mother's was to them. Nanny went back and forth with her light loads, and Sammy tugged with sober energy.

At five o'clock in the afternoon the little house in which the Penns had lived for forty years had emptied itself into the new barn.

Every builder builds somewhat for unknown purposes, and is in a measure a prophet. The architect of Adoniram Penn's barn, while he designed it for the comfort of four-footed animals, had planned better than he knew for the comfort of humans. Sarah Penn saw at a glance its possibilities. These great box-stalls, with quilts hung before them, would make better bedrooms than the one she had occupied for forty years, and there was a tight carriage-room. The harness-room, with its chimney and shelves, would make a kitchen of her dreams. The great middle space would make a parlor, by-and-by, fit for a palace. Up-stairs there was as much room as down. With partitions and windows, what a house would there be! Sarah looked at the row of stanchions before the allotted space for cows, and reflected that she would have her front entry there.

At six o'clock the stove was up in the harness-room, the kettle was boiling, and the table set for tea. It looked almost as home-like as the abandoned house across the yard had ever done. The young hired man milked, and Sarah directed him calmly to bring the milk to the new barn. He came gaping, dropping little blots of foam from the brimming pails on the grass. Before the next morning he had spread the story of Adoniram Penn's wife moving into the new barn all over the little village. Men assembled in the store and talked it over, women with shawls over their heads scuttled into each other's houses before their work was done. Any deviation from the ordinary course of life in this quiet town was enough to stop all progress in it. Everybody paused to look at the staid, independent figure on the side track. There was a difference of opinion with regard to her. Some held her to be insane; some, of a lawless and rebellious spirit.

Friday the minister went to see her. It was in the forenoon, and she was at the barn door shelling pease for dinner. She looked up and returned his salutation with dignity, then she went on with her work. She did not invite him in. The saintly expression of her face remained fixed, but there was an angry flush over it.

The minister stood awkwardly before her, and talked. She handled the pease as if they were bullets. At last she looked up, and her eyes showed the spirit that her meek front had covered for a lifetime.

"There ain't no use talkin', Mr. Hersey," said she. "I've thought it all over an' over, an' I believe I'm doin' what's right. I've made it the subject of prayer, an' it's betwixt me an' the Lord an' Adoniram. There ain't no call for nobody else to worry about it."

"Well, of course, if you have brought it to the Lord in prayer, and feel satisfied that you are doing right, Mrs. Penn," said the minister, helplessly. His thin gray-bearded face was pathetic. He was a sickly man; his youthful confidence had cooled; he had to scourge himself up to some of his pastoral duties as relentlessly as a Catholic ascetic, and then he was prostrated by the smart.

"I think it's right jest as much as I think it was right for our forefathers to come over from the old country 'cause they didn't have what belonged to 'em," said Mrs. Penn. She arose. The barn threshold might have been Plymouth Rock from her bearing. "I don't doubt you mean well, Mr. Hersey," said she, "but there are things people hadn't ought to interfere with. I've been a member of the church for over forty year. I've got my own mind an' my own feet, an' I'm goin' to think my own thoughts an' go my own ways, an' nobody but the Lord is goin' to dictate to me unless I've a mind to have him. Won't you come in an' set down? How is Mis' Hersey?"

"She is well, I thank you," replied the minister. He added some more perplexed apologetic remarks; then he retreated.

He could expound the intricacies of every character study in the Scriptures, he was competent to grasp the Pilgrim Fathers and all historical innovators, but Sarah Penn was beyond him. He could deal with primal cases, but parallel ones worsted him. But, after all, although it was aside from his province, he wondered more how Adoniram Penn would deal with his wife than how the Lord would. Everybody shared the wonder. When Adoniram's four new cows arrived, Sarah ordered three to be put in the old barn, the other in the house shed where the cooking-stove had stood. That added to the excitement. It was whispered that all four cows were domiciled in the house.

Towards sunset on Saturday, when Adoniram was expected home, there was a knot of men in the road near the new barn. The hired man had milked, but he still hung around the premises. Sarah Penn had supper all ready. There were brown bread and baked beans and a custard pie; it was the supper Adoniram loved on a Saturday night. She had a clean calico, and she bore herself imperturbably. Nanny and Sammy kept close at her heels. Their eyes were large, and Nanny was full of nervous tremors. Still there was to them more pleasant excitement than anything else. An inborn confidence in their mother over their father asserted itself.

Sammy looked out of the harness-room window. "There he is," he announced, in an awed whisper. He and Nanny peeped around the casing. Mrs. Penn kept on about her work. The children watched Adoniram leave the new horse standing in the drive while he went to the house door. It was fastened. Then he went around to the shed. That door was seldom locked, even when the family was away. The thought how her father would be confronted by the cow flashed upon Nanny. There was a hysterical sob in her throat. Adoniram emerged from the shed and stood looking about in a dazed fashion. His lips moved; he was saying something, but they could not hear what it was. The hired man was peeping around a corner of the old barn, but nobody saw him.

Adoniram took the new horse by the bridle and led him across the yard to the new barn. Nanny and Sammy slunk close to their mother. The barn doors rolled back, and there stood Adoniram, with the long mild face of the great Canadian farm horse looking over his shoulder.

Nanny kept behind her mother, but Sammy stepped suddenly forward, and stood in front of her.

Adoniram stared at the group. "What on airth you all down here for?" said he. "What's the matter over to the house?"

"We've come here to live, father," said Sammy. His shrill voice quavered out bravely.

"What"—Adoniram sniffed—"what is it smells like cookin'?" said he. He stepped forward and looked in the open door of the harness-room. Then he turned to his wife. His old bristling face was pale and frightened. "What on airth does this mean, mother?" he gasped.

"You come in here, father," said Sarah. She led the way into the harness-room and shut the door. "Now, father," said she, "you needn't be scared. I ain't crazy. There ain't nothin' to be upset over. But we've come here to live, an' we're goin' to live here. We've got jest as good a right here as new horses an' cows. The house wa'n't fit for us to live in any longer, an' I made up my mind I wa'n't goin' to stay there. I've done my duty by you forty year, an' I'm goin' to do it now; but I'm goin' to live here. You've got to put in some windows and partitions; an' you'll have to buy some furniture."

"Why, mother!" the old man gasped.

"You'd better take your coat off an' get washed—there's the wash-basin—an' then we'll have supper."

"Why, mother!"

Sammy went past the window, leading the new horse to the old barn. The old man saw him, and shook his head speechlessly. He tried to take off his coat, but his arms seemed to lack the power. His wife helped him. She poured some water into the tin basin, and put in a piece of soap. She got the comb and brush, and smoothed his thin gray hair after he had washed. The she put the beans, hot bread, and tea on the table. Sammy came in, and the family drew up. Adoniram sat looking dazedly at his plate, and they waited.

"Ain't you goin' to ask a blessin', father?" said Sarah.

And the old man bent his head and mumbled.

All through the meal he stopped eating at intervals, and stared furtively at his wife; but he ate well. The home food tasted good to him, and his old frame was too sturdily healthy to be affected by his mind. But after supper he went out, and sat down on the step of the smaller door at the right of the barn, through which he had meant his Jerseys to pass in stately file, but which Sarah designed for her front house door, and he leaned his head on his hands.

After the supper dishes were cleared away and the milk-pans washed, Sarah went out to him. The twilight was deepening. There was a clear green glow in the sky. Before them stretched the smooth level of field; in the distance was a cluster of hay-stacks like the huts of a village; the air was very cool and calm and sweet. The landscape might have been an ideal one of peace.

Sarah bent over and touched her husband on one of his thin, sinewy shoulders. "Father!"

The old man's shoulders heaved: he was weeping.

"Why, don't do so, father," said Sarah.

"I'll—put up the—partitions, an'—everything you—want, mother."

Sarah put her apron up to her face; she was overcome by her own triumph.

Adoniram was like a fortress whose walls had no active resistance, and went down the instant the right besieging tools were used. "Why, mother," he said, hoarsely, "I hadn't no idee you was so set on't as all this comes to."

Charlotte Perkins Gilman 1860–1935

That Charlotte Perkins Gilman is noted as a feminist activist and important literary figure comes perhaps as some consequence of the influence of her relatives, whose company she frequented: among them, Harriet Beecher Stowe, abolitionist and author of *Uncle Tom's Cabin,* and activists Catherine Beecher and Isabella Beecher Hooker. A staunch supporter of women's rights and a number of feminist concerns—including reform in labor laws—Gilman suffered profoundly after the birth of her daughter with what we would now (and only recently) recognize as postpartum depression. Out of this experience comes Gilman's most well known and anthologized work, "The Yellow Wallpaper" (1899), the story of a woman's descent into madness, following the birth of her child, at the hands of her well-meaning but wholly restrictive physician-husband. Gilman is also known for her utopianlike tales in which men and women are social equals, including *Herland* (1915) and *With Her in Ourland* (1916). In works such as *The Home* (1903), Gilman continued her attempts at fostering social change, arguing that the conventions of domesticity were detrimental to happiness in the home and offering a model of the home as a type of family center in which teaching and child-caring professionals might play important roles. Critic Carl N. Degler, writing in 1956, praised the tract for Gilman's "insights into the position of women and the consequences thereof for the two sexes and society."

THE YELLOW WALLPAPER

It is very seldom that mere ordinary people like John and myself secure ancestral halls for the summer.

A colonial mansion, a hereditary estate, I would say a haunted house, and reach the height of romantic felicity—but that would be asking too much of fate!

Still I will proudly declare that there is something queer about it.

Else, why should it be let so cheaply? And why have stood so long untenanted?

John laughs at me, of course, but one expects that in marriage.

John is practical in the extreme. He has no patience with faith, an intense horror of superstition, and he scoffs openly at any talk of things not to be felt and seen and put down in figures.

John is a physician, and *perhaps*—(I would not say it to a living soul, of course, but this is dead paper and a great relief to my mind—*perhaps* that is one reason I do not get well faster.

You see he does not believe I am sick!

And what can one do?

If a physician of high standing, and one's own husband, assures friends and relatives that there is really nothing the matter with one but temporary nervous depression—a slight hysterical tendency—what is one to do?

My brother is also a physician, and also of high standing, and he says the same thing.

So I take phosphates or phosphites—whichever it is, and tonics, and journeys, and air, and exercise, and am absolutely forbidden to "work" until I am well again.

Personally, I disagree with their ideas.

Personally, I believe that congenial work, with excitement and change, would do me good.

But what is one to do?

I did write for a while in spite of them; but it *does* exhaust me a good deal—having to be so sly about it, or else meet with heavy opposition.

I sometimes fancy that in my condition if I had less opposition and more society and stimulus—but John says the very worst thing I can do is to think about my condition, and I confess it always makes me feel bad.

So I will let it alone and talk about the house.

The most beautiful place! It is quite alone, standing well back from the road, quite three miles from the village. It makes me think of English places that you read about, for there are hedges and walls and gates that lock, and lots of separate little houses for the gardeners and people.

There is a *delicious* garden! I never saw such a garden—large and shady, full of box-bordered paths, and lined with long grape-covered arbors with seats under them.

There were greenhouses, too, but they are all broken now. There was some legal trouble, I believe, something about the heirs and coheirs; anyhow, the place has been empty for years.

That spoils my ghostliness, I am afraid, but I don't care—there is something strange about the house—I can feel it.

I even said so to John one moonlight evening, but he said what I felt was a *draught,* and shut the window.

I get unreasonably angry with John sometimes. I'm sure I never used to be so sensitive. I think it is due to this nervous condition.

But John says if I feel so, I shall neglect proper self-control; so I take pains to control myself—before him, at least, and that makes me very tired.

I don't like our room a bit. I wanted one downstairs that opened on the piazza and had roses all over the window, and such pretty old-fashioned chintz hangings! but John would not hear of it.

He said there was only one window and not room for two beds, and no near room for him if he took another.

He is very careful and loving, and hardly lets me stir without special direction.

I have a schedule prescription for each hour in the day; he takes all care from me, and so I feel basely ungrateful not to value it more.

He said we came here solely on my account, that I was to have perfect rest and all the air I could get. "Your exercise depends on your strength, my dear," said he, "and your food somewhat on your appetite; but air you can absorb all the time." So we took the nursery at the top of the house.

It is a big, airy room, the whole floor nearly, with windows that look all ways, and air and sunshine galore. It was nursery first and then playroom and gymnasium, I should judge; for the windows are barred for little children, and there are rings and things in the walls.

The paint and paper look as if a boys' school had used it. It is stripped off— the paper—in great patches all around the head of my bed, about as far as I can reach, and in a great place on the other side of the room low down. I never saw a worse paper in my life.

One of those sprawling flamboyant patterns committing every artistic sin.

It is dull enough to confuse the eye in following, pronounced enough to constantly irritate and provoke study, and when you follow the lame uncertain curves for a little distance they suddenly commit suicide—plunge off at outrageous angles, destroy themselves in unheard of contradictions.

The color is repellent, almost revolting; a smoldering unclean yellow, strangely faded by the slow-turning sunlight.

It is a dull yet lurid orange in some places, a sickly sulphur tint in others.

No wonder the children hated it! I should hate it myself if I had to live in this room long.

There comes John, and I must put this away,—he hates to have me write a word.

* * *

We have been here two weeks, and I haven't felt like writing before, since that first day.

I am sitting by the window now, up in this atrocious nursery, and there is nothing to hinder my writing as much as I please, save lack of strength.

John is away all day, and even some nights when his cases are serious.

I am glad my case is not serious!

But these nervous troubles are dreadfully depressing.

John does not know how much I really suffer. He knows there is no *reason* to suffer, and that satisfies him.

Of course it is only nervousness. It does weigh on me so not to do my duty in any way!

I meant to be such a help to John, such a real rest and comfort, and here I am a comparative burden already!

Nobody would believe what an effort it is to do what little I am able, — to dress and entertain, and order things.

It is fortunate Mary is so good with the baby. Such a dear baby!

And yet I *cannot* be with him, it makes me so nervous.

I suppose John never was nervous in his life. He laughs at me so about this wallpaper!

At first he meant to repaper the room, but afterwards he said that I was letting it get the better of me, and that nothing was worse for a nervous patient than to give way to such fancies.

He said that after the wallpaper was changed it would be the heavy bedstead, and then the barred windows, and then that gate at the head of the stairs, and so on.

"You know the place is doing you good," he said, "and really, dear, I don't care to renovate the house just for a three months' rental."

"Then do let us go downstairs," I said, "there are such pretty rooms there."

Then he took me in his arms and called me a blessed little goose, and said he would go down to the cellar, if I wished, and have it whitewashed into the bargain.

But he is right enough about the beds and windows and things.

It is an airy and comfortable room as any one need wish, and, of course, I would not be so silly as to make him uncomfortable just for a whim.

I'm really getting quite fond of the big room, all but that horrid paper.

Out of one window I can see the garden, those mysterious deep-shaded arbors, the riotous old-fashioned flowers, and bushes and gnarly trees.

Out of another I get a lovely view of the bay and a little private wharf belonging to the estate. There is a beautiful shaded lane that runs down there from the house. I always fancy I see people walking in these numerous paths and arbors, but John has cautioned me not to give way to fancy in the least. He says that with my imaginative power and habit of story-making, a nervous weakness like mine is sure to lead to all manner of excited fancies, and that I ought to use my will and good sense to check the tendency. So I try.

I think sometimes that if I were only well enough to write a little it would relieve the press of ideas and rest me.

But I find I get pretty tired when I try.

It is so discouraging not to have any advice and companionship about my work. When I get really well, John says we will ask Cousin Henry and Julia down for a long visit; but he says he would as soon put fireworks in my pillow-case as to let me have those stimulating people about now.

I wish I could get well faster.

But I must not think about that. This paper looks to me as if it *knew* what a vicious influence it had!

There is a recurrent spot where the pattern lolls like a broken neck and two bulbous eyes stare at you upside down.

I get positively angry with the impertinence of it and the everlastingness. Up and down and sideways they crawl, and those absurd, unblinking eyes are everywhere. There is one place where two breadths didn't match, and the eyes go all up and down the line, one a little higher than the other.

I never saw so much expression in an inanimate thing before, and we all know how much expression they have! I used to lie awake as a child and get more entertainment and terror out of blank walls and plain furniture than most children could find in a toystore.

I remember what a kindly wink the knobs of our big, old bureau used to have, and there was one chair that always seemed like a strong friend.

I used to feel that if any of the other things looked too fierce I could always hop into that chair and be safe.

The furniture in this room is no worse than inharmonious, however, for we had to bring it all from downstairs. I suppose when this was used as a playroom they had to take the nursery things out, and no wonder! I never saw such ravages as the children have made here.

The wallpaper, as I said before, is torn off in spots, and it sticketh closer than a brother—they must have had perseverance as well as hatred.

Then the floor is scratched and gouged and splintered, the plaster itself is dug out here and there, and this great heavy bed which is all we found in the room, looks as if it had been through the wars.

But I don't mind it a bit—only the paper.

There comes John's sister. Such a dear girl as she is, and so careful of me! I must not let her find me writing.

She is a perfect and enthusiastic housekeeper, and hopes for no better profession. I verily believe she thinks it is the writing which made me sick!

But I can write when she is out, and see her a long way off from these windows.

There is one that commands the road, a lovely shaded winding road, and one that just looks off over the country. A lovely country, too, full of great elms and velvet meadows.

This wallpaper has a kind of sub-pattern in a different shade, a particularly irritating one, for you can only see it in certain lights, and not clearly then.

But in the places where it isn't faded and where the sun is just so—I can see a strange, provoking, formless sort of figure, that seems to skulk about behind that silly and conspicuous front design.

There's sister on the stairs!

Well, the Fourth of July is over! The people are all gone and I am tired out. John thought it might do me good to see a little company, so we just had mother and Nellie and the children down for a week.

Of course I didn't do a thing. Jennie sees to everything now. But it tired me all the same.

John says if I don't pick up faster he shall send me to Weir Mitchell in the fall.

But I don't want to go there at all. I had a friend who was in his hands once, and she says he is just like John and my brother, only more so!

Besides, it is such an undertaking to go so far.

I don't feel as if it was worth while to turn my hand over for anything, and I'm getting dreadfully fretful and querulous.

I cry at nothing, and cry most of the time.

Of course I don't when John is here, or anybody else, but when I am alone.

And I am alone a good deal just now. John is kept in town very often by serious cases, and Jennie is good and lets me alone when I want her to.

So I walk a little in the garden or down that lovely lane, sit on the porch under the roses, and lie down up here a good deal.

I'm getting really fond of the room in spite of the wallpaper. Perhaps *because* of the wallpaper.

It dwells in my mind so!

I lie here on this great immovable bed—it is nailed down, I believe—and follow that pattern about by the hour. It is as good as gymnastics, I assure you. I start, we'll say, at the bottom, down in the corner over there where it has not been touched, and I determine for the thousandth time that I *will* follow that pointless pattern to some sort of a conclusion.

I know a little of the principle of design, and I know this thing was not arranged on any laws of radiation, or alternation, or repetition, or symmetry, or anything else that I ever heard of.

It is repeated, of course, by the breadths, but not otherwise.

Looked at in one way each breadth stands alone, the bloated curves and flourishes—a kind of "debased Romanesque" with *delirium tremens*—go waddling up and down in isolated columns of fatuity.

But, on the other hand, they connect diagonally, and the sprawling outlines run off in great slanting waves of optic horror, like a lot of wallowing seaweeds in full chase.

The whole thing goes horizontally, too, at least it seems so, and I exhaust myself in trying to distinguish the order of its going in that direction.

They have used a horizontal breadth for a frieze, and that adds wonderfully to the confusion.

There is one end of the room where it is almost intact, and there, when the crosslights fade and the low sun shines directly upon it, I can almost fancy radiation after all,—the interminable grotesques seem to form around a common center and rush off in headlong plunges of equal distraction.

It makes me tired to follow it. I will take a nap I guess.

I don't know why I should write this.

I don't want to.

I don't feel able.

And I know John would think it absurd. But I *must* say what I feel and think in some way—it is such a relief.

But the effort is getting to be greater than the relief!

Half the time now I am awfully lazy, and lie down ever so much.

John says I mustn't lose my strength, and has me take cod liver oil and lots of tonics and things, to say nothing of ale and wine and rare meat.

Dear John! He loves me very dearly, and hates to have me sick. I tried to have a real earnest reasonable talk with him the other day, and tell him how I wish he would let me go and make a visit to Cousin Henry and Julia.

But he said I wasn't able to go, nor able to stand it after I got there; and I did not make out a very good case for myself, for I was crying before I had finished.

It is getting to be a great effort for me to think straight. Just this nervous weakness I suppose.

And dear John gathered me up in his arms, and just carried me upstairs and laid me on the bed, and sat by me and read to me till it tired my head.

He said I was his darling and his comfort and all he had, and that I must take care of myself for his sake, and keep well.

He says no one but myself can help me out of it, that I must use my will and self-control and not let any silly fancies run away with me.

There's one comfort, the baby is well and happy, and does not have to occupy this nursery with the horrid wallpaper.

If we had not used it, that blessed child would have! What a fortunate escape! Why, I wouldn't have a child of mine, an impressionable little thing, live in such a room for worlds.

I never thought of it before, but it is lucky that John kept me here after all, I can stand it so much easier than a baby, you see.

Of course I never mention it to them any more—I am too wise,—but I keep watch of it all the same.

There are things in that paper that nobody knows but me, or ever will.

Behind that outside pattern the dim shapes get clearer every day.

It is always the same shape, only very numerous.

And it is like a woman stooping down and creeping about behind that pattern. I don't like it a bit. I wonder—I begin to think—I wish John would take me away from here.

It is so hard to talk with John about my case, because he is so wise, and because he loves me so.

But I tried last night.

It was moonlight. The moon shines in all around just as the sun does.

I hate to see it sometimes, it creeps so slowly, and always comes in by one window or another.

John was asleep and I hated to waken him, so I kept still and watched the moonlight on that undulating wallpaper till I felt creepy.

The faint figure behind seemed to shake the pattern, just as if she wanted to get out.

I got up softly and went to feel and see if the paper *did* move, and when I came back John was awake.

"What is it, little girl?" he said. "Don't go walking about like that—you'll get cold."

I thought it was a good time to talk, so I told him that I really was not gaining here, and that I wished he would take me away.

"Why darling!" said he, "our lease will be up in three weeks, and I can't see how to leave before.

"The repairs are not done at home, and I cannot possibly leave town just now. Of course if you were in any danger, I could and would, but you really are better, dear, whether you can see it or not. I am a doctor, dear, and I know. You are gaining flesh and color, your appetite is better, I feel really much easier about you."

"I don't weigh a bit more," said I, "nor as much; and my appetite may be better in the evening when you are here, but it is worse in the morning when you are away!"

"Bless her little heart!" said he with a big hug, "she shall be as sick as she pleases! But now let's improve the shining hours by going to sleep, and talk about it in the morning!"

"And you won't go away?" I asked gloomily.

"Why, how can I, dear? It is only three weeks more and then we will take a nice little trip of a few days while Jennie is getting the house ready. Really, dear, you are better!"

"Better in body perhaps—" I began, and stopped short, for he sat up straight and looked at me with such a stern, reproachful look that I could not say another word.

"My darling," said he, "I beg of you, for my sake and for our child's sake, as well as for your own, that you will never for one instant let that idea enter your mind! There is nothing so dangerous, so fascinating, to a temperament like yours. It is a false and foolish fancy. Can you not trust me as a physician when I tell you so?"

So of course I said no more on that score, and we went to sleep before long. He thought I was asleep first, but I wasn't, and lay there for hours trying to decide whether that front pattern and the back pattern really did move together or separately.

On a pattern like this, by daylight, there is a lack of sequence, a defiance of law, that is a constant irritant to a normal mind.

The color is hideous enough, and unreliable enough, and infuriating enough, but the pattern is torturing.

You think you have mastered it, but just as you get well under way in following, it turns a back-somersault and there you are. It slaps you in the face, knocks you down, and tramples upon you. It is like a bad dream.

The outside pattern is a florid arabesque, reminding one of a fungus. If you can imagine a toadstool in joints, an interminable string of toadstools, budding and sprouting in endless convolutions—why, that is something like it.

That is, sometimes!

There is one marked peculiarity about this paper, a thing nobody seems to notice but myself, and that is that it changes as the light changes.

When the sun shoots in through the east window—I always watch for that first long, straight ray—it changes so quickly that I never can quite believe it.

That is why I watch it always.

By moonlight—the moon shines in all night when there is a moon—I wouldn't know it was the same paper.

At night in any kind of light, in twilight, candle light, lamplight, and worst of all by moonlight, it becomes bars! The outside pattern I mean, and the woman behind it is as plain as can be.

I didn't realize for a long time what the thing was that showed behind, that dim sub-pattern, but now I am quite sure it is a woman.

By daylight she is subdued, quiet. I fancy it is the pattern that keeps her so still. It is so puzzling. It keeps me quiet by the hour.

I lie down ever so much now. John says it is good for me, and to sleep all I can.

Indeed he started the habit by making me lie down for an hour after each meal.

It is a very bad habit I am convinced, for you see I don't sleep.

And that cultivates deceit, for I don't tell them I'm awake—O no!

The fact is I am getting a little afraid of John.

He seems very queer sometimes, and even Jennie has an inexplicable look.

It strikes me occasionally, just as a scientific hypothesis,—that perhaps it is the paper!

I have watched John when he did not know I was looking, and come into the room suddenly on the most innocent excuses, and I've caught him several times *looking at the paper!* And Jennie too: I caught Jennie with her hand on it once.

She didn't know I was in the room, and when I asked her in a quiet, very quiet voice, with the most restrained manner possible, what she was doing with the paper—she turned around as if she had been caught stealing, and looked quite angry—asked me why I should frighten her so!

Then she said that the paper stained everything it touched, that she had found yellow smooches on all my clothes and John's, and she wished we would be more careful!

Did not that sound innocent? But I know she was studying that pattern, and I am determined that nobody shall find it out but myself!

Life is very much more exciting now than it used to be. You see I have something more to expect, to look forward to, to watch. I really do eat better, and am more quiet than I was.

John is so pleased to see me improve! He laughed a little the other day, and said I seemed to be flourishing in spite of my wallpaper.

I turned it off with a laugh. I had no intention of telling him it was *because* of the wallpaper—he would make fun of me. He might even want to take me away.

I don't want to leave now until I have found it out. There is a week more, and I think that will be enough.

I'm feeling ever so much better! I don't sleep much at night, for it is so interesting to watch developments; but I sleep a good deal in the daytime.

In the daytime it is tiresome and perplexing.

There are always new shoots on the fungus, and new shades of yellow all over it. I cannot keep count of them, though I have tried conscientiously.

It is the strangest yellow, that wallpaper! It makes me think of all the yellow things I ever saw—not beautiful ones like buttercups, but old, foul, bad yellow things.

But there is something else about that paper—the smell! I noticed it the moment we came into the room, but with so much air and sun it was not bad. Now we have had a week of fog and rain, and whether the windows are open or not, the smell is here.

It creeps all over the house.

I find it hovering in the dining-room, skulking in the parlor, hiding in the hall, lying in wait for me on the stairs.

It gets into my hair.

Even when I go to ride, if I turn my head suddenly and surprise it—there is that smell!

Such a peculiar odor, too! I have spent hours in trying to analyze it, to find what it smelled like.

It is not bad—at first, and very gentle, but quite the subtlest, most enduring odor I ever met.

In this damp weather it is awful, I wake up in the night and find it hanging over me.

It used to disturb me at first. I thought seriously of burning the house—to reach the smell.

But now I am used to it. The only thing I can think of that it is like the *color* of the paper! A yellow smell.

There is a very funny mark on this wall, low down, near the mopboard. A streak that runs round the room. It goes behind every piece of furniture, except the bed, a long, straight, even *smooch,* as if it had been rubbed over and over.

I wonder how it was done and who did it, and what they did it for. Round and round and round—round and round and round—it makes me dizzy!

I really have discovered something at last.

Through watching so much at night, when it changes so, I have finally found out.

The front pattern *does* move—and no wonder! The woman behind shakes it!

Sometimes I think there are a great many women behind, and sometimes only one, and she crawls around fast, and her crawling shakes it all over.

Then in the very bright spots she keeps still, and in the very shady spots she just takes hold of the bars and shakes them hard.

And she is all the time trying to climb through. But nobody could climb through that pattern—it strangles so; I think that is why it has so many heads.

They get through, and then the pattern strangles them off and turns them upside down, and makes their eyes white!

If those heads were covered or taken off it would not be half so bad.

I think that woman gets out in the daytime!

And I'll you tell why—privately—I've seen her!

I can see her out of every one of my windows!

It is the same woman, I know, for she is always creeping, and most women do not creep by daylight.

I see her on that long road under the trees, creeping along, and when a carriage comes she hides under the blackberry vines.

I don't blame her a bit. It must be very humiliating to be caught creeping by daylight!

I always lock the door when I creep by daylight. I can't do it at night, for I know John would suspect something at once.

And John is so queer now, that I don't want to irritate him. I wish he would take another room! Besides, I don't want anybody to get that woman out at night but myself.

I often wonder if I could see her out of all the windows at once.

But, turn as fast as I can, I can only see out of one at one time. And though I always see her, she *may* be able to creep faster than I can turn!

I have watched her sometimes away off in the open country, creeping as fast as a cloud shadow in a high wind.

If only that top pattern could be gotten off from the under one! I mean to try it, little by little.

I have found out another funny thing, but I shan't tell at this time! It does not do to trust people too much.

There are only two more days to get this paper off, and I believe John is beginning to notice. I don't like the look in his eyes.

And I heard him ask Jennie a lot of professional questions about me. She had a very good report to give.

She said I slept a good deal in the daytime.

John knows I don't sleep very well at night, for all I'm so quiet!

He asked me all sorts of questions, too, and pretended to be very loving and kind.

As if I couldn't see through him!

Still, I don't wonder he acts so, sleeping under this paper for three months.

It only interests me, but I feel sure John and Jennie are secretly affected by it.

Hurrah! This is the last day, but it is enough. John to stay in town over night, and won't be out until this evening.

Jennie wanted to sleep with me—the sly thing! But I told her I should undoubtedly rest better for a night alone.

That was clever, for really I wasn't alone a bit! As soon as it was moonlight and that poor thing began to crawl and shake the pattern, I got up and ran to help her.

I pulled and she shook, I shook and she pulled, and before morning we had peeled off yards of that paper.

A strip about as high as my head and half round the room. And then when the sun came and that awful pattern began to laugh at me, I declared I would finish it to-day!

We go away to-morrow, and they are moving all the furniture down again to leave things as they were before.

Jennie looked at the wall in amazement, but I told her merrily that I did it out of pure spite at the vicious thing.

She laughed and said she wouldn't mind doing it herself, but I must not get tired.

How she betrayed herself that time!

But I am here, and no person touches this paper but me—not *alive*!

She tried to get me out of the room—it was too patent! But I said it was so quiet and empty and clean now that I believed I would lie down again and sleep all I could; and not to wake me even for dinner—I would call when I woke.

So now she is gone, and the servants are gone, and the things are gone, and there is nothing left but that great bedstead nailed down, with the canvas mattress we found on it.

We shall sleep downstairs to-night, and take the boat home to-morrow.

I quite enjoy the room, now it is bare again.

How those children did tear about here!

This bedstead is fairly gnawed!

But I must get to work.

I have locked the door and thrown the key down into the front path.

I don't want to go out, and I don't want to have anybody come in, till John comes.

I want to astonish him.

I've got a rope up here that even Jennie did not find. If that woman does get out, and tries to get away, I can tie her!

But I forgot I could not reach far without anything to stand on! This bed will *not* move!

I tried to lift and push it until I was lame, and then I got so angry I bit off a little piece at one corner—but it hurt my teeth.

Then I peeled off all the paper I could reach standing on the floor. It sticks horribly and the pattern just enjoys it! All those strangled heads and bulbous eyes and waddling fungus growths just shriek with derision!

I am getting angry enough to do something desperate. To jump out of the window would be admirable exercise, but the bars are too strong even to try.

Besides I wouldn't do it. Of course not. I know well enough that a step like that is improper and might be misconstrued.

I don't like to *look* out of the windows even—there are so many of those creeping women, and they creep so fast.

I wonder if they all come out of that wallpaper as I did?

But I am securely fastened now by my well-hidden rope—you don't get *me* out in the road there!

I suppose I shall have to get back behind the pattern when it comes night, and that is hard!

It is so pleasant to be out in this great room and creep around as I please!

I don't want to go outside. I won't, even if Jennie asks me to.

For outside you have to creep on the ground, and everything is green instead of yellow.

But here I can creep smoothly on the floor, and my shoulder just fits in that long smooch around the wall, so I cannot lose my way.

Why there's John at the door!

It is no use, young man, you can't open it!

How he does call and pound!

Now he's crying for an axe.

It would be a shame to break down that beautiful door!

"John dear!" said I in the gentlest voice, "the key is down by the front steps, under a plantain leaf!"

That silenced him for a few moments.

Then he said—very quietly indeed, "Open the door, my darling!"

"I can't," said I. "The key is down by the front door under a plantain leaf!"

And then I said it again, several times, very gently and slowly, and said it so often that he had to go and see, and he got it of course, and came in. He stopped short by the door.

"What is the matter?" he cried. "For God's sake, what are you doing!"

I kept on creeping just the same, but I looked at him over my shoulder.

"I've got out at last," said I, "in spite of you and Jane. And I've pulled off most of the paper, so you can't put me back!"

Now why should that man have fainted? But he did, and right across my path by the wall, so that I had to creep over him every time!

CLOSED DOORS

When it is night and the house is still,
    When it is day and guests are gone,
When the lights and colors and sounds that fill
    Leave the house empty and you alone:

Then you hear them stir—you hear them shift—   5
    You hear them through the walls and floors—
And the door-knobs turn and the latches lift
    On the closet doors.

Then you try to read and you try to think,
    And you try to work—but the hour is late;   10
No play nor labor nor meat nor drink
    Will make them wait.

Well for you if the locks are good!
    Well for you if the bolts are strong,
And the panels heavy with oaken wood,   15
    And the chamber long.

Even so you can hear them plead—
    Hear them argue—hear them moan—
When the house is very still indeed,
    And you are alone.   20

Blessed then is a step outside,
    Warm hands to hold you, eyes that smile,
The stir and noise of a world that's wide,
    To silence yours for a little while.

Fill your life with work and play!   25
    Fill you heart with joy and pain!
Hold your friends while they will stay,
    Silent so shall these remain.

But you can hear them when you hark—
    Things you wish you had not known—   30
When the house is very still and dark,
    And you are alone.

THE REAL RELIGION

Man, the hunter, Man, the warrior;
Slew for gain and slew for safety,
Slew for rage, for sport, for glory—
    Slaughter was his breath:
So the man's mind, searching inward,   5
Saw in all one red reflection,
Filled the world with dark religions
    Built on Death.

Death and The Fate of The Soul;—
The soul, from the body dissevered;   10
Through the withering failure of age,
Through the horror and pain of disease,
Through raw wounds and destruction and fear:—
In fear, black fear of the dark,
Red fear of terrible gods,   15
Sent forth on its journey, alone,
To eternity, fearful, unknown—
Death, and The Fate of the Soul.

Woman, bearer; Woman, teacher;
Overflowing love and labor,   20
Service of the tireless mother
    Filling all the earth;—
Now her mind, awakening, searching,
Sees a fair world, young and growing,
Sees at last our real religion—   25
    Built on Birth.

Birth, and The Growth of The Soul: —
The Soul, in the body established;
In the ever-new beauty of childhood,
In the wonder of opening power,   30
Still learning, improving, achieving;
In hope, new knowledge and light,
Sure faith in the world's fresh Spring, —
Together we live, we grow,
On the earth that we love and know—   35
Birth, and the Growth of the Soul.

Mary Elizabeth Coleridge 1861–1907

Referred to as "the tail end of the comet S.T.C." because of her status as the great-great-niece of Romantic poet Samuel Taylor Coleridge, Mary Elizabeth may have burned brighter had she allowed all of her work to be published in her lifetime. Although four published novels were successful, most of her verse was not published until a year after her death. She was persuaded by the poet Robert Bridges to permit two small volumes of verse to be printed: *Fancy's Following* (1896) and *Fancy's Guerdon* (1897), both under the pseudonym Anodos. For the most part, however, she would not even consent to discuss her verse. One of her most famous poems, "The Other Side of a Mirror," written in 1882 but published posthumously, reveals images of self-alienation that shed an interesting light on the author's reticence to publish such apparently personal verse. Coleridge, who lived at home with her parents and a sister all of her life, was extremely well educated. Fluent in several languages as well as a scholar of literature and philosophy, Coleridge wrote stories and essays for several journals and frequented the intellectual circles. From 1895 until her death, she taught English literature at a college for working women.

VIII

THE OTHER SIDE OF A MIRROR

I sat before my glass one day,
And conjured up a vision bare,
Unlike the aspects glad and gay,
That erst were found reflected there—
The vision of a woman, wild   5
With more than womanly despair.

Her hair stood back on either side
A face bereft of loveliness.
It had no envy now to hide
What once no man on earth could guess.   10
It formed the thorny aureole
Of hard unsanctified distress.

Her lips were open — not a sound
Came through the parted lines of red.
Whate'er it was, the hideous wound   15
In silence and in secret bled.
No sigh relieved her speechless woe,
She had no voice to speak her dread.

And in her lurid eyes there shone
The dying flame of life's desire,   20
Made mad because its hope was gone,
And kindled at the leaping fire
Of jealousy, and fierce revenge,
And strength that could not change nor tire.

Shade of a shadow in the glass,   25
O set the crystal surface free!
Pass — as the fairer visions pass —
Nor ever more return, to be
The ghost of a distracted hour,
That heard me whisper, "I am she!"   30

MARRIAGE

No more alone sleeping, no more alone waking,
    Thy dreams divided, thy prayers in twain;
Thy merry sisters to-night forsaking,
    Never shall we see thee, maiden, again.

Never shall we see thee, thine eyes glancing,   5
    Flashing with laughter and wild in glee,
Under the mistletoe kissing and dancing,
    Wantonly free.

There shall come a matron walking sedately,
    Low-voiced, gentle, wise in reply.   10
Tell me, O tell me, can I love her greatly?
    All for her sake must the maiden die!

COMPANIONSHIP

The men and women round thee, what are they?
　Frail as the flowers, less lasting than the snow.
If there be angels flitting in the day,
　Who knows those angels? Who shall ever know?
Let them alone and go thou on thy way!　　　　　5
　They came like dreams; like dreams they come and go.

Nay, the companions of thy timeless hours
　Are dreams dreamt first for thee by them of old,
That thou might'st dream them after! These are powers
　Unending and unaging—never cold—　　　　　10
White as the driven snow, fair as the flowers.
　These be thy verities, to have, to hold!

Edith Wharton 1862–1937

Edith Wharton (Edith Newbold Jones) was born in New York City, the youngest child of wealthy and prominent aristocrats. Groomed and educated by tutors in family homes in Paris, New York, and Newport, Rhode Island, she made her society debut at seventeen. At age twenty-three, she married Edward "Teddy" Wharton, a well-to-do Bostonian, thireen years her senior. Although the marriage allowed Edith the luxury to pursue her writing, Teddy did not share her interests in literature and writing nor her intellectual gifts. Three years into her marriage in 1888, Wharton began publishing verses and stories in prestigious periodicals. But the idea of committing to her increasing ambition and productivity became a terrible burden, and by 1897, in a state of "paralyzing melancholy," she underwent S. Weir Mitchell's "rest cure." Wharton recovered by 1899, publishing two collections of short stories and, perhaps more importantly, finally committing herself fully to her craft. From that point on, she published (on average) a book a year for the rest of her life. Wharton, who divorced in 1913, went on to win the Pulitzer Prize for *The Age of Innocence* (1920), a novel that continued her common theme of unconventional women ruined by conventional society, chained to their fates by the "manacles" of society's artificially constructed expectations of women. Artifice is again addressed in "The Other Two" (1904), with a sardonic exploration of how the so-called romantic process molds a woman into the "perfect wife."

THE OTHER TWO[1]

I

Waythorn, on the drawing-room hearth, waited for his wife to come down to dinner.

It was their first night under his own roof, and he was surprised at his thrill of boyish agitation. He was not so old, to be sure—his glass gave him little more than the five-and-thirty years to which his wife confessed—but he had fancied himself already in the temperate zone; yet here he was listening to her step with a tender sense of all it symbolized, with some old trail of verse about the gar-landed nuptial doorposts floating through his enjoyment of the pleasant room and the good dinner just beyond it.

They had been hastily recalled from their honeymoon by the illness of Lily Haskett, the child of Mrs. Waythorn's first marriage. The little girl, at Waythorn's desire, had been transferred to his house on the day of her mother's wedding, and the doctor, on their arrival, broke the news that she was ill with typhoid, but declared that all the symptoms were favorable. Lily could show twelve years of unblemished health, and the case promised to be a light one. The nurse spoke as reassuringly, and after a moment of alarm Mrs. Waythorn had adjusted herself to the situation. She was very fond of Lily—her affection for the child had per-haps been her decisive charm in Waythorn's eyes—but she had the perfectly balanced nerves which her little girl had inherited, and no woman ever wasted less tissue in unproductive worry. Waythorn was therefore quite prepared to see her come in presently, a little late because of a last look at Lily, but as serene and well-appointed as if her good-night kiss had been laid on the brow of health. Her composure was restful to him; it acted as ballast to his somewhat unstable sensibilities. As he pictured her bending over the child's bed he thought how soothing her presence must be in illness: her very step would prognosticate re-covery.

His own life had been a gray one, from temperament rather than circum-stance, and he had been drawn to her by the unperturbed gaiety which kept her fresh and elastic at an age when most woman's activities are growing either slack or febrile. He knew what was said about her; for, popular as she was, there had always been a faint undercurrent of detraction. When she had appeared in New York, nine or ten years earlier, as the pretty Mrs. Haskett whom Gus Varick had unearthed somewhere—was it in Pittsburgh or Utica?—society, while promptly accepting her, had reserved the right to cast a doubt on its own indis-crimination. Inquiry, however, established her undoubted connection with a so-cially reigning family, and explained her recent divorce as the natural result of a runaway match at seventeen; and as nothing was known of Mr. Haskett it was easy to believe the worst of him.

[1] First published by Scribners in the 1904 collection *The Descent of Man and Other Stories*, the source of the present text.

Alice Haskett's remarriage with Gus Varick was a passport to the set whose recognition she coveted, and for a few years the Varicks were the most popular couple in town. Unfortunately the alliance was brief and stormy, and this time the husband had his champions. Still, even Varick's stanchest supporters admitted that he was not meant for matrimony, and Mrs. Varick's grievances were of a nature to bear the inspection of the New York courts.[2] A New York divorce is in itself a diploma of virtue, and in the semi-widowhood of this second separation Mrs. Varick took on an air of sanctity, and was allowed to confide her wrongs to some of the most scrupulous ears in town. But when it was known that she was to marry Waythorn there was a momentary reaction. Her best friends would have preferred to see her remain in the role of the injured wife, which was as becoming to her as crape to a rosy complexion. True, a decent time had elapsed, and it was not even suggested that Waythorn had supplanted his predecessor. People shook their heads over him, however, and one grudging friend, to whom he affirmed that he took the step with his eyes open, replied oracularly: "Yes—and with your ears shut."

Waythorn could afford to smile at these innuendoes. In the Wall Street phrase, he had "discounted" them. He knew that society has not yet adapted itself to the consequences of divorce, and that till the adaptation takes place every woman who uses the freedom the law accords her must be her own social justification. Waythorn had an amused confidence in his wife's ability to justify herself. His expectations were fulfilled, and before the wedding took place Alice Varick's group had rallied openly to her support. She took it all imperturbably: she had a way of surmounting obstacles without seeming to be aware of them, and Waythorn looked back with wonder at the trivialities over which he had worn his nerves thin. He had the sense of having found refuge in a richer, warmer nature than his own, and his satisfaction, at the moment, was humorously summed up in the thought that his wife, when she had done all she could for Lily, would not be ashamed to come down and enjoy a good dinner.

The anticipation of such enjoyment was not, however, the sentiment expressed by Mrs. Waythorn's charming face when she presently joined him. Though she had put on her most engaging teagown she had neglected to assume the smile that went with it, and Waythorn thought he had never seen her look so nearly worried.

"What is it?" he asked. "Is anything wrong with Lily?"

"No; I've just been in and she's still sleeping." Mrs. Waythorn hesitated. "But something tiresome has happened."

He had taken her two hands, and now perceived that he was crushing a paper between them.

"This letter?"

"Yes—Mr. Haskett has written—I mean his lawyer has written."

Waythorn felt himself flush uncomfortably. He dropped his wife's hands.

"What about?"

[2] Divorce in New York State could then be granted only on the grounds of adultery.

"About seeing Lily. You know the courts—"

"Yes, yes," he interrupted nervously.

Nothing was known about Haskett in New York. He was vaguely supposed to have remained in the outer darkness from which his wife had been rescued, and Waythorn was one of the few who were aware that he had given up his business in Utica and followed her to New York in order to be near his little girl. In the days of his wooing, Waythorn had often met Lily on the doorstep, rosy and smiling, on her way "to see papa."

"I am so sorry," Mrs. Waythorn murmured.

He roused himself. "What does he want?"

"He wants to see her. You know she goes to him once a week."

"Well—he doesn't expect her to go to him now, does he?"

"No—he has heard of her illness; but he expects to come here."

"*Here?*"

Mrs. Waythorn reddened under his gaze. They looked away from each other.

"I'm afraid he has the right. . . . You'll see. . . ." She made a proffer of the letter.

Waythorn moved away with a gesture of refusal. He stood staring about the softly-lighted room, which a moment before had seemed so full of bridal intimacy.

"I'm so sorry," she repeated. "If Lily could have been moved—"

"That's out of the question," he returned impatiently.

"I suppose so."

Her lip was beginning to tremble, and he felt himself a brute.

"He must come, of course," he said. "When is—his day?"

"I'm afraid—to-morrow."

"Very well. Send a note in the morning."

The butler entered to announce dinner.

Waythorn turned to his wife. "Come—you must be tired. It's beastly, but try to forget about it," he said, drawing her hand through his arm.

"You're so good, dear. I'll try," she whispered back.

Her face cleared at once, and as she looked at him across the flowers, between the rosy candle-shades, he saw her lips waver back into a smile.

"How pretty everything is!" she sighed luxuriously.

He turned to the butler. "The champagne at once, please. Mrs. Waythorn is tired."

In a moment or two their eyes met above the sparkling glasses. Her own were quite clear and untroubled: he saw that she had obeyed his injunction and forgotten.

II

Waythorn, the next morning, went downtown earlier than usual. Haskett was not likely to come till the afternoon, but the instinct of flight drove him forth. He meant to stay away all day—he had thoughts of dining at his club. As his door closed behind him he reflected that before he opened it again it would have admitted another man who had as much right to enter it as himself, and the thought filled him with a physical repugnance.

He caught the "elevated"[3] at the employees' hour, and found himself crushed between two layers of pendulous humanity. At Eighth Street the man facing him wriggled out, and another took his place. Waythorn glanced up and saw that it was Gus Varick. The men were so close together that it was impossible to ignore the smile of recognition on Varick's handsome overblown face. And after all—why not? They had always been on good terms, and Varick had been divorced before Waythorn's attentions to his wife began. The two exchanged a word on the perennial grievance of the congested trains, and when a seat at their side was miraculously left empty the instinct of self-preservation made Waythorn slip into it after Varick.

The latter drew the stout man's breath of relief. "Lord—I was beginning to feel like a pressed flower." He leaned back, looking unconcernedly at Waythorn. "Sorry to hear that Sellers is knocked out again."

"Sellers?" echoed Waythorn, starting at his partner's name.

Varick looked surprised. "You didn't know he was laid up with the gout?"

"No. I've been away—I only got back last night." Waythorn felt himself reddening in anticipation of the other's smile.

"Ah—yes; to be sure. And Sellers' attack came on two days ago. I'm afraid he's pretty bad. Very awkward for me, as it happens, because he was just putting through a rather important thing for me."

"Ah?" Waythorn wondered vaguely since when Varick had been dealing in "important things." Hitherto he had dabbled only in the shallow pools of speculation, with which Waythorn's office did not usually concern itself.

It occurred to him that Varick might be talking at random, to relieve the strain of their propinquity. That strain was becoming momentarily more apparent to Waythorn, and when, at Cortlandt Street, he caught sight of an acquaintance and had a sudden vision of the picture he and Varick must present to an initiated eye, he jumped up with a muttered excuse.

"I hope you'll find Sellers better," said Varick civilly, and he stammered back: "If I can be of any use to you—" and let the departing crowd sweep him to the platform.

At his office he heard that Sellers was in fact ill with the gout, and would probably not be able to leave the house for some weeks.

"I'm sorry it should have happened so, Mr. Waythorn," the senior clerk said with affable significance. "Mr. Sellers was very much upset at the idea of giving you such a lot of extra work just now."

"Oh, that's no matter," said Waythorn hastily. He secretly welcomed the pressure of additional business, and was glad to think that, when the day's work was over, he would have to call at his partner's on the way home.

---

[3] Elevated railway.

He was late for luncheon, and turned in at the nearest restaurant instead of going to his club. The place was full, and the waiter hurried him to the back of the room to capture the only vacant table. In the cloud of cigar-smoke Waythorn did not at once distinguish his neighbors: but presently, looking about him, he saw Varick seated a few feet off. This time, luckily, they were too far apart for conversation, and Varick, who faced another way, had probably not even seen him; but there was an irony in their renewed nearness.

Varick was said to be fond of good living, and as Waythorn sat dispatching his hurried luncheon he looked across half enviously at the other's leisurely degustation of his meal. When Waythorn first saw him he had been helping himself with critical deliberation to a bit of Camembert at the ideal point of liquefaction, and now, the cheese removed, he was just pouring his *café double* from its little two-storied earthen pot. He poured slowly, his ruddy profile bent over the task, and one beringed white hand steadying the lid of the coffee-pot; then he stretched his other hand to the decanter of cognac at his elbow, filled a liqueur glass, took a tentative sip, and poured the brandy into his coffee-cup.

Waythorn watched him in a kind of fascination. What was he thinking of— only of the flavor of the coffee and the liqueur? Had the morning's meeting left no more trace in his thoughts than on his face? Had his wife so completely passed out of his life that even this odd encounter with her present husband within a week after her remarriage, was no more than an incident in his day? And as Waythorn mused, another idea struck him: had Haskett ever met Varick as Varick and he had just met? The recollection of Haskett perturbed him, and he rose and left the restaurant, taking a circuitous way out to escape the placid irony of Varick's nod.

It was after seven when Waythorn reached home. He thought the footman who opened the door looked at him oddly.

"How is Miss Lily?" he asked in haste.

"Doing very well, sir. A gentleman—"

"Tell Barlow to put off dinner for half an hour," Waythorn cut him off, hurrying upstairs.

He went straight to his room and dressed without seeing his wife. When he reached the drawing-room she was there, fresh and radiant. Lily's day had been good; the doctor was not coming back that evening.

At dinner Waythorn told her of Sellers' illness and of the resulting complications. She listened sympathetically, adjuring him not to let himself be overworked, and asking vague feminine questions about the routine of the office. Then she gave him the chronicle of Lily's day; quoted the nurse and doctor, and told him who had called to inquire. He had never seen her more serene and unruffled. It struck him, with a curious pang, that she was very happy in being with him, so happy that she found a childish pleasure in rehearsing the trivial incidents of her day.

After dinner they went to the library, and the servant put the coffee and liqueurs on a low table before her and left the room. She looked singularly soft and girlish in her rosy pale dress, against the dark leather of one of his bachelor armchairs. A day earlier the contrast would have charmed him.

He turned away now, choosing a cigar with affected deliberation.

"Did Haskett come?" he asked, with his back to her.

"Oh, yes—he came."

"You didn't see him, of course?"

She hesitated a moment. "I let the nurse see him."

That was all. There was nothing more to ask. He swung round toward her, applying a match to his cigar. Well, the thing was over for a week, at any rate. He would try not to think of it. She looked up at him, a trifle rosier than usual, with a smile in her eyes.

"Ready for your coffee, dear?"

He leaned against the mantelpiece, watching her as she lifted the coffee-pot. The lamplight struck a gleam from her bracelets and tipped her soft hair with brightness. How light and slender she was, and how each gesture flowed into the next! She seemed a creature all compact of harmonies. As the thought of Haskett receded, Waythorn felt himself yielding again to the joy of possessorship. They were his, those white hands with their flitting motions, his the light haze of hair, the lips and eyes. . . .

She set down the coffee-pot, and reaching for the decanter of cognac, measured off a liqueur-glass and poured it into his cup.

Waythorn uttered a sudden exclamation.

"What is the matter?" she said, startled.

"Nothing; only—I don't take cognac in my coffee."

"Oh, how stupid of me," she cried.

Their eyes met, and she blushed a sudden agonized red.

III

Ten days later, Mr. Sellers, still house-bound, asked Waythorn to call on his way down town.

The senior partner, with his swaddled foot propped up by the fire, greeted his associate with an air of embarrassment.

"I'm sorry, my dear fellow; I've got to ask you to do an awkward thing for me."

Waythorn waited, and the other went on, after a pause apparently given to the arrangement of his phrases: "The fact is, when I was knocked out I had just gone into a rather complicated piece of business for—Gus Varick."

"Well?" said Waythorn, with an attempt to put him at his ease.

"Well—it's this way: Varick came to me the day before my attack. He had evidently had an inside tip from somebody, and had made about a hundred thousand. He came to me for advice, and I suggested his going in with Vanderlyn."

"Oh, the deuce!" Waythorn exclaimed. He saw in a flash what had happened. The investment was an alluring one, but required negotiation. He listened quietly while Sellers put the case before him, and, the statement ended, he said: "You think I ought to see Varick?"

"I'm afraid I can't as yet. The doctor is obdurate. And this thing can't wait. I hate to ask you, but no one else in the office knows the ins and outs of it."

Waythorn stood silent. He did not care a farthing for the success of Varick's venture, but the honor of the office was to be considered, and he could hardly refuse to oblige his partner.

"Very well," he said, "I'll do it."

That afternoon, apprised by telephone, Varick called at the office. Waythorn waiting in his private room, wondered what the others thought of it. The newspapers, at the time of Mrs. Waythorn's marriage, had acquainted their readers with every detail of her previous matrimonial ventures, and Waythorn could fancy the clerks smiling behind Varick's back as he was ushered in.

Varick bore himself admirably. He was easy without being undignified, and Waythorn was conscious of cutting a much less impressive figure. Varick had no experience of business, and the talk prolonged itself for nearly an hour while Waythorn set forth with scrupulous precision the details of the proposed transaction.

"I'm awfully obliged to you," Varick said as he rose. "The fact is I'm not used to having much money to look after, and I don't want to make an ass of myself—" He smiled, and Waythorn could not help noticing that there was something pleasant about his smile. "It feels uncommonly queer to have enough cash to pay one's bills. I'd have sold my soul for it a few years ago!"

Waythorn winced at the allusion. He had heard it rumored that a lack of funds had been one of the determining causes of the Varick separation, but it did not occur to him that Varick's words were intentional. It seemed more likely that the desire to keep clear of embarrassing topics had fatally drawn him into one. Waythorn did not wish to be outdone in civility.

"We'll do the best we can for you," he said. "I think this is a good thing you're in."

"Oh, I'm sure it's immense. It's awfully good of you—" Varick broke off, embarrassed. "I suppose the thing's settled now—but if—"

"If anything happens before Sellers is about, I'll see you again," said Waythorn quietly. He was glad, in the end, to appear the more self-possessed of the two.

* * *

The course of Lily's illness ran smooth, and as the days passed Waythorn grew used to the idea of Haskett's weekly visit. The first time the day came round, he stayed out late, and questioned his wife as to the visit on his return. She replied at once that Haskett had merely seen the nurse downstairs, as the doctor did not wish any one in the child's sick-room till after the crisis.

The following week Waythorn was again conscious of the recurrence of the day, but had forgotten it by the time he came home to dinner. The crisis of the disease came a few days later, with a rapid decline of fever, and the little girl was pronounced out of danger. In the rejoicing which ensued the thought of Haskett passed out of Waythorn's mind, and one afternoon, letting himself into the house with a latch-key, he went straight to his library without noticing a shabby hat and umbrella in the hall.

In the library he found a small effaced-looking man with a thinnish gray beard sitting on the edge of a chair. The stranger might have been a piano-tuner, or one of those mysteriously efficient persons who are summoned in emergencies to adjust some detail of the domestic machinery. He blinked at Waythorn through a pair of gold-rimmed spectacles and said mildly: "Mr. Waythorn, I presume? I am Lily's father."

Waythorn flushed. "Oh—" he stammered uncomfortably. He broke off, disliking to appear rude. Inwardly he was trying to adjust the actual Haskett to the image of him projected by his wife's reminiscences. Waythorn had been allowed to infer that Alice's first husband was a brute.

"I am sorry to intrude," said Haskett, with his over-the-counter politeness.

"Don't mention it," returned Waythorn, collecting himself. "I suppose the nurse has been told?"

"I presume so. I can wait," said Haskett. He had a resigned way of speaking, as though life had worn down his natural powers of resistance.

Waythorn stood on the threshold, nervously pulling off his gloves.

"I'm sorry you've been detained. I will send for the nurse," he said; and as he opened the door he added with an effort: "I'm glad we can give you a good report of Lily." He winced as the *we* slipped out, but Haskett seemed not to notice it.

"Thank you, Mr. Waythorn. It's been an anxious time for me."

"Ah, well, that's past. Soon she'll be able to go to you." Waythorn nodded and passed out.

In his own room he flung himself down with a groan. He hated the womanish sensibility which made him suffer so acutely from the grotesque chances of life. He had known when he married that his wife's former husbands were both living, and that amid the multiplied contacts of modern existence there were a thousand chances to one that he would run against one or the other, yet he found himself as much disturbed by his brief encounter with Haskett as though the law had not obligingly removed all difficulties in the way of their meeting.

Waythorn sprang up and began to pace the room nervously. He had not suffered half as much from his two meetings with Varick. It was Haskett's presence in his own house that made the situation so intolerable. He stood still, hearing steps in the passage.

"This way, please," he heard the nurse say. Haskett was being taken upstairs, then: not a corner of the house but was open to him. Waythorn dropped into another chair, staring vaguely ahead of him. On his dressing table stood a photograph of Alice, taken when he had first known her. She was Alice Varick then—how fine and exquisite he had thought her! Those were Varick's pearls about her neck. At Waythorn's instance they had been returned before her marriage. Had Haskett ever given her any trinkets—and what had become of them, Waythorn wondered? He realized suddenly that he knew very little of Haskett's past or present situation; but from the man's appearance and manner of speech he could reconstruct with curious precision the surroundings of Alice's first marriage. And it startled him to think that she had, in the background of her life, a phase of existence so different from anything with which he had connected her. Varick, whatever his faults, was a gentleman, in the conventional, traditional sense of the term: the sense which at that moment seemed, oddly enough, to have most meaning to Waythorn. He and Varick had the same social habits, spoke the same language, understood the same allusions. But this other man . . . it was grotesquely uppermost in Waythorn's mind that Haskett had worn a made-up tie attached with an elastic. Why should that ridiculous detail symbolize the whole man? Waythorn was exasperated by his own paltriness, but the fact of the tie expanded, forced itself on him, became as it were the key to Alice's past. He could see her, as Mrs. Haskett, sitting in a "front parlor" furnished in plush, with a pianola, and a copy of "*Ben Hur*"[4] on the center-table. He could see her going to the theater with Haskett—or perhaps even to a "Church Sociable"—she in a "picture hat" and Haskett in a black frock coat, a little creased, with the made-up tie on an elastic. On the way home they would stop and look at the illuminated shop windows, lingering over the photographs of New York actresses. On Sunday afternoons Haskett would take her for a walk, pushing Lily ahead of them in a white enamelled perambulator, and Waythorn had a vision of the people they would stop and talk to. He could fancy how pretty Alice must have looked, in a dress adroitly constructed from the hints of a New York fashion-paper, and how she must have looked down on the other women, chafing at her life, and secretly feeling that she belonged in a bigger place.

For the moment his foremost thought was one of wonder at the way in which she had shed the phase of existence which her marriage with Haskett implied. It was as if her whole aspect, every gesture, every inflection, every allusion, were a studied negation of that period of her life. If she had denied being married to Haskett she could hardly have stood more convicted of duplicity than in this obliteration of the self which had been his wife.

Waythorn started up, checking himself in the analysis of her motives. What right had he to create a fantastic effigy of her and then pass judgment on it? She had spoken vaguely of her first marriage as unhappy, had hinted, with becoming reticence, that Haskett had wrought havoc among her young illusions. . . . It was a pity for Waythorn's peace of mind that Haskett's very inoffensiveness shed a new light on the nature of those illusions. A man would rather think that his wife has been brutalized by her first husband than that the process has been reversed.

---

[4] *Ben Hur, A Tale of the Christ* (1880), an immensely popular, rather melodramatic romance by Lew Wallace (1827–1905).

IV

"Mr. Waythorn, I don't like that French governess of Lily's."

Haskett, subdued and apologetic, stood before Waythorn in the library, revolving his shabby hat in his hand.

Waythorn, surprised in his armchair over the evening paper, stared back perplexedly at his visitor.

"You'll excuse me asking to see you," Haskett continued. "But this is my last visit, and I thought if I could have a word with you it would be a better way than writing to Mrs. Waythorn's lawyer."

Waythorn rose uneasily. He did not like the French governess either; but that was irrelevant.

"I am not so sure of that," he returned stiffly; "but since you wish it I will give your message to—my wife." He always hesitated over the possessive pronoun in addressing Haskett.

The latter sighed. "I don't know as that will help much. She didn't like it when I spoke to her."

Waythorn turned red. "When did you see her?" he asked.

"Not since the first day I came to see Lily—right after she was taken sick. I remarked to her then that I didn't like the governess."

Waythorn made no answer. He remembered distinctly that, after the first visit, he had asked his wife if she had seen Haskett. She had lied to him then, but she had respected his wishes since; and the incident cast a curious light on her character. He was sure she would not have seen Haskett that first day if she had divined that Waythorn would object, and the fact that she did not divine it was almost as disagreeable to the latter as the discovery that she had lied to him.

"I don't like the woman," Haskett was repeating with mild persistency. "She ain't straight, Mr. Waythorn—she'll teach the child to be underhand. I've noticed a change in Lily—she's too anxious to please—and she don't always tell the truth. She used to be the straightest child, Mr. Waythorn—" He broke off, his voice a little thick. "Not but what I want her to have a stylish education," he ended.

Waythorn was touched. "I'm sorry, Mr. Haskett; but frankly, I don't quite see what I can do."

Haskett hesitated. Then he laid his hat on the table, and advanced to the hearth-rug, on which Waythorn was standing. There was nothing aggressive in his manner, but he had the solemnity of a timid man resolved on a decisive measure.

"There's just one thing you can do, Mr. Waythorn," he said. "You can remind Mrs. Waythorn that, by the decree of the courts, I am entitled to have a voice in Lily's bringing-up." He paused, and went on more deprecatingly: "I'm not the kind to talk about enforcing my rights, Mr. Waythorn. I don't know as I think a man is entitled to rights he hasn't known how to hold on to; but this business of the child is different. I've never let go there—and I never mean to."

* * *

The scene left Waythorn deeply shaken. Shamefacedly, in indirect ways, he had been finding out about Haskett; and all that he learned was favorable. The little man, in order to be near his daughter, had sold out his share in a profitable business in Utica, and accepted a modest clerkship in a New York manufacturing house. He boarded in a shabby street and had few acquaintances. His passion for Lily filled his life. Waythorn felt that this exploration of Haskett was like groping about with a dark-lantern in his wife's past; but he saw now that there were recesses his lantern had not explored. He had never enquired into the exact circumstances of his wife's first matrimonial rupture. On the surface all had been fair. It was she who had obtained the divorce, and the court had given her the child. But Waythorn knew how many ambiguities such a verdict might cover. The mere fact that Haskett retained a right over his daughter implied an unsuspected compromise. Waythorn was an idealist. He always refused to recognize unpleasant contingencies till he found himself confronted with them, and then he saw them followed by a spectral train of consequences. His next days were thus haunted, and he determined to try to lay the ghosts by conjuring them up in his wife's presence.

When he repeated Haskett's request a flame of anger passed over her face; but she subdued it instantly and spoke with a slight quiver of outraged motherhood.

"It is very ungentlemanly of him," she said.

The word grated on Waythorn. "That is neither here nor there. It's a bare question of rights."

She murmured: "It's not as if he could ever be a help to Lily—"

Waythorn flushed. This was even less to his taste. "The question is," he repeated, "what authority has he over her?"

She looked downward, twisting herself a little in her seat. "I am willing to see him—I thought you objected," she faltered.

In a flash he understood that she knew the extent of Haskett's claims. Perhaps it was not the first time she had resisted them.

"My objecting has nothing to do with it," he said coldly; "if Haskett has a right to be consulted you must consult him."

She burst into tears, and he saw that she expected him to regard her as a victim.

Haskett did not abuse his rights. Waythorn had felt miserably sure that he would not. But the governess was dismissed, and from time to time the little man demanded an interview with Alice. After the first outburst she accepted the situation with her usual adaptability. Haskett had once reminded Waythorn of the piano-tuner, and Mrs. Waythorn, after a month or two, appeared to class him with that domestic familiar. Waythorn could not but respect the father's tenacity. At first he had tried to cultivate the suspicion that Haskett might be "up to" something, that he had an object in securing a foothold in the house. But in his heart Waythorn was sure of Haskett's singlemindedness; he even guessed in the latter a mild contempt for such advantages as his relation with the Waythorns might offer. Haskett's sincerity of purpose made him invulnerable, and his successor had to accept him as a lien on the property.

* * *

Mr. Sellers was sent to Europe to recover from his gout, and Varick's affairs hung on Waythorn's hands. The negotiations were prolonged and complicated; they necessitated frequent conferences between the two men, and the interests of the firm forbade Waythorn's suggesting that his client should transfer his business to another office.

Varick appeared well in the transaction. In moments of relaxation his coarse streak appeared, and Waythorn dreaded his geniality; but in the office he was concise and clear-headed, with a flattering deference to Waythorn's judgment. Their business relations being so affably established, it would have been absurd for the two men to ignore each other in society. The first time they met in a drawing-room, Varick took up their intercourse in the same easy key, and his hostess's grateful glance obliged Waythorn to respond to it. After that they ran across each other frequently, and one evening at a ball Waythorn, wandering through the remoter rooms, came upon Varick seated beside his wife. She colored a little, and faltered in what she was saying; but Varick nodded to Waythorn without rising, and the latter strolled on.

In the carriage, on the way home, he broke out nervously: "I didn't know you spoke to Varick."

Her voice trembled a little. "It's the first time—he happened to be standing near me; I didn't know what to do. It's so awkward, meeting everywhere—and he said you had been very kind about some business."

"That's different," said Waythorn.

She paused a moment. "I'll do just as you wish," she returned pliantly. "I thought it would be less awkward to speak to him when we meet."

Her pliancy was beginning to sicken him. Had she really no will of her own—no theory about her relation to these men? She had accepted Haskett—did she mean to accept Varick? It was "less awkward," as she had said, and her instinct was to evade difficulties or to circumvent them. With sudden vividness Waythorn saw how the instinct had developed. She was "as easy as an old shoe"—a shoe that too many feet had worn. Her elasticity was the result of tension in too many different directions. Alice Haskett—Alice Varick—Alice Waythorn—she had been each in turn, and had left hanging to each name a little of her privacy, a little of her personality, a little of the inmost self where the unknown god abides.

"Yes—it's better to speak to Varick," said Waythorn wearily.

V

The winter wore on, and society took advantage of the Waythorns' acceptance of Varick. Harassed hostesses were grateful to them for bridging over a social difficulty, and Mrs. Waythorn was held up as a miracle of good taste. Some experimental spirits could not resist the diversion of throwing Varick and his former wife together, and there were those who thought he found a zest in the propinquity. But Mrs. Waythorn's conduct remained irreproachable. She neither avoided Varick nor sought him out. Even Waythorn could not but admit that she had discovered the solution of the newest social problem.

He had married her without giving much thought to that problem. He had fancied that a woman can shed her past like a man. But now he saw that Alice was bound to hers both by the circumstances which forced her into continued relation with it, and by the traces it had left on her nature. With grim irony Waythorn compared himself to a member of a syndicate. He held so many shares in his wife's personality and his predecessors were his partners in the business. If there had been any element of passion in the transaction he would have felt less deteriorated by it. The fact that Alice took her change of husbands like a change of weather reduced the situation to mediocrity. He could have forgiven her for blunders, for excesses; for resisting Haskett, for yielding to Varick; for anything but her acquiescence and her tact. She reminded him of a juggler tossing knives; but the knives were blunt and she knew they would never cut her.

And then, gradually, habit formed a protecting surface for his sensibilities. If he paid for each day's comfort with the small change of his illusions, he grew daily to value the comfort more and set less store upon the coin. He had drifted into a dulling propinquity with Haskett and Varick and he took refuge in the cheap revenge of satirizing the situation. He even began to reckon up the advantages which accrued from it, to ask himself if it were not better to own a third of a wife who knew how to make a man happy than a whole one who had lacked opportunity to acquire the art. For it *was* an art, and made up, like all others, of concessions, eliminations and embellishments; of lights judiciously thrown and shadows skillfully softened. His wife knew exactly how to manage the lights, and he knew exactly to what training she owed her skill. He even tried to trace the source of his obligations, to discriminate between the influences which had combined to produce his domestic happiness: he perceived that Haskett's commonness had made Alice worship good breeding, while Varick's liberal construction of the marriage bond had taught her to value the conjugal virtues; so that he was directly indebted to his predecessors for the devotion which made his life easy if not inspiring.

From this phrase he passed into that of complete acceptance. He ceased to satirize himself because time dulled the irony of the situation and the joke lost its humor with its sting. Even the sight of Haskett's hat on the hall table had ceased to touch the springs of epigram. The hat was often seen there now, for it had been decided that it was better for Lily's father to visit her than for the little girl to go to his boarding-house. Waythorn, having acquiesced in this arrangement, had been surprised to find how little difference it made. Haskett was never obtrusive, and the few visitors who met him on the stairs were unaware of his identity. Waythorn did not know how often he saw Alice, but with himself Haskett was seldom in contact.

One afternoon, however, he learned on entering that Lily's father was waiting to see him. In the library he found Haskett occupying a chair in his usual provisional way. Waythorn always felt grateful to him for not leaning back.

"I hope you'll excuse me, Mr. Waythorn," he said rising. "I wanted to see Mrs. Waythorn about Lily, and your man asked me to wait here till she came in."

"Of course," said Waythorn, remembering that a sudden leak had that morning given over the drawing-room to the plumbers.

He opened his cigar-case and held it out to his visitor, and Haskett's acceptance seemed to mark a fresh stage in their intercourse. The spring evening was chilly, and Waythorn invited his guest to draw up his chair to the fire. He meant to find an excuse to leave Haskett in a moment; but he was tired and cold, and after all the little man no longer jarred on him.

The two were enclosed in the intimacy of their blended cigar smoke when the door opened and Varick walked into the room. Waythorn rose abruptly. It was the first time that Varick had come to the house, and the surprise of seeing him, combined with the singular inopportuneness of his arrival, gave a new edge to Waythorn's blunted sensibilities. He stared at his visitor without speaking.

Varick seemed too preoccupied to notice his host's embarrassment.

"My dear fellow," he exclaimed in his most expansive tone, "I must apologize for tumbling in on you in this way, but I was too late to catch you downtown, and so I thought—"

He stopped short, catching sight of Haskett, and his sanguine color deepened to a flush which spread vividly under his scant blond hair. But in a moment he recovered himself and nodded slightly. Haskett returned the bow in silence, and Waythorn was still groping for speech when the footman came in carrying a tea-table.

The intrusion offered a welcome vent to Waythorn's nerves. "What the deuce are you bringing this here for?" he said sharply.

"I beg your pardon, sir, but the plumbers are still in the drawing-room, and Mrs. Waythorn said she would have tea in the library." The footman's perfectly respectful tone implied a reflection on Waythorn's reasonableness.

"Oh, very well," said the latter resignedly, and the footman proceeded to open the folding tea-table and set out its complicated appointments. While this interminable process continued the three men stood motionless, watching it with a fascinated stare, till Waythorn, to break the silence, said to Varick: "Won't you have a cigar?"

He held out the case he had just tendered to Haskett, and Varick helped himself with a smile. Waythorn looked about for a match, and finding none, proffered a light from his own cigar. Haskett, in the background, held his ground mildly, examining his cigar-tip now and then, and stepping forward at the right moment to knock its ashes into the fire.

The footman at last withdrew, and Varick immediately began: "If I could just say half a word to you about this business—"

"Certainly," stammered Waythorn; "in the dining room—"

But as he placed his hand on the door it opened from without, and his wife appeared on the threshold.

She came in fresh and smiling, in her street dress and hat, shedding a fragrance from the boa which she loosened in advancing.

"Shall we have tea in here, dear?" she began; and then she caught sight of Varick. Her smile deepened, veiling a slight tremor of surprise.

"Why, how do you do?" she said with a distinct note of pleasure.

As she shook hands with Varick she saw Haskett standing behind him. Her smile faded for a moment, but she recalled it quickly, with a scarcely perceptible side-glance at Waythorn.

"How do you do, Mr. Haskett?" she said, and shook hands with him a shade less cordially.

The three men stood awkwardly before her, till Varick, always the most self-possessed, dashed into an explanatory phrase.

"We—I had to see Waythorn a moment on business," he stammered, brick-red from chin to nape.

Haskett stepped forward with his air of mild obstinacy. "I am sorry to intrude; but you appointed five o'clock—" he directed his resigned glance to the timepiece on the mantel.

She swept aside their embarrassment with a charming gesture of hospitality.

"I'm so sorry—I'm always late; but the afternoon was so lovely." She stood drawing off her gloves, propitiatory and graceful, diffusing about her a sense of ease and familiarity in which the situation lost its grotesqueness. "But before talking business," she added brightly, "I'm sure every one wants a cup of tea."

She dropped into her low chair by the tea-table, and the two visitors, as if drawn by her smile, advanced to receive the cups she held out.

She glanced about for Waythorn, and he took the third cup with a laugh.

HER SON

I did not recognize Mrs. Stephen Glenn when I first saw her on the deck of the 'Scythian.'

The voyage was more than half over, and we were counting on Cherbourg within forty-eight hours, when she appeared on deck and sat down beside me. She was as handsome as ever, and not a day older-looking then when we had last met—toward the end of the war, in 1917 it must have been, not long before her only son, the aviator, was killed. Yet now, five years later, I was looking at her as if she were a stranger. Why? Not, certainly, because of her white hair. She had had the American woman's frequent luck of acquiring it while the face beneath was still fresh, and a dozen years earlier, when we used to meet at dinners, at the

Opera, that silver diadem already crowned her. Now, looking more closely, I saw that the face beneath was still untouched; what then had so altered her? Perhaps it was the faint line of anxiety between her dark strongly-drawn eyebrows; or the setting of the eyes themselves, those somber starlit eyes which seemed to have sunk deeper into their lids, and showed like glimpses of night through the arch of a cavern. But what a gloomy image to apply to eyes as tender as Catherine Glenn's! Yet it was immediately suggested by the look of the lady in deep mourning who had settled herself beside me, and now turned to say: 'So you don't know me, Mr. Norcutt — Catherine Glenn?'

The fact was flagrant. I acknowledged it, and added. 'But why didn't I? I can't imagine. Do you mind my saying that I believe it's because you're even more beautiful now than when I last saw you?'

She replied with perfect simplicity: 'No, I don't mind — because I ought to be; that is, if there's any meaning in anything.'

'Any meaning — ?'

She seemed to hesitate; she had never been a woman who found words easily. 'Any meaning in life. You see, since we've met I've lost everything: my son, my husband.' She bent her head slightly, as though the words she pronounced were holy. Then she added, with the air of striving for more scrupulous accuracy: 'Or, at least, almost everything.'

The 'almost' puzzled me. Mrs. Glenn, as far as I knew, had had no child but the son she had lost in the war; and the old uncle who had brought her up had died years earlier. I wondered if, in thus qualifying her loneliness, she alluded to the consolations of religion.

I murmured that I knew of her double mourning; and she surprised me still further by saying: 'Yes; I saw you at my husband's funeral. I've always wanted to thank you for being there.'

'But of course I was there.'

She continued: 'I noticed all of Stephen's friends who came. I was very grateful to them, and especially to the young ones.' (This was meant for me.) 'You see,' she added, 'a funeral is — is a very great comfort.'

Again I looked surprised.

'My son — my son Philip —' (why should she think it necessary to mention his name, since he was her only child?) '— my son Philip's funeral took place just where his airplane fell. A little village in the Somme; his father and I went there immediately after the Armistice. One of our army chaplains read the service. The people from the village were there — they were so kind to us. But there was no one else — no personal friends; at that time only the nearest relations could get passes. Our boy would have wished it. . . . he could have wanted to stay where he fell. But it's not the same as feeling one's friends about one, as I did at my husband's funeral.'

While she spoke she kept her eyes intently, almost embarrassingly, on mine. It had never occurred to me that Mrs. Stephen Glenn was the kind of woman who would attach any particular importance to the list of names at her husband's funeral. She had always seemed aloof and abstracted, shut off from the world behind the high walls of a happy domesticity. But on adding this new indication of character to the fragments of information I had gathered concerning her first appearance in New York, and to the vague impression she used to produce on me when we met, I began to see that lists of names were probably just what she would care about. And then I asked myself what I really knew of her. Very little, I perceived; but no doubt just as much as she wished me to. For, as I sat there, listening to her voice, and catching unguarded glimpses of her crepe-shadowed profile, I began to suspect that what had seemed in her a rather dull simplicity might be the vigilance of a secretive person; or perhaps of a person who had a secret. There is a world of difference between them, for the secretive person is seldom interesting and seldom has a secret; but I felt inclined—though nothing I knew of her justified it—to put her in the other class.

I began to think over the years of our intermittent acquaintance—it had never been more, for I had known the Glenns well. She had appeared in New York when I was a very young man, in the nineties, as a beautiful girl from Kentucky or Alabama—a niece of old Colonel Reamer's. Left an orphan, and penniless, when she was still almost a child, she had been passed about from one reluctant relation to another, and had finally (the legend ran) gone on the stage, and followed a strolling company across the continent. The manager had deserted his troupe in some far-off state, and Colonel Reamer, fatuous, impecunious, and no doubt perplexed as to how to deal with the situation, had yet faced it manfully, and shaking off his bachelor selfishness had taken the girl into his house. Such a past, though it looks dove-colored now, seemed hectic in the nineties, and gave a touch of romance and mystery to the beautiful Catherine Reamer, who appeared so aloof and distinguished, yet had been snatched out of such promiscuities and perils.

Colonel Reamer was a ridiculous old man: everything about him was ridiculous—his 'toupee' (probably the last in existence), his vague military title, his anecdotes about southern chivalry, and duels between other gentlemen with military titles and civilian pursuits, and all the obsolete swagger of a character dropped out of Martin Chuzzlewit. He was the notorious bore of New York; tolerated only because he was old Mrs. So-and-so's second cousin, because he was poor, because he was kindly—and because, out of his poverty, he had managed, with a smile and a gay gesture, to shelter and clothe his starving niece. Old Reamer, I recalled, had always had a passion for lists of names; for seeing his own appear in the society column of the morning papers, for giving you those of the people he had dined with, or been unable to dine with because already bespoken by others even more important. The young people called him 'Old Previous Engagement,' because he was so anxious to have you know that, if you hadn't met him at some particular party, it was because he had been previously engaged at another.

Perhaps, I thought, it was from her uncle that Mrs. Glenn had learned to attach such importance to names, to lists of names, to the presence of certain people on certain occasions, to a social suitability which could give a consecration even to death. The profile at my side, so marble-pure, so marble-sad, did not suggest such preoccupation, neither did the deep entreating gaze she bent on me; yet many details fitted into the theory.

Her very marriage to Stephen Glenn seemed to confirm it. I thought back, and began to reconstruct Stephen Glenn. He was considerably older than myself, and had been a familiar figure in my earliest New York; a man who was a permanent ornament to society, who looked precisely as he ought, spoke, behaved, received his friends, filled his space on the social stage, exactly as his world expected him to. While he was still a young man, old ladies in perplexity over some social problem (there were many in those draconian days) would consult Stephen Glenn as if he had been one of the Ancients of the community. Yet there was nothing precociously old or dry about him. He was one of the handsomest men of his day; a good shot, a leader of cotillions. He practiced at the bar, and became a member of a reputed legal firm chiefly occupied with the management of old ponderous New York estates. In process of time the old ladies who had consulted him about social questions began to ask his advice about investments; and on this point he was considered equally reliable. Only one cloud shadowed his early life. He had married a distant cousin, an effaced sort of woman who bore him no children, and presently (on that account, it was said) fell into suicidal melancholia; so that for a good many years Stephen Glenn's handsome and once hospitable house must have been a grim place to go home to. But at last she died, and after a decent interval the widower married Miss Reamer. No one was greatly surprised. It had been observed that the handsome Stephen Glenn and the beautiful Catherine Reamer were drawn to each other; and though the old ladies thought he might have done better, some of the more caustic remarked that he could hardly have done differently, after having made Colonel Reamer's niece so 'conspicuous.' The attentions of a married man, especially of one unhappily married, and virtually separated from his wife, were regarded in those days as likely to endanger a young lady's future. Catherine Reamer, however, rose above these hints as she had above the perils of her theatrical venture. One had only to look at her to see that, in that smooth marble surface there was no crack in which detraction could take root.

Stephen Glenn's house was opened again, and the couple began to entertain in a quiet way. It was thought natural that Glenn should want to put a little life into the house which had so long been a sort of tomb; but though the Glenn dinners were as good as the most carefully chosen food and wine could make them, neither of the pair had the gifts which make hospitality a success, and by the time I knew them, the younger set had come to regard dining with them as somewhat of a bore. Stephen Glenn was still handsome, his wife still beautiful, perhaps more beautiful than ever; but the apathy of prosperity seemed to have settled down on them, and they wore their beauty and affability like expensive clothes put on for the occasion. There was something static, unchanging in their appearance, as there was in their affability, their conversation, the menus of their carefully planned dinners, the studied arrangement of the drawing room furniture. They had a little boy, born after a year of marriage, and they were devoted parents, given to lengthy anecdotes about their son's doings and sayings; but one could not imagine their tumbling about with him on the nursery floor. Someone said they must go to bed with their crowns on, like the kings and queens on packs of cards; and gradually, from being thought distinguished and impressive, they came to be regarded as wooden, pompous and slightly absurd. But the old ladies still spoke of Stephen Glenn as a man who had done his family credit, and his wife began to acquire his figurehead attributes, and to be consulted, as he was, about the minuter social problems. And all the while—I thought as I looked back—there seemed to have been no one in their lives with whom they were really intimate. . . .

Then, of a sudden, they again became interesting. It was when their only son was killed, attacked alone in mid-sky by a German air squadron. Young Phil Glenn was the first American aviator to fall; and when the news came people saw that the Mr.-and-Mrs. Glenn they had known was a mere façade, and that behind it were a passionate father and mother, crushed, rebellious, agonizing, but determined to face their loss dauntlessly, though they should die of it.

Stephen Glenn did die of it, barely two years later. The doctors ascribed his death to a specific disease; but everybody who knew him knew better. 'It was the loss of the boy,' they said; and added: 'It's terrible to have only one child.'

Since her husband's funeral I had not seen Mrs. Glenn; I had completely ceased to think of her. And now, on my way to take up a post at the American Consulate in Paris, I found myself sitting beside her and remembering these things. 'Poor creatures—it's as if two marble busts had been knocked off their pedestals and smashed,' I thought, recalling the faces of husband and wife after the boy's death; 'and she's been smashed twice, poor woman. . . . Yet she says it has made her more beautiful. . . . Again I lost myself in conjecture.

II

I was told that a lady in deep mourning wanted to see me on urgent business, and I looked out of my private den at the Paris Consulate into the room hung with maps and Presidents, where visitors were sifted out before being passed on to the Vice-consul or the Chief.

The lady was Mrs. Stephen Glenn.

Six or seven months had passed since our meeting on the 'Scythian,' and I had again forgotten her very existence. She was not a person who stuck in one's mind; and once more I wondered why, for in her statuesque weeds she looked nobler, more striking than ever. She glanced at the people awaiting their turn under the maps and the Presidents, and asked in a low tone if she could see me privately.

I was free at the moment, and I led her into my office and banished the typist.

Mrs. Glenn seemed disturbed by the signs of activity about me. 'I'm afraid we shall be interrupted. I wanted to speak to you alone,' she said.

I assured her we were not likely to be disturbed if she could put what she had to say in a few words—

'Ah, but that's just what I can't do. What I have to say can't be put in a few words.' She fixed her splendid nocturnal eyes on me, and I read in them a distress so deep that I dared not suggest postponement.

I said I would do all I could to prevent our being interrupted, and in reply she just sat silent, and looked at me, as if after all she had nothing further to communicate. The telephone clicked, and I rang for my secretary to take the message; then one of the clerks came in with papers for my signature. I said: 'I'd better sign and get it over,' and she sat motionless, her head slightly bent, as if secretly relieved by the delay. The clerk went off, I shut the door again, and when we were alone she lifted her head and spoke, 'Mr. Norcutt,' she asked, 'have you ever had a child?'

I replied with a smile that I was not married. She murmured: 'I'm sorry— excuse me,' and looked down again at her black-gloved hands, which were clasped about a black bag richly embroidered with dull jet. Everything about her was as finished, as costly, as studied, as if she were a young beauty going forth in her joy; yet she looked like a heartbroken woman.

She began again, 'My reason for coming is that I've promised to help a friend, a poor woman who's lost all trace of her son—her only surviving son— and is hunting for him.' She paused, though my expectant silence seemed to encourage her to continue. 'It's a very sad case; I must try to explain. Long ago, as a girl, my friend fell in love with a married man—a man unhappily married.' She moistened her lips, which had become parched and colorless. 'You mustn't judge them too severely. . . . He had great nobility of character—the highest standards—but the situation was too cruel. His wife was insane; at that time there was no legal release in such cases. If you were married to a lunatic only death could free you. It was a most unhappy affair—the poor girl pitied her friend profoundly. Their little boy. . . . ' Suddenly she stood up with a proud and noble movement and leaned to me across the desk. 'I am that woman,' she said.

She straightened herself and stood there, trembling, erect, like a swathed figure of woe on an illustrious grave. I thought: 'What this inexpressive woman was meant to express is grief—' and marveled at the wastefulness of Nature. But suddenly she dropped back into her chair, bowed her face against the desk, and burst into sobs. Her sobs were not violent; they were soft, low, almost rhythmical, with lengthening intervals between, like the last drops of rain after a long downpour; and I said to myself: 'She's cried so much that this must be the very end.'

She opened the jet bag, took out a delicate handkerchief, and dried her eyes. Then she turned to me again. 'It's the first time I've ever spoken of this . . . to any human being except one.'

I laid my hand on hers. 'It was no use—my pretending,' she went on, as if appealing to me for justification.

'Is it ever? And why should you, with an old friend?' I rejoined, attempting to comfort her.

'Ah, but I've had to—for so many years, to be silent has become my second nature.' She paused and then continued in a softer tone: 'My baby was so beautiful . . . do you know, Mr. Norcutt, I'm sure I should know him anywhere. . . . Just two years and one month older than my second boy, Philip . . . the one you know.' Again she hesitated, and then, in a warmer burst of confidence, and scarcely above a whisper: 'We christened the eldest Stephen. We knew it was dangerous: it might give a clue—but I felt I must give him his father's name, the name I loved best. . . . It was all I could keep of my baby. And Stephen understood; he consented. . . . '

I sat and stared at her. What! This child of hers that she was telling me of was the child of Stephen Glenn? The two had had a child two years before the birth of their lawful son Philip? And consequently nearly a year before their marriage? I listened in a stupor, trying to reconstruct in my mind the image of a new, of another, Stephen Glenn, of the suffering reckless man behind the varnished image familiar to me. Now and then I murmured: 'Yes . . . yes. . . ' just to help her to go on.

'Of course it was impossible to keep the baby with me. Think—at my uncle's! My poor uncle—he would have died of it. . . . '

'And so you died instead?'

I had found the right word, her eyes filled again, and she stretched her hands to mine. 'Ah, you've understood! Thank you. Yes; I died.' She added: 'Even when Philip was born I didn't come to life again—not wholly. Because there was always Stevie . . . part of me belonged to Stevie forever.'

'But when you and Glenn were able to marry, why —?'

She hung her head, and the blood rose to her worn temples. 'Ah, why? . . . Listen; you mustn't blame my husband. Try to remember what life was thirty years ago in New York. He had his professional standing to consider. A woman with a shadow on her was damned. . . . I couldn't discredit Stephen. . . . We knew *positively* that our baby was in the best of hands. . . . '

'You never saw him again?'

She shook her head. 'It was part of the agreement—with the persons who took him. They wanted to imagine he was their own. We knew we were fortunate . . . to find such a safe home, so entirely beyond suspicion . . . we had to accept the conditions.' She looked up with a faint flicker of reassurance in her eyes. 'In a way it no longer makes any difference to me—the interval. It seems like yesterday. I know he's been well cared for, and I should recognize him anywhere. No child ever had such eyes. . . . ' She fumbled in her bag, drew out a small morocco case, opened it, and showed me the miniature of a baby a few months old. 'I managed, with the greatest difficulty, to get a photograph of him—and this was done from it. Beautiful? Yes. I shall be able to identify him anywhere. . . . It's only twenty-seven years. . . . '

III

Our talk was prolonged, the next day, at the quiet hotel where Mrs. Glenn was staying; but it led—it could lead—to nothing definite.

The unhappy woman could only repeat and amplify the strange confession stammered out at the Consulate. As soon as her child was born it had been entrusted with the utmost secrecy to a rich childless couple, who at once adopted it, and disappeared forever. Disappeared, that is, in the sense that (as I guessed) Stephen Glenn was as determined as they were that the child's parents should never hear of them again. Poor Catherine had been very ill at her baby's birth. Tortured by the need of concealment, of taking up her usual life at her uncle's as quickly as possible, of explaining her brief absence in such a way as to avert suspicion, she had lived in a blur of fear and suffering, and by the time she was herself again the child was gone, and the adoption irrevocable. Thereafter, I gathered, Glenn made it clear that he wished to avoid the subject, and she learned very little about the couple who had taken her child except that they were of good standing, and came from somewhere in Pennsylvania. They had gone to Europe almost immediately, it appeared, and no more was heard of them. Mrs. Glenn understood that Mr. Brown (their name was Brown) was a painter, and that they went first to Italy, then to Spain—unless it was the other way round. Stephen Glenn, it seemed, had heard of them through an old governess of his sister's, a family confidante, who was the sole recipient of poor Catherine's secret. Soon afterwards the governess died, and with her disappeared the last trace of the mysterious couple; for it was not going to be easy to wander about Europe looking for a Mr. and Mrs. Brown who had gone to Italy or Spain with a baby twenty-seven years ago. But that was what Mrs. Glenn meant to do. She had a fair amount of money, she was desperately lonely, she had no aim or interest or occupation or duty—except to find the child she had lost.

What she wanted was some sort of official recommendation to our consuls in Italy and Spain, accompanied by a private letter hinting at the nature of her errand. I took these papers to her and when I did so I tried to point out the difficulties and risks of her quest, and suggested that she ought to be accompanied by someone who could advise her—hadn't she a man of business, or a relation, a cousin, a nephew? No, she said; there was no one; but for that matter she needed no one. If necessary she could apply to the police, or employ private detectives; and any American consul to whom she appealed would know how to advise her. 'In any case,' she added, 'I couldn't be mistaken—I should always recognize him. He was the very image of his father. And if there were any possibility of my being in doubt, I have the miniature, and photographs of his father as a young man.'

She drew out the little morocco case and offered it again for my contemplation. The vague presentment of a child a few months old—and by its help she expected to identify a man of nearly thirty!

Apparently she had no clue beyond the fact that, all those years ago, the adoptive parents were rumored to have sojourned in Europe. She was starting for Italy because she thought she remembered that they were said to have gone there first—in itself a curious argument. Wherever there was an American consul she meant to apply to him. First at Genoa; then Milan; then Florence, Rome and Naples. In one or the other of these cities she would surely discover some one who could remember the passage there of an American couple named Brown with the most beautiful baby boy in the world. Even the long arm of coincidence could not have scattered so widely over southern Europe American couples of the name of Brown, with a matchlessly beautiful baby called Stephen.

Mrs. Glenn set forth in a mood of almost mystical exaltation. She promised that I should hear from her as soon as she had anything definite to communicate: 'which means that you *will* hear—and soon!' she concluded with a happy laugh. But six months passed without my receiving any direct news, though I was kept on her track by a succession of letters addressed to my chief by various consuls who wrote to say that a Mrs. Stephen Glenn had called with a letter of recommendation, but that unluckily it had been impossible to give her any assistance 'as she had absolutely no data to go upon.' Alas poor lady—

And, then, one day, about eight months after her departure, there was a telegram. 'Found my boy. Unspeakably happy. Long to see you.' It was signed Catherine Glenn, and dated from a mountain cure in Switzerland.

IV

That summer, when the time came for my vacation, it was raining in Paris even harder than it had rained all the preceding winter, and I decided to make a dash for the sun.

I had read in the papers that the French Riviera was suffering from a six months' drought; and though I didn't half believe it, I took the next train for the south. I got out at Les Calanques, a small bathing place between Marseilles and Toulon, where there was a fairish hotel, and pine woods to walk in, and there, that very day, I saw seated on the beach the majestic figure of Mrs. Stephen Glenn. The first thing that struck me was that she had at last discarded her weeds. She wore a thin white dress, and a wide brimmed hat of russet straw shaded the fine oval of her face. She saw me at once, and springing up advanced across the beach with a light step. The sun, striking on her hat brim, cast a warm shadow on her face; and in that semishade it glowed with recovered youth. 'Dear Mr. Norcutt! How wonderful! Is it really you? I've been meaning to write for weeks; but I think happiness has made me lazy and my days are so full,' she declared with a joyous smile.

I looked at her with increased admiration. At the Consulate, I remembered, I had said to myself that grief was what Nature had meant her features to express; but that was only because I had never seen her happy. No; even when her husband and her son Philip were alive, and the circle of her well-being seemed unbroken, I had never seen her look as she looked now. And I understood that, during all those years, the unsatisfied longing for her eldest child, the shame at her own cowardice in disowning and deserting him, and perhaps her secret contempt for her husband for having abetted (or more probably exacted) that desertion, must have been eating into her soul, deeper, far deeper, than satisfied affections could reach. Now everything in her was satisfied; I could see it.

'How happy you look!' I exclaimed.

'But of course.' She took it as simply as she had my former remark on her heightened beauty; and I perceived that what illumined her face when we met on the steamer was not sorrow but the dawn of hope. Even then she had felt certain that she was going to find her boy; now she had found him and was transfigured. I sat down beside her on the sands. 'And now tell me how the incredible thing happened.'

She shook her head. 'Not incredible—inevitable. When one has lived for more than half a life with one object in view it's bound to become a reality. I *had* to find Stevie; and I found him.' She smiled with the inward brooding smile of a Madonna—an image of the eternal mother who, when she speaks of her children in old age, still feels them at the breast.

Of details as I made out there were few; or perhaps she was too confused with happiness to give them. She had hunted up and down Italy for her Mr. and Mrs. Brown, and then suddenly, at Alassio, just as she was beginning to give up hope, and had decided (in a less sanguine mood) to start for Spain, the miracle had happened. Falling into talk, on her last evening, with a lady in the hotel lounge, she had alluded vaguely—she couldn't say why—to the object of her quest; and the lady snatching the miniature from her, and bursting into tears, had identified the portrait as her adopted child's, and herself as the long-sought Mrs. Brown. Papers had been produced, dates compared, all to Mrs. Glenn's complete satisfaction. There could be no doubt that she had found her Stevie (thank heaven, they had kept the name!); and the only shadow on her joy was the discovery that he was lying ill, menaced with tuberculosis, at some Swiss mountain cure. Or rather, that was part of another sadness; of the unfortunate fact that his adopted parents had lost nearly all their money just as he was leaving school, and hadn't been able to do much for him in the way of medical attention or mountain air—the very things he needed as he was growing up. Instead, since he had a passion for painting, they had allowed him to live in Paris, rather miserably, in the Latin Quarter, and work all day in one of those big schools—Julian's wasn't it? The very worst thing for a boy whose lungs were slightly affected; and this last year he had had to give up, and spend several months in a cheap hole in Switzerland. Mrs. Glenn joined him there at once— ah, that meeting!—and as soon as she had seen him, and talked with the doctors, she became convinced that all that was needed to ensure his recovery was comfort, care and freedom from anxiety. His lungs, the doctors assured her, were all right again; and he had such a passion for the sea that after a few weeks in a good hotel at Montana he had persuaded Mrs. Glenn to come with him to the Mediterranean. But she was firmly resolved on carrying him back to Switzerland for another winter, no matter how much he objected; and Mr. and Mrs. Brown agreed that she was absolutely right—

'Ah; there's still a Mr. Brown?'

'Oh, yes.' She smiled at me absently, her whole mind on Stevie. 'You'll see them both—they're here with us. I invited them for a few weeks, poor souls. I can't altogether separate them from Stevie—not yet.' (It was clear that eventually she hoped to.)

No, I assented; I supposed she couldn't; and just then she exclaimed: 'Ah, there's my boy!' and I saw a tall stooping young man approaching us with the listless step of convalescence. As he came nearer I felt that I was going to like him a good deal better than I had expected—though I don't know why I had doubted his likeableness before knowing him. At any rate, I was taken at once by the look of his dark-lashed eyes, deep set in a long thin face which I suspected of being too pale under the carefully acquired sunburn. The eyes were friendly, humorous, ironical; I liked a little less the rather hard lines of the mouth, until his smile relaxed them into boyishness. His body, lank and loose-jointed, was too thin for his suit of light striped flannel, and the untidy dark hair tumbling over his forehead adhered to his temples as if they were perpetually damp. Yes, he looked ill, this young Glenn.

I remembered wondering, when Mrs. Glenn told me her story, why it had not occurred to her that her oldest son had probably joined the American forces and might have remained on the field with his junior. Apparently this tragic possibility had never troubled her. She seemed to have forgotten that there had ever been a war, and that a son of her own, with thousands of young Americans of his generation, had lost his life in it. And now it looked as though she had been gifted with a kind of prescience. The war did not last long enough for America to be called on to give her weaklings, as Europe had, and it was clear that Stephen Glenn, with his narrow shoulders and hectic cheekbones, could never have been wanted for active service. I suspected him of having been ill for longer than his mother knew.

Mrs. Glenn shone on him as he dropped down beside us. 'This is an old friend, Stephen, a very dear friend of your father's.' She added, extravagantly, that but for me she and her son might never have found each other. I protested: 'How absurd,' and young Glenn, stretching out his long limbs against the sand-bank, and crossing his arms behind his head, turned on me a glance of rather weary good humor. 'Better give me a longer trial, my dear, before you thank him.'

Mrs. Glenn laughed contentedly, and continued, her eyes on her son: 'I was telling him that Mr. and Mrs. Brown are with us.'

'Ah, yes—' said Stephen indifferently. I was inclined to like him a little less for his undisguised indifference. Ought he to have allowed his poor and unlucky foster parents to be so soon superseded by this beautiful and opulent new mother? But, after all, I mused, I had not yet seen the Browns, and though I had begun to suspect, from Catherine's tone as well as from Stephen's, that they both felt the presence of that couple to be vaguely oppressive, I decided that I must wait before drawing any conclusions. And then suddenly, Mrs. Glenn said, in a tone of what I can only describe as icy cordiality: 'Ah, here they come now. They must have hurried back on purpose —'

V

Mr. and Mrs. Brown advanced across the beach. Mrs. Brown led the way; she walked with a light springing step, and if I had been struck by Mrs. Glenn's recovered youthfulness, her co-mother, at a little distance, seemed to me positively girlish. She was smaller and much slighter than Mrs. Glenn, and looked so much younger that I had a moment's doubt as to the possibility of her having, twenty-seven years earlier been of legal age to adopt a baby. Certainly she and Mr. Brown must have had exceptional reasons for concluding so early that heaven was not likely to bless their union. I had to admit, when Mrs. Brown came up, that I had overrated her juvenility. Slim, active and girlish she remained; but the freshness of her face was largely due to artifice, and the golden glints in her chestnut hair were a thought too golden. Still, she was a very pretty woman, with the alert cosmopolitan air of one who had acquired her elegance in places where the very best counterfeits are found. It will be seen that my first impression was none too favorable; but for all I knew of Mrs. Brown it might turn out that she had made the best of meager opportunities. She met my name with a conquering smile, said: 'Ah, yes — dear Mr. Norcutt. Mrs. Glenn has told us all we owe you' — and at the 'we' I detected a faint shadow on Mrs. Glenn's brow. Was it only maternal jealousy that provoked it? I suspected an even deeper antagonism. The women were so different, so diametrically opposed to each other in appearance, dress, manner, and the inherited standards, that if they had met as strangers it would have been hard for them to find a common ground of understanding; and the fact of that ground being furnished by Stephen hardly seemed to ease the situation.

'Well, what's the matter with taking some notice of little me?' piped a small dry man dressed in too-smart flannels, and wearing a too-white Panama which he removed with an elaborate flourish.

'Oh, of course! My husband — Mr. Norcutt.' Mrs. Brown laid a jeweled hand on Stephen's recumbent shoulder. 'Steve, you rude boy, you ought to have introduced your dad.' As she pressed his shoulder I noticed that her long oval nails were freshly lacquered with the last new shade of coral, and that the forefinger was darkly yellowed with nicotine. This familiar color scheme struck me at the moment as peculiarly distasteful.

Stephen vouchsafed no answer, and Mr. Brown remarked to me sardonically, 'You know you won't lose your money or your morals in this secluded spot.'

Mrs. Brown flashed a quick glance at him. 'Don't be so silly! It's much better for Steve to be in a quiet place where he can just sleep and eat and bask. His mother and I are going to be firm with him about that — aren't we, dearest?' She transferred her lacquered talons to Mrs. Glenn's shoulder, and the latter, with a just perceptible shrinking, replied gaily: 'As long as we can hold out against him!'

'Oh, this is the very place I was pining for,' said Stephen placidly. ('Gosh — *pining!*' Mr. Brown interpolated.) Stephen tilted his hat forward over his sunburnt nose with the drawn nostrils, crossed his arms under his thin neck, and closed his eyes. Mrs. Brown bent over Mrs. Glenn with one of her quick gestures. 'Darling — before we go in to lunch do let me fluff you out a little: so.' With a flashing hand she loosened the soft white waves under Mrs. Glenn's spreading hat brim. 'There — that's better; isn't it, Mr. Norcutt?'

Mrs. Glenn's face was a curious sight. The smile she had forced gave place to a marble rigidity; the old statuesqueness which had melted to flesh and blood stiffened her features again. 'Thank you . . . I'm afraid I never think. . . . '

'No, you never do; that's the trouble!' Mrs. Brown shot an arch glance at me. 'With her looks, oughtn't she to think? But perhaps it's lucky for the rest of us poor women she didn't — eh, Stevie?'

The color rushed to Mrs. Glenn's face; she was going to retort; to snub the dreadful woman. But the new softness had returned, and she merely lifted a warning finger. 'Oh, don't please . . . speak to him. Can't you see that he's fallen asleep?'

O great King Solomon, I thought — and bowed my soul before the mystery.

I spent a fortnight at Les Calanques, and every day my perplexity deepened. The most conversible member of the little group was undoubtedly Stephen. Mrs. Glenn was as she had always been; beautiful, benevolent and inarticulate. When she sat on the beach beside the dozing Stephen, in her flowing dress, her large white umbrella tilted to shelter him, she reminded me of a carven angel spreading broad wings above a tomb (I could never look at her without being reminded of statuary); and to converse with a marble angel so engaged can never have been easy. But I was perhaps not wrong in suspecting that her smiling silence concealed a reluctance to talk about the Browns. Like many perfectly unegotistical women Catherine Glenn had no subject of conversation except her own affairs; and these at present so visibly hinged on the Browns that it was easy to see why silence was simpler.

Mrs. Brown, I may as well confess, bored me acutely. She was a perfect specimen of the middle-aged flapper, with layers and layers of hard-headed feminine craft under her romping ways. All this I suffered from chiefly because I knew it was making Mrs. Glenn suffer. But after all it was thanks to Mrs. Brown that she had found her son; Mrs. Brown had brought up Stephen, had made him (one was obliged to suppose) the whimsical dreamy charming creature he was; and again and again, when Mrs. Brown outdid herself in girlish archness or middle-aged craft, Mrs. Glenn's wounded eyes said to mine: 'Look at Stephen, isn't that enough?'

Certainly it was enough, enough even to excuse Mr. Brown's jocular allusions and arid anecdotes, his bedroom at Les Calanques, and the too-liberal potations in which he drowned it. Mr. Brown, I may add, was not half as trying as his wife. For the first two or three days I was mildly diverted by his contempt for the quiet watering place in which his women had confined him, and his lordly conception of the life of pleasure, as exemplified by intimacy with the headwaiters of gilt-edged restaurants and the lavishing of large sums on horse racing and cards. 'Damn it, Norcutt, I'm not used to being mewed up in this kind of place. Perhaps it's different with you—all depends on a man's standards, don't it? Now before I lost my money—' and so on. The odd thing was that, though this loss of fortune played a large part in the conversation of both husband and wife, I never somehow believed in it—I mean in the existence of the fortune. I hinted as much one day to Mrs. Glenn, but she only opened her noble eyes reproachfully, as if I had implied that it discredited the Browns to dream of a fortune they had never had. 'They tell me Stephen was brought up with every luxury. And besides—their own tastes seem rather expensive, don't they?' she argued gently.

'That's the very reason.'

'The reason—?'

'The only people I know who are totally without expensive tastes are the overwhelmingly wealthy. You see it when you visit palaces. They sleep on camp beds and live on boiled potatoes.'

Mrs. Glenn smiled. 'Stevie wouldn't have liked that.'

Stephen smiled also when I alluded to these past splendors. 'It must have been before I cut my first teeth. I know Boy's always talking about it; but I've got to take it on faith, just as you have.'

'Boy—?'

'Didn't you know? He's always called "Boy." Boydon Brown—abbreviated by friends and family to "Boy." The Boy Browns. Suits them, doesn't it?'

It did; but I was sure that it suited him to say so.

'And you've always addressed your adopted father in that informal style?'

'Lord, yes; nobody's formal with Boy except headwaiters. They bow down to him; I don't know why. He's got the manner. I haven't. When I go to a restaurant they always give me the worst table and the stupidest waiter.' He leaned back against the sandbank and blinked contentedly seaward. 'Got a cigarette?'

'You know you oughtn't to smoke,' I protested.

'I know; but I do.' He held out a lean hand with prominent knuckles. 'As long as Kit's not about.' He called the marble angel, his mother, 'Kit'! And yet I was not offended—I let him do it, just as I let him have one of my cigarettes. If 'Boy' had a way with headwaiters his adopted son undoubtedly had one with lesser beings; his smile, his faint hoarse laugh would have made me do his will even if his talk had not conquered me. We sat for hours on the sands, discussing and dreaming; not always 'listening in', as she archly called it—('I don't want Stevie to depreciate his poor ex-mamma to you.' she explained one day); and whenever Mrs. Brown (who, even at Les Calanques, had contrived to create a social round for herself) was bathing, dancing, playing bridge, or being waved, massaged or manicured, the other mother, assuring herself from an upper window that the coast was clear, would descend in her gentle majesty and turn our sandbank into a throne by sitting on it. But now and then Stephen and I had a half hour to ourselves and then I tried to lead his talk to the past.

He seemed willing enough that I should, but uninterested, and unable to recover many details. 'I never can remember things that don't matter — and so far nothing about me has mattered,' he said with a humorous melancholy. 'I mean, not till I struck mother Kit.'

He had vague recollections of continental travels as a little boy; had afterward been at a private school in Switzerland; had tried to pass himself off as a Canadian volunteer in 1915, and in 1917 to enlist in the American army, but had failed in each case — one had only to look at him to see why. The war over, he had worked for a time at Julian's and then broken down; and after that it had been a hard row to hoe till mother Kit came along. By George, but he'd never forget what she'd done for him — never!

'Well, it's a way mothers have with their sons,' I remarked.

He flushed under his bronze tanning, and said simply: 'Yes — only you see I didn't know.'

His view of the Browns, while not unkindly, was so detached that I suspected him of regarding his own mother with the same objectivity; but when we spoke of her there was a different note in his voice. 'I didn't know' — it was a new experience to him to be really mothered. As a type, however, she clearly puzzled him. He was too sensitive to class her (as the Browns obviously did) as a simple-minded woman to whom nothing had ever happened: but he could not conceive what sort of thing could happen to a woman of her kind. I gathered that she had explained the strange episode of his adoption by telling him that at the time of his birth she had been 'secretly married' — poor Catherine! — to his father, but that 'family circumstances' had made it needful to conceal his existence till the marriage could be announced; by which time he had vanished with his adopted parents. I guessed how it must have puzzled Stephen to adapt his interpretation of this ingenuous tale to what, in the light of Mrs. Glenn's character, he could make out of her past. Of obvious explanations there were plenty; but evidently none fitted into his vision of her. For a moment (I could see) he had suspected a sentimental lie, a tender past, between Mrs. Glenn and myself; but this his quick perceptions soon discarded, and he apparently resigned himself to regarding her as inscrutably proud and incorrigibly perfect. 'I'd like to paint her some day — if ever I'm fit to,' he said; and I wondered whether his scruples applied to his moral or artistic inadequacy.

At the doctor's orders he had dropped his painting altogether since his last breakdown; but it was manifestly the one thing he cared for, and perhaps the only reason he had for wanting to get well. 'When you've dropped to a certain level, it's so damnably easy to keep on till you're altogether down and out. So much easier than dragging up hill again. But I do want to get well enough to paint mother Kit. She's a subject.'

One day it rained, and he was confined to the house. I went up to sit with him, and he got out some of his sketches and studies. Instantly he was transformed from an amiable mocking dilettante into an absorbed and passionate professional. 'This is the only life I've ever had. All the rest—!' He made a grimace that turned his thin face into a death's-head. 'Cinders!'

The studies were brilliant—there was no doubt of that. The question was—the eternal question—what would they turn into when he was well enough to finish them? For the moment the problem did not present itself and I could praise and encourage him in all sincerity. My words brought a glow into his face, but also, as it turned out, sent up his temperature. Mrs. Glenn reproached me mildly; she begged me not to let him get excited about his pictures. I promised not to, and reassured on that point she asked if I didn't think he had talent—real talent? 'Very great talent, yes,' I assured her, and she burst into tears—not of grief or agitation, but of a deep unwelling joy. 'Oh, what have I done to deserve it all—to deserve such happiness? Yet I always knew if I could find him he'd make me happy!' She caught both my hands, and pressed her wet cheek on mine. That was one of her unclouded hours.

There were others not so radiant. I could see that the Browns were straining at the leash. With the seductions of Juan-les-Pins and Antibes in the offing, why, their frequent allusions implied, must they remain marooned at Les Calanques? Of course, for one thing, Mrs. Brown admitted she hadn't the clothes to show herself on a smart *plage*. Though so few were worn they had to come from the big dressmakers; and the latter's charges, everybody knew, were in inverse ration to the amount of material used. 'So that to be really naked is ruinous,' she concluded, laughing; and I saw the narrowing of Catherine's lips. As for Mr. Brown, he added morosely that if a man couldn't take a hand at baccarat, or offer his friends something decent to eat and drink, it was better to vegetate at Les Calanques, and be done with it. Only, when a fellow'd been used to having plenty of money. . . .

I saw at once what had happened. Mrs. Glenn, whose material wants did not extend beyond the best plumbing and expensive clothes (and the latter were made to do for three seasons), did not fully understand the Brown's aspirations. Her fortune, though adequate, was not large, and she had settled on Stephen's adoptive parents an allowance which, converted into francs, made a generous showing. It was obvious, however, that what they hoped was to get more money. There had been debts in the background, perhaps; who knew but the handsome Stephen had had his share of them? One day I suggested discreetly to Mrs. Glenn that if she wished to be alone with her son she might offer the Browns a trip to Juan-les-Pins, or some such center of gaiety. But I pointed out that the precedent might be dangerous, and advised her first to consult Stephen. 'I suspect he's as anxious to have them go as you are,' I said recklessly; and her flush of pleasure rewarded me. 'Oh, you mustn't say that,' she reproved me, laughing, and added that she would think over my advice, I am not sure if she did consult Stephen, but she offered the Browns a holiday, and they accepted it without false pride.

VI

After my departure from Les Calanques I had no news of Mrs. Glenn till she returned to Paris in October. Then she begged me to call at the hotel where I had previously seen her, and where she was now staying with Stephen—and the Browns.

She suggested, rather mysteriously, my dining with her on a particular evening, when, as she put it, 'everybody' would be out; and when I arrived she explained that Stephen had gone to the country for the week-end, with some old comrades from Julian's, and that the Browns were dining at a smart night-club in Montmartre. 'So we'll have a quiet time all by ourselves.' She added that Steve was so much better that he was trying his best to persuade her to spend the winter in Paris, and let him get back to his painting, but in spite of the good news I thought she looked worn and dissatisfied.

I was surprised to find the Browns still with her, and told her so.

'Well, you see, it's difficult,' she returned with a troubled frown. 'They love Stephen so much that they won't give him up; and how can I blame them? What are my rights, compared to theirs?'

Finding this hard to answer, I put another question 'Did you enjoy your quiet time with Stephen while they were in Juan-les-Pins?'

'Oh, they didn't go; at least Mrs. Brown didn't—Chrissy she likes me to call her,' Mrs. Glenn corrected herself hurriedly. 'She couldn't bear to leave Stephen.'

'So she sacrificed Juan-les-Pins, and that handsome check?'

'Not the check; she kept that. Boy went,' Mrs. Glenn added apologetically. Boy and Chrissy—it had come to that! I looked away from my old friend's troubled face before putting my next question. 'And Stephen—?'

'Well, I can't exactly tell how he feels. But I sometimes think he'd like to be alone with me.' A passing radiance smoothed away her frown. 'He's hinted that, if we decide to stay here, they might be tempted by winter sports, and go to the Engadine later.'

'So that they would have the benefit of the high air instead of Stephen?' She coloured a little, looked down, and then smiled at me. 'What can I do?'

I resolved to sound Stephen on his adopted parents. The present situation would have to be put an end to somehow; but it had puzzling elements. Why had Mrs. Brown refused to go to Juan-les-Pins? Was it, as I had suspected, because there were debts, and more pressing uses for the money? Or was it that she was so much attached to her adopted son as to be jealous of his mother's influence? This was far more to be feared; but it did not seem to fit in with what I knew of Mrs. Brown. The trouble was that what I knew was so little. Mrs. Brown, though in one way so intelligible, was in another as cryptic to me as Catherine Glenn was to Stephen. The surface was transparent enough; but what did the blur beneath conceal? Troubled waters, or just a mud flat? My only hope was to try to get Stephen to tell me.

Stephen had hired a studio—against his doctor's advice, I gathered—and spent most of his hours there, in the company of his old group of painting friends. Mrs. Glenn had been there once or twice, but in spite of his being so sweet and dear to her she had felt herself in the way—as she undoubtedly was. 'I can't keep up with their talk, you know,' she explained. With whose talk could she, poor angel?

I suggested that, for the few weeks of their Paris sojourn, it would be kinder to let Stephen have his fling; and she agreed. Afterward, in the mountains, he could recuperate, youth had such powers of self-healing. But I urged her to insist on his spending another winter in the Engadine; not at one of the big fashionable places—

She interrupted me. 'I'm afraid Boy and Chrissy wouldn't like—'

'Oh, for God's sake; can't you give Boy and Chrissy another check, and send them off to Egypt, or to Monte Carlo?'

She hesitated. 'I could try; but I don't believe she'd go. Not without Stevie.'

'And what does Stevie say?'

'What can he say? She brought him up. She was there—all the years when I'd failed him.'

It was unanswerable, and I felt the uselessness of any advice I could give. The situation could be changed only by some internal readjustment. Still, out of pity for the poor mother, I determined to try a word with Stephen. She gave me the address of his studio, and the next day I went there.

It was in a smart-looking modern building in the Montparnasse quarter; lofty, well-lit and well-warmed. What a contrast to his earlier environment! I climbed to his door, rang the bell and waited. There were sounds of moving about within, but as no one came I rang again; and finally Stephen opened the door. His face lit up pleasantly when he saw me. 'Oh, it's you, my dear fellow!' But I caught a hint of constraint in his voice.

'I'm not in the way? Don't mind throwing me out if I am.'

'I've got a sitter—' he began, visibly hesitating.

'Oh, in that case—'

'No, no; it's only—the fact is, it's Chrissy. I was trying to do a study of her—'

He led me across the passage and into the studio. It was large and flooded with light. Divans against the walls; big oak tables; shaded lamps, a couple of tall screens. From behind one of them emerged Mrs. Brown, hatless, and slim, in a pale summer-like frock, her chestnut hair becomingly tossed about her eyes. 'Dear Mr. Norcutt. So glad you turned up! I was getting such a stiff neck— Stephen's merciless.'

'May I see the result?' I asked; and 'Oh, no,' she protested in mock terror, 'it's too frightful—it really is. I think he thought he was doing a *nature morte*— lemons and a bottle of beer, or something!'

'It's not fit for inspection,' Stephen agreed.

The room was spacious, and not overcrowded. Glancing about, I could see only one easel with a painting on it. Stephen went up and turned the canvas face inward, with the familiar gesture of the artist who does not wish to challenge attention. But before he did so I had remarked that the painting was neither a portrait of Mrs. Brown nor a still-life. It was a rather brilliant three-quarter sketch of a woman's naked back and hips. A model, no doubt—but why did he wish to conceal it?

'I'm so glad you came.' Mrs. Brown repeated, smiling intensely. I stood still, hoping she was about to go; but she dropped down on one of the divans, tossing back her tumbled curls. 'He works too hard, you know; I wish you'd tell him so. Steve, come here and stretch out,' she commanded, indicating the other end of the divan. 'You ought to take a good nap.'

The hint was so obvious that I said; 'In that case I'd better come another time.'

'No, no; wait till I give you a cocktail. We all need cocktails. Where's the shaker, darling?' Mrs. Brown was on her feet again, alert and gay. She dived behind the screen which had previously concealed her, and reappeared with the necessary appliances. 'Bring up that little table, Mr. Norcutt, please. Oh I know—dear Kit doesn't approve of cocktails; and she's right. But look at him—dead-beat! If he will slave at his painting, what's he to do? I was scolding him about it when you came in.'

The shaker danced in her flashing hands, and in a trice she was holding a glass out to me, and another to Stephen, who had obediently flung himself down on the divan. As he took the glass she bent and laid her lips on his damp hair. 'You bad boy, you!'

I looked at Stephen. 'You ought to get out of this, and start straight off for Switzerland,' I admonished him.

'Oh, hell,' he groaned. 'Can't you get Kit to drop all that?'

Mrs. Brown made an impatient gesture. 'Isn't he too foolish? Of course he ought to go away. He looks like nothing on earth. But his only idea of Switzerland is one of those awful places we used to have to go to because they were cheap, where there's nothing to do in the evening but to sit with clergyman's wives looking at stereopticon views of glaciers. I tell him he'll love St. Moritz. There's a thrill there every minute.'

Stephen closed his eyes and sank his head back in the cushions without speaking. His face was drawn and weary; I was startled at the change in him since we had parted at Les Calanques.

Mrs. Brown, following my glance, met it with warning brows and a finger on her painted lips. It was like a parody of Mrs. Glenn's maternal gesture, and I perceived that it meant, 'Can't you see that he's falling asleep? Do be tactful and slip out without disturbing him.'

What could I do but obey? A moment later the studio door had closed on me, and I was going down the long flights of stairs. The worst of it was that I was not at all sure that Stephen was really asleep.

VII

The next morning I received a telephone call from Stephen asking me to lunch. We met at a quiet restaurant near his studio, and when, after an admirably-chosen meal, we settled down to coffee and cigars, he said carelessly: 'Sorry you got thrown out that way yesterday.'

'Oh, well—I saw you were tired, and I didn't want to interfere with your nap.'

He looked down moodily at his plate. 'Tired—yes, I'm tired. But I didn't want a nap. I merely simulated slumber to try and make Chrissy shut up.'

'Ah—' I said.

He shot a quick glance at me, almost resentfully, I thought. Then he went on: 'There are times when aimless talk nearly kills me. I wonder,' he broke out suddenly, 'If you can realize what it feels like for a man who's never—I mean for an orphan—suddenly to find himself with two mothers?'

I said I could see it might be arduous.

'Arduous! It's literally asphyxiating.' He frowned, and then smiled whimsically. 'When I need all the fresh air I can get!'

'My dear fellow—what you need first of all is to get away from cities and studios.'

His frown deepened. 'I know; I know all that. Only, you see—well, to begin with, before I turn up my toes I want to do something for mother Kit.'

'Do something?'

'Something to show her that I was—was worth all this fuss.' He paused, and turned his coffee spoon absently between his long twitching fingers.

I shrugged. 'Whatever you do, she'll always think that. Mothers do.'

He murmured after me slowly: 'Mothers—'

'What she wants you to do now is to get well,' I insisted.

'Yes; I know; I'm pledged to get well. But somehow that bargain doesn't satisfy me. If I don't get well I want to leave something behind me that'll make her think: "If he'd lived a little longer he'd have pulled it off".'

'If you left a gallery of masterpieces it wouldn't help her much.'

His face clouded, and he looked at me wistfully. 'What the devil else can I do?'

'Go to Switzerland, and let yourself be bored for a whole winter. Then you can come back and paint, and enjoy your success instead of having the enjoyment done for you by your heirs.'

'Oh, what a large order—', he sighed, and drew out his cigarettes.

For a moment we were both silent; then he raised his eyes and looked straight at me. 'Supposing I don't get well, there's another thing. . . ' He hesitated a moment. 'Do you happen to know if my mother has made her will?'

I imagine my look must have surprised him, for he hurried on: 'It's only this: if I should drop out—you can never tell—there are Chrissy and Boy, poor, helpless devils. I can't forget what they've been to me . . . done for me . . . though sometimes I daresay I seem ungrateful. . . .'

I listened to his embarrassed phrases with an embarrassment at least as great. 'You may be sure your mother won't forget either,' I said.

'No; I suppose not. Of course not. Only sometimes — you can see for your-self that things are a little breezy. . . . They feel that perhaps she doesn't always remember for how many years . . .' He brought the words out as though he were reciting a lesson. 'I can't forget it . . . of course,' he added, painfully.

I glanced at my watch, and stood up. I wanted to spare him the evident ef-fort of going on. 'Mr. and Mrs. Brown's tastes don't always agree with your mother's. That's evident. If you could persuade them to go off somewhere — or to lead more independent lives when they're with her — mightn't that help?'

He cast a despairing glance at me. 'Lord — I wish you'd try! But you see they're anxious — anxious about their future. . . .'

'I'm sure they needn't be,' I answered shortly, more and more impatient to make an end.

His face lit up with a suddenness that hurt me. 'Oh, well . . . it's sure to be all right if you say so. Of course you know.'

'I know your mother,' I said, holding out my hand for good-bye.

VIII

Shortly after my lunch with Stephen Glenn I was unexpectedly detached from my job in Paris and sent on a special mission to the other side of the world. I was sorry to bid good-bye to Mrs. Glenn, but relieved to be rid of the thankless task of acting as her counselor. Not that she herself was not thankful, poor soul; but the situation abounded in problems, to not one of which could I find a so-lution; and I was embarrassed by her simple faith in my ability to do so. 'Get rid of the Browns; pension them off,' I could only repeat; but since my talk with Stephen I had little hope of his mother's acting on this suggestion. 'You'll proba-bly all end up together in St. Moritz,' I prophesied; and a few months later a be-lated Paris *Herald,* overtaking me in my remote corner of the globe, informed me that among the guests of the new Ice Palace Hotel at St. Moritz were Mrs. Glenn of New York, Mr. Stephen Glenn, and Mr. and Mrs. Boydon Brown. From succeeding numbers of the same sheet I learned that Mr. and Mrs. Boydon Brown were among those entertaining on the opening night of the new *Restau-rant des Glaciers,* that the Boydon Brown cup for the most original costume at the Annual Fancy Ball of the Skiers' Club had been won by Miss Thora Dacy (costume designed by the well-known artist, Stephen Glenn), and that Mr. Boy-don Brown had been one of the stewards of the dinner given to the participants in the ice hockey match between the St. Moritz and Suvretta teams. And on such items I was obliged to nourish my memory of my friends, for no direct news came to me from any of them.

When I bade Mrs. Glenn good-bye I had told her that I had hopes of a post in the State Department at the close of my temporary mission, and she said, a little wistfully; 'How wonderful if we could meet next year in America! As soon as Stephen is strong enough I want him to come back and live with me in his father's house.' This seemed a natural wish; and it struck me that it might be the means of effecting a break with the Browns. But Mrs. Glenn shook her head. 'Chrissy says a winter in New York would amuse them both tremendously.'

I was not so sure that it would amuse Stephen, and therefore did not base much hope on the plan. The one thing Stephen wanted was to get back to Paris and paint: it would presumably be his mother's lot to settle down there when his health permitted.

I heard nothing more until I got back to Washington the following spring; then I had a line from Stephen. The winter in the Engadine had been a deadly bore, but had really done him good, and his mother was just leaving for Paris to look for an apartment. She meant to take one on a long lease, and have the furniture of the New York house sent out—it would be jolly getting it arranged. As for him, the doctors said he was well enough to go on with his painting and, as I knew, it was the one thing he cared for; so I might cast off all anxiety about the family. That was all—and perhaps I should have obeyed if Mrs. Glenn had also written. But no word, no message even, came from her; and as she always wrote when there was good news to give, her silence troubled me.

It was in the course of the same summer, during a visit to Bar Harbor, that one evening, dining with a friend, I found myself next to a slight pale girl with large gray eyes, who suddenly turned them on me reproachfully. 'Then you don't know me? I'm Thora.'

I looked my perplexity, and she added: 'Aren't you Steve Glenn's great friend? He's always talking of you.' My memory struggled with a tangle of oddments, from which I finally extricated the phrase in the *Herald* about Miss Thora Dacy and the fancy-dress ball at St. Moritz. 'You're the young lady who won the Boydon Brown prize in a costume designed by the well-known artist, Mr. Stephen Glenn!'

Her charming face fell. 'If you know me only through that newspaper rubbish. . . . I had an idea the well-known artist might have told you about me.'

'He's not much of a correspondent.'

'No; but I thought—'

'Why won't you tell me yourself instead?'

Dinner was over, and the company had moved out to a wide, starlit verandah looking seaward. I found a corner for two, and installed myself there with my new friend, who was also Stephen's. 'I like him awfully—don't you?' she began at once. I liked her way of saying it; I liked her direct gaze; I found myself thinking: 'But this may turn out to be the solution!' For I felt sure that, if circumstances ever gave her the right to take part in the coming struggle over Stephen, Thora Dacy would be on the side of the angels.

As if she had guessed my thought she continued: 'And I do love Mrs. Glenn too—don't you?'

I assured her that I did, and she added: 'And Steve loves her—I'm sure he does!'

'Well, if he didn't—!' I exclaimed indignantly.

'That's the way I feel; he ought to. Only, you see, Mrs. Brown—the Browns adopted him when he was a baby, didn't they, and brought him up as if he'd been their own child? I suppose they must know him better than any of us do; and Mrs. Brown says he can't help feeling bitter about—I don't know all the circumstances, but his mother did desert him soon after he was born, didn't she? And if it hadn't been for the Browns—'

'The Browns—the Browns! It's a pity they don't leave it to other people to proclaim their merits! And I don't believe Stephen does feel as they'd like you to think. If he does, he ought to be kicked. If—if complicated family reasons obliged Mrs. Glenn to separate herself from him when he was a baby, the way she mourned for him all those years, and her devotion since they've come together again, have atoned a thousand-fold for that old unhappiness; and no one knows it better than Stephen.'

The girl received this without protesting. 'I'm so glad—so glad.' There was a new vibration in her voice; she looked up gravely. 'I've always *wanted* to love Mrs. Glenn the best.'

'Well, you'd better; especially if you love Stephen.'

'Oh, I do love him,' she said simply. 'But of course I understand his feeling as he does about the Browns.'

I hesitated, not knowing how I ought to answer the question I detected under this; but at length I said: 'Stephen, at any rate, must feel that Mrs. Brown has no business to insinuate anything against his mother. He ought to put a stop to that.' She met the suggestion with a sigh, and stood up to join another group. 'Thora Dacy may yet save us!' I thought, as my gaze followed her light figure across the room.

I had half a mind to write of that meeting to Stephen or to his mother; but the weeks passed while I procrastinated, and one day I received a note from Stephen. He wrote (with many messages from Mrs. Glenn) to give me their new address, and to tell me that he was hard at work at his painting, and doing a 'promising portrait of mother Kit.' He signed himself my affectionate Steve, and added underneath: 'So glad you've come across little Thora. She took a most tremendous shine to you. Do please be nice to her; she's a dear child. But don't encourage any illusions about me, please; marrying's not in my program.' 'So that's that,' I thought, and tore the letter up rather impatiently. I wondered if Thora Dacy already knew that her illusions were not to be encouraged.

IX

The months went by, and I heard no more from my friends. Summer came round again, and with it the date of my six weeks' holiday, which I purposed to take that year in Europe. Two years had passed since I had last seen Mrs. Glenn, and during that time I had received only two or three brief notes from her, thanking me for Christmas wishes, or telling me that Stephen was certainly better, though he would take no care of himself. But several months had passed since the date of her last report.

I had meant to spend my vacation in a trip in south-western France and on the way over I decided to invite Stephen Glenn to join me. I therefore made direct for Paris, and the next morning rang him up at Mrs. Glenn's. Mrs. Brown's voice met me in reply, informing me that Stephen was no longer living with his mother. 'Read the riot act to us all a few months ago — said he wanted to be independent. You know his fads. Dear Catherine was foolishly upset. As I said to her . . . yes, I'll give you his address; but poor Steve's not well just now . . . Oh, go on an trip with you? No; I'm afraid there's no chance of that. The truth is, he told us he didn't want to be bothered — rather warned us off the premises; even poor old Boy; and you know he adores Boy. I haven't seen him myself for several days. But you can try . . . Oh, of course you can try . . . No; I'm afraid you can't see Catherine either — not just at present. She's been ill too — feverish; worrying about her naughty Steve, I suspect. I'm mounting guard for a few days, and not letting her see anybody till her temperature goes down. And would you do me a favor? Don't write—-don't let her know you're here. Not for a day or two, I mean. . . . She'd be so distressed at not being able to see you. . . . '

She rang off, and left me to draw my own conclusions.

They were not of the pleasantest. I was perplexed by the apparent sequestration of both my friends, still more so by the disquieting mystery of Mrs. Glenn's remaining with the Brown's while Stephen had left them. Why had she not followed her son? Was it because she had not been allowed to? I conjectured that Mrs. Brown, knowing I was likely to put these questions to the persons concerned, was maneuvering to prevent my seeing them. If she could maneuver, so could I: but for the moment I had to consider what line to take. The fact of her giving me Stephen's address made me suspect that she had taken measures to prevent my seeing him; and if that were so there was not much use in making the attempt. And Mrs. Glenn was in bed, and 'feverish', and not to be told of my arrival. . . .

After a day's pondering I reflected that telegrams sometimes penetrate where letters fail to, and decided to telegraph to Stephen. No reply came, but the following afternoon, as I was leaving my hotel a taxi drove up and Mrs. Glenn descended from it. She was dressed in black, with many hanging scarves and veils, as if she either feared the air or the searching eyes of someone who might be interested in her movements. But for her white hair and heavy stooping lines she might have suggested the furtive figure of a young woman stealing to her lover. But when I looked at her the analogy seemed a profanation.

To women of Catherine Glenn's ripe beauty thinness gives a sudden look of age; and the face she raised among her thrown-back veils was emaciated. Illness and anxiety had scarred her as years and weather scar some beautiful still image on a church front. She took my hand, and I led her into the empty reading-room. 'You've been ill!' I said.

'Not very; just a bad cold.' It was characteristic that while she looked at me with grave beseeching eyes her words were trivial, ordinary. 'Chrissy's so de-voted—takes such care of me. She was afraid to have me go out. The weather's so unsettled, isn't it? But really I'm all right; and as it cleared this morning I just ran off for a minute to see you.' The entreaty in her eyes became a prayer. 'Only don't tell her, will you? Dear Steve's been ill too—did you know? And so I just slipped out while Chrissy went to see him. She sees him nearly every day, and brings me the news.' She gave a sigh and added, hardly above a whisper: 'He sent me your address. She doesn't know.'

I listened with a sense of vague oppression. Why this mystery, this watching, these evasions? Was it because Steve was not allowed to write to me that he had smuggled my address to his mother? Mystery clung about us in damp fog-like coils, like the scarves and veils about Mrs. Glenn's thin body. But I knew that I must let my visitor tell her tale in her own way, and, of course, when it was told, most of the mystery subsisted, for she was in it, enveloped in it, blinded by it. I gathered, however, that Stephen had been very unhappy. He had met at St. Moritz a girl whom he wanted to marry: Thora Dacy—ah, I'd heard of her, I'd met her? Mrs. Glenn's face lit up. She had thought the child lovely; she had known the family in Washington—excellent people; she had been so happy in the prospect of Stephen's happiness. And then something had happened . . . she didn't know, she had an idea that Chrissy hadn't liked the girl. The reason Stephen gave was that in his state of health he oughtn't to marry; but at the time he'd been perfectly well—the doctors had assured his mother that his lungs were sound, and that there was no such scruples, still less why Chrissy should have encouraged them. For Chrissy had also put it on the ground of health; she had approved his decision. And since then he had been unsettled, irritable, diffi-cult—oh, very difficult. Two or three months ago the state of tension in which they had all been living had reached a climax; Mrs. Glenn couldn't say how or why—it was still obscure to her. But she suspected that Stephen had quarreled with the Browns. They had patched it up now, they saw each other; but for a time there had certainly been something wrong. And suddenly, Stephen had left the apartment, and moved into a wretched studio in a shabby quarter. The only reason he gave for leaving was that he had too many mothers—that was a joke, of course, Mrs. Glenn explained . . . but her eyes filled as she said it.

Poor mother—and, alas, poor Stephen! All the sympathy I could spare from the mother went to the son. He had behaved harshly, cruelly, no doubt; the young do; but under what provocation! I understood his saying that he had too many mothers; and I suspected that what he had tried for—and failed to achieve—was a break with the Browns. Trust Chrissy to baffle that attempt, I thought bitterly; she had obviously deflected the dispute, and made the conse-quences fall upon his mother. And at bottom everything was unchanged.

Unchanged—except for that thickening fog. At the moment it was almost as impenetrable to me as to Mrs. Glenn. Certain things I could understand that she could not: for instance, why Stephen had left home. I could guess that the atmosphere had become unbreathable. But if so, it was certainly Mrs. Brown's doing, and what interest had she in sowing discord between Stephen and his mother? With a shock of apprehension my mind reverted to Stephen's enquiry about his mother's will. It had offended me at the time; now it frightened me. If I was right in suspecting that he had tried to break with his adopted parents—over the question of the will, no doubt, or at any rate over their general selfishness and rapacity—then his attempt had failed, since he and the Browns were still on good terms, and the only result of the dispute had been to separate him from his mother. At the thought my indignation burned afresh. 'I mean to see Stephen,' I declared, looking resolutely at Mrs. Glenn.

'But he's not well enough, I'm afraid; he told me to send you his love, and to say that perhaps when you come back—'

'Ah, you've seen him, then?'

She shook her head. 'No; he telegraphed me this morning. He doesn't even write any longer.' Her eyes filled, and she looked away from me.

He too used the telegraph! It gave me more to think about than poor Mrs. Glenn could know. I continued to look at her. 'Don't you want to send him a telegram in return? You could write it here, and give it to me,' I suggested. She hesitated, seemed half to assent, and then stood up abruptly.

'No; I'd better not. Chrissy takes my messages. If I telegraphed she might wonder—she might be hurt—'

'Yes; I see.'

'But I must be off; I've stayed too long.' She cast a nervous glance at her watch. 'When you come back . . . ' she repeated.

When we reached the door of the hotel rain was falling, and I drew her back into the vestibule while the porter went to call a taxi. 'Why haven't you your own motor?' I asked.

'Oh, Chrissy wanted the motor. She had to go to see Stevie—and of course she didn't know I should be going out. You won't tell her, will you?' Mrs. Glenn cried back to me as the door of the taxi closed on her.

The taxi drove off, and I was standing on the pavement looking after it when a handsomely appointed private motor glided up to the hotel. The chauffeur sprang down, and I recognized him as the man who had driven Mrs. Glenn when we had been together at Les Calanques. I was therefore not surprised to see Mrs. Brown, golden haired and slim, descending under his unfurled umbrella. She held a note in her hand, and looked at me with a start of surprise. 'What luck! I was going to try to find out when you were likely to be in—and here you are! Concierges are always so secretive that I'd written as well.' She held the envelope up with her brilliant smile. 'Am I butting in? Or may I come and have a talk?'

I led her to the reading room which Mrs. Glenn had so lately left, and suggested a cup of tea which I had forgotten to offer to her predecessor.

She made a gay grimace. 'Tea? Oh, no—thanks. Perhaps we might go round presently to the Nouveau Luxe grill for a cocktail. But it's rather early yet; there's nobody there at this hour. And I want to talk to you about Stevie.'

She settled herself in Mrs. Glenn's corner, and as she sat there, slender and alert in her perfectly-cut dark coat and skirt, with her silver fox slung at the exact fashion plate angle, I felt the irony of these two women succeeding each other in the same seat to talk to me on the same subject. Mrs. Brown groped in her bag for a jade cigarette case, and lifted her smiling eyes to mine. 'Catherine's just been here, hasn't she? I passed her in a taxi at the corner,' she remarked lightly.

'She's been here; yes. I scolded her for not being in her own motor.' I rejoined with an attempt at the same tone.

Mrs. Brown laughed. 'I knew you would! But I'd taken the motor on purpose to prevent her going out. She has a very bad cold, as I told you; and the doctor has absolutely forbidden—'

'Then why didn't you let me go to see her?'

'Because the doctor forbids her to see visitors. I told you that too. Didn't you notice how hoarse she is?'

I felt my anger rising. 'I noticed how unhappy she is,' I said bluntly.

'Oh, unhappy—why is she unhappy? If I were in her place I should just lie back and enjoy life,' said Mrs. Brown, with a sort of cold impatience.

'She's unhappy about Stephen.'

Mrs. Brown looked at me quickly. 'She came here to tell you so, I suppose? Well—he *has* behaved badly.'

'Why did you let him?'

She laughed again, this time ironically. 'Let him? Ah, you believe in that legend? The legend that I do what I like with Stephen.' She bent her head to light another cigarette. 'He's behaved just as badly to me, my good man—and to Boy. And *we* don't go about complaining!'

'Why should you, when you see him every day?'

At this she bridled, with a flitting smile. 'Can I help it—if it's me he wants?'

'Yes, I believe you can,' I said resolutely.

'Oh, thanks! I suppose I ought to take that as a compliment.'

'Take it as you like. Why don't you make Stephen see his mother?'

'Dear Mr. Norcutt, if I had any influence over Stephen, do you suppose I'd let him quarrel with his bread and butter? To put it on utilitarian grounds, why should I?' She lifted her clear shallow eyes and looked straight into mine—and I found no answer. There was something impenetrable to me beneath that shallowness.

'But why did Stephen leave his mother?' I persisted.

She shrugged, and looked down at her rings, among which I fancied I saw a new one, a dark luminous stone in claws of platinum. She caught my glance. 'You're admiring my brown diamond? A beauty, isn't it? Dear Catherine gave it to me for Christmas. The angel! Do you suppose I wouldn't do anything to

spare her all this misery? I wish I could tell you why Stephen left her. Perhaps
. . . perhaps because she *is* such an angel . . . Young men—you understand?
She was always wrapping him up, lying awake to listen for his latchkey. . . .
Steve's rather a Bohemian; suddenly he struck—that's all I know.'

I saw at once that this contained a shred of truth wrapped round an impenetrable lie; and I saw also that to tell that lie had not been Mrs. Brown's main
object. She had come for a still deeper reason, and I could only wait for her to
reveal it.

She glanced up reproachfully. 'How hard you are on me—always! From the
very first day—don't I know? And never more than now. Don't you suppose I
can guess what you're thinking? You're accusing me of trying to prevent your
seeing Catherine; and in reality I came here to ask you to see her—to beg you
to—as soon as she's well enough. If you'd only trusted me, instead of persuad-
ing her to slip off on the sly and come here in this awful weather. . . . '

It was on the tip of my tongue to declare that I was guiltless of such perfidy;
but it occurred to me that my visitor might be trying to find out how Mrs.
Glenn had known I was in Paris, and I decided to say nothing.

'At any rate, if she's no worse I'm sure she could see you tomorrow. Why not
come and dine? I'll carry Boy off to a restaurant, and you and she can have a
cozy evening together, like old times. You'd like that, wouldn't you?' Mrs.
Brown's face was veiled with a retrospective emotion: I saw that, less acute than
Stephen, she still believed in a sentimental past between myself and Catherine
Glenn. 'She must have been one of the loveliest creatures that ever lived—was-
n't she? Even now no one can come up to her. You don't know how I wish she
liked me better; that she had more confidence in me. If she had, she'd know that
I love Stephen as much as she does—perhaps more. For so many years he was
mine, all mine! But it's all so difficult—at this moment, for instance. . . . ' She
paused, jerked her silver fox back into place, and gave me a prolonged view of
meditative lashes. At last she said: 'Perhaps you don't know that Steve's final folly
has been to refuse his allowance. He returned the last check to Catherine with a
dreadful letter.'

'Dreadful? How?'

'Telling her he was old enough to shift for himself—that he refused to sell
his independence any longer, perfect madness.'

'Atrocious cruelty—'

'Yes; that too. I told him so. But do you realize the result?' The lashes, suddenly lifted, gave me the full appeal of wide, transparent eyes. 'Steve's starving—
voluntarily starving himself. Or would be, if Boy and I hadn't scraped together
our last pennies. . . . '

'If independence is what he wants, why should he take your pennies when
he won't take his mother's?'

'Ah—there's the point. He will.' She looked down again, fretting her rings.
'Ill as he is, how could he live if he didn't take somebody's pennies? If I could sell
my brown diamond without Catherine's missing it I'd have done it long ago,

and you need never have known of all this. But she's so sensitive—and she notices everything. She literally spies on me. I'm at my wits' end. If you'd only help
me!'

'How in the world can I?'

'You're the only person who can. If you'd persuade her, as long as this queer
mood of Stephen's lasts, to draw his monthly check in my name, I'd see that he
gets it—and that he uses it. He would, you know, if he thought it came from
Boy and me.'

I looked at her quickly. 'That's why you want me to see her. To get her to
give you her son's allowance?'

Her lips parted as if she were about to return an irritated answer; but she
twisted them into a smile. 'If you like to describe it in that way—I can't help
your putting an unkind interpretation on whatever I do. I was prepared for that
when I came here.' She turned her bright inclement face on me. 'If you think I
enjoy humiliating myself! After all, it's not so much for Stephen that I ask it as
for his mother. Have you thought of that? If she knew that in his crazy pride he
was depriving himself of the most necessary things, wouldn't she do anything
on earth to prevent it? She's his *real* mother. . . . I'm nothing. . . . '

'You're everything, if he sees you and listens to you.'

She received this with the air of secret triumph that met every allusion to
her power over Stephen. Was she right, I wondered, in saying that she loved him
even more than his mother did? 'Everything?' she murmured deprecatingly. 'It's
you who are everything, who can help us all. What can I do?'

I pondered a moment, and then said, 'You can let me see Stephen.'

The color rushed up under her powder. 'Much good that would do—if I
could! But I'm afraid you'll find his door barricaded.'

'That's a pity,' I said coldly.

'It's very foolish of him,' she assented.

Our conversation had reached a deadlock, and I saw that she was distinctly
disappointed—perhaps even more than I was. I suspected that while I could afford to wait for a solution she could not.

'Of course, if Catherine is willing to sit by and see the boy starve'—she began.

'What else can she do? Shall we go over to the Nouveau Luxe bar and study
the problem from the cocktail angle?' I suggested.

Mrs. Brown's delicately penciled brows gathered over her transparent eyes.
'You're laughing at me—and at Steve. It's rather heartless of you, you know,' she
said, making a movement to rise from the deep armchair in which I had installed her. Her movements, as always, were quick and smooth; she got up and
sat down with the ease of youth. But her face startled me—it had suddenly
shrunk and withered, so that the glitter of cosmetics hung before it like a veil. A
pang of compunction shot through me. I felt that it *was* heartless to make her
look like that. I could no longer endure the part I was playing. 'I'll—see what I
can do to arrange things,' I stammered. 'If only she's not too servile,' I thought,

feeling that my next move hung on the way in which she received my reassurance.

She stood up with a quick smile. 'Ogre!' she just breathed, her lashes dancing. She was laughing at me under her breath—the one thing she could have done just then without offending me. 'Come; we *do* need refreshment, don't we?' She slipped her arm through mine as we crossed the lounge and emerged on the wet pavement.

X

The cozy evening with which Mrs. Brown had tempted me was not productive of much enlightenment. I found Catherine Glenn tired and pale, but happy at my coming, with a sort of furtive schoolgirl happiness which suggested the same secret apprehension as I had seen in Mrs. Brown's face when she found I would not help her to capture Stephen's allowance. I had already perceived my mistake in letting Mrs. Brown see this, and during our cocktail epilogue at the Nouveau Luxe had tried to restore her confidence; but her distrust had been aroused, and in spite of her recovered good humor I felt that I should not be allowed to see Stephen.

In this respect poor Mrs. Glenn could not help me. She could only repeat the lesson which had evidently been drilled into her. 'Why should I deny what's so evident—and so natural? When Stevie's ill and unhappy it's not to me he turns. During so many years he knew nothing of me, never even suspected my existence; and all the while *they* were there, watching over him, loving him, slaving for him. If he concealed his real feelings now it might be only on account of the—the financial inducements; and I like to think my boy's too proud for that. If you see him, you'll tell him so, won't you? You'll tell him that, unhappy as he's making me, mistaken as he is, I enter into his feelings as—as only his mother can.' She broke down, and hid her face from me.

When she regained her composure she rose and went over to the writing table. From the blotting book she drew an envelope. 'I've drawn this check in your name—it may be easier for you to get Stevie to accept a few bank notes than a check. You must try to persuade him—tell him his behavior is making the Browns just as unhappy as it is me, and that he has no right to be cruel to them, at any rate.' She lifted her head and looked into my eyes heroically.

I went home perplexed, and pondering on my next move; but not wholly to my surprise) the question was settled for me the following morning by a telephone call from Mrs. Brown. Her voice rang out cheerfully.

'Good news! I've had a talk with Steve's doctor—on the sly, of course. Steve would kill me if he knew! The doctor says he's really better; you can see him today if you'll promise to stay only a few minutes. Of course I must first persuade Steve himself, the silly boy. You can't think what a savage mood he's in. But I'm sure I can bring him round—he's so fond of you. Only before that I want to see you myself—' ('Of course,' I commented inwardly, feeling that here at last was the gist of the communication.) 'Can I come presently—before you go out? All right; I'll turn up in an hour.'

Within the hour she was at my hotel; but before her arrival I had decided on my course, and she on her side had probably guessed what it would be. Our first phrases however, were noncommittal. As we exchanged them I saw that Mrs. Brown's self-confidence was weakening, and this incited me to prolong the exchange. Stephen's doctor, she assured me, was most encouraging; one lung only was affected, and that slightly; his recovery now depended on careful nursing, good food, cheerful company—all the things of which, in his foolish obstinacy, he had chosen to deprive himself. She paused, expectant—

'And if Mrs. Glenn handed over his allowance to you, you could ensure his accepting what he's too obstinate to take from his mother?'

Under her carefully prepared complexion the blood rushed to her temples. 'I always knew you were Steve's best friend!' she looked away quickly, as if to hide the triumph in her eyes.

'Well, if I am, he's first got to recognize it by seeing me.'

'Of course—of course!' She corrected her impetuosity. 'I'll do all I can. . . .'

'That's a great deal, as we know,' Under their lowered lashes her eyes followed my movements as I turned my coat back to reach an inner pocket. She pressed her lips tight to control their twitching. 'There, then!' I said.

'Oh, you angel, you! I should never have dared to ask Catherine,' she stammered with a faint laugh as the bank notes passed from my hand to her bag.

'Mrs. Glenn understood—she always understands.'

'She understands when *you* ask,' Mrs. Brown insinuated, flashing her lifted gaze on mine. The sense of what was in the bag had already given her a draught of courage, and she added quickly: 'Of course I needn't warn you not to speak of all this to Steve. If he knew of our talk it would wreck everything.'

'I can see that,' I remarked, and she dropped her lids again, as though I had caught her in a blunder.

'Well, I must go; I'll tell him his best friend's coming. . . . I'll reason with him. . . .' she murmured, trying to disguise her embarrassment in emotion. I saw her to the door, and into Mrs. Glenn's motor, from the interior of which she called back: 'You know you're going to make Catherine as happy as I am.'

Stephen Glenn's new habitation was in a narrow and unsavory street, and the building itself contrasted mournfully with the quarters in which he had last received me. As I climbed the greasy stairs I felt as much perplexed as ever. I could not yet see why Stephen's quarrel with Mrs. Glenn should, even partially, have included the Browns, nor, if it had, why he should be willing to accept from their depleted purse the funds he was too proud to receive from his mother. It gave me a feeling of uneasy excitement to know that behind the door at which I stood the answer to these problems awaited me.

No one answered my knock, so I opened the door and went in. The studio was empty, but from the room beyond Stephen's voice called out irritably: 'Who is it?' and then, in answer to my name: 'Oh, Norcutt — come in.'

Stephen Glenn lay in bed, in a small room with a window opening on a dimly-lit inner courtyard. The room was bare and untidy, the bedclothes were tumbled, and he looked at me with the sick man's instinctive resentfulness at any intrusion on his lonely pain. 'Above all,' the look seemed to say, 'don't try to be kind.'

Seeing that moral pillow smoothing would be resented I sat down beside him without any comment on the dismalness of the scene, or on his own aspect, much as it disquietened me.

'Well, old man—' I began, wondering how to go on; but he cut short my hesitation. 'I've been wanting to see you for ever so long,' he said.

In my surprise I had nearly replied: 'That's not what I'd been told'—but, resolved to go warily, I rejoined with a sham gaiety. 'Well, here I am!'

Stephen gave me the remote look which the sick turn on those arch aliens, the healthy. 'Only,' he pursued, 'I was afraid if you did come you'd begin and lecture me; and I couldn't stand that—I can't stand anything. I'm *raw!*' he burst out.

'You might have known me better than to think I'd lecture you.'

'Oh, I don't know. Naturally the one person you care about in all this is— mother Kit.'

'Your mother,' I interposed.

He raised his eyebrows with the familiar ironic movement; then they drew together again over his sunken eyes. 'I wanted to wait till I was up to discussing things. I wanted to get this fever out of me.'

'You don't look feverish now.'

'No; they've brought it down. But I'm down with it. I'm very low,' he said, with a sort of chill impartiality, as though speaking of someone whose disabilities did not greatly move him. I replied that the best way for him to pull himself up again was to get out of his present quarters and let himself be nursed and looked after.

'Oh, don't argue!' he interrupted.

'Argue—?'

'You're going to tell me to go back to—to my mother. To let her fatten me up. Well, it's no use. I won't take another dollar from her—not one.'

I met this in silence, and after a moment perceived that my silence irritated him more than any attempt at argument. I did not want to irritate him, and I began: 'Then why don't you go off again with the Browns? There's nothing you can do that your mother won't understand—'

'And suffer from!' he interjected.

'Oh, as to suffering—she's seasoned.'

He bent his slow feverish stare on me. 'So am I.'

'Well, at any rate, you can spare her by going off at once into good air, and trying your level best to get well. You know as well as I do that nothing else matters to her. She'll be glad to have you go away with the Browns—I'll answer for that.'

He gave a short laugh, so harsh and disenchanted that I suddenly felt he was right: to laugh like that he must be suffering as much as his mother. I laid my hand on his thin wrist. 'Old man—'

He jerked away. 'No, no. Go away with the Browns? Id rather be dead. I'd rather hang on here till I *am* dead.'

The outburst was so unexpected that I sat in silent perplexity. Mrs. Brown had told the truth then, when she said he hated them too? Yet he saw them, he accepted their money. . . . The darkness deepened as I peered into it.

Stephen lay with half-closed lids, and I saw that whatever enlightenment he had to give would have to be forced from him. The perception made me take a sudden resolve.

'When one is physically down and out one *is* raw, as you say: one hates everybody. I know you don't really feel like that about the Browns; but if they've got on your nerves, and you want to go off by yourself, you might at least accept the money they're ready to give you—'

He raised himself on his elbow with an ironical stare. 'Money? They borrow money; they don't give it.'

'Ah—' I thought; but aloud I continued: 'They're prepared to give it now. Mrs. Brown tells me—'

He lifted his hand with a gesture that cut me short; then he leaned back, and drew a painful breath or two. Beads of moisture came out on his forehead. 'If she told you that, it means she's got more out of Kit. Or out of Kit through *you*—is that it?' he brought out roughly.

His clairvoyance frightened me almost as much as his physical distress— and the one seemed, somehow, a function of the other, as though the wearing down of his flesh had made other people's diaphanous to him, and he could see through it to their hearts. 'Stephen—' I began imploringly.

Again his lifted hand checked me. 'No, wait.' He breathed hard again and shut his eyes. Then he opened them and looked into mine. 'There's only one way out of this.'

'For you to be reasonable.'

'Call if that if you like. I've got to see mother Kit—and without their knowing it.'

My perplexity grew, and my agitation with it. Could it be that the end of the Browns was in sight? I tried to remember that my first business was to avoid communicating my agitation to Stephen. In a tone that I did my best to keep steady I said: 'Nothing could make your mother happier. You're all she lives for.'

'She'll have to find something else soon.'

'No, no. Only let her come, and she'll make you well. Mothers work miracles—'

His inscrutable gaze rested on mine. 'So they say. Only, you see, she's not my mother.'

He spoke so quietly, in such a low detached tone, that at first the words carried no meaning to me. If he had been excited I should have suspected fever, delirium, but voice and eyes were clear. 'Now you understand,' he added.

I sat beside him stupidly, speechless, unable to think. 'I don't' understand anything, I stammered. Such a possibility as his words suggested had never once occurred to me. Yet he wasn't delirious, he wasn't raving—it was I whose brain was reeling as if in fever.

'Well, I'm not the long-lost child. The Browns are not *her* Browns. It's all a lie and an imposture. We faked it up between us, Chrissy and I did—her simplicity made it so cruelly easy for us. Boy didn't have much to do with it; poor old Boy! He just sat back and took his share. . . . *Now* you do see,' he repeated, in the cold explanatory tone in which he might have set forth someone else's shortcomings.

My mind was still a blur while he poured out, in broken sentences, the details of the conspiracy—the sordid tale of a trio of society adventurers come to the end of their resources, and suddenly clutching at this unheard-of chance of rescue, affluence, peace. But gradually, as I listened, the glare of horror with which he was blinding me turned into a strangely clear and penetrating light, forcing its way into obscure crannies, elucidating the incomprehensible, picking out one by one the links that bound together his framents of face. I saw—but what I saw my gaze shrank from.

'Well,' I heard him say, between his difficult breaths, 'now do you begin to believe me?'

'I don't know. I can't tell. Why on earth,' I broke out, suddenly relieved at the idea, 'should you want to see your mother if this isn't all a ghastly invention?'

'To tell her what I've just told you—make a clean breast of it. Can't you see?'

'If that's the reason, I see you want to kill her—that's all.'

He grew paler under his paleness. 'Norcutt, I can't go on like this; I've got to tell her. I want to do it at once. I thought I could keep up the lie a little longer—let things go on drifting—but I can't. I held out because I wanted to get well first, and paint her picture—leave her that to be proud of, anyhow! Now that's all over, and there's nothing left but the naked shame. . . . ' He opened his eyes and fixed them again on mine. 'I want you to bring her here today—without *their* knowing it. You've got to manage it somehow. It'll be the first decent thing I've done in years.'

'It will be the most unpardonable,' I interrupted angrily. 'The time's past for trying to square your own conscience. What you've go to do now is to go on lying to her—you've got to get well, if only to go on lying to her!'

A thin smile flickered over his face. 'I can't get well.'

'That's as it may be. You can spare her, anyhow.'

'By letting things go on like this?' He lay for a long time silent; then his lips drew up in a queer grimace. 'It'll be horrible enough to be a sort of expiation —'

'It's the only one.'

'It's the worst.'

He sank back wearily. I saw that fatigue had silenced him, and wondered if I ought to steal away. My presence could not but be agitating; yet in his present state it seemed almost as dangerous to leave him as to stay. I saw a flask of brandy on the table, a glass beside it. I poured out some brandy and held it to his lips. He emptied the glass slowly, and as his head fell back I heard him say: 'Before I knew her I thought I could pull it off. . . . But, you see, her sweetness. . . . '

'If she heard you say that it would make up for everything.'

'Even for what I've just told you?'

'Even for that. For God's sake hold your tongue, and just let her come here and nurse you.'

He made no answer, but under his lids I saw a tear or two.

'Let her come — let her come,' I pleaded taking his dying hand in mine.

XI

Nature does not seem to care for dramatic climaxes. Instead of allowing Stephen to die at once, his secret on his lips, she laid on him the harsher task of living through weary weeks, and keeping back the truth till the end.

As a result of my visit, he consented, the next day, to be carried back in an ambulance to Mrs. Glenn's; and when I saw their meeting it seemed to me that ties of blood were frail compared to what drew those two together. After she had fallen on her knees at his bedside, and drawn his head to her breast, I was almost sure he would not speak; and he did not.

I was able to stay with Mrs. Glenn till Stephen died, then I had to hurry back to my post in Washington. When I took leave of her she told me that she was following on the next steamer with Stephen's body. She wished her son to have a New York funeral, a funeral like his father's, at which all their old friends could be present. 'Not like poor Phil's, you know —' and I recalled the importance she had attached to the presence of her husband's friends at his funeral. 'It's something to remember afterwards,' she said, with dry eyes. 'And it will be their only way of knowing my Stephen. . . . ' It was of course impossible to exclude Mr. and Mrs. Brown from these melancholy rites; and accordingly they sailed with her.

If Stephen had recovered she had meant, as I knew, to reopen her New York house; but now that was not to be thought of. She sold the house, and all it contained, and a few weeks later sailed once more for Paris — again with the Browns.

I had resolved after Stephen's death — when the first shock was over — to do what I could toward relieving her of the Browns' presence. Though I could not tell her the truth about them, I might perhaps help her to effect some transaction which would relieve her of their company. But I soon saw that this was out of the question; and the reason deepened my perplexity. It was simply that the Browns—or at least Mrs. Brown—had become Mrs. Glenn's chief consolation in her sorrow. The two women, so incessantly at odds while Stephen lived were now joined in a common desolation. It seemed like profaning Catherine Glenn's grief to compare Mrs. Brown's to it; yet, in the first weeks after Stephen's death, I had to admit that Mrs. Brown mourned him as genuinely, as inconsolably, as his supposed mother. Indeed, it would be nearer the truth to say that Mrs. Brown's grief was more hopeless and rebellious than the other's. After all, as Mrs. Glenn said, it was much worse for Chrissy. 'She had so little compared to me; and she gave as much, I suppose. Think what I had that she's never known; those precious months of waiting for him, when he was part of me when we were one body and one soul. And then, years afterwards, when I was searching for him, and knowing all the while I should find him; and after that, our perfect life together—our perfect understanding. All that—there's all that left to me! And what did she have? Why, when she shows me his little socks and shoes (she's kept them all so carefully) they're *my* baby's socks and shoes, not hers—and I know she's thinking of it when we cry over them. I see how that I've been unjust to her . . . and cruel . . . For he *did* love me best; and that ought to have made me kinder—'

Yes; I had to recognize that Mrs. Brown's grief was as genuine as her rival's, that she suffered more bleakly and bitterly. Every turn to the strange story had been improbable and incalculable, and this new freak of fate was the most unexpected. But since it brought a softening to my poor friend's affliction, and offered a new pretext for her self-devotion, I could only hold my tongue and be thankful that the Browns were at last serving some humaner purpose.

The next time I returned to Paris the strange trio were still together, and still living in Mrs. Glenn's apartment. Its walls were now hung with Stephen's paintings and sketches—among them many unfinished attempts at a portrait of Mrs. Glenn—and the one mother seemed as eager as the other to tell me that a well-known collector of modern art had been so struck by their quality that there was already some talk of a posthumous exhibition. Mrs. Brown triumphed peculiarly in the affair. It was she who had brought the collector to see the pictures, she who had always known that Stephen had genius; it was with the Browns' meager pennies that he had been able to carry on his studies at Julian's, long before Mrs. Glenn had appeared. 'Catherine doesn't pretend to know much about art. Do you, my dear? But, as I tell her, when you're a picture yourself you don't have to bother about other people's pictures. There—your hat's crooked again! Just let me straighten it, darling—' I saw Mrs. Glenn wince a little, as she had winced the day at Les Calanques when Mrs. Brown, with an arch side glance at me, had given a more artful twist to her friend's white hair.

It was evident that time, in drying up the source which had nourished the two women's sympathy, had revived their fundamental antagonism. It was equally clear, however, that Mrs. Brown was making every effort to keep on good terms with Mrs. Glenn. That substantial benefits thereby accrued to her I had no doubt; but at least she kept up in Catherine's mind the illusion of the tie between them.

Mrs. Brown had certainly sorrowed for Stephen as profoundly as a woman of her kind could sorrow; more profoundly, indeed, than I had thought possible. Even now, when she spoke of him, her metallic voice broke, her metallic mask softened. On the rare occasions when I found myself alone with her (and I had an idea she saw to it that they were rare), she spoke so tenderly of Stephen, so affectionately of Mrs. Glenn that I could only suppose she knew nothing of my last talk with the poor fellow. If she had, she would almost certainly have tried to ensure my silence; unless, as I sometimes imagined, a supreme art led her to feign unawareness. But, as always when I speculated on Mrs. Brown, I ended up against a blank wall.

The exhibition of Stephen's pictures took place, and caused (I learned from Mrs. Glenn) a little flutter in the inner circle of connoisseurs. Mrs. Glenn deluged me with newspaper rhapsodies which she doubtless never imagined had been bought. But presently, as a result of the show, a new difference arose between the two women. The pictures had been sufficiently remarked for several purchasers to present themselves, and their offers were so handsome that Mrs. Brown thought they should be accepted. After all, Stephen would have regarded the sale of the pictures as the best proof of his success, if they remained hidden away at Mrs. Glenn's she, who had the custody of his name, was obviously dooming it to obscurity. Nevertheless she persisted in refusing. If selling her darling's pictures was the price of glory, then she must cherish his genius in secret. Could anyone imagine that she would ever part with a single stroke of his brush? She was his mother; no one else had a voice in the matter. I divined that the struggle between herself and Mrs. Brown had been not only sharp but prolonged, and marked by a painful interchange of taunts. 'If it hadn't been for me,' Mrs. Brown argued, 'the pictures would never have existed'; and 'If it hadn't been for me,' the other retorted, 'my Stephen would never have existed.' It ended—as I had foreseen—in the adoptive parents accepting from Mrs. Glenn a sum equivalent to the value at which they estimated the pictures. The quarrel quieted down, and a few months later Mrs. Glenn was remorsefully accusing herself of having been too hard on Chrissy.

So the months passed. With their passage news came to me more rarely; but I gathered from Mrs. Glenn's infrequent letters that she had been ill, and from her almost illegible writing that her poor hands were stiffening with rheumatism. Finally, a year later, a letter announced that the doctors had warned her against spending her winters in the damp climate of Paris, and that the apartment had been disposed of, and its contents (including, of course, Stephen's pictures) transported to a villa at Nice. The Brown had found the villa and managed the translation—with their usual kindness. After that there was a long silence.

It was not until over two years later that I returned to Europe; and as my short holiday was taken in winter and I meant to spend it in Italy, I took steamer directly to Villefranche. I had not announced my visit to Mrs. Glenn, I was not sure till the last moment of being able to get off; but that was not the chief cause of my silence. Though relations between the incongruous trio seemed to have become harmonious, it was not without apprehension that I had seen Mrs. Glenn leave New York with the Browns. She was old, she was tired and stricken; how long would it be before she became a burden to her beneficiaries? This was what I wanted to find out without giving them time to prepare themselves or their companion for my visit. Mrs. Glenn had written that she wished very particularly to see me, and had begged me to let her know if there were a chance of my coming abroad; but though this increased my anxiety it strengthened my resolve to arrive unannounced, and I merely replied that she could count on seeing me as soon as I was able to get away.

Though some months had since gone by I was fairly sure of finding her still at Nice, for in the newspapers I had bought on landing I had lit on several allusions to Mr. and Mrs. Boydon Brown. Apparently the couple had an active press agent, for an attentive world was daily supplied with a minute description of Mrs. 'Boy' Brown's casino toilets, the value of the golf and pigeon-shooting cups offered to Mr. 'Boy' Brown to various fashionable sporting clubs, and the names of the titled guests whom they entertained at the local 'Lidos' and 'Jardins Fleuris.' I wondered how much of the chronicling of these events was costing Mrs. Glenn, but reminded myself that it was part of the price she had to pay for the hours of communion over Stephen's little socks. At any rate it proved that my old friend was still in the neighborhood; and the next day I set out to find her.

I waited till the afternoon, on the chance of her being alone at the hour when mundane affairs were most likely to engage the Browns; but when my taxi driver had brought me to the address I had given him I found a locked garden gate and a shuttered house. The sudden fear of some new calamity seized me. My first thought was that Mrs. Glenn must have died; yet if her death had occurred before my sailing I could hardly have failed to hear of it, and if it was more recent I must have seen it announced in the papers I had read since landing. Besides, if the Browns had so lately lost their benefactress they would hardly have played such a part in the social chronicles I had been studying. There was no particular reason why a change of address should portend tragedy; and when at length a reluctant portress appeared in answer to my ringing she said, yes, if it was the Americans I was after, I was right: they had moved away a week ago. Moved—and where to? She shrugged and declared she didn't know; but probably not far, she thought, with the old white-haired lady so ill and helpless.

'Ill and helpless—then why did they move?'

She shrugged again. 'When people don't pay their rent, they have to move don't they? When they don't even settle with the butcher and baker before they go, or with the laundress who was fool enough to do their washing—and it's I who speak to you, Monsieur!'

This was worse than I had imagined. I produced a bank note, and in return the victimized concierge admitted that she had secured the fugitive's new address—though they were naturally not anxious to have it known. As I had surmised, they had taken refuge within the kindly bounds of the principality of Monaco; and the taxi carried me to a small shabby hotel in one of the steep streets above the Casino. I could imagine nothing less in harmony with Catherine Glenn or her condition than to be ill and unhappy in such a place. My only consolation was that now perhaps there might be an end to the disastrous adventure. 'After all,' I thought, as I looked up at the cheerless front of the hotel, 'If the catastrophe has come the Browns can't have any reason for hanging on to her.'

A red-faced lady with a false front and false teeth emerged from the back office to receive me.

Madame Glenn—Madame Brown? Oh, yes; they were staying at the hotel—they were both upstairs now, she believed. Perhaps Monsieur was the gentleman that Madame Brown was expecting? She had left word that if he came he was to go up without being announced.

I was inspired to say that I was that gentleman; at which the landlady rejoined that she was sorry the lift was out of order, but that I would find the ladies at number 5 on the third floor. Before she had finished I was halfway up.

A few steps down an unventilated corridor brought me to number 5; but I did not have to knock for the door was ajar—perhaps in expectation of the other gentleman. I pushed it open, and entered a small plushy sitting room, with faded mimosa in ornate vases, newspapers and cigarette ends scattered on the dirty carpet, and a bronzed-over plaster Bayadère posturing before the mantelpiece mirror. If my first glance took such sharp note of these details it is because they seemed almost as much out of keeping with Catherine Glenn as the table laden with gin and bitters, empty cocktail glasses and disks of sodden lemon.

It was not the first time it had occurred to me that I was partly responsible for Mrs. Glenn's unhappy situation. The growing sense of that responsibility had been one of my reasons for trying to keep an eye on her, for wanting her to feel that in case of need she could count on me. But on the whole my conscience had not been oppressed. The impulse which had made me exact from Stephen the promise never to undeceive her had necessarily governed my own conduct. I had only to recall Catherine Glenn as I had first known her to feel sure that, after all, her life had been richer and deeper than if she had spent it, childless and purposeless, in the solemn upholstery of her New York house. I had had nothing to do with her starting on her strange quest; but I was certain that in what had followed she had so far found more happiness than sorrow.

But now? As I stood in that wretched tawdry room I wondered if I had not laid too heavy a burden on my conscience in keeping the truth from her. Suddenly I said to myself: 'The time has come—whatever happens I must get her away from these people.' But then I remembered how Stephen's death had drawn the two ill-sorted women together, and wondered if to destroy that tie would not now be the crowning cruelty.

I was still uneasily deliberating when I heard a voice behind the door opposite the one by which I had entered. The room beyond must have been darkened, for I had not noticed before that this door was also partly open. 'Well,
have you had your nap?' a woman's voice said irritably. 'Is there something you
want before I go out? I told you that the man who's going to arrange for the loan
is coming for me. He'll be here in a minute.' The voice was Mrs. Brown's, but so
sharpened and altered that at first I had not known it. 'This is how she speaks
when she thinks there's no one listening,' I thought.

I caught an indistinct murmur in reply; then the rattle of drawnback curtain rings; then Mrs. Brown continuing: 'Well, you may as well sign the letter
now. Here it is—you've only got to write your name. . . . Your glasses? I
don't know where your glasses are—you're always dropping your things about.
I'm sorry, I can't keep a maid to wait on you—but there's nothing in this letter
you need be afraid of. I've told you before that it's only a formality. Boy's told
you so too, hasn't he? I don't suppose you mean to suggest that we're trying to
do you out of your money, do you? We've got to have enough to keep going.
Here, let me hold your hand while you sign. My hand's shaky too . . . it's
all this beastly worry. . . . Don't you imagine you're the only person who's
had a bad time of it. . . . Why, what's the matter? Why are you pushing me
away—?'

Till now I had stood motionless, unabashed by the fact that I was eaves-
dropping. I was ready enough to stoop to that if there was no other way of getting at the truth. But as the question: 'Why are you pushing me away?' I knocked
hurriedly at the door of the inner room.

There was a silence after my knock. 'There he is! You'll have to sign now,' I
heard Mrs. Brown exclaim; and I opened the door and went in. The room was a
bedroom; like the other, it was untidy and shabby. I noticed a stack of canvases,
framed and unframed, piled up against the wall. In an armchair near the window Mrs. Glenn was seated. She was wrapped in some sort of dark dressing
gown, and a lace cap covered her white hair. The face that looked out from it
had still the same carven beauty; but its texture had dwindled from marble to
worn ivory. Her body too had shrunk, so that, low in her chair, under her loose
garments, she seemed to have turned into a little broken doll. Mrs. Brown on
the contrary, perhaps by contrast, appeared large and almost towering. At first
glance I was more startled by the change in her appearance than in Mrs. Glenn's.
The latter had merely followed more quickly than I had hoped she would, the
natural decline of the years; whereas Mrs. Brown seemed like another woman. It
was not only that she had grown stout and heavy, or that her complexion had
coarsened so noticeably under the skillful make-up. In spite of her good clothes
and studied coiffure there was something haphazard and untidy in her appearance. Her hat, I noticed, had slipped a little sideways on her smartly waved head,
her bright shallow eyes looked blurred and red, and she held herself with a sort
of vacillating erectness. Gradually the incredible fact was borne in on me; Mrs.
Brown had been drinking.

'Why, where on earth—?' she broke out, bewildered, as my identity dawned on her. She put up a hand to straighten her hat, and in doing so dragged it over too far on the other side.

'I beg your pardon. I was told to come to number 5, and as there was no one in the sitting room I knocked on this door.'

'Oh, you knocked? I didn't hear you knock,' said Mrs. Brown suspiciously; but I had no ears for her, for my old friend had also recognized me, and was holding out her trembling hands. 'I knew you'd come—I said you'd come!' she cried out to me.

Mrs. Brown laughed. 'Well, you've said he would often enough. But it's taken some time for it to come true.'

'I knew you'd come,' Mrs. Glenn repeated, and I felt her hand press trembling over my hair as I stooped to kiss her.

'Lovers' meeting!' Mrs. Brown tossed at us with an unsteady gaiety; then she leaned against the door, and stood looking on ironically. 'You didn't expect to find us in this palatial abode, did you?'

'No. I went to the villa first.'

Mrs. Glenn's eyes dwelt on me softly. I sat down beside her, and she put her hand in mine. Her withered fingers trembled incessantly.

'Perhaps,' Mrs. Brown went on, 'if you'd come sooner you might have arranged things so that we could have stayed there. I'm powerless—I can't do anything with her. The fact that for years I looked after the child she deserted weighs nothing with her. She doesn't seem to think she owes us anything.'

Mrs. Glenn listened in silence, without looking at her accuser. She kept her large sunken eyes fixed on mine. 'There's no money left,' she said when the other ended.

'No money! No money! That's always the tune nowadays. There was always plenty of money for her precious—money for all his whims and fancies, for journeys, for motors, for doctors, for—well, what's the use of going on? But not that there's nobody left but Boy and me, who slaved for her darling for years, who spent our last penny on him when his mother'd forgotten his existence—now there's nothing left! Now she can't afford anything; now she won't even pay her own bills; now she'd sooner starve herself to death than let us have what she owes us. . . .'

'My dear—my dear.' Mrs. Glenn murmured, her eyes still on mine.

'Oh, don't "my dear" me,' Mrs. Brown retorted passionately. 'What you mean is: "How can you talk like that before him?" I suppose you think I wish he hadn't come. Well, you never were more mistaken, I'm glad he's here; I'm glad he's found out where you're living, and how you're living. Only this time I mean him to hear our side of the story instead of only yours.'

Mrs. Glenn pressed my hand in her twitching fingers. 'She wants me to sign a paper. I don't understand.'

'You don't understand? Didn't Boy explain it to you? You said you understood then.' Mrs. Brown turned to me with a shrug. 'These whims and capers . . . all I want is money enough to pay the bills. . . . so that we're not turned out of this hole too. . . .'

'There is no money,' Mrs. Glenn softly reiterated.

My heart stood still. The scene must at all costs be ended, yet I could think of no way to silencing the angry woman. At length I said: 'If you'll leave me for a little while with Mrs. Glenn perhaps she'll be able to tell me—'

'How's she to tell you what she says she doesn't understand herself? If I leave her with you all she'll tell you is lies about us—I found that out long ago.' Mrs. Brown took a few steps in my direction, and then, catching at the window curtain, looked at me with a foolish laugh. 'Not that I'm pining for her society. I have a good deal of it in the long run. But you'll excuse me for saying that, as far as this matter is concerned, it's entirely between Mrs. Glenn and me.'

I tightened my hold on Mrs. Glenn's hand, and sat looking at Mrs. Brown in the hope that a silent exchange of glances might lead farther than the vain bandying of arguments. For a moment she seemed dominated; I began to think she had read in my eyes the warning I had tried to put there. If there was any money left I might be able to get it from Catherine after her own attempts had failed; that was what I was trying to remind her of, and what she understood my looks were saying. Once before I had done the trick; supposing she were to trust me to try again? I saw that she wavered; but her brain was not alert, as it had been on that other occasion. She continued to stare at me through a blur of drink and anger; I could see her thoughts clutching uneasily at my suggestion and then losing their hold on it. 'Oh, we all know you think you're God Almighty!' she broke out with a contemptuous toss.

'I think I could help you if I could have a quiet talk with Mrs. Glenn.'

'Well, you can have your quiet talk.' She looked about her, and pulling up a chair plumped down into it heavily. 'I'd love to hear what you've got to say to each other,' she declared.

Mrs. Glenn's hand began to shake again. She turned her head toward Mrs. Brown. 'My dear, I should like to see my friend alone.'

'I should like! I should like! I daresay you would. It's always been what *you'd* like—but now it's going to be what I choose. And I choose to assist at the conversation between Mrs. Glenn and Mr. Norcutt, instead of letting them quietly say horrors about me behind my back.'

'Oh, Chrissy—' my old friend murmured; then she turned to me and said, 'You'd better come back another day.'

Mrs. Brown looked at me with a sort of feeble cunning. 'Oh, you needn't send him away, I've told you my friend's coming—he'll be here in a minute. If you'll sign that letter I'll take it to the bank with him, and Mr. Norcutt can stay here and tell you all the news. Now wouldn't that be nice and cozy?' she concluded coaxingly.

Looking into Mrs. Glenn's pale frightened face I was on the point of saying: 'Well, sign it then, whatever it is—anything to get her to go.' But Mrs. Glenn straightened her drooping shoulders and repeated softly: 'I can't sign it.'

A flush rose to Mrs. Brown's forehead. 'You can't? That's final, is it?' She turned to me. 'It's all money she owed us, mind you—money we've advanced to her—in one way or another. Every penny of it. And now she sits there and says she won't pay us!'

Mrs. Glenn, twisting her fingers, into mine, gave a barely audible laugh. 'Now he's here I'm safe,' she said.

The crimson of Mrs. Brown's face darkened to purple. Her lower lip trembled and I saw she was struggling for words that her dimmed brain could not supply. 'God Almighty—you think he's God Almighty!' She evidently felt the inadequacy of this, for she stood up suddenly, and coming close to Mrs. Glenn's armchair, stood looking down on her in impotent anger. 'Well, I'll show you—' She turned to me, moved by another impulse. 'You know well enough you could make her sign if you chose to.'

My eyes and Mrs. Brown's met again. Hers were saying: 'It's your last chance—it's *her* last chance. I warn you—' and mine replying: 'Nonsense, you can't frighten us, you can't even frighten *her* while I'm here. And if she doesn't want to sign you shan't force her to. I have something up my sleeve that would shut you up in five seconds if you knew.'

She kept her thick stare on mine till I felt as if my silent signal must have penetrated it. But she said nothing, and at last I exclaimed: 'You know well enough the risk you're running—'

Perhaps I had better not have spoken. But that dumb dialogue was getting on my nerves. If she wouldn't see, it was time to make her—

Ah, she saw now—she saw fast enough! My words seemed to have cleared the last fumes from her brain. She gave me back my look with one almost as steady; then she laughed.

'The risk I'm running? Oh, that's it, is it? That's the pull you thought you had over me? Well I'm glad you know—and I'm glad to tell you that I've known all along that you knew. I'm sick and tired of all the humbug—if she won't sign I'm going to tell her everything myself. So now the cards are on the table, and you can take your choice. It's up to you. The risk's on your side now!'

The unaccountable woman—drunkenly incoherent a moment ago, and now hitting the nail on the head with such fiendish precision! I sat silent, meditating her hideous challenge without knowing how to meet it. And then I became aware that a quiver had passed over Mrs. Glenn's face, which had become smaller and more ivory-yellow than before. She leaned towards me as if Mrs. Brown, who stood close above us, could not hear what we were saying.

'What is it she means to tell me? I don't care unless it's something bad about Stevie. And it couldn't be that, could it? How does she know? No one can come between a son and his mother.'

Mrs. Brown gave one of her sudden laughs. 'A son and his mother? I daresay not! Only I'm just about fed up with having you think you're his mother.'

It was the one thing I had not foreseen—that she would possess herself of my threat and turn it against me. The risk was too deadly; and so no doubt she would have felt if she had been in a state to measure it. She was not; and there lay the peril.

Mrs. Glenn sat quite still after the other's outcry, and I hoped it had blown past her like some mere rag of rhetoric. Then I saw that the meaning of the words had reached her, but without carrying conviction. She glanced at me with the flicker of a smile. 'Now she says I'm not his mother—!' It's her last round of ammunition; but don't be afraid—it won't make me sign, the smile seemed to whisper to me.

Mrs. Brown caught the unspoken whisper, and her exasperation rushed to meet it. 'You don't believe me? I knew you wouldn't! Well, ask your friend here; ask Mr. Norcutt; you always believe everything he says. He's known the truth for ever so long—long before Stephen died he knew he wasn't your son.'

I jumped up, as if to put myself between my friends and some bodily harm; but she held fast to my hand with her clinging twitching fingers. 'As if she knew what it is to have a son! All those long months when he's one with you. . . . *Mothers* know,' she said.

'Mothers, yes! I don't say you didn't have a son and desert him. I say that son wasn't Stephen. Don't you suppose I know? Sometimes I've wanted to laugh in your face at the way you went on about him . . . Sometimes I used to have to rush out of the room, just to have my laugh out by myself. . . . '

Mrs. Brown stopped with a gasp, as if the fury of the outburst had shaken her back to soberness, and she saw for the first time what she had done. Mrs. Glenn sat with her head bowed; her hand had grown cold in mine. I looked at Mrs. Brown and said: 'Now won't you leave us? I suppose there's nothing left to say.'

She blinked at me through her heavy lids; I saw she was wavering. But at the same moment Mrs. Glenn's clutch tightened; she drew me down to her, and looked at me out of her deep eyes. 'What does she mean when she says you knew about Stevie?'

I pressed her hand without answering. All my mind was concentrated on the effort of silencing my antagonist and getting her out of the room. Mrs. Brown leaned in the window frame and looked down on us. I could see that she was dismayed at what she had said, and yet exultant; and my business was to work on the dismay before the exultation mastered it. But Mrs. Glenn still held me down; her eyes seemed to be forcing their gaze into me. 'Is it true?' she asked almost inaudibly.

'True?' Mrs. Brown burst out. 'Ask him to swear to you it's not true—see what he looks like then! He was in the conspiracy, you old simpleton.'

Mrs. Glenn's head straightened itself again on her weak neck: her face wore a singular majesty. 'You were my friend—' she appealed to me.

'I've always been your friend.'

'Then I don't have to believe her.'

Mrs. Brown seemed to have been gathering herself up for a last onslaught. She saw that I was afraid to try to force her from the room, and the discovery gave her a sense of hazy triumph, as if all that was left to her was to defy me. 'Tell her I'm lying—why don't you tell her I'm lying?' she taunted me.

I knelt down by my old friend and put my arm about her. 'Will you come away with me now—at once? I'll take you wherever you want to go. . . . I'll look after you. . . . I'll always look after you.'

Mrs. Glenn's eyes grew wider. She seemed to weigh my words till their sense penetrated her; then she said, in the same low voice: 'It is true, then?'

'Come away with me; come away with me,' I repeated.

I felt her trying to rise; but her feet failed under her and she sank back. 'Yes, take me away from her,' she said.

Mrs. Brown laughed. 'Oh, that's it, is it? "Come away from that bad woman, and I'll explain everything, and make it all right" . . . Why don't you adopt *him* instead of Steve? I dare say that's what he's been after all the time. That's the reason he was so determined we shouldn't have your money. . . . ' She drew back, and pointed to the door. 'You can go with him—who's to prevent you? I couldn't if I wanted to. I see now it's for him, and he'll tell you the whole story. . . . ' A strange secretive smile stole over her face. 'All except one bit . . . there's one bit he doesn't know; but *you're* going to know it now.'

She stepped nearer, and I held up my hand; but she hurried on, her eyes on Mrs. Glenn. 'What he doesn't know is why we fixed the thing up. Steve wasn't my adopted son any more than he was your real one. Adopted son, indeed! How old do you suppose I am? He was my lover. There—do you understand? My lover! That's why we faked up that ridiculous adoption story, and all the rest of it—because he was desperately ill, and down and out, and we hadn't a penny, the three of us, and I had to have money for him, and didn't care how I got it, didn't care for anything on earth but seeing him well again, and happy.' She stopped and drew a panting breath. 'There—I'd rather have told you that than have your money. I'd rather you should know what Steve was to me than think any longer that you owned him. . . . '

I was still kneeling by Mrs. Glenn, my arm about her. Once I felt her heart give a great shake; then it seemed to stop altogether. Her eyes were no longer turned to me, but fixed in a wide stare on Mrs. Brown. A tremor convulsed her face; then, to my amazement, it was smoothed into an expression of childish serenity, and a faint smile, half playful, half ironic, stole over it.

She raised her hand and pointed tremulously to the other's disordered headgear. 'My dear—your hat's crooked,' she said.

For a moment, I was bewildered; then I saw that, very gently, she was at last returning the taunt that Mrs. Brown had so often addressed to her. The shot fired, she leaned back against me with the satisfied sigh of a child; and immediately I understood that Mrs. Brown's blow had gone wide. A pitiful fate had darkened Catherine Glenn's intelligence at the exact moment when to see clearly would have been the final anguish.

Mrs. Brown understood too. She stood looking at us doubtfully; then she said in a tone of feeble defiance: 'Well, I had to tell her.'

She turned and went out of the room, and I continued to kneel by Mrs. Glenn. Her eyes had gradually clouded, and I doubted if she still knew me; but her lips nursed their soft smile, and I saw that she must have been waiting for years to launch that little shaft at her enemy.

Mary Austin 1868–1934

After writing more than thirty books and hundreds of articles, Mary Austin is most remembered for her loving depictions of the American West, especially the desert and folk arts of the Native American and Latino populations. Born and raised in Carlinville, Illinois, Austin first encountered the West when, after her graduation from Blackburn College at age twenty, she moved to California with her family. Settling in the Owens Valley, northwest of Bakersfield, the young Mary Hunter began to publish her first short stories and, in 1891, married Stafford Wallace Austin. The unique life she and Stafford led in a series of small Mojave Desert towns inspired Austin to pen her most famous work, *The Land of Little Rain* (1903). *The Basket Woman* (1905), a realistic collection of short stories focusing on American Indian legends, followed. Later novels, such as *A Woman of Genius* (1912), and her 1932 autobiography, *Earth Horizon*, explored the relationship between gender and creativity. Besides her talents as a writer and journalist, Austin is remembered as an ecologist, ethnographer, feminist, and mystic.

THE BASKET WOMAN

The homesteader's cabin stood in a moon-shaped hollow between the hills and the high mesa; and the land before it stretched away golden and dusky green, and was lost in a blue haze about where the river settlements began. The hills had a flowing outline and melted softly into each other and higher hills behind, until the range broke in a ragged crest of thin peaks white with snow. A clean, wide sky bent over that country, and the air that moved in it was warm and sweet.

The homesteader's son had run out on the trail that led toward the spring, with half a mind to go to it, but ran back again when he saw the Basket Woman coming. He was afraid of her, and ashamed because he was afraid, so he did not tell his mother that he had changed his mind.

"There is the mahala coming for the wash," said his mother; "now you will have company at the spring." But Alan only held tighter to a fold of her dress. This was the third time the Indian woman had come to wash for the homesteader's wife; and, though she was slow and quiet and had a pleasant smile, Alan was still afraid of her. All that he had heard of Indians before coming to this country was very frightful, and he did not understand yet that it was not so. Beyond a certain point of hills on clear days he could see smoke rising from the campoodie, and though he knew nothing but his dreams of what went on there, he would not so much as play in that direction.

The Basket Woman was the only Indian that he had seen. She would come walking across the mesa with a great cone-shaped carrier basket heaped with brushwood on her shoulders, stooping under it and easing the weight by a buckskin band about her forehead. Sometimes it would be a smaller basket carried in the same fashion, and she would be filling it with bulbs of wild hyacinth or taboose; often she carried a bottle-necked water basket to and from the spring, and always wore a bowl-shaped basket on her head for a hat. Her long hair hung down from under it, and her black eyes glittered beadily below the rim. Alan had a fancy that any moment she might pick him up with a quick toss as if he had been a bit of brushwood, and drop him over her shoulder into the great carrier, and walk away across the mesa with him. So when he saw her that morning coming down the trail from the spring, he hung close by his mother's skirts.

"You must not be afraid of her, Alan," said his mother; "she is very kind, and no doubt has had a boy of her own."

The Basket Woman showed them her white, even teeth in a smile. "This one very pretty boy," she said; but Alan had made up his mind not to trust her. He was thinking of what the teamster had said when he had driven them up from the railroad station with their belongings the day they came to their new home and found the Basket Woman spying curiously in at the cabin windows.

"You wanter watch out how you behaves yourself, sonny," said the teamster, wagging a solemn jaw, "she's likely to pack you away in that basket o' her'n one of these days." And Alan had watched out very carefully indeed.

It was not a great while after they came to the foothill claim that the homesteader went over to the campoodie to get an Indian to help at fence building, and Alan went with him, holding fast by his father's hand. They found the Indians living in low, foul huts; their clothes were also dirty, and they sat about on the ground, fat and good-natured. The dogs and children lay sleeping in the sun. It was all very disappointing.

"Will they not hurt us, father?" Alan had said at starting.

"Oh, no, my boy; you must not get any such notion as that," said the homesteader; "Indians are not at all now what they were once."

Alan thought of this as he looked at the campoodie, and pulled at his father's hand.

"I do not like Indians the way they are now," he said; and immediately saw that he had made a mistake, for he was standing directly in front of the Basket

Woman's hut, and as she suddenly put her head out of the door he thought by the look of her mysterious, bright eyes that she had understood. He did not venture to say anything more, and all the way home kept looking back toward the campoodie to see if anything came of it.

"Why do you not eat your supper?" said his mother. "I am afraid the long walk in the hot sun was too much for you." Allan dared not say anything to her of what troubled him, though perhaps it would have been better if he had, for that night the Basket Woman came for him.

She did not pick him up and toss him over her shoulder as he expected; but let down the basket, and he stepped into it of his own accord. Alan was surprised to find that he was not so much afraid of her after all.

"What will you do with me?" he said.

"I will show you Indians as they used to be," said she.

Alan could feel the play of her strong shoulders as they went out across the lower mesa and began to climb the hills.

"Where do you go?" said the boy.

"To Pahrump, the valley of Corn Water. It was there my people were happiest in old days."

They went on between the oaks, and smelled the musky sweet smell of the wild grapevines along the water borders. The sagebrush began to fall from the slopes, and buckthorn to grow up tall and thicker; the wind brought them a long sigh from the lowest pines. They came up with the silver firs and passed them, passed the drooping spruces, the wet meadows, and the wood of thimble-cone pines. The air under them had an earthy smell. Presently they came out upon a cleared space very high up where the rocks were sharp and steep.

"Why are there no trees here?" asked Alan.

"I will tell you about that," said the Basket Woman. "In the old flood time, and that is longer ago than is worth counting, the water came up and covered the land, all but the high tops of mountains. Here then the Indians fled and lived, and with them the animals that escaped from the flood. There were trees growing then over all the high places, but because the waters were long on the earth the Indians were obliged to cut them down for firewood. Also they killed all the large animals for food, but the small ones hid in the rocks. After that the waters went down; trees and grass began to grow over all the earth, but never any more on the tops of high mountains. They had all been burned off. You can see that it is so."

From the top of the mountain Alan could see all the hills on the other side shouldering and peering down toward the happy valley of Corn Water.

"Here," said the Basket Woman, "my people came of old time in the growing season of the year; they planted corn, and the streams came down from the hills and watered it. Now we, too, will go down."

They went by a winding trail, steep and stony. The pines stood up around and locked them closely in.

"I see smoke arising," said Alan, "blue smoke above the pines."

"It is the smoke of their hearth fires," said the Basket Woman, and they went down and down.

"I hear a sound of singing," said the boy.

"It is the women singing and grinding at the quern," she said, and her feet went faster.

"I hear laughter," he said again, "it mixes with the running of the water."

"It is the maidens washing their knee-long hair. They kneel by the water and stoop down, they dip in the running water and shake out bright drops in the sun."

"There is a pleasant smell," said Alan.

"It is pine nuts roasting in the cones," said the Basket Woman; "so it was of old time."

They came out of the cleft of the hills in a pleasant place by singing water. "There you will see the rows of wickiups," said the Basket Woman, "with the doors all opening eastward to the sun. Let us sit here and see what we shall see."

The women sat by the wickiups weaving baskets of willow and stems of fern. They made patterns of bright feathers and strung wampum about the rims. Some sewed with sinew and needles of cactus thorn on deerskin white and fine; others winnowed the corn. They stood up tossing it in baskets like grains of gold, and the wind carried away the chaff. All this time the young girls were laughing as they dried their hair in the sun. They bound it with flowers and gay strings of beads, and made their cheeks bright with red earth. The children romped and shouted about the camp, and ran bare-legged in the stream.

"Do they do nothing but play?" said Alan.

"You shall see," said the Basket Woman.

Away up the mountain sounded a faint halloo. In a moment all the camp was bustle and delight. The children clapped their hands; they left off playing and began to drag up brushwood for the fires. The women put away their weaving and brought out the cooking pots; they heard the men returning from the hunt. The young men brought deer upon their shoulders; one had grouse and one held up a great basket of trout. The women made the meat ready for cooking. Some of them took meal and made cakes for baking in the ashes. The men rested in the glow of the fires, feathering arrows and restringing their bows.

"That is well," said the Basket Woman, "to make ready for to-morrow's meat before to-day's is eaten."

"How happy they are!" said the boy.

"They will be happier when they have eaten," said she.

After supper the Indians gathered together for singing and dancing. The old men told tales one after the other, and the children thought each one was the best. Between the tales the Indians all sang together, or one sang a new song that he had made. There was one of them who did better than all. He had streaked his body with colored earth and had a band of eagle feathers in his hair. In his hand was a rattle of wild sheep's horn and small stones; he kept time with it as he leapt and sang in the light of the fire. He sang of old wars, sang of the deer that was killed, sang of the dove and the young grass that grew on the mountain; and the people were well pleased, for when the heart is in the singing it does not matter much what the song is about. The men beat their hands together to keep time to his dancing, and the earth under his feet was stamped to a fine dust.

"He is one that has found the wolf's song," said the Basket Woman.

"What is that?" asked Alan.

"It is an old tale of my people," said she. "Once there was a man who could not make any songs, so he got no praise from the tribe, and it troubled him much. Then, as he was gathering taboose by the river, a wolf went by, and the wolf said to him, 'What will you have me to give you for your taboose?' Then said the man, 'I will have you to give me a song.'

"'That will I gladly,' said the wolf. So the wolf taught him, and that night he sang the wolf's song in the presence of all the people, and it made their hearts to burn within them. Then the man fell down as if he were dead, for the pure joy of singing, and when deep sleep was upon him the wolf came in the night and stole his song away. Neither the man nor any one who had heard it remembered it any more. So we say when a man sings as no other sang before him, 'He has the wolf's song.' It is a good saying. Now we must go, for the children are all asleep by their mothers, and the day comes soon," said the Basket Woman.

"Shall we come again?" said Alan. "And will it all be as it is now?"

"My people come often to the valley of Corn Water," said she, "but it is never as it is now except in dreams. Now we must go quickly." Far up the trail they saw a grayness in the eastern sky where the day was about to come in.

"Hark," said the Basket Woman, "they will sing together the coyote song. It is so that they sing it when the coyote goes home from his hunting, and the morning is near.

"The coyote cries . . .
He cries at daybreak . . .
He cries . . .
The coyote cries" . . .

sang the Basket Woman, but all the spaces in between the words were filled with long howls,—weird, wicked noises that seemed to hunt and double in a half-human throat. It made the hair on Alan's neck stand up, and cold shivers creep along his back. He began to shake, for the wild howls drew near and louder, and he felt the bed under him tremble with his trembling.

"Mother, mother," he cried, "what is that?"

"It is only the coyotes," said she; "they always howl about this time of night. It is nothing; go to sleep again."

"But I am afraid."

"They cannot hurt you," said his mother; "it is only the little gray beasts that you see trotting about the mesa of afternoons; hear them now."

"I am afraid," said Alan.

"Then you must come in my bed," said she; and in a few minutes he was fast asleep again. . . .

THE STREAM THAT RAN AWAY

In a short and shallow cañon on the front of Oppapago running eastward toward the sun, one may find a clear brown stream called the creek of Piñon Pines. That is not because it is unusual to find piñon trees in Oppapago, but because there are so few of them in the cañon of the stream. There are all sorts higher up on the slopes,—long-leaved yellow pines, thimble cones, tamarack, silver fir and Douglas spruce; but here there is only a group of the low-heading, gray nut pines which the earliest inhabitants of that country called piñons.

The cañon of Piñon Pines has a pleasant outlook and lies open to the sun, but there is not much other cause for the forest rangers to remember it. At the upper end there is no more room by the stream border than will serve for a cattle trail; willows grow in it, choking the path of the water; there are brown birches here and ropes of white clematis tangled over thickets of brier rose. Low down the ravine broadens out to inclose a meadow the width of a lark's flight, blossomy and wet and good. Here the stream ran once in a maze of soddy banks and watered all the ground, and afterward ran out at the cañon's mouth across the mesa in a wash of bone-white boulders as far as it could. That was not very far, for it was a slender stream. It had its source really on the high crests and hollows of Oppapago, in the snow banks that melted and seeped downward through the rocks; but the stream did not know any more of that than you know of what happened to you before you were born, and could give no account of itself except that it crept out from under a great heap of rubble far up in the cañon of the Piñon Pines. And because it had no pools in it deep enough for trout, and no trees on its borders but gray nut pines; because, try as it might it could never get across the mesa to the town, the stream had fully made up its mind to run away.

"Pray what good will that do you?" said the pines. "If you get to the town, they will turn you into an irrigating ditch and set you to watering crops."

"As to that," said the stream, "if I once get started I will not stop at the town." Then it would fret between its banks until the spangled frills of the mimulus were all tattered with its spray. Often at the end of the summer it was worn quite thin and small with running, and not able to do more than reach the meadow.

"But some day," it whispered to the stones, "I shall run quite away."

If the stream had been inclined for it, there was no lack of good company on its own borders. Birds nested in the willows, rabbits came to drink; one summer a bobcat made its lair up the bank opposite the brown birches, and often deer fed in the meadow. Then there was a promise of better things. In the spring of one year two old men came up into the cañon of Piñon Pines. They had been miners and partners together for many years, they had grown rich and grown poor, and had seen many hard places and strange times. It was a day when the creek ran clear and the south wind smelled of the earth. Wild bees began to whine among the willows, and the meadow bloomed over with poppy-breasted larks. Then said one of the fold men, "Here is good meadow and water enough; let us build a house and grow trees. We are too old to dig in the mines."

"Let us set about it," said the other; for that is the way with two who have been a long time together: what one thinks of, the other is for doing. So they brought their possessions and made a beginning that day, for they felt the spring come on warmly in their blood; they wished to dig in the earth and handle it.

These two men who, in the mining camps where they were known, were called "Shorty" and "Long Tom," and had almost forgotten that they had other names, built a house by the water border and planted trees. Shorty was all for an orchard, but Long Tom preferred vegetables. So they did each what he liked, and were never so happy as when walking in the garden in the cool of the day, touching the growing things as they walked and praising each other's work.

"This will make a good home for our old age," said Long Tom, "and when we die we can be buried here."

"Under the piñon pines," said Shorty. "I have marked out a place."

So they were very happy for three years. By this time the stream had become so interested it had almost forgotten about running away. But every year it noted that a larger bit of the meadow was turned under and planted, and more and more the men made dams and ditches to govern its running.

"In fact," said the stream, "I am being made into an irrigating ditch before I have had my fling in the world. I really must make a start."

That very winter by the help of a great storm it went roaring down the meadow over the mesa, and so clean away, with only a track of muddy sand to show the way it had gone. All the winter, however, Shorty and Long Tom brought water for drinking from a spring, and looked for the stream to come back. In the spring they hoped still, for that was the season they looked for the orchard to bear. But no fruit set on the trees, and the seeds Long Tom planted shriveled in the earth. So by the end of the summer, when they understood that the water would not come back at all, they went sadly away.

Now what happened to the creek of Piñon Pines is not very well known to any one, for the stream is not very clear on that point, except that it did not have a happy time. It went out in the world on the wings of the storm and was very much tossed about and mixed up with other waters, lost and bewildered. Everywhere it saw water at work, turning mills, watering fields, carrying trade, falling as hail, rain, and snow, and at the last, after many journeys, found itself creeping out from under the rocks of Oppapago in the cañon of Piñon Pines. Immediately the little stream knew itself and recalled clearly all that had happened to it before.

"After all, home is best," said the stream, and ran about in its choked channels looking for old friends. The willows were there, but grown shabby and dying at the top; the birches were quite dead, but stood still in their places; and there was only rubbish where the white clematis had been. Even the rabbits had gone away. The little stream ran whimpering in the meadow, fumbling at the ruined ditches to comfort the fruit-trees which were not quite dead. It was very dull in those days living in the cañon of Piñon Pines.

"But it is really my own fault," said the stream. So it went on repairing the borders with the best heart it could contrive.

About the time the white clematis had come back to hide the ruin of the brown birches, a young man came and camped with his wife and child in the meadow. They were looking for a place to make a home. They looked long at the meadow, for Shorty and Long Tom had taken away their house and it did not appear to belong to any one.

"What a charming place!" said the young wife, "just the right distance from town, and a stream all to ourselves. And look, there are fruit-trees already planted. Do let us decide to stay."

Then she took off the child's shoes and stockings to let it play in the stream. The water curled all about the bare feet and gurgled delightedly.

"Ah, do stay," begged the happy water, "I can be such a help to you, for I know how a garden should be irrigated in the best manner."

The child laughed and stamped the water up to his bare knees. The young wife watched anxiously while her husband walked up and down the stream border and examined the fruit-trees.

"It is a delightful place," he said, "and the soil is rich, but I am afraid the water cannot be depended upon. There are signs of a great drought within the last two or three years. Look, there is a clump of birches in the very path of the stream, but all dead; and the largest limbs of the fruit-trees have died. In this country one must be able to make sure of the water supply. I suppose the people who planted them must have abandoned the place when the stream went dry. We must go on farther." So they took their goods and the child and went on farther.

"Ah, well," said the stream, "that is what is to be expected when one has a reputation for neglecting one's duty. But I wish they stayed. That baby and I understood each other."

He had quite made up his mind not to run away again, though he could not be expected to be quite cheerful after all that had happened; in fact, if you go yourself to the cañon of the Piñon Pines you will notice that the stream, where it goes brokenly about the meadow, has quite a mournful sound.

THE COYOTE-SPIRIT AND THE WEAVING WOMAN

The Weaving Woman lived under the bank of the stony wash that cut through the country of the mesquite dunes. The Coyote-Spirit, which, you understand, is an Indian whose form has been changed to fit with his evil behavior, ranged from the Black Rock where the wash began to the white sands beyond Pahranagat; and the Goat-Girl kept her flock among the mesquites, or along the windy stretch of sage below the campoodie; but as the Coyote-Spirit never came near the wickiups by day, and the Goat-Girl went home the moment the sun dropped behind Pahranagat, they never met. These three are all that have to do with the story.

The Weaving Woman, whose work was the making of fine baskets of split willow and roots of yucca and brown grass, lived alone, because there was nobody found who wished to live with her, and because it was whispered among the wickiups that she was different from other people. It was reported that she had an infirmity of the eyes which caused her to see everything with rainbow fringes, bigger and brighter and better than it was. All her days were fruitful, a handful of pine nuts as much to make merry over as a feast; every lad who went by a-hunting with his bow at his back looked to be a painted brave, and every old woman digging roots as fine as a medicine man in all his feathers. All the faces at the campoodie, dark as the mingled sand and lava of the Black Rock country, deep lined with work and weather, shone for this singular old woman with the glory of the late evening light on Pahranagat. The door of her wickiup opened toward the campoodie with the smoke going up from cheerful hearths, and from the shadow of the bank where she sat to make baskets she looked down the stony wash where all the trails converged that led every way among the dunes, and saw an enchanted mesa covered with misty bloom and gentle creatures moving on trails that seemed to lead to the places where one had always wished to be.

Since all this was so, it was not surprising that her baskets turned out to be such wonderful affairs, and the tribesmen, though they winked and wagged their heads, were very glad to buy them for a haunch of venison or a bagful of mesquite meal. Sometimes, as they stroked the perfect curves of the bowls or traced out the patterns, they were heard to sigh, thinking how fine life would be if it were so rich and bright as she made it seem, instead of the dull occasion they had found it. There were some who even said it was a pity, since she was so clever at the craft, that the weaver was not more like other people, and no one thought to suggest that in that case her weaving would be no better than theirs. For all this the basket-maker did not care, sitting always happily at her weaving or wandering far into the desert in search of withes and barks and dyes, where the wild things showed her many a wonder hid from those who have not rainbow fringes to their eyes; and because she was not afraid of anything; she went farther and farther into the silent places until in the course of time she met the Coyote-Spirit.

Now a Coyote-Spirit, from having been a man, is continually thinking about men and wishing to be with them, and, being a coyote and of the wolf's breed, no sooner does he have his wish than he thinks of devouring. So as soon as this one had met the Weaving Woman he desired to eat her up, or to work her some evil according to the evil of his nature. He did not see any opportunity to begin at the first meeting, for on account of the infirmity of her eyes the woman did not see him as a coyote, but as a man, and let down her wicker water bottle for him to drink, so kindly that he was quite abashed. She did not seem in the least afraid of him, which is disconcerting even to a real coyote; though if he had been, she need not have been afraid of him in any case. Whatever pestiferous beast the Indian may think the dog of the wilderness, he has no reason to fear him except when by certain signs, as having a larger and leaner body, a sharper muzzle, and more evilly pointed ears, he knows him the soul of a bad-hearted man going about in that guise. There are enough of these coyote-spirits ranging in Mesquite Valley and over toward Funeral Mountains and about Pahranagat to give certain learned folk surmise as to whether there may not be a strange breed of wolves in that region; but the Indians know better.

When the coyote-spirit who had met the basket woman thought about it afterward, he said to himself that she deserved all the mischance that might come upon her for that meeting. "She knows," he said, "that this is my range, and whoever walks in a coyote-spirit's range must expect to take the consequences. She is not at all like the Goat-Girl."

The Coyote-Spirit had often watched the Goat-Girl from the top of Pahranagat, but because she was always in the open where no lurking-places were, and never far from the corn lands where the old men might be working, he had made himself believe he would not like that kind of a girl. Every morning he saw her come out of her leafy hut, loose the goats from the corral, which was all of cactus stems and broad leaves of prickly-pear, and lead them out among the wind-blown hillocks of sand under which the trunks of the mesquite flourished for a hundred years, and out of the tops of which the green twigs bore leaves and fruit; or along the mesa to browse on bitterbrush and the tops of scrubby sage. Sometimes she plaited willows for the coarser kinds of basket-work, or, in hot noonings while the flock dozed, worked herself collars and necklaces of white and red and turquoise-colored beads, and other times sat dreaming on the sand. But whatever she did, she kept far enough from the place of the Coyote-Spirit, who, now that he had met the Weaving Woman, could not keep his mind off her. Her hut was far enough from the campoodie so that every morning he went around by the Black Rock to see if she was still there, and there she sat weaving patterns in her baskets of all that she saw or thought. Now it would be the winding wash and the wattled huts beside it, now the mottled skin of the rattlesnake or the curled plumes of the quail.

At last the Coyote-Spirit grew so bold that when there was no one passing on the trail he would go and walk up and down in front of the wickiup. Then the Weaving Woman would look up from her work and give him the news of the season and the tribesmen in so friendly a fashion that he grew less and less troubled in his mind about working her mischief. He said in his evil heart that since the ways of such as he were known to the Indians,—as indeed they were, with many a charm and spell to keep them safe,—it could be no fault of his if they came to harm through too much familiarity. As for the Weaving Woman, he said, "She sees me as I am, and ought to know better," for he had not heard about the infirmity of her eyes.

Finally he made up his mind to ask her to go with him to dig for roots around the foot of Pahranagat, and if she consented,—and of course she did, for she was a friendly soul,—he knew in his heart what he would do. They went out by the mesa trail, and it was a soft and blossomy day of spring. Long wands of the creosote with shining fretted foliage were hung with creamy bells of bloom, and doves called softly from the Dripping Spring. They passed rows of owlets sitting by their burrows and saw young rabbits playing in their shallow forms. The Weaving Woman talked gayly as they went, as Indian women talk, with soft mellow voices and laughter breaking in between the words like smooth water flowing over stones. She talked of how the deer had shifted their feeding grounds and of whether the quail had mated early that year as a sign of a good season, matters of which the Coyote-Spirit knew more than she, only he was not thinking of those things just then. Whenever her back was turned he licked his cruel jaws and whetted his appetite. They passed the level mesa, passed the tumbled fragments of the Black Rock and came to the sharp wall-sided cañons that showed the stars at noon from their deep wells of sombre shade, where no wild creature made its home and no birds ever sang. Then the Weaving Woman grew still at last because of the great stillness, and the Coyote-Spirit said in a hungry, whining voice,—

"Do you know why I brought you here?"

"To show me how still and beautiful the world is here," said the Weaving Woman, and even then she did not seem afraid.

"To eat you up," said the Coyote. With that he looked to see her fall quaking at his feet, and he had it in mind to tell her it was no fault but her own for coming so far astray with one of his kind, but the woman only looked at him and laughed. The sound of her laughter was like water in a bubbling spring.

"Why do you laugh?" said the Coyote, and he was so astonished that his jaws remained open when he had done speaking.

"How could you eat me?" said she. "Only wild beasts could do that."

"What am I, then?"

"Oh, you are only a man."

"I am a coyote," said he.

"Do you think I have no eyes?" said the woman. "Come!" For she did not understand that her eyes were different from other people's, what she really thought was that other people's were different from hers, which is quite another matter, so she pulled the Coyote-Spirit over to a rain-fed pool. In that country the rains collect in basins of the solid rock that grow polished with a thousand years of storm and give back from their shining side a reflection like a mirror. One such lay in the bottom of the black cañon, and the Weaving Woman stood beside it.

Now it is true of coyote-spirits that they are so only because of their behavior; not only have they power to turn themselves to men if they wish—but they do not wish, or they would not have become coyotes in the first place—but other people in their company, according as they think man-thoughts or beast-thoughts, can throw over them such a change that they have only to choose which they will be. So the basket-weaver contrived to throw the veil of her mind over the Coyote-Spirit, so that when he looked at himself in the pool he could not tell for the life of him whether he was most coyote or most man, which so frightened him that he ran away and left the Weaving Woman to hunt for roots alone. He ran for three days and nights, being afraid of himself, which is the worst possible fear, and then ran back to see if the basket-maker had not changed her mind. He put his head in at the door of her wickiup.

"Tell me, now, am I a coyote or a man?"

"Oh, a man," said she, and he went off to Pahranagat to think it over. In a day or two he came back.

"And what now?" he said.

"Oh, a man, and I think you grow handsomer every day."

That was really true, for what with her insisting upon it and his thinking about it, the beast began to go out of him and the man to come back. That night he went down to the campoodie to try and steal a kid from the corral, but it occurred to him just in time that a man would not do that, so he went back to Pahranagat and ate roots and berries instead, which was a true sign that he had grown into a man again. Then there came a day when the Weaving Woman asked him to stop at her hearth and eat. There was a savory smell going up from the cooking-pots, cakes of mesquite meal baking in the ashes, and sugary white buds of the yucca palm roasting on the coals. The man who had been a coyote lay on a blanket of rabbit skin and heard the cheerful snapping of the fire. It was all so comfortable and bright that somehow it made him think of the Goat-Girl.

"That is the right sort of a girl," he said to himself. "She has always stayed in the safe open places and gone home early. She should be able to tell me what I am," for he was not quite sure, and since he had begun to walk with men a little, he had heard about the Weaving Woman's eyes.

Next day he went out where the flock fed, not far from the corn lands, and the Goat-Girl did not seem in the least afraid of him. So he went again, and the third day he said,—

"Tell me what I seem to you."

"A very handsome man," said she.

"Then will you marry me?" said he; and when the Goat-Girl had taken time to think about it she said yes, she thought she would.

Now, when the man who had been a coyote lay on the blanket of the Weaving Woman's wickiup, he had taken notice how it was made of willows driven into the ground around a pit dug in the earth, and the poles drawn together at the top, and thatched with brush, and he had tried at the foot of Pahranagat un-til he had built another like it; so when he had married the Goat-Girl, after the fashion of her tribe, he took her there to live. He was not now afraid of anything except that his wife might get to know that he had once been a coyote. It was during the first month of their marriage that he said to her, "Do you know the basket-maker who lives under the bank of the stony wash? They call her the Weaving Woman."

"I have heard something of her and I have bought her baskets. Why do you ask?"

"It is nothing," said the man, "but I hear strange stories of her, that she asso-ciates with coyote-spirits and such creatures," for he wanted to see what his wife would say to that.

"If that is the case," said she, "the less we see of her the better. One cannot be too careful in such matters."

After that, when the man who had been a coyote and his wife visited the campoodie, they turned out of the stony wash before the reached the wickiup, and came in to the camp by another trail. But I have not heard whether the Weaving Woman noticed it.

Henry Handel Richardson 1870–1946

Ethel Florence Lindsay Richardson left her native Australia when she was seventeen. Though she returned there only once after that, Richardson is considered one of Australia's most celebrated fiction writers. Richardson crafted a trilogy entitled *The Fortunes of Richard Mahony* (1917, 1925, 1929), which dealt with the implications of colonialism for the life of a physician, a character based on her father. Her writing is also known for its frank sexuality and her analysis of society's conventions. Richardson was also trained as a musician, an important part of her life that is reflected in two other novels, *Maurice Guest* (1908) and *The Young Cosima* (1939). But it was the last volume of the trilogy, *Ultima Thule* (1929), that led to her international fame.

TWO HANGED WOMEN

Hand in hand the youthful lovers sauntered along the esplanade. It was a night in midsummer; a wispy moon had set, and the stars glittered. The dark mass of the sea, at flood, lay tranquil, slothfully lapping the shingle.[1]

[1] Beach gravel.

"Come on, let's make for the usual," said the boy.

But on nearing their favorite seat they found it occupied. In the velvety shade of the overhanging sea-wall, the outlines of two figures were visible.

"Oh, blast!" said the lad. "That's torn it. What now, Baby?"

"Why, let's stop here, Pincher, right close up, till we frighten 'em off."

And very soon loud, smacking kisses, amatory pinches and ticklings, and skittish squeals of pleasure did their work. Silently the intruders rose and moved away.

But the boy stood gaping after them, open-mouthed.

"Well, I'm damned! If it wasn't just two hanged[2] women!"

Retreating before a salvo of derisive laughter, the elder of the girls said: "We'll go out on the breakwater."[3] She was tall and thin, and walked with a long stride.

Her companion, shorter than she by a bobbed head of straight flaxen hair, was hard put to it to keep pace. As she pegged along she said doubtfully, as if in self-excuse: "Though I really ought to go home. It's getting late. Mother will be angry."

They walked with finger-tips lightly in contact; and at her words she felt what was like an attempt to get free, on the part of the fingers crooked in hers. But she was prepared for this, and held fast, gradually working her own up till she had a good half of the other hand in her grip.

For a moment neither spoke. Then, in a low, muffled voice, came the question: "Was she angry last night, too?"

The little fair girl's reply had an unlooked-for vehemence. "You know she wasn't!" And, mildly despairing: "But you never will understand. Oh, what's the good of . . . of anything!"

And on sitting down she let the prisoned hand go, even putting it from her with a kind of push. There it lay, palm upwards, the fingers still curved from her hold, looking like a thing with a separate life of its own; but a life that was ebbing.

On this remote seat, with their backs turned on lovers, lights, the town, the two girls sat and gazed wordlessly at the dark sea, over which great Jupiter was flinging a thin gold line. There was no sound but the lapping, sucking, sighing, of the ripples at the edge of the breakwater, and the occasional screech of an owl in the tall trees on the hillside.

But after a time, having stolen more than one side glance at her companion, the younger seemed to take heart of grace. With a childish toss of the head that set her loose hair swaying, she said, in a tone of meaning emphasis: "I like Fred."

The only answer was a faint, contemptuous shrug.

"I tell you I *like* him!"

"Fred? Rats!"

[2] Confounded (British expletive).

[3] Barrier protecting the shore from strong waves.

"No it isn't . . . that's just where you're wrong, Betty. But you think you're so wise. Always."

"I know what I know."

"Or imagine you do! But it doesn't matter. Nothing you can say makes any difference. I like him and always shall. In heaps of ways. He's so big and strong, for one thing: it gives you such a safe sort of feeling to be with him . . . as if nothing could happen while you were. Yes, it's . . . it's . . . well, I can't help it, Betty, there's something *comfy* in having a boy to go about with—like other girls do. One they'd eat their hats to get, too! I can see it in their eyes when we pass; Fred with his great long legs and broad shoulders—I don't nearly come up to them—and his blue eyes with the black lashes, and his shiny black hair. And I like his tweeds, the Harris[4] smell of them, and his dirty old pipe, and the way he shows his teeth—he's got *topping* teeth—when he laughs and says r*ather*! And other people, when they see us, look . . . well I don't quite know how to say it, but they look sort of pleased; and they make room for us and let us into the dark corner-seats at the pictures, just as if we'd a right to them. And they never laugh. (Oh, I can't *stick*[5] being laughed at!—and that's the truth.) Yes, it's so comfy, Betty darling . . . such a warm cosy comfy feeling. Oh, *won't* you understand?

"Gawd! why not make a song of it?" But a moment later, very fiercely: "And who is it's taught you to think all this? Who's hinted it and suggested it till you've come to believe it? . . . believe it's what you really feel."

"She hasn't! Mother's never said a word . . . about Fred."

"Words?—why waste words? . . . when she can do it with a cock of the eye. For your Fred, that!" and the girl called Betty held her fingers aloft and snapped them viciously. "But your mother's a different proposition."

"I think you're simply horrid."

To this there was no reply.

"*Why* have you such a down on her? What's she ever done to you? . . . except not get ratty when I stay out late with Fred. And I don't see how you can expect . . . being what she is . . . and with nobody but me—after all she *is* my mother . . . you can't alter that. I know very well—and you know, too—I'm not *too* putrid-looking. But"—beseechingly—"I'm *nearly* twenty-five now, Betty. And other girls . . . well, she sees them, every one of them, with a boy of their own, even though they're ugly, or fat, or have legs like sausages—they've only got to ogle them a bit—the girls, I mean . . . and there they are. And Fred's a good sort—he is, really!—and he dances well, and doesn't drink, and so . . . so why *shouldn't* I like him? . . . and off my own bat . . . without it having to be all Mother's fault, and me nothing but a parrot, and without any will of my own?"

"Why? Because I know her too well, my child! I can read her as you'd never dare to . . . even if you could. She's sly, your mother is, so sly there's no coming

---

[4] Popular type of tweed clothing made of cloth woven on an island in the Hebrides.
[5] Bear.

to grips with her . . . one might as well try to fill one's hand with cobwebs. But she's got a hold on you, a stranglehold, that nothing'll loosen. Oh! mothers aren't fair—I mean it's not fair of nature to weigh us down with them and yet expect us to be our own true selves. The handicap's too great. All those months, when the same blood's running through two sets of veins—there's no getting away from that, ever after. Take yours. As I say, does she need to open her mouth? Not she! She's only got to let it hang at the corners, and you reek, you drip with guilt."

Something in these words seemed to sting the younger girl. She hit back. "I know what it is, you're jealous, that's what you are! . . . and you've no other way of letting it out. But I tell you this. If ever I marry—yes, *marry!*—it'll be to please myself, and nobody else. Can you imagine me doing it to oblige her?"

Again silence.

"If I only think what it would be like to be fixed up and settled, and able to live in peace, without this eternal dragging two ways . . . just as if I was being torn in half. And see Mother smiling and happy again, like she used to be. Between the two of you I'm nothing but a punch-ball. Oh, I'm fed up with it! . . . fed up to the neck. As for you . . . And yet you can sit there as if you were made of stone! Why don't you *say* something? *Betty!* Why won't you speak?"

But no words came.

"I can *feel* you sneering. And when you sneer I hate you more than any one on earth. If only I'd never seen you!"

"Marry your Fred, and you'll never need to again."

"I will, too! I'll marry him, and have a proper wedding like other girls, with a veil and bridesmaids and bushels of flowers. And I'll live in a house of my own, where I can do as I like, and be left in peace, and there'll be no one to badger and bully me—Fred wouldn't . . . ever! Besides, he'll be away all day. And when he came back at night, he'd . . . I'd . . . I mean I'd—" But here the flying words gave out; there came a stormy breath and a cry of: "Oh, Betty, Betty! . . . I couldn't, no, I couldn't! It's when I think of *that* . . . Yes, it's quite true! I like him all right, I do indeed, but only as long as he doesn't come too near. If he even sits too close, I have to screw myself up to bear it"—and flinging herself down over her companion's lap, she hid her face. "And if he tries to touch me, Betty, or even takes my arm or puts his round me . . . And then his face . . . when it looks like it does sometimes . . . all wrong . . . as if it had gone all wrong—oh! then I feel I shall have to scream—out loud. I'm afraid of him . . . when he looks like that. Once . . . when he kissed me . . . I could have died with the horror of it. His breath . . . his breath . . . and his mouth—like fruit pulp—and the black hairs on his wrists . . . and the way he looked—and . . . and everything! No, I can't, I can't . . . nothing will make me . . . I'd rather die twice over. But what am I to do? Mother'll *never* understand. Oh, why has it got to be like this? I want to be happy, like other girls, and to make her happy, too . . . and everything's all wrong. You tell me, Betty darling, you help me, you're older . . . you *know* . . . and you can help me, if you will . . . if you only will!" And locking her arms round her friend she drove her face deeper into the warmth and darkness, as if, from the very fervor of her clasp, she could draw the aid and strength she needed.

Betty had sat silent, unyielding, her sole movement being to loosen her own arms from her sides and point her elbows outwards, to hinder them touching the arms that lay round her. But at this last appeal she melted; and gathering the young girl to her breast, she held her fast.—And so for long she continued to sit, her chin resting lightly on the fair hair, that was silky and downy as an infant's, and gazing with somber eyes over the stealthily heaving sea.

Amy Lowell 1874–1925

Born to one of Boston's most powerful and important families, Amy Lowell came from a clan of men who became millionaires, scholars, manufacturers, ambassadors, and statesmen. Lowell demonstrated little interest in the expectations of women—raising children, supervising domestics, participating in the social world of the upper crust. Although the Lowell men all attended Harvard, Amy Lowell primarily educated herself and published her first collection of poems at the age of thirty-eight, *A Dome of Many-Coloured Glass* (1912). Her poetry was critically acclaimed and popular from the start. After reading such imagists as Ezra Pound and H.D., she herself became an imagist and wrote two collections of critical works that fostered the movement. Despite her devotion to imagism as a poetic style, she was a follower of Romantic poetry; she also wrote longer narrative and prose poems, as well as standard verse patterns and what has been described as "Whitmanesque free verse." Her work continued to be popular after her death (at fifty-one), but by the 1950s, scholars created an acceptable canon with a limited set of authors, an unofficial "list" that neglected certain writers, particularly women such as Lowell. Her posthumously published volume of poems, *What's O'Clock,* won the Pulitzer Prize. Fortunately, critics in recent years have reestablished her right to prominence in American poetry.

THE LETTER

Little cramped words scrawling all over the paper
Like draggled fly's legs,
What can you tell of the flaring moon
Through the oak leaves?

Or of my uncurtained window and the bare floor   5
Spattered with moonlight?
Your silly quirks and twists have nothing in them
Of blossoming hawthorns,
And this paper is dull, crisp, smooth, virgin of loveliness
Beneath my hand.   10

I am tired, Beloved, of chafing my heart against
The want of you;
Of squeezing it into little inkdrops,
And posting it.
And I scald alone, here, under the fire   15
Of the great moon.

SUMMER RAIN

All night our room was outer-walled with rain.
Drops fell and flattened on the tin roof,
And rang like little disks of metal.
Ping!—Ping!—and there was not a pinpoint of
silence between them.   5
The rain rattled and clashed,
And the slats of the shutters danced and glittered.
But to me the darkness was red-gold and crocus-coloured
With your brightness,
And the words you whispered to me   10
Sprang up and flamed—orange torches against the rain.
Torches against the wall of cool, silver rain!

AFTER A STORM

You walk under the ice trees.
They sway, and crackle,
And arch themselves splendidly
To deck your going.
The white sun flips them into colour   5
Before you.
They are blue,
And mauve,

And emerald.
They are amber,   10
And jade,
And sardonyx.
They are silver fretted to flame
And startled to stillness,
Bunched, splintered, iridescent.   15
You walk under the ice trees
And the bright snow creaks as you step upon it.
My dogs leap about you,
And their barking strikes upon the air
Like sharp hammer-strokes on metal.   20
You walk under the ice trees
But you are more dazzling than the ice flowers,
And the dogs' barking
Is not so loud to me as your quietness.

You walk under the ice trees   25
At ten o'clock in the morning.

THE SISTERS

Taking us by and large, we're a queer lot
We women who write poetry. And when you think
How few of us there've been, it's queerer still.
I wonder what it is that makes us do it,
Singles us out to scribble down, man-wise,   5
The fragments of ourselves. Why are we
Already mother-creatures, double-bearing,
With matrices in body and in brain?
I rather think that there is just the reason
We are so sparse a kind of human being;   10
The strength of forty thousand Atlases
Is needed for our every-day concerns.
There's Sapho, now I wonder what was Sapho.
I know a single slender thing about her:
That, loving, she was like a burning birch-tree   15
All tall and glittering fire, and that she wrote
Like the same fire caught up to Heaven and held there,
A frozen blaze before it broke and fell.
Ah, me! I wish I could have talked to Sapho,

Surprised her reticences by flinging mine   20
Into the wind. This tossing off of garments
Which cloud the soul is none too easy doing
With us to-day. But still I think with Sapho
One might accomplish it, were she in the mood
To bare her loveliness of words and tell   25
The reasons, as she possibly conceived them,
Of why they are so lovely. Just to know
How she came at them, just to watch
The crisp sea sunshine playing on her hair,
And listen, thinking all the while 'twas she   30
Who spoke and that we two were sisters
Of a strange, isolated little family.
And she is Sapho — Sapho — not Miss or Mrs.,
A leaping fire we call so for convenience;
But Mrs. Browning — who would ever think   35
Of such presumption as to call her "Ba."
Which draws the perfect line between sea-cliffs
And a close-shuttered room in Wimpole Street.
Sapho could fly her impulses like bright
Balloons tip-tilting to a morning air   40
And write about it. Mrs. Browning's heart
Was squeezed in stiff conventions. So she lay
Stretched out upon a sofa, reading Greek
And speculating, as I must suppose,
In just this way on Sapho; all the need,   45
The huge, imperious need of loving, crushed
Within the body she believed so sick.
And it was sick, poor lady, because words
Are merely simulacra after deeds
Have wrought a pattern; when they take the place   50
Of actions they breed a poisonous miasma
Which, though it leave the brain, eats up the body.
So Mrs. Browning, aloof and delicate,
Lay still upon her sofa, all her strength
Going to uphold her over-topping brain.   55
It seems miraculous, but she escaped
To freedom and another motherhood
Than that of poems. She was a very woman
And needed both.
        If I had gone to call,   60
Would Wimpole Street have been the kindlier place,
Or Casa Guidi, in which to have met her?

I am a little doubtful of that meeting,
For Queen Victoria was very young and strong
And all-pervading in her apogee   65
At just that time. If we had stuck to poetry,
Sternly refusing to be drawn off by mesmerism
Or Roman revolutions, it might have done.
For, after all, she is another sister,
But always, I rather think, an older sister   70
And not herself so curious a technician
As to admit newfangled modes of writing—
"Except, of course, in Robert, and that is neither
Here nor there for Robert is a genius."
I do not like the turn this dream is taking,   75
Since I am very fond of Mrs. Browning
And very much indeed should like to hear her
Graciously asking me to call her "Ba."
But then the Devil of Verisimilitude
Creeps in and forces me to know she wouldn't.   80
Convention again, and how it chafes my nerves,
For we are such a little family
Of singing sisters, and as if I didn't know
What those years felt like tied down to the sofa.
Confounded Victoria, and the slimy inhibitions   85
She loosed on all us Anglo-Saxon creatures!
Suppose there hadn't been a Robert Browning,
No "Sonnets from the Portuguese" would have been written.
They are the first of all her poems to be,
One might say, fertilized. For, after all,   90
A poet is flesh and blood as well as brain
And Mrs. Browning, as I said before,
Was very, very woman. Well, there are two
Of us, and vastly unlike that's for certain.
Unlike at least until we tear the veils   95
Away which commonly gird souls. I scarcely think
Mrs. Browning would have approved the process
In spite of what had surely been relief;
For speaking souls must always want to speak
Even when bat-eyed, narrow-minded Queens   100
Set prudishness to keep the keys of impulse.
Then do the frowning Gods invent new banes
And make the need of sofas. But Sapho was dead
And I, and others, not yet peeped above
The edge of possibility. So that's an end   105

To speculating over tea-time talks
Beyond the movement of pentameters
With Mrs. Browning.
But I go dreaming on,
In love with these my spiritual relations.   110
I rather think I see myself walk up
A flight of wooden steps and ring a bell
And send a card in to Miss Dickinson.
Yet that's a very silly way to do.
I should have taken the dream twist-ends about   115
And climbed over the fence and found her deep
Engrossed in the doing of a hummingbird
Among nasturtiums. Not having expected strangers,
She might forget to think me one, and holding up
A finger say quite casually: "Take care.   120
Don't frighten him, he's only just begun."
"Now this," I well believe I should have thought,
"Is even better than Sapho. With Emily
You're really here, or never anywhere at all
In range of mind." Wherefore, having begun   125
In the strict centre, we could slowly progress
To various circumferences, as we pleased.
We could, but should we? That would quite depend
On Emily. I think she'd be exacting,
Without intention possibly, and ask   130
A thousand tight-rope tricks of understanding.
But, bless you, I would somersault all day
If by so doing I might stay with her.
I hardly think that we should mention souls
Although they might just round the corner from us   135
In some half-quizzical, half-wistful metaphor.
I'm very sure that I should never seek
To turn her parables to stated fact.
Sapho would speak, I think, quite openly,
And Mrs. Browning guard a careful silence,   140
But Emily would set doors ajar and slam them
And love you for your speed of observation.

Strange trio of my sisters, most diverse,
And how extraordinarily unlike
Each is to me, and which way shall I go?   145
Sapho spent and gained; and Mrs. Browning,
After a miser girlhood, cut the strings

Which tied her money-bags and let them run;
But Emily hoarded—hoarded—only giving
Herself to cold, white paper. Starved and tortured,   150
She cheated her despair with games of patience
And fooled herself by winning. Frail little elf,
The lonely brain-child of a gaunt maturity,
She hung her womanhood upon a bough
And played ball with the stars—too long—too long—   155
The garment of herself hung on a tree
Until at last she lost even the desire
To take it down. Whose fault? Why let us say,
To be consistent, Queen Victoria's.
But really, not to over-rate the queen,   160
I feel obliged to mention Martin Luther,
And behind him the long line of Church Fathers
Who draped their prurience like a dirty cloth
About the naked majesty of God.
Good-bye, my sisters, all of you are great,   165
And all of you are marvellously strange,
And none of you has any word for me.
I cannot write like you, I cannot think
In terms of Pagan or of Christian now.
I only hope that possibly some day   170
Some other woman with an itch for writing
May turn to me as I have turned to you
And chat with me a brief few minutes. How
We lie, we poets! It is three good hours
I have been dreaming. Has it seemed so long   175
To you? And yet I thank you for the time
Although you leave me sad and self-distrustful,
For older sisters are very sobering things.
Put on your cloaks, my dears, the motor's waiting.
No, you have not seemed strange to me, but near.   180
Frightfully near, and rather terrifying.
I understand you all, for in myself—
Is that presumption? Yet indeed it's true—
We are one family. And still my answer
Will not be any one of yours, I see.   185
Well, never mind that now. Good night! Good night!

Gertrude Stein 1874–1946

Hailed as "the Mama of dada" and ridiculed as "the Mother Goose of Montparnasse," Gertrude Stein produced a linguistically experimental body of work that includes short stories, novels, autobiographies, dramas, poems, and portraits. Stein moved from America to Paris with her brother, Leo, in 1902. There, she became an art collector and good friends with such aspiring modernists as Pablo Picasso, Henri Matisse, and Georges Braque, whose philosophies significantly influenced her. Cubists Picasso and Braque believed that representational painting did not depict what people actually saw but, instead, what they had learned to think they saw. Consequently, Stein applied the modernist effort to liberate visual effect from representation, endeavoring to release language from convention by undercutting expectations about the meanings, associations, order, and coherence of words. Stein also experimented with writing in "the continuous present," where time exists as a series of discrete moments rather than as a linear progression. She explains in *The Making of Americans* that "there was a groping for using everything and there was a groping for continuous present and there was an inevitable beginning of beginning again and again and again." She humorously adds, "I went on for a thousand pages of it." In her lesbian love poems and experimental portraits, like *Ada* and *Miss Furr and Miss Skeene,* Stein developed an encoded language of obscure symbolism to describe the eroticism of socially unacceptable feelings. Stein lamented in 1937: "It always did bother me that the American public were more interested in me than in my work."

MISS FURR AND MISS SKEENE

Helen Furr had quite a pleasant home. Mrs. Furr was quite a pleasant woman. Mr. Furr was quite a pleasant man. Helen Furr had quite a pleasant voice a voice quite worth cultivating. She did not mind working. She worked to cultivate her voice. She did not find it gay living in the same place where she had always been living. She went to a place where some were cultivating something, voices and other things needing cultivating. She met Georgine Skeene there who was cultivating her voice which some thought was quite a pleasant one. Helen Furr and Georgine Skeene lived together then. Georgine Skeene liked travelling. Helen Furr did not care about travelling, she liked to stay in one place and be gay there. They were together then and travelled to another place and stayed there and were gay[1] there.

---

[1] The use of the word *gay* to mean "homosexual" was not widespread until the middle of the 20th century.

They stayed there and were gay there, not very gay there, just gay there. They were both gay there, they were regularly working there both of them cultivating their voices there, they were both gay there. Georgine Skeene was gay there and she was regular, regular in being gay, regular in not being gay, regular in being a gay one who was one not being gay longer than was needed to be one being quite a gay one. They were both gay then there and both working there then.

They were in a way both gay there where there were many cultivating something. They were both regular in being gay there. Helen Furr was gay there, she was gayer and gayer there and really she was just gay there, she was gayer and gayer there, that is to say she found ways of being gay there that she was using in being gay there. She was gay there, not gayer and gayer, just gay there, that is to say she was not gayer by using the things she found there that were gay things, she was gay there, always she was gay there.

They were quite regularly gay there, Helen Furr and Georgine Skeene, they were regularly gay there where they were gay. They were very regularly gay.

To be regularly gay was to do every day the gay thing that they did every day. To be regularly gay was to end every day at the same time after they had been regularly gay. They were regularly gay. They were gay every day. They ended every day in the same way, at the same time, and they had been every day regularly gay.

The voice Helen Furr was cultivating was quite a pleasant one. The voice Georgine Skeene was cultivating was, some said, a better one. The voice Helen Furr was cultivating she cultivated and it was quite completely a pleasant enough one then, a cultivated enough one then. The voice Georgine Skeene was cultivating she did not cultivate too much. She cultivated it quite some. She cultivated and she would sometime go on cultivating it and it was not then an unpleasant one, it would not be then an unpleasant one, it would be a quite richly enough cultivated one, it would be quite richly enough to be a pleasant enough one.

They were gay where there were many cultivating something. The two were gay there, were regularly gay there. Georgine Skeene would have liked to do more travelling. They did some travelling, not very much travelling, Georgine Skeene would have liked to do more travelling, Helen Furr did not care about doing travelling, she liked to stay in a place and be gay there.

They stayed in a place and were gay there, both of them stayed there, they stayed together there, they were gay there, they were regularly gay there.

They went quite often, not very often, but they did go back to where Helen Furr had a pleasant enough home and then Georgine Skeene went to a place where her brother had quite some distinction. They both went, every few years, went visiting to where Helen Furr had quite a pleasant home. Certainly Helen Furr would not find it gay to stay, she did not find it gay, she said she would not stay, she said she did not find it gay, she said she would not stay where she did not find it gay, she said she found it gay where she did stay and she did stay there where very many were cultivating something. She did stay there. She always did find it gay there.

She went to see them where she had always been living and where she did not find it gay. She had a pleasant home there, Mrs. Furr was a pleasant enough woman, Mr. Furr was a pleasant enough man, Helen told them and they were not worrying, that she did not find it gay living where she had always been living.

Georgine Skeene and Helen Furr were living where they were both cultivating their voices and they were gay there. They visited where Helen Furr had come from and then they went to where they were living where they were then regularly living.

There were some dark and heavy men there then. There were some who were not so heavy and some who were not so dark. Helen Furr and Georgine Skeene sat regularly with them. They sat regularly with the ones who were dark and heavy. They sat regularly with the ones who were not so dark. They sat regularly with the ones that were not so heavy. They sat with them regularly, sat with some of them. They went with them regularly went with them. They were regular then, they were gay then, they were where they wanted to be then where it was gay to be then, they were regularly gay then. There were men there then who were dark and heavy and they sat with them with Helen Furr and Georgine Skeene and they went with them with Miss Furr and Miss Skeene, and they went with the heavy and dark men Miss Furr and Miss Skeene went with them, and they sat with them, Miss Furr and Miss Skeene sat with them, and there were other men, some were not heavy men and they sat with Miss Furr and Miss Skeene and Miss Furr and Miss Skeene sat with them, and there were other men who were not dark men and they sat with Miss Furr and Miss Skeene and Miss Furr and Miss Skeene sat with them. Miss Furr and Miss Skeene went with them and they went with Miss Furr and Miss Skeene, some who were not heavy men, some who were not dark men. Miss Furr and Miss Skeene sat regularly, they sat with some men. Miss Furr and Miss Skeene went and there were some men with them. There were men and Miss Furr and Miss Skeene went with them, went somewhere with them, went with some of them.

Helen Furr and Georgine Skeene were regularly living where very many were living and cultivating in themselves something. Helen Furr and Georgine Skeene were living very regularly then, being very regular then in being gay then. They did then learn many ways to be gay and they were then being gay being quite regular in being gay, being gay and they were learning little things, little things in ways of being gay, they were very regular then, they were learning very many little things in ways of being gay, they were being and using these little things they were learning to have to be gay with regularly gay with then and they were gay the same amount they had been gay. They were quite gay, they were quite regular, they were learning little things, gay little things, they were gay inside them the same amount they had been gay, they were gay the same length of time they had been gay every day.

They were regular in being gay, they learned little things that are things in being gay, they learned many little things that are things in being gay, they were gay every day, they were regular, they were gay, they were gay the same length of time every day, they were gay, they were quite regularly gay.

Georgine Skeene went away to stay two months with her brother. Helen Furr did not go then to stay with her father and her mother. Helen Furr stayed there where they had been regularly living the two of them and she would then certainly not be lonesome, she would go on being gay. She did go on being gay. She was not any more gay but she was gay longer every day than they had been being gay when they were together being gay. She was gay then quite exactly the same way. She learned a few more little ways of being gay. She was quite gay and in the same way, the same way she had been gay and she was gay a little longer in the day, more of each day she was gay. She was gay longer every day than when the two of them had been being gay. She was gay quite in the way they had been gay, quite in the same way.

She was not lonesome then, she was not at all feeling any need of having Georgine Skeene. She was not astonished at this thing. She would have been a little astonished by this thing but she knew she was not astonished at anything and so she was not astonished at this thing not astonished at not feeling any need of having Georgine Skeene.

Helen Furr had quite a completely pleasant voice and it was quite well enough cultivated and she could use it and she did use it but then there was not any way of working at cultivating a completely pleasant voice when it has become a quite completely well enough cultivated one, and there was not much use in using it when one was not wanting it to be helping to make one a gay one. Helen Furr was not needing using her voice to be a gay one. She was gay then and sometimes she used her voice and she was not using it very often. It was quite completely enough cultivated and it was quite completely a pleasant one and she did not use it very often. She was then, she was quit exactly as gay as she had been, she was gay a little longer in the day then she had been.

She was gay exactly the same way. She was never tired of being gay that way. She had learned very many little ways to use in being gay. Very many were telling about using other ways in being gay. She was gay enough, she was always gay exactly the same way, she was always learning little things to use in being gay, she was telling about using other ways in being gay, she was telling about learning other ways in being gay, she was learning other ways in being gay, she would be using other ways in being gay, she would always be gay in the same way, when Georgine Skeene was there not so long each day as when Georgine Skeene was away.

She came to using many ways in being gay, she came to use every way in being gay. She went on living where many were cultivating something and she was gay, she had used, every way to be gay.

They did not live together then Helen Furr and Georgine Skeene. Helen Furr lived there the longer where they had been living regularly together. Then neither of them were living there any longer. Helen Furr was living somewhere else then and telling some about being gay and she was gay then and she was living quite regularly then. She was regularly gay then. She was quite regular in being gay then. She remembered all the little ways of being gay. She used all the little ways of being gay. She was quite regularly gay. She told many then the way of being gay, she taught very many then little ways they could use in being gay. She was living very well, she was gay then, she went on living then, she was regular in being gay, she always was living very well and was gay very well and was telling about little ways one could be learning to use in being gay, and later was telling them quite often, telling them again and again.

The Gentle Lena

Lena was patient, gentle, sweet and german. She had been a servant for four years and had liked it very well.

Lena had been brought from Germany to Bridgepoint by a cousin and had been in the place there for four years.

This place Lena had found very good. There was a pleasant, unexacting mistress and her children, and they all liked Lena very well.

There was a cook there who scolded Lena a great deal but Lena's german patience held no suffering and the good incessant woman really only scolded so for Lena's good.

Lena's german voice when she knocked and called the family in the morning was as awakening, as soothing, and as appealing, as a delicate soft breeze in midday, summer. She stood in the hallway every morning a long time in her unexpectant and unsuffering german patience calling to the young ones to get up. She would call and wait a long time and then call again, always even, gentle, patient, while the young ones fell back often into that precious, tense, last bit of sleeping that gives a strength of joyous vigor in the young, over them that have come to the readiness of middle age, in their awakening.

Lena had good hard work all morning, and on the pleasant, sunny afternoons she was sent out into the park to sit and watch the little two year old girl baby of the family.

The other girls, all them that make the pleasant, lazy crowd, that watch the children in the sunny afternoons out in the park, all liked the simple, gentle, german Lena very well. They all, too, liked very well to tease her, for it was so easy to make her mixed and troubled, and all helpless, for she could never learn to know just what the other quicker girls meant by the queer things they said.

The two or three of these girls, the ones that Lena always sat with, always worked together to confuse her. Still it was pleasant, all this life for Lena.

The little girl fell down sometimes and cried, and then Lena had to soothe her. When the little girl would drop her hat, Lena had to pick it up and hold it. When the little girl was bad and threw away her playthings, Lena told her she could not have them and took them from her to hold until the little girl should need them.

It was all a peaceful life for Lena, almost as peaceful as a pleasant leisure. The other girls, of course, did tease her, but then that only made a gentle stir within her.

Lena was a brown and pleasant creature, brown as blonde races often have them brown, brown, not with the yellow or the red or the chocolate brown of sun burned countries, but brown with the clear color laid flat on the light toned skin beneath, the plain, spare brown that makes it right to have been made with hazel eyes, and not too abundant straight, brown hair, hair that only later deepens itself into brown from the straw yellow of a german childhood.

Lena had the flat chest, straight back and forward falling shoulders of the patient and enduring working woman, though her body was now still in its milder girlhood and work had not yet made these lines too clear.

The rarer feeling that there was with Lena, showed in all the even quiet of her body movements, but in all it was the strongest in the patient, old-world ignorance, and earth made pureness of her brown, flat, soft featured face. Lena had eyebrows that were a wondrous thickness. They were black, and spread, and very cool, with their dark color and their beauty, and beneath them were her hazel eyes, simple and human, with the earth patience of this working, gentle, german woman.

Yes it was all a peaceful life for Lena. The other girls, of course, did tease her, but then that only made a gentle stir within her.

"What you got on your finger Lena," Mary, one of the girls she always sat with, one day asked her. Mary was good natured, quick, intelligent and Irish.

Lena had just picked up the fancy paper made accordion that the little girl had dropped beside her, and was making it squeak sadly as she pulled it with her brown strong, awkward finger.

"Why, what is it, Mary, paint?" said Lena, putting her finger to her mouth to taste the dirt spot.

"That's awful poison Lena, don't you know?" said Mary, "that green paint that you just tasted."

Lena had sucked a good deal of the green paint from her finger. She stopped and looked hard at the finger. She did not know just how much Mary meant by what she said.

"Ain't it poison, Nellie, that green paint, that Lena sucked just now," said Mary. "Sure it is Lena, its real poison, I ain't foolin' this time anyhow."

Lena was a little troubled. She looked hard at her finger where the paint was, and she wondered if she had really sucked it.

It was still a little wet on the edges and she rubbed it off a long time on the inside of her dress, and in between she wondered and looked at the finger and thought, was it really poison that she had just tasted.

"Ain't it too bad, Nellie, Lena should have sucked that," Mary said.

Nellie smiled and did not answer. Nellie was dark and thin, and looked Italian. She had a big mass of black hair that she wore high up on her head, and that made her face look very fine.

Nellie always smiled and did not say much, and then she would look at Lena to perplex her.

And so they all three sat with their little charges in the pleasant sunshine a long time. And Lena would often look at her finger and wonder if it was really poison that she had just tasted and then she would rub her finger on her dress a little harder.

Mary laughed at her and teased her and Nellie smiled a little and looked queerly at her.

Then it came time, for it was growing cooler, for them to drag together the little ones, who had begun to wander, and to take each one back to its own mother. And Lena never knew for certain whether it was really poison, that green stuff that she had tasted.

During these four years of service, Lena always spent her Sundays out at the house of her aunt, who had brought her four years before to Bridgepoint.

This aunt, who had brought Lena, four years before, to Bridgepoint, was a hard, ambitious, well meaning, german woman. Her husband was a grocer in the town, and they were very well to do. Mrs. Haydon, Lena's aunt, had two daughters who were just beginning as young ladies, and she had a little boy who was not honest and who was very hard to manage.

Mrs. Haydon was a short, stout, hard built, german woman. She always hit the ground very firmly and compactly as she walked. Mrs. Haydon was all a compact and well hardened mass, even to her face, reddish and darkened from its early blonde, with its hearty, shiny, cheeks, and doubled chin well covered over with the up-roll from her short, square neck.

The two daughters, who were fourteen and fifteen, looked like unkneaded, unformed mounds of flesh beside her.

The elder girl, Mathilda, was blonde, and slow, and simple, and quite fat. The younger, Bertha, who was almost as tall as her sister, was dark, and quicker, and she was heavy, too, but not really fat.

These two girls the mother had brought up very firmly. They were well taught for their position. They were always both well dressed, in the same kinds of hats and dresses, as is becoming in two german sisters. The mother liked to have them dressed in red. Their best clothes were red dresses, made of good heavy cloth, and strongly trimmed with braid of a glistening black. They had stiff, red felt hats, trimmed with black velvet ribbon, and a bird. The mother dressed matronly, in a bonnet and in black, always sat between her two big daughters, firm, directing, and repressed.

The only weak spot in this good german woman's conduct was the way she spoiled her boy, who was not honest and who was very hard to manage.

The father of this family was a decent, quiet, heavy, and uninterfering german man. He tried to cure the boy of his bad ways, and make him honest, but the mother could not make herself let the father manage, and so the boy was brought up very badly.

Mrs. Haydon's girls were now only just beginning as young ladies, and so to get her niece, Lena, married, was just then the most important thing that Mrs. Haydon had to do.

Mrs. Haydon had four years before gone to Germany to see her parents, and had taken the girls with her. This visit had been for Mrs. Haydon most successful, though her children had not liked it very well.

Mrs. Haydon was a good and generous woman, and she patronized her parents grandly, and all the cousins who came from all about to see her. Mrs. Haydon's people were of the middling class of farmers. They were not peasants, and they lived in a town of some pretension, but it all seemed very poor and smelly to Mrs. Haydon's american born daughters.

Mrs. Haydon liked it all. It was familiar, and then here she was so wealthy and important. She listened and decided, and advised all of her relations how to do things better. She arranged their present and their future for them, and showed them how in the past they had been wrong in all their methods.

Mrs. Haydon's only trouble was with her two daughters, whom she could not make behave well to her parents. The two girls were very nasty to all their numerous relations. Their mother could hardly make them kiss their grandparents, and every day the girls would get a scolding. But then Mrs. Haydon was so very busy that she did not have time to really manage her stubborn daughters.

These hard working, earth-rough german cousins were to these american born children, ugly and dirty and as far below them as were italian or negro workmen, and they could not see how their mother could ever bear to touch them, and then all the women dressed so funny, and were worked all rough and different.

The two girls stuck up their noses at them all, and always talked in english to each other about how they hated all these people and how they wished their mother would not do so. The girls could talk some german, but they never chose to use it.

It was her eldest brother's family that most interested Mrs. Haydon. Here there were eight children, and out of the eight, five of them were girls.

Mrs. Haydon thought it would be a fine thing to take one of these girls back with her to Bridgepoint and get her well started. Everybody liked that she should do so and they were all willing that it should be Lena.

Lena was the second girl in her large family. She was at this time just seventeen years old. Lena was not an important daughter in the family. She was always sort of dreamy and not there. She worked hard and went very regularly at it, but even good work never seemed to bring her near.

Lena's age just suited Mrs. Haydon's purpose. Lena could first go out to service, and learn how to do things, and then, when she was a little older, Mrs. Haydon could get her a good husband. And then Lena was so still and docile, she would never want to do things her own way. And then, too, Mrs. Haydon, with all her hardness had wisdom, and she could feel the rare strain there was in Lena.

Lena was willing to go with Mrs. Haydon. Lena did not like her german life very well. It was not the hard work but the roughness that disturbed her. The people were not gentle, and the men when they were glad were very boisterous, and would lay hold of her and roughly tease her. They were good people enough around her, but it was all harsh and dreary for her.

Lena did not really know that she did not like it. She did not know that she was always dreamy and not there. She did not think whether it would be different for her away off there in Bridgepoint. Mrs. Haydon took her and got her different kinds of dresses, and then took her with them to the steamer. Lena did not really know what it was that had happened to her.

Mrs. Haydon, and her daughters, and Lena traveled second class on the steamer. Mrs. Haydon's daughters hated that their mother should take Lena. They hated to have a cousin, who was to them, little better than a nigger, and then everybody on the steamer there would see her. Mrs. Haydon's daughters said things like this to their mother, but she never stopped to hear them, and the girls did not dare to make their meaning very clear. And so they could only go on hating Lena hard, together. They could not stop her from going back with them to Bridgepoint.

Lena was very sick on the voyage. She thought, surely before it was over that she would die. She was so sick she could not even wish that she had not started. She could not eat, she could not moan, she was just blank and scared, and sure that every minute she would die. She could not hold herself in, nor help herself in her trouble. She just staid where she had been put, pale, and scared, and weak, and sick, and sure that she was going to die.

Mathilda and Bertha Haydon had no trouble from having Lena for a cousin on the voyage, until the last day that they were on the ship, and by that time they had made their friends and could explain.

Mrs. Haydon went down every day to Lena, gave her things to make her better, held her head when it was needful, and generally was good and did her duty by her.

Poor Lena had no power to be strong in such trouble. She did not know how to yield to her sickness nor endure. She lost all her little sense of being in her suffering. She was so scared, and then at her best, Lena, who was patient, sweet and quiet, had not self-control, nor any active courage.

Poor Lena was so scared and weak, and every minute she was sure that she would die.

After Lena was on land again a little while, she forgot all her bad suffering. Mrs. Haydon got her the good place, with the pleasant unexacting mistress, and her children, and Lena began to learn some English and soon was very happy and content.

All her Sunday's out Lena spent at Mrs. Haydon's house. Lena would have liked much better to spend her Sundays with the girls she always sat with, and who often asked her, and who teased her and made a gentle stir within her, but it never came to Lena's unexpectant and unsuffering german nature to do something different from what was expected of her, just because she would like it that way better. Mrs. Haydon had said that Lena was to come to her house every other Sunday, and so Lena always went there.

Mrs. Haydon was the only one of her family who took any interest in Lena. Mr. Haydon did not think much of her. She was his wife's cousin and he was good to her, but she was for him stupid, and a little simple, and very dull, and sure some day to need help and to be in trouble. All young poor relations, who were brought from Germany to Bridgepoint were sure, before long, to need help and to be in trouble.

The little Haydon boy was always very nasty to her. He was a hard child for any one to manage, and his mother spoiled him very badly. Mrs. Haydon's daughters as they grew older did not learn to like Lena any better. Lena never knew that she did not like them either. She did not know that she was only happy with the other quicker girls, she always sat with in the park, and who laughed at her and always teased her.

Mathilda Haydon, the simple, fat blonde, older daughter felt very badly that she had to say that this was her cousin Lena, this Lena who was little better for her than a nigger. Mathilda was an overgrown, slow, flabby, blonde, stupid, fat girl, just beginning as a woman; thick in her speech and dull and simple in her mind, and very jealous of all her family and of other girls and proud that she could have good dresses and new hats and learn music, and hating very badly to have a cousin who was a common servant. And then Mathilda remembered very strongly that dirty nasty place that Lena came from and that Mathilda had so turned up her nose at, and where she had been made so angry because her mother scolded her and liked all those rough cow-smelly people.

Then, too, Mathilda would get very mad when her mother had Lena at their parties, and when she talked about how good Lena was, to certain german mothers in whose sons, perhaps, Mrs. Haydon might find Lena a good husband. All this would make the dull, blonde, fat Mathilda very angry. Sometimes she would get so angry that she would, in her thick, slow way, and with jealous anger blazing in her light blue eyes, tell her mother that she did not see how she could like that nasty Lena; and then her mother would scold Mathilda, and tell her that she knew her cousin Lena was poor and Mathilda must be good to poor people.

Mathilda Haydon did not like relations to be poor. She told all her girl friends what she thought of Lena, and so the girls would never talk to Lena at Mrs. Haydon's parties. But Lena in her unsuffering and unexpectant patience never really knew that she was slighted. When Mathilda was with her girls in the street or in the park and would see Lena, she always turned up her nose and barely nodded to her, and then she would tell her friends how funny her mother was to take care of people like Lena, and how, back in Germany, all Lena's people lived just like pigs.

The younger daughter, the dark, large, but not fat, Bertha Haydon, who was very quick in her mind, and in her ways, and who was the favorite with her father, did not like Lena, either. She did not like her because for her Lena was a fool and so stupid, and she would let those Irish and Italian girls laugh at her and tease her, and everybody always made fun of Lena, and Lena never got mad, or even had sense enough to know that they were all making an awful fool of her.

Bertha Haydon hated people to be fools. Her father, too, thought Lena was a fool, and so neither the father nor the daughter ever paid any attention to Lena, although she came to their house every other Sunday.

Lena did not know how all the Haydons felt. She came to her aunt's house all her Sunday afternoons that she had out, because Mrs. Haydon had told her she must do so. In the same way Lena always saved all of her wages. She never thought of any way to spend it. The german cook, the good woman who always scolded Lena, helped her to put it in the bank each month, as soon as she got it. Sometimes before it got into the bank to be taken care of, somebody would ask Lena for it. The little Haydon boy sometimes asked and would get it, and sometimes some of the girls, the ones Lena always sat with, needed some more money; but the german cook, who always scolded Lena, saw to it that this did not happen very often. When it did happen she would scold Lena very sharply, and for the next few months she would not let Lena touch her wages, but put it in the bank for her on the same day that Lena got it.

So Lena always saved her wages, for she never thought to spend them, and she always went to her aunt's house for her Sundays because she did not know that she could do anything different.

Mrs. Haydon felt more and more every year that she had done right to bring Lena back with her, for it was all coming out just as she had expected. Lena was good and never wanted her own way, she was learning English, and saving all her wages, and soon Mrs. Haydon would get her a good husband.

All these four years Mrs. Haydon was busy looking around among all the german people that she knew for the right man to be Lena's husband, and now at last she was quite decided.

The man Mrs. Haydon wanted for Lena was a young german-american tailor, who worked with his father. He was good and all the family were very saving, and Mrs. Haydon was sure that this would be just right for Lena, and then too, this young tailor always did whatever his father and his mother wanted.

This old german tailor and his wife, the father and the mother of Herman Kreder, was to marry Lena Mainz, were very thrifty, careful people. Herman was the only child they had left with them, and he always did everything they wanted. Herman was now twenty-eight years old, but he had never stopped being scolded and directed by his father and his mother. And now they wanted to see him married.

Herman Kreder did not care much to get married. He was a gentle soul and a little fearful. He had a sullen temper, too. He was obedient to his father and his mother. He always did his work well. He often went out on Saturday nights and on Sundays, with other men. He liked it with them but he never became really joyous. He liked to be with men and he hated to have women with them. He was obedient to his mother, but he did not care much to get married.

Mrs. Haydon and the elder Kreders had often talked the marriage over. They all three liked it very well. Lena would do anything that Mrs. Haydon wanted, and Herman was always obedient in everything to his father and his mother. Both Lena and Herman were saving and good workers and neither of them ever wanted their own way.

The elder Kreders, everybody knew, had saved up all their money, and they were hard, good german people, and Mrs. Haydon was sure that with these people Lena would never be in any trouble. Mr. Haydon would not say anything about it. He knew old Kreder had a lot of money and owned some good houses, and he did not care what his wife did with that simple, stupid Lena, so long as she would be sure never to need help or to be in trouble.

Lena did not care much to get married. She liked her life very well where she was working. She did not think much about Herman Kreder. She thought he was a good man and she always found him very quiet. Neither of them ever spoke much to the other. Lena did not care much just then about getting married.

Mrs. Haydon spoke to Lena about it very often. Lena never answered anything at all. Mrs. Haydon thought, perhaps Lena did not like Herman Kreder. Mrs. Haydon could not believe that any girl not even Lena, really had no feeling about getting married.

Mrs. Haydon spoke to Lena very often about Herman. Mrs. Haydon sometimes got very angry with Lena. She was afraid that Lena, for once, was going to be stubborn, now when it was all fixed right for her to be married.

"Why you stand there so stupid, why don't you answer, Lena," said Mrs. Haydon one Sunday, at the end of a long talking that she was giving Lena about Herman Kreder, and about Lena's getting married to him.

"Yes ma'am," said Lena, and then Mrs. Haydon was furious with this stupid Lena. "Why don't you answer with some sense, Lena, when I ask you if you don't like Herman Kreder. You stand there so stupid and don't answer just like you ain't heard a word what I been saying to you. I never see anybody like you, Lena. If you going to burst out at all, why don't you burst out sudden instead of standing there so silly and don't answer. And here I am so good to you, and find you a good husband so you can have a place to live in all your own. Answer me, Lena, don't you like Herman Kreder? He is a fine young fellow, almost too good for you, Lena, when you stand there so stupid and don't make no answer. There ain't many poor girls that get the chance you got not to get married."

"Why, I do anything you say, Aunt Mathilda. Yes, I like him. He don't say much to me, but I guess he is a good man, and I do anything you say for me to do."

"Well then Lena, why you stand there so silly all the time and not answer when I asked you."

"I didn't hear you say you wanted I should say anything to you. I didn't know you wanted me to say nothing. I do whatever you tell me it's right for me to do. I marry Herman Kreder, if you want me."

And so for Lena Mainz the match was made.

Old Mrs. Kreder did not discuss the matter with her Herman. She never thought that she needed to talk such things over with him. She just told him about getting married to Lena Mainz who was a good worker and very saving and never wanted her own way, and Herman made his usual little grunt in answer to her.

Mrs. Kreder and Mrs. Haydon fixed the day and made all the arrangements for the wedding and invited everybody who ought to be there to see them married.

In three months Lena Mainz and Herman Kreder were to be married.

Mrs. Haydon attended to Lena's getting all the things that she needed. Lena had to help a good deal with the sewing. Lena did not sew very well. Mrs. Haydon scolded because Lena did not do it better, but then she was very good to Lena, and she hired a girl to come and help her. Lena still stayed on with her pleasant mistress, but she spent all her evenings and her Sundays with her aunt and all the sewing.

Mrs. Haydon got Lena some nice dresses. Lena liked that very well. Lena liked having new hats even better, and Mrs. Haydon had some made for her by a real milliner who made them very pretty.

Lena was nervous these days, but she did not think much about getting married. She did not know really what it was, that, which was always coming nearer.

Lena liked the place where she was with the pleasant mistress and the good cook, who always scolded, and she liked the girls she always sat with. She did not ask if she would like being married any better. She always did whatever her aunt said and expected, but she was always nervous when she saw the Kreders with their Herman. She was excited and she liked her new hats, and everybody teased her and every day her marrying was coming nearer, and yet she did not really know what it was, this that was about to happen to her.

Herman Kreder knew more what it meant to be married and he did not like it very well. He did not like to see girls and he did not want to have to have one always near him. Herman always did everything that his father and his mother wanted and now they wanted that he should be married.

Herman had a sullen temper; he was gentle and he never said much. He liked to go out with other men, but he never wanted that there should be any women with them. The men all teased him about getting married. Herman did not mind the teasing but he did not like very well the getting married and having a girl always with him.

Three days before the wedding day, Herman went away to the country to be gone over Sunday. He and Lena were to be married Tuesday afternoon. When the day came Herman had not been seen or heard from.

The old Kreder couple had not worried much about it. Herman always did everything they wanted and he would surely come back in time to get married. But when Monday night came, and there was no Herman, they went to Mrs. Haydon to tell her what had happened.

Mrs. Haydon got very much excited. It was hard enough to work so as to get everything all ready, and then to have that silly Herman go off that way, so no one could tell what was going to happen. Here was Lena and everything all ready, and now they would have to make the wedding later so that they would know that Herman would be sure to be there.

Mrs. Haydon was very much excited, and then she could not say much to the old Kreder couple. She did not want to make them angry, for she wanted very badly now that Lena should be married to their Herman.

At last it was decided that the wedding should be put off a week longer. Old Mr. Kreder would go to New York to find Herman, for it was very likely that Herman had gone there to his married sister.

Mrs. Haydon sent word around, about waiting until a week from that Tuesday, to everybody that had been invited, and then Tuesday morning she sent for Lena to come down to see her.

Mrs. Haydon was very angry with poor Lena when she saw her. She scolded her hard because she was so foolish, and now Herman had gone off and nobody could tell where he had gone to, and all because Lena always was so dumb and silly. And Mrs. Haydon was just like a mother to her, and Lena always stood there so stupid and did not answer what anybody asked her, and Herman was so silly too, and now his father had to go and find him. Mrs. Haydon did not think that any old people should be good to their children. Their children always were so thankless, and never paid any attention, and older people were always doing things for their good. Did Lena think it gave Mrs. Haydon any pleasure, to work so hard to make Lena happy, and get her a good husband, and then Lena was so thankless and never did anything that anybody wanted. It was a lesson to poor Mrs. Haydon not to do things any more for anybody. Let everybody take care of themselves and never come to her with any troubles; she knew better now than to meddle to make other people happy. It just made trouble for her and her husband did not like it. He always said she was too good, and nobody ever thanked her for it, and there Lena was always standing stupid and not answering anything anybody wanted. Lena could always talk enough to those silly girls she liked so much, and always sat with, but who never did anything for her except to take away her money, and here was her aunt who tried so hard and was so good to her and treated her just like one of her own children and Lena stood there, and never made any answer and never tried to please her aunt, or to do anything that her aunt wanted. "No, it ain't no use your standin' there and cryin', now, Lena. Its too late now to care about that Herman. You should have cared some before, and then you wouldn't have to stand and cry now, and be a disappointment to me, and then I get scolded by my husband for taking care of everybody, and nobody ever thankful. I am glad you got the sense to feel sorry now, Lena, anyway, and I try to do what I can to help you out in your trouble, only you don't deserve to have anybody take any trouble for you. But perhaps you know better next time. You go home now and take care you don't spoil your clothes and that new hat, you had no business to be wearin' that this morning, but you ain't got no sense at all, Lena. I never in my life see anybody be so stupid."

Mrs. Haydon stopped and poor Lena stood there in her hat, all trimmed with pretty flowers, and the tears coming out of her eyes, and Lena did not know what it was that she had done, only she was not going to be married and it was a disgrace for a girl to be left by a man on the very day she was to be married.

Lena went home all alone, and cried in the street car.

Poor Lena cried very hard all alone in the street car. She almost spoiled her new hat with her hitting it against the window in her crying. Then she remembered that she must not do so.

The conductor was a kind man and he was very sorry when he saw her crying. "Don't feel so bad, you get another feller, you are such a nice girl," he said to make her cheerful. "But Aunt Mathilda said now, I never get married," poor Lena sobbed out for her answer. "Why you really got trouble like that," said the conductor, "I just said that now to josh you. I didn't ever think you really was left by a feller. He must be a stupid feller. But don't you worry, he wasn't much good if he could go away and leave you, lookin' to be such a nice girl. You just tell all your trouble to me, and I help you." The car was empty and the conductor sat down beside her to put his arm around her, and to be a comfort to her. Lena suddenly remembered where she was, and if she did things like that her aunt would scold her. She moved away from the man into the corner. He laughed, "Don't be scared," he said, "I wasn't going to hurt you. But you just keep up your spirit. You are a real nice girl, and you'll be sure to get a real good husband. Don't you let nobody fool you. You're all right and I don't want to scare you."

The conductor went back to his platform to help a passenger get on the car. All the time Lena stayed in the street car, he would come in every little while and reassure her, about her not to feel so bad about a man who hadn't no more sense than to go away and leave her. She'd be sure yet to get a good man, she needn't be so worried, he frequently assured her.

He chatted with the other passenger who had just come in, a very well dressed old man, and then with another who came in later, a good sort of a working man, and then another who came in, a nice lady, and he told them all about Lena's having trouble, and it was too bad there were men who treated a poor girl so badly. And everybody in the car was sorry for poor Lena and the workman tried to cheer her, and the old man looked sharply at her, and said she looked like a good girl, but she ought to be more careful and not be so careless, and things like that would not happen to her, and the nice lady went and sat beside her and Lena liked it, though she shrank away from being near her.

So Lena was feeling a little better when she got off the car, and the conductor helped her, and he called out to her, "You be sure you keep up a good heart now. He wasn't no good that feller and you were lucky for to lose him. You'll get a real man yet, one that will be better for you. Don't you be worried, you're a real nice girl as I ever see in such trouble," and the conductor shook his head and went back into his car to talk it over with the other passengers he had there.

The german cook, who always scolded Lena, was very angry when she heard the story. She never did think Mrs. Haydon would do so much for Lena, though she was always talking so grand about what she could do for everybody. The good german cook always had been a little distrustful to her. People who always thought they were so much never did really do things right for anybody. Not that Mrs. Haydon wasn't a good woman. Mrs. Haydon was a real, good, german woman, and she did really mean to do well by her niece Lena. The cook knew that very well, and she had always said so, and she always had liked and respected Mrs. Haydon, who always acted very proper to her, and Lena was so backward, when there was a man to talk to, Mrs. Haydon did have hard work when she tried to marry Lena. Mrs. Haydon was a good woman, only she did talk sometimes too grand. Perhaps this trouble would make her see it wasn't always so easy to do, to make everybody do everything just like she wanted. The cook was very sorry now for Mrs. Haydon. All this must be such a disappointment, and such a worry to her, and she really had always been very good to Lena. But Lena had better go and put on her other clothes and stop with all that crying. That wouldn't do nothing now to help her, and if Lena would be a good girl, and just be real patient, her aunt would make it all come out right yet for her. "I just tell Mrs. Aldrich, Lena, you stay here yet a little longer. You know she is always so good to you, Lena, and I know she let you, and I tell her all about that stupid Herman Kreder. I got no patience, Lena, with anybody who can be so stupid. You just stop now with your crying, Lena, and take off them good clothes and put them away so you don't spoil them when you need them, and you can help me with the dishes and everything will come off better for you. You see if I ain't right by what I tell you. You just stop crying now Lena quick, or else I scold you."

Lena still choked a little and was very miserable inside her but she did everything just as the cook told her.

The girls Lena always sat with were very sorry to see her look so sad with her trouble. Mary the Irish girl sometimes got very angry with her. Mary was always very hot when she talked of Lena's aunt Mathilda, who thought she was so grand, and had such stupid, stuck up daughters. Mary wouldn't be a fat fool like that ugly tempered Mathilda Haydon, not for anything anybody could ever give her. How Lena could keep on going there so much when they all always acted as if she was just dirt to them, Mary never could see. But Lena never had any sense of how she should make people stand round for her, and that was always all the trouble with her. And poor Lena, she was so stupid to be sorry for losing that

gawky fool who didn't ever know what he wanted and just said "ja"[1] to his
mamma and his papa, like a baby, and was scared to look at a girl straight, and
then sneaked away the last day like as if somebody was going to do something to
him. Disgrace, Lena talking about disgrace! It was a disgrace for a girl to be seen
with the likes of him, let alone to be married to him. But that poor Lena, she
never did know how to show herself off for what she was really. Disgrace to have
him go away and leave her. Mary would just like to get a chance to show him. If
Lena wasn't worth fifteen like Herman Kreder, Mary would just eat her own
head all up. It was a good riddance Lena had of that Herman Kreder and his
stingy, dirty parents, and if Lena didn't stop crying about it, — Mary would just
naturally despise her.

Poor Lena, she knew very well how Mary meant it all, this she was always
saying to her. But Lena was very miserable inside her. She felt the disgrace it was
for a decent german girl that a man should go away and leave her. Lena knew
very well that her aunt was right when she said the way Herman had acted to
her was a disgrace to everyone that knew her. Mary and Nellie and the other
girls she always sat with were always very good to Lena but that did not make
her trouble any better. It was a disgrace the way Lena had been left, to any decent family, and that could never be made any different to her.

And so the slow days wore on, and Lena never saw her Aunt Mathilda. At
last on Sunday she got word by a boy to go and see her aunt Mathilda. Lena's
heart beat quick for she was very nervous now with all this that had happened
to her. She went just as quickly as she could to see her Aunt Mathilda.

Mrs. Haydon quick, as soon as she saw Lena, began to scold her for keeping
her aunt waiting so long for her, and for not coming in all the week to see her, to
see if her aunt should need her, and so her aunt had to send a boy to tell her. But
it was easy, even for Lena, to see that her aunt was not really angry with her. It
wasn't Lena's fault, went on Mrs. Haydon, that everything was going to happen
all right for her. Mrs. Haydon was very tired taking all this trouble for her, and
when Lena couldn't even take trouble to come and see her aunt, to see if she
needed anything to tell her. But Mrs. Haydon really never minded things like
that when she could do things for anybody. She was tired now, all the trouble
she had been taking to make things right for Lena, but perhaps now Lena heard
it she would learn a little to be thankful to her. "You get all ready to be married
Tuesday. Lena, you hear me," said Mrs. Haydon to her. "You come here Tuesday
morning and I have everything all ready for you. You wear your new dress I got
you, and your hat with all them flowers on it, and you be very careful coming
you don't get your things all dirty, you so careless all the time, Lena, and not
thinking, and you act sometimes you never got no head at all on you. You go
home now, and you tell your Mrs. Aldrich that you leave her Tuesday. Don't you
go forgetting now, Lena, anything I ever told you what you should do to be care-

[1]Yes (German).

ful. You be a good girl, now Lena. You get married Tuesday to Herman Kreder." And that was all Lena ever knew of what had happened all this week to Herman Kreder. Lena forgot there was anything to know about it. She was really to be married Tuesday, and her Aunt Mathilda said she was a good girl, and now there was no disgrace left upon her.

Lena now fell back into the way she always had of being always dreamy and not there, the way she always had been, except for the few days she was so excited, because she had been left by a man the very day she was to have been married. Lena was a little nervous all these last days, but she did not think much about what it meant for her to be married.

Herman Kreder was not so content about it. He was quiet and was sullen and he knew he could not help it. He knew now he just had to let himself get married. It was not that Herman did not like Lena Mainz. She was as good as any other girl could be for him. She was a little better perhaps than other girls he saw, she was so very quiet, but Herman did not like to always have to have a girl around him. Herman had always done everything that his mother and his father wanted. His father had found him in New York, where Herman had gone to be with his married sister.

Herman's father when he had found him coaxed Herman a long time and went on whole days with his complaining to him, always troubled but gentle and quite patient with him, and always he was worrying to Herman about what was the right way his boy Herman should always do, always whatever it was his mother ever wanted from him, and always Herman never made him any answer.

Old Mr. Kreder kept on saying to him, he did not see how Herman could think now, it could be any different. When you make a bargain you just got to stick right to it, that was the only way old Mr. Kreder could ever see it, and saying you would get married to a girl and she got everything all ready, that was a bargain just like one you make in business and Herman he had made it, and now Herman he would just have to do it, old Mr. Kreder didn't see there was any other way a good boy like his Herman had, to do it. And then too that Lena Mainz was such a nice girl and Herman hadn't ought to really give his father so much trouble and make him pay out all that money, to come all the way to New York just to find him, and they both lose all that time from their working, when all Herman had to do was just to stand up, for an hour, and then he would be all right married, and it would be all over for him, and then everything at home would never be any different to him.

And his father went on; there was his poor mother saying always how her Herman always did everything before she ever wanted, and now just because he got notions in him, and wanted to show people how he could be stubborn, he was making all this trouble for her, and making them pay all that money just to run around and find him. "You got no idea Herman, how bad mama is feeling about the way you been acting Herman," said old Mr. Kreder to him. "She says she never can understand how you can be so thankless Herman. It hurts her very much you been so stubborn, and she find you such a nice girl for you, like Lena Mainz who is always just so quiet and always saves up all her wages, and she never wanting her own way at all like some girls are always all the time to have it, and your mama trying so hard, just so you could be comfortable Herman to be married, and then you act so stubborn Herman. You like all young people Herman, you think only about yourself, and what you are just wanting, and your mama she is thinking only what is good for you to have, for you in the future. Do you think your mama wants to have a girl around to be a bother, for herself, Herman. Its just for you Herman she is always thinking, and she talks always about how happy she will be, when she sees her Herman married to a nice girl, and then when she fixed it all up so good for you, so it never would be any bother to you, just the way she wanted you should like it, and you say yes all right, I do it, and then you go away like this act stubborn, and make all this trouble everybody to take for you, and we spend money, and I got to travel all round to find you. You come home now with me Herman and get married, and I tell your mama she better not say anything to you about how much it cost me to come all the way to look for you—Hey Herman," said his father coaxing, "Hey, you come home now and get married. All you got to do Herman is just to stand up for an hour Herman, and then you don't never to have any more bother to it—Hey Herman!—you come home with me to-morrow and get married. Hey Herman."

Herman's married sister liked her brother Herman, and she had always tried to help him, when there was anything she knew he wanted. She liked it that he was so good and always did everything that their father and their mother wanted, but still she wished it could be that he could have more his own way, if there was anything he ever wanted.

But now she thought Herman with his girl was very funny. She wanted that Herman should be married. She thought it would do him lots of good to get married. She laughed at Herman when she heard the story. Until his father came to find him, she did not know why it was Herman had come just then to New York to see her. When she heard the story she laughed a good deal at her brother Herman and teased him a good deal about his running away, because he didn't want to have a girl to be all the time around him.

Herman's married sister liked her brother Herman, and she did not want him not to like to be with women. He was good, her brother Herman, and it would surely do him good to get married. It would make him stand up for himself stronger. Herman's sister always laughed at him and always she would try to reassure him. "Such a nice man as my brother Herman acting like as if he was afraid of women. Why the girls all like a man like you Herman, if you didn't always run away when you saw them. It do you good really Herman to get married, and then you got somebody you can boss around when you want to. It do you good Herman to get married, you see if you don't like it, when you really done it. You go along home now with papa, Herman and get married to that Lena. You don't know how nice you like it Herman when you try once how you can do it. You just don't be afraid of nothing, Herman. You good enough for any girl to marry, Herman. Any girl be glad to have a man like you to be always with them Herman. You just go along home with papa and try it what I say, Herman. Oh you so funny Herman, when you sit there, and then run away and leave your girl behind you. I know she is crying like anything Herman for to lose you. Don't be bad to her Herman. You go along home with papa now and get married Herman. I'd be awful ashamed Herman, to really have a brother didn't have spirit enough to get married, when a girl is just drying for to have him. You always like me to be with you Herman. I don't see why you say you don't want a girl to be all the time around you. You always been good to me Herman, and I know you always be good to that Lena, and you soon feel just like as if she had always been there with you. Don't act like as if you wasn't a nice strong man, Herman. Really I laugh at you Herman, but you know I like awful well to see you real happy. You go home and get married to that Lena, Herman. She is a real pretty girl and real nice and good and quiet and she make my brother Herman very happy. You just stop your fussing now with Herman, papa. He go with you to-morrow papa, and you see he like it so much to be married, he make everybody laugh just to see him be so happy. Really truly, that's the way it will be with you Herman. You just listen to me what I tell you Herman." And so his sister laughed at him and reassured him, and his father kept on telling what the mother always said about her Herman, and he coaxed him and Herman never said anything in answer, and his sister packed his things up and was very cheerful with him, and she kissed him, and then she laughed and then she kissed him, and his father went and brought the tickets for the train, and at last late on Sunday he brought Herman back to Bridgepoint with him.

It was always very hard to keep Mrs. Kreder from saying what she thought, to her Herman, but her daughter had written her a letter, so as to warn her not to say anything about what he had been doing, to him, and her husband came in with Herman and said, "Here we come home mama, Herman and me, and we are very tired it was so crowded coming," and then he whispered to her. "You be good to Herman, mama, he didn't mean to make us so much trouble," and so old Mrs. Kreder, held in what she felt was so strong in her to say to her Herman. She just said very stiffly to him, "I'm glad to see you come home today, Herman." Then she went to arrange it all with Mrs. Haydon.

Herman was now again just like he always had been, sullen and very good, and very quiet, and always ready to do whatever his mother and his father wanted. Tuesday morning came, Herman got his new clothes on and went with his father and mother to stand up for an hour and get married. Lena was there in her new dress, and her hat with all the pretty flowers, and she was very nervous for now she knew she was really very soon to be married. Mrs. Haydon had everything all ready. Everybody was there just as they should be and very soon Herman Kreder and Lena Mainz were married.

When everything was really over, they went back to the Kreder house together. They were all now to live together, Lena and Herman and the old father and the old mother, in the house where Mr. Kreder had worked so many years as a tailor, with his son Herman always there to help him.

Irish Mary had often said to Lena she never did see how Lena could ever want to have anything to do with Herman Kreder and his dirty stingy parents. The old Kreders were to an Irish nature, a stingy, dirty couple. They had not the free-hearted, thoughtless, fighting, mud bespattered, ragged, peat-smoked cabin dirt that irish Mary knew and could forgive and love. Theirs was the german dirt of saving, of being dowdy and loose and foul in your clothes so as to save them and yourself in washing, having your hair greasy to save it in the soap and drying, having your clothes dirty, not in freedom, but because so it was cheaper, keeping the house close and smelly because so it cost less to get it heated, living so poorly not only so as to save money but so they should never even know themselves that they had it, working all the time not only because from their nature they just had to and because it made them money but also that they never could be put in any way to make them spend their money.

This was the place Lena now had for her home and to her it was very different than it could be for an irish Mary. She too was german and was thrifty, though she was always so dreamy and not there. Lena was always careful with things and she always saved her money, for that was the only way she knew how to do it. She never had taken care of her own money and she never had thought how to use it.

Lena Mainz had been, before she was Mrs. Herman Kreder, always clean and decent in her clothes and in her person, but it was not because she ever thought about it or really needed so to have it, it was the way her people did in the german country where she came from, and her Aunt Mathilda and the good german cook who always scolded, had kept her on and made her, with their scoldings, always more careful to keep clean and to wash real often. But there was no deep need in all this for Lena and so, though Lena did not like the old Kreders, though she really did not know that, she did not think about their being stingy dirty people.

Herman Kreder was cleaner than the old people, just because it was his nature to keep cleaner, but he was used to his mother and his father, and he never thought that they should keep things cleaner. And Herman too always saved all his money, except for that little beer he drank when he went out with other men of an evening the way he always liked to do it, and he never thought of any other way to spend it. His father had always kept all the money for them and he always was doing business with it. And then too Herman really had no money, for he always had worked for his father, and his father had never thought to pay him.

And so they began all four to live in the Kreder house together, and Lena began soon with it to look careless and a little dirty, and to be more lifeless with it, and nobody ever noticed much what Lena wanted, and she never really knew herself what she needed.

The only real trouble that came to Lena with their living all four there together, was the way old Mrs. Kreder scolded. Lena had always been used to being scolded, but this scolding of old Mrs. Kreder was very different from the way she ever before had had to endure it.

Herman, now he was married to her, really liked Lena very well. He did not care very much about her but she never was a bother to him being there around him, only when his mother worried and was nasty to them because Lena was so careless, and did not know how to save things right for them with their eating, and all the other ways with money, that the old woman had to save it.

Herman Kreder had always done everything his mother and his father wanted but he did not really love his parents very deeply. With Herman it was always only that he hated to have any struggle. It was all always all right with him when he could just go along and do the same thing over every day with his working, and not to hear things, and not to have people make him listen to their anger. And now his marriage, and he just knew it would, was making trouble for him. It made him hear more what his mother was always saying, with her scolding. He had to really hear it now because Lena was there, and she was so scared and dull always when she heard it. Herman knew very well with his mother, it was all right if one ate very little and worked hard all day and did not learn her when she scolded, the way Herman always had done before they were so foolish about his getting married and having a girl there to be all the time around him, and now he had to help her so the girl could learn too, not to hear it when his mother scolded, and not to look so scared, and not to eat much, and always to be sure to save it.

Herman really did not know very well what he could do to help Lena to understand it. He could never answer his mother back to help Lena, that never would make things any better for her, and he never could feel in himself any way to comfort Lena, to make her strong not to hear his mother, in all the awful ways she always scolded. It just worried Herman to have it like that all the time around him. Herman did not know much about how a man could make a struggle with a mother, to do much to keep her quiet, and indeed Herman never knew much how to make a struggle against anyone who really wanted to have anything very badly. Herman all his life never wanted anything so badly, that he would really make a struggle against any one to get it. Herman all his life only wanted to live regular and quiet, and not talk much and to do the same way every day like every other with his working. And now his mother had made him get married to this Lena and now with his mother making all that scolding, he had all this trouble and this worry always on him.

Mrs. Haydon did not see Lena now very often. She had not lost her interest in her niece Lena, but Lena could not come much to her house to see her, it would not be right, now Lena was a married woman. And then too Mrs. Haydon had her hands full just then with her two daughters, for she was getting them ready to find them good husbands, and then too her own husband now worried her very often about her always spoiling that boy of hers, so he would be sure to turn out no good and be a disgrace to a german family, and all because his mother always spoiled him. All these things were very worrying now to

Mrs. Haydon, but still she wanted to be good to Lena, though she could not see her very often. She only saw her when Mrs. Haydon went to call on Mrs. Kreder or when Mrs. Kreder came to see Mrs. Haydon, and that never could be very often. Then too these days Mrs. Haydon could not scold Lena, Mrs. Kreder was always there with her, and it would not be right to scold Lena when Mrs. Kreder was there, who had now the real right to do it. And so her aunt always said nice things now to Lena, and though Mrs. Haydon sometimes was a little worried when she saw Lena looking sad and not careful, she did not have time just then to really worry much about it.

Lena now never any more saw the girls she always used to sit with. She had no way now to see them and it was not in Lena's nature to search out ways to see them, nor did she now ever think much of the days when she had been used to see them. They never any of them had come to the Kreder house to see her. Not even Irish Mary had ever thought to come to see her. Lena had been soon forgotten by them. They had soon passed away from Lena and now Lena never thought any more that she had ever known them.

The only one to her old friends who tried to know what Lena liked and what she needed, and who always made Lena come to see her, was the good german cook who had always scolded. She now scolded Lena hard for letting herself go so, and going out when she was looking so untidy. "I know you going to have a baby Lena, but that's no way for you to be looking. I am ashamed most to see you come and sit here in my kitchen, looking so sloppy and like you never used to Lena. I never see anybody like you Lena. Herman is very good to you, you always say so, and he don't treat you bad even though you don't deserve to have anybody good to you, you so careless all the time, Lena, letting yourself go like you never had anybody tell you what was the right way you should know how to be looking. No, Lena, I don't see no reason you should let yourself go so and look so untidy Lena, so I am ashamed to see you sit there looking so ugly, Lena. No Lena that ain't no way ever I see a woman make things come out better, letting herself go so every way and crying all the time like as if you had real trouble. I never wanted to see you marry Herman Kreder, Lena, I knew what you got to stand with that old woman always, and that old man, he is so stingy too and he don't say things out but he ain't any better in his heart than his wife with her bad ways, I know that Lena, I know they don't hardly give you enough to eat, Lena, I am real sorry for you Lena, you know that Lena, but that ain't any way to be going round so untidy Lena, even if you have got all that trouble. You never see me do like that Lena, though sometimes I got a headache so I can't see to stand to be working hardly, and nothing comes right with all my cooking, but I always see Lena, I look decent. That's the only way a german girl can make things come out right Lena. You hear me what I am saying to you Lena. Now you eat something nice Lena, I got it all ready for you, and you wash up and be careful Lena and the baby will come all right to you, and then I make your Aunt Mathilda see that you live in a house soon all alone with Herman and your baby, and then everything go better for you. You hear me what I say to you Lena. Now don't let me ever see you come looking like this any more Lena, and you just stop with that always crying. You ain't got no reason to be sitting there now with all that crying, I never see anybody have trouble it did them any good to be the way you are doing, Lena. You hear me Lena. You go home now and you be good the way I tell you Lena, and I see what I can do. I make sure your Aunt Mathilda make old Mrs. Kreder let you be till you get your baby all right. Now don't you be scared and so silly Lena. I don't like to see you act so Lena when really you got a nice man and so many things really any girl should be grateful to be having. Now you go home Lena to-day and you do the way I say, to you, and I see what I can do to help you."

"Yes Mrs. Aldrich" said the good german woman to her mistress later, "Yes Mrs. Aldrich that's the way it is with them girls when they want so to get married. They don't know when they got it good Mrs. Aldrich. They never know what it is they're really wanting when they got it, Mrs. Aldrich. There's that poor Lena, she just been here crying and looking so careless so I scold her, but that was no good that marrying for that poor Lena, Mrs. Aldrich. She do look so pale and sad now Mrs. Aldrich, it just break my heart to see her. She was a good girl was Lena, Mrs. Aldrich, and I never had no trouble with her like I got with so many young girls nowadays, Mrs. Aldrich, and I never see any girl any better to work right than our Lena, and now she got to stand it all the time with that old woman Mrs. Kreder. My! Mrs. Aldrich, she is a bad old woman to her. I never see Mrs. Aldrich how old people can be so bad to young girls and not have no kind of patience with them. If Lena could only live with her Herman, he ain't so bad the way men are, Mrs. Aldrich, but he is just the way always his mother wants him, he ain't got no spirit in him, and so I don't really see no help for that poor Lena. I know her aunt, Mrs. Haydon, meant it all right for her Mrs. Aldrich, but poor Lena, it would be better for her if her Herman had stayed there in New York that time he went away to leave her. I don't like it the way Lena is looking now, Mrs. Aldrich. She looks like as if she don't have no life left in her hardly, Mrs. Aldrich, she just drags around and looks so dirty and after all the pains I always took to teach her and to keep her nice in her ways and looking. It don't do no good to them, for them girls to get married Mrs. Aldrich, they are much better when they only know it, to stay in a good place when they got it, and keep on regular with their working. I don't like it the way Lena looks now Mrs. Aldrich. I wish I knew some way to help that poor Lena, Mrs. Aldrich, but she is a bad old woman, that old Mrs. Kreder, Herman's mother. I speak to Mrs. Haydon real soon, Mrs. Aldrich, I see what we can do now to help that poor Lena."

These were really bad days for poor Lena. Herman always was real good to her and now he even sometimes tried to stop his mother from scolding Lena. "She ain't well now mama, you let her be now you hear me. You tell me what it is you want she should be doing, I tell her. I see she does it right just the way you want it mama. You let be, I saw now mama, with that always scolding Lena. You let be, I say now, you wait till she is feeling better." Herman was getting really strong to struggle, for he could see that Lena with that baby working hard inside her, really could not stand it any longer with his mother and the awful ways she always scolded.

It was a new feeling Herman now had inside him that made him feel he was strong to make a struggle. It was new for Herman Kreder really to be wanting something, but Herman wanted strongly now to be a father, and he wanted badly that his baby should be a boy and healthy. Herman never had cared really very much about his father and his mother, though always, all his life, he had done everything just as they wanted, and he had never really cared much about his wife, Lena, though he always had been very good to her, and had always tried to keep his mother off her, with the awful way she always scolded, but to be really a father of a little baby, that feeling took hold of Herman very deeply. He was almost ready, so as to save his baby from all trouble, to really make a strong struggle with his mother and with his father, too, if he would not help him to control his mother.

Sometimes Herman even went to Mrs. Haydon to talk all this trouble over. They decided then together, it was better to wait there all four together for the baby, and Herman could make Mrs. Kreder stop a little with her scolding, and then when Lena was a little stronger, Herman should have his own house for her next door to his father, so he could always be there to help him in his working, but so they could eat and sleep in a house where the old woman could not control them and they could not hear her awful scolding.

And so things went on, the same way, a little longer. Poor Lena was not feeling any joy to have a baby. She was scared the way she had been when she was so sick on the water. She was scared now every time when anything would hurt her. She was scared and still and lifeless, and sure that every minute she would die. Lena had no power to be strong in this kind of trouble, she could only sit still and be scared, and dull, and lifeless, and sure that every minute she would die.

Before very long, Lena had her baby. He was a good, healthy little boy, the baby. Herman cared very much to have the baby. When Lena was a little stronger he took a house next door to the old couple, so he and his own family could eat and sleep and do the way they wanted. This did not seem to make much change now for Lena. She was just the same as when she was waiting with her baby. She just dragged around and was careless with her clothes and all lifeless, and she acted always and lived on just as if she had no feeling. She always did everything regular with the work, the way she always had had to do it, but she never got back any spirit in her. Herman was always good and kind, and always helped her with her working. He did everything he knew to help her. He always did all the active new things in the house and for the baby. Lena did what she had to do the way she always had been taught it. She always just kept going now with her working, and she was always careless, and dirty, and a little dazed, and lifeless. Lena never got any better in herself of this way of being that she had had ever since she had been married.

Mrs. Haydon never saw any more of her niece, Lena. Mrs. Haydon had now so much trouble with her own house, and her daughters getting married, and her boy, who was growing up, and who always was getting so much worse to manage. She knew she had done right by Lena. Herman Kreder was a good man, she would be glad to get one so good, sometimes, for her own daughters, and now they had a home to live in together, separate from the old people, who had made their trouble for them. Mrs. Haydon felt she had done very well by her niece, Lena, and she never thought now she needed any more to go and see her. Lena would do very well now without her aunt to trouble herself any more about her.

The good german cook who had always scolded, still tried to do her duty like a mother to poor Lena. It was very hard now to do right by Lena. Lena never seemed to hear now what anyone was saying to her. Herman was always doing everything he could to help her. Herman always, when he was home, took good care of the baby. Herman loved to take care of his baby. Lena never thought to take him out or to do anything she didn't have to.

The good cook sometimes made Lena come to see her. Lena would come with her baby and sit there in the kitchen, and watch the good woman cooking, and listen to her sometimes a little, the way she used to, while the good german woman scolded her for going around looking so careless when now she had no trouble, and sitting there so dull and always being just so thankless. Sometimes Lena would wake up a little and get back into her face her old, gentle, patient, and unsuffering sweetness, but mostly Lena did not seem to hear much when the good german woman scolded. Lena always liked it when Mrs. Aldrich her good mistress spoke to her kindly, and then Lena would seem to go back and feel herself to be like she was when she had been in service. But mostly Lena just lived along and was careless in her clothes, and dull, and lifeless.

By and by Lena had two more little babies. Lena was not so much scared now when she had the babies. She did not seem to notice very much when they hurt her, and she never seemed to feel very much now about anything that happened to her.

They were very nice babies, all these three that Lena had, and Herman took good care of them always. Herman never really cared much about his wife, Lena. The only thing Herman ever really cared for were his babies. Herman always was very good to his children. He always had a gentle, tender way when he held them. He learned to be very handy with them. He spent all the time he was not working, with them. By and by he began to work all day in his own home so that he could have his children always in the same room with him.

Lena always was more and more lifeless and Herman now mostly never thought about her. He more and more took all the care of their three children. He saw to their eating right and their washing, and he dressed them every morning, and he taught them the right way to do things, and he put them to their sleeping, and he was now always every minute with them. Then there was to come to them, a fourth baby. Lena went to the hospital near by to have the baby. Lena seemed to be going to have much trouble with it. When the baby was come out at last, it was like its mother lifeless. While it was coming, Lena had grown very pale and sicker. When it was all over Lena had died, too, and nobody knew just how it had happened to her.

The good german cook who had always scolded Lena, and had always to the last day tried to help her, was the only one who ever missed her. She remembered how nice Lena had looked all the time she was in service with her, and how her voice had been so gentle and sweet-sounding, and how she always was a good girl, and how she never had to have any trouble with her, the way she always had with all the other girls who had been taken into the house to help her. The good cook sometimes spoke so of Lena when she had time to have a talk with Mrs. Aldrich, and this was all the remembering there now ever was of Lena.

Herman Kreder now always lived very happy, very gentle, very quiet, very well content alone with his three children. He never had a woman any more to be all the time around him. He always did all his own work in his house, when he was through every day with the work he was always doing for his father. Herman always was alone, and he always worked alone, until his little ones were big enough to help him. Herman Kreder was very well content now and he always lived very regular and peaceful, and with every day just like the next one, always alone now with his three good, gentle children.

Finis[2]

Alice Moore Dunbar Nelson 1875–1935

Alice Moore Dunbar Nelson's work is as remarkable for its scope as is her life for her other many accomplishments. Dunbar Nelson was a scholar, writing primarily on school curricula and literary topics; a poet and writer of short stories; a cellist and violinist (and a mandolin player); a journalist; a teacher; and an activist in politics and civic affairs. A native of New Orleans, Alice Moore attended public schools and received a degree from Straight College in 1892. (The college is now called Dillard University.) By the time her first book was published in 1895 (*Violets and Other Tales*), Alice Moore was considered a prominent intellectual within the African-American community. Her marriage to writer Paul Laurence Dunbar is considered a study in contrasts: While he wrote in dialect, her work was criticized for being "nonracial." After she and Dunbar

[2]The end (Latin).

divorced, she married Robert John Nelson, publisher of a newspaper dedicated to civil rights, a match for her own political dedication. In addition to her own collections (often with poems, short stories, and sketches), Dunbar Nelson edited several anthologies of African-American writing, worked on local political committees, and prepared a weekly column for the *Washington Eagle* newspaper. Not surprisingly, her stories, journalism, and poems are marked by her unrelenting commitment to constructive activism.

I SIT AND SEW

I sit and sew—a useless task it seems,
My hands grown tired, my head weighed down with dreams—
The panoply of war, the martial tread of men,
Grim-faced, stern-eyed, gazing beyond the ken[1]
Of lesser souls, whose eyes have not seen Death   5
Nor learned to hold their lives but as a breath—
But—I must sit and sew.

I sit and sew—my heart aches with desire—
That pageant terrible, that fiercely pouring fire
On wasted fields, and writhing grotesque things   10
Once men. My soul in pity flings
Appealing cries, yearning only to go
There in that holocaust of hell, those fields of woe—
But—I must sit and sew.

The little useless seam, the idle patch;   15
Why dream I here beneath my homely thatch,
When there they lie in sodden mud and rain,
Pitifully calling me, the quick[2] ones and the slain?
You need me, Christ! It is no roseate dream
That beckons me—this pretty futile seam,   20
It stifles me—God, must I sit and sew?

[1] Range of vision.
[2] Living.

THE GOODNESS OF SAINT ROCQUE

Manuela was tall and slender and graceful, and once you knew her the lithe form could never be mistaken. She walked with the easy spring that comes from a perfectly arched foot. To-day she swept swiftly down Marais Street, casting a quick glance here and there from under her heavy veil as if she feared she was being followed. If you had peered under the veil, you would have seen that Manuela's dark eyes were swollen and discoloured about the lids, as though they had known a sleepless, tearful night.

There had been a picnic the day before, and as merry a crowd of giddy, chattering Creole girls and boys as ever you could see boarded the ramshackle dummy-train that puffed its way wheezily out wide Elysian Fields Street, around the lily-covered bayous, to Milneburg-on-the-Lake. Now, a picnic at Milneburg is a thing to be remembered for ever. One charters a rickety-looking, weather-beaten dancing-pavilion, built over the water, and after storing the children — for your true Creole never leaves the small folks at home — and the baskets and mothers downstairs, the young folk go upstairs and dance to the tune of the best band you ever heard. For what can equal the music of a violin, a guitar, a cornet, and a bass viol to trip the quadrille to at a picnic?

Then one can fish in the lake and go bathing under the prim bath-houses, so severely separated sexually, and go rowing on the lake in a trim boat, followed by the shrill warnings of anxious mamans. And in the evening one comes home, hat crowned with cool gray Spanish moss, hands burdened with fantastic la-tanier baskets woven by the brown bayou boys, hand in hand with your dearest one, tired but happy.

At this particular picnic, however, there had been bitterness of spirit. Theophilé was Manuela's own especial property, and Theophilé had proven false. He had not danced a single waltz or quadrille with Manuela, but had deserted her for Claralie, blonde and petite. It was Claralie whom Theophilé had rowed out on the lake; it was Claralie whom Theophilé had gallantly led to din-ner; it was Claralie's hat that he wreathed with Spanish moss, and Claralie whom he escorted home after the jolly singing ride in town on the little dummy-train.

Not that Manuela lacked partners or admirers. Dear no! she was too grace-ful and beautiful for that. There had been more than enough for her. But Manuela loved Theophilé, you see, and no one could take his place. Still, she had tossed her head and let her silvery laughter ring out in the dance, as though she were the happiest of mortals, and had tripped home with Henri, leaning on his arm, and looking up into his eyes as though she adored him.

This morning she showed the traces of a sleepless night and an aching heart as she walked down Marais Street. Across wide St. Rocque Avenue she hastened. "Two blocks to the river and one below—" she repeated to herself breathlessly. Then she stood on the corner gazing about her, until with a final summoning of a desperate courtage she dived through a small wicket gate into a garden of weed-choked flowers.

There was a hoarse, rusty little bell on the gate that gave querulous tongue as she pushed it open. The house that sat back in the yard was little and old and weather-beaten. Its one-story frame had once been painted, but that was a memory remote and traditional. A straggling morning-glory strove to conceal its time-ravaged face. The little walk of broken bits of brick was reddened carefully, and the one little step was scrupulously yellow-washed, which denoted that the occupants were cleanly as well as religious.

Manuela's timid knock was answered by a harsh "Entrez."

It was a small sombre room within, with a bare yellow-washed floor and ragged curtains at the little widow. In a corner was a diminutive altar draped with threadbare lace. The red glow of the taper lighted a cheap print of St. Joseph and a brazen crucifix. The human element in the room was furnished by a little, wizened yellow woman, who, black-robed, turbaned, and stern, sat before an uncertain table whereon were greasy cards.

Manuela paused, her eyes blinking at the semi-obscurity within. The Wizened One called in croaking tones:

"An 'fo' w'y you come here? Assiez-là, ma'amzelle."

Timidly Manuela sat at the table facing the owner of the voice.

"I want," she began faintly; but the Mistress of the Cards understood: she had had much experience. The cards were shuffled in her long grimy talons and stacked before Manuela.

"Now you cut dem in t'ree part, so — un, deux, trois, bien! You mek' you' weesh wid all you' heart, bien! Yaas, I see, I see!"

Breathlessly did Manuela learn that her lover was true, but "dat light gal, yaas, she mek' nouvena in St. Rocque fo' hees love."

"I give you one lil' charm, yaas," said the Wizened One when the séance was over, and Manuela, all white and nervous, leaned back in the rickety chair. "I give you one lil' charm fo' to ween him back, yaas. You wear h'it 'roun' you' wais', an' he come back. Den you mek prayer at St. Rocque an' burn can'le. Den you come back an' tell me, yaas. Cinquante sous, ma'amzelle. Merci. Good luck go wid you."

Readjusting her veil, Manuela passed out the little wicket gate, treading on air. Again the sun shown, and the breath of the swamps came as healthful seabreeze unto her nostrils. She fairly flew in the direction of St. Rocque.

There were quite a number of persons entering the white gates of the cemetery, for this was Friday, when all those who wish good luck pray to the saint, and wash their steps promptly at twelve o'clock with a wondrous mixture to guard the house. Manuela bought a candle from the keeper of the little lodge at the entrance, and pausing one instant by the great sun-dial to see if the heavens and the hour were propitious, glided into the tiny chapel, dim and stifling with heavy air from myriad wish-candles blazing on the wide table before the altarrail. She said her prayer and lighting her candle placed it with the others.

Mon Dieu! how brightly the sun seemed to shine now, she thought, pausing at the door on her way out. Her small finger-tips, still bedewed with holy water, rested caressingly on a gamin's head. The ivy which enfolds the quaint chapel never seemed so green; the shrines which serve as the Way of the Cross never seemed so artistic; the baby graves, even, seemed cheerful.

Theophilé called Sunday. Manuela's heart leaped. He had been spending his Sundays with Claralie. His stay was short and he was plainly bored. But Manuela knelt to thank the good St. Rocque that night, and fondled the charm about her slim waist. There came a box of bonbons during the week, with a decorative card all roses and fringe, from Theophilé; but being a Creole, and therefore superstitiously careful, and having been reared by a wise and experienced maman to mistrust the gifts of a recreant lover, Manuela quietly thrust bonbons, box, and card into the kitchen fire, and the Friday following placed the second candle of her nouvena in St. Rocque.

Those of Manuela's friends who had watched with indignation Theophilé gallantly leading Claralie home from High Mass on Sundays, gasped with astonishment when the next Sunday, with his usual bow, the young man offered Manuela his arm as the worshippers filed out in step to the organ's march. Claralie tossed her head as she crossed herself with holy water, and the pink in her cheeks was brighter than usual.

Manuela smiled a bright good-morning when she met Claralie in St. Rocque the next Friday. The little blonde blushed furiously, and Manuela rushed post-haste to the Wizened One to confer upon this new issue.

"H'it ees good," said the dame, shaking her turbaned head. "She ees 'fraid, she will work, mais you' charm, h'it weel beat her."

And Manuela departed with radiant eyes.

Theophilé was not at Mass Sunday morning, and murderous glances flashed from Claralie to Manuela before the tinkling of the Host-Bell. Nor did Theophilé call at either house. Two hearts beat furiously at the sound of every passing footstep, and two minds wondered if the other were enjoying the beloved one's smiles. Two pair of eyes, however, blue and black, smiled on others, and their owners laughed and seemed none the less happy. For your Creole girls are proud, and would die rather than let the world see their sorrows.

Monday evening Theophilé, the missing, showed his rather sheepish countenance in Manuela's parlour, and explained that he, with some chosen spirits, had gone for a trip — "over the Lake."

"I did not ask you where you were yesterday," replied the girl, saucily.

Theophilé shrugged his shoulders and changed the conversation.

The next week there was a birthday fête in honour of Louise, Theophilé's young sister. Everyone was bidden, and no one thought of refusing, for Louise was young, and this would be her first party. So, though the night was hot, the dancing went on as merrily as light young feet could make it go. Claralie fluffed her dainty white skirts, and cast mischievous sparkles in the direction of Theophilé, who with the maman and Louise was bravely trying not to look self-conscious. Manuela, tall and calm and proud-looking, in a cool, pale yellow gown was apparently enjoying herself without paying the slightest attention to her young host.

"Have I the pleasure of this dance?" he asked her finally, in a lull of the music.

She bowed assent, and as if moved by a common impulse they strolled out of the dancing-room into the cool, quaint garden, where jessamines gave out an overpowering perfume, and a caged mocking-bird complained melodiously to the full moon in the sky.

It must have been an engrossing tête-a-tête, for the call to supper had sounded twice before they heard and hurried into the house. The march had formed with Louise radiantly leading on the arm of papa. Claralie tripped by with Leon. Of course, nothing remained for Theophilé and Manuela to do but to bring up the rear, for which they received much good-natured chaffing.

But when the party reached the dining-room, Theophilé proudly led his partner to the head of the table, at the right hand of maman, and smiled benignly about at the delighted assemblage. Now you know, when a Creole young man places a girl at his mother's right hand at his own table, there is but one conclusion to be deduced therefrom.

If you had asked Manuela, after the wedding was over, how it happened, she would have said nothing, but looked wise.

If you had asked Claralie, she would have laughed and said she always preferred Leon.

If you had asked Theophilé, he would have wondered that you thought he had ever meant more than to tease Manuela.

If you had asked the Wizened One, she would have offered you a charm.

But St. Rocque knows, for he is a good saint, and if you believe in him and are true and good, and make your nouvenas with a clean heart, he will grant your wish.

Zora Neale Hurston 1881–1960

In addition to her novels, short stories, plays, and essays, Zora Neale Hurston was a student of the anthropologist Franz Boas during her years at Barnard College in New York. Yet despite her important contributions as a writer and documenter of African-American folklore (the stories, as she put it, called "lies" by those who told them), Hurston spent her last years as a maid, her rediscovery in the 1970s prompted almost wholly by writer Alice Walker. It was Walker who placed a prominent tombstone at Hurston's unmarked grave and called Hurston one of the greatest writers of the century. In fact, Walker has said that if she were on a desert island for the rest of her life, allowed only ten books with her, she would "choose, unhesitatingly, two of Zora's": *Mules and Men* (1935) and *Their Eyes Were Watching God* (1937). It is almost universally accepted that these two novels are among the best in African-American literature—or of any literature.

THE GILDED SIX-BITS

It was a Negro yard around a Negro house in a Negro settlement that looked to the payroll of the G. and G. Fertilizer Works for its support.

But there was something happy about the place. The front yard was parted in the middle by a sidewalk from gate to doorstep, a sidewalk edged on either side by quart bottles driven neck down into the ground on a slant. A mess of homey flowers planted without a plan but blooming cheerily from their helter-skelter places. The fence and house were white-washed. The porch and steps scrubbed white.

The front door stood open to the sunshine so that the floor of the front room could finish drying after its weekly scouring. It was Saturday. Everything clean from the front gate to the privy house. Yard raked so that the strokes of the rake would make a pattern. Fresh newspaper cut in fancy edge on the kitchen shelves.

Missie May was bathing herself in the galvanized washtub in the bedroom. Her dark-brown skin glistened under the soapsuds that skittered down from her washrag. Her stiff young breasts thrust forward aggressively like broad-based cones with the tips lacquered in black.

She heard men's voices in the distance and glanced at the dollar clock on the dresser.

"Humph! Ah'm way behind time t'day! Joe gointer be heah 'fore Ah git mah clothes on if Ah don't make haste."

She grabbed the clean meal sack at hand and dried herself hurriedly and began to dress. But before she could tie her slippers, there came the ring of singing metal on wood. Nine times.

Missie May grinned with delight. She had not seen the big, tall man come stealing in the gate and creep up the walk, grinning happily at the joyful mischief he was about to commit. But she knew that it was her husband throwing silver dollars in the door for her to pick up and pile beside her plate at dinner. It was this way every Saturday afternoon. The nine dollars hurled into the open door, he scurried to a hiding place behind the cape jasmine bush and waited.

Missie May promptly appeared at the door in mock alarm.

"Who dat chunkin' money in mah do'way?" she demanded. No answer from the yard. She leaped off the porch and began to search the shrubbery. She peeped under the porch and hung over the gate to look up and down the road. While she did this, the man behind the jasmine darted to the chinaberry tree. She spied him and gave chase.

"Nobody ain't gointer be chunkin' money at me and Ah not do 'em nothin'," she shouted in mock anger. He ran around the house with Missie May at his heels. She overtook him at the kitchen door. He ran inside but could not close it after him before she crowded in and locked with him in a rough and tumble. For several minutes the two were a furious mass of male and female energy. Shouting, laughing, twisting, turning, tussling, tickling each other in the ribs; Missie May clutching onto Joe and Joe trying, but not too hard to get away.

"Missie May, take yo' hand out mah pocket!" Joe shouted out between laughs.

"Ah ain't, Joe, not lessen you gwine gimme whateve' it is good you got in yo' pocket. Turn it go, Joe, do Ah'll tear yo' clothes."

"Go on tear 'em. You de one dat pushes de needles round heah. Move yo' hand, Missie May."

"Lemme git dat paper sack out yo' pocket. Ah bet it's candy kisses."

"Tain't. Move yo' hand. Woman ain't got no business in a man's clothes no-how. Go way."

Missie May gouged way down and gave an upward jerk and triumphed.

"Unhhunh! Ah got it. It 'tis so candy kisses. Ah knowed you had somethin' for me in yo' clothes. Now Ah got to see whut's in every pocket you got."

Joe smiled indulgently and let his wife go through all of his pockets and take out the things that he had hidden there for her to find. She bore off the chewing gum, the cake of sweet soap, the pocket handkerchief as if she had wrested them from him, as if they had not been bought for the sake of this friendly battle.

"Whew! Dat play-fight done got me all warmed up," Joe exclaimed. "Got me some water in de kittle?"

"Yo' water is on de fire and yo' clean things is cross de bed. Hurry up and wash yo'self and git changed so we kin eat. Ah'm hongry." As Missie said this, she bore the steaming kettle into the bedroom.

"You ain't hongry, sugar," Joe contradicted her. "Youse jes' a little empty. Ah'm de one whut's hongry. Ah could eat up camp meetin', back off 'ssociation, and drink Jurdan dry. Have it on de table when Ah git out de tub."

"Don't you mess wid mah business, man. You git in yo' clothes. Ah'm a real wife, not no dress and breath. Ah might not look lak one, but if you burn me, you won't git a thing but wife ashes."

Joe splashed in the bedroom and Missie May fanned around in the kitchen. A fresh red and white checked cloth on the table. Big pitcher of buttermilk beaded with pale drops of butter from the churn. Hot fried mullet, crackling bread, ham hock atop a mound of string beans and new potatoes, and perched on the windowsill, a pone of spicy potato pudding.

Very little talk during the meal, but that little consisted of banter that pretended to deny affection but in reality flaunted it. Like when Missie May reached for a second helping of the tater pone. Joe snatched it out of her reach.

After Missie May had made two or three unsuccessful grabs at the pan, she begged, "Aw, Joe, gimme some mo' dat tater pone."

"Nope, sweetenin' is for us men-folks. Y'all pritty lil frail eels don't need nothin' lak dis. You too sweet already."

"Please, Joe."

"Naw, naw. Ah don't want you to git no sweeter than whut you is already. We goin' down de road a lil piece t'night, so you go put on yo' Sunday-go-to-meetin' things."

Missie May looked at her husband to see if he was playing some prank. "Sho nuff, Joe?"

"Yeah. We goin' to de ice-cream parlor."

"Where de ice-cream parlor at, Joe?"

"A new man done come heah from Chicago and he done got a place and took and opened it up for a ice-cream parlor, and bein' as it's real swell, Ah wants you to be one de first ladies to walk in dere and have some set down."

"Do Jesus. Ah ain't knowed nothin' 'bout it. Who de man done it?"

"Mister Otis D. Slemmons, of spots and places — Memphis, Chicago, Jacksonville, Philadelphia, and so on."

"Dat heavy-set man wid his mouth full of gold teethes?"

"Yeah. Where did you see 'im at?"

"Ah went down to de sto' tuh git a box of lye and Ah seen 'im standin' on de corner talkin' to some of de mens, and Ah come on back and went to scrubbin' de floor, and he passed and tipped his hat whilst Ah was scourin' de steps. Ah thought Ah never seen *him* befo'."

Joe smiled pleasantly. "Yeah, he's up to date. He got de finest clothes Ah ever seen on a colored man's back."

"Aw, he don't look no better in his clothes than you do in yourn. He got a puzzlegut on 'im and he so chuckle-headed, he got a pone behind his neck."

Joe looked down at his own abdomen and said wistfully: "Wisht Ah had a build on me lak he got. He ain't puzzlegutted, honey. He jes' got a corperation. Dat make 'm look lak a rich white man. All rich mens is got some belly on 'em."

"Ah seen de pitchers of Henry Ford and he's a spare-built man, and Rockefeller look lak he ain't got but one gut. But Ford and Rockefeller and dis Slemmons and all de rest kin be as many-gutted as dey please, Ah's satisfied wid you jes' lak you is, baby. God took pattern after a pine tree and built you noble. Youse a pritty man, and if Ah knowed any way to make you mo' pritty still, Ah'd take and do it."

Joe reached over gently and toyed with Missie May's ear. "You jes' say dat cause you love me, but Ah know Ah can't hold no light to Otis D. Slemmons. Ah ain't never been nowhere and Ah ain't got nothin' but you."

Missie May got on his lap and kissed him and he kissed back in kind. Then he went on. "All de womens is crazy 'bout 'im everywhere he go."

"How you know dat, Joe?"

"He told us so hisself."

"Dat don't' make it so. His mouf is cut crossways, ain't it? Well, he kin lie jes' lak anybody else."

"Good Lawd, Missie! You womens sho is hard to sense into things. He's got a five-dollar gold piece for a stickpin and he got a ten-dollar gold piece on his watch chain and his mouf is jes' crammed full of gold teethes. Sho wisht it wuz mine. And whut make it so cool, he got money 'cumulated. And womens give it all to 'im."

"Ah don't see whut de womens see on 'im. Ah wouldn't give 'im a wink if de sheriff wuz after 'im."

"Well, he told us how de white womens in Chicago give 'im all dat gold money. So he don't 'low nobody to touch it at all. Not even put dey finger on it. Dey tole 'im not to. You kin make 'miration at it, but don't tetch it."

"Whyn't he stay up dere where dey so crazy 'bout 'im?"

"Ah reckon dey done made 'im vast-rich and he wants to travel some. He says dey wouldn't leave 'im hit a lick of work. He got mo' lady people crazy 'bout him than he kin shake a stick at."

"Joe, Ah hates to see you so dumb. Dat stray nigger jes' tell y'all anything and y'all b'lieve it."

"Go 'head on now, honey, and put on yo' clothes. He talkin' 'bout his pritty womens—Ah want 'im to see *mine*."

Missie May went off to dress and Joe spent the time trying to make his stomach punch out like Slemmons' middle. He tried the rolling swagger of the stranger, but found that his tall bone-and-muscle stride fitted ill with it. He just had time to drop back into his seat before Missie May came in, dressed to go.

On the way home that night Joe was exultant. "Didn't Ah say ole Otis was swell? Cain't he talk Chicago talk? Wuzn't dat funny whut he said when great big fat ole Ida Armstrong came in? He asted me, 'Who is dat broad wid de forte shake?' Dat's a new word. Us always thought forty was a set of figgers but he showed us where it means a whole heap of things. Sometimes he don't say forty, he jes' say thirty-eight and two, and dat mean de same thing. Know whut he tole me when Ah wuz payin' for our ice cream? He say, 'Ah have to hand it to you, Joe. Dat wife of yours is jes' thirty-eight and two. Yessuh, she's forte!' Ain't he killin'?"

"He'll do in case of a rush. But he sho is got uh heap uh gold on 'im. Dat's de first time Ah ever seed gold money. It lookted good on him show nuff, but it'd look a whole heap better on you."

"Who, me? Missie May, youse crazy! Where would a po'man lak me git gold money from?"

Missie May was silent for a minute, then she said. "Us might find some goin' long de road some time. Us could."

"Who would be losin' gold money round heah? We ain't even seen none dese white folks wearin' no gold money on dey watch chain. You must be figgerin' Mister Packard or Mister Cadillac goin' pass through heah."

"You don't know whut been lost 'round heah. Maybe somebody way back in memorial times lost they gold money and went off and it ain't never been found. And then if we wuz to find it, you could wear some 'thout havin' no gang of womens lak dat Slemmons say he got."

Joe laughed and hugged her. "Don't be so wishful 'bout me. Ah'm satisifed de way Ah is. So long as Ah be yo' husband. Ah don't keer 'bout nothin' else. Ah'd ruther all de other womens in de world to be dead than for you to have de toothache. Less we go to bed and git our night rest."

It was Saturday night once more before Joe could parade his wife in Slemmons' ice-cream parlor again. He worked the night shift, and Saturday was his only night off. Every other evening around six o'clock he left home, and dying dawn saw him hustling home around the lake, where the challenging sun flung a flaming sword from east to west across the trembling water.

That was the best part of life—going home to Missie May. Their white-washed house, the mock battle on Saturday, the dinner and ice-cream parlor afterwards, church on Sunday nights, when Missie outdressed any woman in town—all, everything, was right.

One night around eleven the acid ran out at the G. and G. The foreman knocked off the crew and let the steam die down. As Joe rounded the lake on his way home, a lean moon rode the lake in a silver boat. If anybody had asked Joe about the moon on the lake, he would have said he hadn't paid it any attention. But he saw it with his feelings. It made him yearn painfully for Missie. Creation obsessed him. He thought about children. They had been married more than a year now. They had money put away. They ought to be making little feet for shoes. A little boy-child would be about right.

He saw a dim light in the bedroom and decided to come in through the kitchen door. He could wash the fertilizer dust off himself before presenting himself to Missie May. It would be nice for her not to know that he was there until he slipped into his place in bed and hugged her back. She always liked that.

He eased the kitchen door open slowly and silently, but when he went to set his dinner bucket on the table he bumped into a pile of dishes, and something crashed to the floor. He heard his wife gasp in fright and hurried to reassure her.

"Iss me, honey. Don't git skeered."

There was a quick, large movement in the bedroom. A rustle, a thud, and a stealthy silence. The light went out.

What? Robbers? Murderers? Some varmint attacking his helpless wife, perhaps. He struck a match, threw himself on guard, and stepped over the doorsill into the bedroom.

The great belt on the wheel of Time slipped and eternity stood still. By the match light he could see the man's legs fighting with his breeches in his frantic desire to get them on. He had both chance and time to kill the intruder in his helpless condition—half in and half out of his pants—but he was too weak to take action. The shapeless enemies of humanity that live in the hours of Time had waylaid Joe. He was assaulted in his weakness. Like Samson awakening after his haircut. So he just opened his mouth and laughed.

The match went out, and he struck another and lit the lamp. A howling wind raced across his heart, but underneath its fury he heard his wife sobbing and Slemmons pleading for his life. Offering to buy it with all that he had. "Please, suh, don't kill me. Sixty-two dollars at de sto'. Gold money."

Joe just stood. Slemmons looked at the window, but it was screened. Joe stood out like a rough-backed mountain between him and the door. Barring him from escape, from sunrise, from life.

He considered a surprise attack upon the big clown that stood there, laughing like a chessy cat. But before his fist could travel an inch, Joe's own rushed out to crush him like a battering ram. Then Joe stood over him.

"Git into yo' damn rags, Slemmons, and dat quick."

Slemmons scrambled to his feet and into his vest and coat. As he grabbed his hat, Joe in his fury overrode his intentions and grabbed at Slemmons with his left hand and struck at him with his right. The right landed. The left grazed the front of his vest. Slemmons was knocked a somersault into the kitchen and fled through the open door. Joe found himself alone with Missie May, with the golden watch charm clutched in his left fist. A short bit of broken chain dangled between his fingers.

Missie May was sobbing. Wails of weeping without words. Joe stood, and after a while he found out that he had something in his hand. And then he stood and felt without thinking and without seeing with his natural eyes. Missie May kept on crying and Joe kept on feeling so much; and not knowing what to do with all his feelings, he put Slemmons' watch charm in his pants pocket and took a good laugh and went to bed.

"Missie May, whut you cryin' for?"

"Cause Ah love you so hard and Ah know you don't love *me* no mo'."

Joe sank his face into the pillow for a spell, then he said huskily, "You don't know de feelings of dat yet, Missie May."

"Oh, Joe, honey, he said he wuz gointer give me dat gold money and he jes' kept on after me —"

Joe was very still and silent for a long time. Then he said, "Well, don't cry no mo', Missie May. Ah got yo' gold piece for you."

The hours went past on their rusty ankles. Joe still and quiet on one bed-rail and Missie May wrung dry of sobs on the other. Finally the sun's tide crept up on the shore of night and drowned all its hours. Missie May, with her face, stiff and streaked, towards the window saw the dawn come into her yard. It was day. Nothing more. Joe wouldn't be coming home as usual. No need to fling open the front door and sweep off the porch, making it nice for Joe. Never no more breakfasts to cook; no more washing and starching of Joe's jumper-jackets and pants. No more nothing. So why get up?

With this strange man in her bed, she felt embarrassed to get up and dress. She decided to wait till he had dressed and gone. Then she would get up, dress quickly, and be gone forever beyond reach of Joe's looks and laughs. But he never moved. Red light turned to yellow, then white.

From beyond the no-man's-land between them came a voice. A strange voice that yesterday had been Joe's.

"Missie May, ain't you gonna fix me no breakfus'?"

She sprang out of bed. "Yea, Joe. Ah didn't reckon you wuz hongry."

No need to die today. Joe needed her for a few more minutes anyhow.

Soon there was a roaring fire in the cookstove. Water bucket full and two chickens killed. Joe loved fried chicken and rice. She didn't deserve a thing and good Joe was letting her cook him some breakfast. She rushed hot biscuits to the table as Joe took his seat.

He ate with his eyes in his plate. No laughter, no banter.

"Missie May, you ain't eatin' yo breakfus'."

"Ah don't choose none. Ah thank yuh."

His coffee cup was empty. She sprang to fill it. When she turned from the stove and bent to set the cup beside Joe's plate, she saw the yellow coin on the table between them.

She slumped into her seat and wept into her arms.

Presently Joe said calmly, "Missie May, you cry too much. Don't look back lak Lot's wife and turn to salt."

The sun, the hero of every day, the impersonal old man that beams as brightly on death as on birth, came up every morning and raced across the blue dome and dipped into the sea of fire every evening. Water ran down hill and birds nested.

Missie knew why she didn't leave Joe. She couldn't. She loved him too much, but she could not understand why Joe didn't leave her. He was polite, even kind at times, but aloof.

There were no more Saturday romps. No ringing silver dollars to stack beside her plate. No pockets to rifle. In fact, the yellow coin in his trousers was like a monster hiding in the cave of his pockets to destroy her.

She often wondered if he still had it, but nothing could have induced her to ask nor yet to explore his pockets to see for herself. Its shadow was in the house whether or no.

One night Joe came home around midnight and complained of pains in the back. He asked Missie to rub him down with liniment. It had been three months since Missie had touched his body and it all seemed strange. But she rubbed him. Grateful for the chance. Before morning, youth triumphed and Missie exulted. But the next day, as she joyfully made up their bed, beneath her pillow she found the piece of money with the bit of chain attached.

Alone to herself, she looked at the thing with loathing, but look she must. She took it into her hands with trembling and saw first thing that it was no gold piece. It was a gilded half dollar. Then she knew why Slemmons had forbidden anyone to touch his gold. He trusted village eyes at a distance not to recognize his stickpin as a gilded quarter and his watch charm as a four-bit piece.

She was glad at first that Joe had left it there. Perhaps he was through with her punishment. They were man and wife again. Then another thought came clawing at her. He had come home to buy from her as if she were any woman in the long house. Fifty cents for her love. As if to say that he could pay as well as Slemmons. She slid the coin into his Sunday pants pocket and dressed herself and left his house.

Halfway between her house and the quarters she met her husband's mother, and after a short talk she turned and went back home. Never would she admit defeat to that woman, who prayed for it nightly. If she had not the substance of marriage, she had the outside show. Joe must leave *her.* She let him see she didn't want his old gold four-bits too.

She saw no more of the coin for some time, though she knew that Joe could not help finding it in his pocket. But his health kept poor, and he came home at least every ten days to be rubbed.

The sun swept around the horizon, trailing its robes of weeks and days. One morning as Joe came in from work, he found Missie May chopping wood. Without a word he took the ax and chopped a huge pile before he stopped.

"You ain't got no business choppin' wood, and you know it."

"How come? Ah been choppin' it for de last longest."

"Ah ain't blind. You makin' feet for shoes."

"Won't you be glad to have a li'l baby chile, Joe?"

"You know dat 'thout astin' me."

"Iss gointer be a boy chile and de very spit of you."

"You reckon, Missie May?"

"Who else could it look lak?"

Joe said nothing, but he thrust his hand deep into his pockets and fingered something there.

It was almost six months later Missie May took to bed, and Joe went and got his mother to come wait on the house.

Missie May was delivered of a fine boy. Her travail was over when Joe came in from work one morning. His mother and the old women were drinking great bowls of coffee around the fire in the kitchen.

The minute Joe came into the room his mother called him aside.

"How did Missie May make out?" he asked quickly.

"Who, dat gal? She strong as a ox. She gointer have plenty mo'. We done fixed her wid de sugar and lard to sweeten her for de nex' one."

Joe stood silent for awhile.

"You ain't ast 'bout de baby, Joe. You oughter be mighty proud cause he sho is de spittin' image of yuh, son. Dat's yourn all right, if you never git another one, dat un is yourn. And you know Ah'm might proud too, son, cause Ah never thought well of you marryin' Missie May cause her ma used tuh fan her foot round right smart and Ah been mighty skeered dat Missie May wuz gointer git misput on her road."

Joe said nothing. He fooled around the house till late in the day, then, just before he went to work, he went and stood at the foot of the bed and asked his wife how she felt. He did this every day during the week.

On Saturday he went to Orlando to make his market. It had been a long time since he had done that.

Meat and lard, meal and flour, soap and starch. Cans of corn and tomatoes. All the staples. He fooled around town for a while and bought bananas and apples. Way after a while he went around to the candy store.

"Hello, Joe," the clerk greeted him. "Ain't seen you in a long time."

"Nope, Ah ain't been heah. Been round in spots and places."

"Want some of them molasses kisses you always buy?"

"Yessuh." He threw the gilded half dollar on the counter. "Will dat spend?"

"Whut is it, Joe? Well, I'll be doggone! A gold-plated four-bit piece. Where'd yo git it, Joe?"

"Offen a stray nigger dat come through Eatonville. He had it on his watch chain for a charm—goin' round making out iss gold money. Ha ha! He had a quarter on his tie pin and it wuz all golded up too. Tryin' to fool people. Makin' out he so rich and everything. Ha! Ha! Tryin' to tole off folkses wives from home."

"How did you git it, Joe? Did he fool you, too?"

"Who, me? Naw suh! He ain't fooled me none. Know whut Ah done? He come round me wid his smart talk. Ah hauled off and knocked 'im down and took his old four-bits way from 'im. Gointer buy my wife some good ole lasses kisses wid it. Gimme fifty cents worth of dem candy kisses."

"Fifty cents buys a mighty lot of candy kisses, Joe. Why don't you split it up and take some chocolate bars, too. They eat good, too."

"Yessuh, dey do, but Ah wants all dat in kisses. Ah got a li'l boy chile home now. Tain't a week old yet, but he kin suck a sugar tit and maybe eat one them kisses hisself."

Joe got his candy and left the store. The clerk turned to the next customer. "Wisht I could be like these darkies. Laughin' all the time. Nothin 'worries 'em."

Back in Eatonville, Joe reached his own front door. There was the ring of singing metal on wood. Fifteen times. Missie May couldn't run to the door, but she crept there as quickly as she could.

"Joe Banks, Ah hear you chunkin' money in mah do'way. You wait till Ah got mah strength back and Ah'm gointer fix you for dat."

Sweat

It was eleven o'clock of a Spring night in Florida. It was Sunday. Any other night, Delia Jones would have been in bed for two hours by this time. But she was a washwoman, and Monday morning meant a great deal to her. So she collected the soiled clothes on Saturday when she returned the clean things. Sunday night after church, she sorted them and put the white things to soak. It saved her almost a half day's start. A great hamper in the bedroom held the clothes that she brought home. It was so much neater than a number of bundles lying around.

She squatted in the kitchen floor beside the great pile of clothes, sorting them into small heaps according to color, and humming a song in a mournful key, but wondering through it all where Sykes, her husband, had gone with her horse and buckboard.

Just then something long, round, limp and black fell upon her shoulders and slithered to the floor beside her. A great terror took hold of her. It softened her knees and dried her mouth so that it was a full minute before she could cry out or move. Then she saw that it was the big bull whip her husband liked to carry when he drove.

She lifted her eyes to the door and saw him standing there bent over with laughter at her fright. She screamed at him.

"Sykes, what you throw dat whip on me like dat? You know it would skeer me—looks just like a snake, an' you knows how skeered Ah is of snakes."

"Course Ah knowed it! That's how come Ah done it." He slapped his leg with his hand and almost rolled on the ground in his mirth. "If you such a big fool dat you got to have a fit over a earth worm or a string, Ah don't keer how bad Ah skeer you."

"You aint got no business doing it. Gawd knows it's a sin. Some day Ah'm gointuh drop dead from some of yo' foolishness. 'Nother thing, where you been wid mah rig? Ah feeds dat pony. He aint fuh you to be drivin' wid no bull whip."

"You sho is one aggravatin' nigger woman!" he declared and stepped into the room. She resumed her work and did not answer him at once. "Ah done tole you time and again to keep them white folks' clothes outa dis house."

He picked up the whip and glared down at her. Delia went on with her work. She went out into the yard and returned with a galvanized tub and set it on the washbench. She saw that Sykes had kicked all of the clothes together again, and now stood in her way truculently, his whole manner hoping, *praying*, for an argument. But she walked calmly around him and commenced to re-sort the things.

"Next time, Ah'm gointer kick 'em outdoors," he threatened as he struck a match along the leg of his corduroy breeches.

Delia never looked up from her work, and her thin, stooped shoulders sagged further.

"Ah aint for no fuss t'night, Sykes. Ah just come from taking sacrament at the church house."

He snorted scornfully. "Yeah, you just come from de church house on a Sunday night, but heah you is gone to work on them clothes. You ain't nothing but a hypocrite. One of them amen-corner Christians—sing, whoop, and shout, then come home and wash white folks' clothes on the Sabbath."

He stepped roughly upon the whitest pile of things, kicking them helter-skelter as he crossed the room. His wife gave a little scream of dismay, and quickly gathered them together again.

"Sykes, you quit grindin' dirt into these clothes! How can Ah git through by Sat'day if Ah don't start on Sunday?"

"Ah don't keer if you never git through. Anyhow, Ah done promised Gawd and a couple of other men, Ah aint gointer have it in mah house. Don't gimme no lip neither, else Ah'll throw 'em out and put mah fist up side yo' head to boot."

Delia's habitual meekness seemed to slip from her shoulders like a blown scarf. She was on her feet; her poor little body, her bare knuckly hands bravely defying the strapping hulk before her.

"Looka heah, Sykes, you done gone too fur. Ah been married to you fur fifteen years, and Ah been takin' in washin' fur fifteen years. Sweat, sweat, sweat! Work and sweat, cry and sweat, pray and sweat!"

"What's that got to do with me?" he asked brutally.

"What's it got to do with you, Sykes? Mah tub of suds is filled yo' belly with vittles more times than yo' hands is filled it. Mah sweat is done paid for this house and Ah reckon Ah kin keep on sweatin' in it."

She seized the iron skillet from the stove and struck a defensive pose, which act surprised him greatly, coming from her. It cowed him and he did not strike her as he usually did.

"Naw you won't," she panted, "that ole snaggle-toothed black woman you runnin' with aint comin' heah to pile up on *mah* sweat and blood. You aint paid for nothin' on this place, and Ah'm gointer stay right heah till Ah'm toted out foot foremost."

"Well, you better quit gittin' me riled up, else they'll be totin' you out sooner than you expect. Ah'm so tired of you Ah don't know whut to do. Gawd! how Ah hates skinny wimmen!"

A little awed by this new Delia, he sidled out of the door and slammed the back gate after him. He did not say where he had gone, but she knew too well. She knew very well that he would not return until nearly daybreak also. Her work over, she went on to bed but not to sleep at once. Things had come to a pretty pass!

She lay awake, gazing upon the debris that cluttered their matrimonial trail. Not an image left standing along the way. Anything like flowers had long ago been drowned in the salty stream that had been pressed from her heart. Her tears, her sweat, her blood. She had brought love to the union and he had brought a longing after the flesh. Two months after the wedding, he had given her the first brutal beating. She had the memory of his numerous trips to Orlando with all of his wages when he had returned to her penniless, even before the first year had passed. She was young and soft then, but now she thought of her knotty, muscled limbs, her harsh knuckly hands, and drew herself up into an unhappy little ball in the middle of the big feather bed. Too late now to hope for love, even if it were not Bertha it would be someone else. This case differed from the others only in that she was bolder than the others. Too late for everything except her little home. She had built it for her old days, and planted one by one the trees and flowers there. It was lovely to her, lovely.

Somehow, before sleep came, she found herself saying aloud: "Oh well, whatever goes over the Devil's back, is got to come under his belly. Sometime or ruther, Sykes, like everybody else, is gointer reap his sowing." After that she was able to build a spiritual earthworks against her husband. His shells could no longer reach her. *Amen.* She went to sleep and slept until he announced his presence in bed by kicking her feet and rudely snatching the covers away.

"Gimme some kivah heah, an' git yo' damn foots over on yo' own side! Ah oughter mash you in yo' mouf fuh drawing dat skillet on me."

Delia went clear to the rail without answering him. A triumphant indifference to all that he was or did.

The week was as full of work for Delia as all other weeks, and Saturday found her behind her little pony, collecting and delivering clothes.

It was a hot, hot day near the end of July. The village men on Joe Clarke's porch even chewed cane listlessly. They did not hurl the caneknots as usual. They let them dribble over the edge of the porch. Even conversation had collapsed under the heat.

"Heah come Delia Jones," Jim Merchant said, as the shaggy pony came 'round the bend of the road toward them. The rusty buckboard was heaped with baskets of crisp, clean laundry.

"Yep," Joe Lindsay agreed. "Hot or col', rain or shine, jes ez reg'lar ez de weeks roll 'roun' Delia carries 'em an' fetches 'em on Sat'day."

"She better if she wanter eat," said Moss. "Syke Jones aint wuth de shot an' powder hit would tek tuh kill 'em. Not to *huh* he aint."

"He sho' aint." Walter Thomas chimed in. "It's too bad, too, cause she wuz a right pritty lil trick when he got huh. Ah'd uh mah'ied huh mahseff if he hadnter beat me to it."

Delia nodded briefly at the men as she drove past.

"Too much knockin' will ruin *any* 'oman. He done beat huh 'nough tuh kill three women, let 'lone change they looks," said Elijah Moseley. "How Syke kin stommuck dat big black greasy Mogul he's layin' roun' wid, gits me. Ah swear dat eight-rock couldn't kiss a sardine can Ah done thowed out de back do' 'way las' yeah."

"Aw, she's fat, thass how come. He's allus been crazy 'bout fat women," put in Merchant. "He'd a' been tied up wid one long time ago if he could a' found one tuh have him. Did Ah tell yuh 'bout him come sidlin' roun' *mah* wife—bringin' here a basket uh peecans outa his yard fuh a present? Yes-sir, mah wife! She tol' him tuh take em right straight back home, cause Delia works so hard ovah dat wash tub she reckon everything on de place taste lak sweat an' soapsuds. Ah jus' wisht Ah'd a caught 'im 'roun' dere! Ah'd a' made his hips ketch on fiah down dat shell road."

"Ah know he done it, too. Ah sees 'im grinnin' at every 'oman dat passes," Walter Thomas said. "But even so, he useter eat some mighty big hunks uh humble pie tuh git dat lil' 'oman he got. She wuz ez pritty ez a speckled pup! Dat wuz fifteen yeahs ago. He useter be so skeered uh losin' huh, she could make him do some parts of a husband's duty. Dey never wuz de same in de mind."

"There oughter be a law about him," said Lindsay. "He aint fit tuh carry guts tuh a bear."

Clarke spoke for the first time. "Taint no law on earth dat kin make a man be decent if it aint in 'im. There's plenty men dat takes a wife lak dey do a joint uh sugar-cane. It's round, juicy an' sweet when dey gits it. But dey squeeze an' grind, squeeze an' grind an' wring tell dey wring every drop uh pleasure dat's in 'em out. When dey's satisfied dat dey is wrung dry, dey treats 'em jes lak dey do a cane-chew. Dey throws 'em away. Dey knows whut dey is doin' while dey is at it, an' hates theirselves fuh it but they keeps on hangin' after huh tell she's empty. Den dey hates huh fuh bein' a cane-chew an' in de way."

"We oughter take Syke an' dat stray 'oman uh his'n down in Lake Howell swamp an' lay on de rawhide till they cain't say 'Lawd a' mussy.' He allus wuz uh ovahbearin' niggah, but since dat white 'oman from up north done teached 'im how to run a automobile, he done got too biggety to live—an' we oughter kill 'im," Old Man Anderson advised.

A grunt of approval went around the porch. But the heat was melting their civic virtue and Elijah Moseley began to bait Joe Clarke.

"Come on, Joe, git a melon outa dere an' slice it up for yo' customers. We'se all sufferin' wid de heat. De bear's done got *me!*"

"Thass right, Joe, a watermelon is jes' whut Ah needs tuh cure de eppizu-dicks,"[1] Walter Thomas joined forces with Moseley. "Come on dere, Joe. We all is steady customers an' you aint set us up in a long time. Ah chooses dat long, bowlegged Floridy favorite."

"A god, an' be dough. You all gimme twenty cents and slice way," Clarke retorted. "Ah needs a col' slice m'self. Heah, everybody chip in. Ah'll lend y'll mah meat knife."

The money was quickly subscribed and the huge melon brought forth. At that moment, Sykes and Bertha arrived. A determined silence fell in the porch and the melon was put away again.

Merchant snapped down the blade of his jackknife and moved toward the store door.

"Come on in, Joe, an' gimme a slab uh sow belly an' uh pound uh coffee— almost fuhgot 'twas Sat'day. Got to git on home." Most of the men left also.

Just then Delia drove past on her way home, as Sykes was ordering magnificently for Bertha. It pleased him for Delia to see.

---

[1]"Epizootic," or disease attacking many animals at the same time.

"Git whutsoever yo' heart desires, Honey. Wait a minute, Joe. Give huh two bottles uh strawberry soda-water, uh quart uh parched ground-peas, an' a block uh chewin' gum."

With all this they left the store, with Sykes reminding Bertha that this was his town and she could have it if she wanted it.

The men returned soon after they left, and held their watermelon feast.

"Where did Syke Jones git da 'oman from nohow?" Lindsay asked.

"Ovah Apopka. Guess dey musta been cleanin' out de town when she lef'. She don't look lak a thing but a hunk uh liver wid hair on it."

"Well, she sho' kin squall," Dave Carter contributed. "When she gits ready tuh laff, she jes' opens huh mouf an' latches it back tuh de las' notch. No ole grandpa alligator down in Lake Bell ain't got nothin' on huh."

Bertha had been in town three months now. Sykes was still paying her room rent at Della Lewis'—the only house in town that would have taken her in. Sykes took her frequently to Winter Park to "stomps." He still assured her that he was the swellest man in the state.

"Sho' you kin have dat lil' ole house soon's Ah kin git dat 'oman outa dere. Everything b'longs tuh me an' you sho' kin have it. Ah sho' 'bominates uh skinny 'oman. Lawdy, you sho' is got one portly shape on you! You kin git *anything* you wants. Dis is *mah* town an' you sho' kin have it."

Delia's work-worn knees crawled over the earth in Gethsemane and up the rocks of Calvary many, many times during these months. She avoided the villagers and meeting places in her efforts to be blind and deaf. But Bertha nullified this to a degree, by coming to Delia's house to call Sykes out to her at the gate.

Delia and Sykes fought all the time now with no peaceful interludes. They slept and ate in silence. Two or three times Delia had attempted a timid friendliness, but she was repulsed each time. It was plain that the breaches must remain agape.

The sun had burned July to August. The heat streamed down like a million hot arrows, smiting all things living upon the earth. Grass withered, leaves browned, snakes went blind in shedding and men and dogs went mad. Dog days!

Delia came home one day and found Sykes there before her. She wondered, but started to go on into the house without speaking, even though he was standing in the kitchen door and she must either stoop under his arm or ask him to move. He made no room for her. She noticed a soap box beside the steps, but paid no particular attention to it, knowing that he must have brought it there. As she was stooping to pass under his outstretched arm, he suddenly pushed her backward, laughingly.

"Look in de box dere Delia, Ah done brung yuh somethin'!"

She nearly fell upon the box in her stumbling, and when she saw what it held, she all but fainted outright.

"Syke! Syke, mah Gawd! You take dat rattlesnake 'way from heah! You *gottuh*. Oh, Jesus, have mussy!"

"Ah aint gut tuh do nuthin' uh de kin'—fact is Ah aint got tuh do nothin' but die. Taint no use uh you puttin' on airs makin' out lak you skeered uh dat snake—he's gointer stay right heah tell he die. He wouldn't bite me cause Ah knows how tuh handle 'im. Nohow he wouldn't risk breakin' out his fangs 'gin *yo'* skinny laigs."

"Naw, now Syke, don't keep dat thing 'roun' heah tuh skeer me tuh death. You knows Ah'm even feared uh earth worms. Thass de biggest snake Ah evah did see. Kill 'im Syke, please."

"Doan ast me tuh do nothin' fuh yuh. Goin' 'roun' tryin' tuh be so damn asterperious. Naw, Ah aint gonna kill it. Ah think uh damn sight mo' uh him dan you! Dat's a nice snake an' anybody doan lak 'im kin jes' hit de grit."

The village soon heard that Sykes had the snake, and came to see and ask questions.

"How de hen-fire did you ketch dat six-foot rattler, Syke?" Thomas asked.

"He's full uh frogs so he caint hardly move, thass how Ah eased up on 'im. But Ah'm a snake charmer an' knows how tuh handle 'em. Shux, dat aint nothin'. Ah could ketch one eve'y day if Ah so wanted tuh."

"Whut he needs is a heavy hick'ry club leaned real heavy on his head. Dat's de bes' way tuh charm a rattlesnake."

"Naw, Walt, y'll jes' don't understand dese diamon' backs lak Ah do," said Sykes in a superior tone of voice.

The village agreed with Walter, but the snake stayed on. His box remained by the kitchen door with its screen wire covering. Two or three days later it had digested its meal of frogs and literally came to life. It rattled at every movement in the kitchen or the yard. One day as Delia came down the kitchen steps she saw his chalky-white fangs curved like scimitars hung in the wire meshes. This time she did not run away with averted eyes as usual. She stood for a long time in the doorway in a red fury that grew bloodier for every second that she regarded the creature that was her torment.

That night she broached the subject as soon as Sykes sat down to the table.

"Syke, Ah wants you tuh take dat snake 'way fum heah. You done starved me an' Ah put up widcher, you done beat me an Ah took dat, but you done kilt all mah insides bringin' dat varmint heah."

Sykes poured out a saucer full of coffee and drank it deliberately before he answered her.

"A whole lot Ah keer 'bout how you feels inside uh out. Dat snake aint goin' no damn wheah till Ah gits ready fuh 'im tuh go. So fur as beatin' is concerned, yuh aint took near all dat you gointer take ef yuh stay 'roun' *me*."

Delia pushed back her plate and got up from the table. "Ah hates you, Sykes," she said calmly. "Ah hates you tuh de same degree dat Ah useter love yuh. Ah done took an' took till mah belly is full up tuh mah neck. Dat's de reason Ah got mah letter fum de church an' moved mah membership tuh Woodbridge—so Ah don't haftuh take no sacrament wid yuh. Ah don't wantuh see yuh 'roun' me atall. Lay 'roun' wid dat 'oman all yuh wants tuh, but gwan 'way fum me an' mah house. Ah hates yuh lak uh suck-egg dog."

Sykes almost let the huge wad of corn bread and collard greens he was chewing fall out of his mouth in amazement. He had a hard time whipping himself up to the proper fury to try to answer Delia.

"Well, Ah'm glad you does hate me. Ah'm sho' tiahed uh you hangin' ontuh me. Ah don't want yuh. Look at yuh stringey ole neck! Yo' rawbony laigs an' arms is enough tuh cut uh man tuh death. You looks jes' lak de devvul's doll-baby tuh *me*. You can't hate me no worse dan Ah hates you. Ah been hatin' *you* fuh years."

"Yo' ole black hide don't look lak nothin' tuh me, but uh passle uh wrinkled up rubber, wid yo' big ole yeahs flappin' on each side lak uh paih uh buzzard wings. Don't think Ah'm gointuh be run 'way fum mah house neither. Ah'm goin' tuh de white folks bout *you*, mah young man, de very nex' time you lay yo' han's on me. Mah cup is done run ovah."

Delia said this with no signs of fear and Sykes departed from the house, threatening her, but made not the slightest move to carry out any of them.

That night he did not return at all, and the next day being Sunday, Delia was glad she did not have to quarrel before she hitched up her pony and drove the four miles to Woodbridge.

She stayed to the night service—"love feast"—which was very warm and full of spirit. In the emotional winds her domestic trials were borne far and wide so that she sang as she drove homeward,

"Jurden water, black an' col'
Chills de body, not de soul
An' Ah wantah cross Jurden in uh calm time."

She came from the barn to the kitchen door and stopped.

"Whut's de mattah, ol' satan, you aint kickin' up yo' racket?" She addressed the snake's box. Complete silence. She went on into the house with a new hope in its birth struggles. Perhaps her threat to go to the white folks had frightened Sykes! Perhaps he was sorry! Fifteen years of misery and suppression had brought Delia to the place where she would hope *anything* that looked towards a way over or through her wall of inhibitions.

She felt in the match safe behind the stove at once for a match. There was only one there.

"Dat niggah wouldn't fetch nothin' heah tuh save his rotten neck, but he kin run thew whut Ah brings quick enough. Now he done toted off nigh on tuh haff uh box uh matches. He done had dat 'oman heah in mah house too."

Nobody but a woman could tell how she knew this even before she struck the match. But she did and it put her into a new fury.

Presently she brought in the tubs to put the white things to soak. This time she decided she need not bring the hamper out of the bedroom: she would go in there and do the sorting. She picked up the pot-bellied lamp and went in. The room was small and the hamper stood hard by the foot of the white iron bed.

She could sit and reach through the bedposts—resting as she worked.

"Ah wantah cross Jurden in uh calm time." She was singing again. The mood of the "love feast" had returned. She threw back the lid of the basket almost gaily. Then, moved by both horror and terror, she sprang back toward the door. *There lay the snake in the basket!* He moved sluggishly at first, but even as she turned round and round, jumped up and down in an insanity of fear, he began to stir vigorously. She saw him pouring his awful beauty from the basket upon the bed, then she seized the lamp and ran as fast as she could to the kitchen. The wind from the open door blew out the light and the darkness added to her terror. She sped to the darkness of the yard, slamming the door after her before she thought to set down the lamp. She did not feel safe even on the ground, so she climbed up in the hay barn.

There for an hour or more she lay sprawled upon the hay a gibbering wreck.

Finally she grew quiet, and after that, coherent thought. With this, stalked through her a cold, bloody rage. Hours of this. A period of introspection, a space of retrospection, then a mixture of both. Out of this an awful calm.

"Well, Ah done de bes' Ah could. If things aint right, Gawd knows taint mah fault."

She went to sleep—a twitch sleep—and woke up to a faint gray sky. There was a loud hollow sound below. She peered out. Sykes was at the wood-pile, demolishing a wire-covered box.

He hurried to the kitchen door, but hung outside there some minutes before he entered, and stood some minutes more inside before he closed it after him.

The gray in the sky was spreading. Delia descended without fear now, and crouched beneath the low bedroom window. The drawn shade shut out the dawn, shut in the night. But the thin walls held back no sound.

"Dat ol' scratch is woke up now!" She mused at the tremendous whirr inside, which every woodsman knows, is one of the sound illusions. The rattler is a ventriloquist. His whirr sounds to the right, to the left, straight ahead, behind, close under foot—everywhere but where it is. Woe to him who gueses wrong unless he is prepared to hold up his end of the argument! Sometimes he strikes without rattling at all.

Inside, Sykes heard nothing until he knocked a pot lid off the stove while trying to reach the match safe in the dark. He had emptied his pockets at Bertha's.

The snake seemed to wake up under the stove and Sykes made a quick leap into the bedroom. In spite of the gin he had had, his head was clearing now.

"Mah Gawd!" he chattered, "ef Ah could on'y strack uh light!"

The rattling ceased for a moment as he stood paralyzed. He waited. It seemed that the snake waited also.

"Oh fuh de light! Ah thought he'd be too sick"—Sykes was muttering to himself when the whirr began again, closer, right underfoot this time. Long before this, Sykes' ability to think had been flattened down to primitive instinct and he leaped—onto the bed.

Outside Delia heard a cry that might have come from a maddened chimpanzee, a stricken gorilla. All the terror, all the horror, all the rage that man possibly could express, without a recognizable human sound.

A tremendous stir inside there, another series of animal screams, the intermittent whirr of the reptile. The shade torn violently down from the window, letting in the red dawn, a huge brown hand seizing the window stick, great dull blows upon the wooden floor punctuating the gibberish of sound long after the rattle of the snake had abruptly subsided. All this Delia could see and hear from her place beneath the window, and it made her ill. She crept over to the four-o'clocks[2] and stretched herself on the cool earth to recover.

She lay there. "Delia, Delia!" She could hear Sykes calling in a most despairing tone as one who expected no answer. The sun crept on up, and he called. Delia could not move—her legs were gone flabby. She never moved, he called, and the sun kept rising.

"Mah Gawd!" She heard him moan, "Mah Gawd fum Heben!" She heard him stumbling about and got up from her flower-bed. The sun was growing warm. As she approached the door she heard him call out hopefully, "Delia, is dat you Ah heah?"

She saw him on his hands and knees as soon as she reached the door. He crept an inch or two toward her—all that he was able, and she saw his horribly swollen neck and his one open eye shining with hope. A surge of pity too strong to support bore her away from that eye that must, could not, fail to see the tubs. He would see the lamp. Orlando with its doctors was too far. She could scarcely reach the Chinaberry tree, where she waited in the growing heat while inside she knew the cold river was creeping up and up to extinguish that eye which must know by now that she knew.

Virginia Woolf 1882–1941

It would be difficult to name a more prominent writer of the twentieth century than Virginia Woolf—essayist, novelist, editor, and influential feminist and thinker. Born to a distinguished and well-connected artistic family, Adeline Virginia Stephen became a central figure in the literary life of London, and yet she understood that, as a woman, she was also outside of it. *A Room of One's Own* (1928), her oft-quoted, "extended essay," is considered the "first major achievement of feminist criticism in the English language" and has inspired and served to ground the work of countless writers since. Pieces, including "The Mark on the Wall," demonstrate her

[2] Flowering plant.

experiment with fictive "stream-of-consciousness," a narrator's successive thoughts initiated by her wondering about a spot on the wall across the room from her seat. Her innovative work, exposing the innermost thoughts of her characters, continues in *Mrs. Dalloway* (1925) and *To the Lighthouse* (1927), with her other fiction, essays, and lectures enunciating "the difficulties of any woman who wishes to overcome cultural expectations." Woolf, often haunted by mental illness and fearing a German invasion during the Second World War, took her own life in 1941.

From A ROOM OF ONE'S OWN

[*Shakespeare's Sister*][1]

It was disappointing not to have brought back in the evening some important statement, some authentic fact. Women are poorer than men because—this or that. Perhaps now it would be better to give up seeking for the truth, and receiving on one's head an avalanche of opinion hot as lava, discolored as dishwater. It would be better to draw the curtains; to shut out distractions; to light the lamp; to narrow the inquiry and to ask the historian, who records not opinions but facts, to describe under what conditions women lived, not throughout the ages, but in England, say in the time of Elizabeth.

For it is a perennial puzzle why no woman wrote a word of that extraordinary literature when every other man, it seemed, was capable of song or sonnet. What were the conditions in which women lived, I asked myself; for fiction, imaginative work that is, is not dropped like a pebble upon the ground, as science may be; fiction is like a spider's web, attached ever so lightly perhaps, but still attached to life at all four corners. Often the attachment is scarcely perceptible; Shakespeare's plays, for instance, seem to hang there complete by themselves. But when the web is pulled askew, hooked up at the edge, torn in the middle, one remembers that these webs are not spun in midair by incorporeal creatures, but are the work of suffering human beings, and are attached to grossly material things, like health and money and the houses we live in.

I went, therefore, to the shelf where the histories stand and took down one of the latest, Professor Trevelyan's *History of England*.[2] Once more I looked up

---

[1] This selection is taken from Chapter Three and the conclusion of the final chapter. In the previous chapter Woolf visits the British Museum library in an attempt to trace the different fates of men and women in history.

[2] G. M. Trevelyan's *History of England* (1926), then the standard one-volume history.

Women, found "position of," and turned to the pages indicated. "Wife-beating," I read, "was a recognized right of man, and was practiced without shame by high as well as low. . . . Similarly," the historian goes on, "the daughter who refused to marry the gentleman of her parents' choice was liable to be locked up, beaten, and flung about the room, without any shock being inflicted on public opinion. Marriage was not an affair of personal affection, but of family avarice, particularly in the 'chivalrous' upper classes. . . . Betrothal often took place while one or both of the parties was in the cradle, and marriage when they were scarely out of the nurses' charge." That was about 1470, soon after Chaucer's time. The next reference to the position of women is some two hundred years later, in the time of the Stuarts. "It was still the exception for women of the upper and middle class to choose their own husbands, and when the husband had been assigned, he was lord and master, so far at least as law and custom could make him. Yet even so," Professor Trevelyan concludes, "neither Shakespeare's women nor those of authentic seventeenth-century memoirs, like the Verneys and the Hutchinsons,[3] seem wanting in personality and character." Certainly, if we consider it, Cleopatra must have had a way with her; Lady Macbeth, one would suppose, had a will of her own; Rosalind,[4] one might conclude, was an attractive girl. Professor Trevelyan is speaking no more than the truth when he remarks that Shakespeare's women do not seem wanting in personality and character. Not being a historian, one might go even further and say that women have burned like beacons in all the works of all the poets from the beginning of time—Clytemnestra, Antigone, Cleopatra, Lady Macbeth, Phèdre, Cressida, Rosalind, Desdemona, the Duchess of Malfi, among the dramatists; then among the prose writers: Millamant, Clarissa, Becky Sharp, Anna Karenina, Emma Bovary, Madame de Guermantes[5]—the names flock to mind, nor do they recall women "lacking in personality and character." Indeed, if woman had no existence save in the fiction written by men, one would imagine her a person of the utmost importance; very various; heroic and mean; splendid and sordid; infinitely beautiful and hideous in the extreme; as great as a man, some think

---

[3] Lucy Hutchinson wrote a biography of her husband, Colonel John Hutchinson (1616–1684). "The ideal family life of the period [1640–1650] that ended in such tragic political division has been recorded once and for all in the *Memoirs of the Verney Family*" (Trevelyan, *History of England*).

[4] Heroines of three plays by Shakespeare, *Antony and Cleopatra, Macbeth*, and *As You Like It*, respectively.

[5] Characters in, respectively, Aeschylus's *Agamemnon*, Sophocles' *Antigone*; Shakespeare's *Antony and Cleopatra* and *Macbeth*; Racine's *Phèdre*; Shakespeare's *Troilus and Cressida, As You Like It*, and *Othello*; Webster's *The Duchess of Malfi*; Congreve's *The Way of the World*; Richardson's *Clarissa*; Thackeray's *Vanity Fair*; Tolstoy's *Anna Karenina*; Flaubert's *Madame Bovary*; and Proust's *A la recherche du temps perdu*.

even greater.[6] But this is woman in fiction. In fact, as Professor Trevelyan points out, she was locked up, beaten, and flung about the room.

A very queer, composite being thus emerges. Imaginatively she is of the highest importance; practically she is completely insignificant. She pervades poetry from cover to cover; she is all but absent from history. She dominates the lives of kings and conquerors in fiction; in fact she was the slave of any boy whose parents forced a ring upon her finger. Some of the most inspired words, some of the most profound thoughts in literature fall from her lips; in real life she could hardly read, could scarcely spell, and was the property of her husband.

It was certainly an odd monster that one made up by reading the historians first and the poets afterwards—a worm winged like an eagle; the spirit of life and beauty in a kitchen chopping up suet. But these monsters, however amusing to the imagination, have no existence in fact. What one must do to bring her to life was to think poetically and prosaically at one and the same moment, thus keeping in touch with fact—that she is Mrs. Martin, aged thirty-six, dressed in blue, wearing a black hat and brown shoes; but not losing sight of fiction either—that she is a vessel in which all sorts of spirits and forces are coursing and flashing perpetually. The moment, however, that one tries this method with the Elizabethan woman, one branch of illumination fails; one is held up by the scarcity of facts. One knows nothing detailed, nothing perfectly true and substantial about her. History scarcely mentions her. And I turned to Professor Trevelyan again to see what history meant to him. I found by looking at his chapter headings that it meant—

"The Manor Court and the Methods of Open-Field Agriculture . . . The Cistercians and Sheep-Farming . . . The Crusades . . . The University . . . The House of Commons . . . The Hundred Years' War . . . The Wars of the Roses . . . The Renaissance Scholars . . . The Dissolution of the Monasteries . . . Agrarian and Religious Strife . . . The Origin of English Sea-Power . . . The Armada . . ." and so on. Occasionally an individual woman is mentioned, an Elizabeth, or a Mary; a queen or a great lady. But by no possible means could middle-class women with nothing but brains and character at their command have taken part in any one of the great movements which, brought together, constitute the

[6] "It remains a strange and almost inexplicable fact that in Athena's city, where women were kept in almost Oriental suppression as odalisques or drudges, the stage should yet have produced figures like Clytemnestra and Cassandra, Atossa and Antigone, Phèdre and Medea, and all the other heroines who dominate play after play of the 'misogynist' Euripides. But the paradox of this world where in real life a respectable woman could hardly show her face alone in the street, and yet on the stage woman equals or surpasses man, has never been satisfactorily explained. In modern tragedy the same predominance exists. At all events, a very cursory survey of Shakespeare's work (similarly with Webster, though not with Marlowe or Jonson) suffices to reveal how this dominance, this initiative of women, persists from Rosalind to Lady Macbeth. So too in Racine; six of his tragedies bear their heroines' names; and what male characters of his shall we set against Hermione and Andromaque, Bérénice and Roxane, Phèdre and Athalie? So again with Ibsen; what men shall we match with Solveig and Nora, Hedda and Hilda Wangel and Rebecca West?"—F. L. Lucas, *Tragedy*, pp. 114–15" [Woolf's note].

historian's view of the past. Nor shall we find her in any collection of anecdotes. Aubrey[7] hardly mentions her. She never writes her own life and scarcely keeps a diary; there are only a handful of her letters in existence. She left no plays or poems by which we can judge her. What one wants, I thought—and why does not some brilliant student at Newnham or Girton[8] supply it?—is a mass of information; at what age did she marry; how many children had she as a rule; what was her house like; had she a room to herself; did she do the cooking; would she be likely to have a servant? All these facts lie somewhere, presumably, in parish registers and account books; the life of the average Elizabethan woman must be scattered about somewhere, could one collect it and make a book of it. It would be ambitious beyond my daring. I thought, looking about the shelves for books that were not there, to suggest to the students of those famous colleges that they should rewrite history, though I own that it often seems a little queer as it is, unreal, lopsided; but why should they not add a supplement to history? calling it, of course, by some inconspicuous name so that women might figure there without impropriety? For one often catches a glimpse of them in the lives of the great, whisking away into the background, concealing, I sometimes think, a wink, a laugh, perhaps a tear. And, after all, we have lives enough of Jane Austen; it scarcely seems necessary to consider again the influence of the tragedies of Joanna Baillie upon the poetry of Edgar Allan Poe; as for myself, I should not mind if the homes and haunts of Mary Russell Mitford[9] were closed to the public for a century at least. But what I find deplorable, I continued, looking about the bookshelves again, is that nothing is known about women before the eighteenth century. I have no model in my mind to turn about this way and that. Here am I asking why women did not write poetry in the Elizabethan age, and I am not sure how they were educated; whether they were taught to write; whether they had sitting rooms to themselves; how many women had children before they were twenty-one; what, in short, they did from eight in the morning till eight at night. They had no money evidently; according to Professor Trevelyan they were married whether they liked it or not before they were out of the nursery, at fifteen or sixteen very likely. It would have been extremely odd, even upon this showing, had one of them suddenly written the plays of Shakespeare, I concluded, and I thought of that old gentleman, who is dead now, but was a bishop, I think, who declared that it was impossible for any woman, past, present, or to come, to have the genius of Shakespeare. He wrote to the papers about it. He also told a lady who applied to him for information that cats do not as a matter of fact go to heaven, though they have, he added, souls of a sort. How much thinking those old gentlemen used to save one! How

[7] John Aubrey (1626–1697), English diarist.

[8] The two women's colleges of Cambridge University.

[9] English poet and novelist (1787–1855), best known for her sketches of rural life. Jane Austen (1775–1817), English novelist. Joanna Baillie (1787–1855), English poet and dramatist. Edgar Allan Poe (1809–1849), American poet and short-story writer.

the borders of ignorance shrank back at their approach! Cats do not go to heaven. Women cannot write the plays of Shakespeare.

Be that as it may, I could not help thinking, as I looked at the works of Shakespeare on the shelf, that the bishop was right at least in this; it would have been impossible, completely and entirely, for any woman to have written the plays of Shakespeare in the age of Shakespeare. Let me imagine, since facts are so hard to come by, what would have happened had Shakespeare had a wonderfully gifted sister, called Judith, let us say. Shakespeare himself went, very probably—his mother was an heiress—to grammar school, where he may have learnt Latin—Ovid, Virgil, and Horace[10]—and the elements of grammar and logic. He was, it is well known, a wild boy who poached rabbits, perhaps shot a deer, and had, rather sooner than he should have done, to marry a woman in the neighborhood, who bore him a child rather quicker than was right. That escapade sent him to seek his fortune in London. He had, it seemed, a taste for the theater; he began by holding horses at the stage door. Very soon he got work in the theater, became a successful actor, and lived at the hub of the universe, meeting everybody, knowing everybody, practicing his art on the boards, exercising his wits in the streets, and even getting access to the palace of the queen. Meanwhile his extraordinarily gifted sister, let us suppose, remained at home. She was as adventurous, as imaginative, as agog to see the world as he was. But she was not sent to school. She had no chance of learning grammar and logic, let alone of reading Horace and Virgil. She picked up a book now and then, one of her brother's perhaps, and read a few pages. But then her parents came in and told her to mend the stockings or mind the stew and not moon about with books and papers. They would have spoken sharply but kindly, for they were substantial people who knew the conditions of life for a woman and loved their daughter—indeed, more likely than not she was the apple of her father's eye. Perhaps she scribbled some pages up in an apple loft on the sly, but was careful to hide them or set fire to them. Soon, however, before she was out of her teens, she was to be betrothed to the son of a neighboring wool-stapler.[11] She cried out that marriage was hateful to her, and for that she was severely beaten by her father. Then he ceased to scold her. He begged her instead not to hurt him, not to shame him in this matter of her marriage. He would give her a chain of beads or a fine petticoat, he said; and there were tears in his eyes. How could she disobey him? How could she break his heart? The force of her own gift alone drove her to it. She made up a small parcel of her belongings, let herself down by a rope one summer's night, and took the road to London. She was not seventeen. The birds that sang in the hedge were not more musical than she was. She had the quickest fancy, a gift like her brother's, for the tune of words. Like him, she had a taste for the theater. She stood at the stage door; she

[10] Three Latin poets of the Augustan age (27 B.C.–A.D. 14), whose works were part of the standard curriculum in boys' schools.
[11] A dealer in wool, a "staple" product of 16th-century England.

wanted to act, she said. Men laughed in her face. The manager—a fat, loose-lipped man—guffawed. He bellowed something about poodles dancing and women acting—no woman, he said, could possibly be an actress. He hinted—you can imagine what. She could get no training in her craft. Could she even seek her dinner in a tavern or roam the streets at midnight? Yet her genius was for fiction and lusted to feed abundantly upon the lives of men and women and the study of their ways. At last—for she was very young, oddly like Shakespeare the poet in her face, with the same gray eyes and rounded brows—at last Nick Greene the actor-manager took pity on her; she found herself with child by that gentleman and so—who shall measure the heat and violence of the poet's heart when caught and tangled in a woman's body?—killed herself one winter's night and lies buried at some crossroads where the omnibuses now stop outside the Elephant and Castle![12]

That, more or less, is how the story would run, I think, if a woman in Shakespeare's day had had Shakespeare's genius. But for my part, I agree with the deceased bishop, if such he was—it is unthinkable that any woman in Shakespeare's day should have had Shakespeare's genius. For genius like Shakespeare's is not born among laboring, uneducated, servile people. It was not born in England among the Saxons and the Britons. It is not born today among the working classes. How, then, could it have been born among women whose work began, according to Professor Trevelyan, almost before they were out of the nursery, who were forced to it by their parents and held to it by all the power of law and custom? Yet genius of a sort must have existed among women as it must have existed among the working classes. Now and again an Emily Brontë or a Robert Burns[13] blazes out and proves its presence. But certainly it never got itself on to paper. When, however, one reads of a witch being ducked, of a woman possessed by devils, of a wise woman selling herbs, or even of a very remarkable man who had a mother, then I think we are on the track of a lost novelist, a suppressed poet, of some mute and inglorious[14] Jane Austen, some Emily Brontë who dashed her brains out on the moor or mopped and mowed about the highways crazed with the torture that her gift had put her to. Indeed, I would venture to guess that Anon, who wrote so many poems without signing them, was often a woman. It was a woman Edward Fitzgerald,[15] I think, suggested who made the ballads and the folk songs, crooning them to her children, beguiling her spinning with them, or the length of the winter's night.

This may be true or it may be false—who can say?—but what is true in it, so it seemed to me, reviewing the story of Shakespeare's sister as I had made

[12] A tavern located at a busy crossroads in south London. Suicides were commonly buried at crossroads.

[13] A working-class Scottish poet (1759–1796) who wrote in his native dialect. Emily Brontë (1818–1848), English poet and novelist.

[14] An echo of Thomas Gray's *Elegy Written in a Country Churchyard* (1751): "Some mute inglorious Milton here may rest."

[15] English poet and translator (1809–1883).

it, is that any woman born with a great gift in the sixteenth century would certainly have gone crazed, shot herself, or ended her days in some lonely cottage outside the village, half witch, half wizard, feared and mocked at. For it needs little skill in psychology to be sure that a highly gifted girl who had tried to use her gift for poetry would have been so thwarted and hindered by other people, so tortured and pulled asunder by her own contrary instincts, that she must have lost her health and sanity to a certainty. No girl could have walked to London and stood at a stage door and forced her way into the presence of actor-managers without doing herself a violence and suffering an anguish which may have been irrational—for chastity may be a fetish invented by certain societies for unknown reasons—but were none the less inevitable. Chastity had then, it has even now, a religious importance in a woman's life, and has so wrapped itself round with nerves and instincts that to cut it free and bring it to the light of day demands courage of the rarest. To have lived a free life in London in the sixteenth century would have meant for a woman who was poet and playwright a nervous stress and dilemma which might well have killed her. Had she survived, whatever she had written would have been twisted and deformed, issuing from a strained and morbid imagination. And undoubtedly, I thought, looking at the shelf where there are no plays by women, her work would have gone unsigned. That refuge she would have sought certainly. It was the relic of the sense of chastity that dictated anonymity to women even so late as the nineteenth century. Currer Bell, George Eliot, George Sand,[16] all the victims of inner strife as their writings prove, sought ineffectively to veil themselves by using the name of a man. Thus they did homage to the convention, which if not implanted by the other sex was liberally encouraged by them (the chief glory of a woman is not to be talked of, said Pericles,[17] himself a much-talked-of man), that publicity in women is detestable. Anonymity runs in their blood. The desire to be veiled still possesses them.

* * *

I told you in the course of this paper that Shakespeare had a sister; but do not look for her in Sir Sidney Lee's[18] life of the poet. She died young—alas, she never wrote a word. She lies buried where the omnibuses now stop, opposite the Elephant and Castle. Now my belief is that this poet who never wrote a word and was buried at the crossroads still lives. She lives in you and in me, and in many other women who are not here tonight, for they are washing up the dishes and putting the children to bed. But she lives; for great poets do not die; they are continuing presences; they need only the opportunity to walk among us in the flesh. This opportunity, as I think, it is now coming within your power to give

[16] Male pen names of the novelists Charlotte Brontë, Marian Evans, and Aurore Dupin.
[17] Athenian statesman and orator (495–429 B.C.); this statement comes from his funeral oration (*Thucydides* 2.4).
[18] Biographer of Shakespeare (1859–1926).

her. For my belief is that if we live another century or so—I am talking of the common life which is the real life and not of the little separate lives which we live as individuals—and have five hundred a year each of us and rooms of our own; if we have the habit of freedom and the courage to write exactly what we think; if we escape a little from the common sitting room and see human beings not always in their relation to each other but in relation to reality; and the sky, too, and the trees or whatever it may be in themselves; if we look past Milton's[19] bogey, for no human being should shut out the view; if we face the fact, for it is a fact, that there is no arm to cling to, but that we go alone and that our relation is to the world of reality and not only to the world of men and women, then the opportunity will come and the dead poet who was Shakespeare's sister will put on the body which she has so often laid down. Drawing her life from the lives of the unknown who were her forerunners, as her brother did before her, she will be born. As for her coming without that preparation, without that effort on our part, without that determination that when she is born again she shall find it possible to live and write her poetry, that we cannot expect, for that would be impossible. But I maintain that she would come if we worked for her, and that so to work, even in poverty and obscurity, is worth while.

THE MARK ON THE WALL

Perhaps it was the middle of January in the present year that I first looked up and saw the mark on the wall. In order to fix a date it is necessary to remember what one saw. So now I think of the fire; the steady film of yellow light upon the page of my book; the three chrysanthemums in the round glass bowl on the mantelpiece. Yes, it must have been the winter time, and we had just finished our tea, for I remember that I was smoking a cigarette when I looked up and saw the mark on the wall for the first time. I looked up through the smoke of my cigarette and my eye lodged for a moment upon the burning coals, and that old fancy of the crimson flag flapping from the castle tower came into my mind, and I thought of the cavalcade of red knights riding up the side of the black rock. Rather to my relief the sight of the mark interrupted the fancy, for it is an old fancy, an automatic fancy, made as a child perhaps. The mark was a small round mark, black upon the white wall, about six or seven inches above the mantelpiece.

How readily our thoughts swarm upon a new object, lifting it a little way, as ants carry a blade of straw so feverishly, and then leave it. . . . If that mark was made by a nail, it can't have been for a picture, it must have been for a miniature—the miniature of a lady with white powdered curls, powder-dusted

[19] John Milton (1608–1674), English poet; his epic poem *Paradise Lost* retells the story of Genesis 2–3, and portrays Eve as morally and intellectually secondary to Adam.

cheeks, and lips like red carnations. A fraud of course, for the people who had this house before us would have chosen pictures in that way—an old picture for an old room. That is the sort of people they were—very interesting people, and I think of them so often, in such queer places, because one will never see them again, never know what happened next. They wanted to leave this house because they wanted to change their style of furniture, so he said, and he was in process of saying that in his opinion art should have ideas behind it when we were torn asunder, as one is torn from the old lady about to pour out tea and the young man about to hit the tennis ball in the back garden of the suburban villa as one rushes past in the train.

But for that mark, I'm not sure about it; I don't belive it was made by a nail after all; it's too big, too round, for that. I might get up, but if I got up and looked at it, ten to one I shouldn't be able to say for certain; because once a thing's done, no one ever knows how it happened. Oh! dear me, the mystery of life; the inaccuracy of thought! The ignorance of humanity! To show how very little control of our possessions we have—what an accidental affair this living is after all our civilization—let me just count over a few of the things lost in one lifetime, beginning, for that seems always the most mysterious of losses—what cat would gnaw, what rat would nibble—three pale blue canisters of book-binding tools? Then there were the bird cages, the iron hoops, the steel skates, the Queen Anne coal-scuttle, the bagatelle board, the hand organ—all gone, and jewels, too. Opals and emeralds, they lie about the roots of turnips. What a scraping paring affair it is to be sure! The wonder is that I've any clothes on my back, that I sit surrounded by solid furniture at this moment. Why, if one wants to compare life to anything, one must liken it to being blown through the Tube at fifty miles an hour—landing at the other end without a single hairpin in one's hair! Shot out at the feet of God entirely naked! Tumbling head over heels in the asphodel meadows like brown paper parcels pitched down a shoot in the post office! With one's hair flying back like the tail of a race-horse. Yes, that seems to express the rapidity of life, the perpetual waste and repair; all so casual, all so haphazard. . . .

But after life. The slow pulling down of thick green stalks so that the cup of the flower, as it turns over, deluges one with purple and red light. Why, after all, should one not be born there as one is born here, helpless, speechless, unable to focus one's eyesight, groping at the roots of the grass, at the toes of the Giants? As for saying which are trees, and which are men and women, or whether there are such things, that one won't be in a condition to do for fifty years or so. There will be nothing but spaces of light and dark, intersected by thick stalks, and rather higher up perhaps, rose-shaped blots of an indistinct colour—dim pinks and blues—which will, as time goes on, become more definite, become—I don't know what. . . .

And yet that mark on the wall is not a hole at all. It may even be caused by some round black substance, such as a small rose leaf, life over from the summer, and I, not being a very vigilant housekeeper—look at the dust on the mantelpiece, for example, the dust which, so they say, buried Troy three times over, only fragments of pots utterly refusing annihilation, as one can believe.

The tree outside the window taps very gently on the pane. . . . I want to think quietly, calmly, spaciously, never to be interrupted, never to have to rise from my chair, to slip easily from one thing to another, without any sense of hostility, or obstacle. I want to sink deeper and deeper, away from the surface, with its hard separate facts. To steady myself, let me catch hold of the first idea that passes . . . Shakespeare. . . . Well, he will do as well as another. A man who sat himself solidly in an arm-chair, and looked into the fire, so—A shower of ideas fell perpetually from some very high Heaven down through his mind. He leant his forehead on his hand, and people, looking in through the open door— for this scene is supposed to take place on a summer's evening—But how dull this is, this historical fiction! It doesn't interest me at all. I wish I could hit upon a pleasant track of thought, a track indirectly reflecting credit upon myself, for those are the pleasantest thoughts, and very frequent even in the minds of modest mouse-coloured people, who believe genuinely that they dislike to hear their own praises. They are not thoughts directly praising oneself; that is the beauty of them; they are thoughts like this:

"And then I came into the room. They were discussing botany. I said how I'd seen a flower growing on a dust heap on the site of an old house in Kingsway. The seed, I said, must have been sown in the reign of Charles the First. What flowers grew in the reign of Charles the First?" I asked— (But I don't remember the answer.) Tall flowers with purple tassels to them perhaps. And so it goes on. All the time I'm dressing up the figure of myself in my own mind, lovingly, stealthily, not openly adoring it, for if I did that, I should catch myself out, and stretch my hand at once for a book in self-protection. Indeed, it is curious how instinctively one protects the image of oneself from idolatry or any other handling that could make it ridiculous, or too unlike the original to be believed in any longer. Or is it not so very curious after all? It is a matter of great importance. Suppose the looking-glass smashes, the image disappears, and the romantic figure with the green of forest depths all about it is there no longer, but only that shell of a person which is seen by other people—what an airless, shallow, bald, prominent world it becomes! A world not to be lived in. As we face each other in omnibuses and underground railways we are looking into the mirror; that accounts for the vagueness, the gleam of glassiness, in our eyes. And the novelists in future will realize more and more the importance of these reflections, for of course there is not one reflection but an almost infinite number; those are the depths they will explore, those the phantoms they will pursue, leaving the description of reality more and more out of their stories, taking a knowledge of it for granted, as the Greeks did and Shakespeare perhaps—but these generalizations are very worthless. The military sound of the word is enough. It recalls leading articles, cabinet ministers—a whole class of things indeed which, as a child, one thought the thing itself, the standard thing, the real thing, from which one could not depart save at the risk of nameless damnation. Generalizations bring back somehow Sunday in London, Sunday afternoon walks, Sunday luncheons, and also ways of speaking of the dead, clothes, and habits—like the habit of sitting all together in one room until a certain hour, although nobody liked it. There was a rule for everything. The rule for tablecloths at that particular period was that they should be made of tapestry with little yellow compartments marked upon them, such as you may see in photographs of the carpets in the corridors of the royal palaces. Tablecloths of a different kind were not real tablecloths. How shocking, and yet how wonderful it was to discover that these real things, Sunday luncheons, Sunday walks, country houses, and tablecloths were not entirely real, were indeed half phantoms, and the damnation which visited the disbeliever in them was only a sense of illegitimate freedom. What now takes the place of those things I wonder, those real standard things? Men perhaps, should you be a woman; the masculine point of view which governs our lives, which sets the standard, which establishes Whitaker's Table of Precedency, which has become, I suppose, since the war, half a phantom to many men and women, which soon, one may hope, will be laughed into the dustbin where the phantoms go, the mahogany sideboards and the Landseer prints, Gods and Devils, Hell and so forth, leaving us all with an intoxicating sense of illegitimate freedom—if freedom exists. . . .

In certain lights that mark on the wall seems actually to project from the wall. Nor is it entirely circular. I cannot be sure, but it seems to cast a perceptible shadow, suggesting that if I ran my finger down that strip of the wall it would, at a certain point, mount and descend a small tumulus, a smooth tumulus like those barrows on the South Downs which are, they say, either tombs or camps. Of the two I should prefer them to be tombs, desiring melancholy like most English people, and finding it natural at the end of a walk to think of the bones stretched beneath the turf. . . . There must be some book about it. Some antiquary must have dug up those bones and given them a name. . . . What sort of a man is an antiquary, I wonder? Retired Colonels for the most part, I daresay, leading parties of aged labourers to the top here, examining clods of earth and stone, and getting into correspondence with the neighbouring clergy, which, being opened at breakfast time, gives them a feeling of importance, and the comparison of arrow-heads necessitates cross-country journeys to the county towns, an agreeable necessity both to them and to their elderly wives, who wish to make plum jam or to clean out the study, and have every reason for keeping that great question of the camp or the tomb in perpetual suspension, while the Colonel himself feels agreeably philosophic in accumulating evidence on both sides of the question. It is true that he does finally incline to believe in the camp; and, being opposed, indites a pamphlet which he is about to read at the quarterly meeting of the local society when a stroke lays him low, and his last conscious thoughts are not of wife or child, but of the camp and that arrowhead there, which is now in the case at the local museum, together with the foot of a Chinese murderess, a handful of Elizabethan nails, a great many Tudor clay pipes, a piece of Roman pottery, and the wineglass that Nelson drank out of—proving I really don't know what.

No, no, nothing is proved, nothing is known. And if I were to get up at this very moment and ascertain that the mark on the wall is really— what shall we say?—the head of a gigantic old nail, driven in two hundred years ago, which has now, owing to the patient attrition of many generations of housemaids, revealed its head above the coat of paint, and is taking its first view of modern life in the sight of a white-walled fire-lit room, what should I gain?—Knowledge? Matter for further speculation? I can think sitting still as well as standing up. And what is knowledge? What are our learned men save the descendants of witches and hermits who crouched in caves and in woods brewing herbs, interrogating shrew-mice and writing down the language of the stars? And the less we honour them as our superstitions dwindle and our respect for beauty and health of mind increases. . . . Yes, one could imagine a very pleasant world. A quiet, spacious world, with the flowers so red and blue in the open fields. A world without professors or specialists or house-keepers with the profiles of policemen, a world which one could slice with one's thought as a fish slices the water with his fin, grazing the stems of the water-lilies, hanging suspended over nests of white sea eggs. . . . How peaceful it is down here, rooted in the centre of the world and gazing up through the grey waters, with their sudden gleams of light, and their reflections—if it were not for Whitaker's Almanack—if it were not for the Table of Precedency!

I must jump up and see for myself what that mark on the wall really is—a nail, a rose-leaf, a crack in the wood?

Here is nature once more at her old game of self-preservation. This train of thought, she perceives, is threatening mere waste of energy, even some collision with reality, for who will ever be able to lift a finger against Whitaker's Table of Precedency? The Archbishop of Canterbury is followed by the Lord High Chancellor; the Lord High Chancellor is followed by the Archbishop of York. Everybody follows somebody, such is the philosophy of Whitaker; and the great thing is to know who follows whom. Whitaker knows, and let that, so Nature counsels, comfort you, instead of enraging you; and if you can't be comforted, if you must shatter this hour of peace, think of the mark on the wall.

I understand Nature's game—her prompting to take action as a way of ending any thought that threatens to excite or to pain. Hence, I suppose, comes our slight contempt for men of action—men, we assume, who don't think. Still, there's no harm in putting a full stop to one's disagreeable thoughts by looking at a mark on the wall.

Indeed, now that I have fixed my eyes upon it, I feel that I have grasped a plank in the sea; I feel a satisfying sense of reality which at once turns the two Archbishops and the Lord High Chancellor to the shadows of shades. Here is something definite, something real. Thus, waking from a midnight dream of horror, one hastily turns on the light and lies quiescent, worshipping the chest of drawers, worshipping solidity, worshipping reality, worshipping the impersonal world which is a proof of some existence other than ours. That is what one wants to be sure of. . . . Wood is a pleasant thing to think about. It comes from a tree; and trees grow, and we don't know how they grow. For years and years they grow, without paying any attention to us, in meadows, in forests, and by the side of rivers—all things one likes to think about. The cows swish their tails beneath them on hot afternoons; they paint rivers so green that when a moorhen dives one expects to see its feathers all green when it comes up again. I like to think of the fish balanced against the stream like flags blown out; and of water-beetles slowly raising domes of mud upon the bed of the river. I like to think of the tree itself: first of the close dry sensation of being wood; then the grinding of the storm; then the slow, delicious ooze of sap; I like to think of it, too, on winter's nights standing in the empty field with all leaves close-furled, nothing tender exposed to the iron bullets of the moon, a naked mast upon an earth that goes tumbling, tumbling, all night long. The song of birds must sound very loud and strange in June; and how cold the feet of insects must feel upon it, as they make laborious progresses up the creases of the bark, or sun themselves upon the thin green awning of the leaves, and look straight in front of them with diamond-cut red eyes. . . . One by one the fibres snap beneath the immense cold pressure of the earth, then the last storm comes and, falling, the highest branches drive deep into the ground again. Even so, life isn't done with; there are a million patient, watchful lives still for a tree, all over the world, in bedrooms, in ships, on the pavement, lining rooms, where men and women sit after tea, smoking cigarettes. It is full of peaceful thoughts, happy thoughts, this tree. I should like to take each one separately—but something is getting in the way. . . . Where was I? What has it all beeen about? A tree? A river? The Downs? Whitaker's Almanack? The fields of asphodel? I can't remember a thing. Everything's moving, falling, slipping, vanishing. . . . There is a vast upheaval of matter. Someone is standing over me and saying:

"I'm going out to buy a newspaper."

"Yes?"

"Though it's no good buying newspapers. . . . Nothing ever happens. Curse this war; God damn this war! . . . All the same, I don't see why we should have a snail on our wall."

Ah, the mark on the wall! It was a snail.

Susan Glaspell 1882–1948

While Glaspell is best known as a playwright (with *Trifles* (1916) perhaps the most widely anthologized of her works), she began her writing career as a novelist and also wrote sentimental ("romance") stories for magazines. Born in Davenport, Iowa, she helped to found the Provincetown Players in 1915, a troupe devoted to experimental drama. When the group moved to New York's Greenwich Village in 1916 as the Playwright's Theatre, Glaspell moved as well, serving as a writer, actor, and director for a company that, through her efforts, proved influential in American theatre. Glaspell's best works include *Trifles* and *The Verge* (1921) and feature female protagonists who demonstrate free, spirited independence. Another play, *Allison's House* (1931), based on the life of Emily Dickinson, won the Pulitzer Prize. In all, Glaspell wrote twenty plays, over forty short stories, and ten novels.

TRIFLES

CHARACTERS

GEORGE HENDERSON, *County Attorney*   MRS. PETERS
HENRY PETERS, *Sheriff*   MRS. HALE
LEWIS HALE, *A Neighboring Farmer*

SCENE: *The kitchen in the now abandoned farmhouse of John Wright, a gloomy kitchen, and left without having been put in order—unwashed pans under the sink, a loaf of bread outside the breadbox, a dish towel on the table—other signs of incompleted work. At the rear the outer door opens and the* SHERIFF *comes in followed by the* COUNTY ATTORNEY *and* HALE. *The* SHERIFF *and* HALE *are men in middle life, the* COUNTY ATTORNEY *is a young man; all are much bundled up and go at once to the stove. They are followed by two women—the* SHERIFF's WIFE *first; she is a slight wiry woman, a thin nervous face.* MRS. HALE *is larger and would ordinarily be called more comfortable looking, but she is disturbed now and looks fearfully about as she enters. The women have come in slowly, and stand close together near the door.*

COUNTY ATTORNEY *(Rubbing his hands.)* This feels good. Come up to the fire, ladies.
MRS. PETERS *(After taking a step forward.)* I'm not—cold.
SHERIFF *(Unbuttoning his overcoat and stepping away from the stove as if to mark the beginning of official business.)* Now, Mr. Hale, before we move things about, you explain to Mr. Henderson just what you saw when you came here yesterday morning.
COUNTY ATTORNEY By the way, has anything been moved? Are things just as you left them yesterday?
SHERIFF *(Looking about.)* It's just the same. When it dropped below zero last night I thought I'd better send Frank out this morning to make a fire for us—no use getting pneumonia with a big case on, but I told him not to touch anything except the stove—and you know Frank.

COUNTY ATTORNEY Somebody should have been left here yesterday.

SHERIFF Oh—yesterday. When I had to send Frank to Morris Center for that man who went crazy—I want you to know I had my hands full yesterday, I knew you could get back from Omaha by today and as long as I went over everything here myself—

COUNTY ATTORNEY Well, Mr. Hale, tell just what happened when you came here yesterday morning.

HALE Harry and I had started to town with a load of potatoes. We came along the road from my place and as I got here I said, "I'm going to see if I can't get John Wright to go in with me on a party telephone." I spoke to Wright about it once before and he put me off, saying folks talked too much anyway, and all he asked was peace and quiet—I guess you know about how much he talked himself; but I thought maybe if I went to the house and talked about it before his wife, though I said to Harry that I didn't know as what his wife wanted made much difference to John—

COUNTY ATTORNEY Let's talk about that later, Mr. Hale. I do want to talk about that, but tell now just what happened when you got to the house.

HALE I didn't hear or see anything; I knocked at the door, and still it was all quiet inside. I knew they must be up, it was past eight o'clock. So I knocked again, and I thought I heard somebody say, "Come in." I wasn't sure, I'm not sure yet, but I opened the door—this door (*Indicating the door by which the two women are still standing.*) and there in that rocker—(*Pointing to it.*) sat Mrs. Wright.

(*They all look at the rocker.*)

COUNTY ATTORNEY What—was she doing?

HALE She was rockin' back and forth. She had her apron in her hand and was kind of—pleating it.

COUNTY ATTORNEY And how did she—look?

HALE Well, she looked queer.

COUNTY ATTORNEY How do you mean—queer?

HALE Well, as if she didn't know what she was going to do next. And kind of done up.

COUNTY ATTORNEY How did she seem to feel about your coming?

HALE Why, I don't think she minded—one way or other. She didn't pay much attention. I said, "How do, Mrs. Wright, it's cold, ain't it?" And she said, "Is it?"—and went on kind of pleating at her apron. Well, I was surprised; she didn't ask me to come up to the stove, or to set down, but just sat there, not even looking at me, so I said, "I want to see John." And then she—laughed. I guess you would call it a laugh. I thought of Harry and the team outside, so I said a little sharp: "Can't I see John?" "No," she says, kind o' dull like. "Ain't he home?" says I. "Yes," says she, "he's home." "Then why can't I see him?" I asked her, out of patience. "'Cause he's dead," says she. "*Dead*?" says I. She just nodded her head, not getting a bit excited, but rockin' back and forth. "Why—where is he?" says I, not knowing what to say. She just pointed upstairs—like that *(Himself pointing to the room above).* I got up, with the idea of going up there. I walked from there to here—then I says, "Why, what did he die of?" "He died of a rope round his neck," says she, and just went on pleatin' at her apron. Well, I went out and called Harry. I thought I might— need help. We went upstairs and there he was lyin'—

COUNTY ATTORNEY I think I'd rather have you go into that upstairs, where you can point it all out. Just go on now with the rest of the story.

HALE Well, my first thought was to get that rope off. It looked ... *(Stops, his face twitches.)* ... but Harry, he went up to him, and he said, "No, he's dead all right, and we'd better not touch anything." So we went back down stairs. She was still sitting that same way. "Has anybody been notified?" I asked. "No," says she, unconcerned. "Who did this, Mrs. Wright?" said Harry. He said it businesslike—and she stopped pleatin' of her apron. "I don't know," she says. "You don't *know*?" says Harry. "No," says she. "Weren't you sleepin' in the bed with him?" says Harry. "Yes," says she, "but I was on the inside." "Somebody slipped a rope round his neck and strangled him and you didn't wake up?" says Harry. "I didn't wake up," she said after him. We must 'a looked as if we didn't see how that could be, for after a minute she said, "I sleep sound." Harry was going to ask her more questions but I said maybe we ought to let her tell her story first to the coroner, or the sheriff, so Harry went fast as he could to Rivers' place, where there's a telephone.

COUNTY ATTORNEY And what did Mrs. Wright do when she knew that you had gone for the coroner?

HALE She moved from that chair to this one over here *(Pointing to a small chair in the corner.)* and just sat there with her hands held together and looking down. I got a feeling that I ought to make some conversation, so I said I had come in to see if John wanted to put in a telephone, and at that she started to laugh, and then she stopped and looked at me—scared. *(The* COUNTY ATTORNEY, *who has had his notebook out, makes a note.)* I dunno, maybe it wasn't scared. I wouldn't like to say it was. Soon Harry got back, and then Dr. Lloyd came, and you, Mr. Peters, and so I guess that's all I know that you don't.

COUNTY ATTORNEY *(Looking around.)* I gues we'll go upstairs first—and then out to the barn and around there. *(To the* SHERIFF.) You're convinced that there was nothing important here—nothing that would point to any motive.

SHERIFF Nothing here but kitchen things.

(The COUNTY ATTORNEY, *after again looking around the kitchen, opens the door of a cupboard closet. He gets up on a chair and looks on a shelf. Pulls his hand away, sticky.)*

COUNTY ATTORNEY Here's a nice mess.

(The women draw nearer.)

MRS. PETERS *(To the other woman.)* Oh, her fruit; it did freeze. *(To the* COUNTY ATTORNEY.) She worried about that when it turned so cold. She said the fire'd go out and her jars would break.

SHERIFF Well, can you beat the women! Held for murder and worryin' about her preserves.

COUNTY ATTORNEY I guess before we're through she may have something more serious than preserves to worry about.

HALE Well, women are used to worrying over trifles.

(The two women move a little closer together.)

COUNTY ATTORNEY *(With the gallantry of a young politician.)* And yet, for all their worries, what would we do without the ladies? *(The women do not unbend. He goes to the sink, takes a dipperful of water from the pail and pouring it into a basin, washes his hands. Starts to wipe them on the roller towel, turns it for a cleaner place.)* Dirty towels! *(Kicks his foot against the pans under the sink.)* Not much of a housekeeper, would you say, ladies?

MRS. HALE *(Stiffly.)* There's a great deal of work to be done on a farm.

COUNTY ATTORNEY To be sure. And yet *(With a little bow to her.)* I know there are some Dickson county farmhouses which do not have such roller towels.

(He gives it a pull to expose its full length again.)

MRS. HALE Those towels get dirty awful quick. Men's hands aren't always as clean as they might be.

COUNTY ATTORNEY Ah, loyal to your sex, I see. But you and Mrs. Wright were neighbors. I suppose you were friends, too.

MRS. HALE *(Shaking her head.)* I've not seen much of her of late years. I've not been in this house—it's more than a year.

COUNTY ATTORNEY And why was that? You didn't like her?

MRS. HALE I liked her all well enough. Farmers' wives have their hands full, Mr. Henderson. And then—

COUNTY ATTORNEY Yes—?

MRS. HALE *(Looking about.)* It never seemed a very cheeful place.

COUNTY ATTORNEY No—it's not cheerful. I shouldn't say she had the home-making instinct.

MRS. HALE Well, I don't know as Wright had, either.

COUNTY ATTORNEY You mean that they didn't get on very well?

MRS. HALE No, I don't mean anything. But I don't think a place'd be any cheer-fuller for John Wright's being in it.

COUNTY ATTORNEY I'd like to talk more of that a little later. I want to get the lay of things upstairs now.

(He goes to the left, where three steps lead to a stair door.)

SHERIFF I suppose anything Mrs. Peters does'll be all right. She was to take in some clothes for her, you know, and a few little things. We left in such a hurry yesterday.

COUNTY ATTORNEY Yes, but I would like to see what you take, Mrs. Peters, and keep an eye out for anything that might be of use to us.

MRS. PETERS Yes, Mr. Henderson.

(The women listen to the men's steps on the stairs, then look about the kitchen.)

MRS. HALE I'd hate to have men coming into my kitchen, snooping around and criticizing.

(She arranges the pans under sink which the COUNTY ATTORNEY *had shoved out of place.)*

MRS. PETERS Of course it's no more than their duty.

MRS. HALE Duty's all right, but I guess that deputy sheriff that came out to make the fire might have got a little of this on. *(Gives the roller towel a pull.)* Wish I'd thought of that sooner. Seems mean to talk about her for not having things slicked up when she had to come away in such a hurry.

MRS. PETERS *(Who has gone to a small table in the left rear corner of the room, and lifted one end of a towel that covers a pan.)* She had bread set. *(Stands still.)*

MRS. HALE *(Eyes fixed on a loaf of bread beside the breadbox, which is on a low shelf at the other side of the room. Moves slowly toward it.)* She was going to put this in there. *(Picks up loaf, then abruptly drops it. In a manner of returning to familiar things.)* It's a shame about her fruit. I wonder if it's all gone. *(Gets up on the chair and looks.)* I think there's some here that's all right, Mrs. Peters. Yes—here; *(Holding it toward the window.)* this is cherries, too. *(Looking again.)* I declare I believe that's the only one. *(Gets down, bottle in her hand. Goes to the sink and wipes if off on the outside.)* She'll feel awful bad after all her hard work in the hot weather. I remember the afternoon I put up my cherries last summer.

(She puts the bottle on the big kitchen table, center of the room. With a sigh, is about to sit down in the rocking-chair. Before she is seated realizes what chair it is; with a slow look at it, steps back. The chair which she has touched rocks back and forth.)

MRS. PETERS Well, I must get those things from the front room closet. *(She goes to the door at the right, but after looking into the other room, steps back.)* You coming with me, Mrs. Hale? You could help me carry them.

(They go in the other room; reappear, MRS. PETERS *carrying a dress and skirt,* MRS. HALE *following with a pair of shoes.)*

MRS. PETERS My, it's cold in there.

(She puts the clothes on the big table, and hurries to the stove.)

MRS. HALE *(Examining her skirt.)* Wright was close. I think maybe that's why she kept so much to herself. She didn't even belong to the Ladies Aid. I suppose she felt she couldn't do her part, and then you don't enjoy things when you feel shabby. She used to wear pretty clothes and be lively, when she was Minnie Foster, one of the town girls singing in the choir. But that—oh, that was thirty years ago. This all you was to take in?

MRS. PETERS She said she wanted an apron. Funny thing to want, for there isn't much to get you dirty in jail, goodness knows. But I suppose just to make her feel more natural. She said they was in the top drawer in this cupboard. Yes, here. And then her little shawl that always hung behind the door. *(Opens stair door and looks.)* Yes, here it is.

(Quickly shuts door leading upstairs.)

MRS. HALE *(Abruptly moving toward her.)* Mrs. Peters?

MRS. PETERS Yes, Mrs. Hale?

MRS. HALE Do you think she did it?

MRS. PETERS *(In a frightened voice.)* Oh, I don't know.

MRS. HALE Well, I don't think she did. Asking for an apron and her little shawl. Worrying about her fruit.

MRS. PETERS *(Starts to speak, glances up, where footsteps are heard in the room above. In a low voice.)* Mr. Peters says it looks bad for her. Mr. Henderson is awful sarcastic in a speech and he'll make fun of her sayin' she didn't wake up.

MRS. HALE Well, I guess John Wright didn't wake when they was slipping that rope under his neck.

MRS. PETERS No, it's strange. It must have been done awful crafty and still. They say it was such a—funny way to kill a man, rigging it all up like that.

MRS. HALE That's just what Mr. Hale said. There was a gun in the house. He says that's what he can't understand.

MRS. PETERS Mr. Henderson said coming out that what was needed for the case was a motive; something to show anger, or—sudden feeling.

MRS. HALE *(Who is standing by the table.)* Well I don't see any signs of anger around here. *(She puts her hand on the dish towel which lies on the table, stands looking down at table, one half of which is clean, the other half messy.)* It's wiped to here. *(Makes a move as if to finish work, then turns and looks at loaf of bread outside the breadbox. Drops towel. In that voice of coming back to familiar things.)* Wonder how they are finding things upstairs. I hope she had it a little more red-up up there. You know, it seems kind of sneaking. Locking her up in town and then coming out here and trying to get her own house to turn against her!

MRS. PETERS But Mrs. Hale, the law is the law.

MRS. HALE I s'pose 'tis. *(Unbuttoning her coat.)* Better loosen up your things, Mrs. Peters. You won't feel them when you go out.

(MRS. PETERS takes off her fur tippet, goes to hang it on hook at back of room, stands looking at the under part of the small corner table.)

MRS. PETERS She was piecing a quilt.

(She brings the large sewing basket and they look at the bright pieces.)

MRS. HALE It's log cabin pattern. Pretty, isn't it? I wonder if she was goin' to quilt it or just knot it?

(Footsteps have been heard coming down the stairs. The SHERIFF enters followed by HALE and the COUNTY ATTORNEY.)

SHERIFF They wonder if she was going to quilt it or just knot it!

(The men laugh; the women look abashed.)

COUNTY ATTORNEY *(Rubbing his hands over the stove.)* Frank's fire didn't do much up there, did it? Well, let's go out to the barn and get that cleared up.

(The men go outside.)

MRS. HALE *(Resentfully.)* I don't know as there's anything so strange, our takin' up our time with little things while we're waiting for them to get the evidence. *(She sits down at the big table smoothing out a block with decision.)* I don't see as it's anything to laugh about.

MRS. PETERS *(Apologetically.)* Of course they've got awful important things on their minds.

(Pulls up a chair and joins MRS. HALE at the table.)

MRS. HALE *(Examining another block.)* Mrs. Peters, look at this one. Here, this is the one she was working on, and look at the sewing! All the rest of it has been so nice and even. And look at this! It's all over the place! Why, it looks as if she didn't know what she was about!

(After she has said this they look at each other, then start to glance back at the door. After an instant MRS. HALE has pulled at a knot and ripped the sewing.)

MRS. PETERS Oh, what are you doing, Mrs. Hale?

MRS. HALE *(Mildly.)* Just pulling out a stitch or two that's not sewed very good. *(Threading a needle.)* Bad sewing always made me fidgety.

MRS. PETERS *(Nervously.)* I don't think we ought to touch things.

MRS. HALE I'll just finish up this end. *(Suddenly stopping and leaning forward.)* Mrs. Peters?

MRS. PETERS Yes, Mrs. Hale?

MRS. HALE What do you suppose she was no nervous about?

MRS. PETERS Oh—I don't know. I don't know as she was nervous. I sometimes sew awful queer when I'm just tired. *(MRS. HALE starts to say something, looks at MRS. PETERS, then goes on sewing.)* Well, I must get these things wrapped up. They may be through sooner than we think. *(Putting apron and other things together.)* I wonder where I can find a piece of paper, and string.

MRS. HALE In that cupboard, maybe.

MRS. PETERS *(Looking in cupboard.)* Why, here's a birdcage. *(Holds it up.)* Did she have a bird, Mrs. Hale?

MRS. HALE Why, I don't know whether she did or not—I've not been here for so long. There was a man around last year selling canaries cheap, but I don't know as she took one; maybe she did. She used to sing real pretty herself.

MRS. PETERS *(Glancing around.)* Seems funny to think of a bird here. But she must have had one, or why would she have a cage? I wonder what happened to it.

MRS. HALE I s' pose maybe the cat got it.

MRS. PETERS No, she didn't have a cat. She's got that feeling some people have about cats—being afraid of them. My cat got in her room and she was real upset and asked me to take it out.

MRS. HALE My sister Bessie was like that. Queer, ain't it?

MRS. PETERS *(Examining the cage.)* Why, look at this door. It's broke. One hinge is pulled apart.

MRS. HALE *(Looking too.)* Looks as if someone must have been rough with it.

MRS. PETERS Why, yes.

(She brings the cage forward and puts it on the table.)

MRS. HALE I wish if they're going to find any evidence they'd be about it. I don't like this place.

MRS. PETERS But I'm awful glad you came with me, Mrs. Hale. It would be lone-some for me sitting here alone.

MRS. HALE It would, wouldn't it? *(Dropping her sewing.)* But I tell you what I do wish, Mrs. Peters. I wish I had come over sometimes when she was here. I—*(Looking around the room.)*—wish I had.

MRS. PETERS But of course you were awful busy, Mrs. Hale—your house and your children.

MRS. HALE I could've come. I stayed away because it weren't cheerful—and that's why I ought to have come. I—I've never liked this place. Maybe because it's down in a hollow and you don't see the road. I dunno what it is but it's a lonesome place and always was. I wish I had come over to see Minnie Foster sometimes. I can see now—

(Shakes her head.)

MRS. PETERS Well, you mustn't reproach yourself, Mrs. Hale. Somehow we just don't see how it is with other folks until—something comes up.

MRS. HALE Not having children makes less work—but it makes a quiet house, and Wright out to work all day, and no company when he did come in. Did you know John Wright, Mrs. Peters?

MRS. PETERS Not to know him; I've seen him to town. They say he was a good man.

MRS. HALE Yes—good; he didn't drink, and kept his word as well as most, I guess, and paid his debts. But he was a hard man, Mrs. Peters. Just to pass the time of day with him—*(Shivers.)* Like a raw wind that gets to the bone. *(Pauses, her eye falling on the cage.)* I should think she would 'a wanted a bird. But what do you suppose went with it?

MRS. PETERS I don't know, unless it got sick and died.

(She reaches over and swings the broken door, swings it again. Both women watch it.)

MRS. HALE You weren't raised round here, were you? (MRS. PETERS *shakes her head.*) You didn't know—her?

MRS. PETERS Not till they brought her yesterday.

MRS. HALE She—come to think of it, she was kind of like a bird herself—real sweet and pretty, but kind of timid and—fluttery. How—she—did—change. *(Silence; then as if struck by a happy thought and relieved to get back to every day things.)* Tell you what, Mrs. Peters, why don't you take the quilt in with you? It might take up her mind.

MRS. PETERS Why, I think that's a real nice idea, Mrs. Hale. There couldn't possibly by any objection to it, could there? Now, just what would I take? I wonder if her patches are in here—and her things.

(They look in the sewing basket.)

MRS. HALE Here's some red. I expect this has got sewing things in it. *(Brings out a fancy box.)* What a pretty box. Looks like something somebody would give you. Maybe her scissors are in here. *(Opens box. Suddenly puts her hand to her nose.)* Why—(MRS. PETERS *bends nearer, then turns her face away.)* There's something wrapped up in this piece of silk.

MRS. PETERS Why, this isn't her scissors.

MRS. HALE *(Lifting the silk.)* Oh, Mrs. Peters—it's—

(MRS. PETERS bends closer.)

MRS. PETERS It's the bird.

MRS. HALE *(Jumping up.)* But, Mrs. Peters—look at it! Its neck! Look at its neck! It's all—other side to.

MRS. PETERS Somebody—wrung—its—neck.

(Their eyes meet. A look of growing comprehension, of horror. Steps are heard outside. MRS. HALE slips box under quilt pieces, and sinks into her chair. Enter SHERIFF and COUNTY ATTORNEY. MRS. PETERS rises.)

COUNTY ATTORNEY *(As one turning from serious things to little pleasantries.)* Well, ladies, have you decided whether she was going to quilt it or knot it?

MRS. PETERS We think she was going to—knot it.

COUNTY ATTORNEY Well, that's interesting, I'm sure. *(Seeing the birdcage.)* Has the bird flown?

MRS. HALE *(Putting more quilt pieces over the box.)* We think the—cat got it.

COUNTY ATTORNEY *(Preoccupied.)* Is there a cat?

(MRS. HALE glances in a quick covert way at MRS. PETERS.)

MRS. PETERS Well, not now. They're superstitious, you know. They leave.

COUNTY ATTORNEY *(To SHERIFF PETERS, continuing an interrupted conversation.)* No sign at all of anyone having come from the outside. Their own rope. Now let's go up again and go over it piece by piece. *(They start upstairs.)* It would have to have been someone who knew just the—

(MRS. PETERS sits down. The two women sit there not looking at one another, but as if peering into something and at the same time holding back. When they talk now it is in the manner of feeling their way over strange ground, as if afraid of what they are saying, but as if they can not help saying it.)

MRS. HALE She liked the bird. She was going to bury it in that pretty box.

MRS. PETERS *(In a whisper.)* When I was a girl—my kitten—there was a boy took a hatchet, and before my eyes—and before I could get there— *(Covers her face an instant.)* If they hadn't held me back I would have— *(Catches herself, looks upstairs where steps are heard, falters weakly.)*—hurt him.

MRS. HALE *(With a slow look around her.)* I wonder how it would seem never to have had any children around. *(Pause.)* No, Wright wouldn't like the bird—a thing that sang. She used to sing. He killed that too.

MRS. PETERS *(Moving uneasily.)* We don't know who killed the bird.

MRS. HALE I knew John Wright.

MRS. PETERS It was an awful thing was done in this house that night, Mrs. Hale. Killing a man while he slept, slipping a rope around his neck that choked the life out of him.

MRS. HALE His neck. Choked the life out of him.

(Her hand goes out and rests on the birdcage.)

MRS. PETERS *(With rising voice.)* We don't know who killed him. We don't know.

MRS. HALE *(Her own feeling not interrupted.)* If there'd been years and years of nothing, then a bird to sing to you, it would be awful—still, after the bird was still.

MRS. PETERS *(Something within her speaking.)* I know what stillness is. When we homesteaded in Dakota, and my first baby died—after he was two years old, and me with no other then—

MRS. HALE *(Moving.)* How soon do you suppose they'll be through, looking for the evidence?

MRS. PETERS I know what stillness is. *(Pulling herself back.)* The law has got to punish crime, Mrs. Hale.

MRS. HALE *(Not as if answering that.)* I wish you'd seen Minnie Foster when she wore a white dress with blue ribbons and stood up there in the choir and sang. *(A look around the room.)* Oh, I wish I'd come over here once in a while! That was a crime! That was a crime! Who's going to punish that?

MRS. PETERS *(Looking upstairs.)* We mustn't—take on.

MRS. HALE I might have known she needed help! I know how things can be—for women. I tell you, it's queer, Mrs. Peters. We live close together and we live far apart. We all go through the same things—it's all just a different kind of the same thing. *(Brushes her eyes; noticing the bottle of fruit, reaches out for it.)* If I was you I wouldn't tell her her fruit was gone. Tell her it ain't. Tell her it's all right. Take this in to prove it to her. She—she many never know whether it was broke or not.

MRS. PETERS *(Takes the bottle, looks about for something to wrap it in; takes petticoat from the clothes brought from the other room, very nervously begins winding this around the bottle. In a false voice.)* My, it's a good thing the men couldn't hear us. Wouldn't they just laugh! Getting all stirred up over a little thing like a—dead canary. As if that could have anything to do with—with—wouldn't they laugh!

(The men are heard coming down stairs.)

MRS. HALE *(Under her breath.)* Maybe they would—maybe they wouldn't.

COUNTY ATTORNEY. No, Peters, it's all perfectly clear except a reason for doing it. But you know juries when it comes to women. If there was some definite thing. Something to show—something to make a story about—a thing that would connect up with this strange way of doing it—

(The women's eyes meet for an instant. Enter HALE from outer door.)

HALE Well, I've got the team around. Pretty cold out there.

COUNTY ATTORNEY I'm going to stay here a while by myself. *(To the SHERIFF.)* You can send Frank out for me, can't you? I want to go over everything. I'm not satisfied that we can't do better.

SHERIFF Do you want to see what Mrs. Peters is going to take in?

(The COUNTY ATTORNEY goes to the table, picks up the apron, laughs.)

COUNTY ATTORNEY Oh I guess they're not very dangerous things the ladies have picked out. *(Moves a few things about, disturbing the quilt pieces which cover the box. Steps back.)* No, Mrs. Peters doesn't need supervising. For that matter, a sheriff's wife is married to the law. Even think of it that way, Mrs. Peters?

MRS. PETERS Not—just that way.

SHERIFF (*Chuckling.*) Married to the law. (*Moves toward the other room.*) I just want you to come in here a minute, George. We ought to take a look at these windows.

COUNTY ATTORNEY (*Scoffingly.*) Oh, windows!

SHERIFF We'll be right out, Mr. Hale.

(HALE *goes outside. The* SHERIFF *follows the* COUNTY ATTORNEY *into the other room. Then* MRS. HALE *rises, hands tight together, looking intensely at* MRS. PETERS, *whose eyes make a slow turn, finally meeting* MRS. HALE's. *A moment* MRS. HALE *holds her, then her own eyes point the way to where the box is concealed. Suddenly* MRS. PETERS *throws back quilt pieces and tries to put the box in the bag she is wearing. It is too big. She opens box, starts to take bird out, cannot touch it, goes to pieces, stands there helpless. Sound of a knob turning in the other room* MRS. HALE *snatches the box and puts it in the pocket of her big coat. Enter* COUNTY ATTORNEY *and* SHERIFF.)

COUNTY ATTORNEY (*Facetiously.*) Well, Henry, at least we found out that she was not going to quilt it. She was going to— what is it you call it, ladies?

MRS. HALE (*Her hand against her pocket.*) We call it—knot it, Mr. Henderson.

CURTAIN

Mina Loy 1882–1966

In a situation not unlike that of many women writers of her and other generations, Mina Loy was, it is said, "virtually invisible next to many of her fellow modernists." And, yet, Loy is considered by critics one of the most influential modernist writers of the twentieth century. For instance, Ezra Pound and T. S. Eliot were champions of her work, with critic Kenneth Fields noting, "It may be that [William Carlos] Williams, in a few poems only, surpasses Mina Loy stylistically . . . but the body of his work does not compare with her poems; his subjects are frequently trivial, and hers are not." Loy was born in London, but became a U.S. citizen in 1946. Involved in the avant-garde movement of the 1920s in Paris, living later in self-imposed isolation, Loy was also a painter, connecting herself more with visual arts than with writing. It is believed that Loy's own failure to promote herself was largely responsible for her "disappearance." A critic proposes the following as comparison: If William Carlos Williams had simply stopped sending out his work after 1925, he, too, might have been similarly forgotten.

MOREOVER, THE MOON—

Face of the skies
preside
over our wonder.

Flourescent
truant of heaven   5
draw us under.

Silver, circular corpse
your decease
infects us with unendurable ease,

touching nerve–terminals   10
to thermal icicles

Coercive as coma, frail as bloom
innuendoes of your inverse dawn
suffuse the self;
our every corpuscle become an elf.   15

LUNAR BAEDEKER

A silver Lucifer
serves
cocaine in cornucopia

To some somnambulists
of adolescent thighs   5
draped
in satirical draperies

Peris in livery
prepare
Lethe   10
for posthumous parvenues

Delirious Avenues
lit
with the chandelier souls
of infusoria   15
from Pharoah's tombstones

lead
to mercurial doomsdays
Odious oasis
in furrowed phosphorous—   20

the eye–white sky–light
white–light district
of lunar lusts

—Stellectric signs
"Wing shows on Starway"   25
"Zodiac carrousel"

Cyclones
of ecstatic dust
and ashes whirl
crusaders   30
from hallucinatory citadels
of shattered glass
into evacuate craters

A flock of dreams
browse on Necropolis   35

From the shores
of oval oceans
in the oxidized Orient

Onyx–eyed Odalisques
and ornithologists   40
observe
the flight
of Eros obsolete

And "Immortality"
mildews . . .   45
in the museums of the moon

"Nocturnal cyclops"
"Crystal concubine"

————

Pocked with personification
the fossil virgin of the skies   50
waxes and wanes—

Anne Spencer 1882–1975

A nne Spencer was born on a Virginia plantation to incompatible parents who would separate when she was five years old. After the break-up, Anne moved with her mother to Bramwell, West Virginia, where, at age fourteen, she would attend Virginia Seminary and begin writing poetry. In 1920, her talent was discovered accidentally by James Weldon Johnson, who was staying at her home during a National Association for the Advancement of Colored People (NAACP) business trip aimed at assisting local blacks in forming an organizational chapter. He convinced Spencer to allow *Crisis* to publish "Before the Feast of Shushan." Johnson then introduced her to H. L. Mencken, the renowned editor of *American Mercury* magazine, but Spencer refused Mencken's assistance because she believed that he—as a nonpoet—was unqualified to criticize her work. Regarded as one of the finest poets of the Harlem Renaissance, she lived her life in relative obscurity, publishing fewer than thirty poems in a number of important magazines and anthologies of her time. Praised by critics for its imagistic precision and economy, her verse generally deals with Nature but sometimes veers into an ironic modernism on themes of gender and race. Spencer spent much of life raising three children and cultivating a beautiful garden with her mother and husband, Edward, in Lynchburg, Virginia.

SUBSTITUTION[1]

Is Life itself but many ways to thought,
How real the tropic storm or lambent breeze
Within the slightest convolution wrought
Our mantled world and men-freighted seas?
God thinks . . . and being comes to ardent things: 5
The splendor of the day-spent sun, love's birth,—
Or dreams a little, while creation swings
The circle of His mind and Time's full girth . . .
As here within this noisy peopled room
My thought leans forward . . . quick! you're lifted clear   10
Of brick and frame to moonlit garden bloom,—
Absurdly easy, now, our walking, dear,
Talking, my leaning close to touch your face . . .
His All-Mind bids us keep this sacred place!

[1] Revised in 1973 from the version as first published in Countee Cullen (ed.), *Caroling Dusk: An Anthology of Verse by Negro Poets* (New York: Harper, 1927), 48.

LADY, LADY[2]

Lady, Lady, I saw your face,
Dark as night withholding a star . . .
The chisel fell, or it might have been
You had borne so long the yoke of men.
Lady, Lady, I saw your hands,   5
Twisted, awry, like crumpled roots,
Bleached poor white in a sudsy tub,
Wrinkled and drawn from your rub-a-dub.
Lady, Lady, I saw your heart,
And altared there in its darksome place   10
Were the tongues of flames the ancients knew,
Where the good God sits to spangle through.

Anna Wickham 1884–1947

Underneath the playful, sing-songy verse of Anna Wickham seethes the frustration of an artistic woman struggling to rise above the limitations imposed upon her by the English patriarchy: "If I'd indite an ode or mend a sonnet / I must go choose a dish or tie a bonnet." Like Virginia Woolf, Wickham's cleverly bitter poetry often illustrates the obstacles women must overcome in order to create and achieve in society: "I have to thank God that I'm a woman / For in these ordered days a woman only / Is free to be very hungry, very lonely." Born just outside of London in Wimbledon, Wickham was raised in Australia from the age of six. Returning to Europe at age twenty, she studied opera singing in Paris and then entered into a rather unhappy marriage. Considered a rebellious wife who "lived by her own rules," she transformed her feminist frustrations into 900 poems—all written in an intensely creative four-year period. She is best known for three main collections: *The Contemplative Quarry* (1915), *The Man with a Hammer* (1916), and *The Little Old House* (1921). Wickham, a now largely forgotten feminist pioneer, could never have imagined the ironic proportions that retrospect brings to the following stanza from "The Affinity": "It is sad for Feminism, but still clear / That man, more often than woman, is pioneer. / If I would confide a new thought, / First to a man must it be brought."

[2] First published in the *Survey's Graphic Number*, LIII (March 1, 1925), 661.

THE AFFINITY

I have to thank God I'm a woman,
For in these ordered days a woman only
Is free to be very hungry, very lonely.

It is sad for Feminism, but still clear
That man, more often than woman, is pioneer.   5
If I would confide a new thought,
First to a man must it be brought.

Now, for our sins, it is my bitter fate
That such a man wills soon to be my mate,
And so of friendship is quick end: 10
When I have gained a love I lose a friend.

It is well within the order of things
That man should listen when his mate sings;
But the true male never yet walked
Who liked to listen when his mate talked.   15

I would be married to a full man,
As would all women since the world began;
But from a wealth of living I have proved
I must be silent, if I would be loved.

Now of my silence I have much wealth,   20
I have to do my thinking all by stealth.
My thoughts may never see the day;
My mind is like a catacomb where early Christians pray.

And of my silence I have much pain,
But of these pangs I have great gain;   25
For I must take to drugs or drink,
Or I must write the things I think.

If my sex would let me speak,
I would be very lazy and most weak;
I should speak only, and the things I spoke   30
Would fill the air awhile, and clear like smoke.

The things I think now I write down,
And some day I will show them to the Town.
When I am sad I make thought clear;
I can re-read it all next year.   35

I have to thank God I'm a woman,
For in these ordered days a woman only
Is free to be very hungry, very lonely.

DIVORCE

A voice from the dark is calling me.
In the close house I nurse a fire.
Out in the dark, cold winds rush free,
To the rock heights of my desire.
I smother in the house in the valley below,   5
Let me out to the night, let me go, let me go!

Spirits that ride the sweeping blast,
Frozen in rigid tenderness,
Wait! For I leave the fire at last,
My little-love's warm loneliness.   10
I smother in the house in the valley below,
Let me out in the night, let me go, let me go!

High on the hills are beating drums,
Clear from a line of marching men
To the rock's edge the hero comes.   15
He calls me, and he calls again.
On the hill there is fighting, victory, or quick death,
In the house is the fire, which I fan with sick breath
I smother in the house in the valley below,
Let me out in the dark, let me go, let me go!   20

Anzia Yezierska 1885–1970

Anzia Yezierska's life and work chronicle and speak to the "others" among us, documenting experiences antithetical to the lives of writers such as Virginia Woolf, who are born to privilege. Yezierska's novels and stories reveal the hostile world into which came hopeful immigrants to the United States in the early part of the twentieth century. Her characters are often disillusioned and stifled by their quest for "success," in American terms, finding comfort in a combined set of values from both worlds—the old and the new. Yezierska's stories are "widely regarded as accurate depictions of the entire Jewish immigrant experience," with protagonists who ". . . struggle for acceptance in the New World," characters often based on her own struggles to survive in the United States. Although she died in relative obscurity and poverty, Yezierska "is remembered for the honesty and intensity of her narratives." In the 1950s and 1960s, writes one critic, she focused her work on the problems "facing the wave of Puerto Rican immigrants to the mainland states and on the aged in America," echoing again her fight against prejudice, oppression, and the humiliating treatment afforded immigrants by charitable agencies and other institutions.

From HUNGRY HEARTS

MY OWN PEOPLE

With the suitcase containing all her worldly possessions under her arm, Sophie Sapinsky elbowed her way through the noisy ghetto crowds. Pushcart peddlers and pullers-in shouted and gesticulated. Women with market-baskets pushed and shoved one another, eyes straining with the one thought—how to get the food a penny cheaper. With the same strained intentness, Sophie scanned each tenement, searching for a room cheap enough for her dwindling means.

In a dingy basement window a crooked sign, in straggling, penciled letters, caught Sophie's eye: "Room to let, a bargain, cheap."

The exuberant phrasing was quite in keeping with the extravagant dilapidation of the surroundings. "This is the very place," thought Sophie. "There couldn't be nothing cheaper in all New York."

At the foot of the basement steps she knocked.

"Come in!" a voice answered.

As she opened the door she saw an old man bending over a pot of potatoes on a shoemaker's bench. A group of children in all degrees of rags surrounded him, greedily snatching at the potatoes he handed out.

Sophie paused for an instant, but her absorption in her own problem was too great to halt the question: "Is there a room to let?"

"Hanneh Breineh, in the back, has a room." The old man was so preoccupied filling the hungry hands that he did not even look up.

Sophie groped her way to the rear hall. A gaunt-faced woman answered her inquiry with loquacious enthusiasm. "A grand room for the money. I'll let it down to you only for three dollars a month. In the whole block is no bigger bargain. I should live so."

As she talked, the women led her through the dark hall into an airshaft room. A narrow window looked out into the bottom of a chimney-like pit, where lay the accumulated refuse from a score of crowded kitchens.

"Oi Weh!" gasped Sophie, throwing open the sash. "No air and no light. Outside shines the sun and here it's so dark."

"It ain't so dark. It's only a little shady. Let me only turn up the gas for you and you'll quick see everything like with sunshine."

The claw-fingered flame revealed a rusty, iron cot, an inverted potato barrel that served for a table, and two soap-boxes for chairs.

Sophie felt of the cot. It sagged and flopped under her touch. "The bed has only three feet!" she exclaimed in dismay.

"You can't have Rockefeller's palace for three dollars a month," defended Hanneh Breineh, as she shoved one of the boxes under the legless corner of the cot. "If the bed ain't so steady, so you got good neighbors. Upstairs lives Shprintzeh Gittle, the herring-woman. You can buy by her the biggest bargains in fish, a few days older. . . . What she got left over from the Sabbath, she sells to the neighbors cheap. . . . In the front lives Shmendrik, the shoemaker. I'll tell you the truth, he ain't no real shoemaker. He never yet made a pair of whole shoes in his life. He's a learner from the old country—a tzadik, a saint; but every time he sees in the street a child with torn feet, he calls them in and patches them up. His own eating, the last bite from his mouth, he divides up with them."

"Three dollars," deliberated Sophie, scarcely hearing Hanneh Breineh's chatter. "I will never find anything cheaper. It has a door to lock and I can shut this woman out . . . I'll take it," she said, handing her the money.

Hanneh Breineh kissed the greasy bills gloatingly. "I'll treat you like a mother! You'll have it good by me like in your own home."

"Thanks—but I got no time to shmoos. I got to be alone to get my work done."

The rebuff could not penetrate Hanneh Breineh's joy over the sudden possession of three dollars.

"Long years on you! May we be to good luck to one another!" was Hanneh Breineh's blessing as she closed the door.

Alone in her room—*her* room, securely hers—yet with the flash of triumph, a stab of bitterness. All that was hers—so wretched and so ugly! Had her eager spirit, eager to give and give, no claim to a bit of beauty—a shred of comfort?

Perhaps her family was right in condemning her rashness. Was it worth while to give up the peace of home, the security of a regular job—suffer hunger, loneliness, and want—for what? For something she knew in her heart was beyond her reach. Would her writing ever amount to enough to vindicate the uprooting of her past? Would she ever become articulate enough to express beautifully what she saw and felt? What had she, after all, but a stifling, sweat shop experience, a meager, night-school education, and this wild, blind hunger to release the dumbness that choked her?

Sophie spread her papers on the cot beside her. Resting her elbows on the potato barrel, she clutched her pencil with tense fingers. In the notebook before her were a hundred beginnings, essays, abstractions, outbursts of chaotic moods. She glanced through the titles: "Believe in Yourself," "The Quest of the Ideal."

Meaningless tracings on the paper, her words seemed to her now—a restless spirit pawing at the air. The intensity of experience, the surge of emotion that had been hers when she wrote—where were they? The words had failed to catch the life-beat—had failed to register the passion she had poured into them.

Perhaps she was not a writer, after all. Had the years and years of night-study been in vain? Choked with discouragement, the cry broke from her, "O—God—God help me! I feel—I see, but it all dies in me—dumb!"

Tedious days passed into weeks. Again Sophie sat staring into her notebook. "There's nothing here that's alive. Not a word yet says what's in me . . .

"But it *is* in me!" With clenched fist she smote her bosom. "It must be in me! I believe in it! I got to get it out—even if it tears my flesh in pieces—even if it kills me! . . .

"But these words—these flat, dead words . . .

"Whether I can write or can't write—I can't stop writing. I can't rest. I can't breathe. There's no peace, no running away for me on earth except in the struggle to give out what's in me. The beat from my heart—the blood from my veins—must flow out into my words."

She returned to her unfinished essay, "Believe in Yourself." Her mind groping—clutching at the misty incoherence that clouded her thoughts—she wrote on.

"These sentences are yet only wood—lead; but I can't help it—I'll push on—on—I'll not eat—I'll not sleep—I'll not move from this spot till I get it to say on the paper what I got in my heart!"

Slowly the dead words seemed to begin to breathe. Her eyes brightened. Her cheeks flushed. Her very pencil trembled with the eager onrush of words.

Then a sharp rap sounded on her door. With a gesture of irritation Sophie put down her pencil and looked into the burning, sunken eyes of her neighbor, Hanneh Breineh.

"I got yourself a glass of tea, good friend. It ain't much I got to give away, but it's warm even if it's nothing."

Sophie scowled. "You mustn't bother yourself with me. I'm so busy—thanks."

"Don't thank me yet so quick. I got no sugar." Hanneh Breineh edged herself into the room confidingly. "At home, in Poland, I not only had sugar for tea—but even jelly—a jelly that would lift you up to heaven. I thought in America everything would be so plenty, I could drink the tea out from my sugar-bowl. But ach! Not in Poland did my children starve like in America!"

Hanneh Breineh, in a friendly manner, settled herself on the sound end of the bed, and began her jeremaid.

"Yosef, my man, ain't no bread-giver. Already he got consumption the second year. One week he works and nine weeks he lays sick."

In despair Sophie gathered her papers, wondering how to get the woman out of her room. She glanced through the page she had written, but Hanneh Breineh, unconscious of her indifference, went right on.

"How many times it is tearing the heart out from my body—should I take Yosef's milk to give to the baby, or the baby's milk to give to Yosef? If he was dead the pensions they give to widows would help feed my children. Now I got only the charities to help me. A black year on them! They should only have to feed their own children on what they give me."

Resolved not to listen to the intruder, Sophie debated within herself. "Should I call my essay 'Believe in Yourself,' or wouldn't it be stronger to say, 'Trust Yourself'? But if I say, 'Trust Yourself,' would n't they think that I got the words from Emerson?"

Hanneh Breineh's voice went on, but it sounded to Sophie like a faint buzzing from afar. "Gotteniu! How much did it cost me my life to go and swear myself that my little Fannie—only skin and bones—that she is already fourteen! How it chokes me the tears every morning when I got to wake her and push her out to the shop when her eyes are yet shutting themselves with sleep!"

Sophie glanced at her wrist-watch as it ticked away the precious minutes. She must get rid of the woman! Had she not left her own sister, sacrificed all comfort, all association, for solitude and its golden possibilities? For the first time in her life she had the chance to be by herself and think. And now, the thoughts which a moment ago had seemed like a flock of fluttering birds had come so close—and this woman with her sordid wailing had scattered them.

"I'm a savage, a beast, but I got to ask her to get out—this very minute," resolved Sophie. But before she could summon the courage to do what she wanted to do, there was a timid knock at the door, and the wizened little Fannie, her face streaked with tears, stumbled in.

"The inspector said it's a lie. I ain't yet fourteen," she whimpered.

Hanneh Breineh paled. "Woe is me! Sent back from the shop? God from the world—is there no end to my troubles? Why did n't you hide yourself when you saw the inspector come?"

"I was running to hide myself under the table, but she caught me and she said she'll take me to the Children's Society and arrest me and my mother for sending me to work too soon."

"Arrest me?" shrieked Hanneh Breineh, beating her breast. "Let them only come and arrest me! I'll show America who I am! Let them only begin themselves with me! . . . Black is for my eyes . . . the groceryman will not give us another bread till we pay him the bill!"

"The inspector said . . . " The child's brow puckered in an effort to recall the words.

"What did the inspector said? Gotteniu!" Hanneh Breineh wrung her hands in passionate entreaty. "Listen only once to my prayer! Send on the inspector only a quick death! I only wish her to have her own house with twenty-four rooms and each of the twenty-four rooms should be twenty-four beds and the chills and the fever should throw her from one bed to another!"

"Hanneh Breineh, still yourself a little," entreated Sophie.

"How can I still myself without Fannie's wages? Bitter is me! Why do I have to live so long?"

"The inspector said . . ."

"What did the inspector said? A thunder should strike the inspector! Ain't I as good a mother as other mothers? Would n't I better send my children to school? But who'll give us to eat? And who'll pay us the rent?"

Hanneh Breineh wiped her red-lidded eyes with the corner of her apron.

"The president from America should only come to my bitter heart. Let him go fighting himself with the pushcarts how to get the eating a penny cheaper. Let him try to feed his children on the money the charities give me and we'd see if he would n't better send his littlest ones to the shop better than to let them starve before his eyes. Woe is me! What for did I come to America? What's my life—nothing but one terrible, never-stopping fight with the grocer and the butcher and the landlord . . ."

Suddenly Sophie's resentment for her lost morning was forgotten. The crying waste of Hanneh Breineh's life lay open before her eyes like pictures in a book. She saw her own life in Hanneh Breineh's life. Her efforts to write were like Hanneh Breineh's efforts to feed her children. Behind her life and Hanneh Breineh's life she saw the massed ghosts of thousands upon thousands beating—beating out their hearts against rock barriers.

"The inspector said . . ." Fannie timidly attempted again to explain.

"The inspector!" shrieked Hanneh Breineh, as she seized hold of Fannie in a rage. "Hell-fire should burn the inspector! Tell me again about the inspector and I'll choke the life out from you—"

Sophie sprang forward to protect the child from the mother. "She's only trying to tell you something."

"Why should she yet throw salt on my wounds? If there was enough bread in the house would I need an inspector to tell me to send her to school? If America is so interested in poor people's children, then why don't they give them to eat till they should go to work? What learning can come into a child's head when the stomach is empty?"

A clutter of feet down the creaking cellar steps, a scuffle of broken shoes, and a chorus of shrill voices, as the younger children rushed in from school.

"Mamma—what's to eat?"

"It smells potatoes!"

"Pfui! The pot is empty! It smells over from Cohen's."

"Jake grabbed all the bread!"

"Mamma—he kicked the piece out from my hands!"

"Mamma—it's so empty in my stomach! Ain't there nothing?"

"Gluttons—wolves—thieves!" Hanneh Breineh shrieked. "I should only live to bury you all in one day!"

The children, regardless of Hanneh Breineh's invectives, swarmed around her like hungry bees, tearing at her apron, her skirt. Their voices rose in increased clamor, topped only by their mother's imprecations. "Gotteniu! Tear me away from these leeches on my neck! Send on them only a quick death! . . . Only a minute's peace before I die!"

"Hanneh Breineh—children! What's the matter?" Shmendrik stood at the door. The sweet quiet of the old man stilled the raucous voices as the coming of evening stills the noises of the day.

"There's no end to my troubles! Hear them hollering for bread, and the grocer stopped to give till the bill is paid. Woe is me! Fannie sent home by the inspector and not a crumb in the house!"

"I got something." The old man put his hands over the heads of the children in silent benediction. "All come in by me. I got sent me a box of cake."

"Cake!" The children cried, catching at the kind hands and snuggling about the shabby coat.

"Yes. Cake and nuts and raisins and even a bottle of wine."

The children leaped and danced around him in their wild burst of joy.

"Cake and wine—a box—to you? Have the charities gone crazy?" Hanneh Breineh's eyes sparkled with light and laughter.

"No—no," Shmendrik explained hastily. "Not from the charities—from a friend—for the holidays."

Shmendrik nodded invitingly to Sophie, who was standing in the door of her room. "The roomerkeh will also give a taste with us our party?"

"Sure will she!" Hanneh Breineh took Sophie by the arm. "Who'll say no in this black life to cake and wine?"

Young throats burst into shrill cries. "Cake and wine—wine and cake—raisins and nuts—nuts and raisins!" The words rose in a triumphant chorus. The children leaped and danced in time to their chant, almost carrying the old man bodily into his room in the wildness of their joy.

The contagion of this sudden hilarity erased from Sophie's mind the last thought of work and she found herself seated with the others on the cobbler's bench.

From under his cot the old man drew forth a wooden box. Lifting the cover he held up before wondering eyes a large frosted cake embedded in raisins and nuts.

Amid the shouts of glee Shmendrik now waved aloft a large bottle of grape-juice.

The children could contain themselves no longer and dashed forward.

"Shah—shah! Wait only!" He gently halted their onrush and waved them back to their seats.

"The glasses for the wine!" Hanneh Breineh rushed about hither and thither in happy confusion. From the sink, the shelf, the windowsill, she gathered cracked glasses, cups without handles—anything that would hold even a few drops of the yellow wine.

Sacrificial solemnity filled the basement as the children breathlessly watched Shmendrik cut the precious cake. Mouths—even eyes—watered with the intensity of their emotion.

With almost religious fervor Hanneh Breineh poured the grape-juice into the glasses held in the trembling hands of the children. So overwhelming was the occasion that none dared to taste till the ritual was completed. The suspense was agonizing as one and all waited for Shmendrik's signal.

"Hanneh Breineh—you drink from my Sabbath wine-glass!"

Hanneh Breineh clinked glasses with Schmendrik. "Long years on you— long years on us all!" Then she turned to Sophie, clinked glasses once more. "May you yet marry yourself from our basement to a millionaire!" Then she lifted the glass to her lips.

The spell was broken. With a yell of triumph the children gobbled the cake in huge mouthfuls and sucked the golden liquid. All the traditions of wealth and joy that ever sparkled from the bubbles of champagne smiled at Hanneh Breineh from her glass of California grape-juice.

"Ach!" she sighed. "How good it is to forget your troubles, and only those that's got troubles have the chance to forget them!"

She sipped the grape-juice leisurely, thrilled into ecstacy with each lingering drop. "How it laughs yet in me, the life, the minute I turn my head from my worries!"

With growing wonder in her eyes, Sophie watched Hanneh Breineh. This ragged wreck of a woman—how passionately she clung to every atom of life! Hungrily, she burned through the depths of every experience. How she flared against wrongs—and how every tiny spark of pleasure blazed into joy!

Within a half-hour this woman had touched the whole range of human emotions, from bitterest agony to dancing joy. The terrible despair at the onrush of her starving children when she cried out, "O that I should only bury you all in one day!" And now the leaping light of the words: "How it laughs yet in me, the life, the minute I turn my head from my worries."

"Ach, if I could only write like Hanneh Breineh talks!" thought Sophie. "Her words dance with a thousand colors. Like a rainbow it flows from her lips." Sentences from her own essays marched before her, stiff and wooden. How clumsy, how unreal, were her most labored phrases compared to Hanneh Breineh's spontaneity. Fascinated, she listened to Hanneh Breineh, drinking her words as a thirst-perishing man drinks water. Every bubbling phrase filled her with a drunken rapture to create.

"Up till now I was only trying to write from my head. It wasn't real—it wasn't life. Hanneh Breineh is real. Hanneh Breineh is life."

"Ach! What do the rich people got but dried-up dollars? Pfui on them and their money!" Hanneh Breineh held up her glass to be refilled. "Let me only win a fortune on the lotteree and move myself in my own bought house. Let me only have my first hundred dollars in the bank and I'll lift up my head like a person and tell the charities to eat their own cornmeal. I'll get myself an automobile like the kind rich ladies and ride up to their houses on Fifth Avenue and feed them only once on the eating they like so good for me and my children."

With a smile of benediction Shmendrik refilled the glasses and cut for each of his guests another slice of cake. Then came the handful of nuts and raisins.

As the children were scurrying about for hammers and iron lasts with which to crack their nuts, the basement door creaked. Unannounced, a woman entered — the "friendly visitor" of the charities. Her look of awful amazement swept the group of merry-makers.

"Mr. Shmendrik! — Hanneh Breineh!" Indignation seethed in her voice. "What's this? A feast — a birthday?"

Gasps — bewildered glances — a struggle for utterance!

"I came to make my monthly visit — evidently I'm not needed."

Shmendrik faced the accusing eyes of the "friendly visitor." "Holiday eating . . ."

"Oh — I'm glad you're so prosperous."

Before any one had gained presence of mind enough to explain things, the door had clanked. The "friendly visitor" had vanished.

"Pfui!" Hanneh Breineh snatched up her glass and drained its contents. "What will she do now? Will we get no more dry bread from the charities because once we ate cake?"

"What for did she come?" asked Sophie.

"To see that we don't over-eat ourselves!" returned Hanneh Breineh. "She's a 'friendly visitor'! She learns us how to cook cornmeal. By pictures and lectures she shows us how the poor people should live without meat, without milk, without butter, and without eggs. Always it's on the end of my tongue to ask her, 'You learned us to do without so much, why can't you yet learn us how to eat without eating?'"

The children seized the last crumbs of cake that Shmendrik handed them and rushed for the street.

"What a killing look was on her face," said Sophie. "Could n't she be a little glad for your gladness?"

"Charity ladies — gladness?" The joy of the grape-wine still rippled in Hanneh Breineh's laughter. "For poor people is only cornmeal. Ten cents a day — to feed my children!"

Still in her rollicking mood Hanneh Breineh picked up the baby and tossed it like a Bacchante. "Could you be happy a lot with ten cents in your stomach? Ten cents — half a can of condensed milk — then fill yourself the rest with water! . . . Maybe yet feed you with all water and save the ten-cent pieces to buy you a carriage like the Fifth Avenue babies! . . ."

The soft sound of a limousine purred through the area grating and two well-fed figures in seal-skin coats, led by the "friendly visitor," appeared at the door.

"Mr. Bernstein, you can see for yourself." The "friendly visitor" pointed to the table.

The merry group shrank back. It was as if a gust of icy wind had swept all the joy and laughter from the basement.

"You are charged with intent to deceive and obtain assistance by dishonest means," said Mr. Bernstein.

"Dishonest?" Shmendrik paled.

Sophie's throat strained with passionate protest, but no words came to her release.

"A friend—a friend"—stammered Shmendrik—"sent me the holiday eating."

The superintendent of the Social Betterment Society faced him accusingly. "You told us that you had no friends when you applied to us for assistance."

"My friend—he knew me in my better time." Shmendrik flushed painfully. "I was once a scholar—respected. I wanted by this one friend to hold myself like I was."

Mr. Bernstein had taken from the bookshelf a number of letters, glanced through them rapidly and handed them one by one to the deferential superintendent.

Shmendrik clutched at his heart in an agony of humiliation. Suddenly his bent body straightened. His eyes dilated. "My letters—my life—you dare?"

"Of course we dare!" The superintendent returned Shmendrik's livid gaze, made bold by the confidence that what he was doing was the only scientific method of administering philanthropy. "These dollars, so generously given, must go to those most worthy. . . . I find in these letters references to gifts of fruit and other luxuries you did not report at our office."

"He never kept nothing for himself!" Hanneh Breineh broke in defensively. "He gave it all for the children."

Ignoring the interruption Mr. Bernstein turned to the "friendly visitor." "I'm glad you brought my attention to this case. It's but one of the many impositions on our charity . . . Come . . ."

"Kossacks! Pogromschiks!" Sophie's rage broke at last. "You call yourselves Americans? You dare call yourselves Jews? You bosses of the poor! This man Shmendrik, whose house you broke into, whom you made to shame like a beggar—he is the one Jew from whom the Jews can be proud! He gives all he is—all he has—as God gives. *He is* charity.

"But you—you are the greed—the shame of the Jews! *All-right-niks*—fat bellies in fur coats! What do you give from yourselves? You may eat and bust eating! Nothing you give till you've stuffed yourselves so full that your hearts are dead!"

The door closed in her face. Her wrath fell on indifferent backs as the visitors mounted the steps to the street.

Shmendrik groped blindly for the Bible. In a low, quavering voice, he began the chant of the oppressed—the wail of the downtrodden. "I am afraid, and a trembling taketh hold of my flesh. Wherefore do the wicked live, become old, yea, mighty in power?"

Hanneh Breineh and the children drew close around the old man. They were weeping—unconscious of their weeping—deep-buried memories roused by the music, the age-old music of the Hebrew race.

Through the grating Sophie saw the limousine pass. The chant flowed on: "Their houses are safe from fear; neither is the rod of God upon them."

Silently Sophie stole back to her room. She flung herself on the cot, pressed her fingers to her burning eyeballs. For a long time she lay rigid, clenched— listening to the drumming of her heart like the sea against rock barriers. Presently the barriers burst. Something in her began pouring itself out. She felt for her pencil—paper—and began to write. Whether she reached out to God or man she knew not, but she wrote on and on all through that night.

The gray light entering her grated window told her that beyond was dawn. Sophie looked up: "Ach! At last it writes itself in me!" she whispered triumphantly. "It's not me—it's their cries—my own people—crying in me! Hanneh Breineh, Shmendrik, they will not be stilled in me, till all America stops to listen."

AMERICA AND I

As one of the dumb, voiceless ones I speak. One of the millions of immigrants beating, beating out their hearts at your gates for a breath of understanding.

Ach! America! From the other end of the earth where I came, America was a land of living hope, woven of dreams, aflame with longing and desire.

Choked for ages in the airless oppression of Russia, the Promised Land rose up—wings for my stifled spirit—sunlight burning through my darkness— freedom singing to me in my prison—deathless songs turning prison-bars into strings of a beautiful violin.

I arrived in America. My young, strong body, my heart and soul pregnant with the unlived lives of generations clamoring for expression.

What my mother and father and their mother and father never had a chance to give out in Russia, I would give out in America. The hidden sap of centuries would find release; colors that never saw light—songs that died unvoiced—romance that never had a chance to blossom in the black life of the Old World.

In the golden land of flowing opportunity I was to find my work that was denied me in the sterile village of my forefathers. Here I was to be free from the dead drudgery for bread that held me down in Russia. For the first time in America, I'd cease to be a slave of the belly. I'd be a creator, a giver, a human being! My work would be the living joy of fullest self-expression.

But from my high visions, my golden hopes, I had to put my feet down on earth. I had to have food and shelter. I had to have the money to pay for it.

I was in America, among the Americans, but not of them. No speech, no common language, no way to win a smile of understanding from them, only my young, strong body and my untried faith. Only my eager, empty hands, and my full heart shining from my eyes!

God from the world! Here I was with so much richness in me but my mind was not wanted without the language. And my body, unskilled, untrained, was not even wanted in the factory. Only one of two chances was left open to me: the kitchen, or minding babies.

My first job was as a servant in an Americanized family. Once, long ago, they came from the same village from where I came. But they were so well-dressed, so well-fed, so successful in America, that they were ashamed to remember their mother tongue.

"What were to be my wages?" I ventured timidly, as I looked up to the well-fed, well-dressed "American" man and woman.

They looked at me with a sudden coldness. What have I said to draw away from me their warmth? Was it so low from me to talk of wages? I shrank back into myself like a low-down bargainer. Maybe they're so high up in well-being they can't any more understand my low thoughts for money.

From his rich height the man preached down to me that I must not be so grabbing for wages. Only just landed from the ship and already thinking about money when I should be thankful to associate with "Americans."

The woman, out of her smooth, smiling fatness assured me that this was my chance for a summer vacation in the country with her two lovely children. My great chance to learn to be a civilized being, to become an American by living with them.

So, made to feel that I was in the hands of American friends, invited to share with them their home, their plenty, their happiness, I pushed out from my head the worry for wages. Here was my first chance to begin my life in the sunshine, after my long darkness. My laugh was all over my face as I said to them: "I'll trust myself to you. What I'm worth you'll give me." And I entered their house like a child by the hand.

The best of me I gave them. Their house cares were my house cares. I got up early. I worked till late. All that my soul hungered to give I put into the passion with which I scrubbed floors, scoured pots, and washed clothes. I was so grateful to mingle with the American people, to hear the music of the American language, that I never knew tiredness.

There was such a freshness in my brains and such a willingness in my heart that I could go on and on—not only with the work of the house, but work with my head—learning new words from the children, the grocer, the butcher, the iceman. I was not even afraid to ask for words from the policeman on the street. And every new word made me see new American things with American eyes. I felt like a Columbus, finding new worlds through every new word.

But words alone were only for the inside of me. The outside of me still branded me for a steerage immigrant. I had to have clothes to forget myself that I'm a stranger yet. And so I had to have money to buy these clothes.

The month was up. I was so happy! Now I'd have money. *My own, earned* money. Money to buy a new shirt on my back—shoes on my feet. Maybe yet an American dress and hat!

Ach! How high rose my dreams! How plainly I saw all that I would do with my visionary wages shining like a light over my head!

In my imagination I already walked in my new American clothes. How beautiful I looked as I saw myself like a picture before my eyes! I saw how I would throw away my immigrant rags tied up in my immigrant shawl. With money to buy—free money in my hands—I'd show them that I could look like an American in a day.

Like a prisoner in his last night in prison, counting the seconds that will free him from his chains, I trembled breathlessly for the minute I'd get the wages in my hand.

Before dawn I rose.

I shined up the house like a jewel-box.

I prepared breakfast and waited with my heart in my mouth for my lady and gentleman to rise. At last I heard them stirring. My eyes were jumping out of my head to them when I saw them coming in and seating themselves by the table.

Like a hungry cat rubbing up to its boss for meat, so I edged and simpered around them as I passed them the food. Without my will, like a beggar, my hand reached out to them.

The breakfast was over. And no word yet from my wages.

"*Gottuniu!*" I thought to myself. Maybe they're so busy with their own things they forgot it's the day for my wages. Could they who have everything know what I was to do with my first American dollars? How could they, soaking in plenty, how could they feel the longing and the fierce hunger in me, pressing up through each visionary dollar? How could they know the gnawing ache of my avid fingers for the feel of my own, earned dollars? *My* dollars that I could spend like a free person. *My* dollars that would make me feel with everybody alike!

Breakfast was long past.

Lunch came. Lunch past.

Oi-i weh! Not a word yet about my money.

It was near dinner. And not a word yet about my wages.

I began to set the table. But my head—it swam away from me. I broke a glass. The silver dropped from my nervous fingers. I couldn't stand it any longer. I dropped everything and rushed over to my American lady and gentleman.

"*Oi Weh*! The money—my money—my wages!" I cried breathlessly. Four cold eyes turned on me.

"Wages? Money?" The four eyes turned into hard stone as they looked me up and down. "Haven't you a comfortable bed to sleep, and three good meals a day? You're only a month here. Just came to America. And you already think about money. Wait till you're worth any money. What use are you without knowing English? You should be glad we keep you here. It's like a vacation for you. Other girls pay money yet to be in the country."

It went black for my eyes. I was so choked no words came to my lips. Even the tears went dry in my throat.

I left. Not a dollar for all my work.

For a long, long time my heart ached and ached like a sore wound. If murderers would have robbed me and killed me it wouldn't have hurt me so much. I couldn't think through my pain. The minute I'd see before me how they looked at me, the words they said to me—then everything began to bleed in me. And I was helpless.

For a long, long time the thought of ever working in an "American" family made me tremble with fear, like the fear of wild wolves. No—never again would I trust myself to an "American" family, no matter how fine their language and how sweet their smile.

It was blotted out in me all trust in friendship from "Americans." But the life in me still burned to live. The hope in me still craved to hope. In darkness, in dirt, in hunger and want, but only to live on!

There had been no end to my day—working for the "American" family.

Now rejecting false friendships from higher-ups in America, I turned back to the Ghetto. I worked on a hard bench with my own kind on either side of me. I knew before I began what my wages were to be. I knew what my hours were to be. And I knew the feeling of the end of the day.

From the outside my second job seemed worse than the first. It was in a sweat-shop of a Delancey Street basement, kept up by an old, wrinkled woman that looked like a black witch of greed. My work was sewing on buttons. While the morning was still dark I walked into a dark basement. And darkness met me when I turned out of the basement.

Day after day, week after week, all the contact I got with America was handling dead buttons. The money I earned was hardly enough to pay for bread and rent. I didn't have a room to myself. I didn't even have a bed. I slept on a mattress on the floor in a rat-hole of a room occupied by a dozen other immigrants. I was always hungry—oh, so hungry! The scant meals I could afford only sharpened my appetite for real food. But I felt myself better off than working in the "American" family, where I had three good meals a day and a bed to myself. With all the hunger and darkness of the sweat-shop, I had at least the evening to myself. And all night was mine. When all were asleep, I used to creep up on the roof of the tenement and talk out my heart in silence to the stars in the sky.

"Who am I? What am I? What do I want with my life? Where is America? Is there an America? What is this wilderness in which I'm lost?"

I'd hurl my questions and then think and think. And I could not tear it out of me, the feeling that America must be somewhere, somehow—only I couldn't find it—*my America*, where I would work for love and not for a living. I was like a thing following blindly after something far off in the dark!

"*Oi weh!*" I'd stretch out my hand up in the air. "My head is so lost in America! What's the use of all my working if I'm not in it? Dead buttons is not me."

Then the busy season started in the shop. The mounds of buttons grew and grew. The long day stretched out longer. I had to begin with the buttons earlier and stay with them till later in the night. The old witch turned into a huge greedy maw for wanting more and more buttons.

For a glass of tea, for a slice of herring over black bread, she would buy us up to stay another and another hour, till there seemed no end to her demands.

One day, the light of self-assertion broke into my cellar darkness.

"I don't want the tea. I don't want your herring," I said with terrible boldness. "I only want to go home. I only want the evening to myself!"

"You fresh mouth, you!" cried the old witch. "You learned already too much in America. I want no clock-watchers in my shop. Out you go!"

I was driven out to cold and hunger. I could no longer pay for my mattress on the floor. I no longer could buy the bite in the mouth. I walked the streets. I knew what it is to be alone in a strange city, among strangers.

But I laughed through my tears. So I learned too much already in America because I wanted the whole evening to myself? Well America has yet to teach me still more: how to get not only the whole evening to myself, but a whole day a week like the American workers.

That sweat-shop was a bitter memory but a good school. It fitted me for a regular factory. I could walk in boldly and say I could work at something, even if it was only sewing on buttons.

Gradually, I became a trained worker. I worked in a light, airy factory, only eight hours a day. My boss was no longer a sweater and a bloodsqueezer. The first freshness of the morning was mine. And the whole evening was mine. All day Sunday was mine.

Now I had better food to eat. I slept on a better bed. Now, I even looked dressed up like the American-born. But inside of me I knew that I was not yet an American. I choked with longing when I met an American-born, and I could say nothing.

Something cried dumb in me. I couldn't help it. I didn't know what it was I wanted. I only knew I wanted. I wanted. Like the hunger in the heart that never gets food.

An English class for foreigners started in our factory. The teacher had such a good, friendly face, her eyes looked so understanding, as if she could see right into my heart. So I went to her one day for an advice:

"I don't know what is with me the matter," I began. "I have no rest in me. I never yet done what I want."

"What is it you want to do, child?" she asked me.

"I want to do something with my head, my feelings. All day long, only with my hands I work."

"First you must learn English." She patted me as if I was not yet grown up. "Put your mind on that, and then we'll see."

So for a time I learned the language. I could almost begin to think with English words in my head. But in my heart the emptiness still hurt. I burned to give, to give something, to do something, to be something. The dead work with my hands was killing me. My work left only hard stones on my heart.

Again I went to our factory teacher and cried to her: "I know already to read and write the English language, but I can't put it into words what I want. What is it in me so different that can't come out?"

She smiled at me down from her calmness as if I were a little bit out of my head. "What *do you want* to do?"

"I feel. I see. I hear. And I want to think it out. But I'm like dumb in me. I only feel I'm different—different from everybody."

She looked at me close and said nothing for a minute. "You ought to join one of the social clubs of the Women's Association," she advised.

"What's the Women's Association?" I implored greedily.

"A group of American women who are trying to help the working-girl find herself. They have a special department for immigrant girls like you."

I joined the Women's Association. On my first evening there they announced a lecture: "The Happy Worker and His Work," by the Welfare director of the United Mills Corporation.

"Is there such a thing as a happy worker at his work?" I wondered. Happiness is only by working at what you love. And what poor girl can ever find it to work at what she loves? My old dreams about my America rushed through my mind. Once I thought that in America everybody works for love. Nobody has to worry for a living. Maybe this welfare man came to show me the *real* America that till now I sought in vain.

With a lot of polite words the head lady of the Women's Association introduced a higher-up that looked like the king of kings of business. Never before in my life did I ever see a man with such a sureness in his step, such power in his face, such friendly positiveness in his eye as when he smiled upon us.

"Efficiency is the new religion of business," be began. "In big business houses, even in up-to-date factories, they no longer take the first comer and give him any job that happens to stand empty. Efficiency begins at the employment office. Experts are hired for the one purpose, to find out how best to fit the worker to his work. It's economy for the boss to make the worker happy." And then he talked a lot more on efficiency in educated language that was over my head.

I didn't know exactly what it meant—efficiency—but if it was to make the worker happy at his work, then that's what I had been looking for since I came to America. I only felt from watching him that he was happy by his job. And as I looked on this clean, well-dressed, successful one, who wasn't ashamed to say he rose from an office-boy, it made me feel that I, too, could lift myself up for a person.

He finished his lecture, telling us about the Vocational-Guidance Center that the Women's Association started.

The very next evening I was at the Vocational-Guidance Center. There I found a young, college-looking woman. Smartness and health shining from her eyes! She, too, looked as if she knew her way in America. I could tell at the first glance: here is a person that is happy by what she does.

"I feel you'll understand me," I said right away.

She leaned over with pleasure in her face: "I hope I can."

"I want to work by what's in me. Only, I don't know what's in me. I only feel I'm different."

She gave me a quick, puzzled look from the corner of her eyes. "What are you doing now?"

"I'm the quickest shirtwaist hand on the floor. But my heart wastes away by such work. I think and think, and my thoughts can't come out."

"Why don't you think out your thoughts in shirtwaists? You could learn to be a designer. Earn more money."

"I don't want to look on waists. If my hands are sick from waists, how could my head learn to put beauty into them?"

"But you must earn your living at what you know, and rise slowly from job to job."

I looked at her office sign: "Vocational Guidance," "What's your vocational guidance?" I asked. "How to rise from job to job—how to earn more money?"

The smile went out from her eyes. But she tried to be kind yet. "What *do* you want?" she asked, with a sigh of last patience.

"I want America to want me."

She fell back in her chair, thunderstruck with my boldness. But yet, in a low voice of educated self-control, she tried to reason with me:

"You have to *show* that you have something special for America before America has need of you."

"But I never had a chance to find out what's in me, because I always had to work for a living. Only, I feel it's efficiency for America to find out what's in me so different, so I could give it out by my work."

Her eyes half closed as they bored through me. Her mouth opened to speak, but no words came from her lips. So I flamed up with all that was choking in me like a house on fire:

"America gives free bread and rent to criminals in prison. They got grand houses with sunshine, fresh air, doctors and teachers, even for the crazy ones.

Why don't they have free boarding-schools for immigrants—strong people—willing people? Here you see us burning up with something different, and America turns her head away from us."

Her brows lifted and dropped down. She shrugged her shoulders away from me with the look of pity we give to cripples and hopeless lunatics.

"America is no Utopia. First you must become efficient in earning a living before you can indulge in your poetic dreams."

I went away from the vocational-guidance office with all the air out of my lungs. All the light out of my eyes. My feet dragged after me like dead wood.

Till now there had always lingered a rosy veil of hope over my emptiness, a hope that a miracle would happen. I would open my eyes some day and suddenly find the America of my dreams. As a young girl hungry for love sees always before her eyes the picture of lover's arms around her, so I saw always in my heart the vision of Utopian America.

But now I felt that the America of my dreams never was and never could be. Reality had hit me on the head as with a club. I felt that the America that I sought was nothing but a shadow—an echo—a chimera of lunatics and crazy immigrants.

Stripped of all illusion, I looked about me. The long desert of wasting days of drudgery stared me in the face. The drudgery that I had lived through, and the endless drudgery still ahead of me rose over me like a withering wilderness of sand. In vain were all my cryings, in vain were all frantic efforts of my spirit to find the living waters of understanding for my perishing lips. Sand, sand was everywhere. With every seeking, every reaching out I only lost myself deeper and deeper in a vast sea of sand.

I knew now the American language. And I knew now, if I talked to the Americans from morning till night, they could not understand what the Russian soul of me wanted. They could not understand *me* anymore than if I talked to them in Chinese. Between my soul and the American soul were worlds of difference that no words could bridge over. What was that difference? What made the Americans so far apart from me?

I began to read the American history. I found from the first pages that America started with a band of Courageous Pilgrims. They had left their native country as I had left mine. They had crossed an unknown ocean and landed in an unknown country, as I.

But the great difference between the first Pilgrims and me was that they expected to make America, build America, create their own world of liberty. I wanted to find it ready made.

I read on. I delved deeper down into the American history. I saw how the Pilgrim Fathers came to a rocky desert country, surrounded by Indian savages on all sides. But undaunted, they pressed on—through danger—through famine, pestilence, and want—they pressed on. They did not ask the Indians for sympathy, for understanding. They made no demands on anybody, but on their own indomitable spirit of persistence.

And I—I was forever begging a crumb of sympathy, a gleam of understanding from strangers who could not sympathize, who could not understand.

I, when I encountered a few savage Indian scalpers, like the old witch of the sweat-shop, like my "Americanized" countryman, who cheated me of my wages—I, when I found myself on the lonely, untrodden path through which all seekers of the new world must pass, I lost heart and said: "There is no America!"

Then came a light—a great revelation! I saw America—a big idea—a deathless hope—a world still in the making. I saw that it was the glory of America that it was not yet finished. And I, the last comer, had her share to give, small or great, to the making of America, like those Pilgrims who came in the *Mayflower*.

Fired up by this revealing light, I began to build a bridge of understanding between the American-born and myself. Since their life was shut out from such as me, I began to open up my life and the lives of my people to them. And life draws life. In only writing about the Ghetto I found America.

Great chances have come to me. But in my heart is always a deep sadness. I feel like a man who is sitting down to a secret table of plenty, while his near ones and dear ones are perishing before his eyes. My very joy in doing the work I love hurts me like secret guilt, because all about me I see so many with my longings, my burning eagerness, to do and to be, wasting their days in drudgery they hate, merely to buy bread and pay rent. And America is losing all that richness of the soul.

The Americans of to-morrow, the America that is every day nearer coming to be, will be too wise, too open-hearted, too friendly-handed, to let the least last-comer at their gates knock in vain with his gifts unwanted.

Radclyffe Hall 1886–1943

Facts concerning Marguerite Radclyffe-Hall's life are sketchy at best, but her biographer, Una, Lady Troubridge (also Hall's lover for over two decades), notes that the English writer was neglected by both her parents; her maternal grandmother proved to be the only member of the family who was attentive and affectionate towards Hall. Considered a pioneering lesbian novelist, Hall published two novels and several volumes of poetry before her book, *Adam's Breed* (1926), won several significant prizes, including the James Tait Black Memorial Book Prize. She became famous, however, because of the scandal that resulted from her next novel, *The Well of Loneliness* (1928), which protests against the persecution of lesbians. After the book was banned in England, Hall wrote several religious novels; but her place in literary history was secured nonetheless by her depiction of the androgynous, heroic Stephen in *The Well of Loneliness.*

MISS OGILVY FINDS HERSELF

Miss Ogilvy stood on the quay at Calais and surveyed the disbanding of her Unit, the Unit that together with the coming of war[1] had completely altered the complexion of her life, at all events for three years.

Miss Ogilvy's thin, pale lips were set sternly and her forehead was puckered in an effort of attention, in an effort to memorize every small detail of every old war-weary battered motor on whose side still appeared the merciful emblem[2] that had set Miss Ogilvy free.

Miss Ogilvy's mind was jerking a little, trying to regain its accustomed balance, trying to readjust itself quickly to this sudden and paralyzing change. Her tall, awkward body with its queer look of strength, its broad, flat bosom and thick legs and ankles, as though in response to her jerking mind, moved uneasily, rocking backwards and forwards. She had this trick of rocking on her feet in moments of controlled agitation. As usual, her hands were thrust deep into her pockets, they seldom seemed to come out of her pockets unless it were to light a cigarette, and as though she were still standing firm under fire while the wounded were placed in her ambulances, she suddenly straddled her legs very slightly and lifted her head and listened. She was standing firm under fire at that moment, the fire of a desperate regret.

Some girls came towards her, young, tired-looking creatures whose eyes were too bright from long strain and excitement. They had all been members of that glorious Unit, and they still wore the queer little forage-caps[3] and the short, clumsy tunics of the French Militaire. They still slouched in walking and smoked Caporals in emulation of the Poilus.[4] Like their founder and leader these girls were all English, but like her they had chosen to serve England's ally, fearlessly thrusting right up to the trenches in search of the wounded and dying. They had seen some fine things in the course of three years, not the least fine of which was the cold, hard-faced woman who, commanding, domineering, even hectoring at times, had yet been possessed of so dauntless a courage and of so insistent a vitality that it vitalized the whole Unit.

---

[1]World War I, in 1914.
[2]A Red Cross symbol of the ambulance corps.
[3]Caps worn by infantry soldiers.
[4]French soldiers.

"It's rotten!' Miss Ogilvy heard someone saying. "It's rotten, this breaking up of our Unit!" And the high, rather childish voice of the speaker sounded perilously near to tears.

Miss Ogilvy looked at the girl almost gently, and it seemed, for a moment, as though some deep feeling were about to find expression in words. But Miss Ogilvy's feelings had been held in abeyance so long that they seldom dared become vocal, so she merely said "Oh?" on a rising inflection—her method of checking emotion.

They were swinging the ambulance cars in midair, those of them that were destined to go back to England, swinging them up like sacks of potatoes, then lowering them with much clanging of chains to the deck of the waiting steamer. The porters were showing and shouting and quarreling, pausing now and again to make meaningless gestures; while a pompous official was becoming quite angry as he pointed at Miss Ogilvy's own special car—it annoyed him, it was bulky and difficult to move.

"Bon Dieu! Mais dépêchez-vous donc!"[5] he bawled, as though he were bullying the motor.

Then Miss Ogilvy's heart gave a sudden, thick thud to see this undignified, pitiful ending; and she turned and patted the gallant old car as though she were patting a well-beloved horse, as though she would say: "Yes, I know how it feels—never mind, we'll go down together."

2

Miss Ogilvy sat in the railway carriage on her way from Dover to London. The soft English landscape sped smoothly past: small homesteads, small churches, small pastures, small lanes with small hedges; all small like England itself, all small like Miss Ogilvy's future. And sitting there still arrayed in her tunic, with her forage-cap resting on her knees, she was conscious of a sense of complete frustration; thinking less of those glorious years at the Front and of all that had gone to the making of her, than of all that had gone to the marring of her from the days of her earliest childhood.

She saw herself as a queer little girl, aggressive and awkward because of her shyness; a queer little girl who loathed sisters and dolls, preferring the stableboys as companions, preferring to play with footballs and tops, and occasional catapults. She saw herself climbing the tallest beech trees, arrayed in old breeches illicitly come by. She remembered insisting with tears and some temper that her real name was William and not Wilhelmina. All these childish pretences and illusions she remembered, and the bitterness that came after. For Miss Ogilvy had found as her life went on that in this world it is better to be one with the herd, that the world has no wish to understand those who cannot conform to its stereotyped pattern. True enough, in her youth she had gloried in her strength,

[5]Good God! Move along, then! (French).

lifting weights, swinging clubs and developing muscles, but presently this had grown irksome to her; it had seemed to lead nowhere, she being a woman, and then as her mother had often protested: muscles looked so appalling in evening dress—a young girl ought not to have muscles.

Miss Ogilvy's relation to the opposite sex was unusual and at that time added much to her worries, for no less than three men had wished to propose, to the genuine amazement of the world and her mother. Miss Ogilvy's instinct made her like and trust men, for whom she had a pronounced fellow-feeling; she would always have chosen them as her friends and companions in preference to girls or women; she would dearly have loved to share in their sports, their business, their ideas and their wide-flung interests. But men had not wanted her, except the three who had found in her strangeness a definite attraction, and those would-be suitors she had actually feared, regarding them with aversion. Towards young girls and women she was shy and respectful, apologetic and sometimes admiring. But their fads and their foibles, none of which she could share, while amusing her very often in secret, set her outside the sphere of their intimate lives, so that in the end she must blaze a lone trail through the difficulties of her nature.

"I can't understand you," her mother had said, "you're a very odd creature—now when I was your age . . ."

And her daughter had nodded, feeling sympathetic. There were two younger girls who also gave trouble, though in their case the trouble was fighting for husbands who were scarce enough even in those days. It was finally decided, at Miss Ogilvy's request, to allow her to leave the field clear for her sisters. She would remain in the country with her father when the others went up for the Season.[6]

Followed long, uneventful years spent in sport, while Sarah and Fanny toiled, sweated and gambled in the matrimonial market. Neither ever succeeded in netting a husband, and when the Squire died leaving very little money, Miss Ogilvy found to her great surprise that they looked upon her as a brother. They had so often jibed at her in the past, that at first she could scarcely believe her senses, but before very long it became all too real: she it was who must straighten out endless muddles, who must make the dreary arrangements for the move, who must find a cheap but genteel house in London and, once there, who must cope with the family accounts which she only, it seemed, could balance.

It would be: "You might see to that, Wilhelmina: you write, you've got such a good head for business." Or: "I wish you'd go down and explain to that man that we really can't pay his account till next quarter." Or: "This money for the grocer is five shillings short. Do run over my sum, Wilhelmina."

Her mother, grown feeble, discovered in this daughter a staff upon which she could lean with safety. Miss Ogilvy genuinely loved her mother, and was

[6] The social season.

therefore quite prepared to be leaned on; but when Sarah and Fanny began to lean too with the full weight of endless neurotic symptoms incubated in resentful virginity, Miss Ogilvy found herself staggering a little. For Sarah and Fanny were grown hard to bear, with their mania for telling their symptoms to doctors, with their unstable nerves and their acrid tongues and the secret dislike they now felt for their mother. Indeed, when old Mrs. Ogilvy died, she was unmourned except by her eldest daughter who actually felt a void in her life—the unforeseen void that the ailing and weak will not infrequently leave behind them.

At about this time an aunt also died, bequeathing her fortune to her niece Wilhelmina who, however, was too weary to gird up her loins and set forth in search of exciting adventure—all she did was to move her protesting sisters to a little estate she had purchased in Surrey. This experiment was only a partial success, for Miss Ogilvy failed to make friends of her neighbors; thus at fifty-five she had grown rather dour, as is often the way with shy, lonely people.

When the war came she had just begun settling down—people do settle down in their fifty-sixth year—she was feeling quite glad that her hair was gray, that the garden took up so much of her time, that, in fact, the beat of her blood was slowing. But all this was changed when war was declared; on that day Miss Ogilvy's pulses throbbed wildly.

"My God! If only I were a man!" she burst out, as she glared at Sarah and Fanny, "if only I had been born a man!" Something in her was feeling deeply defrauded.

Sarah and Fanny were soon knitting socks and mittens and mufflers and Jaeger trench-helmets.[7] Other ladies were busily working at depots, making swabs at the Squire's, or splints at the Parson's; but Miss Ogilvy scowled and did none of these things—she was not at all like other ladies.

For nearly twelve months she worried officials with a view to getting a job out in France—not in their way but in hers, and that was the trouble. She wished to go up to the front-line trenches, she wished to be actually under fire, she informed the harassed officials.

To all her enquiries she received the same answer: "We regret that we cannot accept your offer." But once thoroughly roused she was hard to subdue, for her shyness had left her as though by magic.

Sarah and Fanny shrugged angular shoulders: "There's plenty of work here at home," they remarked, "though of course it's not quite so melodramatic!"

"Oh . . . ?" queried their sister on a rising note of impatience—and she promptly cut off her hair: "That'll jar them!" she thought with satisfaction.

Then she went up to London, formed her admirable unit and finally got it accepted by the French, despite renewed opposition.

In London she had found herself quite at her ease, for many another of her kind was in London doing excellent work for the nation. It was really surprising

---

[7] Woolen caps worn in the trenches, where much of World War I was fought.

how many cropped heads had suddenly appeared as it were out of space; how many Miss Ogilvies, losing their shyness, had come forward asserting their right to serve, asserting their claim to attention.

There followed those turbulent years at the front, full of courage and hardship and high endeavor; and during those years Miss Ogilvy forgot the bad joke that Nature seemed to have played her. She was given the rank of a French lieutenant and she lived in a kind of blissful illusion; appalling reality lay on all sides and yet she managed to live in illusion. She was competent, fearless, devoted and untiring. What then? Could any man hope to do better? She was nearly fifty-eight, yet she walked with a stride, and at times she even swaggered a little.

Poor Miss Ogilvy sitting so glumly in the train with her manly trench-boots and her forage-cap! Poor all the Miss Ogilvies back from the war with their tunics, their trench-boots, and their childish illusions! Wars come and wars go but the world does not change: it will always forget an indebtedness which it thinks it expedient not to remember.

3

When Miss Ogilvy returned to her home in Surrey it was only to find that her sisters were ailing from the usual imaginary causes, and this to a woman who had seen the real thing was intolerable, so that she looked with distaste at Sarah and then at Fanny. Fanny was certainly not prepossessing, she was suffering from a spurious attack of hay fever.

"Stop sneezing!" commanded Miss Ogilvy, in the voice that had so much impressed the Unit. But as Fanny was not in the least impressed, she naturally went on sneezing.

Miss Ogilvy's desk was piled mountain-high with endless tiresome letters and papers: circulars, bills, months-old correspondence, the gardener's accounts, an agent's report on some fields that required land-draining. She seated herself before this collection; then she sighed, it all seemed so absurdly trivial.

"Will you let your hair grow again?" Fanny enquired . . . she and Sarah had followed her into the study. "I'm certain the Vicar would be glad if you did."

"Oh?" murmured Miss Ogilvy, rather too blandly.

"Wilhelmina!"

"Yes?"

"You will do it, won't you?"

"Do what?"

"Let your hair grow; we all wish you would."

"Why should I?"

"Oh, well, it will look less odd, especially now that the war is over—in a small place like this people notice such things."

"I entirely agree with Fanny;" announced Sarah.

Sarah had become very self-assertive, no doubt though having mismanaged the estate during the years of her sister's absence. They had quite a heated dispute one morning over the south herbaceous border.

"Whose garden is this?" Miss Ogilvy asked sharply. "I insist on auricula-eyed sweet Williams! I even took the trouble to write from France, but it seems that my letter has been ignored."

"Don't shout," rebuked Sarah, "you're not in France now!"

Miss Ogilvy could gladly have boxed her ears: "I only wish to God I were," she muttered.

Another dispute followed close on its heels, and this time it happened to be over the dinner. Sarah and Fanny were living on weeds—at least that was the way Miss Ogilvy put it.

"We've become vegetarians," Sarah said grandly.

"You've become two damn tiresome cranks!" snapped their sister.

Now it never had been Miss Ogilvy's way to indulge in acid recriminations, but somehow, these days, she forgot to say: "Oh?" quite so often as expediency demanded. It may have been Fanny's perpetual sneezing that had got on her nerves; or it may have been Sarah, or the gardener, or the Vicar, or even the canary; though it really did not matter very much what it was just so long as she found a convenient peg upon which to hang her growing irritation.

"This won't do at all," Miss Ogilvy thought sternly, "lilfe's not worth so much fuss, I must pull myself together." But it seemed this was easier said than done; not a day passed without her losing her temper and that over some trifle: "No, this won't do at all—it just mustn't be," she thought sternly.

Everyone pitied Sarah and Fanny: "Such a dreadful, violent odd thing," said the neighbors.

But Sarah and Fanny had their revenge: "Poor darling, it's shell shock,[8] you know," they murmured.

Thus Miss Ogilvy's prowess was whittled away until she herself was beginning to doubt it. Had she ever been that courageous person who had faced death in France with such perfect composure? Had she ever stood tranquilly under fire, without turning a hair, while she issued her orders? Had she ever been treated with marked respect? She herself was beginning to doubt it.

Sometimes she would see an old member of the Unit, a girl who more faithful to her than the others, would take the trouble to run down to Surrey. These visits, however were seldom enlivening.

"Oh, well . . . here we are. . ." Miss Ogilvy would mutter.

But one day the girl smiled and shook her blond head: "I'm not—I'm going to be married."

Strange thoughts had come to Miss Ogilvy, unbidden, thoughts that had stayed for many an hour after the girl's departure. Alone in her study she had suddenly shivered, feeling a sense of complete desolation. With cold hands she had lighted a cigarette.

"I must be ill or something," she had mused, as she stared at her trembling fingers.

[8] A mental illness suffered by some soldiers during World War I, brought on by combat experience (i.e. posttraumatic stress disorder).

After this she would sometimes cry out in her sleep, living over in dreams God knows what emotions; returning, maybe to the battlefield of France. Her hair turned snow-white; it was not unbecoming yet she fretted about it.

"I'm growing very old," she would sigh as she brushed her thick mop before the glass; and then she would peer at her wrinkles.

For now that it had happened she hated being old; it no longer appeared such an easy solution of those difficulties that had always beset her. And this she resented most bitterly, so that she became the prey of self-pity, and of other undesirable states in which the body will torment the mind, and the mind, in its turn, the body. Then Miss Ogilvy straightened her ageing back, in spite of the fact that of late it had ached with muscular rheumatism, and she faced herself squarely and came to a resolve.

"I'm off!" she announced abruptly one day; and that evening she packed her kit-bag.

4

Near the south coast of Devon there exists a small island that is still very little known to the world, but which nevertheless can boast an hotel, the only building upon it. Miss Ogilvy had chosen this place quite at random, it was marked on her map by scarcely more than a dot, but somehow she had liked the look of that dot and had set forth alone to explore it.

She found herself standing on the mainland one morning looking at a vague blur of green through the mist, a vague blur of green that rose out of the Channel like a tidal wave suddenly suspended. Miss Ogilvy was filled with a sense of adventure; she had not felt like this since the ending of war.

"I was right to come here, very right indeed. I'm going to shake off my troubles," she decided.

A fisherman's boat was parting the mist, and before it was properly beached, in she bundled.

"I hope they're expecting me?" she said gaily.

"They du be expecting you," the man answered.

The sea, which is generally rough off that coast, was indulging itself in an oily ground-swell; the broad glossy swells struck the side of the boat, then broke and sprayed over Miss Ogilvy's ankles.

The fisherman grinned: "Feeling all right?" he queried. "It du be tiresome most times about these parts." But the mist had suddenly drifted away and Miss Ogilvy was staring wide-eyed at the island.

She saw a long shoal of jagged black rocks, and between them the curve of a small sloping beach, and above that the lift of the island itself, and above that again, blue heaven. Near the beach stood the little two-storied hotel which was thatched, and built entirely of timber; for the rest she could make out no signs of life apart from a host of white sea-gulls.

Then Miss Ogilvy said a curious thing. She said: "On the south-west side of that place there was once a cave—a very large cave. I remember that it was some way from the sea."

"There du be a cave still," the fisherman told her, "But it's just above high-water level."

"A-ah," murmured Miss Ogilvy thoughtfully, as though to herself; then she looked embarrassed.

The little hotel proved both comfortable and clean, the hostess both pleasant and comely. Miss Ogilvy started unpacking her bag, changed her mind and went for a stroll round the island. The island was covered with turf and thistles and traversed by narrow green paths thick with daisies. It had four rock-bound coves of which the south-western was by far the most difficult of access. For just here the island descended abruptly as though it were hurtling down to the water; and just here the shale was most treacherous and the tide-swept rocks most aggressively pointed. Here it was that the seagulls, grown fearless of man by reason of his absurd limitations, built their nests on the ledges and reared countless young who multiplied, in their turn, every season. Yes, and here it was that Miss Ogilvy, greatly marveling, stood and stared across at a cave; much too near the crumbling edge for her safety, but by now completely indifferent to caution.

"I remember . . . I remember. . ." she kept repeating. Then: "That's all very well, but what do I remember?"

She was conscious of somehow remembering all wrong, of her memory being distorted and colored—perhaps by the endless things she had seen since her eyes had last rested upon that cave. This worried her sorely, far more than the fact that she should be remembering the cave at all, she who had never set foot on the island before that actual morning. Indeed, except for the sense of wrongness when she struggled to piece her memories together, she was steeped in a very profound contentment which surged over her spirit, wave upon wave.

"It's extremely odd," pondered Miss Ogilvy. Then she laughed, so pleased did she feel with its oddness.

5

That night after supper she talked to her hostess who was only too glad, it seemed, to be questioned. She owned the whole island and was proud of the fact, as she very well might be, decided her boarder. Some curious things had been found on the island, according to comely Mrs. Nanceskivel: bronze arrow-heads, pieces of ancient stone celts;[9] and once they had dug up a man's skull and thigh bone—this had happened while they were sinking a well. Would Miss Ogilvy care to have a look at the bones? They were kept in a cupboard in the scullery.

Miss Ogilvy nodded.

"Then I'll fetch him this moment," said Mrs. Nanceskivel, briskly.

In less than two minutes she was back with the box that contained those poor remnants of a man, and Miss Ogilvy, who had risen from her chair, was

[9]Prehistoric stone axes.

gazing down at those remnants. As she did so her mouth was sternly compressed, but her face and her neck flushed darkly.

Mrs. Nanceskivel was pointing to the skull: "Look miss, he was killed," she remarked rather proudly, "and they tell me that the axe that killed him was bronze. He's thousands and thousands of years old, they tell me. Our local doctor knows a lot about such things and he wants me to send these bones to an expert; they ought to belong to the Nation, he says. But I know what would happen, they'd come digging up my island, and I won't have people digging up my island, I've got enough worry with the rabbits as it is." But Miss Ogilvy could no longer hear the words for the pounding of the blood in her temples.

She as filled with a sudden, inexplicable fury against the innocent Mrs. Nanceskivel: "You . . . you. . ." she began, then checked herself, fearful of what she might say to the woman.

For her sense of outrage was overwhelming as she stared at those bones that were kept in the scullery; moreover, she knew how such men had been buried, which made the outrage seem all the more shameful. They had buried such men in deep, well-dug pits surmounted by four stout stones at their corners—four stout stones there had been and a covering stone. And all this Miss Ogilvy knew as by instinct, having no concrete knowledge on which to draw. But she knew it right down in the depths of her soul, and she hated Mrs. Nanceskivel.

And now she was swept by another emotion that was even more strange and more devastating: such a grief as she had not conceived could exist; a terrible unassuageable grief, without hope, without respite, without palliation, so that with something akin to despair she touched the long gash in the skull. Then her eyes, that had never wept since her childhood, filled slowly with large, hot, difficult tears. She must blink very hard, then close her eyelids, turn away from the lamp and say rather loudly:

"Thanks, Mrs. Nanceskivel. It's past eleven—I think I'll be going upstairs."

6

Miss Ogilvy closed the door of her bedroom, after which she stood quite still to consider: "Is it shell shock?" she muttered incredulously. "I wonder, can it be shell shock?"

She began to pace slowly about the room, smoking a Caporal. As usual her hands were deep in her pockets; she could feel small, familiar things in those pockets and she gripped them, glad of their presence. Then all of a sudden she was terribly tired, so tired that she flung herself down on the bed, unable to stand any longer.

She thought that she lay there struggling to reason, that her eyes were closed in the painful effort, and that as she closed them she continued to puff the inevitable cigarette. At least that was what she thought at one moment—the next, she was out in a sunset evening, and a large red sun was sinking slowly to the rim of a distant sea.

Miss Ogilvy knew that she was herself, that is to say she was conscious of her being, and yet she was not Miss Ogilvy at all, nor had she a memory of her. All that she now saw was very familiar, all that she now did was what she should do, and all that she now was seemed perfectly natural. Indeed, she did not think of these things; there seemed no reason for thinking about them.

She was walking with bare feet on turf that felt springy and was greatly enjoying the sensation; she had always enjoyed it, ever since as an infant she had learned to crawl on this turf. On either hand stretched rolling green uplands, while at her back she knew that there were forests; but in front, far away, lay the gleam of the seas towards which the big sun was sinking. The air was cool and intensely still, with never so much as a ripple or bird song. It was wonderfully pure—one might also say young—but Miss Ogilvy thought of it merely as air. Having always breathed it she took it for granted, as she took the soft turf and the uplands.

She pictured herself as immensely tall; she was feeling immensely tall at the moment. As a matter of fact she was five feet eight which, however, was quite a considerable height when compared to that of her fellow tribesmen. She was wearing a single garment of pelts which came to her knees and left her arms sleeveless. Her arms and her legs, which were closely tattooed with blue zig-zag lines, were extremely hairy. From a leathern thong twisted about her waist there hung a clumsily made stone weapon, a celt, which in spite of its clumsiness was strongly hafted and useful for killing.

Miss Ogilvy wanted to shout aloud from a glorious sense of physical well-being, but instead she picked up a heavy, round stone which she hurled with great force at some distant rocks.

"Good! Strong!" she exclaimed. "See how far it goes!"

"Yes, strong. There is no one so strong as you. You are surely the strongest man in our tribe," replied her little companion.

Miss Ogilvy glanced at this little companion and rejoiced that they two were all alone together. The girl at her side had a smooth brownish skin, oblique black eyes and short, sturdy limbs. Miss Ogilvy marveled because of her beauty. She also was wearing a single garment of pelts, new pelts, she had made it that morning. She had stitched at it diligently for hours with short lengths of gut and her best bone needle. A strand of black hair hung over her bosom, and this she was constantly stroking and fondling; then she lifted the strand and examined her hair.

"Pretty," she remarked with childish complacence.

"Pretty," echoed the young man at her side.

"For you," she told him, "all of me is for you and none other. For you this body has ripened."

He shook back his own coarse hair from his eyes; he had sad brown eyes like those of a monkey. For the rest he was lean and steel-strong of loin, broad of chest, and with features not too uncomely. His prominent cheekbones were set rather high, his nose was blunt, his jaw somewhat bestial; but his mouth though full-lipped, contradicted his jaw, being very gentle and sweet in expression. And now he smiled, showing big, square, white teeth.

"You . . . woman," he murmured contentedly, and the sound seemed to come from the depths of his being.

His speech was slow and lacking in words when it came to expressing a vital emotion, so one word must suffice and this he now spoke, and the word that he spoke had a number of meanings. It meant: "Little spring of exceedingly pure water." It meant: "Hut of peace for a man after battle." It meant: "Ripe red berry sweet to the taste." It meant: "Happy small home of future generations." All these things he must try to express by a word, and because of their loving she understood him.

They paused, and lifting her up he kissed her. Then he rubbed his large shaggy head on her shoulder; and when he released her she knelt at his feet.

"My master; blood of my body," she whispered. For with her it was different, love had taught her love's speech, so that she might turn her heart into sounds that her primitive tongue could utter.

After she had pressed her lips to his hands, and her cheeks to his hairy and powerful forearm, she stood up and they gazed at the setting sun, but with bowed heads, gazing under their lids because this was very sacred.

A couple of mating bears padded toward them from a thicket, and the female rose to her haunches. But the man drew his celt and menaced the beast, so that she dropped down noiselessly and fled, and her mate also fled, for here was the power that few dared to withstand by day or by night, on the uplands or in the forests. And now from across to the left where a river would presently lose itself in the marshes, came a rhythmical thudding, as a herd of red deer with wide nostrils and starting eyes thundered past, disturbed in their drinking by the bears.

After this the evening returned to its silence, and the spell of its silence descended on the lovers, so that each felt very much alone, yet withal more closely united to the other. But the man became restless under that spell, and he suddenly laughed; then grasping the woman he tossed her above his head and caught her. This he did many times for his own amusement and because he knew that his strength gave her joy. In this manner they played together for a while, he with his strength and she with her weakness. And they cried out, and made many guttural sounds which were meaningless save only to themselves. And the tunic of pelts slipped down from her breasts, and her two little breasts were pear-shaped.

Presently, he grew tired of their playing, and he pointed toward a cluster of huts and earthworks that lay to the eastward. The smoke from these huts rose in thick straight lines, bending neither to right nor to left in its rising, and the thought of sweet burning rushes and brushwood touched his consciousness, making him feel sentimental.

"Smoke," he said.

And she answered: "Blue smoke."

He nodded: "Yes, blue smoke—home."

Then she said: "I have ground much corn since the full moon. My stones are too smooth. You make me new stones."

"All you have need of, I make," he told her.

She stole closer to him, taking his hand: "My father is still a black cloud full of thunder. He thinks that you wish to be head of our tribe in his place, because he is now very old. He must not hear of these meetings of ours, if he did I think he would beat me!"

So he asked her: "Are you unhappy, small berry?"

But at this she smiled: "What is being unhappy? I do not know what that means any more."

"I do not either," he answered.

Then as though some invisible force had drawn him, his body swung around and he stared at the forests where they lay and darkened, fold upon fold; and his eyes dilated with wonder and terror, and he moved his head quickly from side to side as a wild thing will do that is held between bars and whose mind is pitifully bewildered.

"Water!" he cried hoarsely, "great water—look, look! Over there. This land is surrounded by water!"

"What water?" she questioned.

He answered: "The sea." And he covered his face with his hands.

"Not so," she consoled, "big forests, good hunting. Big forests in which you hunt boar and aurochs.[10] No sea over there but only the trees."

He took his trembling hands from his face: "You are right . . . only trees," he said dully.

But now his face had grown heavy and brooding and he started to speak of a thing that oppressed him: "The Roundheaded-ones, they are devils," he growled, while his bushy black brows met over his eyes, and when this happened it changed his expression which became a little sub-human.

"No matter," she protested, for she saw that he forgot her and she wished him to think and talk only of love. "No matter. My father laughs at your fears. Are we not friends with the Roundheaded-ones? We are friends, so why should we fear them?"

"Our forts, very old, very weak," he went on, "and the Roundheaded-ones have terrible weapons. Their weapons are not made of good stone like ours, but of some dark, devilish substance."

"What of that?" she said lightly. "They would fight on our side, so why need we trouble about their weapons?"

But he looked away, not appearing to hear her. "We must barter all, all for their celts and arrows and spears, and then we must learn their secret. They lust after our women, they lust after our lands. We must barter all, all for their sly brown celts."

[10]Extinct long-horned wild oxen.

"Me . . . bartered?" she queried, very sure of his answer, otherwise she had not dared to say this.

"The Roundheaded-ones may destroy my tribe and yet I will not part with you," he told her. Then he spoke very gravely: "But I think they desire to slay us, and me they will try to slay first because they well know how much I mistrust them—they have seen my eyes fixed many times on their camps."

She cried: "I will bite out the throats of these people if they so much as scratch your skin!"

And at this his mood changed and he roared with amusement: "You . . . woman!" he roared. "Little foolish white teeth. Your teeth were made for nibbling wild cherries, not for tearing the throats of the Roundheaded-ones!"

"Thoughts of war always made me afraid," she whimpered, still wishing him to talk about love.

He turned his sorrowful eyes upon her, the eyes that were sad even when he was merry, and although his mind was often obtuse, yet he clearly perceived how it was with her then. And his blood caught fire from the flame in her blood, so that he strained her against his body.

"You . . . mine. . ." he stammered.

"Love," she said, trembling, "this is love."

And he answered: "Love."

Then their faces grew melancholy for a moment, because dimly, very dimly in their dawning souls, they were conscious of a longing for something more vast than their earthly passion could compass.

Presently, he lifted her like a child and carried her quickly southward and westward till they came to a place where a gentle descent led down to a marshy valley. Far way, at the line where the marshes ended, they discerned the misty line of the sea; but the sea and the marshes were become as one substance, merging, blending, folding together; and since they were lovers they also would be one, even as the sea and the marshes.

And now they reached the mouth of a cave that was set in the quiet hillside. There was bright green verdure beside the cave, and a number of small, pink, thick-stemmed flowers that when they were crushed smelt of spices. And within the cave there was bracken newly gathered and heaped together for a bed; while beyond, from some rocks, came a low liquid sound as a spring dripped out through a crevice. Abruptly, he set the girl on her feet, and she knew that the days of her innocence were over. And she thought of the anxious virgin soil that was rent and sown to bring forth fruit in season, and she gave a quick little gasp of fear.

"No . . . no . . ." she gasped. For, divining his need, she was weak with longing to be possessed, yet the terror of love lay heavy upon her. "No . . . no . . ." she gasped.

But he caught her wrist and she felt the great strength of his rough, gnarled fingers, the great strength of the urge that leapt in his loins, and again she must give the quick gasp of fear, the while she clung close to him lest he should spare her.

The twilight was engulfed and possessed by darkness, which in turn was transfigured by the moonrise, which in turn was fulfilled and consumed by dawn. A mighty eagle soared up from his eyrie,[11] cleaving the air with his masterful wings, and beneath him from the rushes that harbored their nests, rose other great birds, crying loudly. Then the heavy-horned elks appeared on the uplands, bending their burdened heads to the sod; while beyond in the forests the fierce wild aurochs stamped as they bellowed their love songs.

But within the dim cave the lord of these creatures had put by his weapon and his instinct for slaying. And he lay there defenseless with tenderness, thinking no longer of death but of life as he murmured the word that had so many meanings. That meant: "Little spring of exceedingly pure water." That meant: "Hut of peace for a man after battle." That meant: "Ripe red berry sweet to the taste." That meant: "Happy small home of future generations."

7

They found Miss Ogilvy the next morning; the fisherman saw her and climbed to the ledge. She was sitting at the mouth of the cave. She was dead, with her hands thrust deep into her pockets.

H.D. (Hilda Doolittle) 1886–1961

H.D.'s writing has been called a "personal, spiritual quest for resurrection," an attempt to find "personal realism" in a nightmarish, modern universe. Her poems are complex, with interpretations challenged by her deliberately multilayered, associative meanings of words. H.D. is primarily known both for her short poetry that helped to formulate the literary movement called Imagism and for her association with another key figure of the movement, Ezra Pound. However, critics have also traced her development as a poet to her other work in the 1920s and 1930s: her translations of texts in Greek and her film criticism and prose. Her interest in spiritualism and her poetic experiments have influenced a number of contemporary poets, among them Denise Levertov, who commented that H.D's work presents "doors . . . tunnels through . . . before which man must shed his arrogance."

---

[11]Nest on a cliff or mountaintop.

SEA ROSE

Rose, harsh rose,
marred and with stint of petals,
meagre flower, thin,
sparse of leaf,

more precious   5
than a wet rose
single on a stem—
you are caught in the drift.

Stunted, with small leaf,
you are flung on the sand,   10
you are lifted
in the crisp sand
that drives in the wind.

Can the spice-rose
drip such acrid fragrance   15
hardened in a leaf?

OREAD[1]

Whirl up, sea—
whirl your pointed pines,
splash your great pines
on our rocks,
hurl your green over us,   5
cover us with your pools of fir.

HELEN[2]

All Greece hates
the still eyes in the white face,
the lustre as of olives
where she stands,
and the white hands.   5

---

[1] A nymph of the mountains and hills.
[2] Beautiful wife of Menelaus whose abduction by Paris brought on the Trojan War.

All Greece reviles
the wan face when she smiles,
hating it deeper still
when it grows wan and white,
remembering past enchantments   10
and past ills.

Greece sees unmoved,
God's daughter, born of love,
the beauty of cool feet
and slenderest knees,   15
could love indeed the maid,
only if she were laid,
white ash amid funereal cypresses.

Marianne Moore 1887–1972

Marianne Moore earned the so-called triple crown of prestigious awards for poetry for her 1951 *Collected Poems:* the National Book Award, the Pulitzer Prize, and the Bollingen Prize. This lifelong Brooklyn Dodgers fan (where the team played before moving to Los Angeles in 1957) was also a translator, essayist, short-story writer, dramatist, editor, and writer of children's books. One of the most important writers of the twentieth century, Moore was recognized as a "clever, scornful" writer with "avant-garde intelligence." She was graduated from Bryn Mawr College in 1909 and began to make her mark as a poet in 1915. In 1925, she became editor of the prestigious literary magazine *Dial* and associated with groups of writers that included William Carlos Williams and Wallace Stevens. Moore counted Emily Dickinson as one of her models, but also credited English poets, including religious poets such as George Herbert, with having influenced her work. Called a "radically inventive" modern, Moore's work is marked by precise observations and language, complex stanza patterns (she also said that she wrote in stanzas, not lines), and eloquent diction.

POETRY

I, too, dislike it.
    Reading it, however, with a perfect contempt for it, one dis-
                                                    covers in
    it, after all, a place for the genuine.

When I Buy Pictures

or what is closer to the truth,
when I look at that of which I may regard myself as the
                                    imaginary possessor,
I fix upon what would give me pleasure in my average moments:
the satire upon curiosity in which no more is discernible
than the intensity of the mood;   5
or quite the opposite—the old thing, the medieval decorated
                                    hat-box,
in which there are hounds with waists diminishing like the
                                    waist of the hour-glass,
and deer and birds and seated people;
it may be no more than a square of parquetry; the literal
                                    biography perhaps,
in letters standing well apart upon a parchment-like expanse;   10
an artichoke in six varieties of blue; the snipe-legged
                                    hieroglyphic in three parts;
the silver fence protecting Adam's grave, or Michael taking
                                    Adam by the wrist.
Too stern an intellectual emphasis upon this quality or that
                                    detracts from one's enjoyment.
It must not wish to disarm anything; nor may the approved
                                    triumph easily be honored—
that which is great because something else is small.   15
It comes to this: of whatever sort it is,
it must be "lit with piercing glances into the life of things";
it must acknowledge the spiritual forces which have made it.

Hometown Piece For Messrs. Alston And Reese

To the tune:
"Li'l baby, don't say a word: Mama goin' to buy you a
                                    mocking-bird.
Bird don't sing: Mama goin' to sell it and buy a brass ring."

"Millennium," yes; "pandemonium"!
Roy Campanella leaps high. Dodgerdom

crowned, had Johnny Podres on the mound.
Buzzie Bavasi and the Press gave ground;

the team slapped, mauled, and asked the Yankees' match,   5
"How did you feel when Sandy Amoros made the catch?"

"I said to myself"—pitcher for all innings—
"as I walked back to the mound I said, 'Everything's

getting better and better.'" (Zest: they've zest.
"'Hope springs eternal in the Brooklyn breast.'"   10

And would the Dodger Band in 8, row 1, relax
if they saw the collector of income tax?

Ready with a tune if that should occur:
"Why Not Take All of Me—All of Me, Sir?")

Another series. Round-tripper Duke at bat,   15
"Four hundred feet from home-plate"; more like that.

A neat bunt, please; a cloud-breaker, a drive
like Jim Gilliam's great big one. Hope's alive.

Homered, flied out, fouled? Our "stylish stout"
so nimble Campanella will have him out.   20

A-squat in double-headers four hundred times a day,
he says that in a measure the pleasure is the pay:

catcher to pitcher, a nice easy throw
almost as if he'd just told it to go.

Willie Mays should be a Dodger. He should—   25
a lad for Roger Craig and Clem Labine to elude;

but you have an omen, pennant-winning Peewee,
on which we are looking superstitiously.

Ralph Branca has Preacher Roe's number; recall?
and there's Don Bessent; he can really fire the ball.   30

As for Gil Hodges, in custody of first—
"He'll do it by himself." Now a specialist—versed

in an extension reach far into the box seats—
he lengthens up, leans and gloves the ball. He defeats

expectation by a whisker. The modest star,   35
irked by one misplay, is no hero by a hair;

in a strikeout slaughter when what could matter more,
he lines a homer to the signboard and has changed the score.

Then for his nineteenth season, a home run—
with four of six runs batted in—Carl Furillo's the big gun;   40

almost dehorned the foe—has fans dancing in delight.
Jake Pitler and his Playground "get a Night" —

Jake, that hearty man, made heartier by a harrier
who can bat as well as field—Don Demeter.

Shutting them out for nine innings—hitter too—   45
Carl Erskine leaves Cimoli nothing to do.

Take off the goat-horns, Dodgers, that egret
which two very fine base-stealers can offset.

You've got plenty: Jackie Robinson
and Campy and big Newk, and Dodgerdom again   50
watching everything you do. You won last year. Come on.

Katherine Mansfield 1888–1923

Born Kathleen Beauchamp, Katherine Mansfield seems to have led a divided life: From a conventional New Zealand, Victorian family, Mansfield called herself a "child" who liked to play with imaginary children, but who lived unconventionally. Devoted to her husband, she nonetheless retained a close relationship with the woman she called her "wife," Ida Baker. When she was not traveling, Mansfield became friends with important novelists in London, particularly Virginia Woolf, with whom she collaborated, and D. H. Lawrence. In 1911, after suffering a miscarriage and a stay in a German convent, Mansfield wrote sketches and stories, which were collected as *In a German Pension*. After that, she published a number of stories in literary magazines, and, in 1916, Mansfield embarked on a series of pieces based on her early years in New Zealand. Her most noted collections include *Bliss and Other Stories* (1918), *The Garden Party and Other Stories* (1922), and *The Dove's Nest and Other Stories* (1923). In 1918, Mansfield contracted tuberculosis, which led to her death at only thirty-five.

BLISS

Although Bertha Young was thirty she still had moments like this when she wanted to run instead of walk, to take dancing steps on and off the pavement, to bowl a hoop, to throw something up in the air and catch it again, or to stand still and laugh at—nothing—at nothing, simply.

What can you do if you are thirty and, turning the corner of your own street, you are overcome, suddenly, by a feeling of bliss—absolute bliss!—as though you'd suddenly swallowed a bright piece of that late afternoon sun and it burned in your bosom, sending out a little shower of sparks into every particle, into every finger and toe . . . ?

Oh, is there no way you can express it without being "drunk and disorderly"? How idiotic civilization is! Why be given a body if you have to keep it shut up in a case like a rare, rare fiddle?

"No, that about the fiddle is not quite what I mean," she thought, running up the steps and feeling in her bag for the key—she'd forgotten it, as usual—and rattling the letter-box. "It's not what I mean, because—Thank you, Mary"—she went into the hall. "Is nurse back?"

"Yes, M'm."

"And has the fruit come?"

"Yes, M'm. Everything's come."

"Bring the fruit up to the dining-room, will you? I'll arrange it before I go upstairs."

It was dusky in the dining-room and quite chilly. But all the same Bertha threw off her coat; she could not bear the tight clasp of it another moment, and the cold air fell on her arms.

But in her bosom there was still that bright glowing place—that shower of little sparks coming from it. It was almost unbearable. She hardly dared to breath for fear of fanning it higher, and yet she breathed deeply, deeply. She hardly dared to look into the cold mirror—but she did look, and it gave her back a woman, radiant, with smiling, trembling lips, with big, dark eyes and an air of listening, waiting for something . . . divine to happen . . . that she knew must happen . . . infallibly.

Mary brought in the fruit on a tray and with it a glass bowl, and a blue dish, very lovely, with a strange sheen on it as though it had been dipped in milk.

"Shall I turn on the light, M'm?"

"No, thank you. I can see quite well."

There were tangerines and apples stained with strawberry pink. Some yellow pears, smooth as silk, some white grapes covered with a silver bloom and a big cluster of purple ones. These last she had bought to tone in with the new living-room carpet. Yes, that did sound rather far-fetched and absurd, but it was really why she had bought them. She had thought in the shop: "I must have some purple ones to bring the carpet up to the table." And it had seemed quite sense at the time.

When she had finished with them and had made two pyramids of these bright round shapes, she stood away from the table to get the effect—and it really was most curious. For the dark table seemed to melt into the dusky light and the glass dish and the blue bowl to float in the air. This, of course in her present mood, was so incredibly beautiful. . . . She began to laugh.

"No, no. I'm getting hysterical." And she seized her bag and coat and ran upstairs to the nursery.

* * *

Nurse sat at a low table giving Little B her supper after her bath. The baby had on a white flannel gown and a blue wollen jacket, and her dark, fine hair was brushed up into a funny little peak. She looked up when she saw her mother and began to jump.

"Now, my lovey, eat it up like a good girl," said Nurse, setting her lips in a way that Bertha knew, and that meant she had come into the nursery at another wrong moment.

"Has she been good, Nanny?"

"She's been a little sweet all the afternoon," whispered Nanny. "We went to the park and I sat down on a chair and took her out of the pram and a big dog came along and put its head on my knee and she clutched its ear, tugged it. Oh, you should have seen her."

Bertha wanted to ask if it wasn't rather dangerous to let her clutch at a strange dog's ear. But she did not dare to. She stood watching them, her hands by her side, like the poor little girl in front of the rich little girl with the doll.

The baby looked up at her again, stared, and then smiled so charmingly that Bertha couldn't help crying:

"Oh, Nanny, do let me finish giving her her supper while you put the bath things away."

"Well, M'm, she oughtn't to be changed hands while she's eating," said Nanny, still whispering, "It unsettles her; it's very likely to upset her."

How absurd it was. Why have a baby if it has to be kept—not in a case like a rare, rare fiddle—but in another woman's arms?

"Oh, I must!" said she.

Very offended, Nanny handed her over.

"Now, don't excite her after her supper. You know you do, M'm. And I have such a time with her after!"

Thank heaven! Nanny went out of the room with the bath towels.

"Now I've got you to myself, my little precious," said Bertha, as the baby leaned against her.

She ate delightfully, holding up her lips for the spoon and then waving her hands. Sometimes she wouldn't let the spoon go; and sometimes, just as Bertha had filled it, she waved it away to the four winds.

When the soup was finished Bertha turned round to the fire.

"You're nice—you're very nice!" said she, kissing her warm baby. "I'm fond of you. I like you."

And, indeed, she loved Little B so much—her neck as she bent forward, her exquisite toes as they shone transparent in the firelight—that all her feeling of bliss came back again, and again she didn't know how to express it—what to do with it.

"You're wanted on the telephone," said Nanny, coming back in triumph and seizing *her* Little B.

* * *

Down she flew. It was Harry.

"Oh, is that you, Ber? Look here. I'll be late. I'll take a taxi and come along as quickly as I can, but get dinner put back ten minutes—will you? All right?"

"Yes, perfectly. Oh, Harry!"

"Yes?"

What had she to say? She'd nothing to say. She only wanted to get in touch with him for a moment. She couldn't absurdly cry: "Hasn't it been a divine day!"

"What is it?" rapped out the little voice.

"Nothing. *Entendu*,"[1] said Bertha, and hung up the receiver, thinking how more than idiotic civilization was.

They had people coming to dinner. The Norman Knights—a very sound couple—he was about to start a theatre, and she was awfully keen on interior decoration, a young man, Eddie Warren, who had just published a little book of poems and whom everybody was asking to dine, and a "find" of Bertha's called Pearl Fulton. What Miss Fulton did, Bertha didn't know. They had met at the club and Bertha had fallen in love with her, as she always did fall in love with beautiful women who had something strange about them.

The provoking thing was that, though they had been about together and met a number of times and really talked, Bertha couldn't yet make her out. Up to a certain point Miss Fulton was rarely, wonderfully frank, but the certain point was there, and beyond that she would not go.

Was there anything beyond it? Harry said "No." Voted her dullish, and "cold like all blond women, with a touch, perhaps, of anæmia of the brain." But Bertha wouldn't agree with him; not yet, at any rate.

"No, the way she has of sitting with her head a little on one side, and smiling, has something behind it, Harry, and I must find out what that something is."

"Most likely it's a good stomach," answered Harry.

He made a point of catching Bertha's heels with replies of that kind . . . "liver frozen, my dear girl," or "pure flatulence," or "kidney disease," . . . and so on. For some strange reason Bertha liked this, and almost admired it in him very much.

She went into the drawing-room and lighted the fire; then, picking up the cushions, one by one, that Mary had disposed so carefully, she threw them back on to the chairs and the couches. That made all the difference; the room came alive at once. As she was about to throw the last one she surprised herself by suddenly hugging it to her, passionately, passionately. But it did not put out the fire in her bosom. Oh, on the contrary!

The windows of the drawing-room opened on to a balcony overlooking the garden. At the far end, against the wall, there was a tall, slender pear tree in fullest, richest bloom; it stood perfect, as though becalmed against the jade-green sky. Bertha couldn't help feeling, even from this distance, that it

[1] Understood.

had not a single bud or a faded petal. Down below, in the garden beds, the red and yellow tulips, heavy with flowers, seemed to lean upon the dusk. A grey cat, dragging its belly, crept across the lawn, and a black one, its shadow, trailed after. The sight of them, so intent and so quick, gave Bertha a curious shiver.

"What creepy things cats are!" she stammered, and she turned away from the window and began walking up and down. . . .

How strong the jonquils smelled in the warm room. Too strong? Oh, no. And yet, as though overcome, she flung down on a couch and pressed her hands to her eyes.

"I'm too happy—too happy!" she murmured.

And she seemed to see on her eyelids the lovely pear tree with its wide open blossoms as a symbol of her own life.

Really—really—she had everything. She was young. Harry and she were as much in love as ever, and they got on together splendidly and were really good pals. She had an adorable baby. They didn't have to worry about money. They had this absolutely satisfactory house and garden. And friends—modern, thrilling friends, writers and painters and poets or people keen on social questions—just the kind of friends they wanted. And then there were books, and there was music, and she had found a wonderful little dressmaker, and they were going abroad in the summer, and their new cook made the most superb omelettes. . . .

"I'm absurd. Absurd!" She sat up; but she felt quite dizzy, quite drunk. It must have been the spring.

Yes, it was the spring. Now she was so tired she could not drag herself upstairs to dress.

A white dress, a string of jade beads, green shoes and stockings. It wasn't intentional. She had thought of this scheme hours before she stood at the drawing-room window.

Her petals rustled softly into the hall, and she kissed Mrs. Norman Knight, who was taking off the most amusing orange coat with a procession of black monkeys round the hem and up the fronts.

". . . Why! Why! Why is the middle-class so stodgy—so utterly without a sense of humour! My dear, it's only by a fluke that I am here at all—Norman being the protective fluke. For my darling monkeys so upset the train that it rose to a man and simply ate me with its eyes. Didn't laugh—wasn't amused—that I should have loved. No, just stared—and bored me through and through."

"But the cream of it was," said Norman, pressing a large tortoise-shell-rimmed monocle into his eye, "you don't mind me telling this, Face, do you?" (In their home and among their friends they called each other Face and Mug.) "The cream of it was when she, being full fed, turned to the woman beside her and said: 'Haven't you ever seen a monkey before?'"

"Oh, yes!" Mrs. Norman Knight joined in the laughter. "Wasn't that too absolutely creamy?"

And a funnier thing still was that now her coat was off she did look like a very intelligent monkey—who had even made that yellow silk dress out of scraped banana skins. And her amber ear-rings; they were like little dangling nuts.

"This is a sad, sad fall!" said Mug, pausing in front of Little B's perambulator. "When the perambulator comes into the hall—" and he waved the rest of the quotation away.

The bell rang. It was lean, pale Eddie Warren (as usual) in a state of acute distress.

"It *is* the right house, *isn't* it?" he pleaded.

"Oh, I think so—I hope so," said Bertha brightly.

"I have had such a *dreadful* experience with a taxi-man; he was *most* sinister. I couldn't get him to *stop*. The *more* I knocked and called the *faster* he went. And *in* the moonlight this *bizarre* figure with the *flattened* head *crouching* over the *lit-tle* wheel. . . ."

He shuddered, taking off an immense white silk scarf. Bertha noticed that his socks were white, too—most charming.

"But how dreadful!" she cried.

"Yes, it really was," said Eddie, following her into the drawing-room. "I saw myself *driving* through Eternity in a *timeless* taxi."

He knew the Norman Knights. In fact, he was going to write a play for N. K. when the theatre scheme came off.

"Well, Warren, how's the play?" said Norman Knight, dropping his monocle and giving his eye a moment in which to rise to the surface before it was screwed down again.

And Mrs. Norman Knight: "Oh, Mr. Warren, what happy socks!"

"I *am* so glad you like them," said he, staring at his feet. "They seem to have got so *much* whiter since the moon rose." And he turned his lean sorrowful young face to Bertha. "There *is* a moon, you know."

She wanted to cry: "I am sure there is—often—often!"

He really was a most attractive person. But so was Face, crouched before the fire in her banana skins, and so was Mug, smoking a cigarette and saying as he flicked the ash: "Why doth the bridegroom tarry?"

"There he is, now."

Bang went the front door open and shut. Harry shouted: "Hullo, you people. Down in five minutes." And they heard him swarm up the stairs. Bertha couldn't help smiling; she knew how he loved doing things at high pressure. What, after all, did an extra five minutes matter? But he would pretend to himself that they mattered beyond measure. And then he would make a great point of coming into the drawing-room, extravagantly cool and collected.

Harry had such a zest for life. Oh, how she appreciated it in him. And his passion for fighting—for seeking in everything that came up against him another test of his power and of his courage—that, too, she understood. Even when it made him just occasionally, to other people, who didn't know him well, a little ridiculous perhaps. . . . For there were moments when he rushed into battle where no battle was. . . . She talked and laughed and positively forgot until he had come in (just as she had imagined) that Pearl Fulton had not turned up.

"I wonder if Miss Fulton has forgotten?"

"I expect so," said Harry. "Is she on the 'phone?"

"Ah! There's a taxi, now." And Bertha smiled with that little air of proprietorship that she always assumed while her women finds were new and mysterious. "She lives in taxis."

"She'll run to fat if she does," said Harry coolly, ringing the bell for dinner. "Frightful danger for blond women."

"Harry—don't," warned Bertha, laughing up at him.

Came another tiny moment, while they waited, laughing and talking, just a trifle too much at their ease, a trifle too unaware. And then Miss Fulton, all in silver, with a silver fillet binding her pale blond hair, came in smiling, her head a little on one side.

"Am I late?"

"No, not at all," said Bertha. "Come along." And she took her arm and they moved into the dining-room.

What was there in the touch of that cool arm that could fan—fan—start blazing—blazing—the fire of bliss that Bertha did not know what to do with?

Miss Fulton did not look at her; but then she seldom did look at people directly. Her heavy eyelids lay upon her eyes and the strange half smile came and went upon her lips as though she lived by listening rather than seeing. But Bertha knew, suddenly, as if the longest, most intimate look had passed between them—as if they had said to each other: "You, too?"—that Pearl Fulton, stirring the beautiful red soup in the grey plate, was feeling just what she was feeling.

And the others? Face and Mug, Eddie and Harry, their spoons rising and falling—dabbing their lips with their napkins, crumbling bread, fiddling with the forks and glasses and talking.

"I met her at the Alpha show—the weirdest little person. She'd not only cut off her hair, but she seemed to have taken a dreadfully good snip off her legs and arms and her neck and her poor little nose as well."

"Isn't she very *liée*[2] with Michael Oat?"

"The man who wrote *Love in False Teeth*?"

"He wants to write a play for me. One act. One man. Decides to commit suicide. Gives all the reasons why he should and why he shouldn't. And just as he has made up his mind either to do it or not to do it—curtain. Not half a bad idea."

"What's he going to call it—'Stomach Trouble'?"

"I *think* I've come across the *same* idea in a lit-tle French review, *quite* unknown in England."

No, they didn't share it. They were dears—dears—and she loved having them there, at her table, and giving them delicious food and wine. In fact, she longed to tell them how delightful they were, and what a decorative group they

[2] Involved.

made, how they seemed to set one another off and how they reminded her of a play by Tchekof![3]

Harry was enjoying his dinner. It was part of his—well, not his nature, exactly, and certainly not his pose—his—something or other—to talk about food and to glory in his "shameless passion for the white flesh of the lobster" and "the green of pistachio ices—green and cold like the eyelids of Egyptian dancers."

When he looked up at her and said: "Bertha, this is a very admirable soufflé!" she almost could have wept with child-like pleasure.

Oh, why did she feel so tender towards the whole world tonight? Everything was good—was right. All that happened seemed to fill again her brimming cup of bliss.

And still, in the back of her mind, there was the pear tree. It would be silver now, in the light of poor dear Eddie's moon, silver as Miss Fulton, who sat there turning a tangerine in her slender fingers that were so pale a light seemed to come from them.

What she simply couldn't make out—what was miraculous—was how she should have guessed Miss Fulton's mood so exactly and so instantly. For she never doubted for a moment that she was right, and yet what had she to go on? Less than nothing.

"I believe this does happen very, very rarely between women. Never between men," thought Bertha. "But while I am making the coffee in the drawing-room perhaps she will 'give a sign.'"

What she meant by that she did not know, and what would happen after that she could not imagine.

While she thought like this she saw herself talking and laughing. She had to talk because of her desire to laugh.

"I must laugh or die."

But when she noticed Face's funny little habit of tucking something down the front of her bodice—as if she kept a tiny, secret hoard of nuts there, too—Bertha had to dig her nails into her hands—so as not to laugh too much.

It was over at last. And: "Come and see my new coffee machine," said Bertha.

"We only have a new coffee machine once a fortnight," said Harry. Face took her arm this time; Miss Fulton bent her head and followed after.

The fire had died down in the drawing-room to a red, flickering "nest of baby phœnixes," said Face.

"Don't turn up the light for a moment. It is so lovely." And down she crouched by the fire again. She was always cold . . . "without her little red flannel jacket, of course," thought Bertha.

At that moment, Miss Fulton "gave the sign."

"Have you a garden?" said the cool, sleepy voice.

[3] Variant spelling for Chekhov, Russian playwright and short-story writer (1860–1904).

This was so exquisite on her part that all Bertha could do was to obey. She crossed the room, pulled the curtains apart, and opened those long windows.

"There!" she breathed.

And the two women stood side by side looking at the slender, flowering tree. Although it was so still it seemed, like the flame of a candle, to stretch up, to point, to quiver in the bright air, to grow taller and taller as they gazed— almost to touch the rim of the round, silver moon.

How long did they stand there? Both, as it were, caught in that circle of unearthly light, understanding each other perfectly, creatures of another world, and wondering what they were to do in this one with all this blissful treasure that burned in their bosoms and dropped, in silver flowers, from their hair and hands?

For ever—for a moment? And did Miss Fulton murmur: "Yes. Just *that*." Or did Bertha dream it?

Then the light was snapped on and Face made the coffee and Harry said: "My dear Mrs. Knight, don't ask me about my baby. I never see her. I shan't feel the slightest interest in her until she has a lover," and Mug took his eye out of the conservatory for a moment and then put it under glass again and Eddie Warren drank his coffee and set down the cup with a face of anguish as though he had drunk and seen the spider.

"What I want to do is to give the young men a show. I believe London is simply teeming with first-chop, unwritten plays. What I want to say to 'em is: 'Here's the theatre. Fire ahead.'"

"You know, my dear, I am going to decorate a room for the Jacob Nathans. Oh, I am so tempted to do a fried-fish scheme, with the backs of the chairs shaped like frying pans and lovely chip potatoes embroidered all over the curtains."

"The trouble with our young writing men is that they are still too romantic. You can't put out to sea without being seasick and wanting a basin. Well, why won't they have the courage of those basins?"

"A *dreadful* poem about a *girl* who was *violated* by a beggar *without* a nose in a lit-tle wood...."

Miss Fulton sank into the lowest, deepest chair and Harry handed round the cigarettes.

From the way he stood in front of her shaking the silver box and saying abruptly: "Egyptian? Turkish? Virginian? They're all mixed up," Bertha realized that she not only bored him; he really disliked her. And she decided from the way Miss Fulton said: "No, thank you, I won't smoke," that she felt it, too, and was hurt.

"Oh, Harry, don't dislike her. You are quite wrong about her. She's wonderful, wonderful. And, besides, how can you feel so differently about someone who means so much to me. I shall try to tell you when we are in bed to-night what has been happening. What she and I have shared."

* * *

At those last words something strange and almost terrifying darted into Bertha's mind. And this something blind and smiling whispered to her: "Soon these people will go. The house will be quiet — quiet. The lights will be out. And you and he will be alone together in the dark room — the warm bed. . . ."

She jumped up from her chair and ran over to the piano.

"What a pity someone does not play!" she cried. "What a pity somebody does not play."

For the first time in her life Bertha Young desired her husband.

Oh, she'd loved him — she'd been in love with him, of course, in every other way, but just not in that way. And, equally, of course, she'd understood that he was different. They'd discussed it so often. It had worried her dreadfully at first to find that she was so cold, but after a time it had not seemed to matter. They were so frank with each other — such good pals. That was the best of being modern.

But now — ardently! ardently! The word ached in her ardent body! Was this what that feeling of bliss had been leading up to? But then, then —

"My dear," said Mrs. Norman Knight, "you know our shame. We are the victims of time and train. We live in Hampstead.[4] It's been so nice."

"I'll come with you into the hall," said Bertha. "I loved having you. But you must not miss the last train. That's so awful, isn't it?"

"Have a whisky, Knight, before you go?" called Harry.

"No, thanks, old chap."

Bertha squeezed his hand for that as she took it.

"Good night, good-bye," she cried from the top step, feeling that this self of hers was taking leave of them for ever.

When she got back into the drawing-room the others were on the move.

". . . Then you can come part of the way in my taxi."

"I shall be *so* thankful *not* to have to face *another* drive *alone* after my *dreadful* experience."

"You can get a taxi at the rank[5] just at the end of the street. You won't have to walk more than a few yards."

"That's comfort. I'll go and put on my coat."

Miss Fulton moved towards the hall and Bertha was following when Harry almost pushed past.

"Let me help you."

Bertha knew that he was repenting his rudeness — she let him go. What a boy he was in some ways — so impulsive — so — simple.

And Eddie and she were left by the fire.

"I *wonder* if you have seen Bilks' *new* poem called *Table d'Hôte*," said Eddie softly. "It's *so* wonderful. In the last Anthology. Have you got a copy? I'd *so* like

---

[4] A suburb of London.

[5] Stand.

to *show* it to you. It begins with an *incredibly* beautiful line: 'Why Must it Always be Tomato Soup?'"

"Yes," said Bertha. And she moved noiselessly to a table opposite the drawing-room door and Eddie glided noiselessly after her. She picked up the little book and gave it to him; they had not made a sound.

While he looked it up she turned her head towards the hall. And she saw . . . Harry with Miss Fulton's coat in his arms and Miss Fulton with her back turned to him and her head bent. He tossed the coat away, put his hands on her shoulders and turned her violently to him. His lips said: "I adore you," and Miss Fulton laid her moonbeam fingers on his cheeks and smiled her sleepy smile. Harry's nostrils quivered; his lips curled back in a hideous grin while he whispered. "Tomorrow," and with her eyelids Miss Fulton said: "Yes."

"Here it is," said Eddie. "'Why Must it Always be Tomato Soup?' It's so *deeply* true, don't you feel? Tomato soup is so *dreadfully* eternal."

"If you prefer," said Harry's voice, very loud, from the hall. "I can phone you a cab to come to the door."

"Oh, no. It's not necessary," said Miss Fulton, and she came up to Bertha and gave her the slender fingers to hold.

"Good-bye. Thank you so much."

"Good-bye," said Bertha.

Miss Fulton held her hand a moment longer.

"Your lovely pear tree!" she murmured.

And then she was gone, with Eddie following, like the black cat following the grey cat.

"I'll shut up shop," said Harry, extravagantly cool and collected.

"Your lovely pear tree—pear tree—pear tree!"

Bertha simply ran over to the long windows.

"Oh, what is going to happen now?" she cried.

But the pear tree was as lovely as ever and as full of flower and as still.

THE GARDEN-PARTY

And after all the weather was ideal. They could not have had a more perfect day for a garden-party if they had ordered it. Windless, warm, the sky without a cloud. Only the blue was veiled with a haze of light gold, as it is sometimes in early summer. The gardener had been up since dawn, mowing the lawns and sweeping them, until the grass and the dark flat rosettes where the daisy plants had been seemed to shine. As for the roses, you could not help feeling they understood that roses are the only flowers that impress people at garden-parties; the only flowers that everybody is certain of knowing. Hundreds, yes, literally hundreds, had come out in a single night; the green bushes bowed down as though they had been visited by archangels.

Breakfast was not yet over before the men came to put up the marquee.[1]

"Where do you want the marquee put, mother?"

"My dear child, it's no use asking me. I'm determined to leave everything to you children this year. Forget I am your mother. Treat me as an honoured guest."

But Meg could not possibly go and supervise the men. She had washed her hair before breakfast, and she sat drinking her coffee in a green turban, with a dark wet curl stamped on each cheek. Jose, the butterfly, always came down in a silk petticoat and a kimono jacket.

"You'll have to go, Laura; you're the artistic one."

Away Laura flew, still holding her piece of bread-and-butter. It's so delicious to have an excuse for eating out of doors, and besides, she loved having to arrange things; she always felt she could do it so much better than anybody else.

Four men in their shirt-sleeves stood grouped together on the garden path. They carried staves covered with rolls of canvas, and they had big tool-bags slung on their backs. They looked impressive. Laura wished now that she had not got the bread-and-butter, but there was nowhere to put it, and she couldn't possibly throw it away. She blushed and tried to look severe and even a little bit short-sighted as she came up to them.

"Good morning," she said, copying her mother's voice. But that sounded so fearfully affected that she was ashamed, and stammered like a little girl, "Oh — er — have you come — is it about the marquee?"

"That's right, miss," said the tallest of the men, a lanky, freckled fellow, and he shifted his tool-bag, knocked back his straw hat and smiled down at her. "That's about it."

His smile was so easy, so friendly that Laura recovered. What nice eyes he had, small, but such a dark blue! And now she looked at the others, they were smiling too. "Cheer up, we won't bite," their smile seemed to say. How very nice workmen were! And what a beautiful morning! She musn't mention the morning; she must be businesslike. The marquee.

"Well, what about the lily-lawn? Would that do?"

And she pointed to the lily-lawn with the hand that didn't hold the bread-and-butter. They turned, they stared in the direction. A little fat chap thrust out his under-lip, and the tall fellow frowned.

"I don't fancy it," said he. "Not conspicuous enough. You see, with a thing like a marquee," and he turned to Laura in his easy way, "you want to put it somewhere where it'll give you a bang slap in the eye, if you follow me."

Laura's upbringing made her wonder for a moment whether it was quite respectful of a workman to talk to her of bangs slap in the eye. But she didn't quite follow him.

"A corner of the tennis-court," she suggested. "But the band's going to be in one corner."

---

[1] Canvas shelter set up for outdoor parties.

"H'm, going to have a band, are you?" said another of the workmen. He was pale. He had a haggard look as his dark eyes scanned the tennis-court. What was he thinking?

"Only a very small band," said Laura gently. Perhaps he wouldn't mind so much if the band was quite small. But the tall fellow interrupted.

"Look here, miss, that's the place. Against those trees. Over there. That'll do fine."

Against the karakas. Then the karaka trees would be hidden. And they were so lovely, with their broad, gleaming leaves, and their clusters of yellow fruit. They were like trees you imagined growing on a desert island, proud, solitary, lifting their leaves and fruits to the sun in a kind of silent splendour. Must they be hidden by a marquee?

They must. Already the men had shouldered their staves and were making for the place. Only the tall fellow was left. He bent down, pinched a sprig of lavender, put his thumb and forefinger to his nose and snuffed up the smell. When Laura saw that gesture she forgot all about the karakas in her wonder at him caring for things like that—caring for the smell of lavender. How many men that she knew would have done such a thing? Oh, how extraordinarily nice workmen were, she thought. Why couldn't she have workmen for friends rather than the silly boys she danced with and who came to Sunday night supper? She would get on much better with men like these.

It's all the fault, she decided, as the tall fellow drew something on the back of an envelope, something that was to be looped up or left to hang, of these absurd class distinctions. Well, for her part, she didn't feel them. Not a bit, not an atom. . . . And now there came the chock-chock of wooden hammers. Some one whistled, some one sang out, "Are you right there, matey?" "Matey!" The friendliness of it, the—the—Just to prove how happy she was, just to show the tall fellow how at home she felt, and how she despised stupid conventions, Laura took a big bite of her bread-and-butter as she stared at the little drawing. She felt just like a work-girl.

"Laura, Laura, where are you? Telephone, Laura!" a voice cried from the house.

"Coming!" Away she skimmed, over the lawn, up the path, up the steps, across the verandah, and into the porch. In the hall her father and Laurie were brushing their hats ready to go to the office.

"I say, Laura," said Laurie very fast, "you might just give a squiz at my coat before this afternoon. See if it wants pressing."

"I will," said she. Suddenly she couldn't stop herself. She ran at Laurie and gave him a small, quick squeeze. "Oh, I do love parties, don't you?" gasped Laura.

"Rather," said Laurie's warm, boyish voice, and he squeezed his sister too, and gave her a gentle push. "Dash off to the telephone, old girl."

The telephone. "Yes, yes; oh yes. Kitty? Good morning, dear. Come to lunch? Do, dear. Delighted of course. It will only be a very scratch meal—just the sandwich crusts and broken meringue-shells and what's left over. Yes, isn't it a perfect morning? Your white? Oh, I certainly should. One moment—hold the line. Mother's calling." And Laura sat back. "What, mother? Can't hear."

Mrs. Sheridan's voice floated down the stairs. "Tell her to wear that sweet hat she had on last Sunday."

"Mother says you're to wear that *sweet* hat you had on last Sunday. Good. One o'clock. Bye-bye."

Laura put back the receiver, flung her arms over her head, took a deep breath, stretched and let them fall. "Huh," she sighed, and the moment after the sigh she sat up quickly. She was still listening. All the doors in the house seemed to open. The house was alive with soft, quick steps and running voices. The green baize door that led to the kitchen regions swung open and shut with a muffled thud. And now there came a long, chuckling absurd sound. It was the heavy piano being moved on its stiff castors. But the air! If you stopped to notice, was the air always like this? Little faint winds were playing chase, in at the tops of the windows, out at the doors. And there were two tiny spots of sun, one on the inkpot, one on a silver photograph frame, playing too. Darling little spots. Especially the one on the inkpot lid. It was quite warm. A warm little silver star. She could have kissed it.

The front door bell pealed, and there sounded the rustle of Sadie's print skirt on the stairs. A man's voice murmured; Sadie answered, careless, "I'm sure I don't know. Wait. I'll ask Mrs. Sheridan."

"What is it, Sadie?" Laura came into the hall.

"It's the florist, Miss Laura."

It was, indeed. There, just inside the door, stood a wide, shallow tray full of pots of pink lilies. No other kind. Nothing but lilies—canna lilies, big pink flowers, wide open, radiant, almost frighteningly alive on bright crimson stems.

"O-oh, Sadie!" said Laura, and the sound was like a little moan. She crouched down as if to warm herself at that blaze of lilies; she felt they were in her fingers, on her lips, growing in her breast.

"It's some mistake," she said faintly. "Nobody ever ordered so many. Sadie, go and find mother."

But at that moment Mrs. Sheridan joined them.

"It's quite right," she said calmly. "Yes, I ordered them. Aren't they lovely?" She pressed Laura's arm. "I was passing the shop yesterday, and I saw them in the window. And I suddenly thought for once in my life I shall have enough canna lilies. The garden-party will be a good excuse."

"But I thought you said you didn't mean to interfere," said Laura. Sadie had gone. The florist's man was still outside at his van. She put her arm round her mother's neck and gently, very gently, she bit her mother's ear.

"My darling child, you wouldn't like a logical mother, would you? Don't do that. Here's the man."

He carried more lilies still, another whole tray.

"Bank them up, just inside the door, on both sides of the porch, please," said Mrs. Sheridan. "Don't you agree, Laura?"

"Oh, I *do* mother."

In the drawing-room Meg, Jose and good little Hans had at last succeeded in moving the piano.

"Now, if we put this chesterfield against the wall and move everything out of the room except the chairs, don't you think?"

"Quite."

"Hans, move these tables into the smoking-room, and bring a sweeper to take these marks off the carpet and—one moment, Hans—" Jose loved giving orders to the servants, and they loved obeying her. She always made them feel they were taking part in some drama. "Tell mother and Miss Laura to come here at once."

"Very good, Miss Jose."

She turned to Meg. "I want to hear what the piano sounds like, just in case I'm asked to sing this afternoon. Let's try over 'This life is Weary.'"

Pom! Ta-ta-ta *Tee*-ta! The piano burst out so passionately that Jose's face changed. She clasped her hands. She looked mournfully and enigmatically at her mother and Laura as they came in

> This Life is *Wee*-ary,
> A Tear—a Sigh.
> A Love that *Chan*-ges,
> This life is *Wee*-ary,
> A Tear—a Sigh.
> A Love that *Chan*-ges,
> And then . . . Good-bye!

But at the word "Good-bye," and although the piano sounded more desperate than ever, her face broke into a brilliant, dreadfully unsympathetic smile.

"Aren't I in good voice, mummy?" she beamed.

> This Life is *Wee*-ary,
> Hope comes to Die.
> A Dream—a *Wa*-kening.

But now Sadie interrupted them. "What is it, Sadie?"

"If you please, m'm, cook says have you got the flags[2] for the sandwiches?"

"The flags for the sandwiches, Sadie?" echoed Mrs. Sheridan dreamily. And the children knew by her face that she hadn't got them. "Let me see." And she said to Sadie firmly, "Tell cook I'll let her have them in ten minutes."

---

[2]Toothpick and paper decorations.

Sadie went.

"Now, Laura," said her mother quickly. "Come with me into the smoking-room. I've got the names somewhere on the back of an envelope. You'll have to write them out for me. Meg, go upstairs this minute and take that wet thing off your head. Jose, run and finish dressing this instant. Do you hear me, children, or shall I have to tell your father when he comes home to-night? And—and, Jose, pacify cook if you do go into the kitchen, will you? I'm terrified of her this morning."

The envelope was found at last behind the dining-room clock, though how it had got there Mrs. Sheridan could not imagine.

"One of you children must have stolen it out of my bag, because I remember vividly—cream cheese and lemon-curd. Have you done that?"

"Yes."

"Egg and—" Mrs. Sheridan held the envelope away from her. "It looks like mice. It can't be mice, can it?"

"Olive, pet," said Laura, looking over her shoulder.

"Yes, of course, olive. What a horrible combination it sounds. Egg and olive."

They were finished at last, and Laura took them off to the kitchen. She found Jose there pacifying the cook, who did not look at all terrifying.

"I have never seen such exquisite sandwiches," said Jose's rapturous voice. "How many kinds did you say there were, cook? Fifteen?"

"Fifteen, Miss Jose."

"Well, cook, I congratulate you."

Cook swept up crusts with the long sandwich knife, and smiled broadly.

"Godber's has come," announced Sadie, issuing out of the pantry. She had seen the man pass the window.

That meant the cream puffs had come. Godber's were famous for their cream puffs. Nobody ever thought of making them at home.

"Bring them in and put them on the table, my girl," ordered cook.

Sadie brought them in and went back to the door. Of course Laura and Jose were far too grown-up to really care about such things. All the same, they couldn't help agreeing that the puffs looked very attractive. Very. Cook began arranging them, shaking off the extra icing sugar.

"Don't they carry one back to all one's parties?" said Laura.

"I suppose they do," said practical Jose, who never liked to be carried back. "They look beautifully light and feathery, I must say."

"Have one each, my dears," said cook in her comfortable voice. "Yer ma won't know."

Oh, impossible. Fancy cream puffs so soon after breakfast. The very idea made one shudder. All the same, two minutes later Jose and Laura were licking their fingers with that absorbed inward look that only comes from whipped cream.

"Let's go into the garden, out by the back way," suggested Laura. "I want to see how the men are getting on with the marquee. They're such awfully nice men."

But the back door was blocked by cook, Sadie, Godber's man and Hans.

Something had happened.

"Tuk-tuk-tuk," clucked cook like an agitated hen. Sadie had her hand clapped to her cheek as though she had toothache. Han's face was screwed up in the effort to understand. Only Godber's man seemed to be enjoying himself; it was his story.

"What's the matter? What's happened?"

"There's been a horrible accident," said cook. "A man killed."

"A man killed! Where? How? When?"

But Godber's man wasn't going to have his story snatched from under his very nose.

"Know those little cottages just below here, miss?" Know them? Of course, she knew them. "Well, there's a young chap living there, name of Scott, a carter. His horse shied at a traction-engine, corner of Hawke Street this morning, and he was thrown out on the back of his head. Killed."

"Dead!" Laura stared at Godber's man.

"Dead when they picked him up," said Godber's man with relish. They were taking the body home as I come up here." And he said to the cook, "He's left a wife and five little ones."

"Jose, come here." Laura caught hold of her sister's sleeve and dragged her through the kitchen to the other side of the green baize door. There she paused and leaned against it. "Jose!" she said, horrified, "however, are we going to stop everything?"

"Stop everything, Laura!" cried Jose in astonishment. "What do you mean?"

"Stop the garden-party, of course." Why did Jose pretend?

But Jose was still more amazed. "Stop the garden-party? My dear Laura, don't be so absurd. Of course we can't do anything of the kind. Nobody expects us to. Don't be so extravagant."

"But we can't possibly have a garden-party with a man dead just outside the front gate."

That really was extravagant, for the little cottages were in a lane to themselves at the very bottom of a steep rise that led up to the house. A broad road ran between. True, they were far too near. They were the greatest possible eyesore, and they had no right to be in that neighbourhood at all. They were little mean dwellings painted a chocolate brown. In the garden patches there was nothing but cabbage stalks, sick hens and tomato cans. The very smoke coming out of their chimneys was poverty-stricken. Little rags and shreds of smoke, so unlike the great silvery plumes that uncurled from the Sheridans' chimneys. Washerwomen lived in the lane and sweeps and a cobbler, and a man whose house-front was studded all over with minute birdcages. Children swarmed. When the Sheridans were little they were forbidden to set foot there because of the revolting language and of what they might catch. But since they were grown up, Laura and Laurie on their prowls sometimes walked through. It was disgusting and sordid. They came out with a shudder. But still one must go everywhere; one must see everything. So through they went.

"And just think of what the band would sound like to that poor woman," said Laura.

"Oh, Laura!" Jose began to be seriously annoyed. "If you're going to stop a band playing every time some one has an accident, you'll lead a very strenuous life. I'm every bit as sorry about it as you. I feel just as sympathetic." Her eyes hardened. She looked at her sister just as she used to when they were little and fighting together. "You won't bring a drunken workman back to life by being sentimental," she said softly.

"Drunk! Who said he was drunk?" Laura turned furiously on Jose. She said, just as they had used to say on those occasions, "I'm going straight up to tell mother."

"Do, dear," cooed Jose.

"Mother, can I come into your room?" Laura turned the big glass door-knob.

"Of course, child. Why, what's the matter? What's given you such a colour?" And Mrs. Sheridan's turned round from her dressing table. She was trying on a new hat.

"Mother, a man's been killed," began Laura.

"*Not* in the garden?" interrupted her mother.

"No, no!"

"Oh, what a fright you gave me!" Mrs. Sheridan sighed with relief, and took off the big hat and held it on her knees.

"But listen, mother," said Laura. Breathless, half-choking, she told the dreadful story. "Of course, we can't have our party, can we?" she pleaded. "The band and everybody arriving. They'd hear us, mother; they're nearly neighbours!"

To Laura's astonishment, her mother behaved just like Jose, it was harder to bear because she seemed amused. She refused to take Laura seriously.

"But, my dear child, use your common sense. It's only by accident we've heard of it. If some one had died there normally—and I can't understand how they keep alive in those poky little holes—we should still be having our party, shouldn't we?"

Laura had to say "yes" to that, but she felt it was all wrong. She sat down on her mother's sofa and pinched the cushion frill.

"Mother, isn't it really terribly heartless of us?" she asked.

"Darling!" Mrs. Sheridan got up and came over to her, carrying the hat. Before Laura could stop her she had popped it on. "My child!" said her mother, "the hat is yours. It's made for you. It's much too young for me. I have never seen you look such a picture. Look at yourself!" And she held up her hand-mirror.

"But, mother," Laura began again. She couldn't look at herself; she turned aside.

This time Mrs. Sheridan lost patience just as Jose had done.

"You are being very absurd, Laura," she said coldly. "People like that don't expect sacrifices from us. And it's not very sympathetic to spoil everybody's enjoyment as you're doing now."

"I don't understand," said Laura, and she walked quickly out of the room into her own bedroom. There, quite by chance, the first thing she saw was this charming girl in the mirror, in her black hat trimmed with gold daisies, and a long black velvet ribbon. Never had she imagined she could look like that. Is mother right? she thought. And now she hoped her mother was right. Am I being extravagant? Perhaps it was extravagant. Just for a moment she had another glimpse of that poor woman and those little children, and the body being carried into the house. But it all seemed blurred, unreal, like a picture in the newspaper. I'll remember it again after the party's over, she decided. And somehow that seemed quite the best plan. . . .

Lunch was over by half past one. By half past two they were all ready for the fray. The green-coated band had arrived and was established in a corner of the tennis-court.

"My dear!" trilled Kitty Maitland, "aren't they too like frogs for words? You ought to have arranged them round the pond with the conductor in the middle on a leaf."

Laurie arrived and hailed them on his way to dress. At the sign of him Laura remembered the accident again. She wanted to tell him. If Laurie agreed with the others, then it was bound to be all right. And she followed him into the hall.

"Laurie!" Hallo!" He was half-way upstairs, but when he turned round and saw Laura he suddenly puffed out his cheeks and goggled his eyes at her. "My word, Laura; you do look stunning," said Laurie. "What an absolutely topping hat!"

Laura said faintly "Is it?" and smiled up at Laurie, and didn't tell him after all.

Soon after that people began coming in streams. The band struck up; the hired waiters ran from the house to the marquee. Wherever you looked there were couples strolling, bending to the flowers, greeting moving on over the lawn. They were like bright birds that had alighted in the Sheridans' garden for this one afternoon, on their way to — where? Ah, what happiness it is to be with people who all are happy, to press hands, press cheeks, smile into eyes.

"Darling Laura, how well you look!"

"What a becoming hat, child!"

"Laura, you look quite Spanish. I've never seen you look so striking."

And Laura, glowing, answered softly, "Have you had tea? Won't you have an ice? The passion-fruit ices really are rather special." She ran to her father and begged him. "Daddy darling, can't the band have something to drink?"

And the perfect afternoon slowly ripened, slowly faded, slowly its petals closed.

"Never a more delightful garden-party. . ." "The greatest success. . ." "Quite the most. . ."

Laura helped her mother with the good-byes. They stood side by side in the porch till it was all over.

"All over, all over, thank heaven," said Mrs. Sheridan. "Round up the others, Laura. Let's go and have some fresh coffee. I'm exhausted. Yes, its been very successful. But oh, these parties, these parties! Why will you children insist on giving parties!" And they all of them sat down in the deserted marquee.

"Have a sandwich, daddy dear. I wrote the flag."

"Thanks." Mr. Sheridan took a bite and the sandwich was gone. He took another. "I suppose you didn't hear of a beastly accident that happened to-day?" he said.

"My dear," said Mrs. Sheridan, holding up her hand, "we did. It nearly ruined the party. Laura insisted we should put it off."

"Oh, mother!" Laura didn't want to be teased about it.

"It was a horrible affair all the same," said Mrs. Sheridan. "The chap was married too. Lived just below in the lane, and leaves a wife and half a dozen kiddies, so they say."

An awkward little silence fell. Mrs. Sheridan fidgeted with her cup. Really, it was very tactless of father . . .

Suddenly she looked up. There on the table were all those sandwiches, cakes, puffs, all uneaten, all going to be wasted. She had one of her brilliant ideas.

"I know," she said. "Let's make up a basket. Let's send that poor creature some of this perfectly good food. At any rate, it will be the greatest treat for the children. Don't you agree? And she's sure to have neighbours calling in and so on. What a point to have it all ready prepared. Laura!" She jumped up. "Get me the big basket out of the stairs cupboard."

"But, mother, do you really think it's a good idea?" said Laura.

Again, how curious, she seemed to be different from them all. To take scraps from their party. Would the poor woman really like that?

"Of course! What's the matter with you to-day? An hour or two ago you were insisting on us being sympathetic, and now—"

Oh, well! Laura ran for the basket. It was filled, it was heaped by her mother.

"Take it yourself, darling," said she. "Run down just as you are. No, wait, take the arum lilies too. People of that class are so impressed by arum lilies."

"The stems will ruin her lace frock," said practical Jose.

So they would. Just in time. "Only the basket, then. And, Laura!"—her mother followed her out of the marquee—"don't on any account—"

"What, mother?"

No, better not put such ideas into the child's head! "Nothing! Run along."

It was just growing dusky as Laura shut their garden gates. A big dog ran by like a shadow. The road gleamed white, and down below in the hollow the little cottages were in deep shade. How quiet it seemed after the afternoon. Here she was going down the hill to somewhere where a man lay dead, and she couldn't realize it. Why couldn't she? She stopped a minute. And it seemed to her that kisses, voices, tinkling spoons, laughter, the smell of crushed grass were somehow inside her. She had no room for anything else. How strange! She looked up at the pale sky, and all she thought was, "Yes, it was the most successful party."

Now the broad road was crossed. The lane began, smoky and dark. Women in shawls and men's tweed caps hurried by. Men hung over the palings; the children played in the doorways. A low hum came from the mean little cottages. In some of them there was a flicker of light, and a shadow, crab-like, moved across the window. Laura bent her head and hurried on. She wished now she had put on a coat. How her frock shone! And the big hat with the velvet streamer—if only it was another hat! Were the people looking at her? They must be. It was a mistake to have come; she knew all along it was a mistake. Should she go back even now?

No, too late. This was the house. It must be. A dark knot of people stood outside, Beside the gate an old, old woman with a crutch sat in a chair, watching. She had her feet on a newspaper. The voices stopped as Laura drew near. The group parted. It was as though she was expected, as though they had known she was coming here.

Laura was terribly nervous. Tossing the velvet ribbon over her shoulder, she said to a woman standing by, "Is this Mrs. Scott's house?" and the woman, smiling queerly, said, "It is, my lass."

Oh, to be away from this! She actually said, "Help me, God," as she walked up the tiny path and knocked. To be away from those staring eyes, or to be covered up in anything, one of those women's shawls even. I'll just leave the basket and go, she decided I shan't even wait for it to be emptied.

Then the door opened. A little woman in black showed in the gloom.

Laura said, "Are you Mrs. Scott?" But to her horror the woman answered, "Walk in please, miss," and she was shut in the passage.

"No," said Laura, "I don't want to come in. I only want to leave this basket. Mother sent—"

The little woman in the gloomy passage seemed not to have heard her. "Step this way, please, miss," she said in an oily voice, and Laura followed her.

She found herself in a wretched little low kitchen, lighted by a smoky lamp. There was a woman sitting before the fire.

"Em," said the little creature who had let her in. "Em! It's a young lady." She turned to Laura. She said meaningly. "I'm 'er sister, miss. You'll excuse 'er, won't you?"

"Oh, but of course!" said Laura. "Please, don't disturb her. I—I only want to leave—"

But at that moment the woman at the fire turned round. Her face, puffed up, red, with swollen eyes and swollen lips, looked terrible. She seemed as though she couldn't understand why Laura was there. What did it mean? Why was this stranger standing in the kitchen with a basket? What was it all about? And the poor face puckered up again.

"All right, my dear, "said the other. "I'll thank the young lady."

And again she began, "You'll excuse her, miss, I'm sure," and her face swollen too, tried an oily smile.

Laura only wanted to get out, to get away. She was back in the passage. The door opened. She walked straight through into the bedroom, where the dead man was lying.

"You'd like a look at 'im, wouldn't you?" said Em's sister, and she brushed past Laura over to the bed. "Don't be afraid, my lass,—" and now her voice sounded fond and sly, and fondly she drew down the sheet—"'e looks a picture. There's nothing to show. Come along, my dear."

Laura came.

There lay a young man, fast asleep—sleeping so soundly, so deeply, that he was far, far away from them both. Oh, so remote, so peaceful. He was dreaming. Never wake him up again. His head was sunk in the pillow, his eyes were closed; they were blind under the closed eyelids. He was given up to his dream. What did garden-parties and baskets and lace frocks matter to him? He was far from all those things. He was wonderful, beautiful. While they were laughing and while the band was playing, this marvel had come to the lane. Happy . . . happy. . . . All is well, said that sleeping face. This is just as it should be. I am content.

But all the same you had to cry, and she couldn't go out of the room without saying something to him. Laura gave a loud childish sob.

"Forgive my hat," she said.

And this time she didn't wait for Em's sister. She found her way out of the door, down the path, past all those dark people. At the corner of the lane she met Laurie.

He stepped out of the shadow. "Is that you, Laura?"

"Yes."

"Mother was getting anxious. Was it all right?"

"Yes, quite. Oh, Laurie!" She took his arm, she pressed up against him.

"I say, you're not crying, are you?" asked her brother.

Laura shook her head. She was.

Laurie put his arm round her shoulder. "Don't cry," he said in his warm, loving voice. "Was it awful?"

"No," sobbed Laura. "It was simply marvellous. But. Laurie—" She stopped, she looked at her brother. "Isn't life," she stammered, "Isn't life—" But what life was she couldn't explain. No matter. He quite understood.

"*Isn't* it, darling?" said Laurie.

Anna Akhmatova 1888–1966

Considered to be Russia's finest woman poet, Anna Akhmatova (pseudonym of Anna Andreyevna Gorenko) experienced a tumultuous life as poet and translator. From 1910 to 1917, she and her husband were main figures in the Acmeist movement, a reaction against the mysticism and vagueness of the symbolists. In 1921, her husband was executed as a counterrevolutionary, and in the 1930s, their son was banished to a prison camp where he stayed until Stalin's death in 1953. After the execution of her husband, Akhmatova was not allowed to officially publish until 1940. During this time, she burned many of her poems while new poems were memorized by friends. In 1946, Soviet cultural leader Zhdanov proclaimed Akhmatova's writing dangerous and subversive; she did not publish again until Stalin's death. She was a candidate for the Nobel Prize in 1958 and 1965 and received an honorary doctorate from Oxford University in 1965. Critics remember Akhmatova's poetry for its accessibility, economy of style, and concrete imagery. Her main theme of love, whether it regarded nature, Russia, or love itself, was consistently intimate and authentically rendered. Judith Hemschemeyer writes, "She has lately come to symbolize for the world even beyond Russia the power of art to survive and transcend the terrors of our century."

IN MEMORY OF M. B.

Here is my gift, not roses on your grave,
not sticks of burning incense.
You lived aloof, maintaining to the end
Your magnificent disdain.
You drank wine, and told the wittiest jokes,   5
and suffocated inside stifling walls.
Alone you let the terrible stranger in,
and stayed with her alone.

Now you're gone, and nobody says a word
about your troubled and exalted life.   10
Only my voice, like a flute, will mourn
at your dumb funeral feast.
Oh, who would have dared believe that half-crazed I,
I, sick with grief for the buried past,
I, smoldering on a slow fire,   15
having lost everything and forgotten all,
would be fated to commemorate a man
so full of strength and will and bright inventions,
who only yesterday it seems, chatted with me,
hiding the tremor of his mortal pain.   20

REDWINGED BIRDS

I hear always the sad voices
of summer
passing like red winged birds
over the high grass

where peasants gather   5
skirts lifted, blouses open.
If only the old voices would linger
in the evening air!

I do not need your loving words
or hurried kiss   10
as night comes down
in the place where we once lived

innocent as children,
and happier.

THE GUEST

Everything is
as it was. Metallic snow
and I am the same.
A woman comes to me.

What do you want   5
of me? "To be in hell
with you," she says, standing
at the window.

She touches the flower,
the vase. "Tell me   10
how you kissed me,
how you took me to bed."

Her eyes never waver
from my ring.
Nothing moves   15
in her face.

I know that she wants
all that I have.
She will give me
nothing.   20

Miriam Raskin 1889–1973

Born in Slonim, White Russia, Miriam Raskin was a member of the *Bund* as a young woman. Imprisoned for a year in St. Petersburg because of her political activities, Raskin left Russia in 1920 and came to the United States. In America, her short stories appeared in *Tsukunft* and her serialized novels in *Der forverts*, portraying life as a Jew in czarist Russia and the immigrant experience in America. Her *Bundist* politics and perspective carried over into three published volumes: *Tsen yor lebn* (Ten Years of Life), a series of diary entries; *Zlatke*, a novel depicting Jewish revolutionary politics and life on the verge of change in czarist Russia; and *Shtile lebns* (Quiet Lives), a compassionate collection of short stories about working-class people of various backgrounds, races, and ethnicities struggling to make a living.

AT A PICNIC

TRANSLATED BY HENIA REINHARTZ

The protagonist of this story had been a member of the *Bund* in czarist Russia. Like most other Jews, she came to North America to escape the pogroms and persecution of the regime. In America thousands of Jews continued to devote their lives to the goals of the *Bund,* working and organizing within the trade union and progressive political movements. For the most part, however, the children of these Jewish immigrants, like those of the protagonist, moved into business and the professions, dramatically changing the character of Jewish class structure in North America.

That morning Sadie hadn't slept since dawn. When she pushed the curtain on her window aside she saw the sun rising red and her heart gladdened.

"A great day for a picnic!"

For Sadie, a socialist picnic was a holiday better than any other. Sadie was proud that in the old country she had been part of the heroic past of the *Bund.* Then she had been known as Zeldke the dressmaker, the first to do dangerous underground work and the first to sing at holidays; so too her late husband Arontshik the gaiter-maker. Heroic and courageous in those great struggles, his name was known in all of Berezin and in all the towns around Minsk.

Nowadays Sadie was forever busy with the work she brought home from the shop to support her household and her three children. She had a hard life, Sadie, but drew strength from the firm heartfelt belief that in the society of the future people would not have to suffer so much.

On the day of the picnic Sadie was in a holiday mood from early morning. She made her house beautiful for the holiday, dusting the photographs on the walls, the innocent faces of boys and girls standing in heroic poses; among them

Karl Marx with his rabbi's beard and clear face. Sadie stared at her pictures. It seemed to her that through them she was united with her ideals and with the memory of her husband.

Sadie herself then seemed happy. Her pale, tired face was serious and devout, and in the dark depths of her eyes a spark glowed.

Her three sons, all of whom attended college, were good-naturedly patronizing but proud of their mother. The youngest son lovingly lectured her.

"You'd do better to rest up on a Sunday, Ma!"

Sadie sadly nodded her head. Her heart quietly ached. Those sons of hers, her own flesh and blood, she would do anything for them; she would have them educated so they would grow up important people. But they were so Americanized, not the least bit "class conscious."

In difficult moments, when hardship touched their young lives and they lost courage, Sadie taught them not to surrender, not to give in.

"Imagine how it was for me at your age. We were hungry and we were put in jail . . . in the old country. . . . "

They didn't answer, Sadie's sons, but exchanged glances silently. Her lessons didn't stick. And this hurt her very much. The field that led to the picnic grounds was green and bright. Throngs of people were converging on the field from all sides and all directions.

A socialist picnic is like a great migration. From the Bronx and from Brooklyn whole families set out on the journey, their movements imprinted with the feverish pace of New York and the shop. People carried huge bags of food in hairy hands, sleeves pushed up, everyone lively and animated. The July sun played overhead and the gang laughingly exchanged banter.

"Say *landsman!*" Say there, hard worker!"

"Stop—what's the hurry? This isn't piece-work."

Sadie kept pace with everyone else. They were her kind of people, one big family. She heard the friendly conversation and the laughter, and it was sweet music to her ears. And as one thinks one's own thoughts listening to good music, so Sadie took stock of herself, seeing her youth, her husband Arontshik the gaiter-maker, thinking about her children and her whole life.

"Hello, Sadie!" she would hear every few minutes and would turn hastily and answer merrily, "What kind of *Sadie* am I to you? *Zeldke* is my name, did you already forget!"

She felt thrilled to see her dear old friends Dvoyrele the lanky one, Bertshik the tailor and Avreml the scribe. In this country Dvoyrele had grown fat, and Bertshik very much wanted to speak only English to Sadie; Avreml the scribe had learned here in America to be a union leader and had become very pompous. But in Sadie's eyes they hadn't changed a bit. She still remembered their features as they had been in the past.

"You see? Uncle Sam's country!" she said to them, smiling knowingly.

The holiday was already in full swing in the big shady park. Like tribes of common ancestry, the celebrants divided according to their town or group. At the tables the loud, lively conversation was accompanied by a sandwich and a tasty beer. Someone was already involved in a heated dispute; someone else had already set up a choir to sing proletarian songs.

Sadie and her old friend Tsaytl the sock maker stood to the side leaning against a tree and pouring out their hearts to each other about all the long years that had passed. Tsaytl had become in this country a bourgeoise who called herself Celia Kaufman, but she was still drawn to her warm old friends.

"Tsaytele darling, if I would start telling you . . . ," Sadie said in a singsong voice. "You know my Arontshik *olevasholem*. . . ."

The traditional *"olevasholem"* slipped out unwittingly and Sadie immediately hid her mouth with two fingers.

Now Sadie talked about her children, holding her friend tightly by the sleeve.

"The oldest, the doctor, has a golden heart, may he only be well. And the other, he will soon be a lawyer and is still involved in sports. Sports, only sports, what else? He's not at all class conscious," Sadie finished somewhat sadly.

Tsaytl quickly responded with great authority.

"He's probably growing up to be an American *dope* already!"

But Sadie would not allow anyone to think badly of her children.

"Well, let it be, Tsaytl, he'll still have time to come to his senses. Let him play a while longer. The good life we ourselves had with *our* parents . . . !"

"*Nu*, and the youngest?" her friend wanted to know.

"Kling-klong, kling-klong." Sadie in the meanwhile caught a tune coming from another corner of the park and recognized the proletarian song immediately.

"You mean the youngest?" she continued the interrupted conversation. And her face lit up in a special way. "May he live long. An artist, that's what he is. Plays the violin; that's what he plays."

"Is that so?"

"What else? You can certainly believe me: it's murder to pay for the lessons every time."

"Why didn't you make at least one of your sons a worker?"

"You listen to me, they are growing up to be only professionals," Sadie pronounced with special pride.

The sun was nearing the horizon and the whole park rejoiced with life and human noise. Sadie was sitting among a group of her friends, her face enraptured, eyes half-closed. She was singing. In her hand she held a yellow-paged booklet with all the songs they used to sing in the movement.

"Akh, ti dolya moya dolya!"

Her voice trembled with great emotion, and it seemed as if the song were part of her own life.

A crowd gathered around her: handsome grey heads, seasoned old fighters joined in the chorus with their strong bass voices. And it was as though they were singing out some far-away secret desires, some longing for beautiful times, for their youth. . . .

And Sadie, surrounded by such people, was overwhelmed with joy. She felt protected against all the evils of the world by a strong wall.

The singing was often interrupted. Someone would throw in a familiar saying. Someone else would answer with a juicy joke. The bygone movement, the *Bund* in the old country, immediately came to mind. Sadie remained seated, pensive, to hold on to that wonderful time.

Just as Jews read from the *hagode* every year at *Peysekh* at the table, so everyone who ever belonged to the *Bund* knows how to tell beautiful stories about it, without ever tiring of them.

There were in the crowd former leaders of the *Bund*; wise, learned heads, a youthful fire still in their eyes, and Sadie listened to their conversation with respect. She herself was silent like a simple Jew in the presence of scholars. She sat, her hands folded, mute joy in her heart. But all her senses participated in their conversation, and her face was aglow.

That wonderful evening songs rose from all corners of the park. And among them the youth with their exuberant new revolutionary songs. But as she listened to those new songs, Sadie did not find any to her taste. She looked at her old friends again and with fear in her heart thought: What will happen to the world when this strong old army will, God forbid, die out?

It was late at night and the picnic was almost over. People said goodbye to each other as they hurried home. Very few people were left in the park. But Sadie liked to stay to the end. She had to see everyone, to exchange a word with everyone. She felt a kind of sweet sadness in her heart, like a pious Jew at the end of *Shabes. . . .*

Sadie walked through the field to the train station almost alone. Her friends dispersed in all directions but this didn't bother Sadie. She was overflowing with what she had just experienced.

In the subway Sadie sat completely alone. Her face was flushed, her hat slipped to the back of her neck. Strangers looked at her but Sadie was oblivious to everything around her. She rocked to the rhythm of the moving train, her thoughts far away. And she saw now before her her wonderful youth and her husband Arontshik the gaiter-maker, and she thought about her house and about her children and about her whole rich, unusual life.

Jean Rhys 1890–1979

Jean Rhys is perhaps best known for what is now termed a "prequel"—in this case, the story of how the fictional Bertha Mason Rochester, the "madwoman in the attic," came to England and ultimately to her characterization in *Jane Eyre.* The novel, *Wide Sargasso Sea* (1966), is a retelling of the first novel from

Bertha's perspective, providing an alternative, compelling context that gives an additionally disturbing edge to Bertha's fate. Like Bertha, Rhys was born in the West Indies and reveals in her writing what Ford Madox Ford called her "passion for stating the case of the underdog." Her prose—encompassing five novels and many short stories—has been described as understated, even spare, with "dreamlike imagery" and an "ironic, often embittered tone." Educated in a convent school, she studied at the Royal Academy of Dramatic Art in London and led what was to many an unconventional life, one not without its ironies: Despite her championing of "forgotten" and dependent women, she herself was victimized and exploited by men, contributing to what Ford—one of her victimizers— interestingly called Rhys's "terrifying insight" into the lives of those who are oppressed.

From WIDE SARGASSO SEA

'They knew that he was in Jamaica when his father and his brother died,' Grace Poole said. 'He inherited everything, but he was a wealthy man before that. Some people are fortunate, they said, and there were hints about the woman he brought back to England with him.' Next day Mrs Eff wanted to see me and she complained about gossip. I don't allow gossip. I told you that when you came. Servants will talk and you can't stop them, I said. And I am not certain that the situation will suit me, madam. First when I answered your advertisement you said that the person I had to look after was not a young girl. I asked if she was an old woman and you said no. Now that I see her I don't know what to think. She sits shivering and she is so thin. If she dies on my hands who will get the blame? Wait, Grace, she said. She was holding a letter. Before you decide will you listen to what the master of the house has to say about this matter. "If Mrs Poole is satisfactory why not give her double, treble the money," she read, and folded the letter away but not before I had seen the words on the next page, "but for God's sake let me hear no more of it." There was a foreign stamp on the envelope. "I don't serve the devil for no money," I said. She said, "If you imagine that when you serve this gentlemen you are serving the devil you never made a greater mistake in your life. I knew him as a boy. I knew him as a young man. He was gentle, generous, brave. His stay in the West Indies has changed him out of all knowledge. He has grey in his hair and misery in his eyes. Don't ask me to pity anyone who had a hand in that. I've said enough and too much. I am not prepared to treble your money, Grace, but I am prepared to double it. But there must be no more gossip. If there is I will dismiss you at once. I do not think it will be impossible to fill your place. I'm sure you understand." Yes, I understand, I said.

'Then all the servants were sent away and she engaged a cook, one maid and you, Leah. They were sent away but how could she stop them talking? If you ask me *the whole county knows. The rumours I've heard—very far from the truth. But I don't contradict, I know better than to say a word. After all the house is big and safe, a shelter from the world outside which, say what you like, can be a black and cruel world to a woman. Maybe that's why I stayed on.'*

The thick walls, she thought. Past the lodge gate a long avenue of trees and inside the house the blazing fires and the crimson and white rooms. But above all the thick walls, keeping away all the things that you have fought till you can fight no more. Yes, maybe that's why we all stay—Mrs Eff and Leah and me. All of us except that girl who lives in her own darkness. I'll say one thing for her, she hasn't lost her spirit. She's still fierce. I don't turn my back on her when her eyes have that look. I know it.

In this room I wake early and lie shivering for it is very cold. At last Grace Poole, the woman who looks after me, lights a fire with paper and sticks and lumps of coal. She kneels to blow it with bellows. The paper shrivels, the sticks crackle and spit, the coal smoulders and glowers. In the end flames shoot up and they are beautiful. I get out of bed and go close to watch them and to wonder why I have been brought here. For what reason? There must be a reason. What is it that I must do? When I first came I thought it would be for a day, two days, a week perhaps. I thought that when I saw him and spoke to him I would be wise as serpents, harmless as doves. 'I give you all I have freely,' I would say, 'and I will not trouble you again if you will let me go.' But he never came.

The woman Grace sleeps in my room. At night I sometimes see her sitting at the table counting money. She holds a gold piece in her hand and smiles. The she puts it all into a little canvas bag with a drawstring and hangs the bag round her neck so that it is hidden in her dress. At first she used to look at me before she did this but I always pretended to be asleep, now she does not trouble about me. She drinks from a bottle on the table then she goes to bed, or puts her arms on the table, her head on her arms, and sleeps. But I lie watching the fire die out. When she is snoring I get up and I have tasted the drink without colour in the bottle. The first time I did this I wanted to spit it out but managed to swallow it. When I got back into bed I could remember more and think again. I was not so cold.

There is one window high up—you cannot see out of it. My bed had doors but they have been taken away. There is not much else in the room. Her bed, a black press, the table in the middle and two black chairs carved with fruit and flowers. They have high backs and no arms. The dressing-room is very small, the room next to this one is hung with tapestry. Looking at the tapestry one day I recognized my mother dressed in an evening gown but with bare feet. She looked away from me, over my head just as she used to do. I wouldn't tell Grace this. Her name oughtn't to be Grace. Names matter, like when he wouldn't call me Antoinette, and I saw Antoinette drifting out of the window with her scents, her pretty clothes and her looking-glass.

There is no looking-glass here and I don't know what I am like now. I remember watching myself brush my hair and how my eyes looked back at me. The girl I saw was myself yet not quite myself. Long ago when I was a child and very lonely I tried to kiss her. But the glass was between us—hard, cold and misted over with my breath. Now they have taken everything away. What am I doing in this place and who am I?

The door of the tapestry room is kept locked. It leads, I know, into a passage. That is where Grace stands and talks to another women whom I have never seen. Her name is Leah. I listen but I cannot understand what they say.

So there is still the sound of whispering that I have heard all my life, but these are different voices.

When night comes, and she has had several drinks and sleeps, it is easy to take the keys. I know now where she keeps them. Then I open the door and walk into their world. It is, as I always knew, made of cardboard. I have seen it before somewhere, this cardboard world where everything is coloured brown or dark red or yellow that has no light in it. As I walk along the passages I wish I could see what is behind the cardboard. They tell me I am in England but I don't believe them. We lost our way to England. When? Where? I don't remember, but we lost it. Was it that evening in the cabin when he found me talking to the young man who brought me my food? I put my arms round his neck and asked him to help me. He said, 'I didn't know what to do, sir.' I smashed the glasses and plates against the porthole. I hoped it would break and the sea come in. A woman came and then an older man who cleared up the broken things on the floor. He did not look at me while he was doing it. The third man said drink this and you will sleep. I drank it and I said, 'It isn't like it seems to be.' — 'I know. It never is,' he said. And then I slept. When I woke it was a different sea. Colder. It was that night, I think, that we changed course and lost our way to England. This cardboard house where I walk at night is not England.

One morning when I woke I ached all over. Not the cold, another sort of ache. I saw that my wrists were red and swollen. Grace said, 'I suppose you're going to tell me that you don't remember anything about last night.'

'When was last night?' I said.

'Yesterday.'

'I don't remember yesterday.'

'Last night a gentleman came to see you,' she said.

'Which of them was that?'

Because I knew that there were strange people in the house. When I took the keys and went into the passage I heard them laughing and talking in the distance, like birds, and there were lights on the floor beneath.

Turning a corner I saw a girl coming out of her bedroom. She wore a white dress and she was humming to herself. I flattened myself against the wall for I did not wish her to see me, but she stopped and looked round. She saw nothing but shadows, I took care of that, but she didn't walk to the head of the stairs. She ran. She met another girl and the second girl said, 'Have you seen a ghost?' — 'I didn't see anything but I thought I felt something.'— 'That is the ghost,' the second one said and they went down the stairs together.

'Which of these people came to see me, Grace Poole?' I said.

He didn't come. Even if I was asleep I would have known. He hasn't come yet. She said, 'It's my belief that you remember much more than you pretend to remember. Why did you behave like that when I had promised you would be quiet and sensible? I'll never try and do you a good turn again. Your brother came to see you.'

'I have no brother.'

'He said he was your brother.'

A long long way my mind reached back.

'Was his name Richard?'

'He didn't tell me what his name was.'

'I know him,' I said, and jumped out of bed. 'It's all here, it's all here, but I hid it from your beastly eyes as I hide everything. But where is it? Where did I hide it? The sole of my shoes? Underneath the mattress? On top of the press? In the pocket of my red dress? Where, where is this letter? It was short because I remembered that Richard did not like long letters. Dear Richard please take me away from this place where I am dying because it is so cold and dark.'

Mrs Poole said, 'It's no use running around and looking now. He's gone and he won't come back—nor would I in his place.'

I said, 'I can't remember what happened. I can't remember.'

'When he came in,' said Grace Poole, 'he didn't recognize you.'

'Will you light the fire,' I said, 'because I'm so cold.'

'This gentleman arrived suddenly and insisted on seeing you and that was all the thanks he got. You rushed at him with a knife and when he got the knife away you bit his arm. You won't see him again. And where did you get that knife? I told them you stole it from me but I'm much too careful. I'm used to your sort. You got no knife from me. You must have bought it that day when I took you out. I told Mrs Eff you ought to be taken out.'

'When we went to England,' I said.

'You fool,' she said, 'this is England.'

'I don't believe it,' I said, 'and I never will believe it.'

(That afternoon we went to England. There was grass and olive-green water and tall trees looking into the water. This, I thought, is England. If I could be here I could be well again and the sound in my head would stop. Let me stay a little longer, I said, and she sat down under a tree and went to sleep. A little way off there was a cart and horse—a woman was driving it. It was she who sold me the knife. I gave her the locket round my neck for it.)

Grace Poole said, 'So you don't remember that you attacked this gentleman with a knife? I said that you would be quiet. "I must speak to her," he said. Oh he was warned but he wouldn't listen. I was in the room but I didn't hear all he said except "I cannot interfere legally between yourself and your husband." It was when he said "legally" that you flew at him and when he twisted the knife out of your hand you bit him. Do you mean to say that you don't remember any of this?'

I remember now that he did not recognize me. I saw him look at me and his eyes went first to one corner and then to another, not finding what they expected. He looked at me and spoke to me as though I were a stranger. What do you do when something happens to you like that? Why are you laughing at me? 'Have you hidden my red dress too? If I'd been wearing that he'd have known me.'

'Nobody's hidden your dress,' she said. 'It's hanging in the press.'

She looked at me and said, 'I don't believe you know how long you've been here, you poor creature.'

'On the contrary,' I said, 'only I know how long I have been here. Nights and days and days and nights, hundreds of them slipping through my fingers. But that does not matter. Time has no meaning. But something you can touch and hold like my red dress, that has a meaning. Where is it?'

She jerked her head towards the press and the corners of her mouth turned down. As soon as I turned the key I saw it hanging, the colour of fire and sunset. The colour of flamboyant flowers. 'If you are buried under a flamboyant tree,' I said, 'your soul is lifted up when it flowers. Everyone wants that.'

She shook her head but she did not move or touch me.

The scent that came from the dress was very faint at first, then it grew stronger. The smell of vetivert and frangipanni, of cinnamon and dust and lime trees when they are flowering. The smell of the sun and the smell of the rain.

. . . I was wearing a dress of that colour when Sandi came to see me for the last time.

'Will you come with me?' he said. 'No,' I said, 'I cannot.'

'So this is good-bye?'

Yes, this is good-bye.

'But I can't leave you like this,' he said, 'you are unhappy.'

'You are wasting time,' I said, 'and we have so little.'

Sandi often came to see me when that man was away and when I went out driving I would meet him. I could go out driving then. The servants knew, but none of them told.

Now there was no time left so we kissed each other in that stupid room. Spread fans decorated the walls. We had often kissed before but not like that. That was the life and death kiss and you only know a long time afterwards what it is, the life and death kiss. The white ship whistled three times, once gaily, once calling, once to say good-bye.

I took the red dress down and put it against myself. 'Does it make me look intemperate and unchaste?' I said. That man told me so. He had found out that Sandi had been to the house and that I went to see him. I never knew who told. 'Infamous daughter of an infamous mother,' he said to me.

'Oh put it away,' Grace Poole said, 'come and eat your food. Here's your grey wrapper. Why they can't give you anything better is more than I can understand. They're rich enough.'

But I held the dress in my hand wondering if they had done the last and worst thing. If they had *changed* it when I wasn't looking. If they had changed it and it wasn't my dress at all—but how could they get the scent?

'Well don't stand there shivering,' she said, quite kindly for her.

I let the dress fall on the floor, and looked from the fire to the dress and from the dress to the fire.

I put the grey wrapper round my shoulders, but I told her I wasn't hungry and she didn't try to force me to eat as she sometimes does.

'It's just as well that you don't remember last night,' she said. 'The gentleman fainted and a fine outcry there was up here. Blood all over the place and I was blamed for letting you attack him. And the master is expected in a few days. I'll never try to help you again. You are too far gone to be helped.'

I said, 'If I had been wearing my red dress Richard would have known me.'

'Your red dress,' she said, and laughed.

But I looked at the dress on the floor and it was as if the fire had spread across the room. It was beautiful and it reminded me of something I must do. I will remember I thought. I will remember quite soon now.

That was the third time I had my dream, and it ended. I know now that the flight of steps leads to this room where I lie watching the woman asleep with her head on her arms. In my dream I waited till she began to snore, then I got up, took the keys and let myself out with a candle in my hand. It was easier this time than ever before and I walked as though I were flying.

All the people who had been staying in the house had gone, for the bedroom doors were shut, but it seemed to me that someone was following me, someone was chasing me, laughing. Sometimes I looked to the right or to the left but I never looked behind me for I did not want to see that ghost of a woman whom they say haunts this place. I went down the staircase. I went further than I had ever been before. There was someone talking in one of the rooms. I passed it without noise, slowly.

At last I was in the hall where a lamp was burning. I remember that when I came. A lamp and the dark staircase and the veil over my face. They think I don't remember but I do. There was a door to the right. I opened it and went in. It was a large room with a red carpet and red curtains. Everything else was white. I sat down on a couch to look at it and it seemed sad and cold and empty to me, like a church without an altar. I wished to see it clearly so I lit all the candles, and there were many. I lit them carefully from the one I was carrying but I couldn't reach up to the chandelier. Then I looked round for the altar for with so many candles and so much red, the room reminded me of a church. Then I heard a clock ticking and it was made of gold. Gold is the idol they worship.

Suddenly I felt very miserable in that room, though the couch I was sitting on was so soft that I sank into it. It seemed to me that I was going to sleep. Then I imagined that I heard a footstep and I thought what will they say, what will they do if they find me here? I held my right wrist with my left hand and waited. But it was nothing. I was very tired after this. Very tired. I wanted to get out of the room but my own candle had burned down and I took one of the others. Suddenly I was in Aunt Cora's room. I saw the sunlight coming through the window, the tree outside and the shadows of the leaves on the floor, but I saw the wax candles too and I hated them. So I knocked them all down. Most of them went out but one caught the thin curtains that were behind the red ones. I laughed when I saw the lovely colour spreading so fast, but I did not stay to watch it. I went into the hall again with the tall candle in my hand. It was then that I saw her—the ghost. The woman with streaming hair. She was surrounded by a gilt frame but I knew her. I dropped the candle I was carrying and it caught the end of a tablecloth and I saw flames shoot up. As I ran or perhaps floated or flew I called help me Christophine help me and looking behind me I saw that I had been helped. There was a wall of fire protecting me but it was too hot, it scorched me and I went away from it.

There were more candles on a table and I took one of them and ran up the first flight of stairs and the second. On the second floor I threw away the candle. But I did not stay to watch. I ran up the last flight of stairs and along the passage. I passed the room where they brought me yesterday or the day before yesterday, I don't remember. Perhaps it was quite long ago for I seemed to know the house quite well. I knew how to get away from the heat and the shouting, for there was shouting now. When I was out on the battlements it was cool and I could hardly hear them. I sat there quietly. I don't know how long I sat. Then I turned round and saw the sky. It was red and all my life was in it. I saw the grandfather clock and Aunt Cora's patchwork, all colours, I saw the orchids and the stephanotis and the jasmine and the tree of life in flames. I saw the chandelier and the red carpet downstairs and the bamboos and the tree ferns, the gold ferns and the silver, and the soft green velvet of the moss on the garden wall. I saw my doll's house and the books and the picture of the Miller's Daughter. I heard the parrot call as he did when he saw a stranger, *Qui est là? Qui est là?* and the man who hated me was calling too, Bertha! Bertha! The wind caught my hair and it streamed out like wings. It might bear me up, I thought, if I jumped to those hard stones. But when I looked over the edge I saw the pool at Coulibri. Tia was there. She beckoned to me and when I hesitated, she laughed. I heard her say, You frightened? And I heard the man's voice, Bertha! Bertha! All this I saw and heard in a fraction of a second. And the sky so red. Someone screamed and I thought, *Why did I scream?* I called 'Tia!' and jumped and woke.

Grace Poole was sitting at the table but she had heard the scream too, for she said, 'What was that?' She got up, came over and looked at me. I lay still, breathing evenly with my eyes shut. 'I must have been dreaming,' she said. Then she went back, not to the table but to her bed. I waited a long time after I heard her snore, then I got up, took the keys and unlocked the door. I was outside holding my candle. Now at last I know why I was brought here and what I have to do. There must have been a draught for the flame flickered and I thought it was out. But I shielded it with my hand and it burned up again to light me along the dark passage.

Edna St. Vincent Millay 1892–1950

Born in Rockland, Maine, Edna St. Vincent Millay's writing career began in high school when she published poetry in *St. Nicholas*, a children's magazine. Millay attracted attention three years later when her poem "Renaissance" (later re-titled "Renascence") won a writing competition sponsored by the magazine *Lyric Year*. In the three years following her graduation from Vassar in 1917, she published the books *Renascence and Other Poems* and *A Few Figs from Thistles*. She also wrote and directed the play *Aria da Capo* for the Province-town Players. Throughout Millay's career she continued to explore the four major themes put forth in these early works: social, political, and sexual equality; "local color" and nature as inspired by her childhood on the coast of Maine; dramatic literature and related political concerns; and lyric poetry in traditional forms. Commenting on Millay's impact on a generation of women, Dorothy Parker wrote, "We all wandered in after Miss Millay. We were all being dashing and gallant, declaring that we weren't virgins, whether we were or not." Originally regarded as reckless, naughty, and cynical, her work was considered dated when she died in 1950. Currently, Millay's writing is appreciated for anticipating feminism and the "new formalism" of the 1970s and 1980s.

[I, BEING BORN A WOMAN]

I, being born a woman and distressed
By all the needs and notions of my kind,
Am urged by your propinquity to find
Your person fair, and feel a certain zest
To bear your body's weight upon my breast: 5
So subtly is the fume of life designed,
To clarify the pulse and cloud the mind,
And leave me once again undone, possessed.
Think not for this, however, the poor treason
Of my stout blood against my staggering brain,   10
I shall remember you with love, or season

My scorn with pity,—let me make it plain:
I find this frenzy insufficient reason
For conversation when we meet again.

APOSTROPHE TO MAN

(On reflecting that the world is ready to go to war again)

Detestable race, continue to expunge yourself, die out.
Breed faster, crowd, encroach, sing hymns, build bombing airplanes;
Make speeches, unveil statues, issue bonds, parade;
Convert again into explosives the bewildered ammonia and the
    distracted cellulose;
Convert again into putrescent matter drawing flies   5
The hopeful bodies of the young; exhort,
Pray, pull long faces, be earnest, be all but overcome, be photographed;
Confer, perfect your formulae, commercialize
Bacteria harmful to human tissue,
Put death on the market;   10
Breed, crowd, encroach, expand, expunge yourself, die out,
Homo called *sapiens*.

THE SNOW STORM

No hawk hangs over in this air:
The urgent snow is everywhere.
The wing adroiter than a sail
Must lean away from such a gale,
Abandoning its straight intent,   5
Or else expose tough ligament
And tender flesh to what before
Meant dampened feathers, nothing more.

Forceless upon our backs there fall
Infrequent flakes hexagonal,   10
Devised in many a curious style
To charm our safety for a while,
Where close to earth like mice we go
Under the horizontal snow.

[I WILL PUT CHAOS INTO FOURTEEN LINES]

I will put Chaos into fourteen lines
And keep him there; and let him thence escape
If he be lucky; let him twist, and ape
Flood, fire, and demon—his adroit designs
Will strain to nothing in the strict confines   5
Of this sweet Order, where, in pious rape,
I hold his essence and amorphous shape,
Till he with Order mingles and combines.
Past are the hours, the years, of our duress,
His arrogance, our awful servitude: 10
I have him. He is nothing more nor less
Than something simple not yet understood;
I shall not even force him to confess;
Or answer. I will only make him good.

UNTITLED SONNET I

Love is not all: it is not meat nor drink
Nor slumber nor a roof against the rain;
Nor yet a floating spar to men that sink
And rise and sink and rise and sink again;
Love can not fill the thickened lung with breath,   5
Nor clean the blood, nor set the fractured bone;
Yet many a man is making friends with death
Even as I speak, for lack of love alone.
It well may be that in a difficult hour,
Pinned down by pain and moaning for release,   10
Or nagged by want past resolution's power,
I might be driven to sell your love for peace,
Or trade the memory of this night for food.
It well may be. I do not think I would.

Dorothy Parker 1893–1967

Known for her acerbic wit and her membership in the famous Algonquin Hotel literary "club," Dorothy Parker coined such memorable lines as "Men don't make passes at girls who wear glasses." Parker wrote for *The New Yorker* and *Vanity Fair* magazines and was acclaimed as a poet, critic, and short-story writer. Parker won the prestigious O. Henry Award for *Big Blonde* (1929), and throughout the 1930s she published short fiction dealing with a variety of themes, often focusing on the contrast between outward appearance and the realities of emptiness and loneliness. Two notable collections appeared in 1930 and 1933, respectively: *Laments for the Living* and *After Such Pleasures*. In similar fashion to other writers and intellectuals of her time, Parker was involved in radical politics and was included with her husband and screenplay collaborator, actor Alan Campbell, in the McCarthy Era blacklists, making it impossible for them to work.

INDIAN SUMMER

In youth, it was a way I had
    To do my best to please,
And change, with every passing lad,
    To suit his theories.

But now I know the things I know,   5
    And do the things I do;
And if you do not like me so,
    To hell, my love, with you!

THE LITTLE OLD LADY IN LAVENDER SILK

I was seventy-seven, come August,
    I shall shortly be losing my bloom;
I've experienced zephyr and raw gust
    And (symbolical) flood and simoom.

When you come to this time of abatement,   5
    To this passing from Summer to Fall,
It is manners to issue a statement
    As to what you got out of it all.

So I'll say, though reflection unnerves me
  And pronouncements I dodge as I can,   10
That I think (if my memory serves me)
  There was nothing more fun than a man!

In my youth, when the crescent was too wan
  To embarrass with beams from above,
By the aid of some local Don Juan   15
  I fell into the habit of love.

And I learned how to kiss and be merry—an
  Education left better unsung.
My neglect of the waters Pierian
  Was a scandal, when Grandma was young.   20

Though the shabby unbalanced the splendid,
  And the bitter outmeasured the sweet,
I should certainly do as I then did,
  Were I given the chance to repeat.

For contrition is hollow and wraithful,   25
  And regret is no part of my plan,
And I think (if my memory's faithful)
  There was nothing more fun than a man!

Marita Bonner 1899–1971

Born in Boston and educated at Radcliffe, Marita Bonner was a multitalented individual who, in the 1920s, won significant prizes for her essays, dramas, music, and short stories. In 1924, while teaching high school in Washington, D.C., playwright and poet Georgia Douglas Johnson became a mentor to Bonner. Being included in Johnson's esteemed weekly salon, which featured the likes of Langston Hughes, Willis Richardson, Jean Toomer, and Alain Locke, subsequently launched Bonner's literary career. During this time, Bonner left her mark on the literary movement in Harlem, publishing prize-winning works in *Crisis* and *Opportunity*, two premier journals of the Harlem Renaissance. Bonner focused her acute awareness of being an African American woman in the midst of major social change and, in 1925, produced her landmark essay, "On Being Young— a Woman—and Colored." In 1930, she met and married William Occomy, an accountant, and moved to Chicago where she would live the rest of her life. While in Chicago, she continued to publish until 1941 when she resumed her teaching career. Most notably though, her work in the 1930s, mainly short stories, concentrates on the challenges of poverty, prejudice, and violence and their effect on black families in Chicago.

ON BEING YOUNG—A WOMAN— AND COLORED

You start out after you have gone from kindergarten to sheepskin covered with sundry Latin phrases.

At least you know what you want life to give you. A career as fixed and as calmly brilliant as the North Star. The one real thing that money buys. Time. Time to do things. A house that can be as delectably out of order and as easily put in order as the doll-house of "playing-house" days. And of course, a husband you can look up to without looking down on yourself.

Somehow you feel like a kitten in a sunny catnip field that sees sleek, plump brown field mice and yellow baby chicks sitting coyly, side by side, under each leaf. A desire to dash three or four ways seizes you.

That's Youth.

But you know that things learned need testing—acid testing—to see if they are really after all, an interwoven part of you. All your life you have heard of the debt you owe "Your Pepole" because you have managed to have the things they have not largely had.

So you find a spot where there are hordes of them—of course below the Line—to be your catnip field while you close your eyes to mice and chickens alike.

If you have never lived among your own, you feel prodigal. Some warm untouched current flows through them—through you—and drags you out into the deep waters of a new sea of human foibles and mannerisms; of a peculiar psychology and prejudices. And one day you find yourself entangled—enmeshed—pinioned in the seaweed of a Black Ghetto.

Not a Ghetto, placid like the Strasse[1] that flows, outwardly unperturbed and calm in a stream of religious belief, but a peculiar group. Cut off, flung together, shoved aside in a bundle because of color and with no more in common.

Unless color is, after all, the real bond.

Milling around like live fish in a basket. Those at the bottom crushed into a sort of stupid apathy by the weight of those on top. Those on top leaping, leaping; leaping to scale the sides; to get out.

[1] Street (German).

There are two "colored" movies, innumerable parties—and cards. Cards played so intensely that it fascinates and repulses at once.

Movies.

Movies worthy and worthless—but not even a low-caste spoken stage.

Parties, plentiful. Music and dancing and much that is wit and color and gaiety. But they are like the richest chocolate; stuffed costly chocolates that make the taste go stale if you have too many of them. That make plain whole bread taste like ashes.

There are all the earmarks of a group within a group. Cut off all around from ingress from or egress to other groups. A sameness of type. The smug self-satisfaction of an inner measurement; a measurement by standards known within a limited group and not those of an unlimited, seeing, world. . . . Like the blind, blind mice. Mice whose eyes have been blinded.

Strange longing seizes hold of you. You wish yourself back where you can lay your dollar down and sit in a dollar seat to hear voices, strings, reeds that have lifted the World out, up, beyond things that have bodies and walls. Where you can marvel at new marbles and bronzes and flat colors that will make men forget that things exist in a flesh more often than in spirit. Where you can sink your body in a cushioned seat and sink your soul at the same time into a section of life set before you on the boards for a few hours.

You hear that up at New York this is to be seen; that, to be heard.

You decide the next train will take you there.

You decide the next second that that train will not take you, nor the next— nor the next for some time to come.

For you know that—being a woman—you cannot twice a month or twice a year, for that matter, break away to see or hear anything in a city that is supposed to see and hear too much.

That's being a woman. A woman of any color.

You decide that something is wrong with a world that stifles and chokes; that cuts off and stunts; hedging in, pressing down on eyes, ears and throat. Somehow all wrong.

You wonder how it happens there that—say five hundred miles from the Bay State[2]—Anglo Saxon intelligence is so warped and stunted.

How judgment and discernment are bred out of the race. And what has become of discrimination? Discrimination of the right sort. Discrimination that the best minds have told you weighs shadows and nuances and spiritual differences before it catalogues. The kind they have taught you all of your life was best: that looks clearly past generalization and past appearance to dissect, to dig down to the real heart of matters. That casts aside rapid summary conclusions, drawn from primary inference, as Daniel did the spiced meats.[3]

---

[2] Massachusetts.

[3] See Daniel 1:8–16, where he refused to "defile himself with the portion of the king's meat."

Why can't they then perceive that there is a difference in the glance from a pair of eyes that look, mildly docile, at "white ladies" and those that, impersonally and perceptively—aware of distinctions—see only women who happen to be white?

Why do they see a colored woman only as a gross collection of desires, all uncontrolled, reaching out for their Apollos and the Quasimodos[4] with avid indiscrimination?

Why unless you talk in staccato squawks—brittle as seashells—unless you "champ" gum—unless you cover two yards square when you laugh—unless your taste runs to violent colors—impossible perfumes and more impossible clothes—are you a feminine Caliban craving to pass for Ariel?[5]

An empty imitation of an empty invitation. A mime; a sham; a copy-cat. A hollow re-echo. A froth, a foam. A fleck of the ashes of superficiality?

Everything you touch or taste now is like the flesh of an unripe persimmon.

... Do you need to be told what that is being ... ?

Old ideas, old fundamentals seem worm-eaten, out-grown, worthless, bitter; fit for the scrap-heap of Wisdom.

What you had thought tangible and practical has turned out to be a collection of "blue-flower" theories.

If they have not discovered how to use their accumulation of facts, they are useless to you in Their world.

Every part of you becomes bitter.

But—"In Heaven's name, do not grow bitter. Be bigger than they are"—exhort white friends who have never had to draw breath in a Jim-Crow train. Who have never had petty putrid insult dragged over them—drawing blood—like pebbled sand on your body where the skin is tenderest. On your body where the skin is thinnest and tenderest.

You long to explode and hurt everything white; friendly; unfriendly. But you know that you cannot live with a chip on your shoulder even if you can manage a smile around your eyes—without getting steely and brittle and losing the softness that makes you a woman.

For chips make you bend your body to balance them. And once you bend, you lose your poise, your balance, and the chip gets into you. The real you. You get hard.

... And many things in you can ossify ...

And you know, being a woman, you have to go about it gently and quietly, to find out and to discover just what is wrong. Just what can be done.

You see clearly that they have acquired things.

Money; money. Money to build with, money to destroy. Money to swim in. Money to drown in. Money.

---

[4] Quasimodo is the central character in Victor Hugo's novel *The Hunchback of Notre Dame* (1831).

[5] Savage and ugly trying to pass as noble and beautiful. Caliban and Ariel are characters in Shakespeare's *The Tempest*.

An ascendancy of wisdom. An incalculable hoard of wisdom in all fields, in all things collected from all quarters of humanity.

A stupendous mass of things.

Things.

So, too, the Greeks . . . Things.

And the Romans. . . .

And you wonder and wonder why they have not discovered how to handle deftly and skillfully, Wisdom, stored up for them—like the honey for the Gods on Olympus—since time unknown.

You wonder and you wonder until you wander out into Infinity, where—if it is to be found anywhere—Truth really exists.

The Greeks had possessions, culture. They were lost because they did not understand.

The Romans owned more than anyone else. Trampled under the heel of Vandals and Civilization, because they would not understand.

Greeks. Did not understand.

Romans. Would not understand.

"They." Will not understand.

So you find they have shut Wisdom up and have forgotten to find the key that will let her out. They have trapped, trammeled, lashed her to themselves with thews and thongs and theories. They have ransacked sea and earth and air to bring every treasure to her. But she sulks and will not work for a world with a whitish hue because it has snubbed her twin sister, Understanding.

You see clearly—off there is Infinity—Understanding. Standing alone, waiting for someone to really want her.

But she is so far out there is no way to snatch at her and really drag her in.

So—being a woman—you can wait.

You must sit quietly without a chip. Not sodden—and weighted as if your feet were cast in the iron of your soul. Not wasting strength in enervating gestures as if two hundred years of bonds and whips had really tricked you into nervous uncertainty.

But quiet; quiet. Like Buddha—who brown like I am—sat entirely at ease, entirely sure of himself; motionless and knowing, a thousand years before the white man knew there was so very much difference between feet and hands.

Motionless on the outside. But on the inside?

Silent.

Still . . . "Perhaps Buddha is a woman."

So you too. Still; quiet; with a smile, ever so slight, at the eyes so that Life will flow into and not by you. And you can gather, as it passes, the essences, the overtones, the tints, the shadows; draw understanding to yourself.

And then you can, when Time is ripe, swoop to your feet—at your full height—at a single gesture.

Ready to go where?

Why . . . Wherever God motions.

Meridel Le Sueur 1900–1996

The best-known woman among the proletarian writers of the 1930s, Meridel Le Sueur was born in Murray, Iowa. Her mother left an abusive husband in 1910 and later married Alfred Le Sueur, a lawyer who founded the Industrial Workers of the World. The new family's Midwestern kitchen soon became the stomping ground of labor organizers, Marxists, and eloquent radicals whose influence contributed to Le Sueur's decision to drop out of high school at age sixteen and pursue political activism. Moving to New York, she lived with Emma Goldman in an anarchist commune and studied at the Academy of Dramatic Arts. She eventually went to Hollywood, earning $25 a day as a stuntwoman on the serial *The Perils of Pauline* but left disgusted by the corruption of the movie business. Marrying a labor organizer, she gave birth to two daughters and began to publish her journal writings in the late 1920s. Soon thereafter, she left her husband and lived communally with a group of women and their children in an abandoned warehouse. From this experience, she gathered material for her first novel, *Girl,* which was written in 1939 but not published until 1978. While her acclaimed fiction depicted obscure lives lived in poverty, her reporting covered breadlines, strikes, unemployment struggles, and the plight of farmers. She was blacklisted during the McCarthy years because of her association with the Communist party and had great difficulty publishing her work for nearly thirty years. Due in part to the women's movement in the early 1970s, her work enjoyed a revival, and she continued to publish well into her nineties.

From SALUTE TO SPRING

A Hungry Intellectual

Andrew Hobbs was an intellectual. He continually said he was an intellectual, an idealist. Before the depression he had had a job as an advertising writer, and had a stenographer of his own, that's what he said. He was always telling us what a good position he had had and how he was getting on in the world. Of course he was just going into advertising until he got started with his writing, he said, but he seemed to get farther and farther into debt, so he never could stop his job. That was before the depression scooped him out, with no so much as a by-your-leave, and left him without any of the gadgets he had bought, and dumped him on the street.

The first time I saw him he was talking against God down at Gateway Park, standing very tall, his narrow head showing above the crowd of workmen. The old gospel-monger was holding forth across the street, and Hobbs was talking

Ingersoll atheism on the opposite corner, and he would take up a collection afterwards which would sometimes amount to even fifty cents. Anyhow he could
eat off it. But he said he didn't really care for the collection, it was just the principle of the thing, if a person didn't pay for a thing they didn't appreciate it,
even a few dimes like that.

I always had an awful time keeping the children quiet, waiting for the
speaking to be over and the boys to come home to dinner. Karen was only two
and Sybil just nine months. There was fifteen months between them. Somebody
brought him over and introduced him and he stood back very modestly and
tried to keep his shoes in the dark. He looked like he was trying to step back
through a door that wasn't there. He seemed to be stepping back away from
something, away from any one touching him so that his face and even his body
seemed to have a receding look about them as if he would presently disappear
into something behind him. For all that, he was well-meaning, anyone could see
that. And he had his own pride.

When Karl introduced him, he took off his hat and bowed a little, like a
Southern gentleman, and sure enough I found out he had been raised in Georgia, the lower middle class, always trying to get up further, always thinking
themselves ascending a little on the social ladder and really descending frightfully from generation to generation. This continual lowering and defeat gave
him a sad gentility. He took off his hat and bowed a little and seemed to recede.

Karl went back to the corner with the boys to distribute some leaflets about
the mass meeting the next night, and Hobbs sat down in the car with me and
politely asked about the children, but he was ignoring them. The pigeons walked
around the feet of the unemployed men sitting in the park, getting the last
breath of summer air before going to their flops. "You know," Hobbs said, "I
don't have to do this."

"Listen!" I shouted at Karen, "sit still just a minute and I'll get you a cone.
What?" I said.

"I graduated from the University of Georgia," he said delicately.

"Yeah? Listen!" I shouted between my teeth. "I'll get you a tooth brush with
Mickey Mouse on it." I couldn't keep them quiet. Hobbs looked offended as if he
had smelled something bad. He jerked up his pants over his knee and I could see
his awfully white shanks and he had no socks on. He jerked down his pants
again and I felt sorry because I could see his poor feet, in somebody else's shoes
and one shoe had a big place like a carbuncle where the guy who had had them
before kept his bunion.

"I don't know what I am going to do," I said. "I can't wait around at these
meetings all the time because the milk gets sour."

He smiled abstractedly, and looked out past the tattered top of the Ford at
the sky. He had a thin face. He looked hungry. I remember the way I had seen
his pants bag down over his rumps as if he had filled them more at some time.

"Why don't you come along and have supper with us?" I said. "We're going
to have a swell stew."

"Well," he said, vaguely, so very delicate and evasive, "I don't know, I was supposed to meet a fellow over here." He waved his long white hand. "I don't know I might . . . Wait a minute . . . I'll see if I can find him."

He swung his long thin shanks out the door. "O.K.," I said, swatting Sybil's hands so they wouldn't catch in the door. I watched him take a walk behind the statue of the unknown solider, duck a few seconds on the other side and come back. He didn't have to meet anybody. He didn't have anybody to meet.

He came to our house often just about supper time. He never came right in and had something to eat like others. He always stood vaguely in the door, and bowing a little, and my lord he got thinner and thinner until he seemed like a wraith and his pants hung on his poor shanks like an old sack. "Well, well," he would say, politely, "you're just having supper. No . . . no, I don't want to spoil your evening meal."

"We're just having supper," I would say. "Come on in and have supper."

"No. No," he would say, flapping his white hands. "I just ate." And he would brush his face off with his hands as if he had walked through cobwebs. He would sit on the step and we would whisper inside about it.

"I know he hasn't had any supper."

"The poor guy," Karl would say.

"Why doesn't he say . . . just say he's hungry and come in and eat."

"It's pride."

"My God, everyone is hungry."

"I know, but he's an intellectual."

"Ohhhhh!"

Then all who were eating would fall against each other sniggering.

"Shut up," I'd say. "He'll hear."

Afterwards, when the boys went out to the meeting, he'd come in sometimes and help me with the children. If I went out of the room for something, I could see that he took things off the table, and when I would come back, he wouldn't chew a bit but sit there smiling vaguely, with his mouth full of food, so I would have to go out again so he could chew it up.

He never once said he was hungry. He always had mysterious places where he said he slept and ate. Yet we all knew that he slept at the mission and ate that slop. Lots of the boys saw him there, but he never said a word about it, never said that he did, as if not saying so made it not so.

He seemed to like better to be with me than with the boys. He was raised by women I guess and felt easier with them, and the boys made fun of his high-fa-lutin' ideas. He would say all sorts of great high-sounding phrases he must have remembered from school. "We must all struggle," he would say, "life is progress." And yet he seemed neither to struggle nor to make any progress. You could see he felt fine when he was talking. I would feed the babies or change them for the night, and you could see in a few minutes he made the world a place it was easy for him to be in. He kept saying that change must come without violence, that it must be intellectual.

I said, "When you have a baby, birth is violent."

"No. No," he said. "Change must come from the intellect with understanding and non-violence, non-resistance."

"I don't think it's that way," I said. "From having a baby I think it's different. It comes out violently."

I could see him eyeing the last chop left on the plate. "Why don't you eat that chop?" I said. I wanted to give the bone to the baby to chew anyway; besides, one chop is nothing to fix another meal with.

He said, "Oh, I had plenty, plenty," and he went on talking, telling about how you must educate everyone and then they would understand.

"Understanding comes in the stomach," I said, turning the baby up for powder.

When I went out to put the baby to bed he ate the chop. Then he cleared the table so I wouldn't notice and washed all the dishes. I didn't say anything about it until later when I talked it over with Karl. "Why wouldn't he eat the chop?" I asked Karl.

"Damned if I know," Karl said.

"I guess it was too simple a way to do it," I said.

"If your belly's empty, it's empty," Karl said. "That's all there is to it to me."

"But it's different with him," I said. "It must be something more to him, something subtle."

"Well, the point is," Karl said, "he did eat the chop. He did actually eat the chop, that's the point."

"But he didn't say so."

"No, the say is worth something to that guy."

"Sure, the say is everything. . ."

"What the hell's the say worth? The point is he ate the chop," and Karl went off into a huge howl of laughter. I had to make him promise he wouldn't tell anyone so they wouldn't guy Hobbs about it.

"Yeah, he ate the chop," Karl howled.

Sometimes Hobbs would look like he had some mysterious grievance and wouldn't speak for days. He would come to the meetings or do some typing, but he wouldn't say a word and acted very polite and mysterious as if he had some great secret tragedy connected with him that he couldn't speak of. He would hardly speak to the boys, but he would come and take care of the babies while I did some work. It got awful hot and he would roll the babies out to the park.

He was always awfully clean. Once his collar was torn a little and he tried to mend it but he couldn't do anything with his hands. They didn't seem to have any life in them. We used to talk about it sometimes, how that fellow always had a clean shirt and his feet never stank. It's something to be able to do that when you never have a place to wash or a bed alone but he always looked scrubbed. I don't know how he did it, but no one ever asked him outright because he wouldn't have told anything, he would have had something mysterious to say, as if he had been washed in the blood of the lamb or something. Nothing natural and outright seemed to happen to him. Once I asked him if he ever had a woman.

"Didn't you ever have a woman?" I asked him because I couldn't imagine it, everything seemed so ideal and delicate to him. The boys always laughed at the way he came and sat with me like another woman. Once he helped me move and even if I did most of the work I felt delicate and precious. I had to laugh. The boys said, "Well, I suppose Sir Walter Raleigh helped you move." I had to laugh.

When I asked him if he ever had a woman, he blushed and spread out his long thin hands, "Well, if you mean have I ever been in love?"

"Well, all right, have you ever been in love?"

He looked at his hands a long time. I felt it as plain as your face that he was having a struggle between what had really happened when he was in love and what he wished to tell me had happened. I felt an awful disgust and pity for him, like shouting at him, "Go on tell, tell me all the dirt, don't fix it up into the ideal, get it all out of your poor lean body, spit it out, vile and awful." But I knew he wouldn't tell me what had happened. There was something vague all over him. I saw the shanks of the poor guy, his shoes a little hard from being damp so much, turned up at the toes and hardened in the leather, living for the glorious mind and sitting, pawing webs over his own face.

He told me a long tale about his wife. I couldn't look at him at all. He said he had made five hundred dollars a month and had a pretty wife, and it seems she had fallen in love, he said, with a race track man, a driver of a fast car, and she had gone off with him, and then he said, and I was astonished, I couldn't believe it, that they had been killed, both of them, together. He seemed to like that almost and licked his thin lips over something. Yes, they had gone around the track together, driving very, very fast, he wasn't sure how fast, and they had both been killed.

About this time they were organizing a Hunger March to the state Capitol of all the farmers and unemployed to demand bread and milk for their children. Karl had been telling me that Hobbs never seemed to be there when anything actual was happening. He would talk or write plenty but somehow or other he never seemed to be at a meeting, where there was danger. I said to Karl, I couldn't believe it.

"That's the way it turns out," he said. "I don't believe it," I told him. "He's trying. He feels timid. He's sore from being alone."

"Just the same you'll see," Karl said. "Wait till the Hunger March and you'll see what I say is so, all right."

Before that we had a picnic down at the grove along the Mississippi. It was a fine summer afternoon in harvest, a good summer day with the wind blowing the heavy trees and the water like the sky and the little curl of beach golden in the bright sun. A day when you like to see your fat children running naked in the sun and water. Rose was there with her baby one month off and we all felt happy sitting on the beach with the tiny waves curling up and the sound of summer wind and the sun beating down into our pores like golden fire and the rosy naked children. Rose said, "Gee, I can't wait to see mine. I feel all the time like taking it out to look at it." Karl laughed and we all looked, laughing at each other through the sunlight.

Hobbs was sitting by himself and had taken off his awful shoes showing his long white toes but he wouldn't go in the water. We all put on our suits in the bushes and went into the river, but Hobbs wouldn't go in. He sat on the beach and that day somehow his eyes looked so cunning and dead I could hardly speak to him. And he somehow made Rose being so heavy with child seem out of place although we all liked it. "A woman," he said, "shouldn't come out like that." It made me kind of mad.

After we had lunch and Sybil and Karen were lying under a spotted beach tree sleeping with the shadows splotched on them, he said, "I don't see why people have children. We have no right to bring children into the world until we know more about it." Perpetuating the race, he called it. He got quite excited talking to me about it until I went to sleep too. I sort of dozed off, but I could hear Karl and Rose's husband talking very earnestly planning the Hunger March where they squatted down on their heels at the edge of the water as if they didn't quite have time to sit down even. Somehow the drone of their voices, earnest, real, coming through the heat and wind, filled me with assurance. I wasn't afraid. The sun seemed to pour down on us expanding over and in and through the water and sky, sand and bodies and the lovely full mound of Rose sitting in the sand over her beautiful stomach.

"The masses won't stand together," Hobbs was saying, writing words with a stick in the sand. "They'll betray one another," he said. "They won't stick together . . . You can't make a silk purse out of a sow's ear."

I could hear the lovely drone of the men's voices and the life and dream singing in the heat, and our bodies intertwined together . . . "Look what the masses read. . ." I heard his dry voice going on and on.

A long time later I heard him say, "My wife and I might have had a child once but we got rid of it."

The afternoon of the Hunger March, Hobbs came over and stuck pretty close to me. He seemed silent and then he would talk very fast and loud. I kept thinking he would go but he helped me put on Karen's sun hat and said he would carry Sybil. It was a hot day but I was going to push the carriage up to the Capitol. I thought we could sit across in the park anyway and see what happened. The walks were sizzling, but Hobbs helped me push up the steepest hills. I was used to pushing them until I felt like a dray horse. We sat down on the grass on the mound across from the Capitol. We sat where we could see the marchers coming down University Avenue. The heat was like a falling curtain you couldn't look through. Hobbs had been telling me about a girl he saw at the Busy Bee cafeteria and what a pure face she had. It got to be past time for the marchers who were coming from the heart of the city. Hobbs got nervous and stopped talking and wrung his hands together in his lap. A dog lifted its leg right on the bench he was sitting on, but he didn't pay any attention. I let the children out of the buggy to play on the fine freshly mowed green grass. They don't get to see green grass too often.

Hobbs said, "What time is it?"

I said, "It's three o'clock."

After a while I said, "You keep yourself pretty safe all right." A slow color mounted his neck and half up his cheeks. He didn't say a word.

"Listen," I said, but then I could see the dark clot of men down the highway like a mass of angry bees moving swiftly towards the Capitol. "There they are," I cried, trying to see Karl, but they all looked like the same man, loose dirty clothes, angry pressing-forward faces, and all lean as a soup bone, but they came in a thick swift cloud, black and angry, bearing banners saying, WE WANT BREAD. WE WANT MILK. OUR CHILDREN ARE HUNGRY.

I began jumping up and down with a cry in my throat and my children climbing up my thighs. "Listen," I said. "You can still go. You can still join them . . . Look . . . Run. . ." But he never moved.

He didn't come around for a long time after that. I felt sorry for the poor guy after all. I knew it hit him pretty hard, in a way, not being able to go that day.

We got kicked out of where we were living and moved into a kind of shack down the river. And one day there was Hobbs in the doorway making a bow, clean as ever, with his hair plastered down on his head as if he had been ducked in the river. He said that he had swum four miles down the river and walked back, but looking at him I thought he hadn't done it at all, that he had just wet his hair and then come up and told me a tale. It would be a daring, clean thing to do, to take off your clothes and go down a swift river. . .

Then he says that he got a boat for twelve dollars and that he expects to hear from his old advertising company in Detroit any day now and they will have a place for him in January, so he thinks he will go down the river alone for a spell and have an adventure until then. He sat very delicately in the room keeping his pants legs down so as not to show his bare shanks.

But, my lord, I even thought that maybe he would go down the river. A woman has always got faith and hope certainly. I felt glad and thought now maybe he will do it, maybe he will go down that river.

He sat on the couch telling about the books he had been reading. Pretty soon he got up and said he was going down to the river now and see about that scow he was dickering for and he stooped over and drew a diagram on the back of a leaflet, how he would fix it up for himself. It was all quite clear, there on paper.

Then he made a little bow, backed off into that space that would never protect him and went down to the river.

I didn't tell Karl anything about his having been there, but the very next day we got back from trying to get an extra quart of milk from the relief which they wouldn't give us, and we felt pretty discouraged because many that were demonstrating needed it worse than us and it didn't seem we got very far with all our organizing—and there was a note on the table, held down by the butcher knife stuck into it very dramatic, and scrawled on it with an elegant hand, it said:

AM GOING DOWN THE RIVER. SAVE ALL MY LETTERS. WILL WRITE MY ADVENTURES AND WE WILL PUBLISH THEM. IT WILL BE THE ONLY RECORD OF THE TRIP. SAVE ALL.

We never heard of him again.

THE GIRL

She was going the inland route because she had been twice on the coast route. She asked three times at the automobile club how far it was through the Tehachapi Mountains, and she had the route marked on the map in red pencil. The car was running like a T, the garage man told her. All her dresses were back from the cleaners, and there remained only the lace collar to sew on her black crepe so that they would be all ready when she got to San Francisco. She had read up on the history of the mountains and listed all the Indian tribes and marked the route of the Friars from the Sacramento Valley. She was glad now that Clara Robbins, the math teacher, was not going with her. She liked to be alone, to have everything just the way she wanted it, exactly.

There was nothing she wanted changed. It was a remarkable pleasure to have everything just right, to get into her neat fine-looking little roadster, start out in the fine morning, with her map tucked into the seat, every road marked. She was lucky too, how lucky she was. She had her place secure at Central High, teaching history. On September 18, she knew she would be coming back to the same room, to teach the same course in history. It was a great pleasure. Driving along, she could see her lean face in the windshield. She couldn't help but think that she had no double chin, and her pride rode in her, a lean thing. She saw herself erect, a little caustic and severe, and the neat turnover collar of her little blue suit. Her real lone self. This was what she wanted. Nothing messy. She had got herself up in the world. This was the first summer she had not taken a summer course, and she felt a little guilty; but she had had a good summer just being lazy, and now she was going to San Francisco to see her sister and would come back two days before school opened. She had had thought in the spring that her skin was getting that papyrus look so many teachers had, and she had a little tired droop to her shoulders and was a little bit too thin. It was fine to be thin but not too thin. Now she looked better, brown, and she had got the habit of a little eye shadow, a little dry rouge, and just a touch of lipstick. It was really becoming.

Yes, everything was ideal.

But before long she was sorry she had come through the Tehachapi Mountains. Why hadn't someone told her they were like that? They did her in. Frightening. Mile after mile in the intense September heat, through fierce mountains of sand, and bare gleaming rock faces jutting sheer from the road. Her eyes burned, her throat was parched, and there was mile after mile of lonely road without a service station and not a soul passing. She wished, after all, that Miss Robbins had come with her. It would have been nice to be able to say, "What an interesting formation, Miss Robbins! We really should make sketches of it, so we could look up the geological facts when we get back." Everything would have seemed normal then.

She drove slowly through the hot yellow swells, around the firm curves; and the yellow light shone far off in the tawny valleys, where black mares, delicate-haunched, grazed, flesh shining as the sun struck off them. The sun beat down like a golden body about to take form on the road ahead of her. She drove very slowly, and something began to loosen in her, and her eyes seemed to dilate and darken as she looked into the fold upon fold of earth flesh lying clear to the horizon. She saw she was not making what is called "good time." In fact, she was making very bad time.

She had been driving five hours. She looked at her wrist watch and decided she would stop, even if it was only eleven-thirty, and have lunch. So when she saw a little service station far down, tucked into the great folds of dun hill, she was glad. Her car crept closer circling out of sight of it and then circling back until her aching eyes could read the sign — Half Way Station — and she drew up to the side and stopped. Her skin felt as if it were shriveling on her bones. She saw a man — or was it a boy? — with a pack, standing by the gas pump probably waiting to catch a ride; she wouldn't pick him up, that was certain. These hills were certainly forsaken.

She went in at the door marked Ladies. The tiny cubicle comforted her. She opened her vanity case and took out some tissue, made little pads and put them over her eyes. But still all she could see were those terrifying great mounds of the earth and the sun thrusting down like arrows. What a ghastly country! Why hadn't someone told her? It was barbarous of the automobile club to let her come through this country. She couldn't think of one tribe of Indians.

She really felt a kind of fright and stayed there a long time, and then she got a fright for fear she had left her keys in the car, and with that boy out there — she could see his sharp piercing glance out of his brown face — and she had to go pouncing all through her bag, and at last she found them, of all places, in her coin purse and she always put them into the breast pocket of her suit. She did think people were nuisances who had to go looking in all their pockets for keys. Habit was an excellent thing and saved nobody knew how much time.

But at last she drew a deep breath, opened the door onto the vast terrible bright needles of light, and there she saw through the heavy down-pouring curtain the boy still standing there exactly as he had been standing before, half leaning, looking from under his black brows. He looked like a dark stroke in the terrible light, and he seemed to be still looking at her. She fumbled the collar at her throat, brushed off the front of her skirt, and went into the lunch room.

"My, it's certainly hot," she said to the thin man behind the counter. She felt strange hearing her voice issue from her.

"It is," said the proprietor, "but a little cooler in here." He was a thin, shrewd man.

She sat down in the booth. "Yes," she said, and saw that the boy had followed her in and sat down on the stool at the lunch counter, but he seemed to be still looking at her. He looked as if he had been roasted, slowly turned on a spit until he seemed glowing, like phosphorus, as if the sun were in him, and his black eyes were a little bloodshot as if the whites had been burned, and his broad chest fell down easily to his hips as he ground out a cigarette with his heel. The thin man brought her a glass of water. "What will you have, ma'am?" he said with respect. "I'll have a lettuce sandwich," she said. "I'm afraid we ain't got any proper lettuce ma'am," he said bowing a little. "We can't get it fresh out here. We have peanut butter, sliced tongue. . ." "All right," she said quickly, "peanut butter and, well, a glass of beer." She felt that the boy was somehow laughing at her. She felt angry.

"This the first time you been in these parts?" called out the thin man from behind the counter. "Yes," she said, and her own voice sounded small to her. "It is." The boy at the counter turned his head, still with it lowered, so that his eyes looked up at her even though she was sitting down in the booth, and a soft charge went through her, frightening. She felt herself bridling, and she said in a loud, cool voice: "This is a very interesting country. Do you know anything about the formation of these curious rocks that jut out of the hills? They are so bare and then suddenly this rock —"

Was she imagining it only, that the boy seemed to smile and shift his weight?

"No'm," said the thin man, drawing the beer, "I can't say I ever thought about it." She felt as if something passed between the two men, and it made her angry, as if they were subtly laughing at her. "I know it's hard to grow anything here, unless you got a deep well," he said.

"Oh, I can imagine," she sang out too loud; she felt her voice ringing like metal. The boy seemed not to be touched by what she was saying, but he attended curiously to every word, standing silent but alert like a horse standing at a fence waiting for something. So she began to tell the lunch room proprietor the history of the country, and he seemed amazed but not impressed. It made her feel vindicated somehow. Still the boy drooped alert on the stool, his half face turned toward her, his huge burned ear springing from his head. She stayed half an hour and so cut her time still further, but she felt much better and thought she would make up for it. She got up and paid her bill. "I'll send you a book about the Indians," she said to the thin man.

He smiled, "That will be very nice," he said. "Thank you, I'm sure," and the two men looked at each other again, and she was amazed at the anger that gushed like a sudden fountain in her breast. She sailed out and got into the car. The thin man came after her. "Oh, by the way," he said, "the lad in there has had an awful time this morning catching a ride. He's got to get up the bridge, about fifty miles." She felt they were putting something over on her. "I'll vouch for him," the thin man said. "He lives here, and I know his folks now for eighteen years. He's been to the harvest fields, and it would be something for him to ride with an educated lady like you," he added cunningly. The boy came out and was smiling at her now very eagerly. "Now they want something," she thought and was suddenly amazed to find out that she despised men and always had.

"I don't like to drive with a strange man," she said, stubborn.

"Oh, this boy is harmless," the thin man said, and that look passed between the two of them again. "I can vouch for him—good as gold his family is. I thought maybe anyhow you might give a mite of education on the way." A pure glint of malice came into the thin man's eyes that frightened her. He hates me, too, she thought. Men like that hate women with brains.

"All right," she said, "get in."

"Get right in there," the thin man said. "It's only a piece."

The boy rose towards her, and she drew away, and he sat down in a great odor of milk and hay, right beside her, stifling. Without speaking she threw the car in, and they plunged up the bald brow of the hill and began to climb slowly. The sun was in the central sky, and the heat fell vertically. She wouldn't look at him and wished she could get out her handkerchief—such a nauseating odor of sweat and something like buttermilk. She couldn't help but be conscious of the side of his overall leg beside her and his big shoes, and she felt he never took his eyes off her, like some awful bird—and that curious little smile on his mouth as if he knew something about her that she didn't know herself. She knew without looking that he was bending his head towards her with that curious awful little glimmer of a smile.

He said in a soft cajoling voice, "It's pretty hot, and it's nice of you to take me. I had a hard time."

It disarmed her. She felt sorry for him, wanting to be helpful. She always wanted to help men, do something for them, and then really underneath she could hate them. "Oh," she said, "that was all right. You know one hates to pick up just anyone."

"Sure enough," he said. "I heard in Colorado a fellow got killed."

"Yes," she said, but she was on her guard. His words seemed to mean nothing to him. He was like the heat, in a drowse. "My, you must have been in the sun," she said.

"Yes," he said, "I've been as far as Kansas—looking for work."

"The conditions are pretty bad," she said.

"There ain't no work," he said simply.

"Oh," she said, "that's too bad," and felt awkward and inane. He seemed in such a sun-warmed ease, his legs stretching down. He had his coat in his arms and his shirt sleeves were torn off, showing his huge roasted arms. She could see the huge turn of the muscles of his arms, out of the corner of her eye.

They went climbing in gear up that naked mountain, and it began to affect her curiously. The earth seemed to turn on the bone rich and shining, the great mounds burning in the sun, the great golden body, hard and robust, and the sun striking hot and dazzling.

"These mountains," she began to tell him, "are thousands of years old."

"Yeah," he said looking at her sharply, "I'll bet." He lounged down beside her. "I'm sleepy," he said. "I slept on a bench in L. A. las' night." She felt he was moving slowly towards her as if about to touch her leg. She sat as far over as she could, but she felt him looking at her, taking something for granted.

"Yes," she said, "it would be an interesting study, these mountains."

He didn't answer and threw her into confusion. He lounged down, looking up at her. She drew her skirt sharply down over her leg. Something became very alert in her, and she could tell what he was doing without looking at him.

They didn't stop again. The country looked the same every minute. They rose on that vast naked curve into the blue blue sky, and dropped into the crevasse and rose again on the same curve. Lines and angles, and bare earth curves, tawny and rolling in the heat. She thought she was going a little mad and longed to see a tree or a house.

"I could go on to San Francisco with you," he said and she could feel her heart suddenly in her.

"Why would you do that?" she said drawing away, one hand at her throat.

"Why shouldn't I?" he said insolently. "It would be kind of nice for both of us," he was smiling that insolent knowing smile. She didn't know how to answer. If she took him seriously it would implicate her, and if she didn't it might also. "It would be kind of nice now, wouldn't it?" he said again with his curious soft imprudence. "Wouldn't it?"

"Why, of course, I'm going to San Francisco anyway," she said evasively.

"Oh, sure," he said, "I know that. But it isn't so hot going alone. And we get along, don't we?" He didn't move, but his voice drove into her.

"Why, I don't know," she said coldly, "I'm only taking you to the bridge."

He gave a little grunt and put his cap on his head, pulling the beak over his eyes which only concentrated his awful power. She pulled her blouse up over her shoulders. She had never noticed before that it fell so low in front. She felt terribly. And to her horror he went on talking to her softly.

"You wouldn't kid me, would you? You know I like you. I like you, You're pretty."

She couldn't say a word. She felt her throat beating. He was making love to her just as if she was any common slut. She felt her throat beating and swelling.

He kept on his soft drowsy talk, "The times is sure hard." His words seemed to be very tiny falling from the enormous glow of his presence, wonderful, as if he had been turned naked, roasted in the sun. You could smell his sunburnt flesh. And you could smell the earth turning on its spit under the mighty sun. If only he were not so near; the car threw them close together, and she tried to go easy around the curves so that his big body would not lounge down upon her like a mountain. She couldn't remember when she had been so close to a man. It was as frightening as some great earth cataclysm. She prided herself on knowing men. She was their equal in every way, she knew that.

If only she could see something familiar, then she could get back her normal feelings about men. She felt as if she were in a nightmare.

"I worked when I was twenty," he went on softly. "Made good money, blew it in on Saturday night. Made big money when I was twenty—Jesus, I've got something to look forward to, haven't I."

She sat over as far as she could. "Where did you work?" she managed to say. She prided herself on always getting information about people. They talked about Roosevelt and the New Deal. She always had strong views, but for the first time in her life she felt as if what she was saying was no good, like talking when some gigantic happening is silently going on. She didn't know what was happening, but she felt that every moment he won, was slowly overcoming her, and that her talk gave him a chance silently to overcome her. She was frightened as if they were about to crack up in a fearful accident. She relaxed on the seat, and the heat stroked down her body. She wished she wasn't driving a car. The great body of the earth seemed to touch her, and she began looking where the shadows were beginning to stroke down the sides of the mounds as if she might sleep there for a little while. An awful desire to sleep drugged her, as if she hadn't slept for years and years. She felt warm and furred and dangerously drugged.

It was as if a little rocket exploded in front of her face when he said, "Let's don't talk about that," and he leaned closer than he had. "Let's talk about you." She could see suddenly his whole face thrust to her, the gleaming strong teeth, the roasted young cheeks, and he had long single whiskers growing out like a mandarin. She laughed a little. "Who do you think I am?" she asked nervously. "Why, I guess you're a pretty good-looking girl," he said. "You look pretty good to me." She bridled at this common language, as if she were nothing but any girl you pick up anywhere.

"Why, I'm a schoolteacher," she cried.

He didn't seem surprised. "O.K.," he said, laughing into her face.

"Why, I could almost be your mother," she cried.

"Aw, that's a new one," he said, and he put his great hand straight on her arm. "Never heard of a girl wanting to make out she was old before."

She had an awful desire to make him say more; she was frightened. Swift thoughts, habitual thoughts, came into her head, and they seemed like frail things that the heat pounded down. Was it because they were so far out in these strange, rising, mounded hills?

"Are those cigarettes?" he said, pointing to the pocket beside her. "Let's stop and have a smoke."

"Oh, no," she cried, "I haven't time. I'm behind now. I've got to make up a lot of time."

"O.K.," he said. "We can smoke here."

"All right," she said, handing him the package. "You keep the package."

"All right," he said and took one out and put the package into his pocket.

The sun moved to her side and fell on her shoulder and breast and arm. It was as if all her blood sprang warm out of her. The sun moved slowly and fell along her whole side.

"Oh," he said, "I know you like me."

"How do you know?" she said offended, trying to see the road. She felt fatuous indulging in this adolescent conversation. She let her skirt slip up a little. She knew she had good legs, tapering down swiftly to her ankles. But he didn't seem actually to be looking at her; a heat came out of his great lax body and enveloped her. He seemed warmly to include her, close to himself.

"What kind of a wheel is that?" he said and put his large thick hand beside her own small one on the wheel. "Oh, it turns easy," he said. "I haven't driven a car since I left home. A good car is a pretty sweet thing," he said, and leaned over and began to fondle the gadgets on the front, and she looked fascinated at his huge wrist joint covered with golden hair bleached in the sun. She had to look and saw that his hair was black on his skull but also burnt around the edges. Looking at him she met his gaze and felt her face flush.

They fell down the valley, yellow as a dream. The hills lifted themselves out on the edge of the light. The great animal flesh jointed mountains wrought a craving in her. There was not a tree, not a growth, just the bare swelling rondures of the mountains, the yellow hot swells, as if they were lifting and being driven through an ossified torrent.

The Tehachapis rolled before them, with only their sharp primeval glint, warm and fierce. They didn't say anything about that in the books. She felt suddenly as if she had missed everything. She should say something more to her classes. Suppose she should say—The Tehachapi Mountains have warmed and bloomed for a thousand years. After all, why not? This was the true information.

She stopped the car. She turned and looked directly at him. "What is your name?" she asked.

Puzzled, he leaned towards her, that tender warm glint on his face. "Thom Beason," he said. The hot light seemed to fall around them like rain.

"Listen," he said gripping her hands, twisting them a little, "let's get out. Wouldn't it be swell to lie down over there in the hills. Look there's a shadow just over there. It's cool in those shadows if you dig down a little."

She saw his wrists, his giant breast, his knees, and behind him the tawny form and heat of the great earth woman, basking yellow and plump in the sun, her cliffs, her joints gleaming yellow rock, her ribs, her sides warm and full. The rocks that skirted the road glistened like bone, a sheer precipice and dazzle of rock, frightening and splendid, like the sheer precipice of his breast looming towards her so that she could feel the heat come from him and envelop her like fire, and she felt she was falling swiftly down the sides of him, and for the first time in her life she felt the sheer sides of her own body dropping swift and fleet down to her dreaming feet, and an ache, like lightning piercing stone, struck into her between the breasts.

She let her head fall over their hands and pulled back from him in hard resistance. She could not go to his breast that welcomed her. All my delicacy, my purity, she thought. He will not see me. I must not change. I must not change. The tears came to her eyes, and at the same time a canker of self-loathing, terrible, festered in her.

The moment had passed. He withdrew from her. "O.K.," he said. "You don't need to be scared. Only if you wanted to. O.K. Let's go. You can make up your time. We're only about a half-hour from the bridge where I blow."

She began driving very fast, very well. He withdrew completely from her, just waiting to get out. It hurt her, as if there had been before some sumptuous feast she had been unable to partake of, the lush passional day, the wheaty boy, some wonderful, wonderful fruit.

"I'll swan," he said. "There's old Magill going with a load of melons. Hi!" he shouted.

She wished he was gone already. She wildly began thinking what she could say to him. She thought she would say, casually—Well, good luck. She felt easier knowing what she was going to say. She stopped the car. He got out and stood by the car. She wanted to do something for him. She really would have liked to give him something. She thought she would buy him a melon. "How much are they?" she said nodding towards the melons and hunting for her pocketbook. He ran over. "You pick out a good one," she called after him.

He came back with a large one with yellow crevasses. His strong talons curved around it, and he kept pressing it, leaving a dent which swelled out after his fingers. He held up the great melon with its half-moon partitions, grading golden towards the sun. She fumbled with her purse to pay for it, and suddenly she saw that he was holding it towards her, that he was giving it to her, and she was ashamed and held the quarter she had taken out, in her hand. He was smiling at her as if he felt sad for her. She smiled foolishly and sat pressing her wet hands together.

"Well, good-bye," he said. "And good luck."

"Good-bye," she said. Now she could not say good luck. He had beat her to it. Why should he wish her good luck when she had it?

He turned and ran towards the wagon, climbed in and did not look back. She drove around the curve, stopped, turned down the mirror and looked at her face. She felt like a stick and looked like a witch. Now she was safe—safe. She would never, never change, pure and inviolate forever; and she began to cry.

After five minutes she saw a car rounding the mountain to her right. It would pass her soon. She got out her whisk broom, brushed her suit, brushed off the seat where he had sat, opened the back window to air out the smell of buttermilk and hay, started the car and drove to San Francisco because that was where she was going.

ANNUNCIATION[1]

For Rachel

Ever since I have known I was going to have a child I have kept writing things down on these little scraps of paper. There is something I want to say, something I want to make clear for myself and others. One lives all one's life in a sort of way, one is alive and that is about all that there is to say about it. Then something happens.

There is the pear tree I can see in the afternoons as I sit on this porch writing these notes. It stands for something. It has had something to do with what has happened to me. I sit here all afternoon in the autumn sun and then I begin to write something on this yellow paper; something seems to be going on like a buzzing, a flying and circling within me, and then I want to write it down in some way. I have never felt this way before, except when I was a girl and was first in love and wanted then to set things down on paper so that they would not be lost. It is something perhaps like a farmer who hears the swarming of a host of bees and goes out to catch them so that he will have honey. If he does not go out right away, they will go, and he will hear the buzzing growing more distant in the afternoon.

My sweater pocket is full of scraps of paper on which I have written. I sit here many afternoons while Karl is out looking for work, writing on pieces of paper, unfolding, reading what I have already written.

We have been here two weeks at Mrs. Mason's boarding house. The leaves are falling and there is a golden haze over everything. This is the fourth month for me and it is fall. A rich powerful haze comes down from the mountains over the city. In the afternoon I go out for a walk. There is a park just two blocks from here. Old men and tramps lie on the grass all day. It is hard to get work. Many people beside Karl are out of work. People are hungry just as I am hungry. People are ready to flower and they cannot. In the evenings we go there with a sack of old fruit we can get at the stand across the way quite cheap, bunches of grapes and old pears. At noon there is a hush in the air and at evening there are stirrings of wind coming from the sky, blowing in the fallen leaves, or perhaps there is a light rain, falling quickly on the walk. Early in the mornings the sun comes up hot in the sky and shines all day through the mist. It is strange, I notice all these things, the sun, the rain falling, the blowing of the wind. It is as if they had a meaning for me as the pear tree has come to have.

In front of Mrs. Mason's house there is a large magnolia tree with its blossoms yellow, hanging over the steps almost within reach. Its giant leaves are mo-

---

[1] The angel Gabriel's announcement to Mary that she is to give birth to the son of God (Luke 1:26–38).

tionless and shining in the heat, occasionally as I am going down the steps towards the park one falls heavily on the walk.

This house is an old wooden one, that once was quite a mansion I imagine.
There are glass chandeliers in the hall and fancy tile in the bathrooms. It was
owned by the rich once and now the dispossessed live in it with the rats. We
have a room three flights up. You go into the dark hallway and up the stairs.
Broken settees and couches sit in the halls. About one o'clock the girls come
down stairs to get their mail and sit on the front porch. The blinds go up in the
old wooden house across the street. It is always quite hot at noon.

Next to our room lies a sick woman in what is really a kind of closet with
no windows. As you pass you see her face on the pillow and a nauseating odor of
sickness comes out the door. I haven't asked her what is the matter with her but
everyone knows she is waiting for death. Somehow it is not easy to speak to her.
No one comes to see her. She has been a housemaid all her life tending other
people's children; now no one comes to see her. She gets up sometimes and
drinks a little from the bottle of milk that is always sitting by her bed covered
with flies.

Mrs. Mason, the landlady, is letting us stay although we have only paid a
week's rent and have been here over a week without paying. But it is a bad season and we may be able to pay later. It is better perhaps for her than having an
empty room. But I hate to go out and have to pass her door and I am always
fearful of meeting her on the stairs. I go down as quietly as I can but it isn't easy,
for the stairs creak frightfully.

The room we have on the top floor is a back room, opening out onto an old
porch which seems to be actually tied to the wall of the house with bits of wire
and rope. The floor of it slants downward to a rickety railing. There is a box
perched on the railing that has geraniums in it. They are large, tough California
geraniums. I guess nothing can kill them. I water them since I have been here
and a terribly red flower has come. It is on this porch I am sitting. Just over the
banisters stand the top branches of a pear tree.

Many afternoons I sit here. It has become a kind of alive place to me. The
room is dark behind me, with only the huge walnut tree scraping against the one
window over the kitchenette. If I go to the railing and look down I can see far below the back yard which has been made into a garden with two fruit trees and I
can see where a path has gone in the summer between a small bed of flowers,
now only dead stalks. The ground is bare under the walnut tree where little sun
penetrates. There is a dog kennel by the round trunk but there doesn't ever seem
to be a dog. An old wicker chair sits outdoors in rain or shine. A woman in an
old wrapper comes out and sits there almost every afternoon. I don't know who
she is, for I don't know anybody in this house, having to sneak downstairs as I do.

Karl says I am foolish to be afraid of the landlady. He comes home drunk
and makes a lot of noise. He said she's lucky in these times to have anybody in
her house, but I notice in the mornings he goes down the stairs quietly and often goes out the back way.

I'm alone all day so I sit on this rickety porch. Straight out from the rail so that I can almost touch it is the radiating frail top of the pear tree that has opened a door for me. If the pears were still hanging on it each would be alone and separate with a kind of bloom upon it. Such a bloom is upon me at this moment. Is it possible that everyone, Mrs. Mason who runs this boarding house, the woman next door, the girls downstairs, all in this dead wooden house have hung at one time, each separate in a mist and bloom upon some invisible tree? I wonder if it is so.

I am in luck to have this high porch to sit on and this tree swaying before me through the long afternoons and the long nights. Before we came here, after the show broke up in S.F.[2] we were in an old hotel, a foul smelling place with a dirty chambermaid and an old cat in the halls, and night and day we could hear the radio going in the office. We had a room with a window looking across a narrow way into another room where a lean man stood in the mornings looking across, shaving his evil face. By leaning out and looking up I could see straight up the sides of the tall building and above the smoky sky.

Most of the time I was sick from the bad food we ate. Karl and I walked the streets looking for work. Sometimes I was too sick to go. Karl would come in and there would be no money at all. He would go out again to perhaps borrow something. I know many times he begged although we never spoke of it, but I could tell by the way he looked when he came back with a begged quarter. He went in with a man selling Mexican beans but he didn't make much. I lay on the bed bad days feeling sick and hungry, sick too with the stale odor of the foul walls. I would lie there a long time listening to the clang of the city outside. I would feel thick with this child. For some reason I remember that I would sing to myself and often became happy as if mesmerised there in the foul room. It must have been because of this child. Karl would come back perhaps with a little money and we would go out to a dairy lunch[3] and there have food I could not relish. The first alleyway I must give it up with the people all looking at me.

Karl would be angry. He would walk on down the street so people wouldn't think he was with me. Once we walked until evening down by the docks. "Why don't you take something?" he kept saying. "Then you wouldn't throw up your food like that. Get rid of it. That's what everybody does nowadays. This isn't the time to have a child. Everything is rotten. We must change it." He kept on saying, "Get rid of it. Take something why don't you?" And he got angry when I didn't say anything but just walked along beside him. He shouted too loud at me that some stevedores loading a boat for L.A. laughed at us and began kidding us, thinking perhaps we were lovers having a quarrel.

Some time later, I don't know how long it was, for I hadn't any time except the nine months I was counting off, but one evening Karl sold enough Mexican jumping beans at a carnival to pay our fare, so we got on a river boat and went

[2] San Francisco.

[3] In Jewish dietary custom, a meal containing only fish and dairy products.

up the river to a delta town. There might be a better chance of a job. On this boat you can sit up all night if you have no money to buy a berth. We walked all evening along the deck and then when it got cold we went into the saloon because we had pawned our coats. Already at that time I had got the habit of carrying slips of paper around with me and writing on them, as I am doing now. I had a feeling then that something was happening to me of some kind of loveliness I would want to preserve in some way. Perhaps that was it. At any rate I was writing things down. Perhaps it had something to do with Karl wanting me all the time to take something. "Everybody does it," he kept telling me. "It's nothing, then it's all over." I stopped talking to him much. Everything I said only made him angry. So writing was a kind of conversation I carried on with myself and with the child.

Well, on the river boat that night after we had gone into the saloon to get out of the cold, Karl went to sleep right away in a chair. But I couldn't sleep. I sat watching him. The only sound was the churning of the paddle wheel and the lap of the water. I had on then this sweater and the notes I wrote are still in the breast pocket. I would look up from writing and see Karl sleeping like a young boy.

"Tonight, the world into which you are coming" — then I was speaking to the invisible child — "is very strange and beautiful. That is, the natural world is beautiful. I don't know what you will think of man, but the dark glisten of vegetation and the blowing of the fertile land wind and the delicate strong step of the sea wind, these things are familiar to me and will be familiar to you. I hope you will be like these things. I hope you will glisten with the glisten of ancient life, the same beauty that is in a leaf or a wild rabbit, wild sweet beauty of limb and eye. I am going on a boat between dark shores, and the river and the sky are so quiet that I can hear the scurryings of tiny animals on the shores and their little breathings seem to be all around. I think of them, wild, carrying their young now, crouched in the dark underbrush with the fruit-scented land wind in their delicate nostrils, and they are looking out at the moon and the fast clouds. Silent, alive, they sit in the dark shadow of the greedy world. There is something wild about us too, something tender and wild about my having you as a child, about your crouching so secretly here. There is something very tender and wild about it. We, too, are at the mercy of many hunters. On this boat I act like the other human beings, for I do not show that I have you, but really I know we are as helpless, as wild, as at bay as some tender wild animals who might be on the ship.

"I put my hand where you lie so silently. I hope you will come glistening with life power, with it shining upon you as upon the feathers of birds. I hope you will be a warrior and fierce for change, so all can live."

Karl woke at dawn and was angry with me for sitting there looking at him. Just to look at me makes him angry now. He took me out and made me walk along the deck although it was hardly light yet. I gave him the "willies" he said, looking at him like that. We walked round and round the decks and he kept talking to me in a low voice, trying to persuade me. It was hard for me to listen. My teeth were chattering with cold, but anyway I found it hard to listen to anyone talking, especially Karl. I remember I kept thinking to myself that a child should be made by machinery now, then there would be no fuss. I kept thinking of all the places I had been with this new child, traveling with the show from Tia Juana to S. F. In trains, over mountains, through deserts, in hotels and rooming houses, and myself in a trance of wonder. There wasn't a person I could have told it to, that I was going to have a child. I didn't want to be pitied. Night after night we played in the tent and the faces were all dust to me, but traveling, through the window the many vistas of the earth meant something—the bony skeleton of the mountains, like the skeleton of the world jutting through its flowery flesh. My child too would be made of bone. There were the fields of summer, the orchards fruiting, the berry fields and the pickers stooping, the oranges and the grapes. Then the city again in September and the many streets I walk looking for work, stopping secretly in doorways to feel beneath my coat.

It is better in this small town with the windy fall days and the sudden rain falling out of a sunny sky. I can't look for work any more. Karl gets a little work washing dishes at a wienie place.[4] I sit here on the porch as if in a deep sleep waiting for this unknown child. I keep hearing this far flight of strange birds going on in the mysterious air about me. This time has come without warning. How can it be explained? Everything is dead and closed, the world a stone, and then suddenly everything comes alive as it has for me, like an anemone on a rock, opening itself, disclosing itself, and the very stones themselves break open like bread. It has all got something to do with the pear tree too. It has come about some way as I have sat here with this child so many afternoons, with the pear tree murmuring in the air.

The pears are all gone from the tree but I imagine them hanging there, ripe curves within the many scimitar leaves, and within them many pears of the coming season. I feel like a pear. I hang secret within the curling leaves, just as the pear would be hanging on its tree. It seems possible to me that perhaps all people at some time feel this, round and full. You can tell by looking at most people that the world remains a stone to them and a closed door. I'm afraid it will become like that to me again. Perhaps after this child is born, then everything will harden and become small and mean again as it was before. Perhaps I would even have a hard time remembering this time at all and it wouldn't seem wonderful. That is why I would like to write it down.

How can it be explained? Suddenly many movements are going on within me, many things are happening, there is an almost unbearable sense of sprouting, of bursting encasements, of moving kernels, expanding flesh. Perhaps it is such an activity that makes a field come alive with millions of sprouting shoots of corn or wheat. Perhaps it is something like that that makes a new world.

---

[4] Hotdog stand.

I have been sitting here and it seems as if the wooden houses around me had become husks that suddenly as I watched began to swarm with livening seed. The house across becomes a fermenting seed alive with its own movements. Everything seems to be moving along a curve of creation. The alley below and all the houses are to me like an orchard abloom, shaking and trembling, moving outward with shouting. The people coming and going seem to hang on the tree of life, each blossoming from himself. I am standing here looking at the blind windows of the house next door and suddenly the walls fall away, the doors open, and within I see a young girl making a bed from which she had just risen having dreamed of a young man who became her lover . . . she stands before her looking-glass in love with herself.

I see in another room a young man sleeping, his bare arm thrown over his head. I see a woman lying on a bed after her husband has left her. There is a child looking at me. An old woman sits rocking. A boy leans over a table reading a book. A woman who has been nursing a child comes out and hangs clothes on the line, her dress in front wet with milk. A young woman comes to an open door looking up and down the street waiting for her young husband. I get up early to see this woman come to the door in a pink wrapper and wave to her husband. They have only been married a short time, she stands waving until he is out of sight and even then she stands smiling to herself, her hand upraised.

Why should I be excited? Why should I feel this excitement, seeing a woman waving to her young husband, or a woman who has been nursing a child, or a young man sleeping? Yet I am excited. The many houses have become like an orchard blooming soundlessly. The many people have become like fruits to me, the young girl in the room alone before her mirror, the young man sleeping, the mother, all are shaking with their inward blossoming, shaken by the windy blooming, moving along a future curve.

I do not want it all to go away from me. Now many doors are opening and shutting, light is falling upon darkness, closed places are opening, still things are now moving. But there will come a time when the doors will close again, the shouting will be gone, the sprouting and the movement and the wondrous opening out of everything will be gone. I will be only myself. I will come to look like the women in this house. I try to write it down on little slips of paper, trying to preserve this time for myself so that afterwards when everything is the same again I can remember what all must have.

This is the spring there should be in the world, so I say to myself, "Lie in the sun with the child in your flesh shining like a jewel. Dream and sing, pagan, wise in your vitals. Stand still like a fat budding tree, like a stalk of corn athrob and aglisten in the heat. Lie like a mare panting with the dancing feet of colts against her sides. Sleep at night as the spring earth. Walk heavily as a wheat stalk at its full time bending towards the earth waiting for the reaper. Let your life swell downward so you become like a vase, a vessel. Let the unknown child knock and knock against you and rise like a dolphin within."

I look at myself in the mirror. My legs and head hardly make a difference, just a stem my legs. My hips are full and tight in back as if bracing themselves. I look like a pale and shining pomegranate, hard and tight, and my skin shines like crystal with the veins showing beneath blue and distended. Children are playing outside and girls are walking with young men along the walk. All that seems over for me. I am a pomegranate hanging from an invisible tree with the juice and movement of seed within my hard skin. I dress slowly. I hate the smell of clothes. I want to leave them off and just hang in the sun ripening . . . ripening.

It is hard to write it down so that it will mean anything. I've never heard anything about how a woman feels who is going to have a child, or about how a pear tree feels bearing its fruit. I would like to read these things many years from now, when I am barren and no longer trembling like this, when I get like the women in this house; or like the woman in the closed room, I can hear her breathing through the afternoon.

When Karl has no money he does not come back at night. I go out on the street walking to forget how hungry I am. This is an old town and along the streets are many old strong trees. Night leaves hang from them ready to fall, dark and swollen with their coming death. Trees, dark, separate, heavy with their down hanging leaves, cool surfaces hanging on the dark. I put my hand among the leaf sheaves. They strike with a cool surface, their glossy surfaces surprising me in the dark. I feel like a tree swirling upwards too, muscular sap alive, with rich surfaces hanging from me, flaring outward rocket-like and falling to my roots, a rich strong power in me to break through into a new life. And dark in me as I walk the streets of this decayed town are the buds of my child. I walk alone under the dark flaring trees. There are many houses with the lights shining out but you and I walk on the skirts of the lawns amidst the downpouring darkness. Houses are not for us. For us many kinds of hunger, for us a deep rebellion.

Trees come from a far seed walking the wind, my child too from a far seed blowing from last year's rich and revolutionary dead. My child budding secretly from far walking seed, budding secretly and dangerously in the night.

The woman has come out and sits in the rocker, reading, her fat legs crossed. She scratches herself, cleans her nails, picks her teeth. Across the alley lying flat on the ground is a garage. People are driving in and out. But up here it is very quiet and the movement of the pear tree is the only movement and I seem to hear its delicate sound of living as it moves upon itself silently, and outward and upward.

The leaves twirl and twirl all over the tree, the delicately curving tinkling leaves. They twirl and twirl on the tree and the tree moves far inward upon its stem, moves in an invisible wind, gently swaying. Far below straight down the vertical stem like a stream, black and strong into the ground, runs the trunk; and invisible, spiraling downward and outwards in powerful radiation, lie the roots. I can see it spiraling upwards from below, its stem straight, and from it, spiraling the branches season by season, and from the spiraling branches moving out in quick motion, the forked stems, and from the stems twirling fragilely the tinier stems holding outward until they fall, the half curled pear leaves.

Far below lies the yard, lying flat and black beneath the body of the up-shooting tree, for the pear tree from above looks as if it had been shot instanta-neously from the ground, shot upward like a rocket to break in showers of leaves and fruits twirling and falling. Its movement looks quick, sudden and rocketing. My child when grown can be looked at in this way as if it suddenly existed . . . but I know the slow time of making. The pear tree knows.

Far inside the vertical stem there must be a movement, a river of sap rising from below and radiating outward in many directions clear to the tips of the leaves. The leaves are the lips of the tree speaking in the wind or they move like many tongues. The fruit of the tree you can see has been a round speech, speak-ing in full tongue on the tree, hanging in ripe body, the fat curves hung within the small curves of the leaves. I imagine them there. The tree has shot up like a rocket, then stops in midair and its leaves flow out gently and its fruit curves roundly and gently in a long slow curve. All is gentle on the pear tree after its strong upward shooting movement.

I sit here all the afternoon as if in its branches, midst the gentle and curving body of the tree. I have looked at it until it has become more familiar to me than Karl. It seems a strange thing that a tree might come to mean more to one than one's husband. It seems a shameful thing even. I am ashamed to think of it but it is so. I have sat here in the pale sun and the tree has spoken to me with its many tongued leaves, speaking through the afternoon of how to round a fruit. And I listen through the slow hours. I listen to the whisperings of the pear tree, speaking to me, speaking to me. How can I describe what is said by a pear tree? Karl did not speak to me so. No one spoke to me in any good speech.

There is a woman coming up the stairs, slowly. I can hear her breathing. I can hear her behind me at the screen door.

She came out and spoke to me. I know why she was looking at me so closely. "I hear you're going to have a child," she said. "It's too bad." She is the same color as the dead leaves in the park. Was she once alive too?

I am writing on a piece of wrapping paper now. It is about ten o'clock. Karl didn't come home and I had no supper. I walked through the streets with their heavy, heavy trees bending over the walks and the lights shining from the houses and over the river the mist rising.

Before I came into this room I went out and saw the pear tree standing mo-tionless, its leaves curled in the dark, its radiating body falling darkly, like a stream far below into the earth.

Stevie Smith 1902–1971

Because of her relatively small size, Florence Margaret Smith was nicknamed "Stevie," after the jockey Steve Donoghue. Described as "one of the absolute originals of English literature," she first published as a novelist: *Novel on Yellow Paper* appeared in 1936, with two other novels and nine collections of poetry to follow. Her own sketches often accompany her poems. Despite her unique voice, Smith's is also an educated poetry, echoing Blake, T. S. Eliot, Yeats, and others, her tone often lambasting their self-importance and high seriousness. Smith's stylistic technique varies from traditional verse forms to the experimental. Her work often reveals an obsession with darkness (death, for instance) cloaked in wry, almost ironic humor.

NOT WAVING BUT DROWNING

Nobody heard him, the dead man,
But still he lay moaning:
I was much further out than you thought
And not waving but drowning.

Poor chap, he always loved larking   5
And now he's dead
It must have been too cold for him his heart gave way,
They said.

Oh, no no no, it was too cold always
(Still the dead one lay moaning)   10
I was much too far out all my life
And not waving but drowning.

THE NEW AGE

Shall I tell you the signs of a New Age coming?
It is a sound of drubbing and sobbing
Of people crying, We are old, we are old
And the sun is going down and becoming cold
Oh sinful and sad and the last of our kind   5
If we turn to God now do you think He will mind?

Then they fall on their knees and begin to whine
That the state of Art itself presages decline
As if Art has anything or ever had
To do with civilization whether good or bad.   10
Art is wild as a cat and quite separate from civilization
But that is another matter that is not now under consideration.
Oh these people are fools with their sighing and sinning
Why should Man be at an end? he is hardly beginning.
This New Age will slip in under cover of their cries   15
And be upon them before they have opened their eyes.
Well, say geological time is a one-foot rule
Then Man's only been here about half an inch to play the fool
Or be wise if he likes, as he often has been
Oh heavens how these crying people spoil the beautiful
    geological scene.   20

Sylvia Regan 1908–

B efore discovering her calling as a playwright, Sylvia Regan assumed a variety of roles in the theater. Besides working for the Theater Union in publicity and public relations, the native New Yorker and American Academy of Dramatic Arts student contributed costumes, choreography, and her acting abilities to Saturday night productions at Camp Tamamint, an adult resort that earned a reputation as a training ground for future headliners. In the summer of 1937, Regan was forced to leave her position upholstering seats in Orson Welles and John Houseman's Mercury Theater when she suffered a severe sunburn. During her recovery she created a dramatic script, *Everyday but Friday*, from a story told to her by a childhood friend. Regan went on to write *A Hundred Million Nickles, Morning Star, Safe Harbor, 44 West, The Twelfth Hour,* and *Zelda. The Fifth Season,* which chronicled the ups and downs of the garment industry, debuted in 1953 and ran 654 performances—her biggest commercial achievement. *Morning Star,* although not as commercially successful, has enjoyed a long career in stock, amateur, and off-Broadway productions for its quintessential portrayal of the American Jewish experience. A favorite of critics and renowned for its international appeal, it has played to packed houses throughout Europe, Israel, Australia, and South America.

MORNING STAR

Morning Star was produced for the first time by George Kondolf at the Longacre Theatre, New York, April 16, 1940, with the following cast:

Fanny
Becky Felderman
Aaron Greenspan
Esther
Hymie (*as a boy*)
Harry Engel
Sadie
Irving Tashman
Benjamin Brownstein
Myron Engel
Hymie (*as a young man*)
Pansy
Hymie Tashman

SYNOPSIS OF SCENES

The action takes place in Becky Felderman's home, on the lower East Side of New York.

ACT I

SCENE 1: A December afternoon, 1910.
SCENE 2: A month later.

ACT II

SCENE 1: Early morning, March 25th, 1911. (During this scene the curtain will be lowered twice to denote a passage of time.)
SCENE 2: Early April, six years later.
SCENE 3: Eighteen months later.

ACT III

Thirteen years later, November, 1931.

AUTHOR'S NOTE

Since the language of the play is rich in Jewish idiom and speech color, there is a danger of caricaturing the lines should the accent be used. Therefore, with the possible exception of Aaron's speech, it is suggested that no other accent be used throughout.

NOTE: The songs "We'll Bring the Rue de la Paix" and "Under a Painted Smile," by Abraham Ellstein and Robert Sour, are reprinted by permission of Sylvia Regan (Mrs. Abraham Ellstein).

ACT I

SCENE 1

Late afternoon in December, 1910. The scene is the combination living room-dining room of the Felderman household, on the lower East Side, New York. A door up L. leads to hall. Two doors at R. lead to bedrooms. Door L. leads to kitchen and door up L. to bathroom. There is a neatly curtained window up R., which faces on the street. An old leather couch stands downstage R. A round table C., several hideous straight-backed chairs and a heavy buffet at upstage wall. An old upright piano, the one note of luxury, stands down L. At the moment, a dressmaker's form stands in front of window. The fancy calendar of the type given away free by tradesmen, bric-a-brac, and other decoration may be left to the discretion of the director.

AT RISE: A general feeling of disorder. It is ironing day. A number of freshly ironed petticoats of the period, stiff with starch, stand around the room as though on legs, and take up all the available floor space between table and chairs.

ESTHER FELDERMAN is at ironing board. She is a frail girl, no more than sixteen. Enormous eyes set off her thin, fair-complexioned face. BECKY FELDERMAN, her mother, is at dressmaker's form, working on a much-flowered dress. BECKY is about thirty-seven, with a girlish alive quality.

FANNY FELDERMAN, her second daughter, is at piano, hammering out a tune with one finger. She is a little over seventeen, a dark, buxom peasant beauty, with a vivacious and excitable manner. AARON GREENSPAN, the boarder, a man of about forty, is stretched out on couch, sleeping the sleep of the dead, snoring occasionally. BECKY hums as she works.

FANNY *(Looking up. Good-naturedly.)* Mama, those aren't the words.
BECKY *(Singing off-key.)* Ta-ta-ta—ta-ta-ta— It's just like you sing it, no?
FANNY No, Mama. It goes like this— Ta-ta-ta-ta—ta-ta—

(BECKY joins in. By this time they are making a terrific racket.)

AARON *(Sits up.)* In Grand Central Station it's more quiet!
BECKY In Grand Central they take in boarders?
FANNY *(Of the song she has been playing.)* Is this new song beautiful! *(Laughing.)* In "Alma, Where Do You Live?" the man in the music store told me Kitty Gordon takes off all her clothes when she sings it!

BECKY Such a song you are singing?

FANNY Mama, please—don't get excited—

BECKY To ruin your life singing in the Apollo Nickelette every night—

FANNY If that's how you felt, why'd you have to go to the contest with me?

BECKY Because I didn't think you could win—

FANNY What!

BECKY To sing in a place where they throw on the actors eggs—

FANNY *(Cutting in hotly.)* On me they throw eggs? They *love* me—

BECKY Every night I am taking you from the theatre, a dozen bums standing by the back door. Even to me, an old woman, they are making "Hello, baby." That's *love*? That's *respect*?

FANNY *(As she starts to exit.)* You make me so nervous, I can't even practice! *(She is gone.)*

AARON Aye, Becky, Becky, you need a *man* in the house.

ESTHER *(Accidentally dropping the iron onto the board.)* Ouch!

BECKY You burned yourself?

AARON You can't wear it without pressing? Who sees it?

BECKY And if, God forbid, an accident, you get run down from a horse-car—they take you to the hospital, it looks nice the petticoat should be with wrinkles?

AARON The trouble is, Becky, you are a *pessimist*.

BECKY What?

AARON You can only see from everything the *bad* side!

ESTHER Mama is always making us feel good when *we* are seeing the bad side—

AARON All right! She is always seeing the *good* side! You are satisfied? So, if you'll excuse me!

(The picture of AARON *treading gingerly between the petticoats as he exits into bathroom is too much for* BECKY *and* ESTHER. *They start to laugh.)*

ESTHER *(Picking up the much-flowered dress.)* For what Mrs. Smith is paying, without seam binding would be good enough. In Sadie's shop they never sew a piece of seam binding.

BECKY What can you expect in ready-made? *(A clock strikes.)* Hymie is late from school—

ESTHER *(Hesitating.)* Mama, please, can I go with Sadie tomorrow?

BECKY Where?

ESTHER To the Triangle Shop.

BECKY Again you ask me? Esther—

ESTHER When Fanny was in the shop you didn't mind. Sadie, you don't mind. Only me—

BECKY You're too young.

ESTHER Mrs. O'Shaughnessy's Annie is only fifteen.

BECKY Mrs. O'Shaughnessy has also cockroaches in the sink!

ESTHER   Six, seven dollars a week—

BECKY   Esther, what did I tell you yesterday?

ESTHER   You told me "no"—

BECKY   And the day before?

ESTHER   "No" also—

BECKY   And this morning?

ESTHER   "No"—

BECKY   So?

ESTHER   *(Eagerly.)* So I can?

BECKY   No! *(BECKY gets up, starts to take away ironing board.)*

ESTHER   But, Mama, Sadie says to work gives a girl independence.

BECKY   What?

ESTHER   You have money in your pocket, you are the boss!

BECKY   The boss is not the boss? *You* are the boss?

ESTHER   Over yourself, Mama! You don't need to go to anybody for something! *(Inspired.)* You are free!

BECKY   *(Settling the matter.)* In America everybody is free! Something is on your mind, Esther. Mama can tell—

ESTHER   Mama, please—sometimes I would like to have a pair of lisle stockings! Not cotton—

BECKY   *(Smiling.)* That's all? So I'll buy you a pair of lisle stockings— *(Touching* ESTHER's *face, as though seeking the source of her apparent upset.)* Will that make you happier?

(BECKY exits into kitchen with ironing board. ESTHER looks after her a moment, then starts to gather petticoats together, placing one over the other on dressmaker's form. AARON enters. ESTHER looks away, embarrassed, but he calmly goes on pulling up his suspenders.)

ESTHER   Aaron, please, try to remember, *women* live in this house!

AARON   It's my fault conditions is crowded? I'm not exactly complaining, but a boarder has some rights, too! I pay my rent, no?

ESTHER   No!

AARON   *(Abashed.)* Well—it is my *intention* to pay! It's my fault I'm a millinery worker on straw and the season is late this year? A man can suddenly get hard up! *(ESTHER stares at him skeptically.)* If you have to know, little lady, right this minute, I could be in the millinery business for myself, a boss—if I wanted!

ESTHER   *(Still skeptical.)* It doesn't cost money to go into business?

AARON   Who says no? My friend Van Brett the blocker—*he* has the money. He begs me! With his thousand dollars and my brains, the sky is the limitation!

ESTHER   So what stops you?

AARON   Because I have a conscience! On one side of me, Van Brett! He says to me, "Become a boss, make a million. It's America—one, two, three."

ESTHER   Then why don't you do it?

AARON Because on the other side of me is my friend Brownstein the radical. He says to me, "Exploiter! On the backs of the workers you don't climb to success." Can I help it if I have a conscience? I'm completely confused.

ESTHER *(Impressed.)* Please don't tell Mama I said anything about—the rent. I apologize.

AARON *(Grandly.)* I accept— *(BECKY enters.)*

BECKY I didn't study the lesson for today—and Mr. Engel will be here any minute— *(She takes a book from buffet, starts to glance through it.)*

AARON The whole house English lessons! Does a woman have to vote for the President? What does she need citizna papers for?

BECKY My children and I should have a place in the world. To belong here.

AARON Listen, Becky, why should you bother with examinations, lessons? If you would listen to my proposition—after all—I'm a citizen and in America the law is—

BECKY You're starting up again?

AARON What's the use, Becky, you need a man in the house!

BECKY *(Playfully.)* So you live here, no?

AARON A boarder ain't the same thing? *(BECKY stares at him.)* All right! I'm not starting up again! But a man can put in a good word for himself?

BECKY You're not ashamed in front of the world—

ESTHER *(Giggling.)* Should I go into the kitchen, Mama?

AARON What I have to say to your mother, I'm not ashamed the world to hear! *(To BECKY, directly.)* Nu? *(BECKY laughs.)* You ever saw such a woman? Can you tell me please, one objection you could have to me? I'm an honest man, I don't drink, I don't gamble. Thank God, I make a good living— *(He breaks off, embarrassed by this obvious overstatement.)* When I'm working— *(Pause.)* Becky, say the word, I go into partnership with Van Brett, in no time I could dress you up in Hudson sealskin from head to toe! *(BECKY pays no attention.)* You are exactly my type.

BECKY Aaron, please—

AARON A beautiful woman like you—a woman full of life. To live out your days without a husband, ain't—ain't natural!

BECKY Aaron, please, once and for all—to me it's natural a woman should know her responsibility to her four children—

AARON Children! You can't fool me, Becky! It's Jacob. Jacob Felderman. A man is dead so many years, but in your heart he's lucky! He'll live forever! *(BECKY continues to read her book. A pause. AARON on couch dejectedly. Suddenly he jumps up, goes to door, puts on his overcoat and hat.)* Ask me where I'm going? *(He exits.)*

BECKY *(To ESTHER.)* So—where was I?

ESTHER You're on Columbus, Mama.

BECKY That's right—Columbus— *(Turning over pages.)* In 1492 Columbus discovered America. *(A knock at door. ESTHER remains at table, trying to contain her excitement. HARRY ENGEL enters. He is about twenty-three, a slender young man with a gentle scholarly manner.)* Hello, Mr. Engel. Come in—

428 Sylvia Regan 1908–

HARRY How do you do? And Miss Esther?

ESTHER Very, very fine, thank you—

BECKY I'm ashamed of myself. I didn't hardly study the lesson today. *(They get set-tled,* HARRY *and* BECKY *at table,* ESTHER *on couch where she follows his every movement. Occasionally he glances in her direction.* BECKY *puts on spectacles.)* This minute I was looking up when did Columbus discover America. Oy! *(Giggles.)* I forgot it already. Wait! Don't tell me—fourteen, fourteen is right, yes?

HARRY That's right. Fourteen what?

BECKY You have to give the exact *minute* when they ask you?

HARRY I think they'll want to know the year. Shall I tell you?

BECKY What can I do?

HARRY Mrs. Felderman, I'll tell you and when I do, you'll never forget it again. Listen—

"In fourteen hundred and ninety-two
Columbus sailed the ocean blue."

BECKY

"In fourteen hundred and ninety-two
Columbus sailed the ocean blue."

That's wonderful. I'll never forget it. *(Pause.)* I better write it down. *(Writing laboriously, she looks up.)* Mr. Engel, what do you think? Am I passing for my "citizna papers"?

HARRY It means a lot to you, doesn't it?

BECKY The world. *(She laughs.)* I could die laughing when I think how many times they caught us by the border. My Sadie used to say, "Mama, there is no America. It's only a dream in your head." But the dream came true. Mr. Engel, I could kiss George Washington's feet for chopping down the cherry tree, we should be free.

ESTHER *(Laughing.)* Mama, he chopped it down and didn't tell a lie.

BECKY Mr. Engel knows what I mean—

HARRY Now tell me, when was the Declaration of Independence signed?

BECKY July the fourth, 1776!

HARRY Good!

BECKY I should say it's good! In Russia when my brother Abraham used to say "Revolution," I laughed, but now I have different ideas—if a Revolution could make a country like this, maybe Abraham was right? *(*HARRY *looks doubtful.)* Was he?

HARRY *(With a smile.)* Not exactly, Mrs. Felderman. It's never war that makes a country great. It's the work of her people during peace times—

BECKY You explain things so good—please don't be mad on me, Mr Engel, but I have to thank you for what you're doing.

HARRY Mrs. Felderman, it's nothing—

BECKY Free lessons to Sadie and Esther and me is nothing?

HARRY I couldn't take money from you. It would be like taking it from my own family—

BECKY Yes?

HARRY *(Afraid he has said too much.)* It's good experience for me, too. I'm taking an examination myself in a few weeks. To teach school—

BECKY That's wonderful—

HARRY I think so. To me, it's the most important job in the whole world— *(With some enthusiasm.)* Matter of fact, I intend to specialize in American History.

BECKY Columbus and Lincoln?

HARRY That's right. *(Enthusiastically.)* Some day I expect to write a textbook for children. A new kind of history book that doesn't glorify "war"!

BECKY You're so smart, Mr. Engel. Your mother must be proud of you.

HARRY I have only my father. I think he's proud of me, but not to my face— *(HYMIE FELDERMAN enters. He is not quite thirteen—a thin kid with a sensitive face.)*

HYMIE *(Going directly to BECKY at table.)* Hello, Mama—

BECKY You're late from school!

HYMIE The teacher kept us— *(Hesitating.)* Mama, could you come now with me to the Rabbi, to get my speech?

BECKY My Hymie is being Bar Mitzvah next month, Mr. Engel. I would be very happy if you and your papa could come—

HARRY Thank you very much—

HYMIE Mama, could you come now?

BECKY Mr. Engel, would you please excuse me—I've been promising him for a week already—

HARRY Certainly—of course— *(Glancing toward ESTHER.)* We'll give Miss Esther a little more time for her lesson.

BECKY *(Putting on a shawl.)* Well, good-bye and thank you, Mr. Engel. I'll be back soon, Esther— *(Calling out.)* Fanny, get dressed!

HARRY And, Mrs. Felderman, WHEN did Columbus discover America?

BECKY *(Delightedly.)*

"In fourteen hundred and ninety-two
Columbus sailed the blue ocean."

(BECKY and HYMIE exit. The moment they are gone, HARRY and ESTHER quickly go toward one another. His manner changes from the pedantic school teacher of the moment before to a young boy in love. They are about to embrace, think better of it as ESTHER reminds him by gestures of FANNY's presence in next room. They stare at one another for a moment.)

HARRY Esther, darling—

ESTHER You were five minutes late—

HARRY I ran all the way from Canal Street. Can you meet me tonight? Delancey Park, near the fence, like yesterday?

ESTHER *(Giggling.)* Mama can't understand why I'm always wanting to go down for a walk after supper!

HARRY The minute I pass my examination, we'll tell them— *(Tenderly.)* So sweet—

ESTHER Harry, do you think Mama will be mad when we tell her? I'm the youngest. A mother always likes it better when the *oldest* gets married first.

HARRY *(Upset.)* But you told me yourself your mother was only sixteen and three months when Sadie was born, so how can she be mad? Please, Esther, maybe we ought to tell her right away—

ESTHER Oh, no—please—it wouldn't look nice. We don't know each other so long—

HARRY You mean you're not sure? *(They draw apart quickly as* FANNY *enters, still in her kimono. She makes a beeline for bathroom.)* As I was saying— *(Discovering* FANNY.*)* Oh—how do you do, Miss Fanny?

FANNY *(Wrapping kimono around her modestly.)* Very fine, thank you. *(With exaggerated politeness.)* Pardon the appearance— *(She is gone, banging door behind her.)*

HARRY *(When* FANNY *has gone.)* You didn't answer me. Aren't you sure? About us?

ESTHER Please Harry, I'm sure—I—I— would die for you, so sure I am—

HARRY Gosh, for a minute you had me scared— *(Glancing around.)* If—if I kissed you somebody might see. Look at me. *(Pause.)* I have just kissed you.

ESTHER *(Slowly.)* I felt it— *(Giggling.)* This is a fine English lesson—

HARRY *(Laughing happily.)* And did you hear your mother invite us to the Bar Mitzvah? Like being in the family already!

ESTHER I was holding my breath!

HARRY I can hardly wait for my father to meet you. I have already told him about you.

ESTHER *(Frightened.)* Oh—what did he say?

HARRY He said, "If you love her, I love her." According to my father we could get married tomorrow.

ESTHER *(Frightened again.)* So soon?

HARRY In one month I'll be able to support a wife—

ESTHER Mama'll be so mad on me—

HARRY Then we better tell her right away—

ESTHER Oh, Harry, please—no— *(SADIE FELDERMAN enters. She is about nineteen, thin and sallow-complexioned, with a forceful drive in her manner that belies her slight frame.)*

SADIE *(Pleased to see him.)* Oh—how do you do, Mr. Engel—?

HARRY Very well. And you?

SADIE Simply exhausted. The last minute they brought in a hundred and fifty new waists to finish up! Please pardon my appearance—I must look a sight— *(As she goes toward bedroom.)* I'll be back in a moment— *(She exits into bedroom.)*

ESTHER   Harry, please, maybe you better go—

HARRY   But we didn't settle anything. About when we are getting married.

ESTHER   Please, Harry, we can't talk about it now—somebody'll hear.

HARRY   You'll have to meet me tonight so we can talk.

ESTHER   Maybe Mama won't let me go out—

HARRY   *(Adamant.)* I'll wait for you. Same time tonight.

ESTHER   I'll try my best. Good-bye—

HARRY   Until tonight—darling— *(He is at door.)* Mrs. Engel— *(He is gone.* ESTHER *runs to window.)*

FANNY   *(Calling out.)* Esther! He's gone?

ESTHER   Yes—

FANNY   *(Entering, comes toward* ESTHER.*)* Esther, I—I couldn't help myself, honest, but I heard what you and your boy friend were talking about.

ESTHER   Oh—

FANNY   Don't get scared. I won't tell anyone, darling. Can you keep a secret?

ESTHER   Surely— *(*FANNY *nods her head vigorously.)* You mean *you*, too?

FANNY   That's right.

ESTHER   Oh, Fanny, Fanny—both of us— *(The girls embrace, giggling happily.)* Is he nice?

FANNY   He's *wonderful*! The way he dresses—you should just see him!

ESTHER   I'm thinking what Mama will say—

FANNY   She'll have to get used to it. We ain't babies! *(Excitedly.)* He's an usher in the Apollo, where I work. But he's only doing it *temporary*. He writes songs!

ESTHER   No!

FANNY   Honest! He's writing a song for me to sing—

ESTHER   Oh, Fanny please, let's have a double wedding.

FANNY   He didn't *ask* me yet!

ESTHER   Oh— *(Cheerily.)* But don't worry! Harry didn't *really* ask me right away! Maybe he's bashful?

FANNY   *(Laughing.)* Him bashful? He wouldn't be bashful to tell President William Howard Taft to go to the dickens—

ESTHER   Fanny—

FANNY   I mean it. He's got some mouth on him!

ESTHER   What's his name?

FANNY   Irving. Irving Tashman. I'll be *Mrs.* Irving Tashman—if he asks me—

ESTHER   Oh—he will—how could he help it? You're so beautiful. And you sing so beautiful—

FANNY   *(Pleased.)* Go on— *(She surveys herself in mirror over buffet, wrapping kimono tightly about her.)* Maybe you're right. I don't know— *(Trying to be modest and hardly succeeding.)* Everybody tells me I'm beautiful. And when I sing everybody *whistles*! *(As though telling a great secret.)* I'm going to tell you something I wouldn't tell a soul— (AARON *enters, disconsolately. The girls draw apart quickly.*)

AARON (*As he goes toward couch.*) A man can go crazy when he's not working. Sit in the house, it's on your nerves. Take a walk—so where are you going? Aye, confusion! (*He lies full-length on couch.*)

FANNY (*Whispering to* ESTHER.) Tonight, he's taking me to a *restaurant!*

ESTHER Mama won't let you go— (BECKY *enters with* HYMIE.)

BECKY (*To* FANNY.) You're not dressed yet?

FANNY I'm getting dressed now— (*She exits, making gesture for secrecy to* ESTHER.)

BECKY Mr. Engel is gone already?

ESTHER He had to leave— (HYMIE *goes into kitchen.* SADIE *enters.*)

SADIE (*Looking around disappointed.*) Mr. Engel is gone already?

ESTHER He had to leave—

SADIE (*Disappointed, she takes it out on* AARON, *now lying on couch.*) You have to use the living room for a bedroom even in the daytime?

AARON (*Sitting up.*) Oh, *you're* here.

SADIE Mama, I asked you—

BECKY But the living room *is* his bedroom—

SADIE Even when he don't pay rent weeks already?

BECKY Sadie!

AARON Never mind, Miss Smarty.— These humiliations! Why do I stand for it? These—these insults! If I had money you would speak to me with kid gloves! I ask you, would Brownstein be such a Socialist, if he had my opportunity to go into business and be treated like a gentleman?

SADIE And hereafter on a Wednesday night, be so kind as to take a walk for yourself! Last night when I'm taking my lesson, he lays there on the couch talking to himself the whole time!

AARON Engel doesn't care if I sit here. Who do I hurt?

SADIE I care! Like living in the middle of Castle Garden,[1] this house! (*She exits lower bedroom.*)

AARON What did I come to America for? To be insulted I could have stayed in Russia.

BECKY Don't be mad on her, Aaron. She can't help it—she's the nervous type.

AARON How is it *you* ain't the nervous type? I know those skinny women already!

BECKY In her heart is something which pushes her—to build herself up—to improve her life—

AARON She should learn first to improve her temper!

(FANNY *enters, wearing an evening dress, obviously home-made, but very becoming.* SADIE *follows her in.*)

---

[1] Huge, busy reception center for immigrants arriving in the port of New York.

SADIE Mama, look at Fanny—

BECKY The stage dress for eating supper in the kitchen?

FANNY *(Excitedly.)* Mama, please don't get excited—tonight I am not eating supper home. I am eating in a restaurant.

BECKY A restaurant?

FANNY *(Anxious.)* I was invited!

BECKY *(Quietly.)* Who invited you?

FANNY *(Almost hysterical now.)* Mr. Irving Tashman, he invited me!

BECKY Who?

FANNY Mama, please don't get excited! He's a Jewish boy!

BECKY All day you're home you couldn't tell me—

FANNY I was afraid to tell you, you might say "no."

BECKY It's still not too late to say "no."

FANNY *(Screaming.)* Mama!

SADIE And who is this Mr. Tashman?

FANNY He works in my theatre and he's a very nice fellow!

SADIE An actor?

FANNY An usher. His Uncle Abe owns the place. And the usher is only *temporary*— *(Anxiously to* BECKY.) Mama, please, he's taking me to a French restaurant!

BECKY French? American ain't good enough?

AARON Aye, Becky, if you had a man in the house!

FANNY *(To* AARON.) Your two cents, too? The company I am keeping is plenty good enough.

SADIE Fine company! With tramps!

FANNY It's *my* life! I should give a care what you think! When I'm a big star, you'll be kissing my feet! *(To* BECKY.) Gee, Mom—you got to get used to it. In America a girl don't wait till the *Shotchun*[2] comes. Here we gotta meet our own fellows, or how are we going to get a husband?

BECKY From husbands you are thinking already? *(Doorbell rings.)*

FANNY It's him! *(The house is suddenly galvanized into action.* FANNY *runs to window, opens it, calling out.)* Yoo-hoo—I'll be right down!

BECKY He's not coming upstairs?

FANNY Mama, please—

BECKY You don't go with him one step unless he comes upstairs first. Mama should take a look at him! (HYMIE *has entered a moment before.)*

FANNY *(Tearfully.)* In this dump? What will he think of me?

BECKY *(Pointing to window, sternly.)* Upstairs first!

FANNY *(Reluctantly calling down again.)* Irving! Mr. Tashman! Please come upstairs, will you! *(She comes away from window unhappily, spots* AARON *on couch.)* Aaron, please—

[2] Or *shadchen,* a professional matchmaker.

AARON *(Sitting up.)* All right, all right! It's not so terrible he should find me on the couch!

ESTHER Maybe I'll go into the bedroom, the house won't be so crowded?

FANNY *(Gently.)* Please stay, Esther. I want *you* to meet him. *(They all stand around in stiff, expectant attitudes, waiting for* IRVING TASHMAN's *arrival. There is a knock at door.* IRVING *enters. A slender fellow, with a breezy manner. His clothes are sporty and perhaps a little too colorful, his hat a little too cocked to one side.)* Hello. This—this is my family. And Mr. Greenspan—a *friend.*

IRVING Pleased to meet ya—everybody— *(Looking around.)* Nice little place you got here.

FANNY It's not fancy exactly.

IRVING But it's home. No place like home, I always say— *(Spotting piano.)* Say, you didn't tell me you had a piano in the house.

BECKY You play the piano?

IRVING *(Trying to be modest.)* Do I play? Tell her.

FANNY Like Paderewski—

IRVING *(About to demonstrate.)* Would you like me to show you something I just knocked out—it's a beaut—

FANNY *(Drawing his attention away from piano.)* Irving—I'm all ready—

IRVING Ready for the big time? Taking her out big-time tonight. Didja tell 'em?

BECKY A *French* place. She told us—

IRVING Best place in town. I always say, you gonna take a girl out? Then take her to the best! That's my motto.

FANNY And, Mama, tonight it's not necessary for you to take me home from the Apollo.

BECKY I'll let you go home alone, Jack the Ripper should catch you?

FANNY *(Looking at* IRVING *shyly.)* Mr. Tashman is escorting me home tonight.

IRVING Don't you worry, Mom—I'll take good care of your little girl. Wouldn't let anything happen to her for the world—

FANNY Irving, are we going?

IRVING *(Breezily.)* Well—glad to 'a' metya—everybody— *(To* AARON.*)* Have a cigar. Havana. Have 'em made up special for me—

AARON Thanks. It's a pleasure.

IRVING Don't even mention it— *(He and* FANNY *exit.)*

SADIE Cigars made special for him! Two for three cents, I betcha. Candy-store sport! (HYMIE *exits into kitchen.* AARON *has lighted cigar and now inhales the aroma.)*

AARON If you have to know, Miss Smarty, this cigar costs at least ten cents!

SADIE And how would you know?

BECKY I like him. He's a nice boy. A little bit fresh, but nice!

SADIE *(Laughing.)* Mama, you meet a fellow two minutes, and you know already he's nice?

BECKY One look and I can tell. He's a good boy.

ESTHER *(As she exits into kitchen.)* I think he is very nice.

SADIE   Another party heard from—

AARON   Well, in my opinion—

BECKY   *(Nastily.)* Oh! So you have an opinion, too—

AARON   Well, that settles it! *(Jumps up and starts to put on his coat.)*

BECKY   Where are you going?

AARON   I'm taking myself for a walk to the Bronx to see Van Brett! And believe me, I'm going to tell it to Brownstein. To hell with my conscience! *(He exits, banging door.* SADIE *remains behind, absorbed.)*

SADIE   *(After a pause, quietly.)* Mama, he was here again today—and again I didn't get a chance to talk to him. *(Bursting out passionately.)* If I could only have more time with him alone!

BECKY   He's bashful—

SADIE   What could *any* man say with Aaron on the couch, people walking in and out— *(Pause—then quietly.)* All week I wait on pins till Wednesday when he comes to give me the lesson. I have figured out what I am going to say—how I am going to say it— *(Ruefully.)* Comes the time—I sit, shivering, afraid to open my mouth.

BECKY   He said something today, makes me wonder—

SADIE   What?

BECKY   I was thanking him for what he was doing, lessons for nothing, so he said, money he couldn't take, like from his own family.

SADIE   He really said that?

BECKY   It's a good sign—

SADIE   *(Throwing her arms around* BECKY.*)* Oh, Mama—

BECKY   *(Smiling.)* So maybe now you'll feel better?

SADIE   *(Gaily.)* I should say so. What's for supper, Mama?

*(*SADIE *exits. Clock strikes six.* BECKY *steps on a chair, about to turn on gas.* ESTHER *enters.)*

ESTHER   Mama, I don't feel so hungry. I—I think I'll take a little walk—

BECKY   Now?

ESTHER   I was in the house all day. I need a little air—

BECKY   So take a walk. Don't stay long. *(*ESTHER *quickly takes her coat from rack and exits.* BECKY *lights gas. A warm glow of light suffuses the room.* BECKY *steps down, glances at book on table. Reciting, half to herself.)*

"In fourteen hundred and ninety-two
            Columbus sailed the ocean blue—"

(She exits into kitchen as)

CURTAIN

SCENE 2

The same. A month later. The house has a festive air. There are candles in the brass candelabra on buffet. Table is covered with a white cloth and there are new curtains at window.

AT RISE: IRVING TASHMAN *is at piano, playing. He is in his shirtsleeves, and is by now completely "at home."* BECKY *and* FANNY, *in new silk dresses, are busy setting table.* HYMIE, *in a stiff new suit, is on floor studying a paper in his hand.*

HYMIE *(Half to himself.)* "My dear mama and sisters and brother-in-law and— friends— Today I yam a man. I—I—" *(His nose is back in paper.)*

FANNY Mama, you're putting the knives on the wrong side.

BECKY What's the difference? A person can tell it's a knife.

HYMIE *(Laughing.)* Oh boy, was the Rabbi sore when I told him I'm makin' the speech in English!

BECKY I told him to tell the Rabbi he shouldn't be mad. After all, God can understand English and in America you have to do like the Romans do. *(To* FANNY.) Oh, I forgot! We have to make another setting. I told Aaron to invite his friend Brownstein.

FANNY Him? Tonight? Gee, Mom—why?

BECKY The poor man— God knows when he gets something homemade to eat—

FANNY So we have to listen a whole night to his politics? Hymie, get out of the way!

BECKY Hymie, your new suit—

*(*HYMIE *exits into upper bedroom, holding paper behind his back, muttering.)*

IRVING *(As he plays.)* What's it sound like to you, Mom?

BECKY Beautiful—

IRVING *(To* FANNY.) C'mon, Kiddo, let's sing the chorus for Mom. *(*FANNY *and* IRVING *sing as he plays,* "Under a Painted Smile." *They finish song with great aplomb.)*

BECKY Beautiful—

IRVING And whose little sweetheart am I writing it for?

FANNY *(Giggling.)* Yours!

IRVING And what's her name?

FANNY Mrs. Fanny Tashman!

BECKY For that I am not forgiving you so easy!

IRVING *(Getting up, playfully putting his arms around her.)* Whatsa matter, Mom! Still sore? I didn't wanna elope. Fanny made me. She took one look at the way I look at you and she got jealous—

BECKY *(Fighting him off good-naturedly.)* Go away, you loafer, you! I'll go with the broom to you!

FANNY Irv, let's fix up the cake like you said— *(They exit into kitchen, laughing.* SADIE *and* ESTHER *enter from street.)*

ESTHER *(Excitedly, as they remove their wraps.)* We ran all the way home!

SADIE We tried to get off a few minutes early, so the foreman wouldn't let us—

ESTHER *(Laughing.)* I went up to him and I said, "We don't feel so good—we're sick"—so he says, "Only one of you is allowed to be sick at one time. Make up your mind—" *(ESTHER exits into lower bedroom. SADIE goes to window, looks out pensively.)*

BECKY *(Noticing SADIE's absorption.)* Last night he didn't say anything? *(SADIE shakes her head despondently.)* You'll see. He will—

SADIE What's the use—? *(She turns suddenly.)* All he knows is, I'm a shop girl and he's a school teacher— Why should he even look at me?

BECKY He's a bashful type boy—

SADIE I bet if I was a secretary or a bookkeeper—he would look at me then, all right. *(Directly.)* Is Mrs. Gold's Dora smarter than me, Mama?

BECKY I should say not—

SADIE That's all I want to know— *(Pause.)* Mama, help me—I want to quit the shop and go to secretary school. I know it's a lot of money, but if you give me thirty dollars I'll pay you back—

BECKY Why not? Of course I'll give it to you—

SADIE Oh, Mama, Mama, thank you! And the minute I get job in an office, have I got plans! The first thing I'm going to do is—throw out that couch—I'm ashamed every time he walks into the house—it's so homely—

BECKY I don't think it makes a difference to Mr. Engel. He's a very plain boy. He don't expect to get rich.

SADIE Don't be foolish, Mama. Everybody cares about getting rich. You should see the way people live uptown. You should see what they eat and the way they dress— *(Giggling.)* Honest, Mama, I think he's afraid of girls. He's so polite he still calls me "Miss" Sadie. I'm afraid a boy like him you have to *push* into saying something.

BECKY *(Smiling.)* So—you want Mama to give him a push for you? *(A knock at door. BECKY goes to answer it. SADIE exits. BENJAMIN BROWNSTEIN enters. He is a large man with a bald head and enormous mustachios. His clothes are those of a poor working man, and he has made no concessions in dress to the occasion.)* Come in, Mr. Brownstein. *(HYMIE enters.)*

BENJAMIN *(Looking around.)* Greenspan is not home yet?

BECKY Any minute. Take off your coat.

BENJAMIN *(Removing coat, he finds a place on couch.)* He told me six o'clock we're eating.

HYMIE Hello, Mr. Brownstein.

BENJAMIN *(To HYMIE, whom he favors.)* How are you, my boy? *(IRVING and FANNY enter.)*

IRVING *(Holding cake under BECKY's nose.)* Rector's[3] comes to Broome Street! *(Placing cake on buffet.)* How'ya, Brownstein—

[3] A high-class restaurant.

(IRVING *goes back to piano, starts to play.*)

BENJAMIN Excuse me if I am insulting you, Mrs. Felderman, but this celebration, to me, it's a barbaric bourgeois custom! Gefilte fish and kugel on a boy's thirteenth birthday does not make a man!

HYMIE (*Listening with all ears.*) What's a bourgeois, Mr. Brownstein?

BENJAMIN (*About to hold forth.*) A bourgeois—

FANNY Mr. Browstein, if it is not too much trouble, *tonight* could we live without a discussion of politics?

BENJAMIN (*To* HYMIE.) You see, Hymie? That's a bourgeois!

HYMIE (*Puzzled.*) I see—

FANNY Honest, I betcha this song sells a million copies!

IRVING And when it does, you and me'll be living on Riverside Drive and Mama'll be living with us—with a colored cook!

BECKY I would starve first!

BENJAMIN Ambitions! To lay a head on a pillow on Riverside Drive when millions ain't got straw to sleep on.

IRVING That's my fault? Listen to him! I say a man's got one life to live. Make your mark and live it easy. That's my motto.

BENJAMIN Aye, boychick, boychick, comes the Revolution, ideas like yours will not be popular. (ESTHER *enters, wearing new dress.*)

ESTHER (*Pirouetting.*) So—how do I look?

BECKY Even if I made it myself, it looks good!

IRVING Now *that's* what I call class—

FANNY Like a doll! I could get you a job in my theatre any time—

IRVING Seeing as how you don't work there any more?

FANNY (*Petulantly.*) It's just *temporary*—

BECKY When did this happen?

IRVING Yesterday. And it's as permanent as Christmas!

FANNY Ish kabibble,[4] what you say! Monday I'll go see Mr. Shubert and ask him to try me out for the new Winter Garden—

IRVING You'll see Shubert over my dead body—

FANNY You make me sick! The way you carry on, you'd think I was undressing in front of the audience—

IRVING You don't have to undress in front of them! Those guys out front are doin' it for you!

FANNY You just want to ruin my life! All I want is to give pleasure to people—

BECKY You have it in your heart to sing, so sing for Irving's pleasure—for mine— (BECKY *exits into kitchen.*)

FANNY You and Irving are going to make a star outta me? (*Dramatically.*) Can I help it if I have it in my nature to be loved and admired by the world? Do you know what it means to sing for an *audience*? To hear them *whistling* for you?

IRVING Aw, cut it out, Sarah Bernhardt—I'll whistle for you any time—

[4] Comic character whose name became synonymous with "I should worry."

FANNY Go away from me—you—you— *(She sniffles unhappily.* SADIE *enters, goes to window, looks out anxiously.)*

IRVING *(Taking* FANNY *in his arms.)* If it will make you feel better Uncle Abe fired me, too.

FANNY What?

IRVING That's right. I ain't workin' for him any more—

FANNY Why didn't you tell me?

BENJAMIN Aha! I told you, workers of the world unite!

IRVING So I'm *united* with Fanny. So we both lost our jobs! *(*BECKY *enters with a challis bread wrapped in napkin.)*

FANNY Did you hear, Mama? Irving lost his job, too!

BECKY That's terrible. How did it happen?

IRVING Uncle Abe is selling the Apollo to Jack Greenfal—so he had to fire us on account Greenfal will have to hire *his own* relatives.

BECKY He's selling the theatre?

IRVING *(Laughing skeptically.)* To go to California to make those moving pictures!

FANNY Gee—Irv—maybe he'll take us with him?

IRVING You looney? Go all the way out there, we should have to walk back?

FANNY In the meantime we'll starve—

BECKY What are you talking about? Tomorrow you move out of the furnished room into the house—

SADIE *(Who has been listening, all ears, unhappier by the moment.)* The house isn't already overstuffed?

BECKY *(Firmly.)* We'll find room. Tomorrow you move in—

IRVING Gee, thanks. You'll get it back. With interest. See if you don't. *(*AARON *enters from street, dressed in what he considers the well-dressed businessman should wear.)*

SADIE *(Disappointed.)* Oh—it's you.

AARON Hello. Hello. Mazeltuff! And how is my friend Brownstein?

BENJAMIN You said six o'clock—we're eating— *(*ESTHER *sticks her head through door.)*

ESTHER *(Disappointed.)* Oh—it's you—

AARON What is this? They are expecting the King of England and it's only me? *(He hands* HYMIE *a package, ostentatiously.)* For you, Hymie. On the occasion of your thirteenth birthday! That's why I was late!

BECKY Aaron—you shouldn't—

AARON *(Grandly.)* Why not? I can afford it!

HYMIE *(Fingering package shyly.)* Should I open it up now? *(*SADIE *and* ESTHER *exit lower bedroom.)*

BECKY Why not? *(All eyes are on him as he opens package. It contains a large white silk handkerchief.)*

AARON I asked the fellow, "For the Bar Mitzvah of a boy who is playing the violin, what would be suitable?" So he said, "For under the chin when you play violin, a white silk handkerchief is very suitable."

HYMIE Gee—thanks—

BENJAMIN (*Reluctantly taking package from his coat pocket.*) You might as well take this, too.

HYMIE (*Opening it quickly.*) Thank you, Mr. Brownstein—

BECKY You shouldn't—

BENJAMIN (*Angrily.*) Why not? From *him* is all right and not from me? (HYMIE *opens package.*)

BECKY A book!

BENJAMIN (*Looking directly at* AARON.) I asked *myself*, for the Bar Mitzvah of a boy who wants to be a *man!* Take a look, Mr. Greenspan! *The Writings of Karl Marx*—by Marx! (AARON *takes a large envelope from his pocket, nonchalantly throws it on table.*)

AARON And *furthermore*—open this up, Mrs. Felderman, mine darling, and get yourself an excitement.

BECKY What is this?

AARON Open it up!

BECKY (*Opening envelope, takes out sheaf of money.*) I'm dying! Look what he throws on the table like a newspaper!

AARON (*Pompously to* BENJAMIN.) Seventy-five dollars, cash money! (*Sorting bills, hands* BECKY *several.*) And this, mine sweet Becky, is yours. In full payment of my just debts!

BENJAMIN (*Bursting out violently.*) Blood money!

BECKY (*Disregarding* BENJAMIN's *outburst. She fingers bills, worried.*) That means you're moving out?

AARON Who said? Even if the couch is not so comfortable, the landlady is one in a million! For the rest of my life, you can count on me! (BENJAMIN *continues to glare at* AARON.) And out of next month's profits, the first thing I am going to buy is a new couch. A comfortable bed is a good investment. (*To* BECKY *pointedly.*) Unless, Mrs. Becky, you are changing your mind. Mine proposition is still good! (BECKY *glares at him.*) All right! All right! Forget I said it! (ESTHER *and* SADIE *enter.* SADIE *carries small package, which she gives to* HYMIE.)

SADIE Hymie!

HYMIE (*Overwhelmed.*) I'm getting a present from you, too? (*Hastily opens package, takes out a small watch.*)

SADIE From Esther and Mama and me—

HYMIE (*Putting it to his ear.*) It ticks! Mama—it ticks!

BECKY (*Proudly.*) Sure it ticks. (HYMIE *swallows hard, trying to contain his emotion and pleasure. He gathers his bundles together and runs into bedroom.*)

ESTHER (*Laughing, exiting after him.*) Hymie! Don't cry! You have to laugh, not cry! (SADIE, FANNY *and* ESTHER *exit after him, laughing.*)

BECKY (*Sniffing.*) The fish! (*She exits into kitchen. A moment's pause.* BENJAMIN *glares at* AARON.)

BENJAMIN (*Unable to contain himself.*) Exploiter!

AARON Please! You are starting up again? Don't confuse me now! A man is entitled to make a living!

BENJAMIN Five hundred percent profit is a *living* for you and a *dying* for the man on the machine who does all the work!

IRVING Don't you guys ever get tired? *(He exits into kitchen.)*

AARON Don't exaggerate! Five hundred percent profit I'm not making—yet! And even if I was, who is stopping anybody from doing the same? You'll excuse me, it's a free country!

BENJAMIN A free country, you'll excuse *me*, to starve!

AARON You're starving? You been working steady in a bakery since the first day you came here!

BENJAMIN Fourteen hours a day in a dirty bakery cellar—Five men side by side in a room half like this. No windows. Every five minutes somebody mops the floor. Water? No! Sweat! Sweat I said? Blood! The blood of the workers is in every piece of bread you eat!

AARON I don't taste it!

BENJAMIN *(Almost apoplectic.)* You will! *(A knock on door.* BECKY *enters to answer it.)*

BECKY Aaron—Mr. Brownstein—please, the company! *(She opens door.* HARRY ENGEL *and his father,* MYRON *enter.* MYRON ENGEL *is a fifty-year-old edition of his son. Quiet, pedantic, scholarly.)*

HARRY Papa, this is Mrs. Felderman. And this is my father, Myron Engel.

MYRON How do you do?

BECKY I'm glad you came— *(Calling out.)* Girls! Sadie! The company is here! *(*HYMIE *and the girls enter.* IRVING *comes out of kitchen.)* Meet my family. This is Mr. Engel's father—and this is my Fanny's husband, Mr. Tashman—and Mr. Greenspan and Benjamin Brownstein—

HYMIE How about me? It's my birthday—

BECKY The most important one we forgot—this is my Hymie— *(Laughing.)* If you'll excuse me, I have to see to the dinner— Fanny! Esther! *(*BECKY *exits.* ESTHER *glances at* HARRY *shyly, then she and* FANNY *follow their mother into kitchen.)*

SADIE *(Trying to gain* HARRY's *attention.)* Won't you be seated, Mr. Engel? *(To* MYRON.*)* And you, Mr. Engel—won't you make yourself comfortable?

MYRON *(As he sits.)* Thank you.

AARON What line are you in, Mr. Engel?

MYRON You might call it the *hospital* line.

AARON A doctor?

MYRON I am in what you might call the cleaning up line in the hospital. *(With a smile.)* Not exactly a professional man—but my son, Harry, is— *(Proudly.)* He has just passed his examination to teach public school.

SADIE Congratulations!

HARRY Thank you!

BENJAMIN A worthy profession, teaching. But, unfortunately, the school system is a tool of the bosses!

AARON My friend is slightly inclined toward the Socialistic system— *(*BECKY *enters.* FANNY *and* ESTHER *follow her in, carrying plates of food.)*

BECKY It's ready, gentlemen. The dinner.

MYRON A pleasure to sit at the table with such a nice family—

IRVING C'mon, folks! Let's dig in!

MYRON Everything looks delicious. *(HARRY whispers into ESTHER's ear.)*

SADIE Secrets, Mr. Engel?

ESTHER You're going to tell them now?

HARRY You said tonight at the Bar Mitzvah—

ESTHER *(Looking around embarrassed, then suddenly.)* All right—now.

HARRY *(He clears his throat nervously.)* My dear friends—

AARON Hear! Hear! He's going to make a speech!

HARRY I—we—that is to say—Esther and I—well—well—I can't make a speech, but Esther and I—well—

MYRON *(Beaming.)* Don't be nervous, son— *(HARRY looks around tongue-tied.)* They are engaged!

HARRY Thank you, Papa, for telling it for me. *(SADIE stares straight ahead, trying to contain herself during following.)*

FANNY *(Screaming happily.)* I knew it all the time, but I didn't tell. Not even to Irving!

BECKY *(Her voice choked.)* It's a great surprise—

AARON Those quiet fellows certainly put it over on us.   *(Simultaneously.)*

FANNY *(Embracing IRVING.)* They'll love married life, won't they, Irving?

ESTHER *(To BECKY.)* You're not mad we kept it a secret?

BECKY How could I be mad?— He's a fine boy—

MYRON *(Shaking BECKY's hand, solemnly.)* Your daughter is a lovely girl. My son is lucky.

BECKY *(Glancing toward SADIE, words do not come easily.)* My daughter is lucky too.

HARRY *(To SADIE.)* I can't thank you enough for bringing me into the house to teach you, Miss Sadie.

SADIE *(Dryly.)* You can call me Sadie now, without the *Miss*—

MYRON You have settled on a day for wedding? *(HARRY and ESTHER nod vigorously.)*

ESTHER *(Shyly.)* Harry wants it soon.

HARRY And you are all invited to the wedding!

AARON Right away is the best. Once I was engaged to a girl, I found out so much about her, I didn't marry her! *(General congratulations and laughter.)* So kiss the bride!

(They all tap on glasses with silverware. The tinkling sound continues as HARRY kisses her tenderly. Everyone applauds.)

MYRON Aren't you forgetting something, my son?

HARRY Oh, for goodness' sakes! In my pocket— *(He tenderly extracts a small box, taking out ring.)* It's for you— *(He puts it on ESTHER's finger.)*

ESTHER Oh, Harry—you shouldn't—

HARRY My father went with me to pick it out.

ESTHER It must have cost so much—

HARRY In Greenhut's they have inaugurated a new system. If you are reliable, they give it to you for a dollar a week for two years!

FANNY Listen to that—

AARON The man who thought it up will make a million. They charge ten percent interest— (HYMIE, *completely neglected, has been watching proceedings with great interest.*)

HYMIE Don't anybody want to hear my speech? (*No one pays any attention to him.*)

ESTHER Sadie, isn't the ring wonderful! You didn't say anything!

SADIE I—I wish you everything.

ESTHER I can't tell you how happy I am—

SADIE (*Dryly.*) You should be!

MYRON (*Getting up.*) Let us drink a toast to the bride-to-be— (*Holding up his glass.*) To Esther, my future daughter. A long life and a happy one! (*They all drink, exclaim happily.*)

FANNY Now you, Mama—you make a toast!

BECKY Me?

IRVING C'mon, Mom—it ain't hard—

MYRON Just say what's in your heart, Mrs. Felderman.

BECKY (*Getting up.*) I—I don't know what— (*She clears her throat.*)

AARON (*Applauding.*) Hear! Hear! (*They are seated now, as follows:* BECKY, *table* R., AARON, FANNY, IRVING, *from* R. *to* L., *backs facing audience,* HYMIE *at table* L., MYRON, SADIE, HARRY, ESTHER *and* BENJAMIN *from* R. *to* L., *facing audience.*)

BECKY A lifetime it would take to say what's in my heart— (*They are quiet now.* BECKY *looks from one to other, then last at* SADIE. *In an effort to give* SADIE *courage,* BECKY *decides to make speech. Quietly.*) I look around this table and I see: My Fanny has a good husband who loves her— (FANNY *takes* IRVING'S *hand.*) For my Esther and her Harry . . . life is just beginning— (*Pause.*) Then I see my Hymie sitting in the place where his father would be sitting— and I think, today he is a man. I remember, where we came from was chances only for a man to die—and here—here they beg you to take the chances for living— (*She pauses, then fixes her gaze on* SADIE, *who sits, head bowed.*) Then I look at my Sadie, and for her, too, my heart is happy. (SADIE *looks up sharply.*) Oh, yes! She also has an important announcement surprise. My Sadie is going to give up working in the shop and will go to a school to become a secretary! (*General exclamation, "A secretary"—"That's wonderful!" etc.*) Oh, yes! My Sadie knows in America are chances for everybody to be somebody! (*She lifts her glass.*) So, if it is allowed we should drink, not to a person, but to a place—then please—to America! (*Pause.*) Because we know only good can come to us here! (*She looks around.*) Now should we drink?

(They are all visibly affected by BECKY's *speech.* BENJAMIN *has taken out his handkerchief and chooses at this point to blow his nose vigorously. The spell is broken. They begin to drink and eat, all except* SADIE, *who continues to stare straight ahead, as though in a trance.)*

HYMIE   *(Suddenly.)* Mama! Please! *Now* can I make my speech? *(He gets up.)* My dear mother and sisters and brother-in-law and friends! Today I yam a man— *(As)*

CURTAIN

ACT II

SCENE 1

The same. Early morning of Saturday, March 25, 1911. AARON's *couch is disheveled, sheets thrown in a lump, etc.* SADIE *is at window, wan and dispirited.* BECKY *enters from kitchen. She goes to upper bedroom door and knocks.*

BECKY   Fanny!

FANNY   *(Off.)* I'm up! *(Yelling.)* Irving! Get up—

BECKY   Let him sleep.

FANNY   *(Entering.)* If I can get up at six, he can get up at six! (BECKY, *folding* AARON's *sheets, watches* SADIE *in deep concern.* FANNY *making a beeline for bathroom.)* I'm first— *(She is gone.)*

BECKY   *(To* SADIE.) Maybe you won't go to the *shop* today!

SADIE   *(Wearily.)* I'm all right.

BECKY   Sadie, please, do me a favor, don't go.

SADIE   Why shouldn't I go? It's *my* wedding? Tell her to stay home. She's the bride! *(A pause.)* I know. You're afraid I'll say something—

BECKY   Did I say it?

SADIE   That's what you're thinking, isn't it? *(Getting up wearily.)* Don't worry, I won't say anything. *(Passionately.)* But you can't stop a person's *thoughts!* Today I'll be sitting at the machine, biting my tongue to keep from running to the window and throwing myself out of it!

BECKY   You don't go to the shop today! I'll tie you with ropes to the bed—

SADIE   Don't worry. They say when a person talks about it, he doesn't do it.

BECKY   Sadie—please—I'll give you breakfast.

SADIE   I'm not hungry.

BECKY   You're killing yourself! A whole month not to eat—

SADIE   I don't know what you want from me.— Leave me alone— *(She exits into bedroom.* BECKY *stares unhappily at her retreating form.)*

FANNY   *(Entering.)* I'm out! Who's next? *(She stops when she sees* BECKY's *expression.)* What's the matter? (BECKY *nods toward door.)* Sadie? She'll get over it.

BECKY It's easy for somebody else to say it.

FANNY *(Calling out as she exits into upper bedroom.)* Irving! Get up! *(BECKY continues to fold sheets as ESTHER enters. She is half dressed.)*

ESTHER Sadie is sick?

BECKY She didn't sleep so good—

ESTHER *(She laughs.)* I guess I made her nervous. Pinching myself all night— *(With a sigh.)* Today, the last day in the shop. Tomorrow I'm getting married. Me! *(Pause.)* Mama, could I ask you a question?

BECKY Why not?

ESTHER Were you scared, Mama—when the time came? *(She runs to BECKY.)* Last night when Harry was here, I got so frightened, I wanted to say, "Please excuse me, but I can't do it." I wanted to run away— Is that how you felt?

BECKY *(Smiling gently.)* If you want to know, I *did* run away. I got up early in the morning and I ran into the fields. I buried my head in the grass and I said to myself, no—no—I wouldn't go back! *(Laughing.)* An hour later, I got hungry, I went back.

ESTHER *(Laughing, incredulous.)* No!

BECKY That evening I married Papa—

ESTHER Mama, Mama, I'm so nervous, I wish it were tomorrow already!

BECKY Hurry up, get dressed; you'll be late!

ESTHER *(Gaily, as she exits into bathroom.)* If I'm late today, the foreman can fire me! *(BECKY looks after her a moment, then at door where SADIE is. With a sigh she exits into kitchen. FANNY enters dressed for street.)*

FANNY *(In high agitation.)* You'll see if I'll stand for it!

IRVING *(Coming to door, in his bathrobe.)* Give me one good reason why I have to get up at six-thirty?

FANNY It's the principle!

IRVING What principle? Six-thirty you have to hand me four-syllable words?

FANNY All right—I don't mind working in the shop again. I know it's only *temporary.* But when my back is breaking over the machine, I feel ten times worse if I know you're laying in bed!

IRVING Have a heart—darling. I'm dead on my feet.

FANNY The thing that tears me up—this minute I could be turning over on the other side! If you'd only let me go back on the stage . . . Milton Glaser, the agent, came looking for me—

IRVING *(Angrily.)* All over again? Half the night wasn't enough? I'm a mild man, Fanny, but—

FANNY Go ahead! Hit me, why don't you!

IRVING *(Falling into chair, half asleep.)* I'm too tired—

FANNY If I knew I'd have to give up my career when I married you, I wouldn't— *(breaking off hotly.)* Irving! You're not listening!

IRVING *(Wearily.)* I'm listening.

FANNY That man will drive me wild! *(IRVING gets up.)* Where are you going?

IRVING Back to sleep.

FANNY That's all the appreciation—

IRVING Look, baby, I know we're having a hard time. But, honey—look at me—c'mon—look at me— *(His arms on her shoulders.)* Do I look like the kinda fellow that likes his wife to work for him? Do I?

FANNY *(Reluctantly.)* No—

IRVING You know it's only *temporary*— *(Reasoning with her.)* And if I go to a publishing house early, I gotta buy lunch outside and lunch means a quarter. So you think I'm gonna spend your hard-earned quarters buying myself lunch? See the point? *(Pause.)*

FANNY I see it—

IRVING *(Sitting next to her, arm about her.)* Now you're talking! You know it's just a question of minutes! Kitty Gordon is *positively* trying out my song at the new Roseland Palace! It's as good as published already—

FANNY *(Jumping up. Tearfully.)* And you wrote that song for me!

IRVING *(Whistling impatiently.)* Sure I did. And I'm even gonna make 'em print it on the sheet! "For My Wife"—just like that! Gee, baby, don't cry— *(Holding her close.)* I'm crazy about you—

FANNY *(Through her tears.)* Are you?

IRVING You've got the most beautiful nose in the whole world! *(Kisses her nose.)*

FANNY Have I?

IRVING I'll kill anybody says "no"— *(Pause, as he and* FANNY *embrace.)* As if I don't appreciate what you're doin'— and never, *never* throwin' it up to me— *(He breaks off.)* Well—hardly ever. And, baby, will I make it up to you! You'll have so many dresses hangin' in your closet, it'll take you an hour to make up your mind which one to wear.

FANNY Oh, Irving— *(They embrace again.)*

IRVING Now can I go back to sleep?

FANNY *(Tenderly.)* Go back to sleep, Poppy— *(Pause as she watches him go toward door.)* Today is pay day. Should I bring you home something, darling? *(*ESTHER *enters, dressed for street.)*

IRVING *(Yawning.)* Cuppla Havana Burns Specials—Am I sleepy— *(He is gone.)*

BECKY *(Calling out from kitchen.)* Girls, come eat breakfast—

ESTHER Come on, Fanny, we'll be late—

FANNY *(Still filled with spell of* IRVING's *presence.)* Married life is wonderful! It's so legitimate! *(*SADIE *enters.)*

ESTHER Are you feeling any better, Sadie?

SADIE This is a wonderful day for you—

ESTHER I feel—like on air—Fanny, did you feel that way?

FANNY To tell you the truth, I don't remember *how* I felt! I was so scared Mama would be mad—

ESTHER I—I feel so empty—

SADIE *(Quietly.)* You feel empty—?

ESTHER *(Gaily.)* Wouldn't you? *(She is about to exit into kitchen.)* I don't know how I'll live through this day—

SADIE You don't know how *you'll* live through this day— *(Forcing* ESTHER's *attention to her.)* And how do you think *I'll* live through this day? And tomorrow? And for days and days and years after that? For the rest of my life! (ESTHER *stares at her, still uncomprehending.)* That's right! Stand there looking at me as if I were crazy! *(Her voice reaching a wild crescendo.)* You took him away from me! I brought him into the house! He would have married *me!* You took him away from me, do you hear me?—I hate you? I wish you were dead! (BECKY *has entered at sounds of* SADIE's *hysteria.)*

BECKY Sadie! No! No! (ESTHER *has been staring at* SADIE—*the full implication of her words dawning gradually. Suddenly, with a cry of deep hurt, she runs from the house.* FANNY *looks at* SADIE *as if she could strike her, quickly takes* ESTHER's *wraps and her own from rack, exits after* ESTHER.)

SADIE *(Falling into chair.)* Mama, please—do something—help me! I can't stand it— *(She weeps—dry hacking sobs escaping her.* BECKY *looks on—bewildered and unhappy—as—the curtain is lowered to show the lapse of several hours.)*

TIME: *Four-thirty same afternoon.*

BECKY *is at table, kneading dough.* AARON *watches her.*

HYMIE *is at piano, playing "Here Comes the Bride" on his violin.*

AARON Cakes! Wedding! One by one they'll get married and leave you alone. (BECKY *looks at him, sharply.)* All right! All right! I didn't say it. *(He goes to couch, sits down.)* A double wedding we could make it. They would even put it in the *Forwartz.* Mother and daughter marry on the same day. (BECKY *continues her work, not looking at him. He lies full-length on couch.)*

BECKY Hymie! Go downstairs and play! What are you doing, hanging around the house on such a nice day?

HYMIE I was practicing for tomorrow, I shouldn't make a mistake.

BECKY If you make one little mistake, who will notice? (HYMIE *puts away violin and exits.* IRVING *enters, yawning.)*

IRVING To the "Wedding March" I was dreaming. You know, Mom, the kid's got a nice touch. (SADIE *enters from street as* IRVING *nears bathroom.)*

SADIE Good morning, Mr. Tashman! Sleep till four-thirty in the afternoon with his wife slaving in the shop! *(As she goes toward bedroom.)* If I had a man like you, I would throw him out of the window. *(She exits.)*

IRVING *(As he exits into bathroom.)* I believe you! In your house murder would be an everyday occurrence! *(He is gone.* AARON *starts fussing with baking utensils on table.)*

BECKY Aaron! What are you doing?

AARON Why not? Somebody else helps you around this house?

BECKY It's very nice of you.

AARON Becky, Becky, if you would only let me . . . (BECKY *does not answer. He changes his tack.)* Listen, Mrs. Felderman—lately, since I am doing business with the outside world, I am subject to *embarrassment!* How can I explain to my friends that I'm not married? Am I twenty-one? A schoolboy? They think there's something the matter with me.

BECKY Maybe your friends are right, Aaron. A man like you should be married. . . .

AARON So?

BECKY Take my advice, look around. You'll find a good woman who can give you a heart one hundred percent for yourself! *(She looks around at doors of her house in concern.)*

AARON Tell me the truth—if I took your advice, you mean to say you wouldn't miss me? *(A knock at door.)*

BECKY Answer the door, Aaron. (AARON *opens door.* BENJAMIN *enters, greatly perturbed.)*

BENJAMIN *(Banging on a newspaper.)* What did I tell you American justice? Hello, Mrs. Felderman— On the side of the bosses!

AARON Brownstein, do you ever give yourself a minute's peace?

BENJAMIN In war how can there be peace?

AARON What war?

BENJAMIN *(Banging on paper again.)* They're not ashamed to print the decision in the paper! The New York State ten-hour-a-day legislation for bakers is unconstitutional! Mr. Justice Peckham! The *Supreme* Court! *(Snorting.)* That's justice?

AARON I don't know about you, Brownstein, but I'm hungry.

BENJAMIN Don't change the subject.

AARON It's easier to change the subject than to change the world. The only thing a sensible man can do is take care of himself. (BENJAMIN *glares at him.)* That makes me a criminal? Brownstein, I wouldn't hurt a fly.

BENJAMIN *(Angrily.)* Boss of a nonunion sweat shop, and he wouldn't hurt a fly!

AARON Tell them to get a union, and I'll have a union! I'm stopping them? (BENJAMIN *looks at* AARON, *unable to face force of his logic.)* The trouble is, Brownstein, you are not looking for a system. You are looking for a Heaven! (BECKY *has been listening, all ears.)*

BECKY Mr. Brownstein! My three girls work in the Triangle Shop, and they are not complaining and I am not complaining, so why should you? *(Suddenly.)* Tell me, where you and I came from did we have even a *chance* to work? If you ask me, in America it's a "Paradise" for the workingman.

BENJAMIN *(Almost apoplectic.)* Paradise! Excuse me for insulting you, but you're crazy! *(Watching her as she kneads dough.)* Furthermore, you make me nervous. With the fingers you don't do it! With the hands—the *palms* of the hands— *(He goes at dough.* BECKY *pushes him away.)*

BECKY Wash your hands first!

BENJAMIN *(Examining his hands.)* To hell with it! *(He walks away, brooding.* SADIE *enters.)*

AARON I'm still hungry.

BENJAMIN I could eat myself.

BECKY *(Good-naturedly.)* Two grown men, you can't help yourself? The icebox is full.

AARON Come, Brownstein, I'll make you a sandwich like in Delmonico's Restaurant.

BENJAMIN It doesn't have to be so fancy— *(AARON and BENJAMIN exit into kitchen. A moment of pause. From street we hear dimly sounds of fire engines and bells.)*

SADIE Well, why don't you say something?

BECKY What should I say?

SADIE Haven't you any curiosity? Don't you want to know where I went in such a rush?

BECKY I'm hoping in my heart you went to the shop to apologize to your sister Esther for what you did this morning.

SADIE If you have to know, I took myself for a walk to the secretary school! I enrolled! *(BECKY does not answer.)* Nobody in this world will ever have the satisfaction of seeing Sadie Felderman crying her eyes out over a man! From now on, it's something else in my life! You said in America are chances for everybody to be somebody! Well, I'm going to be somebody! And I won't stop at secretary school, either! That's just the beginning! I'll show them! I'll show— *(She breaks completely, dropping into a chair, weeping.)*

BECKY *(Gently, going to her.)* Kind, kind, as if I don't know how you're feeling. Don't I know what it means for a woman to lose the man she loves? I lived with Papa for ten years—and when I lost him, I wanted to die— *(Sounds of engines, sirens and bells playing a strange counterpoint to her voice.)* But I remembered I had other things to live for. I said to myself, "I cannot take out on my innocent children what I feel." Sadie, Sadie, a family is something you have to hold on to with all your strength! You don't tear it to pieces because you lost a man you never had!

SADIE Didn't I try? Did I say something all month? But when I see you making preparations, wedding cake, wedding dresses—a stone couldn't stand it!

BECKY *Kind, kind,* what is the trick in being strong when everything is going your way? *(Firmly.)* Be a *mensch*, Sadie!

(Door bursts open. HYMIE is there gesticulating, wildly, breathlessly.)

HYMIE Mama—Mama— *(His voice trails off in a wail. Finding his voice, he screams the words.)* The shop—the Triangle Shop—Mama—it's on fire—

SADIE *(Screaming the word.)* No!

(IRVING has entered from bathroom, face covered with shaving lather.)

HYMIE *(Hysterically.)* It's burning—

(They stand shocked, unable to believe their ears.)

BECKY The girls!

(Following action happens simultaneously: IRVING *grabs his coat from rack, wiping his face with it as he rushes out of door, followed by* BECKY. HYMIE, *breathless, stands staring at* SADIE, *then quickly exits after them hurriedly.* SADIE *stands alone, looking at open door, not daring to move as—the curtain is lowered to show the lapse of several hours.)*

TIME: *Midnight.*

SADIE *is at table, her head buried in her arms.*

HYMIE *is at window. Restlessly, he looks out.*

HYMIE Sadie, please, can't I go downstairs?

SADIE Hymie, I asked you not to— *(From outside we hear sounds of wailing.)* It's Mrs. O'Shaughnessy—her Annie, she worked in the shop—

HYMIE *(Frightened.)* I don't care. I'm gonna go. I'm going downstairs to look for Mama— *(He exits quickly.)*

SADIE *(Calling after him.)* Hymie! Come back— *(Exhausted, she sits, head in arms again. A moment's pause.* IRVING *enters, grimy, disheveled.)* No news? *(*IRVING *shakes his head. He sits, suddenly doubles up as if in physical pain. She goes toward him.)* Maybe no news is good news—

IRVING If they're all right, why aren't they *home? (The horror pouring out of him.)* Maybe they jumped! The way I seen 'em jump. Cracking the sidewalks! At the windows screaming at you. All you could do was watch 'em burn up in front of your eyes— *(He weeps dryly, silently.)* This morning I held her in my arms—she was laughing—

SADIE Stop it—

IRVING *One* fire escape for eight hundred people. It broke in the middle—with twenty—thirty people on it—

(A pause, both SADIE *and* IRVING *lost in their own grief. Door opens.* FANNY *is there. She stands still, half demented, her clothes hanging about her, wildly.* IRVING *throws his arms around her, hardly believing she is there.)*

FANNY *(In a dull flat tone, almost unrecognizable.)* Where's Esther?

IRVING Fanny—Fanny— *(He kisses her hand over and over again.)*

SADIE She'll be home right away—Didn't you come home? Irving—go quick— find Mama—tell her Fanny is home—

IRVING *(Shaking her, trying to impress his words on her.)* Fanny—listen to me— I'm going to look for Mama—tell her you're here— *(He suddenly begins to laugh hysterically.)* Fanny—you're home—you're home, darling—laugh! Laugh, Fanny! *(He continues to laugh, his hysteria mounting.)*

FANNY Where's Esther?

SADIE *(Breaking.)* We don't know where she is!

FANNY *(Quietly, after pause.)* I am downstairs. Walking, walking—I ask every-body, where is Esther? Nobody knows. *(She notices* SADIE.)*

IRVING Sadie, please, I'll stay here with her. Go try to find Mama—please—

FANNY *(Suddenly, pointing to* SADIE.*) She* did it—she put the curse on her! I heard you! This morning you said to her, "I wish you were dead—"

(SADIE, *frightened, runs to door, exits quickly.* IRVING *holds* FANNY *close, quieting her.*)

IRVING Look, Fanny—it's me, Irving. Remember Irving? Just like yesterday and the day before—your piece of candy—

FANNY *(Quietly.)* I forgot—the pay envelope. Here— *(She takes small envelope out of her pocket, miraculously safe. Suddenly rational.)* The bell is ringing. Everybody talking and laughing. We are going home. Then—we are running—like crazy we are running—screaming. I am near a wall and somebody is pushing me up a ladder. *(Her voice trails off.)* Who is pushing me—Oh, yes— Piney—

IRVING *(Weeping unashamedly.)* I'm going to kiss Piney for that, you'll see, I'll kiss him for pushing you—

FANNY *(Suddenly she breaks away from* IRVING *and starts running around, pushing* IRVING *aside as though he were in the way. She starts screaming.)* I gotta get out! Out—out—help—out—Esther—Esther—

(IRVING *picks her up, carries her into upper bedroom, where her moans resound for a moment.* AARON *and* BECKY *enter.* BECKY *is near collapse.* SADIE *follows them in.*)

BECKY Oh— *(She quickly exits into upper bedroom.* AARON *sits, exhausted.* MYRON *enters.)*

AARON *(Looking up.)* Fanny is home—

MYRON Thank God!

AARON We left Harry in our place in the line—thousands waiting to get into the morgue. All of them had relatives or friends? No. Curiosity seekers. At a time like this, curiosity seekers!

MYRON *(Quietly.)* They'll know soon enough. The morgue has no secrets. Tomorrow the whole East Side will be in mourning— *(Pause,* SADIE *enters.)* For eight hours I have been making the rounds of the hospitals. After what I saw the first five minutes I prayed in my heart I would not find them—better off dead. Better off— *(A pause. The men look at one another.)* You have to hope. Fanny came home.

AARON A child—a baby. (BECKY *enters from bedroom.)*

BECKY Asleep. It's good she can sleep—

AARON *(Placating, to* BECKY.*)* Becky, where was Fanny all day? Maybe Esther is also walking around like Fanny. They'll find her—they'll bring her home—

BECKY *(In a daze.)* She *got* to come home—tomorrow is the wedding—everything is ready— *(Looking around.)* I didn't finish the challis— *(She touches *dough, still resting on table where she left it.)* Mrs. O'Shaughnessy's Annie. They found her there— *(Looking around suddenly.)* Where's Hymie?

SADIE   He went downstairs—I'll go find him. *(She exits quickly.)*

BECKY   *(Dazed.)* Mrs. Pomerantz's two boys and her husband— *(Suddenly she runs to rack, grabs her shawl.)*

AARON   *(Gently taking her arm.)* Where are you going?

BECKY   Esther is there—somewhere—I have to find her—

AARON   *(Gently drawing her away from door.)* Please, you have to wait—

BECKY   *(To* MYRON *as she walks toward table.)* I have to wait—wait— *(Dropping into chair, exhausted.)* Wait— *(A pause. A moment later door opens and* HARRY *enters. He is too quiet. They all look at him with pleading eyes.* HARRY *goes toward* BECKY. *Taking her hand, he opens it, placing* ESTHER'S *ring in it.* HARRY *turns away, goes to buffet quietly, his back to them. He suddenly doubles up in a spasm of dry, hacking sobs.* BECKY *continues to stare at ring in her hand. Quietly, dazed, unbelieving.)* A dollar a week for two years— *(Her voice breaks as)*

CURTAIN

SCENE 2

The same. Early April, 1917. Six years later. Late afternoon. The set is changed only in so far as six years of living in one place will bring about the inevitable changes of a different set of curtains, a new calendar, perhaps a new chair or two. The old couch has been exchanged for a new sofa in the best Grand Rapids manner of the period. Otherwise everything remains the same.

AT RISE: HYMIE *and* HARRY *in heated discussion.* HARRY *is now close to thirty, he wears glasses and has developed a more scholarly manner.* HYMIE *is now nineteen, a good-looking young man with a vivacious excitable manner.*

HYMIE   I tell you it's any minute now, Harry. Did you see where we handed the German Ambassador his walking papers?

HARRY   *(Unnerved.)* Severing of diplomatic relations doesn't necessarily mean war! *(HYMIE takes up violin and plays a bar of scales.)* The *Illinois*'s not the first ship that went down. They can still send a note of regret.

HYMIE   Not this time. She told us six weeks ago she's starting unrestricted submarine warfare! They're calling National Guardsmen up for Federal Service already!

(A knock at door. HYMIE *answers it.* BENJAMIN *enters. The years have made little change in his appearance.)*

BENJAMIN   Greenspan is home?

HYMIE   Not yet—

BENJAMIN   *(Ill at ease, not in his usual manner.)* If it's all right with you, I'll wait.

HYMIE How'ya, Brownstein?

BENJAMIN *(Absorbed in his own thoughts.)* All right—

HYMIE *(With a laugh.)* You *should* be all right! Kerensky and your boyfriends sure fixed the Czar!

BENJAMIN Kerensky! When I think of him, with my two hands I could— *(He makes gesture of choking.)*

HYMIE You're complaining?

BENJAMIN The workers made a Revolution to reestablish the old order? No! *(He gets up, agitated.)* Any minute they'll start sweeping again—they'll sweep him out with the rest of the dirt!

HARRY *(Suddenly, out of his own absorption.)* Benjamin, do you think America will enter the war?

BENJAMIN Wall Street, you should excuse me, will sit on its fat behind, and let Germany win? And lose their investment in the Allies?

HYMIE *(Laughing.)* Speech! Speech! (BECKY *enters from kitchen.)*

BENJAMIN Go ahead! Make fun! The propaganda presses will start rolling, before you know it you'll be sporting a uniform and acting like it was your own idea! You give your life. Wall Street gets back its money! Fifty-fifty! Fine America! *(He spits disgustedly.)*

BECKY Mr. Brownstein! This is a free country, but about America please don't spit in my house!

BENJAMIN What did I tell you? Propaganda presses!

HARRY *(More and more disturbed.)* I'll never go to war. I'll go to jail first!

HYMIE *(Laughing.)* I think I'll give up the violin and start playing the bugle!

BECKY Nothing is settled yet, so Hymie is playing the bugle and Harry is sitting in jail already!

BENJAMIN *(Quietly.)* And I am on my way to Russia.

BECKY Russia?

BENJAMIN Saturday I am sailing.

BECKY *(Concerned.)* Why should you go to Russia? You're an American citizen—

BENJAMIN *(Solemnly.)* They *need* me.

BECKY Without you they made it— How about a bite supper with us, Mr. Brownstein?

BENJAMIN *(Getting up instantly, follows* BECKY *into kitchen.)* Supper? I wouldn't care if I did. *(They are gone.* HARRY, *greatly upset, continues to read paper, anxiously.)*

HYMIE *(Putting violin back into case. Noticing* HARRY's *absorption.)* Got you worried, hasn't it—

HARRY *(Picking up newspaper.)* Seven thousand dead—like they were describing a baseball game— Everything I've tried to teach, all being destroyed in front of my eyes! *(Pleading suddenly.)* Wilson was re-elected because he kept us out of it— He can't suddenly turn turkey on us—

HYMIE He'll do what he has to do! *(Pause as he sees* HARRY's *expression.)* They're fighting our battle, Harry. How can we avoid it? This is a war to end war!

HARRY War to end war? Man! There's no such thing!

HYMIE   *(After a pause.)* Well—I'm enlisting—

HARRY   Hymie, my God—why?

HYMIE   Sh—Mom doesn't know yet—

HARRY   Do you mean to say you could go out and kill a man?

HYMIE   About such things you have to be strictly impersonal—

HARRY   What's impersonal about killing a man who wants to live as much as you do?

HYMIE   I don't like that part of it any more than you do! But fellows like you take too much for granted! Freedom, Democracy—just words in a dictionary to you! When I think of that guy and what he's doing over there—I see red!

HARRY   Listen to me, Hymie—you're not going to preserve Freedom and Democracy by killing! You're going to *destroy* it! Just look at your history books—even the rotten books they gave you to read. The books I've had to teach all my life— *(Breaks off.)* Maybe it's my fault. Maybe if I and others like me had done our parts better—maybe if I had *fought* for the things I stood for— *(Pause.)* But I lost interest— *(Pause.)* Do I talk this way because I'm afraid to die? God knows I've thought of death often enough, as a way out—

HYMIE   *(Quietly.)* Harry, don't talk like a fool—

HARRY   Don't do it, Hymie.

HYMIE   *(Quietly.)* Please, I've made up my mind—a man's gotta do what he has to do—

HARRY   *(After pause.)* All right. We see things differently. You want to go—I can't stop you. But I won't go, because I don't believe in it! I have no faith in violence as a means of settling anything.

BECKY   *(Calling out from kitchen.)* Boys! Come eat supper—

(HARRY exits into kitchen. HYMIE remains behind absorbed in thought. AARON enters. The six years have dealt kindly with him. A few gray hairs add distinction to his appearance.)

HYMIE   Hello, Mr. Greenspan—

BECKY   *(Calling out again.)* That's you, Aaron?

AARON   Who else?

BECKY   *(Through kitchen door.)* Mr. Brownstein, Aaron is here—

AARON   *(To HYMIE.)* Some warm day for this time of year— (HYMIE *grabs his hat, and exits suddenly.)* Where are you going in such a hurry? (BENJAMIN *enters. To BENJAMIN.)* And how is the world treating you, Brownstein?

BENJAMIN   *(Coming to point.)* Greenspan, I won't waste your time and my time with preliminaries! You can answer "yes" or "no" and I won't be insulted. Last week I told you I am going to Russia. Well—there is a small matter of two hundred dollars for expenses. I need a loan. (AARON *is taken by surprise. Suddenly implication of* BENJAMIN's *words dawns on him.* AARON *starts to laugh.)* What's the joke?

AARON *(Laughing heartily.)* You are asking *me*, the dirtiest capitalist exploiter in America, by your own words, to lend you the money to go to Russia to fight a revolution?

BENJAMIN I thought you wouldn't see it my way. Never mind—

AARON Wait a minute! Did I say "no"? *(BENJAMIN stops in his tracks.)* Give a man at least a good laugh for his two hundred dollar investment?

BENJAMIN Please—I don't see the joke!

AARON Aye, Brownstein, one reason I like you is because you can always be depended on *not* to see the joke!

BENJAMIN Greenspan, yes or no, do I get the money?

AARON *(With a smile.)* I'll lend you the money, on *one* condition—

BENJAMIN *(Almost apoplectic.)* Conditions?

AARON Yes. On condition that— *(Pretending to be serious.)* comes the Revolution in America, when they are putting me against the wall, you'll tell them, if it weren't for *me*—you would never—

BENJAMIN *(Cutting in.)* Never! You can't buy your immunity with two hundred dollars, Greenspan.

AARON *(Laughing.)* Brownstein, Brownstein, you are worth the price of an admission! *(Suddenly serious.)* You want to know the *truth?* Comes the Revolution in America— *(Forcefully.)* they can line me against the wall and to hell with your immunity!

BENJAMIN So? *(AARON takes out checkbook, makes out check.)*

AARON *(As he writes.)* Believe it or not, I will miss you, Brownstein.

BENJAMIN A man must go where his principles send him. *(Ostentatiously, blows his nose. It is evident that AARON's generosity has touched him. AARON solemnly hands check to BENJAMIN.)*

AARON *(Holding out his hand.)* Will I see you again in my life?

BENJAMIN Where I am going, a man can't make plans for the future.

AARON So it's good-bye— *(They shake hands.)*

BENJAMIN Well— *(He fingers check, then shoves it into his pocket, and goes toward kitchen door.)* On good-byes and thank-yous, I'm not so good— *(Pause.)* You tell her— *(BENJAMIN is gone.)*

BECKY *(Entering.)* Aaron, supper is ready—where's Brownstein? *(AARON looks after him a moment.)*

AARON He went to Russia— Becky, would you call me a fool? I gave him two hundred dollars to go there.

BECKY Oh— *(Slowly, after a moment.)* I think if a man believes in something so strong he's willing to give up his life for it— *(Shaking her head.)* a person shouldn't stand in his way.

AARON *(Gently.)* That's what I thought, too. *(They smile each other, a look of understanding passing between them. HARRY enters from kitchen, goes to window, pensively.)* What's for supper, mine dear lady? *(AARON exits. BECKY remains behind, watching HARRY. She is about to exit into kitchen when FANNY and IRVING enter from street.)*

BECKY How was the picture?

IRVING I never saw such trash—

FANNY Maybe it's trash, but in the meantime your Uncle Abe is in California making thousands out of it, and you're starving to death!

IRVING I'm starving?

FANNY That's right! Take me literal—

IRVING *(As they go toward kitchen.)* The public wants live shows! Movies are a novelty. There's no *future* in it!

FANNY I suppose there's a big future for you in a forty-cent table de hote restaurant! Singing for *tips! (She is gone.)*

IRVING If you don't stop nagging me, I'll go out of the house, I won't come back! What's for supper? *(He exits after her.)*

BECKY *(Smiling gently.)* They talk like they mean it— *(Going to window, she opens it, sniffing the air.)* It's spring on Broome Street already, Harry— *(BECKY comes away from window, humming.)* "I didn't raise my boy to be a soldier. I raised him up to be my pride and—" *(She stops short, alarm in her voice.)* Harry!

HARRY *(Out of his absorption.)* Yes?

BECKY If—if they declare war—will my Hymie have to go? *(HARRY does not answer. BECKY is suddenly filled with the realization that War is the personal business of one's son going.)* Of course he'll have to go. Mrs. Strong's boy is only eighteen and he's a sailor— *(Pause.)* I'm so mixed up, Harry. When I took out my papers I swore to hold up the Constitution—to give my life— my life—gladly—but—but Hymie— *(She breaks off, tries to throw off her mood, hardly succeeding.)* You know what I am? Aaron calls me a pessimist. A Calamity Jane—that's me. *(Pleading with HARRY for confirmation.)* I bet in a few days the whole things is over and I'm worrying about Hymie—

HARRY We stayed out of it so far—there's not a chance in the world— *(Pause.)*

BECKY *(Seeing HARRY's absorption.)* After all these years, Harry—I think of you as if you were my own—

HARRY *(Looks up, caught by her tone.)* Yes?

BECKY *(Shaking her head.)* It's no good—Harry—what you have made of your life. *(With some force.)* A man mustn't dig a hole in the ground beside the loved one and lie down in it for the rest of his life! No! Six years of death for the living is a sin!

HARRY When she died the life went out of me—as if I were blinded—

BECKY Maybe it's because you have eyes in your head but you won't see what's right under your nose— *(She breaks off, looks closely at him.)* Sadie.

HARRY You mean Sadie—and me? *(BECKY nods gently. Disquieted.)* But—I never thought of Sadie that way—I—

BECKY Maybe if you did think about? *(HARRY turns away.)* I worry about you, Harry. I think what you were like, six, seven years ago! You were going to *do* so much! The world was yours—I look at you today, I get frightened. A young man and you never smile. Sitting for hours with your nose in a book,

looking for companionship with people who aren't real. Who never lived—
Tell me, is that a way for a man to live? Is it healthy? What will become of
you? *(Pause.)* My Sadie—I can see how she buries her feelings in the *job.*
Why? Because she has to have something to fill up her life—it's no way for a
woman to live, either! *(Quietly.)* Believe me, Harry, there is still time for you
to make a life for yourself. But you can't do it alone. I think to myself—two
fine young people—if they were *together,* they would be living for each other,
and they would both be happy— *(She breaks off.)* Harry—if you can't do
what I said—please forget I said it—

(Door opens and SADIE *enters. In six years she has gained a successful, satisfied
look. She is well-dressed and her manner is brisk.)*

SADIE Good evening.

HARRY How are you?

SADIE *(Taking off wraps.)* Same as I was last evening and the evening before.
Exhausted!

BECKY The shop is still going overtime? Aaron is home a while already—
(She exits to kitchen.)

SADIE He can leave. He's the boss— *(*AARON *comes to door.)*

AARON Where's the ketchup?

SADIE *(Laughing.)* Did you see today's papers, Greenspan? The shop'll be going
overtime plenty.

AARON *(Pompously.)* We're equipped!

SADIE Aaron, please, put me in charge of production. I'll make a fortune for
you! Don't leave me rotting behind that cage!

AARON What will I do with Van Brett?

SADIE Get rid of him. What do you need him for?

AARON *(Angrily.)* What are you talking about—? *(To no one in particular.)*
Did you ever see such a hard-boiled—I'm in partners with a man—my
friend—

SADIE *(Cutting in.)* He'll still be your friend when he bankrupts you? *(Sarcastically.)* Production manager! Buys ribbons when they wear feathers,
and feathers when they wear flowers and flowers when they want ribbons,
and when you ask him *why,* he says he *likes* it!

AARON We're making enough for a few mistakes. He's an old man—By the way,
make a note, I gave Benjamin Brownstein two hundred dollars. A loan.

SADIE What?

AARON Don't get excited! I shouldn't have told you.

SADIE I'm the bookkeeper so I wouldn't find out? Of course, the three hundred
dollars you owe me—

AARON *(Angrily.)* You don't trust me? I'm going to skip town with it?

SADIE Aaron, Aaron—sometimes, if you weren't my boss I would lose my
temper.

AARON That stops you? *(He exits into kitchen, ketchup bottle in his hand.* HARRY *is at window again, his back to* SADIE. *Her manner softens. We sense her old feeling for this man is still an active part of her.)*

SADIE *(As she takes some silver out of buffet drawer and sets a place for herself at table.)* Do you think I'm hard-boiled? When all I'm doing is protecting his interests. In business you have to follow the rules of *good* business.

HARRY I don't understand much about such things—

SADIE *(After pause.)* Did you have your supper?

HARRY Yes, thanks. Earlier—

SADIE And how is the teaching business?

HARRY It's all right— *(Awkward pause.* HARRY *suddenly looks at* SADIE *as though seeing her for the first time. Pointing to her dress.)* Is that what they call violet color?

SADIE *(Pleased.)* More on the purple side. Do you like it? I got it wholesale. *(She laughs.)* For as many years as I know you, never once did you remark on something I wore. You surprised me.

HARRY Sadie—I was wondering if you— *(He breaks off.)*

SADIE *(Starting to eat, newspaper by her side, she glances through it.)* Yes?

HARRY I—I wanted to ask you something—

SADIE *(After pause.)* You were saying—?

HARRY In—in all the years I have been practically living in the house—you know—eating here every night since Papa died—well—what I'd like to know is— *(Suddenly.)* What do you think of me—that is to say—if you think of me at all? *(From street we hear the faint call of newsboys shouting "Extry"— "Extry." The two pay no attention.)*

SADIE That's a funny question. We think of you as *belonging* in the house. Like a fixture—

HARRY I see. *(Simply.)* I guess I feel that way, too. *(Rationalizing, more for his own benefit than hers.)* This is my home. The only home I've known for a long time. I—I guess somehow I've attached myself to the family— *(Clears his throat.)* I feel very close to *all* of you. *(Pause.)* Do I make myself clear?

(We now make out cries of "Extry, Extry" as being quite close.)

SADIE Harry Engel, what are you trying to say to me?

*(*AARON *enters.)*

AARON They're calling "Extra"—

*(*BECKY, FANNY, *and* IRVING *have now entered, rush to window excitedly.)*

IRVING Wait a minute—

AARON *(To* IRVING.*)* Run down and get a paper.

BECKY *(Frightened.)* What could the Extra say? *(*IRVING *is at door, about to exit.* HYMIE *bursts into room. He carries a newspaper. They crowd around him.)* What is the Extra?

HYMIE *(Throwing paper on table.)* Listen, everybody! Wilson just called another session of Congress—

*(*HARRY *has picked paper up, scans it anxiously.)*

AARON An emergency?

HYMIE Just wants to talk a few things over with them.

SADIE I thought for a minute war was declared—

IRVING This means war, sure as there's hair on my head—

AARON Why should you care? You're a married man—

*(*FANNY, IRVING, *and* AARON *exit into kitchen, chattering excitedly.)*

HARRY Sadie—how—how would you like to take a walk—

SADIE *(Pleased.)* Why—that would be very nice. *(She goes toward rack, taking her jacket.* BECKY *has picked up newspaper which* HARRY *has dropped.)*

HARRY *(Pointedly, as he helps* SADIE *on with her coat.)* We'll be back in a little while, Mama—

*(*BECKY *looks up, torn between her realization that war is imminent and her pleasure that* HARRY *has asked* SADIE *to take a walk, perhaps more may come of it.* HARRY *and* SADIE *exit.)*

BECKY Come, I'll give you supper, Hymie—

HYMIE Mom—

BECKY Yes—

HYMIE First—I—I—gotta tell you something. *(Goes toward her, takes her hand in his, looking at her.)* Now, Mom, please don't be mad on me—

BECKY *(A frightened tone in her voice.)* Wait! don't tell me— *(She glances at paper on table, then quietly.)* I know—

CURTAIN

SCENE 3

The same. A year and a half later. November, 1918. About six-thirty in the evening.

AT RISE: FANNY *and* BECKY *enter from street. They take off their wraps, put their bundles down.*

FANNY *(Calling out.)* Irving! We're home! I don't feel my feet any more. *(She waits for his response.)* Asleep! Sometimes I get so mad at that man I could— *(She goes to bedroom door.)* Irving! He's not home. *(FANNY sits disconsolately.)*

BECKY He said he was going to see Mr. Strauss, the publisher—

FANNY That's what he tells you. How—how do I know he's not with some—some—?

BECKY You're not ashamed to think such a thing? What's got into you—?

FANNY I could swear—lately, he's *different.* Mama, I'm going crazy—

BECKY Foolish girl—he loves you like—I don't know what— *(Sternly.)* You know why he's never in the house? It's because you are making his life miserable, nagging and picking on him— *(Shaking head.)* All because he didn't make a million dollars—

FANNY *(Defensively.)* Who wants a *million*—just a living—

BECKY *(Gently.)* Fanny, Fanny, in your condition, a woman always imagines things ten times worse—

FANNY I'm giving him one last chance! If something doesn't happen by the time the baby comes, we're packing up! *(Pacing nervously.)* Right this minute he could be making fifty dollars a week with his Uncle Abe! Has he the right to bring a third person into the world when he can't take care of himself?

BECKY The boy hasn't luck—

FANNY If he found a horseshoe in front of the door, it would be his luck to trip on it, and break his neck!

BECKY *(Knocking on wood.)* God forbid! *(FANNY sits, exhausted by her tirade. Pause.)* Fanny—

FANNY Yes, Mama?

BECKY I believe in Irving. *(Simply.)* When he plays me one of his songs, I sing it in my head for a week. And if I could sing it—somebody else will—

FANNY *(Suddenly bitter again.)* Mama, Mama—I get so discouraged sometimes—I—I could die!

BECKY Sh! Don't say it. Never. Even if you feel it, *don't* say it. *(Gently patting* FANNY's *head.)*

FANNY *(After pause.)* Mama, are my feet *supposed* to hurt—?

(FANNY gets up. She kisses her mother gently, then exits into bedroom. BECKY remains behind looking after her. BECKY goes to window, raises shade. The raised shade discloses a service flag with a single gold star on it. A moment's pause. BECKY goes to buffet and takes a small watch from drawer. She winds it, puts it to her ear. After a moment, a knock at door. Hastily she puts it back into drawer—runs to open door. HARRY and SADIE enter. A year and a half of marriage has given SADIE added confidence in herself. Her manner is brisk, poised. HARRY, by contrast, is quieter than ever.)

SADIE *(Pecking BECKY's cheek.)* How are you, Mom?
BECKY All right. Hello, Harry.

HARRY Hello, Mama—

SADIE (*As she takes off her wraps.*) I'm starved. So busy today, I didn't eat lunch. (*As she comes down* C.) How's Fanny?

BECKY Fine. She's resting now.

SADIE Some people can *afford* to have babies. (*Pause.*) Well, Mama—we have wonderful news!

BECKY Yes?

SADIE We are going into business for ourselves! Today we settled everything! (HARRY *does not look particularly happy about this, but he nods when* BECKY *looks in his direction.*)

BECKY You're quitting Aaron?

SADIE That's right.

BECKY Now is a good time to go into business? Everybody says the war will be over any minute—

SADIE So the millinery business will be better than ever. The girls will be so happy the boys are coming home, they'll be dressed to kill!

BECKY What did Aaron say?

SADIE I didn't ask his opinion! (*Gaily to* HARRY.) And Harry is going to be my sales manager—

BECKY Harry? (*She turns toward him.*) You're giving up teaching?

SADIE Foolish to pay a stranger sixty a week when we can keep it in the family— (BECKY *looks at* HARRY, *searchingly, aware how painful this business must be to him.*) And, Mama—speaking of keeping it in the family, how much money do you have?

BECKY You know what I have— (*A catch in her throat.*) Hymie's—the college money—

SADIE Well, I'm borrowing two hundred—

HARRY (*Cutting in.*) Sadie, I asked you not to—

SADIE She's using it? I'll pay her back with interest! We need cash, don't we? Come on—let's eat—

(SADIE *and* HARRY *exit into kitchen.* BECKY *is about to exit.* AARON *enters from street, visibly shaken.* BECKY *follows his every movement, deeply concerned. He walks to couch, sits down, buries face in his hands.*)

BECKY Aaron—what's the matter?

AARON Mrs. Felderman, you see before you a man at the end of his senses. That daughter of yours, Sadie—if—if I am arrested for committing murder on her, please, you should excuse me, but I am *entitled* to it!

BECKY What are you talking about?

AARON With her own hands to stick the knife in my back— (*Mops his brow.*) Today she quit Van Brett and Greenspan. A woman has a *right* to quit— (*Quietly, a catch in his throat.*) Just now I find out why she quit! To open a millinery factory next door!

BECKY *(Softly.)* Oh—

AARON Would you call that ethical? A woman works for us seven years—gets on friendly terms with all our customers—gets them all in the bag—and quits us to open up next door! *(Pause.)* To take away our business. For myself, to hell with it! But Van Brett—over sixty years old—a man with a wife and four children— (SADIE *comes to door.)* Oh! There you are!

BECKY *(To* SADIE *forcibly.)* Sadie! Is he telling me the truth?

SADIE *(Coldly, without emotion.)* Did you also tell her why I haven't a cent in cash? How much money you owe me in five and ten dollar bills, out of my salary every other week—six hundred dollars! *(Directly to* AARON.*)* Would you like it better if I put you into bankruptcy? I am entitled to it! But I am simply going into legitimate competition with you!

AARON Competition to ruin our business?

SADIE A man like you doesn't have the *right* to be in business! You're an old fool! Now I can tell it to you!

AARON *(Almost apoplectic.)* I'm a fool? What I forgot about the millinery business, you don't have in your little finger! *(To* BECKY.*)* You know what she can't stand? Because I have a *union* in my shop!

SADIE To be the *only* manufacturer on Grand Street with a union shop is to be in the charity business, not the millinery business!

AARON In my shop I don't want to be ashamed my workingmen should look me in the face! (HARRY *is at door watching proceedings with distaste.* AARON, *in a daze.)* You know what this will do to Van Brett? It will kill him. *(Pleading.)* Please, so I owe you a few cents. *(Pause.)* A man has a season's hard luck. Notes I'll give you—with my life's blood, I'll pay you back—

SADIE Hard luck? To lose a fortune in a boom period? If you have to know, you're the laughing stock in the whole trade!

AARON *(Screaming.)* What I forgot about the millinery business—

SADIE *(Cutting in.)* In my little finger—I know! *(Laughing.)* You shouldn't be afraid of a little competition! It's the life and spirit of American business! On that principle, my dear man, there is room for everybody! I am quoting you, Mr. Greenspan!

(SADIE *exits into kitchen.* HARRY *and* BECKY *remain behind, watching* AARON. *He takes a much-battered suitcase from behind couch, opens buffet drawer and starts to throw his clothes into it.)*

BECKY What are you doing?

AARON How will I face Van Brett! *(Paying no attention. Pursues his own train of thought. He throws more clothes into suitcase.)* Van Brett never liked her. But I said to him, "Let's hire her. She's not so good-natured, but she's smart. And she's the daughter of my best friend." So we hired her. *(Goes to bedroom door, takes two suits which hang behind it, packs them into suitcase through the next.)* How can I tell him we had behind our cage a snake in the grass!

(Addressing HARRY *and* BECKY *directly.)* You heard her! "Room for everybody." Me she was quoting! My own words come home to slap me in the face! *(He continues to pack. Quietly, with resignation.)* America I wanted. In a potato barrel I escaped to come here. For five days and five nights it rained. When they pulled me out on the other side of the border, I was half drowned. *(He laughs, a thin laugh, with no mirth in it.)* You know what, Mrs. Felderman, my darling? I *should* have drowned.

BECKY *(A frightened strain in her voice.)* You're moving out—

AARON *(Gently.)* I'll visit you, Becky. She's your daughter. You can't refuse her the house. To meet her accidentally, ten years from now, would be too soon— *(Picks up his suitcase. With nod to* HARRY *and gentle look in* BECKY's *direction, he exits.* BECKY *looks at* HARRY, *then in direction of kitchen door, as though making up her mind. Suddenly calls out, a forceful dominant quality in her voice.)*

BECKY Sadie!

SADIE *(Coming to door.)* He's gone?

BECKY You didn't tell me going into business would mean this—

SADIE Mama, please, take care of your own life. And I'll take care of mine! In business it's the survival of the *fittest!*

BECKY With not one penny of mine! *(Pleading.)* Sadie, Sadie, with such ideas— to go through life— *(FANNY enters from bedroom.)*

HARRY *(Has been listening, now speaks suddenly, agitated.)* I never wanted to go into business, anyway!

SADIE *(Sharply.)* I'll stay home and bake a cake waiting for your twenty-seven dollar pay envelope from the City of New York?

HARRY But business is not in my nature—I like to teach school. It's useful, important work—

SADIE Where *promotion* is something the *kids* get! You took the examination, they threw you into 5-B—to sit there till you rot! Well, I want something better from life than a three-room flat in the Bronx, even if it has got an elevator! *(BECKY turns away, the picture of* HARRY *at the mercy of* SADIE's *bitter tongue too much for her.* SADIE *putting coat on, impatiently.)* I did all the arguing in one day I'm going to— *(To* HARRY.) Get your coat. We're going home. *(To* BECKY.) Never mind your money. I'll get what I need from the bank! *(SADIE is gone. A pause.)*

BECKY *(Quietly, in self-castigation.)* I begged Aaron to give her the job. *(Pause, as she closes buffet drawer, breaks off.)* And worst of all, Harry, what did I do to you?

HARRY Don't blame youself, Mama. A man should be able to face his life like— like a *man. (Pause, then wryly.)* I guess I'm a pretty poor excuse for one— *(Taking his coat from rack. With a level glance in* BECKY's *direction, he exits.)*

FANNY *(When he is gone.)* Why does he stand for it? If I was him, I'd leave and I'd never come back! *(Torn,* BECKY *goes to window.* IRVING *enters, morose, his appearance has changed considerably. He looks tired, seedy.)*

IRVING *(With no spirit.)* How'ya, Mom? Hello, honey— *(Managing a wry smile.)* Well—I saw Strauss today— *(IRVING looks at FANNY.)* You win, baby! We're packing for California the minute the kid comes!

BECKY Something happened, Irving—I can tell—

IRVING He told me the truth! He can't publish my stuff. And you wanna know why? Because they're *too* sad. They want happy songs! Optimistic songs! Songs that'll make 'em forget we're still fightin' a war— *(Breaking out.)* How in hell can I *write* happy, if I don't feel happy?

FANNY *(Gently.)* You hate to leave New York, don't you?

IRVING Like taking poison—

FANNY Then we *don't* go! No! No! *(To BECKY.)* I'm not doing to my Irving what she's doing to Harry! No, sir! *(Going to IRVING.)* You want to stay here, you stay here, darling! Even if you don't make a million dollars, if *you're* happy, I'm happy! *(BECKY looks on, fighting tears. From outside we hear faint cries and a whistle blowing.)*

IRVING *(Hugging FANNY.)* God! What a woman! What a woman!

FANNY Irving, sweetheart, only one thing I'm going to ask you— Promise me, when you become a big songwriter, you'll let me sing your songs.

IRVING *(Laughing affectionately.)* Okay, I swear! When I write my hit, you can sing it all you want.

FANNY Oh, Irving—

IRVING Except on the stage!

FANNY You rotten thing! *(BECKY goes to window, opens it. Sounds from outside grow louder. She looks out.)*

BECKY What's all the blowing, Irving? I can't see what—

IRVING *(Going to window.)* Something in the street—

FANNY *(She too is at window now. Excitedly.)* It's coming from across the way. Look! Mrs. Gold! She's going crazy! She's banging on the window with a pot!

BECKY Mr. Sullivan is hanging with his head out yelling— *(Calling down.)* Mr. Sullivan! What's the noise? *(A pause as she listens for his answer.)* What? Did you hear him? It's over! IT'S OVER!

(BECKY, IRVING and FANNY, now hysterical, hang over window yelling "Hooray" — "Hooray" — "It's over — "It's over." Street noises, whistles, sirens, voices have grown to tremendous proportions. The three embrace for a moment, dancing around. Suddenly BECKY disengages herself, walks away, lost in her own grief.)

FANNY Irving! Quick! Let's go downstairs!

IRVING *(Rushing to piano.)* Wait a minute! Wait a minute!

FANNY The war is over and he's at the piano!

IRVING *(Excitedly, plays something with a stirring martial quality.)* He said he wants it happy, didn't he? Didn't he?

FANNY Irving, please, take me downstairs!

IRVING *(Playing four bars over again.)* Just listen to this, will ya? The same tune I wrote last week. I change it from a major key to a minor key—and put it in four, four time! *(FANNY suddenly begins to double over with pain, a surprised look on her face.)* And what a title! "We'll Bring the Rue de la Paix Back to Old Broadway, and Make the Boys Forget Paree"— *(He repeats four bars, playing while he sings.)*

FANNY *(Calling out suddenly.)* Irving! *(He pays no attention to her. Sounds of sirens, whistles are now joined by a brass band, filling room. FANNY screams again.)* Mama!

(In a moment BECKY's grief is forgotten in FANNY's need of her. BECKY rushes to FANNY's side.)

BECKY Irving! Quick! Run for the doctor! It's her time!

IRVING *(Frightened.)* Oh, my God—

BECKY Stop swearing and run for the doctor! You'll talk to God later— *(The room is filled with the sounds of Armistice as)*

CURTAIN

ACT III

NOTE ON SET DECORATION: *It is suggested that a simple change can be effected by the substitution of two wallpaper plugs, one at upstage wall and one at lower L. wall.*

SCENE: *Late afternoon, November, 1931. Thirteen years later. While the set remains the same, considerable change has taken place in its furnishings. The old furniture is gone and a heterogeneous assortment of modern and overstuffed pieces takes its place. The old upright piano has been exchanged for a radio. This is still BECKY's home, however, so that the whole suggests a comfortable living atmosphere, in spite of IRVING and FANNY's overgenerosity in the matter of "buying Mama a nice thing occasionally." The table C. is elaborately set with a complete service for seven, including shining glassware and silver.*

AT RISE: PANSY, *the Tashman's colored maid, finishing setting table. She is about fifty, inclined to fat, with a broad good-humored smile. She hums a tune. Goes to a drawer, takes some linen out of it. SADIE and HARRY enter. Both are now definitely middle-aged. SADIE is thinner, drier, her voice more carping than ever. HARRY, now forty-five, looks closer to fifty. The years have taken their toll of his health and spirit.*

SADIE *(As they enter.)* I told Mama the minute I laid eyes on that fellow— *(Breaks off when she sees PANSY.)* What are you doing here?

PANSY Mis' Fanny sent me. (*Pompously.*) I'm supposed to be helpin' with the dinner for Mr. Hymie's birthday— (*Exits into kitchen.*)

HARRY (*Coming down to couch.*) In spite of what the papers say—I never met a finer, more generous fellow than Irving—

SADIE Why shouldn't he be? Mama didn't do enough for him? (*Laughing.*) Some generous. Carrying on with that Hope—Hope whatever-her-name-is—

HARRY (*As he sits.*) Please, Sadie—

SADIE All right! There's nobody around— (*Placing package on buffet which she has brought in with her.*) You think he deserves it, the fresh kid! Image of his father—

HARRY For his Bar Mitzvah, you could have bought him something better than two shirts. There are a hundred things a boy would enjoy more—

SADIE Let his father watch out for his son's enjoyment. Eighty-five dollar Erector sets, hundred dollar trains—if I spent my hard-earned money on foolishness like his father— (HARRY *looks at her. She goes to table, sits down.*) I hope Aaron shows up! It's our only chance. Four times I got him to the phone. When I tell him who it is, he hangs up—

HARRY He can't do anything anyway—

SADIE (*Getting up impatiently.*) He's influential in the union, isn't he? You'll have to talk to him, Harry—

HARRY What could I say? He'd be on their side, not yours—

SADIE Tell him, with thirty-two stores all canceling our orders because the union threatens to picket them, it absolutely ain't fair!

HARRY They catch you where it hurts the most, so you have to sign with them—

SADIE What I want to know is, what side are *you* on? (PANSY *enters with seltzer bottle, places it on table.*)

HARRY (*Cutting in, patiently.*) Sadie, I've had a hard day. I don't feel well—I'm going to lie down. (*Exits up. R.*)

SADIE (*Following him in.*) I was in the office three hours before you came in—I can hardly stand on my feet—and you don't feel well—

(*They are gone. A moment later* BECKY *enters, carrying a number of bundles. Well preserved, nicely dressed, she still retains her youthful vivacity.*)

PANSY Lordy, Lordy—what you got there? I thought you was jes' goin' 'cross the street to show Mrs. Gold your dress—

BECKY (*Handing her bundles.*) A few extra things I figured we would need— (*Surveying herself happily.*) She says I look like a girl in it.

PANSY Sure do! Cake's finished, ma'am. Stuck a straw in it. It come out clean, so I took it outta the stove—

BECKY (*Smiling.*) On Broome Street you can *smell* a cake is done, Pansy.

PANSY (*Near kitchen door.*) Miss Sadie and Mr. Harry, they're here—and Mr. Tashman, he brung the liquor— (*Whispering.*) And, ma'am—he gimme a note for you— (BECKY *takes it.*) He said nobody else was to see it—

(BECKY *reads note.* PANSY *exits into kitchen.* BECKY *goes to phone. She is about to make a call, when voices of* FANNY *and* YOUNG HYMIE *are heard in hall.* BECKY *puts down receiver, drops note in her pocket, opens door.* FANNY *and* YOUNG HYMIE *enter. She is now thirty-eight, smartly dressed, inclined to plumpness.* HYMIE *is thirteen—a cute, spoiled kid.)*

FANNY   I don't feel my feet any more.

BECKY   How was the parade, Hymie?

HYMIE   *(In a bored tone.)* It was all right—

FANNY   Every time I go, I vow never again! If it wasn't for the kid— *(She is sitting now and has removed one shoe.)* Everything is ready, Mama? Pansy was a help to you?

BECKY   *(Laughing.)* If somebody told me thirteen years ago Pansy would be making gefilte fish for Hymie's Bar Mitzvah—

FANNY   *(Rubbing the aching foot.)* With a bunch of dummies pushing you around like you were nothing! I don't know if it's from walking or because it's going to rain!

HYMIE   *(Speaking up.)* Not enough we gotta *watch* the parade, Mom makes us *follow* it from 34th Street to 59th Street—

FANNY   *(Defensively.)* What's the matter? Don't I do it for you?

HYMIE   *(Trying to be patient.)* Mom, in my whole life did I ever ask you to take me to a parade?

FANNY   Will you listen to that kid, Mama? That's all the appreciation—

HYMIE   Well, did I? *(BECKY starts to laugh.)* She's always saying we go to the parade on account of *me.* I don't even *like* parades. *She* likes them, that's why we go.

FANNY   *(Laughing.)* I'll kill that kid! You're not ashamed to embarrass me in front of Grandma? *(FANNY makes playful dash for him. He eludes her, laughing.)* Hurry up, take your bath—

HYMIE   Gee, I had a bath this morning, didn't I—?

FANNY   My hair is turning white—

HYMIE   Okay, okay— *(As he walks toward kitchen door.)* Hey, Mom—do I have to make the speech tonight?

FANNY   I should say so!

HYMIE   Gee—it's so dumb—I don't wanna—

FANNY   What did I tell you out of respect for Grandma?

HYMIE   So can't I make it for her *alone?*

FANNY   You have to make it for everybody, or it's not good luck!

HYMIE   *(As he exits into kitchen.)* Today I yam a man! Crap!

FANNY   *(Laughing.)* I'll die with that kid! Where he picks up those words! *(SADIE enters.)* Hello.

BECKY   How is Harry feeling?

SADIE   I made him lay down a while.

BECKY   He saw the doctor last week?

SADIE *(Sitting.)* If he were really sick, he'd run! *(Sighing.)* Mama—have I trouble—times are terrible. They've been picketing my place for three weeks already—

BECKY   I thought you were going to settle with them?

SADIE   They should live so, if I'll let a union dictate how my business should be run! I'll starve first!

FANNY   You won't starve

SADIE   *(Sharply.)* What do you mean by that? *(Hotly.)* Every cent I have is frozen in real estate. Maybe you are not aware we are up to our ears in a depression, the worst in the history—

FANNY   People still pay you rent, or they'd get a dispossess. *(Laughing.)* I should know. Any minute I expect to find them sticking one under *my* door—

SADIE   You're certainly very cheerful about it—

FANNY   Why shouldn't I be cheerful? Even if Irving's royalties only came to a couple of hundred last month, a son's Bar Mitzvah doesn't happen every day in the week. *(Cheerfully rubbing the offending member.)* I bet I walked a hundred blocks today. Oh—those high heels. (HARRY *enters, stands at doorway, stretching.*)

SADIE   *(Relentlessly pursuing subject.)* For a man who's making so little money, he certainly allows himself expensive *pastimes*—

FANNY   *(Hotly.)* Well—we're not like *some* people! We like to live!

SADIE   Evidently you don't read the papers, or you wouldn't be so cheerful—

FANNY   *(Suddenly looking from one to other.)* Wait a minute. What was that remark? *(An embarrassed pause.)*

SADIE   It just struck me funny you don't read the newspapers.

FANNY   *(Beseechingly to* BECKY.*)* Mama, what is she talking about?

SADIE   *(Casually.)* Turn to page 26 in the *Graphic*—

FANNY   Where's the paper, Mama?

BECKY   I don't know—

SADIE   *(Pointing to table.)* I brought one in— (FANNY *grabs paper, hastily scans it.*)

HARRY   Did you have to tell her?

SADIE   *(Defensively.)* Better to hear it from her sister than her poker-playing girl friends!

(BECKY *looks on, fear growing in her expression.* FANNY *reads item, thrusts paper into* BECKY's *hand. She exits quickly, lower* R., *a sob escaping her.* BECKY *reads item quickly.*)

BECKY   *(Exiting after* FANNY, *calling out as she goes.)* Fanny! Don't believe it! It's not true—

HARRY   *(Too quietly.)* Well, I guess we can go home now.

SADIE   We're staying right here for our family obligations! *(We hear* FANNY's *voice in hysterical weeping.)*

HARRY   Was that a family obligation, too?

SADIE The *Graphic* has a circulation of a million, so she wouldn't find out? *(HARRY stares at her a moment, turns on his heels.)* Where are you going?

HARRY Home.

SADIE You're staying right here to speak to Greenspan tonight!

HARRY *(With quiet determination.)* This is as good a time as any to tell you, Monday morning won't see me in that shop again. I'm re-applying for my license to teach school, and I'm going back!

SADIE *(Startled.)* The fact that I need you in the shop more than ever—

HARRY *(Quietly but with strange force.)* For my part, lock it up, throw the key in the river!

SADIE This is my reward, my thanks for fighting to build up some security for our old age?

HARRY I don't need security for my old age. I'm a sick man, Sadie. I want to live the last few years of my life in *peace!*

(BECKY enters distracted and upset.)

SADIE Did you hear him, Mama? After all these years he wants to go back to 5-B again!

HARRY *(Cutting in.)* Do we have to talk about it here?

SADIE Anything I have to say to you, my mother can hear! *(With self-assurance.)* Make up your mind to it, Engel. Monday morning finds you in the office as usual!

HARRY *(Quietly.)* I'll see you in hell first!

SADIE *(Aghast.)* Who do you think you are, to talk to me—?

HARRY *(With a new kind of determination.)* I'm a man! I know you don't think I'm much of a man—but *once* I had a heart and a spirit and a head! I didn't ask for much. A decent useful life with a woman—

SADIE Well, you had it, so what do you want?

HARRY No! No! Now I can say it! Never with you! Not for one minute— *(Pause.)* When I married you I was lost and I wanted to find myself again. I thought I could find myself with you! I wanted to love you! For fifteen years I tried! For fifteen years I've watched you violate every code of human behavior—putting money before human decency—playing one dirty trick after another on people who trusted you—what you did to Fanny just now—I just can't take it any longer! Ask me why I'm telling you now! I could have told you when you murdered Van Brett—

BECKY Harry—no—

HARRY *(Relentlessly pursuing subject.)* A coincidence—wasn't it, his jumping out of a window just thirteen years ago today! The Armistice bells were still ringing when we got the news! I didn't tell you then because I was afraid of your tongue. Afraid of that cyclone in you that goes through life tearing people up by the roots! Ask me why I'm telling you now! Why I'm no longer afraid— *(Pause.)* Because I'm dying, Sadie. As surely as I stand here.

BECKY *(Taking step toward* HARRY, *horrified.)* It's not true—you'll see a doctor—

HARRY It's no use, Mama. On Saturday I saw the best heart specialist in the country. At the most I've got one, maybe two years—

BECKY *(Heartbroken.)* Harry—Harry—

HARRY And I'm not sorry, Sadie. No. I deserved what I got. I gave in to you because it was easier than fighting with you. It took me all these years to learn that men who don't fight for the things they believe in deserve to die—

SADIE *(Turning.)* I hope you're being paid back for what you did to me. You think you fooled me all these years? You think a woman doesn't know when she lives with a man who's in love with a memory? The joke is on me! Break my heart over a man for the best years of my life! I finally get him! What do I get? A weak—spineless—impotent—

(She breaks off. With look of complete contempt, HARRY *turns, takes his hat, exits without a backward glance.)*

BECKY Harry, come back—

SADIE He'll come back. *(After pause.)* Well, we put on a fine show for you, didn't we? Trying to scare me that way—

BECKY *(Stonily.)* He was telling the truth—

SADIE Oh, go on—

BECKY I know Harry. Only if he were dying could he tell you the truth about yourself!

SADIE That's right—go ahead—

BECKY *(Flaring out.)* The outside world doesn't do enough to tear a family to pieces, you have to tear it apart from the *inside!* I ask you, can a string of tenement properties and a boxful of printed papers in a bank bring you an ounce of happiness, when there's not a human soul in the world cares if they never saw you again—

SADIE *(Waving hand grandly.)* My sentiments are ditto for them—

BECKY All these years watching what you did to Harry—every time I saw you together, my heart broke—*because I told him to marry you!* (SADIE *sits, stunned.)* I didn't have to tell you, but I did it so you would know how it feels to be hurt for no reason—the way you hurt Fanny just now! I should have recognized this terrible thing in you when you were a child! I should have *beat* it out of you! *When*—when will you learn there are other things in life besides building up a fortune! Decency—human decency—

SADIE *(Going toward rack.)* If you think I'm going to stay here to be insulted!

BECKY Oh, no, you don't! *(With authority.)* You will sit here tonight at this table, eating Hymie's Bar Mitzvah supper if it kills you. You will talk and be friendly like nothing happened— *(Quietly.)* When you go home tonight—you do not have to come back here again. Never. (SADIE *makes move toward door.* BECKY *shouts.)* You will do as I say!

(Reluctant and frightened, SADIE *drops into a chair, weeping.* BECKY *exits into kitchen, a tiny, unhappy figure, torn by her participation in the scene.* FANNY *enters, looks at* SADIE. *Unable to face her gaze,* SADIE *exits into upper bedroom.)*

FANNY *(Calling out.)* Mama! *(*BECKY *enters.)* Well, Mama, I've made up my mind!

BECKY *(Her voice choked.)* Yes?

FANNY I'm leaving for Reno in the morning!

BECKY *(Frightened.)* Reno? In the magazines where they get divorces?

FANNY Not only in magazines. In real life too! *(Pause.)* Well, *say* something! You stand there like the Sphinx in Egypt!

BECKY Don't do it, Fanny—

FANNY Mama, Mama, I can't tell you how miserable I've been!

BECKY Fanny, darling, don't believe it! It's not true—

FANNY Mama, don't be naive! This isn't the first time! Three years ago when I read he was seen out with that dancer, I didn't believe it either! I let him get away with it. How long can I keep on closing my eyes—when Hope Robert's husband is suing her for divorce and naming Irving co-respondent?

BECKY The man says in the column he only *thinks* so—

FANNY He wouldn't dare to print it if it weren't true! He could be sued! *(Pause.)* Why should it happen to me? Am I ugly? Am I like some women married twenty years? I'm still beautiful, even if I do say so myself! *(Her voice breaks. Summoning her courage.)* Well, he won't get away with it! I'm leaving for Reno in the morning and he'll pay alimony through the nose!

BECKY With what? No song in a show for two years—

FANNY *(Heatedly.)* Right this minute he could be making three, four hundred a week in Hollywood with his Uncle Abe. *(Determined.)* Anyway, I don't need his money. I'm going back on the stage!

BACKY Thirty-eight years old, you do not start a career—

FANNY I'm thirty-seven.

BECKY If a year could make a difference to your voice— Maybe if you *still* had a voice—

FANNY All my friends think my voice is grand!

BECKY *(Firmly.)* They don't *pay* to hear you— *(Sadly.)* It makes me sad to say it, but you sound, you should excuse me, like a duck. *(*FANNY *stares at* BECKY. *Suddenly she understands* BECKY *is telling her the truth. In a daze she sits, then crumples up, dissolved in tears.)* Fanny—Fanny—

FANNY *(Miserably.)* Leave me alone—

BECKY I'm sorry I had to be the one to tell you. *(Pause.)* Hymie will not be so happy when he hears you are leaving Irving. *(No response from* FANNY.*)* I suppose he'll live through it. Children live through worse. *(*BECKY *has been making up her mind to say something. Now she finds courage to do so.)* You asked me before to say something— *(Quietly.)* What could I say? You see— once I came to my mother with a story— *(The words do not come easily.)* The *same* story—

FANNY *(Incredulous.)* Our papa? You're lying— *(Heatedly.)* You always said he was the finest, the most wonderful—

BECKY *(Cutting in.)* He *was*—the finest, the sweetest man a woman ever had— *(Quickly.)* But he was a *man*—

FANNY A man can't be wonderful in one breath and a cheater in the other!

BECKY *(Angrily.)* Don't you say such a thing about Papa!

FANNY I can't understand it. All these years you talked about him like he was God—

BECKY And he was! Even if he was dead he was alive enough in my heart to help me keep the family together— *(Pleading suddenly.)* Fanny, please, don't do it! I know he loves you— *(FANNY exits lower bedroom in tears. Pause. Torn, BECKY goes to phone. Consulting note, dials number. After a pause.)* Hello? Irving? It's Mama. I—just talked to Fanny. She—she didn't sound so—so—encouraging. . . . Sure she knows. *(Pause.)* It's not exactly a *secret.* Irving, I know how you feel. Right now I don't feel so hot myself. But never mind that. It's Hymie's birthday. I think if you came down and brought his mother a little present—or even a *big* one— *(Pause.)* No, not over the telephone. You'll kiss my feet when you get here. *(BECKY hangs up. In a daze, she walks toward kitchen. Halfway she changes her mind. Goes toward buffet, examines bottle of liquor. Making up her mind quickly, she pours some rye into glass, adds seltzer from table. PANSY enters. When she notices PANSY's expression.)* There is always a first time for everything. *(She takes sip, makes a wry face.)* People drink this for pleasure? *(Pause.)* It tastes terrible.

PANSY My James says it feels mighty good after.

BECKY *(Like a hurt child.)* That's what I want. To feel good after. *(Pause.)* I think I'll sit a while. Have a seat, Pansy.

PANSY Lordy, no, ma'am—I got work to do.

BECKY Sit, sit—on Mr. Tashman's time you can take a little rest—maybe you'll have a drink?

PANSY Lordy, no—not while I'm on the job, ma'am.

BECKY *(Smiling gently.)* When I went to Paris, France, five years ago, I was the only Gold Star mother on the boat who didn't drink cocktails—

PANSY You been that far, ma'am? To Paris, France?

BECKY *(Proudly.)* Oh, yes. My son-in-law, Mr. Tashman, sent me— *(Breaking suddenly.)* Pansy, Pansy—I did a terrible thing tonight—

PANSY You couldn't do anything terrible, Mis' Becky.

BECKY *(Pause.)* Yes, I did. I told a lie—I spoiled Jacob's memory. The only thing I had left, and I spoiled it. *(She is weeping now, unashamedly. A strange new BECKY, for whom a first drink of hard liquor has meant a loosening of her tongue and her emotions as well.)* I'm afraid all the perfumes in Arabia won't wash away my sin. *(Pause.)* Lady Macbeth said it.

PANSY *(Admiringly.)* I could lissen to you talkin' all day, Mis' Becky. You sure are powerful eddicated—

BECKY Oh, yes, I am a high school graduate from Night School— *(Her mood changes.)* I went to Washington with my Night School Delegation. I shook hands with President Harding. Afterwards, they said he was a crook. But I never believed it. Such a fine looking man— *(Slightly tipsy now, she is in a reminiscent mood.)* In Washington they took us in buses to Arlington Cemetery. Beautiful. Like a park. Only instead of trees, millions of little crosses growing up from the ground. And flags! So many little American flags on the graves, and when the wind blows, they wave in the breeze like this— *(Waves hand in front of her dizzily. Suddenly getting up.)* I looked for my Hymie there. *(Staring straight ahead, her body erect.)* Then they showed us the place where one soldier is buried. And him they call the Unknown Soldier. And him they never leave alone. Always, day and night, two live soldiers are walking up and down—day and night— *(Breaks off, then simply.)* I think of this place and I am glad they don't leave him alone. Please, Pansy, don't tell anybody, but *that's* the place where my Hymie is! *(Pause.)* I lost my Esther in the Triangle Fire. After that the inspector came and made me take my plants off the fire escape. It was the law. And after that, the committee from the Garment Workers came to tell me that she didn't die for nothing. And after that—my Sadie got her husband—

PANSY *(Incredulously.)* Lordy, Lordy— *(A pause.)*

BECKY Tell me, Pansy, do *you* think everything in this world happens for the best?

PANSY Hard to say for sure, ma'am—but if you believes it, it makes you feel mighty good when the bad is happenin'.

BECKY I wanted my family to have *life.* That's why I brought them here. They sing about it. "The Land of the Free and the Home of the Brave." *(Pause.)* My Hymie was brave. The day before he went away he said to me, "Mama, don't be a Calamity Jane. Here's my watch. When you get lonely, just wind it. When it ticks, it'll be me, talking to you." Then he went away! *(Pause.)* What is left, Pansy? Nothing— not even Jacob's memory—

PANSY *(After pause.)* You sure feel bad, don't you, Mis' Becky? (BECKY *looks up, tries to smile. The smile does not come.)* Down home the ole folks use'n to say, "The Morning Star, she always shines brighter after a real dark night." Yes, Ma'am—guess as long as she's there every morning, the end a the world ain't come yet—

BECKY *(Sitting suddenly, exhausted.)* Life is very hard, but life is wonderful, no?

PANSY *(Wiping a tear from her eye.)* It sure is, Mis' Becky—

BECKY *(Slowly as though this were a revelation.)* I guess a person has to have patience to live through history while they are making it— (IRVING *enters. Goes toward* BECKY *like a frightened child.)*

IRVING Mama—what am I going to do?

*(*PANSY *exits into kitchen.)*

BECKY Now you're asking? She's inside. Go—go in to her, look her straight in the eye and tell him he printed a lie. That you are going to *sue* him for it!

IRVING But, Mama—

BECKY I know it's true—but she'll believe you because she *wants* to believe you, and if she doesn't— (*Forcefully.*) Make her! Slap her face! Do something—anything—but if you let her get away, I'll never talk to you again as long as I live! You heard me?

IRVING I heard you— (*Takes off coat, goes to rack, hangs it up.*)

BECKY (*With great authority.*) And furthermore, tomorrow morning you will go downtown and buy yourself three tickets to Hollywood, California!

IRVING (*Coming toward her.*) Me?

BECKY (*Continuing firmly.*) Yes, you! You will take a job with your Uncle Abe once and for all. You will keep yourself so busy day and night writing songs for the all-singing pictures, you won't have time to get yourself in the papers— (*Winking.*) And if you live in California, how can you sue him in New York?

IRVING Mom—the only brains in the family—thanks, Mom—

BECKY I am not through yet— (*Roughly.*) Come here! (IRVING *goes toward her.* BECKY *slaps him sharply across face.*) That's for being a bad boy! (*She slaps him again.*) And *that's* in *advance*—if you ever hurt my Fanny again—I, myself, personally will— (*Breaks off, contrite.*) Did I hurt you?

IRVING (*Throwing arms around* BECKY, *bursting with laughter.*) Mom, do I love you, do I love you— (*Pause.*) Becky Felderman! What in hell have you been drinking?

BECKY A cocktail! What's wrong with it?

IRVING (*Shouting with laughter.*) Where's my wife? (*Goes toward upper bedroom.*)

BECKY Not in there. Sadie is in there.

(IRVING *exits lower* R. BECKY *looks after him, smiling, then looks at her* R. *hand, which has so gloriously told* IRVING *off. She salutes it, with a nod of her head.* YOUNG HYMIE *comes out of kitchen.*)

HYMIE Did I hear my pop?

BECKY Don't go in there now, Hymela—

(*Her tone seems odd to* HYMIE. *He exits into kitchen, looking back at her with a puzzled expression.* BECKY *goes to buffet, takes out a small package, placing it at head of table. A knock at door. Out of habit,* BECKY *starts to answer it, but* PANSY *rushes through to door, from kitchen.* AARON GREENSPAN *enters. He is now sixty, hair turned white, a tall, straight boyish figure for his years. Takes off coat and hat, hangs them up.*)

AARON (*Coming toward* BECKY, *hands outstretched.*) Becky, Becky, Mazeltuff—

BECKY Thanks, Aaron, thanks. You are looking very well.

AARON You don't look so bad yourself—

BECKY (*Laughing.*) Thank you—

AARON (*Touching couch.*) Aye, Becky—where is my old good friend— (*Pause.*) It's a great day for you, Becky—

BECKY *(Looking up meaningfully.)* They have an old saying, "Never say a man lived a happy life till he's dead." Anything could happen the last minute.

AARON *(Laughing.)* Aye, Becky, Becky—still the pessimist!

BECKY I'm a pessimist? If you have to know, I am the world's biggest optimist. If I wasn't, I would have been dead long ago— *(Pause. BECKY's manner softens.)* A fine way for me to treat a guest. Five minutes in the house, and I'm fighting with you—

AARON *(Feeling sorry for himself.)* It's all right. Fight all you want. Even a fight is a pleasure for a lonely old man— *(After pause.)* Oh—I knew I had to tell you something funny. The other night I went to a newsreel. I could swear, on my life, standing next to Stalin on the platform was—guess who?

BECKY Who?

AARON Benjamin Brownstein!

BECKY No! Time flies— *(Pause.)* And otherwise, how do you spend your time?

AARON Work all day. Comes the night, *again* to a movie or a pinochle. Some life for a man, yes? *(Stares at her. She turns away.)* Oh, yes—last night for a change, in Gold's house, we played guess what, a game! That's the style today—to play games. Well, in this game they ask you questions. So, they asked me, "Who would I rather be, in the whole world, if I could positively *not* be Aaron Greenspan?" *(Turning toward her.)* Should I tell you what I answered? *(Pause.)* I said, I would rather be Jacob Felderman.

BECKY *(Breaking completely.)* Oh—Aaron—Aaron—

AARON Becky, please—I didn't mean to hurt your feelings— *(Pause.)*

BECKY *You*—you didn't hurt my feelings, Aaron.

AARON So—what's wrong?

BECKY Plenty! *(Slowly.)* Sadie—after tonight, she does not step foot in this house. Irving and Fanny and Hymie? To California. As they say, "New worlds to conquer"—and Harry— *(Shaking head.)* Harry is a sick boy—very sick— *(Pause.)* My world! The reason I lived and breathed. Finished—done—

AARON Aye, Becky, still the Calamity Jane—

BECKY *(Angrily.)* If a woman doesn't have the right to have heartache—

AARON *(Going toward her.)* If it's a family you want— *(Suddenly angry.)* For years I have been waiting to be your family! As long as you had them— damned kids— *(BECKY looks at him sharply. Looks around, afraid he has been overheard.)* We—we could have such a fine sweet life together. We talk a little—we laugh a little—all right—we *fight* a little— *(Pause.)* Well! Why don't you *say* something?

BECKY I—I don't know what to say—

AARON *(Incredulous.)* You mean, you didn't say "no"?

BECKY Please—Aaron—I have to think—

AARON If you didn't shut me up with "no"—it's—it's practically a declaration of love!

BECKY   Stop hollering—they'll hear—

AARON   Once in a lifetime a man is entitled to holler! *(Pause.)* Nu? *(A moment of pause.)*

BECKY   *(Quietly.)* Well, consider I said it. *(AARON stares at her, hardly believing his success. Completely overcome with emotion, takes out handkerchief.)*

AARON   All my life I pictured this moment and all I can do is blow my nose— Becky, Becky darling—

BECKY   *(Smiles gently. AARON goes toward her, kissing her hand.)* But first, I have a favor to ask—

AARON   Already?

BECKY   Tonight—*no* announcements!

AARON   Your slightest wish is my command, madam!

(Bows low, takes her hand in his, kissing it in cavalier fashion. Suddenly, as one person, they start to laugh. They are still laughing when PANSY enters. She wears a fresh apron and cap and is beaming.)

PANSY   Dinner's ready to serve now, Mis' Becky—

BECKY   Knock on the door and tell the others—

(PANSY knocks on upper bedroom door, calling out, "Supper's ready." IRVING, FANNY and YOUNG HYMIE enter arm-in-arm, smiling happily. PANSY exits into kitchen.)

FANNY   *(Showing BECKY a bracelet.)* Mama! Look at this! Hello, Aaron—

BECKY   It's beautiful—

FANNY   Irving, darling, you shouldn't have done it!

IRVING   What else have I got to do, except make you happy?

(SADIE enters, slightly the worse for a crying fit, in which she has obviously been indulging.)

FANNY   *(Throwing arms around IRVING.)* I wouldn't care if I never saw another bracelet in my life! It's you I love, not the bracelet! *(To BECKY, proudly.)* Irving is bringing suit first thing next week!

IRVING   *(With a wink toward BECKY.)* I should say so! For damages to my reputation and happiness! And, Mom—how'd you like to come to California to live?

FANNY   He's doing a musical for his Uncle Abe!

IRVING   He sold me a bill of goods this afternoon— *(Winking to BECKY again.)* I didn't want it, but you don't sneeze at five hundred a week!

AARON   *(Whistling.)* I wouldn't sneeze at it—

FANNY   *(To SADIE.)* You see, it doesn't pay to believe everything you read in the papers! *(Goes toward kitchen.)*

BECKY *(Giving* HYMIE *small package.)* For you, Hymela— *(*HYMIE *opens package, takes out watch.)*

HYMIE Gee, thanks, Grandma— *(Reading inscription.)* "To Hymie, from Mama and Esther and Sadie"—was that Tanta Esther?

BECKY Yes. Tanta Esther. The watch belonged to your Uncle Hymie.

*(*HARRY *has entered quietly through the last. Looks up at mention of* ESTHER*'s name, quietly takes his place near others. They gather around table. Speaking as they seat themselves in following order:* HYMIE, *head of table* L. BECKY, *head of table* R. AARON *and* SADIE *facing audience.* HARRY *next to* SADIE. FANNY *and* IRVING *with backs facing audience.)*

IRVING Tonight Mama and Hymie sit at the heads. This is their night.

AARON Believe me, Irving, judging from the talking moving pictures I seen lately, your mediocrity will be rewarded by great success—

IRVING My what?

SADIE And how are you, Greenspan?

AARON I never felt better in my life!

SADIE The world is having a depression, but on you evidently it doesn't make a dent!

AARON Not even a pin scratch. The union scale is very good. That is, for *us*— but not for you, when you'll have to pay it!

SADIE Never! I'll move to Jersey first!

*(*PANSY *enters with tray of food.)*

FANNY You may serve now, Pansy—

PANSY Ain't we gonna hear Mr. Hymie's speech first?

HYMIE Aw, gee, didja have to remind her?

FANNY Hymie! Remember what I said!

HYMIE *(Getting up reluctantly, takes out crumpled paper, consults it.)* Well—dear Grandma and Mama and Papa and everything—I mean everybody— *(In a sing-song manner.)* Today I yam a man. I am thirteen years old. I promise to be a good boy, I mean man—and, well— *(Quickly.)* If it's true I'm a man, I guess I better be getting more than a dollar and a quarter a week spending money—

FANNY *(Horrified.)* Hymie! That's not in the speech!

HYMIE Well—I put it in— *(Continuing.)* And, dear God, we thank you for all the blessings—and please bless Grandma and my dear mother and my dear father— *(As the)*

CURTAIN SLOWLY DESCENDS

UNDER A PAINTED SMILE

LYRICS BY ROBERT SOUR   MUSIC BY ABRAHAM ELLSTEIN

Under a painted smile there is a heart that's breaking
Clothes of the latest style tell of the step she's taking
Powder and paint won't hide the tears that she's shedding the while
For there is a heart that's breaking
Under a painted smile.   5

WE'LL BRING THE RUE DE LA PAIX!

LYRICS BY ROBERT SOUR   MUSIC BY ABRAHAM ELLSTEIN

We'll bring the Rue de la Paix back to old Broadway
and make the boys forget Paree
We'll change the farm back home into the Place Vendôme
And teach the girls to par-ley-voo that old oui-oui
There'll be a plenty of jazzin' and razz-a-ma-tazz—   5
when they come home from across the sea
We'll bring the Rue de la Paix back to old Broadway
and make the soldierboys forget Paree.

Eudora Welty 1909–

One of the best-known and most respected writers of the United States in general, and the southern United States in particular, Eudora Welty has produced celebrated short fiction, novels, essays, and her memoir, *One Writer's Beginnings* (1984). Welty has spoken of her indebtedness to her birth region: "It's my source of knowledge. It tells me the important things. It steers me and keeps me going straight, because place is a definer and a confiner of what I'm doing." Born in Jackson, Mississippi, Welty was educated at Mississippi State College for Women and transferred to the University of Wisconsin, graduating in 1929; she later attended Columbia University in New York, albeit briefly, to study advertising. In addition to her writing, Welty was a photographer of southern poverty as part of her role as a publicist for the WPA. Her photographs were shown in 1936 and again in 1973 at the Museum of Modern Art as part of a one-woman show. Welty's work is graced by strongly drawn, engaging women, and she herself has written, "I have been told, both in approval and in accusation, that I seem to love all my characters."

A WORN PATH

It was December—a bright frozen day in the early morning. Far out in the country there was an old Negro woman with her head tied in a red rag, coming along a path through the pinewoods. Her name was Phoenix Jackson. She was very old and small and she walked slowly in the dark pine shadows, moving a little from side to side in her steps, with the balanced heaviness and lightness of a pendulum in a grandfather clock. She carried a thin, small cane made from an umbrella, and with this she kept tapping the frozen earth in front of her. This made a grave and persistent noise in the still air, that seemed meditative like the chirping of a solitary little bird.

She wore a dark striped dress reaching down to her shoe tops, and an equally long apron of bleached sugar sacks, with a full pocket: all neat and tidy, but every time she took a step she might have fallen over her shoelaces, which dragged from her unlaced shoes. She looked straight ahead. Her eyes were blue with age. Her skin had a pattern all its own of numberless branching wrinkles and as though a whole little tree stood in the middle of her forehead, but a golden color ran underneath, and the two knobs of her cheeks were illumined by a yellow burning under the dark. Under the red rag her hair came down on her neck in the frailest of ringlets, still black, and with an odor like copper.

Now and then there was a quivering in the thicket. Old Phoenix said, "Out of my way, all you foxes, owls, beetles, jack rabbits, coons and wild animals! . . . Keep out from under these feet, little bobwhites. . . . Keep the big wild hogs out of my path. Don't let none of those come running my direction. I got a long way." Under her small black-freckled hand her cane, limber as a buggy whip, would switch at the brush as if to rouse up any hiding things.

On she went. The woods were deep and still. The sun made the pine needles almost too bright to look at, up where the wind rocked. The cones dropped as light as feathers. Down in the hollow was the mourning dove—it was not too late for him.

The path ran up a hill. "Seem like there is chains about my feet, time I get this far," she said, in the voice of argument old people keep to use with themselves. "Something always take a hold of me on this hill—pleads I should stay."

After she got to the top she turned and gave a full, severe look behind her where she had come. "Up through pines," she said at length. "Now down through oaks."

Her eyes opened their widest, and she started down gently. But before she got to the bottom of the hill a bush caught her dress.

Her fingers were busy and intent, but her skirts were full and long, so that before she could pull them free in one place they were caught in another. It was not possible to allow the dress to tear. "I in the thorny bush," she said. "Thorns, you doing your appointed work. Never want to let folks pass, no sir. Old eyes thought you was a pretty little *green* bush."

Finally, trembling all over, she stood free, and after a moment dared to stoop for her cane.

"Sun so high!" she cried, leaning back and looking, while the thick tears went over her eyes. "The time getting all gone here."

At the foot of this hill was a place where a log was laid across the creek.

"Now comes the trial," said Phoenix.

Putting her right foot out, she mounted the log and shut her eyes. Lifting her skirt, leveling her cane fiercely before her, like a festival figure in some parade, she began to march across. Then she opened her eyes and she was safe on the other side.

"I wasn't as old as I thought," she said.

But she sat down to rest. She spread her skirts on the bank around her and folded her hands over her knees. Up above her was a tree in a pearly cloud of mistletoe. She did not dare to close her eyes, and when a little boy brought her a plate with a slice of marble-cake on it she spoke to him. "That would be acceptable," she said. But when she went to take it there was just her own hand in the air.

So she left that tree, and had to go through a barbed-wire fence. There she had to creep and crawl, spreading her knees and stretching her fingers like a baby trying to climb the steps. But she talked loudly to herself: she could not let her dress be torn now, so late in the day, and she could not pay for having her arm or her leg sawed off if she got caught fast where she was.

At last she was safe through the fence and risen up out in the clearing. Big dead trees, like black men with one arm, were standing in the purple stalks of the withered cotton field. There sat a buzzard.

"Who you watching?"

In the furrow she made her way along.

"Glad this not the season for bulls," she said, looking sideways, "and the good Lord made his snakes to curl up and sleep in the winter. A pleasure I don't see no two-headed snake coming around that tree, where it come once. It took a while to get by him, back in the summer."

She passed through the old cotton and went into a field of dead corn. It whispered and shook and was taller than her head. "Through the maze now," she said, for there was no path.

There was something tall, black, and skinny there, moving before her.

At first she took it for a man. It could have been a man dancing in the field. But she stood still and listened, and it did not make a sound. It was as silent as a ghost.

"Ghost," she said sharply, "who be you the ghost of? For I have heard of nary death close by."

But there was no answer—only the ragged dancing in the wind.

She shut her eyes, reached out her hand, and touched a sleeve. She found a coat and inside that an emptiness, cold as ice.

"You scarecrow," she said. Her face lighted. "I ought to be shut up for good," she said with laughter. "My senses is gone. I too old. I the oldest people I ever know. Dance, old scarecrow," she said, "while I dancing with you."

She kicked her foot over the furrow, and with mouth drawn down, shook her head once or twice in a little strutting way. Some husks blew down and whirled in streamers about her skirts.

Then she went on, parting her way from side to side with the cane, through the whispering field. At last she came to the end, to a wagon track where the silver grass blew between the red ruts. The quail were walking around like pullets, seeming all dainty and unseen.

"Walk pretty," she said. "This the easy place. This the easy going."

She followed the track, swaying through the quiet bare fields, through the little strings of trees silver in their dead leaves, past cabins silver from weather, with the doors and windows boarded shut, all like old women under a spell sitting there. "I walking in their sleep," she said, nodding her head vigorously.

In a ravine she went where a spring was silently flowing through a hollow log. Old Phoenix bent and drank. "Sweet-gum makes the water sweet," she said, and drank more. "Nobody know who made this well, for it was here when I was born."

The track crossed a swampy part where the moss hung as white as lace from every limb. "Sleep on, alligators, and blow your bubbles." Then the track went into the road.

Deep, deep the road went down between the high green-colored banks. Overhead the live-oaks met, and it was as dark as a cave.

A black dog with lolling tongue came up out of the weeds by the ditch. She was meditating, and not ready, and when he came at her she only hit him a little with her cane. Over she went in the ditch, like a little puff of milkweed.

Down there, her senses drifted away. A dream visited her, and she reached her hand up, but nothing reached down and gave her a pull. So she lay there and presently went to talking. "Old woman," she said to herself, "that black dog come up out of the weeds to stall you off, and now there he sitting on his fine tail, smiling at you."

A white man finally came along and found her—a hunter, a young man, with his dog on a chain.

"Well, Granny!" he laughed. "What are you doing there?"

"Lying on my back like a June-bug waiting to be turned over, mister," she said, reaching up her hand.

He lifted her up, gave her a swing in the air, and set her down. "Anything broken, Granny?"

"No sir, them old dead weeds is springy enough," said Phoenix, when she had got her breath. "I thank you for your trouble."

"Where do you live, Granny?" he asked, while the two dogs were growling at each other.

"Away back yonder, sir, behind the ridge. You can't even see it from here."

"On your way home?"

"No sir, I going to town."

"Why, that's too far! That's as far as I walk when I come out myself, and I get something for my trouble." He patted the stuffed bag he carried, and there hung down a little closed claw. It was one of the bob-whites, with its beak hooked bitterly to show it was dead. "Now you go on home, Granny!"

"I bound to go to town, mister," said Phoenix. "The time come around."

He gave another laugh, filling the whole landscape. "I know you old colored people! Wouldn't miss going to town to see Santa Claus!"

But something held old Phoenix very still. The deep lines in her face went into a fierce and different radiation. Without warning, she had seen with her own eyes a flashing nickel fall out of the man's pocket onto the ground.

"How old are you, Granny?" he was saying.

"There is no telling, mister," she said, "no telling."

Then she gave a little cry and clapped her hand and said, "Git on away from here, dog! Look! Look at that dog!" She laughed as if in admiration. "He ain't scared of nobody. He a big black dog." She whispered, "Sic him!"

"Watch me get rid of that cur," said the man. "Sic him, Pete! Sic him!"

Phoenix heard the dogs fighting, and heard the man running and throwing sticks. She even heard a gunshot. But she was slowly bending forward by that time, further and further forward, the lids stretched down over her eyes, as if she were doing this in her sleep. Her chin was lowered almost to her knees. The yellow palm of her hand came out from the fold of her apron. Her fingers slid down and along the ground under the piece of money with the grace and care they would have in lifting an egg from under a setting hen. Then she slowly straightened up, she stood erect, and the nickel was in her apron pocket. A bird flew by. Her lips moved. "God watching me the whole time. I come to stealing."

The man came back, and his own dog panted about them. "Well, I scared him off that time," he said, and then he laughed and lifted his gun and pointed it at Phoenix.

She stood straight and faced him.

"Doesn't the gun scare you?" he said, still pointing it.

"No, sir, I seen plenty go off closer by, in my day, and for less than what I done," she said, holding utterly still.

He smiled, and shouldered the gun. "Well Granny," he said, "you must be a hundred years old, and scared of nothing. I'd give you a dime if I had any money with me. But you take my advice and stay home, and nothing will happen to you."

"I bound to go on my way, mister," said Phoenix. She inclined her head in the red rag. Then they went in different directions, but she could hear the gun shooting again and again over the hill.

She walked on. The shadows hung from the oak trees to the road like curtains. Then she smelled wood-smoke, and smelled the river, and she saw a steeple and the cabins on their steep steps. Dozens of little black children whirled around her. There ahead was Natchez shining. Bells were ringing. She walked on.

In the paved city it was Christmas time. There were red and green electric lights strung and crisscrossed everywhere, and all turned on in the daytime. Old Phoenix would have been lost if she had not distrusted her eyesight and depended on her feet to know where to take her.

She paused quietly on the sidewalk where people were passing by. A lady came along in the crowd, carrying an armful of red-, green- and silver-wrapped presents; she gave off perfume like the red roses in hot summer, and Phoenix stopped her.

"Please, missy, will you lace up my shoe?" She held up her foot.

"What do you want, Grandma?"

"See my shoe," said Phoenix. "Do all right for out in the country, but wouldn't look right to go in a big building."

"Stand still then, Grandma," said the lady. She put her packages down on the sidewalk beside her and laced and tied both shoes tightly.

"Can't lace 'em with a cane," said Phoenix. "Thank you, missy. I doesn't mind asking a nice lady to tie up my shoe, when I gets out on the street."

Moving slowly and from side to side, she went into the big building, and into a tower of steps, where she walked up and around and around until her feet knew to stop.

She entered a door, and there she saw nailed up on the wall the document that had been stamped with the gold seal and framed in the gold frame, which matched the dream that was hung up in her head.

"Here I be," she said. There was a fixed and ceremonial stiffness over her body.

"A charity case, I suppose," said an attendant who sat at the desk before her. But Phoenix only looked above her head. There was sweat on her face, the wrinkles in her skin shone like a bright net.

"Speak up, Grandma," the women said. "What's your name? We must have your history, you know. Have you been here before? What seems to be the trouble with you?"

Old Phoenix only gave a twitch to her face as if a fly were bothering her.

"Are you deaf?" cried the attendant.

But then the nurse came in.

"Oh, that's just old Aunt Phoenix," she said. "She doesn't come for herself—she has a little grandson. She makes these trips just as regular as clockwork. She lives away back off the Old Natchez Trace."[1] She bent down. "Well, Aunt Phoenix, why don't you just take a seat? We won't keep you standing after your long trip." She pointed.

The old woman sat down, bolt upright in the chair.

"Now, how is the boy?" asked the nurse.

Old Phoenix did not speak.

"I said, how is the boy?"

But Phoenix only waited and stared straight ahead, her face very solemn and withdrawn into rigidity.

"Is his throat any better?" asked the nurse. "Aunt Phoenix, don't you hear me? Is your grandson's throat any better since the last time you came for the medicine?"

With her hands on her knees, the old woman waited, silent, erect and motionless, just as if she were in armor.

"You mustn't take up our time this way, Aunt Phoenix," the nurse said. "Tell us quickly about your grandson, and get it over. He isn't dead, is he?"

At last there came a flicker and then a flame of comprehension across her face, and she spoke.

"My grandson. It was my memory had left me. There I sat and forgot why I made my long trip."

"Forgot?" The nurse frowned. "After you came so far?"

Then Phoenix was like an old woman begging a dignified forgiveness for waking up frightened in the night. "I never did go to school, I was too old at the Surrender,"[2] she said in a soft voice. "I'm an old woman without an education. It was my memory fail me. My little grandson, he is just the same, and I forgot it in the coming."

"Throat never heals, does it?" said the nurse, speaking in a loud, sure voice to old Phoenix. By now she had a card with something written on it, a little list. "Yes. Swallowed lye. When was it?—January—two, three years ago—"

Phoenix spoke unasked now. "No, missy, he not dead, he just the same. Every little while his throat begin to close up again, and he not able to swallow. He not get his breath. He not able to help himself. So the time come around, and I go on another trip for the soothing medicine."

"All right. The doctor said as long as you came to get it, you could have it," said the nurse. "But it's an obstinate case."

"My little grandson, he sit up there in the house all wrapped up, waiting by himself," Phoenix went on. "We is the only two left in the world. He suffer and it

---

[1] A 19th-century pioneer road between Natchez, Mississippi, and Nashville, Tennessee.

[2] I.e., the surrender of Robert E. Lee at Appomattox in 1865, which ended the Civil War.

don't seem to put him back at all. He got a sweet look. He going to last. He wear a little patch quilt and peep out holding his mouth open like a little bird. I re-members so plain now. I not going to forget him again, no, the whole enduring time. I could tell him from all the others in creation."

"All right." The nurse was trying to hush her now. She brought her a bottle of medicine. "Charity," she said, making a check mark in a book.

Old Phoenix held the bottle close to her eyes, and then carefully put it into her pocket.

"I thank you," she said.

"It's Christmas time, Grandma," said the attendant. "Could I give you a few pennies out of my purse?"

"Five pennies is a nickel," said Phoenix stiffly.

"Here's a nickel," said the attendant.

Phoenix rose carefully and held out her hand. She received the nickel and then fished the other nickel out of her pocket and laid it beside the new one. She stared at her palm closely, with her head on one side.

Then she gave a tap with her cane on the floor.

"This is what come to me to do," she said. "I going to the store and buy my child a little windmill they sells, made out of paper. He going to find it hard to believe there such a thing in the world. I'll march myself back where he waiting, holding it straight up in this hand."

She lifted her free hand, gave a little nod, turned around, and walked out of the doctor's office. Then her slow step began on the stairs, going down.

Elizabeth Bishop 1911–1979

Considered by her peers to be, as critic Sibyl Estess writes, "a virtuoso of de-scriptive poetry," the work of Elizabeth Bishop has, since her death, become increasingly regarded as meditative, visionary, and exceedingly sensitive to the nuance of inner perception and the details of external objects. Born in Worcester, Massachusetts, Bishop's father died when she was eight months old. Soon after, her mother was hospitalized for mental illness, and Elizabeth was subsequently raised by two sets of grandparents in Nova Scotia and England. At nineteen she enrolled at Vassar, and with the help of aspiring author Mary McCarthy and oth-ers, she founded the literary magazine *Con Spirito*. By her senior year, Bishop was publishing poems and short stories in nationally known periodicals. As fate would have it, she was befriended by Marianne Moore, who persuaded her not to attend medical school, instead advising that all energies be put into writing. Bishop won the Pulitzer Prize in 1956 and the National Book Award in 1970.

THE FISH

I caught a tremendous fish
and help him beside the boat
half out of water, with my hook
fast in a corner of his mouth.
He didn't fight.   5
He hadn't fought at all.
He hung a grunting weight,
battered and venerable
and homely. Here and there
his brown skin hung in strips   10
like ancient wallpaper,
and its pattern of darker brown
was like wallpaper:
shapes like full-blown roses
stained and lost through age.   15
He was speckled with barnacles,
fine rosettes of lime,
and infested
with tiny white sea-lice,
and underneath two or three   20
rags of green weed hung down.
While his gills were breathing in
the terrible oxygen
—the frightening gills,
fresh and crisp with blood,   25
that can cut so badly—
I thought of the coarse white flesh
packed in like feathers,
the big bones and the little bones,
the dramatic reds and blacks   30
of his shiny entrails,
and the pink swim bladder
like a big peony.
I looked into his eyes
which were far larger than mine   35
but shallower, and yellowed,
the irises backed and packed
with tarnished tinfoil
seen through the lenses
of old scratched isinglass.[1]   40

---

[1] Semitransparent substance, originally obtained from the swim bladders of some freshwater fishes. Used for windows.

They shifted a little, but not
to return my stare.
—It was more like the tipping
of an object toward the light.
I admired his sullen face,   45
the mechanism of his jaw,
and then I saw
that from his lower lip
—if you could call it a lip—
grim, wet, and weaponlike,   50
hung five old pieces of fish-line,
or four and a wire leader
with the swivel still attached,
with all their five big hooks
grown firmly in his mouth.   55
A green line, frayed at the end
where he broke it, two heavier lines,
and a fine black thread
still crimped from the strain and snap
when it broke and he got away.   60
Like medals with their ribbons
frayed and wavering,
a five-haired beard of wisdom
trailing from his aching jaw.
I stared and stared   65
and victory filled up
the little rented boat,
from the pool of bilge
where oil had spread a rainbow
around the rusted engine   70
to the bailer rusted orange,
the sun-cracked thwarts,
the oarlocks on their strings,
the gunnels—until everything
was rainbow, rainbow, rainbow!   75
And I let the fish go.

INVITATION TO MISS MARIANNE MOORE[1]

From Brooklyn, over the Brooklyn Bridge, on this fine morning,
    please come flying.
In a cloud of fiery pale chemicals,
    please come flying.
to the rapid rolling of thousands of small blue drums   5
descending out of the mackerel sky
over the glittering grandstand of harbor-water,
    please come flying.

Whistles, pennants and smoke are blowing. The ships
are signaling cordially with multitudes of flags   10
rising and falling like birds all over the harbor.
Enter: two rivers, gracefully bearing
countless little pellucid jellies
in cut-glass epergnes[2] dragging with silver chains.
The flight is safe; the weather is all arranged   15
The waves are running in verses this fine morning.
    Please come flying.

Come with the pointed toe of each black shoe
trailing a sapphire highlight,
with a black capeful of butterfly wings and bon-mots,[3]   20
with heaven knows how many angels all riding
on the broad black brim of your hat,
    please come flying.

Bearing a musical inaudible abacus,
a slight censorious frown, and blue ribbons,   25
    please come flying.
Facts and skyscrapers glint in the tide; Manhattan
is all awash with morals this fine morning,
    so please come flying.

Mounting the sky with natural heroism,   30
above the accidents, above the malignant movies,
the taxicabs and injustices at large,
while horns are resounding in your beautiful ears
that simultaneously listen to

[1] American poet (1887–1972).

[2] Compartmented serving dishes.

[3] Clever remarks.

a soft uninvented music, fit for the musk deer,   35
     please come flying.

For whom the grim museums will behave
like courteous male bower birds,
for whom the agreeable lions lie[4] in wait
on the steps of the Public Library,   40
eager to rise and follow through the doors
up into the reading rooms,
     please come flying.

We can sit down and weep; we can go shopping,
or play at a game of constantly being wrong   45
with a priceless set of vocabularies,
or we can bravely deplore, but please
     please come flying.

With dynasties of negative constructions
darkening and dying around you,   50
with grammar that suddenly turns and shines
like flocks of sandpipers flying,
     please come flying.

Come like a light in the white mackerel sky,
come like a daytime comet   55
with a long unnebulous train of words,
from Brooklyn, over the Brooklyn Bridge, on this fine morning,
     please come flying.

May Sarton 1912–1995

Born in Belgium, May Sarton was a prolific writer with more than fifty books to her credit, including poetry, novels, essays, journals, and children's books. Due to the outbreak of World War I, she and her family spent six years trying to find a place to settle down until at last putting down roots in Cambridge, Massachusetts. Declining a scholarship to Vassar, Sarton chose instead to apprentice at the Civic Repertory Theater in New York, eventually founding and directing her own theater before turning to a career in writing three years later. Publishing her first verse in *Poetry* magazine in 1929, Sarton became famous for the theme of solitude so evident in the journal writing that described her solitary life in Nelson, New Hampshire. She was also renowned for such novels as *The Small*

---

[4] Large stone lions flank the entrance to the main branch of the New York Public Library.

Room (1961), *Joanna and Ulysses* (1963), and *Kinds of Love* (1970), which portray the female friendships and love affairs that rescue women from isolation and loneliness. Before she died, Sarton received seventeen honorary Doctor of Letters degrees.

THE MUSE AS MEDUSA

I saw you once, Medusa; we were alone.
I looked you straight in the cold eye, cold.
I was not punished, was not turned to stone—
How to believe the legends I am told?

I came as naked as any little fish,   5
Prepared to be hooked, gutted, caught;
But I saw you, Medusa, made my wish,
And when I left you I was clothed in thought . . .

Being allowed, perhaps, to swim my way
Through the great deep and on the rising tide,   10
Flashing wild streams, as free and rich as they,
Though you had power marshaled on your side.

The fish escaped to many a magic reef;
The fish explored many a dangerous sea—
The fish, Medusa, did not come to grief,   15
But swims still in a fluid mystery.

Forget the image: your silence is my ocean,
And even now it teems with life. You chose
To abdicate by total lack of motion,
But did it work, for nothing really froze?   20

It is all fluid still, that world of feeling
Where thoughts, those fishes, silent, feed and rove;
And fluid, it is also full of healing,
For love is healing, even rootless love.

I turn your face around! It is my face.   25
That frozen rage is what I must explore—
Oh secret, self-enclosed, and ravaged place!
This is the gift I thank Medusa for.

DER ABSCHIED

Now frost has broken summer like a glass,
This house and I resume our conversations;
The floors whisper a message as I pass,
I wander up and down these empty rooms
That have become my intimate relations,   5
Brimmed with your presence where your absence blooms—
And did you come at last, come home, to tell
How all fulfillment tastes of a farewell?

Here is the room where you lay down full length
That whole first day, to read, and hardly stirred,   10
As if arrival had taken all your strength;
Here is the table where you bent to write
The morning through, and silence spoke its word;
And here beside the fire we talked, as night
Came slowly from the wood across the meadow   15
To frame half of our brilliant world in shadow.

The rich fulfillment came; we held it all;
Four years of struggle brought us to this season,
Then in one week our summer turned to fall;
The air chilled and we sensed the chill in us,   20
The passionate journey ending in sweet reason.
The autumn light was there, frost on the grass.
And did you come at last, come home, to tell
How all fulfillment tastes of a farewell?

Departure is the constant at this stage;   25
And all we know is that we cannot stop,
However much the childish heart may rage.
We are still outward-bound to obligations
And, radiant centers, life must drink us up;
Devour our strength in multiple relations.   30
Yet I still question in these empty rooms
Brimmed with your presence where your absence blooms,

What stays that can outlast these deprivations?
Now, peopled by the dead, and ourselves dying,
The house and I resume old conversations: 35
What stays? Perhaps some autumn tenderness,
A different strength that forbids youthful sighing.
Though frost has broken summer like a glass,
Know, as we hear the thudding apples fall,
Not ripeness but the suffering change is all.   40

Mary Lavin 1912–1966

Born in Massachusetts and taken by her parents to live in Ireland when she was nine, Mary Lavin has said, "It is in the short story that a writer distills the essence of . . . thought. . . . Short-story writing—for me—is only looking closer than normal into the human heart." Lavin began as a literary critic, turning her talents to fiction after graduate studies at University College, Dublin. Although Lavin has published several novels, including *Mary O'Grady* (1950), she is best known for her many collections of short stories focusing on women's lives and subjects "distinctively Irish."

THE NUN'S MOTHER

Well, it was all over now, anyway. Mrs. Latimer closed her eyes and laid her head back against the horsehair cushions in the taxi. It was all over now, anyway, and she was certainly glad of that much. She kept her eyes closed as they drove down the convent avenue. And what is more, she decided childishly, she would keep them closed, keep them closed at any rate until they reached the gate lodge. In the main road she might perhaps open them. But then, would she know when that was: when they were in the main road, she meant; of course she would, the taxi would go up with a little bump and then down with a little bump. Inside Luke and herself would joggle about no matter how hard they clung to the leather straps. Their elbows would come together and, like corks on a wave-wash, their feet would lift a little from the rubber flooring and fall into place again. Her hair would catch on the loose threads of the cushions, or on one of the uncovered buttons. It would hurt for a second. Cat hairs. Only cat hairs. Her plaited bun kept the rest of her hair too taut to drag. Although, indeed, it would not matter a terrible lot if any of it got pulled. She could get Luke to free them. Or jerk her head and free them herself. What harm if they broke. Her hair was thick enough to stand it. And since it got gray there was no sense in being too particular.

It wasn't so very gray, of course, considering her age and that. Indeed, most people thought she was the youngest of her family, instead of the eldest. She was much younger looking than Luke. (She opened her eyes a little and looked at him.) This last week had told on him too. Worn him out. But it had taken more effect on herself all the same. Until lately her underneath hairs had been as brown as when she was a girl, but only this morning she had seen a fleck or two of gray reflected in the mirror when the brush sprayed out her hair upon her shoulder. It had been a great strain, a great strain for both of them.

Poor Luke. His hand was on her knee now. They must be coming to the gate lodge. Up with a little bump. Down with a little bump. Out over the paving stones into the main road. They joggled together. He steadied himself with his hand on her knee, and when they wheeled into the tar road he left it on her knee. That was for sympathy. Sympathy with her sorrow. He was waiting for her to open her eyes until he told her how badly he felt for her.

Oh, so that was it! She had not realized. That was why she had hesitated to open them. Instinct. She had hesitated to shock Luke by letting him see her eyes empty of hurt, empty of sorrow. Empty, that was to say, of all appropriate expression. For she felt, at the moment, absolutely nothing. Nothing but relief that it was all over.

She certainly was not suffering. No matter how unnatural it might seem, it was nevertheless true that she was not suffering a bit. And Luke, poor Luke, he was not only hurt, but frightened and perplexed. Men had such an irrational horror of the cloister, the very word they used—"nunnery"—was so medieval. Really and truly she quite believed that Luke had been more hurt and repulsed by what Angela had done than he would have been had she got into some serious scrape or other. Yes, even *that* kind of scrape. If anything like *that* had happened he would have been shocked and grieved, angered and worried, but he would, underneath it all, have been infinitely gentle and understanding. For that would have been something within the orbit of his instincts. This, on the other hand, was completely alien to his nature. This was treasonable. This was abnormal.

A woman felt different. Women had a curious streak of chastity in them, no matter how long they were married, or how ardently they loved. And so, for most women, when they heard that a young girl was entering a convent, there was a strange triumph in their hearts at once; and during the day, as they moved around the house, they felt a temporary hostility to their husbands, towards the things of his household, towards his tables and chairs; yes, indeed, down even to his dishes and dishcloths. They flicked the dishcloths from them, from time to time, sending fans of filigree spray into the warm kitchen air, and all the time their minds were filled with conquering visions of glad young girls (who might have been themselves) going garlanded with lilies down a cool green cloisteral arch ivied over by the centuries; and, what was more, those glad young girls were going without once looking back at the blazing lawns, lit with brightly burning sun and hotly flaming flowers where lovers with lutes were lying. Yes, that was undoubtedly how most women felt. Or how else could one account for the success of novels like *The White Sister* that were always appearing in the shop windows? But *she* didn't feel like that. Of course, she could understand the feeling. She would admit that much: she could understand it. And Luke's grief, that too, she could understand. She could even imagine just how the pain of grief would have felt had it seized her, too, and dug into her with its claws. She could summon the feeling at once as if it were real and sincere. She could bare her breast and draw down the stroke of the pitiless beak. If she wished. But she didn't. Hadn't she always been sincere?

If asked, in all sincerity, how the loss of Angela affected her, she would have to answer truthfully and say that it meant no more fun out shopping, no more flippancies, no more visits to the Small Women shops (matrons and outsize now forever), no more angling to get new young men for parties (bridge and sandwiches now forever), no more need to lay aside linen, no more need to be on the lookout for bargains in silver spoons and forks (even when they were going for a song). No need, in short, to remain young.

Now, no longer, need she dream of riding down the years and passing under the arch of age, with a prancing two-in-hand. It would be a single gallop from now on. And one that would get faster with the years. Faster and faster she would go from now on, throwing up choking dust in the air and crazed by the cries from the wayside, cries of weary, childless women calling out after her: "Well for you, Mrs. Latimer, well for you, with a daughter a nun to pray for you."

A nun to pray for her. That meant the prayers of her daughter Angela. She had faith, of course. She believed in prayer to a certain extent, prayers of praise and prayers of remorse. Not what they meant—petition-prayers to find a ten-shilling note that was lost, prayers that it would not rain on the day of the tennis tournament. That was not real prayer. That she discounted. But real prayer, for her soul's salvation, from Angela, it was absurd! Her daughter Angela!—with plaits down her back until last spring and always sitting so immodestly with her bare thighs showing—it was, as she said at first, absurd.

There now. That was the truth. That was what she really felt about it. Not grief or sorrow in her loss, and not pride and joy either in the fact that the Lord had chosen the fruit of her tree. To be quite honest, she didn't believe He *had* chosen Angela. Angela had *gone*. But why? There was the mystery. Angela had made her choice and gone away without thinking of them, without caring how they felt, it seemed. And now there was Luke with tears in his eyes. And there was she herself—a nun's mother.

It was quite a title. A nun's mother. "Mrs. Latimer has a daughter a nun." "Meet Mrs. Latimer, who has a daughter in the convent." She would be quite an exhibit at church bazaars and charity whist drives. She might even have to assume an attitude. Would she, perhaps, have to dress in black? to smoke only in a cupboard, to put up holy pictures, even in the downstairs rooms, to write S.A.G. on the back of her envelopes, to . . . to . . . what else do the mothers of nuns have to do? . . . to donate settees to the convent parlor? It was enough to give anyone mixed emotions. All very well for Luke. There was no notoriety attached to being the father of a nun. And when he went to visit her he would be treated quite normally. Angela would not criticize him nor blush if his tie was rather bright. She would talk to him gladly and freely and not be afraid that Reverend Mother would come into the room and notice this, or speak afterwards about that, or comment, even ever so lightly, on the other. It was all very well for him. When he got used to the idea he would quite like going up to Mount St. Joseph and walking around with his cool, stately daughter in black-pleated gabardine with a high, firm, virgin bust. He'd grow to love it, and gradually give up going to the club, give up wanting to go abroad for the summers . . . But she must not allow her resentment to include him too, because this resignation was yet a long way from him, might, indeed, never come to him, for how could she tell? She must be understanding with him. But it was very difficult when she did not know exactly how he felt. He was so silent.

He was always so silent when he was hurt. When she had first told him about Angela he had hardly said a word. Certainly nothing important or memorable. Had he said anything at all? She couldn't remember. Quite possible that he had not. Or perhaps he had just said "Angela?" like that, with a question in the word and a swift lift of his head to the light. "Angela?"—like that. As if they had half a dozen daughters, and that she had possibly mixed the names. He could be most irritating. There was no doubt about it. Most irritating. Look at him now straining back to see if he could catch another glimpse of the convent through the trees. His eyes were probably still filled with tears. She must shut her own eyes quickly before he turned around. It would be unspeakably annoying to think he was crying. There was his hand on her knee again, saying as clearly as words, "just a little while longer, Maud, silence and sympathy just a little while longer, the length of the drive home, and then we will talk." About other things, of course. Not about Angela. That would be understood.

It was odd that he never could talk about Angela without great difficulty. And his efforts to do so during the last month had been unbearably irritating. Heavily, from time to time he would gulpingly ask a question about her.

"Are you sure she knows her own mind?"

He had asked that at least six nights running, coming into their bedroom without mentioning a name. Through sheer annoyance and strain she had said, "Who are you talking about?" Just to hurt him because he was so clumsy and helpless. The fact that he was so pathetic had made her torment him deliberately. Why, she did not know. Unless perhaps that she felt impatient that he could not take up where she had failed and find out why their lovely Angela was going away from them for ever and ever. He had made such desperate attempts to find out from her, without ever once thinking of going directly to Angela. "Does she know what she is giving up?" He would ask that at the oddest times. She knew what he meant, of course, what any man would have meant, and what any but Luke would have put so much more clearly. "Oh, yes," she had heard herself answer always, moving a chair, or twitching across a curtain. "Her mind is quite made up, I assure you." Why had she not gone to him and caught at the lapels of his coat and said, "I don't know, I don't know. . . . I'm afraid to ask her."

For that had been so. Hadn't it? She had been impatient with Luke only because she saw that he was suffering as she was, and that, what was worse, he was depending on her to ease his suffering. Why had she done nothing? Why?

It was queer that she who was so extraordinarily free with her tongue talking to most people should have been afraid to ask her own daughter one simple question. One small fact was all they both wanted to find out, and yet she could not rouse herself to ask outright, nor calm herself to employ the subtlety of trivial questions whose answers would weave together into the information she was seeking. In either case, Angela might give her a rebuff. If it had been a son instead of a daughter it would have been easier, she felt sure. But then, if it had been a son it would all have been out of her hands, anyway. Luke would have been so efficient then. Men were so straight with each other. No nonsense. "Look here, boy . . ." and "Tell me frankly, son . . ." and "Have you thought about this, my boy . . ." The "this" would be sex and love and the bodies of men and women. It would all be spoken of lightly, easily, even, indeed, with a slight flavor of humor, and the question would be settled once and for all. The boy would go ahead with his own idea, or he would think over what had been said. In either case they would know that he was equipped with knowledge enough to make an adult choice. But was Angela so equipped? Should she have spoken to her, straight out, about her body and the bodies of men?

It was so hard for women to be frank with each other. With men it was easy. With each other impossible. Or so she had found. Always. At school even. Women were so covert and sly when they were alone, so prudish, so guarded. All that awful, lumpy shuffling and protruding of elbows that went on under slips and nightdresses in order to dress or undress. No simplicity, no grace. And that was what it was to be a modest woman, to shuffle and clutch at straps and buttons. . . . Men were so much more normal. Why! they'd think nothing of walking around with nothing on. And if they were given any encouragement they'd never wear bathing suits. A bit startling perhaps at first, when you thought it would have been the other way round. Women's bodies were so much more graceful; molded so secretively, so subtly. In art it actually was the other way round, as if women were the franker sex. If only they were how handy everything would be; no falsity; no clutching at sheets when the door knob rattled; no "turn around for a minute, dear"; no nonsense. But most of all, none of the terrible reticence about the body between mothers and daughters, a reticence based on revulsion, and not, as with mothers and sons, upon respect and mystery. She was conscious of this revulsion every time she was alone with her daughter during the last month. It seemed to her sometimes that Angela assumed a defiance every time they were together as much as to say, "Speak now, if you dare, about me and my private affairs. . . ." It could have been only imagination, of course, but it kept her lips closed as surely as if the words had been really spoken. Luke knew nothing of all this. She would have to give him credit for that much. She could have thrown something at him when he inquired every night as they undressed, "Well, dear? Did you have a word with her?"

A word with her! It was in irony she had first said that she had. "A nice long chat," she had said sneeringly. But he had been bending down taking off his slippers and he had heard the words and missed the sneer. His face had lit up with such relief and she had been so repentant of her unkindness that she did not tell him she had been sarcastic. After that he had somehow relied on her to talk to Angela. He had lost his uneasy look and stopped asking clumsy questions. Instead, he got the more irritating habit of throwing them together at every possible moment. "Wouldn't you like to run along. I'll be after you in a few minutes." And if by any chance he came into a room when they were talking (about getting the poodle's hair cut or putting more sugar in the rhubarb) he would scuttle out again with apologies, like a visitor who got up too early, saying, "Don't let me disturb you." It was a wonder she had not run after him and beat at him with a newspaper. She had wanted so badly to be cruel or crude or vulgar. Poor Luke. She loved him so much but why, *oh why*, had he not kept his nose out of this.

Poor Luke. That was unfair. He was more sincere than she was, that was all. And he had been so worried about Angela. He was certain they had had a long talk and that Angela had assured her that she knew exactly what she was doing. That accounted for the strange way he treated the girl towards the end, as if she were a bit frightening, somebody not quite real, a little too unworldly, too precious, to be treated like a daughter. Because, of course, there was only one real difference for Luke between the cloister and the world—the difference of the flesh and the flesh denied. Poverty and obedience didn't matter a rap to him. He said as much twenty times a day.

"Poverty? Haven't the nuns more money than anyone in the country? Haven't they bought up all the fine castles and demesnes there are? Isn't there always a good smell of meat boiling in a convent no matter what hour you may call? And central heating? Poverty did you say? Nonsense!" She wanted to say "Nonsense yourself" when she saw Angela giving away her little blue velvet toque to one of her friends and telling the chambermaid she could take all her pictures of film stars. For a girl like Angela who stored up such rubbish, ribbons and programs and post cards and letters and goodness knows how much other stuff, the poverty of community possessions would be terrible. But of course she hadn't wanted to add to Luke's sorrow, and so she let him talk away as much as he wanted. He had a few words about obedience too.

"You'd have to be a lot more obedient in a office," he would assure her, "and no roses in heaven after it either." But about chastity Luke had nothing to say. That was what floored him. That a daughter of his should choose a life of chastity—a daughter of his—the child of his own delight. It was beyond his power to comprehend how such a choice existed for a woman. Poor Luke. He had looked at her sometimes as she sat brushing her hair, for all the world as if he were longing to ask, "Would you have done it? . . . Would you have given it all up?" But of course he never said anything of the kind.

Mrs. Latimer felt panic rise in her again. What would he say if he knew that she had not said one word to Angela about what she was giving up.

Men were so complacent. What could she have said? Yes! What could she have said to her own daughter that would not have been sickeningly embarrassing for them both.

It would have been no use saying anything. No matter what she had said she would be as much in doubt as she was at this minute about Angela's knowledge of life. Of course, she had not said a word to her. And it was all over now, anyway. She must remember that. From now on it was no use worrying. She must tell Luke that too. For better or worse it was all over now.

What an unfortunate choice of phrase—for better or worse. . . . And yet marriage, after all, was more worse than better, more of a cross than a crown. She herself had not found it so. Far from it . . . dear Luke . . . but so most of her married friends told her. They didn't even need to tell her, she could see for herself. In fact, when she thought about them she felt relieved that Angela had taken the veil. It was only when she thought about herself and Luke that she felt sorry. Sorry? Yes, so sorry she could cry with pity.

Angela was going to miss it all; the heavy weight of the hard male breast, the terror, the pain, the soft delirium seeping through. She clutched the hand strap tightly. Better not to remember those far-back years. She must forget them if she was to assume a role. And assume a role she must. She must singe the edges of the past and its dear delight with a religious remorse. She must seal the memories of her love into a casket of stern taciturnity. She must let her fate fall into its natural folds, and she must act and think like a nun's mother. For Luke's sake. She must be able to turn to him and smile and press his hand, tell him that the Lord had been good to them, had chosen them above others, had sent them a cross of sweet lebanon wood embossed with flowers and foliage. Yes. That was the way she should feel. She would discipline herself to feel so. She would make her brazen soul seek shame in the joys of its past. She would search into the dimmest hours of the days and nights gone by, hours most misted over by the languors of love, and find some memory to blush her cheeks.

But she could find nothing. She had no shame for herself. Wait a minute. Perhaps there was a moment when she had reddened for Luke's shame? Perhaps by thinking of him she could see some foolishness in their love.

She thought of him, as she had often seen him, with his head bent back, eyes heavy and breath unsure, answering her questions reluctantly and incoherently, a vein in his forehead throbbing. Then she turned deliberately and stared at him where he sat beside her in the taxi. She looked at him sitting bolt upright on the edge of the taxi seat, his hands folded firmly and an umbrella across his knees.

Now, was she not repulsed? Now, did she not feel compunction, to think that she had reduced this nattiness in a bowler hat to the small indignity of a dressing gown and urgently feeling fingers? No; she did not.

It was better to be honest to the end. She felt instead a pride and potency that made her press her shoulder blades into the horsehair cushioned seat while her breast rose high and firm, carrying a coral cameo brooch up from the depths of sepia lace and down again to its hollows. None of all the women she knew had lived with love as long and as intimately as she had done. No one knew what love was as well as she.

And now her own daughter would have her hair shorn and hide her body with twenty-five yards of black. Her daughter would never know anything about it. Should she have told her?

But with what words? She would have no words different from those the sisters had used to draw her into the cloister. She could hear their gentle voices saying with St. Paul that love was the fulfilling of the law, and speaking too of the greater love that no man hath than he . . . What chance had a few words from her against the power of quotations a thousand years old? Anything she could say would sound weak. "What do you know, Angela, of the love of a man for a woman?" Just suppose that Angela had listened and answered that she knew nothing. Supposing she had been gentle and trusting and said, "Tell me, Mother." It was extremely unlikely, but just suppose, for a moment, that it had happened. What would she have said love was? Not generous. Not kind. Not gentle. Not dignified. Not humble. Not to be described, in short, by any adjective that would appeal to a young girl straight from school. There were no words to describe it. Those who had tried were exiled and their books were burned on the quayside. It couldn't be described. And yet Luke had asked if she had "had a word with her." How irritating. Such a lack of understanding. Why didn't he try himself. Mrs. Latimer kicked the car rug.

Even if she could have described the peace and beauty of marriage, perhaps she would not have done so. For why, after all, should she take the responsibility of interfering with a vocation. Just because she didn't put a lot of faith in the idea of a personal call was no reason, when she came to think of it, for interfering with the life of someone who did. Wasn't there a girl in her own mother's town who wanted to be a nun? And, when her parents interfered, she went up on the roof one night in a nightdress, with a crucifix in her hand and her hair all down her back. The poor girl was saved, if she had intended jumping down, but her mind had gone. Interference was dangerous. It was not right to accept the responsibility of another soul.

Nonsense. There she was again trying to delude herself. She had accepted that responsibility twenty years ago when she brought her daughter into the world. Even at the time she had been aware of it. She had lain in her darkened room and tried to gaze down the widening wedge of the years ahead. She had seen her child and her child's children, and their children's children, wandering wider and wider over the world as year followed year; strange, terrifying people; lawyers, doctors, soldiers, nurses, deans with rolled parchments, drunkards, men of business, cheats, liars . . . along they trudged over the land while she lay in her grave, and from time to time they turned back with frightened faces, and each face had the cast of hers; her features, her skin, her hair, her eyes. They all seemed to stream out from her as she had often seen people stream out of a cinema, coming singly through the doors, joining into pairs, going on to the pavements and walking there in threes and fours, then five, then six abreast. On, on, widening out into twenties, fifties, hundreds, thousands, as they spread like a ray over the city.

A great weariness came over her at this thought of the future in which she had played so short but so significant a part. She became panic-stricken and it seemed to her that all those people were aware of her part in their birth, even those who were generations away in the hidden years, and that they called a vision of her face to mind and reproached her and said, "If only you . . . if only you . . . You alone could have saved us from life." For the lives they led had suddenly seemed evil in every case. Some were prising open drawers and looking over their shoulders. Some were stealthily crossing the "t's" of letters that were forged. Some were creeping down dark stairs and waiting in hallways for a silent, empty street before they ventured out with turned-up collars. All were better never born. All were born because she had shaken a bough and let down the fertile pollen of life over flowers she would never see bloom—wicked dark blossoms that were better left unbudded. Why had she done it? Why had she not gone away one summer afternoon like her daughter Angela, in black gabardine, with no nail varnish and a clean face washed with soap?

Angela would never have such responsibility. She would never be an old woman sitting in a taxi dreading the pointed finger of the unborn. With Angela life would end like a bud blown onto the river and carried away in its beauty. Life would end? End with Angela? But she had forgotten, she had been inattentive, she had been so depressed . . . why had she not realized what Angela's going would mean? Up through her body into her eyes flew the blue bird of happiness that had cowered afraid and out with a flutter of smiles it flew from her lips. How had she been so stupid? Why had she not thought of it sooner? It seemed so obvious now. Angela had freed her from the future. Angela had cut them both adrift from the shore of the menacing future. There would be no people branching out into armies of evil in the years beyond control. There would be no pointing fingers. She had received some grace. Her flower had shed its seed and the seed had flowered to beauty, but beyond that beauty it had not blown. Down into the dark clay both petals, hers and Angela's, would fall together. Suddenly she felt happy again, happy and carefree. Angela had freed her from her only fear.

Had she perhaps been conscious of this freedom somewhere in the pools of her thought without having brought it up to the light? Had the feeling of happiness lurked in her eyes the day her daughter had come to her and told her of her decision? For if it had (though she certainly had not been conscious of it), that would account for the strange antagonism in Angela's eyes as she held out a paper and said:—

"Here's a list of what I've to get."

The list had made everything seem so certain, so definite, that even then, even before Luke began to worry, she had felt it was too late to do anything. The list had filled the weeks, crowding out everything else. It was hard to believe it was written on a half sheet of note paper. It took up the whole day every day. It took away the leisure they had always had downtown for a cup of coffee or tea. It made it impossible to stop, even for ten minutes, and run into a news theater.

Such peculiar things as it called for! Her feet ached walking, and Angela was irritable and cross. White corsets, for instance! Where would you go for them? *She* hadn't known. They tried about twenty places before they got them. The sales girl had thought it so odd. "I don't know where you would get them, madam. Pink are all we are ever asked for." They spoke as if *she* wanted them. As if *she* wore them. Good Lord, did they think she looked like someone who wore white corsets? She had been furious. Poor Angela. But it had been intensely irritating. "It's outlandish," she had said to the poor girl every other ten minutes. And Angela had not answered, had pretended not to hear, but her cheeks had burned up red. And no wonder. It was enough to make anyone blush. White seemed so immodest, like something you'd see on the seashore, sticking out from under a bathing sheet while a fat woman got ready for a dip; a silly woman who would hold hands and flop up and down in the water edge without wetting her top. White corsets—disgusting! Once as they came through the swing doors of the twelfth shop into a blazing city sun, Angela had ventured to say in a quiet voice that the list said white *or* black. "Black?" she had screamed (the people had turned and stared at them). "Black?" Out of the question. Bad enough to be taken for a fool, without being taken for a prostitute as well.

Yes. She had said prostitute. What if Angela had been shocked, she was going far enough from the world where such words were said. And in any case she probably did not know what the word meant. She was going into a sanctuary of lisle stockings and flannel petticoats three deep.

They had to have a dressmaker fix up the petticoats. There was no use trying the shops for them. "And you'll have to tell her what you want them for, too," she had said to the reluctant Angela, "or else she will think you are mad." That had been unkind. Everything she said those days seemed sharp and bitter. But every hour brought a fresh annoyance. Even the old dressmaker had become a pest. She had showered them with leaflets and medals and medallions. She had given them memorial cards of fathers and aunts and cousins and sisters, all of whom had looked most alive in their pictures, with waxed whiskers or tight buns and their shoulders stiffened as if to say, "I'm not dead. She just thinks I am." And she had asked them to pray for this and for that, and promised her own prayers in return. Then, worst of all, there was the dreadful day that she had come back with the petticoats while Benny Trench was visiting them and had started all that shocking nonsense about the bandages and the statue. She would never forget it. Poor Angela reddening and Benny getting ready to go so that he could spread the story all over the city. He would probably pretend that it was Angela who had told the story. Or she herself. Well, he would hardly go that far. No one would believe him. He would say it was Angela who told it—Angela, who was always so reserved and sceptical, always, even there on the convent steps.

That last week had been one of constant humiliation; tactless remarks every other minute; presents arriving by every post. And such presents, holy pictures, holy water fonts, prayer books, quartz angels, rosary beads . . . and, of course, the thought that came first to mind as you watched her untie the parcels was that the poor child should have been getting wedding presents; finger bowls and glass decanters, boudoir cushions and silver salvers. Did Angela never think that, at times, herself? Did she never have regrets? You could not tell by her face.

What in the world had come over her? It was, of course, sheer nonsense to say that she did not know what she was giving up. Hadn't she read books? Hadn't she been to the cinema often enough? Hadn't she gone to parties? And hadn't they, surely, surely, hadn't they played postman's knock at any of those parties? And, whether they did or not, there were countless ways that girls became accustomed to life and learned its implications. How was this she herself had got the first inklings? She couldn't remember exactly. There was one very clear memory of gay Cousin Charlie that might have been important. He had kissed her the night she came home from school as she was going through the kitchen door with a tray of coffee in her hands. She hadn't been able to do anything to stop him. "On your way now, Crybaby," he had said to her, "and tell your ma." But she hadn't told her ma. She had gone up to her room instead and sat in the dusk thinking of him until it was time to light the lamps. And before she had gone to bed that night she had carefully set up stitches in canary colored wool to knit him a sweater. Poor Cousin Charlie. He had gone to America before she had the front finished, and it wasn't a year until she was engaged to Luke and starting to knit the jumper again, beginning the back, to give it to him. Poor Charlie. Who knows what would have happened to her had it not been for him? She could not remember much about those early days before she put her hair up, but she had vague memories of being rather a prude, and her sisters had some joke or other, that they kept up to this day, about the way she looked at Papa when he spoke about the heifer. . . . She didn't know what it was even now, but it proved what a ridiculous girl she must have seemed to them. Poor Charlie, he had done more harm than good with his kisses, but not in her case.

Had nobody ever kissed Angela? Angela who was as pretty as a cool, wet flower. What flower did she always remind you of? Not a summer one, but some spring chalice flower. What one? Perhaps no one had ever dared kiss her, she looked so inaccessible, like a water lily, still and pale and beautiful, but cool and clear and remote as well.

Should they have given more parties for her, or sent her away on holidays with a girl friend? Yet all around them were people who had been bitterly sorry for giving their girls too much liberty. It was hard to know just what to do. Even if no one had ever kissed her she had her imagination, hadn't she? Although the other was far the simplest way to learn, still, when it came to a fine point one could justly ask what nice girl, brought up in a convent, had any experience of boys. Yet that did not prevent them from having a healthy curiosity. Could there be anything, after all, in the idea of a Personal Call, a Divine Choice? It was so hard not to be sceptical when you had traveled a bit and read a lot. But how else could you account for a lovely girl like Angela going away like that so suddenly? If she were plain, or delicate, or even aggressive about women's rights, she would not have worried. But a girl as fitted for love as Angela, decked out with petals, you would think, to attract and to draw men towards her. She was so beautifully balanced and reasonable for a girl, so normal and so calm, that the shock of this sudden fanaticism (what else was it?) overcame you completely.

Never had a child been as normal. Right up to this very summer her room had been hung all over with pictures of film stars. And, as a child, no one ever needed to tell her to pull up her socks or wash her hands. She kept herself pretty and neat by instinct to please and attract. She was always in trouble with her nurse for looking around in church to smile at the boys in the choir, and as for frizzing her hair with her fingers, nothing would stop her. People told her since (thank God she had not known at the time) that when the child was six or seven she used to spend hours at the foot of the drive holding up her dress and calling to the bread men and messenger boys to look at her lovely new dress with bloomers to match.

What had changed her? Why had she turned aside from such a simple and happy vanity? Whatever it was that made her change, it was not religion. That might be a terrible thing for a Catholic woman to say, but wasn't it clear to be seen? When had Angela ever been pious? No beads at Mass, no prayer book, looking around her all the time, yawning during the sermon and pushing going out of the door, as if she were coming out from a football match. Since she had made up her mind to go away she had been worse than ever. She wouldn't come near the house if she saw the curate's car at the door, and she had lost her temper completely with Luke the day he asked her to go to twelve o'clock mass with Aunt Helen in case she got dizzy in the heated atmosphere. "Haven't I been to mass already?" she asked as irritably as if no one were ever known to go twice, much less three or four times, like some people.

At moments like that it seemed that there was some queer reason at the back of her idea. But then at other times she seemed anxious enough to go, and eager for the time to come.

Well, it had come, and there was no use worrying now. While there had been times she had lain awake for nights and thought about nothing else till dawn. All to no good. Angela was gone. Now she must reconcile herself to the inevitable and help Luke to form new dreams. How proud he would become of her again in a new and reverent way as she came towards him across the polished floors, swinging her beads and swaying her skirts, tall, aloof and proud, with the firm high bust of a virgin.

There had been no mention of brassières on the list. She only remembered that now. Yet all the nuns had the same young line of bosom, even the oldest of them. No strain of bearing children probably, and an erect carriage at all times. And then those stiff old-fashioned corsets. She would never forget them. She would never get the simple pleasure that Luke would get from looking at Angela in her habit. She would be filled with petty feelings of disgust and irritation about some trivial thing like a corset. But perhaps after a time she would not care. As long as Angela herself did not care . . .

But that was the mystery. Did Angela care? Flannel nightdresses with ruffles around the neck and long sleeves for a girl like a cool water lily. How did she bear it? Why did she go through with it? Things like that were the real test, not the big things like leaving home and obeying a superior. Flannel next your skin and wearing a bathing suit in the bath, things like that were the test. Why had she gone through with it? What had given her the idea in the first place?

"Luke?" (She must ask him that, whether or not he guessed that she had not spoken to Angela about it.)

"Luke?"

"Just a minute, dear." He was leaning back and looking out the little window at the back of the car. Not at the convent still, she hoped; that would be insincere and theatrical. He turned round with a frown.

"Did you see that man at the lamppost?" he asked.

(How like a man to switch from one thing to another.)

"No, I didn't notice."

"Well, I did, and what is more I've seen him before, off and on since Easter. Up to no good I should say; a bit off. I think I'll give the police a ring and have them watch him. He might give someone a nasty fright, school children or the like, not properly dressed and that kind of thing. . . ."

The taxi drew up at the house. Luke began to pay the driver in the light of the headlamps. Suddenly she felt weary. And she went wearily up the steps. But the weariness was all in her heart. It was hard to be a mother. Hard to be vigilant night and day and at the end of it not to know whether you had failed or triumphed. She looked down the dark green avenue and thought with fear of the maniac a few yards down the road. His face, that she had not seen, came clear before her frightened eyes. He was bending down among rushes on a river bank and reaching out with cruel fingers to pluck at a floating lily, a water lily, cool, clear and remote, whose petals folded up with the rancidness of his breath. But whether he reached it or not she didn't have time to see in her dream, because the door was flung open by Hetty, who hurried her into the lighted hall.

"The tea is wet, ma'am. I heard the car on the drive."

Hetty spoke with a wonderful gentleness. The fire was piled with logs. The silver shone. Her slippers, as well as Luke's, were warming on the fender. There was some change in the atmosphere. Hetty was so kindly and like an old friend. What was it? And then she knew with a sinking of heart and another vision of fear. Everyone would be kind to her now and treat her with high respect as well. For she had proved herself. She was the mother of a nun.

Tillie Olsen 1912–

Had Tillie Olsen possessed Woolf's idyllic "room of one's own" in which to write, there's no telling how much work she might have produced. Then again, it is exactly this absence of creative time and economic status in her life that led to the groundbreaking essays in *Silences* (1978), a collection that explores the relationship of circumstances regarding race, class, sex, and "the unnatural thwarting of what struggles to come into being." Born to Russian immigrants in Omaha, Nebraska, Tillie Lerner left high school after the eleventh grade to enter the world of "everyday jobs," but continued to educate herself claiming, "Public libraries were my college." In 1934, she published in *Partisan Review* what forty years later would become the first chapter of her only novel, *Yonnondio: From the Thirties* (1974). Unfortunately, the responsibilities of raising and supporting four children during the depression provided Olsen with little time to write for the next twenty years. She came back strong in 1953 with the classic story "I Stand Here Ironing," and in 1961 published her only collection of fiction, *Tell Me a Riddle* (1961), the title story winning the O. Henry Award for best American short story. Summing up her writing, *The Harper American Literature* states: "Olsen's work is especially unforgettable for its poor, forgotten female characters—archetypal in their ordinariness—who struggle to claim a dignified place for themselves in circumstances that nurture but also restrain the creative self."

I STAND HERE IRONING

I stand here ironing, and what you asked me moves tormented back and forth with the iron.

"I wish you would manage the time to come in and talk with me about your daughter. I'm sure you can help me understand her. She's a youngster who needs help and whom I'm deeply interested in helping."

"Who needs help." . . . Even if I came, what good would it do? You think because I am her mother I have a key, or that in some way you could use me as a key? She has lived for nineteen years. There is all that life that has happened outside of me, beyond me.

And when is there time to remember, to sift, to weigh, to estimate, to total? I will start and there will be an interruption and I will have to gather it all together again. Or I will become engulfed with all I did or did not do, with what should have been and what cannot be helped.

She was a beautiful baby. The first and only one of our five that was beautiful at birth. You do not guess how new and uneasy her tenancy in her now-loveliness. You did not know her all those years she was thought homely, or see her poring over her baby pictures, making me tell her over and over how beautiful she had been—and would be, I would tell her—and was now, to the seeing eye. But the seeing eyes were few or nonexistent. Including mine.

I nursed her. They feel that's important nowadays. I nursed all the children, but with her, with all the fierce rigidity of first motherhood, I did like the books then said. Though her cries battered me to trembling and my breasts ached with swollenness, I waited till the clock decreed.

Why do I put that first? I do not even know if it matters, or if it explains anything.

She was a beautiful baby. She blew shining bubbles of sound. She loved motion, loved light, loved color and music and textures. She would lie on the floor in her blue overalls patting the surface so hard in ecstasy her hands and feet would blur. She was a miracle to me, but when she was eight months old I had to leave her daytimes with the woman downstairs to whom she was no miracle at all, for I worked or looked for work and for Emily's father, who "could no longer endure" (he wrote in his good-bye note) "sharing want with us."

I was nineteen. It was the pre-relief, pre-WPA world of the depression. I would start running as soon as I got off the streetcar, running up the stairs, the place smelling sour, and awake or asleep to startle awake, when she saw me she would break into a clogged weeping that could not be comforted, a weeping I can hear yet.

After a while I found a job hashing at night so I could be with her days, and it was better. But it came to where I had to bring her to his family and leave her.

It took a long time to raise the money for her fare back. Then she got chicken pox and I had to wait longer. When she finally came, I hardly knew her, walking quick and nervous like her father, looking like her father, thin, and dressed in a shoddy red that yellowed her skin and glared at the pockmarks. All the baby loveliness gone.

She was two. Old enough for nursery school they said, and I did not know then what I know now—the fatigue of the long day, and the lacerations of group life in the kinds of nurseries that are only parking places for children.

Except that it would have made no difference if I had known. It was the only place there was. It was the only way we could be together, the only way I could hold a job.

And even without knowing, I knew. I knew the teacher that was evil because all these years it has curdled into my memory, the little boy hunched in the corner, her rasp, "why aren't you outside, because Alvin hits you? that's no reason, go out, scaredy." I knew Emily hated it even if she did not clutch and implore "don't go Mommy" like the other children, mornings.

She always had a reason why we should stay home. Momma, you look sick. Momma, I feel sick. Momma, the teachers aren't there today, they're sick. Momma, we can't go, there was a fire there last night. Momma, it's a holiday today, no school, they told me.

But never a direct protest, never rebellion. I think of our others in their three-, four-year-oldness—the explosions, the tempers, the denunciations, the demands—and I feel suddenly ill. I put the iron down. What in me demanded that goodness in her? And what was the cost, the cost to her of such goodness?

The old man living in the back once said in his gentle way: "You should smile at Emily more when you look at her." What *was* in my face when I looked at her? I loved her. There were all the acts of love.

It was only with the others I remembered what he said, and it was the face of joy, and not of care or tightness or worry I turned to them—too late for Emily. She does not smile easily, let alone almost always as her brothers and sisters do. Her face is closed and sombre, but when she wants, how fluid. You must have seen it in her pantomimes, you spoke of her rare gift for comedy on the stage that rouses a laughter out of the audience so dear they applaud and applaud and do not want to let her go.

Where does it come from, that comedy? There was none of it in her when she came back to me that second time, after I had had to send her away again. She had a new daddy now to learn to love, and I think perhaps it was a better time.

Except when we left her alone nights, telling ourselves she was old enough.

"Can't you go some other time, Mommy, like tomorrow?" she would ask. "Will it be just a little while you'll be gone? Do you promise?"

The time we came back, the front door open, the clock on the floor in the hall. She rigid awake. "It wasn't just a little while. I didn't cry. Three times I called you, just three times, and then I ran downstairs to open the door so you could come faster. The clock talked loud. I threw it away, it scared me what it talked."

She said the clock talked loud again that night I went to the hospital to have Susan. She was delirious with the fever that comes before red measles, but she was fully conscious all the week I was gone and the week after we were home when she could not come near the new baby or me.

She did not get well. She stayed skeleton thin, not wanting to eat, and night after night she had nightmares. She would call for me, and I would rouse from exhaustion to sleepily call back: "You're all right, darling, go to sleep, it's just a dream," and if she still called, in a sterner voice, "Now go to sleep, Emily, there's nothing to hurt you." Twice, only twice, when I had to get up for Susan anyhow, I went in to sit with her.

Now when it is too late (as if she would let me hold and comfort her like I do the others) I get up and go to her at once at her moan or restless stirring. "Are you awake, Emily? Can I get you something?" And the answer is always the same: "No, I'm all right, go back to sleep, Mother."

They persuaded me at the clinic to send her away to a convalescent home in the country where "she can have the kind of food and care you can't manage for her, and you'll be free to concentrate on the new baby." They still send children to that place. I see pictures on the society page of sleek young women planning affairs to raise money for it, or dancing at the affairs, or decorating Easter eggs or filling Christmas stockings for the children.

They never have a picture of the children so I do not know if the girls still wear those gigantic red bows and the ravaged looks on the every other Sunday when parents can come to visit "unless otherwise notified"—as we were notified the first six weeks.

Oh it is a handsome place, green lawns and tall trees and fluted flower beds. High up on the balconies of each cottage the children stand, the girls in their red bows and white dresses, the boys in white suits and giant red ties. The parents stand below shrieking up to be heard and the children shriek down to be heard, and between them the invisible wall "Not To Be Contaminated by Parental Germs or Physical Affection."

There was a tiny girl who always stood hand in hand with Emily. Her parents never came. One visit she was gone. "They moved her to Rose Cottage" Emily shouted in explanation. "They don't like you to love anybody here."

She wrote once a week, the labored writing of a seven-year-old. "I am fine. How is the baby. If I write my leter nicly I will have a star. Love." There never was a star. We wrote every other day, letters she could never hold or keep but only hear read—once. "We simply do not have room for children to keep any personal possessions," they patiently explained when we pieced one Sunday's shrieking together to plead how much it would mean to Emily, who loved so to keep things, to be allowed to keep her letters and cards.

Each visit she looked frailer. "She isn't eating," they told us.

(They had runny eggs for breakfast or mush with lumps, Emily said later, I'd hold it in my mouth and not swallow. Nothing ever tasted good, just when they had chicken.)

It took us eight months to get her released home, and only the fact that she gained back so little of her seven lost pounds convinced the social worker.

I used to try to hold and love her after she came back, but her body would stay stiff, and after a while she'd push away. She ate little. Food sickened her, and I think much of life too. Oh she had physical lightness and brightness, twinkling by on skates, bouncing like a ball up and down up and down over the jump rope, skimming over the hill; but these were momentary.

She fretted about her appearance, thin and dark and foreign-looking at a time when every little girl was supposed to look or thought she should look a chubby blond replica of Shirley Temple. The doorbell sometimes rang for her, but no one seemed to come and play in the house or be a best friend. Maybe because we moved so much.

There was a boy she loved painfully through two school semesters. Months later she told me how she had taken pennies from my purse to buy him candy. "Licorice was his favorite and I brought him some every day, but he still liked Jennifer better'n me. Why, Mommy?" The kind of question for which there is no answer.

School was a worry to her. She was not glib or quick in a world where glibness and quickness were easily confused with ability to learn. To her overworked and exasperated teachers she was an overconscientious "slow learner" who kept trying to catch up and was absent entirely too often.

I let her be absent, though sometimes the illness was imaginary. How different from my now-strictness about attendance with the others. I wasn't working. We had a new baby, I was home anyhow. Sometimes, after Susan grew old enough, I would keep her home from school, too, to have them all together.

Mostly Emily had asthma, and her breathing, harsh and labored, would fill the house with a curiously tranquil sound. I would bring the two old dresser mirrors and her boxes of collections to her bed. She would select beads and single earrings, bottle tops and shells, dried flowers and pebbles, old postcards and scraps, all sorts of oddments; then she and Susan would play Kingdom, setting up landscapes and furniture, peopling them with action.

Those were the only times of peaceful companionship between her and Susan. I have edged away from it, that poisonous feeling between them, that terrible balancing of hurts and needs I had to do between the two, and did so badly, those earlier years.

Oh there are conflicts between the others too, each one human, needing, demanding, hurting, taking—but only between Emily and Susan, no, Emily toward Susan that corroding resentment. It seems so obvious on the surface, yet it is not obvious. Susan, the second child, Susan, golden- and curly-haired and chubby, quick and articulate and assured, everything in appearance and manner Emily was not; Susan, not able to resist Emily's precious things, losing or sometimes clumsily breaking them; Susan telling jokes and riddles to company for applause while Emily sat silent (to say to me later: that was *my* riddle, Mother, I told it to Susan); Susan, who for all the five years' difference in age was just a year behind Emily in developing physically.

I am glad for that slow physical development that widened the difference between her and her contemporaries, though she suffered over it. She was too vulnerable for that terrible world of youthful competition, of preening and parading, of constant measuring of yourself against every other, of envy, "If I had that copper hair," "If I had that skin. . . . " She tormented herself enough about not looking like the others, there was enough of the unsureness, the having to be conscious of words before you speak, the constant caring—what are they thinking of me? without having it all magnified by the merciless physical drives.

Ronnie is calling. He is wet and I change him. It is rare there is such a cry now. That time of motherhood is almost behind me when the ear is not one's own but must always be racked and listening for the child cry, the child call. We sit for a while and I hold him, looking out over the city spread in charcoal with its soft aisles of light. "*Shoogily*," he breathes and curls closer. I carry him back to bed, asleep. *Shoogily*. A funny word, a family word, inherited from Emily, invented by her to say: *comfort*.

In this and other ways she leaves her seal, I say aloud. And startle at my saying it. What do I mean? What did I start to gather together, to try and make coherent? I was at the terrible, growing years. War years. I do not remember them well. I was working, there were four smaller ones now, there was not time for her. She had to help be a mother, and housekeeper, and shopper. She had to set her seal. Mornings of crisis and near hysteria trying to get lunches packed, hair combed, coats and shoes found, everyone to school or Child Care on time, the baby ready for transportation. And always the paper scribbled on by a smaller one, the book looked at by Susan then mislaid, the homework not done. Running out to that huge school where she was one, she was lost, she was a drop; suffering over her unpreparedness, stammering and unsure in her classes.

There was so little time left at night after the kids were bedded down. She would struggle over books, always eating (it was in those years she developed her enormous appetite that is legendary in our family) and I would be ironing, or preparing food for the next day, or writing V-mail to Bill, or tending the baby. Sometimes, to make me laugh, or out of her despair, she would imitate happenings or types at school.

I think I said once: "Why don't you do something like this in the school amateur show?" One morning she phoned me at work, hardly understandable through the weeping: "Mother, I did it. I won, I won; they gave me first prize; they clapped and clapped and wouldn't let me go."

Now suddenly she was Somebody, and as imprisoned in her difference as she had been in her anonymity.

She began to be asked to perform at other high schools, even in colleges, then at city and statewide affairs. The first one we went to, I only recognized her that first moment when thin, shy, she almost drowned herself into the curtains. Then: Was this Emily? The control, the command, the convulsing and deadly clowning, the spell, then the roaring, stamping audience, unwilling to let this rare and precious laughter out of their lives.

Afterwards: You ought to do something about her with a gift like that—but without money or knowing how, what does one do? We have left it all to her, and the gift has as often eddied inside, clogged and clotted, as been used and growing.

She is coming. She runs up the stairs two at a time with her light graceful step, and I know she is happy tonight. Whatever it was that occasioned your call did not happen today.

"Aren't you ever going to finish the ironing, Mother? Whistler painted his mother in a rocker. I'd have to paint mine standing over an ironing board." This is one of her communicative nights and she tells me everything and nothing as she fixes herself a plate of food out of the icebox.

She is so lovely. Why did you want me to come in at all? Why were you concerned? She will find her way.

She starts up the stairs to bed. "Don't get *me* up with the rest in the morning." "But I thought you were having midterms." "Oh, those," she comes back in, kisses me, and says quite lightly, "in a couple of years when we'll all be atom-dead they won't matter a bit."

She has said it before. She *believes* it. But because I have been dredging the past, and all that compounds a human being is so heavy and meaningful in me, I cannot endure it tonight.

I will never total it all. I will never come in to say: She was a child seldom smiled at. Her father left me before she was a year old. I had to work her first six years when there was work, or I sent her home and to his relatives. There were years she had care she hated. She was dark and thin and foreign-looking in a world where the prestige went to blondness and curly hair and dimples; she was slow where glibness was prized. She was a child of anxious, not proud, love. We were poor and could not afford for her the soil of easy growth. I was a young mother, I was a distracted mother. There were the other children pushing up, demanding. Her younger sister seemed all that she was not. There were years she did not let me touch her. She kept too much in herself, her life was such she had to keep too much in herself. My wisdom came too late. She has much to her and probably little will come of it. She is a child of her age, of depression, of war, of fear.

Let her be. So all that is in her will not bloom—but in how many does it? There is still enough left to live by. Only help her to know—help make it so there is cause for her to know—that she is more than this dress on the ironing board, helpless before the iron.

Muriel Rukeyser 1913–1980

Poet Muriel Rukeyser, according to author Erica Jong, was "the mother of us all." With a tremendous breadth of knowledge and the passions requisite of the iconoclast, she explored subjects ranging from architecture to eroticism to politics and physics, alienating critics with her radical social convictions and actions in the process. Because her work was censured, ignored, and misunderstood during her peak years of creativity, much of the recognition she has received as a major American poet has been late in coming—not that she was ignored in her lifetime. Her first collection of poetry, *Theory of Flight*, won the prestigious Yale Younger Poets Prize in 1935. From 1938 to 1948, Rukeyser published six more collections of verse, much of it dealing with social inequality and the atrocities of World War II. Her Jewishness and involvement in the anti-fascism movement in Spain fired her passion for these subjects. After the war, as a single mother, she taught and lectured part-time and still wrote the occasional collection of poetry. Always an unabashedly subjective writer of great intensity, she was radical feminism's most articulate spokesperson during periods of national struggle.

STUDY IN A LATE SUBWAY

The moon revolves outside; possibly, black air
turns so around them facing night's concave,
momentum the slogan of their hurling brains
swung into speed, crying for stillness   high
    suspended and rising on time's wave.   5

Did these tracks have a wilder life in the ground?
beaten from streams of metal in secret earth   :
energy travels along the veins of steel,
their faces rush forward, missiles of discontent
    thrown vaguely to the south and north.   10

That head is jointed loosely on his neck,
his glossy eyes turn on the walls and floor   :
her face is a blank breast with sorrow
spouting at the mouth's nipple.   All eyes move
    heavily to the opening door,   15

regarding in dullness how we also enter.
An angle of track charges up to us, swings
out and past in a firework of signals.
Sleepily others dangle by one hand
    tense and semi-crucified things.   20

Speed welcomes us in explosions of night   :   here
is wrath and fortitude and motion's burning   :
the world buries the directionless, until
the heads are sprung in awareness or drowned in peace.
    Sleep will happen.   We must give them morning. 25

ECCENTRIC MOTION

Dashing in glass we race,
New York to Washington   :
encased with bubbles lie

in emerald spa   :
upholstered promenades   5
convey us far.
Have we reached the last limits?
What have we not done?

Shut into velvet we
survey the scene,   10
the locked-up building,
the frozen pier   :
before and before the events,
we loved our minds in fear   :
they wriggle into worms.   15
We watch.   We turn.   Surrounded,
we are at last closed in.

Coated in learning, do we
cause its crown to fall?
the plane, the bath, the car   20
extend our protection   :
(But have we seen it all?
Shall we continue
in this direction?   :   )

This is not the way
to save the day.   25
Get up and dress and go
nobly to and fro   :
Dashing in glass we race,
New York to Mexico. . . .   30

To Be a Jew in the Twentieth Century

To be a Jew in the twentieth century
Is to be offered a gift.   If you refuse,
Wishing to be invisible, you choose
Death of the spirit, the stone insanity.
Accepting, take full life, full agonies: 5
Your evening deep in labyrinthine blood
Of those who resist, fail and resist; and God
Reduced to a hostage among hostages.
The gift is torment.   Not alone the still
Torture, isolation; or torture of the flesh.   10

That may come also.   But the accepting wish,
The whole and fertile spirit as guarantee
For every human freedom, suffering to be free,
Daring to live for the impossible.

Ruth Stone 1915–

Claiming that poetry came with "this mysterious feeling . . . of peculiar ecstasy," Ruth Stone has gone through life crafting wide-ranging and elegant aesthetic visions. Born in Roanoke, Virginia, and raised in Indiana and Illinois, her poetry consistently focuses on diverse situations involving women, addressing metaphysical meditations and philosophical questions from a distinctly feminist perspective. Educated at the University of Illinois and Harvard, she supported herself by teaching and as a poet-in-residence at institutions such as the University of Illinois, the University of Wisconsin, Indiana University, the University of California at Davis, Brandeis University, Wellesley College, and SUNY at Binghamton. She is the author of five collections of poetry: *In an Iridescent Time* (1958), *Topography* (1970), *Cheap* (1975), *Second-Hand Coat: New and Selected Poems* (1987), and *Simplicity* (1995). Her awards and honors include two Guggenheim fellowships, a Radcliffe Institute fellowship, a PEN award, and the Bess Hokin Prize from *Poetry* magazine.

THINGS I SAY TO MYSELF WHILE HANGING LAUNDRY

If an ant, crossing on the clothesline
from apple tree to apple tree,
would think and think,
it probably could not dream up Albert Einstein.
Or even his sloppy mustache;   5
or the wrinkled skin bags under his eyes
that puffed out years later,
after he dreamed up that maddening relativity.[1]

---

[1] The idea that time and motion are relative to the observer, if the speed of light is constant in all frames of reference. Albert Einstein (1879–1955) was only in his twenties when he published his papers on the special theory of relativity.

Even laundry is three dimensional.
The ants cross its great fibrous forests   10
from clothespin to clothespin
carrying the very heart of life in their sacs or mandibles,
the very heart of the universe in their formic acid molecules.
And how refreshing the linens are,
lying in the clean sheets at night,   15
when you seem to be the only one on the mountain,
and your body feels the smooth touch of the bed
like love against your skin;
and the heavy sac of yourself relaxes into its embrace.
When you turn out the light,   20
you are blind in the dark
as perhaps the ants are blind,
with the same abstract leap out of this limiting dimension.
So that the very curve of light,
as it is pulled in the dimple of space,[2]   25
is relative to your own blind pathway across the abyss.
And there in the dark is Albert Einstein
with his clever formula[3] that looks like little mandibles
digging tunnels into the earth
and bringing it up, grain by grain,   30
the crystals of sand exploding
into white hot radiant turbulence,
smiling at you, his shy bushy smile,
along an imaginary line from here to there.

Margaret Walker 1915–

M argaret Walker is best known for her 1942 book, *For My People*, a collection
of poems that she finished while pursuing a master's degree at the Iowa
Writers' Workshop. As her first book, it won the Yale University Younger Poets
Award and was the only volume of American poetry published by a black woman
since Georgia Douglass Johnson's *The Heart of a Woman and Other Poems*
in 1918. Describing the title poem of *For My People* as a "signature piece" for
black audiences, a critic commented, "We knew the poem. It was ours. . . . And
as [it] moved on, rhythmically piling image after image of our lives . . . mirroring

---

[2] I.e., by gravity. According to Einstein's general theory of relativity, which predicted such curvature
of light, gravity is a curved field created by mass.

[3] Expressing the equivalence of mass and energy in the famous equation $E = mc^2$.

our collective selves . . . we cried out in deep response." Walker, born the
daughter of a Methodist minister and music teacher in Birmingham, Alabama, received encouragement in her writing from W. E. B. Du Bois, Langston Hughes,
and Richard Wright. It was while working for the WPA Federal Writers' Project
that Walker became friends with Wright and subsequently started a three-year
relationship in which Wright would respond to Walker's poetry while she helped
him to revise *Almos' a Man* and the posthumously published *Lawd Today*.
Walker went on to publish the controversial biography *Richard Wright: A
Daemonic Genius* (1989). After *For My People*, Walker did not publish again
until 1966 when her historical novel, *Jubilee*, broke the silence. Walker has
taught at a variety of colleges and universities and is the recipient of numerous
fellowships and honorary degrees.

FOR MY PEOPLE

For my people everywhere singing their slave songs
    repeatedly: their dirges and their ditties and their blues
    and jubilees, praying their prayers nightly to an
    unknown god, bending their knees humbly to an
    unseen power;   5

For my people lending their strength to the years, to the
    gone years and the now years and the maybe years,
    washing ironing cooking scrubbing sewing mending
    hoeing plowing digging planting pruning patching
    dragging along never gaining never reaping never   10
    knowing and never understanding;

For my playmates in the clay and dust and sand of Alabama
    backyards playing baptizing and preaching and doctor
    and jail and soldier and school and mama and cooking
    and playhouse and concert and store and hair and Miss   15
    Choomby and company;

For the cramped bewildered years we went to school to learn
    to know the reasons why and the answers to and the
    people who and the places where and the days when, in
    memory of the bitter hours when we discovered we   20
    were black and poor and small and different and nobody
    cared and nobody wondered and nobody understood;

For the boys and girls who grew in spite of these things to
    be man and woman, to laugh and dance and sing and
    play and drink their wine and religion and success, to   25
    marry their playmates and bear children and then die
    of consumption and anemia and lynching;

For my people thronging 47th Street in Chicago and Lenox
    Avenue in New York and Rampart Street in New
    Orleans, lost disinherited dispossessed and happy   30
    people filling the cabarets and taverns and other
    people's pockets needing bread and shoes and milk and
    land and money and something—something all our own;

For my people walking blindly spreading joy, losing time
    being lazy, sleeping when hungry, shouting when   35
    burdened, drinking when hopeless, tied, and shackled
    and tangled among ourselves by the unseen creatures
    who tower over us omnisciently and laugh;

For my people blundering and groping and floundering in
    the dark of churches and schools and clubs and   40
    societies, associations and councils and committees and
    conventions, distressed and disturbed and deceived and
    devoured by money-hungry glory-craving leeches,
    preyed on by facile force of state and fad and novelty, by
    false prophet and holy believer;   45

For my people standing staring trying to fashion a better way
    from confusion, from hypocrisy and misunderstanding,
    trying to fashion a world that will hold all the people,
    all the faces, all the adams and eves and their countless
    generations;   50

Let a new earth rise. Let another world be born. Let a
    bloody peace be written in the sky. Let a second
    generation full of courage issue forth; let a people
    loving freedom come to growth. Let a beauty full of
    healing and a strength of final clenching be the pulsing   55
    in our spirits and our blood. Let the martial songs be
    written, let the dirges disappear. Let a race of men now
    rise and take control.

CHICAGO

One day I saw Chicago river move
through milky dusk of twilight's lighted lamps.
I saw the avenues of moving lights
pour over Wacker Drive's slow blinking ramps.
I saw through fiery glow of foundry blasts   5
the river squatting low at dawn for steel.
Then in a filthy noon of stench-filled air
I saw the fouling river touch the slaughter pens.
I saw the freighted river moving on
through belching smoke of mill and boiler room   10
her river fingers washing in their hold
her lake and all its throngs of people fold
within their living and their daily toil
Her ancient meaning in their ageless tide.

SOUTHERN SONG

I want my body bathed again by southern suns, my soul
    reclaimed again from southern land. I want to rest
    again in southern fields, in grass and hay and clover
    bloom; to lay my hand again upon the clay baked by a
    southern sun, to touch the rain-soaked earth and smell   5
    the smell of soil.

I want my rest unbroken in the fields of southern earth;
    freedom to watch the corn wave silver in the sun and
    mark the splashing of a brook, a pond with ducks and
    frogs and count the clouds.   10

I want no mobs to wrench me from my southern rest; no
    forms to take me in the night and burn my shack and
    make for me a nightmare full of oil and flame.

I want my careless song to strike no minor key; no fiend to
    stand between my body's southern song—the fusion of   15
    the South, my body's song and me.

Judith Wright 1915–

A ustralia's most heralded twentieth-century female poet, Judith Wright has perhaps not received the attention she deserves outside of her native land. Although her work may be decidedly and proudly Australian in terms of its respect for the land and its endemic slant, Wright is nevertheless a socially conscious writer whose social concern and love of country are universal themes. She has been described by the critic S. E. Lee as "a rare combination of metaphysical thinker and down-to-earth realist . . . Her best poems integrate the intellect, passion, imagination and common sense of the thinker-mystic-poet-country wife." Her first collection of verse, *The Moving Image* (1946), introduced her recurring theme of a search for meaning amidst the chaos of modern life. She received high praise for her next collection, *Woman to Man* (1949), regarded as a positive and highly profound celebration of womanhood. Other notable collections include *The Gateway* (1953), *The Two Fires* (1955), *Birds* (a collection of poems for young readers, 1962), and *The Other Half* (1966).

THE SISTERS

In the vine-shadows on the veranda,
under the yellow leaves, in the cooling sun,
sit the two sisters. Their slow voices run
like little winter creeks dwindled by frost and wind,
and the square of sunlight moves on the veranda.   5

They remember the gay young men on their tall horses
who came courting; the dancing and the smells of leather
and wine, the girls whispering by the fire together:
even their dolls and ponies, all they have left behind
moves in the yellow shadows on the veranda.   10

Thinking of their lives apart and the men they married,
thinking of the marriage-bed and the birth of the first child,
they look down smiling. "My life was wide and wild,
and who can know my heart? There in that golden jungle
I walk alone," say the old sisters on the veranda.   15

To Another Housewife

Do you remember how we went,
on duty bound, to feed the crowd
of hungry dogs your father kept
as rabbit-hunters? Lean and loud,
half-starved and furious, how they leapt   5
against their chains, as though they meant
in mindless rage for being fed,
to tear our childish hands instead!

With tomahawk and knife we hacked
the flyblown tatters of old meat,   10
gagged at their carcass-smell, and threw
the scraps and watched the hungry eat.
Then turning faint, we made a pact,
(two greensick girls), crossed hearts and swore
to touch no meat forever more.   15

How many cuts of choice and prime
our housewife hands have dressed since then —
these hands with love and blood imbrued —
for daughters, sons, and hungry men!
How many creatures bred for food   20
we've raised and fattened for the time
they met at last the steaming knife
that serves the feast of death-in-life!

And as the evening meal is served
we hear the turned-down radio   25
begin to tell the evening news
just as the family joint[1] is carved.
O murder, famine, pious wars. . . .
Our children shrink to see us so,
in sudden meditation, stand   30
with knife and fork in either hand.

---

[1] I.e., Joint of roast meat.

NAKED GIRL AND MIRROR

This is not I. I had no body once—
only what served my need to laugh and run
and stare at stars and tentatively dance
on the fringe of foam and wave and sand and sun.
Eyes loved, hands reached for me, but I was gone   5
on my own currents, quicksilver, thistledown.
Can I be trapped at last in that soft face?

I stare at you in fear, dark brimming eyes.
Why do you watch me with that immoderate plea—
"Look under these curled lashes, recognize   10
that you were always here; know me—be me."
Smooth once-hermaphrodite[2] shoulders, too tenderly
your long slope runs, above those sudden shy
curves furred with light that spring below your space.

No, I have been betrayed. If I had known   15
that this girl waited between a year and a year,
I'd not have chosen her bough to dance upon.
Betrayed, by that little darkness here, and here
this swelling softness and that frightened stare
from eyes I will not answer; shut out here   20
from my own self, by its new body's grace—

for I am betrayed by someone lovely. Yes,
I see you are lovely, hateful naked girl.
Your lips in the mirror tremble as I refuse
to know or claim you. Let me go—let me be gone.   25
You are half of some other who may never come.
Why should I tend you? You are not my own;
you seek that other—he will be your home.

Yet I pity your eyes in the mirror, misted with tears;
I lean to your kiss. I must serve you; I will obey.   30
Some day we may love. I may miss your going, some day,
though I shall always resent your dumb and fruitful years.
Your lovers shall learn better, and bitterly too,
if their arrogance dares to think I am part of you.

---

[2] With both female and male characteristics.

COUNTING IN SEVENS

Seven ones are seven.
I can't remember that year
or what presents I was given.

Seven twos are fourteen.
That year I found my mind,   5
swore not to be what I had been.

Seven threes are twenty-one.
I was sailing my own sea,
first in love, the knots undone.

Seven fours are twenty-eight;   10
three false starts had come and gone;
my true love came, and not too late.

Seven fives are thirty-five.
In her cot my daughter lay,
real, miraculous, alive.   15

Seven sixes are forty-two.
I packed her sandwiches for school,
I loved my love and time came true.

Seven sevens are forty-nine.
Fruit loaded down my apple-tree,   20
near fifty years of life were mine.

Seven eights are fifty-six.
My lips still cold from a last kiss,
my fire was ash and charcoal-sticks.

Seven nines are sixty-three; seven tens are seventy.   25
Who would that old woman be?
She will remember being me,

but what she is I cannot see.
Yet with every added seven,
some strange present I was given.   30

Lili Berger 1916–

L ili Berger was born in Eastern Poland's Malkin, Bialystok region. A prolific
and versatile writer, her genres include literary criticism, journal articles, novels, short stories, plays, and translations. As a critic of classical and contemporary literature, she is lauded for her insights regarding the work of Sholom Ale-
ichem; her novels and short stories of real people in unreal circumstances have
been called Kafkaesque *sans* the bizarre characteristics. In 1933, Berger completed the Polish-Jewish *gymnasium* in Warsaw, went on to study pedagogy in
Brussels, and, in 1936, settled in Paris where she taught in Yiddish supplemen-
tary schools. She later wrote for *Oyfsney* and *Di vokh*, important Yiddish publications in Paris, as well as contributing to the *Naye prese*. Berger was active in
the Resistance movement during the Nazi occupation of France but returned to
Warsaw after the war. In 1968, she relocated to Paris where she currently resides.

On Saint Katerine's Day

TRANSLATED BY FRIEDA FORMAN AND ETHEL RAICUS

Hundreds of thousands of Jewish children were murdered in the Holocaust. As
the war escalated in the early Forties and Jews were sent to ghettos, and to
work and death camps, parents tried every imaginable way to save their children. Many gave them away for hiding, hoping to come back for them after
the war. Children were taken to convents. Some Christian families were willing
to risk their own lives to save a child, others were bribed and still others
turned over the children to the authorities while keeping the remuneration.

The hidden children were usually raised as Christians. Those who were given
away as babies did not remember their parents after the war and often were
reluctant to leave the only family they knew. If no mother or father survived,
the child's background was withheld. Today, particularly in Eastern Europe,
thousands of middle-aged adults know nothing of their true parentage or religion. Writer Lili Berger tells a not uncommon story of a teenage girl who dis-
covers an identity hidden from her for fifteen years.

"From '42 to '57 is fifteen . . . and one is sixteen . . . no, it doesn't add up, perhaps it was later, she said 'from '42,' then I'd be . . . She also said 'perhaps almost
two,' I would now be . . . the years are probably also fabricated, everything,
everything is false . . . ."

The more Katerine calculated, the more entangled she became and the
more numerous her doubts. Straining her memory, she tried to remember
things, events, experiences; in her head everything became a jumble; everything
now appeared strange. Things that once seemed simple, natural, were now

523

suspect. "Why didn't I catch on at the time? Why was I such a foolish idiot? Why did I let them pull the wool over my eyes?"

She saw her saddened face in the wall mirror opposite. The thought ran through her mind that she was now entirely other. She rose from her chair, went over to the old, worn mirror, sought her former, familiar likeness there, regarded her face—the hair, eyes, nose—as though they were not her own, as though they had, within the last few hours, been pulled over her own former face. She drew her thick hair back with both hands, looked at her face with surprise as if it were a stranger's, then wearily dropped her hands. Her face was once more framed in a cascade of black curly hair.

How often had she heard, "What beautiful hair!" They always smiled when they complemented her beautiful hair, complemented and smiled enigmatically. "Why did I not catch on? Why was I such a foolish cow?"

"You don't have to wave your hair, you have naturally curly hair," Marilla used to say to her.

"Would *you* like hair like this?" she had asked her best friend.

"No," she'd answered shyly, "yours is right for . . . for your face, right for you. For me . . . ours is better."

That's how Marilla had spoken at the time but she had paid no attention, she soon forgot about it. Katerine never thought that her hair, her face, were different. Now she looked at the mirror and she seemed to be someone else; she felt her eyes beginning to fill with tears, something stuck in her throat; she held back from crying, questions swirling in her head, a cluster of questions: "Who am I? Who? Why do they say that I'm. . . . Would they make it up? And my mother, how did they. . . . "

"Katerine, Katerine, of all things, playing in front of the mirror? I thought you weren't home. What's the matter with you? Has something happened?"

Katerine didn't hear her mother come in from work, she hadn't heated the mid-day meal her mother had prepared that morning before going to the office. Head lowered, she followed her mother into the kitchen and saw a box of cakes and a bunch of chrysanthemums; she looked away, they went unappreciated, now none of this belonged to her. . . .

"Dear God, it's your saint's day and you look like you've seen a ghost. Did you quarrel with someone? Have you been to see Sister Katerine yet?"

"I've been. . . . "

"Put the flowers in the water, they're for you; aren't you at all pleased?"

"No. . . . Yes, I'm pleased. . . . "

"I see you're not . . . probably something happened in class, probably you forgot to prepare something—" her mother probed.

"No, no," Katerine answered with a contrary scowl.

"What then? What happened? Why so down at the mouth?"

"I want . . . I must speak with you, I must . . . ," Katerine stammered in a voice not her own.

Fifty year old Magdalena Vrublevska, a former teacher, now an office worker, turned from the kitchen perplexed, looked at her daughter and, after a short pause, asked, "Just to 'speak' with me? Is that a reason for such a face? And of all days, today? On your saint's day?"

"I must, today, now . . . I must."

"At this very moment? Will it run away? Lunch is ready, sit down, eat; you haven't even put the flowers in water, you're not yourself . . . give me a smile, come on. Come, let's eat."

"I won't eat, I'm not hungry."

Her mother sat down, pretending not to concern herself with her daughter's whims; "It'll pass, then she'll sit down on her own and eat; at that age she won't be able to stay hungry for long." But Katerine didn't sit at the table. She went to her room, once again stood before the mirror and scrutinized her face. Everything in the room looked changed; hundreds of questions once again sprang to mind. No, she wouldn't be fooled any longer. This time she would have to find out everything, everything, everything, and today before the day was out. . . .

Katerine Vrublevska had thick black curly hair, large, dark velvet eyes, a pale, dreamy, longish face and was fifteen years old.

Her classmates described her skin colour as "café au lait." She knew she was a beauty, how could she not know since they always told her so. Among her school-friends she looked like an exotic rose by some chance growing amidst wild flowers. Ever since she could remember she had been called "black beauty," and when her Uncle Karol, a pharmacist from Warsaw, came to visit, he brought gifts for the "pretty gypsy." Uncle Karol loved her dearly, her aunt did too, but now their love seemed so strange to Katerine, so distant, even her mother's love. Why did she hide it from her? Everyone knew, but she didn't. That's why Fat Theresa felt free to make fun of her. Probably everyone, everyone was laughing at her; she had understood nothing, now she understood very well, now she remembered everything. Sundays, at church, she would feel them looking at her strangely. "Because you are a beauty," her mother would tell her. Not true, it was because of something else, all of them, all of them were always looking at her; she had never guessed, was never suspicious. Now she knew, this morning she finally understood everything, now she remembered how they would sometimes say to her, "You're different, somehow." Why hadn't she caught on? She probably wouldn't have caught on, even now, if it weren't for Fat Theresa, that red-faced girl always blurted out what others wouldn't say, she'd often dropped hints.

What did Theresa have against her? She never did her any harm—on the contrary, while others ridiculed her, disliked her, imitated her duck's waddle, Katerine wouldn't. That one was so silly and fat as a barrel, her face puffy, red as a beet; learning was hard for her, she couldn't absorb it. But was it Theresa's fault? Wouldn't she have wanted to be pretty and clever? Katerine had always sympathized with her, had never done her any wrong, and still Theresa never had a good word for her, only barbs, insinuations, always resentment, until finally Theresa had blurted out,

"You shouldn't bring flowers to Sister Katerine! It's not your place! It has nothing to do with you!"

"Why not with me?"

"Because . . . because . . . you're a Jew!"

"You're one yourself!" Katerine answered impulsively and immediately regretted it. Everyone laughed and Fat Theresa with the red face laughed the loudest of all, gasping with laughter, jeering.

"Who's a Jew? Me or her?" the fat girl asked triumphantly and again burst out with mocking laughter.

That laughter had cut and stung Katerine like a whip. She fled, escaping their laughter, found her way to the convent which wasn't far from the forest. She didn't feel the cold wind on her face, walked quickly, almost running, as though pursued by their laughter. The flowers' wrapping came apart, she paid no attention. Every year she brought flowers to Sister on her saint's day, it had always been a pleasure for her. Now she arrived at the convent out of breath, distraught, and nervously rang the bell. When Sister Katerine appeared at the door, she fell into her arms weeping.

"My child, what happened to you? You're crying on such a day? On the day of our patron saint? Tell me, what happened to you?"

"They . . . they . . . said that it's not my saint's day, Saint Katerine's Day, that . . . it doesn't belong to me, that . . . that I'm a Jew."

"Don't listen to such foolish talk, my child. People like to smear others, they don't have God in their hearts, they fill their time with evil talk. . . . "

"Why do they think I'm a . . . ? Why? I ask you, tell me, I want to know why, I want to know what I am." Katerine pleaded tearfully.

"What are you? You're a good Christian, a Christian for a long time now, since 1942. You were probably a year old, certainly not two; foolishness . . . not worth talking about, people love to babble—" the nun held herself back, sorry that she'd said this much.

"Once . . . was I a Jew once?" Katerine persisted with a new question and her eyes, full of tears, begged for an answer.

"You're good Christian like your mother. Go, my child, go home, I'm busy now, it's our name day. Remember, today you mustn't cry; on Saint Katerine's Day, one doesn't cry; a great day, she was a great saint. Thank you for the flowers; you always remember, you're a good Christian . . . go home, my child. . . . "

The way home from the convent could be shortened by going through a small field, then across a little bridge over the stream. Katerine didn't like that path; this time she took the back road, walking quickly, gasping for air, over-whelmed. Only at home did she calm down a bit, began to make sense of Sister's vague words, counting the years, remembering various insinuations, overheard conversations about Jewish children protected in convents. She did know something about these things but never gave it much thought, had read several books about how those people perished. Her mother wouldn't let her read such books;

"You'll get sick, you mustn't read that." Now she understood why her mother had taken *Maria's Farewell* from her hands, why her mother always avoided questions, didn't answer, squirming exactly the way Sister Katerine had. She wouldn't put up with it any longer; she would have to find everything out, figure it all out herself, and she'd force her mother, her mother would have to tell her the truth, she'd beg with tears, she would have to know today, today her mother would have to. . . .

"I thought you were lying down, but here you are sitting staring; you said you had a headache, so why are you fretting?"

Her mother's voice interrupted Katerine's thoughts. She let her finish, raised her head, and looked at her mother suspiciously, the way you look at a stranger whose closed face you want to decipher, but she was immediately ashamed of herself and lowered her head.

"What's wrong, daughter? I can tell that something's happened; tell your mother; you've always told me everything. You trust your mother after all; tell the truth; you've never held back from me."

"And you, mother, have never withheld anything from me? Told the truth?"

"I think . . . why should I hide, when you ask, if it's appropriate, I tell you . . . but what kind of talk is this, my daughter? You're not speaking nicely to your mother," said Magdalena tenderly and with wily humour.

"I want to know . . . I want to know . . . who I am; they said that . . . that I'm a Jew, everyone, everyone knows it, they look at me. . . . "

Magdalena Vrublevska turned pale, held on to the bed railing with both hands. It was suddenly difficult for her to remain standing. Slowly she sat down beside her daughter, sat mute as though the power of speech had been taken from her, and then she quietly answered,

"You accept all this gossip and take it seriously, fuss over every foolishness. . . . "

"I want to know who I am," Katerine interrupted her. "I want to know the truth!" By now she was shouting.

"Who drummed such thoughts into your head?" her mother tried raising her voice.

"Everyone, everyone knows; Sister Katerine also told me a while ago that I'm . . . no, Sister also didn't want to tell me everything, didn't want to answer . . . put me off with—" Katerine burst into tears, holding her face in both hands and sobbing. Magdalena moved closer to her, holding her, pressing her against herself, trying to convince her in a soft, shaking voice,

"Who are you? You're my daughter, my whole life. I love you as you love me, your mother. Why pay attention to . . . ? Why? Why listen to foolish prattle?"

"I want to know . . . I must know. Tell me the truth! Tell me!"

"Fine, I will . . . tomorrow. First, calm down, my foolish child. Come and eat, my little fool."

"To you I'm still a child, a 'little fool.' I want you to tell me everything right now!" And Katerine burst into even more violent weeping.

"So, good, let it be, but stop crying. That's why I didn't want to tell you in the first place. You make a fuss about any little trifle. I beg you, daughter, there's nothing to cry about. Promise me, my child, that you won't exaggerate things. You're a grown girl now, and crying is unbecoming. Is life so bad for us?"

Magdalena caught her breath, silent for a while, thinking of how to go on with this painful conversation with her daughter.

"If you want, I'll tell everything. But it mustn't change anything between us. What can it possibly mean to us? Isn't that so? Do you promise me, daughter dear?"

Katerine nodded and blurted through her tears, "I promise, but tell me everything, tell me the whole truth."

Mother and daughter sat clinging to one another. Katerine, sobbing quietly from time to time, dried her eyes. Magdalena Vrublevska was silent for some time. What she had feared of late had come to pass. Katerine was an intelligent girl, but so sensitive; she felt everythig so intensely. Now she could no longer pull the wool over her eyes. She must tell her the truth, but how? She had thought about it many times; in her imagination, that daybreak reappeared. She covered her eyes with her hands, steeled herself, and began,

"I adopted you, Sister Katerine probably told you that. You were tiny, really tiny; you were with Sister Katerine. I adopted you and from that time on you've been my daughter and I your mother."

"From the beginning, start at the beginning. Where did Sister Katerine get me? Tell me, tell me from the beginning, everything, everything, I beg of you."

Magdalena remained silent, her face clouded over. She clasped her daughter more tightly to herself, stroking her hair, and then began again.

"It was in 1942, dawn, still dark. They were being driven on this road, the back road that leads to the forest; they passed close to our house. I lay in bed shaking as if I had a fever. The wailing and howling was unbearable, wailing and howling, then an echo of gunshot, then—silence. There was no question of sleep after that; my heart was heavy, in my ears the wailing rang but outside it was as silent as the graveyard. Suddenly, I heard whimpering, like a sick kitten, then something like the choked cry of a baby. I got out of bed to listen at the door. Everything was quiet; I stood there a few minutes and went back to bed.

"It was daylight at last but the town was lifeless; people were still afraid to go out. It was a Sunday; no-one went to work, they stayed indoors. It was very stuffy and I wanted some air, so I carefully opened the front shutter and stuck my head out and . . . a parcel at the door, some sort of strange parcel, a kind of bundle. I panicked; we were afraid of everything. I closed the window but, recalling the whimpering earlier on, I opened the door a crack. The bundle stirred. I looked around to see whether anyone was watching, pulled the bundle in and untied it . . . a child . . . seemingly smothered; the sop had fallen out of the little mouth. I put my ear to the child; it was breathing. I took it out of the knotted little quilt; it looked frail. It occurred to me to pour warm, sweet water into the little mouth; it wasn't long before it began to cry, first quite softly, then louder and louder. Oh my God, a catastrophe! Then I really panicked; such a risk, everyone knew I was a widow, alone; my child had died three years earlier, and here a child, and one so dark, my God. I quickly stopped your mouth with the sop; packed it with wet sugar. I was so terrified that it would cry; I was almost out of my mind with fright, what to do with the child? It was then that I remembered Sister Katerine, she was so compassionate and wise, gave good advice; she wouldn't refuse. I dressed quickly, put the child into the vegetable basket, packing the sop with wet sugar, covered the basket with an old towel, put the flowers from the vase on top, as well as some vegetables I had prepared to take to the convent on Sunday. Fortunately you didn't cry, you were hungry and sucked on the sugar. When Sister Katerine removed your clothing to bathe you a note fell out of your little right sock: 'Merciful people, save this child; God will reward you.' Then the name. Date of birth wasn't given, probably forgotten. Sister Katerine fed you, then made out a certificate of baptism. It was Saint Katerine's Day, just like today; you were given her name and I was forbidden to come to see you, just as well. After that, difficult times befell me."

Magdalena Vrublevska stopped as though the telling had exhausted her and looking at Katerine saw her strange expression: the girl was staring straight ahead, mouth open, not a muscle in her face moving, as though everything had frozen from shock. Magdalena waited for her to respond, then could wait no longer "My child, should I go on to the end?" Katerine only nodded and two full, round tears rolled down from her dark eyes. Magdalena, now hurrying to finish, spoke in chaotic, unfinished sentences.

"Told myself that if I survived, you'd be my child; my little girl died, God sent an unfortunate child, had to wait. After the war my situation was difficult, had to come back to myself; thanks to Uncle Karol, he helped me a lot, always loved you; according to the baptismal certificate, you were four years old. Sister Katerine led me to a dark little girl and, pointing to me, said to her, 'This is your mother, a good mother, you must love her. . . . ' Since then, I have been so happy; grew to love you like my own child, what's the difference? You really are my own child, my only daughter. I was so. . . ."

The words stuck in her throat, choking. Both were silent now, their heartbeats could be heard in the stillness. Magdalena became alarmed at Katerine's silence and said,

"You see, my child, I've told everything, hidden nothing; you know everything now."

"Not everything yet."

"What more do you want to know?"

"What was my name?"

"Miriam. Miriam Zack."

"And my parents?"

"Sister Katerine may know."

"The note, my note? I want to see. . . ."

"I'll ask Sister, perhaps she has it, perhaps. . . . But be patient, better I go myself, it's more fitting."

"And family? Relatives? Do I have someone . . . ?"

"How can we know that? You have . . . me, Uncle Karol, Auntie, aren't we your family? Am I not a mother to you and you a daughter to me?"

"Yes, yes, you are, of course you are, but—" and Katerine broke into tears again.

Shortly after Saint Katerine's Day, mother and daughter together composed and mailed the following notice to the Red Cross, Missing Relatives Division: "Miriam Zack, daughter of Leyzer and Rivke Zack from the city of T., seeks relatives, wherever they may be, within the country or abroad. Reply."

Gwendolyn Brooks 1917–

When Gwendolyn Brooks was five weeks old, her parents brought her from Topeka, Kansas, to the south side of Chicago. Growing up in "Bronzeville," a name journalists gave the black ghetto where Brooks was raised, provided the subject matter for the area with which she would always be identified. After graduation from Chicago's Wilson Junior College in 1936, Brooks enrolled in a poetry workshop where, under the guidance of Chicago socialite Inez Cunningham Stark, she studied the intricacies of poetry. A tremendous facility for language was immediately apparent in the young poet as she began to combine European forms, such as the sonnet, with street slang, jazz rhythm, and black idioms. In 1945, she earned a Guggenheim Fellowship and an award from the American Academy of Arts and Letters for her first volume of poetry, *A Street Named Bronzeville*. Five years later, she published *Annie Allen* and became the first African American to win the Pulitzer Prize. In 1967, at the urging of a number of young black poets, Brooks consciously committed herself to their idea that black poets need to write *as* blacks, addressing themselves specifically *to* blacks. In doing so, she became an activist leader who, through her work, fought to create "an expression relevant to all manner of blacks, poems I could take into a tavern, into a street, into the halls of a housing project."

FIVE MEN
AGAINST THE THEME
"MY NAME IS RED HOT.
YO NAME AIN DOODLEY SQUAT."

HOYT AND LERONE, DUDLEY
AND HAKI AND LU.

This is the time of the crit, the creeple, and the makeiteer.

Our warfare is through the trite traitors, through
the ice-committees, through
the mirages, through
the suburban petals, through   5
toss-up, and tin-foil.

Therefore we are thankful for steel.
We
are thanful
for steel.   10

FRIEND

Walking with you
shuts off shivering.
Here we are.
Here we are.

I am with you to share and to bear and to care.   5

This is warm.
I want you happy, I want you warm.

Your Friend for our forever is what I am.
Your Friend in thorough thankfulness.

It is the evening of our love.   10
Evening is hale and whole.
Evening shall not go out.
Evening is comforting flame.
Evening is comforting flame.

THE MOTHER

Abortions will not let you forget.
You remember the children you got that you did not get,
The damp small pulps with a little or with no hair,
The singers and workers that never handled the air.
You will never neglect or beat   5
Them, or silence or buy with a sweet.
You will never wind up the sucking-thumb
Or scuttle off ghosts that come.
You will never leave them, controlling your luscious sigh,
Return for a snack of them, with gobbling mother-eye   10

I have heard in the voices of the wind the voices of my dim
      killed children.
I have contracted. I have eased
My dim dears at the breasts they could never suck.
I have said, Sweets, if I sinned, if I seized
Your luck   15
And your lives from your unfinished reach,
If I stole your births and your names,
Your straight baby tears and your games,
Your stilted or lovely loves, your tumults, your marriages,
      aches, and your deaths,
If I poisoned the beginnings of your breaths,   20
Believe that even in my deliberateness I was not deliberate.
Though why should I whine,
Whine that the crime was other than mine?—
Since anyhow you are dead.
Or rather, or instead,   25
You were never made.

But that too, I am afraid,
Is faulty: oh, what shall I say, how is the truth to be said?
You were born, you had body, you died.
It is just that you never giggled or planned or cried   30

Believe me, I loved you all.
Believe me, I knew you, though faintly, and I loved, I loved you
All.

Mary Tallmountain 1918–1994

A uthor of six collections of poetry and widely published in anthologies and periodicals, Mary Tallmountain was born of Athapascan-Russian and Scotch-Irish descent in a rural Alaskan village near the Arctic Circle. At the age of six, her idyllic existence along the Yukon River tragically came to an end when her mother died of tuberculosis. Adopted by a non-Native-American family, she was subsequently traumatized by the loss of her family, homeland, and the shocking adjustment to American mainstream culture. In 1945, Tallmountain became employed as a legal secretary and began publishing in literary journals around 1960. She developed a friendship with Native-American poet and scholar, Paula Gunn Allen, who tutored Tallmountain weekly. During this time, she wrote sixteen hours a day, reaching back through the alcoholism, the frequent depression, and her adoptive mother's suicide to reclaim in her writings the magical childhood along the Yukon River. Bill Moyers commented, "Her poetry is a permanent testament to the rich tapestry of experience that was her life." Living for many years in San Francisco's Tenderloin district, Tallmountain served as a continual voice of encouragement to aspiring writers from San Francisco's inner city to remote Alaskan villages where, in her later years, she taught poetry to children.

THE LAST WOLF

the last wolf hurried toward me
through the ruined city
and I heard his baying echoes
down the steep smashed warrens
of Montgomery Street and past   5
the few ruby-crowned highrises
left standing
their lighted elevators useless

passing the flicking red and green
of traffic signals   10
baying his way eastward
in the mystery of his wild loping gait
closer the sounds in the deadly night
through clutter and rubble of quiet blocks

I heard his voice ascending the hill   15
and at last his low whine as he came
floor by empty floor to the room

where I sat
in my narrow bed looking west, waiting
I heard him snuffle at the door and   20
I watched
he trotted across the floor

he laid his long gray muzzle
on the spare white spread
and his eyes burned yellow   25
his small dotted eyebrows quivered

Yes, I said.
I know what they have done.

THE IVORY DOG FOR MY SISTER

oh sister
how those Nulato sled dogs howl
at sunset it

haunted me a lifetime
by river's edge they mourn   5
passing the hours
of summer

all day
they lie chained
bury their noses under   10
fluffy Malemute tail plumes
grey-blue eyes watch the People
getting ready the nets and
fishwheels

under strong skulls they   15
remember winter
the rushing freedom how they
leap and bark and when the
harness tangles
how the whip whistles down to nudge   20
their furry backs

Clem says fifty years ago he
and a half wolf husky named Moose
worked the team how
icy the air   25
how white

the flowing breaths
of men and dogs

the ivory dog
from Nulato a piece of my life   30
I thought he could tell you
about the moving of time and
what it is to wait
he's done it so long now
sister   35
the ivory dog is true

Now watching you in lamplight,
I see scarlet berries
Ripened,
Your sunburned fingers plucking them.   40
With hesitant words,
With silence,
From inmost space
I call you
Out of the clay.   45

It is time at last,
This dawn.
Stir. Wake. Rise.
Glide gentle between my bones,
Grasp my heart. Now   50
Walk beside me. Feel
How these winds move, the way
These mornings breathe.
Let me see you new
In this light.   55

You—
Wrapped in brown,
Myself repeated
Out of dark and different time.

THERE IS NO WORD FOR GOODBYE

Sokoya,[1] I said, looking through
        the net of wrinkles into
        wise black pools
        of her eyes.

---

[1] *Sokoya:* Aunt (mother's sister)

What do you say in Athabaskan   5
   when you leave each other?
   What is the word
   for goodbye?

A shade of feeling rippled
   the wind-tanned skin.   10
   Ah, nothing, she said,
   watching the river flash.

She looked at me close.
   We just say, Tłaa. That means,
   See you.   15
   We never leave each other.
   When does your mouth
   say goodbye to your heart?

She touched me light
   as a bluebell.   20
   You forget when you leave us;
   you're so small then.
   We don't use that word.

We always think you're coming back,
   but if you don't,   25
   we'll see you some place else.
   You understand.
   There is no word for goodbye.

May Swenson 1919–1989

Though she enjoyed success as a dramatist, critic, translator, and author of children's books, it is her highly praised poetry for which May Swenson is best remembered. Nature and animals are dominant subject matter among her poems, but unlike the postromanticist who uses such subject matter metaphorically for the purpose of social comment, Swenson reveled in the beauty of nature for its own sake. Swenson's poems are widely read in schools, perhaps because she enjoyed employing so many of the literary devices commonly found in textbook glossaries: alliteration, personification, assonance, dissonance, metaphor, and frequent use of concrete poetry. Her skills at observation and her great facility with word play ensure that such devices seem neither contrived nor pretentious. No mere gimmicks, they are central to the core, theme, and visceral impact of each poem. Born and educated in Utah, Swenson was as devoted to the cause of education as she was to writing and taught and/or lectured at more than fifty universities in her lifetime. She was writer-in-residence at Purdue University and the University of North Carolina, as well as the recipient of numerous awards, honorary degrees, and fellowships. Noted collections of her poetry include *Another Animal* (1954), *A Cage of Spines* (1958), *Iconographs* (1970), *New Poems to Solve* (1971), *In Other Words* (1988), and *Nature: Poems Old and New* (1994).

SLEEPING WITH BOA

I show her how to put her arms around me,
but she's much too small.
What's worse, she doesn't understand.
And
although she lies beside me, sticking   5
out her tongue, it's herself she licks.

She likes my stroking hand.
And
even lets me kiss.
But at my demand: 10
"Now, do it to me, like this,"
she backs off with a hiss.

What's in her little mind?
Jumping off the bed,
she shows me her behind,   15
but curls up on the rug instead.
I beg her to return. At first, she did,
then went and hid

under the covers. She's playing with my feet!
"Oh, Boa, come back. Be sweet,   20
Lie against me here where I'm nice and warm.
Settle down. Don't claw, don't bite.
Stay with me tonight."
Seeming to consent, she gives a little whine.

Her deep, deep pupils meet mine   25
with a look that holds a flood . . .
But not my brand.
Not at all.
And,
what's worse, she's much too small.   30

VIEW TO THE NORTH

As you grow older, it gets colder.
You see through things.
I'm looking through the trees,

their torn and thinning leaves,
to where chill blue water   5
is roughened by wind.

Day by day the scene opens,
enlarges, rips of space
appear where full branches

used to snug the view.   10
Soon it will be wide, stripped,
entirely unobstructed:

I'll see right through
the twining waves, to
the white horizon, to the place   15

where the North begins.
Magnificent! I'll be thinking
while my eyeballs freeze.

HOW TO BE OLD

It is easy to be young. (Everybody is,
at first.) It is not easy
to be old. It takes time.
Youth is given; age is achieved.
One must work a magic to mix with time   5
in order to become old.

Youth is given. One must put it away
like a doll in a closet,
take it out and play with it only
on holidays. One must have many dresses   10
and dress the doll impeccably
(but not to show the doll, to keep it hidden).

It is necessary to adore the doll,
to remember it in the dark on the ordinary

days, and every day congratulate   15
one's aging face in the mirror.

In time one will be very old.
In time, one's life will be accomplished.
And in time, in time, the doll—
like new, though ancient—may be found.   20

Doris Lessing 1919–

D oris Lessing is recognized as one of the most important writers of the
twentieth century. Born in Persia (now Iran) and raised and educated in
Southern Rhodesia (now Zimbabwe), Lessing is primarily known as a novelist
and writer of short fiction, although she has also written four plays and a collection of poems. Critic Gail Caldwell writes that "Lessing has written prolifically
on everything from British colonialism . . . to the failure of ideology." Caldwell
continues, attemping to sum up this complex, thematically wide-ranging writer:
"In more than thirty books, she's taken on the apocalyptic potential of a futuristic,
Blade Runner London, the perils of the color bar in Africa, the life of a young
girl growing up on the veld" (an Africaans term for "hill"). Consequently, Lessing's
work is difficult to characterize: Lessing has described herself as an "architect of
the soul," with all of her books examining what she has called "the individual
conscience in its relation with the collective."

TO ROOM NINETEEN

This is a story, I suppose, about a failure in intelligence: the Rawlings' marriage
was grounded in intelligence.

They were older when they married than most of their married friends: in
their well-seasoned late twenties. Both had had a number of affairs, sweet rather
than bitter; and when they fell in love—for they did fall in love—had known
each other for some time. They joked that they had saved each other "for the
real thing." That they had waited so long (but not too long) for this real thing
was to them a proof of their sensible discrimination. A good many of their
friends had married young, and now (they felt) probably regretted lost opportunities; while others, still unmarried, seemed to them arid, self-doubting, and
likely to make desperate or romantic marriages.

Not only they, but others, felt they were well-matched: their friends' delight was an additional proof of their happiness. They had played the same roles, male and female, in this group or set, if such a wide, loosely connected, constantly changing constellation of people could be called a set. They had both become, by virtue of their moderation, their humour, and their abstinence from painful experience, people to whom others came for advice. They could be, and were, relied on. It was one of those cases of a man and a woman linking themselves whom no one else had ever thought of linking, probably because of their similarities. But then everyone exclaimed: Of course! How right! How was it we never thought of it before!

And so they married amid general rejoicing, and because of their foresight and their sense for what was probable, nothing was a surprise to them.

Both had well-paid jobs. Matthew was a subeditor on a large London newspaper, and Susan worked in an advertising firm. He was not the stuff of which editors or publicised journalists are made, but he was much more than "a subeditor," being one of the essential background people who in fact steady, inspire and make possible the people in the limelight. He was content with this position. Susan had a talent for commercial drawing. She was humorous about the advertisements she was responsible for, but she did not feel strongly about them one way or the other.

Both, before they married, had had pleasant flats, but they felt it unwise to base a marriage on either flat, because it might seem like a submission of personality on the part of the one whose flat it was not. They moved into a new flat in South Kensington[1] on the clear understanding that when their marriage had settled down (a process they knew would not take long, and was in fact more a humorous concession to popular wisdom than what was due to themselves) they would buy a house and start a family.

And this is what happened. They lived in their charming flat for two years, giving parties and going to them, being a popular young married couple, and then Susan became pregnant, she gave up her job, and they bought a house in Richmond.[2] It was typical of this couple that they had a son first, then a daughter, then twins, son and daughter. Everything right, appropriate, and what everyone would wish for, if they could choose. But people did feel these two had chosen; this balanced and sensible family was no more than what was due to them because of their infallible sense for *choosing* right.

And so they lived with their four children in their gardened house in Richmond and were happy. They had everything they had wanted and had planned for.

And yet . . .

Well, even this was expected, that there must be a certain flatness. . . .

Yes, yes, of course, it was natural they sometimes felt like this. Like what?

---

[1] Part of the fashionable West End of London.

[2] One of the outer boroughs of Greater London.

Their life seemed to be like a snake biting its tail. Matthew's job for the sake of Susan, children, house, and garden—which caravanserai needed a well-paid job to maintain it. And Susan's practical intelligence for the sake of Matthew, the children, the house and the garden—which unit would have collapsed in a week without her.

But there was no point about which either could say: "For the sake of *this* is all the rest." Children? But children can't be a centre of life and a reason for being. They can be a thousand things that are delightful, interesting, satisfying, but they can't be a wellspring to live from. Or they shouldn't be. Susan and Matthew knew that well enough.

Matthew's job? Ridiculous. It was an interesting job, but scarcely a reason for living. Matthew took pride in doing it well, but he could hardly be expected to be proud of the newspaper; the newspaper he read, *his* newspaper, was not the one he worked for.

Their love for each other? Well, that was nearest it. If this wasn't a centre, what was? Yes, it was around this point, their love, that the whole extraordinary structure revolved. For extraordinary it certainly was. Both Susan and Matthew had moments of thinking so, of looking in secret disbelief at this thing they had created: marriage, four children, big house, garden, charwomen, friends, cars . . . and this *thing*, this entity, all of it had come into existence, been blown into being out of nowhere, because Susan loved Matthew and Matthew loved Susan. Extraordinary. So that was the central point, the wellspring.

And if one felt that it simply was not strong enough, important enough, to support it all, well whose fault was that? Certainly neither Susan's nor Matthew's. It was in the nature of things. And they sensibly blamed neither themselves nor each other.

On the contrary, they used their intelligence to preserve what they had created from a painful and explosive world: they looked around them, and took lessons. All around them, marriages collapsing, or breaking, or rubbing along (even worse, they felt). They must not make the same mistakes, they must not.

They had avoided the pitfall so many of their friends had fallen into—of buying a house in the country *for the sake of the children*, so that the husband became a weekend husband, a weekend father, and the wife always careful not to ask what went on in the town flat which they called (in joke) a bachelor flat. No, Matthew was a full-time husband, a full-time father, and at night, in the big married bed in the big married bedroom (which had an attractive view of the river), they lay beside each other talking and he told her about his day, and what he had done, and whom he had met; and she told him about her day (not as interesting, but that was not her fault), for both knew of the hidden resentments and deprivations of the woman who has lived her own life—and above all, has earned her own living—and is now dependent on a husband for outside interests and money.

Nor did Susan make the mistake of taking a job for the sake of her independence, which she might very well have done, since her old firm, missing her qualities of humour, balance, and sense, invited her often to go back. Children needed their mother to a certain age, that both parents knew and agreed on; and when these four healthy wisely brought up children were of the right age, Susan would work again, because she knew, and so did he, what happened to women of fifty at the height of their energy and ability, with grownup children who no longer needed their full devotion.

So here was this couple, testing their marriage, looking after it, treating it like a small boat full of helpless people in a very stormy sea. Well, of course, so it was. . . . The storms of the world were bad, but not too close—which is not to say they were selfishly felt: Susan and Matthew were both well-informed and responsible people. And the inner storms and quicksands were understood and charted. So everything was all right. Everything was in order. Yes, things were under control.

So what did it matter if they felt dry, flat? People like themselves, fed on a hundred books (psychological, anthropological, sociological), could scarcely be unprepared for the dry, controlled wistfulness which is the distinguishing mark of the intelligent marriage. Two people, endowed with education, with discrimination, with judgement, linked together voluntarily from their will to be happy together and to be of use to others—one sees them everywhere, one knows them, one even is that thing oneself: sadness because so much is after all so little. These two, unsurprised, turned towards each other with even more courtesy and gentle love: this was life, that two people, no matter how carefully chosen, could not be everything to each other. In fact, even to say so, to think in such a way, was banal; they were ashamed to do it.

It was banal, too, when one night Matthew came home late and confessed he had been to a party, taken a girl home and slept with her. Susan forgave him, of course. Except that forgiveness is hardly the word. Understanding, yes. But if you understand something, you don't forgive it you are the thing itself; forgiveness is for what you *don't* understand. Nor had he *confessed*—what sort of word is that?

The whole thing was not important. After all, years ago they had joked: Of course I'm not going to be faithful to you, no one can be faithful to one other person for a whole lifetime. (And there was the word "faithful"—stupid, all these words, stupid, belonging to a savage old world.) But the incident left both of them irritable. Strange, but they were both bad-tempered, annoyed. There was something unassimilable about it.

Making love splendidly after he had come home that night, both had felt that the idea that Myra Jenkins, a pretty girl met at a party, could be even relevant was ridiculous. They had loved each other for over a decade, would love each other for years more. Who, then, was Myra Jenkins?

Except, thought Susan, unaccountably bad-tempered, she was (is?) the first. In ten years. So either the ten year's fidelity was not important, or she isn't. (No, no, there is something wrong with this way of thinking, there must be.) But if she isn't important, presumably it wasn't important either when Matthew and I first went to bed with each other that afternoon whose delight even now (like a very long shadow at sundown) lays a long, wandlike finger over us. (Why did I say sundown?) Well, if what we felt that afternoon was not important, nothing is important, because if it hadn't been for what we felt, we wouldn't be Mr. and Mrs. Rawlings with four children, et cetera, et cetera. The whole thing is *absurd*—for him to have come home and told me was absurd. For him not to have told me was absurd. For me to care or, for that matter, not to care, is absurd . . . and who is Myra Jenkins? Why, no one at all.

There was only one thing to do, and of course these sensible people did it; they put the thing behind them, and consciously, knowing what they were doing, moved forward into a different phase of their marriage, giving thanks for past good fortune as they did so.

For it was inevitable that the handsome, blond, attractive, manly man, Matthew Rawlings, should be at times tempted (oh, what a word!) by the attractive girls at parties she could not attend because of the four children; and that sometimes he would succumb (a word even more repulsive, if possible) and that she, a goodlooking woman in the big well-tended garden at Richmond, would sometimes be pierced as by an arrow from the sky with bitterness. Except that bitterness was not in order, it was out of court. Did the casual girls touch the marriage? They did not. Rather it was they who knew defeat because of the handsome Matthew Rawlings' marriage body and soul to Susan Rawlings.

In that case why did Susan feel (though luckily not for longer than a few seconds at a time) as if life had become a desert, and that nothing mattered, and that her children were not her own?

Meanwhile her intelligence continued to assert that all was well. What if her Matthew did have an occasional sweet afternoon, the odd affair? For she knew quite well, except in her moments of aridity, that they were very happy, that the affairs were not important.

Perhaps that was the trouble? It was in the nature of things that the adventures and delights could no longer be hers, because of the four children and the big house that needed so much attention. But perhaps she was secretly wishing, and even knowing that she did, that the wildness and the beauty could be his. But he was married to her. She was married to him. They were married inextricably. And therefore the gods could not strike him with the real magic, not really. Well, was it Susan's fault that after he came home from an adventure he looked harassed rather than fulfilled? (In fact, that was how she knew he had been *unfaithful*, because of his sullen air, and his glances at her, similar to hers at him: What is it that I share with this person that shields all delight from me?) But none of it by anybody's fault. (But what did they feel ought to be somebody's fault?) Nobody's fault, nothing to be at fault, no one to blame, no one to offer or to take it . . . and nothing wrong, either, except that Matthew never was really struck, as he wanted to be, by joy; and that Susan was more and more often threatened by emptiness. (It was usually in the garden that she was invaded by this feeling: she was coming to avoid the garden, unless the children or Matthew were with her.) There was no need to use the dramatic words "un-faithful," "forgive," and the rest: intelligence forbade them. Intelligence barred, too, quarrelling, sulking, anger, silences of withdrawal, accusations and tears. Above all, intelligence forbids tears.

A high price has to be paid fo the happy marriage with the four healthy children in the large white gardened house.

And they were paying it, willingly, knowing what they were doing. When they lay side by side or breast to breast in the big civilised bedroom overlooking the wild sullied river, they laughed, often, for no particular reason; but they knew it was really because of these two small people, Susan and Matthew, sup-porting such an edifice on their intelligent love. The laugh comforted them; it saved them both, though from what, they did not know.

They were now both fortyish. The older children, boy and girl, were ten and eight, at school. The twins, six, were still at home. Susan did not have nurses or girls to help her: childhood is short; and she did not regret the hard work. Often enough she was bored, since small children can be boring; she was often very tired; but she regretted nothing. In another decade, she would turn herself back into being a woman with a life of her own.

Soon the twins would go to school, and they would be away from home from nine until four. These hours, so Susan saw it, would be the preparation for her own slow emancipation away from the role of hub-of-the-family into woman-with-her-own-life. She was already planning for the hours of freedom when all the children would be "off her hands." That was the phrase used by Matthew and by Susan and by their friends, for the moment when the youngest child went off to school. "They'll be off your hands, darling Susan, and you'll have time to yourself." So said Matthew, the intelligent husband, who had often enough commended and consoled Susan, standing by her in spirit during the years when her soul was not her own, as she said, but her children's.

What it amounted to was that Susan saw herself as she had been at twenty-eight, unmarried; and then again somewhere about fifty, blossoming from the root of what she had been twenty years before. As if the essential Susan were in abeyance, as if she were in cold storage. Matthew said something like this to Susan one night: and she agreed that it was true—she did feel something like that. What, then, was this essential Susan? She did not know. Put like that it sounded ridiculous, and she did not really feel it. Anyway, they had a long discussion about the whole thing before going off to sleep in each other's arms.

So the twins went off to their school, two bright affectionate children who had no problems about it, since their older brother and sister had trodden this path so successfully before them. And now Susan was going to be alone in the big house, every day of the school term, except for the daily woman who came in to clean.

It was now, for the first time in this marriage, that something happened which neither of them had foreseen.

This is what happened. She returned, at nine-thirty, from taking the twins to the school by car, looking forward to seven blissful hours of freedom. On the first morning she was simply restless, worrying about the twins "naturally enough" since this was their first day away at school. She was hardly able to contain herself until they came back. Which they did happily, excited by the world of school, looking forward to the next day. And the next day Susan took them, dropped them, came back, and found herself reluctant to enter her big and beautiful home because it was as if something was waiting for her there that she did not wish to confront. Sensibly, however, she parked the car in the garage, entered the house, spoke to Mrs. Parkes, the daily woman, about her duties, and went up to her bedroom. She was possessed by a fever which drove her out again, downstairs, into the kitchen, where Mrs. Parkes was making cake and did not need her, and into the garden. There she sat on a bench and tried to calm herself looking at trees, at a brown glimpse of the river. But she was filled with tension, like a panic: as if an enemy was in the garden with her. She spoke to herself severely, thus: All this is quite natural. First, I spent twelve years of my adult life working, *living my own life*. Then I married, and from the moment I became pregnant for the first time I signed myself over, so to speak, to other people. To the children. Not for one moment in twelve years have I been alone, had time to myself. So now I have to learn to be myself again. That's all.

And she went indoors to help Mrs. Parkes cook and clean, and found some sewing to do for the children. She kept herself occupied every day. At the end of the first term she understood she felt two contrary emotions. First: secret astonishment and dismay that during those weeks when the house was empty of children she had in fact been more occupied (had been careful to keep herself occupied) than ever she had been when the children were around her needing her continual attention. Second: that now she knew the house would be full of them, and for five weeks, she resented the fact she would never be alone. She was already looking back at those hours of sewing, cooking (but by herself) as at a lost freedom which would not be hers for five long weeks. And the two months of term which would succeed the five weeks stretched alluringly open to her—freedom. But what freedom—when in fact she had been so careful *not* to be free of small duties during the last weeks? She looked at herself, Susan Rawlings, sitting in a big chair by the window in the bedroom, sewing shirts or dresses, which she might just as well have bought. She saw herself making cakes for hours at a time in the big family kitchen: yet usually she bought cakes. What she saw was a woman alone, that was true, but she had not felt alone. For instance, Mrs. Parkes was always somewhere in the house. And she did not like being in the garden at all, because of the closeness there of the enemy— irritation, restlessness, emptiness, whatever it was—which keeping her hands occupied made less dangerous for some reason.

Susan did not tell Matthew of these thoughts. They were not sensible. She did not recognize herself in them. What should she say to her dear friend and husband, Matthew? "When I go into the garden, that is, if the children are not there, I feel as if there is an enemy there waiting to invade me." "What enemy, Susan darling?" "Well I don't know, really. . . ." "Perhaps you should see a doctor?"

No, clearly this conversation should not take place. The holidays began and Susan welcomed them. Four children, lively, energetic, intelligent, demanding: she was never, not for a moment of her day, alone. If she was in a room, they would be in the next room, or waiting for her to do something for them; or it would soon be time for lunch or tea, or to take one of them to the dentist. Something to do: five weeks of it, thank goodness.

On the fourth day of these so welcome holidays, she found she was storming with anger at the twins; two shrinking beautiful children who (and this is what checked her) stood hand in hand looking at her with sheer dismayed disbelief. This was their calm mother, shouting at them. And for what? They had come to her with some game, some bit of nonsense. They looked at each other, moved closer for support, and went off hand in hand, leaving Susan holding on to the windowsill of the livingroom, breathing deep, feeling sick. She went to lie down, telling the older childen she had a headache. She heard the boy Harry telling the little ones: "It's all right, Mother's got a headache." She heard that *It's all right* with pain.

That night she said to her husband: "Today I shouted at the twins, quite unfairly." She sounded miserable, and he said gently: "Well, what of it?"

"It's more of an adjustment than I thought, their going to school."

"But Susie, Susie darling. . . ." For she was crouched weeping on the bed. He comforted her: "Susan, what is all this about? You shouted at them? What of it? If you shouted at them fifty times a day it wouldn't be more than the little devils deserve." But she wouldn't laugh. She wept. Soon he comforted her with his body. She became calm. Calm, she wondered what was wrong with her, and why she should mind so much that she might, just once, have behaved unjustly with the children. What did it matter? They had forgotten it all long ago: Mother had a headache and everything was all right.

It was a long time later that Susan understood that that night, when she had wept and Matthew had driven the misery out of her with his big solid body, was the last time, ever in their married life, that they had been—to use their mutual language—with each other. And even that was a lie, because she had not told him of her real fears at all.

The five weeks passed, and Susan was in control of herself, and good and kind, and she looked forward to the end of the holidays with a mixture of fear and longing. She did not know what to expect. She took the twins off to school (the elder children took themselves to school) and she returned to the house determined to face the enemy wherever he was, in the house, or the garden or—where?

She was again restless, she was possessed by restlessness. She cooked and sewed and worked as before, day after day, while Mrs. Parkers remonstrated: "Mrs. Rawlings, what's the need for it? I can do that, it's what you pay me for."

And it was so irrational that she checked herself. She would put the car into the garage, go up to her bedroom, and sit, hands in her lap, forcing herself to be quiet. She listened to Mrs. Parkes moving around the house. She looked out into the garden and saw the branches shake the trees. She sat defeating the enemy, restlessness. Emptiness. She ought to be thinking about her life, about herself. But she did not. Or perhaps she could not. As soon as she forced her mind to think about Susan (for what else did she want to be alone for?), it skipped off to thoughts of butter or school clothes. Or it thought of Mrs. Parkes. She realised that she sat listening for the movements of the cleaning woman, following her every turn, bend, thought. She followed her in her mind from kitchen to bathroom, from table to oven, and it was as if the duster, the cleaning cloth, the saucepan, were in her own hand. She would hear herself saying: No, not like that, don't put that there. . . . Yet she did not give a damn what Mrs. Parkes did, or if she did it at all. Yet she could not prevent herself from being conscious of her, every minute. Yes, this was what was wrong with her: she needed, when she was alone, to be really alone, with no one near. She could not endure the knowledge that in ten minutes or in half an hour Mrs. Parkes would call up the stairs: "Mrs. Rawlings, there's no silver polish. Madam, we're out of flour."

So she left the house and went to sit in the garden where she was screened from the house by trees. She waited for the demon to appear and claim her, but he did not.

She was keeping him off, because she had not, after all, come to an end of arranging herself.

She was planning how to be somewhere where Mrs. Parkes would not come after her with a cup of tea, or a demand to be allowed to telephone (always irritating, since Susan did not care who she telephoned or how often), or just a nice talk about something. Yes, she needed a place, or a state of affairs, where it would not be necessary to keep reminding herself: In ten minutes I must telephone Matthew about . . . and at half past three I must leave early for the children because the car needs cleaning. And at ten o'clock tomorrow I must remember. . . . She was possessed with resentment that the seven hours of freedom in every day (during weekdays in the school term) were not free, that never, not for one second, ever, was she free from the pressure of time, from having to remember this or that. She could never forget herself; never really let herself go into forgetfulness.

Resentment. It was poisoning her. (She looked at this emotion and thought it was absurd. Yet she felt it.) She was a prisoner. (She looked at this thought too, and it was no good telling herself it was a ridiculous one.) She must tell Matthew—but what? She was filled with emotions that were utterly ridiculous, that she despised, yet that nevertheless she was feeling so strongly she could not shake them off.

The school holidays came round, and this time they were for nearly two months, and she behaved with a conscious controlled decency that nearly drove her crazy. She would lock herself in the bathroom, and sit on the edge of the bath, breathing deep, trying to let go into some kind of calm. Or she went up into the spare room, usually empty, where no one would expect her to be. She heard the children calling "Mother, Mother," and kept silent, feeling guilty. Or she went to the very end of the garden, by herself, and looked at the slow-moving brown river; she looked at the river and closed her eyes and breathed slow and deep, taking it into her being, into her veins.

Then she returned to the family, wife and mother, smiling and responsible, feeling as if the pressure of these people—four lively children and her husband—were a painful pressure on the surface of her skin, a hand pressing on her brain. She did not once break down into irritation during these holidays, but it was like living out a prison sentence, and when the children went back to school, she sat on a white stone seat near the flowing river, and she thought: It is not even a year since the twins went to school, since *they were off my hands* (What on earth did I think I meant when I used that stupid phrase?), and yet I'm a different person. I'm simply not myself. I don't understand it.

Yet she had to understand it. For she knew that this structure—big white house, on which the mortgage still cost four hundred[3] a year, a husband, so good and kind and insightful; four children, all doing so nicely; and the garden where she sat; and Mrs. Parkes, the cleaning woman—all this depended on her, and yet she could not understand why, or even what it was she contributed to it.

She said to Matthew in their bedroom: "I think there must be something wrong with me."

And he said: "Surely not, Susan? You look marvellous— you're as lovely as ever."

She looked at the handsome blond man, with his clear, intelligent, blue-eyed face, and thought: Why is it I can't tell him? Why not? And she said: "I need to be alone more than I am."

At which he swung his slow blue gaze at her, and she saw what she had been dreading: Incredulity. Disbelief. And fear. An incredulous blue stare from a stranger who was her husband, as close to her as her own breath.

He said: "But the children are at school and off your hands."

She said to herself: I've got to force myself to say: Yes, but do you realize that I never feel free? There's never a moment I can say to myself: There's nothing I have to remind myself about, nothing I have to do in half an hour, or an hour, or two hours. . . .

But she said: "I don't feel well."

He said: "Perhaps you need a holiday."

She said, appalled: "But not without you, surely?" For she could not imagine herself going off without him. Yet that was what he meant. Seeing her face, he laughed, and opened his arms, and she went into them, thinking: Yes, yes, but why can't I say it? And what is it I have to say?

---

[3] I.e., four hundred pounds.

She tried to tell him, about never being free. And he listened and said: "But Susan, what sort of freedom can you possibly want—short of being dead! Am I ever free? I go to the office, and I have to be there at ten—all right, half past ten, sometimes. And I have to do this or that, don't I? Then I've got to come home at a certain time—I don't mean it, you know I don't—but if I'm not going to be back home at six I telephone you. When can I ever say to myself: I have nothing to be responsible for in the next six hours?"

Susan, hearing this, was remorseful. Because it was true. The good marriage, the house, the children, depended just as much on his voluntary bondage as it did on hers. But why did he not feel bound? Why didn't he chafe and become restless? No, there was something really wrong with her and this proved it.

And that word "bondage"—Why had she used it? She had never felt marriage, or the children, as bondage. Neither had he, or surely they wouldn't be together lying in each other's arms content after twelve years of marriage.

No, her state (whatever it was) was irrelevant, nothing to do with her real good life with her family. She had to accept the fact that, after all, she was an irrational person and to live with it. Some people had to live with crippled arms, or stammers, or being deaf. She would have to live knowing she was subject to a state of mind she could not own.

Nevertheless, as a result of this conversation with her husband, there was a new regime next holidays.

The spare room at the top of the house now had a cardboard sign saying: PRIVATE! DO NOT DISTURB! on it. (This sign had been drawn in coloured chalks by the children, after a discussion between the parents in which it was decided this was psychologically the right thing.) The family and Mrs. Parkes knew this was "Mother's Room" and that she was entitled to her privacy. Many serious conversations took place between Matthew and the children about not taking Mother for granted. Susan overheard the first, between father and Harry, the older boy, and was surprised at her irritation over it. Surely she could have a room somewhere in that big house and retire into it without such a fuss being made? Without it being so solemnly discussed? Why couldn't she simply have announced: "I'm going to fit out the little top room for myself, and when I'm in it I'm not to be disturbed for anything short of fire"? Just that, and finished; instead of long earnest discussions. When she heard Harry and Matthew explaining it to the twins with Mrs. Parkes coming in—"Yes, well, a family sometimes gets on top of a woman"—she had to go right away to the bottom of the garden until the devils of exasperation had finished their dance in her blood.

But now there was a room, and she could go there when she liked, she used it seldom: she felt even more caged there than in her bedroom. One day she had gone up there after a lunch for ten children she had cooked and served because Mrs. Parkes was not there, and had sat alone for a while looking into the garden. She saw the children stream out from the kitchen and stand looking up at the window where she sat behind the curtains. They were all—her children and their friends—discussing Mother's Room. A few minutes later, the chase of children in some game came pounding up the stairs, but ended as abruptly as if they had fallen over a ravine, so sudden was the silence. They had remembered she was there, and had gone silent in a great gale of "Hush! Shhhhh! Quiet, you'll disturb her. . . ." And they went tiptoeing downstairs like criminal conspirators. When she came down to make tea for them, they all apologised. The twins put their arms around her, from front and back, making a human cage of loving limbs, and promised it would never occur again. "We forgot, Mummy, we forgot all about it!"

What it amounted to was that Mother's Room, and her need for privacy, had become a valuable lesson in respect for other people's rights. Quite soon Susan was going up to the room only because it was a lesson it was a pity to drop. Then she took sewing up there, and the children and Mrs. Parkes came in and out: it had become another family room.

She sighed, and smiled, and resigned herself—she made jokes at her own expense with Matthew over the room. That is, she did from the self she liked, she respected. But at the same time, something inside her howled with impatience, with rage. . . . And she was frightened. One day she found herself kneeling by her bed and praying: "Dear God, keep it away from me, keep him away from me." She meant the devil, for she now thought of it, not caring if she was irrational, as some sort of demon. She imagined him, or it, as a youngish man, or perhaps a middle-aged man pretending to be young. Or a man young-looking from immaturity? At any rate, she saw the young-looking face which, when she drew closer, had dry lines about mouth and eyes. He was thinnish, meagre in build. And he had a reddish complexion, and ginger hair. That was he—a gingery, energetic man, and he wore a reddish hairy jacket, unpleasant to the touch.

Well, one day she saw him. She was standing at the bottom of the garden, watching the river ebb past, when she raised her eyes and saw this person, or being, sitting on the white stone bench. He was looking at her, and grinning. In his hand was a long crooked stick, which he had picked off the ground, or broken off the tree above him. He was absent-mindedly, out of an absent-minded or freakish impulse of spite, using the stick to stir around in the coils of a blind-worm or a grass snake (or some kind of snakelike creature: it was whitish and unhealthy to look at, unpleasant). The snake was twisting about, flinging its coils from side to side in a kind of dance of protest against the teasing prodding stick.

Susan looked at him thinking: Who is the stranger? What is he doing in our garden? Then she recognised the man around whom her terrors had crystallised. As she did so, he vanished. She made herself walk over to the bench. A shadow from a branch lay across thin emerald grass, moving jerkily over its roughness, and she could see why she had taken it for a snake, lashing and twisting. She went back to the house thinking: Right, then, so I've seen him with my own eyes, so I'm not crazy after all—there *is* a danger because I've seen him. He is lurking in the garden and sometimes even in the house, and he wants to *get into me and to take me over.*

She dreamed of having a room or a place, anywhere, where she could go and sit, by herself, no one knowing where she was.

Once, near Victoria,[4] she found herself outside a news agent that had Rooms to Let advertised. She decided to rent a room, telling no one. Sometimes she could take the train into Richmond and sit alone in it for an hour or two. Yet how could she? A room would cost three or four pounds a week, and she earned no money, and how could she explain to Matthew that she needed such a sum? What for? It did not occur to her that she was taking it for granted she wasn't going to tell him about the room.

Well, it was out of the question, having a room; yet she knew she must.

One day, when a school term was well established, and none of the children had measles or other ailments, and everything seemed in order, she did the shopping early, explained to Mrs. Parkes she was meeting an old school friend, took the train to Victoria, searched until she found a small quiet hotel, and asked for a room for the day. They did not let rooms by the day, the manageress said, looking doubtful, since Susan so obviously was not the kind of woman who needed a room for unrespectable reasons. Susan made a long explanation about not being well, being unable to shop without frequent rests for lying down. At last she was allowed to rent the room provided she paid a full night's price for it. She was taken up by the manageress and a maid, both concerned over the state of the health . . . which must be pretty bad if, living at Richmond (she had signed her name and address in the register), she needed a shelter at Victoria.

The room was ordinary and anonymous, and was just what Susan needed. She put a shilling in the gas fire, and sat, eyes shut, in a dingy armchair with her back to a dingy window. She was alone. She was alone. She was alone. She could feel pressures lifting off her. First the sounds of traffic came very loud; then they seemed to vanish; she might even have slept a little. A knock on the door: it was Miss Townsend, the manageress, bringing her a cup of tea with her own hands, so concerned was she over Susan's long silence and possible illness.

Miss Townsend was a lonely woman of fifty, running this hotel with all the rectitude expected of her, and she sensed in Susan the possibility of understanding companionship. She stayed to talk. Susan found herself in the middle of a fantastic story about her illness, which got more and more improbable as she tried to make it tally with the large house at Richmond, well-off husband, and four children. Suppose she said instead: Miss Townsend, I'm here in your hotel because I need to be alone for a few hours, above all *alone and with no one knowing where I am.* She said it mentally, and saw, mentally, the look that would inevitably come on Miss Townsend's elderly maiden's face. "Miss Townsend, my four children and my husband are driving me insane, do you understand that? Yes, I can see from the gleam of hysteria in your eyes that comes from loneliness

[4] One of the main railway stations in central London.

controlled but only just contained that I've got everything in the world you've ever longed for. Well, Miss Townsend, I don't want any of it. You can have it, Miss Townsend. I wish I was absolutely alone in the world, like you. Miss Townsend, I'm besieged by seven devils, Miss Townsend, Miss Townsend, let me stay here in your hotel where the devils can't get me. . . ." Instead of saying all this, she described her anaemia, agreed to try Miss Townsend's remedy for it, which was raw liver, minced, between whole-meal bread, and said yes, perhaps it would be better if she stayed at home and let a friend do shopping for her. She paid her bill and left the hotel, defeated.

At home Mrs. Parkes said she didn't really like it, no, not really, when Mrs. Rawlings was away from nine in the morning until five. The teacher had telephoned from school to say Joan's teeth were paining her, and she hadn't known what to say; and what was she to make for the children's tea, Mrs. Rawlings hadn't said.

All this was nonsense, of course. Mrs. Parkes's complaint was that Susan had withdrawn herself spiritually, leaving the burden of the big house on her.

Susan looked back at her day of "freedom" which had resulted in her becoming a friend of the lonely Miss Townsend, and in Mrs. Parkes's remonstrances. Yet she remembered the short blissful hour of being alone, really alone. She was determined to arrange her life, no matter what it cost, so that she could have that solitude more often. An absolute solitude, where no one knew her or cared about her.

But how? She thought of saying to her old employer: I want you to back me up in a story with Matthew that I am doing part-time work for you. The truth is that . . . But she would have to tell him a lie too, and which lie? She could not say: I want to sit by myself three or four times a week in a rented room. And besides, he knew Matthew, and she could not really ask him to tell lies on her behalf, apart from being bound to think it meant a lover.

Suppose she really took a part-time job, which she could get through fast and efficiently, leaving time for herself. What job? Addressing envelopes? Canvassing?

And there was Mrs. Parkes, working widow, who knew exactly what she was prepared to give to the house, who knew by instinct when her mistress withdrew in spirit from her responsibilities. Mrs. Parkes was one of the servers of this world, but she needed someone to serve. She had to have Mrs. Rawlings, her madam, at the top of the house or in the garden, so that she could come and get support from her: "Yes, the bread's not what it was when I was a girl. . . . Yes, Harry's got a wonderful appetite, I wonder where he puts it all. . . . Yes, it's lucky the twins are so much of a size, they can wear each other's shoes, that's saving in these hard times. . . . Yes, the cherry jam from Switzerland is not a patch on the jam from Poland, and three times the price . . ." And so on. That sort of talk Mrs. Parkes must have, every day, or she would leave, not knowing herself why she left.

Susan Rawlings, thinking these thoughts, found that she was prowling through the great thicketed garden like a wild cat: she was walking up the stairs, down the stairs, through the rooms into the garden, along the brown running river, back, up through the house, down again. . . . It was a wonder Mrs. Parkes did not think it strange. But, on the contrary, Mrs. Rawlings could do what she liked, she could stand on her head if she wanted, provided she was *there*. Susan Rawlings prowled and muttered through her house, hating Mrs. Parkes, hating poor Miss Townsend, dreaming of her hour of solitude in the dingy respectability of Miss Townsend's hotel bedroom, and she knew quite well she was mad. Yes, she was mad.

She said to Matthew that she must have a holiday. Matthew agreed with her. This was not as things had been once—how they had talked in each other's arms in the marriage bed. He had, she knew, diagnosed her finally as *unreasonable*. She had become someone outside himself that he had to manage. They were living side by side in this house like two tolerably friendly strangers.

Having told Mrs. Parkes—or rather, asked for her permission— she went off on a walking holiday in Wales. She chose the remotest place she knew of. Every morning the children telephoned her before they went off to school, to encourage and support her, just as they had over Mother's Room. Every evening she telephoned them, spoke to each child in turn, and then to Matthew. Mrs. Parkes, given permission to telephone for instructions or advice, did so every day at lunchtime. When, as happened three times, Mrs. Rawlings was out on the mountainside, Mrs. Parkes asked that she should ring back at such-and-such a time, for she would not be happy in what she was doing without Mrs. Rawlings' blessing.

Susan prowled over wild country with the telephone wire holding her to her duty like a leash. The next time she must telephone, or wait to be telephoned, nailed her to her cross. The mountains themselves seemed trammelled by her unfreedom. Everywhere on the mountains, where she met on one at all, from breakfast time to dusk, excepting sheep, or a shepherd, she came face to face with her own craziness, which might attack her in the broadest valleys, so that they seemed too small, or on a mountaintop from which she could see a hundred other mountains and valleys, so that they seemed too low, too small, with the sky pressing down too close. She would stand gazing at a hillside brilliant with ferns and bracken, jewelled with running water, and see nothing but her devil, who lifted inhuman eyes at her from where he leaned negligently on a rock, switching at his ugly yellow boots with a leafy twig.

She returned to her home and family, with the Welsh emptiness at the back of her mind like a promise of freedom.

She told her husband she wanted to have an *au pair* girl.[5]

---

[5] Young woman, usually foreign, who lives in with a family, doing housework and babysitting in exchange for room and board.

They were in their bedroom, it was late at night, the children slept. He sat, shirted and slippered, in a chair by the window, looking out. She sat brushing her hair and watching him in the mirror. A time-hallowed scene in the connubial bedroom. He said nothing, while she heard the arguments coming into his mind, only to be rejected because every one was *reasonable.*

"It seems strange to get one now; after all, the children are in school most of the day. Surely the time for you to have help was when you were stuck with them day and night. Why don't you ask Mrs. Parkes to cook for you? She's even offered to—I can understand if you are tired of cooking for six people. But you know that an *au pair* girl means all kinds of problems, it's not like having an ordinary char in during the day. . . ."

Finally he said carefully: "Are you thinking of going back to work?"

"No," she said, "no, not really." She made herself sound vague, rather stupid. She went on brushing her black hair and peering at herself so as to be oblivious of the short uneasy glances her Matthew kept giving her. "Do you think we can't afford it?" she went on vaguely, not at all the old efficient Susan who knew exactly what they could afford.

"It's not that," he said, looking out of the window at dark trees, so as not to look at her. Meanwhile she examined a round, candid, pleasant face with clear dark brows and clear grey eyes. A sensible face. She brushed thick healthy black hair and thought: Yet that's the reflection of a madwoman. How very strange! Much more to the point if what looked back at me was the gingery green-eyed demon with his dry meagre smile. . . . Why wasn't Matthew agreeing? After all, what else could he do? She was breaking her part of the bargain and there was no way of forcing her to keep it: that her spirit, her soul, should live in this house, so that the people in it could grow like plants in water, and Mrs. Parkes remain content in their service. In return for this, he would be a good loving husband, and responsible towards the children. Well, nothing like this had been true of either of them for a long time. He did his duty, perfunctorily; she did not even pretend to do hers. And he had become like other husbands, with his real life in his work and the people he met there, and very likely a serious affair. All this was her fault.

At last he drew heavy curtains, blotting out the trees, and turned to force her attention: "Susan, are you really sure we need a girl?" But she would not meet his appeal at all. She was running the brush over her hair again and again, lifting fine black clouds in a small hiss of electricity. She was peering in and smiling as if she were amused at the clinging hissing hair that followed the brush.

"Yes, I think it would be a good idea, on the whole," she said, with the cunning of a madwoman evading the real point.

In the mirror she could see her Matthew lying on his back, his hands behind his head, staring upwards, his face sad and hard. She felt her heart (the old heart of Susan Rawlings) soften and call out to him. But she set it to be indifferent.

He said: "Susan, the children?" It was an appeal that *almost* reached her. He opened his arms, lifting them palms up, empty. She had only to run across and fling herself into them, onto his hard, warm chest, and melt into herself, into Susan. But she could not. She would not see his lifted arms. She said vaguely: "Well, surely it'll be even better for them? We'll get a French or a German girl and they'll learn the language."

In the dark she lay beside him, feeling frozen, a stranger. She felt as if Susan had been spirited away. She disliked very much this woman who lay here, cold and indifferent beside a suffering man, but she could not change her.

Next morning she set about getting a girl, and very soon came Sophie Traub from Hamburg, a girl of twenty, laughing, healthy, blue-eyed, intending to learn English. Indeed, she already spoke a good deal. In return for a room—"Mother's Room"—and her food, she undertook to do some light cooking, and to be with the children when Mrs. Rawlings asked. She was an intelligent girl and understood perfectly what was needed. Susan said: "I go off sometimes, for the morning or for the day—well, sometimes the children run home from school, or they ring up, or a teacher rings up. I should be here, really. And there's the daily woman. . . ." And Sophie laughed her deep fruity *Fräulein*'s laugh, showed her fine white teeth and her dimples, and said: "You want some person to play mistress of the house sometimes, not so?"

"Yes, that is just so," said Susan, a bit dry, despite herself, thinking in secret fear how easy it was, how much nearer to the end she was than she thought. Healthy Fräulein Traub's instant understanding of their position proved this to be true.

The *au pair* girl, because of her own commonsense, or (as Susan said to herself, with her new inward shudder) because she had been *chosen* so well by Susan, was a success with everyone, the children liking her, Mrs. Parkes forgetting almost at once that she was German, and Matthew finding her "nice to have around the house." For he was now taking things as they came, from the surface of life, withdrawn both as a husband and a father from the household.

One day Susan saw how Sophie and Mrs. Parkes were talking and laughing in the kitchen, and she announced that she would be away until tea time. She knew exactly where to go and what she must look for. She took the District Line to South Kensington, changed to the Circle, got off at Paddington,[6] and walked around looking at the smaller hotels until she was satisfied with one which had FRED'S HOTEL painted on windowpanes that needed cleaning. The facade was a faded shiny yellow, like unhealthy skin. A door at the end of a passage said she must knock; she did, and Fred appeared. He was not at all attractive, not in any way, being fattish, and run-down, and wearing a tasteless striped suit. He had small sharp eyes in a white creased face, and was quite prepared to let Mrs. Jones (she chose the farcical name deliberately, staring him out) have a room three days a week from ten until six. Provided of course that she paid in advance each time she came? Susan produced fifteen shillings (no price had been set by

---

[6] Railway and subway station in London. The Circle is the Circle Line of the subway.

him and held it out, still fixing him with a bold unblinking challenge she had not known until then she could use at will. Looking at her still, he took up a ten-shilling note from her palm between thumb and forefinger, fingered it; then shuffled up two half-crowns,[7] held out his own palm with these bits of money displayed thereon, and let his gaze lower broodingly at them. They were standing in the passage, a red-shaded light above, bare boards beneath, and a strong smell of floor polish rising about them. He shot his gaze up at her over the still-extended palm, and smiled as if to say: What do you take me for? "I shan't," said Susan, "be using this room for the purposes of making money." He still waited. She added another five shillings, at which he nodded and said: "You pay, and I ask no questions." "Good," said Susan. He now went past her to the stairs, and there waited a moment: the light from the street door being in her eyes, she lost sight of him momentarily. Then she saw a sober-suited, white-faced, white-balding little man trotting up the stairs like a waiter, and she went after him. They proceeded in utter silence up the stairs of this house where no questions were asked — Fred's Hotel, which could afford the freedom for its visitors that poor Miss Townsend's hotel could not. The room was hideous. It had a single window, with thin green brocade curtains, a three-quarter bed that had a cheap green satin bedspread on it, a fireplace with a gas fire and a shilling meter by it, a chest of drawers, and a green wicker armchair.

"Thank you," said Susan, knowing that Fred (if this was Fred, and not George, or Herbert or Charlie) was looking at her, not so much with curiosity, an emotion he would not own to, for professional reasons, but with a philosophical sense of what was appropriate. Having taken her money and shown her up and agreed to everything, he was clearly disapproving of her for coming here. She did not belong here at all, so his look said. (But she knew, already, how very much she did belong: the room had been waiting for her to join it.) "Would you have me called at five o'clock, please?" and he nodded and went downstairs.

It was twelve in the morning. She was free. She sat in the armchair, she simply sat, she closed her eyes and sat and let herself be alone. She was alone and no one knew where she was. When a knock came on the door she was annoyed, and prepared to show it: but it was Fred himself, it was five o'clock and he was calling her as ordered. He flicked his sharp little eyes over the room — bed, first. It was undisturbed. She might never have been in the room at all. She thanked him, said she would be returning the day after tomorrow, and left. She was back home in time to cook supper, to put the children to bed, to cook a second supper for her husband and herself later. And to welcome Sophie back from the pictures where she had gone with a friend. All these things she did cheerfully, willingly. But she was thinking all the time of the hotel room; she was longing for it with her whole being.

---

[7] Coins worth 5 shillings each.

Three times a week. She arrived promptly at ten, looked Fred in the eyes, gave him twenty shillings, followed him up the stairs, went into the room, and shut the door on him with gentle firmness. For Fred, disapproving of her being here at all, was quite ready to let friendship, or at least acquaintanceship, follow his disapproval, if only she would let him. But he was content to go off on her dismissing nod, with the twenty shillings in his hand.

She sat in the armchair and shut her eyes.

What did she *do* in the room? Why, nothing at all. From the chair, when it had rested her, she went to the window, stretching her arms, smiling, treasuring her anonymity, to look out. She was no longer Susan Rawlings, mother of four, wife of Matthew, employer of Mrs. Parkes and of Sophie Traub, with these and those relations with friends, school-teachers, tradesmen. She no longer was mistress of the big white house and garden, owning clothes suitable for this and that activity or occasion. She was Mrs. Jones, and she was alone, and she had no past and no future. Here I am, she thought, after all these years of being married and having children and playing those roles of responsibility—and I'm just the same. Yet there have been times I thought that nothing existed of me except the roles that went with being Mrs. Matthew Rawlings. Yes, here I am, and if I never saw any of my family again, here I would still be . . . how very strange that is! And she leaned on the still, and looked into the street, loving the men and women who passed, because she did not know them. She looked at the down-trodden buildings over the street, and at the sky, wet and dingy, or sometimes blue, and she felt she had never seen buildings or sky before. And then she went back to the chair, empty, her mind a blank. Sometimes she talked aloud, saying nothing—an exclamation, meaningless, followed by a comment about the floral pattern on the thin rug, or a stain on the green satin coverlet. For the most part, she wool-gathered—what word is there for it?—brooded, wandered, simply went dark, feeling emptiness run deliciously through her veins like the movement of her blood.

This room had become more her own than the house she lived in. One morning she found Fred taking her a flight higher than usual. She stopped, refusing to go up, and demanded her usual room, Number 19. "Well, you'll have to wait half an hour, then," he said. Willingly she descended to the dark disinfectant-smelling hall, and sat waiting until the two, man and woman, came down the stairs, giving her swift indifferent glances before they hurried out into the street, separating at the door. She went up to the room, *her* room, which they had just vacated. It was no less hers, though the windows were set wide open, and a maid was straightening the bed as she came in.

After these days of solitude, it was both easy to play her part as mother and wife, and difficult—because it was so easy: she felt an impostor. She felt as if her shell moved here, with her family, answering to Mummy, Mother, Susan, Mrs. Rawlings. She was surprised no one saw through her, that she wasn't turned out of doors, as a fake. On the contrary, it seemed the children loved her more; Matthew and she "got on" pleasantly, and Mrs. Parkes was happy in her work under (for the most part, it must be confessed) Sophie Traub. At night she lay beside her husband, and they made love again, apparently just as they used to, when they were really married. But she, Susan, or the being who answered so readily and improbably to the name of Susan, was not there: she was in Fred's Hotel, in Paddington, waiting for the easing hours of solitude to begin.

Soon she made a new arrangement with Fred and with Sophie. It was for five days a week. As for the money, five pounds, she simply asked Matthew for it. She saw that she was not even frightened he might ask what for: he would give it to her, she knew that, and yet it was terrifying it could be so, for this close couple, these partners, had once known the destination of every shilling they must spend. He agreed to give her five pounds a week. She asked for just so much, not a penny more. He sounded indifferent about it. It was as if he were paying her, she thought: *paying her off*—yes, that was it. Terror came back for a moment when she understood this, but she stilled it: things had gone too far for that. Now, every week, on Sunday nights, he gave he five pounds, turning away from her before their eyes could meet on the transaction. As for Sophie Traub, she was to be somewhere in or near the house until six at night, after which she was free. She was not to cook or to clean; she was simply to be there. So she gardened or sewed, and asked friends in, being a person who was bound to have a lot of friends. If the children were sick, she nursed them. If teachers telephoned, she answered them sensibly. For the five daytimes in the school week, she was altogether the mistress of the house.

One night in the bedroom, Matthew asked: "Susan, I don't want to interfere—don't think that, please—but are you sure you are well?"

She was brushing her hair at the mirror. She made two more strokes on either side of her head, before she replied: "Yes, dear, I am sure I am well."

He was again lying on his back, his blond head on his hands, his elbows angled up and part-concealing his face. He said: "Then Susan, I have to ask you this question, though you must understand, I'm not putting any sort of pressure on you." (Susan heard the word "pressure" with dismay, because this was inevitable; of course she could not go on like this.) "Are things going to go on like this?"

"Well," she said, going vague and bright and idiotic again, so as to escape: "Well, I don't see why not."

He was jerking his elbows up and down, in annoyance or in pain, and, looking at him, she saw he had got thin, even gaunt; and restless angry movements were not what she remembered of him. He said: "Do you want a divorce, is that it?"

At this, Susan only with the greatest difficulty stopped herself from laughing: she could hear the bright bubbling laughter she *would* have emitted, had she let herself. He could only mean one thing: she had a lover, and that was why she spent her days in London, as lost to him as if she had vanished to another continent.

Then the small panic set in again: she understood that he hoped she did have a lover, he was begging her to say so, because otherwise it would be too terrifying.

She thought this out as she brushed her hair, watching the fine black stuff fly up to make its little clouds of electricity, hiss, hiss, hiss. Behind her head, across the room, was a blue wall. She realised she was absorbed in watching the black hair making shapes against the blue. She should be answering him. "Do *you* want a divorce, Matthew?"

He said: "That surely isn't the point, is it?"

"You brought it up, I didn't," she said, brightly, suppressing meaningless tinkling laughter.

Next day she asked Fred: "Have enquiries been made for me?"

He hesitated, and she said: "I've been coming here a year now. I've made no trouble, and you've been paid every day. I have a right to be told."

"As a matter of fact, Mrs. Jones, a man did come asking."

"A man from a detective agency?"

"Well, he could have been, couldn't he?"

"I was asking you. . . . Well, what did you tell him?"

"I told him a Mrs. Jones came every weekday from ten until five or six and stayed in Number 19 by herself."

"Describing me?"

"Well, Mrs. Jones, I had no alternative. Put yourself in my place."

"By rights I should deduct what that man gave you for the information."

He raised shocked eyes: she was not the sort of person to make jokes like this! Then he chose to laugh: a pinkish wet slit appeared across his white crinkled face; his eyes positively begged her to laugh, otherwise he might lose some money. She remained grave, looking at him.

He stopped laughing and said: "You want to go up now?"— returning to the familiarity, the comradeship, of the country where no questions are asked, on which (and he knew it) she depended completely.

She went up to sit in her wicker chair. But it was not the same. Her husband had searched her out. (The world had searched her out.) The pressures were on her. She was here with his connivance. He might walk in at any moment, here, into Room 19. She imagined the report from the detective agency: "A woman calling herself Mrs. Jones, fitting the description of your wife (et cetera, et cetera, et cetera), stays alone all day in Room No. 19. She insists on this room, waits for it if it is engaged. As far as the proprietor knows, she receives no visitors there, male or female." A report something on these lines Matthew must have received.

Well, of course he was right: things couldn't go on like this. He had put an end to it all simply by sending the detective after her.

She tried to shrink herself back into the shelter of the room, a snail pecked out of its shell and trying to squirm back. But the peace of the room had gone. She was trying consciously to revive it, trying to let go into the dark creative trance (or whatever it was) that she had found there. It was no use, yet she craved for it, she was as ill as a suddenly deprived addict.

Several times she returned to the room, to look for herself there, but instead she found the unnamed spirit of restlessness, a pricking fevered hunger for movement, an irritable self-consciousness that made her brain feel as if it had coloured lights going on and off inside it. Instead of the soft dark that had been the room's air, were now waiting for her demons that made her dash blindly about, muttering words of hate; she was impelling herself from point to point like a moth dashing itself against a windowpane, sliding to the bottom, fluttering off on broken wings, then crashing into the invisible barrier again. And again and again. Soon she was exhausted, and she told Fred that for a while she would not be needing the room, she was going on holiday. Home she went, to the big white house by the river. The middle of a weekday, and she felt guilty at returning to her own home when not expected. She stood unseen, looking in at the kitchen window. Mrs. Parkes, wearing a discarded floral overall of Susan's, was stooping to slide something into the oven. Sophie, arms folded, was leaning her back against a cupboard and laughing at some joke made by a girl not seen before by Susan—a dark foreign girl, Sophie's visitor. In an armchair Molly, one of the twins, lay curled, sucking her thumb and watching the grownups. She must have some sickness, to be kept from school. The child's listless face, the dark circles under her eyes, hurt Susan: Molly was looking at the three grownups working and talking in exactly the same way Susan looked at the four through the kitchen window: she was remote, shut off from them.

But then, just as Susan imagined herself going in, picking up the little girl, and sitting in an armchair with her, stroking her probably heated forehead, Sophie did just that: she had been standing on one leg, the other knee flexed, its foot set against the wall. Now she let her foot in its ribbon-tied red shoe slide down the wall, stood solid on two feet, clapping her hands before and behind her, and sang a couple of lines in German, so that the child lifted her heavy eyes at her and began to smile. Then she walked, or rather skipped, over to the child, swung her up, and let her fall into her lap at the same moment she sat herself. She said "Hopla! Hopla! Molly . . ." and began stroking the dark untidy young head that Molly laid on her shoulder for comfort.

Well. . . . Susan blinked the tears of farewell out of her eyes, and went quietly up through the house to her bedroom. There she sat looking at the river through the trees. She felt at peace, but in a way that was new to her. She had no desire to move, to talk, to do anything at all. The devils that had haunted the house, the garden, were not there; but she knew it was because her soul was in Room 19 in Fred's Hotel; she was not really here at all. It was a sensation that should have been frightening: to sit at her own bedroom window, listening to Sophie's rich young voice sing German nursery songs to her child, listening to Mrs. Parkes clatter and move below, and to know that all this had nothing to do with her: she was already out of it.

Later, she made herself go down and say she was home: it was unfair to be here unannounced. She took lunch with Mrs. Parkes, Sophie, Sophie's Italian friend Maria, and her daughter Molly, and felt like a visitor.

A few days later, at bedtime, Matthew said: "Here's your five pounds," and pushed them over at her. Yet he must have known she had not been leaving the house at all.

She shook her head, gave it back to him, and said, in explanation, not in accusation: "As soon as you knew where I was, there was no point."

He nodded, not looking at her. He was turned away from her: thinking, she knew, how best to handle this wife who terrified him.

He said: "I wasn't trying to . . . It's just that I was worried."

"Yes, I know."

"I must confess that I was beginning to wonder . . ."

"You thought I had a lover?"

"Yes, I am afraid I did."

She knew that he wished she had. She sat wondering how to say: "For a year now I've been spending all my days in a very sordid hotel room. It's the place where I'm happy. In fact, without it I don't exist." She heard herself saying this, and understood how terrified he was that she might. So instead she said: "Well, perhaps you're not far wrong."

Probably Matthew would think the hotel proprietor lied: he would want to think so.

"Well," he said, and she could hear his voice spring up, so to speak, with relief, "in that case I must confess I've got a bit of an affair on myself."

She said, detached and interested: "Really? Who is she?" and saw Matthew's startled look because of this reaction.

"It's Phil. Phil Hunt."

She had known Phil Hunt well in the old unmarried days. She was thinking: No, She won't do, she's too neurotic and difficult. She's never been happy yet. Sophie's much better. Well, Matthew will see that himself, as sensible as he is.

This line of thought went on in silence, while she said aloud: "It's no point in telling you about mine, because you don't know him."

Quick, quick, invent, she thought. Remember how you invented all that nonsense for Miss Townsend.

She began slowly, careful not to contradict herself: "His name is Michael" (*Michael What?*)—"Michael Plant." (What a silly name!) "He's rather like you—in looks, I mean." And indeed, she could imagine herself being touched by no one but Matthew himself. He's a publisher," (Really? Why?) "He's got a wife already and two children."

She brought out this fantasy, proud of herself.

Matthew said: "Are you two thinking of marrying?"

She said, before she could stop herself: "Good God, *no!*"

She realised, if Matthew wanted to marry Phil Hunt, that this was too emphatic, but apparently it was all right, for his voice sounded relieved as he said: "It is a bit impossible to imagine oneself married to anyone else, isn't it?" With which he pulled her to him, so that her head lay on his shoulder. She turned her face into the dark of his flesh, and listened to the blood pounding through her ears saying: I am alone, I am alone, I am alone.

In the morning Susan lay in bed while he dressed.

He had been thinking things out in the night, because now he said: "Susan, why don't we make a foursome?"

Of course, she said to herself, of course he would be bound to say that. If one is sensible, if one is reasonable, if one never allows oneself a base thought or an envious emotion, natually one says: Let's make a foursome!

"Why not?" she said.

"We could all meet for lunch. I mean, it's ridiculous, you sneaking off to filthy hotels, and me staying late at the office, and all the lies everyone has to tell."

What on earth did I say his name was?—she panicked then said: "I think it's a good idea, but Michael is away at the moment. When he comes back, though—and I'm sure you two would like each other."

"He's away, is he? So that's why you've been . . ." Her husband put his hand to the knot of his tie in a gesture of male coquetry she would not before have associated with him; and he bent to kiss her cheek with the expression that goes with the words: Oh you naughty little puss! And she felt its answering look, naughty and coy, come onto her face.

Inside she was dissolving in horror at them both, at how far they had both sunk from honesty of emotion.

So now she was saddled with a lover, and he had a mistress! How ordinary, how reassuring, how jolly! And now they would make a foursome of it, and go about to theatres and restaurants. After all, the Rawlings could well afford that sort of thing, and presumably the publisher Michael Plant could afford to do himself and his mistress quite well. No, there was nothing to stop the four of them developing the most intricate relationship of civilised tolerance, all enveloped in a charming afterglow of autumnal passion. Perhaps they would all go off on holidays together? She had known people who did. Or perhaps Matthew would draw the line there? Why should he, though, if he was capable of talking about "foursomes" at all?

She lay in the empty bedroom, listening to the car drive off with Matthew in it, off to work. Then she heard the children clattering off to school to the accompaniment of Sophie's cheerfully ringing voice. She slid down into the hollow of the bed, for shelter against her own irrelevance. And she stretched out her hand to the hollow where her husband's body had lain, but found no comfort there: he was not her husband. She curled herself up in a small tight ball under the clothes: she could stay here all day, all week, indeed, all her life.

But in a few days she must produce Michael Plant, and—but how? She must presumably find some agreeable man prepared to impersonate a publisher called Michael Plant. And in return for which she would—what? Well, for one thing they would make love. The idea made her want to cry with sheer exhaustion. Oh no, she had finished with all that—the proof of it was that the words "make love," or even imagining it, trying hard to revive no more than the pleasures of sensuality, let alone affection, or love, made her want to run away and hide from the sheer effort of the thing. . . . Good Lord, why make love at all? Why make love with anyone? Or if you are going to make love, what does it matter who with? Why shouldn't she simply walk into the street, pick up a man and have a roaring sexual affair with him? Why not? Or even with Fred? What difference did it make?

But she had let herself in for it—an interminable stretch of time with a lover, called Michael, as part of a gallant civilised foursome. Well, she could not, and she would not.

She got up, dressed, went down to find Mrs. Parkes, and asked her for the loan of a pound, since Matthew, she said, had forgotten to leave her money. She exchanged with Mrs. Parkes variations on the theme that husbands are all the same, they don't think, and without saying a word to Sophie, whose voice could be heard upstairs from the telephone, walked to the underground, travelled to South Kensington, changed to the Inner Circle, got out at Paddington, and walked to Fred's Hotel. There she told Fred that she wasn't going on holiday after all, she needed the room. She would have to wait an hour, Fred said. She went to a busy tearoom-cum-restaurant around the corner, and sat watching the people flow in and out the door that kept swinging open and shut, watched them mingle and merge, and separate, felt her being flow into them, into their movement. When the hour was up, she left a half-crown for her pot of tea, and left the place without looking back at it, just as she had left her house, the big, beautiful white house, without another look, but silently dedicating it to Sophie. She returned to Fred, received the key of Number 19, now free, and ascended the grimy stairs slowly, letting floor after floor fall away below her, keeping her eyes lifted, so that floor after floor descended jerkily to her level of vision, and fell away out of sight.

Number 19 was the same. She saw everything with an acute, narrow, checking glance: the cheap shine of the satin spread, which had been replaced carelessly after the two bodies had finished their convulsions under it; a trace of powder on the glass that topped the chest of drawers; an intense green shade in a fold of the curtain. She stood at the window, looking down, watching people pass and pass and pass until her mind went dark from the constant movement. Then she sat in the wicker chair, letting herself go slack. But she had to be careful, because she did not want, today, to be surprised by Fred's knock at five o'clock.

The demons were not here. They had gone forever, because she was buying her freedom from them. She was slipping already into the dark fructifying dream that seemed to caress her inwardly, like the movement of her blood . . . but she had to think about Matthew first. Should she write a letter for the coroner? But what should she say? She would like to leave him with the look on his face she had seen this morning—banal, admittedly, but at least confidently healthy. Well, that was impossible, one did not look like that with a wife dead from suicide. But how to leave him believing she was dying because of a man—because of the fascinating publisher Michael Plant? Oh, how ridiculous! How absurb! How humiliating! But she decided not to trouble about it, simply not to think about the living. If he wanted to believe she had a lover, he would believe it. And he *did* want to believe it. Even when he had found out that there was no publisher in London called Michael Plant, he would think: Oh poor Susan, she was afraid to give me his real name.

And what did it matter whether he married Phil Hunt or Sophie? Though it ought to be Sophie, who was already the mother of those children . . . and what hypocrisy to sit here worrying about the children, when she was going to leave them because she had not got the energy to stay.

She had about four hours. She spent them delightfully, darkly, sweetly, letting herself slide gently, gently, to the edge of the river. Then, with hardly a break in her consciousness, she got up, pushed the thin rug against the door, made sure the windows were tight shut, put two shillings in the meter, and turned on the gas. For the first time since she had been in the room she lay on the hard bed that smelled stale, that smelled of sweat and sex.

She lay on her back on the green satin cover, but her legs were chilly. She got up, found a blanket folded in the bottom of the chest of drawers, and carefully covered her legs with it. She was quite content lying there, listening to the faint soft hiss of the gas that poured into the room, into her lungs, into her brain, as she drifted off into the dark river.

Hisaye Yamamoto 1921–

The daughter of Japanese immigrants, Hisaye Yamamoto was born in Redondo Beach, California. Her writing, intimately connected with events from her own life, often explores the relationship between issei and nisei (first generation Japanese immigrants and their children). "Seventeen Syllables" (1949), her most widely anthologized story, deals with a mother-daughter relationship made difficult not only because of the language difference but because of the mysteries of the mother's previous life in Japan. While attending Compton Junior College in California, Yamamoto and her family were sent to a Japanese-American internment camp in Poston, Arizona, where they remained until the end of World War II. During this time, she wrote columns and news reports for the camp newspaper, the *Poston Chronicle*. After the war, she worked for the *Los Angeles Tribune*, an African-American weekly publication that aspired to create an inter-ethnic readership, and the socially conscious *Catholic Worker* in New York. In addition to "Seventeen Syllables," Yamamoto wrote three other stories that were also included in the yearly *Best American Short Stories:* "The Brown House" (1951), "Epithalamium" (1960), and "Yoneko's Earthquake" (1952). Her collection of fiction, *Seventeen Syllables*, was published in Japan in 1985 and in the United States in 1988.

SEVENTEEN SYLLABLES

The first Rosie knew that her mother had taken to writing poems was one evening when she finished one and read it aloud for her daughter's approval. It was about cats, and Rosie pretended to understand it thoroughly and appreciate it no end, partly because she hesitated to disillusion her mother about the quantity and quality of Japanese she had learned in all the years now that she had been going to Japanese school every Sunday (and Wednesday, too, in the summer). Even so, her mother must have been skeptical about the depth of Rosie's understanding, because she explained afterwards about the kind of poem she was trying to write.

See, Rosie, she said, it was a *haiku*, poem in which she must pack all her meaning into seventeen syllables only, which were divided into three lines of five, seven, and five syllables. In the one she had just read, she had tried to capture the charm of a kitten, as well as comment on the superstition that owning a cat of three colors meant good luck.

"Yes, yes, I understand. How utterly lovely," Rosie said, and her mother, either satisfied or seeing through the deception and resigned, went back to composing.

The truth was that Rosie was lazy; English lay ready on the tongue but Japanese had to be searched for and examined, and even then put forth tentatively (probably to meet with laughter). It was so much easier to say yes, yes, even when one meant no, no. Besides, this was what was in her mind to say: I was looking through one of your magazines from Japan last night, Mother, and towards the back I found some *haiku* in English that delighted me. There was one that made me giggle off and on until I fell asleep—

It is morning, and lo!
I lie awake, comme il faut.
sighing for some dough.

Now, how to reach her mother, how to communicate the melancholy song? Rosie knew formal Japanese by fits and starts, her mother had even less English, no French. It was much more possible to say yes, yes.

It developed that her mother was writing the *haiku* for a daily newspaper, the *Mainichi Shimbun*, that was published in San Francisco. Los Angeles, to be sure, was closer to the farming community in which the Hayashi family lived and several Japanese vernaculars were printed there, but Rosie's parents said they preferred the tone of the northern paper. Once a week, the *Mainichi* would have a section devoted to *haiku,* and her mother became an extravagant contributor, taking for herself the blossoming pen name, Ume Hanazono.

So Rosie and her father lived for awhile with two women, her mother and Ume Hanazono. Her mother (Tome Hayashi by name) kept house, cooked, washed, and, along with her husband and the Carrascos, the Mexican family hired for the harvest, did her ample share of picking tomatoes out in the sweltering fields and boxing them in tidy strata in the cool packing shed. Ume Hanazono, who came to life after the dinner dishes were done, was an earnest, muttering stranger who often neglected speaking when spoken to and stayed busy at the parlor table as late as midnight scribbling with pencil on scratch paper or carefully copying characters on good paper with her fat, pale green Parker.

The new interest had some repercussions on the household routine. Before, Rosie had been accustomed to her parents and herself taking their hot baths early and going to bed almost immediately afterwards, unless her parents challenged each other to a game of flower cards or unless company dropped in. Now if her father wanted to play cards, he had to resort to solitaire (at which he always cheated fearlessly), and if a group of friends came over, it was bound to contain someone who was also writing *haiku,* and the small assemblage would be split in two, her father entertaining the non-literary members and her mother comparing ecstatic notes with the visiting poet.

If they went out, it was more of the same thing. But Ume Hanazono's life span, even for a poet's, was very brief—perhaps three months at most.

One night they went over to see the Hayano family in the neighboring town to the west, an adventure both painful and attractive to Rosie. It was attractive because there were four Hayano girls, all lovely and each one named after a season of the year (Haru, Natsu, Aki, Fuyu), painful because something had been wrong with Mrs. Hayano ever since the birth of the first child. Rosie would sometimes watch Mrs. Hayano, reputed to have been the belle of her native village, making her way about a room, stooped, slowly shuffling, violently trembling (*always* trembling), and she would be reminded that this woman, in this same condition, had carried and given issue to three babies. She would look wonderingly at Mr. Hayano, handsome, tall, and strong, and she would look at her four pretty friends. But it was not a matter she could come to any decision about.

On this visit, however, Mrs. Hayano sat all evening in the rocker, as motionless and unobtrusive as it was possible for her to be, and Rosie found the greater part of the evening practically anaesthetic. Too, Rosie spent most of it in the girls' room, because Haru, the garrulous one, said almost as soon as the bows and other greetings were over, "Oh, you must see my new coat!"

It was a pale plaid of grey, sand, and blue, with an enormous collar, and Rosie, seeing nothing special in it, said, "Gee, how nice."

"Nice?" said Haru, indignantly, "Is that all you can say about it? It's gorgeous! And so cheap, too. Only seventeen-ninety-eight, because it was a sale. The saleslady said it was twenty-five dollars regular."

"Gee," said Rosie. Natsu, who never said much and when she said anything said it shyly, fingered the coat covetously and Haru pulled it away.

"Mine," she said, putting it on. She minced in the aisle between the two large beds and smiled happily. "Let's see how your mother likes it."

She broke into the front room and the adult conversation and went to stand in front of Rosie's mother, while the rest watched from the door. Rosie's mother was properly envious. "May I inherit it when you're through with it?"

Haru, pleased, giggled and said yes, she could, but Natsu remained gravely from the door, "You promised me, Haru."

Everyone laughed but Natsu, who shamefacedly retreated into the bedroom. Haru came in laughing, taking off the coat. "We were only kidding, Natsu," she said. "Here, you try it on now."

After Natsu buttoned herself into the coat, inspected herself solemnly in the bureau mirror, and reluctantly shed it, Rosie, Aki, and Fuyu got their turns, and Fuyu, who was eight, drowned in it while her sisters and Rosie doubled up in amusement. They all went into the front room later, because Haru's mother quaveringly called to her to fix the tea and rice cakes and open a can of sliced peaches for everybody. Rosie noticed that her mother and Mr. Hayano were talking together at the little table—they were discussing a *haiku* that Mr. Hayano was planning to send to the *Mainichi*, while her father was sitting at one end of the sofa looking through a copy of *Life*, the new picture magazine. Occasionally, her father would comment on a photograph, holding it toward Mrs. Hayano and speaking to her as he always did—loudly, as though he thought someone such as she must surely be at least a trifle deaf also.

The five girls had their refreshments at the kitchen table, and it was while Rosie was showing the sisters her trick of swallowing peach slices without chewing (she chased each slipper crescent down with a swig of tea) that her father brought his empty teacup and untouched saucer to the sink and said, "Come on, Rosie, we're going home now."

"Already?" asked Rosie.

"Work tomorrow," he said.

He sounded irritated, and Rosie, puzzled, gulped one last yellow slice and stood up to go, while the sisters began protesting, as was their wont.

"We have to get up at five-thirty," he told them, going into the front room quickly, so that they did not have their usual chance to hang onto his hands and plead for an extension of time.

Rosie, following, saw that her mother and Mr. Hayano were sipping tea and still talking together, while Mrs. Hayano concentrated, quivering, on raising the handleless Japanese cup to her lips with both her hands and lowering it back to her lap. Her father, saying nothing, went out the door, onto the bright porch, and down the steps. Her mother looked up and asked, "Where is he going?"

"Where is he going?" Rosie said. "He said we were going home now."

"Going home?" Her mother looked with embarrassment at Mr. Hayano and his absorbed wife and then forced a smile. "He must be tired," she said.

Haru was not giving up yet. "May Rosie stay overnight?" she asked, and Natsu, Aki, and Fuyu came to reinforce their sister's plea by helping her make a circle around Rosie's mother. Rosie, for once having no desire to stay, was relieved when her mother, apologizing to the perturbed Mr. and Mrs. Hayano for her father's abruptness at the same time, managed to shake her head no at the quartet, kindly but adamant, so that they broke their circle and let her go.

Rosie's father looked ahead into the windshield as the two joined him. "I'm sorry," her mother said. "You must be tired." Her father, stepping on the starter, said nothing. "You know how I get when it's *haiku*," she continued. "I forget what time it is." He only grunted.

As they rode homeward silently, Rosie, sitting between, felt a rush of hate for both—for her mother for begging, for her father for denying her mother. I wish this old Ford would crash, right now, she thought, then immediately, no, no, I wish my father would laugh, but it was too late: already the vision had passed through her mind of the green pick-up crumpled in the dark against one of the mighty eucalyptus trees they were just riding past, of the three contorted bleeding bodies, one of them hers.

Rosie ran between two patches of tomatoes, her heart working more rambunctiously than she had ever known it to. How lucky it was that Aunt Taka and Uncle Gimpachi had come tonight, though, how very lucky. Otherwise she might not have really kept her half-promise to meet Jesus Carrasco. Jesus was going to be a senior in September at the same school she went to, and his parents were the ones helping with the tomatoes this year. She and Jesus, who hardly remembered seeing each other at Cleveland High where there were so many other people and two whole grades between them, had become great friends this summer—he always had a joke for her when he periodically drove the loaded pick-up up from the fields to the shed where she was usually sorting while her mother and father did the packing, and they laughed a great deal together over infinitesimal repartee during the afternoon break for chilled watermelon or ice cream in the shade of the shed.

What she enjoyed most was racing him to see who could finish picking a double row first. He, who could work faster, would tease her by slowing down until she thought she would surely pass him this time, then speeding up furiously to leave her several sprawling vines behind. Once he had made her screech hideously be crossing over, while her back was turned, to place atop the tomatoes in her green-stained bucket a truly monstrous, pale green worm (it had looked more like an infant snake). And it was when they had finished a contest this morning, after she had pantingly pointed a green finger at the immature tomatoes evident in the lugs at the end of his row and he had returned the accusation (with justice), that he had startlingly brought up the matter of their possible meeting outside the range of both their parents' dubious eyes.

"What for?" she had asked.

"I've got a secret I want to tell you," he said.

"Tell me now," she demanded.

"It won't be ready till tonight," he said.

She laughed. "Tell me tomorrow then."

"It'll be gone tomorrow," he threatened.

"Well, for seven hakes, what is it?" she had asked, more than twice, and when he had suggested that the packing shed would be an appropriate place to find out, she had cautiously answered maybe. She had not been certain she was going to keep the appointment until the arrival of mother's sister and her husband. Their coming seemed a sort of signal of permission, of grace, and she had definitely made up her mind to lie and leave as she was bowing them welcome.

So as soon as everyone appeared settled back for the evening, she announced loudly that she was going to the privy outside. "I'm going to the *benjo!*" and slipped out the door. And now that she was actually on her way, her heart pumped in such an undisciplined way that she could hear it with her ears. It's because I'm running, she told herself, slowing to a walk. The shed was up ahead, one more patch away, in the middle of the fields. Its bulk, looming in the dimness, took on a sinisterness that was funny when Rosie reminded herself that it was only a wooden frame with a canvas roof and three canvas walls that made a slapping noise on breezy days.

Jesus was sitting on the narrow plank that was the sorting platform and she went around to the other side and jumped backwards to seat herself on the rim of a packing stand. "Well, tell me," she said without greeting, thinking her voice sounded reassuringly familiar.

"I saw you coming out the door," Jesus said. "I heard you running part of the way, too."

"Uh-huh," Rosie said. "Now tell me the secret."

"I was afraid you wouldn't come," he said.

Rosie delved around on the chicken-wire bottom of the stall for number two tomatoes, ripe, which she was sitting beside, and came up with a left-over that felt edible. She bit into it and began sucking out the pulp and seeds. "I'm here," she pointed out.

"Rosie, are you sorry you came?"

"Sorry? What for?" she said. "You said you were going to tell me something."

"I will, I will," Jesus said, but his voice contained disappointment, and Rosie fleetingly felt the older of the two, realizing a brand new power which vanished without category under her recognition.

"I have to go back in a minute," she said. "My aunt and uncle are here from Wintersburg, I told them I was going to the privy."

Jesus laughed. "You funny thing," he said. "You slay me!"

"Just because you have a bathroom *inside*," Rosie said. "Come on, tell me."

Chuckling, Jesus came around to lean on the stand facing her. They still could not see each other very clearly, but Rosie noticed that Jesus became very sober again as he took the hollow tomato from her hand and dropped it back into the stall. When he took hold of her empty hand, she could find no words to protest; her vocabulary had become distressingly constricted and she thought desperately that all that remained intact now was yes and no and oh, and even these few sounds would not easily come out. Thus, kissed by Jesus, Rosie fell for the first time entirely victim to a helplessness delectable beyond speech. But the terrible, beautiful sensation lasted no more than a second, and the reality of Jesus' lips and tongue and teeth and hands made her pull away with such strength that she nearly tumbled.

Rosie stopped running as she approached the lights from the windows of home. How long since she had left? She could not guess, but gasping yet, she went to the privy in back and locked herself in. Her own breathing deafened her in the dark, close space, and she sat and waited until she could hear at last the nightly calling of the frogs and crickets. Even then, all she could think to say was oh, my, and the pressure of Jesus' face against her face would not leave.

No one had missed her in the parlor, however, and Rosie walked in and through quickly, announcing that she was next going to take a bath. "Your father's in the bathhouse," her mother said, and Rosie, in her room, recalled that she had not seen him when she entered. There had been only Aunt Taka and Uncle Gimpachi with her mother at the table, drinking tea. She got her robe and straw sandals and crossed the parlor again to go outside. Her mother was telling them about the *haiku* competition in the *Mainichi* and the poem she had entered.

Rosie met her father coming out of the bathhouse. "Are you through, Father?" she asked. "I was going to ask you to scrub my back."

"Scrub your own back," he said shortly, going toward the main house.

"What have I done now?" she yelled after him. She suddenly felt like doing a lot of yelling. But he did not answer, and she went into the bathhouse. Turning on the dangling light, she removed her denims and T shirt and threw them in the big carton for dirty clothes standing next to the washing machine. Her other things she took with her into the bath compartment to wash after her bath. After she had scooped a basin of hot water from the square wooden tub, she sat on the grey cement of the floor and soaped herself at exaggerated leisure, singing "Red Sails in the Sunset" at the top of her voice and using da-da-da where she suspected her words. Then, standing up, still singing, for she was possessed by the notion that any attempt now to analyze would result in spoilage and she believed that the larger her volume the less she would be able to hear herself think, she obtained more hot water and poured it on until she was free of lather. Only then did she allow herself to step into the steaming vat, one leg first, then the remainder of her body inch by inch until the water no longer stung and she could move around at will.

She took a long time soaking, afterwards remembering to go around outside to stoke the embers of the tin-lined fireplace beneath the tub and to throw on a few more sticks so that the water might keep its heat for her mother, and when she finally returned to the parlor, she found her mother still talking *haiku* with her aunt and uncle, the three of them on another round of tea. Her father was nowhere in sight.

At Japanese school the next day (Wednesday, it was), Rosie was grave and giddy by turns. Preoccupied at her desk in the row for students on Book Eight, she made up for it at recess by performing wild mimicry for the benefit of her friend Chizuko. She held her nose and whined a witticism or two in what she considered was the manner of Fred Allen; she assumed intoxication and a British accent to go over the climax of the Rudy Vallee recording of the pub conversation about William Ewart Galdstone; she was the child Shirley Temple piping, "On the Good Ship Lollipop"; she was the gentleman soprano of the Four Inkspots trilling, "If I Didn't Care." And she felt reasonably satisfied when Chizuko wept and gasped. "Oh, Rosie, you ought to be in the movies!"

Her father came after her at noon, bringing her sandwiches of minced ham and two nectarines to eat while she rode, so that she could pitch right into the sorting when they got home. The lugs were piling up, he said, and the ripe tomatoes in them would probably have to be taken to the cannery tomorrow if they were not ready for the produce haulers tonight. "This heat's not doing them any good. And we've got no time for a break today."

It *was* hot, probably the hottest day of the year, and Rosie's blouse stuck damply to her back even under the protection of the canvas. But she worked as efficiently as a flawless machine and kept the stalls heaped, with one part of her mind listening in to the parental murmuring about the heat and the tomatoes and with another part planning the exact words she would say to Jesus when he drove up with the first load of the afternoon. But when at last she saw that the pick-up was coming, her hands went berserk and the tomatoes started falling in the wrong stalls, and her father said, "Hey, hey! Rosie, watch what you're doing!"

"Well, I have to go to the *benjo*," she said, hiding panic.

"Go in the weeds over there," he said, only half-joking.

"Oh, Father!" she protested.

"Oh, go on home," her mother said. "We'll make out for awhile."

In the privy Rosie peered through a knothole toward the fields, watching as much as she could of Jesus. Happily she thought she saw him look in the direction of the house from time to time before he finished unloading and went back toward the patch where his mother and father worked. As she was heading for the shed, a very presentable black car purred up the dirt driveway to the house and its driver motioned to her. Was this the Hayashi home, he wanted to know. She nodded. Was she a Hayashi? Yes, she said, thinking that he was a good-looking man. He got out of the car with a huge, flat package and she saw that he warmly wore a business suit. "I have something here for your mother then," he said, in a more elegant Japanese than she was used to.

She told him where her mother was and he came along with her, patting his face with an immaculate white handkerchief and saying something about the coolness of San Francisco. To her surprised mother and father, he bowed and introduced himself as, among other things, the *haiku* editor of the *Mainichi Shimbun,* saying that since he had been coming as far as Los Angeles anyway, he had decided to bring her the first prize she had won in the recent contest.

"First prize?" her mother echoed, believing and not believing, pleased and overwhelmed. Handed the package with a bow, she bobbed her head up and down numerous times to express her utter gratitude.

"It is nothing much," he added, "but I hope it will serve as a token of our great appreciation for your contributions and our great admiration of your considerable talent."

"I am not worthy," she said, falling easily into his style. "It is I who should make some sign of my humble thanks for being permitted to contribute."

"No, no, to the contrary," he said, bowing again.

But Rosie's mother insisted, and then saying that she knew she was being unorthodox, she asked if she might open the package because her curiosity was so great. Certainly she might. In fact, he would like her reaction to it, for personally, it was one of his favourite *Hiroshiges.*

Rosie thought it was a pleasant picture, which looked to have been sketched with delicate quickness. There were pink clouds, containing some graceful calligraphy, and a sea that was a pale blue except at the edges, containing four sampans with indications of people in them. Pines edged the water and on the far-off beach there was a cluster of thatched huts towered over by pin-dotted mountains of grey and blue. The frame was scalloped and gilt.

After Rosie's mother pronounced it without peer and somewhat prodded her father into nodding agreement, she said Mr. Kuroda must at least have a cup of tea after coming all this way, and although Mr. Kuroda did not want to impose, he soon agreed that a cup of tea would be refreshing and went along with her to the house, carrying the picture for her.

"Ha, your mother's crazy!" Rosie's father said, and Rosie laughed uneasily as she resumed judgment on the tomatoes. She had emptied six lugs when he broke into an imaginary conversation with Jesus to tell her to go and remind her mother of the tomatoes, and she went slowly.

Mr. Kuroda was in his shirtsleeves expounding some *haiku* theory as he munched a rice cake, and her mother was rapt. Abashed in the great man's presence, Rosie stood next to her mother's chair until her mother looked up inquiringly, and then she started to whisper the message, but her mother pushed her gently away and reproached, "You are not being very polite to our guest."

"Father says the tomatoes . . ." Rosie said aloud, smiling foolishly.

"Tell him I shall only be a minute," her mother said, speaking the language of Mr. Kuroda.

When Rosie carried the reply to her father, he did not seem to hear and she said again, "Mother says she'll be back in a minute."

"All right, all right," he nodded, and they worked again in silence. But suddenly, her father uttered an incredible noise, exactly like the cork of a bottle popping, and the next Rosie knew, he was stalking angrily toward the house, almost running in fact, and she chased after him crying, "Father! Father! What are you going to do?"

He stopped long enough to order her back to the shed. "Never mind!" he shouted. "Get on with the sorting!"

And from the place in the fields where she stood, frightened and vacillating, Rosie saw her father enter the house. Soon Mr. Kuroda came out alone, putting on his coat. Mr. Kuroda got into his car and backed out down the driveway onto the highway. Next her father emerged, also alone, something in his arms (it was the picture, she realized), and, going over to the bathhouse woodpile, he threw the picture on the ground and picked up the axe. Smashing the picture, glass and all (she heard the explosion faintly), he reached over for the kerosene that was used to encourage the bath fire and poured it over the wreckage. I am dreaming, Rosie said to herself, I am dreaming, but her father, having made sure that his act of cremation was irrevocable, was even then returning to the fields.

Rosie ran past him and toward the house. What had become of her mother? She burst into the parlor and found her mother at the back window watching the dying fire. They watched together until there remained only a feeble smoke under the blazing sun. Her mother was very calm.

"Do you know why I married your father?" she said without turning.

"No," said Rosie. It was the most frightening question she had ever been called upon to answer. Don't tell me now, she wanted to say, tell me tomorrow, tell me next week, don't tell me today. But she knew she would be told now, that the telling would combine with the other violence of the hot afternoon to level her life, her world to the very ground.

It was like a story out of the magazines illustrated in sepia, which she had consumed so greedily for a period until the information had somehow reached her that those wretchedly unhappy autobiographies, offered to her as the testimonials of living men and women, were largely inventions: Her mother, at nineteen, had come to America and married her father as an alternative to suicide.

At eighteen she had been in love with the first son of one of the well-to-do families in her village. The two had met whenever and wherever they could secretly, because it would not have done for his family to see him favor her—

her father had no money, he was a drunkard and a gambler besides. She had learned she was with child; an excellent match had already been arranged for her lover. Despised by her family, she had given premature birth to a stillborn son, who would be seventeen now. Her family did not turn her out, but she could no longer project herself in any direction without refreshing in them the memory of her indiscretion. She wrote to Aunt Taka, her favorite sister in America, threatening to kill herself if Aunt Taka would not send for her. Aunt Taka hastily arranged a marriage with a young man of whom she knew, but lately arrived from Japan, a young man of simple mind, it was said, but of kindly heart. The young man was never told why his unseen betrothed was so eager to hasten the day of meeting.

The story was told perfectly, with neither groping for words nor untoward passion. It was as though her mother had memorized it by heart, reciting it to herself so many times over that its nagging vileness had long since gone.

"I had a brother then?" Rosie asked, for this was what seemed to matter now; she would think about the other later, she assured herself, pushing back the illumination which threatened all that darkness that had hitherto been merely mysterious or even glamorous. "A half-brother?"

"Yes."

"I would have liked a brother," she said.

Suddenly, her mother knelt on the floor and took her by the wrists. "Rosie," she said urgently, "Promise me you will never marry!" Shocked more by the request than the revelation, Rosie stared at the mother's face. Jesus, Jesus, she called silently, not certain whether she was invoking the help of the son of the Carrascos or of God, until there returned sweetly the memory of Jesus' hand, how it had touched her and where. Still her mother waited for an answer, holding her wrists so tightly that her hands were going numb. She tried to pull free. Promise, her mother whispered fiercely, promise. Yes, yes, I promise, Rosie said. But for an instant she turned away, and her mother, hearing the familiar glib agreement, released her. Oh, you, you, you, her eyes and twisted mouth said, you fool. Rosie, covering her face, began at last to cry, and the embrace and consoling hand came much later than she expected.

Grace Paley 1922–

Short-story writer and essayist Grace Paley, often referred to as a "writer's writer," grew up in the Bronx, the daughter of Russian immigrants who spoke both Russian and Yiddish. Influenced by Old and New World cultures, Paley would later draw upon these experiences as she developed stories of humor and sadness about multicultural street life in New York. In an inventive style that is often fragmented, open-ended, and that disregards conventional development of characterization and plot, Paley frequently portrays politically oriented female characters struggling to keep their families intact or persevering on their own. Ivan Gold described Paley's serio-comic stories as ". . . quirky, anguished, funny, loving, deep and antic glimpses into the hearts and lives of children, mothers, lovers, spouses divorced and abandoned, the aging and the old, in a prose as re-silient and unpredictable as one imagines the fate of her characters to be." Paley is the author of three collections of stories: *The Little Disturbances of Man* (1959), *Enormous Changes at the Last Minute* (1974), and *Later the Same Day* (1985). "It may come from my political feelings," Paley told *Ms.* magazine, "but I think art, literature, fiction, poetry, whatever it is, makes justice in the world. That's why it almost always has to be on the side of the underdog." She recently published *Just as I Thought* (1998), a collection of articles, reports, and talks covering thirty years of political and literary activity.

ENORMOUS CHANGES AT THE LAST MINUTE

A young man said he wanted to go to bed with Alexandra because she had an interesting mind. He was a cabdriver and she *had* admired the curly back of his head. Still, she was surprised. He said he would pick her up again in about an hour and a half. Because she was fair and a responsible person, she placed between them a barrier of truthful information. She said, I suppose you don't know many middle-aged women.

You don't look so middle-aged to me. I mean, everyone likes what they like. That is, I'm interested in your point of view, your way of life. Anyway, he said, peering into the mirror, your face is nice and your eyebrows are out of sight!

Make it two hours, she said. I'm visiting my father whom I happen to love.

I love mine too, he said. He just doesn't love me. Too too bad.

O.K. That's enough, she said. Because they had already *had* the following factual and introductory conversation.

How old are your kids?

I have none.

Sorry. Then what do you do for a living?

Children. Early teenage. Adoptions, foster homes. Probation. Troubles— well . . .

Where'd you go to school?

City colleges. What about you?

Oh, me. Lots of places. Antioch. Wisconsin. California. I might go back someday. Some place else though. Maybe Harvard. Why not?

He leaned on his horn to move a sixteen-wheel trailer truck delivering Kleenex to the A & P.

I wish you'd stop that, she said. I hate that kind of driving.

Why? Oh! You're an idealist! He looked through his rearview mirror straight into her eyes. But were you married? Ever?

Once. For years.

Who to?

It's hard to describe. A revolutionist.

Really? Could I know him? What's his name? We say revolutionary nowadays. Oh?

By the way, my name's Dennis. I probably like you, he said.

You do, do you? Well, why should you? And let me ask you something. What do you mean by nowadays?

By the birdseed of St. Francis[1] he said, taking a tiny brogue to the tip of his tongue. I meant no harm.

Nowadays! she said. What does that mean? I guess you think you're kind of brand-new. You're not so brand-new. The telephone was brand-new. The airplane was brand-new. *You've* been seen on earth before.

Wow! he said. He stopped the cab just short of the hospital entrance. He turned to look at her and make decisions. But you're right, he said sweetly. You know the mind *is* an astonishing, long-living, erotic thing.

Is it? she asked. Then she wondered: What is the life expectancy of the mind?

Eighty years, said her father, glad to be useful. Once he had explained electrical storms before you could find the Book of Knowledge. Now in the cave of old age, he continued to amass wonderful information. But he was sick with oldness. His arteries had a hopeless future, and conversation about all that obsolescent tubing often displaced very interesting subjects.

One day he said, Alexandra! Don't show me the sunset again. I'm not interested any more. You know that. She had just pointed to a simple sunset happening outside his hospital window. It was a red ball—all alone, without its evening streaking clouds—a red ball falling hopelessly west, just missing the Hudson River, Jersey City, Chicago, the Great Plains, the Golden Gate—falling, falling.

Then in Russian he sighed some Pushkin.[2] Not for me, the spring. *Nye dyla menya.* . . . He slept. She read the large-print edition of *The Guns of August.*[3] A half hour later, he opened his eyes and told her how, in that morning's *Times,* the Phoenicians had sailed to Brazil in about 500 B.C. A remarkable people. The Vikings too were remarkable. He spoke well of the Chinese, the Jews, the Greeks, the Indians—all the old commercial people. Actually he had never knocked an entire nation. International generosity had been started in him during the late

---

[1] St. Francis of Assisi (1182?–1226) is traditionally depicted preaching to birds.

[2] Aleksandr Pushkin (1799–1837), Russian poet.

[3] A history of the beginning of World War I by Barbara Tuchman, published in 1962.

nineteenth century by his young mother and father, candleholders inside the dark tyranny of the czars. It was childhood training. Thoughtfully, he passed it on.

In the hospital bed next to him, a sufferer named John feared the imminent rise of the blacks of South Africa, the desperate blacks of Chicago, the yellow Chinese, and the Ottoman Turks. He had more reason than Alexandra's father to dread the future because his heart was strong. He would probably live to see it all. He believed the Turks when they came would bring to New York City diseases like cholera, virulent scarlet fever, and particularly leprosy.

Leprosy! for God's sakes! said Alexandra. John! Upset yourself with reality for once! She read aloud from the *Times* about the bombed, burned lepers' colonies in North Vietnam. Her father said, Please, Alexandra, today, no propaganda. Why do you constantly pick on the United States? He remembered the first time he'd seen the American flag on wild Ellis Island. Under its protection and working like a horse, he'd read Dickens,[4] gone to medical school, and shot like a surface-to-air missile right into the middle class.

Then he said, But they shouldn't put a flag in the middle of the chocolate pudding. It's ridiculous.

It's Memorial Day, said the nurse's aide, removing his tray.

In the early evening Dennis stood at the door of each room of Alexandra's apartment. He looked this way and that. Underuse in a time of population stress, he muttered. He entered the kitchen and sniffed the kitchen air. It doesn't matter, he said aloud. He took a fingerful of gravy out of the pot on the stove. Beef stew, he whispered. Then he opened the door to the freezer compartment and said, Sweet Jesus! because there were eleven batches of the same, neatly stacked and frozen. They were for Alexandra's junkies, whose methadone required lots of protein and carbohydrates.

I wouldn't have them in my house. It's a wonder you got a cup and saucer left. Creeps, said Dennis. However, yes indeed, I will eat this stuff. Why? Does it make me think of home or of something else? he asked. I think, a movie I once saw.

Apple turnovers! You know I have to admit it, our commune isn't working too well. Probably because it's in Brooklyn and the food coop[5] isn't together. But it's cool, they've accepted the criticism.

You have lots of junk in here, he pointed out after dinner. He had decided to give the place some respectful attention. He meant armchairs, lamps, desk sets, her grandmother's wedding portrait, and an umbrella stand with two of her father's canes.

Um, said Alexandra, it's rent-controlled.[6]

---

[4] Charles Dickens (1812–1870), English novelist. Ellis Island, in the harbor of New York City, where new immigrants were processed.

[5] Organization for the cooperative purchase of food.

[6] An apartment whose rent is controlled by the city government.

You know what I like to do, Alexandra? I like to sit with a girl and look at a late movie, he said. It's an experience common to Americans at this hour. It's important to be like others, to dig the average dude, you have to be him. Be HIM. It's groovier than a lot of phony gab. You'd be surprised how friendly you get.

I'm not against friendliness, she said, I'm not even against Americans.

They watched half of *A Day at the Races*.[7] This is very relaxing, he said. It's kind of long though, isn't it? Then he began to undress. He held out his arms. He said, Alexandra I really can't wait any more. I'm a sunrise person. I like to go to bed early. Can I stay a few days?

He gave reasons: 1. It was a Memorial Day weekend, and the house in Brooklyn was full of tripping visitors. 2. He was disgusted with them anyway because they'd given up the most beautiful batik work for fashionable tie-dying. 3. He and Alexandra could take some good walks in the morning because all the parks to walk in were the lightest green. He had noticed that the tree on the corner though dying of buses was green at the beginning of many twigs. 4. He could talk to her about the kids, help her to understand their hangups, their incredible virtues. He had missed being one of them by about seven useless years.

So many reasons are not essential, Alexandra said. She offered him a brandy. Holy toads! he said furiously. You *know* I'm not into that. Touched by gloom, he began to remove the heavy shoes he wore for mountain walking. He dropped his pants and stamped on them a couple of times to make sure he and they were disengaged.

Alexandra, in the first summer dress of spring, stood still and watched. She breathed deeply because of having been alone for a year or two. She put her two hands over her ribs to hold her heart in place and also out of modesty to quiet its immodest thud. Then they went to bed in the bedroom and made love until that noisy disturbance ended. She couldn't hear one interior sound. Therefore they slept.

In the morning she became interested in reality again, which she had always liked. She wanted to talk about it. She began with a description of John, her father's neighbor in the hospital.

Turks? Far out! Well he's right. And another thing. Leprosy is coming. It's coming to the Forest Hills Country Fair, the Rikers Island Jamboree, the Fillmore East, and the Ecolocountry Gardens in Westchester.[8] In August.

Reality? A lesson in reality? Am I a cabdriver? No. I drive a cab but I am not a cabdriver. I'm a song hawk. A songmaker. I'm a poet, in other words. Do you know that every black man walking down the street today is a poet? But only one white honky devil in ten. One in ten.

Nowadays I write for the Lepers all the time. Fuck poetry. The Lepers dig me. I dig them.

---

[7] A 1936 comedy starring the Marx Brothers.
[8] All locations in the New York area.

The Lepers? Alexandra said.

Cool! You know them? No? Well, you may have known them under their old name. They used to be called The Split Atom. But they became too popular and their thing is anonymity. That's what they're known for. They'll probably change their name after the summer festivals. They might move to the country and call themselves Winter Moss.

Do you really make a living now?

Oh yes. I do. I do. Among technicians like myself I do.

Now: I financially carry one third of a twelve-person, three-children commune. I only drive a cab to keep on top of the world of illusion, you know, Alexandra, to rap with the bourgeoisies, the fancy whores, the straight ladies visiting their daddies. Oh, excuse me, he said.

Now, Alexandra, imagine this: two bass guitars, a country violin, one piccolo, and drums. The Lepers' theme song! He sat up in bed. The sun shone on his chest. He had begun to think of breakfast, but he sang so that Alexandra could know him better and dig his substantialness.

> *ooooh*
> *first my finger goes goes goes*
> *then my nose*
>   *then baby my toes*
>
> *If you love me this way anyway any day*
> *I'll go your way*
>   *my Little Neck[9] rose*

Well? he asked. He looked at Alexandra. Was she going to cry? I thought you were such a reality freak. Alexandra. That's the way it is in the real world. Anyway! He then said a small prose essay to explain and buttress the poem:

> The kids! the kids! Though terrible troubles hang over them, such as the absolute end of the known world quickly by detonation or slowly through the easygoing destruction of natural resources, they are still, even now, optimistic, humorous, and brave. In fact, they intend enormous changes at the last minute.

Come on, said Alexandra, hardhearted, an enemy of generalization, there are all kinds. My boys aren't like that.

Yes, they are, he said, angry. You bring them around. I'll prove it. Anyway, I love them. He tried for about twenty minutes, forgetting breakfast, to show Alexandra how to look at things in this powerful last-half-of-the-century way. She tried. She had always had a progressive if sometimes reformist disposition, but at that moment, listening to him talk, she could see straight ahead over the thick hot rod of love to solitary age and lonesome death.

But there's nothing to fear my dear girl, her father said. When you get there you will not want to live a hell of a lot. Nothing to fear at all. You will be used

---

[9] A residential section of Queens (in New York City).

up. You are like a coal burning, smoldering. Then there's nothing left to burn. Finished. Believe me, he said, although he hadn't been there yet himself, at that moment you won't mind. Alexandra's face was a bit rumpled, listening.

Don't look at me like that! he said. He was too sensitive to her appearance. He hated her to begin to look older the way she'd had to in the last twenty years. He said, Now *I* have seen people die. A large number. Not one or two. Many. They are good and ready. Pain. Despair. Unconsciousness, nightmares. Perfectly good comas, wrecked by nightmares. They are ready. You will be too, Sashka.[10] Don't worry so much.

Ho ho ho, said John in the next bed listening through the curtains. Doc, I'm not ready. I feel terrible, I got lousy nightmares. I don't sleep a wink. But I'm not ready. I can't piss without this tube. Lonesomeness! Boy! Did you ever see *one* of my kids visiting? No! Still I am *not* ready NOT READY. He spelled it out, looking at the ceiling or through it, to the roof garden for incurables, and from there to God.

The next morning Dennis said, I would rather die than go to the hospital.
For God's sakes why?
Why? Because I hate to be in the hands of strangers. They don't let you take the pills you got that you know work, then if you need one of their pills, even if you buzz, they don't come. The nurse and three interns are making out in the information booth. I've seen it. It's a high counter, she's answering questions, and they're taking turns banging her from behind.

Dennis! You're too dumb. You sound like some superstitious old lady with rape dreams.

That's cool, he said. I *am* an old lady about my health. I mean I like it. I want my teeth to go right on. Right on sister. He began to sing, then stopped. Listen! Your destiny's in their hands. It's up to them. Do you live? Or are you a hippie crawling creep from their point of view? Then die!

Really. Nobody ever decides to let you die. In fact, that's what's wrong. They decide to keep people alive for years after death has set in.

You mean like your father?

Alexandra leaped out of bed stark naked. My father! Why he's got twenty times your zip.

Cool it! he said. Come back. I was just starting to fuck you and you get so freaked.

And another thing. Don't use that word. I hate it. When you're with a woman you have to use the language that's right for her.

What do you want me to say?

I want you to say, I was just starting to make love to you, etc.

Well, that's true, said Dennis, I was. When she returned to him, he only touched the tips of her fingers, though all of her was present. He kissed each

---

[10] Russian diminutive for Alexandra.

finger and said right after each kiss, I want to make love to you. He did this sweetly, not sarcastically.

Dennis, Alexandra said in an embarrassment of recognition, you look like one of my placements, in fact you look like a kid, Billy Platoon. His real name is Platon but he calls himself Platoon so he can go to Vietnam and get killed like his stepbrother. He's a dreamy boy.

Alexandra, you talk a lot, now hush, no politics.

Alexandra continued for a sentence or two. He carries a stick with a ball full of nails attached, like some medieval weapon, in case an enemy from Suffolk Street CIA's him. That's what they call it.

Never heard that before. Besides I'm jealous. And also I'm the enemy from Suffolk Street.

No, no, said Alexandra. Then she noticed in her mother's bedroom bureau mirror across the room a small piece of her naked self. She said, Ugh!

There, there! said Dennis lovingly, caressing what he thought she'd looked at, a couple of rippled inches between her breast and belly. It's natural, Alexandra. Men don't change as much as women. Among all the animals, human females are the only ones to lose estrogen as they get older.

Is that it? she said.

Then there was nothing to talk about for half an hour.

But how come you knew that? she asked. The things you know, Dennis. What for?

Why—for my art, he said. And despite his youth he rested from love the way artists often do in order to sing. He sang:

> Camp out
>   out in the forest daisy
>   under the gallows tree
> with the
>   ace of pentacles[11]
>   and me.
>   daisy flower
> What of the
>   earth's ecology
> you're drivin too fast
> Daisy you're drivin alone
>   Hey Daisy   cut the ignition
>   let the oil
>   back in the stone.

Oh, I like that one. I admire it! Alexandra said. But in fact, is ecology a good word for a song? It's technical. . . .

Any word is good, it's the big word today anyway, said Dennis. It's what you do with the word. The language and the idea, they work it out together.

[11] Card in the mystical Tarot deck.

Really? Where do you get most of your ideas?

I don't know if I want to eat or sleep, he said. I think I just want to nuzzle your titty. Talk talk talk. Most? Well, I would say the majority are from a magazine, the *Scientific American*.

During breakfast, language remained on his mind. Because of this, he was silent. After the pancakes, he said, Actually Alexandra, I *can* use any words I want. And I have. I proved it last week in a conversation just like this one. I asked these blue-eyed cats to give me a dictionary. I just flipped the pages and jabbed and the word I hit was *ophidious*.[12] But I did it, because the word does the dreaming for you. The WORD.

To a tune that was probably "On Top of Old Smoky" he sang:

> The ophidious garden
> was invented by Freud
>
> where three ladies murdered
> oh three ladies murdered
>
> the pricks of the birds
>
> the cobra is buried
> the rattlesnake writhes
>
> in the black snaky garden
> in the blue snaky garden
>
> in the hairs of my wives.[13]

More coffee, please, he said with pride and modesty.

It's better than most of your songs, Alexandra said. It's a poem, isn't it? It is better.

What? What? It is *not* better, it is not, goddamn. It is not. . . . It just isn't . . . oh, excuse me for losing my cool like that.

Forget it sonny, Alexandra said respectfully. I only meant I liked it, but I know, I'm too frank from living alone so much I think. Anyway, how come you always think about wives? Wives, mothers?

Because that's me, said peaceful Dennis. Haven't you noticed it yet? That's my bag. I'm a motherfucker.

Oh, she said, I see. But I'm not a mother, Dennis.

Yes, you are, Alexandra. I've figured out a lot about you. I know. I act like the weekend stub sometimes. But I wrote you a song. Just last night in the cab.

---

[12] Involving snakes.

[13] An allusion to the Gorgons, three sisters in Greek mythology with snakes for hair. Sigmund Freud (1856–1939) interprets this myth as containing phallic symbolism.

I think about you. The Lepers'll never dig it. They don't know too much about life. They're still baby bees trying to make it to the next flower, but some old-timer'll tape it, some sore dude who's been out of it for a couple of years who wants to grow. He'll smell the shit in it.

> Oh
> I know something about you baby
>
> that's sad
> don't be mad
>   baby
> That you will never have children at
>   rest
>   at that beautiful breast
>   my love
>
> But see
>   everywhere you go, children follow you
>   for more
>   many more
>   are the children of your life
>   than the children of the married wife.

That one is out of the Bible, he said.[14] Pa, Alexandra said, don't you think a woman in this life ought to have at least one child?

No doubt about it, he said. You should have when you were married to Granofsky, the Communist. We disagreed. He had no sense of humor. He's probably boring the Cubans to death this minute. But he was an intelligent person otherwise. I would have brilliant grandchildren. They would not necessarily have the same politics.

Then he looked at her, her age and possibilities. He softened. You don't look so bad. You could still marry, dear girl. Then he softened further, thinking of hopeless statistics he had just read about the ratio of women to men. Actually! So what! It's not important, Alexandra. According to the Torah,[15] only the man is commanded to multiply. You are not commanded. You have a child, you don't have, God doesn't care. You don't have one, you call in the maid. You say to your husband, Sweetie, get my maid with child.[16] O.K. Well, your husband has anyway been fooling around with the maid for a couple of years, but now it's a respectable business. Good. You don't have to go through the whole thing, nine months, complications, maybe a Caesarean, no no pronto, a child for the Lord, Hosanna.

[14] Sing, O barren, thou that didst not bear; break forth into singing, and cry aloud, thou that didst not travail with child: for more are the children of the desolate than the children of the married wife" (Isaiah 54:1).

[15] The first five books of the Bible, i.e., according to Judaic law.

[16] A brief retelling of the story of Sarah, Abraham, and Hagar (Genesis 16:1–3).

Pa, she said, several weeks later, but what if I did have a baby?

Don't be a fool, he said. Then he gave her a terrible long medical look, which included her entire body. He said, Why do you ask this question? He became red in the face, which had never happened. He took hold of his chest with his right hand, the hospital buzzer with the left. First, he said, I want the nurse! Now! Then he ordered Alexandra: marry!

Dennis said, I don't know how I got into this shit. It's not right, but because your habits and culture are different, I will compromise. What I suggest is this, Alexandra. The three children in our commune belong to us all. No one knows who the father is. It's far out. I swear—by the cock of our hard-up gods, I swear it's beautiful. One of them might be mine. But she doesn't have any distinguishing marks. Why don't you come and live with us and we'll all raise that kid up to be a decent human and humane being in this world. We need a slightly older person, we really do, with a historic sense. We lack that.

Thank you, Alexandra replied. No.

Her father said, Explain it to me, please. For what purpose did you act out this nonsense? For love? At your age. Money? Some conniver flattered you. You probably made him supper. Some starving ne'er-do-well probably wanted a few meals and said, Why not? This middle-aged fool is an easy mark. She'll give me pot roast at night, bacon and eggs in the morning.

No Pa, no, Alexandra said. Please, you'll get sicker.

John in the next bed dying with a strong heart wrote a little note to him. Doc, you're crazy. Don't leave enemies. That girl is loyal! She hasn't missed a Tues., Thurs., or Sat. Did you ever see one of my kids visit? Something else. I feel worse and worse. But I'm still *not ready*.

I want to tell you one more thing, her father said. You are going to embitter my last days and ruin my life.

After that, Alexandra hoped every day for her father's death, so that she could have a child without ruining his interesting life at the very end of it when ruin is absolutely retroactive.

Finally, Dennis said, Then let me at least share the pad with you. It'll be to *your* advantage.

No, Alexandra said. Please, Dennis. I've got to go to work early. I'm sleepy.

I dig. I've been a joke to you. You've used me in a bad way. That's not cool. That smells under heaven.

No, Alexandra said. Please, shut up. Anyway, how do you know you're the father?

Come on, he said, who else would be?

Alexandra smiled, bit her lip to the edge of blood to show pain politely. She was thinking about the continuity of her work, how to be proud and not lose a productive minute. She thought about the members of her case load one by one.

She said, Dennis, I know exactly what I'm going to do.

In that case, this is it, I'm splitting.

This is what Alexandra did in order to make good use of the events of her life. She invited three pregnant clients who were fifteen and sixteen years old to live with her. She visited each one and explained to them that she was pregnant too, and that her apartment was very large. Although they had disliked her because she'd always worried more about the boys, they moved out of the homes of their bad-tempered parents within a week. At the very first evening meal they began to give Alexandra good advice about men, which she did appreciate years later. She ensured their health and her own and she took notes as well. She established a precedent in social work which would not be followed or even mentioned in state journals for about five years.

Alexandra's father's life was not ruined, nor did he have to die. Shortly before the baby's birth, he fell hard on the bathroom tiles, cracked his skull, dipped the wires of his brain into his heart's blood. Short circuit! He lost twenty, thirty years in the flood, the faces of nephews, in-laws, the names of two Presidents, and a war. His eyes were rounder, he was often awestruck, but he was smart as ever, and able to begin again with fewer scruples to notice and appreciate.

The baby was born and named Dennis for his father. Of course his last name was Granofsky because of Alexandra's husband, Granofsky the Communist.

The Lepers, who had changed their name to the Edible Amanita, taped the following song in his tiny honor. It was called "Who? I."

The lyrics are simple. They are:

Who is the father?
Who is the father
Who is the father

I!   I!   I!   I!

I am the father
I am the father
I am the father

Dennis himself sang the solo which was I! I! I! I! in a hoarse enraged prophetic voice. He had been brave to acknowledge the lyrics. After a thirty-eight-hour marathon encounter at his commune, he was asked to leave. The next afternoon he moved to a better brownstone about four blocks away where occasional fatherhood was expected.

On the baby's third birthday, Dennis and the Fair Fields of Corn produced a folk-rock album because that was the new sound and exciting. It was called *For Our Son*. Tuned-in listeners could hear how taps played by the piccolo about forty times a verse flitted in and out of the long dark drum rolls, the ordinary banjo chords, and the fiddle tune which was something but not exactly like "Lullaby and Good Night."

Will you come to see me Jack
        When I'm old and very shaky?
Yes I will for you're my dad
        And you've lost your last old lady
        Though you traveled very far
To the highlands and the badlands
        And ripped off the family car
Still, old dad, I won't forsake you.

Will you come to see me Jack?
        Though I'm really not alone.
Still I'd like to see my boy
        For we're lonesome for our own.
        Yes I will for you're my dad
Though you dumped me and my brothers
        And you sizzled down the road
Loving other fellows' mothers.

Will you come to see me Jack?
        Though I look like time boiled over.
Growing old is not a lark.
        Yes I will for you're my dad
        Though we never saw a nickel
As we struggled up life's ladder
        I will call you and together
We will cuddle up and see
        What the weather's like in Key West
On the old-age home TV.

This song was sung coast to coast and became famous from the dark Maine woods to Texas's shining gulf. It was responsible for a statistical increase in visitors to old-age homes by the apprehensive middle-aged and the astonished young.

Denise Levertov 1923–1997

Born in England, Denise Levertov began writing poetry at the age of twelve, when she mailed several poems to T. S. Eliot, who responded with encouragement. At fifteen, she was regularly corresponding with poet-critic Herbert Read. And it is said that her poetry often demonstrates her knowledge and appreciation of those whom she studied: Her early poems are often called neo-Romantic, while her later writing reflects the modernism of Ezra Pound, Wallace Stevens, H.D., and William Carlos Williams. Poet Kenneth Rexroth notes that Levertov's style is ". . . characterized by its low visibility. Her poems are so carefully wrought that the workmanship goes by unnoticed. They seem like speech, heightened and purified." An essayist as well as poet, Levertov has been described by critic Doris Earnshaw as "fitted by birth and political destiny to voice the terrors and pleasures of the twentieth century. . . . She has published poetry since the 1940s that speaks of the great contemporary themes: Eros, solitude, community, war."

THE ACHE OF MARRIAGE

The ache of marriage:

thigh and tongue, beloved,
are heavy with it,
it throbs in the teeth

We look for communion   5
and are turned away, beloved,
each and each

It is leviathan[1] and we
in its belly
looking for joy, some joy   10
not to be known outside it

two by two in the ark[2] of
the ache of it.

DIVORCING

One garland
of flowers, leaves, thorns
was twined round our two necks.
Drawn tight, it could choke us,
yet we loved its scratchy grace,   5
our fragrant yoke.

[1] A reference to the story of Jonah, who was swallowed by a sea monster, or leviathan (Book of Jonah).

[2] A reference to Noah's ark, in which animals of every species were preserved from the flood that destroyed all other life (Genesis).

We were Siamese twins.
Our blood's not sure
if it can circulate,
now we are cut apart.   10
Something in each of us is waiting
to see if we can survive,
severed.

BEDTIME

We are a meadow where the bees hum,
mind and body are almost one

as the fire snaps in the stove
and our eyes close,

and mouth to mouth, the covers   5
pulled over our shoulders,

we drowse as horses drowse afield,
in accord; though the fall cold

surrounds our warm bed, and though
by day we are singular and often lonely.   10

Nadine Gordimer 1923–

A short-story writer, novelist, essayist, and critic, Nadine Gordimer's work has made her the "conscience" of South Africa, where she was born, raised, and where she still lives. In 1991, she was awarded the Nobel Prize in Literature, which verified the role of Gordimer's fiction in challenging the doctrine of apartheid and policies related to it. So compelling were Gordimer's critiques of apartheid that several of her novels were actually banned from her own country. Her novels and short stories include *The Lying Days* (1953), *Occasion for Loving* (1963), *A Sport of Nature* (1987), *Not for Publication and Other Stories* (1965), and *Jump and Other Stories* (1991). Critics write that her fiction often portrays "individuals who struggle to avoid, confront, or change the conditions under which they live," and "ordinary people defying apartheid in their daily lives." Critic

Edith Milton suggests that Gordimer "looks beyond political and social outrage to the sad contradiction of the human spirit, which delivers to those in power an even worse sentence of pain than they themselves can pass upon their victims."

TOWN AND COUNTRY LOVERS[1]

Dr. Franz-Josef von Leinsdorf is a geologist absorbed in his work; wrapped up in it, as the saying goes—year after year the experience of this work enfolds him, swaddling him away from the landscapes the cities and the people, wherever he lives: Peru, New Zealand, the United States. He's always been like that, his mother could confirm from their native Austria. There, even as a handsome small boy he presented only his profile to her: turned away to his bits of rock and stone. His few relaxations have not changed much since then. An occasional skiing trip, listening to music, reading poetry—Rainer Maria Rilke[2] once stayed in his grandmother's hunting lodge in the forests of Styria and the boy was introduced to Rilke's poems while very young.

Layer upon layer, country after country, wherever his work takes him— and now he has been almost seven years in Africa. First the Côte d'Ivoire, and the past five years, South Africa. The shortage of skilled manpower brought about his recruitment here. He has no interest in the politics of the countries he works in. His private preoccupation-within-the-preoccupation of his work has been research into underground water-courses, but the mining company that employs him in a senior though not executive capacity is interested only in mineral discovery. So he is much out in the field—which is the veld,[3] here— seeking new gold, copper, platinum and uranium deposits. When he is at home—on this particular job, in this particular country, this city—he lives in a two-roomed flat in a suburban block with a landscaped garden, and does his shopping at a supermarket conveniently across the street. He is not married— yet. That is how his colleagues, and the typists and secretaries at the mining company's head office, would define his situation. Both men and women would describe him as a good-looking man, in a foreign way, with the lower half of the face dark and middle-aged (his mouth is thin and curving, and no matter how close-shaven his beard shows like fine shot embedded in the skin round mouth and chin) and the upper half contradictorily young, with deep-set eyes (some would say gray, some black), thick eyelashes and brows. A tangled gaze: through which concentration and gleaming thoughtfulness perhaps

---

[1] This is the first of two stories that Gordimer published as a sequence, under the title *Town and Country Lovers. One and Two;* this selection originally appeared in *The New Yorker* as *City Lovers.*

[2] German poet (1875–1926).

[3] Open grassland in southern Africa.

appear as fire and languor. It is this that the women in the office mean when they remark he's not unattractive. Although the gaze seems to promise, he has never invited any one of them to go out with him. There is the general assumption he probably has a girl who's been picked for him, he's bespoken by one of his own kind, back home in Europe where he comes from. Many of these well-educated Europeans have no intention of becoming permanent immigrants; neither the remnant of white colonial life nor idealistic involvement with Black Africa appeals to them.

One advantage, at least, of living in underdeveloped or half-developed countries is that flats are serviced. All Dr. von Leinsdorf has to do for himself is buy his own supplies and cook an evening meal if he doesn't want to go to a restaurant. It is simply a matter of dropping in to the supermarket on his way from his car to his flat after work in the afternoon. He wheels a trolley up and down the shelves, and his simple needs are presented to him in the form of tins, packages, plastic-wrapped meat, cheeses, fruit and vegetables, tubes, bottles. . . . At the cashiers counters where customers must converge and queue[4] there are racks of small items uncategorized, for last-minute purchase. Here, as the colored girl cashier punches the adding machine, he picks up cigarettes and perhaps a packet of salted nuts or a bar of nougat. Or razor-blades, when he remembers he's running short. One evening in winter he saw that the cardboard display was empty of the brand of blades he preferred, and he drew the cashier's attention to this. These young colored girls are usually pretty unhelpful, taking money and punching their machines in a manner that asserts with the time-serving obstinacy of the half-literate the limit of any responsibility towards customers, but this one ran an alert glance over the selection of razor-blades, apologized that she was not allowed to leave her post, and said she would see that the stock was replenished "next time." A day or two later she recognized him, gravely, as he took his turn before her counter—"I ahssed them, but it's out of stock. You can't get it. I did ahss about it." He said this didn't matter. "When it comes in, I can keep a few packets for you." He thanked her.

He was away with the prospectors the whole of the next week. He arrived back in town just before nightfall on Friday, and was on his way from car to flat with his arms full of briefcase, suitcase and canvas bags when someone stopped him by standing timidly in his path. He was about to dodge round unseeingly on the crowded pavement but she spoke. "We got the blades in now. I didn't see you in the shop this week, but I kept some for when you come. So . . . "

He recognized her. He had never seen her standing before, and she was wearing a coat. She was rather small and finely-made, for one of them. The coat was skimpy but no big backside jutted. The cold brought an apricot-graining of warm color to her cheekbones, beneath which a very small face was quite delicately hollowed, and the skin was smooth, the subdued satiny color of certain yellow wood. That crêpey hair, but worn drawn back flat and in a little knot

---

[4] Form lines.

pushed into one of the cheap wool chignons that (he recognized also) hung in the miscellany of small goods along with the razor-blades, at the supermarket. He said thanks, he was in a hurry, he'd only just got back from a trip—shifting the burdens he carried, to demonstrate. "Oh shame." She acknowledged his load. "But if you want I can run in and get it for you quickly. If you want."

He saw at once it was perfectly clear that all the girl meant was that she would go back to the supermarket, buy the blades and bring the packet to him there where he stood, on the pavement. And it seemed that it was this certainty that made him say, in the kindly tone of assumption used for an obliging under-ling, "I live just across there—*Atlantis*—that flat building. Could you drop them by, for me—number seven-hundred-and-eighteen, seventh floor—"

She had not before been inside one of these big flat buildings near where she worked. She lived a bus- and train-ride away to the West of the city, but this side of the black townships, in a township for people her tint. There was a pool with ferns, not plastic, and even a little waterfall pumped electrically over rocks, in the entrance of the building *Atlantis;* she didn't wait for the lift marked goods but took the one meant for whites and a white woman with one of those sausage-dogs on a lead got in with her but did not pay her any attention. The corridors leading to the flats were nicely glassed-in, not draughty.

He wondered if he should give her a twenty-cent piece for her trouble—ten cents would be right for a black; but she said, "Oh no—please, here—" standing outside his open door and awkwardly pushing back at his hand the change from the money he'd given her for the razor-blades. She was smiling, for the first time, in the dignity of refusing a tip. It was difficult to know how to treat these people, in this country, to know what they expected. In spite of her embarrass-ing refusal of the coin, she stood there, completely unassuming, fists thrust down the pockets of her cheap coat against the cold she'd come in from, rather pretty thin legs neatly aligned, knee to knee, ankle to ankle.

"Would you like a cup of coffee or something?"

He couldn't very well take her into his study-cum-living-room and offer her a drink. She followed him to his kitchen, but at the sight of her pulling out the single chair to drink her cup of coffee at the kitchen table, he said, "No—bring it in here—" and led the way into the big room where, among his books and his papers, his files of scientific correspondence (and the cigar boxes of stamps from the envelopes), his racks of records, his specimens of minerals and rocks, he lived alone.

It was no trouble to her; she saved him the trips to the supermarket and brought him his groceries two or three times a week. All he had to do was to leave a list and the key under the doormat, and she would come up in her lunch-hour to collect them, returning to put his supplies in the flat after work. Sometimes he was home and sometimes not. He bought a box of chocolates and left it, with a note, for her to find; and that was acceptable, apparently, as a gratuity.

Her eyes went over everything in the flat although her body tried to conceal its sense of being out of place by remaining as still as possible, holding its contours in the chair offered her as a stranger's coat is set aside and remains exactly as left until the owner takes it up to go. "You collect?"

"Well, these are specimens—connected with my work."

"My brother used to collect. Miniatures. With brandy and whisky and that, in them. From all over. Different countries."

The second time she watched him grinding coffee for the cup he had offered her she said, "You always do that? Always when you make coffee?"

"But of course. Is it no good, for you? Do I make it too strong?"

"Oh it's just I'm not used to it. We buy it ready—you know, it's in a bottle, you just add a bit to the milk or water."

He laughed, instructive: "That's not coffee, that's a synthetic flavoring. In my country we drink only real coffee, fresh, from the beans—you smell how good it is as it's being ground?"

She was stopped by the caretaker and asked what she wanted in the building. Heavy with the *bona fides*[5] of groceries clutched to her body, she said she was working at number 718, on the seventh floor. The caretaker did not tell her not to use the whites' lift; after all, she was not black; her family was very light-skinned.

There was the item "gray button for trousers" on one of his shopping lists. She said as she unpacked the supermarket carrier, "Give me the pants, so long, then," and sat on his sofa that was always gritty with fragments of pipe tobacco, sewing in and out through the four holes of the button with firm, fluent movements of the right hand, gestures supplying the articulacy missing from her talk. She had a little yokel's, peasant's (he thought of it) gap between her two front teeth when she smiled that he didn't much like, but, face ellipsed to three-quarter angle, eyes cast down in concentration with soft lips almost closed, this didn't matter. He said, watching her sew, "You're a good girl"; and touched her.

She remade the bed every late afternoon when they left it and she dressed again before she went home. After a week there was a day when late afternoon became evening, and they were still in the bed.

"Can't you stay the night?"

"My mother," she said.

"Phone her. Make an excuse." He was a foreigner. He had been in the country five years, but the didn't understand that people don't usually have telephones in their houses, where she lived. She got up to dress. He didn't want that tender body to go out in the night cold and kept hindering her with the interruption of his hands; saying nothing. Before she put on her coat, when the body had already disappeared, he spoke. "But you must make some arrangement."

"Oh my mother!" Her face opened to fear and vacancy he could not read.

He was not entirely convinced the woman would think of her daughter as some pure and unsullied virgin. . . . "Why?"

The girl said, "S'e'll be scared. S'e'll be scared we get caught."

---

[5] In good faith (Latin, literal trans.); evidence of qualifications or genuineness.

"Don't tell her anything. Say I'm employing you." In this country he was working in now there were generally rooms on the roofs of flat buildings for tenants' servants.

She said: "That's what I told the caretaker."

She ground fresh coffee beans every time he wanted a cup while he was working at night. She never attempted to cook anything until she had watched in silence while he did it the way he liked, and she learned to reproduce exactly the simple dishes he preferred. She handled his pieces of rock and stone, at first admiring the colors— "It'd make a beautiful ring or a necklace, ay." Then he showed her the striations, the formation of each piece, and explained what each was, and how, in the long life of the earth, it had been formed. He named the mineral it yielded, and what that was used for. He worked at his papers, writing, writing, every night, so it did not matter that they could not go out together to public places. On Sundays she got into his car in the basement garage and they drove to the country and picnicked away up in the Magaliesberg, where there was no one. He read or poked about among the rocks; they climbed together, to the mountain pools. He taught her to swim. She had never seen the sea. She squealed and shrieked in the water, showing the gap between her teeth, as—it crossed his mind—she must do when among her own people. Occasionally he had to go out to dinner at the houses of colleagues from the mining company; she sewed and listened to the radio in the flat and he found her in the bed, warm and already asleep, by the time he came in. He made his way into her body without speaking; she made him welcome without a word. Once he put on evening dress for a dinner at his country's consulate; watching him brush one or two fallen hairs from the shoulders of the dark jacket that sat so well on him, she saw a huge room, all chandeliers and people dancing some dance from a costume film—stately, hand-to-hand. She supposed he was going to fetch, in her place in the car, a partner for the evening. They never kissed when either left the flat; he said, suddenly, kindly, pausing as he picked up cigarettes and keys, "Don't be lonely." And added, "Wouldn't you like to visit your family sometimes, when I have to go out?"

He had told her he was going home to his mother in the forests and mountains of his country near the Italian border (he showed her on the map) after Christmas. She had not told him how her mother, not knowing there was any other variety, assumed he was a medical doctor, so she had talked to her about the doctor's children and the doctor's wife who was a very kind lady, glad to have someone who could help out in the surgery as well as the flat.

She remarked wonderingly on his ability to work until midnight or later, after a day at work. She was so tired when she came home from her cash register at the supermarket that once dinner was eaten she could scarcely keep awake. He explained in a way she could understand that while the work she did was repetitive, undemanding of any real response from her intelligence, requiring little mental or physical effort and therefore unrewarding, his work was his greatest interest, it taxed his mental capacities to their limit, exercised all his concentration, and rewarded him constantly as much with the excitement of a problem presented as with the satisfaction of a problem solved. He said later, putting away his papers, speaking out of a silence: "Have you done other kinds of work?" She said, "I was in a clothing factory before. Sportbeau shirts; you know? But the pay's better in the shop."

Of course. Being a conscientious newspaper-reader in every country he lived in, he was aware that it was only recently that the retail consumer trade in this one had been allowed to employ coloreds as shop assistants; even punching a cash register represented advancement. With the continuing shortage of semi-skilled whites a girl like this might be able to edge a little farther into the white-collar category. He began to teach her to type. He was aware that her English was poor, even though, as a foreigner, in his ears her pronounciation did not offend, nor categorize her as it would in those of someone of his education whose mother tongue was English. He corrected her grammatical mistakes but missed the less obvious ones because of his own sometimes exotic English usage—she continued to use the singular pronoun "it" when what was required was the plural "they." Because he was a foreigner (although so clever, as she saw) she was less inhibited than she might have been by the words she knew she misspelled in her typing. While she sat at the typewriter she thought how one day she would type notes for him, as well as making coffee the way he liked it, and taking him inside her body without saying anything, and sitting (even if only through the empty streets of quiet Sundays) beside him in his car, like a wife.

On a summer night near Christmas—he had already bought and hidden a slightly showy but nevertheless good watch he thought she would like—there was a knocking at the door that brought her out of the bathroom and him to his feet, at his work-table. No one over came to the flat at night; he had no friends intimate enough to drop in without warning. The summons was an imperious banging that did not pause and clearly would not stop until the door was opened.

She stood in the open bathroom doorway gazing at him across the passage into the living-room; her bare feet and shoulders were free of a big bath-towel. She said nothing, did not even whisper. The flat seemed to shake with the strong unhurried blows.

He made as if to go to the door, at last, but now she ran and clutched him by both arms. She shook her head wildly; her lips drew back but her teeth were clenched, she didn't speak. She pulled him into the bedroom, snatched some clothes from the clean laundry laid out on the bed and got into the wall-cupboard thrusting the key at his hand. Although his arms and calves felt weakly cold he was horrified, distastefully embarrassed at the sight of her pressed back crouching there under his suits and coat; it was horrible and ridiculous. *Come out!* he whispered. *No! Come out!* She hissed: *Where? Where can I go?*

Never mind! Get out of there!

He put out his hand to grasp her. At bay, she said with all the force of her terrible whisper, baring the gap in her teeth: *I'll throw myself out the window.*

She forced the key into his hand like the handle of a knife. He closed the door on her face and drove the key home in the lock, then dropped it among coins in his trouser pocket.

He unslotted the chain that was looped across the flat door. He turned the serrated knob of the Yale lock. The three policemen, two in plain clothes, stood there without impatience although they had been banging on the door for several minutes. The big dark one with an elaborate moustache held out in a hand wearing a plaited gilt ring some sort of identity card.

Dr. von Leinsdorf said quietly, the blood coming strangely back to legs and arms, "What is it?"

The sergeant told him they knew there was a colored girl in the flat. They had had information; "I been watching this flat three months, I know."

"I am alone here." Dr. von Leinsdorf did not raise his voice.

"I know, I know who is here. Come — " And the sergeant and his two assistants went into the living-room, the kitchen, the bathroom (the sergeant picked up a bottle of after-shave cologne, seemed to study the French label) and the bedroom. The assistants removed the clean laundry that was laid upon the bed and then turned back the bedding, carrying the sheets over to be examined by the sergeant under the lamp. They talked to one another in Afrikaans, which the Doctor did not understand. The sergeant himself looked under the bed, and lifted the long curtains at the window. The wall cupboard was of the kind that has no knobs; he saw that it was locked and began to ask in Afrikaans, then politely changed to English, "Give us the key."

Dr. von Leinsdorf said, "I'm sorry, I left it at my office — I always lock and take my keys with me in the mornings."

"It's no good, man, you better give me the key."

He smiled a little, reasonably. "It's on my office desk."

The assistants produced a screwdriver and he watched while they inserted it where the cupboard doors met, gave it quick, firm but not forceful leverage. He heard the lock give.

She had been naked, it was true, when they knocked. But now she was wearing a long-sleeved T-shirt with an appliquéd butterfly motif on one breast, and a pair of jeans. Her feet were still bare; she had managed, by feel, in the dark, to get into some of the clothing she had snatched from the bed, but she had no shoes. She had perhaps been weeping behind the cupboard door (her cheeks looked stained) but now her face was sullen and she was breathing heavily, her diaphragm contracting and expanding exaggeratedly and her breasts pushing against the cloth. It made her appear angry; it might simply have been that she was half-suffocated in the cupboard and needed oxygen. She did not look at Dr. von Leinsdorf. She would not reply to the sergeant's questions.

They were taken to the police station where they were at once separated and in turn led for examination by the district surgeon. The man's underwear was taken away and examined, as the sheets had been, for signs of his seed. When the girl was undressed, it was discovered that beneath her jeans she was wearing a pair of men's briefs with his name on the neatly-sewn laundry tag; in her haste, she had taken the wrong garment to her hiding-place.

Now she cried, standing there before the district surgeon in a man's underwear.

He courteously pretended not to notice. He handed briefs, jeans and T-shirt round the door, and motioned her to lie on a white-sheeted high table where he placed her legs apart, resting in stirrups, and put into her where the other had made his way so warmly a cold hard instrument that expanded wider and wider. Her thighs and knees trembled uncontrollably while the doctor looked into her and touched her deep inside with more hard instruments, carrying wafers of gauze.

When she came out of the examining room back to the charge office, Dr. von Leinsdorf was not there; they must have taken him somewhere else. She spent what was left of the night in a cell, as he must be doing; but early in the morning she was released and taken home to her mother's house in the colored township by a white man who explained he was the clerk of the lawyer who had been engaged for her by Dr. von Leinsdorf. Dr. von Leinsdorf, the clerk said, had also been bailed out that morning. He did not say when, or if, she would see him again.

A statement made by the girl to the police was handed in to Court when she and the man appeared to meet charges of contravening the Immorality Act in a Johannesburg flat on the night of—December, 19—. *I lived with the white man in his flat. He had intercourse with me sometimes. He gave me tablets to take to prevent me becoming pregnant.*

Interviewed by the Sunday papers, the girl said, "I'm sorry for the sadness brought to my mother." She said she was one of nine children of a female laundry worker. She had left school in Standard Three[6] because there was no money at home for gym clothes or a school blazer. She had worked as a machinist in a factory and a cashier in a supermarket. Dr. von Leinsdorf taught her to type his notes.

Dr. Franz-Josef von Leinsdorf, described as the grandson of a baroness, a cultured man engaged in international mineralogical research, said he accepted social distinctions between people but didn't think they should be legally imposed. "Even in my own country it's difficult for a person from a higher class to marry one from a lower class."

The two accused gave no evidence. They did not greet or speak to each other in Court. The Defense argued that the sergeant's evidence that they had been living together as man and wife was hearsay. (The woman with the dachshund, the caretaker?) The magistrate acquitted them because the State failed to prove carnal intercourse had taken place on the night of—December, 19—.

The girl's mother was quoted, with photograph, in the Sunday papers: "I won't let my daughter work as a servant for a white man again."

---

[6] South African equivalent of eighth grade.

Jane Cooper 1924–

Born in Atlantic City, New Jersey, Jane Cooper attended Vassar College from 1942–1944, received her B.A. from the University of Wisconsin and her M.A. from the University of Iowa. Beginning as poet-in-residence and professor of creative writing and literature at Sarah Lawrence College in 1950, Cooper has garnered numerous honors and awards in her career, including fellowships from the National Endowment for the Arts, Guggenheim Foundation, Ingram Merrill Foundation, and Bunting Institute of Radcliffe College. Additionally, she received the Award in Literature from the American Academy of Arts and Letters, the Shelley Memorial Award, and was the 1996–97 New York State Poet. Cooper's books of poetry include *Green Notebook, Winter Road* (1994), a finalist for the Lenore Marshall Poetry Prize; *Scaffolding: Selected Poems* (1993); *Maps and Windows* (1974); and *The Weather of Six Mornings* (1969), winner of the Lamont award. She is a visiting faculty member to the Iowa Writers' Workshop.

RENT

If you want my apartment, sleep in it
but let's have a clear understanding:
the books are still free agents.

If the rocking chair's arms surround you
they can also let you go,   5
they can shape the air like a body.

I don't want your rent, I want
a radiance of attention
like the candle's flame when we eat,

I mean a kind of awe   10
attending the spaces between us—
Not a roof but a field of stars.

Flannery O'Connor 1925–1964

Considered one of the finest short-story writers of the twentieth century, Flannery O'Connor chose the South as the backdrop of her fiction. Sometimes referred to as "the maker of grotesques," her dark humor often highlights the distortions of contemporary religion and is filled with keen mockery of her characters' banal lives and their cliché-ridden conversations about life, death, and the universe. Many of her characters face a violent spiritual struggle or are confronted by violence for which their ingrained, habitual behavior is completely unprepared. Born in Savannah, Georgia, O'Connor was educated at Georgia State College for Women and the University of Iowa's Writers' Workshop. At Iowa she won the Rinehart-Iowa prize for work-in-progress, which eventually became her first novel, *Wise Blood* (1952), a masterpiece of black humor about a religious fanatic who preaches "a church without Christ, where the blind stay blind, the lame stay lame and them that's dead stay that way." In 1950, at the age of twenty-five, O'Connor was diagnosed with lupus erythematosus, an incurable degenerative blood disease that had slowly killed her father ten years earlier. She spent the last fourteen years of her life writing and raising peacocks on her mother's farm in Milledgeville, Georgia. Her other works include short-story collection *A Good Man Is Hard to Find* (1955) and *The Violent Bear It Away*, a novel published in 1960. Her second collection of short stories, *Everything That Rises Must Converge*, was published posthumously in 1965.

GOOD COUNTRY PEOPLE

Besides the neutral expression that she wore when she was alone, Mrs. Freeman had two others, forward and reverse, that she used for all her human dealings. Her forward expression was steady and driving like the advance of a heavy truck. Her eyes never swerved to left or right but turned as the story turned as if they followed a yellow line down the center of it. She seldom used the other expression because it was not often necessary for her to retract a statement, but when she did, her face came to a complete stop, there was an almost imperceptible movement of her black eyes, during which they seemed to be receding, and then the observer would see that Mrs. Freeman, though she might stand there as real as several grain sacks thrown on top of each other, was no longer there in spirit. As for getting anything across to her when this was the case, Mrs. Hopewell had given it up. She might talk her head off. Mrs. Freeman could never be brought to admit herself wrong on any point. She would stand there and if she could be brought to say anything, it was something like, "Well, I wouldn't of said it was and I wouldn't of said it wasn't," or letting her gaze range over the top kitchen shelf where there was an assortment of dusty bottles, she might remark, "I see you ain't ate many of them figs you put up last summer."

They carried on their important business in the kitchen at breakfast. Every morning Mrs. Hopewell got up at seven o'clock and lit her gas heater and Joy's. Joy was her daughter, a large blonde girl who had an artificial leg. Mrs. Hopewell thought of her as a child though she was thirty-two years old and highly educated. Joy would get up while her mother was eating and lumber into the bathroom and slam the door, and before long, Mrs. Freeman would arrive at the back door. Joy would hear her mother call, "Come on in," and then they would talk for a while in low voices that were indistinguishable in the bathroom. By the time Joy came in, they had usually finished the weather report and were on one or the other of Mrs. Freeman's daughters, Glynese or Carramae. Joy called them Glycerin and Caramel. Glynese, a redhead, was eighteen and had many admirers; Carramae, a blonde, was only fifteen but already married and pregnant. She could not keep anything on her stomach. Every morning Mrs. Freeman told Mrs. Hopewell how many times she had vomited since the last report.

Mrs. Hopewell liked to tell people that Glynese and Carramae were two of the finest girls she knew and that Mrs. Freeman was a *lady* and that she was never ashamed to take her anywhere or introduce her to anybody they might meet. Then she would tell how she had happened to hire the Freemans in the first place and how they were a godsend to her and how she had had them four years. The reason for her keeping them so long was that they were not trash. They were good country people. She had telephoned the man whose name they had given as a reference and he had told her that Mr. Freeman was a good farmer but that his wife was the nosiest woman ever to walk the earth. "She's got to be into everything," the man said. "If she don't get there before the dust settles, you can bet she's dead, that's all. She'll want to know all your business. I can stand him real good," he had said, "but me nor my wife neither could have stood that woman one more minute on this place." That had put Mrs. Hopewell off for a few days.

She had hired them in the end because there were no other applicants but she had made up her mind beforehand exactly how she would handle the woman. Since she was the type who had to be into everything, then, Mrs. Hopewell had decided, she would not only let her be into everything, she would *see to it* that she was into everything—she would give her the responsibility of everything, she would put her in charge. Mrs. Hopewell had no bad qualities of her own but she was able to use other people's in such a constructive way that she never felt the lack. She had hired the Freemans and she had kept them four years.

Nothing is perfect. This was one of Mrs. Hopewell's favorite sayings. Another was: that is life! And still another, the most important, was: well, other people have their opinions too. She would make these statements, usually at the table, in a tone of gentle insistence as if no one held them but her, and the large hulking Joy, whose constant outrage had obliterated every expression from her face, would stare just a little to the side of her, her eyes icy blue, with the look of someone who has achieved blindness by an act of will and means to keep it.

When Mrs. Hopewell said to Mrs. Freeman that life was like that, Mrs. Freeman would say, "I always said so myself." Nothing had been arrived at by anyone that had not first been arrived at by her. She was quicker than Mr. Freeman. When Mrs. Hopewell said to her after they had been on the place a while, "You know, you're the wheel behind the wheel, and winked," Mrs. Freeman had said, "I know it. I've always been quick. It's some that are quicker than others."

"Everybody is different," Mrs. Hopewell said.

"Yes, most people is," Mrs. Freeman said.

"It takes all kinds to make the world."

"I always said it did myself."

The girl was used to this kind of dialogue for breakfast and more of it for dinner; sometimes they had it for supper too. When they had no guest they ate in the kitchen because that was easier. Mrs. Freeman always managed to arrive at some point during the meal and to watch them finish it. She would stand in the doorway if it were summer but in the winter she would stand with one elbow on top of the refrigerator and look down on them, or she would stand by the gas heater, lifting the back of her skirt slightly. Occasionally she would stand against the wall and roll her head from side to side. At no time was she in any hurry to leave. All this was very trying on Mrs. Hopewell but she was a woman of great patience. She realized that nothing is perfect and that in the Freemans she had good country people and that if, in this day and age, you get good country people, you had better hang onto them.

She had had plenty of experience with trash. Before the Freemans she had averaged one tenant family a year. The wives of these farmers were not the kind you would want to be around you for very long. Mrs. Hopewell, who had divorced her husband long ago, needed someone to walk over the fields with her; and when Joy had to be impressed for these services, her remarks were usually so ugly and her face so glum that Mrs. Hopewell would say, "If you can't come pleasantly, I don't want you at all," to which the girl, standing square and rigid-shouldered with her neck thrust slightly forward, would reply, "If you want me, here I am—LIKE I AM."

Mrs Hopewell excused this attitude because of the leg (which had been shot off in a hunting accident when Joy was ten). It was hard for Mrs. Hopewell to realize that her child was thirty-two now and that for more than twenty years she had had only one leg. She thought of her still as a child because it tore her heart to think instead of the poor stout girl in her thirties who had never danced a step or had any *normal* good times. Her name was really Joy but as soon as she was twenty-one and away from home, she had had it legally changed. Mrs. Hopewell was certain that she had thought and thought until she had hit upon the ugliest name in any language. Then she had gone and had the beautiful name, Joy, changed without telling her mother until after she had done it. Her legal name was Hulga.

When Mrs. Hopewell thought the name, Hulga, she thought of the broad blank hull of a battleship. She would not use it. She continued to call her Joy to which the girl responded but in a purely mechanical way.

Hulga had learned to tolerate Mrs. Freeman who saved her from taking walks with her mother. Even Glynese and Carramae were useful when they occupied attention that might otherwise have been directed at her. At first she had thought she could not stand Mrs. Freeman for she had found that it was not possible to be rude to her. Mrs. Freeman would take on strange resentments and for days together she would be sullen but the source of her displeasure was always obscure; a direct attack, a positive leer, blatant ugliness to her face—these never touched her. And without warning one day, she began calling her Hulga.

She did not call her that in front of Mrs. Hopewell who would have been incensed but when she and the girl happened to be out of the house together, she would say something and add the name Hulga to the end of it, and the big spectacled Joy-Hulga would scowl and redden as if her privacy had been intruded upon. She considered the name her personal affair. She had arrived at it first purely on the basis of its ugly sound and then the full genius of its fitness had struck her. She had a vision of the name working like the ugly sweating Vulcan who stayed in the furnace and to whom, presumably, the goddess had to come when called.[1] She saw it as the name of her highest creative act. One of her major triumphs was that her mother had not been able to turn her dust into Joy, but the greater one was that she had been able to turn it herself into Hulga. However, Mrs. Freeman's relish for using the name only irritated her. It was as if Mrs. Freeman's beady steel-pointed eyes had penetrated far enough behind her face to reach some secret fact. Something about her seemed to fascinate Mrs. Freeman and then one day Hulga realized that it was the artificial leg. Mrs. Freeman had a special fondness for the details of secret infections, hidden deformities, assaults upon children. Of diseases, she preferred the lingering or incurable. Hulga had heard Mrs. Hopewell give her the details of the hunting accident, how the leg had been literally blasted off, how she had never lost consciousness. Mrs. Freeman could listen to it any time as if it had happened an hour ago.

When Hulga stumped into the kitchen in the morning (she could walk without making the awful noise but she made it—Mrs. Hopewell was certain—because it was ugly-sounding), she glanced at them and did not speak. Mrs. Hopewell would be in her red kimono with her hair tied around her head in rags. She would be sitting at the table, finishing her breakfast and Mrs. Freeman would be hanging by her elbow outward from the refrigerator, looking down at

[1] Vulcan was the Greek god of fire whom Venus, goddess of love, "presumably" obeyed as her consort.

the table. Hulga always put her eggs on the stove to boil and then stood over them with her arms folded, and Mrs. Hopewell would look at her—a kind of indirect gaze divided between her and Mrs. Freeman—and would think that if she would only keep herself up a little, she wouldn't be so bad looking. There was nothing wrong with her face that a pleasant expression wouldn't help. Mrs. Hopewell said that people who looked on the bright side of things would be beautiful even if they were not.

Whenever she looked at Joy this way, she could not help but feel that it would have been better if the child had not taken the Ph.D. It had certainly not brought her out any and now that she had it, there was no more excuse for her to go to school again. Mrs. Hopewell thought it was nice for girls to go to school to have a good time but Joy had "gone through." Anyhow, she would not have been strong enough to go again. The doctors had told Mrs. Hopewell that with the best of care, Joy might see forty-five. She had a weak heart. Joy had made it plain that if it had not been for this condition, she would be far from these red hills and good country people. She would be in a university lecturing to people who knew what she was talking about. And Mrs. Hopewell could very well picture her there, looking like a scarecrow and lecturing to more of the same. Here she went about all day in a six-year-old skirt and a yellow sweat shirt with a faded cowboy on a horse embossed on it. She thought this was funny; Mrs. Hopewell thought it was idiotic and showed simply that she was still a child. She was brilliant but she didn't have a grain of sense. It seemed to Mrs. Hopewell that every year she grew less like other people and more like herself—bloated, rude, and squint-eyed. And she said such strange things! To her own mother she had said—without warning, without excuse, standing up in the middle of a meal with her face purple and her mouth half full—"Woman! do you ever look inside? Do you ever look inside and see what you are *not*? God!" she had cried sinking down again and staring at her plate, "Malebranche[2] was right: we are not our own light. We are not our own light!" Mrs. Hopewell had no idea to this day what brought that on. She had only made the remark, hoping Joy would take it in, that a smile never hurt anyone.

The girl had taken the Ph.D. in philosophy and this left Mrs. Hopewell at a complete loss. You could say, "My daughter is a nurse," or "My daughter is a school teacher," or even, "My daughter is a chemical engineer." You could not say, "My daughter is a philosopher." That was something that had ended with the Greeks and Romans. All day Joy sat on her neck in a deep chair, reading. Sometimes she went for walks but she didn't like dogs or cats or birds or flowers or nature or nice young men. She looked at nice young men as if she could smell their stupidity.

One day Mrs. Hopewell had picked up one of the books the girl had just put down and opening it at random, she read, "Science, on the other hand, has to assert its soberness and seriousness afresh and declare that it is concerned

---

[2] Nicolas Malebranche (1638–1715), French philosopher.

solely with what-is. Nothing—how can it be for science anything but a horror and a phantasm? If science is right, then one thing stands firm: science wishes to know nothing of nothing. Such is after all the strictly scientific approach to Nothing. We know it by wishing to know nothing of Nothing." These words had been underlined with a blue pencil and they worked on Mrs. Hopewell like some evil incantation in gibberish. She shut the book quickly and went out of the room as if she were having a chill.

This morning when the girl came in, Mrs. Freeman was on Carramae. "She thrown up four times after supper," she said, "and was up twict in the night after three o'clock. Yesterday she didn't do nothing but ramble in the bureau drawer. All she did. Stand up there and see what she could run up on."

"She's got to eat," Mrs. Hopewell muttered, sipping her coffee, while she watched Joy's back at the stove. She was wondering what the child had said to the Bible salesman. She could not imagine what kind of a conversation she could possibly have had with him.

He was a tall gaunt hatless youth who had called yesterday to sell them a Bible. He had appeared at the door, carrying a large black suitcase that weighted him so heavily on one side that he had to brace himself against the door facing. He seemed on the point of collapse but he said in a cheerful voice. "Good morning, Mrs. Cedars!" and set the suitcase down on the mat. He was not a bad-looking young man though he had on a bright blue suit and yellow socks that were not pulled up far enough. He had prominent face bones and a streak of sticky-looking brown hair falling across his forehead.

"I'm Mrs. Hopewell," she said.

"Oh!" he said, pretending to look puzzled but with his eyes sparkling, "I saw it said 'The Cedars' on the mailbox so I thought you was Mrs. Cedars!" and he burst out in a pleasant laugh. He picked up the satchel and under cover of a pant, he fell forward into her hall. It was rather as if the suitcase had moved first, jerking him after it. "Mrs. Hopewell!" he said and grabbed her hand. "I hope you are well!" and he laughed again and then all at once his face sobered completely. He paused and gave her a straight earnest look and said, "Lady, I've come to speak of serious things."

"Well, come in," she muttered, none too pleased because her dinner was almost ready. He came into the parlor and sat down on the edge of a straight chair and put the suitcase between his feet and glanced around the room as if he were sizing her up by it. Her silver gleamed on the two sideboards; she decided he had never been in a room as elegant as this.

"Mrs. Hopewell," he began, using her name in a way that sounded almost intimate, "I know you believe in Chrustian service."

"Well yes," she murmured.

"I know," he said and paused, looking very wise with his head cocked on one side, "that you're a good woman. Friends have told me."

Mrs. Hopewell never liked to be taken for a fool. "What are you selling?" she asked.

"Bibles," the young man said and his eye raced around the room before he added, "I see you have no family Bible in your parlor, I see that is the one lack you got!"

Mrs. Hopewell could not say, "My daughter is an atheist and won't let me keep the Bible in the parlor." She said, stiffening slightly, "I keep my Bible by my bedside." This was not the truth. It was in the attic somewhere.

"Lady," he said, "the word of God ought to be in the parlor."

"Well, I think that's a matter of taste," she began. "I think . . ."

"Lady," he said, "for a Christian, the word of God ought to be in every room in the house besides in his heart. I know you're a Christian because I can see it in every line of your face."

She stood up and said, "Well, young man, I don't want to buy a Bible and I smell my dinner burning."

He didn't get up. He began to twist his hands and looking down at them, he said softly, "Well lady, I'll tell you the truth—not many people want to buy one nowadays and besides, I know I'm real simple. I don't know how to say a thing but to say it. I'm just a country boy." He glanced up into her unfriendly face. "People like you don't like to fool with country people like me!"

"Why!" she cried, "good country peope are the salt of the earth! Besides, we all have different ways of doing, it takes all kinds to make the world go 'round. That's life!"

"You said a mouthful," he said.

"Why, I think there aren't enough good country people in the world!" she said, stirred. "I think that's what's wrong with it!"

His face had brightened. "I didn't intraduce myself," he said. "I'm Manley Pointer from out in the country around Willohobie, not even from a place, just from near a place."

"You wait a minute," she said. "I have to see about my dinner." She went out to the kitchen and found Joy standing near the door where she had been listening.

"Get rid of the salt of the earth," she said, "and let's eat."

Mrs. Hopewell gave her a pained look and turned the heat down under the vegetables. "*I* can't be rude to anybody," she murmured and went back into the parlor.

He had opened the suitcase and was sitting with a Bible on each knee.

"You might as well put those up," she told him. "I don't want one."

"I appreciate your honesty," he said. "You don't see any more real honest people unless you go way out in the country."

"I know," she said, "real genuine folks!" Through the crack in the door she heard a groan.

"I guess a lot of boys come telling you they're working their way through college," he said, "but I'm not going to tell you that. Somehow," he said, "I don't want to go to college. I want to devote my life to Chrustian service. See," he said, lowering his voice, "I got this heart condition. I may not live long. When you know it's something wrong with you and you may not live long, well then, lady . . ." He paused, with his mouth open, and stared at her.

He and Joy had the same condition! She knew that her eyes were filling with tears but she collected herself quickly and murmured, "Won't you stay for dinner? We'd love to have you!" and was sorry the instant she heard herself say it.

"Yes mam," he said in an abashed voice, "I would sher love to do that!"

Joy had given him one look on being introduced to him and then throughout the meal had not glanced at him again. He had addressed several remarks to her, which she had pretended not to hear. Mrs. Hopewell could not understand deliberate rudeness, although she lived with it, and she felt she had always to overflow with hospitality to make up for Joy's lack of courtesy. She urged him to talk about himself and he did. He said he was the seventh child of twelve and that his father had been crushed under a tree when he himself was eight years old. He had been crushed very badly, in fact, almost cut in two and was practically not recognizable. His mother had got along the best she could by hard working and she had always seen that her children went to Sunday School and that they read the Bible every evening. He was now nineteen years old and he had been selling Bibles for four months. In that time he had sold seventy-seven Bibles and had the promise of two more sales. He wanted to become a missionary because he thought that was the way you could do most for people. "He who losest his life shall find it," he said simply and he was so sincere, so genuine and earnest that Mrs. Hopewell would not for the world have smiled. He prevented his peas from sliding onto the table by blocking them with a piece of bread which he later cleaned his plate with. She could see Joy observing sidewise how he handled his knife and fork and she saw too that every few minutes, the boy would dart a keen appraising glance at the girl as if he were trying to attract her attention.

After dinner Joy cleared the dishes off the table and disappeared and Mrs. Hopewell was left to talk with him. He told her again about his childhood and his father's accident and about various things that had happened to him. Every five minutes or so she would stifle a yawn. He sat for two hours until finally she told him she must go because she had an appointment in town. He packed his Bibles and thanked her and prepared to leave, but in the doorway he stopped and wrung her hand and said that not on any of his trips had he met a lady as nice as her and he asked if he could come again. She had said she would always be happy to see him.

Joy had been standing in the road, apparently looking at something in the distance, when he came down the steps toward her, bent to the side with his heavy valise. He stopped where she was standing and confronted her directly. Mrs. Hopewell could not hear what he said but she trembled to think what Joy would say to him. She could see that after a minute Joy said something and that then the boy began to speak again, making an excited gesture with his free hand. After a minute Joy said something else at which the boy began to speak once more. Then to her amazement, Mrs. Hopewell saw the two of them walk off together, toward the gate. Joy had walked all the way to the gate with him and Mrs. Hopewell could not imagine what they had said to each other, and she had not yet dared to ask.

Mrs. Freeman was insisting upon her attention. She had moved from the refrigerator to the heater so that Mrs. Hopewell had to turn and face her in order to seem to be listening. "Glynese gone out with Harvey Hill again last night," she said. "She had this sty."

"Hill," Mrs. Hopewell said absently, "is that the one who works in the garage?"

"Nome, he's the one that goes to chiropracter school," Mrs. Freeman said. "She had this sty. Been had it two days. So she says when he brought her in the other night he says, 'Lemme get rid of that sty for you,' and she says, 'How?' and he says, 'You just lay yourself down acrost the seat of that car and I'll show you.' So she done it and he popped her neck. Kept on a-popping it several times until she made him quit. This morning," Mrs. Freeman said, "she ain't got no sty. She ain't got no traces of a sty."

"I never heard of that before," Mrs. Hopewell said.

"He ast her to marry him before the Ordinary,"[3] Mrs. Freeman went on, "and she told him she wasn't going to be married in no *office*."

"Well, Glynese is a fine girl," Mrs. Hopewell said. "Glynese and Carramae are both fine girls."

"Carramae said when her and Lyman was married Lyman said it sure felt sacred to him. She said he said he wouldn't take five hundred dollars for being married by a preacher."

"How much would he take?" the girl asked from the stove.

"He said he wouldn't take five hundred dollars," Mrs. Freeman repeated.

"Well we all have work to do," Mrs. Hopewell said.

"Lyman said it just felt more sacred to him." Mrs. Freeman said. "The doctor wants Carramae to eat prunes. Says instead of medicine. Says them cramps is coming from pressure. You know where I think it is?"

"She'll be better in a few weeks," Mrs. Hopewell said.

"In the tube," Mrs. Freeman said. "Else she wouldn't be as sick as she is."

Hulga had cracked her two eggs into a saucer and was bringing them to the table along with a cup of coffee that she had filled too full. She sat down carefully and began to eat, meaning to keep Mrs. Freeman there by questions if for any reason she showed an inclination to leave. She could perceive her mother's eye on her. The first round-about question would be about the Bible salesman and she did not wish to bring it on. "How did he pop her neck?" she asked.

Mrs. Freeman went into a description of how he had popped her neck. She said he owned a '55 Mercury but that Glynese said she would rather marry a man with only a '36 Plymouth who would be married by a preacher. The girl

[3] Justice of the peace who performs the marriage ceremony in chambers rather than in public.

asked what if he had a '32 Plymouth and Mrs. Freeman said what Glynese had said was a '36 Plymouth.

Mrs. Hopewell said there were not many girls with Glynese's common sense. She said what she admired in those girls was their common sense. She said that reminded her that they had a nice visitor yesterday, a young man selling Bibles. "Lord," she said, "he bored me to death but he was so sincere and genuine I couldn't be rude to him. He was just good country people, you know," she said, "—just the salt of the earth."

"I seen him walk up," Mrs. Freeman said, "and then later—I seen him walk off," and Hulga could feel the slight shift in her voice, the slight insinuation, that he had not walked off alone, had he? Her face remained expressionless but the color rose into her neck and she seemed to swallow it down with the next spoonful of egg. Mrs. Freeman was looking at her as if they had a secret together.

"Well, it takes all kinds of people to make the world go 'round," Mrs. Hopewell said. "It's very good we aren't all alike."

"Some people are more alike than others," Mrs. Freeman said.

Hulga got up and stumped, with about twice the noise that was necessary, into her room and locked the door. She was to meet the Bible salesman at ten o'clock at the gate. She had thought about it half the night. She had started thinking of it as a great joke and then she had begun to see profound implications in it. She had lain in bed imagining dialogues for them that were insane on the surface but that reached below to depths that no Bible salesman would be aware of. Their conversation yesterday had been of this kind.

He had stopped in front of her and had simply stood there. His face was bony and sweaty and bright, with a little pointed nose in the center of it, and his look was different from what it had been at the dinner table. He was gazing at her with open curiosity, with fascination, like a child watching a new fantastic animal at the zoo, and he was breathing as if he had run a great distance to reach her. His gaze seemed somehow familiar but she could not think where she had been regarded with it before. For almost a minute he didn't say anything. Then on what seemed an insuck of breath, he whispered, "You ever ate a chicken that was two days old?"

The girl looked at him stonily. He might have just put this question up for consideration at the meeting of a philosophical association. "Yes," she presently replied as if she had considered it from all angles.

"It must have been mighty small!" he said triumphantly and shook all over with little nervous giggles, getting very red in the face, and subsiding finally into his gaze of complete admiration, while the girl's expression remained exactly the same.

"How old are you?" he asked softly.

She waited some time before she answered. Then in a flat voice she said, "Seventeen."

His smiles came in succession like waves breaking on the surface of a little lake. "I see you got a wooden leg." he said. "I think you're brave. I think you're real sweet."

The girl stood blank and solid and silent.

"Walk to the gate with me," he said. "You're a brave sweet little thing and I liked you the minute I seen you walk in the door."

Hulga began to move forward.

"What's your name?" he asked, smiling down on the top of her head.

"Hulga," she said.

"Hulga," he murmured, "Hulga. Hulga. I never heard of anybody name Hulga before. You're shy, aren't you, Hulga?" he asked.

She nodded, watching his large red hand on the handle of the giant valise.

"I like girls that wear glasses," he said. "I think a lot. I'm not like these people that a serious thought don't ever enter their heads. It's because I may die."

"I may die too," she said suddenly and looked up at him. His eyes were very small and brown, glittering feverishly.

"Listen," he said, "don't you think some people was meant to meet on account of what all they got in common and all? Like they both think serious thoughts and all?" He shifted the valise to his other hand so that the hand nearest her was free. He caught hold of her elbow and shook it a little. "I don't work on Saturday," he said. "I like to walk in the woods and see what Mother Nature is wearing. O'er the hills and far away. Pic-nics and things. Couldn't we go on a pic-nic tomorrow? Say yes, Hulga," he said and gave her a dying look as if he felt his insides about to drop out of him. He had even seemed to sway slightly toward her.

During the night she had imagined that she seduced him. She imagined that the two of them walked on the place until they came to the storage barn beyond the two back fields and there, she imagined, that things came to such a pass that she very easily seduced him and that then, of course, she had to reckon with his remorse. True genius can get an idea across even to an inferior mind. she imagined that she took his remorse in hand and changed it into a deeper understanding of life. She took all his shame away and turned it into something useful.

She set off for the gate at exactly ten o'clock, escaping without drawing Mrs. Hopewell's attention. She didn't take anything to eat, forgetting that food is usually taken on a picnic. She wore a pair of slacks and a dirty white shirt, and as an afterthought, she had put some Vapex on the collar of it since she did not own any perfume. When she reached the gate no one was there.

She looked up and down the empty highway and had the furious feeling that she had been tricked, that he had only meant to make her walk to the gate after the idea of him. Then suddenly he stood up, very tall, from behind a bush on the opposite embankment. Smiling, he lifted his hat which was new and wide-brimmed. He had not worn it yesterday and she wondered if he had bought it for the occasion. It was toast-colored with a red and white band around it and was slightly too large for him. He stepped from behind the bush still carrying the black valise. He had on the same suit and the same yellow socks sucked down in his shoes from walking. He crossed the highway and said, "I knew you'd come!"

The girl wondered acidly how he had known this. She pointed to the valise and asked, "Why did you bring your Bibles?"

He took her elbow, smiling down on her as if he could not stop. "You can never tell when you'll need the word of God, Hulga," he said. She had a moment in which she doubted that this was actually happening and then they began to climb the embankment. They went down into the pasture toward the woods. The boy walked lightly by her side, bouncing on his toes. The valise did not seem to be heavy today; he even swung it. They crossed half the pasture without saying anything and then, putting his hand easily on the small of her back, he asked softly, "Where does your wooden leg join on?"

She turned an ugly red and glared at him and for an instant the boy looked abashed. "I didn't mean you no harm," he said. "I only meant you're so brave and all. I guess God takes care of you."

"No," she said, looking forward and walking fast, "I don't even believe in God."

At this he stopped and whistled. "No!" he exclaimed as if he were too astonished to say anything else.

She walked on and in a second he was bouncing at her side, fanning with his hat. "That's very unusual for a girl," he remarked, watching her out of the corner of his eye. When they reached the edge of the wood, he put his hand on her back again and drew her against him without a word and kissed her heavily.

The kiss, which had more pressure than feeling behind it, produced that extra surge of adrenalin in the girl that enables one to carry a packed trunk out of a burning house, but in her, the power went at once to the brain. Even before he released her, her mind, clear and detached and ironic anyway, was regarding him from a great distance, with amusement but with pity. She had never been kissed before and she was pleased to discover that it was an unexceptional experience and all a matter of the mind's control. Some people might enjoy drain water if they were told it was vodka. When the boy, looking expectant but uncertain, pushed her gently away, she turned and walked on, saying nothing as if such business, for her, were common enough.

He came along panting at her side, trying to help her when he saw a root that she might trip over. He caught and held back the long swaying blades of thorn vine until she had passed beyond them. She led the way and he came breathing heavily behind her. Then they came out on a sunlit hillside, sloping softly into another one a little smaller. Beyond, they could see the rusted top of the old barn where the extra hay was stored.

The hill was sprinkled with small pink weeds. "Then you ain't saved?" he asked suddenly, stopping.

The girl smiled. It was the first time she had smiled at him at all. "In my economy," she said, "I'm saved and you are damned but I told you I didn't believe in God."

Nothing seemed to destroy the boy's look of admiration. He gazed at her now as if the fantastic animal at the zoo had put its paw through the bars and given him a loving poke. She thought he looked as if he wanted to kiss her again and she walked on before he had the chance.

"Ain't there somewheres we can sit down sometime?" he murmured, his voice softening toward the end of the sentence.

"In that barn," she said.

They made for it rapidly as if it might slide away like a train. It was a large two-story barn, cool and dark inside. The boy pointed up the ladder that led into the loft and said, "It's too bad we can't go up there."

"Why can't we?" she asked.

"Yer leg," he said reverently.

The girl gave him a contemptuous look and putting both hands on the ladder, she climbed it while he stood below, apparently awestruck. She pulled herself expertly through the opening and then looked down at him and said, "Well, come on if you're coming," and he began to climb the ladder, awkwardly bringing the suitcase with him.

"We won't need the Bible," she observed.

"You never can tell," he said, panting. After he had got into the loft, he was a few seconds catching his breath. She had sat down in a pile of straw. A wide sheath of sunlight, filled with dust particles, slanted over her. She lay back against a bale, her face turned away, looking out the front opening of the barn where hay was thrown from a wagon into the loft. The two pink-speckled hillsides lay back against a dark ridge of woods. The sky was cloudless and cold blue. The boy dropped down by her side and put one arm under her and the other over her and began methodically kissing her face, making little noises like a fish. He did not remove his hat but it was pushed far enough back not to interfere. When her glasses got in his way, he took them off of her and slipped them into his pocket.

The girl at first did not return any of the kisses but presently she began to and after she had put several on his cheek, she reached his lips and remained there, kissing him again and again as if she were trying to draw all the breath out of him. His breath was clear and sweet like a child's and the kisses were sticky like a child's. He mumbled about loving her and about knowing when he first seen her that he loved her. but the mumbling was like the sleepy fretting of a child being put to sleep by his mother. Her mind, throughout this, never stopped or lost itself for a second to her feelings. "You ain't said you loved me none," he whispered finally, pulling back from her. "You got to say that."

She looked away from him off into the hollow sky and then down at a black ridge and then down farther into what appeared to be two green swelling lakes.

She didn't realize he had taken her glasses but this landscape could not seem exceptional to her for she seldom paid any close attention to her surroundings.

"You got to say it," he repeated. "You got to say you love me."

She was always careful how she committed herself. "In a sense," she began, "if you use the word loosely, you might say that. But it's not a word I use. I don't have illusions. I'm one of those people who see *through* to nothing."

The boy was frowning. "You got to say it. I said it and you got to say it," he said.

The girl looked at him almost tenderly. "You poor baby," she murmured. "It's just as well you don't understand," and she pulled him by the neck, face-down against her. "We are all damned," she said, "but some of us have taken off our blindfolds and see that there's nothing to see. It's a kind of salvation."

The boy's astonished eyes looked blankly through the ends of her hair. "Okay," he almost whined, "but do you love me or don'tcher?"

"Yes," she said and added, "in a sense. But I must tell you something. There mustn't be anything dishonest between us." She lifted his head and looked him in the eye. "I am thirty years old." she said. "I have a number of degrees."

The boy's look was irritated by dogged. "I don't care," he said. "I don't care a thing about what all you done. I just want to know if you love me or don'tcher?" and he caught her to him and wildly planted her face with kisses until she said, "Yes, yes."

"Okay then," he said, letting her go. "Prove it."

She smiled, looking dreamily out on the shifty landscape. She had seduced him without even making up her mind to try. "How?" she asked, feeling that he should be delayed a little.

He leaned over and put his lips to her ear. "Show me where your wooden leg joins on," he whispered.

The girl uttered a sharp little cry and her face instantly drained of color. The obscenity of the suggestion was not what shocked her. As a child she had sometimes been subject to feelings of shame but education had removed the last traces of that as a good surgeon scrapes for cancer; she would no more have felt it over what he was asking than she would have believed in his Bible. But she was as sensitive about the artificial leg as a peacock about his tail. No one ever touched it but her. She took care of it as someone else would his soul, in private and almost with her own eyes turned away. "No," she said.

"I known it," he muttered, sitting up. "You're just playing me for a sucker."

"Oh no no!" she cried. "It joins on at the knee. Only at the knee. Why do you want to see it?"

The boy gave her a long penetrating look. "Because," he said, "it's what makes you different. You ain't like anybody else."

She sat staring at him. There was nothing about her face or her round freezing-blue eyes to indicate that this had moved her; but she felt as if her heart had stopped and left her mind to pump her blood. She decided that for the first time in her life she was face to face with real innocence. This boy, with an instinct that came from beyond wisdom, had touched the truth about her. When after a minute, she said in a hoarse high voice, "All right," it was like surrendering to him completely. It was like losing her own life and finding it again, miraculously, in his.

Very gently he began to roll the slack leg up. The artificial limb, in a white sock and brown flat shoe, was bound in a heavy material like canvas and ended in an ugly jointure where it was attached to the stump. The boy's face and his voice were entirely reverent as he uncovered it and said, "Now show me how to take it off and on."

She took it off for him and put it back on again and then he took it off himself, handling it as tenderly as if it were a real one. "See!" he said with a delighted child's face. "Now I can do it myself!"

"Put it back on," she said. She was thinking that she would run away with him and that every night he would take the leg off and every morning put it back on again. "Put it back on," she said.

"Not yet," he murmured, setting it on its foot out of her reach. "Leave it off for a while. You got me instead."

She gave a cry of alarm but he pushed her down and began to kiss her again. Without the leg she felt entirely dependent on him. Her brain seemed to have stopped thinking altogether and to be about some other function that it was not very good at. Different expressions raced back and forth over her face. Every now and then the boy, his eyes like two steel spikes, would glance behind him where the leg stood. Finally she pushed him off and said, "Put it back on me now."

"Wait," he said. He leaned the other way and pulled the valise toward him and opened it. It had a pale blue spotted lining and there were only two Bibles in it. He took one of these out and opened the cover of it. It was hollow and contained a pocket flask of whiskey, a pack of cards, and a small blue box with printing on it. He laid these out in front of her one at a time in an evenly-spaced row, like one presenting offerings at the shrine of a goddess. He put the blue box in her hand. THIS PRODUCT TO BE USED ONLY FOR THE PREVENTION OF DISEASE, she read, and dropped it. The boy was unscrewing the top of the flask. He stopped and pointed, with a smile, to the deck of cards. It was not an ordinary deck but one with an obscene picture on the back of each card. "Take a swig," he said, offering her the bottle first. He held it in front of her, but like one mesmerized, she did not move.

Her voice when she spoke had an almost pleading sound. "Aren't you," she murmured, "are'nt you just good country people?"

The boy cocked his head. He looked as if he were just beginning to understand that she might be trying to insult him. "Yeah," he said, curling his lip slightly, "but it ain't held me back none. I'm as good as you any day in the week."

"Give me my leg," she said.

He pushed it farther away with his foot. "Come on now, let's begin to have us a good time." he said coaxingly. "We ain't got to know one another good yet."

"Give me my leg!" she screamed and tried to lunge for it but he pushed her down easily.

"What's the matter with you all of a sudden?" he asked, frowning as he screwed the top on the flask and put it quickly back inside the Bible. "You just a while ago said you didn't believe in nothing. I thought you was some girl!"

Her face was almost purple. "You're a Christian!" she hissed. "You're a fine Christian!" You're just like them all—say one thing and do another. You're a perfect Christian, you're . . ."

The boy's mouth was set angrily. "I hope you don't think," he said in a lofty indignant tone, "that I believe in that crap! I may sell Bibles but I know which end is up and I wasn't born yesterday and I know where I'm going!"

"Give me my leg!" she screeched. He jumped up so quickly that she barely saw him sweep the cards and the blue box into the Bible and throw the Bible into the valise. She saw him grab the leg and then she saw it for an instant slanted forlornly across the inside of the suitcase with a Bible at either side of its opposite ends. He slammed the lid shut and snatched up the valise and swung it down the hole and then stepped through himself.

When all of him had passed but his head, he turned and regarded her with a look that no longer had any admiration in it. "I've gotten a lot of interesting things," he said. "One time I got a woman's glass eye this way. And you needn't to think you'll catch me because Pointer ain't really my name. I use a different name at every house I call at and don't stay nowhere long. And I'll tell you another thing. Hulga," he said, using the name as if he didn't think much of it, "you ain't so smart. I been believing in nothing every since I was born!" and then the toast-colored hat disappeared down the hole and the girl was left, sitting on the straw in the dusty sunlight. When she turned her churning face toward the opening, she saw his blue figure struggling successfully over the green speckled lake.

Mrs. Hopewell and Mrs. Freeman, who were in the back pasture, digging up onions, saw him emerge a little later from the woods and head across the meadow toward the highway. "Why, that looks like that nice dull young man that tried to sell me a Bible yesterday," Mrs. Hopewell said, squinting. "He must have been selling them to the Negroes back in there. He was so simple," she said, "but I guess the world would be better off if we were all that simple."

Mrs. Freeman's gaze drove forward and just touched him before he disappeared under the hill. Then she returned her attention to the evil-smelling onion shoot she was lifting from the ground. "Some can't be that simple," she said. "I know I never could."

Carolyn Kizer 1925–

Carolyn Kizer is co-founder of the important poetry journal *Poetry Northwest* and served as its editor from its inception in 1959 until 1965. From 1966 until 1970, she directed literary programs for the National Endowment for the Arts; in 1985, Kizer was awarded the Pulitzer Prize for her collection, *Yin. New Poems.* Born in Spokane, Washington, and educated at Sarah Lawrence College in New York, Kizer's work demonstrates what critics have called ". . . a sense of irony and restrained emotion wedded to a mastery of form traditional and free." While her poetry has evolved to include social issues and contemplative musings about the world, Kizer has been praised for her "tough wisdom," her sharp focus on the rising and falling fortunes of women, and her "technical control and admiration for human resilience."

THE INTRUDER

My mother—preferring the strange to the tame:
Dove-note, bone marrow, deer dung,
Frog's belly distended with finny young,
Leaf-mould wilderness, hare-bell, toadstool,
Odd, small snakes roving through the leaves,   5
Metallic beetles rambling over stones: all
Wild and natural!—flashed out her instinctive love, and quick, she
Picked up the fluttering, bleeding bat the cat laid at her feet,
And held the little horror to the mirror, where
He gazed on himself, and shrieked like an old screen door far off.   10

Depended from her pinched thumb, each wing
Came clattering down like a small black shutter.
Still tranquil, she began, "It's rather sweet. . . ."
The soft mouse body, the hard feral glint
In the caught eyes. Then we saw,   15
And recoiled, lice, pallid, yellow,
Nested within the wing-pits, cosily sucked and snoozed.
The thing dropped from her hands, and with its thud,
Swiftly, the cat, with a clean careful mouth
Closed on the soiled webs, growling, took them out to the back
                                stoop.   20

But still, dark blood, a sticky puddle on the floor
Remained, of all my mother's tender, wounding passion
For a whole wild, lost, betrayed and secret life
Among its dens and burrows, its clean stones,
Whose denizens can turn upon the world   25
With spitting tongue, an odor, talon, claw,
To sting or soil benevolence, alien
As our clumsy traps, our random scatter of shot.
She swept to the kitchen. Turning on the tap,
She washed and washed the pity from her hands.   30

A WIDOW IN WINTERTIME

Last night a baby gargled in the throes
Of a fatal spasm. My children are all grown
Past infant strangles; so, reassured, I knew
Some other baby perished in the snow.
But no. The cat was making love again.   5

Later, I went down and let her in.
She hung her tail, flagging from her sins.
Though she'd eaten, I forked out another dinner,
Being myself hungry all ways, and thin
From metaphysic famines she knows nothing of,   10

The feckless beast! Even so, resemblances
Were on my mind: female and feline, though
She preens herself from satisfaction, and does
Not mind lying even in snow. She is
Lofty and bedraggled, without need to choose.   15

As an ex-animal, I look fondly on
her excesses and simplicities, and would not return
To them; taking no marks for what I have become,
Merely that my nine lives peal in my ears again
And again, ring in these austerities,   20

These arbitrary disciplines of mine,
Most of them trivial: like covering
The children on my way to bed, and trying
To live well enough alone, and not to dream
Of grappling in the snow, claws plunged in fur,   25

Or waken in a caterwaul of dying.

THRALL

The room is sparsely furnished:
A chair, a table and a father.

He sits in the chair by the window.
There are books on the table.
The time is always just past lunch.   5

You tiptoe past as he eats his apple
And reads. He looks up, angry.
He has heard your asthmatic breathing.

He will read for years without looking up
Until your childhood is over: 10

Smells, untidiness and boring questions;
Blood, from the first skinned knees

To the first stained thighs;
The foolish tears of adolescent love.

One day he looks up, pleased   15
At the finished product.
Now he is ready to love you!

So he coaxes you in the voice reserved
For reading Keats. You agree to everything.

Drilled in silence and duty,   20
You will give him no cause for reproach.
He will boast of you to strangers.

When the afternoon is older
Shadows in a smaller room
Fall on the bed, the books, the father.   25

You read aloud to him
"La Belle Dame sans Merci."
You feed him his medicine.
You tell him you love him.

You wait for his eyes to close at last   30
So you may write this poem.

Maxine Kumin 1925–

Novelist, short-story writer, essayist, and author of children's books, Maxine Kumin is best known for her poetry, which celebrates the ordinary aspects of everyday life: children, friends, family, animals, vegetables, and the seasons. Like Thoreau, she has been labeled a transcendentalist for extolling the natural world's redemptive qualities while exploring humanity's relationship to nature. She has also been compared to her late friend, Anne Sexton, as being a "confessional" poet. As housewives with children, Kumin and Sexton assisted in each other's development, analyzing and revising their poems and writing four children's books together. Kumin has published eleven books of poetry, including *Connecting the Dots* (1996) and *Up Country: Poems of New England* (1972), which won the Pulitzer Prize. In addition, she has authored four novels, a collection of short stories, more than twenty children's books, and three books of essays. She is the recipient of numerous awards, grants, and fellowships, and was poetry consultant to the Library of Congress in 1981–82, a post now called Poet Laureate of the United States. She resides on her farm in New Hampshire.

REGRET

The field's no longer simple; it's a soul's crossing time.
                                        —Roethke

All those elusive berries
that run like hen tracks
through this field of daisies
through this field of larks' nests
paintbrush, quack grass;   5

all those tag ends of human
speech the insects imitate
hanging their odd inflected
buzz, free-standing and misheard
in still air over this field;   10

all those annulled connections
all those missed chances
and time running out untested
hot and headlong like the voles'
slim tunnels in this field   15

running out like summer
into the mouths of immense frogs
into the blowing field and leaf clatter
calling to me and me crossing over
as if nothing were the matter.   20

BY HEART

Dear Miss Bloomberg in your
rusty purple Eleanor Roosevelt dress
drumming your thimbled finger
on a bad child's skull
calling us up to recite one by one   5
from the Vision of Sir Launfal
what is so rare as a day in June?

here I stand declaiming
in that chalk-eraser-clapping clime
cowslips flutter in meadows green   10
when up out of the poem they come again
—marsh marigolds in proper nomenclature—
come puddling their chrome
across our still-drab wetland and pasture.

How your eyelids flutter to see the mess   15
of young leaves chopped and steamed
swimming in butter,
you in your Depression dress
buttoned to the chin with mother-of-pearl—
eat, eat, Miss Bloomberg! It's   20
spring tonic for a scurvied world.

Anne Sexton 1928–1974

Anne Sexton's career seems fairly brief, given that she began writing poetry at the relatively advanced age of twenty-eight. However, she received a number of prestigious literary awards during her short life: Her collection *Live or Die* (1967) won the Pulitzer Prize, and she also was awarded the American Academy of Arts and Letters traveling fellowship. With emotional problems that evidently originated in her childhood, Sexton suffered successive breakdowns and yet was brilliantly prolific and a dramatic, exciting reader of her work, her poetry marked by "surrealistic verve and sardonic wit." She was hospitalized periodically, attempting to escape voices that "urged her to die." Her volumes also include *All My Pretty Ones* (1962), *Love Poems* (1969), *Transformations* (1971), *The Book of Folly* (1972), and *The Death Notebooks* (1974). Most of her poems are about the personal, her family life and physical state serving as larger metaphors for humankind—sexuality, motherhood, illegitimacy, guilt, and madness among them. In similar fashion to her friend Sylvia Plath more than a decade earlier, Sexton took her own life, the suicide coming a month before her forty-sixth birthday.

SAID THE POET TO THE ANALYST

My business is words. Words are like labels,
or coins, or better, like swarming bees.
I confess I am only broken by the sources of things;
as if words were counted like dead bees in the attic,
unbuckled from their yellow eyes and their dry wings.   5
I must always forget how one word is able to pick
out another, to manner another, until I have got
something I might have said . . .
but did not.

Your business is watching my words. But I   10
admit nothing. I work with my best, for instance,
when I can write my praise for a nickel machine,
that one night in Nevada: telling how the magic jackpot
came clacking three bells out, over the lucky screen.
But if you should say this is something it is not,   15
then I grow weak, remembering how my hands felt funny
and ridiculous and crowded with all
the believing money.

HER KIND

I have gone out, a possessed witch,
haunting the black air, braver at night;
dreaming evil, I have done my hitch
over the plain houses, light by light:
lonely thing, twelve-fingered, out of mind.   5
A woman like that is not a woman, quite.
I have been her kind.

I have found the warm caves in the woods,
filled them with skillets, carvings, shelves,
closets, silks, innumerable goods;   10
fixed the suppers for the worms and the elves:
whining, rearranging the disaligned.
A woman like that is misunderstood.
I have been her kind.

I have ridden in your cart, driver,   15
waved my nude arms at villages going by,
learning the last bright routes, survivor
where your flames still bite my thigh
and my ribs crack where your wheels wind.
A woman like that is not ashamed to die.   20
I have been her kind.

Maya Angelou 1928–

In 1970, at the age of 42, Maya Angelou burst on the literary scene with her best-selling *I Know Why the Caged Bird Sings*, the first of many autobiographical volumes. Before becoming an immensely popular writer, Angelou was a singer and dancer who performed on and off-Broadway, as well as in cinema and television. At the encouragement of friends, including James Baldwin who had heard her tell stories of her childhood, Angelou began to write. Born Marguerite Johnson in St. Louis, Missouri, the three-year-old Angelou was sent to live with her grandmother in Stamps, Arkansas. The author describes her rural town as being so segregated that the black children "didn't really, absolutely know what whites looked like." At the age of eight, she returned to St. Louis to live with her mother, but soon returned to Stamps after being sexually abused by her mother's lover. Back in Arkansas, the traumatized Angelou refused to speak for five years. In the midst of her psychological crisis, Angelou's life was profoundly affected by her introduction to books by a sympathetic white woman. Angelou writes, "She had given me her secret world which called forth a djinn [supernatural being] who was to serve me all my life." In January of 1993, Angelou recited her poem "On the Pulse of Morning" at the inauguration of President Bill Clinton.

From I KNOW WHY THE CAGED BIRD SINGS

The school band struck up a march and all classes filed in as had been rehearsed. We stood in front of our seats, as assigned, and on a signal from the choir director, we sat. No sooner had this been accomplished than the band started to play the national anthem. We rose again and sang the song, after which we recited the pledge of allegiance. We remained standing for a brief minute before the choir director and the principal signaled to us, rather desperately I thought, to take our seats. The command was so unusual that our carefully rehearsed and smooth-running machine was thrown off. For a full minute we fumbled for our chairs and bumped into each other awkwardly. Habits change or solidify under pressure, so in our state of nervous tension we had been ready to follow our usual assembly pattern: the American national anthem, then the pledge of allegiance, then the song every Black person I knew called the Negro National Anthem. All done in the same key, with the same passion and most often standing on the same foot.

Finding my seat at last, I was overcome with a presentiment of worse things to come. Something unrehearsed, unplanned, was going to happen, and we were going to be made to look bad. I distinctly remember being explicit in the choice of pronoun. It was "we," the graduating class, the unit, that concerned me then.

The principal welcomed "parents and friends" and asked the Baptist minister to lead us in prayer. His invocation was brief and punchy, and for a second I thought we were getting back on the high road to right action. When the principal came back to the dais, however, his voice had changed. Sounds always affected me profoundly and the principal's voice was one of my favorites. During assembly it melted and lowed weakly into the audience. It had not been in my plan to listen to him, but my curiosity was piqued and I straightened up to give him my attention.

He was talking about Booker T. Washington, our "late great leader," who said we can be as close as the fingers on the hand, etc. . . . Then he said a few vague things about friendship and the friendship of kindly people to those less fortunate than themselves. With that his voice nearly faded, thin, away. Like a river diminishing to a stream and then to a trickle. But he cleared his throat and said, "Our speaker tonight, who is also our friend, came from Texarkana to deliver the commencement address, but due to the irregularity of the train schedule, he's going to, as they say, 'speak and run.'" He said that we understood and wanted the man to know that we were most grateful for the time he was able to give us and then something about how we were willing always to adjust to another's program, and without more ado— "I give you Mr. Edward Donleavy."

Not one but two white men came throught the door offstage. The shorter one walked to the speaker's platform, and the tall one moved over to the center seat and sat down. But that was our principal's seat, and already occupied. The dislodged gentleman bounced around for a long breath or two before the Baptist minister gave him his chair, then with more diginty than the situation deserved, the minister walked off the stage.

Donleavy looked at the audience once (on reflection, I'm sure that he wanted only to reassure himself that we were really there), adjusted his glasses and began to read from a sheaf of papers.

He was glad "to be here and to see the work going on just as it was in the other schools."

At the first "Amen" from the audience I willed the offender to immediate death by choking on the word. But Amens and Yes, sir's began to fall around the room like rain through a ragged umbrella.

He told us of the wonderful changes we children in Stamps had in store. The Central School (naturally, the white school was Central) had already been granted improvements that would be in use in the fall. A well-known artist was coming from Little Rock to teach art to them. They were going to have the newest microscopes and chemistry equipment for their laboratory. Mr. Donleavy didn't leave us long in the dark over who made these improvements available to Central High. Nor were we to be ignored in the general betterment scheme he had in mind.

He said that he had pointed out to people at a very high level that one of the first-line football tacklers at Arkansas Agricultural and Mechanical College had graduated from good old Lafayette County Training School. Here fewer Amen's were heard. Those few that did break through lay dully in the air with the heaviness of habit.

He went on to praise us. He went on to say how he had bragged that "one of the best basketball players at Fisk sank his first ball right here at Lafayette County Training School."

The white kids were going to have a chance to become Galileos and Madame Curies and Edisons and Gauguins, and our boys (the girls weren't even in on it) would try to be Jesse Owenses and Joe Louises.

Owens and the Brown Bomber were great heroes in our world, but what school official in the white-goddom of Little Rock had the right to decide that those two men must be our only heroes? Who decided that for Henry Reed to become a scientist he had to work like George Washington Carver, as a boot-black, to buy a lousy microscope? Bailey was obviously always going to be too small to be an athlete, so which concrete angel glued to what country seat had decided that if my brother wanted to become a lawyer he had to first pay penance for his skin by picking cotton and hoeing corn and studying correspondence books at night for twenty years?

The man's dead words fell like bricks around the auditorium and too many settled in my belly. Constrained by hard-learned manners I couldn't look behind me, but to my left and right the proud graduating class of 1940 had dropped their heads. Every girl in my row had found something new to do with her handkerchief. Some folded the tiny squares into love knots, some into triangles, but most were wadding them, then pressing them flat on their yellow laps.

On the dais, the ancient tragedy was being replayed. Professor Parsons sat, a sculptor's reject, rigid. His large, heavy body seemed devoid of will or willingness, and his eyes said he was no longer with us. The other teachers examined the flag (which was draped stage right) or their notes, or the windows which opened on our now-famous playing diamond.

Graduation, the hush-hush magic time of frills and gifts and congratulations and diplomas, was finished for me before my name was called. The accomplishment was nothing. The meticulous maps, drawn in three colors of ink, learning and spelling decasyllabic words, memorizing the whole of *The Rape of Lucrece*—it was for nothing. Donleavy had exposed us.

We were maids and farmers, handymen and washerwomen, and anything higher that we aspired to was farcical and presumptuous.

Then I wished that Gabriel Prosser and Nat Turner had killed all whitefolks in their beds and that Abraham Lincoln had been assassinated before the signing of the Emancipation Proclamation, and that Harriet Tubman had been killed by that blow on her head and Christopher Columbus had drowned in the *Santa María*.

It was awful to be Negro and have no control over my life. It was brutal to be young and already trained to sit quietly and listen to charges brought against my color with no chance of defense. We should all be dead. I thought I should like to see us all dead, one on top of the other. A pyramid of flesh with the whitefolks on the bottom, as the broad base, then the Indians with their silly tomahawks and teepees and wigwams and treaties, the Negroes with their mops and recipes and cotton sacks and spirituals sticking out of their mouths. The Dutch children should all stumble in their wooden shoes and break their necks. The French should choke to death on the Louisiana Purchase (1803) while silkworms ate all the Chinese with their stupid pigtails. As a species, we were an abomination. All of us.

Donleavy was running for election, and assured our parents that if he won we could count on having the only colored paved playing field in that part of Arkansas. Also—he never looked up to acknowledge the grunts of acceptance—also, we were bound to get some new equipment for the home economics building and the workshop.

He finished, and since there was no need to give any more than the most perfunctory thank-you's, he nodded to the men on the stage, and the tall white man who was never introduced joined him at the door. They left with the attitude that now they were off to something really improtant. (The graduation ceremonies at Lafayette County Training School had been a mere preliminary.)

The ugliness they left was palpable. An uninvited guest who wouldn't leave. The choir was summoned and sang a modern arrangement of "Onward, Christian Soldiers," with new words pertaining to graduates seeking their place in the world. But it didn't work. Elouise, the daughter of the Baptist minister, recited "Invictus," and I could have cried at the impertinence of "I am the master of my fate, I am the captain of my soul."

My name had lost its ring of familiarity and I had to be nudged to go and receive my diploma. All my preparations had fled. I neither marched up to the stage like a conquering Amazon, nor did I look in the audience for Bailey's nod of approval. Marguerite Johnson, I heard the name again, my honors were read, there were noises in the audience of appreciation, and I took my place on the stage as rehearsed.

I thought about colors I hated: ecru, puce, lavender, beige and black.

There was shuffling and rustling around me, then Henry Reed was giving his valedictory address, "To Be or Not to Be." Hadn't he heard the whitefolks? We couldn't *be*, so the question was a waste of time. Henry's voice came out clear and strong. I feared to look at him. Hadn't he got the message? There was no "nobler in the mind" for Negroes because the world didn't think we had minds, and they let us know it. "Outrageous fortune"? Now, that was a joke. When the ceremony was over I had to tell Henry Reed some things. That is, if I still cared. Not "rub," Henry, "erase." "Ah, there's the erase." Us.

Henry had been a good student in elocution. His voice rose on tides of promise and fell on waves of warnings. The English teacher had helped him to create a sermon winging through Hamlet's soliloquy. To be a man, a doer, a builder, a leader, or to be a tool, an unfunny joke, a crusher of funky toadstools. I marveled that Henry could go through with the speech as if we had a choice.

I had been listening and silently rebutting each sentence with my eyes closed; then there was a hush, which in an audience warns that something unplanned is happening. I looked up and saw Henry Reed, the conservative, the proper, the A student, turn his back to the audience and turn to us (the proud graduating class of 1940) and sing, nearly speaking,

> "Lift ev'ry voice and sing
> Till earth and heaven ring
> Ring with the harmonies of Liberty . . ."

It was the poem written by James Weldon Johnson. It was the music composed by J. Rosamond Johnson. It was the Negro national anthem. Out of habit we were singing it.

Our mothers and fathers stood in the dark hall and joined the hymn of encouragement. A kindergarten teacher led the small children onto the stage and the buttercups and daisies and bunny rabbits marked time and tried to follow:

> "Stony the road we trod
> Bitter the chastening rod
> Felt in the days when hopes, unborn, had died.
> Yet with a steady beat
> Have not our weary feet
> Come to the place for which our fathers sighed?"

Every child I knew had learned that song with his ABC's and along with "Jesus Loves Me This I Know." But I personally had never heard it before. Never heard the words, despite the thousands of times I had sung them. Never thought they had anything to do with me.

On the other hand, the words of Patrick Henry had made such an impression on me that I had been able to stretch myself tall and trembling and say, "I know not what course others may take, but as for me, give me liberty or give me death."

And now I heard, really for the first time:

> "We have come over a way that with tears
> has been watered,
> We have come, treading our path through
> the blood of the slaughtered."

While echoes of the song shivered in the air, Henry Reed bowed his head, said "Thank you," and returned to his place in the line. The tears that slipped down many faces were not wiped away in shame.

We were on top again. As always, again. We survived. The depths had been icy and dark, but now a bright sun spoke to our souls. I was no longer simply a member of the proud graduating class of 1940; I was a proud member of the wonderful, beautiful Negro race.

Oh, Black known and unknown poets, how often have your auctioned pains sustained us? Who will compute the lonely nights made less lonely by your songs, or by the empty pots made less tragic by your tales?

If we were a people much given to revealing secrets, we might raise monuments and sacrifice to the memories of our poets, but slavery cured us of that weakness. It may be enough, however, to have it said that we survive in exact relationship to the dedication of our poets (include preachers, musicians and blues singers).

A Good Woman Feeling Bad

The blues may be the life you've led
Or midnight hours in
An empty bed. But persecuting
Blues I've known
Could stalk   5
Like tigers, break like bone,

Pend like rope in
A gallows tree,
Make me curse
My pedigree,   10

Bitterness thick on
A rankling tongue,
A psalm to love that's
Left unsung,

Rivers heading north   15
But ending South,
Funeral music
In a going-home mouth.

All riddles are blues,
And all blues are sad,   20
And I'm only mentioning
Some blues I've had.

A Georgia Song

We swallow the odors of Southern cities,
Fatback boiled to submission,
Tender evening poignancies of
Magnolia and the great green
smell of fresh sweat.   5
In Southern fields,
The sound of distant
Feet running, or dancing,
And the liquid notes of
Sorrow songs,   10
Waltzes, screams and

French quadrilles float over
The loam of Georgia.

Sing me to sleep, Savannah.

Clocks run down in Tara's halls and dusty   15
Flags droop their unbearable
Sadness.

Remember our days, Susannah.

Oh, the blood-red clay,
Wet still with ancient   20
Wrongs, and Abenaa
Singing her Creole airs to
Macon.
We long, dazed, for winter evenings
And a whitened moon,   25
And the snap of controllable fires.

Cry for our souls, Augusta.

We need a wind to strike
Sharply, as the thought of love
Betrayed can stop the heart.   30
An absence of tactile
Romance, no lips offering
Succulence, nor eyes
Rolling, disconnected from
A Sambo face.   35

Dare us new dreams, Columbus.

A cool new moon, a
Winter's night, calm blood,
Sluggish, moving only
Out of habit, we need   40
Peace.

O Atlanta, O deep, and
Once-lost city,

Chant for us a new song. A song
Of Southern peace.   45

Cynthia Ozick 1928–

"What does concern Cynthia Ozick is that her fiction retain an authentically Jewish nature," writes critic Sarah Blacher Cohen. "Moreover," Cohen continues, Ozick ". . . laments the American Jews' abandonment of Yiddish for English, a language they consider more secular and thus more aesthetic." Short-story writer, translator, novelist, critic, essayist, and poet, Cynthia Ozick frequently centers her work on the predicament of the transplant—the immigrant in America—with language marked by eloquence and intricacy. *The Shawl* (1990) is one of Ozick's most renowned works, an intense short story about the Holocaust, which moved eminent writer Elie Wiesel to comment, "Non-survivor [of the Holocaust] novelists who treat the Holocaust ought to learn from Ozick the art of economy and what the French call *pudeur* (modesty)." Ozick's has been called an important voice in American fiction, with one critic calling her "a woman whose intellect . . . is so impressive that it pervades the words she chooses, the stories she elects to tell, and every careful phrase and clause in which they are conveyed."

THE SHAWL

Stella, cold, cold, the coldness of hell. How they walked on the roads together, Rosa with Magda curled up between sore breasts, Magda wound up in the shawl. Sometimes Stella carried Magda. But she was jealous of Magda. A thin girl of fourteen, too small, with thin breasts of her own, Stella wanted to be wrapped in a shawl, hidden away, asleep, rocked by the march, a baby, a round infant in arms. Magda took Rosa's nipple, and Rosa never stopped walking, a walking cradle. There was not enough milk; sometimes Magda sucked air; then she screamed. Stella was ravenous. Her knees were tumors on sticks, her elbows chicken bones.

Rosa did not feel hunger; she felt light, not like someone walking but like someone in a faint, in trance, arrested in a fit, someone who is already a floating angel, alert and seeing everything, but in the air, not there, not touching the road. As if teetering on the tips of her fingernails. She looked into Magda's face through a gap in the shawl: a squirrel in a nest, safe, no one could reach her inside the little house of the shawl's windings. The face, very round, a pocket mirror of a face: but it was not Rosa's bleak complexion, dark like cholera, it was another kind of face altogether, eyes blue as air, smooth feathers of hair nearly as yellow as the Star sewn into Rosa's coat. You could think she was one of *their* babies.[1]

Rosa, floating, dreamed of giving Magda away in one of the villages. She could leave the line for a minute and push Magda into the hands of any woman on the side of the road. But if she moved out of line they might shoot. And even if she fled the line for half a second and pushed the shawl-bundle at a stranger, would the woman take it? She might be surprised, or afraid; she might drop the shawl, and Magda would fall out and strike her head and die. The little round head. Such a good child, she gave up screaming, and sucked now only for the taste of the drying nipple itself. The neat grip of the tiny gums. One mite of a tooth tip sticking up in the bottom gum, how shining, an elfin tombstone of white marble gleaming there. Without complaining, Magda relinquished Rosa's teats, first the left, then the right; both were cracked, not a sniff of milk. The duct-crevice extinct, a dead volcano, blind eye, chill hole, so Magda took the corner of the shawl and milked it instead. She sucked and sucked, flooding the threads with wetness. The shawl's good flavor, milk of linen.

It was a magic shawl, it could nourish an infant for three days and three nights. Magda did not die, she stayed alive, although very quiet. A peculiar smell, of cinnamon and almonds, lifted out of her mouth. She held her eyes open every moment, forgetting how to blink or nap, and Rosa and sometimes Stella studied their blueness. On the road they raised one burden of a leg after another and studied Magda's face. "Aryan," Stella said, in a voice grown as thin as a string; and Rosa thought how Stella gazed at Magda like a young cannibal. And the time that Stella said "Aryan," it sounded to Rosa as if Stella had really said "Let us devour her."

But Magda lived to walk. She lived that long, but she did not walk very well, partly because she was only fifteen months old, and partly because the spindles of her legs could not hold up her fat belly. It was fat with air, full and round. Rosa gave almost all her food to Magda, Stella gave nothing; Stella was ravenous, a growing child herself, but not growing much. Stella did not menstruate. Rosa did not menstruate. Rosa was ravenous, but also not; she learned from Magda how to drink the taste of a finger in one's mouth. They were in a place without pity, all pity was annihilated in Rosa, she looked at Stella's bones without pity. She was sure that Stella was waiting for Magda to die so she could put her teeth into the little thighs.

Rosa knew Magda was going to die very soon; she should have been dead already, but she had been buried away deep inside the magic shawl, mistaken there for the shivering mound of Rosa's breasts; Rosa clung to the shawl as if it covered only herself. No one took it away from her. Magda was mute. She never cried. Rosa hid her in the barracks, under the shawl, but she knew that one day

---

[1] The Nazi "Aryan" ideal of beauty included blond hair and blue eyes. Under the Nazis, Jews in Germany and German-occupied countries were made to wear yellow Stars of David.

someone would inform; or one day someone, not even Stella, would steal Magda to eat her. When Magda began to walk Rosa knew that Magda was going to die very soon, something would happen. She was afraid to fall asleep; she slept with the weight of her thigh on Magda's body; she was afraid she would smother Magda under her thigh. The weight of Rosa was becoming less and less; Rosa and Stella were slowly turning into air.

Magda was quiet, but her eyes were horribly alive, like blue tigers. She watched. Sometimes she laughed—it seemed a laugh, but how could it be? Magda had never seen anyone laugh. Still, Magda laughed at her shawl when the wind blew its corners, the bad wind with pieces of black in it, that made Stella's and Rosa's eyes tear. Magda's eyes were always clear and tearless. She watched like a tiger. She guarded her shawl. No one could touch it; only Rosa could touch it. Stella was not allowed. The shawl was Magda's own baby, her pet, her little sister. She tangled herself up in it and sucked on one of the corners when she wanted to be very still.

Then Stella took the shawl away and made Magda die.

Afterward Stella said: "I was cold."

And afterward she was always cold, always. The cold went into her heart: Rosa saw that Stella's heart was cold. Magda flopped onward with her little pencil legs scribbling this way and that, in search of the shawl; the pencils faltered at the barracks opening, where the light began. Rosa saw and pursued. But already Magda was in the square outside the barracks, in the jolly light. It was the roll-call arena. Every morning Rosa had to conceal Magda under the shawl against a wall of the barracks and go out and stand in the arena with Stella and hundreds of others, sometimes for hours, and Magda, deserted, was quiet under the shawl, sucking on her corner. Every day Magda was silent, and so she did not die. Rosa saw that today Magda was going to die, and at the same time a fearful joy ran in Rosa's two palms, her fingers were on fire, she was astonished, febrile: Magda, in the sunlight, swaying on her pencil legs, was howling. Ever since the drying up of Rosa's nipples, ever since Magda's last scream on the road, Magda had been devoid of any syllable; Magda was a mute. Rosa believed that something had gone wrong with her vocal cords, with her windpipe, with the cave of her larynx; Magda was defective, without a voice; perhaps she was deaf; there might be something amiss with her intelligence; Magda was dumb. Even the laugh that came when the ash-stippled wind made a clown out of Magda's shawl was only the air-blown showing of her teeth. Even when the lice, head lice and body lice, crazed her so that she became as wild as one of the big rats that plundered the barracks at daybreak looking for carrion, she rubbed and scratched and kicked and bit and rolled without a whimper. But now Magda's mouth was spilling a long viscous rope of clamor.

"Maaaa—"

It was the first noise Magda had ever sent out from her throat since the drying up of Rosa's nipples.

"Maaaa . . . aaa!"

Again! Magda was wavering in the perilous sunlight of the arena, scribbling on such pitiful little bent shins. Rosa saw. She saw that Magda was grieving for the loss of her shawl, she saw that Magda was going to die. A tide of commands hammered in Rosa's nipples: Fetch, get, bring! But she did not know which to go after first, Magda or the shawl. If she jumped out into the arena to snatch Magda up, the howling would not stop, because Magda would still not have the shawl; but if she ran back into the barracks to find the shawl, and if she found it, and if she came after Magda holding it and shaking it, then she would get Magda back, Magda would put the shawl in her mouth and turn dumb again.

Rosa entered the dark. It was easy to discover the shawl. Stella was heaped under it, asleep in her thin bones. Rosa tore the shawl free and flew—she could fly, she was only air—into the arena. The sunheat murmured of another life, of butterflies in summer. The light was placid, mellow. On the other side of the steel fence, far away, there were green meadows speckled with dandelions and deep-colored violets; beyond them, even farther, innocent tiger lilies, tall, lifting their orange bonnets. In the barracks they spoke of "flowers," of "rain": excrement, thick turd-braids, and the slow stinking maroon waterfall that slunk down from the upper bunks, the stink mixed with a bitter fatty floating smoke that greased Rosa's skin. She stood for an instant at the margin of the arena. Sometimes the electricity inside the fence would seem to hum; even Stella said it was only an imagining, but Rosa heard real sounds in the wire: grainy sad voices. The farther she was from the fence, the more clearly the voices crowded at her. The lamenting voices strummed so convincingly, so passionately, it was impossible to suspect them of being phantoms. The voices told her to hold up the shawl, high; the voices told her to shake it, to whip with it, to unfurl it like a flag. Rosa lifted, shook, whipped, unfurled. Far off, very far, Magda leaned across her air-fed belly, reaching out with the rods of her arms. She was high up, elevated, riding someone's shoulder. But the shoulder that carried Magda was not coming toward Rosa and the shawl, it was drifting away, the speck of Magda was moving more and more into the smoky distance. Above the shoulder a helmet glinted. The light tapped the helmet and sparkled in into a goblet. Below the helmet a black body like a domino and a pair of black boots hurled themselves in the direction of the electrified fence. The electric voices began to chatter wildly. "Maamaa, maaa-maaa," they all hummed together. How far Magda was from Rosa now, across the whole square, past a dozen barracks, all the way on the other side! She was no bigger than a moth.

All at once Magda was swimming through the air. The whole of Magda traveled through loftiness. She looked like a butterfly touching a silver vine. And the moment Magda's feathered round head and her pencil legs and balloonish belly and zigzag arms splashed against the fence, the steel voices went mad in their growling, urging Rosa to run and run to the spot where Magda had fallen from her flight against the electrified fence; but of course Rosa did not obey them. She only stood, because if she ran they would shoot, and if she tried to pick up the sticks of Magda's body they would shoot, and if she let the wolf's screech ascending now through the ladder of her skeleton break out, they would shoot; so she took Magda's shawl and filled her own mouth with it, stuffed it in and stuffed it in, until she was swallowing up the wolf's screech and tasting the cinnamon and almond depth of Magda's saliva; and Rosa drank Magda's shawl until it dried.

Lore Segal 1928–

L ore Segal, a short-story writer, translator, and novelist, was educated at Bedford College, University of London, after her escape from Nazi-era Austria. Her autobiographical novel, *Other People's Houses* (1964), documents this difficult period in her life and is perhaps her best-known work. Her other works include *Tell Me a Mitzi* (1970), *All the Way Home* (1973), and *The Story of Mrs. Brubeck and Trouble* (1981). She contributes regularly to such periodicals as *The New Yorker, Commentary, The New Republic,* and other publications. Her many honors include a Guggenheim Fellowship and a National Council for the Arts and Humanities Grant. Segal, also a professor of creative writing, is noted for stories that often "reflect the warmth and naturalness of family life with a gentle mirth. Hers is seemingly effortless storytelling. . . ."

THE REVERSE BUG

"Let's get the announcements out of the way," said Ilka, the teacher, to her foreigners in Conversational English for Adults. "Tomorrow evening the institute is holding a symposium. Ahmed," she asked the Turkish student with the magnificently drooping mustache, who also wore the institute's janitorial keys hooked to his belt, "where are they holding the symposium?"

"In the New Theatre," said Ahmed.

"The theme," said the teacher, "is 'Should there be a statute of limitations on genocide?' with a wine-and-cheese reception —"

"In the lounge," said Ahmed.

"To which you are all invited. Now," Ilka said in the bright voice of a hostess trying to make a sluggish dinner party go, "what shall we talk about? Doesn't do me a bit of good, I know, to ask you all to come forward and sit in a nice cozy clump. Who would like to start us off? Tell us a story, somebody. We love stories. Tell the class how you came to America."

The teacher looked determinedly past the hand, the arm, with which Gerti

Gruner stirred the air—death, taxes, and Thursdays, Gerti Gruner in the front row center. Ilka's eye passed over Paulino, who sat in the last row, with his back to the wall. Matsue, a pleasant, older Japanese from the university's engineering department, smiled at Ilka and shook his head, meaning "Please, not me!" Matsue was sitting in his usual place by the window, but Ilka had to orient herself as to the whereabouts of Izmira, the Cypriot doctor, who always left two empty rows between herself and Ahmed, the Turk. Today it was Juan, the Basque, who sat in the rightmost corner, and Eduardo, the Spaniard from Madrid, in the leftmost.

Ilka looked around for someone too shy to self-start who might enjoy talking if called upon, but Gerti's hand stabbed the air immediately underneath Ilka's chin, so she said, "Gerti wants to start. Go, Gerti. When did you come to the United States?"

"In last June," said Gerti.

Ilka corrected her, and said, "Tell the class where you came from, and, everybody, please speak in whole sentences."

Gerti said, "I have lived before in Uruguay."

"We would say, '*Before that I lived*,'" said Ilka, and Gerti said, "And *before that* in Vienna."

Gerti's story bore a family likeness to the teacher's own superannuated, indigestible history of being sent out of Hitler's Europe as a little girl.

Gerti said, "In the Vienna train station has my father told to me . . ."

"*Told me.*"

"*Told me* that so soon as I am coming to Montevideo . . ."

Ilka said, "As soon as I *come*, or more colloquially, *get* to Montevideo . . ."

Gerti said, "*Get* to Montevideo, I should tell to all the people . . ."

Ilka corrected her. Gerti said, "*Tell* all the people to bring my father out from Vienna before come the Nazis and put him in concentration camp."

Ilka said, "In 'the' or 'a' concentration camp."

"Also my mother," said Gerti, "and my Opa, and my Oma, and my Onkel Peter, and the twins, Hedi and Albert. My father has told, 'Tell to the foster mother, "Go, please, with me, to the American Consulate."'"

"My father went to the American Consulate," said Paulino, and everybody turned and looked at him. Paulino's voice had not been heard in class since the first Thursday, when Ilka had got her students to go around the room and introduce themselves to one another. Paulino had said that his name was Paulino Patillo and that he was born in Bolivia. Ilka was charmed to realize it was Danny Kaye of whom Paulino reminded her—fair, curly, middle-aged, smiling. He came punctually every Thursday. Was he a very sweet or a very simple man?

Ilka said, "Paulino will tell us his story after Gerti has finished. How old were you when you left Europe?" Ilka asked, to reactivate Gerti, who said, "Eight years," but she and the rest of the class, and the teacher herself, were watching Paulino put his right hand inside the left breast pocket of his jacket, withdraw an envelope, turn it upside down, and shake out onto the desk before him a pile of news clippings. Some looked sharp and new, some frayed and yellow; some seemed to be single paragraphs, others the length of several columns.

"You got to Montevideo . . ." Ilka prompted Gerti.

"And my foster mother has fetched me from the ship. I said, 'Hello, and will you please bring out from Vienna my father before come the Nazis and put him in—a concentration camp!'" Gerti said triumphantly.

Paulino had brought the envelope close to his eyes and was looking inside. He inserted a forefinger, loosened something that was stuck, and shook out a last clipping. It broke at the fold when Paulino flattened it onto the desk top. Paulino brushed away the several paper crumbs before beginning to read: "La Paz, September 19."

"Paulino," said Ilka, "You must wait till Gerti is finished."

But Paulino read, "Señora Pilar Patillo has reported the disappearance of her husband, Claudio Patillo, after a visit to the American Consulate in La Paz on September 15."

"Gerti, go on," said Ilka.

"The foster mother has said, 'When comes home the Uncle from the office, we will ask.' I said, 'And bring out, please, also my mother, my Opa, my Oma, my Onkel Peter . . .'"

Paulino read, "A spokesman for the American Consulate contacted in La Paz states categorically that no record exists of a visit from Señor Patillo within the last two months. . . ."

"Paulino, you really *have* to wait your turn," Ilka said.

Gerti said, " 'Also the twins.' The foster mother has made such a desperate face with her lips."

Paulino read, "Nor does the consular calendar for September show any appointment made with Señor Patillo. Inquiries are said to be under way with the Consulate at Sucre." And Paulino folded his column of newsprint and returned it to the envelope.

"O.K., thank you, Paulino," Ilka said.

Gerti said, "When the foster father has come home, he said, 'We will see, tomorrow,' and I said, 'And will you go, please, with me, to the American Consulate?' and the foster father has made a face."

Paulino was flattening the second column of newsprint on his desk. He read, "New York, December 12 . . ."

"*Paulino*," said Ilka, and caught Matsue's eye. He was looking expressly at her. He shook his head ever so slightly and with his right hand, palm down, he patted the air three times. In the intelligible language of charade with which humankind frustrated God at Babel, Matsue was saying, "Calm down, Ilka. Let Paulino finish. Nothing you can do will stop him." Ilka was grateful to Matsue.

"A spokesman for the Israeli Mission to the United Nations," read Paulino, "denies a report that Claudio Patillo, missing after a visit to the American Consulate in La Paz since September 15, is en route to Israel. . . ." Paulino finished reading this column also, folded it into the envelope, and unfolded the next column. "U.P.I., January 30. The car of Pilar Patillo, wife of Claudio Patillo, who was reported missing from La Paz last September, has been found at the bottom of a ravine in the eastern Andes. It is not known whether any bodies were found inside the wreck," Paulino read with the blind forward motion of a tank that receives no message from any sound or movement in the world outside. The students had stopped looking at Paulino; they were not looking at the teacher. They looked into their laps. Paulino read one column after the other, returning each to his envelope before he took the next, and when he had read and returned the last, and returned the envelope to his breast pocket, he leaned his back against the wall and turned to the teacher his sweet, habitual smile of expectant participation.

Gerti said, "In that same night have I woken up . . ."

"That night I *woke* up," the teacher helplessly said.

"*Woke* up," Gerti Gruner said, "and I have thought, What if it is even now, this exact minute, that one Nazi is knocking at the door, and I am here lying not telling to anybody anything, and I have stood up and gone into the bedroom where were sleeping the foster mother and father. Next morning has the foster mother gone with me to the refugee committee, and they found for me a different foster family."

"Your turn, Matsue," Ilka said. "How, when, and why did you come to the States? We're all here to help you!" Matsue's written English was flawless, but he spoke with an accent that was almost impenetrable. His contribution to class conversation always involved a communal interpretative act.

"Aisutudieddu attoza unibashite innu munhen," Matsue said.

A couple of stabs and Eduardo, the madrileño, got it: "You studied at the university in Munich!"

"You studied acoustics?" ventured Izmira, the Cypriot doctor.

"The war trapped you in Germany?" proposed Ahmed, the Turk.

"You have been working in the ovens," suggested Gerti, the Viennese.

"Acoustic ovens?" marvelled Ilka. "Do you mean stoves? Ranges?"

No, what Matsue meant was that he had got his first job with a Munich firm employed in soundproofing the Dachau ovens so that what went on inside could not be heard on the outside. "I made the tapes," said Matsue. "Tapes?" they asked him. They figured out that Matsue had returned to Japan in 1946. He had collected Hiroshima "tapes." He had been brought to Washington as an acoustical consultant to the Kennedy Center, and had come to Connecticut to design the sound system of the New Theatre at Concordance University, where he subsequently accepted a research appointment in the department of engineering. He was now returning home, having finished his work—Ilka thought he said—on the reverse bug.

Ilka said, "I thought, ha ha, you said 'the reverse bug'!"

"The reverse bug" was what everybody understood Matsue to say that he had said. With his right hand he performed a row of air loops, and, pointing at the wall behind the teacher's desk, asked for, and received, her O.K. to explain himself in writing on the blackboard.

Chalk in hand, he was eloquent on the subject of the regular bug, which can be introduced into a room to relay to those outside what those inside want them not to hear. A sophisticated modern bug, explained Matsue, was impossible to locate and deactivate. Buildings had had to be taken apart in order to rid them of alien listening devices. The reverse bug, equally impossible to locate and deactivate, was a device whereby those outside were able to relay *into* a room what those inside would prefer not to have to hear.

"And how would such a device be used?" Ilka asked him.

Matsue was understood to say that it could be useful in certain situations to certain consulates, and Paulino said, "My father went to the American Consulate," and put his hand into his breast pocket. Here Ilka stood up, and, though there was still a good fifteen minutes of class time, said, "So! I will see you all next Thursday. Everybody—be thinking of subjects you would like to talk about. Don't forget the symposium tomorrow evening!" She walked quickly out the door.

Ilka entered the New Theatre late and was glad to see Matsue sitting on the aisle in the second row from the back with an empty seat beside him. The platform people were already settling into their places. On the right, an exquisite golden-skinned Latin man was talking, in a way people talk to people they have known a long time, with a heavy, rumpled man, whom Ilka pegged as Israeli. "Look at the thin man on the left," Ilka said to Matsue. "He has to be from Washington. Only a Washingtonian's hair gets to be that particular white color." Matsue laughed. Ilka asked him if he knew who the woman with the oversized glasses and the white hair straight to the shoulders might be, and Matsue said something that Ilka did not understand. The rest of the panelists were institute people, Ilka's colleagues—little Joe Bernstine from philosophy, Yvette Gordot, a mathematician, and Leslie Shakespere, an Englishman, the institute's new director, who sat in the moderator's chair.

Leslie Shakespere had the soft weight of a man who likes to eat and the fine head of a man who thinks. It had not as yet occurred to Ilka that she was in love with Leslie. She watched him fussing with the microphone. "Why do we need this?" she could read Leslie's lips saying. "Since when do we use microphones in the New Theatre?" Now he quieted the hall with a grateful welcome for this fine attendance at a discussion of one of our generation's unmanageable questions—the application of justice in an era of genocides.

Here Rabbi Shlomo Grossman rose from the floor and wished to take exception to the plural formulation: "All killings are not murders; all murders are not 'genocides.'"

Leslie said, "Shlomo, could you hold your remarks until question time?"

Rabbi Grossman said, "Remarks? Is that what I'm making? Remarks! The death of six million—is it in the realm of a question?"

Leslie said, "I give you my word that there will be room for the full expression of what you want to say when we open the discussion to the floor." Rabbi Grossman acceded to the evident desire of the friends sitting near him that he should sit down.

Director Leslie Shakespere gave the briefest of accounts of the combined federal and private funding that had enabled the Concordance Institute to invite these very distinguished panelists to take part in the institute's Genocide Project. "The institute, as you know, has a long-standing tradition of 'debriefings,' in which the participants in a project that is winding down sum up their thinking for the members of the institute, the university, and the public. But this evening's panel has agreed, by way of an experiment, to talk in an informal way of our notions, of the history of the interest each of us brings to this question— problem—at the point of entry. I want us to interest ourselves in the *nature of inquiry:* Will we come out of this project with our original notions reinforced? Modified? Made over?

"I imagine that this inquiry will range somewhere between the legal concept of a statute of limitations that specifies the time within which human law must respond to a specific crime, and the Biblical concept of the visitation of punishment of the sins of the fathers upon the children. One famous version plays itself out in the 'Oresteia,' where a crime is punished by an act that is itself a crime and punishable, and so on, down the generations. Enough. Let me introduce our panel, whom it will be our very great pleasure to have among us in the coming months."

The white-haired man turned out to be the West German ex-mayor of Obernpest, Dieter Dobelmann. Ilka felt the prompt conviction that she had known all along—that one could tell from a mile—that that mouth, that jaw, had to be German. Leslie dwelled on Dobelmann's persuasive anti-Nazi credentials. The woman with the glasses was on loan to the institute from Georgetown University. ("The white hair! You see!" Ilka whispered to Matsue, who laughed.) She was Jerusalem-born Shulamit Gershon, professor of international law, and longtime adviser to Israel's ongoing project to identify Nazi war criminals and bring them to trial. The rumpled man was the English theologian William B. Thayer. The Latin really was a Latin—Sebastian Maderiaga, who was taking time off from his consulate in New York. Leslie squeezed his eyes to see past the stage lights into the well of the New Theatre. There was a rustle of people turning to locate the voice that had said, "My father went to the American Consulate," but it said nothing further and the audience settled back. Leslie introduced Yvette and Joe, the institute's own fellows assigned to Genocide.

Ilka and Matsue leaned forward, watching Paulino across the aisle. Paulino was withdrawing the envelope from his breast pocket. "Without a desk?" whispered Ilka anxiously. Paulino upturned the envelope onto the slope of his lap. The young student sitting beside him got on his knees to retrieve the sliding batch of newsprint and held onto it while Paulino arranged his coat across his thighs to create a surface.

"My own puzzle," said Leslie, "with which I would like to puzzle our panel, is this: Where do I, where do we all, get these feelings of moral malaise when wrong goes unpunished and right goes unrewarded?"

Paulino had brought his first newspaper column up to his eyes and read, "La Paz, September 19. Señora Pilar Patillo has reported the disappearance of her husband, Claudio Patillo . . ."

"Where," Leslie was saying, "does the human mind derive its expectation of a set of consequences for which it finds no evidence whatsoever in nature or in history, or in looking around its own autobiography? . . . Could I *please* ask for quiet from the floor until we open the discussion?" Leslie was once again peering out into the hall.

The audience turned and looked at Paulino reading, "Nor does the consular calendar for September show any appointment . . ." Shulamit Gershon leaned toward Leslie and spoke to him for several moments while Paulino read, "A spokesman for the Israeli Mission to the United Nations denies a report . . ."

It was after several attempts to persuade him to stop that Leslie said, "Ahmed? Is Ahmed in the hall? Ahmed, would you be good enough to remove the unquiet gentleman as gently as necessary force will allow. Take him to my office, please, and I will meet with him after the symposium."

Everybody watched Ahmed walk up the aisle with a large and sheepish-looking student. The two lifted the unresisting Paulino out of his seat by the armpits. They carried him reading, "The car of Pilar Patillo, wife of Claudio Patillo . . ."—backward, out the door.

The action had something about it of the classic comedy routine. There was a cackling, then the relief of general laughter. Leslie relaxed and sat back, understanding that it would require some moments to get the evening back on track, but the cackling did not stop. Leslie said, "Please." He waited. He cocked his head and listened: it was more like a hiccupping that straightened and elongated into a sound drawn on a single breath. Leslie looked at the panel. The panel looked. The audience looked all around. Leslie bent his ear down to the microphone. It did him no good to turn the button off and on, to put his hand over the mouthpiece, to bend down as if to look it in the eye. "Anybody know— is the sound here centrally controlled?" he asked. The noise was growing incrementally. Members of the audience drew their heads back and down into their shoulders. It came to them—it became impossible to not know—that it was not laughter to which they were listening but somebody yelling. Somewhere there was a person, and the person was screaming.

Ilka looked at Matsue, whose eyes were closed. He looked an old man.

The screaming stopped. The relief was spectacular, but lasted only for that same unnaturally long moment in which a howling child, having finally exhausted its strength, is fetching up new breath from some deepest source for a new onslaught. The howl resumed at a volume that was too great for the small theatre; the human ear could not accommodate it. People experienced a physical distress. They put their hands over their ears.

Leslie had risen. He said, "I'm going to suggest an alteration in the order of this evening's proceedings. Why don't we clear the hall—everybody, please, move into the lounge, have some wine, have some cheese while we locate the source of the trouble."

Quickly, while people were moving along their rows, Ilka popped out into the aisle and collected the trail of Paulino's news clippings. The young student who had sat next to Paulino found and handed her the envelope.

Ilka walked down the hall in the direction of Leslie Shakespere's office, diagnosing in herself an inappropriate excitement at having it in her power to throw light.

Ilka looked into Leslie's office. Paulino sat on a hard chair with his back to the door, shaking his head violently from side to side. Leslie stood facing him. He and Ahmed and all the panelists, who had disposed themselves about Leslie's office, were screwing their eyes up as if wanting very badly to close every bodily opening through which unwanted information is able to enter. The intervening wall had somewhat modified that volume, but not the variety—length, pitch, and pattern—of the sounds that continually altered as in response to a new and continually changing cause.

Leslie said, "We know this stuff goes on whether we are hearing it or not, but this. . . ." He saw Ilka at the door and said, "Mr. Patillo is your student, no? He refuses to tell us how to locate the screaming unless they release his father."

Ilka said, "*Paulino?* Does Paulino *say* he 'refuses'?"

Leslie said to Paulino, "Will you please tell us how to find the source of this noise so we can shut it off?"

Paulino shook his head and said, "It is my father screaming."

"Ilka followed the direction of Leslie's eye. Maderiaga was perched with a helpless elegance on the corner of Leslie's desk, speaking Spanish into the telephone. Through the open door that led into a little outer office, Ilka saw Shulamit Gershon hang up the phone. She came back in and said, "Patillo is the name this young man's father adopted from his Bolivian wife. He's Klaus Herrmann, who headed the German Census Bureau. After the Anschluss they sent him to Vienna to put together the registry of Jewish names and addresses. Then on to Budapest, and so on. After the war we traced him to La Paz. I think he got into trouble with some mines or weapons deals. We put him on the back burner when it turned out the Bolivians were after him as well."

Now Maderiaga hung up and said, "Hasn't he been the busy little man! My office is going to check if it's the Gonzales people who got him for expropriating somebody's tin mine, or the R.R.N. If they suspect Patillo of connection with the helicopter crash that killed President Barrientos, they'll have more or less killed him."

"It is my father screaming," said Paulino.

"It's got nothing to do with his father," said Ilka. While Matsue was explaining the reverse bug on the blackboard the previous evening, Ilka had grasped the principle. It disintegrated as she was explaining it to Leslie. She was distracted, moreover, by a retrospective image: Last night, hurrying down the corridor, Ilka had turned her head and must have seen, since she was now able to recollect, young Ahmed and Matsue moving away together down the hall. If Ilka had thought them a curious couple, the thought, having nothing to feed on, had died before her lively wish to maneuver Gerti and Paulino into one elevator just as the doors were closing, so she could come down in the other.

Now Ilka asked Ahmed, "Where did you and Matsue go after class last night?"

Ahmed said, "He wanted to come into the New Theatre."

Leslie said, "Ahmed, forgive me for ordering you around all evening, but will you go and find me Matsue and bring him here to my office?"

"He has gone," said Ahmed. "I saw him leave by the front door with a suitcase on wheels."

"He is going home," said Ilka. "Matsue has finished his job."

Paulino said, "It is my father screaming."

"No, it's not, Paulino," said Ilka. "Those screams are from Dachau and they are from Hiroshima."

"It is my father," said Paulino, "and my mother."

Leslie asked Ilka to come with him to the airport. They caught up with Matsue queuing, with only five passengers ahead of him, to enter the gangway to his plane.

Ilka said, "Matsue, you're not going away without telling us how to shut the thing off!"

Matsue said, "Itto dozunotto shattoffu."

Ilka and Leslie said, "Excuse me?"

With the hand that was not holding his boarding pass, Matsue performed a charade of turning a faucet and he shook his head. Ilka and Leslie understood him to be saying, "It does not shut off." Matsue stepped out of the line, kissed Ilka on the cheek, stepped back, and passed through the door.

When Concordance Institute takes hold of a situation, it deals humanely with it. Leslie found funds to pay a private sanitarium to evaluate Paulino. Back at the New Theatre, the police, a bomb squad, and a private acoustics company from Washington set themselves to locate the source of the screaming.

Leslie looked haggard. His colleagues worried when their director, a sensible man, continued to blame the microphone after the microphone had been removed and the screaming continued. The sound seemed not to be going to loop back to any familiar beginning, so that the hearers might have become familiar— might, in a manner of speaking, have made friends—with one particular roar or screech, but to be going on to perpetually new and fresh howls of pain.

Neither the Japanese Embassy in Washington nor the American Embassy in Tokyo had got anywhere with the tracers sent out to locate Matsue. Leslie called in a technician. "Look into the wiring!" he said, and saw in the man's eyes that look experts wear when they have explained something and the layman says what he said in the beginning all over again. The expert had another go. He talked to Leslie about the nature of the sound wave; he talked about cross-Atlantic phone calls and about the electric guitar. Leslie said, "Could you look *inside* the wiring?"

Leslie fired the first team of acoustical experts, found another company, and asked them to check inside the wiring. The new man reported back to Leslie: He thought they might start by taking down the stage portion of the theatre. If the sound people worked closely with the demolition people, they might be able to avoid having to mess with the body of the hall.

The phone call that Maderiaga had made on the night of the symposium had, in the meantime, set in motion a series of official acts that were bringing to America—to Concordance—Paulino Patillo's father, Claudio/Klaus Patillo/Herrmann. The old man was eighty-nine, missing an eye by an act of man and a lung by an act of God. On the plane he suffered a collapse and was rushed from the airport straight to Concordance University's Medical Center.

Rabbi Grossman walked into Leslie's office and said, "Am I hearing things? You've approved a house, on this campus, for the accomplice of the genocide of Austrian and Hungarian Jewry?"

"And a private nurse!" said Leslie.

"Are you out of your mind?" asked Rabbi Grossman.

"Practically. Yes," said Leslie.

"You look terrible," said Shlomo Grossman, and sat down.

"What," Leslie said, "am I the hell to do with an old Nazi who is postoperative, whose son is in the sanitarium, who doesn't know a soul, doesn't have a dime, doesn't have a roof over his head?"

"Send him home to Germany," shouted Shlomo.

"I tried. Dobelmann says they won't recognize Claudio Patillo as one of their nationals."

"So send him to his comeuppance in Israel!"

"Shulamit says they're no longer interested, Shlomo! They have other things on hand!"

"Put him back on the plane and turn it around."

"For another round of screaming? Shlomo!" cried Leslie, and put his hands over his ears against the noise that, issuing out of the dismembered building materials piled in back of the institute, blanketed the countryside for miles around, made its way down every street of the small university town, into every back yard, and filtered in through Leslie's closed and shuttered windows. "Shlomo," Leslie said, "come over tonight. I promise Eliza will cook you something you can eat. I want you, and I want Ilka—and we'll see who all else—to help me think this thing through."

* * *

"We . . . I," said Leslie that night, "need to understand how the scream of Dachau is the same, and how it is a different scream from the scream of Hiroshima. And after that I need to learn how to listen to the selfsame sound that rises out of the Hell in which the torturer is getting what he's got coming. . . ."

His wife called, "Leslie, can you come and talk to Ahmed?"

Leslie went out and came back in carrying his coat. A couple of young punks with an agenda of their own had broken into Patillo/Herrmann's new American house. They had gagged the nurse and tied her and Klaus up in the new American bathroom. Here Ilka began to laugh. Leslie buttoned his coat and said, "I'm sorry, but I have to go on over. Ilka. Shlomo, please, I leave for Washington tomorrow, early, to talk to the Superfund people. While I'm there I want to get a Scream Project funded. Ilka? Ilka, what is it?" But Ilka was helplessly giggling and could not answer him. Leslie said, "What I need is for you two to please sit down, here and now, and come up with a formulation I can take with me to present to Arts and Humanities."

The Superfund granted Concordance an allowance, for scream disposal, and the dismembered stage of the New Theatre was loaded onto a flatbed truck and driven west. The population along Route 90 and all the way down to Arizona came out into the street, eyes squeezed together, heads pulled back and down into shoulders. They buried the thing fifteen feet under, well away from the highway, and let the desert howl.

Ursula K. Le Guin 1929–

Though most frequently labeled a science-fiction or fantasy writer, Ursula K. Le Guin's works defy categorization. "Some of my fiction is 'science fiction,' some of it is 'fantasy,' some of it is 'realist,' and some of it is "magical realism,'" she has stated. Her approach allows her to invent new worlds, societies, and cultures, often presenting an idealized view of human potential combined with a sharp criticism of the current human condition. Making strong use of symbolism and literary devices, Le Guin advocates chaos and rebellion for the well-balanced society. Her more highly praised efforts include the novels *Rocannon's World* (1966), *Planet of Exile* (1966), *City of Illusions* (1967), *The Left Hand of Darkness* (1969), and *The Dispossessed: An Ambiguous Utopia* (1974), as well as numerous short stories, essays, screenplays, and children's books. Her *Earthsea Trilogy* (1968–72) has been compared to J. R. R. Tolkien's *The Lord of the Rings* in terms of subject and scope and helped LeGuin reach a large young adult audience.

SOME APPROACHES TO THE PROBLEM OF THE SHORTAGE OF TIME

The Little Tiny Hole Theory

The hypothesis put forward by James Osbold of the Lick Observatory, though magnificently comprehensive, presents certain difficulties to agencies seeking practical solutions to the problem. Divested of its mathematical formulation, Dr. Osbold's theory may be described in very approximate terms as positing the existence of an anomaly in the space-time continuum. The cause of the anomaly is a failure of reality to meet the specifications of the General Theory of Relativity, although only in one minor detail. Its effect on the actual constitution of the universe is a local imperfection or flaw, that is, a hole in the continuum.

The hole, according to Osbold's calculations, is a distinctly spacelike hole. In this spatiality lies its danger, since the imbalance thus constituted in the continuum causes a compensatory influx from the timelike aspect of the cosmos. In other words, time is running out of the hole. This has probably been going on ever since the origin of the universe 12 to 15 billion years ago, but only lately has the leak grown to noticeable proportions.

The propounder of the theory is not pessimistic, remarking that it might be even worse if the anomaly were in the timelike aspect of the continuum, in which case space would be escaping, possibly one dimension at a time, which would cause untold discomfort and confusion; although, Osbold adds, "In that event we might have time enough to do something about it."

Since the theory posits the hole's location somewhere or other, Lick and two Australian observatories have arranged a coordinated search for local variations in the red shift which might aid in pinpointing the point/instant. "It may still be a very small hole," Osbold says. "Quite tiny. It would not need to be very large to do a good deal of damage. But since the effect is so noticeable here on Earth, I feel we have a good chance of finding the thing perhaps no farther away than the Andromeda Galaxy, and then all we'll need is what you might call a Dutch boy."

The Nonbiodegradable Moment

A totally different explanation of the time shortage is offered by a research team of the Interco Development Corporation. Their approach to the problem, as presented by N. T. Chaudhuri, an internationally recognised authority on the ecology and ethology of the internal combustion engine, is chemical rather than cosmological. Chaudhuri has proved that the fumes of incompletely burned petroleum fuel, under certain conditions—diffused anxiety is the major predisposing factor—will form a chemical bond with time, "tying down" instants in the same manner as a nucleating agent "ties down" free atoms into molecules. The process is called chronocrystallisation or (in the case of acute anxiety) chronoprecipitation. The resulting compact arrangement of instants is far more orderly than the preexistent random "nowness," but unfortunately this decrease in entropy is paid for by a very marked increase in bioinsupportability. In fact the petroleum/time compound appears to be absolutely incompatible with life in any form, even anaerobic bacteria, of which so much was hoped.

The present danger, then, as described by team member F. Gonzales Park, is that so much of our free time, or radical time properly speaking, will be locked into this noxious compound (which she refers to as petropsychotoxin or PPST) that we will be forced to bring up the vast deposits of PPST which the U.S. Government has dumped or stored in various caves, swamps, holes, oceans, and back yards, and deliberately break down the compound, thus releasing free temporal radicals. Senator Helms and several Sunbelt Democrats have already protested. Certainly the process of reclaiming time from PPST is risky, requiring so much oxygen that we might end up, as O. Heiko, a third member of the team, puts it, with plenty of free time but no air.

Feeling that time is running out even faster than the oil wells, Heiko himself favors an "austerity" approach to the problem, beginning with a ban on aircraft flying in excess of the speed of sound, and working steadily on down through prop planes, racing cars, standard cars, ships, motorboats, etc., until if necessary, all petroleum-powered vehicles have been eliminated. Speed serves as the standard of priority, since the higher the velocity of the petroleum-fueled vehicle, and hence the more concentrated the conscious or subliminal anxiety of the driver/passengers, the more complete is the petrolisation of time, and the more poisonous the resultant PPST. Heiko, believing there is no "safe level" of contamination, thinks that probably not even mopeds would eventually escape the ban. As he points out, a single gas-powered lawnmower moving at less than 3 mph can petrolise three solid hours of a Sunday afternoon in an area of one city block.

A ban on gas guzzlers may, however, solve only half the problem. An attempt by the Islamic League to raise the price of crude time by $8.50/hr was recently foiled by prompt action by the Organisation of Time Consuming States; but West Germany is already paying $18.75/hr—twice what the American consumer expects to pay for his time.

Bleeding Hearts? The Temporal Conservation Movement

Willing to listen to the cosmological and chemical hypotheses but uncommitted to either is a growing consortium of scientists and laypersons, many of whom have grouped themselves into organisations such as Le Temps Perdu (Brussels), Protestants Concerned at the Waste of Time (Indianapolis), and the driving, widespread Latin-American action group Mañana. A Mañanista spokesperson, Dolores Guzman McIntosh of Buenos Aires, states the group's view: "We have—

all of us—almost entirely wasted our time. If we do not save it, we are lost. There is not much time left." The Mañanistas have so far carefully avoided political affiliation, stating bluntly that the time shortfall is the fault of Communist and Capitalist governments equally. A growing number of priests from Mexico to Chile have joined the movement, but the vatican recently issued an official denunciation of those "who, while they talk of saving time, lose their own souls." In Italy a Communist temporal-conservation group, Eppur Si Muove, was recently splintered by the defection of its president, who after a visit to Moscow stated in print: "Having watched the bureaucracy of the Soviet Union in action I have lost faith in the arousal of class consciousness as the principal means towards our goal."

A group of social scientists in Cambridge, England, continues meanwhile to investigate the as yet unproven link of the time shortage with shortage of temper. "If we could show the connection," says psychologist Derrick Groat, "the temporal conservation groups might be able to act more effectively. As it is they mostly quarrel. Everybody wants to save time before it's gone forever, but nobody really knows how, and so we all get cross. If only there were a substitute, you know, like solar and geothermal for petroleum, it would ease the strain. But evidently we have to make do with what we've got." Groast mentioned the "time stretcher" marketed by General Substances under the trademark Sudokron, withdrawn last year after tests indicated that moderate doses caused laboratory mice to turn into Kleenex. Informed that the Rand Corporation was devoting massive funding to research into a substitute for time, he said, "I wish them luck. But they may have to work longer hours at it!" The British scientist was referring to the fact that the United States has shortened the hour by ten minutes while retaining twenty-four per day, while the EEC countries, foreseeing increasing shortages, have chosen to keep sixty minutes to the hour but allow only twenty hours to the "devalued" European day.

Meantime, the average citizen in Moscow or Chicago, while often complaining about the shortage of time or the deteriorating quality of what remains, seems inclined to scoff at the doomsday prophets, and to put off such extreme measures as rationing as long as possible. Perhaps he feels, along with Ecclesiastes and the president, that when you've seen one day, you've seen 'em all.

SHE UNNAMES THEM

Most of them accepted namelessness with the perfect indifference with which they had so long accepted and ignored their names. Whales and dolphins, seals and sea otters consented with particular grace and alacrity, sliding into anonymity as into their element. A faction of yaks, however, protested. They said that "yak" sounded right, and that almost everyone who knew they existed called them that. Unlike the ubiquitous creatures such as rats and fleas, who had been called by hundreds or thousands of different names since Babel, the yaks could truly say, they said, that they had a *name*. They discussed the matter all summer. The councils of the elderly females finally agreed that though the name might be useful to others it was so redundant from the yak point of view that they never spoke it themselves and hence might as well dispense with it. After they presented the argument in this light to their bulls, a full consensus was delayed only by the onset of severe early blizzards. Soon after the beginning of the thaw, their agreement was reached and the designation "yak" was returned to the donor.

Among the domestic animals, few horses had cared what anybody called them since the failure of Dean Swift's[1] attempt to name them from their own vocabulary. Cattle, sheep, swine, asses, mules and goats, along with chickens, geese, and turkeys, all agreed enthusiastically to give their names back to the people to whom—as they put it—they belonged.

A couple of problems did come up with pets. The cats, of course, steadfastly denied ever having had any name other than those self-given, unspoken, ineffably personal names which, as the poet named Eliot[2] said, they spend long hours daily contemplating—though none of the contemplators has ever admitted that what they contemplate is their names and some onlookers have wondered if the object of that meditative gaze might not in fact be the Perfect, or Platonic, Mouse.[3] In any case, it is a moot point now. It was with the dogs, and with some parrots, lovebirds, ravens and mynahs, that the trouble arose. These verbally talented individuals insisted that their names were important to them, and flatly refused to part with them. But as soon as they understood that the issue was precisely one of individual choice, and that anybody who wanted to be called Rover, or Froufrou, or Polly, or even Birdie in the personal sense, was perfectly free to do so, not one of them had the least objection to parting with the lower-case (or, as regards German creatures, uppercase) generic appellations "poodle," "parrot," "dog," or "bird," and all the Linnaean[4] qualifiers that had trailed along behind them for two hundred years like tin cans tied to a tail.

The insects parted with their names in vast clouds and swarms of ephemeral[5] syllables buzzing and stinging and humming and flitting and crawling and tunneling away.

---

[1] The last section of *Gulliver's Travels* (1726) by Jonathan Swift (1667–1745), dean of St. Patrick's, Dublin, describes the country and language of the Houyhnhnms, who were rational horses.

[2] T. S. Eliot, in *The Naming of Cats* (1939).

[3] The Greek philosopher Plato (4th century B.C.) argued that there exist ideal forms or archetypes of all material things (these perfect Ideas gurantee the existance of the phenomenal world).

[4] Swiss botanist Karl Linnaeus (1701–1778) devised the modern system of binomial scientific nomenclature for plants and animals.

[5] Existing only for a day.

As for the fish of the sea, their names dispersed from them in silence throughout the oceans like faint, dark blurs of cuttlefish ink, and drifted off on the currents without a trace.

None were left now to unname, and yet how close I felt to them when I saw one of them swim or fly or trot or crawl across my way or over my skin, or stalk me in the night, or go along beside me for a while in the day. They seemed far closer than when their names had stood between myself and them like a clear barrier: so close that my fear of them and their fear of me became one same fear. And the attraction that many of us felt, the desire to smell one another's smells, feel or rub or caress one another's scales or skin or feather or fur, taste one another's scales or skin or feathers or fur, taste one another's blood or flesh, keep one another warm—that attraction was now all one with the fear, and the hunter could not be told from the hunted, nor the eater from the food.

This was more or less the effect I had been after. It was somewhat more powerful than I had anticipated, but I could not now, in all conscience, make an exception for myself. I resolutely put anxiety away, went to Adam,[6] and said, "You and your father lent me this—gave it to me, actually. It's been really useful but it doesn't exactly seem to fit very well lately. But thanks very much! It's really been very useful."

It is hard to give back a gift without sounding peevish or ungrateful, and I did not want to leave him with that impression of me. He was not paying much attention, as it happened, and said only, "Put it down there, O.K.?" and went on with what he was doing.

One of my reasons for doing what I did was that talk was getting us nowhere, but all the same I felt a little down. I had been prepared to defend my decision. And I thought that perhaps when he did notice he might be upset and want to talk. I put some things away and fiddled around a little, but he continued to do what he was doing and to take no notice of anything else. At last I said, "Well, goodbye, dear. I hope the garden key turns up."

He was fitting parts together, and said, without looking around, "O.K., fine dear. When's dinner?"

"I'm not sure," I said. "I'm going now. With the—" I hesitated, and finally said, "With them, you know," and went on out. In fact, I had only just then realized how hard it would have been to explain myself. I could not chatter away as I used to do, taking it all for granted. My words now must be as slow, as new, as single, as tentative as the steps I took going down the path away from the house, between the dark-branched, tall dancers motionless against the winter shining.

[6] In Genesis 2:19, God brings all the beasts to Adam for naming; in Genesis 3:20, shortly before their expulsion from the Garden of Eden, Adam gives his wife the name Eve.

THE PROFESSOR'S HOUSES

The professor has two houses, one inside the other. He lived with his wife and child in the outer house, which was comfortable, clean, disorderly, not quite big enough for all his books, her papers, their daughter's bright deciduous treasures. The roof leaked after heavy rains early in the fall before the wood swelled, but a bucket in the attic sufficed. No rain fell upon the inner house, where the professor lived without his wife and child, or so he said jokingly sometimes: "Here's where I live. My house." His daughter often added, without resentment, for the visitor's information, "It started out to be for me, but it's really his." And she might reach in to bring forth an inch-high table lamp with fluted shade, or a blue bowl the size of her little fingernail, marked "Kitty" and half full of eternal milk; but she was sure to replace these, after they had been admired, pretty near exactly where they had been. The little house was very orderly, and just big enough for all it contained, though to some tastes the bric-a brac in the parlor might seem excessive. The daughter's preference was for the store-brought gimmicks and appliances, the toasters and carpet sweepers of Lilliput, but she knew that most adult visitors would admire the perfection of the furnishings her father himself had so delicately and finely made and finished. He was inclined to be a little shy of showing off his own work, so she would point out the more ravishing elegances: the glass-fronted sideboard, the hardwood parquetry and the dadoes, the widow's walk. No visitor, child or adult, could withstand the fascination of the Venetian blinds, the infinitesimal slats that slanted and slid in perfect order on their cords of double-weight sewing thread. "Do you know how to make a Venetian blind?" the professor would inquire, setting up the visitor for his daughter, who would forestall or answer the hesitant negative with a joyful "Put his eyes out!" Her father, who was entertained by involutions and, like all teachers, willing to repeat a good thing, would then remark that after working for two weeks on those blinds he had established that a Venetian blind can also make an American blind.

"I did that awful rug in the nursery," the professor's wife, Julia, might say, evidencing her participation in the inner house, her approbation, her incompetence. "It's not up to Ian's standard, but he accepted the intent." The crocheted rug was, in fact, coarse-looking and curly edged; the needlepoint rugs in the other rooms, miniature Orientals and a gaudy floral in the master bedroom, lay flat and flawless.

The inner house stood on a low table in an open alcove, called "the bookshelf end," of the long living room of the outer house. Friends of the family checked the progress of its construction, furnishing, and fitting out as they came to dinner or for a drink from time to time, from year to year. Occasional visitors assumed that it belonged to the daughter and was kept downstairs on display because it was a really fine doll's house, a regular work of art, and miniatures were coming into or recently had been in vogue. To certain rather difficult guests, including the dean of his college, the professor, without affirming or denying his part as architect, cabinet-maker, roofer, glazier, electrician, and *tapissier,* might quote Claude Lévi-Strauss.[1] "It's in *La Pensée Sauvage,* I think," he would say. "His idea is that the reduced model—the miniature—allows a knowledge of the whole to precede the knowledge of the parts. A reversal of the usual process of knowing. Essentially, all the arts proceed that way, reducing a material dimension in favor of an intellectual dimension." He found that persons entirely incapable of, and averse to, the kind of concrete thought that was his chief pleasure in working on the house went rigid as bird dogs at the name of the father of structuralism, and sometimes continued to gaze at the doll's house for some minutes with the tense and earnest gaze of a pointer at a sitting duck. The professor's wife had to entertain a good many strangers when she became state coordinator of the conservation organization for which she worked, but her guests, with urgent business on their minds, admired the doll's house perfunctorily if they noticed it at all.

As the daughter, Victoria, passed through the Vickie period and, at thirteen, entered upon the Tori period, her friends no longer had to be restrained or distracted from fiddling with the fittings of the little house, wearing out the fragile mechanisms, sometimes handling the furniture carelessly in their story games with its occupants. For there was, or had been, a family living in it. Victoria at eight had requested and received for Christmas a rather expensive European mama, papa, brother, sister, and baby all cleverly articulated so that they could sit in the armchairs, and reach up to the copper-bottom saucepans hung above the stove, and hit or clasp one another in moments of passion. Family dramas of great intensity were enacted from time to time in the then incompletely furnished house. The brother's left leg came off at the hip and was never properly mended. Papa Bendsky received a marking-pen mustache and eyebrows that gave him an evil squint, like the half-breed lascar in an Edwardian thriller. The baby got lost. Victoria no longer played with the survivors; and the professor gratefully put them into the drawer of the table on which the house stood. He had always hated them, invaders, especially the papa, so thin, so flexible, with his nasty little Austrian-looking green jackets and his beady lascar eyes.

Victoria had recently bought with her earnings from babysitting a gift to the house and her father: a china cat to drink the eternal milk form the blue bowl marked "Kitty." The professor did not put the cat in the drawer. He believed it to be worthy of the house, as the Bendsky family had never been. It was a finely modelled little figure, glazed tortoiseshell on white. Curled on the hearth rug at twilight in the ruddy glow of the flames (red cellophane and a penlight bulb), it looked very comfortable indeed. But since it lay curled up, it could never go into the kitchen to drink from the blue bowl; and this was evidently a trouble or burden to the professor's unconscious mind, for he had not exactly a dream about

[1]*Lévi-Strauss:* Claude Lévi-Strauss (b. 1908), professor of social anthropology in the Collège de France and "the father of structuralism," published *La Pensée Sauvage* in 1962. It was translated as *The Savage Mind* in 1966. For his theory that in the case of miniatures, "knowledge of the whole precedes knowledge of the parts," see *The Savage Mind* (Chicago, 1966), 23–24.

it, one night while he was going to sleep after working late on a complex and difficult piece of writing, a response he was to give to a paper to be presented later in the year at the A.A.A.S.; not a dream but a kind of half-waking experience. He was looking into or was in the kitchen of the inner house. That was not unusual, for when fitting the cabinets and wall panelling and building in the sink, he had become deeply familiar with the proportions and aspects of the kitchen from every angle, and had frequently and deliberately visualized it from the perspective of a six-inch person standing by the stove or at the pantry door. But in this case he had no sense of volition; he was merely there; and while standing there, near the big wood-burning stove, he saw the cat come in, look up at him, and settle itself down to drink the milk, The experience include the auditory: he heard the neat and amusing sound a cat makes lapping.

Next day he remembered this little vision clearly. His mind ran upon it, now and then. Walking across campus after a lecture, he thought with some intensity that it would be very pleasant to have an animal in the house, a live animal. Not a cat, of course. Something very small. But his precise visual imagination at once presented him with a gerbil the size of the sofa, a monstrous hamster in the master bedroom, like the dreadful Mrs. Bhoolabhoy in *Staying On,* billowing in the bed, immense, and he laughed inwardly, and winced away from the spectacle.

Once, indeed, when he had been installing the pull-chain toilet—the house and its furnishings were generally Victorian; that was the original eponymous joke—he had glanced up to see that a moth had got into the attic, but only after a moment of shock did he recognize it as a moth, the marvellous, soft-winged, unearthly owl beating there beneath the rafters. Flies, however, which often visited the house, brought only thoughts of horror movies and about professors who tampered with what man was not meant to know and ended up buzzing at the windowpane, crying vainly, "Don't! No!" as the housewife's inexorable swatter fell. And serve them right. Would a ladybug do for a tortoise? The size was right, the colors wrong. The Victorians did not hesitate to paint live tortoises' shells. But tortoises do not raise their shells and fly away home. There was no pet suitable for the house. Lately he had not been working much on the house; weeks and months went by before he got the tiny Lamdseer framed, and then it was a plain gilt frame fitted up on a Sunday afternoon, not the scrollwork masterpiece he had originally planned. Sketches for a glassed-in sun porch were never, as his dean would have put it, implemented. The personal and professional stresses in his department at the university, which had first driven him to this small escape hatch, were considerably eased under the new chairman; he and Julia had worked out their problems well enough to go on; and anyway the house and all its furnishings were done, in place, complete. Every armchair its antimacassars. Now that the Bendskys were gone, nothing got lost or broken, nothing even got moved. And no rain fell. The outer house was in real need of reroofing; it had required three attic buckets this October, and even so there had been some damage to the study ceiling. But the cedar shingles on the inner house were still blond, virginal. They knew little of sunlight, and nothing of the rain.

I could, the professor thought, pour water on the roof, to weather the shingles a bit. It ought to be sprinkled on, somehow, so it would be more like rain. He saw himself stand with Julia's green plastic half-gallon watering can at the low table in the book-lined alcove of the living room; he saw water falling on the little shingles, pooling on the table, dripping to the ancient but serviceable Oriental rug. He saw a mad professor watering a toy house. Will it grow, Doctor? Will it grow?

That night he dreamed that the inner house, his house, was outside. It stood in a garden patch on a rickety support of some kind. The ground around it had been partly dug up as if for planting. The sky was low and dingy, though it was not raining yet. Some slats had come away from the back of the house, and he was worried about the glue. "I'm worried about the glue," he said to the gardener or whoever it was that was there with a short-handled shovel, but the person did not understand. The house should not be outside, but it was outside, and it was too late to do anything about it.

He woke in great distress from this dream and could not find rest from it until his mind came upon the notion of, as it were, obeying the dream: actually moving the inner house outdoors, into the garden, which would then become the garden of both houses. An inner garden within the outer garden could be designed. Julia's advice would be needed for that. Miniature roses for hawthorn trees, surely. Scotch moss for the lawn? What could you use for hedges? She might know. A fountain? . . . He drifted back to sleep contentedly planning the garden of the house. And for months, even years, after that he amused or consoled himself from time to time, on troubled nights or in boring meetings, by reviving the plans for the miniature garden. But really it was not a practicable idea, given the rainy weather of his part of the world.

He and Julia got their house reroofed eventually, and brought the buckets down from the attic. The inner house was moved upstairs into Victoria's room when she went off to college. Looking into that room toward dusk of a November evening, the professor saw the peaked roofs and widow's walk sharp against the window light. They were still dry. Dust falls here, not rain, he thought. It isn't fair. He opened the front of the house and turned on the fireplace. The little cat lay curled up on the rug before the ruddy glow, the illusion of warmth, the illusion of shelter. And the dry milk in the half-full bowl marked "Kitty" by the kitchen door. And the child gone.

Paule Marshall 1929–

Paule Marshall's writing reflects not only her concern with issues surrounding social justice, colonialism, immigration, and racism, but also the often conflicting cultural and physical environments of her heritage—the Carribbean, her parents' home, and Brooklyn, New York, to which they emigrated. These themes, along with the importance of "women's voices," prevail in four novels:

Brown Girl, Brownstones (1959), *The Chosen Place, the Timeless People* (1969), *Praisesong for the Widow* (1983), and *Daughters* (1991). Along with these, Marshall has also published a collection of novellas, numerous short stories, and her influential essay, "The Making of a Writer: From the Poets in the Kitchen" (1983), which explores the relationship between and among the women in her mother's kitchen—where the rhythms of their speech "liberated their powers of expression"—and her own creative powers. With her last two novels, Marshall also began to enjoy more pronounced acclaim from critics and the public, as well as commercial success. Marshall is also the recipient of numerous significant awards, including a Guggenheim Fellowship, a Rosenthal Award, a Before Columbus Foundation American Book Award, and the highly prestigious MacArthur Fellowship (1992).

BARBADOS

This is another of the novellas from SOUL CLAP HANDS AND SING. The four long stories which make up the collection all have to do with old men. They are—the men—of different backgrounds and cultures, yet they share a common predicament: their lives have been essentially empty. They have failed to commit themselves to anyone or anything in a meaningful way. When confronted with this truth or when their long-suppressed need for love finally surfaces, they reach out in a desperate, last-ditch effort to the women in the stories. (While the women are not major characters, they are nonetheless important as "bringers of the truth," and also because they come to realize their own strength as a result of the encounter. I saw this as a second motif.)

One of the reasons I undertook SOUL was to see if I could write convincingly of men. More important, I wanted to use the relationships between the old men and the young women in the stories to suggest themes of a political nature. These were of increasing interest to me at the time.

"Barbados" came to me practically ready-made during a year I spent on Barbados overhauling BROWN GIRL, BROWNSTONES for publication. It was 1958. The owner of the house where I had rented a room was, like the main character in the story, a solitary, taciturn old bachelor who had returned home after having worked most of his life in the United States. (He was a carbon copy of the stern-faced West Indian custodian of my neighborhood library when I was a child, and I merged them into a single character.) The man scarcely said two words to me the whole time I was there. His house, which served as a model for the one in the story, called to mind Tara in GONE WITH THE WIND. Large, white, with tall columns at the front, it was a plantation house for a black man "playing white." My aging landlord had built it with money he had accumulated while in the States.

There was even a young servant girl, just as in the story, whom he hired to cook and clean for me. She never said two words either. (I changed this though when I got around to writing about her. She evolves from a silent, submerged, anonymous creature into a young woman with a growing sense of herself and her rights.)

There was scarcely anything for me to invent in other words. All I did with "Barbados" was to exclude myself from the "big house" and to provide my two ready-made characters with background, a psychology, and a plot. I never had it so easy.

Dawn, like the night which had preceded it, came from the sea. In a white mist tumbling like spume over the fishing boats leaving the island and the hunched, ghost shapes of the fishermen. In a white, wet wind breathing over the villages scattered amid the tall canes. The cabbage palms roused, their high headdresses solemnly saluting the wind, and along the white beach which ringed the island the casuarina trees began their moaning—a sound of women lamenting their dead within a cave.

The wind, smarting of the sea, threaded a wet skein through Mr. Watford's five hundred dwarf coconut trees and around his house at the edge of the grove. The house, Colonial American in design, seemed created by the mist—as if out of the dawn's formlessness had come, magically, the solid stone walls, the blind, broad windows and the portico of fat columns which embraced the main story. When the mist cleared, the house remained—pure, proud, a pristine white— disdaining the crude wooden houses in the village outside its high gate.

It was not the dawn settling around his house which awakened Mr. Watford, but the call of his Barbary doves from their hutch in the yard. And it was more the feel of that sound than the sound itself. His hands had retained, from the many times a day he held the doves, the feel of their throats swelling with that murmurous, mournful note. He lay abed now, his hands—as cracked and calloused as a cane cutter's—filled with the sound, and against the white sheet which flowed out to the white walls he appeared profoundly alone, yet secure in loneliness, contained. His face was fleshless and severe, his black skin sucked deep into the hollow of his jaw, while under a high brow, which was like a bastion raised against the world, his eyes were indrawn and pure. It was as if during all his seventy years, Mr. Watford had permitted nothing to sight which could have affected him.

He stood up, and his body, muscular but stripped of flesh, appeared to be absolved from time, still young. Yet each clenched gesture of his arms, of his lean shank as he dressed in a faded shirt and work pants, each vigilant, snapping motion of his head betrayed tension. Ruthlessly he spurred his body to perform like a younger man's. Savagely he denied the accumulated fatigue of the years. Only sometimes when he paused in his grove of coconut trees during the day, his eyes tearing and the breath torn from his lungs, did it seem that if he could find a place hidden from the world and himself he would give way to exhaustion and weep from weariness.

Dressed, he strode through the house, his step tense, his rough hand touching the furniture from Grand Rapids which crowded each room. For some reason, Mr. Watford had never completed the house. Everywhere the walls were raw and unpainted, the furniture unarranged. In the drawing room with its coffered ceiling, he stood before his favorite piece, an old mantel clock which eked out the time. Reluctantly it whirred five and Mr. Watford nodded. His day had begun.

It was no different from all the days which made up the five years since his return to Barbados. Downstairs in the unfinished kitchen, he prepared his morning tea—tea with canned milk and fried bakes—and ate standing at the stove while lizards skittered over the unplastered walls. Then, belching and snuffling the way a child would, he put on a pith helmet, secured his pants legs with bicycle clasps and stepped into the yard. There he fed the doves, holding them so that their sound poured into his hands and laughing gently—but the laugh gave way to an irritable grunt as he saw the mongoose tracks under the hutch. He set the trap again.

The first heat had swept the island like a huge tidal wave when Mr. Watford, with that tense, headlong stride, entered the grove. He had planted the dwarf co-conut trees because of their quick yield and because, with their stunted trunks, they always appeared young. Now as he worked, rearranging the complex of pipes which irrigated the land, stripping off the dead leaves, the trees were like cool, moving presences; the stiletto fronds wove a protective dome above him and slowly, as the day soared toward noon, his mind filled with the slivers of sunlight through the trees and the feel of earth in his hands, as it might have been filled with thoughts.

Except for a meal at noon, he remained in the grove until dusk surged up from the sea; then returning to the house, he bathed and dressed in a medical doctor's white uniform, turned on the lights in the parlor and opened the tall doors to the portico. Then the old women of the village on their way to church, the last hawkers caroling, "Fish, flying fish, a penny, my lady," the roistering saga-boys lugging their heavy steel drums to the crossroad where they would rehearse under the street lamp—all passing could glimpse Mr. Watford, stiff in his white uniform and with his head bent heavily over a Boston newspaper. The papers reached him weeks late but he read them anyway, giving a little savage chuckle at the thought that beyond his world that other world went its senseless way. As he read, the night sounds of the village welled into a joyous chorale against the sea's muffled cadence and the hollow, haunting music of the steel band. Soon the moths, lured in by the light, fought to die on the lamp, the bee-tles crashed drunkenly against the walls and the night—like a woman offering herself to him—became fragrant with the night-blooming cactus.

Even in America Mr. Watford had spent his evenings this way. Coming home from the hospital, where he worked in the boiler room, he would dress in his white uniform and read in the basement of the large rooming house he owned. He had lived closeted like this, detached, because America—despite the money and property he had slowly accumulated—had meant nothing to him. Each morning, walking to the hospital along the rutted Boston streets, through the smoky dawn light, he had known—although it had never been a thought—that his allegiance, his place, lay elsewhere. Neither had the few acquaintances he had made mattered. Nor the women he had occasionally kept as a younger man.

After the first months their bodies would grow coarse to his hand and he would begin edging away. . . . So that he had felt no regret when, the year before his retirement, he resigned his job, liquidated his properties and, his fifty-year exile over, returned home.

The clock doled out eight and Mr. Watford folded the newspaper and brushed the burnt moths from the lamp base. His lips still shaped the last words he had read as he moved through the rooms, fastening the windows against the night air, which he had dreaded even as a boy. Something palpable but unseen was always, he believed, crouched in the night's dim recess, waiting to snare him. . . . Once in bed in his sealed room, Mr. Watford fell asleep quickly.

The next day was no different except that Mr. Goodman, the local shop-keeper, sent the boy for coconuts to sell at the race track and then came that evening to pay for them and to herald—although Mr. Watford did not know this—the coming of the girl.

That morning, taking his tea, Mr. Watford heard the careful tap of the mule's hoofs and looking out saw the wagon jolting through the dawn and the boy, still lax with sleep, swaying on the seat. He was perhaps eighteen and the muscles packed tightly beneath his lustrous black skin gave him a brooding strength. He came and stood outside the back door, his hands and lowered head performing the small, subtle rites of deference.

Mr. Watford's pleasure was full, for the gestures were those given only to a white man in his time. Yet the boy always nettled him. He sensed a natural arro-gance like a pinpoint of light within his dark stare. The boy's stance exhumed a memory buried under the years. He remembered, staring at him, the time when he had worked as a yard boy for a white family, and had had to assume the same respectful pose while their flat, raw, Barbadian voices assailed him with orders. He remembered the muscles in his neck straining as he nodded deeply and a taste like alum on his tongue as he repeated the "Yes, please," as in a litany. But, because of their whiteness and wealth, he had never dared hate them. Instead his rancor, like a boomerang, had rebounded, glancing past him to strike all the dark ones like himself, even his mother with her spindled arms and her stomach sagging with a child who was, invariably, dead at birth. He had been the only one of ten to live, the only one to escape. But he had never lost the sense of being pursued by the same dread presence which had claimed them. He had never lost the fear that if he lived too fully he would tire and death would quickly close the gap. His only defense had been a cautious life and work. He had been almost broken by work at the age of twenty when his parents died, leaving him enough money for the passage to America. Gladly had he fled the island. But nothing had mattered after his flight.

The boy's foot stirred the dust. He murmured, "Please, sir, Mr. Watford, Mr. Goodman at the shop send me to pick the coconuts."

Mr. Watford's head snapped up. A caustic word flared; but died as he no-ticed a political button pinned to the boy's patched shirt with "Vote for the Barbados People's Party" printed boldly on it, and below that the motto of the party: "The Old Order Shall Pass." At this ludicrous touch (for what could this boy, with his splayed and shigoed feet and blunted mind, understand about politics?) he became suddenly nervous, angry. The button and its motto seemed, somehow, directed at him. He said roughly, "Well, come then. You can't pick any coconuts standing there looking foolish!"—and he led the way to the grove.

The coconuts, he knew, would sell well at the booths in the center of the track, where the poor were penned in like cattle. As the heat thickened and the betting grew desperate, they would clamor: "Man, how you selling the water coconuts?" and hacking off the tops they would pour rum into the water within the hollow centers, then tilt the coconuts to their heads so that the rum-sweetened water skimmed their tongues and trickled bright down their dark chins. Mr. Watford had stood among them at the track as a young man, as poor as they were, but proud. And he had always found something unutterably graceful and free in their gestures, something which had roused contradictory feelings in him: admiration, but just as strong, impatience at their easy ways, and shame . . .

That night, as he sat in his white uniform reading, he heard Mr. Goodman's heavy step and went out and stood at the head of the stairs in a formal, pro-prietary pose. Mr. Goodman's face floated up into the light—the loose folds of flesh, the skin slick with sweat as if oiled, the eyes scribbled with veins and mottled, bold—as if each blemish there was a sin he proudly displayed or a scar which proved he had met life head-on. His body, unlike Mr Watford's, was corpulent and, with the trousers caught up around his full crotch, openly con-cupiscent. He owned the one shop in the village which gave credit and a booth which sold coconuts at the race track, kept a wife and two outside women, drank a rum with each customer at his bar, regularly caned his fourteen chil-dren, who still followed him everywhere (even now they were waiting for him in the darkness beyond Mr. Watford's gate) and bet heavily at the races, and when he lost gave a loud hacking laugh which squeezed his body like a pain and left him gasping.

The laugh clutched him now as he flung his pendulous flesh into a chair and wheezed, "Watford, how? Man, I near lose house, shop, shirt and all at races today. I tell you, they got some horses from Trinidad in this meet that's making ours look like they running backwards. Be-Jese, I wouldn't bet on a Bajan horse tomorrow if Christ heself was to give me the tip. Those bitches might look good but they's nothing 'pon a track."

Mr. Watford, his back straight as the pillar he leaned against, his eyes unstained, his gaunt face planed by contempt, gave Mr. Goodman his cold, measured smile, thinking that the man would be dead soon, bloated with rice and rum—and somehow this made his own life more certain.

Sputtering with his amiable laughter, Mr. Goodman paid for the coconuts, but instead of leaving then as he usually did, he lingered, his eyes probing for a glimpse inside the house. Mr. Watford waited, his head snapping warily; then, impatient, he started toward the door and Mr. Goodman said, "I tell you, your coconut trees bearing fast enough even for dwarfs. You's lucky, man."

Ordinarily Mr. Watford would have waved both the man and his remark aside, but repelled more than usual tonight by Mr. Goodman's gross form and immodest laugh, he said—glad of the cold edge his slight American accent gave the words—"What luck got to do with it? I does care the trees properly and they bear, that's all. Luck! People, especially this bunch around here, is always looking to luck when the only answer is a little brains and plenty of hard work. . . ." Suddenly remembering the boy that morning and the political button, he added in loud disgust, "Look that half-foolish boy you does send here to pick the coconuts. Instead of him learning a trade and going to England where he might find work he's walking about with a political button. He and all in politics now! But that's the way with these down in here. They'll do some of everything but work. They don't want work!" He gestured violently, almost dancing in anger. "They too busy spreeing."

The chair creaked as Mr. Goodman sketched a pained and gentle denial. "No, man," he said, "you wrong. Things is different to before. I mean to say, the young people nowadays is different to how we was. They not just sitting back and taking things no more. They not so frighten for the white people as we was. No man. Now take that said same boy, for an example. I don't say he don't like a spree, but he's serious, you see him there. He's a member of this new Barbados People's Party. He wants to see his own color running the government. He wants to be able to make a living right here in Barbados instead of going to any cold England. And he's right!" Mr. Goodman paused at a vehement pitch, then shrugged heavily. "What the young people must do, nuh? They got to look to something. . . ."

"Look to work!" And Mr. Watford thrust out a hand so that the horned knuckles caught the light.

"Yes, that's true—and it's up to we that got little something to give them work," Mr. Goodman said, and a sadness filtered among the dissipations in his eyes. "I mean to say we that got little something got to help out. In a manner of speaking, we's responsible . . ."

"Responsible!" The word circled Mr. Watford's head like a gnat and he wanted to reach up and haul it down, to squash it underfoot.

Mr. Goodman spread his hands; his breathing rumbled with a sigh. "Yes, in a manner of speaking. That's why, Watford man, you got to provide little work for some poor person down in here. Hire a servant at least! 'Cause I gon tell you something . . ." And he hitched forward his chair, his voice dropped to a wheeze. "People talking. Here you come back rich from big America and build a swell house and plant 'nough coconut trees and you still cleaning and cooking and thing like some woman? Man, it don't look good!" His face screwed in emphasis and he sat back. "Now there's this girl, the daughter of a friend that just dead, and she need work bad enough. But I wouldn't like to see she working for these white people 'cause you know how those men will take advantage of she. And she'd make a good servant, man. Quiet and quick so, and nothing a-tall to feed and she can sleep anywhere about the place. And she don't have no boys always around her either. . . ." Still talking, Mr. Goodman eased from his chair and reached the stairs with surprising agility. "You need a servant," he whispered, leaning close to Mr. Watford as he passed. "It don't look good, man. People talking. I gon send she."

Mr. Watford was overcome by nausea. Not only from Mr. Goodman's smell—a stench of salt fish, rum and sweat, but from an outrage which was like a sediment in his stomach. For a long time he stood there almost kecking from disgust, until his clock struck eight, reminding him of the sanctuary within—and suddenly his cold laugh dismissed Mr. Goodman and his proposal. Hurrying in, he locked the doors and windows against the night air and still laughing, he slept.

The next day, coming from the grove to prepare his noon meal, he saw her. She was standing in his driveway, her bare feet like strong dark roots amid the jagged stones, her face tilted toward the sun—and she might have been standing there always waiting for him. She seemed of the sun, of the earth. The folktale of creation might have been true with her: that along a river bank a god had scooped up the earth—rich and black and warmed by the sun—and molded her poised head with its tufted braids and then with a whimsical touch crowned it with a sober brown felt hat which should have been worn by some stout English matron in a London suburb, had sculpted the passionless face and drawn a screen of gossamer across her eyes to hide the void behind. Beneath her bodice her small breasts were smooth at the crest. Below her waist, her hips branched wide, the place prepared for its load of life. But it was the bold and sensual strength of her legs which completely unstrung Mr. Watford. He wanted to grab a hoe and drive her off.

"What it 'tis you want?" he called sharply.

"Mr. Goodman send me."

"Send you for what?" His voice was shrill in the glare.

She moved. Holding a caved-in valise and a pair of white sandals, her head weaving slightly as though she bore a pail of water there or a tray of mangoes, she glided over the stones as if they were smooth ground. Her bland expression did not change, but her eyes, meeting his, held a vague trust. Pausing a few feet away, she curtsied deeply. "I's the new servant."

Only Mr. Watford's cold laugh saved him from anger. As always it raised him to a height where everything below appeared senseless and insignificant— especially his people, whom the girl embodied. From this height, he could even be charitable. And thinking suddenly of how she had waited in the brutal sun since morning without taking shelter under the nearby tamarind tree, he said, not unkindly, "Well, girl, go back and tell Mr. Goodman for me that I don't need no servant."

"I can't go back."

"How you mean can't?" His head gave its angry snap.

"I'll get lashes," she said simply. "My mother say I must work the day and then if you don't wish me, I can come back. But I's not to leave till night falling, if not I get lashes."

He was shaken by her dispassion. So much so that his head dropped from its disdaining angle and his hands twitched with helplessness. Despite anything he might say or do, her fear of the whipping would keep her there until nightfall, the valise and shoes in hand. He felt his day with its order and quiet rhythms threatened by her intrusion—and suddenly waving her off as if she were an evil visitation, he hurried into the kitchen to prepare his meal.

But he paused, confused, in front of the stove, knowing that he could not cook and leave her hungry at the door, nor could he cook and serve her as though he were the servant.

"You know anything about cooking?" he shouted finally.

"Yes, please."

They said nothing more. She entered the room with a firm step and an air almost of familiarity, placed her valise and shoes in a corner and went directly to the larder. For a time Mr. Watford stood by, his muscles flexing with anger and his eyes bounding ahead of her every move, until feeling foolish and frighteningly useless, he went out to feed his doves.

The meal was quickly done and as he ate he heard the dry slap of her feet behind him—a pleasant sound—and then silence. When he glanced back she was squatting in the doorway, the sunlight aslant the absurd hat and her face bent to a bowl she held in one palm. She ate slowly, thoughtfully, as if fixing the taste of each spoonful in her mind.

It was then that he decided to let her work the day and at nightfall to pay her a dollar and dismiss her. His decision held when he returned later from the grove and found tea awaiting him, and then through the supper she prepared. Afterward, dressed in his white uniform, he patiently waited out the day's end on the portico, his face setting into a grim mold. Then just as dusk etched the first dark line between the sea and sky, he took out a dollar and went downstairs.

She was not in the kitchen, but the table was set for his morning tea. Muttering at her persistence, he charged down the corridor, which ran the length of the basement, flinging open the doors to the damp, empty rooms on either side, and sending the lizards and the shadows long entrenched there scuttling to safety.

He found her in the small slanted room under the stoop, asleep on an old cot he kept there, her suitcase turned down beside the bed, and the shoes, dress and the ridiculous hat piled on top. A loose night shift muted the outline of her body and hid her legs, so that she appeared suddenly defenseless, innocent, with a child's trust in her curled hand and in her deep breathing. Standing in the doorway, with his own breathing snarled and his eyes averted. Mr. Watford felt like an intruder. She had claimed the room. Quivering with frustration, he slowly turned away, vowing that in the morning he would shove the dollar at her and lead her like a cow out of his house. . . .

Dawn brought rain and a hot wind which set the leaves rattling and swiping

at the air like distraught arms. Dressing in the dawn darkness, Mr. Watford
again armed himself with the dollar and, with his shoulders at an uncompromising set, plunged downstairs. He descended into the warm smell of bakes and
this smell, along with the thought that she had been up before him, made his
hand knot with exasperation on the banister. The knot tightened as he saw her,
dust swirling at her feet as she swept the corridor, her face bent solemn to the
task. Shutting her out with a lifted hand, he shouted, "Don't bother sweeping.
Here's a dollar. G'long back."

The broom paused and although she did not raise her head, he sensed her
groping through the shadowy maze of her mind toward his voice. Behind the
dollar which he waved in her face, her eyes slowly cleared. And, surprisingly,
they held no fear. Only anticipation and a tenuous trust. It was as if she expected
him to say something kind.

"G'long back!" His angry cry was a plea.

Like a small, starved flame, her trust and expectancy died and she said,
almost with reproof, "The rain falling."

To confirm this, the wind set the rain stinging across the windows and he
could say nothing, even though the words sputtered at his lips. It was useless.
There was nothing inside her to comprehend that she was not wanted. His
shoulders sagged under the weight of her ignorance, and with a futile gesture he
swung away, the dollar hanging from his hand like a small sword gone limp.

She became as fixed and familiar a part of the house as the stones—and as
silent. He paid her five dollars a week, gave her Mondays off and in the evenings,
after a time, even allowed her to sit in the alcove off the parlor, while he read
with his back to her, taking no more notice of her than he did the moths on the
lamp.

But once, after many silent evenings together, he detected a sound apart
from the night murmurs of the sea and village and the metallic tuning of the
steel band, a low, almost inhuman cry of loneliness which chilled him. Frightened, he turned to find her leaning hesitantly toward him, her eyes dark with
urgency, and her face tight with bewilderment and a growing anger. He started,
not understanding, and her arm lifted to stay him. Eagerly she bent closer. But
as she uttered the low cry again, as her fingers described her wish to talk, he
jerked around, afraid that she would be foolish enough to speak and that once
she did they would be brought close. He would be forced then to acknowledge
something about her which he refused to grant; above all, he would be called
upon to share a little of himself. Quickly he returned to his newspaper, rustling
it to settle the air, and after a time he felt her slowly, bitterly, return to her
silence. . . .

Like sand poured in a careful measure from the hand, the weeks flowed
down to August and on the first Monday, August Band holiday, Mr. Watford
awoke to the sound of the excursion buses leaving the village for the annual
outing, their backfire pelleting the dawn calm and the ancient motors protesting
the overcrowding. Lying there, listening, he saw with disturbing clarity his
mother dressed for an excursion—the white head tie wound above her dark

face and her head poised like a dancer's under the heavy outing basket of food. That set of her head had haunted his years, reappearing in the girl as she walked toward him the first day. Aching with the memory, yet annoyed with himself for remembering, he went downstairs.

The girl had already left for the excursion, and although it was her day off, he left vaguely betrayed by her eagerness to leave him. Somehow it suggested ingratitude. It was as if his doves were suddenly to refuse him their song or his trees their fruit, despite the care he gave them. Some vital part which shaped the simple mosaic of his life seemed suddenly missing. An alien silence curled like coal gas throughout the house. To escape it he remained in the grove all day and, and upon his return to the house, dressed with more care than usual, putting on a fresh, starched uniform, and solemnly brushing his hair until it lay in a smooth bush above his brow. Leaning close to the mirror, but avoiding his eyes, he cleaned the white rheum at their corners, and afterward pried loose the dirt under his nails.

Unable to read his papers, he went out on the portico to escape the unnatural silence in the house, and stood with his hands clenched on the balustrade and his taut body straining forward. After a long wait he heard the buses return and voices in gay shreds upon the wind. Slowly his hands relaxed, as did his shoulders under the white uniform; for the first time that day his breathing was regular. She would soon come.

But she did not come and dusk bloomed into night, with a fragrant heat and a full moon which made the leaves glint as though touched with frost. The steel band at the crossroads began the lilting songs of sadness and seduction, and suddenly—like shades roused by the night and the music—images of the girl flitted before Mr. Watford's eyes. He saw her lost amid the carousings in the village, despoiled; he imagined someone like Mr. Goodman clasping her lewdly or tumbling her in the canebrake. His hand rose, trembling, to rid the air of her; he tried to summon his cold laugh. But, somehow, he could not dismiss her as he had always done with everyone else. Instead, he wanted to punish and protect her, to find and lead her back to the house.

As he leaned there, trying not to give way to the desire to go and find her, his fist striking the balustrade to deny his longing, he saw them. The girl first, with the moonlight like a silver patina on her skin, then the boy whom Mr. Goodman sent for the coconuts, whose easy strength and the political button—"The Old Order Shall Pass"—had always mocked and challenged Mr. Watford. They were joined in a tender battle: the boy in a sport shirt riotous with color was reaching for the girl as he leaped and spun, weightless, to the music, while she fended him off with a gesture which was lovely in its promise of surrender. Her protests were little scattered bursts: "But, man, why you don't stop, nuh? ... But, you know, you getting on like a real-real idiot. . . .

Each time she chided him he leaped higher and landed closer, until finally he eluded her arm and caught her by the waist. Boldly he pressed a leg between her tightly closed legs until they opened under his pressure. Their bodies cleaved into one whirling form and while he sang she laughed like a wanton with her hat cocked over her ear. Dancing, the stones moiling underfoot, they claimed the night. More than the night. The steel band played for them alone. The trees were their frivolous companions, swaying as they swayed. The moon rode the sky because of them.

Mr. Watford, hidden by a dense shadow, felt the tendons which strung him together suddenly go limp; above all, an obscure belief which, like rare china, he had stored on a high shelf in his mind began to tilt. He sensed the familiar specter which hovered in the night reaching out to embrace him, just as the two in the yard were embracing. Utterly unstrung, incapable of either speech or action, he stumbled into the house, only to meet there an accusing silence from the clock, which had missed its eight o'clock winding, and his newspapers lying like ruined leaves over the floor.

He lay in bed in the white uniform, waiting for sleep to rescue him, his hands seeking the comforting sound of his doves. But sleep eluded him and instead of the doves, their throats tremulous with sound, him scarred hands filled with the shape of a woman he had once kept: her skin, which had been almost bruising in its softness; the buttocks and breasts spread under his hands to inspire both cruelty and tenderness. His bands closed to softly crush those forms, and the searing thrust of passion, which he had not felt for years, stabbed his dry groin. He imagined the two outside, their passion at a pitch by now, lying together behind the tamarind tree, or perhaps—and he sat up sharply—they had been bold enough to bring their lust into the house. Did he not smell their taint on the air? Restored suddenly, he rushed downstairs. As he reached the corridor, a thread of light beckoned him from her room and he dashed furiously toward it, rehearsing the angry words which would jar their bodies apart. He neared the door, glimpsed her through the small opening, and his step faltered; the words collapsed.

She was seated alone on the cot, tenderly holding the absurd felt hat in her lap, one leg tucked under her while the other trailed down. A white sandal, its strap broken, dangled from the foot and gently knocked the floor as she absently swung her leg. Her dress was twisted around her body—and pinned to the bodice, so that it gathered the cloth between her small breasts, was the political button the boy always wore. She was dreamily fingering it, her mouth shaped by a gentle, ironic smile and her eyes strangely acute and critical. What had transpired on the cot had not only, it seemed, twisted the dress around her, tumbled her hat and broken her sandal, but had also defined her and brought the blurred forms of life into focus for her. There was a woman's force in her aspect now, a tragic knowing and acceptance in her bent head, a hint about her of Cassandra watching the future wheel before her eyes.

Before those eyes which looked to another world, Mr. Watford's anger and strength failed him and he held to the wall for support. Unreasonably, he felt that he should assume some hushed and reverent pose, to bow as she had the day she had come. If he had known their names, he would have pleaded forgiveness for the sins he had committed against her and the others all his life, against himself. If he could have borne the thought, he would have confessed that it had been love, terrible in its demand, which he had always fled. And that love had been the reason for his return. If he had been honest he would have whispered—his head bent and a hand shading his eyes—that unlike Mr. Good-man (whom he suddenly envied for his full life) and the boy with his political button (to whom he had lost the girl), he had not been willing to bear the weight of his own responsibility. . . . But all Mr. Watford could admit, clinging there to the wall, was, simply, that he wanted to live—and that the girl held life within her as surely as she held the hat in her hands. If he could prove himself better than the boy, he could win it. Only then, he dimly knew, would he shake off the pursuer which had given him no rest since birth. Hopefully, he staggered forward, his step cautious and contrite, his hands quivering along the wall.

She did not see or hear him as he pushed the door wider. And for some time he stood there, his shoulders hunched in humility, his skin stripped away to reveal each flaw, his whole self offered in one outstretched hand. Still unaware of him, she swung her leg, and the dangling shoe struck a derisive note. Then, just as he had turned away that evening in the parlor when she had uttered her low call, she turned away now, refusing him.

Mr. Watford's body went slack and then stiffened ominously. He knew that he would have to wrest from her the strength needed to sustain him. Slamming the door, he cried, his voice cracked and strangled, "What you and him was doing in here? Tell me! I'll not have you bringing nastiness round here. Tell me!"

She did not start. Perhaps she had been aware of him all along and had expected his outburst. Or perhaps his demented eye and the desperation rising from him like a musk filled her with pity instead of fear. Whatever, her benign smile held and her eyes remained abstracted until his hand reached out to fling her back on the cot. Then, frowning, she stood up, wobbling a little on the broken shoe and holding the political button as if it was a new power which would steady and protect her. With a cruel flick of her arm she struck aside his hand and, in a voice as cruel, halted him. "But you best move and don't come holding on to me, you nasty, pissy old man. That's all you is, despite yuh big house and fancy furnitures and yuh newspapers from America. You ain't people, Mr. Watford, you ain't people!" And with a look and a lift of her head which made her condemnation final, she placed the hat atop her braids, and turning aside picked up the valise which had always lain, packed, beside the cot—as if even on the first day she had known that this night would come and had been prepared against it. . . .

Mr. Watford did not see her leave, for a pain squeezed his heart dry and the driven blood was a bright, blinding cataract over his eyes. But his inner eye was suddenly clear. For the first time it gazed mutely upon the waste and pretense which had spanned his years. Flung there against the door by the girl's small blow, his body slowly crumpled under the weariness he had long denied. He sensed that dark but unsubstantial figure which roamed the nights searching for him wind him in its chill embrace. He struggled against it, his hands clutching the air with the spastic eloquence of a drowning man. He moaned—and the anguished sound reached beyond the room to fill the house. It escaped to the yard, and his doves swelled their throats, moaning with him.

Adrienne Rich 1929–

O ne of the most important poets and essayists in the United States, Adrienne Rich was formally educated at Radcliffe College; it was during the year of her graduation, 1951, that celebrated poet W. H. Auden selected her first collection for the prestigious Yale Series of Younger Poets. Resisting the assimilationist drive of her Jewish father, Rich has often used her poetry to explore new stylistic forms and to examine relationships with those in her family (her father and her husband, both deceased) who represent her Jewish heritage. Rich, a lesbian and feminist, has published over fifteen books of poetry, a tract on motherhood, and several collections of her speeches and essays. She has gathered numerous, significant honors, including several Guggenheim fellowships, the Fund for Human Dignity Award for the National Gay and Lesbian Task Force, the Fellowship of the Academy of American Poets, and others.

WHEN WE DEAD AWAKEN: WRITING AS RE-VISION (1971)[1]

The Modern Language Association is both marketplace and funeral parlor for the professional study of Western literature in North America. Like all gatherings of the professions, it has been and remains a "procession of the sons of educated men" (Virginia Woolf)[2] a congeries of old-boys' networks, academicians rehearsing their numb canons in sessions dedicated to the literature of white males, junior scholars under the lash of "publish or perish" delivering papers in the bizarrely lit drawing- rooms of immense hotels: a ritual competition veering between cynicism and desperation.

However, in the interstices of these gentlemanly rites (or, in Mary Daly's words, on the boundaries of this patriarchal space),[3] some feminist scholars, teachers, and graduate students, joined by feminist writers, editors, and publishers, have for a decade been creating more subversive occasions, challenging the sacredness of the gentlemanly canon, sharing the rediscovery of buried works by women, asking women's questions, bringing literary history and criticism back to life in both senses. The Commission on the Status of Women in the Profession was formed in 1969, and held its first public event in 1970. In 1971 the Commission asked Ellen Peck Killoh, Tillie Olsen, Elaine Reuben, and myself, with Elaine Hedges as moderator, to talk on "The Woman Writer in the

---

[1] As Rich explains, this essay—written in 1971—was first published in 1972 and then included in her volume *On Lies, Secrets, and Silence* (1978). At that time she added the introductory note reprinted here, as well as some notes beginning, "A.R. 1978."

[2] The phrase is a quote from Woolf's *Three Guineas* (1938).

[3] Mary Daly, *Beyond God the Father* (Boston: Beacon, 1971), pp. 40–41 [Rich's note].

Twentieth Century." The essay that follows was written for that forum, and later published, along with the other papers from the forum and workshops, in an issue of College English *edited by Elaine Hedges ("Women Writing and Teaching," vol. 34, no. 1, October 1972). With a few revisions, mainly updating, it was reprinted in* American Poets in 1976, *edited by William Heyen (New York: Bobbs-Merrill, 1976). That later text is the one published here.*

The challenge flung by feminists at the accepted literary canon, at the methods of teaching it, and at the biased and astigmatic view of male "literary scholarship," has not diminished in the decade since the first Women's Forum; it has become broadened and intensified more recently by the challenges of black and lesbian feminists pointing out that feminist literary criticism itself has overlooked or held back from examining the work of black women and lesbians. The dynamic between a political vision and the demand for a fresh vision of literature is clear: without a growing feminist movement, the first inroads of feminist scholarship could not have been made; without the sharpening of a black feminist consciousness, black women's writing would have been left in limbo between misogynist black male critics and white feminists still struggling to unearth a white women's tradition; without an articulate lesbian/feminist movement, lesbian writing would still be lying in that closet where many of us used to sit reading forbidden books "in a bad light."

Much, much more is yet to be done; and university curricula have of course changed very little as a result of all this. What *is* changing is the availability of knowledge, of vital texts, the visible effects on women's lives of seeing, hearing our wordless or negated experience affirmed and pursued further in language.

Ibsen's[4] *When We Dead Awaken* is a play about the use that the male artist and thinker—in the process of creating culture as we know it—has made of women, in his life and in his work; and about a woman's slow struggling awakening to the use to which her life has been put. Bernard Shaw wrote in 1900 of this play:

> [Ibsen] shows us that no degradation ever devized or permitted is as disastrous as this degradation; that through it women can die into luxuries for men and yet can kill them; that men and women are becoming conscious of this; and that what remains to be seen as perhaps the most interesting of all imminent social developments is what will happen "when we dead awaken."[5]

It's exhilarating to be alive in a time of awakening consciousness; it can also be confusing, disorienting, and painful. This awakening of dead or sleeping consciousness has already affected the lives of millions of women, even those who don't know it yet. It is also affecting the lives of men, even those who deny its

---

[4] Henrik Ibsen (1828–1906), Norwegian poet and playwright.

[5] G. B. Shaw, *The Quintessence of Ibsenism* (New York: Hill & Wang, 1922), p. 139 [Rich's note].

claims upon them. The argument will go on whether an oppressive economic class system is responsible for the oppressive nature of male/female relations, or whether, in fact, patriarchy—the domination of males—is the original model of oppression on which all others are based. But in the last few years the women's movement has drawn inescapable and illuminating connections between our sexual lives and our political institutions. The sleepwalkers are coming awake, and for the first time this awakening has a collective reality; it is no longer such a lonely thing to open one's eyes.

Re-vision—the act of looking back, of seeing with fresh eyes, of entering an old text from a new critical direction—is for women more than a chapter in cultural history: it is an act of survival. Until we can understand the assumptions in which we are drenched we cannot know ourselves. And this drive to self-knowledge, for women, is more than a search for identity: it is part of our refusal of the self-destructiveness of male-dominated society. A radical critique of literature, feminist in its impulse, would take the work first of all as a clue to how we live, how we have been living, how we have been led to imagine ourselves, how our language has trapped as well as liberated us, how the very act of naming has been till now a male prerogative, and how we can begin to see and name—and therefore live—afresh. A change in the concept of sexual identity is essential if we are not going to see the old political order reassert itself in every new revolution. We need to know the writing of the past, and know it differently than we have ever known it; not to pass on a tradition but to break its hold over us.

For writers, and at this moment for women writers in particular, there is the challenge and promise of a whole new psychic geography to be explored. But there is also a difficult and dangerous walking on the ice, as we try to find language and images for a consciousness we are just coming into, and with little in the past to support us. I want to talk about some aspect of this difficulty and this danger.

Jane Harrison, the great classical anthropologist, wrote in 1914 in a letter to her friend Gilbert Murray:

> By the by, about "Women," it has bothered me often—why do women never
> want to write poetry about Man as a sex—why is Woman a dream and a terror
> to man and not the other way around? . . . Is it mere convention and propriety,
> or something deeper?[6]

I think Jane Harrison's question cuts deep into the myth-making tradition, the romantic tradition; deep into what women and men have been to each other; and deep into the psyche of the woman writer. Thinking about that question, I began thinking of the work of two twentieth-century women poets, Sylvia Plath and Diane Wakoski. It strikes me that in the work of both Man appears as, if not a dream, a fascination and a terror; and that the source of the fascination and

[6] J. G. Stewart, *Jane Ellen Harrison: A Portrait from Letters* (London: Merlin, 1959), p. 140 [Rich's note].

the terror is, simply, Man's power—to dominate, tyrannize, choose, or reject the woman. The charisma of Man seems to come purely from his power over her and his control of the world by force, not from anything fertile or life-giving in him. And, in the work of both these poets, it is finally the woman's sense of *herself*—embattled, possessed—that gives the poetry its dynamic charge, its rhythms of struggle, need, will, and female energy. Until recently this female anger and this furious awareness of the Man's power over her were not available materials to the female poet, who tended to write of Love as the source of her suffering, and to view that victimization by Love as an almost inevitable fate. Or, like Marianne Moore and Elizabeth Bishop,[7] she kept sexuality at a measured and chiseled distance in her poems.

One answer to Jane Harrison's question has to be that historically men and women have played very different parts in each others' lives. Where woman has been a luxury for man, and has served as the painter's model and the poet's muse, but also as comforter, nurse, cook, bearer of his seed, secretarial assistant, and copyist of manuscripts, man has played a quite different role for the female artist. Henry James repeats an incident which the writer Prosper Mérimée described, of how, while he was living with George Sand,

> he once opened his eyes, in the raw winter dawn, to see his companion, in a dressing-gown, on her knees before the domestic hearth, a candle-stick beside her and a red *madras* round her head, making bravely, with her own hands the fire that was to enable her to sit down betimes to urgent pen and paper. The story represents him as having felt that the spectacle chilled his ardor and tried his taste; her appearance was unfortunate, her occupation an inconsequence, and her industry a reproof— the result of all which was a lively irritation and an early rupture.[8]

The specter of this kind of male judgment, along with the misnaming and thwarting of her needs by a culture controlled by males, has created problems for the woman writer: problems of contact with herself, problems of language and style, problems of energy and survival.

In rereading Virginia Woolf's *A Room of One's Own* (1929) for the first time in some years, I was astonished at the sense of effort, of pains taken, of dogged tentativeness, in the tone of that essay. And I recognized that tone. I had heard it often enough, in myself and in other women. It is the tone of a woman almost in touch with her anger, who is determined not to appear angry, who is *willing* herself to be calm, detached, and even charming in a roomful of men where things have been said which are attacks on her very integrity. Virginia Woolf is addressing an audience of women, but she is acutely conscious—as she always was—of being overheard by men: by Morgan and Lytton and Maynard Keynes[9]

---

[7] Plath, Wakoski, Moore, and Bishop are all included in this anthology.

[8] Henry James, "Notes on Novelists," in *Selected Literary Criticism of Henry James*, Morris Shapira, ed. (London: Heinemann, 1965), pp. 157–58 [Rich's note].

[9] I.e., E. M. Forster, Lytton Strachey, and John Maynard Keynes, all members of Woolf's Bloomsbury circle.

and for that matter by her father, Leslie Stephen.[10] She drew the language out into an exacerbated thread in her determination to have her own sensibility yet protect it from those masculine presences. Only at rare moments in that essay do you hear the passion in her voice; she was trying to sound as cool as Jane Austen, as Olympian as Shakespeare, because that is the way the men of the culture thought a writer should sound.

No male writer has written primarily or even largely for women, or with the sense of women's criticism as a consideration when he chooses his materials, his theme, his language. But to a lesser or greater extent, every woman writer has written for men even when, like Virginia Woolf, she was supposed to be addressing women. If we have come to the point when this balance might begin to change, when women can stop being haunted, not only by "convention and propriety" but by internalized fears of being and saying themselves, then it is an extraordinary moment for the woman writer—and reader.

I have hesitated to do what I am going to do now, which is to use myself as an illustration. For one thing, it's a lot easier and less dangerous to talk about other women writers. But there is something else. Like Virginia Woolf, I am aware of the women who are not with us here because they are washing the dishes and looking after the children. Nearly fifty years after she spoke, that fact remains largely unchanged. And I am thinking also of women whom she left out of the picture altogether—women who are washing other people's dishes and caring for other people's children, not to mention women who went on the streets last night in order to feed their children. We seem to be special women here, we have liked to think of ourselves as special, and we have known that men would tolerate, even romanticize us as special, as long as our words and actions didn't threaten their privilege of tolerating or rejecting us and our work according to *their* ideas of what a special woman ought to be. An important insight of the radical women's movement has been how divisive and how ultimately destructive is this myth of the special woman, who is also the token woman. Every one of us here in this room has had great luck—we are teachers, writers, academicians; our own gifts could not have been enough, for we all know women whose gifts are buried or aborted. Our struggles can have meaning and our privileges—however precarious under patriarchy—can be justified only if they can help to change the lives of women whose gifts—and whose very being—continue to be thwarted and silenced.

My own luck was being born white and middle-class into a house full of books, with a father who encouraged me to read and write. So for about twenty

---

[10] "A. R., 1978: This intuition of mine was corroborated when, early in 1978, I read the correspondence between Woolf and Dame Ethel Smyth (Henry W. and Albert A. Berg Collection, The New York Public Library, Astor, Lenox and Tilden Foundations); in a letter dated June 8, 1933, Woolf speaks of having kept her own personality out of *A Room of One's Own* lest she not be taken seriously: '. . . how personal, so will they say, rubbing their hands with glee, women always are; *I even hear them as I write.*' (Italics mine.)" [Rich's note]. Leslie Stephen (1832–1904), a distinguished man of letters.

years I wrote for a particular man, who criticized and praised me and made me feel I was indeed "special." The obverse side of this, of course, was that I tried for a long time to please him, or rather, not to displease him. And then of course there were other men—writers, teachers—the Man, who was not a terror or a dream but a literary master and a master in other ways less easy to acknowledge. And there were all those poems about women, written by men: it seemed to be a given that men wrote poems and women frequently inhabited them. These women were almost always beautiful, but threatened with the loss of beauty, the loss of youth—the fate worse than death. Or, they were beautiful and died young, like Lucy and Lenore. Or, the woman was like Maud Gonne,[11] cruel and disastrously mistaken, and the poem reproached her because she had refused to become a luxury for the poet.

A lot is being said today about the influence that the myths and images of women have on all of us who are products of culture. I think it has been a peculiar confusion to the girl or woman who tries to write because she is peculiarly susceptible to language. She goes to poetry or fiction looking for *her* way of being in the world, since she too has been putting words and images together; she is looking eagerly for guides, maps, possibilities; and over and over in the "words' masculine persuasive force" of literature she comes up against something that negates everything she is about: she meets the image of Woman in books written by men. She finds a terror and a dream, she finds a beautiful pale face, she finds La Belle Dame Sans Merci, she finds Juliet or Tess or Salomé,[12] but precisely what she does not find is that absorbed, drudging, puzzled, sometimes inspired creature, herself, who sits at a desk trying to put words together.

So what does she do? What did I do? I read the older women poets with their peculiar keenness and ambivalence: Sappho, Christina Rossetti, Emily Dickinson, Elinor Wylie, Edna Millay, H. D.[13] I discovered that the woman poet most admired at the time (by men) was Marianne Moore, who was maidenly, elegant, intellectual, discreet. But even in reading these women I was looking in them for the same things I had found in the poetry of men, because I wanted women poets to be the equals of men, and to be equal was still confused with sounding the same.

I know that my style was formed first by male poets: by the men I was reading as an undergraduate—Frost, Dylan Thomas, Donne, Auden, MacNeice,

---

[11] Irish revolutionary activist (1865–1953), beautiful beloved of William Butler Yeats, and subject of many of his poems. "Lucy and Lenore": in poems written by William Wordsworth and Edgar Allan Poe.

[12] Dancer responsible for killing John the Baptist in Oscar Wilde's play. "La Belle Dame Sans Merci": title of a poem by John Keats (the beautiful lady without pity; French). "Juliet": tragic heroine of Shakespeare's *Romeo and Juliet*. "Tess": doomed heroine in Thomas Hardy's *Tess of the D'Urbervilles*.

[13] Rossetti, Dickinson, Wylie, Millay, and H. D. are included in this anthology. Sappho (c. 600 B.C.), Greek poet.

Stevens, Yeats. What I chiefly learned from them was craft.[14] But poems are like
dreams: in them you put what you don't know you know. Looking back at poems
I wrote before I was twenty-one, I'm startled because beneath the conscious
craft are glimpses of the split I even then experienced between the girl who
wrote poems, who defined herself in writing poems, and the girl who was to
define herself by her relationships with men. "Aunt Jennifer's Tigers" (1951),
written while I was a student, looks with deliberate detachment at this split.[15]
In writing this poem, composed and apparently cool as it is, I thought I was
creating a portrait of an imaginary woman. But this woman suffers from the
opposition of her imagination, worked out in tapestry, and her life-style, "ringed
with ordeals she was mastered by." It was important to me that Aunt Jennifer
was a person as distinct from myself as possible—distanced by the formalism of
the poem, by its objective, observant tone—even by putting the woman in a
different generation.

In those years formalism was part of the strategy—like asbestos gloves, it
allowed me to handle materials I couldn't pick up bare-handed. A later strategy
was to use the persona of a man, as I did in "The Loser" (1958):

A man thinks of the woman he once loved: first, after her
wedding, and then nearly a decade later.

I
I kissed you, bride and lost, and went
home from that bourgeois sacrament,
your cheek still tasting cold upon
my lips that gave you benison
with all the swagger that they knew—
as losers somehow learn to do.

Your wedding made my eyes ache; soon
the world would be worse off for one
more golden apple dropped to ground
without the least protesting sound,
and you would windfall lie, and we
forget your shimmer on the tree.

Beauty is always wasted: if
not Mignon's song[16] sung to the deaf,
at all events to the unmoved.

---

[14] A. R., 1978: Yet I spent months, at sixteen, memorizing and writing imitations of Millay's sonnets;
and in notebooks of that period I find what are obviously attempts to imitate Dickinson's metrics
and verbal compression. I knew H. D. only through anthologized lyrics; her epic poetry was not
then available to me. [Rich's note].

[15] For the text of the poem, see p. 1955.

[16] From Ambroise Thomas's *Mignon* (1866), an opera based on Goethe's *Wilhelm Meister*.

A face like yours cannot be loved
long or seriously enough.
Almost, we seem to hold it off.

II
Well, you are tougher than I thought.
Now when the wash with ice hangs taut
this morning of St. Valentine,
I see you strip the squeaking line,
you body weighed against the load,
and all my groans can do no good.

Because you are still beautiful,
though squared and stiffened by the pull
of what nine windy years have done.
You have three daughters, lost a son.
I see all your intelligence
flung into that unwearied stance.

My envy is of no avail.
I turn my head and wish him well
who chafed your beauty into use
and lives forever in a house
lit by the friction of your mind.
You stagger in against the wind.

I finished college, pubished my first book by a fluke, as it seemed to me, and broke off a love affair. I took a job, lived alone, went on writing, fell in love. I was young, full of energy, and the book seemed to mean that others agreed I was a poet. Because I was also determined to prove that as a woman poet I could also have what was then defined as a "full" woman's life, I plunged in my early twenties into marriage and had three children before I was thirty. There was nothing overt in the environment to warn me: these were the fifties, and in reaction to the earlier wave of feminism, middle-class women were making careers of domestic perfection, working to send their husbands through professional schools, then retiring to raise large families. People were moving out to the suburbs, technology was going to be the answer to everything, even sex; the family was in its glory. Life was extremely private; women were isolated from each other by the loyalties of marriage. I have a sense that women didn't talk to each other much in the fifties—not about their secret emptinesses, their frustrations. I went on trying to write; my second book and first child appeared in the same month. But by the time that book came out I was already dissatisfied with those poems, which seemed to me mere exercises for poems I hadn't written. The book was praised, however, for its "gracefulness"; I had a marriage and a child. If there were doubts, if there were periods of null depression or active despairing, these could only mean that I was ungrateful, insatiable, perhaps a monster.

About the time my third child was born, I felt that I had either to consider myself a failed woman and a failed poet, or to try to find some synthesis by which to understand what was happening to me. What frightened me most was the sense of drift, of being pulled along on a current which called itself my destiny, but in which I seemed to be losing touch with whoever I had been, with the girl who had experienced her own will and energy almost ecstatically at times, walking around a city or riding a train at night or typing in a student room. In a poem about my grandmother I wrote (of myself): "A young girl, thought sleeping, is certified dead" ("Halfway"). I was writing very little, partly from fatigue, that female fatigue of suppressed anger and loss of contact with my own being; partly from the discontinuity of female life with its attention to small chores, errands, work that others constantly undo, small children's constant needs. What I did write was unconvincing to me; my anger and frustration were hard to acknowledge in or out of poems because in fact I cared a great deal about my husband and my children. Trying to look back and understand that time I have tried to analyze the real nature of the conflict. Most, if not all, human lives are full of fantasy—passive day-dreaming which need not be acted on. But to write poetry or fiction, or even to think well, is not to fantasize, or to put fantasies on paper. For a poem to coalesce, for a character or an action to take shape, there has to be an imaginative transformation of reality which is no way passive. And a certain freedom of the mind is needed—freedom to press on, to enter the currents of your thought like a glider pilot, knowing that your motion can be sustained, that the buoyancy of your attention will not be suddenly snatched away. Moreover, if the imagination is to transcend and transform experience it has to question, to challenge, to conceive of alternatives, perhaps to the very life you are living at that moment. You have to be free to play around with the notion that day might be night, love might be hate; nothing can be too sacred for the imagination to turn into its opposite or to call experimentally by another name. For writing is re-naming. Now, to be maternally with small children all day in the old way, to be with a man in the old way of marriage, requires a holding-back, a putting-aside of that imaginative activity, and demands instead a kind of conservatism. I want to make it clear that I am *not* saying that in order to write well, or think well, it is necessary to become unavailable to others, or to become a devouring ego. This has been the myth of the masculine artist and thinker; and I do not accept it. But to be a female human being trying to fulfill traditional female functions in a traditional way *is* in direct conflict with the subversive function of the imagination. The word traditional is important here. There must be ways, and we will be finding out more and more about them, in which the energy of creation and the energy of relation can be united. But in those years I always felt the conflict as a failure of love in myself. I had thought I was choosing a full life: the life available to most men, in which sexuality, work, and parenthood could coexist. But I felt, at twenty-nine, guilt toward the people closest to me, and guilty toward my own being.

I wanted, then, more than anything, the one thing of which there was never enough: time to think, time to write. The fifties and early sixties were years of rapid revelations: the sit-ins and marches in the South, the Bay of Pigs,[17] the early antiwar movement, raised large questions—questions for which the masculine world of the academy around me seemed to have expert and fluent answers. But I needed to think for myself—about pacifism and dissent and violence, about poetry and society, and about my own relationship to all these things. For about ten years I was reading in fierce snatches, scribbling in notebooks, writing poetry in fragments; I was looking desperately for clues, because if there were no clues then I thought I might be insane. I wrote in a notebook about this time:

> Paralyzed by the sense that there exists a mesh of relationships—e.g., between my anger at the children, my sensual life, pacifism, sex (I mean sex in its broadest significance, not merely sexual disire)—an interconnectedness which, if I could see it, make it valid, would give me back myself, make it possible to function lucidly and passionately. Yet I grope in and out among these dark webs.

I think I began at this point to feel that politics was not something "out there" but something "in here" and of the essence of my condition.

In the late fifties I was able to write, for the first time, directly about experiencing myself as a woman. The poem was jotted in fragments during children's naps, brief hours in a library, or at 3:00 A.M. after rising with a wakeful child. I despaired of doing any continuous work at this time. Yet I began to feel that my fragments and scraps had a common consciousness and a common theme, one which I would have been very unwilling to put on paper at an earlier time because I had been taught that poetry should be "universal," which meant, of course, nonfemale. Until then I had tried very much *not* to identify myself as a female poet. Over two years I wrote a ten-part poem called "Snapshots of a Daughter-in-Law" (1958–1960), in a longer looser mode than I'd ever trusted myself with before. It was an extraordinary relief to write that poem. It strikes me now as too literary, too dependent on allusion; I hadn't found the courage yet to do without authorities, or even to use the pronoun "I"—the woman in the poem is always "she." One section of it, No. 2, concerns a woman who thinks she is going mad; she is haunted by voices telling her to resist and rebel, voices which she can hear but not obey.

> 2.
> Banging the coffee-pot into the sink
> she hears the angels chiding, and looks out
> past the raked gardens to the sloppy sky.
> Only a week since They said: *Have no patience.*

---

[17] A 1961 abortive invasion of Cuba by CIA-trained anti-Castro exiles—financed and supported by the U.S. government—which was a fiasco. Like the other "revelations" mentioned, it fed the growing distrust of the government among some Americans.

The next time it was: *Be insatiable.*
Then: *Save yourself*; others you cannot save.
Sometimes she's let the tapstream scald her arm,
a match burn to her thumbnail,

or held her hand above the kettle's snout
right in the woolly steam. They are probably angels,
since nothing hurts her anymore, except
each morning's grit blowing into her eyes.

The poem "Orion," written five years later, is a poem of reconnection with a part of myself I had felt I was losing—the active principle, the energetic imagination, the "half-brother" whom I projected, as I had for many years, into the constellation Orion. It's no accident that the words "cold and egotistical" appear in this poem, and are applied to myself.

Far back when I went zig-zagging
through tamarack[18] pastures
you were my genius, you
my cast-iron Viking, my helmed
lion-heart king in prison.
Years later now you're young

my fierce half-brother, staring
down from that simplified west
your breast open, your belt dragged down
by an oldfashioned thing, a sword
the last bravado you won't give over
though it weighs you down as you stride

and the stars in it are dim
and maybe have stopped burning.
But you burn, and I know it;
as I throw back my head to take you in
an old transfusion happens again:
divine astronomy is nothing to it.

Indoors I bruise and blunder,
break faith, leave ill enough
alone, a dead child born in the dark.
Night cracks up over the chimney,
pieces of time, frozen geodes
come showering down in the grate.

A man reaches behind my eyes
and finds them empty
a woman's head turns away
from my head in the mirror

---

[18] Larch.

children are dying my death
and eating crumbs of my life.

Pity is not your forte.
Calmly you ache up there
pinned aloft in your crow's nest,
my speechless pirate!
You take it all for granted
and when I look you back

it's with a starlike eye
shooting its cold and egotistical spear
where it can do least damage.
Breathe deep! No hurt, no pardon
out here in the cold with you
you with your back to the wall.

The choice still seemed to be between "love"—womanly, maternal love, altruistic love—a love defined and ruled by the weight of an entire culture; and egotism—a force directed by men into creation, achievement, ambition, often at the expense of others, but justifiably so. For weren't they men, and wasn't that their destiny as womanly, selfless love was ours? We know now that the alternatives are false ones—that the word "love" is itself in need of revision.

There is a companion poem to "Orion," written three years later, in which at last the woman in the poem and the woman writing the poem become the same person. It is called "Planetarium," and it was written after a visit to a real planetarium, where I read an account of the work of Caroline Herschel, the astronomer, who worked with her brother William, but whose name remained obscure, as his did not.

A woman in the shape of a monster
a monster in the shape of a woman
the skies are full of them

a woman   'in the snow
among the Clocks and instruments
or measuring the ground with poles'
in her 98 years to discover
8 comets

she whom the moon ruled
likes us
levitating into the night sky
riding the polished lenses

Galaxies of women, there
doing penance for impetuousness
ribs chilled
in those spaces   of the mind

An eye,

　　　　'virile, precise and absolutely certain'
　　　　from the mad webs of Uranusborg

　　　　　　encountering the NOVA

every impulse of light exploding
from the core
as life flies out of us

　　　　Tycho whispering at last
　　　　'Let me not seem to have lived in vain'

What we see, we see
and seeing is changing

the light that shrivels a mountain
and leaves a man alive

Heartbeat of the pulsar
heart sweating through my body

The radio impulse
pouring in from Taurus

　　　　I am bombarded yet　　　I stand

I have been standing all my life in the
direct path of a battery of signals
the most accurately transmitted most
untranslatable language in the universe
I am a galactic cloud so deep　　so invo-
luted that a light wave could take 15
years to travel through me　　And has
taken　　I am an instrument in the shape
of a woman trying to translate pulsations
into images　　for the relief of the body
and the reconstruction of the mind.

In closing I want to tell you about a dream I had last summer. I dreamed I was asked to read my poetry at a mass women's meeting, but when I began to read, what came out were the lyrics of a blues song. I share this dream with you because it seemed to me to say something about the problems and the future of the woman writer, and probably of women in general. The awakening of consciousness is not like the crossing of a frontier—one step and you are in another country. Much of woman's poetry has been of the nature of the blues song: a cry of pain, of victimization, or a lyric of seduction.[19] And today, much

---

[19] A. R., 1978: When I dreamed that dream, was I wholly ignorant of the tradition of Bessie Smith and other women's blues lyrics which transcended victimization to sing of resistance and indepen-dence? [Rich's note].

poetry by women—and prose for that matter—is charged with anger. I think we need to go through that anger, and we will betray our own reality if we try, as Virginia Woolf was trying, for an objectivity, a detachment, that would make us sound more like Jane Austen or Shakespeare. We know more than Jane Austen or Shakespeare knew: more than Jane Austen because our lives are more complex, more than Shakespeare because we know more about the lives of women—Jane Austen and Virginia Woolf included.

Both the victimization and the anger experienced by women are real, and have real sources, everywhere in the environment, built into society, language, the structures of thought. They will go on being tapped and explored by poets, among others. We can neither deny them, nor will we rest there. A new generation of women poets is already working out of the psychic energy released when women begin to move out towards what the feminist philosopher Mary Daly has described as the "new space" on the boundaries of patriarchy.[20] Women are speaking to and of women in these poems, out of a newly released courage to name, to love each other, to share risk and grief and celebration.

To the eye of a feminist, the work of Western male poets now writing reveals a deep, fatalistic pessimism as to the possibilities of change, whether societal or personal, along with a familiar and threadbare use of women (and nature) as redemptive on the one hand, threatening on the other; and a new tide of phallocentric sadism and overt woman-hating which matches the sexual brutality of recent films. "Political" poetry by men remains stranded amid the struggles for power among male groups; in condemning U.S. imperialism or the Chilean junta the poet can claim to speak for the oppressed while remaining, as male, part of a system of sexual oppression. The enemy is always outside the self, the struggle somewhere else. The mood of isolation, self-pity, and self-imitation that pervades "nonpolitical" poetry suggests that a profound change in masculine consciousness will have to precede any new male poetic—or other—inspiration. The creative energy of patriarchy is fast running out; what remains is its self-generating energy for destruction. As women, we have our work cut out for us.

WHEN WE DEAD AWAKEN

—*for E. Y.*

> Trying to tell you how
> the anatomy of the park
> through stained panes, the way
> guerrillas are advancing

[20] Mary Daly, *Beyond God the Father: Towards a Philosophy of Women's Liberation* (Boston: Beacon, 1973) [Rich's note].

through minefields, the trash   5
burning endlessly in the dump
to return to heaven like a stain—
everything outside our skins is an image
of this affliction:
stones on my table, carried by hand   10
from scenes I trusted
souvenirs of what I once described
as happiness
everything outside my skin
speaks of the fault that sends me limping   15
even the scars of my decisions
even the sunblaze in the mica-vein
even you, fellow-creature, sister,
sitting across from me, dark with love,
working like me to pick apart   20
working with me to remake
this trailing knitted thing, this cloth of darkness,
this woman's garment, trying to save the skein.

2.

The fact of being separate
enters your livelihood like a piece of furniture   25
—a chest of seventeenth-century wood
from somewhere in the North.
It has a huge lock shaped like a woman's head
but the key has not been found.
In the compartments are other keys   30
to lost doors, an eye of glass.
Slowly you begin to add
things of your own.
You come and go reflected in its panels.
You give up keeping track of anniversaries,   35
you begin to write in your diaries
more honestly than ever.

3.

The lovely landscape of southern Ohio
betrayed by strip mining, the
thick gold band on the adulterer's finger   40
the blurred programs of the offshore pirate station
are causes for hesitation.

Here in the matrix of need and anger, the
disproof of what we thought possible
failures of medication   45
doubts of another's existence
—tell it over and over, the words
get thick with unmeaning—
yet never have we been closer to the truth
of the lies we were living, listen to me: 50
the faithfulness I can imagine would be a weed
flowering in tar, a blue energy piercing
the massed atoms of a bedrock disbelief.

SISTERS

Can I easily say,
I know you of course now,
no longer the fellow-victim,
reader of my diaries, heir
to my outgrown dresses,   5
ear for my poems and invectives?
Do I know you better
than that blue-eyed stranger
self-absorbed as myself
raptly knitting or sleeping   10
through a thirdclass winter journey?
Face to face all night
her dreams and whimpers
tangled with mine,
sleeping but not asleep   15
behind the engine drilling
into dark Germany,
her eyes, mouth, head
reconstructed by dawn
as we nodded farewell.   20
Her I should recognize
years later, anywhere.

PEELING ONIONS

Only to have a grief
equal to all these tears!

There's not a sob in my chest.
Dry-hearted as Peer Gynt

I pare away, no hero   5
merely a cook.

Crying was labor, once
when I'd good cause.
Walking, I felt my eyes like wounds
raw in my head,   10
so postal-clerks, I thought, must stare.
A dog's look, a cat's, burnt to my brain—
yet all that stayed
stuffed in my lungs like smog.

These old tears in the chopping-bowl.   15

FROM A SURVIVOR

The pact that we made was the ordinary pact
of men & women in those days

I don't know who we thought we were
that our personalities
could resist the failures of the race   5

Lucky or unlucky, we didn't know
the race had failures of that order
and that we were going to share them

Like everybody else, we thought of ourselves as special

Your body is as vivid to me   10
as it ever was: even more

since my feeling for it is clearer:
I know what it could and could not do

it is no longer
the body of a god   15
or anything with power over my life

Next year it would have been 20 years
and you are wastefully dead
who might have made the leap
we talked, too late, of making   20

which I live now
not as a leap
but a succession of brief, amazing movements

each one making possible the next

Toni Morrison 1931–

Toni Morrison is not only one of the best writers of her generation and one of the best African-American authors of the twentieth century, but undoubtedly she is also one of the finest writers of this century. Indeed, over twenty years Morrison has published a collection of essays and six novels that, it has been written, have completely changed "our view of American history and literature." Morrison has said that ". . . the best art is political and you ought to make it unquestionably political and irrevocably beautiful at the same time," a point of view about the relationship between writer and reader that has made Morrison both popular and critically acclaimed. Unlike many examples of African-American fiction that take place in the South or urban North, Morrison's takes us to the Midwest, especially Ohio, where Morrison was raised. According to the author, Ohio serves as a crucial "escape from stereotyped black settings," as it is ". . . neither plantation nor ghetto" and also was a major stop on the Underground Railroad. Formally educated and influenced by great writers from Europe, including Flaubert and Austen, Morrison attended Howard University and Cornell University; she wrote a master's thesis at Cornell on the idea of alienation in works by Virginia Woolf and William Faulkner. Her novels include *The Bluest Eye* (1970), *Sula* (1974), *The Song of Solomon* (1977), for which Morrison earned the National Book Critics Circle Award, and *Beloved* (1984), which won the Pulitzer Prize for fiction. Along with Alice Walker, she is noted for having changed the central focus of fiction about African Americans to issues of women from those of men, along with persistently examining the diversity of African-American communities. In 1993, Toni Morrison became the first African American to be awarded the Nobel Prize in Literature.

RECITATIF

My mother danced all night and Roberta's was sick. That's why we were taken to St. Bonny's. People want to put their arms around you when you tell them you were in a shelter, but it really wasn't bad. No big long room with one hundred beds like Bellevue. There were four to a room, and when Roberta and me came, there was a shortage of state kids, so we were the only ones assigned to 406 and could go from bed to bed if we wanted to. And we wanted to, too. We changed beds every night and for the whole four months we were there we never picked one out as our own permanent bed.

It didn't start out that way. The minute I walked in and the Big Bozo introduced us, I got sick to my stomach. It was one thing to be taken out of your own bed early in the morning—it was something else to be stuck in a strange place with a girl from a whole other race. And Mary, that's my mother, she was right. Every now and then she would stop dancing long enough to tell me something important and one of the things she said was that they never washed their hair and they smelled funny. Roberta sure did. Smell funny, I mean. So when the Big Bozo (nobody ever called her Mrs. Itkin, just like nobody ever said St. Bonaventure)—when she said, "Twyla, this is Roberta. Roberta, this is Twyla. Make each other welcome," I said, "My mother won't like you putting me in here."

"Good," said Bozo. "Maybe then she'll come and take you home."

How's that for mean? If Roberta had laughed I would have killed her, but she didn't. She just walked over to the window and stood with her back to us.

"Turn around," said the Bozo. "Don't be rude. Now Twyla. Roberta. When you hear a loud buzzer, that's the call for dinner. Come down to the first floor. Any fights and no movie." And then, just to make sure we knew what we would be missing, "*The Wizard of Oz.*"

Roberta must have thought I meant that my mother would be mad about my being put in the shelter. Not about rooming with her, because as soon as Bozo left she came over to me and said, "Is your mother sick too?"

"No," I said. "She just likes to dance all night."

"Oh." She nodded her head and I liked the way she understood things so fast. So for the moment it didn't matter that we looked like salt and pepper standing there and that's what the other kids called us sometimes. We were eight years old and got F's all the time. Me because I couldn't remember what I read or what the teacher said. And Roberta because she couldn't read at all and didn't even listen to the teacher. She wasn't good at anything except jacks, at which she was a killer: pow scoop pow scoop pow scoop.

We didn't like each other all that much at first, but nobody else wanted to play with us because we weren't real orphans with beautiful dead parents in the sky. We were dumped. Even the New York City Puerto Ricans and the upstate Indians ignored us. All kinds of kids were in there, black ones, white ones, even two Koreans. The food was good, though. At least I thought so. Roberta hated it and left whole pieces of things on her plate: Spam, Salisbury steak—even Jell-O with fruit cocktail in it, and she didn't care if I ate what she wouldn't. Mary's idea of supper was popcorn and a can of Yoo-Hoo. Hot mashed potatoes and two weenies was like Thanksgiving for me.

It really wasn't bad, St. Bonny's. The big girls on the second floor pushed us around now and then. But that was all. They wore lipstick and eyebrow pencil and wobbled their knees while they watched TV. Fifteen, sixteen, even, some of them were. They were put-out girls, scared runaways most of them. Poor little girls who fought their uncles off but looked tough to us, and mean. God, did they look mean. The staff tried to keep them separate from the younger children, but sometimes they caught us watching them in the orchard where they played radios and danced with each other. They'd light out after us and pull our hair or twist our arms. We were scared of them, Roberta and me, but neither of us wanted the other one to know it. So we got a good list of dirty names we could shout back when we ran from them through the orchard. I used to dream a lot and almost always the orchard was there. Two acres, four maybe, of these little apple trees. Hundreds of them. Empty and crooked like beggar women when I first came to St. Bonny's but fat with flowers when I left. I don't know why I dreamt about that orchard so much. Nothing really happened there. Nothing all that important, I mean. Just the big girls and playing the radio. Roberta and me watching. Maggie fell down there once. The kitchen woman with legs like parentheses. And the big girls laughed at her. We should have helped her up, I know, but we were scared of those girls with lipstick and eyebrow pencil. Maggie couldn't talk. The kids said she had her tongue cut out, but I think she was just born that way: mute. She was old and sandy-colored and she worked in the kitchen. I don't know if she was nice or not. I just remember her legs like parentheses and how she rocked when she walked. She worked from early in the morning till two o'clock, and if she was late, if she had too much cleaning and didn't get out till two-fifteen or so, she'd cut through the orchard so she wouldn't miss her bus and have to wait another hour. She wore this really stupid little hat—a kid's hat with ear flaps—and she wasn't much taller than we were. A really awful little hat. Even for a mute, it was dumb—dressing like a kid and never saying anything at all.

"But what about if somebody tries to kill her?" I used to wonder about that. "Or what if she wants to cry? Can she cry?"

"Sure," Roberta said. "But just tears. No sounds come out."

"She can't scream?"

"Nope. Nothing."

"Can she hear?"

"I guess."

"Let's call her," I said. And we did.

"Dummy! Dummy!" She never turned her head.

"Bow legs! Bow legs!" Nothing. She just rocked on, the chin straps of her baby-boy hat swaying from side to side. I think we were wrong. I think she could hear and didn't let on. And it shames me even now to think there was somebody in there after all who heard us call her those names and couldn't tell on us.

We got along all right, Roberta and me. Changed beds every night, got F's in civics and communication skills and gym. The Bozo was disappointed in us, she said. Out of 130 of us state cases, 90 were under twelve. Almost all were real orphans with beautiful dead parents in the sky. We were the only ones dumped and the only ones with F's in three classes including gym. So we got along— what with her leaving whole pieces of things on her plate and being nice about not asking questions.

I think it was the day before Maggie fell down that we found out our mothers were coming to visit us on the same Sunday. We had been at the shelter twenty-eight days (Roberta twenty-eight and a half) and this was their visit with us. Our mothers would come at ten o'clock in time for chapel, then lunch with us in the teacher's lounge. I thought if my dancing mother met her sick mother it might be good for her. And Roberta thought her sick mother would get a big bang out of a dancing one. We got excited about it and curled each other's hair. After breakfast we sat on the bed watching the road from the window. Roberta's socks were still wet. She washed them the night before and put them on the radiator to dry. They hadn't, but she put them on anyway because their tops were so pretty—scalloped in pink. Each of us had a purple construction-paper basket that we had made in craft class. Mine had a yellow crayon rabbit on it. Roberta's had eggs with wiggly lines of color. Inside were cellophane grass and just the jelly beans because I'd eaten the two marshmallow eggs they gave us. The Big Bozo came herself to get us. Smiling she told us we looked very nice and to come downstairs. We were so surprised by the smile we'd never seen before, neither of us moved.

"Don't you want to see your mommies?"

I stood up first and spilled the jelly beans all over the floor. Bozo's smile disappeared while we scrambled to get the candy up off the floor and put it back in the grass.

She escorted us downstairs to the first floor, where the other girls were lining up to file into the chapel. A bunch of grown-ups stood to one side. Viewers mostly. The old biddies who wanted servants and the fags who wanted company looking for children they might want to adopt. Once in a while a grandmother. Almost never anybody young or anybody whose face wouldn't scare you in the night. Because if any of the real orphans had young relatives they wouldn't be real orphans. I saw Mary right away. She had on those green slacks I hated and hated even more now because didn't she know we were going to chapel? And that fur jacket with the pocket linings so ripped she had to pull to get her hands out of them. But her face was pretty—like always—and she smiled and waved like she was the little girl looking for her mother, not me.

I walked slowly, trying not to drop the jelly beans and hoping the paper handle would hold. I had to use my last Chiclet because by the time I finished cutting everything out, all the Elmer's was gone. I am left-handed and the scissors never worked for me. It didn't matter, though; I might just as well have chewed the gum. Mary dropped to her knees and grabbed me, mashing the basket, the jelly beans, and the grass into her ratty fur jacket.

"Twyla, baby. Twyla, baby!"

I could have killed her. Already I heard the big girls in the orchard the next time saying, "Twyyyyyla, baby!" But I couldn't stay mad at Mary while she was smiling and hugging me and smelling of Lady Esther dusting powder. I wanted to stay buried in her fur all day.

To tell the truth I forgot about Roberta. Mary and I got in line for the traipse into chapel and I was feeling proud because she looked so beautiful even in those ugly green slacks that made her behind stick out. A pretty mother on earth is better than a beautiful dead one in the sky even if she did leave you all alone to go dancing.

I felt a tap on my shoulder, turned, and saw Roberta smiling. I smiled back, but not too much lest somebody think this visit was the biggest thing that ever happened in my life. Then Roberta said, "Mother, I want you to meet my roommate, Twyla. And that's Twyla's mother."

I looked up it seemed for miles. She was big. Bigger than any man and on her chest was the biggest cross I'd ever seen. I swear it was six inches long each way. And in the crook of her arm was the biggest Bible ever made.

Mary, simpleminded as ever, grinned and tried to yank her hand out of the pocket with the raggedy lining—to shake hands, I guess. Roberta's mother looked down at me and then looked down at Mary too. She didn't say anything, just grabbed Roberta with her Bible-free hand and stepped out of line, walking quickly to the rear of it. Mary was still grinning because she's not too swift when it comes to what's really going on. Then this light bulb goes off in her head and she says "That bitch!" really loud and us almost in the chapel now. Organ music whining; the Bonny Angels singing sweetly. Everybody in the world turned around to look. And Mary would have kept it up—kept calling names if I hadn't squeezed her hands as hard as I could. That helped a little, but she still twitched and crossed and uncrossed her legs all through service. Even groaned a couple of times. Why did I think she would come there and act right? Slacks. No hat like the grandmothers and viewers, and groaning all the while. When we stood for hymns she kept her mouth shut. Wouldn't even look at the words on the page. She actually reached in her purse for a mirror to check her lipstick. All I could think of was that she really needed to be killed. The sermon lasted a year, and I knew the real orphans were looking smug again.

We were supposed to have lunch in the teacher's lounge, but Mary didn't bring anything, so we picked fur and cellophane grass off the mashed jelly beans and ate them. I could have killed her. I sneaked a look at Roberta. Her mother had brought chicken legs and ham sandwiches and oranges and a whole box of chocolate-covered grahams. Roberta drank milk from a thermos while her mother read the Bible to her.

Things are not right. The wrong food is always with the wrong people. Maybe that's why I got into waitress work later—to match up the right people with the right food. Roberta just let those chicken legs sit there, but she did bring a stack of grahams up to me later when the visit was over. I think she was sorry that her mother would not shake my mother's hand. And I liked that and I liked the fact that she didn't say a word about Mary groaning all the way through the service and not bringing any lunch.

Roberta left in May when the apple trees were heavy and white. On her last day we went to the orchard to watch the big girls smoke and dance by the radio. It didn't matter that they said, "Twyyyyyla, baby." We sat on the ground and breathed. Lady Esther. Apple blossoms. I still go soft when I smell one or the other. Roberta was going home. The big cross and the big Bible was coming to get her and she seemed sort of glad and sort of not. I thought I would die in that room of four beds without her and I knew Bozo had plans to move some other dumped kid in there with me. Roberta promised to write every day, which was really sweet of her because she couldn't read a lick so how could she write anybody? I would have drawn pictures and sent them to her but she never gave me her address. Little by little she faded. Her wet socks with the pink scalloped tops and her big serious-looking eyes—that's all I could catch when I tried to bring her to mind.

I was working behind the counter at the Howard Johnson's on the Thruway just before the Kingston exit. Not a bad job. Kind of a long ride from Newburgh, but okay once I got there. Mine was the second night shift, eleven to seven. Very light until a Greyhound checked in for breakfast around six-thirty. At that hour the sun was all the way clear of the hills behind the restaurant. The place looked better at night—more like shelter— but I loved it when the sun broke in, even if it did show all the cracks in the vinyl and the speckled floor looked dirty no matter what the mop boy did.

It was August and a bus crowd was just unloading. They would stand around a long while: going to the john, and looking at gifts and junk-for-sale machines, reluctant to sit down so soon. Even to eat. I was trying to fill the coffeepots and get them all situated on the electric burners when I saw her. She was sitting in a booth smoking a cigarette with two guys smothered in head and facial hair. Her own hair was so big and wild I could hardly see her face. But the eyes. I would know them anywhere. She had on a powder-blue halter and shorts outfit and earrings the size of bracelets. Talk about lipstick and eyebrow pencil. She made the big girls look like nuns. I couldn't get off the counter until seven o'clock, but I kept watching the booth in case they got up to leave before that. My replacement was on time for a change, so I counted and stacked my receipts as fast as I could and signed off. I walked over to the booth, smiling and wondering if she would remember me. Or even if she wanted to remember me. Maybe she didn't want to be reminded of St. Bonny's or to have anybody know she was ever there. I know I never talked about it to anybody.

I put my hands in my apron pockets and leaned against the back of the booth facing them.

"Roberta? Roberta Fisk?"

She looked up. "Yeah?"

"Twyla."

She squinted for a second and then said, "Wow."

"Remember me?"

"Sure. Hey. Wow."

"It's been awhile," I said, and gave a smile to the two hairy guys.

"Yeah. Wow. You work here?"

"Yeah," I said. "I live in Newburgh."

"Newburgh? No kidding?" She laughed then, a private laugh that included the guys but only the guys, and they laughed with her. What could I do but laugh too and wonder why I was standing there with my knees showing out from under that uniform. Without looking I could see the blue-and-white triangle on my head, my hair shapeless in a net, my ankles thick in white oxfords. Nothing could have been less sheer than my stockings. There was this silence that came down right after I laughed. A silence it was her turn to fill up. With introductions, maybe, to her boyfriends or an invitation to sit down and have a Coke. Instead she lit a cigarette off the one she'd just finished and said, "We're on our way to the Coast. He's got an appointment with Hendrix." She gestured casually toward the boy next to her.

"Hendrix? Fantastic," I said. "Really fantastic. What's she doing now?"

Roberta coughed on her cigarette and the two guys rolled their eyes up at the ceiling.

"Hendrix. Jimi Hendrix, asshole. He's only the biggest—Oh, wow. Forget it."

I was dismissed without anyone saying good-bye, so I thought I would do it for her.

"How's your mother?" I asked. Her grin cracked her whole face. She swallowed. "Fine," she said. "How's yours?"

"Pretty as a picture," I said and turned away. The backs of my knees were damp. Howard Johnson's really was a dump in the sunlight.

James is as comfortable as a house slipper. He liked my cooking and I liked his big loud family. They have lived in Newburgh all of their lives and talk about it the way people do who have always known a home. His grandmother has a porch swing older than his father and when they talk about streets and avenues and buildings they call them names they no longer have. They still call the A&P Rico's because it stands on property once a mom-and-pop store owned by Mr. Rico. And they call the new community college Town Hall because it once was. My mother-in-law puts up jelly and cucumbers and buys butter wrapped in cloth from a dairy. James and his father talk about fishing and baseball and I can see them all together on the Hudson in a raggedy skiff. Half the population of Newburgh is on welfare now, but to my husband's family it was still some upstate paradise of a time long past. A time of ice houses and vegetable wagons, coal furnaces and children weeding gardens. When our son was born my mother-in-law gave me the crib blanket that had been hers.

But the town they remembered had changed. Something quick was in the air. Magnificent old houses, so ruined they had become shelter for squatters and rent risks, were bought and renovated. Smart IBM people moved out of their suburbs back into the city and put shutters up and herb gardens in their backyards. A brochure came in the mail announcing the opening of a Food Emporium. Gourmet food, it said—and listed items the rich IBM crowd would want. It was located in a new mall at the edge of town and I drove out to shop there one day—just to see. It was late in June. After the tulips were gone and the Queen Elizabeth roses were open everywhere. I trailed my cart along the aisle tossing in smoked oysters and Robert's sauce and things I knew would sit in my cupboard for years. Only when I found some Klondike ice cream bars did I feel less guilty about spending James's fireman's salary so foolishly. My father-in-law ate them with the same gusto little Joseph did.

Waiting in the checkout line I heard a voice say, "Twyla!"

The classical music piped over the aisles had affected me and the woman leaning toward me was dressed to kill. Diamonds on her hand, a smart white summer dress. "I'm Mrs. Benson," I said.

"Ho. Ho. The Big Bozo," she sang.

For a split second I didn't know what she was talking about. She had a bunch of asparagus and two cartons of fancy water.

"Roberta!"

"Right."

"For heaven's sake. Roberta."

"You look great," she said.

"So do you. Where are you? Here? In Newburgh?"

"Yes. Over in Annandale."

We both giggled. Really giggled. Suddenly, in just a pulse beat, twenty years disappeared and all of it came rushing back. The big girls (whom we called gar girls—Roberta's misheard word for the evil stone faces described in a civics class) there dancing in the orchard, the ploppy mashed potatoes, the double weenies, the Spam with pineapple. We went into the coffee shop holding on to one another and I tried to think why we were glad to see each other this time and not before. Once, twelve years ago, we passed like strangers. A black girl and a white girl meeting in a Howard Johnson's on the road and having nothing to say. One in a blue-and-white triangle waitress hat, the other on her way to see Hendrix. Now we were behaving like sisters separated for much too long. Those four short months were nothing in time. Maybe it was the thing itself. Just being there, together. Two little girls who knew what nobody else in the world knew—how not to ask questions. How to believe what had to be believed. There was politeness in that reluctance and generosity as well. Is your mother sick too? No, she dances all night. Oh—and an understanding nod.

We sat in a booth by the window and fell into recollection like veterans.

"Did you ever learn to read?"

"Watch." She picked up the menu. "Special of the day. Cream of corn soup. Entrées. Two dots and a wriggly line. Quiche. Chef salad, scallops . . ."

I was laughing and applauding when the waitress came up.

"Remember the Easter baskets?"

"And how we tried to *introduce* them?"

"Your mother with that cross like two telephone poles."

"And yours with those tight slacks."

We laughed so loudly heads turned and made the laughter hard to suppress.

"What happened to the Jimi Hendrix date?"

Roberta made a blow-out sound with her lips.

"When he died I thought about you."

"Oh, you heard about him finally?"

"Finally. Come on, I was a small-town country waitress."

"And I was a small-town country dropout. God, were we wild. I still don't know how I got out of there alive."

"But you did."

"I did. I really did. Now I'm Mrs. Kenneth Norton."

"Sounds like a mouthful."

"It is."

"Servants and all?"

Roberta held up two fingers.

"Ow! What does he do?"

I was opening my mouth to say more when the cashier called my attention to her empty counter.

"Meet you outside." Roberta pointed her finger and went into the express line.

I placed the groceries and kept myself from glancing around to check Roberta's progress. I remembered Howard Johnson's and looking for a chance to speak only to be greeted with a stingy "wow." But she was waiting for me and her huge hair was sleek now, smooth around a small, nicely shaped head. Shoes, dress, everything lovely and summery and rich. I was dying to know what happened to her, how she got from Jimi Hendrix to Annandale, a neighborhood full of doctors and IBM executives. Easy, I thought. Everything is so easy for them. They think they own the world.

"How long," I asked her. "How long have you been here?"

"A year. I got married to a man who lives here. And you, you're married too, right? Benson, you said."

"Yeah. James Benson."

"And is he nice?"

"Oh, is he nice?"

"Well, is he?" Roberta's eyes were steady as though she really meant the question and wanted an answer.

"He's wonderful, Roberta. Wonderful."

"So you're happy."

"Very."

"That's good," she said and nodded her head. "I always hoped you'd be happy. Any kids? I know you have kids."

"One. A boy. How about you?"

"Four."

"Four?"

She laughed. "Step kids. He's widower."

"Oh."

"Got a minute? Let's have a coffee."

I thought about the Klondikes melting and the inconvenience of going all the way to my car and putting the bags in the trunk. Served me right for buying all that stuff I didn't need. Roberta was ahead of me.

"Put them in my car. It's right here."

And then I saw the dark blue limousine.

"You married a Chinaman?"

"No." She laughed. "He's the driver."

"Oh, my. If the Big Bozo could see you now."

"Computers and stuff. What do I know?"

"I don't remember a hell of a lot from those days, but Lord, St. Bonny's is as clear as daylight. Remember Maggie? The day she fell down and those gar girls laughed at her?"

Roberta looked up from her salad and stared at me. "Maggie didn't fall," she said.

"Yes, she did. You remember."

"No, Twyla. They knocked her down. Those girls pushed her down and tore her clothes. In the orchard."

"I don't—that's not what happened."

"Sure it is. In the orchard. Remember how scared we were?"

"Wait a minute. I don't remember any of that."

"And Bozo was fired."

"You're crazy. She was there when I left. You left before me."

"I went back. You weren't there when they fired Bozo."

"What?"

"Twice. Once for a year when I was about ten, another for two months when I was fourteen. That's when I ran away."

"You ran away from St. Bonny's?"

"I had to. What do you want? Me dancing in that orchard?"

"Are you sure about Maggie?"

"Of course I'm sure. You've blocked it, Twyla. It happened. Those girls had behavior problems, you know."

"Didn't they, though. But why can't I remember the Maggie thing?"

"Believe me. It happened. And we were there."

"Who did you room with when you went back?" I asked her as if I would know her. The Maggie thing was troubling me.

"Creeps. They tickled themselves in the night."

My ears were itching and I wanted to go home suddenly. This was all very well but she couldn't just comb her hair, wash her face, and pretend everything was hunky-dory. After the Howard Johnson's snub. And no apology. Nothing.

"Were you on dope or what that time at Howard Johnson's?" I tried to make my voice sound friendlier than I felt.

"Maybe, a little. I never did drugs much. Why?"

"I don't know, you acted sort of like you didn't want to know me then."

"Oh, Twyla, you know how it was in those days: black—white. You know how everything was."

But I didn't know. I thought it was just the opposite. Busloads of blacks and whites came into Howard Johnson's together. They roamed together then: students, musicians, lovers, protesters. You got to see everything at Howard Johnson's, and blacks were very friendly with whites in those days. But sitting there with nothing on my plate but two hard tomato wedges wondering about the melting Klondikes it seemed childish remembering the slight. We went to her car and, with the help of the driver, got my stuff into my station wagon.

"We'll keep in touch this time," she said.

"Sure," I said. "Sure. Give me a call."

"I will," she said, and then, just as I was sliding behind the wheel, she leaned into the window. "By the way. Your mother. Did she ever stop dancing?"

I shook my head. "No. Never."

Roberta nodded.

"And yours? Did she ever get well?"

She smiled at tiny sad smile. "No. She never did. Look, call me, okay?"

"Okay," I said, but I knew I wouldn't. Roberta had messed up my past somehow with that business about Maggie. I wouldn't forget a thing like that. Would I?

Strife came to us that fall. At least that's what the paper called it. Strife. Racial strife. The word made me think of a bird—a big shrieking bird out of 1,000,000,000 B.C. Flapping its wings and cawing. Its eye with no lid always bearing down on you. All day it screeched and at night it slept on the rooftops. It woke you in the morning, and from the *Today* show to the eleven o'clock news it kept you an awful company. I couldn't figure it out from one day to the next. I knew I was supposed to feel something strong, but I didn't know what, and James wasn't any help. Joseph was on the list of kids to be transferred from the junior high school to another one at some far-out-of-the-way place and I thought it was a good thing until I heard it was a bad thing. I mean I didn't know. All the schools seemed dumps to me, and the fact that one was nicer looking didn't hold much weight. But the papers were full of it and then the kids began to get jumpy. In August, mind you. Schools weren't even open yet. I thought Joseph might be frightened to go over there, but he didn't seem scared so I forgot about it, until I found myself driving along Hudson Street out there by the school they were trying to integrate and saw a line of women marching. And who do you suppose was in line, big as life, holding a sign in front of her bigger than her mother's cross? MOTHERS HAVE RIGHTS TOO! it said.

I drove on and then changed my mind. I circled the block, slowed down, and honked my horn.

Roberta looked over and when she saw me she waved. I didn't wave back, but I didn't move either. She handed her sign to another woman and came over to where I was parked.

"Hi."

"What are you doing?"

"Picketing. What's it look like?"

"What for?"

"What do you mean, 'What for?' They want to take my kids and send them out of the neighborhood. They don't want to go."

"So what if they go to another school? My boy's being bussed too, and I don't mind. Why should you?"

"It's not about us, Twyla. Me and you. It's about our kids."

"What's more *us* than that?"

"Well, it is a free country."

"Not yet, but it will be."

"What the heck does that mean? I'm not doing anything to you."

"You really think that?"

"I know it."

"I wonder what made me think you were different."

"I wonder what made me think you were different."

"Look at them," I said. "Just look. Who do they think they are? Swarming all over the place like they own it. And now they think they can decide where my child goes to school. Look at them, Roberta. They're Bozos."

Roberta turned around and looked at the women. Almost all of them were standing still now, waiting. Some were even edging toward us. Roberta looked at me out of some refrigerator behind her eyes. "No, they're not. They're just mothers."

"And what am I? Swiss cheese?"

"I used to curl your hair."

"I hated your hands in my hair."

The women were moving. Our faces looked mean to them of course and they looked as though they could not wait to throw themselves in front of a police car or, better yet, into my car and drag me away by my ankles. Now they surrounded my car and gently, gently began to rock it. I swayed back and forth like a sideways yo-yo. Automatically I reached for Roberta, like the old days in the orchard when they saw us watching them and we had to get out of there, and if one of us fell the other pulled her up and if one of us was caught the other stayed to kick and scratch, and neither would leave the other behind. My arm shot out of the car window but no receiving hand was there. Roberta was looking at me sway from side to side in the car and her face was still. My purse slid from the car seat down under the dashboard. The four policemen who had been drinking Tab in their car finally got the message and strolled over, forcing their way through the women. Quietly, firmly they spoke. "Okay, ladies. Back in line or off the streets."

Some of them went away willingly; others had to be urged away from the car doors and the hood. Roberta didn't move. She was looking steadily at me. I was fumbling to turn on the ignition, which wouldn't catch because the gearshift was still in drive. The seats of the car were a mess because the swaying had thrown my grocery coupons all over and my purse was sprawled on the floor.

"Maybe I am different now, Twyla. But you're not. You're the same little state kid who kicked a poor old black lady when she was down on the ground. You kicked a black lady and you have the nerve to call me a bigot."

The coupons were everywhere and the guts of my purse were bunched under the dashboard. What was she saying? Black? Maggie wasn't black.

"She wasn't black," I said.

"Like hell she wasn't, and you kicked her. We both did. You kicked a black lady who couldn't even scream."

"Liar!"

"You're the liar! Why don't you just go on home and leave us alone, huh?"

She turned away and I skidded away from the curb.

The next morning I went into the garage and cut the side out of the carton our portable TV had come in. It wasn't nearly big enough, but after a while I had a decent sign: red spray-painted letters on a white background—AND SO DO CHILDREN****. I meant just to go down to the school and tack it up somewhere so those cows on the picket line across the street could see it, but when I got there, some ten or so others had already assembled—protesting the cows across the street. Police permits and everything. I got in line and we strutted in time on our side while Roberta's group strutted on theirs. That first day we were all dignified, pretending the other side didn't exist. The second day there was name calling and finger gestures. But that was about all. People changed signs from time to time, but Roberta never did and neither did I. Actually my sign didn't make sense without Roberta's. "And so do children what?" one of the women on my side asked me. Have rights, I said, as though it was obvious.

Roberta didn't acknowledge my presence in any way, and I got to thinking maybe she didn't know I was there. I began to pace myself in the line, jostling people one minute and lagging behind the next, so Roberta and I could reach the end of our respective lines at the same time and there would be a moment in our turn when we would face each other. Still, I couldn't tell whether she saw me and knew my sign was for her. The next day I went early before we were scheduled to assemble. I waited until she got there before I exposed my new creation. As soon as she hoisted her MOTHERS HAVE RIGHTS TOO I began to wave my new one, which said, HOW WOULD YOU KNOW? I know she saw that one, but I had gotten addicted now. My signs got crazier each day, and the women on my side decided that I was a kook. They couldn't make heads or tails out of my brilliant screaming posters.

I brought a painted sign in queenly red with huge black letters that said, IS YOUR MOTHER WELL? Roberta took her lunch break and didn't come back for the rest of the day or any day after. Two days later I stopped going too and couldn't have been missed because nobody understood my signs anyway.

It was a nasty six weeks. Classes were suspended and Joseph didn't go to anybody's school until October. The children—everybody's children—soon got bored with that extended vacation they thought was going to be so great. They looked at TV until their eyes flattened. I spent a couple of mornings tutoring my son, as the other mothers said we should. Twice I opened a text from last year that he had never turned in. Twice he yawned in my face. Other mothers organized living room sessions so the kids would keep up. None of the kids could concentrate, so they drifted back to *The Price Is Right* and *The Brady Bunch*. When the school finally opened there were fights once or twice and some sirens roared through the streets every once in a while. There were a lot of photographers from Albany. And just when ABC was about to send up a news crew, the kids settled down like nothing in the world had happened. Joseph hung my HOW WOULD YOU KNOW? sign in his bedroom. I don't know what became of AND SO DO CHILDREN****. I think my father-in-law cleaned some fish on it. He was always puttering around in our garage. Each of his five children lived in Newburgh, and he acted as though he had five extra homes.

I couldn't help looking for Roberta when Joseph graduated from high school, but I didn't see her. It didn't trouble me much what she had said to me in the car. I mean the kicking part. I know I didn't do that, I couldn't do that. But I was puzzled by her telling me Maggie was black. When I thought about it I actually couldn't be certain. She wasn't pitch-black, I knew, or I would have remembered that. What I remember was the kiddie hat and the semicircle legs. I tried to reassure myself about the race thing for a long time until it dawned on me that the truth was already there, and Roberta knew it. I didn't kick her, I didn't join in with the gar girls and kick that lady, but I sure did want to. We watched and never tried to help her and never called for help. Maggie was my dancing mother. Deaf, I thought, and dumb. Nobody inside. Nobody who would hear you if you cried in the night. Nobody who could tell you anything important that you could use. Rocking, dancing, swaying as she walked. And when the gar girls pushed her down and started roughhousing, I knew she wouldn't scream, couldn't—just like me—and I was glad about that.

We decided not to have a tree, because Christmas would be at my mother-in-law's house, so why have a tree at both places? Joseph was at SUNY New Paltz and we had to economize, we said. But at the last minute, I changed my mind. Nothing could be that bad. So I rushed around town looking for a tree, something small but wide. By the time I found a place, it was snowing and very late. I dawdled like it was the most important purchase in the world and the tree man was fed up with me. Finally I chose one and had it tied onto the trunk of the car. I drove away slowly because the sand trucks were not out yet and the streets could be murder at the beginning of a snowfall. Downtown the streets were wide and rather empty except for a cluster of people coming out of the Newburgh Hotel. The one hotel in town that wasn't built out of cardboard and Plexiglas. A party, probably. The men huddled in the snow were dressed in tails and the women had on furs. Shiny things glittered from underneath their coats. It made me tired to look at them. Tired, tired, tired. On the next corner was a small diner with loops and loops of paper bells in the window. I stopped the car and went in. Just for a cup of coffee and twenty minutes of peace before I went home and tried to finish everything before Christmas Eve.

"Twyla?"

There she was. In a silvery evening gown and dark fur coat. A man and another woman were with her, the man fumbling for change to put in the cigarette machine. The woman was humming and tapping on the counter with her fingernails. They all looked a little bit drunk.

"Well. It's you."

"How are you?"

I shrugged. "Pretty good. Frazzled. Christmas and all."

"Regular?" called the woman from the counter.

"Fine," Roberta called back and then, "Wait for me in the car."

She slipped into the booth beside me. "I have to tell you something, Twyla. I made up my mind if I ever saw you again, I'd tell you."

"I'd as soon not hear anything, Roberta. It doesn't matter now, anyway."

"No," she said. "Not about that."

"Don't be long," said the woman. She carried two regulars to go and the man peeled his cigarette pack as they left.

"It's about St. Bonny's and Maggie."

"Oh, please."

"Listen to me. I really did think she was black. I didn't make that up. I really thought so. But now I can't be sure. I just remember her as old, so old. And because she couldn't talk—well, you know, I thought she was crazy. She'd been brought up in an institution like my mother was and like I thought I would be too. And you were right. We didn't kick her. It was the gar girls. Only them. But, well, I wanted to. I really wanted them to hurt her. I said we did it, too. You and me, but that's not true. And I don't want you to carry that around. It was just that I wanted to do it so bad that day—wanting to is doing it."

Her eyes were watery from the drinks she'd had, I guess. I know it's that way with me. One glass of wine and I start bawling over the littlest thing.

"We were kids, Roberta."

"Yeah. Yeah. I know, just kids."

"Eight."

"Eight."

"And lonely."

"Scared, too."

She wiped her cheeks with the heel of her hand and smiled. "Well, that's all I wanted to say."

I nodded and couldn't think of any way to fill the silence that went from the diner past the paper bells on out into the snow. It was heavy now. I thought I'd better wait for the sand trucks before starting home.

"Thanks, Roberta."

"Sure."

"Did I tell you? My mother, she never did stop dancing."

"Yes. You told me. And mine, she never got well." Roberta lifted her hands from the tabletop and covered her face with her palms. When she took them away she really was crying. "Oh, shit, Twyla. Shit, shit, shit. What the hell happened to Maggie?"

Alice Munro 1931–

Although Alice Munro is one of Canada's most celebrated authors, she counts as her most significant influences writers of the southern United States—Flannery O'Connor and Eudora Welty, in particular. Critic Catherine Sheldrick notes that Munro, in her stories, presents "ordinary experiences so that they appear extraordinary, invested with a kind of magic." Munro's stories often offer no resolution to overt moral crises, leaving readers to conclude for themselves what will become of her unpredictable central characters. Her collections of stories include *Lives of Girls and Women* (1971), *Who Do You Think You Are?: Stories* (1978), *Friend of My Youth* (1991), and *Open Secrets: Stories* (1994). Writer-critic Joyce Carol Oates has said that readers will be "most impressed by the feeling behind [the] stories—the evocation of emotions, ranging from bitter hatred to love, from bewilderment and resentment to awe."

VISITORS

Mildred had just come into the kitchen and was looking at the clock, which said five to two. She had thought it might be at least half past. Wilfred came in from the back, through the utility room, and said, "Hadn't you ought to be out there keeping them company?"

His brother Albert's wife, Grace, and her sister, Vera, were sitting out in the shade of the carport making lace tablecloths. Albert was out at the back of the house, sitting beside the patch of garden where Wilfred grew beans, tomatoes, and cucumbers. Every half-hour Wilfred checked to see which tomatoes were ripe enough to pick. He picked them half-ripe and spread them out on the kitchen windowsill, so the bugs wouldn't get them.

"I was," said Mildred. She ran a glass of water. "I maybe might take them for a drive," she said when she had finished drinking it.

"That's a good idea."

"How is Albert?"

Albert had spent most of the day before, the first full day of the visit, lying down.

"I can't figure out."

"Well surely if he felt sick he'd say so."

"That's just it," said Wilfred. "That's just what he wouldn't."

This was the first time Wilfred had seen his brother in more than thirty years.

Wilfred and Mildred were retired. Their house was small and they weren't, but they got along fine in the space. They had a kitchen not much wider than a hallway, a bathroom about the usual size, two bedrooms that were pretty well filled up when you got a double bed and a dresser into them, a living room where a large sofa sat five feet in front of a large television set, with a low table about the size of a coffin in between, and a small glassed-in porch.

Mildred had set up a table on the porch to serve meals on. Ordinarily, she and Wilfred ate at the table under the kitchen window. If one of them was up and moving around, the other always stayed sitting down. There was no way five people could have managed there, even when three of them were as skinny as these visitors were.

Fortunately there was a daybed on the porch, and Vera, the sister-in-law, slept on that. The sister-in-law had been a surprise to Mildred and Wilfred. Wilfred had done the talking on the phone (nobody in his family, he said, had ever written a letter); according to him, no sister-in-law had been mentioned, just Albert and his wife. Mildred thought Wilfred might not have heard, because he was so excited. Talking to Albert on the phone, from Logan, Ontario, to Elder, Saskatchewan, taking in the news that his brother proposed to visit him, Wilfred had been in a dither of hospitality, reassurances, amazement.

"You come right ahead," he yelled over the phone to Saskatchewan. "We can put you up as long as you want to stay. We got plenty of room. We'll be glad to. Never mind your return tickets. You get on down here and enjoy the summer." It might have been while he was going on like this that Albert was explaining about the sister-in-law.

"How do you tell them apart?" said Wilfred on first meeting Grace and Vera. "Or do you always bother?" He meant it for a joke.

"They're not twins," said Albert, without a glance at either of them. Albert was a short, thin man in dark clothes, who looked as if he might weigh heavy, like dense wood. He wore a string tie and a westerner's hat, but these did not give him a jaunty appearance. His pale cheeks hung down on either side of his chin.

"You look like sisters, though," said Mildred genially to the two dried-out, brown-spotted, gray-haired women. Look what the prairie did to a woman's skin, she was thinking. Mildred was vain of her own skin; it was her compensation for being fat. Also, she put an ash-gold rinse on her hair and wore coordinated pastel pants and tops. Grace and Vera wore dresses with loose pleats over their flat chests and cardigans in summer. "You look a lot more like sisters than those two look like brothers."

It was true. Wilfred had a big head as well as a big stomach, and an anxious, eager, changeable face. He looked like a man who put a high value on joking and chatting, and so he did.

"It's lucky there's none of you too fleshy," Wilfred said. "You can all fit into the one bed. Naturally Albert gets the middle."

"Don't pay attention to him," said Mildred. "There's a good daybed if you don't mind sleeping on the porch," she said to Vera. "It's got blinds on the windows and it gets the best breeze of anywhere."

God knows if the women even caught on to what Wilfred was joking about.

"That'll be fine," said Albert.

With Albert and Grace sleeping in the spare room, which was where Mildred usually slept, Mildred and Wilfred had to share a double bed. They weren't used to it. In the night, Wilfred had one of his wild dreams, which were the reason Mildred had moved to the spare room in the first place.

"Grab ahold!" yelled Wilfred, in terror. Was he on a lake boat, trying to pull somebody out of the water?

"Wilfred, wake up! Stop hollering and scaring everybody to death."

"I am awake," said Wilfred. "I wasn't hollering."

"Then I'm Her Majesty the Queen."

They were lying on their backs. They both heaved, and turned to face the outside. Each kept a courteous but firm hold on the top sheet.

"Is it whales that can't turn over when they get up on the beach?" Mildred said.

"I can still turn over," said Wilfred. They aligned backsides. "Maybe you think that's the only thing I can do."

"Keep still, now, you've got them all listening."

In the morning she said, "Did Wilfred wake you up? He's a terrible hollerer in his sleep."

"I hadn't got to sleep anyway," Albert said.

She went and got the two ladies into the car. "We'll take a little drive and raise a breeze to cool us off," she said. They sat in the back, because there wasn't really room left over in the front, even for two such skinnies.

"I'm the chauffeur!" said Mildred merrily. "Where to, your ladyships?"

"Just anyplace you'd like," said one of them. When she wasn't looking at them Mildred couldn't be sure which was talking.

She drove them around Winter Court and Chelsea Drive to look at the new houses with their landscaping and swimming pools. Then she took them to the Fish and Game Club, where they saw the ornamental fowl, the family of deer, the raccoons, and the caged bobcat. She felt as tired as if she had driven to Toronto, and in need of refreshment, so she headed out to the place on the highway to buy ice-cream cones. They both asked for a small vanilla. Mildred had a mixed double: rum-raisin and praline cream. They sat at a picnic table licking their ice-cream cones and looking at a field of corn.

"They grow a lot of corn around here," Mildred said. Albert had been the manager of a grain elevator before he retired, so she supposed they might be interested in crops. "Do they grow a lot of corn out west?"

They thought about it. Grace said, "Well. Some."

Vera said, "I was wondering."

"Wondering what?" said Mildred cheerfully.

"You wouldn't have a Pentecostal Church here in Logan?"

They set out in the car again, and after some blundering, Mildred found the Pentecostal Church. It was not one of the handsomer churches in town. It was a plain building, of cement blocks, with the doors and the window-trim painted orange. A sign told the minister's name and the times of service. There was no shade tree near it and no bushes or flowers, just a dry yard. Maybe that would remind them of Saskatchewan.

"Pentecostal Church," said Mildred, reading the sign. "Is that the church you people go to?"

"Yes."

"Wilfred and I are not regular churchgoers. If we went, I guess we would go to the United. Do you want to get out and see if it's unlocked?"

"Oh, no."

"If it was locked, we could try and locate the minister. I don't know him, but there's a lot of Logan people I don't know yet. I know the ones that bowl and the ones that play euchre at the Legion. Otherwise, I don't know many. Would you like to call on him?"

They said no. Mildred was thinking about the Pentecostal Church, and it seemed to her that it was the one where people spoke in tongues. She thought she might as well get something out of the afternoon, so she went ahead and asked them: was that true?

"Yes, it's true."

"But what are tongues?"

A pause. One said, with difficulty, "It's the voice of God."

"Heavens," said Mildred. She wanted to ask more—did they speak in tongues themselves?—but they made her nervous. It was clear that she made them nervous, too. She let them look a few minutes more, then asked if they had seen enough. They said they had, and thanked her.

* * *

If she had married Wilfred when they were young, Mildred thought, she would have known something about his family and what to expect of them. Mildred and Wilfred had married in late middle age, after a courtship of only six weeks. Neither of them had been married before. Wilfred had moved around too much, or so he said. He had worked on the lake boats and in lumber camps, he had helped build houses and had pumped gas and had pruned trees; he had worked from California to the Yukon and from the east coast to the west. Mildred had spent most of her life in the town of McGaw, twenty miles from Logan, where she now lived. She had been an only child, and had been given tap-dancing lessons and then sent to business school. From business school she went into the office of the Toll Shoe Factory, in McGaw, and shortly became the sweetheart of Mr. Toll, who owned it. There she stayed.

It was during the last days of Mr. Toll's life that she met Wilfred. Mr. Toll was in the psychiatric hospital overlooking Lake Huron. Wilfred was working there as a groundsman and guard. Mr. Toll was eighty-two years old and didn't know who Mildred was, but she visited him anyway. He called her Sadie, that being the name of his wife. His wife was dead now but she had been alive all the time Mr. Toll and Mildred were taking their little trips together, staying at hotels together, staying in the cottage Mr. Toll had bought for Mildred at Amberley Beach. In all the time she had known him, Mildred had never heard him speak of his wife except in a dry, impatient way. Now she had to listen to him tell Sadie he loved her, ask Sadie's forgiveness. Pretending she was Sadie, Mildred said she forgave him. She dreaded some confession regarding a brassy-headed floozy named Mildred. Nevertheless, she kept on visiting. She hadn't the heart to deprive him. That had been her trouble all along. But when the sons or daughters or Sadie's sisters showed up, she had to make herself scarce. Once, taken by surprise, she had to get Wilfred to let her out a back way. She sat down on a cement wall by the back door and had a cigarette, and Wilfred asked her if anything was the matter. Being upset, and having nobody in McGaw to talk to, she told him what was going on, even about the letter she had received from a lawyer telling her she had to get out of the Amberley cottage. She had thought all along it was in her name, but it wasn't.

Wilfred took her side. He went in and spied on the visiting family, and reported that they were sitting staring at the poor old man like crows on a fence. He didn't pout out to Mildred what she already knew: that she should have seen the writing on the wall. She herself said it.

"I should've gotten out while I still had something going for me."

"You must've been fond of him," said Wilfred reasonably.

"It was never love," said Mildred sadly. Wilfred scowled with deep embarrassment. Mildred had the sense not to go on, and couldn't have explained, anyway, how she had been transfixed by Mr. Toll in his more vigorous days, when his need for her was so desperate she thought he would turn himself inside out.

Mr. Toll died in the middle of the night. Wilfred phoned Mildred at seven in the morning.

"I didn't want to wake you up," he said. "But I wanted to make sure you knew before you heard it out in public."

Then he asked her to have supper with him in a restaurant. Being used to Mr. Toll, she was surprised at Wilfred's table manners. He was nervous, she decided. He got upset because the waitress hadn't brought their glasses of water. Mildred told him she was going to quit her job, she wanted to get clear of Mc-Gaw, she might end up out west.

"Why not end up in Logan?" Wilfred said. "I've got a house there. It's not so big a house, but it'll take two."

So it dawned on her. His nervousness, his bad temper with the waitress, his sloppiness, must all relate to her. She asked if he had ever been married before, and if not, why not?

He said he had always been on the go, and besides, it wasn't often you met a good-hearted woman. She was about to make sure he had things straight, by pointing out that she expected nothing from Mr. Toll's will (nothing was what she got), but she saw in the nick of time that Wilfred was the kind of man who would be insulted.

Instead, she said, "You know I'm secondhand goods?"

"None of that," he said. "We won't have any of that kind of talk around the house. Is it settled?"

Mildred said yes. She was glad to see an immediate improvement in his behavior to the waitress. In fact, he went overboard, apologizing for his impatience earlier, telling her he had worked in a restaurant himself. He told her where the restaurant was, up on the Alaska Highway. The girl had trouble getting away to serve coffee at the other tables.

No such improvement took place in Wilfred's table manners. She guessed that this was one of his bachelor ways she would just have to learn to live with.

"You better tell me a bit about where you were born, and so on," Mildred said.

He told her he had been born on a farm in Hullett Township, but left there when he was three days old.

"Itchy feet," he said, and laughed. Then he sobered, and told her that his mother had died within a few hours of his birth, and his aunt had taken him. His aunt was married to a man who worked on the railway. They moved around, and when he was twelve his aunt died. Then the man she was married to looked at Wilfred and said, "You're a big boy. What size shoe do you wear?"

"Number nine," said Wilfred.

"Then you're big enough to earn your own living."

"Him and my aunt had eight kids of their own," said Wilfred. "So I don't blame him."

"Did you have any brothers and sisters in your real family?" Mildred thought cozily of her own life long ago: her mother fixing her curls in the morning, the kitten, named Pansy, that she used to dress up in doll's clothes and wheel round the block in the doll buggy.

"I had two older sisters, married. Both dead now. And one brother. He went out to Saskatchewan. He has a job managing a grain elevator. I don't know what he gets paid but I imagine it's pretty good. He went to business college, like yourself. He's a different person than me, way different."

The day that Albert had stayed in bed, he wanted the curtains shut. He didn't want a doctor. Wilfred couldn't get out of him what was wrong. Albert said he was just tired.

"Then maybe he is tired," said Mildred. "Let him rest."

But Wilfred was in and out of the spare room all day. He was talking, smoking, asking Albert how he felt. He told Albert he had cured himself of migraine headaches by eating fresh leeks from the bush in the spring. Albert said he didn't have a migraine headache, even if he did want the curtains closed. He said he had never had a bad headache in his life. Wilfred explained that you could have migraine headaches without knowing it—that is, without having the actual ache—so that could be what Albert had. Albert said he didn't see how that was possible.

Early that afternoon Mildred heard Wilfred crashing around in the clothes closet. He emerged calling her name.

"Mildred! Mildred! Where is the Texas mickey?"

"In the buffet," said Mildred, and she got it out for him so he wouldn't be rummaging around in there in her mother's china. It was in a tall box, gold-embossed, with the Legion crest on it. Wilfred bore it into the bedroom and set it on the dressed for Albert to see.

"What do you think that is and how do you think I come by it?"

It was a bottle of whiskey, a gallon bottle of whiskey, 140-proof, that Wilfred had won playing darts at the tournament in Owen Sound. The tournament had taken place in February three years before. Wilfred described the terrible drive from Logan to Owen Sound, himself driving, the other members of the dart team urging him to stop in every town they reached, and not to try to get farther. A blizzard blew off Lake Huron, they were enveloped in whiteouts, trucks and buses loomed up in front of their eyes out of the wall of snow, there was no room to maneuver because the road was walled with drifts ten feet high. Wilfred kept driving; driving blind, driving through skids and drifts across the road. At last, on Highway No. 6, a blue light appeared ahead of him, a twirling blue light, a beacon, a rescue-light. It was the snowplow, travelling ahead of them. The road was filling in almost as fast as the snowplow cleared it, but by keeping close behind the plow they were guided safe into Owen Sound. There they played in the tournament, and were victorious.

"Do you ever play darts yourself?" Mildred heard Wilfred ask his brother.

"As a rule they play darts in places that serve liquor," Albert said. "As a rule I don't go into those places."

"Well, this here is liquor I would never consider drinking. I keep it for the honor of it."

* * *

Their sitting took on a regular pattern. In the afternoon Grace and Vera sat in the driveway crocheting their tablecloths. Mildred sat with them off and on. Albert and Wilfred sat at the back of the house, by the vegetables. After supper they all sat together, moving their chairs to the lawn in front of the flower beds, which was then in the shade. Grace and Vera went on crocheting as long as they could see.

Wilfred admired the crocheting.

"How much would you get for one of those things?"

"Hundreds of dollars," Albert said.

"It's sold for the church," said Grace.

"Blanche Black," said Wilfred, "was the greatest crocheter, knitter, sewer, what-all, and cook of any girl I ever knew."

"What a name," said Mildred.

"She lived in the state of Michigan. It was when I got fed up with working on the boats and I had a job over there working on a farm. She could make quilts or anything. And bake bread, fancy cake, anything. But not very good-looking. In fact, she was about as good-looking as a turnip, and about the shape."

Now came a story that Mildred had heard before. It was told when the subject of pretty girls and homely girls came up, or baking, or box socials, or pride. Wilfred told how he and a friend went to a box social, where at an intermission in the dancing you bid on a box, and the box contained a lunch, and you ate lunch with the girl whose box you had bought. Blanche Black brought a box lunch and so did a pretty girl, a Miss Buchanan, and Wilfred and his friend got into the back room and switched all the wrappings around on these two boxes. So when it came time to bid, a fellow named Jack Fleck, who had a very good opinion of himself and a case on Miss Buchanan, bid for the box he thought was hers, and Wilfred and his friend bid for the box that everybody thought was Blanche Black's. The boxes were given out, and to his consternation Jack Fleck was compelled to sit down with Blanche Black. Wilfred and his friend were set up with Miss Buchanan. Then Wilfred looked in the box and saw there was nothing but sandwiches with a kind of pink paste on them.

"So over I go to Jack Fleck and I say, 'Trade you the lunch and the girl.' I didn't do it entirely on account of the food but because I saw how he was going to treat that poor creature. He agreed like a shot and we sat down. We ate fried chicken. Home-cured ham and biscuits. Date pie. Never fed better in my life. And tucked down in the bottom of the box she had a mickey of whiskey. So I sat eating and drinking and looking at him over there with his paste sandwiches."

Wilfred must have started that story as a tribute to ladies whose crocheting or baking or whatever put them away ahead of ladies who had better looks to offer, but Mildred didn't think even Grace and Vera would be pleased to be put in the category of Blanche Black, who looked like a turnip. And mentioning the mickey of whiskey was a mistake. It was a mistake as far as she was concerned, too. She thought of how much she would like a drink at this moment. She thought of Old Fashioneds, Brown Cows, Pink Ladies, every fancy drink you could imagine.

"I better go and see if I can fix that air-conditioner," Wilfred said. "We'll roast tonight if I don't."

Mildred sat on. Over in the next block there was a blue light that sizzled loudly, catching bugs.

"I guess those things make a difference with the flies," she said.

"Fries them," said Albert.

"I don't like the noise, though."

She thought he wasn't going to answer but he finally said, "If it doesn't make a noise it can't destroy the bugs."

When she went into the house to put on some coffee (a good thing Pentecostals had no ban on that), Mildred could hear the air-conditioner humming away. She looked into the bedroom and saw Wilfred stretched out asleep. Worn out.

"Wilfred?"

He jumped. "I wasn't asleep."

"They're still sitting out front. I thought I'd make us some coffee." Then she couldn't resist adding, "I'm glad it isn't anything too serious the matter with the air-conditioner."

On the next-to-last day of the visit, they decided to drive forty-five miles over to Hullett Township to see the place where Wilfred and Albert were born. This was Mildred's idea. She had thought Albert might suggest it, and she was waiting for that, because she didn't want to push Albert into doing anything he was too tired to do. But at last she mentioned it. She said she had been trying for a long time to get Wilfred to take her, but he said he wouldn't know where to go, since he had never been back after being taken away as a baby. The buildings were all gone, the farms were gone; that whole part of the township had become a conservation area.

Grace and Vera brought along their tablecloths. Mildred wondered why they didn't get sick, working with their heads down in a moving car. She sat between them in the back seat, feeling squashed, although she knew she was the one doing the squashing. Wilfred drove and Albert sat beside him.

Wilfred always got into an argumentative mood when driving.

"Now what is so wrong with taking a bet?" he said. "I don't mean gambling. I don't mean you go down to Las Vegas and you throw all your money away on those games and machines. With betting you can sometimes be lucky. I had a free winter in the Soo on a bet."

"Sault Ste. Marie," Albert said.

"We always said The Soo. I was off the *Kamloops,* I was in for the winter. The old *Kamloops,* that was a terrible boat. One night in the bar they were listening to the hockey game on the radio. Before television. Playing Sudbury. Sudbury four, the Soo nothing."

"We're getting to where we turn off the highway," Albert said.

Mildred said, "Watch for the turn, Wilfred."

"I am watching."

Albert said, "Not this one but the next one."

"I was helping them out in there, I was slinging beer for tips because I didn't have a union card, and this grouchy fellow was cursing at the Soo. They might come out of it yet, I said, the Soo might beat them yet."

"Right here," said Albert.

Wilfred made a sharp turn. "Put your money where your mouth is! Put your money where your mouth is! That's what he said to me. Ten to one. I didn't have the money, but the fellow that owned the hotel was a good fellow, and I was helping him out, so he says, take the bet, Wilfred! He said, you go ahead and take the bet!"

"The Hullett Conservation Area," Mildred read from a sign. They drove along the edge of a dark swamp.

"Heavens, it's gloomy in there!" she said. "And water standing, at this time of the year."

"The Hullett Swamp," said Albert. "It goes for miles."

They came out of the swamp and on either side was wasteland, churned-up black earth, ditches, uprooted trees. The road was very rough.

"I'll back you, he said. So I went ahead and took the bet."

Mildred read the crossroad signs: "Dead end. No winter maintenance beyond this point."

Albert said, "Now we'll want to turn south."

"South?" said Wilfred. "South. I took it and you know what happened? The Soo came through and beat Sudbury seven to four!"

There was a large pond and a lookout stand, and a sign saying "Wildfowl Observation Point."

"Wildfowl," said Mildred. "I wonder what there is to see?"

Wilfred was not in the mood to stop. "You wouldn't know a crow from a hawk, Mildred! The Soo beat Sudbury seven to four and I had my bet. That fellow sneaked out when I was busy but the manager knew where he lived and next day I had a hundred dollars. When I got called to go back on the *Kamloops* I had exactly to the penny the amount of money I had when I got off before Christmas. I had the winter free in the Soo."

"This looks like it," Albert said.

"Where?" asked Wilfred.

"Here."

"Here? I had the winter free, all from one little bet."

They turned off the road into a rough sort of lane, where there were wooden arrows on a post. "Hawthorn Trail. Sugar Bush Trail. Tamarack Trail. No motor vehicles beyond this point." Wilfred stopped the car and he and Albert got out. Grace got out to let Mildred out and then got back in. The arrows were all pointing in the same direction. Mildred thought some children had probably tampered with them. She didn't see any trails at all. They had climbed out of the low swampland and were among rough little hills.

"This where your farm was?" she asked Albert.

"The house was up there," said Albert, pointing uphill. "The lane ran up there. The barn was behind."

There was a brown wooden box on the post under the arrows. She opened it up and took out a handful of brightly colored pamphlets. She looked through them.

"These tell about the different trails."

"Maybe they'd like something to read if they aren't going to get out," said Wilfred, nodding toward the women in the car. "Maybe you should go and ask them."

"They're busy," Mildred said. She thought she should go and tell Grace and Vera to roll down the windows so they wouldn't suffocate, but she decided to let them figure that out for themselves. Albert was setting off up the hill and she and Wilfred followed him, plowing through goldenrod, which, to her surprise, was easier than grass to walk in. It didn't tangle you so, and felt silky. Goldenrod she knew, and wild carrot, but what were these little white flowers on a low bush, and this blue one with coarse petals, and this feathery purple? You always heard about the spring flowers, the buttercups and the trilliums and marsh marigolds, but here were just as many, names unknown, at the end of summer. There were also little frogs leaping from underfoot, and small white butterflies, and hundreds of bugs she couldn't see that nibbled at and stung her bare arms.

Albert walked up and down in the grass. He made a turn, he stopped and looked around and started again. He was trying to get the outline of the house. Wilfred frowned at the grass, and said, "They don't leave you much."

"Who?" said Mildred faintly. She fanned herself with goldenrod.

"Conservation people. They don't leave one stone of the foundation, or the cellar hole, or one brick or beam. They did it all out and fill it all in and haul it all away."

"Well, they couldn't leave a pile of rubble, I guess, for people to fall over."

"You sure this is where it would have been?" Wilfred said.

"Right about here," said Albert, "facing south. Here would've been the front door."

"You could be standing on the step, Albert," said Mildred, with as much interest as she had energy for.

But Albert said, "We never had a step at the front door. We only opened it once that I can remember, and that for Mother's coffin. We put some chunks of wood down then, to make a temporary step."

"That's a lilac," said Mildred, noticing a bush near where he was standing. "Was that there then? It must have been there then."

"I think it was."

"Is it a white one or a purple?"

"I can't say."

That was the difference between him and Wilfred, she thought. Wilfred would have said. Whether he remembered or not, he would have said, and then believed himself. Brothers and sisters were a mystery to her. There were Grace and Vera, speaking like two mouths out of the same head, and Wilfred and Albert without a thread of connection between them.

They ate lunch in a café down the road. It wasn't licensed, or Mildred would have ordered beer, never mind how she shocked Grace and Vera or how Wilfred glared at her. She was hot enough. Albert's face was a bright pink and his eyes had a fierce, concentrating look. Wilfred looked cantankerous.

"It used to be a lot bigger swamp," Albert said. "They've drained it."

"That's so people can get in and walk and see different things," said Mildred. She still had the red and green and yellow pamphlets in her hand, and she smoothed them out and looked at them.

"Squawks, calls, screeches, and cries echo throughout this bush," she read. "Do you recognize any of them? Most are made by birds." What else would they be made by? she wondered.

"A man went into the Hullett Swamp and remained there," Albert said.

Wilfred made a mess of his ketchup and gravy, then dipped his french fries into it with his fingers.

"For how long?" he said.

"Forever."

"You going to eat them?" said Wilfred, indicating Mildred's french fries.

"Forever?" said Mildred, dividing them and sliding half onto Wilfred's plate. "Did you know him, Albert?"

"No. It was too long ago."

"Did you know his name?"

"Lloyd Sallows."

"Who?" said Wilfred.

"Lloyd Sallows," said Albert. "He worked on a farm."

"I never heard of him," Wilfred said.

"How do you mean, he went into the swamp?" said Mildred.

"They found his clothes on the railway tracks and that's what they said, he went into the swamp."

"Why would he go in there without his clothes on?"

Albert thought for a few minutes and said, "He could have wanted to go wild."

"Did he leave his shoes, too?"

"I would think so."

"He might have committed suicide," Mildred said briskly. "Did they look for a body?"

"They did look."

"Or might have been murdered. Did he have any enemies? Was he in trouble? Maybe he was in debt or in trouble about a girl."

"No," said Albert.

"So they never found a trace of him?"

"No."

"Was there any suspicious sort of person around at the time?"

"No."

"Well, there must be some explanation," said Mildred. "A person, if they're not dead, they go on living somewhere."

Albert forked the hamburger patty out of his bun onto his plate, where he proceeded to cut it up into little pieces. He had not yet eaten anything.

"He was thought to be living in the swamp."

"They should've looked in the swamp, then," Wilfred said.

"They went in at both ends and said they'd meet in the middle but they didn't."

"Why not?" said Mildred.

"You can't just walk your way through that swamp. You couldn't then."

"So they thought he was in there?" Wilfred persisted. "Is that what they thought?"

"Most did," said Albert, rather grudgingly. Wilfred snorted.

"What was he living on?"

Albert put down his knife and fork and said somberly, "Flesh."

All of a sudden, after being so hot, Mildred's arms came out in goose bumps.

"Did anybody ever see him?" she asked, in a more subdued and thoughtful voice than before.

"Two said so."

"Who were they?"

"One was a lady that when I knew her, she was in her fifties. She had been a little girl at the time. She saw him when she was sent back to get the cows. She saw a long white person running behind the trees."

"Near enough that she could tell if it was a boy or a girl?" said Wilfred.

Albert took the question seriously.

"I don't know how near."

"That was one person," Mildred said. "Who was the other?"

"It was a boy fishing. This was years later. He looked up and saw a white fellow watching him from the other bank. He thought he'd seen a ghost."

"Is that all?" said Wilfred. "They never found out what happened?"

"No."

"I guess he'd be dead by now anyway," Mildred said.

"Dead long ago," said Albert.

If Wilfred had been telling that story, Mildred thought, it would have gone someplace, there would have been some kind of ending to it. Lloyd Sallows might reappear stark naked to collect on a bet, or he would come back dressed as a millionaire, maybe having tricked some gangsters who had robbed him. In Wilfred's stories you could always be sure that the gloomy parts would give way to something better, and if somebody behaved in a peculiar way there was an explanation for it. If Wilfred figured in his own stories, as he usually did, there was always a stroke of luck for him somewhere, a good meal or a bottle of whiskey or some money. Neither luck nor money played a part in this story. She wondered why Albert had told it, what it meant to him.

"How did you happen to remember that story, Albert?"

As soon as she said that, she knew she shouldn't have spoken. It was none of her business.

"I see they have apple or raisin pie," she said.

"No apple or raisin pie in the Hullett Swamp!" said Wilfred raucously. "I'm having apple."

Albert picked up a cold piece of hamburger and put it down and said, "It's not a story. It's something that happened."

Mildred had stripped the bed the visitors had slept in, and hadn't got it made up again, so she lay down beside Wilfred, on their first night by themselves.

Before she went to sleep she said to Wilfred, "Nobody in their right mind would go and live in a swamp."

"If you did want to live someplace like that," said Wilfred, "the place to live would be the bush, where you wouldn't have so much trouble making a fire if you wanted one."

He seemed restored to good humor. But in the night she was wakened by his crying. She was not badly startled, because she had known him to cry before, usually at night. It was hard to tell how she knew. He wasn't making any noise and he wasn't moving. Maybe that in itself was the unusual thing. She knew that he was lying beside her on his back with tears welling up in his eyes and wetting his face.

"Wilfred?"

Any time before, when he had consented to tell her why he was crying, the reason had seemed to her very queer, something thought up on the spur of the moment, or only distantly connected with the real reason. But maybe it was as close as he could get.

"Wilfred."

"Albert and I will probably never see each other again," said Wilfred in a loud voice with no trace of tears, or any clear indication of either satisfaction or regret.

"Unless we did go to Saskatchewan," said Mildred. An invitation had been extended, and she had thought at the time she would be as likely to visit Siberia.

"Eventually," she added.

"Eventually, maybe," Wilfred said. He gave a prolonged, noisy sniff that seemed to signal content. "Not next week."

Sylvia Plath 1932–1963

A Boston poet, scholar, and posthumous cult figure whose best works were published after her suicide, Sylvia Plath's short, intense life was marred by manic-depression. *The Bell Jar* (1963), published only four weeks before her death, has been likened to J. D. Salinger's *The Catcher in the Rye* for its insight into the superficiality, hypocrisy, and corruption of adult society. Originally published under the pseudonym Victoria Lucas, this autobiographical novel draws largely from her summer internship in Manhattan as a guest editor for *Mademoiselle*, which was immediately followed by a suicide attempt, electric shock therapy, and one year institutionalization at the age of nineteen. There is prevailing opinion that Plath was never able to get over the grief induced by her father's death that occurred when she was eight. She explains "Daddy," perhaps the most powerful of her last poems, as an "awful little allegory" that had to be acted out before she could free herself of it. Of Plath's final death-haunted poems, A. Alvarez noted that the "poetry and death [are] inseparable. The one could not exist without the other. . . . In a curious way, the poems read as if they were written posthumously." Anne Sexton wrote, "These last poems stun me. They eat time."

CONVERSATION AMONG THE RUINS

Through portico of my elegant house you stalk
With your wild furies, disturbing garlands of fruit
And the fabulous lutes and peacocks, rending the net
Of all decorum which holds the whirlwind back.
Now, rich order of walls is fallen; rooks croak   5
Above the appalling ruin; in bleak light
Of your stormy eye, magic takes flight
Like a daunted witch, quitting castle when real days break.

Fractured pillars frame prospects of rock;
While you stand heroic in coat and tie, I sit   10
Composed in Grecian tunic and psyche-knot,
Rooted to your black look, the play turned tragic:
With such blight wrought on our bankrupt estate,
What ceremony of words can patch the havoc?

CHANNEL CROSSING

On storm-struck deck, wind sirens caterwaul;
With each tilt, shock and shudder, our blunt ship
Cleaves forward into fury; dark as anger,
Waves wallop, assaulting the stubborn hull.
Flayed by spray, we take the challenge up,   5
Grip the rail, squint ahead, and wonder how much longer

Such force can last; but beyond, the neutral view
Shows, rank on rank, the hungry seas advancing.
Below, rocked havoc-sick, voyagers lie
Retching in bright orange basins; a refugee   10
Sprawls, hunched in black, among baggage, wincing
Under the strict mask of his agony.

Far from the sweet stench of that perilous air
In which our comrades are betrayed, we freeze
And marvel at the smashing nonchalance   15
Of nature: what better way to test taut fiber
Than against this onslaught, these casual blasts of ice
That wrestle with us like angels; the mere chance

Of making harbor through this racketing flux
Taunts us to valor. Blue sailors sang that our journey   20
Would be full of sun, white gulls, and water drenched
With radiance, peacock-colored; instead, bleak rocks
Jutted early to mark our going, while sky
Curded over with clouds and chalk cliffs blanched

In sullen light of the inauspicious day.   25
Now, free, by hazard's quirk, from the common ill
Knocking our brothers down, we strike a stance
Most mock-heroic, to cloak our waking awe
At this rare rumpus which no man can control:
Meek and proud both fall; stark violence   30

Lays all walls waste; private estates are torn,
Ransacked in the public eye. We forsake
Our lone luck now, compelled by bond, by blood,
To keep some unsaid pact; perhaps concern
Is helpless here, quite extra, yet we must make   35
The gesture, bend and hold the prone man's head.

And so we sail toward cities, streets and homes
Of other men, where statues celebrate

Brave acts played out in peace, in war; all dangers
End: green shores appear; we assume our names,   40
Our luggage, as docks halt out brief epic; no debt
Survives arrival; we walk the plank with strangers.

LADY LAZARUS

I have done it again.
One year in every ten
I manage it————

A sort of walking miracle, my skin
Bright as a Nazi lampshade,   5
My right foot

A paperweight,
My face a featureless, fine
Jew linen.

Peel off the napkin   10
O my enemy.
Do I terrify?————

The nose, the eye pits, the full set of teeth?
The sour breath
Will vanish in a day.   15

Soon, soon the flesh
The grave cave ate will be
At home on me

And I a smiling woman.
I am only thirty.   20
And like the cat I have nine times to die.

This is Number Three.
What a trash
To annihilate each decade.

What a million filaments.   25
The peanut-crunching crowd
Shoves in to see

Them unwrap me hand and foot————
The big strip tease.
Gentlemen, ladies   30

These are my hands
My knees.
I may be skin and bone,

Nevertheless, I am the same, identical woman.
The first time it happened I was ten.   35
It was an accident.

The second time I meant
To last it out and not come back at all.
I rocked shut

As a seashell.   40
They had to call and call
And pick the worms off me like sticky pearls.

Dying
Is an art, like everything else.
I do it exceptionally well.   45

I do it so it feels like hell.
I do it so it feels real.
I guess you could say I've a call.

It's easy enough to do it in a cell.
It's easy enough to do it and stay put.   50
It's the theatrical

Comeback in broad day
To the same place, the same face, the same brute
Amused shout:

'A miracle!'   55
That knocks me out.
There is a charge

For the eyeing of my scars, there is a charge
For the hearing of my heart———
It really goes.   60

And there is a charge, a very large charge
For a word or a touch
Or a bit of blood

Or a piece of my hair or my clothes.
So, so, Herr Doktor.   65
So, Herr Enemy.

I am your opus,
I am your valuable,
The pure gold baby

That melts to a shriek.   70
I turn and burn.
Do not think I underestimate your great concern.

Ash, ash—
You poke and stir.
Flesh, bone, there is nothing there————   75

A cake of soap,
A wedding ring,
A gold filling.

Herr God, Herr Lucifer
Beware   80
Beware.

Out of the ash
I rise with my red hair
And I eat men like air.

DADDY

You do not do, you do not do
Any more, black shoe
In which I have lived like a foot
For thirty years, poor and white,
Barely daring to breather or Achoo.   5

Daddy, I have had to kill you
You died before I had time————
Marble-heavy, a bag full of God,
Ghastly statue with one gray toe
Big as a Frisco seal   10

And a head in the freakish Atlantic
Where it pours bean green over blue
In the waters off beautiful Nauset.
I used to pray to recover you.
Ach, du.   15

In the German tongue, in the Polish town
Scraped flat by the roller
Of wars, wars, wars.
But the name of the town is common.
My Polack friend   20

Says there are a dozen or two.
So I never could tell where you
Put your foot, your root,
I never could talk to you.
The tongue stuck in my jaw. 25

It stuck in a barb wire snare.
Ich, ich, ich, ich,
I could hardly speak.
I thought every German was you.
And the language obscene 30

An engine, an engine
Chuffing me off like a Jew.
A Jew to Dachau, Auschwitz, Belsen.
I began to talk like a Jew.
I think I may well be a Jew. 35

The snows of the Tyrol, the clear beer of Vienna
Are not very pure or true.
With my gipsy ancestress and my weird luck
And my Taroc pack and my Taroc pack
I may be a bit of a Jew. 40

I have always been scared of *you,*
With your Luftwaffe, your gobbledygoo.
And your neat mustache
And your Aryan eye, bright blue.
Panzer-man, panzer-man, O You——— 45

Not Got but a swastika
So black no sky could squeak through.
Every woman adores a Fascist,
The boot in the face, the brute
Brute heart of a brute like you. 50

You stand at the blackboard, daddy,
In the picture I have of you,
A cleft in your chin instead of your foot
But no less a devil for that, no not
Any less the black man who 55

Bit my pretty red heart in two.
I was ten when they buried you.
At twenty I tried to die
And get back, back, back to you.
I thought even the bones would do. 60

But they pulled me out of the sack,
And they stuck me together with glue.
And then I knew what to do.
I made a model of you,
A man in black with a Meinkampf look   65

And a love of the rack and the screw.
And I said I do, I do.
So daddy, I'm finally through.
The black telephone's off at the root,
The voices just can't worm through.   70

If I've killed one man, I've killed two——
The vampire who said he was you
And drank my blood for a year,
Seven years, if you want to know.
Daddy, you can lie back now.   75

There's a stake in your fat black heart
And the villagers never liked you.
They are dancing and stamping on you.
They always *knew* it was you.
Daddy, daddy, you bastard, I'm through.   80

Edna O'Brien 1932–

Playwright, screenwriter, short-story writer, and novelist, Edna O'Brien's Catholic upbringing and her Irish childhood are prevalent in much of her work. Much of her fiction centers on women who deeply hope for love and acceptance, but who usually find only disappointment. Men in her work are often irresponsible, drunken, and heartless; the women who depend on them are unhappy, betrayed, or tragic, but most often they are also survivors. Divorced and the mother of two sons, O'Brien has used many of her own personal experiences as the sources for her writing. Her frankness about women's sexuality has led to her books being banned in her native country. Said O'Brien, ". . . I must have sensed . . . that [using material from life] would bring me into conflict with parents, friends, and indeed the Irish establishment." Critics agree, however, that O'Brien's already compelling work is particularly ". . . effective when it recreates the Ireland of her childhood," telling of "people and places close to her heart."

NUMBER TEN

Everything began to be better for Mrs. Reinhardt from the moment she started to sleepwalk. Every night her journey yielded a fresh surprise. First it was that she saw sheep—not sheep as one sees them in life, a bit sooty and bleating away, but sheep as one sees them in a dream. She saw myriads of white fleece on a hilltop, surrounded by little lambs frisking and suckling to their hearts' content.

Then she saw pictures such as she had not seen in life. Her husband owned an art gallery and Mrs. Reinhardt had the opportunity to see many pictures, yet the ones she saw at night were much more satisfying. For one thing she was inside them. She was not an outsider looking in, making idiotic remarks, she was part of the picture: an arm or a lily or the grey mane of a horse. She did not have to compete, did not have to say anything. All her movements were preordained. She was simply aware of her own breath, a soft steady, sustaining breath.

In the mornings her husband would say she looked a bit frayed or a bit intense, and she would say, "Nonsense," because in fifteen years of marriage she had never felt better. Her sleeping life suited her and, of course, she never knew what to expect. Her daily life had a pattern to it. Weekday mornings she spent at home, helping or supervising Fatima, the Spanish maid. She gave two afternoons a week to teaching autistic children, two afternoons were devoted to an exercise class, and on Fridays she shopped in Harrods and got all the groceries for the weekend. Mr. Reinhardt had bought a farm two years before, and weekends they spent in the country, in their newly renovated cottage. In the country she did not sleepwalk, and Mrs. Reinhardt wondered if it might be that she was inhibited by the barbed-wire fence that skirted their garden. But there are gates, she thought, and I should open them. She was a little vexed with herself for not being more venturesome.

Then one May night, in her house in London, she had an incredible dream. She walked over a field with her youngest son—in real life he was at university—and all of a sudden, and in unison, the two of them knelt down and began scraping the earth up with their bare hands. It was a rich red earth and easy to crumble. They were so eager because they knew that treasure was about to be theirs. Sure enough, they found bits of gold, tiny specks of it, which they put in a handkerchief, and then to crown her happiness Mrs Reinhardt found the loveliest little gold key, and held it up to the light while her son laughed and in a baby voice said, "Mama."

Soon after this dream Mrs. Reinhardt embarked on a bit of spring cleaning. Curtains and carpets for the dry cleaners, drawers depleted of all the old useless odds and ends that had been piling up. Her husband's clothing, too, she must put in order. A little rift had sprung up between them and was widening day by day. He was moody. He got home later than usual and, though he did not say so, she knew that he had stopped at the corner and had a few drinks. Once of late he had pulled her down beside him on the living-room sofa and stroked her thighs and started to undress her within hearing distance of Fatima, who was in the kitchen chopping and singing. Always chopping and singing or humming. For the most part, though, Mr. Reinhardt went straight to the liquor cabinet and gave them both a gin, pouring himself a bigger one because, as he said, all her bloody fasting made Mrs. Reinhardt light-headed.

She was sorting Mr. Reinhardt's shirts—tee shirts, summer sweaters, thick crew-neck sweaters—and putting them each in a neat pile, when out of his seersucker jacket there tumbled a little gold key that caused her to let out a cry. The first thing she felt was a jet of fear. Then she bent down and picked it up. It was exactly like the one in her sleepwalk. She held it in her hand, promising herself never to let it go. What fools we are to pursue in daylight what we should leave for night-time.

Her next sleepwalking brought Mrs. Reinhardt out of her house into a waiting taxi and, some distance away, to a mews house. Outside the mews house was a black and white tub filled with pretty flowers. She simply put her hand under a bit of foliage and there was the latchkey. Inside was a little nest. The wallpaper in the hall was the very one she had always wanted for their house, a pale gold with the tiniest white flowers—mere suggestions of flowers, like those of the wild strawberry. The kitchen was immaculate. On the landing upstairs was a little fretwork bench. The cushions in the sitting room were stiff and stately, and so was the upholstery, but the bedroom—ah, the bedroom.

It was everything she had ever wanted their own to be. In fact, the bedroom *was* the very room she had envisaged over and over again and had described to her husband down to the last detail. Here it was—a brass bed with a little lace canopy above it, the entire opposite wall a dark metallic mirror in which dark shadows seemed to swim around; a light-blue velvet chaise longue, a hanging plant with shining leaves and a floor lamp with a brown-fringed shade that gave off the softest of light.

She sat on the edge of the bed, marvelling, and saw the other things that she had always wanted. She saw, for instance, the photo of a little girl in First Communion attire; she saw the paperweight that when shaken yielded a miniature snowstorm; she saw the mother-of-pearl tray with the two champagne glasses—and all of a sudden she began to cry because her happiness was so immense. Perhaps, she thought, he will come to me here, he will visit, and it will be like the old days and he won't be irritable and he won't be tapping with his fingers or fiddling with the lever of his fountain pen. He will smother me with hugs and kisses and we will tumble about on the big foamy bed.

She sat there in the bedroom and she touched nothing, not even the two white irises in the tall glass vase. The little key was in her hand and she knew it was for the wardrobe and that she had only to open it to find there a nightdress with a pleated top, a voile dance dress, a silver fox cape, and a pair of sling-back shoes. But she did not open it. She wanted to leave something a secret. She crept away and was home in her own bed without her husband being aware of her absence. He had complained on other occasions about her cold feet as she got back into bed, and asked in Christ's name what was she doing—making tea or what? That morning her happiness was so great that she leaned over, unknotted his pyjamas, and made love to him very sweetly, very slowly and to his apparent delight. Yet when he wakened he was angry, as if a wrong had been done him.

Naturally, Mrs. Reinhardt now went to the mews house night after night and her heart would light up as she saw the pillar of the house with its number, ten, lettered in gold edged with black. The nought was a little slanted. Sometimes she got into the brass bed and she knew it was only a question of time before Mr. Reinhardt followed her there.

One night as she lay in the bed, a little breathless, he came in very softly, closed the door, removed his dressing gown, and took possession of her with such a force that afterward she suspected she had a broken rib. They used words that they had not used for years. She was young and wild. A lovely fever took hold of her. She was saucy while he kept imploring her to please marry him, to please give up her independence, to please be his—adding that even if she said no he was going to whisk her off. Then to prove his point he took possession of her again. She almost died, so deep and so thorough was her pleasure, and each time as she came back to her senses she saw some little object or trinket that was intended to add to her pleasure—once it was a mobile in which silver horses chased one another around, once it was a sound as of a running stream. He gave her some champagne and they drank in utter silence.

But when she wakened from this idyll she was in fact in her own bed and so was he. She felt mortified. Had she cried out in her sleep? Had she moaned? There was no rib broken. She reached for the hand mirror and saw no sign of wantonness on her face, no tossed hair, and the buttons of her nightdress were neatly done up to the throat.

He was a solid mass of sleep. He opened his eyes. She said something to him, something anxious, but he did not reply. She got out of bed and went down to the sitting room to think. Where would it all lead to? Should she tell him? She thought not. All morning she tried the key in different locks, but it was too small. In fact, once she nearly lost it because it slipped into a lock and she had to tease it out with the prong of a fork. Of course she did not let Fatima, the maid, see what she was doing.

It was Friday, their day to go to the country, and she was feeling reluctant about it. She knew that when they arrived they would rush around their garden and look at their plants to see if they'd grown a bit, and look at the rose leaves to make sure there were no greenfly. Then, staring out across the fields to where the cows were, they would tell each other how lucky they were to have such a nice place, and how clever. The magnolia flowers would be fully out and she would stand and stare at the tree as if by staring at it she could imbue her body with something of its whiteness.

The magnolia was out when they arrived—like little white china eggcups, each bloom with its leaves lifted to the heavens. Two of the elms definitely had the blight, Mr. Reinhardt said, as the leaves were withering away. The elms would have to be chopped, and Mr. Reinhardt estimated that there would be enough firewood for two winters. He would speak to the farm manager, who lived down the road, about this. They carried in the shopping, raised the blinds, and switched on the central heating. The little kitchen was just as they had left it, except that the primroses in the jar had faded and were like bits of yellow skin. She unpacked the food they had brought, put some things in the fridge, and began to peel the carrots and potatoes for the evening meal. Mr. Reinhardt hammered four picture hooks into the wall for the new prints that he had brought down. From time to time he would call her to ask what order he should put them in, and she would go in, her hands covered with flour and rather absently suggest a grouping.

She had the little key with her in her purse and would open the purse from time to time to make sure that it was there. Then she would blush.

At dusk she went out to get a branch of apple wood for the fire, in order to engender a lovely smell. A bird chirped from a tree. It was more sound than song. She could not tell what bird it was. The magnolia tree was a mass of white in the surrounding darkness. The dew was falling and she bent for a moment to touch the wet grass. She wished it were Sunday, so that they could be going home. In London the evenings seemed to pass more quickly and they each had more chores to do. She felt in some way she was deceiving him.

They drank some red wine as they sat by the fire. Mr. Reinhardt was fidgety but at the very same time accused her of being fidgety. He was being adamant about the Common Market. Why did he expound on the logistics of it when she was not even contradicting him? He got carried away, made gestures, said he loved England, loved it passionately, that England was going to the dogs. When she got up to push in a log that had fallen from the grate, he asked her for God's sake to pay attention.

She sat down at once, and hoped that there was not going to be one of those terrible, unexpected, meaningless rows. But blessedly they were distracted. She heard him say, "Crikey!" and then she looked up and saw what he had just seen. There was a herd of cattle staring in at them. She jumped up. Mr. Reinhardt rushed to the phone to call the farm manager, since he himself knew nothing about country life, certainly not how to drive away cattle.

She grabbed a walking stick and went outside to prevent the cows from falling in the swimming pool. It was cold out of doors and the wind rustled in all the trees. The cows looked at her, suspicious. Their ears pricked. She made tentative movements with the stick, and at that moment four of them leaped over the barbed wire and back into the adjoining field. The remaining cow began to race around. From the field the four cows began to bawl. The fifth cow was butting against the paling. Mrs. Reinhardt thought, I know what you are feeling—you are feeling lost and muddled and you have gone astray.

Her husband came out in a frenzy because when he rang the farm manager no one was there.

"Bloody never there!" he said. His loud voice so frightened the fifth cow that she made a leap for it and got stuck in the barbed wire. Mrs. Reinhardt could see the barb in her huge udder and thought what a place for it to have landed. They must rescue her. Very cautiously they both approached the animal, and the intention was that Mr. Reinhardt would hold the cow while Mrs. Reinhardt freed the flesh. She tried to be gentle. The cow's smell was milky, and soft compared with her roar, which was beseeching. Mr. Reinhardt caught hold of the hindquarters and told his wife to hurry up. The cow was obstreperous. As Mrs. Reinhardt lifted the bleeding flesh away, the cow took a huge jump and was over the fence and down the field, where she hurried to the river to drink.

The others followed her and suddenly the whole meadow was the scene of bawling and mad commotion. Mr. Reinhardt rubbed his hands and let out a sigh of relief. He suggested that they open a bottle of champagne. Mrs. Reinhardt was delighted. Of late he had become very thrifty and did not permit her any extravagances. In fact he had been saying that they would soon have to give up wine because of the state of the country. As they went indoors he put an arm around her. And back in the room she sat and felt like a mistress as she drank the champagne, smiled at him and felt the stuff coursing through her body. The champagne put them in a nice mood and they linked as they went up the narrow stairs to bed. Nevertheless, Mrs. Reinhardt did not feel like any intimacy; she wanted it reserved for the hidden room.

They returned to London on Sunday evening, and that night Mrs. Reinhardt did not sleep. Consequently she walked nowhere in her dreams. In the morning she felt fidgety. She looked in the mirror. She was getting old. After breakfast, as Mr. Reinhardt was hurrying out of the house, she held up the little key.

"What is it?" she said.

"How would I know," he said. He looked livid.

She called and made an appointment at the hairdresser's. She looked in the mirror. She must not get old. Later, when her hair was set she would surprise him—she would drop in at his gallery and ask him to take her to a nice pub. On the way she would buy a new scarf and knot it at the neck and she would be youthful.

When she got to the gallery, Mr. Reinhardt was not there. Hans, his assistant, was busy with a client from the Middle East. She said she would wait. The new secretary went off to make some tea. Mrs. Reinhardt sat at her husband's desk brooding, and then idly she began to flick through his desk diary, just to pass the time. Lunch with this one and that one. A reminder to buy her a present for their anniversary—which he had done. He had brought her a beautiful ring with a sphinx on it.

Then she saw it—the address that she went to night after night. Number ten. The digits danced before her eyes as they had danced when she drove up in the taxi the very first time. All her movements became hurried and mechanical. She gulped her tea, she gave a distracted handshake to the Arab gentleman, she ate the ginger biscuit and gnashed her teeth, so violently did she chew. She paced the floor, she went back to the diary. The same address—three, four, or five times a week. She flicked back to see how long it had been going on. It was no use. She simply had to go there.

At the mews, she found the key in the flower tub. In the kitchen were eggshells and a pan in which an omelette had been cooked. There were two brown eggshells and one white. She dipped her finger in the fat; it was still warm. Her heart went ahead of her up the stairs. It was like a pellet in her body. She had her hand on the doorknob, when all of a sudden she stopped in her tracks and became motionless. She crept away from the door and went back to the landing seat.

She would not intrude, no. It was perfectly clear why Mr. Reinhardt went there. He went by day to keep his tryst with her, be unfaithful with her, just as she went by night. One day or one night, if they were very lucky, they might meet and share their secret, but until then Mrs. Reinhardt was content to leave everything just as it was. She tiptoed down the stairs and was pleased that she had not acted rashly, that she had not lost her head.

Audre Lorde 1934–1992

Believing that she must claim the many aspects of her personality, "black, lesbian, feminist, mother, lover, poet," Audre Lorde contributed a major theoretical reevaluation of "difference" in her poetry and essays. Rather than a threat, she saw difference as a dialogue and energizing force, emphasizing in works like *Sister Outsider* (1984) the need for those marginalized by society to "speak" in order to empower themselves. Born in Harlem, the painfully shy daughter of Caribbean immigrants, Lorde did not speak until she was five years old and not in full sentences until she was twenty. Ironically, Lorde created a poetry that wages "a war against the tyrannies of silence," her voice angrily cutting through politeness, denial, and fear. "My Black woman's anger is a molten pond at the core of me, my most fiercely guarded secret." Married with two children, the "guarded secret" of her lesbianism was first revealed in her early poetry of the late 1960s and later in her "biomythography," *Zami: A New Spelling of My Name* (1982), which presented a fictionalized memoir of growing up a black lesbian in a homophobic world. Her most popular poetry was written in the 1970s and includes National Book Award nominee *From a Land Where Other People Live* (1973), *Coal* (1976), and the critically acclaimed *The Black Unicorn* (1978). Overall, Lorde is best known for *The Cancer Journals* (1980), the triumphant account of her successful battle against breast cancer. *A Burst of Light,* winner of the 1989 National Book Award, provides sad counterpoint of her relapse that resulted in fatal liver cancer. Lorde was poet-in-residence at Mississippi's Tougaloo College in the early sixties and later taught English at a variety of colleges.

FUTURE PROMISE

This house will not stand forever.
The windows are sturdy
but shuttered
like individual solutions
that match one at a time.   5

The roof leaks.
On persistent rainy days
I look up to see
the gables weeping
quietly.   10

The stairs are sound
beneath my children
but from time to time
a splinter leaves
imbedded in a childish foot.   15

I dream of stairways
sagging
into silence
well used and satisfied
with no more need   20
for changelessness

Once
freed from constancy
this house
will not stand   25
forever.

THIS URN CONTAINS EARTH FROM GERMAN CONCENTRATION CAMPS

Plotensee Memorial, West Berlin, 1984

Dark grey
the stone wall hangs
self-conscious wreaths
the heavy breath of gaudy Berlin roses
"The Vice Chancellor Remembers   5
The Heroic Generals Of The Resistance"
and before a well-trimmed hedge
unpolished granite
tall as my daughter and twice around
Neatness   10
wiping memories   payment
from the air.

Midsummer's Eve beside a lake
keen   the smell of quiet
children straggling homeward   15
the rough precisions of earth
beneath my rump
in a hollow root of the dead elm
a brown rabbit kindles.

The picnic is over   20
reluctantly
I stand   pick up my blanket
and flip into the bowl of still-warm corn
a writhing waterbug
cracked open   pale eggs oozing   25
quiet
from the smash

Earth
not the unremarkable ash
of fussy thin-boned infants   30
and adolescent Jewish girls
liming the Ravensbruck potatoes
careful and monsterless
this urn makes nothing
easy   35
to say.

Joan Didion 1934–

N ovelist, essayist, journalist, and screenwriter, Joan Didion is as widely praised for her precise, controlled style as for the content of her work. *Newsweek's* Peter S. Prescott states that Didion is "able to condense into a paragraph what others would take three pages to expound. Unerringly, she seizes the exact phrase that not only describes but comments on a scene." Born a sixth-generation Californian in Sacramento, Didion began her career editing *Vogue* magazine in New York and writing essays for the *National Review, Saturday Evening Post,* and *Mademoiselle.* After the publication of her first novel, *Run River* (1963), Didion married writer John Gregory Dunne with whom she has recently collaborated on screenplays. Two collections of essays followed: *Slouching Towards Bethlehem* (1968), described by Dan Wakefield as "a rich display of some of the best prose written today," and *The White Album* (1979). *Salvador* (1983) is a book-length essay based on her experiences in war-torn El Salvador, and *Miami* (1987) examines the Cuban exiles in Florida. Her novels include the National Book Award nominee *Play It as It Lays* (1971), *A Book of Common Prayer* (1977), *Democracy* (1984), and *The Last Thing He Wanted* (1996).

HOLY WATER

Some of us who live in arid parts of the world think about water with a reverence others might find excessive. The water I will draw tomorrow from my tap in Malibu is today crossing the Mojave Desert from the Colorado River, and I like to think about exactly where that water is. The water I will drink tonight in a restaurant in Hollywood is by now well down the Los Angeles Aqueduct from the Owens River, and I also think about exactly where that water is: I particularly like to imagine it as it cascades down the 45-degree stone steps that aerate Owens water after its airless passage through the mountain pipes and siphons. As it happens my own reverence for water has always taken the form of this constant meditation upon where the water is, of an obsessive interest not in the politics of water but in the waterworks themselves, in the movement of water through aqueducts and siphons and pumps and forebays and afterbays and weirs and drains, in plumbing on the grand scale. I know the data on water projects I will never see. I know the difficulty Kaiser had closing the last two sluiceway gates on the Guri Dam in Venezuela. I keep watch on evaporation behind the Aswan in Egypt. I can put myself to sleep imagining the water dropping a thousand feet into the turbines at Churchill Falls in Labrador. If the Churchill Falls Project fails to materialize, I fall back on waterworks closer at hand—the tailrace at Hoover on the Colorado, the surge tank in the Tehachapi Mountains that receives California Aqueduct water pumped higher than water has ever been pumped before—and finally I replay a morning when I was seventeen years old and caught, in a military-surplus life raft, in the construction of the Nimbus Afterbay Dam on the American River near Sacramento. I remember that at the moment it happened I was trying to open a tin of anchovies with capers. I recall the raft spinning into the narrow chute through which the river had been temporarily diverted. I recall being deliriously happy.

I suppose it was partly the memory of that delirium that led me to visit, one summer morning in Sacramento, the Operations Control Center for the California State Water Project. Actually so much water is moved around California by so many different agencies that maybe only the movers themselves know on any given day whose water is where, but to get a general picture it is necessary only to remember that Los Angeles moves some of it, San Francisco moves some of it, the Bureau of Reclamation's Central Valley Project moves some of it, and the California State Water Project moves most of the rest of it, moves a vast amount of it, moves more water farther than has ever been moved anywhere. They collect this water up in the granite keeps of the Sierra Nevada and they store roughly a trillion gallons of it behind the Oroville Dam and every morning, down at the Project's headquarters in Sacramento, they decide how much of their water they want to move the next day. They make this morning decision according to supply and demand, which is simple in theory but rather more complicated in practice. In theory each of the Project's five field divisions—the Oroville, the Delta, the San Luis, the San Joaquin, and the Southern divisions—places a call to headquarters before nine A.M. and tells the dispatchers how much water is needed by its local water contractors, who have in turn based their morning estimates on orders from growers and other big users. A schedule is made. The gages open and close according to schedule. The water flows south and the deliveries are made.

In practice this requires prodigious coordination, precision, and the best efforts of several human minds and that of a Univac 418. In practice it might be necessary to hold large flows of water for power production, or to flush out encroaching salinity in the Sacramento–San Joaquin Delta, the most ecologically sensitive point on the system. In practice a sudden rain might obviate the need for a delivery when that delivery is already on its way. In practice what is being delivered here is an enormous volume of water, not quarts of milk or spools of thread, and it takes two days to move such a delivery down through Oroville into the Delta, which is the great pooling place for California water and has been for some years alive with electronic sensors and telemetering equipment and men blocking channels and diverting flows and shoveling fish away from the pumps. It takes perhaps another six days to move this same water down the California Aqueduct from the Delta to the Tehachapi and put it over the hill to Southern California. "Putting some over the hill" is what they say around the Project Operations Control Center when they want to indicate that they are pumping Aqueduct water from the floor of the San Joaquin Valley up and over the Tehachapi Mountains. "Pulling it down" is what they say when they want to indicate that they are lowering a water level somewhere in the system. They can put some over the hill by remote control from this room in Sacramento with its Univac and its big board and its flashing lights. They can pull down a pool in the San Joaquin by remote control from this room in Sacramento with its locked doors and its ringing alarms and its constant printouts of data from sensors out there in the water itself. From this room in Sacramento the whole system takes on the aspect of a perfect three-billion-dollar hydraulic toy, and in certain ways it is. "LET'S START DRAINING QUAIL AT 12:00" was the 10:51 A.M. entry on the electronically recorded communications log the day I visited the Operations Control Center. "Quail" is a reservoir in Los Angeles County with a gross capacity of 1,636,018,000 gallons. "OK" was the response recorded in the log. I knew at that moment that I had missed the only vocation for which I had any instinctive affinity: I wanted to drain Quail myself.

Not many people I know carry their end of the conversation when I want to talk about water deliveries, even when I stress that these deliveries affect their lives, indirectly, every day. "Indirectly" is not quite enough for most people I know. This morning, however, several people I know were affected not "indirectly" but "directly" by the way the water moves. They had been in New Mexico shooting a picture, one sequence of which required a river deep enough to sink a truck, the kind with a cab and a trailer and fifty or sixty wheels. It so happened that no river near the New Mexico location was running that deep this year. The production was therefore moved today to Needles, California, where the Colorado River normally runs, depending upon releases from Davis Dam, eighteen to twenty-five feet deep. Now. Follow this closely: Yesterday we had a freak tropical storm in Southern California, two inches of rain in a normally dry month, and because this rain flooded the fields and provided more irrigation than any grower could possibly want for several days, no water was ordered from Davis Dam.

No orders, no releases.

Supply and demand.

As a result the Colorado was running only seven feet deep past Needles today, Sam Peckinpah's[1] desire for eighteen feet of water in which to sink a truck not being the kind of demand anyone at Davis Dam is geared to meet. The production closed down for the weekend. Shooting will resume Tuesday, providing some grower orders water and the agencies controlling the Colorado release it. Meanwhile many gaffers, best boys, cameramen, assistant directors, script supervisors, stunt drivers, and maybe even Sam Peckinpah are waiting out the weekend in Needles, where it is often 110 degrees at five P.M. and hard to get dinner after eight. This is a California parable, but a true one.

---

[1] **Sam Peckinpah** American film director.

* * *

I have always wanted a swimming pool, and never had one. When it became generally known a year or so ago that California was suffering severe drought, many people in water-rich parts of the country seemed obscurely gratified, and made frequent reference to Californians having to brick up their swimming pools. In fact a swimming pool requires, once it has been filled and the filter has begun its process of cleaning and recirculating the water, virtually no water, but the symbolic content of swimming pools has always been interesting: A pool is misapprehended as a trapping of affluence, real or pretended, and of a kind of hedonistic attention to the body. Actually a pool is, for many of us in the West, a symbol not of affluence but of order, of control over the uncontrollable. A pool is water, made available and useful, and is, as such, infinitely soothing to the western eye.

It is easy to forget that the only natural force over which we have any control out here is water, and that only recently. In my memory California summers were characterized by the coughing in the pipes that meant the well was dry, and California winters by all-night watches on rivers about to crest, by sandbagging, by dynamite on the levees, and flooding on the first floor. Even now the place is not all that hospitable to extensive settlement. As I write a fire has been burning out of control for two weeks in the ranges behind the Big Sur coast. Flash floods last night wiped out all major roads into Imperial County. I noticed this morning a hairline crack in a living-room tile from last week's earthquake, a 4.4 I never felt. In the part of California where I now live aridity is the single most prominent feature of the climate, and I am not pleased to see, this year, cactus spreading wild to the sea. There will be days this winter when the humidity will drop to ten, seven, four. Tumbleweed will blow against my house and the sound of the rattlesnake will be duplicated a hundred times a day by dried bougainvillea drifting in my driveway. The apparent ease of California life is an illusion, and those who believe the illusion real live here in only the most temporary way. I know as well as the next person that there is considerable transcendent value in a river running wild and undammed, a river running free over granite, but I have also lived beneath such a river when it was running in flood, and gone without showers when it was running dry.

"The West begins," Bernard DeVoto wrote, "where the average annual rainfall drops below twenty inches." This is maybe the best definition of the West I have ever read, and it goes a long way toward explaining my own passion for seeing the water under control, but many people I know persist in looking for psychoanalytical implications in this passion. As a matter of fact I have explored, in an amateur way, the more obvious of these implications, and come up with nothing interesting. A certain external reality remains, and resists interpretation. The West begins where the average annual rainfall drops below twenty inches. Water is important to people who do not have it, and the same is true of control. Some fifteen years ago I tore a poem by Karl Shapiro from a magazine and pinned it on my kitchen wall. This fragment of paper is now on the wall of a sixth kitchen, and crumbles a little whenever I touch it, but I keep it there for the last stanza, which has for me the power of a prayer:

> It is raining in California, a straight rain
> Cleaning the heavy oranges on the bough,
> Filling the gardens till the gardens flow,
> Shining the olives, tiling the gleaming tile,
> Waxing the dark camellia leaves more green,
> Flooding the daylong valleys like the Nile.

I thought of those lines constantly on the morning in Sacramento when I went to visit the California State Water Project Operations Control Center. If I had wanted to drain Quail at 10:51 that morning, I wanted, by early afternoon, to do a great deal more. I wanted to open and close the Clifton Court Forebay intake gate. I wanted to produce some power down at the San Luis Dam. I wanted to pick a pool at random on the Aqueduct and pull it down and then refill it, watching for the hydraulic jump. I wanted to put some water over the hill and I wanted to shut down all flow from the Aqueduct into the Bureau of Reclamation's Cross Valley Canal, just to see how long it would take somebody over at Reclamation to call up and complain. I stayed as long as I could and watched the system work on the big board with the lighted checkpoints. The Delta salinity report was coming in on one of the teletypes behind me. The Delta tidal report was coming in on another. The earthquake board, which has been desensitized to sound its alarm (a beeping tone for Southern California, a high-pitched tone for the north) only for those earthquakes which register at least 3.0 on the Richter Scale, was silent. I had no further business in this room and yet I wanted to stay the day. I wanted to be the one, that day, who was shining the olives, filling the gardens, and flooding the daylong valleys like the Nile. I want it still.

Sonia Sanchez 1934–

Poet, playwright, fiction writer, and essayist—with many published collections to her credit—Sonia Sanchez has been called one ". . . among the strongest voices in black nationalism" and one of the most "admired . . . poets of the Black Arts movement." Sanchez emphasizes poetry as a spoken art, linking her to African oral traditions. Critic and poet Haki Madhubuti has written that Sanchez, an "intense and meticulous poet who has not compromised craft or skill for message," has also legitimized ". . . the use of urban Black English in written form," putting ". . . Black speech . . . in the context of world literature." She has also written books for children and is considered an innovator in education. Recipient

of numerous awards and honors, Sanchez notes that her writing ". . . must serve
a dual purpose. It must be a clarion call to the values of change while it also
speaks to the beauty of a nonexploitative age."

AFTER SATURDAY NIGHT COMES SUNDAY

It had all started at the bank. She wuzn't sure, but she thot it had. At that
crowded bank where she had gone to clear up the mistaken notion that she wuz
$300.00 overdrawn in her checking account.

Sandy had moved into that undersized/low expectation of niggahs/being
able to save anything bank/meanly. She wuz tired of people charging her fo they
own mistakes. She had seen it wid her own eyes, five checks: four fo $50 the
other one fo $100 made out to an Anthony Smith. It wuz Winston's signature.
Her stomach jumped as she added and re-added the figures. Finally she dropped
the pen and looked up at the business/suited/man sitten across from her wid
crossed legs and eyes. And as she called him faggot in her mind, watermelon
tears gathered round her big eyes and she just sat.

Someone had come for her at the bank. A friend of Winston's helped her to
his car. It wuz the wite/dude who followed Winston constantly wid his eyes.
Begging eyes she had once called 'em, half in jest, half seriously. They wuz
begging now, along wid his mouth, begging Sandy to talk. But she cudn't. The
words had gone away, gotten lost, drowned by the warm/april/rain dropping in
on her as she watched the car move down the long/unbending/street. It was her
first spring in Indianapolis. She wondered if it wud be beautiful.

He wuz holding her. Crying in her ear. Loud cries, almost louder than the
noise already turning in her head. Yeh. He sed between the cries that he had
messed up the money. He had . . . he had . . . oh babee. *C'mon, Sandy, and talk.
Talk to me. Help me, babee. Help me to tell you what I got to tell you for both our
sakes.* He stretched her out on the green/oversized/couch that sat out from the
wall like some displaced trailer waiting to be parked.

*I'm hooked, he sed. I'm hooked again on stuff. It's not like befo though when I wuz
17 and just beginning. This time it's different. I mean it has to do now wid me and
all my friends who are still on junk. You see I got out of the joint and looked around
and saw those brothers who are my friends all still on the stuff and I cried inside. I
cried long tears for some beautiful dudes who didn't know how the man had 'em by
they balls. Baby, I felt so sorry for them and they wuz so turned around that one
day over to Tony's crib I got high wid 'em. That's all, babee. I know I shouldn't have
done that. You and the kids and all. But they wuz dudes I wuz in the joint wid. My
brothers who wuz still unaware. I can git clean, babee. I mean, I don't have a long*

jones. I ain't been on it too long. I can kick now. Tomorrow. You just say it. Give me the word/sign that you understand, forgive me for being one big asshole and I'll start kicking tomorrow. For you, babee. I know I been laying some heavy stuff on you. Spending money we ain't even got—I'll git a job, too, next week—staying out all the time. Hitting you fo telling me the truth 'bout myself. My actions. Babee, it's you I love in spite of my crazy actions. It's you I love. Don't nobody else mean to me what you do. It's just that I been acting crazy but I know I can't keep on keepin' on this way and keep you and the children. Give me a whole lot of slack during this time and I can kick it, babee. I love you. You so good to me. The meanest thing that done ever happened to me. You the best thing that ever happened to me in all of my 38 years and I'll take better care of you. Say something, Sandy. Say you understand it all. Say you forgive me. At least that, babee.

He raised her head from the couch and kissed her. It was a short cooling kiss. Not warm. Not long. A binding kiss. She opened her eyes and looked at him, and the bare room that somehow now complemented their lives, and she started to cry again. And as he grabbed her and rocked her, she spoke fo the first time since she had told that wite/collar/man in the bank that the bank was wrong.

The-the-the-the bab-bab-bab-ies. Ar-ar-ar-are th-th-th-they o-o-okay? Oh my god. I'm stuttering. Stuttering, she thot. Just like when I wuz little. Stop talking. Stop talking, girl. Write what you have to say. Just like you used to when you wuz little and you got tired of people staring at you while you pushed words out of an unaccommodating mouth. Yeh. That was it, she thot. Stop talking and write what you have to say. Nod yo/head to all of this madness. But rest yo/head and use yo/hands till you git it all straight again.

She pointed to her bag and he handed it to her. She took out a pen and note-book and wrote that she wuz tired, that her head hurt and wuz spinning, and that she wanted to sleep fo a while. She turned and held his face full of little sores where he had picked fo ingrown hairs the nite befo. She kissed them and let her tongue move over his lips, wetting them. He smiled at her and sed he wud git her a coupla sleeping pills. He wud also pick up some dollies fo himself cuz Saturday was kicking time fo him. As he went out the door he turned and sed, *Lady, you some lady. I'm a lucky M.F. to have found you.* She watched him from the window and the sun hit the gold of his dashiki and made it bleed yellow raindrops.

She must have dozed. She knew it wuz late. It was dark outside. The room was dark also and she wondered if he had come in and gone upstairs where the children were napping. What a long nap the boys were taking. They wud be up all nite tonite if they didn't wake up soon. Maybe she shud wake them up, but she decided against it. Her body wuz still tired and she heard footsteps on the porch.

His voice was light and cracked a little as he explained his delay. He wuz high. She knew it. He sounded like he sounded on the phone when he called her late in the nite from some loud place and complimented her fo understanding his late hours. She hadn't understood them, she just hated to be a complaining bitch. He had no sleeping pills, but he had gotten her something as good. A morphine tablet. She watched his face as he explained that she cud swallow it or pop it into the skin. He sed it worked better if you stuck it in yo/arm. As he took the tablet out of the cellophane paper of his cigarettes, she closed her eyes and, fo a moment, she thot she heard someone crying outside the house. She opened her eyes.

His body hung loose as he knelt by the couch. He took from his pocket a manila envelope. It had little spots of blood on it and, as he undid the rubber bands, she saw two needles, a black top wid two pieces of dirty, wite cotton balls in it. She knew this wuz what he used to git high wid.

I-I-I-I-I don-don-don-don't wa-wa-want none o-o-o-of that stuff, ma-a-a-a-a-n. Ain't th-th-th-that do-do-do-dope, too? I-I-I-I-I just just just just wa-wa-wa-nnnt-ted to sleep. I'm o-o-o-kay now. She picked up her notebook and pen and started to write again.

I slept while you wuz gone, man. I drifted on off as I looked for you to walk up the steps. I don't want that stuff. Give me a cold beer though, if there's any in the house. I'll drink that. But no stuff man, she wrote. I'm yo/woman. You shudn't be giving me any of that stuff. Throw the pill away. We don't need it. You don't need it any mo. You gon kick and we gon move on. Keep on being baddDDD togetha. I'll help you, man, cuz I know you want to kick. Flush it down the toilet! You'll start kicking tomorrow and I'll get a babysitter and take us fo a long drive in the country and we'll move on the grass and make it move wid us, cuz we'll be full of living/alive/thots and we'll stop and make love in the middle of nowhere, and the grass will stop its wintry/brown/chants and become green as our Black bodies sing. Heave. Love each other. Throw that stuff away, man, cuz we got more important/beautiful/things to do.

As he read the note his eyes looked at hers in a half/clear/way and he got up and walked slowly to the john. She heard the toilet flushing and she heard the refrigerator door open and close. He brought two cold beers and, as she opened hers, she sat up to watch him rock back and forth in the rocking chair. And his eyes became small and sad as he sed, half-jokingly, *Hope I don't regret throwing that stuff in the toilet,* and he learned back and smiled sadly as he drank his beer. She turned the beer can up to her lips and let the cold evening foam wet her mouth and drown the gathering stutters of her mind.

The sound of cries from the second floor made her move. As she climbed the stairs she waved to him. But his eyes were still closed. He wuz somewhere else, not in this house she thot. He wuz somewhere else, floating among past dreams she had never seen or heard him talk about. As she climbed the stairs, the boy's screams grew louder. *Wow. Them boys got some strong lungs*, she thot. And smiled.

It wuz 11:30 and she had just put the boys in their cribs. She heard them sucking on their bottles, working hard at nourishing themselves. She knew the youngest twin wud finish his bottle first and cry out fo more milk befo he slept. She laughed out loud. He sho cud grease.

He wuz in the bathroom. She knocked on the door, but he sed for her not to come in. She stood outside the door, not moving, and knocked again. *Go and turn on the TV,* he said, *I'll be out in a few minutes.*

It wuz 30 minutes later when he came out. His walk wuz much faster than befo and his voice wuz high, higher than the fear moving over her body. She ran to him, threw her body against him and held on. She kissed him hard and moved her body 'gainst him til he stopped and paid attention to her movements. They fell to the floor. She felt his weight on her as she moved and kissed him. She wuz feeling good and she cudn't understand why he stopped. In the midst of pulling off her dress he stopped and took out a cigarette and lit it while she undressed to her bra and panties. She felt naked all of a sudden and sat down and drew her legs up against her chest and closed her eyes. She reached for a cigarette and lit it.

He stretched out next to her. She felt very ashamed, as if she had made him do something wrong. She wuz glad that she cudn't talk cuz that way she didn't have to explain. He ran his hand up and down her legs and touched her soft wet places.

It's just, babee, that this stuff kills any desire for THAT! I mean, I want you and all that but I can't quite git it up to perform. He lit another cigarette and sat up. *Babee, you sho know how to pick 'em. I mean, wuz you born under an unlucky star or sumthin'? First, you had a nigguh who preferred a rich/wite/woman to you and Blackness. Now you have a junkie who can't even satisfy you when you need satisfying.* And his laugh wuz harsh as he sed again, *You sho know how to pick 'em, lady.* She didn't know what else to do so she smiled a nervous smile that made her feel, remember times when she wuz little and she had stuttered thru a sentence and the listener had acknowledged her accomplishment wid a smile and all she cud do was smile back.

He turned and held her and sed, *Stay up wid me tonite, babee. I got all these memories creeping in on me. Bad ones. They's the things that make kicking hard, you know. You begin remembering all the mean things you've done to yo/family/friends who dig you. I'm remembering now all the heavee things I done laid on you in such a short time. You hardly had a chance to catch yo/breath when I'd think of sum new game to lay on you. Help me, Sandy. Listen to my talk. Hold my hand when I git too sad. Laugh at my fears that keep poppin' out on me like some childhood disease. Be my vaccine, babee. I need you. Don't ever leave me, babee, cuz I'll never have a love like you again. I'll never have another woman again if you leave me.* He picked up her hands and rubbed them in his palms as he talked, and she listened until he finally slept and morning crept in through the shades and covered them.

He threw away his works when he woke up. He came over to where she wuz feeding the boys and kissed her and walked out to the backyard and threw the manila envelope into the middle can. He came back inside, smiled and took a dollie wid a glass of water, and fell on the couch.

Sandy put the boys in their strollers in the backyard where she cud watch them as she cleaned the kitchen. She saw Snow, their big/wite/dog, come round the corner of the house to sit in front of them. They babbled words to him but he sat still guarding them from the backyard/evils of the world.

She moved fast in the house, had a second cup of coffee, called their babysitter and finished straightening up the house. She put on a short dress which showed her legs, and she felt good about her black/hairy legs. She laughed as she remembered that the young brothers on her block used to call her a big/legged/momma as she walked in her young ways.

They never made the country. Their car refused to start and Winston wuz too sick to push it to the filling station for a jump. So they walked to the park. He pushed her in the swing and she pumped herself higher and higher and higher till he told her to stop. She let the swing come slowly to a stop and she jumped out and hit him on the behind and ran. She heard him gaining on her and she tried to dodge him but they fell laughing and holding each other. She looked at him and her eyes sed, *I wish you cud make love to me, man.* As she laughed and pushed him away she thot, *but just you wait til you all right, Winston, I'll give you a workout you'll never forget,* and they got up and walked till he felt badly and went home.

He stayed upstairs while she cooked. When she went upstairs to check on him, he was curled up, wrapped tight as a child in his mother's womb. She wiped his head and body full of sweat and kissed him and thought how beautiful he wuz and how proud she wuz of him. She massaged his back and went away. He called fo her as she wuz feeding the children and asked for the wine. He needed somethin' else to relieve this saturday/nite/pain that was creeping up on him. He looked bad, she thot, and raced down the stairs and brought him the sherry. He thanked her as she went out the door and she curtsied, smiled and sed, *Any ol time, man.* She noticed she hadn't stuttered and felt good.

By the time she got back upstairs he was moaning and turning back and forth on the bed. He had drunk half the wine in the bottle, now he wuz getting up to bring it all up. When she came back up to the room he sed he was cold, so she got another blanket for him. He wuz still cold, so she took off her clothes and got under the covers wid him and rubbed her body against him. She wuz scared. She started to sing a Billie Holiday song. Yeh. God bless the child that's got his own. She cried in between the lyrics as she felt his big frame trembling and heaving. *Oh god,* she thot, *am I doing the right thing?* He soon quieted down and got up to go to the toilet. She closed her eyes as she waited fo him. She closed her eyes and felt the warmth of the covers creeping over her. She remembered calling his name as she drifted off to sleep. She remembered how quiet everything finally wuz.

One of the babies woke her up. She went into the room, picked up his bottle and got him more milk. It wuz while she wuz handing him the milk that she heard the silence. She ran to their bedroom and turned on the light. The bed wuz empty. She ran down the stairs and turned on the lights. He was gone. She saw her purse on the couch. Her wallet wuz empty. Nothing was left. She opened the door and went out on the porch, and she remembered the lights were on and that she wuz naked. But she stood fo a moment looking out at the flat/Indianapolis/street and she stood and let the late/nite/air touch her body and she turned and went inside.

POEM NO. 2

my puertorican
husband who feeds me
cares for me and loves me
is trying to under
stand my Blackness.   5
so he is taking up
watercolors.

BLUES

in the night
in my half hour
negro dreams
i hear voices knocking at the door
i see walls dripping screams up   5
and down the halls
               won't someone open
the door for me? won't some
one schedule my sleep
and don't ask no questions?   10
noise.
       like when he took me to his
home away from home place
and i died the long sought after

death he'd planned for me.   15
and two days later
when i was talking
i started to grin.
as everyone knows
i am still grinning.   20

HAIKU

did ya ever cry
Black man, did ya ever cry
til you knocked all over?

TO ALL BROTHERS: FROM ALL SISTERS

each nite without you.

and I give birth to myself.

who am i to be touched at random?

to be alone so long. to see you move
in this varicose country   5
like silhouettes passing in apprenticeship,
from slave to slavery to pimp
to hustler to murderer to negro
to nigguhdom to militant to revolutionary
to Blackness to faggot with the same   10
shadings of disrespect covering your voice.

and the nite, playing a maiden tune,
singes my eyes.

who am i to have loved you in rooms
lit by a single wall?   15
who am i to have loved at all as the
years come like water and the
madness of my blood drains rivers.

Lucille Clifton 1936–

L ucille Clifton once wrote: "I am not interested if anyone knows whether or not I am familiar with big words, I am interested in trying to render big ideas in a simple way. I am interested in being understood not admired." Nonetheless, Lucille Clifton *is* admired for two Pulitzer Prize nominations, one Emmy award, twenty-one books of juvenile fiction, seven volumes of poetry, and teaching appointments at several universities. Born in DePew, New York, to parents who instilled a love of literature, Clifton attended Howard University and gained her teacher's degree from Fredonia State Teachers' College. Encouraged to publish by poet Robert Hayden, Clifton responded with the critically acclaimed poetry collection *Good Times* (1969), from which the 1970s sitcom about life in Chicago's black community took its name. Although she passionately discards what she calls "white ways," malice is not evident in her writing. Instead, one encounters an intense, terse style that champions the extraordinary in ordinary black folk and celebrates the deep spiritual traditions created despite considerable hardship.

POEM

them bones
them bones will
rise again
them bones
them bones will   5
walk again
them bones
them bones will
talk again
now hear   10
the word of The Lord.

Traditional

atlantic is a sea of bones.
my bones.
my elegant afrikans   15
connecting whydah and new york,
a bridge of ivory.

seabed they call it.
in its arms my early mothers sleep.
some women leapt with babies in their arms.   20
some women wept and threw the babies in.

maternal armies pace the atlantic floor.
i call my name into the roar of surf
and something awful answers.

ALBUM

for lucille chan hall

1. it is 1939.
    our mothers are turning our hair
    around rags.
    our mothers
    have filled our shirley temple cups.   5
    we drink it all.

2. 1939 again.
    our shirley temple curls.
    shirley yellow.
    shirley black.   10
    our colors are fading.

later we had to learn ourselves.
back across 2 oceans
into bound feet and nappy hair.

3. 1958 and 9.   15
    we have dropped daughters,
    afrikan and chinese.
    we think
    they will be beautiful
    we think   20
    they will become themselves

4. it is 1985.
    she is.
    she is.
    they are.   25

Marge Piercy 1936–

A highly political and often controversial writer, Marge Piercy is a novelist and poet whose central theme is the struggle of the individual to attain full potential in the face of societal constraints. Alternately raw and angry, tender and humorous, her work ranges from urban realism to science fiction and fantasy. She eschews any dividing line between personal and political poetry; her chief antagonist is the society that humans have created, and all conflict is simultaneously personal and political. Her first novel, *Going Down Fast* (1969), attacks real-estate developers, social scientists, and higher education, which are all seen as enemies of the urban poor. Her most acclaimed novel is probably *Woman on the Edge of Time* (1976), set in a utopian society of 2137 in which racism, sexism, and classism no longer exist. Other major works include the novels *The High Cost of Living* (1978), *Braided Lives* (1982), and *Summer People* (1989), as well as the poetry collections *Breaking Camp* (1968), *The Moon Is Always Female* (1980), and *Available Light* (1988).

BARBIE DOLL

This girlchild was born as usual
and presented dolls that did pee-pee
and miniature GE stoves and irons
and wee lipsticks the color of cherry candy.
Then in the magic of puberty, a classmate said: 5
You have a great big nose and fat legs.

She was healthy, tested intelligent,
possessed strong arms and back,
abundant sexual drive and manual dexterity.
She went to and fro apologizing.   10
Everyone saw a fat nose on thick legs.

She was advised to play coy,
exhorted to come on hearty,
exercise, diet, smile and wheedle.
Her good nature wore out   15
like a fan belt.
So she cut off her nose and her legs
and offered them up.

In the casket displayed on satin she lay
with the undertaker's cosmetics painted on,   20

a turned-up putty nose,
dressed in a pink and white nightie.
Doesn't she look pretty? everyone said.
Consummation at last.
To every woman a happy ending.   25

THE WOMAN IN THE ORDINARY

The woman in the ordinary pudgy downcast girl
is crouching with eyes and muscles clenched.
Round and pebble smooth she effaces herself
under ripples of conversation and debate.
The woman in the block of ivory soap   5
has massive thighs that neigh,
great breasts that blare and strong arms that trumpet.

The woman of the golden fleece
laughs uproariously from the belly
inside the girl who imitates   10
a Christmas card virgin with glued hands,
who fishes for herself in other's eyes,
who stoops and creeps to make herself smaller.
In her bottled up is a woman peppery as curry,
a yam of a woman of butter and brass,   15
compounded of acid and sweet like a pineapple,
like a handgrenade set to explode,
like goldenrod ready to bloom.

Bessie Head 1937–1986

Tormented by the realities of apartheid that plagued her in her birthplace of South Africa and her adopted land of Botswana, Bessie Head produced fiction that explored how racism affects the lives of South African people. Born in a mental hospital because her white mother was labeled insane for conceiving a child with a Zulu stable worker, she was reared by a black foster family and educated in a South African mission orphanage. In 1964, after a brief marriage that ended in divorce, Head moved to a refugee community in Botswana with her son. Making money by selling vegetables and guava jam, Head began her first novel, *When Rain Clouds Gather* (1969), typing by candlelight because she had no electricity. Head would eventually produce three novels, a collection of short stories, and two historical chronicles. One critic writes that "Her novels rise above the bitterness common to much protest literature in that Head strives to understand not only the effects of prejudice but also the causes."

SNAPSHOTS OF A WEDDING

Wedding days always started at the haunting, magical hour of early dawn when there was only a pale crack of light on the horizon. For those who were awake, it took the earth hours to adjust to daylight. The cool and damp of the night slowly arose in shimmering waves like water and even the forms of the people who bestirred themselves at this unearthly hour were distorted in the haze; they appeared to be dancers in slow motion, with fluid, watery forms. In the dim light, four men, the relatives of the bridegroom, Kegoletile, slowly herded an ox before them towards the yard of MmaKhudu, where the bride, Neo, lived. People were already astir in MmaKhudu's yard, yet for a while they all came and peered closely at the distorted fluid forms that approached, to ascertain if it were indeed the relatives of the bridegroom. Then the ox, who was a rather stupid fellow and unaware of his sudden and impending end as meat for the wedding feast, bellowed casually his early morning yawn. At this, the beautiful ululating of the women rose and swelled over the air like water bubbling rapidly and melodiously over the stones of a clear, sparkling stream. In between ululating all the while, the women began to weave about the yard in the wedding dance; now and then they bent over and shook their buttocks in the air. As they handed over the ox, one of the bridegroom's relatives joked:

'This is going to be a modern wedding.' He meant that a lot of the traditional courtesies had been left out of the planning for the wedding day; no one had been awake all night preparing diphiri or the traditional wedding breakfast of pounded meat and samp; the bridegroom said he had no church and did not care about such things; the bride was six months pregnant and showing it, so there was just going to be a quick marriage ceremony at the police camp.

'Oh, we all have our own ways,' one of the bride's relatives joked back. 'If the times are changing, we keep up with them.' And she weaved away ululating joyously.

Whenever there was a wedding the talk and gossip that preceded it were appalling, except that this time the relatives of the bride, Neo, kept their talk a strict secret among themselves. They were anxious to be rid of her; she was an impossible girl with haughty, arrogant ways. Of all her family and relatives, she was the only one who had completed her 'O' levels and she never failed to rub in this fact. She walked around with her nose in the air; illiterate relatives were beneath her greeting—it was done in a clever way, she just turned her head to one side and smiled to herself or when she greeted it was like an insult; she stretched her hand out, palm outspread, swung it down laughing with a gesture that plainly said: 'Oh, that's you!' Only her mother seemed bemused by her education. At her own home Neo was waited on hand and foot. Outside her home nasty remarks were passed. People bitterly disliked conceit and pride.

'That girl has no manners!' the relatives would remark. 'What's the good of education if it goes to someone's head so badly they have no respect for the people? Oh, she is not a person.'

Then they would nod their heads in that fatal way, with predictions that one day life would bring her down. Actually, life had treated Neo rather nicely. Two months after completing her 'O' levels she became pregnant by Kegoletile with their first child. It soon became known that another girl, Mathata, was also pregnant by Kegoletile. The difference between the two girls was that Mathata was completely uneducated; the only work she would ever do was that of a housemaid, while Neo had endless opportunities before her—typist, book-keeper, or secretary. So Neo merely smiled; Mathata was no rival. It was as though the decision had been worked out by circumstance because when the families converged on Kegoletile at the birth of the children—he was rich in cattle and they wanted to see what they could get—he of course immediately proposed marriage to Neo; and for Mathata, he agreed to a court order to pay a maintenance of R10.00 a month until the child was twenty years old. Mathata merely smiled too. Girls like her offered no resistance to the approaches of men; when they lost them, they just let things ride.

'He is of course just running after the education and not the manners,' Neo's relatives commented, to show they were not fooled by human nature. 'He thinks that since she is as educated as he is they will both get good jobs and be rich in no time . . .'

Educated as he was, Kegoletile seemed to go through a secret conflict during that year he prepared a yard for his future married life with Neo. He spent most of his free time in the yard of Mathata. His behaviour there wasn't too alarming but he showered Mathata with gifts of all kinds—food, fancy dresses, shoes and underwear. Each time he came, he brought a gift and each time Mathata would burst out laughing and comment: 'Ow, Kegoletile, how can I wear all these dresses? It's just a waste of money! Besides, I manage quite well with the R10.00 you give every month for the child . . .'

She was a very pretty girl with black eyes like stars; she was always smiling and happy; immediately and always her own natural self. He knew what he was marrying—something quite the opposite, a new kind of girl with false postures and acquired, grand-madame ways. And yet, it didn't pay a man these days to look too closely into his heart. They all wanted as wives, women who were big money-earners and they were so ruthless about it! And yet it was as though the society itself stamped each of its individuals with its own particular brand of wealth and Kegoletile had not yet escaped it; he had about him an engaging humility and eagerness to help and please that made him loved and respected by all who knew him. During those times he sat in Mathata's yard, he communicated nothing of the conflict he felt but he would sit on a chair with his arms spread out across its back, turn his head sideways and stare at what seemed to be an empty space beside him. Then he would smile, stand up and walk away. Nothing dramatic. During the year he prepared the huts in his new yard, he frequently slept at the home of Neo.

Relatives on both sides watched this division of interest between the two yards and one day when Neo walked patronizingly into the yard of an aunt, the aunt decided to frighten her a little.

'Well aunt,' she said, with the familiar careless disrespect which went with her so-called, educated, status. 'Will you make me some tea? And how's things?'

The aunt spoke very quietly.

'You may not know it, my girl, but you are hated by everyone around here. The debate we have going is whether a nice young man like Kegoletile should marry bad-mannered rubbish like you. He would be far better off if he married a girl like Mathata, who though uneducated, still treats people with respect.'

The shock the silly girl received made her stare for a terrified moment at her aunt. Then she stood up and ran out of the house. It wiped the superior smile off her face and brought her down a little. She developed an anxiety to greet people and also an anxiety about securing Kegoletile as a husband—that was why she became pregnant six months before the marriage could take place. In spite of this, her own relatives still disliked her and right up to the day of the wedding they were still debating whether Neo was a suitable wife for any man. No one would have guessed it though with all the dancing, ululating and happiness expressed in the yard and streams of guests gaily ululated themselves along the pathways with wedding gifts precariously balanced on their heads. Neo's maternal aunts, all sedately decked up in shawls, sat in a select group by themselves in a corner of the yard. They sat on the bare ground with their legs stretched out before them but they were served like queens the whole day long. Trays of tea, dry white bread, plates of meat, rice, and salad were constantly placed before them. Their important task was to formally hand over the bride to Kegoletile's maternal aunts when they approached the yard at sunset. So they sat the whole day with still, expressionless faces, waiting to fulfill this ancient rite.

Equally still and expressionless were the faces of the long column of women, Kegoletile's maternal aunts, who appeared outside the yard just as the sun sank low. They walked slowly into the yard indifferent to the ululating that greeted them and seated themselves in a group opposite Neo's maternal aunts. The yard became very silent while each group made its report. Kegoletile had provided all the food for the wedding feast and a maternal aunt from his side first asked:

'Is there any complaint? Has all gone well?'

'We have no complaint,' the opposite party replied.

'We have come to ask for water,' Kegoletile's side said, meaning that from times past the bride was supposed to carry water at her in-law's home.

'It is agreed to,' the opposite party replied.

Neo's maternal aunts then turned to the bridegroom and counselled him: 'Son, you must plough and supply us with corn each year.'

Then Kegoletile's maternal aunts turned to the bride and counselled her: 'Daughter, you must carry water for your husband. Beware, that at all times, he is the owner of the house and must be obeyed. Do not mind if he stops now and then and talks to other ladies. Let him feel free to come and go as he likes . . .'

The formalities over, it was now time for Kegoletile's maternal aunts to get up, ululate and weave and dance about the yard. Then, still dancing and ululating, accompanied by the bride and groom they slowly wound their way to the yard of Kegoletile where another feast had been prepared. As they approached his yard, an old woman suddenly dashed out and chopped at the ground with a hoe. It was all only a formality. Neo would never be the kind of wife who went to the lands to plough. She already had a well-paid job in an office as a secretary. Following on this another old woman took the bride by the hand and led her to a smeared and decorated courtyard wherein had been placed a traditional animal-skin Tswana mat. She was made to sit on the mat and a shawl and kerchief were placed before her. The shawl was ceremonially wrapped around her shoulders; the kerchief tied around her head—the symbols that she was now a married woman.

Guests quietly moved forward to greet the bride. Then two girls started to ululate and dance in front of the bride. As they both turned and bent over to shake their buttocks in the air, they bumped into each other and toppled over. The wedding guests roared with laughter. Neo, who had all this time been stiff, immobile and rigid, bent forward and her shoulders shook with laughter.

The hoe, the mat, the shawl, the kerchief, the beautiful flute-like ululating of the women seemed in itself a blessing on the marriage but all the guests were deeply moved when out of the crowd, a woman of majestic, regal bearing slowly approached the bride. It was the aunt who had scolded Neo for her bad manners and modern ways. She dropped to her knees before the bride, clenched her fists together and pounded the ground hard with each clenched fist on either side of the bride's legs. As she pounded her fists she said loudly:

'Be a good wife! Be a good wife!'

Joyce Carol Oates 1938–

Joyce Carol Oates brings a new meaning to the word "prolific." In 1998, at the age of fifty, she had published more than eighty books, including novels, poetry, short stories, plays, and essays, as well as editing thirteen anthologies. In her spare time, she teaches in the Princeton University creative writing program and, with her husband, operates a small press and publishes a literary magazine, *The Ontario Review*. Born in a small town in upstate New York, much like the

"Eden County" country depicted in so much of her work, Oates found success early, winning the prestigious *Mademoiselle* fiction contest while attending Syracuse University on a scholarship. She would eventually evolve a style that portrays the basic disposition of contemporary culture as one ruled by violence and psychic dislocation. "Typical activities in Oates's novels," asserts critic Marvin Mudrick, "are arson, rape, riot, mental breakdown, murder (plain and fancy, with excursions into patricide, matricide, uxoricide, mass filicide), and suicide." Much of her violent vision traces its genesis to the mid 1960s in Detroit when, as a teacher, she witnessed the race riots. "Detroit, my 'great subject,'" Oates writes, "made me the person I am, consequently the writer I am—for better or worse." The National Book Award winner for fiction, *them* (1969), came out of her Detroit experience.

UNMAILED, UNWRITTEN LETTERS

Dear Mother and Father,

The weather is lovely here. It rained yesterday. Today the sky is blue. The trees are changing colors, it is October 20, I have got to buy some new clothes sometime soon, we've changed dentists, doctors, everything is lovely here and I hope the same with you. Greg is working hard as usual. The doctor we took Father to see, that time he hurt his back visiting here, has died and so we must change doctors. Dentists also. I want to change dentists because I can't stand to go back to the same dentist any more. He is too much of a fixed point, a reference point. It is such a chore, changing doctors and dentists.

Why are you so far away in the Southwest? Is there something about the Southwest that lures old people? Do they see images there, shapes in the desert? Holy shapes? Why are you not closer to me, or farther away? In an emergency it would take hours or days for you to get to me. I think of the two of you in the Southwest, I see the highways going off into space and wonder at your courage, so late in life, to take on space. Father had all he could do to manage that big house of yours, and the lawn. Even with workers to help him it was terrifying, all that space, because he owned it. Maybe that was why it terrified him, because he owned it. Out in the Southwest I assume that no one owns anything. Do people even live there? Some people live there, I know. But I think of the Southwest as an optical illusion, sunshine and sand and a mountainous (mountainous?) horizon, with highways perfectly divided by their white center lines, leading off to Mars or the moon, unhurried. And there are animals, the designs of animals, mashed into the highways! The shape of a dog, a dog's pelty shadow, mashed into the hot, hot road—in mid-flight, so to speak, mid-leap, run over again and again by big trucks and retired people seeing America. That vastness would terrify me. I think of you and I think of protoplasm being drawn off into space, out there, out in the West, with no human limits to keep it safe.

Dear Marsha Katz,

   Thank you for the flowers, white flowers, but why that delicate hint of death, all that fragrance wasted on someone like myself who is certain to go on living? Why are you pursuing me? Why in secrecy? (I see all the letters you write to your father, don't forget; and you never mention me in them.) Even if your father were my lover, which is not true and cannot be verified, why should you pursue me? Why did you sign the card with the flowers *Trixie?* I don't know anyone named Trixie! How could I know anyone named Trixie? It is a dog's name, a high school cheerleader's name, an aunt's name . . . why do you play these games, why do you pursue me?

   Only ten years old, and too young for evil thoughts—do you look in your precocious heart and see only grit, the remains of things, a crippled shadow of a child? Do you see in all this the defeat of your Daughterliness? Do you understand that a Daughter, like a Mistress, must be feminine or all is lost, must keep up the struggle with the demonic touch of matter-of-fact irony that loses us all our men . . . ? I think you have lost, yes. A ten-year-old cannot compete with a thirty-year-old. Send me all the flowers you want. I pick them apart one by one, getting bits of petals under my fingernails, I throw them out before my husband gets home.

   Nor did I eat that box of candies you sent. Signed "Uncle Bumble"!

   Are you beginning to feel terror at having lost? Your father and I are not lovers, we hardly see each other any more, since last Wednesday and today is Monday, still you've lost because I gather he plans on continuing the divorce proceedings, long distance, and what exactly can a child do about that . . . ? I see all the letters you write him. No secrets. Your Cape Cod sequence was especially charming. I like what you did with that kitten, the kitten that is found dead on the beach! Ah, you clever little girl, even with your I.Q. of uncharted heights, you couldn't quite conceal from your father and me your attempt to make him think 1) the kitten suggests a little girl, namely you 2) its death suggests your pending, possible death, if Father does not return. Ah, how we laughed over that! . . . Well, no, we didn't laugh, he did not laugh, perhaps he did not even understand the trick you were playing . . . your father can be a careless, abrupt man, but things stick in his mind, you know that and so you write of a little white kitten, alive one day and dead the next, so you send me flowers for a funeral parlor, you keep me in your thoughts constantly so that I can feel a tug all the way here in Detroit, all the way from Boston, and I hate it, I hate that invisible pulling, tugging, that witch's touch of yours. . . .

Dear Greg,

   We met about this time years ago. It makes me dizzy, it frightens me to think of that meeting. Did so much happen, and yet nothing? Miscarriages, three or four, one loses count, and eight or nine sweet bumbling years—why do I use the word *bumbling*, it isn't a word I would ever use—and yet there is nothing there, if I go to your closet and open the door your clothes tell me as much as you do. You are a good man. A faithful husband. A subdued and excellent husband. The way you handled my parents alone would show how good you are, how excellent. . . . My friend X, the one with the daughter said to be a genius and the wife no one has ever seen, X couldn't handle my parents, couldn't put up with my father's talk about principles, the Principles of an Orderly Universe, which he sincerely believes in though he is an intelligent man. . . . X couldn't handle anything, anyone. He loses patience. He is vulgar. He watches himself swerve out of control but can't stop. Once, returning to his car, we found a ticket on the windshield. He snatched it and tore it up, very angry, and then when he saw my surprise he thought to make a joke of it—pretending to be tearing it with his teeth, a joke. And he is weak, angry men are weak. He lets me close doors on him. His face seems to crack with sorrow, but he lets me walk away, why is he so careless and weak . . . ?

But I am thinking of us, our first meeting. An overheated apartment, graduate school . . . a girl in dark stockings, myself, frightened and eager, trying to be charming in a voice that didn't carry, a man in a baggy sweater, gentle, intelligent, a little perplexed, the two of us gravitating together, fearful of love and fearful of not loving, of not being loved. . . . So we met. The evening falls away, years fall away. I count only three miscarriages, really. The fourth a sentimental miscalculation.

My darling,

I am out somewhere, I see a telephone booth on a corner, the air is windy and too balmy for October. I won't go in the phone booth. Crushed papers, a beer bottle, a close violent stench. . . . I walk past it, not thinking of you. I am out of the house so that you can't call me and so that I need not think of you. Do you talk to your wife every night, still? Does she weep into your ear? How many nights have you lain together, you and that woman now halfway across the country, in Boston, weeping into a telephone? Have you forgotten all those nights?

Last night I dreamed about you mashed into a highway. More than dead. I had to wake Greg up, I couldn't stop trembling, I wanted to tell him of the waste, the waste of joy and love, your being mashed soundlessly into a road and pounded into a shape no one would recognize as yours. . . . Your face was gone. What will happen to me when your face is gone from this world?

I parked the car down here so that I could go shopping at Saks but I've been walking, I'm almost lost. The streets are dirty. A tin can lies on the sidewalk, near a vacant lot. Campbell's Tomato Soup. I am dressed in the suit you like, though it is a little baggy on me, it would be a surprise for someone driving past to see a lady in such a suit bend to pick up a tin can. . . . I pick the can up. The edge is jagged and rusty. No insects inside. Why would insects be inside, why bother with an empty can? Idly I press the edge of the lid against my wrist; it isn't sharp, it makes only a fine white line on my skin, not sharp enough to penetrate the skin.

Dear Greg,

I hear you walking downstairs. You are going outside, out into the back yard. I am tempted, heart pounding, to run to the window and spy on you. But everything is tepid, the universe is dense with molecules, I can't get up. My legs won't move. You said last night, "The Mayor told me to shut up in front of Arthur Grant. He told me to shut up." You were amused and hurt at the same time, while I was furious, wishing you were . . . were someone else, someone who wouldn't be amused and hurt, a good man, a subdued man, but someone else who would tell that bastard to go to hell. I am a wife, jealous for her husband.

Three years you've spent working for the Mayor, His Honor, dodging reporters downtown. Luncheons, sudden trips, press conferences, conferences with committees from angry parts of Detroit, all of Detroit angry, white and black, bustling, ominous. Three years. Now he tells you to shut up. All the lies you told for him, not knowing how to lie with dignity, he tells you to shut up, my body suffers as if on the brink of some terrible final expulsion of our love, some blood-smear of a baby. When a marriage ends, who is left to understand it? No witnesses. No young girl in black stockings, no young man, all those witnesses gone, grown up, moved on, lost.

Too many people know you now, your private life is dwindling. You are dragged back again and again to hearings, commission meetings, secret meetings, desperate meetings, television interviews, interviews with kids from college newspapers. Everyone has a right to know everything! *What Detroit Has Done to Combat Slums. What Detroit Has Done To Prevent Riots*, updated to *What Detroit Has Done to Prevent a Recurrence of the 1967 Riot*. You people are rewriting history as fast as history happens. I love you, I suffer for you, I lie here in a paralysis of love, sorrow, density, idleness, lost in my love for you, my shame for having betrayed you. . . . Why should slums be combatted? Once I wept to see photographs of kids playing in garbage heaps, now I weep at crazy sudden visions of my lover's body become only a body, I have no tears left for anyone else, for anything else. Driving in the city I have a sudden vision of my lover dragged along by a stranger's car, his body somehow caught up under the bumper or the fender and dragged along, bleeding wildly in the street. . . .

My dear husband, betraying you was the most serious act of my life. Far more serious than marrying you. I knew my lover better when he finally became my lover than I knew you when you became my husband. I know him better now than I know you. You and I have lived together for eight years. Smooth coins, coins worn smooth by constant handling. . . . I am a woman trapped in love, in the terror of love. Paralysis of love. Like a great tortoise, trapped in a heavy deathlike shell, a mask of the body pressing the body down to earth. . . . I went for a week without seeing him, an experiment. The experiment failed. No husband can keep his wife's love. So you walk out in the back yard, admiring the leaves, the sky, the flagstone terrace, you are a man whom betrayal would destroy and yet your wife betrayed you, deliberately.

To The Editor:

Anonymously and shyly I want to ask—why are white men so weak, so feeble? The other day I left a friend at his hotel and walked quickly, alone, to my car, and the eyes of black men around me moved onto me with a strange hot perception, seeing everything. They knew, seeing me, what I was. Tension rose through the cracks in the sidewalk. Where are white men who are strong, who see women in this way? The molecules in the air of Detroit are humming. I wish I could take a knife and cut out an important piece of my body, my insides, and hold it up . . . on a street corner, an offering. Then will they let me alone? The black men jostle one another on street corners, out of work and not wanting work, content to stare at me, knowing everything in me, not surprised. My lover, a white man, remains back in the hotel, his head in his hands because I have walked out, but he won't run after me, he won't follow me. *They* follow me. One of them bumped into me, pretending it was an accident. I want to cut up my body, I can't live in this body.

Next door to us a boy is out in his driveway, sitting down, playing a drum. Beating on a drum. Is he crazy? A white boy of about sixteen pounding on a drum. He wants to bring the city down with that drum and I don't blame him. I understand that vicious throbbing.

Dear Marsha Katz,

Thank you for the baby clothes. Keep sending me things, test your imagination. I feel that you are drowning. I sense a tightness in your chest, your throat. Are your eyes leaden with defeat, you ten-year-old wonder? How many lives do children relive at the moment of death?

Dear Mother and Father,

The temperature today is _____. Yesterday at this time, _____. Greg has been very busy as usual with _____, _____, _____. This weekend we must see the _____'s, whom you have met. How is the weather there? How is your vacation? Thank you for the postcard from _____. I had not thought lawns would be green there.

. . . The Mayor will ask all his aides for resignations, signed. Some he will accept and others reject. A kingly man, plump and alcoholic. Divorced. Why can't I tell you about my husband's job, about my life, about anything real? Scandals fall on the head of my husband's boss, reading the paper is torture, yet my husband comes home and talks seriously about the future, about improvements, as if no chaos is waiting. No picketing ADC mothers, no stampede to buy guns, no strangled black babies found in public parks. In the midst of this my husband is clean and untouched, innocent, good. He has dedicated his life to helping others. I love him but cannot stop betraying him, again and again, having reclaimed my life as my own to throw away, to destroy, to lose. My life is my own. I keep on living.

My darling,

It is one-thirty and if you don't call by two, maybe you won't call; I know that you have a seminar from two to four, maybe you won't call; I know that you have a seminar from two to four, maybe you won't call today and everything will end. My heart pounds bitterly, in fear, in anticipation? Your daughter sent me some baby clothes, postmarked Boston. I understand her hatred, but one thing: how much did you tell your wife about me? About my wanting children? You told her you no longer loved her and couldn't live with her, that you loved another woman who could not marry you, but . . . did you tell her this other woman had no children? And what else?

I will get my revenge on you.

I walk through the house in a dream, in a daze. I am sinking slowly through the floor of this expensive house, a married woman in a body grown light as a shell, empty as a shell. My body has no other life in it, only its own. What you discharge in me is not life but despair. I can remember my body having life, holding it. It seemed a trick, a feat that couldn't possibly work: like trying to retain liquid up a reed, turning the reed upside down. The doctor said, "Babies are no trouble. Nothing." But the liquid ran out. All liquid runs out of me. That first week, meeting with you at the Statler, everything ran out of me like blood. I alarmed you, you with your nervous sense of fate, your fear of getting cancer, of having a nervous breakdown. I caused you to say stammering *But what if you get pregnant?* I am not pregnant but I feel a strange tingling of life, a tickling, life at a distance, as if the spirit of your daughter is somehow in me, lodged in me. She sucks at my insides with her pinched jealous lips, wanting blood. My body seeks to discharge her magically.

My dear husband,

I wanted to test being alone. I went downtown to the library, the old library. I walked past the hotel where he and I have met, my lover and I, but we were not meeting today and I was alone, testing myself as a woman alone, a human being alone. The library was filled with old men. Over seventy, dressed in black, with white shirts. Black and white: a reading room of old men, dressed in black and white.

I sat alone at a table. Some of the old men glanced at me. In a dream I began to leaf through a magazine, thinking, *Now I am leafing through a magazine: this is expected.* Why can't I be transformed to something else—to a mask, a shell, a statue? I glance around shyly, trying to gauge the nature of the story I am in. Is it tragic or only sad? The actors in this play all seem to be wearing masks, even I am wearing a mask, I am never naked. My nakedness, with my lover, is a kind of mask—something he sees, something I can't quite believe in. Women who are loved are in perpetual motion, dancing. We dance and men follow to the brink of madness and death, but what of us, the dancers?—when the dancing ends we stand back upon our heels, back upon our heels, dazed and hurt. Beneath the golden cloth on our thighs is flesh, and flesh hurts. Men are not interested in the body, which feels pain, but in the rhythm of the body as it goes about its dance, the body of a woman who cannot stop dancing.

A confession. In Ann Arbor last April, at the symposium, I fell in love with a man. The visiting professor from Boston University—a man with black-rimmed glasses, Jewish, dark-eyed, dark-haired, nervous and arrogant and restless. Drumming his fingers. Smoking too much. (And you, my husband, were sane enough to give up smoking five years ago.) A student stood up in the first row and shouted out something and it was he, my lover, the man who would become my lover, who stood up in turn and shouted something back . . . it all happened so fast, astounding everyone, even the kid who reported for the campus newspaper didn't catch the exchange. How many men could handle a situation like that, being wilder and more profane than a heckler? . . . He was in the group at the party afterward, your friend Bryan's house. All of you talked at once, excited and angry over the outcome of the symposium, nervous at the sense of agitation in the air, the danger, and he and I wandered to the hostess's table, where food was set out. We made pigs of ourselves, eating. He picked out the shrimp and I demurely picked out tiny flakes of dough with miniature asparagus in them. Didn't you notice us? Didn't you notice this dark-browed man with the glasses that kept slipping down his nose, with the untidy black hair? We talked. We ate. I could see in his bony knuckles a hunger that would never be satisfied. And I, though I think I am starving slowly to death now, I leaped upon the food as if it were a way of getting at him, of drawing him into me. We talked. We wandered around the house. He looked out a window, drawing a curtain aside, at the early spring snowfall, falling gently outside, and he said that he didn't know why he had come to this part of the country, he was frightened of traveling, of strangers. He said that he was very tired. He seduced me with the slump of his shoulders. And when he turned back to me we entered another stage of the evening, having grown nervous and brittle with each other, the two of us suddenly conscious of being together. My eyes grew hot and searing. I said carelessly that he must come over to Detroit sometime, we could have lunch, and he said at once, "I'd like that very much. . . ." and then paused. Silence.

Later, in the hotel, in the cheap room he rented, he confessed to me that seeing my face had been an experience for him—did he believe in love at first sight, after all? Something so childish? It had been some kind of love, anyway. We talked about our lives, about his wife, about my husband, and then he swung onto another subject, talking about his daughter for forty-five minutes . . . a genius, a ten-year-old prodigy. I am brought low, astounded. I want to cry out to him, *But what about me! Don't stop thinking about me!* At the age of six his daughter was writing poems, tidy little poems, like Blake's. *Like Blake's? Yes.* At the age of eight she was publishing those poems.

No, I don't want to marry him. I'm not going to marry him. What we do to each other is too violent, I don't want it brought into marriage and domesticated, nor do I want him to see me at unflattering times of the day . . . getting up at three in the morning to be sick, a habit of mine. He drinks too much. He reads about the connection between smoking and death, and turns the page of the newspaper quickly. Superstitious, stubborn. In April he had a sore throat, that was why he spoke so hoarsely on the program . . . but a month later he was no better: "I'm afraid of doctors," he said. This is a brilliant man, the father of a brilliant child? We meet nowhere, at an unimaginative point X, in a hotel room, in the anonymous drafts of air from blowers that never stop blowing, the two of us yearning to be one, in this foreign dimension where anything is possible. Only later, hurrying to my car, do I feel resentment and fury at him . . . why doesn't he buy me anything, why doesn't he get a room for us, something permanent? And hatred for him rises in me in long shuddering surges, overwhelming me. I don't want to marry him. Let me admit the worst—anxious not to fall in love with him, I think of not loving him at the very moment he enters me, I think of him already boarding a plane and disappearing from my life, with relief, I think with pity of human beings and this sickness of theirs, this desire for unity. Why this desire for unity, why? We walk out afterward, into the sunshine or into the smog. Obviously we are lovers. Once I saw O'Leary, from the Highway Commission, he nodded and said a brisk hello to me, ignored my friend; obviously we are lovers, anyone could tell. We walked out in the daylight, looking for you. That day, feverish and aching, we were going to tell you everything. He was going to tell his wife everything. But nothing happened . . . we ended up in a cocktail lounge, we calmed down. The air conditioning calmed us. On the street we passed a Negro holding out pamphlets to other Negroes but drawing them back when whites passed. I saw the headline—*Muslim Killed in Miami Beach by Fascist Police.* A well-dressed Negro woman turned down a pamphlet with a toothy, amused smile—none of that junk for her! My love didn't even notice.

Because he is not my husband I don't worry about him. I worry about my own husband, whom I own. I don't own this man. I am thirty and he is forty-one; to him I am young—what a laugh. I don't worry about his coughing, his drinking (sometimes over the telephone I can hear ice cubes tinkling in a glass—he drinks to get the courage to call me), his loss of weight, his professional standing. He didn't return to his job in Boston, but stayed on here. A strange move. The department at Michigan considered it a coup to get him, this disintegrating, arrogant man, they were willing to pay him well, a man who has already made enemies there. No, I don't worry about him.

On a television program he was moody and verbose, moody and silent by turns. Smokes too much. Someone asked him about the effect of something on something—Vietnam on the presidential election, I think—and he missed subtleties, he sounded distant, vague. Has lost passion for the truth. He has lost his passion for politics, discovering in himself a passion for me. It isn't my fault.

On the street he doesn't notice things, he smiles slowly at me, complimenting me, someone brushes against him and he doesn't notice, what am I doing to this man? Lying in his arms I am inspired to hurt him. I say that we will have to give this up, these meetings; too much risk, shame. What about my husband, what about his wife? (A deliberate insult—I know he doesn't love his wife.) I can see at once that I've hurt him, his face shows everything, and as soon as this registers in both of us I am stunned with the injustice of what I've done to him, I must erase it, cancel it out, undo it; I caress his body in desperation. . . . Again and again. A pattern. What do I know about caressing the bodies of men? I've known only two men in my life. My husband and his successor. I have never wanted to love anyone, the strain and risk are too great, yet I have fallen in love for the second time in my life and this time the sensation is terrifying, bitter, violent. It ends the first cycle, supplants all that love, erases all that affection— destroys everything. I stand back dazed, flat on my heels, the dance being over. I will not move on into another marriage. I will die slowly in this marriage rather than come to life in another.

Dear Mrs. Katz,

I received your letter of October 25 and I can only say

I don't know how to begin this letter except to tell you

Your letter is here on my desk. I've read it over again and again all morning. It is true, yes, that I have made the acquaintance of a man who is evidently your husband, though he has not spoken of you. We met through mutual friends in Ann Arbor and Detroit. Your informant at the University is obviously trying to upset you, for her own reasons. I assume it is a woman—who else would write you such a letter? I know nothing of your personal affairs. Your husband and I have only met a few times, socially. What do you want from me?

And your daughter, tell your daughter to let me alone!

Thank you both for thinking of me. I wish I could be equal to your hatred. But the other day an old associate of my husband's, a bitch of a man, ran into me in the Fisher lobby and said, "What's happened to you—you look terrible! You've lost weight!" He pinched the waist of my dress, drawing it out to show how it hung loose on me, he kept marveling over how thin I am, not releasing me. A balding, pink-faced son of a bitch who has made himself rich by being on the board of supervisors for a country north of here, stuffing himself at the trough. I know all about him. A subpolitician, never elected. But I trust the eyes of these submen, their hot keen perception. Nothing escapes them. "One month ago," he said, "you were a beautiful woman." Nothing in my life has hurt me as much as that remark, *One month ago you were a beautiful woman.* . . .

Were you ever beautiful? He says not. So he used you, he used you up. That isn't my fault. You say in your letter—thank you for typing it, by the way—that I could never understand your husband, his background of mental instability, his weaknesses, his penchant (your word) for blaming other people for his own faults. Why tell me this? He isn't going to be my husband. I have a husband.

Why should I betray my husband for yours, your nervous, guilty, hypochondriac husband? The first evening we met, believe it or not, he told me about his *hurts*—people who've hurt him deeply! "The higher you go in a career, the more people take after you, wanting to bring you down," he told me. And listen: "The worst hurt of my life was when my first book came out, and an old professor of mine, a man I had idolized at Columbia, reviewed it. He began by saying, *Bombarded as we are by prophecies in the guise of serious historical research . . .* and my heart was broken." We were at a party but apart from the other people, we ate, he drank, we played a game with each other that made my pulse leap, and certainly my pulse leaped to hear a man, a stranger, speak of his heart being broken—where I come from men don't talk like that! I told him a *hurt* of my own, which I've never told anyone before: "The first time my mother saw my husband, she took me aside and said, *Can't you tell him to stand up straighter?* and my heart was broken. . . ."

And so, with those words, I had already committed adultery, betraying my husband to a stranger.

Does he call you every night? I am jealous of those telephone calls. What if he changes his mind and returns to you, what then? When he went to the Chicago convention I'm sure he telephoned you constantly (he telephoned me only three times, the bastard) and joked to you about his fear of going out into the street. "Jesus, what if somebody smashes in my head, there goes my next book!" he said over the phone, but he wasn't kidding me. I began to cry, imagining him beaten up, bloody, far away from me. Why does he joke like that? Does he joke like that with you?

Dear Mother and Father,

My husband Greg is busy with _____. Doing well. Not fired. Pressure on, pressure off. Played golf with _____. I went to a new doctor yesterday, a woman. I had made an appointment to go to a man but lost my courage, didn't show up. Better a woman. She examined me, she looked at me critically and said, "Why are you trying to starve yourself?" *To keep myself from feeling love, from feeling lust, from feeling anything at all.* I told her I didn't know I was starving myself. I had no appetite. Food sickened me . . . how could I eat? She gave me a vitamin shot that burned me, like fire. Things good for you burn like fire, shot up into you, no escape. You would not like my lover, you would take me aside and say, *Jews are very brilliant and talented, yes, but. . . .*

I am surviving at half-tempo. A crippled waltz tempo. It is only my faith in the flimsiness of love that keeps me going—I know this will end. I've been waiting for it to end since April, having faith. Love can't last. Even lust can't last. I loved my husband and now I do not love him, we never sleep together, that's through. Since he isn't likely to tell you that, I will.

Lloyd Burt came to see my husband the other day, downtown. Eleven in the morning and already drunk. His kid had been stopped in Grosse Pointe, speeding. The girl with him knocked out on pills. *He* had no pills on him, luckily. Do you remember Lloyd? Do you remember any of us? I am your daughter. Do you regret having had a daughter? I do not regret having no children, not now. Children, more children, children upon children, protoplasm upon protoplasm. . . . Once I thought I couldn't bear to live without having children, now I can't bear to live at all. I must be the wife of a man I can't have, I don't even want children from him. I sit here in my room with my head and body aching with a lust that has become metaphysical and skeptical and bitter, living on month after month, cells dividing and heating endlessly. I don't regret having no children. I don't thank you for having me. No gratitude in me, nothing. No, I feel no gratitude. I can't feel gratitude.

My dear husband,

I want to tell you everything. I am in a motel room, I've just taken a bath. How can I keep a straight face telling you this? Sat in the bathtub for an hour, not awake, not asleep, the water was very hot. . . .

I seem to want to tell you something else, about Sally Rodgers. I am light-headed, don't be impatient. I met Sally at the airport this afternoon, she was going to New York, and she saw me with a man, a stranger to her, the man who is the topic of this letter, the crucial reason for this letter. . . . Sally came right up to me and started talking, exclaiming about her bad fortune, her car had been stolen last week! Then, when she and a friend took her boat out of the yacht club and docked it at a restaurant on the Detroit River, she forgot to take the keys out and someone stole her boat! Twenty thousand dollars' worth of boat, a parting gift from her ex-husband, pirated away down-river. She wore silver eye-lids, silver stockings, attracting attention not from men but from small children, who stared. My friend, my lover, did not approve of her—her clanking jewelry made his eye twitch.

I am thirty miles from Detroit. In Detroit the multiplication of things is too brutal, I think it broke me down. Weak, thin, selfish, a wreck, I have become oblivious to the deaths of other people. (Robert Kennedy was murdered since I became this man's mistress, but I had no time to think of him—I put the thought of his death aside, to think of later. No time now.) Leaving him and walking in Detroit, downtown, on those days we met to make love, I began to understand what love is. Holding a man between my thighs, my knees, in my arms, one single man out of all this multiplication of men, this confusion, this din of human beings. So it is we choose someone. Someone chooses us. I admit that if he did not love me so much I couldn't love him. It would pass. But a woman has no choice, let a man love her and she must love him, if the man is strong enough. I stopped loving you, I am a criminal. . . . I see myself sinking again and again beneath his body, those heavy shoulders with tufts of dark hair on them, again and again pressing my mouth against his, wanting something from him, betraying you, giving myself up to that throbbing that arises out of my heartbeat and builds to madness and then subsides again, slowly, to become my ordinary heartbeat again, the heartbeat of an ordinary body from which divinity has fled.

Flesh with an insatiable soul. . . .

You would hear in a few weeks, through your innumerable far-flung cronies, that my lover's daughter almost died of aspirin poison, a ten-year-old girl with an I.Q. of about 200. But she didn't die. She took aspirin because her father was leaving her, divorcing her mother. The only gratitude I can feel is for her not having died. . . . My lover, whom you hardly know (he's the man of whom you said that evening, "He certainly can talk!") telephoned me to give me this news, weeping over the phone. A man weeping. A man weeping turns a woman's heart to stone. I told him I would drive out at once, I'd take him to the airport. He had to catch the first plane home and would be on stand-by at the airport. So I drove to Ann Arbor to get him. I felt that we were already married and that passion had raced through us and left us years ago, as soon as I saw him lumbering to the car, a man who has lost weight in the last few months but who carries himself a little clumsily, out of absent-mindedness. He wore a dark suit, rumpled. His necktie pulled away from his throat. A father distraught over his daughter belongs to mythology. . . .

Like married people, like conspirators, like characters in a difficult scene hurrying their lines, uncertain of the meaning of lines . . . "It's very thoughtful of you to do this," he said, and I said, "What else can I do for you? Make telephone calls? Anything?" *Should I go along with you?* So I drive him to the airport. I let him out at the curb, he hesitates, not wanting to go without me. He says, "But aren't you coming in . . . ?" and I see fear in his face. I tell him yes, yes, but I must park the car. This man, so abrupt and insulting in his profession, a master of whining rhetoric, stares at me in bewilderment as if he cannot remember why I have brought him here to let him out at the United Air Lines terminal, why I am eager to drive away. "I can't park here," I tell him sanely, "I'll get a ticket." He respects all minor law; he nods and backs away. It takes me ten minutes to find a parking place. All this time I am sweating in the late October heat, thinking that his daughter is going to win after all, has already won. Shouldn't I just drive home and leave him, put an end to it? A bottle of aspirin was all it took. The tears I might almost shed are not tears of shame or regret but tears of anger—that child has taken my lover from me. That child! I don't cry, I don't allow myself to cry, I drive all the way through a parking lot without finding a place and say to the girl at the booth, who puts her hand out expecting a dime, "But I couldn't find a place! I've driven right through! This isn't fair!" Seeing my hysteria, she relents, opens the gate, lets me through. *Once a beautiful woman*, she is thinking. I try another parking lot.

Inside the terminal, a moment of panic—what if he has already left? Then he hurries to me. I take his arm. He squeezes my hand. Both of us very nervous, agitated. "They told me I can probably make the two-fifteen, can you wait with me?" he says. His face, now so pale, is a handsome man's face gone out of control; a pity to look upon it. In a rush I feel my old love for him, hopeless. I begin to cry. Silently, almost without tears. A girl in a very short skirt passes us with a smile—lovers, at their age! "You're not to blame," he says, very nervous, "she's just a child and didn't know what she was doing—please don't blame yourself!

It's my fault—" But a child tried to commit suicide, shouldn't someone cry? I am to blame. She is hurting me across the country. I have tried to expel her from life and she, the baby, the embryo, stirs with a will of her own and chooses death calmly. . . . "But she's going to recover," I say to him for the twentieth time, "isn't she? You're sure of that?" He reassures me. We walk.

The airport is a small city. Outside the plate glass, airplanes rise and sink without effort. Great sucking vacuums of power, enormous wings, windows brilliant with sunlight. We look on unamazed. To us these airplanes are un-spectacular. We walk around the little city, walking fast and then slowing down, wandering, holding hands. It is during one of those strange lucky moments that lovers have—he lighting a cigarette—that Sally comes up to us. We are not holding hands at that moment. She talks, bright with attention for my friend, she herself being divorced and not equipped to live without a man. He smiles nervously, ignoring her, watching people hurry by with their luggage. She leaves. We glance at each other, understanding each other. Nothing to say. *My darling! . . .*

Time does not move quickly. I am sweating again, I hope he won't notice, he is staring at me in that way . . . the way that frightens me. I am not equal to your love, I want to tell him. Not equal, not strong enough. I am ashamed. Better for us to say good-by. A child's corpse between us? A few hundred miles away, in Boston, are a woman and a child I have wronged, quite intentionally; aren't these people real? But he stares at me, the magazine covers on a newsstand blur and wink, I feel that everything is becoming a dream and I must get out of here, must escape from him, before it is too late. . . . "I should leave," I tell him. He seems not to hear. He is sick. Not sick; frightened. He shows too much. He takes my hand, caresses it, pleading in silence. A terrible sensation of desire rises in me, suprising me. I don't want to feel desire for him! I don't want to feel it for anyone, I don't want to feel anything at all! I don't want to be drawn to an act of love, or even to think about it; I want freedom, I want the smooth sterility of coins worn out from friendly handling, rubbing together, I want to say good-by to love at the age of thirty, not being strong enough for it. A woman in the act of love feels no joy but only terror, a parody of labor, giving birth. Torture. Heartbeat racing at 160, 180 beats a minute, where is joy in this, what is this deception, this joke. Isn't the body itself a joke?

He leads me somewhere, along a corridor. Doesn't know where he is going. People head toward us with suitcases. A soldier on leave from Vietnam, we don't notice, a Negro woman weeping over another soldier, obviously her son, my lover does not see. A man brushes against me and with exaggerated fear I jump to my lover's side . . . but the man keeps on walking, it is nothing. My lover strokes my damp hand. "You won't. . . . You're not thinking of. . . . What are you thinking of?" he whispers. Everything is open in him, everything. He is not ashamed of the words he says, of his fear, his pleading. No irony in him, this ironic man. And I can hear myself saying that we must put an end to this, it's driving us both crazy and there in no future, nothing ahead of us, but I don't say these words or anything like them. We walk along. I am stunned. I feel a heavy, ugly desire for him, for his body. I want him as I've wanted him many times before, when our lives seemed simpler, when we were both deluded about what we were doing . . . both of us thought, in the beginning, that no one would care if we fell in love . . . not my husband, not his family. I don't know why. Now I want to say good-by to him but nothing comes out, nothing. I am still crying a little. It is not a weapon of mine—it is an admission of defeat. I am not a woman who cries well. Crying is a confession of failure, a giving in. I tell him no, I am not thinking of anything, only of him. I love him. I am not thinking of anything else.

We find ourselves by Gate 10. What meaning has Gate 10 to us? People are lingering by it, obviously a plane has just taken off, a stewardess is shuffling papers together, everything is normal. I sense normality and am drawn to it. We wander on. We come to a doorway, a door held open by a large block of wood. Where does that lead to? A stairway. The stairway is evidently not open. We can see that it leads up to another level, a kind of runway, and though it is not open he takes my hand and leads me to the stairs. In a delirium I follow him, why not? The airport is so crowded that we are alone and anonymous. He kicks the block of wood away, wisely. We are alone. On this stairway—which smells of disinfectant and yet is not very clean—my lover embraces me eagerly, wildly, he kisses me, kisses my damp cheeks, rubs his face against mine. I half-fall, half-sit on the stairs. He begins to groan, or to weep. He presses his face against me, against my breasts, my body. It is like wartime—a battle is going on outside, in the corridor. Hundreds of people! A world of people jostling one another! Here, in a dim stairway, clutching each other, we are oblivious to their deaths. But I want to be good! What have I wanted in my life except to be good? To lead a simple, good, intelligent life? He kisses my knees, my thighs, my stomach. I embrace him against me. Everything has gone wild, I am seared with the desire to be unfaithful to a husband who no longer exists, nothing else matters except this act of unfaithfulness. I feel that I am a character in a story, a plot, who has not understood until now exactly what is going to happen to her. Selfish, eager, we come together and do not breathe, we are good friends and anxious to help each other, I am particularly anxious to help him, my soul is sweated out of me in those two or three minutes that we cling together in love. Then, moving from me, so quickly exhausted, he puts his hands to his face and seems to weep without tears, while I feel my eyelids closing slowly upon the mangled length of my body. . . .

This is a confession but part of it is blacked out. Minutes pass in silence, mysteriously. It is those few minutes that pass after we make love that are most mysterious to me, uncanny. And then we cling to each other again, like people too weak to stand by ourselves; we are sick in our limbs but warm with affection, very good friends, the kind of friends who tell each other only good news. He helps me to my feet. We laugh. Laughter weakens me, he has to hold me, I put my arms firmly around his neck and we kiss, I am ready to give up all my life for him, just to hold him like this. My body is all flesh. There is nothing empty about us, only a close space, what appears to be a stairway in some public place. . . . He draws my hair back from my face, he stares at me. It is obvious that he loves me.

When we return to the public corridor no one has missed us. It is strangely late, after three. This is a surprise, I am really surprised, but my lover is more businesslike and simply asks at the desk—the next plane? to Boston? what chance of his getting on? His skin is almost ruddy with pleasure. I can see what pleasure does to a man. But now I must say good-by, I must leave. He holds my hand. I linger. We talk seriously and quietly in the middle of the great crowded floor about his plans—he will stay in Boston as long as he must, until things are settled; he will see his lawyer; he will talk it over, *talk it over*, with his wife and his daughter, he will not leave until they understand why he has to leave. . . . I want to cry out at him, *Should you come back?* but I can't say anything. Everything in me is a curving to submission, in spite of what you, my husband, have always thought.

Finally . . . he boards a plane at four. I watch him leave. He looks back at me, I wave, the plane taxis out onto the runway and rises . . . no accident, no violent ending. There is nothing violent about us, everything is natural and gentle. Walking along the long corridor I bump into someone, a woman my own age. I am suddenly dizzy. She says, "Are you all right?" I turn away, ashamed. I am on fire! My body is on fire! I feel his semen stirring in my loins, that rush of heat that always makes me pause, staring into the sky or at a wall, at something blank to mirror the blankness in my mind . . . stunned, I feel myself so heavily a body, so lethargic with the aftermath of passion. How did I hope to turn myself into a statue, into the constancy of a soul? No hope. The throbbing in my loins has not yet resolved itself into the throbbing of my heart. A woman does not forget so quickly, nothing lets her forget. I am transparent with heat. I walk on, feeling my heart pound weakly, feeling the moisture between my legs, wondering if I will ever get home. My vision seems blotched. The air—air conditioning—is humming, unreal. It is not alien to me but a part of my own confusion, a long expulsion of my own breath. What do I look like making love? Is my face distorted, am I ugly? Does he see me? Does he judge? Or does he see nothing but beauty, transported in love as I am, helpless?

I can't find the car. Which parking lot? The sun is burning. A man watches me, studies me. I walk fast to show that I know what I'm doing. And if the car is missing, stolen . . . ? I search through my purse, noting how the lining is soiled, ripped. Fifty thousand dollars in the bank and no children and I can't get around to buying a new purse; everything is soiled, ripped, worn out . . . the keys are missing . . . only wadded tissue, a sweetish smell, liquid stiffening on the tissue . . . everything hypnotized me. . . . I find the keys, my vision swims, I will never get home.

My knees are trembling. There is an ocean of cars here at Metropolitan Airport. Families stride happily to cars, get in, drive away. I wander around, staring.

I must find my husband's car in order to get home. . . . I check in my purse again, panicked. No, I haven't lost the keys. I take the keys out of my purse to look at them. The key to the ignition, to the trunk, to the front door of the house. All there. I look around slyly and see, or think I see, a man watching me. He moves behind a car. He is walking away. My body still throbs from the love of another man, I can't concentrate on a stranger, I lose interest and forget what I am afraid of. . . .

The heat gets worse. Thirty, forty, forty-five minutes pass . . . I have given up looking for the car . . . I am not lost, I am still heading home in my imagination, but I have given up looking for the car. I turn terror into logic. I ascend the stairway to the wire-guarded overpass that leads back to the terminal, walking sensibly, and keep on walking until I come to one of the airport motels. I ask them for a room. A single. Why not? Before I can go home I must bathe, I must get the odor of this man out of me, I must clean myself. I take a room, I close the door to the room behind me; alone, I go to the bathroom and run a tubful of water. . . .

And if he doesn't call me from Boston then all is finished, at an end. What good luck, to be free again and alone, the way I am alone in this marvelous empty motel room! the way I am alone in this bathtub, cleansing myself of him, of every cell of him!

My darling,
You have made me so happy. . . .

Toni Cade Bambara 1939–1995

Toni Cade, who added "Bambara" after finding it in the sketchbook of her great-grandmother's trunk, has worked as a social worker, professor, writing instructor, dancer, critic, and activist. Growing up in Harlem, Queens, and Jersey City, Bambara was exposed to black oral tradition, which she dubbed "Our Great Kitchen Tradition." She went on to uphold African-American communal tradition and "our high standards governing the rap." In 1970, she edited and contributed to an early and pivotal collection of feminist writing, *The Black Woman*. A year later she edited a second anthology, *Tales and Stories for Black Folks*, which, in addition to contributions from Langston Hughes, Alice Walker, and Ernest Gaines, contained stories from her Livingston College first-year composition students and her favorite "subversive" black fairy tales. Two representative short-story collections, *Gorilla My Love* (1972) and *The Sea Birds Are Still Alive* (1977), describe racial, sexual, and economic inequality, as well as black women's political conflicts among themselves and in the male-dominated nuclear family. In 1981, Bambara wrote the introduction for *This Bridge Called My Back*, a groundbreaking anthology edited by Chicana writers and theorists. With regard to her writing and that of women of color, Bambara claims that the motive behind the work is to "make revolution irresistible." Until her death in Philadelphia, she remained intensely involved as an activist in community media.

THE LESSON

Back in the days when everyone was old and stupid or young and foolish and me and Sugar were the only ones just right, this lady moved on our block with nappy hair and proper speech and no makeup. And quite naturally we laughed at her, laughed the way we did at the junk man who went about his business like he was some big-time president and his sorry-ass horse his secretary. And we kinda hated her too, hated the way we did the winos who cluttered up our parks and pissed on our handball walls and stank up our hallways and stairs so you couldn't halfway play hide-and-seek without a goddamn gas mask. Miss Moore was her name. The only woman on the block with no first name. And she was black as hell, cept for her feet, which were fish-white and spooky. And she was always planning these boring-ass things for us to do, us being my cousin, mostly, who lived on the block cause we all moved North the same time and to the same apartment then spread out gradual to breathe. And our parents would yank our heads into some kinda shape and crisp up our clothes so we'd be presentable for travel with Miss Moore, who always looked like she was going to church, though she never did. Which is just one of the things the grownups talked about when they talked behind her back like a dog. But when she came calling with some sachet she'd sewed up or some gingerbread she'd made or some book, why then they'd all be too embarrassed to turn her down and we'd get handed over all spruced up. She'd been to college and said it was only right that she should take responsibility for the younger ones' education, and she not even related by marriage or blood. So they'd go for it. Specially Aunt Gretchen. She was the main gofer in the family. You got some ole dumb shit foolishness you want somebody to go for, you send for Aunt Gretchen. She been screwed into the go-along for so long, it's a blood-deep natural thing with her. Which is how she got saddled with me and Sugar and Junior in the first place while our mothers were in a la-de-da apartment up the block having a good ole time.

So this one day Miss Moore rounds us all up at the mailbox and it's puredee hot and she's knockin herself out about arithmetic. And school suppose to let up in summer I heard, but she don't never let up. And the starch in my pinafore scratching the shit outta me and I'm really hating this nappy-head bitch and her goddamn college degree. I'd much rather go to the pool or to the show where it's cool. So me and Sugar leaning on the mailbox being surly, which is a Miss

Moore word. And Flyboy checking out what everybody brought for lunch. And Fat Butt already wasting his peanut-butter-and-jelly sandwich like the pig he is. And Junebug punching on Q.T.'s arm for potato chips. And Rosie Giraffe shifting from one hip to the other waiting for somebody to step on her foot or ask her if she from Georgia so she can kick ass, preferably Mercedes'. And Miss Moore asking us do we know what money is, like we a bunch of retards. I mean real money, she say, like it's only poker chips or monopoly papers we lay on the grocer. So right away I'm tired of this and say so. And would much rather snatch Sugar and go to the Sunset and terrorize the West Indian kids and take their hair ribbons and their money too. And Miss Moore files that remark away for next week's lesson on brotherhood, I can tell. And finally I say we oughta get to the subway cause it's cooler and besides we might meet some cute boys. Sugar done swiped her mama's lipstick, so we ready.

So we heading down the street and she's boring us silly about what things cost and what our parents make and how much goes for rent and how money ain't divided up right in this country. And then she gets to the part about we all poor and live in the slums, which I don't feature. And I'm ready to speak on that, but she steps out in the street and hails two cabs just like that. Then she hustles half the crew in with her and hands me a five-dollar bill and tells me to calculate 10 percent tip for the driver. And we're off. Me and Sugar and Junebug and Flyboy hangin out the window and hollering to everybody, putting lipstick on each other cause Flyboy a faggot anyway, and making farts with our sweaty armpits. But I'm mostly trying to figure how to spend this money. But they all fascinated with the meter ticking and Junebug starts laying bets as to how much it'll read when Flyboy can't hold his breath no more. Then Sugar lays bets as to how much it'll be when we get there. So I'm stuck. Don't nobody want to go for my plan, which is to jump out at the next light and run off to the first bar-b-que we can find. Then the driver tells us to get the hell out cause we there already. And the meter reads eight-five cents. And I'm stalling to figure out the tip and Sugar say give him a dime. And I decide he don't need it bad as I do, so later for him. But then he tries to take off with Junebug still in the door so we talk about his mama something ferocious. Then we check out that we on Fifth Avenue and everybody dressed up in stockings. One lady in a fur coat, hot as it is. White folks crazy.

"This is the place," Miss Moore say, presenting it to us in the voice she uses at the museum. "Let's look in the windows before we go in."

"Can we steal?" Sugar asks very serious like she's getting the ground rules squared away before she plays. "I beg your pardon," say Miss Moore, and we fall out. So she leads us around the windows of the toy store and me and Sugar screamin, "This is mine, that's mine, I gotta have that, that was made for me, I was born for that," till Big Butt drowns us out.

"Hey, I'm going to buy that there."

"That there? You don't even know what it is, stupid."

"I do so," he say punchin on Rosie Giraffe. "It's a microscope."

"Whatcha gonna do with a microscope, fool?"

"Look at things."

"Like what, Ronald?" asks Miss Moore. And Big Butt ain't got the first no-tion. So here go Miss Moore gabbing about the thousands of bacteria in a drop of water and the somethinorother in a speck of blood and the million and one living things in the air around us is invisible to the naked eye. And what she say that for? Junebug go to town on that "naked" and we rolling. Then Miss Moore ask what it cost. So we all jam into the window smudgin it up and the price tag say $300. So then she ask how long'd take for Big Butt and Junebug to save up their allowances. "Too long," I say. "Yeh," adds Sugar, "outgrown it by that time." And Miss Moore say no, you never outgrow learning instruments. "Why, even medical students and interns and," blah, blah, blah. And we ready to choke Big Butt for bringing it up in the first damn place.

"This here costs four hundred eighty dollars," say Rosie Giraffe. So we pile up all over her to see what she pointin out. My eyes tell me it's a chunk of glass cracked with something heavy, and different-color inks dripped into the splits, then the whole thing put into a oven or something. But for $480 it don't make sense.

"That's a paperweight made of semi-precious stones fused together under tremendous pressure," she explains slowly, with her hands doing the mining and all the factory work.

"So what's a paperweight?" asks Rosie Giraffe.

"To weigh paper with, dumbbell," say Flyboy, the wise man from the East.

"Not exactly," say Miss Moore, which is what she say when you warm or way off too. "It's to weigh paper down so it won't scatter and make your desk un-tidy." So right away me and Sugar curtsey to each other and then to Mercedes who is more the tidy type.

"We don't keep paper on top of the desk in my class," say Junebug, figuring Miss Moore crazy or lyin one.

"At home, then," she say. "Don't you have a calendar and a pencil case and a blotter and a letter-opener on your desk at home where you do your home-work?" And she knew damn well what our homes look like cause she nosys around in them every chance she gets.

"I don't even have a desk," say Junebug. "Do we?"

"No. And I don't get no homework neither," say Big Butt.

"And I don't even have a home," say Flyboy like he do at school to keep the white folks off his back and sorry for him. Send this poor kid to camp posters, is his specialty.

"I do," says Mercedes. "I have a box of stationery on my desk and a picture of my cat. My godmother bought the stationery and the desk. There's a big rose on each sheet and the envelopes smell like roses."

"Who wants to know about your smelly-ass stationery," say Rosie Giraffe fore I can get my two cents in.

"It's important to have a work area all your own so that. . . "

"Will you look at this sailboat, please," say Flyboy, cuttin her off and pointin to the thing like it was his. So once again we tumble all over each other to gaze at this magnificent thing in the toy store which is just big enough to maybe sail two kittens across the pond if you strap them to the posts tight. We all start reciting the price like we in assembly. "Handcrafted sailboat of fiberglass at one thousand one hundred ninety-five dollars."

"Unbelievable," I hear myself say and am really stunned. I read it again for myself just in case the group recitation put me in a trance. Same thing. For some reason this pisses me off. We look at Miss Moore and she lookin at us, waiting for I dunno what.

Who'd pay all that when you can buy a sailboat set for a quarter at Pop's, a tube of glue for a dime, and a ball of string for eight cents? It must have a motor and a whole lot else besides, I say. "My sailboat cost me about fifty cents."

"But will it take water?" say Mercedes with her smart ass.

"Took mine to Alley Pond Park once," say Flyboy. "String broke. Lost it. Pity."

"Sailed mine in Central Park and it keeled over and sank. Had to ask my father for another dollar."

"And you got the strap," laughs Big Butt. "The jerk didn't even have a string on it. My old man wailed on his behind."

Little Q.T. was staring hard at the sailboat and you could see he wanted it bad. But he too little and somebody'd just take it from him. So what the hell. "This boat for kids, Miss Moore?"

"Parents silly to buy something like that just to get all broke up," say Rosie Giraffe.

"That much money it should last forever," I figure.

"My father'd buy it for me if I wanted it."

"Your father, my ass," say Rosie Giraffe getting a chance to finally push Mercedes.

"Must be rich people shop here," say Q.T.

"You are a very bright boy," say Flyboy. "What was your first clue?" And he rap him on the head with the back of his knuckles, since Q.T. the only one he could get away with. Though Q.T. liable to come up behind you years later and get his licks in when you half expect it.

"What I want to know is," I says to Miss Moore though I never talk to her, I wouldn't give the bitch that satisfaction, "is how much a real boat costs? I figure a thousand'd get you a yacht any day."

"Why don't you check that out," she says, "and report back to the group?" Which really pains my ass. If you gonna mess up a perfect good swim day least you could do is have some answers. "Let's go in," she say like she got something up her sleeve. Only she don't lead the way. So me and Sugar turn the corner to where the entrance is, but when we get there I kinda hang back. Not that I'm scared, what's there to be afraid of, just a toy store. But I feel funny, shame. But what I got to be shamed about? Got as much right to go in as anybody. But somehow I can't seem to get hold of the door, so I step away from Sugar to lead. But she hangs back too. And I look at her and she looks at me and this is ridiculous. I mean, damn, I have never ever been shy about doing nothing or going nowhere. But then Mercedes steps up and then Rosie Giraffe and Big Butt crowd in behind and shove, and next thing we all stuffed into the doorway with only Mercedes squeezing past us, smoothing out her jumper and walking right down the aisle. Then the rest of us tumble in like a glued-together jigsaw done all wrong. And people lookin at us. And it like the time me and Sugar crashed into the Catholic church on a dare. But once we got in there and everything so hushed and holy and the candles and the bowin and the handkerchiefs on all the drooping heads, I just couldn't go through with the plan. Which was for me to run up to the altar and do a tap dance while Sugar played the nose flute and messed around in the holy water. And Sugar kept giving me the elbow. Then later teased me so bad I tied her up in the shower and turned it on and locked her in. And she'd be there till this day if Aunt Gretchen hadn't finally figured I was lying about the boarder takin a shower.

Same thing in the store. We all walkin on tiptoe and hardly touchin the games and puzzles and things. And I watched Miss Moore who is steady watchin us like she waitin for a sign. Like Mama Drewery watches the sky and sniffs the air and takes note of just how much slant is in the bird formation. Then me and Sugar bump smack into each other, so busy gazing at the toys, 'specially the sailboat. But we don't laugh and go into our fat-lady bump-stomach routine. We just stare at that price tag. Then Sugar run a finger over the whole boat. And I'm jealous and want to hit her. Maybe not her, but I sure want to punch somebody in the mouth.

"Watcha bring us here for, Miss Moore?"

"You sound angry, Sylvia. Are you mad about something?" Givin me one of them grins like she telling a grown-up joke that never turns out to be funny. And she's lookin very closely at me like maybe she plannin to do my portrait from memory. I'm mad, but I won't give her that satisfaction. So I slouch around the store bein very bored and say, "Let's go."

Me and Sugar at the back of the train watchin the tracks whizzin by large then small then getting gobbled up in the dark. I'm thinkin about this tricky toy I saw in the store. A clown that somersaults on a bar then does chin-ups just cause you yank lightly at his leg. Cost $35. I could see me askin my mother for a $35 birthday clown. "You wanna who that costs what?" she'd say, cocking her head to the side to get a better view of the hole in my head. Thirty-five dollars could buy new bunk beds for Junior and Gretchen's boy. Thirty-five dollars and the whole household could go visit Granddaddy Nelson in the country. Thirty-five dollars would pay for the rent and the piano bill too. Who are these people that spend that much for performing clowns and $1000 for toy sailboats? What kinda work they do and how they live and how come we ain't in on it? Where we are is who we are, Miss Moore always pointin out. But it don't necessarily have to be that way, she always adds then waits for somebody to say that poor people have to wake up and demand their share of the pie and don't none of us know what kind of pie she talking about in the first damn place. But she ain't so smart cause I still got her four dollars from the taxi and she sure ain't gettin it. Messin up my day with this shit. Sugar nudges me in my pocket and winks.

Miss Moore lines us up in front of the mailbox where we started from, seem like years ago, and I got a headache for thinkin so hard. And we lean all over each other so we can hold up under the draggy-ass lecture she always finishes us off with at the end before we thank her for borin us to tears. But she just looks at us like she readin tea leaves. Finally she say, "Well, what did you think of F.A.O. Schwartz?"

Rosie Giraffe mumbles, "White folks crazy."

"I'd like to go there again when I get my birthday money," says Mercedes, and we shove her out the pack so she has to lean on the mailbox by herself.

"I'd like a shower. Tiring day," say Flyboy.

Then Sugar surprises me by sayin, "You know, Miss Moore, I don't think all of us here put together eat in a year what that sailboat costs." And Miss Moore lights up like somebody goosed her. "And?" she say, urging Sugar on. Only I'm standin on her foot so she don't continue.

"Imagine for a minute what kind of society it is in which some people can spend on a toy what it would cost to feed a family of six or seven. What do you think?"

"I think," say Sugar pushing me off her feet like she never done before, cause I whip her ass in a minute, "that this is not much of a democracy if you ask me. Equal chance to pursue happiness means an equal crack at the dough, don't it?" Miss Moore is besides herself and I am disgusted with Sugar's treachery. So I stand on her foot one more time to see if she'll shove me. She shuts up, and Miss Moore looks at me, sorrowfully I'm thinkin. And something weird is goin on, I can feel it in my chest.

"Anybody else learn anything today?" lookin dead at me. I walk away and Sugar has to run to catch up and don't even seem to notice when I shrug her arm off my shoulder.

"Well, we got four dollars anyway," she says.

"Uh-hunh."

"We could go to Hascombs and get half a chocolate layer and then go to the Sunset and still have plenty money for potato chips and ice cream sodas."

"Uh hunh."

"Race you to Hascombs," she say.

We start down the block and she gets ahead which is O.K. by me cause I'm goin to the West End and then over to the Drive to think this day through. She can run if she want to and even run faster. But ain't nobody gonna beat me at nuthin.

Margaret Atwood 1939–

Noted, prolific writer of poetry (including prose poems), criticism, novels, and short stories, Margaret Atwood frequently parallels the theme that she finds pivotal to life for all Canadians: survival. Raised in Ottawa, Ontario, Atwood graduated from the University of Toronto in 1962; it was then that she published her first book of poems, *Double Persephone*. She received a master's degree from Radcliffe College and continued literary studies at Harvard, publishing six volumes of poetry and two novels between 1966 and 1974. Many critics note Atwood's attempts in her poetry to reunite the "split self," to find a hidden self beyond the commercialism of modern life. In the novels *Surfacing* (1972), *Lady Oracle* (1976), and *Life Before Man* (1979), for instance, she also delineates characters who attempt to take control of their alienating surroundings in a search for personal integrity. Atwood's poetry and fiction provide what she has called "procedures for underground" (also a 1970 book title), where the underground refers to alternative ways of existing to those prescribed by a particular society.

RAPE FANTASIES

The way they're going on about it in the magazines you'd think it was just invented, and not only that but it's something terrific, like a vaccine for cancer. They put it in capital letters on the front cover, and inside they have these questionnaires like the ones they used to have about whether you were a good enough wife or an endomorph or an ectomorph, remember that? with the scoring upside down on page 73, and then these numbered do-it-yourself dealies, you know? RAPE, TEN THINGS TO DO ABOUT IT, like it was ten new hairdos or something. I mean, what's so new about it?

So at work they all have to talk about it because no matter what magazine you open, there it is, staring you right between the eyes, and they're beginning to have it on the television, too. Personally I'd prefer a June Allyson movie anytime but they don't make them any more and they don't even have them that much on the Late Show. For instance, day before yesterday, that would be Wednesday, thank god it's Friday as they say, we were sitting around in the women's lunch room—the *lunch* room, I mean you'd think you could get some peace and quiet in there—and Chrissy closes up the magazine she's been reading and says, "How about it girls, do you have rape fantasies?"

The four of us were having our game of bridge the way we always do, and I had a bare twelve points counting the singleton with not that much of a bid in anything. So I said one club, hoping Sondra would remember about the one club convention, because the time before when I used that she thought I really meant clubs and she bid us up to three, and all I had was four little ones with nothing higher than a six, and we went down two and on top of that we were vulnerable. She is not the world's best bridge player. I mean, neither am I but there's a limit.

Darlene passed but the damage was done, Sondra's head went round like it was on ball bearings and she said, "*What* fantasies?"

"Rape fantasies," Chrissy said. She's a receptionist and she looks like one; she's pretty but cool as a cucumber, like she's been painted all over with nail polish, if you know what I mean. Varnished. "It says here all women have rape fantasies."

"For Chrissake, I'm eating an egg sandwich," I said, "and I bid one club and Darlene passed."

"You mean, like some guy jumping you in an alley or something," Sondra said. She was eating her lunch, we all eat our lunches during the game, and she bit into a piece of that celery she always brings and started to chew away on it with this thoughtful expression in her eyes and I knew we might as well pack it in as far as the game was concerned.

"Yeah, sort of like that," Chrissy said. She was blushing a little, you could see it even under her makeup.

"I don't think you should go out alone at night," Darlene said, "you put yourself in a position," and I may have been mistaken but she was looking at me. She's the oldest, she's forty-one though you wouldn't know it and neither does she, but I looked it up in the employees' file. I like to guess a person's age and then look it up to see if I'm right. I let myself have an extra pack of cigarettes if I am, though I'm trying to cut down. I figure it's harmless as long as you don't tell. I mean, not everyone has access to that file, it's more or less confidential. But it's all right if I tell you, I don't expect you'll ever meet her, though you never know, it's a small world. Anyway.

"For *heaven's* sake, it's only *Toronto*," Greta said. She worked in Detroit for three years and she never lets you forget it, it's like she thinks she's a war hero or something, we should all admire her just for the fact that she's still walking this earth, though she was really living in Windsor the whole time, she just worked in Detroit. Which for me doesn't really count. It's where you sleep, right?

"Well, do you?" Chrissy said. She was obviously trying to tell us about hers but she wasn't about to go first, she's cautious, that one.

"I certainly don't," Darlene said, and she wrinkled up her nose, like this, and I had to laugh. "I think it's disgusting." She's divorced, I read that in the file too, she never talks about it. It must've been years ago anyway. She got up and went over to the coffee machine and turned her back on us as though she wasn't going to have anything more to do with it.

"Well," Greta said. I could see it was going to be between her and Chrissy. They're both blondes, I don't mean that in a bitchy way but they do try to out-dress each other. Greta would like to get out of Filing, she'd like to be a receptionist too so she could meet more people. You don't meet much of anyone in

Filing except other people in Filing. Me, I don't mind it so much, I have outside interests.

"Well," Greta said, "I sometimes think about, you know my apartment? It's got this little balcony, I like to sit out there in the summer and I have a few plants out there. I never bother that much about locking the door to the balcony, it's one of those sliding glass ones, I'm on the eighteenth floor for heaven's sake, I've got a good view of the lake and the CN Tower and all. But I'm sitting around one night in my housecoat, watching TV with my shoes off, you know how you do, and I see this guy's feet, coming down past the window, and the next thing you know he's standing on the balcony, he's let himself down by a rope with a hook on the end of it from the floor above, that's the nineteenth, and before I can even get up off the chesterfield he's inside the apartment. He's all dressed in black with black gloves on"—I knew right away what show she got the black gloves off because I saw the same one—"and then he, well, you know."

"You know what?" Chrissy said, but Greta said, "And afterwards he tells me that he goes all over the outside of the apartment building like that, from one floor to another, with his rope and his hook . . . and then he goes out to the balcony and tosses his rope, and he climbs up it and disappears."

"Just like Tarzan," I said, but nobody laughed.

"Is that all?" Chrissy said. "Don't you ever think about, well, I think about being in the bathtub, with no clothes on . . ."

"So who takes a bath in their clothes?" I said, you have to admit it's stupid when you come to think of it, but she just went on, ". . . with lots of bubbles, what I use is Vitabath, it's more expensive but it's so relaxing, and my hair pinned up, and the door opens and this fellow's standing there. . . ."

"How'd he get in?" Greta said.

"Oh, I don't know, through a window or something. Well, I can't very well get out of the bathtub, the bathroom's too small and besides he's blocking the doorway, so I just *lie* there, and he starts to very slowly take his own clothes off, and then he gets into the bathtub with me."

"Don't you scream or anything?" said Darlene. She'd come back with her cup of coffee, she was getting really interested. "I'd scream like bloody murder."

"Who'd hear me?" Chrissy said. "Besides, all the articles say it's better not to resist, that way you don't get hurt."

"Anyway you might get bubbles up your nose," I said, "from the deep breathing," and I swear all four of them looked at me like I was a bad taste, like I'd insulted the Virgin Mary or something. I mean, I don't see what's wrong with a little joke now and then. Life's too short, right?

"Listen," I said, "those aren't *rape* fantasies. I mean, you aren't getting *raped*, it's just some guy you haven't met formally who happens to be more attractive than Derek Cummins"—he's the Assistant Manager, he wears elevator shoes or at any rate they have these thick soles and he has this funny way of talking, we call him Derek Duck—"and you have a good time. Rape is when they've got a knife or something and you don't want to."

"So what about you, Estelle," Chrissy said, she was miffed because I laughed at her fantasy, she thought I was putting her down. Sondra was miffed too, by this time she'd finished her celery and she wanted to tell about hers, but she hadn't got in fast enough.

"All right, let me tell you one," I said, "I'm walking down this dark street at night and this fellow comes up and grabs my arm. Now it so happens that I have a plastic lemon in my purse, you know how it always says you should carry a plastic lemon in your purse? I don't really do it, I tried it once but the darn thing leaked all over my checkbook, but in this fantasy I have one, and I say to him, 'You're intending to rape me, right?' and he nods, so I open my purse to get the plastic lemon, and I can't find it! My purse is full of all this junk, Kleenex and cigarettes and my change purse and my lipstick and my driver's license, you know the kind of stuff; so I ask him to hold out his hands, like this, and I pile all this junk into them and down at the bottom there's the plastic lemon, and I can't get the top off. So I hand it to him and he's very obliging, he twists the top off and hands it back to me, and I squirt him in the eye."

I hope you don't think that's too vicious. Come to think of it, it is a bit mean, especially when he was so polite and all.

"*That's* your rape fantasy?" Chrissy says. "I don't believe it."

"She's a card," Darlene says, she and I are the ones that've been here the longest and she never will forget the time I got drunk at the office party and insisted I was going to dance under the table instead of on top of it, I did a sort of Cossack number but then I hit my head on the bottom of the table—actually it was a desk—when I went to get up, and I knocked myself out cold. She's decided that's the mark of an original mind and she tells everyone new about it and I'm not sure that's fair. Though I did do it.

"I'm being totally honest," I say. I always am and they know it. There's no point in being anything else, is the way I look at it, and sooner or later the truth will out so you might as well not waste the time, right? "You should hear the one about the Easy-Off Oven Cleaner."

But that was the end of the lunch hour, with one bridge game shot to hell, and the next day we spent most of the time arguing over whether to start a new game or play out the hands we had left over from the day before, so Sondra never did get a chance to tell about her rape fantasy.

It started me thinking though, about my own rape fantasies. Maybe I'm abnormal or something, I mean I have fantasies about handsome strangers coming in through the window too, like Mr. Clean, I wish one would, please god somebody without flat feet and big sweat marks on his shirt, and over five feet five, believe me being tall is a handicap though it's getting better, tall guys are starting to like someone whose nose reaches higher than their belly button. But if you're being totally honest you can't count those as rape fantasies. In a real rape fantasy, what you should feel is this anxiety, like when you think about your apartment building catching on fire and whether you should use the elevator or the stairs or maybe just stick your head under a wet towel, and you try to remember everything you've read about what to do but you can't decide.

For instance, I'm walking along this dark street at night and this short, ugly fellow comes up and grabs my arm, and not only is he ugly, you know, with a sort of puffy nothing face, like those fellows you have to talk to in the bank when your account's overdrawn—of course I don't mean they're all like that—but he's absolutely covered in pimples. So he gets me pinned against the wall, he's short but he's heavy, and he starts to undo himself and the zipper gets stuck. I mean, one of the most significant moments in a girl's life, it's almost like getting married or having a baby or something, and he sticks the zipper.

So I say, kind of disgusted, "Oh for Chrissake," and he starts to cry. He tells me he's never been able to get anything right in his entire life, and this is the last straw, he's going to go jump off a bridge.

"Look," I say, I feel so sorry for him, in my rape fantasies I always end up feeling sorry for the guy, I mean there has to be something *wrong* with them, if it was Clint Eastwood it'd be different but worse luck it never is. I was the kind of little girl who buried dead robins, know what I mean? It used to drive my mother nuts, she didn't like me touching them, because of the germs I guess. So I say, "Listen, I know how you feel. You really should do something about those pimples, if you got rid of them you'd be quite good looking, honest; then you wouldn't have to go around doing stuff like this. I had them myself once," I say, to comfort him, but in fact I did, and it ends up I give him the name of my old dermatologist, the one I had in high school, that was back in Leamington, except I used to go to St. Catharines for the dermatologist. I'm telling you, I was really lonely when I first came here; I thought it was going to be such a big adventure and all, but it's a lot harder to meet people in a city. But I guess it's different for a guy.

Or I'm lying in bed with this terrible cold, my face is all swollen up, my eyes are red and my nose is dripping like a leaky tap, and this fellow comes in through the window and *he* has a terrible cold too, it's a new kind of flu that's been going around. So he says, "I'b goig do rabe you"—I hope you don't mind me holding my nose like this but that's the way I imagine it—and he lets out this terrific sneeze, which slows him down a bit, also I'm no object of beauty myself, you'd have to be some kind of pervert to want to rape someone with a cold like mine, it'd be like raping a bottle of LePages mucilage the way my nose is running. He's looking wildly around the room, and I realize it's because he doesn't have a piece of Kleenex! "Id's ride here," I say, and I pass him the Kleenex, god knows why he even bothered to get out of bed, you'd think if you were going to go around climbing in windows you'd wait till you were healthier, right? I mean, that takes a certain amount of energy. So I ask him why doesn't he let me fix him a Neo-Citran and scotch, that's what I always take, you still have the cold but you don't feel it, so I do and we end up watching the Late Show together. I mean, they aren't all sex maniacs, the rest of the time they must lead a normal life. I figure they enjoy watching the Late Show just like anybody else.

I do have a scarier one though . . . where the fellow says he's hearing angel voices that're telling him he's got to kill me, you know, you read about things like that all the time in the papers. In this one I'm not in the apartment where I live now, I'm back in my mother's house in Leamington and the fellow's been hiding in the cellar, he grabs my arm when I go downstairs to get a jar of jam and he's got hold of the axe too, out of the garage, that one is really scary. I mean, what do you say to a nut like that?

So I start to shake but after a minute I get control of myself and I say, is he sure the angel voices have got the right person, because I hear the same angel voices and they've been telling me for some time that I'm going to give birth to the reincarnation of St. Anne who in turn has the Virgin Mary and right after that comes Jesus Christ and the end of the world, and he wouldn't want to interfere with that, would he? So he gets confused and listens some more, and then he asks for a sign and I show him my vaccination mark, you can see it's sort of an odd-shaped one, it got infected because I scratched the top off, and that does it, he apologizes and climbs out the coal chute again, which is how he got in in the first place, and I say to myself there's some advantage in having been brought up a Catholic even though I haven't been to church since they changed the service into English, it just isn't the same, you might as well be a Protestant. I must write to Mother and tell her to nail up that coal chute, it always has bothered me. Funny, I couldn't tell you at all what this man looks like but I know exactly what kind of shoes he's wearing, because that's the last I see of him, his shoes going up the coal chute, and they're the old-fashioned kind that lace up the ankles, even though he's a young fellow. That's strange, isn't it?

Let me tell you though I really sweat until I see him safely out of there and I go upstairs right away and make myself a cup of tea. I don't think about that one much. My mother always said you shouldn't dwell on unpleasant things and I generally agree with that, I mean, dwelling on them doesn't make them go away. Though not dwelling on them doesn't make them go away either, when you come to think of it.

Sometimes I have these short ones where the fellow grabs my arm but I'm really a Kung-Fu expert, can you believe it, in real life I'm sure it would just be a conk on the head and that's that, like getting your tonsils out, you'd wake up and it would be all over except for the sore places, and you'd be lucky if your neck wasn't broken or something, I could never even hit the volleyball in gym and a volleyball is fairly large, you know?—and I just go *zap* with my fingers into his eyes and that's it, he falls over, or I flip him against a wall or something. But I could never really stick my fingers in anyone's eyes, could you? It would feel like hot jello and I don't even like cold jello, just thinking about it gives me the creeps. I feel a bit guilty about that one, I mean how would you like walking around knowing someone's been blinded for life because of you?

But maybe it's different for a guy.

The most touching one I have is when the fellow grabs my arm and I say, sad and kind of dignified, "You'd be raping a corpse." That pulls him up short and I explain that I've just found out I have leukemia and the doctors have only given me a few months to live. That's why I'm out pacing the streets alone at night, I need to think, you know, come to terms with myself. I don't really have leukemia but in the fantasy I do, I guess I chose that particular disease because a girl in my grade four class died of it, the whole class sent her flowers when she was in the hospital. I didn't understand then that she was going to die and I wanted to have leukemia too so I could get flowers. Kids are funny, aren't they? Well, it turns out that he has leukemia himself, and he only has a few months to live, that's why he's going around raping people, he's very bitter because he's so young and his life is being taken from him before he's really lived it. So we walk along gently under the street lights, it's spring and sort of misty, and we end up going for coffee, we're happy we've found the only other person in the world who can understand what we're going through, it's almost like fate, and after a while we just sort of look at each other and our hands touch, and he comes back with me and moves into my apartment and we spend our last months together before we die, we just sort of don't wake up in the morning, though I've never decided which one of us gets to die first. If it's him I have to go on and fantasize about the funeral, if it's me I don't have to worry about that, so it just about depends on how tired I am at the time. You may not believe this but sometimes I even start crying. I cry at the ends of movies, even the ones that aren't all that sad, so I guess it's the same thing. My mother's like that too.

The funny thing about these fantasies is that the man is always someone I don't know, and the statistics in the magazines, well most of them anyway, they say it's often someone you do know, at least a little bit, like your boss or something—I mean, it wouldn't be *my* boss, he's over sixty and I'm sure he couldn't rape his way out of a paper bag, poor old thing, but it might be someone like Derek Duck, in his elevator shoes, perish the thought—or someone you just met, who invites you up for a drink, it's getting so you can hardly be sociable any more, and how are you supposed to meet people if you can't trust them even that basic amount? You can't spend your whole life in the Filing Department or cooped up in your own apartment with all the doors and windows locked and the shades down. I'm not what you would call a drinker but I like to go out now and then for a drink or two in a nice place, even if I am by myself, I'm with Women's Lib on that even though I can't agree with a lot of other things they say. Like here for instance, the waiters all know me and if anyone, you know, bothers me. . . . I don't know why I'm telling you all this, except I think it helps you get to know a person, especially, at first, hearing some of the things they think about. At work they call me the office worry wart, but it isn't so much like worrying, it's more like figuring out what you should do in an emergency, like I said before.

Anyway, another thing about it is that there's a lot of conversation, in fact I spend most of my time, in the fantasy that is, wondering what I'm going to say and what he's going to say, I think it would be better if you could get a conversation going. Like, how could a fellow do that to a person he's just had a long conversation with, once you let them know you're human, you have a life too, I don't see how they could go ahead with it, right? I mean, I know it happens but I just don't understand it, that's the part I really don't understand.

Lynne Sharon Schwartz 1939–

It has been said that Lynne Sharon Schwartz's fiction magnifies ". . . the subtleties of human relationships." One critic notes that "She writes of those things that constitute our lives," things that "show us how what we do and what's done to us slowly accumulate to make us what we are." Born in Brooklyn, New York, Schwartz attended Barnard College, earning a B.A. in 1959, with graduate study at Bryn Mawr College and New York University. She has received a number of awards, including the Guggenheim Fellowship. In addition to her fiction, she has also written a children's book and a nonfictional account that concerns her landlord-tenant dispute with Columbia University. In a review of Schwartz's collection *The Melting Pot and Other Subversive Stories* (1987), one critic writes that Schwartz ". . . writes cleanly and with compassion. Her voice is strong, even as her stories are varied, and her images are compelling."

THE MELTING POT

Rita suffers from nightmares. This morning's: she is summoned from San Francisco to New York for her grandfather's funeral, where she causes a catastrophe. She enters the chapel with her Russian-born grandmother, Sonia, on her arm, she sees the sea of men and women segregated by a carpeted aisle—solid people, bearers of durable wisdom—and her legs become immovable weights. Everything in her hardens, refusing to move towards the women's side, where she belongs. Even her teeth harden. Sonia, a scrawny, vinegary woman in perpetual haste, tries to drag her along, but Rita cannot be moved. Suddenly from the closed coffin comes a choked, rising moan almost like a tune, the voice trying to break out in protest. Rita's grandmother gasps in horror, clutches her chest, and collapses. All the mourners look at Rita and gasp in unison, like the string section opening a great symphony. One by one, they topple over in shock, both sexes heaped together, mingling. Rita's teeth clench in the dream, biting the hands that fed her.

She wakes up and holds on to Sanjay, who grunts in his sleep. The nightmares dissipate more quickly when he is there. He is a very large, smooth man and she clings to him like a rock climber. In the limbo of waking she cannot even remember which house they are in, his or hers—for they are next-door neighbors, only a wall between them for six years. They live in similar narrow row houses with luscious little flower beds in front, on a sunny San Francisco street lined with eucalyptus trees.

Sanjay, a seeker of practical solutions, thinks the ideal solution to Rita's nightmares would be for them to marry. Why should they live on opposite sides of the wall, like those silly lovers of legend? They are not children, there are no watchful parents hindering them.

"One day soon it will strike you," he says now and then in half-humorous, half-cajoling way, a man of many charms, "that it is the right thing to do. It won't happen when we are making love, but at a more trustworthy moment. Maybe after you have asked me for the fifth time to fix your dishwasher, or after I have consulted you for the ninth time on how some fourth cousin can satisfy the immigration authorities. Some very banal moment between us, and you'll suddenly know. You will want to belong to me forever."

Rita usually laughs. "You've seen too many Fred Astaire movies." But she is afraid. She doesn't want to belong to anyone forever. She has grown up watching that. And she is afraid she won't know how to fit herself in, fit with another life. She looks at their bodies, which do fit sleekly together. Parts of them are the very same color, side by side. The palms of his hands are the color of her thighs, his cheeks the color of her nipples. "What would our children be like?" she says lightly. "What would they call themselves?"

She is not really worried about possible children or what they would call themselves. She mentions it only to deflect his yearnings, because Sanjay has three children already, grown and married. The oldest, who has gone back to India to study his roots, is Rita's age, twenty-eight. It is only natural that Sanjay's fatherliness should appeal to her, a fatherless child—that and his size and bulk, his desire to possess and protect, his willingness to fix her dishwasher and to accept the silences during which she tried to extricate herself from her history. His willingness to accept her history itself. But marrying him seems so definitive.

Now she sits up, leaning on her elbows. The room is suffused with a pre-dawn tinge of lavender. It is Sanjay's house. Of course. There are the faint smells of cumin, coriander, anise—bitter and lush. They are strongest in the kitchen but waft through the other rooms as well. Sanjay's daughter comes two afternoons a week to cook for him. She was born right here on Russian Hill, but she cooks the way her mother did. She doesn't know that her father and Rita eat her food in bed. Sanjay cannot bring himself to tell his children he sleeps with the young woman next door, although he is ready to present her as his wife.

"Why do you let her do that?" Rita asked at the beginning, three years ago. "Doesn't she have enough to do, with the baby and all?"

"I don't ask her to. She insists, ever since her mother died. She's very old-fashioned." A soulful pause. "And she's such a good cook."

"What do you cook when you're alone?"

He made a wry face. "Hamburgers. Tuna fish."

Besides the lush smell, she sees it is Sanjay's house by the shadowy bulk of the large chest of drawers, the darkened sheen of the gilded mirror above it, the glint of the framed photograph of his wife on the chest. When Rita first came to his bedroom Sanjay used to turn the photograph to the wall. As a courtesy, she assumed, for he is a man of delicate feelings, of consummate discretion; but she wasn't sure if the courtesy was directed to her or to his late wife. Now, grown familiar and cozy, he sometimes forgets. Rita has always imagined that she reminds him of his wife, that he wants her because of a resemblance. With the picture facing front, perhaps they are communing through her body.

Well, all right. Rita is used to being a link, endlessly malleable. She is used to reminding people of someone, and to being loved as a link to the true loved one. Even at work, she helps people locate their relatives, and at times she is present at the reunion and watches them embrace. When they finish embracing each other they often embrace her too, as the link. She helps them find ways to stay here. If they succeed in becoming citizens, then Rita is the bridge they pass over to their new identity.

"Immigration law!" Her grandfather, Sol, expected the worst when she started. "You'll see," he grumbled over the phone, wheezing long-distance. "You'll be always with those refugees, you'll wind up marrying one, you with your bleeding heart. And who knows where they come from, what they—"

"Enough already, Sol!" Sonia's rough voice in the background. "Enough!"

"Sometimes these people have to marry someone just to stay in this country," he explains to his granddaughter, the immigration lawyer. "They see a pretty young girl with a profession, what could be better?"

True enough. In three years Rita has had several tentative suggestions of marriage. But she tries to find those desperate souls a better way. She reminds them that they came here to be free, free, and that marriage to a stranger is no freedom. Besides, there is Sanjay.

Sanjay works all day in a laboratory, or la*bor*atory, as he calls it; he wants to cure hemophiliacs, bleeders. (Contrary to popular notion, hemophiliacs do not bleed more intensely than most people, only longer.) Sanjay knows almost all there is to know about genes and blood. Indeed, he has the exile's air of knowing all there is to know about everything. Yet he has been here for nearly thirty years, is a citizen, and, unlike Rita's jittery clients, seems very much at home. His face has taken on a West Coast transparency. His courtly speech is sprinkled with the local argot. Still, Rita suspects, even knowing all there is to know about her, he sees her as his entryway to the land of dreams. His bridge. His American girl.

Rita's present life is, in her grandfather's view, one of disobedience (like her nightmares), but as a small child she was quite obedient. She submitted when he found her costuming paper dolls in her bedroom on a Saturday afternoon and unhooked the scissors from her thumb and forefinger, reminding her that Jews do not cut on the Sabbath. Nor do they color in coloring books, trace pictures from magazines, turn on the lights, the toaster, the radio, or the television, use the phone, cook, sew, drive. . . . The way Sol explains it, they are defined by what they are forbidden. There are things they must not eat and not wear, not do and not utter. The most constricted people are the most holy, relieved from confronting the daily unknown with bare instinct, for happily, every conceivable pattern of human event and emotion was foreseen centuries ago and the script is at hand, in old books in an old tongue. She submitted. But she was allowed to read. *A Little Princess* was her favorite story, where the orphaned and hungry heroine is forced to live in a lonely freezing garret, until a kindly Indian gentleman feeds her and lights a fire in her room and finally rescues her altogether, restoring her to a life of abundance.

For the most holy people, the most holy season is fall, the most beautiful. Also the most allusive and most amenable to introspection, with its amber light, its sounds of leaves scuttling, brittle as death, on the pavement, its eerie chills at sundown, and its holidays calling for renewal, guilt, atonement, remembrance, hope, and pride, one after the other in breathless succession. It is the season to think over your past deeds and ask forgiveness of anyone you might have injured, for only after asking a fellow creature's forgiveness may you ask God's. God has a big book and keeps his accounts: Your fortunes in the year to come depend on your actions in the year just passed. (Karma, thinks Rita years later, when she knows Sanjay.) It is the season when Rita is required to get out of her jeans and beads and into a dress. Shoes instead of sneakers. Sweating great beads of boredom, resistance seeping from every pore to form a second skin beneath her proper clothing, she trails her grandfather to the synagogue to sit with the women in the balcony (so as not to distract the men) and listen to him sing the prayers in a language she cannot understand.

Her grandmother the atheist also conforms, sits in the women's balcony behind a curtain and fasts on the Day of Atonement, and this not merely out of obedience, like Rita. Sonia finds her identity in opposition. She conforms in order to assert her difference in the New World, as in the Old World others asserted it for her, in the form of ostracism and pogroms. But within the family's little conforming circle she has to assert her difference too, and so while her husband is out at the synagogue she fixes herself a forbidden glass of tea. Her wiry body moves quickly around the kitchen, as if charged with electrical current. Snickering like a child, she raises the steaming glass by the rim and drinks, immensely pleased with her mischief, her high cheekbones gleaming.

"You might as well have a sandwich while you're at it," says Rita, at eleven years old not yet required to fast, to choose between her grandparents, obedience in bed with defiance.

A sandwich would be going too far. They destroy the evidence, wash and dry the glass and spoon and put them away; luckily he doesn't count the tea bags, hardly the province of a holy man.

What is the province of a holy man? God, of course, Wrong. Rules. Sanjay could have told her that. His family's rules fill at least as many books. Rita's grandfather loves rules, constrictions, whatever narrows the broad path of life and disciplines the meandering spirit for its own good. The lust to submit is his ruling passion. It is part of the covenant with God: Obey all the rules and you will be safe. Sol takes this literally. He seeks out arcane rules to obey and seizes upon them, appropriates them with the obsessiveness of a Don Juan appropriating new women. Nor is that enough; his passion requires that others obey them too. His wife. His granddaughter. For the family is the pillar of society. The family is the society. And if a member disobeys, strays too far beyond the pillars, he becomes an outcast. At risk in the wide world, the world of the others. "Them."

So Rita rarely hears him speak of God. And Sonia mentions God with contempt, as one would speak of the meanest enemy, too mean even to contend with. "What God says I'm not interested in!" she shouts bitterly when Sol nags her back onto the little path of submission. "I'm interested in what people do right here on earth!" Alone together, Sonia and Rita never tire of cataloguing the discrepancies between God's reputation and his manifest deeds. They, obey in their hearts? It is to laugh. And laugh they do, showing their perfect teeth, as enduring as rocks. Of course they are women, their minds fixed on the specific. Perhaps they cannot grasp the broader scheme of things.

"What would be sins?" Rita asks her grandfather, thinking of Sonia's tea.

He pats his soft paunch thoughtfully with both hands. "Lying to your grandparents. Thinking wicked thoughts. Being unkind to people."

This sounds fairly mild. She tries to enumerate her greater sins but can think of none that any God worthy of the name would take notice of. With a new assassination almost yearly, the portraits of the dead promptly appearing on the walls at school, can God care that she listens to the Supremes on a Saturday afternoon, she and the radio muffled under a blanket? She asks her grandmother about sins but Sonia waves her arm dismissively, an arc of contempt scything the air. Rita infers that God, rather than mortals, has a lot to answer for, though she doesn't know what in particular is on her grandmother's mind besides the general wretchedness abounding. Poor people ride to Washington on mules. Long-haired students in Chicago get beaten by police. Rita passes the time in the balcony constructing cases against God on their behalf. Her father was a lawyer, she had managed to glean; she invokes his help. The cases are very good, watertight, with evidence starting from Abraham; no, Abel. But no matter what the jury decides, God remains. That is his nature, she gathers, to be there watching and judging, always alert for a misstep, but not helping.

Light is coming in at the window, a Pacific coast autumn light, creamy, soft-edged. As it slides up his face, Sanjay wakes, and Rita tells him about her bad dream, for she cannot shake it. She tells him how in the dream her father's father, the most obedient servant of his Lord, is taken, even so. How his obedience did not shield him in the end, and how she, by her disobedience rooted in a certain juxtaposition of genes, causes a shocking event, rivaling the one that convulsed the family twenty-six years ago.

"Heredity," says Sanjay sleepily, "doesn't work that way. You make too much of it." He has exchanged the faith in karma for the science of genetics. And he wants to help. He wants her to turn around and live facing front. Odd, since he comes from a country imprisoned in history, while she is the young West Coast lawyer. Sometimes it seems they have changed places.

"And don't you make much of it? Don't you tell me you get glimpses of your father's face in the mirror when you shave, but with a peeled, American expression? I feel my mother when I brush my hair. In the texture of the hair."

"That's different. You can inherit hair but not destinies."

He sounds so sure. . . . "I think in the dream he was trying to sing. Did I ever tell you that my grandfather used to sing in the synagogue?"

"I thought your mother was the singer."

"Her too. That was a different kind of song. He ran the store all week, but on Saturday mornings he was a cantor, he led the prayers. Then when I was about seventeen, he had some minor surgery in his throat and he never sang again."

"Why, what happened?"

"Nothing. He was afraid."

"Of what?"

"Well that's exactly it. Something cosmic. That his head might burst, I don't know. It was just too risky. The absurd thing was, he had the operation to restore his voice. We never heard him sing again. So what do you make of a man who loves to sing and sings for the glory of God, then refuses to sing out of fear?"

"In his heart he still sings. He sings, Safe, safe." Sanjay composes a little tune on the word.

Rita smiles. "I thought immigrants always sang, Free, free."

"Not always. We"—he means his brother and himself, who came here to be educated and returned home only to visit—"we sing, Away, away. New, new." He yawns, and then, in a lower key, "Guilt, guilt."

All the indigenous American tunes, thinks Rita. But she is still smiling. He has a way of making heavy things feel lighter. He has a mild grace that buoys him through life. Maybe she should marry him after all. She is so malleable an American, she could become anyone with ease. And it would be a way to live; it would be safe, safe. She might even let her hair grow long and smooth it down with coconut oil, start frying wheat cakes and clarifying butter and stepping delicately down the hills of San Francisco as Sanjay's wife did, holding up her long skirts.

That was how Rita first saw them, the Indian gentleman and his wife. It was the day of her graduation from college, which her grandparents flew west to attend. Afterwards, she took them across the bay to San Francisco, to show them her new apartment. For she was staying on. Through a friend, she had found a summer job in a Spanish record store, and in the fall she would start law school.

While Sonia tore through the rooms like a high wind, Sol stood at the front window, holding the curtain to one side and peering out as though he were in a hostile country, a place you could get yourself killed. Though not much of a traveler, he had been here once before, briefly.

"Who are your neighbors?" he asks, gesturing with his chin.

"I don't know. Which ones?" Rita comes over to peer out too.

It is an Indian couple, the man tall and broad, with heavy eyebrows and longish hair, dressed impeccably, even a bit flamboyantly, in a light gray suit. Rita likes the suit and likes his walk, stately, meditative, achieving a look that is both scholarly and debonair. By his side is a slight woman in a green and gold sari, holding his arm. Her head is lowered, so Rita can barely see her face. She holds the sari up skillfully, climbing the hill.

"I guess they're an Indian couple."

"Indians?" Her grandfather's voice rises. Bows and arrows?

"From India. You know, Gandhi, Nehru, no eating cows. That's what the women wear."

"I know what India is. I read the papers too, Rita. I'm not as ignorant as you think."

"Sorry, Papa."

"How do they live? Nice?"

She shrugs. "I guess so."

"Yes. They're not the same as the colored."

"Oh, Papa, don't start."

The Indian couple is moving unusually slowly, their heads cast down. They look like a devoted pair; they walk in step, rhythmically. As they turn into the front yard next door, to the left, he swings the gate open for her.

Much later, when Rita tells Sanjay about the first time she saw him, he says they might have been coming from the doctor; it was the month when his wife had some tests. The tests said yes, but it would probably not get really bad till the end.

It is strange, Rita thinks now, that she was with her grandfather when she first saw Sanjay.

A scene from one of Rita's silences: Her great-uncle Peter, her grandfather's twin brother, is a philanthropic dentist—he fills the cavities of Orthodox Jewish orphans for free. Also he checks Rita's teeth. Her grandmother drives her to his office for a checkup every six months, on a Sunday morning. The tiny waiting room is crowded with old people—fifty years old at least; where are the orphans of legend? They wait in the little waiting room which smells of dental supplies—sweet, medicinal, like wintergreen—until all the paying customers have had their turns, which may take an entire Sunday morning. Rita and Sonia share many qualities of temperament, notably the impatience gene. They wait with difficulty. Though they like to talk, they find no solace in the small talk that accompanies waiting. They leaf through magazines, they go to the superbly clean bathroom smelling of mouthwash, they pace the tiny waiting room. Sonia, unable to be confined, goes out to walk around the block. Rita cannot take such liberties since it's her mouth waiting to be examined, and her uncle might take a notion to sneak her in between the creaky patients. Her grandmother walks fast, round and round the block; Rita imagines her tense, bony body crackling like November twigs. Sonia's short auburn hair is alive in the breeze, and her fierce mind works on the fabric of the past, ripping stitches, patching.

At last it is Rita's turn. Her great-uncle, bald and moon-faced, rotund in his sparkling white jacket, round-collared like a priest's, beckons, the outstretched hand making a swift fluttering motion, giving the impression that she has been dilatory, that she has kept him waiting. He greets her using a Hebrew name that no one ever uses. She feels he is talking to some invisible person in the room. "What a pretty complexion," he says, in a way that suggests perhaps it is not, a consoling way. And, "What strong white teeth!" In a stage whisper, over her head: "She must get those from her mother."

"I have strong white teeth too," Sonia says with savage energy. "When have you ever had to fix anything in my mouth?"

Sonia dislikes her brother-in-law passionately. All the dislike she cannot expend on her husband she transfers to his twin brother. Peter and Sol are cautious people, supremely timid in the face of life. Yet they came to the New World as infants and know only by hearsay what they escaped. Sonia, who came later, remembers, and finds their timidities an indulgence. Her family are extravagant-tempered Russians whom Russians never accepted as such, which is why they journeyed so far. Genetically defiant people with hyperactive brains, willful, angry, ebullient. Their bones snap, the veins in their temples throb. There is nothing they cannot feel passionate about, and so they lavish huge and frightful energies on life and live long, propelled by their exuberant indignation. Rita is fascinated by them and bored by her grandfather's docile family. She sees the two sides of the family as opposing teams, opposing stances towards life. When she is older she sees her grandparents in an incessant game of running bases: they throw the ball back and forth—the ball is truth, how to live—and she, Rita, must run between them, pulled now to the safety of rules and traditions, now back to the thrills of defiance and pride.

Once she is in the funny chair, Peter gives her avuncular rides up and down, chattering affectionately, almost too affectionately, as if he is trying extra hard. There are whispered words with her grandmother, exchanges Rita doesn't grasp except that Sonia wants none of his proffered commiseration. "You can't trust one of them, not one," he mumbles. "That's the way it is, that's the way it will always be."

"Shh, shh," Sonia hushes him in disgust. "Just do her teeth, no speeches." Sonia always sticks up for her; with crackling Sonia she is utterly safe.

"Such beautiful dark hair." He does seem to like her, in the brief time he has available. Yet he calls her by the wrong name, which you do not do to someone you like. That's not who I am, Rita wants to cry out, but there is something peculiar and mysterious about who she is that keeps her silent, openmouthed like an idiot. She sometimes gets glimmerings of losses below the surface, like sunken jewels that divers plunge and grope for in vain. They might be memories of a different climate, or the feel of an embrace, or a voice, feelings so fleeting and intangible she can hardly call them memories. But they have been with her since she can remember—wispy vapors of another way she might once have been, another mode of feeling the world, as believers in reincarnation sense their past lives.

That's not who I am, she wants to cry out, but she can offer no more, she knows nothing more, and anyway he is all frothing joviality and patter, while his hands nimbly prepare the instruments. Rita is enthralled by the rows of false teeth lined up on the cabinet, pink gums and ivory teeth, the many different shapes waiting like orphans to be adopted, for mouths to come by and take them in, ready to be pressed into service chewing and forming the dental consonants. Unspoken words and stories are hiding in the teeth.

"So. Are you going to play Queen Esther this year?"

"No." She rinses and spits. "The teacher said I should be Vashti."

"Well, Vashti is good too. She was very beautiful."

"She gets killed in the beginning. I was Vashti last year."

"Finished?" asks Sonia impatiently.

Fortunately Rita's teeth are excellent, she can be disposed of in five minutes. Rocks, he says every time. She has rocks in her head. And he tells her that her teeth, like her grandmother's, will last a lifetime. Good news. Sharp and hard, they bite, they grip, grind, gnash, and clench. They make the words come out clear. Sonia grinds her teeth all night, Sol remarks at breakfast. Good, Rita thinks. They will be useful in times of stress. They will help her chew hard things, and grind them down, make them fit for swallowing.

———

When Sanjay's wife died, Rita paid a neighborly call, as her grandfather taught her to do. Solomon was conscientious about visiting the bereaved. He would enter their houses with no greeting (that was the rule), seat himself in a corner, open a book, and pray as though he were alone in the room and the universe, which in a sense he was, for all around him people continued to speak, eat, and even make merry as survivors will.

The rules behind her, no book to guide her, Rita brings a rich, fruity cake to Sanjay and greets him. They have exchanged greetings on the street, she has inquired with concern about his wife, but she has never been in his house before. She notices he has some Indian things—a big brass tray, a lacquered vase with an array of peacock feathers, and several photos of Allahabad, his home town, a very holy place, he tells her, where two holy rivers meet. One photo shows masses of people, the tops of heads, mostly, bathing in a holy river banked by two fantastical buildings, castles out of a tale of chivalry. Otherwise it is a San Francisco kind of house—airy, with thriving plants and colorful pillows. It smells spicy.

They become friends. They go to an occasional movie, a restaurant. He asks her advice about relatives who need green cards. She asks if he can fix her dishwasher. She loves the way he moves, his great weight treading softly, the smooth sound of his voice and the way after all these years he keeps pronouncing certain words in the British fashion—"dance," "record," "laboratory"—his slow, very inquisitive eyes and hard mouth.

Finally, after several months of decorous behavior they meet by chance on the street one evening and get to talking. Something feels different. Ripe. His eyes and his speech are slower, more judicious than usual, almost ponderous. He asks her into his house and she smells the sharp spices. He gives her some stuffed chapattis his daughter brought over that morning; he insists on warming them in the oven first. Delicious. The bread is important; it is, she understands, part of the seduction. Standing very erect, shoulders squared, like a man about to deliver a speech, he says, "Well, Rita, I have never courted an American young woman before, so you'll have to forgive my . . . ineptness. But it seems time, to me. And you? Will you?" She nods. He looks so safe.

Upstairs, the furniture in the bedroom is weighty, built for the ages. It reminds her of the furniture in her grandparents' apartment. Married furniture. The first thing Sanjay does is turn his wife's photograph to the wall.

Rita lets herself be undressed. "Oh. Oh," he says, touching her, When he takes her in his arms she feels an immense relief—at last!—as if she has been freezing for years and suddenly a fur coat is thrown over her, the kind of coat shown in photos of Russian winters, and she realizes she has wanted him from the moment she saw him from the window three years ago, looking out with her grandfather. She can feel his immense relief too, but that, she imagines, is because he has not held anyone in his arms in months. Oh God, she hopes it will not be . . . like that.

No, he is in no hurry. He proves to know a lot about women. Maybe in a past incarnation he was a woman—she can almost believe it. Also, from the way he touches her, she feels how he must have loved his wife. She wonders if she feels like his wife, if maybe all women feel alike, after a certain point. In his arms, Rita forgets who she is. She could almost be his wife. And then she falls immediately asleep.

When she wakes, the bedside lamp is on and Sanjay is weeping into the pillow. He looks up and sees her watching.

"I'm sorry. Forgive me." He stops abruptly.

Is this all she will ever be, a link to the beloved dead?

"Really, I'm terribly sorry, Rita. I thought you were sleeping."

"It's all right, Sanjay, it's all right." What else can she say?

She does not sleep much that night but watches him sleep. For hours, it seems. She has shielded herself so far, but now it envelops her like a shower of gold threads. Of red powder, and she sees that love is the greatest defiance of all. She is afraid of it.

She has to leave early, go home to the other side of the wall and change, pick up her cap and gown. She is graduating from law school that very day. Sanjay says he wants to be there, so she gives him a ticket—she has them to spare since her grandparents are not flying out this time. Sol's heart is too irregular.

Just before she leaves to take her place in the line, he slips her a tiny candy wrapped in silver paper. "For luck."

She starts to unwrap it.

"No, no. You eat the paper too."

She trusts him infinitely. She eats the paper. Silver, sweet, delicious. Bits of it stick in her teeth, making the taste linger.

When he announces months later that he loves her and wants to marry her, that he has thought it over and waited to speak until he was quite sure, she takes the information skeptically.

"Why? Can't you believe that I loved her and now I love you?"

"I don't know."

"You must have loved other people. I don't think about them."

"But I haven't."

"Maybe, maybe not. You do love me, though," Sanjay says. "I know. Must I see a problem in that, perhaps?" This is comical, she thinks, this interrogation. He can be so matter-of-fact, even imperious. There is a sliver of amusement in his eyes, too. Whatever he is, she loves.

"I never felt this before. I don't know what to make of it."

"Come now. You must have. American girls . . ."

"I was busy with other things."

"What things?"

She can't tell him how she spent her college years. It's too crazy. Not yet, anyway. So instead she says something hurtful. "You're too old for me."

He seems impervious, tilts his head carelessly. "That can't be helped. And anyway, you don't really mind."

It's true, she doesn't. Quite the contrary.

Rita and Sanjay find that their backgrounds have a number of things in common. A preponderance of rules for proper behavior is one, especially rules about not consorting—eating or sleeping—with members of another caste. This, like pioneers, they have both left behind. Arranged marriages is another. This one does not seem so far behind.

"So you never really knew her before you were married?"

"We knew each other, but not in the way that you mean. The families met several times. We spoke. It's not really so preposterous. The idea is that you come to love each other. We trust in proximity to breed love."

Rita frowns. He is still trusting.

"It sounds very unromantic, I know. But it doesn't exclude romance of a kind."

"Does it work? I mean, for most people?"

"Well, more than you'd expect. Some love each other with a goodwill kind of love. Some even have passionate love. But there are other ways to love besides those, more ways than are recognized here. You can love someone simply because she's yours, part of you. You've accepted each other and you don't question it. My parents were like that. Are still like that."

"And what about you? What kind of love was it?"

He closes his eyes. The pain of loss, regret? Or merely impatience. "Why do you keep asking? You know the answer."

She knows. The goodwill kind, the passionate kind, the totally accepting kind. Often, those first three years, she saw them walking arm in arm down the street, their steps falling together in rhythm. Belonging.

"You were lucky. Did she know, the first night, what she was supposed to do?"

"Not precisely. She was a very sheltered girl."

"But you knew, I presume?"

Sanjay takes a deep breath and his face begins a little performance—his face has a great repertoire of expressions. His eyes roll, his forehead wrinkles, his lips curl. "What do you think?"

"Was she appalled?"

"No."

Rita would like to know, in graphic detail, exactly how Sanjay made it clear what was expected. She is not a voyeur by nature; rather, she is mystified by the transmutations of love—how indifference turns into love, love into indifference and even worse. But it is useless to ask. He doesn't tell. It must be too precious. Yes, because he does love to tell stories about his parents, his brothers and sisters and cousins. She has heard comic stories about bicycles capsized in the mud and a flirtatious widowed aunt, stories of school pranks and festival antics, and painful stories about a baby sister who died of diphtheria on the day Gandhi was shot. But no stories about his wife.

"I know what you're thinking. But people can love more than once, Rita. After all . . ."

"I know, I know." Yet she knows only in the abstract. She feels generally ignorant on the subject. She thinks that what she saw, growing up, was not love but a species of belonging.

Her grandparents' marriage took place in 1927 and was also arranged, though not as strictly as Sanjay's. The couple was introduced; they took several walks together over the Brooklyn Bridge; they went to a few movies and even to an opera, *Madame Butterfly*. This was all quite ordinary. But the wedding itself was extraordinary. The father of the groom had collapsed and died two days before. No matter; the rules say ceremonies must take place as scheduled, like Broadway shows. And the bride did not refuse; she had not yet learned how. But she had her doubts, surely, Rita thinks. For it is hard to imagine the Sonia she knows being so compliant. Surely she must have been astounded, felt that such a beginning did not augur well and maybe she had better pull out before it was too late? But it was already too late.

"Can you picture that wedding?" she queries Sanjay.

"Well, quiet, I'd imagine. Very quiet."

No doubt. A dearth of dancing, the musicians laboring to rouse an unap-preciative crowd. Rita's various aunts and uncles, disguised as young people, gathered around linen-covered tables, eating sweetbreads and drinking sweet wine while salt streams down their faces. The children fretful and confused— no one is urging delicacies on them or swinging them through the air. Her own father not yet an outcast, not even born, a gleam, as they say, in his father's very gleaming eye. As her grandparents toast their life together, the groom weeps under the harshness of his own discipline. He can barely drink and cannot eat. He does not need to eat. Self-pity and self-satisfaction are his feast—for this ordeal will make him a better person, bring him favor in the eyes of his God. What kind of eyes could they be?

Very quickly the couple has an indissoluble connection, a son. Sonia's first decade of marriage is a depression, then comes the war.

Throughout their married life there are many changes in the world. The maps of Europe, Africa, and Asia change drastically. There are immense shifts of population, new technologies, cures for diseases; wonders and horrors as usual. The twentieth century. But—and she has to admire his tenacity—Rita's grandfather's world remains the world he grew up in, a small world left over from the youth of the century, a bit cramped and crowded, like a room to which new pieces are added but from which nothing is ever thrown away, a thoroughly benign and safe world, according to his stories—for he is, yes, a storyteller, with a magnetic eye, bluest of blues, and a magnetic voice.

"Our house was the place where all immigrants stopped first," he says. "And no matter how crowded we were, when they opened the door, whoever came in I welcomed them with open arms. I was only a child. But I felt the call of blood."

Open arms. He lives, Rita comes to understand, by appropriation. He takes in, processes, categorizes, labels, and provides a commentary. To have any act unexplained or unexcused, anyone left out of the scheme, can put the world in an imbalanced state, as taunting and intolerable as an unresolved chord in his singer's ear.

So he narrates the fortunes of each arrival, one by one: loves, travels, business ventures, progeny. And in his stories—long, highly dramatized, and gripping— never a harsh word is spoken between sister and brother, parent and child, hus- band and wife, only happy grateful immigrants making good in the promised land, learning the customs and the lingo. He has an instinctive way of skimming over pain or crisis, a lighting mostly on moments of epiphany when generosity and breadth of spirit are revealed, moments when virtue triumphs over self- interest. What everyone fled from is never mentioned above a whisper, and never at all in the presence of "them," the others, the ones who can never be trusted, who pursue and destroy. The moral is always the same: The family is the pillar of society. There are no distinctions when it comes to family. A cousin? "Like my own brother!" (A granddaughter? "Like my own daughter!") And when a member strays beyond the pillars he becomes an outcast. Formerly appropriated, now vomited up.

Since Sol's stories extol righteousness, Rita asks why, then, he and his brother don't go out, this minute, and work for civil rights and for an end to the war in Vietnam. If they fled from the draft on one continent, shouldn't they protest it on another? Sol listens because she is a clever speaker, and when she becomes too annoying he waves her away like a mosquito. Her uncle the dentist points out that all the boys in the immediate neighborhood are going to college, not Asia. Once, her great-aunt, the dentist's wife, loses patience. "Protest, protest!" she mocks, eyeing Rita as she would a stranger who had jumped the line at the bakery. "She should be glad she has a roof over her head."

What could it mean? Rita knows her parents are . . . well . . . dead, it must be. The subject is taboo. It is as if she is Sol's and Sonia's child. This is her roof, isn't it? Her grandfather tells his sister-in-law to shut her big mouth. Sonia goes further and throws her out of the house, and the incident is closed. Everyone goes to bed with a headache.

Undaunted, at fourteen years old Rita thinks she too can appropriate the world, make it over to fit her vision. Not all immigrants are so well assimilated, she finds out. She feels for those beyond the pillars, maybe because she is darker than any Jew she knows and has never had a chance to play Queen Esther. With an adolescent's passion to convert, she wants her grandfather to feel for them too, and to agree that breadth of spirit does not mean obeying the most rules but scorning them all, except for the rules of the heart. She wants him to thrill to the uneven rhythms of heroic outcasts, anarchists: "I might have lived out my life talking at street corners, to scorning men. I might have died unmarked, unknown, a failure. Now we are not a failure. This is our career and our triumph. Never in our full life could we hope to do so much work for tolerance, for justice, for man's understanding of man as we do now by accident. Our words—our lives—our pains—nothing! The taking of our lives—lives of a good shoemaker and a poor fish-peddler—all! That last moment belongs to us—that agony is our triumph!" She finds this in a book about famous trials of the century, and shivers with passion.

But Solomon hears it impassively, and in response, launches into one of his own speeches—clears his throat and prepares his oratorical voice. "Ours, Rita, is a religion of ethics. A man's devotion to God is shown in how he treats his fellow man, beginning with his own—his children, his grandchildren"—he smiles fondly, justly pleased with himself on this score—"his neighbors." (Sonia puts down the skirt she is hemming, tosses aside her glasses and stalks out of the room.) "In other words, *mamaleh*, charity begins at home."

Very well, and where is home? Everywhere, she lectures him in turn. He calls her a bleeding heart. Whatever he cannot appropriate, whatever refuses to go down and be assimilated—outsiders, heinous deeds, gross improprieties—he ignores, which means it ceases to exist.

He has been unable to appropriate, for instance, his son's marriage to a Mexican immigrant, which took place in far-off San Francisco, California, in 1955. This Rita learns through piecing together family whispers. If Sol had had his way, ostracism—the tool of his enemies—would not have sufficed; according to the rules, his son would have been interred in absentia and mourned for a week, and neighbors would have visited him and Sonia while they sat on wooden boxes, wearing bedroom slippers, with the mirrors in the house covered by bed sheets. But he didn't have his way. Sonia refused to do it. It was the beginning of her refusals.

That her mother was Mexican is one of four or five facts Rita knows about her. Her name was Carmen. She was a singer—strangely enough, like Rita's grandfather, but singing a different kind of song. Rita would like to know what kind of love her parents had and how they came to marry, but she never will. It was certainly not arranged.

————

Rita's dream foresees her grandfather's funeral because he is not well, Sanjay suggests reasonably. Perhaps; she shrugs. She is not really seeking explanations. It is certainly true that Sol's fears have caught up with him, and that there are not enough rules to cover them adequately. Once sturdy, he has become in old age what he calls "nervous." He sees death coming, and his nervous system is in a twit. He has spells of weakness, shortness of breath, panic; all activities have to be gauged in advance as to how taxing they will be and the chance of mishaps. He monitors his vital signs with loving care, as solicitous of himself as a mother. The path has narrowed till on the vast new continent there is hardly room to place one foot in front of the other. Safe, safe. Rita hates the way he lives. She wants him to get up and do something—sing, pray, sell sportswear, anything but pave the way for death, be the advance man.

But for safety he must keep himself as confined as possible, especially since Rita and Sonia have slipped out of his control. He would not be so "nervous," he claims, if he could oversee what they were doing at all times. Of course, this cannot be. Rita is far away, doing God knows what and with whom, and Sonia has to manage the store. Sonia began to elude him long ago anyhow. For the first three decades of their marriage she obeyed, and then something happened. It was as if she had sealed up her disobedience the way pioneer women canned fruits and vegetables for a later season, and then she broke it out in abundance, jar after jar releasing its briny fumes. Years ago, members of the congregation reported that they saw the cantor's wife, her granddaughter beside her, driving his car on the Sabbath, a cigarette in her invincible teeth! Where could they be going? There was even talk of replacing him, but it came to nothing—they pitied him, first his great tragedy with his son and now unable to control his family.

Sonia, once tame, has reverted to the ways of her family. Anarchists, though not the grand kind. No, they fit very well into the elastic New World. Except that they argue passionately with the clerks of bureaucracies, they walk on the grass, they refuse to wait on lines, they smoke in nonsmoking areas, they open doors labeled authorized personnel only, they zip through traffic jams on the shoulders of roads or in lanes blocked off by orange stanchions. It is part of their passion, their brand of civil disobedience. Sol is horrified and Rita is amused, even though these are gestures only, to show they will not take the law from anyone, for they know who the lawgivers are. Clay like all the rest. They obey what they like, laws unto themselves. They are in fact (some of them, at any rate) lawyers. They came here in installments, three boys and three girls from Kiev. The girls became seamstresses, the boys lawyers. The girls went to factories, to sit on a cushion and sew a fine seam, while the boys were sent to school—the New World not so unlike the Old in that regard.

Three dressmakers make three lawyers: stitch, stitch. The dressmakers live in small apartments in Jewish ghettos with their husbands, small businessmen like Rita's grandfather, while their brothers prosper in modern assimilated suburbs. Then in 1959, the only child—a son—of one of the girls is stabbed to death in far-off San Francisco, California. That is truly lawless. The family, convulsed, will grieve in unison. That is not the kind of lawlessness, the kind of anarchy they intended, no, never, never! His mother will stop recognizing the world, any world, New, Old, all the same to her.

The family fears she may never return to the realm of the living. Days go by while she sits on a hard kitchen chair with her eyes fixed on nothing. She will not change her clothing or eat or sleep. When spoken to she will not respond, or else shakes her head, or at the most says, "Not now." It seems she is waiting for something, someone. Perhaps she is remembering how she refused to mourn her son when he married out of his faith—was it for this, so she could mourn him now?

Meanwhile her husband, accompanied by his twin brother the dentist, will fly out to the unknown western territories to settle his son's affairs and see that justice is done—a most adventurous trip, which he would not undertake for any other reason, but shock has made him a father again. The former outcast as a corpse is unobjectionable. And what, of all things, will he discover in the shadow of the Golden Gate but a child! Just two years old. If he had known, maybe . . . The child has been staying with her maternal uncle and his wife (her mother being in no condition to take care of her), but really, it is very difficult. They own a bar, a nightclub, actually—he is the bartender, his wife the waitress. (And there Rita's mother sang her Spanish songs. A vision in sequins? A floozy? She will never know.) No place for a baby. Without a moment's hesitation, Solomon transcends himself (possibly for the baby's blue eyes, which reflect his own), to perform the one daring act of his life—he takes her back. He takes her in. It is an act that could speak best for itself, but he cannot resist the ready phrase, a Jewish Polonius.

"It was the call of blood," he explains to Sonia as he enters carrying the child on one arm, suitcase and briefcase dangling from the other. She stares at him in the stupor that has become her mode of existence. Nothing surprises her. "Here," he says more naturally, holding out his burden like an offering. "Better take her to the bathroom. Her name is Rita." He thrusts her at Sonia. "Take a look at her eyes. Like skies."

A good name, Rita. It can derive from either set of genes. And there are plenty of dark Jews, her grandfather will declaim, presenting her to the family and the neighbors, the little bilingual prodigy. Yemenites. Ethiopians. The sons of

Ham. Anyway, she is not all that dark. Some regular Jews are swarthy. Anyway, there she is, and her grandmother takes her to the bathroom, feeds her, clothes her, and low, a miracle sprung from tragedy, Sonia returns to life like Sarah in Genesis, fertilized in old age. Soon the neighborhood women start coming back to the house for fittings. They stand stiffly, only their mouths moving, as she pins folds of fabric around them, the pins stuck in her tough teeth. Rita plays with dolls at their feet, and not all her dolls are blonde. One is quite dark, with glossy black hair—Sonia understands the demands of a pluralistic society. That doll is not Rita's best baby, however. Her best baby is a blue-eyed blonde she calls Nita, to rhyme. The clients fuss over her, how cute, how bright, congratulate her grandmother on this unexpected boon, but their tone is very odd, not utterly pure. Ambiguous, like Rita.

For Sonia, though, there is no ambiguity. She accepts their goodwill with nonchalance—the pins in her mouth make it hard to speak in any case—and in their presence ignores Rita. When they leave she clasps her close, then talks, talks, low and fast like someone who has saved up words over a lifetime. She talks as if she is talking to herself—much of it a small child can hardly understand. So many things that she thinks and feels, but not the one thing. Of Rita's parents she never speaks, but she returns to life, and best of all, learns to drive. She neglects the housework that exasperates her, and together they breeze through the tangled city like tourists. Even when Rita is a big schoolgirl, she will wait for her and greet her at the door at three-fifteen: "Let's take a ride, okay?"

They ride through exotic neighborhoods of Greeks, Asians, blacks, Hispanics, Russians—there they eat pirogen and caviar and borscht. A passionately discontented woman, angular and veiny, Sonia is most content at the wheel of the dark green Pontiac. A born voyager. Short, straight-backed, she sits on a pillow and stretches her neck like a swan to peruse the traffic. Her driving style is aggressive, arrogant, anarchic. And Rita by her side is her natural passenger. Nothing can shock or frighten her, so thoroughly does she trust her grandmother, so closely are they twined, having accepted each other on first sight with no questions asked, like Sanjay's parents—neither the U-turns in tunnels nor the sprinting across intersections nor the sparring with buses and trucks. Sonia is omnipotent, fearless. Queen of the Road. Defying the rules about the Sabbath, she takes Rita to, of all places, the beach, where in all kinds of weather they wet their feet in the surf and build sand castles and Sonia tells stories—not morality tales like Sol's but true stories without morals—of what lies across the openness of the Atlantic, and she tells Rita that they came here to be free, free.

Now Rita longs for those forbidden afternoons at the edge of the Atlantic. Like a child, she would like to incorporate her grandmother, swallow her, as her grandfather lived by appropriating. Appropriation is the tactic of the lost and the scared. Oh, if only Rita could swallow her whole, if only she would go down, she could have Sonia forever with her. Safe at last. Then she would never clutch her heart and die as in the nightmare, leaving Rita standing alone, severed.

———

While Sanjay and Rita are watching a Fred Astaire and Ginger Rogers movie on television one evening, her phone rings. Rita speaks to her friend who still works in the Spanish record store in the Mission district. When she hangs up she says, "I've just been invited to a wedding. Rosalia's brother Luis. Would you like to come?"

"I never knew you could speak Spanish like that." They have been lovers for almost a year.

"Oh. Well, I need it, you know, for my clients."

"But you speak it like a native. I thought you were only two years old . . ."

"I learned when I was in college. Do you want to go to the wedding? It'll be fun. Lots of music and dancing."

"Sure."

She sits down and touches his hand. "I used to go out with her brother, years ago. He's very nice. Gentle, you know, like Rosalia. I'm glad he's getting married."

"You never mentioned it before."

"Well, it was nothing, really. We were kids. There's no way it should bother you."

"It doesn't. Only I sometimes realize I know so little about you. You tell me so little."

Sanjay develops an interest in her past loves. Like her curiosity about his wife, his is not lascivious in nature. Rather, he wants coherent social history. What has her life been all about? And generically, what are young American women's lives all about? A question that has never occupied him before.

She is not a typical case, Rita tries to explain. But it's a matter of optics, of the precision of the lens. To a fifty-year-old naturalized Indian widower, she is representative enough. He wants his American girl, Rita thinks. And he wants the real thing.

"Did you ever sleep with any of your clients?"

"No! Anyway, by the time I had clients I already knew you."

"Well, what about at law school?"

"One student." She grins, teasing. "One professor."

"A professor!"

"Is there any more paratha?"

Sanjay reaches for the plate on the floor. "Yes, but they're cold by now."

All during these absurd conversations they eat his daughter's food. Rita feels funny about that, but Sanjay says nonsense, his daughter made it to be enjoyed. Food is for whoever is hungry.

"I don't mind them cold. Thanks. You'll be relieved to know I wasn't in his class at the time."

"But a law professor. A jurist! He must have been so much older."

"He was seven years older, Sanjay. What about you?"

"I may be old, but at least I'm pure!" He laughs loud belly laughs. His whole body shakes. The bed shakes. Rita feels safe, wrapped up warm in his laughter. He is so domesticated, so easy to entertain. Pure: he says he never knew any women besides his wife. Before he was married, two prostitutes. They don't count.

"We'd better start at the beginning. What about in college?"

"This is getting very silly. Stop."

"Aha! Now we're getting somewhere."

"Just Luis, for a while."

"Why a Chicano?"

"Why not? Now stop. Really. It's annoying."

"Because there's something you're not telling me. Why won't you marry me? You're footloose. Then you'd know where you belong."

The Indian gentleman next door wants to rescue the poor orphan girl, give her food and warm clothes and light a fire in her garret. And she would not be cast out if she married him, as her father was. It's thirty years later. And it's Rita. What can you expect? They are prepared for almost anything from her. They believe in nature, not nurture, and she believes with them.

But she has never told anyone. She shakes her head.

"It is terrible?" Sanjay asks. He is not fooling around anymore. She sees his age in the set of his face. His lips are parted. His cheeks are sagging in a kind of resigned expectation.

"Yes."

He hands her more stuffed bread. "Well, eat something while you tell me, then." To her surprise, his eyes, however old and sympathetic, have turned lustful. He is waiting to hear about a frenzied, tragic love affair. Rita stares right into them as she speaks.

She was seventeen. There was talk in the house about where she would be sent to college. Oh, how she kept them young, kept them abreast of things. She said to her grandmother in the kitchen, making the fish for Friday night, "You have to tell me now. Or I'll go away forever, I swear it."

"Big shot!" Sonia says, her fingers plunged deep in the bowl of chopped fish. "Where will you go? And with what?"

"There's always a way for a girl to make a living, Grandma. This is 1974, after all," and she smirks brazenly. "I know plenty of places I can stay."

A look of doom streaks over Sonia's face, and it is not so much prostitution she is thinking of as certain types of irregular living conditions: dope fiends, drifters, hippies, pads. Rita is bad enough already, with her ideas, her gypsy clothes, her unexplained forays into Manhattan, her odd-looking inky newspapers, the closely typed petitions she brings home indefatigably for them to sign; but at least she sleeps in her bed every night and takes showers. . . . At the same time, the vision of such irregularity holds a fascination for her grandmother, Rita can tell. She sees enticement seasoning the horror in her eyes, orange flecks against the green. Sonia might have tried it herself if she hadn't been so tired, sewing in the factory. Sometimes she even signs the petitions, after Sol goes to bed.

"You're not going anywhere," Sonia says confidently, blinking away her enticement, slapping the fish into ovals, and she shoves the bowl in Rita's direction for help. "Just to college like all your cousins."

"But I'm not the same as them. I have a right to know what I am, don't I? All these years you would never answer me. But I'm not a child anymore. It's my life."

There is something different, this time, in the way she says it, or maybe Sonia is simply worn down—Sol will be going to the hospital for his throat operation very soon; there have been doctors' appointments, consultations; he lays down the law in an ever hoarser voice. "You can't ask this of me!" she groans, but they both understand she means the opposite. Rita waits, her hands growing cold in the bowl of fish. She forms an oval and places it in the baking pan.

"They were separated. They never could get along. I knew. I used to speak to him all the time. No one could stop me from using the phone." She looks at Rita curiously. "I even knew about you."

"What about me?"

"That they had you! But I didn't tell him. That's what he wanted, not to know anything. Like he was dead. So let him not know, I thought." Sonia sits silent, not moving, a hostile witness in the box.

"So?"

She sighs as though she had hoped for a reprieve, that this much would be enough. "So he went over there to get something. They had an argument."

"And?"

She wipes her hands carefully on a dish towel. Then she takes the towel and holds it up to her face, covering her face. Her words come muffled through the towel. "She stabbed him."

"She what?"

"With a knife." She weeps behind the towel.

Rita is weirdly calm. Of all the scenes she has invented, never anything like this. Much more romantic, her visions were. Lost at sea. Activists kidnapped by the Klan. Wasting disease. Cult suicide. Yes, her nights have been busy, but all wrong. "I don't believe it."

"Don't, then. You asked. You pestered me for years."

"It's not possible. He must have been stronger than her."

"But he didn't have the knife," she wails. "Oh, my baby." Shoulders heaving, towel over her face.

Suddenly Rita cannot bear that towel anymore and snatches it away. Her grandmother's hollowed face is wet and blotched and smells of fish. "No. That can't be the whole story. He must have attacked her first."

Sonia gives the maddest laugh, a witch's cackle. "He? The gentlest boy who ever breathed?"

Rita could almost laugh too. Their child, gentle! But she also knows they do not attack. A picture is coming into focus, a kitchen, a hysterical woman who looks like an older version of herself, waving a bread knife; a pale man trying to wrest it from her. But she's too quick, too fierce. . . . Oh God, already she's becoming a type, a caricature. Leave her be. Leave that room altogether, before it gets bloody. . . . What about the baby . . . ? What about the baby . . . ? The baby is in another room, mercifully sleeping, yes. Go back, try again, try it in the living room. The scene has endless possibilities, bloody ones, Rita could labor over it for years. Give up the rest of her life to screening it every possible way: He said . . . No, she said . . . She grabbed . . . No, he . . .

"Wasn't there a trial? Didn't the facts come out at the trial? I bet she was a battered wife." Yes, lately even juries have learned to sympathize. Her poor mother, black and blue? Sonia looks baffled—this is beyond her imaginings. "I'll find out the truth" Rita shouts. "I'll visit her in jail." Where she languishes, thinking only of her lost baby.

"She's not in jail."

"No?"

"Finished. Six years and out. Good behavior! Rita, everyone said it, even her brother, what kind of woman she was, how she treated him so terrible. He was a good man, the brother. He wrote us a letter about . . . I felt sorry for him."

The outrage. She killed Rita's gentle father and she walks the streets free. "She never looked for me?" Now, now, she feels tears. This is the real outrage. Sonia feels it too.

"We wouldn't have given you up anyway. You were my reason to go on living. Two years I waited to see you." She covers her face again, this time with her hand and only for an instant. "And then I got you for good." As she gazes at Rita, her brow, for once, is calm. "You're just like him."

Me! thinks Rita, with my murderer's face? It must be a torment to have me around, reminding everyone. And what is just like him? They never say. Now more than ever she wants so badly to see him, it is almost like a sexual longing— she will die, just shrink and evaporate, if she cannot see him, touch him. She does not recognize the feeling till much later, though, when she knows Sanjay.

("When I know you," she says. "When I know you.")

For her mother Rita does not long—she feels she has her already, in her bones, her blood, the coarseness of her hair. In some essential, inescapable way, she carries her around.

"Why did they get married?" she whispers to Sonia. Why does anyone?

"Ha!" Sonia is recovered now, is getting back to her work. She must know these spasms of grief intimately after so many years, the way people know their attacks of epilepsy or asthma—the shape of their parabolas, and the intensity. She must have learned how to assimilate them into her days and proceed. It strikes Rita that she has never seen her grandmother idle. From dawn onwards Sonia scurries about, shopping, cooking, sewing, driving. Then at ten o'clock she falls exhausted into her old stuffed chair in the living room to read novels under a solitary lamp, while Sol calls every ten minutes, "Come to bed already!"

"Why did they have me?"

"Come on with the fish, Rita. It'll be midnight at this rate before we eat."

There is only one place she wants to go to college: Berkeley. Her grandfather is sure it is because they have the most hippies there. Her grandmother knows better, but in the end Rita gets her way. They are old and weary, no match for her in her new wisdom. For what scope and vision she suddenly possesses! Now she understands why her grandfather cleaves to the rules and her grandmother cleaves to him, all the while raging against God and driving like a maniac. She understands why the family, those stolidly decent people, look at her with a blend of pity and suspicion—it's not the color she is, no, it's that at any moment she may show her true colors. . . . She understands so much, it feels at night as if her head will burst with understanding and with blood. Only the one thing she wants to understand she doesn't.

She will find her and make her tell how it was. How to think about it. Until she knows, between her and the rest of the world is a wall of blood, ever fresh, never clotting, and she will never cross it into a life.

Her mother must have been a Catholic; as a girl she must have knelt and confessed to puny childish sins—lying, being unkind, thinking wicked thoughts. Maybe the Christ in her village church dripped with crimson paint and so she got used to spilled blood, it didn't seem alien and horrifying. It doesn't to Sanjay; he is used to handling it, but what does it tell him?

("Stop torturing yourself. It's only a physical substance, a liquid. It carries things, but not the kinds of things you mean. Don't tell me I traveled halfway across the world to find a mystic."

He's getting to sound like a Jew, thinks Rita. They are changing places.)

When she goes away to school her grandparents are afraid she will become a hippie, a druggie, but instead she spends her free time in San Francisco, the Mission district, where the Mexicans and Chicanos live, looking and waiting. A deranged sort of looking—she doesn't really want to find. She wants to be found. She learns Spanish—relearns—and it nestles lovingly in her mouth. Her tongue wraps around the syllables like a lover returning from exile to embrace his beloved, feeling the familiar contours. People say she sounds like a native speaker. She learns it so she can ask around for her, but she never asks. She doesn't even know her mother's name. Carmen, yes, but not her last name. Useless to ask for her own last name. Her mother does not seem one of the family. She would not have kept it.

("How did you expect to find her? What did you think you were doing?" Sanjay is incredulous. The Rita he knows is so sane, so sensible, aside from the nightmares. So presentable. It would be his pleasure to bring her home to meet his family, once they had gotten used to the idea of a half-Jewish, half-Mexican American lawyer twenty-two years younger.)

What did she think she was doing? Wandering around the Mission looking for a woman who looked like her, who would be looking in turn for a girl like Rita. Only the woman isn't looking. She has never looked. Luncheonettes, candy stores, bars—Rita can't get to like the food she buys as her excuse for being there, heavy and beany, maybe because for her it is the food of despair. She reads the names of singers on posters outside cafés, she reads the personal ads in newspapers, she even studies the names alongside doorbells in dingy, flaking old buildings. Crazy, she knows it. No explanation or story could change the fact. Like God in the trials she staged as a child, it remains: One lives having killed the other. It would be the same fact if the roles were reversed.

Nothing ever happens except some men try to pick her up, and once her pocket is picked in a movie line, and she makes friends with a girl who works in a record store and goes out with her brother for a few months. Rita is drawn by the easy friendliness of the family. She sees a life there that she might retreat into, but she would have to tell so many lies, and even so she would never fit, never feel quite right. By what right is she anywhere, she the most contingent of contingencies, a superfluous mystery? So she breaks it off. And with that, the quest breaks off as well. Enough. She is worn out, like a soldier after battle, like a battleground in the night. For a month, over Christmas vacation of her junior year, she goes home to do nothing but sleep, grinding her teeth.

When Sonia asks anxiously what she plans to do after college, she says she will apply to law school. Because she is tired of her obsessions, tired of the parents she can't remember and who have left her this hard inheritance to swallow, tired of breaking her teeth on it. However hard she gnaws, the mystery won't crack. World without end, she is two years old, and in the next room is some kind of dreadful racket going on that will not let her sleep, some kind of screeching not at all like the singing she is used to, and maybe it is all a bad dream, but the next thing she knows she is in an airplane with two strange men who are interchangeable and who weep, and it is a miserable trip, she wets her pants, she throws up.

"Rita, Rita." Sanjay takes her in his arms. "Lie down and rest. Give it up."

Lying there, Rita wonders once again who she would be had she been left with her aunt and uncle in the bar. Maybe then her mother would have rushed to her when she got out of jail, like a doe flying to her fawn, and sheltered her and told her . . . everything. Or would she have done as the mother eel, who flees to the other end of the world and leaves its young behind, groping in slime? Maybe she could have become a nightclub singer too? But she has no voice— she would probably work in a store like Rosalia. Or go off to New York to search for her father's family, who would appear exotic and a little alluring. She might speak English with a rippling musical accent and move and dress and feel about the world in a different way. She could be almost anyone, and anywhere. Even now, there are times when she thinks of her name and who it stands for, and it feels like looking in a mirror and seeing a blank sheet, the sheet covering a mirror in a house of the bereaved. But she is this, and here, this person in Sanjay's arms.

She thought he would be horrified, repelled by her. Instead he has fallen asleep holding her, his arm draped across her middle like a sash. She watches him sleep for a while, then gets up and tiptoes around the bedroom. She takes a good look at the photograph of his wife. Yes, there is a certain resemblance. The result of nature, history, the migrations of people, and love.

It is strange that with all the hours she has spent in this bedroom she has never poked around. She opens the dresser drawers, one after another, but all she sees are Sanjay's socks and underwear and handkerchiefs neatly and predictably folded. Then, on a shelf in the closet she finds a pile of saris, also neatly folded, all colors, generous, deep colors, gold threads running through the fabrics. She chooses a red one, the bridal color. But she can't figure out how to get it on right. It is fun, this dressing up; she did it as a child. Vashti. Finally she gets the sari on in a makeshift fashion, not the way Sanjay's wife used to wear it. In the bottom drawer of the night table she finds little jars of powders—red, amber, green, blue—and she plays with them, dabs them on her hands, puts some green on her eyelids. She has seen women with a spot of red in the center of the forehead, but she is not sure what it means, maybe a symbol of Hindu caste or rank; she doesn't dare do it. She appraises herself in the mirror. Queen Esther, at last. Behind her in the mirror she sees Sanjay roll over and open his eyes. He blinks and the color drains away, leaving him yellowish.

"Rita? What are you doing?"

"How do I look?"

"That's not how it goes. Don't, anyway. Take it off. It's not right."

She steps to the edge of the bed, presenting herself. "Fix it. You must know how it goes. You must have seen it done a million times."

"I don't. Do you know how to tie a tie?"

She tries to dab some red powder on him, but he moves out of reach. He won't play. "Please, Rita. Stop."

She yanks off the red sari, the bridal color, rolls it into a ball, and weeps into it.

"But I love you," he protests, a frightening look of middle-aged acceptance on his face. He does not show any shock at what she has told him—that is what is frightening. Will time do that to her too, and then what will she have left? "I do, Rita." If she didn't know him, his smile might seem simpleminded. "You don't have to masquerade for me to love you."

But she cannot believe it. It costs so much.

Angela (Olive) Carter 1940–1992

Writer of children's books, essays, newspaper articles, poetry, and fiction, Angela Carter often combined genres, winning the Somerset Maugham Award in 1969 for her novel *Several Perceptions*. Carter also demonstrated a pronounced interest in fantasy and mythology, especially in one of her novels, *The War of Dreams* (1983), and in story collections such as *The Bloody Chamber* (1979). The latter features adult versions of fairy tales, such as *Little Red Riding Hood;* Carter also wrote several adult novels that explore her interest in female desire. Critic James Brockway comments that Carter, "like all geniuses . . . walks one tightrope on one side of which yawns the chasm of madness, and the other the chasm of bathos. . . ." Carter attended the University of Bristol, graduating in 1965. Her intriguing proclamation regarding herself has been widely quoted: She was the progeny, in her words, of "witch blood on . . . father's side; solid radical trade-unionists on mother's."

THE LOVES OF LADY PURPLE

The Notorious Amours of Lady Purple
The Shameless Oriental Venus

When she was only a few days old, her mother wrapped her in a tattered blanket and abandoned her on the doorstep of a prosperous merchant and his barren wife. These respectable *bourgeois* were to become the siren's first dupes. They lavished upon her all the attentions which love and money could devise and yet they reared a flower which, although perfumed, was carnivorous. At the age of twelve, she seduced her foster-father. Utterly besotted with her, he trusted to her the key of the safe where he kept all his money and she immediately robbed it of every farthing.

Packing his treasure in a laundry basket together with the clothes and jewellery he had already given her, she then stabbed her first lover and his wife, her foster mother, in their bellies with a knife used in the kitchen to slice fish. Then she set fire to their house to cover the traces of her guilt. She annihilated her own childhood in the blaze that destroyed her first home and, springing like a corrupt phoenix from the pyre of her crime, she rose again in the pleasure quarters, where she at once hired herself out to the madame of the most imposing brothel.

In the pleasure quarters, life passed entirely in artificial day for the bustling noon of those crowded alleys came at the time of drowsing midnight for those who lived outside that inverted, sinister, abominable world which functioned only to gratify the whims of the senses. Every rococo desire the mind of man might, in its perverse ingenuity, devise found ample gratification here, amongst the hall of mirrors, the flagellation parlours, the cabarets of nature-defying copulations and the ambiguous soirées held by men-women and female men. Flesh was the speciality of every house and it came piping hot, served up with all the garnishes imaginable. The Professor's puppets dryly and perfunctorily performed these tactical manœuvres like toy soldiers in a mock battle of carnality.

Along the streets, the women for sale, the mannequins of desire, were displayed in wicker cages so that potential customers could saunter past inspecting them at leisure. These exalted prostitutes sat motionless as idols. Upon their real features had been painted symbolic abstractions of the various aspects of allure and the fantastic elaboration of their dress hinted it covered a different kind of skin. The cork heels of their shoes were so high they could not walk but only totter and the sashes round their waists were of brocade so stiff the movements of the arms were cramped and scant so they presented attitudes of physical unease which, though powerfully moving, derived partly, at least, from the deaf assistant's lack of manual dexterity, for his apprenticeship had not as yet reached even the journeyman stage. Therefore the gestures of these *hetaerae* were as stylized as if they had been clockwork. Yet, however fortuitously, all worked out so well it seemed each one was as absolutely circumscribed as a figure in rhetoric, reduced by the rigorous discipline of her vocation to the nameless essence of the idea of woman, a metaphysical abstraction of the female which could, on payment of a specific fee, be instantly translated into an oblivion either sweet or terrible, depending on the nature of her talents.

Lady Purple's talents verged on the unspeakable. Booted, in leather, she became a mistress of the whip before her fifteenth birthday. Subsequently, she graduated in the mysteries of the torture chamber, where she thoroughly researched all manner of ingenious mechanical devices. She utilized a baroque apparatus of funnel, humiliation, syringe, thumbscrew, contempt and spiritual anguish; to her lovers, such severe usage was both bread and wine and a kiss from her cruel mouth was the sacrament of suffering.

Soon she became successful enough to be able to maintain her own establishment. When she was at the height of her fame, her slightest fancy might cost a young man his patrimony and, as soon as she squeezed him dry of fortune, hope and dreams, for she was quite remorseless, she abandoned him; or else she might, perhaps, lock him up in her closet and force him to watch her while she took for nothing to her usually incredibly expensive bed a beggar encountered by chance on the street. She was no malleable, since frigid, substance upon which desires might be executed; she was not a true prostitute for she was the object on which men prostituted themselves. She, the sole perpetrator of desire, proliferated malign fantasies all around her and used her lovers as the canvas on which she executed boudoir masterpieces of destruction. Skins melted in the electricity she generated.

Soon, either to be rid of them or, simply, for pleasure, she took to murdering her lovers. From the leg of a politician she poisoned she cut out the thigh bone and took it to a craftsman who made it into a flute for her. She persuaded succeeding lovers to play tunes for her on this instrument and, with the supplest and most serpentine grace, she danced for them to its unearthly music. At this point, the dumb girl put down her samisen and took up a bamboo pipe from which issued weird cadences and, though it was by no means the climax of the play, this dance was the apex of the Professor's performance for the numinous pavane progressed like waves of darkness and, as she stamped, wheeled and turned to the sound of her malign chamber music, Lady Purple became entirely the image of irresistible evil.

She visited men like a plague, both bane and terrible enlightenment, and she was as contagious as the plague. The final condition of all her lovers was this: they went clothed in rags held together with the discharge of their sores, and their eyes held an awful vacancy, as if their minds had been blown out like candles. A parade of ghastly spectres, they trundled across the stage, their passage implemented by medieval horrors for, here, an arm left its socket and whisked up out of sight into the flies and, there, a nose hung in the air after a gaunt shape that went tottering noseless forward.

So foreclosed Lady Purple's pyrotechnical career, which ended as if it had been indeed a firework display, in ashes, desolation and silence. She became more ghastly than those she had infected. Circe at last became a swine herself and, seared to the bone by her own flame, walked the pavements like a dessicated shadow. Disaster obliterated her. Cast out with stones and oaths by those who had once adulated her, she was reduced to scavenging on the seashore, where she plucked hair from the heads of the drowned to sell to wigmakers who catered to the needs of more fortunate since less diabolic courtesans.

Now her finery, her paste jewels and her enormous superimposition of black hair hung up in the green room and she wore a drab rag of coarse hemp for the final scene of her desperate decline, when, outrageous nymphomaniac, she practised extraordinary necrophilies on the bloated corpses the sea tossed contemptuously at her feet for her dry rapacity had become entirely mechanical and still she repeated her former actions though she herself was utterly other. She abrogated her humanity. She became nothing but wood and hair. She became a marionette herself, herself her own replica, the dead yet moving image of the shameless Oriental Venus.

The professor was at last beginning to feel the effects of age and travel. Sometimes he complained in noisy silence to his nephew of pains, aches, stiffening muscles, tautening sinews, and shortness of breath. He began to limp a little and left to the boy all the rough work of mantling and dismantling. Yet the balletic mime of Lady Purple grew all the more remarkable with the passage of the years, as though his energy, channelled for so long into a single purpose, refined itself more and more in time and was finally reduced to a single, purified, concentrated essence which was transmitted entirely to the doll; and the Professor's mind attained a condition not unlike that of the swordsman trained in Zen, whose sword is his soul, so that neither sword nor swordsman has meaning without the presence of the other. Such swordsmen, armed, move towards their victims like automata, in a state of perfect emptiness, no longer aware of any distinction between self or weapon. Master and marionette had arrived at this condition.

Age could not touch Lady Purple for, since she had never aspired to mortality, she effortlessly transcended it and, though a man who was less aware of the expertise it needed to make her so much as raise her left hand might, now and then, have grieved to see how she defied ageing, the Professor had no fancies of that kind. Her miraculous inhumanity rendered their friendship entirely free from the anthropomorphic, even on the night of the Feast of All Hallows when, the mountain-dwellers murmured, the dead held masked balls in the graveyards while the devil played the fiddle for them.

The rough audience received their copeck's worth of sensation and filed out into a fairground which still roared like a playful tiger with life. The foundling girl put away her samisen and swept out the booth while the nephew set the stage afresh for next day's matinée. Then the Professor noticed Lady Purple had ripped a seam in the drab shroud she wore in the final act. Chattering to himself with displeasure, he undressed her as she swung idly, this way and that way, from her anchored strings and then he sat down on a wooden property stool on the stage and plied his needle like a good housewife. The task was more difficult than it seemed at first for the fabric was also torn and required an embroidery of darning so he told his asistants to go home together to the lodging house and let him finish his task alone.

A small oil-lamp hanging from a nail at the side of the stage cast an insufficient but tranquil light. The white puppet glimmered fitfully through the mists which crept into the theatre from the night outside through all the chinks and gaps in the tarpaulin and now began to fold their chiffon drapes around her as if to decorously conceal her or else to render her more translucently enticing. The mist softened her painted smile a little and her head dangled to one side. In the last act, she wore a loose, black wig, the locks of which hung down as far as her softly upholstered flanks, and the ends of her hair flickered with her random movements, creating upon the white blackboard of her back one of those fluctuating optical effects which make us question the veracity of our vision. As he often did when he was alone with her, the Professor chatted to her in his native language, rattling away an intimacy of nothings, of the weather, of his rheumatism, of the unpalatability and expense of the region's coarse, black bread, while the small winds took her as their partner in a scarcely perceptible *valse triste* and the mist grew minute by minute thicker, more pallid and more viscous.

The old man finished his mending. He rose and, with a click or two of his old bones, he went to put the forlorn garment neatly on its green room hanger beside the glowing, winey purple gown splashed with rosy peonies, sashed with carmine, that she wore for her appalling dance. He was about to lay her, naked, in her coffin-shaped case and carry her back to their chilly bedroom when he paused. He was seized with the childish desire to see her again in all her finery once more that night. He took her dress off its hanger and carried it to where she drifted, at nobody's volition but that of the wind. As he put her clothes on her, he murmured to her as if she were a little girl for the vulnerable flaccidity of her arms and legs made a six-foot baby of her.

'There, there, my pretty; this arm here, that's right! Oops a daisy, easy does it . . .'

Then he tenderly took off her penitential wig and clicked his tongue to see how defencelessly bald she was beneath it. His arms cracked under the weight of her immense chignon and he had to stretch up on tiptoe to set it in place because, since she was as large as life, she was rather taller than he. But then the ritual of apparelling was over and she was complete again.

Now she was dressed and decorated, it seemed her dry wood had all at once put out an entire springtime of blossoms for the old man alone to enjoy. She could have acted as the model for the most beautiful of women, the image of that woman whom only memory and imagination can devise, for the lamplight fell too mildly to sustain her air of arrogance and so gently it made her long nails look as harmless as ten fallen petals. The Professor had a curious habit; he always used to kiss his doll good night.

A child kisses its toy before he pretends it sleeps although, even though he is only a child, he knows its eyes are not constructed to close so it will always be a sleeping beauty no kiss will waken. One in the grip of savage loneliness might kiss the face he sees before him in the mirror for want of any other face to kiss. These are kisses of the same kind; they are the most poignant of caresses, for they are too humble and too despairing to wish or seek for any response.

Yet, in spite of the Professor's sad humility, his chapped and withered mouth opened on hot, wet, palpitating flesh.

The sleeping wood had wakened. Her pearl teeth crashed against his with the sound of cymbals and her warm, fragrant breath blew around him like an Italian gale. Across her suddenly moving face flashed a whole kaleidoscope of expression, as though she were running instantaneously through the entire repertory of human feeling, practising, in an endless moment of time, all the scales of emotion as if they were music. Crushing vines, her arms, curled about the Professor's delicate apparatus of bone and skin with the insistent pressure of an actuality by far more authentically living than that of his own, time-desiccated flesh. Her kiss emanated from the dark country where desire is objectified and lives. She gained entry into the world by a mysterious loophole in its metaphysics and, during her kiss, she sucked his breath from his lungs so that her own bosom heaved with it.

So, unaided, she began her next performance with an apparent improvisation which was, in reality, only a variation upon a theme. She sank her teeth into his throat and drained him. He did not have the time to make a sound. When he was empty, he slipped straight out of her embrace down to her feet with a dry rustle, as of a cast armful of dead leaves, and there he sprawled on the floor-boards as empty, useless and bereft of meaning as his own tumbled shawl.

She tugged impatiently at the strings which moored her and out they came in bunches from her head, her arms and her legs. She stripped them off her fingertips and stretched out her long, white hands, flexing and unflexing them again and again. For the first time for years, or, perhaps, for ever, she closed her bloodstained teeth thankfully, for her cheeks still ached from the smile her maker had carved into the stuff of her former face. She stamped her elegant feet to make the new blood flow more freely there.

Unfurling and unravelling itself, her hair leapt out of its confinements of combs, cords and lacquer to root itself back into her scalp like cut grass bounding out of the stack and back again into the ground. First, she shivered with pleasure to feel the cold, for she realized she was experienceing a physical sensation; then either she remembered or else she believed she remembered that the sensation of cold was not a pleasurable one so she knelt and, drawing off the old man's shawl, wrapped it carefully about herself. Her every motion was instinct with a wonderful, reptilian liquidity. The mist outside now seemed to rush like a tide into the booth and broke against her in white breakers so that she looked like a baroque figurehead, lone survivor of a shipwreck, thrown up on a shore by the tide.

But whether she was renewed or newly born, returning to life or becoming alive, awakening from a dream or coalescing into the form of a fantasy generated in her wooden skull by the mere repetition so many times of the same invariable actions, the brain beneath the reviving hair contained only the scantiest notion of the possibilities now open to it. All that had seeped into the wood was the notion that she might perform the forms of life not so much by the skill of another as by her own desire that she did so, and she did not possess enough equipment to comprehend the complex circularity of the logic which inspired her for she had only been a marionette. But, even if she could not perceive it, she could not escape the tautological paradox in which she was trapped; had the marionette all the time parodied the living or was she, now living, to parody her own performance as a marionette? Although she was now manifestly a woman, young and extravagantly beautiful, the leprous whiteness of her face gave her the appearance of a corpse animated solely by demonic will.

Deliberately, she knocked the lamp down from its hook on the wall. A puddle of oil spread at once on the boards of the stage. A little flame leapt across the fuel and immediately began to eat the curtains. She went down the aisle between the benches to the little ticket booth. Already, the stage was an inferno and the corpse of the Professor tossed this way and that on an uneasy bed of fire. But she did not look behind her after she slipped out into the fairground although soon the theatre was burning like a paper lantern ignited by its own candle.

Now it was so late that the sideshows, gingerbread stalls and liquor booths were locked and shuttered and only the moon, half obscured by drifting cloud, gave out a meagre, dirty light, which sullied and deformed the flimsy pasteboard façades, so the place, deserted with curds of vomit, refuse of revelry, underfoot, looked utterly desolate.

She walked rapidly past the silent roundabouts, accompanied only by the fluctuating mists, towards the town, making her way like a homing pigeon, out of logical necessity, to the single brothel it contained.

Judy Grahn 1940–

G rahn, a poet and fiction writer, identifies herself as a lesbian feminist. In 1969, she co-founded the first all-women's press, the Oakland Women's Press Collective, which published a variety of "new voices," featuring her own *Edward the Dyke and Other Poems* (1971) and *A Woman Is Talking to Death* (1974). Grahn is also an essayist and critic; she has edited an anthology, *Really Reading Gertrude Stein* (1989), and has written several novels and a "verse play," *Queen of Swords* (1987). She currently teaches creative writing and literature in the Bay Area.

CAROL, IN THE PARK, CHEWING ON STRAWS

She has taken a woman lover
whatever shall we do
she has taken a woman lover
how lucky it wasn't you
And all the day through she smiles and lies   5
and grits her teeth and pretends to be shy,
or weak, or busy. Then she goes home
and pounds her own nails, makes her own
bets, and fixes her own car, with her friend.
She goes as far   10
as women can go without protection
from men.
On weekends she dreams of becoming a tree;
a tree that dreams it is ground up
and sent to the paper factory, where it   15
lies helpless in sheets, until it dreams
of becoming a paper airplane, and rises
on its own current; where it turns into a
bird, a great coasting bird that dreams of becoming
more free, even, than that—a feather, finally, or   20
a piece of air with lightning in it.
    she has taken a woman lover
    whatever can we say
She walks around all day
quietly, but underneath it   25
she's electric;
angry energy inside a passive form.

The common woman is as common
as a thunderstorm.

II. Ella, in a square apron, along Highway 80

She's a copperheaded waitress,
tired and sharp-worded, she hides
her bad brown tooth behind a wicked
smile, and flicks her ass
out of habit, to fend off the pass   5
that passes for affection.
She keeps her mind the way men
keep a knife—keen to strip the game
down to her size. She has a thin spine,
swallows her eggs cold, and tells lies.   10
She slaps a wet rag at the truck drivers
if they should complain. She understands
the neccessity for pain, turns away
the smaller tips, out of pride, and
keeps a flask under the counter. Once,   15
she shot a lover who misused her child.
Before she got out of jail, the courts had pounced
and given the child away. Like some isolated lake,
her flat blue eyes take care of their own stark
bottoms. Her hands are nervous, curled, ready   20
to scrape.
The common woman is as common
as a rattlesnake.

Maxine Hong Kingston 1940–

Maxine Hong Kingston auspiciously burst on the literary scene with her first book, *The Woman Warrior: Memoirs of a Girlhood Among Ghosts* in 1976. Winner of the National Book Critics Circle Award, the book combines fiction with autobiography as it embodies the clash of two cultures and addresses the cultural conflicts Chinese Americans must confront. The 1980 American Book Award winner, *China Men*, continues the theme of Asian identity, with Kingston portraying her relationship with her father, her early ancestors who came to America to build the railroads, and her brother's Naval experience in Vietnam. Other works on Asian identity include *Hawaii: One Summer* (1987), *Through the Black Curtain* (1988), and P.E.N. West award winner *Tripmaster Monkey: His Fake Book* (1989). Born the eldest child of Chinese immigrant parents who operated a laundry in Stockton, California, Kingston's writing would eventually draw from the stories told by the Chinese families who regularly gathered at the laundry. A recipient of Guggenheim and NEA writing fellowships, Kingston has taught at a variety of high schools and universities throughout Hawaii and California, including the University of California at Berkeley.

NO NAME WOMAN

"You must not tell anyone," my mother said, "what I am about to tell you. In China your father had a sister who killed herself. She jumped into the family well. We say that your father has all brothers because it is as if she had never been born.

"In 1924 just a few days after our village celebrated seventeen hurry-up weddings—to make sure that every young man who went 'out on the road' would responsibly come home—your father and his brothers and your grandfather and his brothers and your aunt's new husband sailed for America, the Gold Mountain. It was your grandfather's last trip. Those lucky enough to get contracts waved good-bye from the decks. They fed and guarded the stowaways and helped them off in Cuba, New York, Bali, Hawaii. 'We'll meet in California next year,' they said. All of them sent money home.

"I remember looking at your aunt one day when she and I were dressing; I had not noticed before that she had such a protruding melon of a stomach. But I did not think, 'She's pregnant,' until she began to look like other pregnant women, her skirt pulling and the white tops of her black pants showing. She could not have been pregnant, you see, because her husband had been gone for years. No one said anything. We did not discuss it. In early summer she was ready to have the child, long after the time when it could have been possible.

"The village had also been counting. On the night the baby was to be born the villagers raided our house. Some were crying. Like a great saw, teeth strung with lights, files of people walked zigzag across our land, tearing the rice. Their lanterns doubled in the disturbed black water, which drained away through the broken bunds. As the villagers closed in, we could see that some of them, probably men and women we knew well, wore white masks. The people with long hair hung it over their faces. Women with short hair made it stand up on end. Some had tied white bands around their foreheads, arms, and legs.

"At first they threw mud and rocks at the house. Then they threw eggs and began slaughtering our stock. We could hear the animals scream their deaths— the roosters, the pigs, a last great roar from the ox. Familiar wild heads flared in our night windows; the villagers encircled us. Some of the faces stopped to peer at us, their eyes rushing like searchlights. The hands flattened against the panes, framed heads, and left red prints.

"The villagers broke in the front and the back doors at the same time, even though we had not locked the doors against them. Their knives dripped with the blood of our animals. They smeared blood on the doors and walls. One woman swung a chicken, whose throat she had slit, splattering blood in red arcs about her. We stood together in the middle for our house, in the family hall with the pictures and tables of the ancestors around us, and looked straight ahead.

"At that time the house had only two wings. When the men came back, we would build two more to enclose our courtyard and a third one to begin a second courtyard. The villagers pushed through both wings, even your grand-parents' rooms, to find your aunt's, which was also mine until the men returned. From this room a new wing for one of the younger families would grow. They ripped up her clothes and shoes and broke her combs, grinding them under-foot. They tore her work from the loom. They scattered the cooking fire and rolled the new weaving in it. We could hear them in the kitchen breaking our bowls and banging the pots. They overturned the great waist-high earthenware jugs; duck eggs, picked fruits, vegetables burst out and mixed in acrid torrents. The old woman from the next field swept a broom through the air and loosed the spirits-of-the-broom over our heads. 'Pig.' 'Ghost.' 'Pig,' they sobbed and scolded while they ruined our house.

"When they left, they took sugar and oranges to bless themselves. They cut pieces from the dead animals. Some of them took bowls that were not broken and clothes that were not torn. Afterward we swept up the rice and sewed it back up into sacks. But the smells from the spilled preserves lasted. Your aunt gave birth in the pigsty that night. The next morning when I went for the water, I found her and the baby plugging up the family well.

"Don't let your father know that I told you. He denies her. Now that you have started to menstruate, what happened to her could happen to you. Don't humiliate us. You wouldn't like to be forgotten as if you had never been born. The villagers are watchful."

Whenever she had to warn us about life, my mother told stories that ran like this one, a story to grow up on. She tested our strength to establish realities. Those in the emigrant generations who could not reassert brute survival died young and far from home. Those of us in the first American generations have had to figure out how the invisible world the emigrants built around our child-hoods fit in solid America.

The emigrants confused the gods by diverting their curses, misleading them with crooked streets and false names. They must try to confuse their offspring as well, who, I suppose, threaten them in similar ways—always trying to get things straight, always trying to name the unspeakable. The Chinese I know hide their names; sojourners take new names when their lives change and guard their real names with silence.

Chinese-Americans, when you try to understand what things in you are Chinese, how do you separate what is peculiar to childhood, to poverty, insanities, one family, your mother who marked your growing with stories, from what is Chinese? What is Chinese tradition and what is the movies?

If I want to learn what clothes my aunt wore, whether flashy or ordinary, I would have to begin, "Remember Father's drowned-in-the-well sister?" I cannot ask that. My mother has told me once and for all the useful parts. She will add nothing unless powered by Necessity, a riverbank that guides her life. She plants vegetable gardens rather than lawns; she carries the odd-shaped tomatoes home from the fields and eats food left for the gods.

Whenever we did frivolous things, we used up energy; we flew high kites. We children came up off the ground over the melting cones our parents brought home from work and the American movie on New Year's Day—*Oh, You Beautiful Doll* with Betty Grable one year, and *She Wore A Yellow Ribbon* with John Wayne another year. After the one carnival ride each, we paid in guilt; our tired father counted his change on the dark walk home.

Adultery is extravagance. Could people who hatch their own chicks and eat the embryos and the heads for delicacies and boil the feet in vinegar for party food, leaving only the gravel, eating even the gizzard lining—could such people engender a prodigal aunt? To be a woman, to have a daughter in starvation time was a waste enough. My aunt could not have been the lone romantic who gave up everything for sex. Women in the old China did not choose. Some man had commanded her to lie with him and be his secret evil. I wonder whether he masked himself when he joined the raid on her family.

Perhaps she encountered him in the fields or on the mountain where the daughters-in-law collected fuel. Or perhaps he first noticed her in the marketplace. He was not a stranger because the village housed no strangers. She had to have dealings with him other than sex. Perhaps he worked an adjoining field, or he sold her the cloth for the dress she sewed and wore. His demand must have surprised, then terrified her. She obeyed him; she always did as she was told.

When the family found a young man in the next village to be her husband, she stood tractably beside the best rooster, his proxy, and promised before they met that she would be his forever. She was lucky that he was her age and she would be the first wife, an advantage secure now. The night she first saw him, he had sex with her. Then he left for America. She had almost forgotten what he looked like. When she tried to envision him, she only saw the black and white face in the group photograph the men had had taken before leaving.

The other man was not, after all, much different from her husband. They both gave orders: she followed. "If you tell your family, I'll beat you. I'll kill you. Be here again next week." No one talked sex, ever. And she might have separated the rapes from the rest of living if only she did not have to buy her oil from him or gather wood in the same forest. I want her fear to have lasted just as long as rape lasted so that the fear could have been contained. No drawn-out fear. But women at sex hazarded birth and hence lifetimes. The fear did not stop but permeated everywhere. She told the man, "I think I'm pregnant." He organized the raid against her.

On nights when my mother and father talked about their life back home, sometimes they mentioned an "outcast table" whose business they still seemed to be settling, their voices tight. In a commensal tradition, where food is precious, the powerful older people made wrongdoers eat alone. Instead of letting them start separate new lives like the Japanese, who could become samurais and geishas, the Chinese family, faces averted but eyes glowering sideways, hung on to the offenders and fed them leftovers. My aunt must have lived in the same house as my parents and eaten at an outcast table. My mother spoke about the raid as if she had seen it, when she and my aunt, a daughter-in-law to a different household, should not have been living together at all. Daughters-in-law lived with their husbands' parents, not their own; a synonym for marriage in Chinese is "taking a daughter-in-law." Her husband's parents could have sold her, mortgaged her, stoned her. But they had sent her back to her own mother and father, a mysterious act hinting at disgraces not told me. Perhaps they had thrown her out to deflect the avengers.

She was the only daughter; her four brothers went with her father, husband, and uncles "out on the road" and for some years became Western men. When the goods were divided among the family, three of the brothers took land, and the youngest, my father, chose an education. After my grandparents gave their daughter away to her husband's family, they had dispensed all the adventure and all the property. They expected her alone to keep the traditional ways, which her brothers, now among the barbarians, could fumble without detection. The heavy, deep-rooted women were to maintain the past against the flood, safe for returning. But the rare urge west had fixed upon our family, and so my aunt crossed boundaries not delineated in space.

The work of preservation demands that the feelings playing about in one's guts not be turned into action. Just watch their passing like cherry blossoms. But perhaps my aunt, my forerunner, caught in a slow life, let dreams grow and fade and after some months or years went toward what persisted. Fear at the enormities of the forbidden kept her desires delicate, wire and bone. She looked at a man because she liked the way the hair was tucked behind his ears, or she liked the question-mark line of a long torso curving at the shoulder and straight at the hip. For warm eyes or a soft voice or a slow walk—that's all—a few hairs, a line, a brightness, a sound, a pace, she gave up family. She offered us up for a charm that vanished with tiredness, a pigtail that didn't toss when the wind died. Why, the wrong lighting could erase the dearest thing about him.

It could very well have been, however, that my aunt did not take subtle enjoyment of her friend, but, a wild woman, kept rollicking company. Imagining her free with sex doesn't fit, though. I don't know any women like that, or men either. Unless I see her life branching into mine, she gives me no ancestral help.

To sustain her being in love, she often worked at herself in the mirror, guessing at the colors and shapes that would interest him, changing them frequently in order to hit on the right combination. She wanted him to look back.

On a farm near the sea, a woman who tended her appearance reaped a reputation for eccentricity. All the married women blunt-cut their hair in flaps about their ears or pulled it back in tight buns. No nonsense. Neither style blew easily into heart-catching tangles. And at their weddings they displayed themselves in their long hair for the last time. "It brushed the backs of my knees," my mother tells me. "It was braided, and even so, it brushed the backs of my knees."

At the mirror my aunt combed individuality into her bob. A bun could have been contrived to escape into black streamers blowing in the wind or in quiet wisps about her face, but only the older women in our picture album wear buns. She brushed her hair back from her forehead, tucking the flaps behind her ears. She looped a piece of thread, knotted into a circle between her index fingers and thumbs, and ran the double strand across her forehead. When she closed her fingers as if she were making a pair of shadow geese bite, the string twisted together catching the little hairs. Then she pulled the thread away from her skin, ripping the hairs out neatly, her eyes watering from the needles of pain. Opening her fingers, she cleaned the thread, then rolled it along her hairline and the tops of her eyebrows. My mother did the same to me and my sisters and herself. I used to believe that the expression "caught by the short hairs" meant a captive held with a depilatory string. It especially hurt at the temples, but my mother said we were lucky we didn't have to have our feet bound when we were seven. Sisters used to sit on their beds and cry together, she said, as their mothers or their slave removed the bandages for a few minutes each night and let the blood gush back into their veins. I hope that the man my aunt loved appreciated a smooth brow, that he wasn't just a tits-and-ass man.

Once my aunt found a freckle on her chin, at a spot that the almanac said predestined her for unhappiness. She dug it out with a hot needle and washed the wound with peroxide.

More attention to her looks than these pullings of hairs and pickings at spot would have caused gossip among the villagers. They owned work clothes and good clothes, and they wore good clothes for feasting the new seasons. But since a woman combing her hair hexes beginnings, my aunt rarely found an occasion to look her best. Women looked like great sea snails—the corded wood, babies, and laundry they carried were the whorls on their backs. The Chinese did not admire a bent back; goddesses and warriors stood straight. Still there must have been a marvelous freeing of beauty when a worker laid down her burden and stretched and arched.

Such commonplace loveliness, however, was not enough for my aunt. She dreamed of a lover for the fifteen days of New Year's, the time for families to exchange visits, money, and food. She plied her secret comb. And sure enough she cursed the year, the family, the village, and herself.

Even as her hair lured her imminent lover, many other men looked at her. Uncles, cousins, nephews, brothers would have looked, too, had they been home between journeys. Perhaps they had already been restraining their curiosity, and they left, fearful that their glances, like a field of nesting birds, might be startled and caught. Poverty hurt, and that was their first reason for leaving. But another, final reason for leaving the crowded house was the never-said.

She may have been unusually beloved, the precious only daughter, spoiled and mirror gazing because of the affection the family lavished on her. When her husband left, they welcomed the chance to take her back from the in-laws; she could live like the little daughter for just a while longer. There are stories that my grandfather was different from other people, "crazy ever since the little Jap bayoneted him in the head." He used to put his naked penis on the dinner table, laughing. And one day he brought home a baby girl, wrapped up inside his brown western-style greatcoat. He had traded one of his sons, probably my father, the youngest, for her. My grandmother made him trade back. When he finally got a daughter of his own, he doted on her. They must have all loved her, except perhaps my father, the only brother who never went back to China, having once been traded for a girl.

Brothers and sisters, newly men and women, had to efface their sexual color and present plain miens. Disturbing hair and eyes, a smile like no other, threatened the ideal of five generations living under one roof. To focus blurs, people shouted face to face and yelled from room to room. The immigrants I know have loud voices, unmodulated to American tones even after years away from the village where they called their friendships out across the fields. I have not been able to stop my mother's screams in public libraries or over telephones. Walking erect (knees straight, toes pointed forward, not pigeon-toed, which is Chinese-feminine), and speaking in an inaudible voice, I have tried to turn myself American-feminine. Chinese communication was loud, public. Only sick people had to whisper. But at the dinner table, where the family members came nearest one another, no one could talk, not the outcasts nor any eaters. Every word that falls from the mouth is a coin lost. Silently they gave and accepted food with both hands. A preoccupied child who took his bowl with one hand got a sideways glare. A complete moment of total attention is due everyone alike. Children and lovers have no singularity here, but my aunt used a secret voice, a separate attentiveness.

She kept the man's name to herself throughout her labor and dying; she did not accuse him that he be punished with her. To save her inseminator's name she gave silent birth.

He may have been somebody in her own household, but intercourse with a man outside the family would have been no less abhorrent. All the village were kinsmen, and the titles shouted in loud country voices never let kinship be forgotten. Any man within visiting distance would have been neutralized as a lover—"brother," "younger brother," "older brother"—one hundred and fifteen relationship titles. Parents researched birth charts probably not so much to assure good fortune as to circumvent incest in a population that has but one hundred surnames. Everybody has eight million relatives. How useless then sexual mannerisms, how dangerous.

As if it came from an atavism deeper than fear, I used to add "brother" silently to boy's names. It hexed the boys, who would or would not ask me to dance, and made them less scary and as familiar and deserving of benevolence as girls.

But, of course, I hexed myself also—no dates. I should have stood up, both arms waving, and shouted out across libraries, "Hey you! Love me back." I had no idea, though, how to make attraction selective, how to control its direction and magnitude. If I made myself American-pretty so that the five or six Chinese boys in the class fell in love with me, everyone else—the Caucasian, Negro, and Japanese boys—would too. Sisterliness, dignified and honorable, made much more sense.

Attraction eludes control so stubbornly that whole societies designed to organize relationships among people cannot keep order, not even when they bind people to one another from chilhood and raise them together. Among the very poor and the wealthy, brothers married their adopted sisters, like doves. Our family allowed some romance, paying adult brides' prices and providing dowries so that their sons and daughters could marry strangers. Marriage promises to turn strangers into friendly relatives—a nation of siblings.

In the village structure, spirits shimmered among the live creatures, balanced and held in equilibrium by time and land. But one human being flaring up into violence could open up a black hole, a maelstrom that pulled in the sky. The frightened villagers, who depended on one another to maintain the real, went to my aunt to show her a personal, physical representation of the break she had made in the "roundness." Misallying couples snapped off the future, which was to be embodied in true offspring. The villagers punished her for acting as if she could have a private life, secret and apart from them.

If my aunt had betrayed the family at a time of large grain yields and peace, when many boys were born, and wings were being built on many houses, perhaps she might have escaped such severe punishment. But the men—hungry, greedy, tired of planting in dry soil, cuckolded—had had to leave the village in order to send food-money home. There were ghost plagues, bandit plagues, wars with the Japanese, floods. My Chinese brother and sister had died of an unknown sickness. Adultery, perhaps only a mistake during good times, became a crime when the village needed food.

The round moon cakes and round doorways, the round tables of graduated size that fit one roundness into another, round windows and rice bowls—these talismans had lost their power to warn this family of the law: A family must be whole, faithfully keeping the descent line by having sons to feed the old and the dead, who in turn look after the family. The villagers came to show my aunt and her lover-in-hiding a broken house. The villagers were speeding up the circling of events because she was too shortsighted to see that her infidelity had already harmed the village, that waves of consequences would return unpredictably, sometimes in disguise, as now, to hurt her. This roundness had to be made coin-sized so that she would see its circumference: Punish her at the birth of her baby. Awaken her to the inexorable. People who refused fatalism because they could invest small resources insisted on culpability. Deny accidents and wrest fault from the stars.

After the villagers left, their lanterns now scattering in various directions toward home, the family broke their silence and cursed her. "Aiaa, we're going to die. Death is coming. Death is coming. Look what you've done. You've killed us. Ghost! Dead ghost! Ghost! You've never been born." She ran out into the fields, far enough from the house so that she could no longer hear their voices, and pressed herself against the earth, her own land no more. When she felt the birth coming, she thought that she had been hurt. Her body seized together. "They've hurt me too much," she thought. "This is gall, and it will kill me." With forehead and knees against the earth, her body convulsed and then relaxed. She turned on her back, lay on the ground. The black well of sky and stars went out and out and out forever; her body and her complexity seemed to disappear. She was one of the stars, a bright dot in blackness, without home, without a companion, in eternal cold and silence. An agoraphobia rose in her, speeding higher and higher, bigger and bigger; she would not be able to contain it; there would be no end to fear.

Flayed, unprotected against space, she felt pain return, focusing her body. This pain chilled her—a cold, steady kind of surface pain. Inside, spasmodically, the other pain, the pain of the child, heated her. For hours she lay on the ground, alternately body and space. Sometimes a vision of normal comfort obliterated reality: she saw the family in the evening gambling at the dinner table, the young people massaging their elders' backs. She saw them congratulating one another, high joy on the mornings the rice shoots came up. When these pictures burst, the stars drew yet further apart. Black space opened.

She got to her feet to fight better and remembered that old-fashioned women gave birth in their pigsties to fool the jealous, pain-dealing gods, who do not snatch piglets. Before the next spasms could stop her, she ran to the pigsty, each step a rushing out into emptiness. She climbed over the fence and knelt in the dirt. It was good to have a fence enclosing her, a tribal person alone.

Laboring, this woman who had carried her child as a foreign growth that sickened her every day, expelled it at last. She reached down to touch the hot, wet, moving mass, surely smaller than anything human, and could feel that it was human after all—fingers, toes, nails, nose. She pulled it up on to her belly, and it lay curled there, butt in the air, feet precisely tucked one under the other. She opened her loose shirt and buttoned the child inside. After resting, it squirmed and thrashed and she pushed it up to her breast. It turned its head this way and that until it found her nipple. There, it made little snuffling noises. She clenched her teeth at its preciousness, lovely as a young calf, a piglet, a little dog.

She may have gone to the pigsty as a last act of responsibility: She would protect this child as she had protected its father. It would look after her soul, leaving supplies on her grave. But how would this tiny child without family find her grave when there would be no marker for her anywhere, neither in the earth nor the family hall? No one would give her a family hall name. She had taken the child with her into the wastes. At its birth the two of them had felt the same raw pain of separation, a wound that only the family pressing tight could close. A child with no descent line would not soften her life but only trail after her, ghostlike, begging her to give it purpose. At dawn the villagers on their way to the fields would stand around the fence and look.

Full of milk, the little ghost slept. When it awoke, she hardened her breasts against the milk that crying loosens. Toward morning she picked up the baby and walked to the well.

Carrying the baby to the well shows loving. Otherwise abandon it. Turn its face into the mud. Mothers who love their children take them along. It was probably a girl; there is some hope of forgiveness for boys.

"Don't tell anyone you had an aunt. Your father does not want to hear her name. She has never been born." I have believed that sex was unspeakable and words so strong and fathers so frail that "aunt" would do my father mysterious harm. I have thought that my family, having settled among immigrants who had also been their neighbors in the ancestral land, needed to clean their name, and a wrong word would incite the kinspeople even here. But there is more to this silence: they want me to participate in her punishment. And I have.

In the twenty years since I heard this story I have not asked for details nor said my aunt's name; I do not know it. People who can comfort the dead can also chase after them to hurt them further—a reverse ancestor worship. The real punishment was not the raid swiftly inflicted by the villagers, but the family's deliberately forgetting her. Her betrayal so maddened them, they saw to it that she should suffer forever, even after death. Always hungry, always needing, she would have to beg food from other ghosts, snatch and steal it from those whose living descendants give them gifts. She would have to fight the ghosts massed at crossroads for the buns a few thoughtful citizens leave to decoy her away from village and home so that the ancestral spirits could feast unharassed. At peace, they could act like gods, not ghosts, their descent lines providing them with paper suits and dresses, spirit money, paper houses, paper automobiles, chicken, meat, and rice into eternity—essences delivered up in smoke and flames, steam and incense rising from each rice bowl. In an attempt to make the Chinese care for people outside the family, Chairman Mao encourages us now to give our paper replicas to the spirits of outstanding soldiers and workers, no matter whose ancestors they may be. My aunt remains forever hungry. Goods are not distributed evenly among the dead.

My aunt haunts me—her ghost drawn to me because now, after fifty years of neglect, I alone devote pages of paper to her, though not origamied into houses and clothes. I do not think she always means me well. I am telling on her, and she was a spite suicide, drowning herself in the drinking water. The Chinese are always very frightened of the drowned one, whose weeping ghost, wet hair hanging and skin bloated, waits silently by the water to pull down a substitute.

Bobbie Ann Mason 1940–

Hailed by writer Anne Tyler and others as an outstanding writer of the short story, Bobbie Ann Mason parades before us a cast of characters steeped in the southern regionalism of rural Kentucky, which she describes as "southern Gothic going to the supermarket." The working-class people of her stories stand perplexed at the crossroads between permanence and transience, constantly feeling a "tension between their rural traditional past and the modern world." This ambivalence is backlit by the societal changes produced by such popular culture phenomena as television, supermarkets, fast-food restaurants, vocational training centers, and popular music. Raised on a dairy farm in Mayfield, Kentucky, Mason claims to "identify with people who are ambivalent about their situation," and imagines herself "as I would have felt if I had not gotten away and gotten a different perspective on things." She took her Ph.D. at the University of Connecticut and did her dissertation on Vladimir Nabakov, subsequently publishing *Nabokov's Garden: A Nature Guide to "Ada"* (1974). She followed with an analysis of pop-culture fiction aimed at girls called *The Girl Sleuth: A Feminist Guide to the Bobbsey Twins, Nancy Drew, and Their Sisters* (1975). By 1982, heavily committed to fiction writing, Mason won the Ernest Hemingway Award for First Fiction for *Shiloh and Other Stories*. Other major works include the novel *In Country* (1985) and a second collection of stories, *Love Life: Stories* (1989). The recipient of both NEA and Guggenheim fellowships, Mason currently lives in rural Pennsylvania.

PRIVATE LIES

"If you don't want to hear about it, why don't you say so?" Mickey asked his wife. He was lying in bed with a glass of Scotch balanced on his navel.

"I thought I made myself plain," Tina said. "If you want to go find your long-lost daughter, please just leave me out of it. I don't want the kids to find out about your past."

"What if she needs a kidney transplant? Or has a hereditary disease?"

"What disease?" Tina asked. She snapped off a length of dental floss.

Mickey closed his eyes and breathed so that his drink tilted slightly. He inched it to his lips. "I want to find her," he said.

"I don't know how you expect to find her. Those adoption people guard them kids like the gold in Fort Knox."

"The gold in Fort Knox doesn't mean the same thing anymore," Mickey said, sipping his drink. "It's an outdated comparison."

He wasn't supposed to drink, because he was preulcerous, but he compromised by drinking Scotch with half-and-half. His brother swore a doctor had told him it was harmless that way—Scotch tranquilized the stomach muscles; half-and-half blotted out the acid. Tina told him he would have a heart attack from the milk fat. She was a nurse. Mickey and Tina had been together for more than a dozen years, and they had a boy and a girl; Ricky and Kelly. The furniture was paid for, and the final installment on the car was due next month. Mickey sold real estate, and he hadn't sold a house in six weeks, but with interest rates going down, he was optimistic. If Mickey hadn't had a daughter born out of wedlock eighteen years ago next Tuesday, he'd have nothing on his mind now worse than the recession.

Tina turned down the corner of a page of her book, something called *Every Secret Thing*, and put it on the night table. She said, "What if she don't want to see you?"

"I think I've got a right."

"The law will tell you you lost your rights a long time ago."

Mickey saw the child once, through the window at the hospital. Donna, the mother, got to hold the baby, but he did not. No one was supposed to know he was the father. The little creature was shrimp-colored, with fuzzy black hair. Mickey could not believe what he had done. They let Donna hold her for about two minutes. Donna checked her all over, counted her fingers and toes, looked inside her diaper. "I wanted to make sure she was all there," Donna said later. "I didn't want to give away a defective baby."

Mickey sometimes felt that marriage to Tina was like riding a bus. She was the driver and he was a passenger. She made all the decisions—food, furniture, Kelly's braces, his socks. If he weren't married to Tina, he might be alone in a rented room, living on canned soup and Tang. Tina rescued him. With her, life had a regularity that was almost dogmatic. But now Tina was working a night shift, and her schedule was disrupted. She hated to miss "M*A*S*H," her favorite program. When she watched it, she always scrutinized the surgical procedures and pointed out when the action was inauthentic. "B.J. shouldn't ask for the retractor at that point," she would say.

Without Tina at night, Mickey had to keep the schedule rolling. One evening, before "M*A*S*H" came on, he helped Ricky with his arithmetic.

"I have to be in a special class," Ricky said suddenly, between problems.

"What class?"

"I have to have a tutor."

"What for? You're already in the Enrichment Class."

"I can't say my *s*'s right."

"What's wrong with your *s*'s? I don't hear anything wrong with your *s*'s."

"The teacher said so."

"Say something with an *s*. Say 'snake.' Say 'sports special.'"

"Snake. Sports special."

"That teacher has her head up her butt," said Mickey, tilting his glass of beer and then trying to peer at Ricky through the rim. It made him cross-eyed to do that.

Beer with half-and-half wasn't drinkable. It was too much like the barium milk shake he had had to drink when they X-rayed his stomach. The chalky liquid had made him gag. After swallowing it, he had watched on a screen as the dancing dots went through his system. Now he tried an experiment. First he took a swig of beer, then a sip of half-and-half. He leaned back in his La-Z-Boy and watched his children watching TV. When the commercial for Federal Express popped on, Mickey turned the volume up with the remote control. Ricky and Kelly loved the fast-talking businessman, making deals on the telephone. No one could talk that fast. Yet it didn't seem to be a trick, like a speeded-up tape, because the man didn't sound like a chipmunk.

"You should learn to talk that fast, Daddy," said Kelly.

"Why?"

"So you could sell lots of houses. It would save time."

Mickey rehearsed ways of telling Ricky and Kelly that they had a half-sister. Tina would kill him.

Mickey was uncomfortable whenever he appraised houses. The owners hovered over him while he measured the rooms and ran through his checklist of FHA-approved specifications. They resented the intrusion, but later, when he brought strangers in, the owners seemed resigned to their loss. The prospective buyers explored the houses, opening closets and cabinets. Tina snooped around like that, as a nurse, taking temperatures, washing people's private parts. Yet she wouldn't tolerate anyone knowing how much insurance they had, or how much they owed on their car. The ultimate in privacy, though, was guaranteed by adoption agencies. Like the CIA, they created new identities. Mickey didn't even know his daughter's name. If they were to meet, how would she view him? If she could appraise his life, as he would a house, she might find its dimensions too narrow, its ceilings too high, its basement cluttered and dank with memories and secrets. A dangerous basement. Not a good selling point. She would see a grouchy, preulcerous, balding bore. But that was not really true. He had his comic moments. He liked to clown around, singing "The Star-Spangled Banner" in a mock-operatic style; he would pretend to forget the words and then shift abruptly into "Carry Me Back to Old Virginny." He was a riot at parties.

Mickey and his ex-wife, Donna, had both stayed around the small town where they grew up, but he had not talked to her in three years, since the time they ran into each other at McDonald's. She was getting a hamburger and French fries to go. They made small talk. Not long after that, her second husband, Bill Jackson, died of a heart attack, and Mickey felt guilty about not sending her flowers. Mickey detested Bill Jackson—a loud-mouthed fool with a violent streak—and he thought Donna was better off without him. Mickey had entertained the idea that finding their daughter would be more for Donna's sake than for his own, because she had never had other children. She had had only her husband, Bill, and, before him, three years of a bad marriage to Mickey. The marriage had dried up and died, without the baby. In fact, they did not marry until after the baby was gone. It all seemed like a cruel mistake, as though they lived in some fascist state where illegitimate babies were rounded up and taken away. When Donna got pregnant, her parents sent her to Florida to stay with her aunt temporarily. Her parents, who had money, pressured her into giving the baby up for adoption, arguing that if she kept the child, she would have to quit school in disgrace. Mickey worked after school at a feed mill to pay for a bus trip to Florida to see her when the baby was born. When he got there, Donna convinced him that giving up the baby was the only choice they had if they ever wanted to return to Kentucky. Later, after she graduated, they did marry—an afterthought, a desperate way of making amends or maybe just to spite her parents. For their honeymoon, they drove to Florida. It was the wrong time of year, unbearably hot. They stayed in an air-conditioned room in a cheap motel. Donna got her period. It seemed such a vicious irony. The marriage didn't work. Mickey often got drunk and left Donna alone at night. He blamed her for giving up the baby. After a while, he blamed her parents. In a later period, he blamed society. And more recently, he blamed himself.

Donna was expecting him. On the telephone, she seemed hesitant, but she agreed to see him. Her apartment was in a low brick building with sliding-glass entrances facing a patio and a pool, like a Holiday Inn. As he rang her bell, Mickey wondered if he could sell her a house.

"Come in if you can get in," she said, shoving away a large grocery box near the doorway. "Clothes for the Salvation Army," she said. She looked up, smiling at him. Her smile was different. "Bridgework," she explained, noticing his look.

As he sank into her white-wicker love seat, she stood over him expectantly. Her eyelids were blue. Her light-brown hair was cut in curly layers that stuck out in fluffy bunches. She worked at Lucille's Beauty Bar.

"Do you know why I'm here?" he asked, feeling suddenly weak.

"Let me guess."

"I bet you can."

"Mickey, I thought we settled everything years ago."

"Tomorrow's her birthday."

Donna went to the kitchen. She gave Mickey some lemon icebox pie and Coke. Both Coke and lemons were on his list of forbidden substances, so he picked at the pie and sipped the Coke. Donna watched him and smoked a cigarette. She never used to smoke. The dishes clattered on her glass coffee table. Mickey had to study her ashtray a long time before he realized that it was a model of Mount St. Helens. Maybe his daughter had been on a camping trip on that mountain when it blew up. He would never know.

Watching Donna emerge from the bathroom, looking stylish and aloof in pants and high heels, Mickey felt a burning pain in his stomach. Donna seemed different, prettier and more assured. Her voice had grown husky, as though she had spent years on the stage. She used to be a whiner. When they were married, she threw tantrums. When a friend gave them a starter set of stoneware as a wedding present, she grew so impatient to finish the set that she sometimes cried about it. She wasn't used to being poor, and she loathed living in a trailer.

"Do you want some more Coke?" Donna asked.

"No." He laid down the fork and blurted out, "I can't think about anything but her. Knowing she's eighteen now—it's made me stop and think. And I want to find her. Donna, they've got to tell us where she is."

"There's no way on God's green earth we can find her," said Donna. "You know that." She lit a cigarette and offered Mickey one, but he waved the pack away.

"I've been quit four years on July first," he said.

"You have everything measured."

Donna's smoke traveled in front of his face. "Anyone else would have praised me for quitting," he said. "Look, Donna. All I'm saying is, the girl's eighteen now, and she just might be wondering who her mama and daddy are. Why don't we try to find her? I can't afford a lawyer, but together we could—"

"I don't want to find her," said Donna, sucking deeply on her cigarette. "She wouldn't mean anything to me. I don't know her. That's all way in the past."

The pain seized Mickey's stomach. "I don't think you mean that, Donna."

"I would be just asking for trouble," she said, looking straight into his eyes. She stood up and took the plate with the unfinished pie into the kitchen. She even looked taller now, Mickey realized, amazed. "She wouldn't want to see us," Donna said from the kitchen. "Not after what we did."

"Here, sign this," Tina said, shoving a paper at Mickey.

"What is it?" asked Mickey suspiciously. On "M*A*S*H," Radar always tricked the colonel into signing for things.

"The permission to let Ricky take special classes for his s's."

"I don't hear nothing wrong with his s's."

"You don't? Did you hear him say 'Southside'?" Their street was Southside Drive. Tina went to the foot of the stairs and called Ricky.

Ricky obediently said "Southside."

"Say 'sports special,'" said Mickey.

"Sports special."

"Can't you hear it?" Tina asked.

"No. You never heard it either till the experts thought this up."

"Experts," said Ricky, lisping on both *s* sounds.

"You're exaggerating," Mickey said.

He signed the paper. Once, he had signed a kid away completely.

If Mickey had some money, he'd hire a detective. If he sold a house, he would go to Florida to search for his daughter. He would kidnap Donna and take her with him. He couldn't get over her bridgework. It made her smile sexy and mysterious. Nobody was thinking seriously of buying. Mickey had a feeling that the prime rate was going to go down, but when he took clients around in the big company Buick to view houses, he felt like a museum guide. People seemed to be looking at interiors aesthetically, as though the Formica counters and bay windows with imitation leaded glass were priceless antiquities. One day, Mickey showed a sixty-thousand-dollar house to a young couple who drove a ten-year-old Ford with a noisy muffler. They were spending an unusual amount of time in the house. The man was crawling around in the attic, inspecting the insulation, and the woman was measuring rooms. Mickey forgot where he was. He stared out the picture window. It was raining lightly. A bird was in the street, hopping just ahead of a downhill rivulet, then letting it overtake him and splashing his wings in it. "Are you on the way to loving me?" the woman with the tape measure asked. Mickey shook himself out of his trance. The woman was smiling. "I love that song, don't you?" she was referring to a song playing on the radio. She wasn't even talking to Mickey. She was talking to her husband, who had cobwebs on his nose.

When Mickey arrived at home that afternoon, after the couple had said they would think about the house, he punched the remote control for the garage door. Too late, he saw that the robin that had been building a nest on the ledge above the door was at it again. The vibration from the door sent springs of dry grass wafting to the ground. He turned around and drove to Donna's.

"You can't get rid of me that easy," he said. When she laughed, he said clumsily, "I like your apartment."

She smiled with her gums showing, like Lily Tomlin. "Try this tea," she said. "It's herb tea. It'll help you relax."

Donna had red-striped wallpaper that he could see on his eyelids when he closed his eyes. She said she had chartered a plane with some "crazy business types" and had flown over Mount St. Helens. That explained the ashtray. She had been out in Seattle at a hairdressers' convention. Beauticians were no longer called beauticians. Now they were called hairdressers, or, better still, cosmetologists, which sounded like a group Carl Sagan would be president of.

"Tell me what else you've been doing with your life," said Mickey, burning his tongue on his tea. He admired a woman who would charter a plane.

"Just crazy things," she said. "Since Bill died, I've been thrown back on my own resources, you might say. I run around with some girls and we go to Lexington and mess around. Or we go to Memphis and mess around."

Mickey listened, fascinated.

Donna said, "That tea's good for your stomach. I'm getting into herbs. Chamomile, tansy, chervil, lots of them. And mugwort!" She broke out laughing. "You put mugwort under your pillow to make you dream more intensely. But I had to take it out. With all those wild dreams, I wasn't getting any rest! It's a very *female* herb, they say." She laughed again. "Whatever that means."

"I dreamed somebody dumped forty newborn kittens at my house—all orange, with two black mamas. What do you think that means?"

"I'm not going to answer that." Donna turned her back on him and rummaged in a kitchen drawer. "I think you dreamed that deliberately," she said.

"Did you love Bill?"

"What kind of question is that? Do *you* love Tina?"

"Well, yes and no." Mickey sipped the tea. It was watery, with a taste of licorice.

"Let's change the subject," Donna said, almost whispering as she brushed past him.

"Do you have any half-and-half?"

"No, just milk."

"How about Scotch?"

"Are you still drinking? Isn't the tea any good?"

"It's too hot." He set the mug down. "I'll come back to it."

Donna gave him some gin, with a milk chaser. The tea grew cold. Donna had a drink with him, the first they had ever had together. Growing giggly, she told him several wacky episodes from her trips to Lexington and Memphis. She and a friend planned to move to Lexington and open a little teashop that sold gourmet items and herbs—*if* her friend could make up her mind about leaving her husband.

"It's a bad time to start a new business," Mickey warned her. "Are you going to buy or rent? Do you know how to do your own taxes?"

"I wasn't born yesterday," Donna said.

She gave him another drink and they watched *Hangar 18* on HBO. She sat beside him on the couch, so close he could smell her perfume. Mickey hardly noticed the movie. He was thinking about Donna's teeth, her formidable high-heeled boots, the way she stuck her cigarette in the volcano.

When the movie ended, Donna said, "I feel cheated. The idea that human life originated on another planet is old stuff."

"I feel cheated, too," Mickey said, before realizing she was talking about the movie. But she was already in his arms.

Mickey and Donna got in the habit of talking on the telephone late at night, when Tina was working and the children were asleep. Tina complained about the line being busy when she tried to call from the hospital, but Mickey blamed it on the party line. Mickey didn't remember having conversations with Donna when they were married. Now he liked the way long silences on the telephone seemed so natural. Donna wouldn't say, "Are you still there?" She just waited for him to talk. She wouldn't talk about their daughter, though. When he brought up the subject, she said "Hush," in her new, throaty voice. Mickey reviewed his life for her. Tina and the kids. Houses. He said Tina was the sort of person who had separate garbage bags for everything, even tiny ones for scraps from each meal. He told her about Ricky's speech therapy, and Donna said authorities were trying to make everyone sound like John Chancellor. You couldn't make Tina see that, he said, feeling elated.

When he could get free in the afternoons, he went to Donna's apartment. There was nothing about making love with Donna that was familiar. She seemed to have learned all new techniques. Her body was different, lighter, more flexible. Her striped wallpaper burned his eyelids. They heard piano lessons coming from the floor above them, pupils jerking their way through John Thompson. Later, they watched HBO and drank herb tea.

On the news, the prime rate dropped half a percentage point. Housing starts were holding steady. Mickey expected to sell a house any day. He was sure he had fought off the ulcer.

One night at McDonald's with Ricky and Kelly, Mickey saw Donna with a blond woman in a back booth, and he felt a twinge in his duodenum. She waved, and the children stared at her. When Donna walked by their booth, he nodded and said, "How ya doing, Donna," as though she were any old secretary or store clerk he used to know. He bought a milk shake to go, so he could take it home and put Scotch in it.

When Mickey finally sold a house—a brick ranch with a two-car garage, owner-financed—he knew immediately that he wanted to take Donna to Florida. When he told Tina he wanted to go search for his daughter, she said, "I don't care, but I can't have the children knowing what you're up to. That's all I ask. The things they learn in school are bad enough."

Tina was trying to get the cellophane off a box containing a frozen deep-dish peach pie. Mickey stared at the uncharacteristically helpless way she was opening the package, pawing at the cellophane like a declawed cat. Kelly rushed in then, pummeling his stomach and saying, "You *have* to get me new sneakers for gym. I can't live like a grubbo!"

Mickey planned to leave Tina half the commission money. He told Donna, "We'll still have enough to have a blast. We'll stay in a fancy hotel this time."

He knew she loved to travel. She had been to Yosemite with Bill once, and on a package tour to New York with a girlfriend, as well as on the recent trip to Seattle, which she was still paying VISA for.

Donna said, "I'd go with you if you went to Hawaii instead."

"Too far. Too expensive."

"Bermuda, then. Or Acapulco."

"Those are all tropical resorts," he said. "I can tell that's where you really want to go. And Florida is the closest."

Donna studied the map of Florida that he gave her. She made a list of places she wouldn't mind seeing: Disney World, Sea World, anything with "world" in it. "Alligator Alley!" she sang out on the telephone when he said "Hello" one evening.

"I knew you'd see it my way," Mickey said.

"Why don't you get Tina a subscription to HBO?" Donna suggested. "That will keep her busy."

Mickey wondered if he was leaving Tina for good. He was not really making that clear. Kelly and Ricky didn't enter into his plans yet. It was too complicated. Tina was so orderly. She thought of all the details. She asked questions. Would he promise to stay in hotels that had smoke alarms? Did he know how ridiculous it was to set out for Florida with no inkling of how to find the girl? Tina followed him around as he tended to last-minute chores. He cleaned the leaves out of the gutters for her, then almost wept at the poignancy of that final gesture. He was up on the ladder and she was talking, talking. She told him that her niece, who had a paper route, was accosted on her bike by a weirdo who wanted her to stick a newspaper in his pants. He had on pants with a stretch waistband, and he pulled the band out for her to poke the rolled newspaper in. Tina's niece escaped, pedaling like crazy. Then Tina described an operation for breast cancer, explaining the way the doctors inserted a probe into a bleeding duct. Was that hereditary? Mickey wanted to know.

On the lawn, a robin fluttered its wings, rose in the air like a helicopter, and snatched a slim green caterpillar glinting in the sun.

"You can't just up and leave all you've worked so hard for," Tina said, finally breaking into tears.

"Tina's no fool," Donna said. "I bet she knows what's going on." They were driving her Mazda to the Nashville airport. Mickey had told Tina he had a ride with a client, and met Donna at his office.

"Don't worry," he said. "This is *our* trip. It's none of her business. We're going to have us some fun." He started singing "The Star-Spangled Banner" in his fake operatic style. Donna howled with laughter. He realized she had never heard his act before. When he pretended to forget the words and shifted into "Carry Me Back to Old Virginny," she went to pieces.

Florida was balmy, the right season this time. The plane ride was thrilling, and Mickey was giddy. He had graduated to Brandy Alexanders. The herb tea, he was convinced, had cured his stomach problem. The hotel was a beachfront high-rise with pink balconies—first class, to compensate for the depressing motel years ago. Mickey had intended to pay for Donna's trip but at the hotel desk she slapped down her credit card.

"I insist on paying my own way," she said.

"No. I didn't mean for you to do that."

"I insist. Don't forget I owe you for that plane ticket."

The desk clerk ran the credit cards through the machine.

"This is the eighties," Donna said. "Nobody gives a hoot if we're not married."

From the balcony of their third-floor room, they watched the swarm of people on the beach. The sunshine felt like a warm glow of approval.

"Look at all the fat people," Donna said. "Some people just shouldn't be allowed to wear bathing suits."

"I'm glad I lifted weights this winter," said Mickey.

He brought a bucket of ice and a can of Coke to the balcony and sat down in a canvas chair. As he poured the Coke into plastic glasses, he said, "Cokes are sixty cents in that machine. I couldn't believe it."

When he handed Donna the glass, she burst into tears.

"All I can imagine is that we will just somehow run into her down here and recognize her," she sobbed. "I've heard of that happening with separated twins."

Mickey found a Kleenex and nervously dabbed at her cheeks. "She'd look just like you," he said.

"She had your mouth." Donna stopped crying and shed her beach jacket. Her skin was pale and freckled. Mickey thought of two springer spaniels he had known in his life, both named Freckles.

Donna blew her nose and said, "I should have gotten an abortion back then, but I was too chicken. I knew of a girl in Bowling Green who died suddenly from a strange hemorrhage. I was a sophomore. She was such a nice girl, and real popular. Everybody was so naive back then. They all believed she really died from a hemorrhage, out of the blue. I was terrified that any month I might bleed to death, without warning. But a couple of years later, when I got pregnant and my parents wanted me to have an abortion, I put two and two together, and I realized what had happened to her. That's why I wouldn't have an abortion. But later I thought I should have. Then the whole thing would have been over with."

"That's a terrible thing to say. You'd feel worse."

"I think death is a whole lot easier to get over than the mess people make of their lives. Bill's been dead three years. I'm over *him*." Donna lit a cigarette and blew out a deliberate cloud of smoke. "It's all so messy," she said. "I didn't want to dig up the past. She's got her own life."

"But we could find her."

"I don't see how."

"What if she wants to find us?" asked Mickey. "Where would she look?"

Donna didn't answer. Mickey watched a flock of sea birds fly between him and a palm tree, like a line crossing it out.

On the beach, Donna scooped up some sand and put it in Mickey's hand. "Feel," she said, "Feel how scratchy it is."

"Why's that?"

"It's teeny bits of coral. It's not smooth, the way other sand is. It's hell on your feet."

"I didn't know that." He had on tennis shoes and Donna had on flip-flops. "I remember that from when we were in Florida before."

Mickey found a little white shell and handed it to Donna, but she wouldn't take it.

"I don't want to collect shells," she said. "When you look inside them, sometimes you find creepy little things living in there."

Mickey let the shell fall. He did not remember the sand from before. Looking out at the bright ocean coming to meet it, in whispers, he felt, with a sense of relief, that nothing private was left here. The thousands of people were all exposed—like underwear in the wrong room, like a lisp. Mickey saw himself and Donna years from now, holding hands, still walking on this beach. They stepped back, then forward, like dancers. They were moving like this along the beach, crunching the fragments of skeletons.

Bharati Mukherjee 1940–

B orn the daughter of a Brahmin pharmaceutical chemist in Calcutta, India, Bharati Mukherjee was educated in English-speaking schools as a child, earned graduate and postgraduate degrees in English at universities in India, and eventually received her M.F.A. from the University of Iowa Writers' Workshop in 1963. Mukherjee rejects the label "Third-World woman writer" in order to escape the confinement of "a narrow, airless, tightly roofed arena." Her fiction is often informed by personal experience, presenting immigrant protagonists, alienated by racism, sexism, and other forms of social prejudice, who experience the world through the disorder of "broken identities and discarded languages." In a *Los Angeles Times* interview, Mukherjee commented, "I truly appreciate the special qualities that America and American national myths offer me. I've lived everywhere [and] I'm truly touched and moved by the idea of America. It *includes you* [and] allows you to think of yourself as American. Other countries in Europe and Canada deliberately exclude you." An author of more than ten books, Mukherjee is the recipient of numerous honors and awards and has taught at many American colleges and universities. *Leave It to Me*, her most recent novel, was published in 1997.

THE MANAGEMENT OF GRIEF

A women I don't know is boiling tea the Indian way in my kitchen. There are a lot of women I don't know in my kitchen, whispering, and moving tactfully. They open doors, rummage through the pantry, and try not to ask me where things are kept. They remind me of when my sons were small, on Mother's Day or when Vikram and I were tired, and they would make big, sloppy omelets. I would lie in bed pretending I didn't hear them.

Dr. Sharma, the treasurer of the Indo-Canada Society, pulls me into the hallway. He wants to know if I am worried about money. His wife, who has just come up from the basement with a tray of empty cups and glasses, scolds him. "Don't bother Mrs. Bhave with mundane details." She looks so monstrously pregnant her baby must be days overdue. I tell her she shouldn't be carrying heavy things. "Shaila," she says, smiling, "this is the fifth." Then she grabs a teenager by his shirttails. He slips his Walkman off his head. He has to be one of her four children, they have the same domed and dented foreheads. "What's the official word now?" she demands. The boy slips the headphones back on. "They're acting evasive, Ma. They're saying it could be an accident or a terrorist bomb."

All morning, the boys have been muttering, Sikh Bomb, Sikh Bomb. The men, not using the word, bow their heads in agreement. Mrs. Sharma touches her forehead at such a word. At least they've stopped talking about space debris and Russian lasers.

Two radios are going in the dining room. They are tuned to different stations. Someone must have brought the radios down from my boys' bedrooms. I haven't gone into their rooms since Kusum came running across the front lawn in her bathrobe. She looked so funny, I was laughing when I opened the door.

The big TV in the den is being whizzed through American networks and cable channels.

"Damn!" some man swears bitterly. "How can these preachers carry on like nothing's happened?" I want to tell him we're not that important. You look at the audience, and at the preacher in his blue robe with his beautiful white hair, the potted palm trees under a blue sky, and you know they care about nothing.

The phone rings and rings. Dr. Sharma's taken charge. "We're with her," he keeps saying. "Yes, yes, the doctor has given calming pills. Yes, yes, pills are having necessary effect." I wonder if pills alone explain this calm. Not peace, just a deadening quiet. I was always controlled, but never repressed. Sound can reach me, but my body is tensed, ready to scream. I hear their voices all around me. I hear my boys and Vikram cry, "Mommy, Shaila!" and their screams insulate me, like headphones.

The women boiling water tells her story again and again. "I got the news first. My cousin called from Halifax before six A.M., can you imagine? He'd gotten up for prayers and his son was studying for medical exams and he heard on a rock channel that something had happened to a plane. They said first it had disappeared from the radar, like a giant eraser just reached out. His father called me, so I said to him, what do you mean, 'something bad'? You mean a hijacking? And he said, *behn*, there is no confirmation of anything yet, but check with your neighbors because a lot of them must be on that plane.[1] So I called poor Kusum straightaway. I knew Kusum's husband and daughter were booked to go yesterday."

Kusum lives across the street from me. She and Satish had moved in less than a month ago. They said they needed a bigger place. All these people, the Sharmas and friends from the Indo-Canada Society, had been there for the housewarming. Satish and Kusum made homemade tandoori on their big gas grill and even the white neighbors piled their plates high with that luridly red, charred, juicy chicken. Their younger daughter had danced, and even our boys had broken away from the Stanley Cup telecast to put in a reluctant appearance. Everyone took pictures for their albums and for the community newspapers—another of our families had made it big in Toronto—and now I wonder how many of those happy faces are gone. "Why does God give us so much if all along He intends to take it away?" Kusum asks me.

I nod. We sit on carpeted stairs, holding hands like children. "I never once told him that I loved him," I say. I was too much the well brought up woman. I was so well brought up I never felt comfortable calling my husband by his first name.

"It's all right," Kusum says. "He knew. My husband knew. They felt it. Modern young girls have to say it because what they feel is fake."

Kusum's daughter, Pam, runs in with an overnight case. Pam's in her McDonald's uniform. "Mummy! You have to get dressed!" Panic makes her cranky. "A reporter's on his way here."

"Why?"

"You want to talk to him in your bathrobe?" She starts to brush her mother's long hair. She's the daughter whose always in trouble. She dates Canadian boys and hangs out in the mall, shopping for tight sweaters. The younger one, the goody-goody one according to Pam, the one with a voice so sweet that when she sang *bhajans*[2] for Ethiopian relief even a frugal man like my husband wrote out a hundred dollar check, *she* was on that plane. *She* was going to spend July and August with grandparents because Pam wouldn't go. Pam said she'd rather waitress at McDonald's. "If it's a choice between Bombay and Wonderland, I'm picking Wonderland," she'd said.

"Leave me alone," Kusum yells. "You know what I want to do? If I didn't have to look after you now, I'd hang myself."

---

[1] In June 1985, an Air India flight from Toronto to Bombay crashed off the coast of Ireland, apparently as the result of an explosion caused by a bomb. All 329 people on board were killed.

[2] Devotional songs, hymns (Hindi).

Pam's young face goes blotchy with pain. "Thanks," she says, "don't let me stop you."

"Hush," pregnant Mrs. Sharma scolds Pam. "Leave your mother alone. Mr. Sharma will tackle the reporters and fill out the forms. He'll say what has to be said."

Pam stands her ground. "You think I don't know what Mummy's thinking? *Why her?* that's what. That's sick! Mummy wishes my little sister were alive and I were dead."

Kusum's hand in mine is trembly hot. We continue to sit on the stairs.

She calls before she arrives, wondering if there's anything I need. Her name is Judith Templeton and she's an appointee of the provincial government. "Multiculturalism?" I ask, and she says, "partially," but that her mandate is bigger. "I've been told you knew many of the people on the flight," she says. "Perhaps if you'd agree to help us reach the others . . . ?"

She gives me time at least to put on tea water and pick up the mess in the front room. I have a few *samosas*[3] from Kusum's housewarming that I could fry up, but then I think, Why prolong this visit?

Judith Templeton is much younger than she sounded. She wears a blue suit with white blouse and a polka dot tie. Her blond hair is cut short, her only jewelry is pearl drop earrings. Her briefcase is new and expensive looking, a gleaming cordovan leather. She sits with it across her lap. When she looks out the front windows onto the street, her contact lenses seem to float in front of her light blue eyes.

"What sort of help do you want from me?" I ask. She has refused the tea, out of politeness, but I insist, along with some slightly stale biscuits.

"I have no experience," she admits. "That is, I have an MSW and I've worked in liaison with accident victims, but I mean I have no experience with a tragedy of this scale—"

"Who could?" I ask.

"—and with the complications of culture, language, and customs. Someone mentioned that Mrs. Bhave is a pillar—because you've taken it more calmly."

At this, perhaps, I frown, for she reaches forward, almost to take my hand. "I hope you understand my meaning, Mrs. Bhave. There are hundreds of people in Metro directly affected, like you, and some of them speak no English. There are some widows who've never handled money or gone on a bus, and there are old parents who still haven't eaten or gone outside their bedrooms. Some houses and apartments have been looted. Some wives are still hysterical. Some husbands are in shock and profound depression. We want to help, but our hands are tied in so many ways. We have to distribute money to some people, and there are legal documents—these things can be done. We have interpreters, but we don't

---

[3] Deep fried pastries filled with vegetables or meat.

always have the human touch, or maybe the right human touch. We don't want to make mistakes, Mrs. Bhave, and that's why we'd like to ask you to help us."

"More mistakes, you mean," I say.

"Police matters are not in my hands," she answers.

"Nothing I can do will make any difference," I say. "We must all grieve in our own way."

"But you are coping very well. All the people said, Mrs. Bhave is the strongest person of all. Perhaps if the others could see you, talk with you, it would help them."

"By the standards of the people you call hysterical, I am behaving very oddly and very badly, Miss Templeton." I want to say to her, *I wish I could scream, starve, walk into Lake Ontario, jump from a bridge.* "They would not see me as a model. I do not see myself as a model."

I am a freak. No one who has ever known me would think of me reacting this way. This terrible calm will not go away.

She asks me if she may call again, after I get back from a long trip that we all must make. "Of course," I say. "Feel free to call, anytime."

Four days later, I find Kusum squatting on a rock overlooking a bay in Ireland. It isn't a big rock, but it juts sharply out over water. This is as close as we'll ever get to them. June breezes balloon out her sari and unpin her knee-length hair. She has the bewildered look of a sea creature whom the tides have stranded.

It's been one hundred hours since Kusum came stumbling and screaming across my lawn. Waiting around the hospital, we've heard many stories. The police, the diplomats, they tell us things thinking that we're strong, that knowledge is helpful to the grieving, and maybe it is. Some, I know, prefer ignorance, or their own versions. The plane broke into two, they say. Unconsciousness was instantaneous. No one suffered. My boys must have just finished their breakfasts. They loved eating on planes, they loved the smallness of plates, knives, and forks. Last year they saved the airline salt and pepper shakers. Half an hour more and they would have made it to Heathrow.

Kusum says that we can't escape our fate. She says that all those people — our husbands, my boys, her girl with the nightingale voice, all those Hindus, Christians, Sikhs, Muslims, Parsis, and atheists on that plane — were fated to die together off this beautiful bay. She learned this from a swami in Toronto.

I have my Valium.

Six of us "relatives" — two widows and four widowers — choose to spend the day today by the waters instead of sitting in a hospital room and scanning photographs of the dead. That's what they call us now: relatives. I've looked through twenty-seven photos in two days. They're very kind to us, the Irish are very understanding. Sometimes understanding means freeing a tourist bus for this trip to the bay, so we can pretend to spy our loved ones through the glassiness of waves or in sun-speckled cloud shapes.

I could die here, too, and be content.

"What is that, out there?" She's standing and flapping her hands and for a moment I see a head shape bobbing in the waves. She's standing in the water, I, on the boulder. The tide is low, and a round, black, head-sized rock has just risen from the waves. She returns, her sari end dripping and ruined and her face is a twisted remnant of hope, the way mine was a hundred hours ago, still laughing but inwardly knowing that nothing but the ultimate tragedy could bring two women together at six o'clock on a Sunday morning. I watch her face sag into blankness.

"That water felt warm, Shaila," she says at length.

"You can't," I say. "We have to wait for our turn to come."

I haven't eaten in four days, haven't brushed my teeth.

"I know," she says. "I tell myself I have no right to grieve. They are in a better place than we are. My swami says I should be thrilled for them. My swami says depression is a sign of our selfishness."

Maybe I'm selfish. Selfishly I break away from Kusum and run, sandals slapping against stones, to the water's edge. What if my boys aren't lying pinned under the debris? What if they aren't stuck a mile below that innocent blue chop? What if, given the strong currents. . . .

Now I've ruined my sari, one of my best. Kusum has joined me, knee-deep in water that feels to me like a swimming pool. I could settle in the water, and my husband would take my hand and the boys would slap water in my face just to see me scream.

"Do you remember what good swimmers my boys were, Kusum?"

"I saw the medals," she says.

One of the widowers, Dr. Ranganathan from Montreal, walks out to us, carrying his shoes in one hand. He's an electrical engineer. Someone at the hotel mentioned his work is famous around the world, something about the place where physics and electricity come together. He has lost a huge family, something indescribable. "With some luck," Dr. Ranganathan suggests to me, "a good swimmer could make it safely to some island. It is quite possible that there may be many, many microscopic islets scattered around."

"You're not just saying that?" I tell Dr. Ranganathan about Vinod, my elder son. Last year he took diving as well.

"It's a parent's duty to hope," he says. "It is foolish to rule out possibilities that have not been tested. I myself have not surrendered hope."

Kusum is sobbing once again. "Dear lady," he says, laying his free hand on her arm, and she calms down.

"Vinod is how old?" he asks me. He's very careful, as we all are. *Is*, not was.

"Fourteen. Yesterday he was fourteen. His father and uncle were going to take him down to the Taj and give him a big birthday party. I couldn't go with them because I couldn't get two weeks off from my stupid job in June." I process bills for a travel agent. June is a big travel month.

Dr. Ranganathan whips the pockets of his suit jacket inside out. Squashed roses, in darkening shades of pink, float on the water. He tore the roses off creepers in somebody's garden. He didn't ask anyone if he could pluck the roses, but now there's been an article about it in the local papers. When you see an Indian person, it says, please give him or her flowers.

"A strong youth of fourteen," he says, "can very likely pull to safety a younger one."

My sons, though four years apart, were very close. Vinod wouldn't let Mithun drown. *Electrical engineering*, I think, foolishly perhaps: this man knows important secrets of the universe, things closed to me. Relief spins me light-headed. No wonder my boys' photographs haven't turned up in the gallery of photos of the recovered dead. "Such pretty roses," I say.

"My wife loved pink roses. Every Friday I had to bring a bunch home. I used to say, Why? After twenty odd years of marriage you're still needing proof positive of my love?" He has identified his wife and three of his children. Then others from Montreal, the lucky ones, intact families with no survivors. He chuckles as he wades back to shore. Then he swings around to ask me a question. "Mrs. Bhave, you are wanting to throw in some roses for your loved ones? I have two big ones left."

But I have other things to float: Vinod's pocket calculator; a half-painted model B-52 for my Mithun. They'd want them on their island. And for my husband? For him I let fall into the calm, glassy waters a poem I wrote in the hospital yesterday. Finally he'll know my feelings for him.

"Don't tumble, the rocks are slippery," Dr. Ranganathan cautions. He holds out a hand for me to grab.

Then it's time to get back on the bus, time to rush back to our waiting posts on hospital benches.

Kusum is one of the lucky ones. The lucky ones flew here, identified in multiplicate their loved ones, then will fly to India with the bodies for proper ceremonies. Satish is one of the few males who surfaced. The photos of faces we saw on the walls in an office at Heathrow and here in the hospital are mostly of women. Women have more body fat, a nun said to me matter-of-factly. They float better.

Today I was stopped by a young sailor on the street. He had located bodies, he'd gone into the water when—he checks my face for signs of strength—when the sharks were first spotted. I don't blush, and he breaks down. "It's all right," I say. "Thank you." I had heard about the sharks from Dr. Ranganathan. In his orderly mind, science brings understanding, it holds no terror. It is the shark's duty. For every deer there is a hunter, for every fish a fisherman.

The Irish are not shy; they rush to me and give me hugs and some are crying. I cannot imagine reactions like that on the streets of Toronto. Just strangers, and I am touched. Some carry flowers with them and give them to any Indian they see.

After lunch, a policeman I have gotten to know quite well catches hold of me. He says he thinks he has a match for Vinod. I explain what a good swimmer Vinod is.

"You want me with you when you look at photos?" Dr. Ranganathan walks ahead of me into the picture gallery. In these matters, he is a scientist, and I am grateful. It is a new perspective. "They have performed miracles," he says. "We are indebted to them."

The first day or two the policeman showed us relatives only one picture at a time; now they're in a hurry, they're eager to lay out the possibles, and even the probables.

The face on the photo is of a boy much like Vinod; the same intelligent eyes, the same thick brows dipping into a V. But this boy's features, even his cheeks, are puffier, wider, mushier.

"No." My gaze is pulled by other pictures. There are five other boys who look like Vinod.

The nun assigned to console me rubs the first picture with a fingertip.

"When they've been in the water for a while, love, they look a little heavier." The bones under the skin are broken, they said on the first day—try to adjust your memories. It's important.

"It's not him. I'm his mother. I'd know."

"I know this one!" Dr. Ranganathan cries out suddenly from the back of the gallery. "And this one!" I think he senses that I don't want to find my boys. "They are the Kutty brothers. They were also from Montreal." I don't mean to be crying. On the contrary, I am ecstatic. My suitcase in the hotel is packed heavy with dry clothes for my boys.

The policeman starts to cry. "I am so sorry, I am so sorry, ma'am. I really thought we had a match."

With the nun ahead of us and the policeman behind, we, the unlucky ones without our children's bodies, file out of the makeshift gallery.

From Ireland most of us go on to India. Kusum and I take the same direct flight to Bombay, so I can help her clear customs quickly. But we have to argue with a man in uniform. He has large boils on his face. The boils swell and glow with sweat as we argue with him. He wants Kusum to wait in line and he refuses to take authority because his boss is on a tea break. But Kusum won't let her coffins out of sight, and I shan't desert her though I know that my parents, elderly and diabetic, must be waiting in a stuffy car in a scorching lot.

"You bastard!" I scream at the man with the popping boils. Other passengers press closer. "You think we're smuggling contraband in those coffins!"

Once upon a time we were well brought up women; we were dutiful wives who kept our heads veiled, our voices shy and sweet.

In India, I become, once again, an only child of rich, ailing parents. Old friends of the family come to pay their respects. Some are Sikh, and inwardly, involuntarily, I cringe. My parents are progressive people; they do not blame communities for a few individuals.

In Canada it is a different story now.

"Stay longer," my mother pleads. "Canada is a cold place. Why would you want to be all by yourself?" I stay.

Three months pass. Then another.

"Vikram wouldn't have wanted you to give up things!" they protest. They call my husband by the name he was born with. In Toronto he'd changed to Vik so the men he worked with at his office would find his name as easy as Rod or Chris. "You know, the dead aren't cut off from us!"

My grandmother, the spoiled daughter of a rich *zamindar*,[4] shaved her head with rusty razor blades when she was widowed at sixteen. My grandfather died of childhood diabetes when was nineteen, and she saw herself as the harbinger of bad luck. My mother grew up without parents, raised indifferently by an uncle, while her true mother slept in a hut behind the main estate house and took her food with the servants. She grew up a rationalist. My parents abhor mindless mortification.

The zamindar's daughter kept stubborn faith in Vedic rituals;[5] my parents rebelled. I am trapped between two modes of knowledge. At thirty-six, I am too old to start over and too young to give up. Like my husband's spirit, I flutter between worlds.

Courting aphasia, we travel. We travel with our phalanx of servants and poor relatives. To hill stations and to beach resorts. We play contract bridge in dusty gymkhana clubs.[6] We ride stubby ponies up crumbly mountain trails. At tea dances, we let ourselves be twirled twice round the ballroom. We hit the holy spots we hadn't made time for before. In Varanasi, Kalighat, Rishikesh, Hardwar, astrologers and palmists seek me out and for a fee offer me cosmic consolations.

Already the widowers among us are being shown new bride candidates. They cannot resist the call of custom, the authority of their parents and older brothers. They must marry; it is the duty of a man to look after a wife. The new wives will be young widows with children, destitute but of good family. They will make loving wives, but the men will shun them. I've had calls from the men over crackling Indian telephone lines. "Save me," they say, these substantial, educated, successful men of forty. "My parents are arranging a marriage for me." In a month they will have buried one family and returned to Canada with a new bride and partial family.

I am comparatively lucky. No one here thinks of arranging a husband for an unlucky widow.

Then, on the third day of the sixth month into this odyssey, in an abandoned temple in a tiny Himalayan village, as I make my offering of flowers and sweetmeats to the god of a tribe of animists, my husband descends to me. He is

---

[4] Landholder.

[5] The *Vedas* are the oldest scriptures in Hinduism.

[6] Athletic facilities.

squatting next to a scrawny *sadhu*[7] in moth-eaten robes. Vikram wears the vanilla suit he wore the last time I hugged him. The *sadhu* tosses petals on a butter-fed flame, reciting Sanskrit mantras[8] and sweeps his face of flies. My husband takes my hands in his.

You're beautiful, he starts. Then, *What are you doing here?*

Shall I stay? I ask. He only smiles, but already the image is fading. *You must finish alone what we started together.* No seaweed wreathes his mouth. He speaks too fast just as he used to when we were an envied family in our pink split-level. He is gone.

In the windowless altar room, smoky with *joss*[9] sticks and clarified butter lamps, a sweaty hand gropes for my blouse. I do not shriek. The *sadhu* arranges his robe. The lamps hiss and sputter out.

When we come out of the temple, my mother says, "Did you feel something weird in there?"

My mother has no patience with ghosts, prophetic dreams, holy men, and cults.

"No," I lie. "Nothing."

But she knows that she's lost me. She knows that in days I shall be leaving.

Kusum's put her house up for sale. She wants to live in an ashram[10] in Hardwar. Moving to Hardwar was her swami's idea. Her swami runs two ashrams, the one in Hardwar and another here in Toronto.

"Don't run away," I tell her.

"I'm not running away," she says. "I'm pursuing inner peace. You think you or that Ranganathan fellow are better off?"

Pam's left for California. She wants to do some modeling, she says. She says when she comes into her share of the insurance money she'll open a yoga-cum-aerobics studio in Hollywood. She sends me postcards so naughty I daren't leave them on the coffee table. Her mother has withdrawn from her and the world.

The rest of us don't lose touch, that's the point. Talk is all we have, says Dr. Ranganathan, who has also resisted his relatives and returned to Montreal and to his job, alone. He says, whom better to talk with than other relatives? We've been melted down and recast as a new tribe.

He calls me twice a week from Montreal. Every Wednesday night and every Saturday afternoon. He is changing jobs, going to Ottawa. But Ottawa is over a hundred miles away, and he is forced to drive two hundred and twenty miles a day. He can't bring himself to sell his house. The house is a temple, he says; the king-sized bed in the master bedroom is a shrine. He sleeps on a folding cot. A devotee.

---

[7] A Hindu holy man (a mendicant ascetic).

[8] Mystic words used in ritual and meditation.

[9] Incense.

[10] Hindu religious retreat.

* * *

There are still some hysterical relatives. Judith Templeton's list of those needing help and those who've "accepted" is in nearly perfect balance. Acceptance means you speak of your family in the past tense and you make active plans for moving ahead with your life. There are courses at Seneca and Ryerson we could be taking. Her gleaming leather briefcase is full of college catalogs and lists of cultural societies that need our help. She has done impressive work, I tell her.

"In the textbooks on grief management," she replies—I am confidante, I realize, one of the few whose grief has not sprung bizarre obsessions—"there are stages to pass through: rejection, depression, acceptance, reconstruction." She has compiled a chart and finds that six months after the tragedy, none of us still reject reality, but only a handful are reconstructing. "Depressed Acceptance" is the plateau we've reached. Remarriage is a major step in reconstruction (though she's a little surprised, even shocked, over *how* quickly some of the men have taken on new families). Selling one's house and changing jobs and cities is healthy.

How do I tell Judith Templeton that my family surrounds me, and that like creatures in epics, they've changed shapes? She sees me as calm and accepting but worries that I have no job, no career. My closest friends are worse off than I. I cannot tell her my days, even my nights, are thrilling.

She asks me to help with families she can't reach at all. An elderly couple in Agincourt whose sons were killed just weeks after they had brought their parents over from a village in Punjab. From their names, I know they are Sikh. Judith Templeton and a translator have visited them twice with offers of money for air fare to Ireland, with bank forms, power-of-attorney forms, but they have refused to sign, or to leave their tiny apartment. Their sons' money is frozen in the bank. Their sons' investment apartments have been trashed by tenants, the furnishings sold off. The parents fear that anything they sign or any money they receive will end the company's or the country's obligations to them. They fear they are selling their sons for two airline tickets to a place they've never seen.

The high-rise apartment is a tower of Indians and West Indians, with a sprinkling of Orientals. The nearest bus stop kiosk is lined with women in saris. Boys practice cricket in the parking lot. Inside the building, even I wince a bit from the ferocity of onion fumes, the distinctive and immediate Indianness of frying *ghee*,[11] but Judith Templeton maintains a steady flow of information. These poor old people are in imminent danger of losing their place and all their services.

I say to her, "They are Sikh. They will not open up to a Hindu woman." And what I want to add is, as much as I try not to, I stiffen now at the sight of beards and turbans. I remember a time when we all trusted each other in this new country, it was only the new country we worried about.

The two rooms are dark and stuffy. The lights are off, an oil lamp sputters on the coffee table. The bent old lady has let us in, and her husband is wrapping a white turban over his oiled, hip-length hair. She immediately goes to the

[11] Clarified butter.

kitchen, and I hear the most familiar sound of an Indian home, tap water hitting and filling a teapot.

They have not paid their utility bills, out of fear and the inability to write a check. The telephone is gone; electricity and gas and water are soon to follow. They have told Judith their sons will provide. They are good boys, and they have always earned and looked after their parents.

We converse a bit in Hindi. They do not ask about the crash and I wonder if I should bring it up. If they think I am here merely as a translator, then they may feel insulted. There are thousands of Punjabi-speakers, Sikhs, in Toronto to do a better job. And so I say to the old lady, "I too have lost my sons, and my husband, in the crash."

Her eyes immediately fill with tears. The man mutters a few words which sound like a blessing. "God provides and God takes away," he says.

I want to say, But only men destroy and give back nothing. "My boys and my husband are not coming back," I say. "We have to understand that."

Now the old woman responds. "But who is to say? Man alone does not decide these things." To this her husband adds his agreement.

Judith asks about the bank papers, the release forms. With a stroke of the pen, they will have a provincial trustee to pay their bills, invest their money, send them a monthly pension.

"Do you know this woman?" I ask them.

The man rises his hand from the table, turns it over and seems to regard each finger separately before he answers. "This young lady is always coming here, we make tea for her and she leaves papers for us to sign." His eyes scan a pile of papers in the corner of the room. "Soon we will be out of tea, then will she go away?"

The old lady adds, "I have asked my neighbors and no one else gets *angrezi*[12] visitors. What have we done?"

"It's her job," I try to explain. "The government is worried. Soon you will have no place to stay, no lights, no gas, no water."

"Government will get its money. Tell her not to worry, we are honorable people."

I try to explain the government wishes to give money, not take. He raises his hand. "Let them take," he says. "We are accustomed to that. That is no problem."

"We are strong people," says the wife. "Tell her that."

"Who needs all this machinery?" demands the husband. "It is unhealthy, the bright lights, the cold air on a hot day, the cold food, the four gas rings. God will provide, not government."

"When our boys return," the mother says. Her husband sucks his teeth. "Enough talk," he says.

Judith breaks in. "Have you convinced them?" The snaps on her cordovan briefcase go off like firecrackers in that quiet apartment. She lays the sheaf of

[12] An English speaker, a Westerner.

legal papers on the coffee table. "If they can't write their names, an X will do—I've told them that."

Now the old lady has shuffled to the kitchen and soon emerges with a pot of tea and two cups. "I think my bladder will go first on a job like this," Judith says to me, smiling. "If only there was some way of reaching them. Please thank her for the tea. Tell her she's very kind."

I nod in Judith's direction and tell them in Hindi, "She thanks you for the tea. She thinks you are being very hospitable but she doesn't have the slightest idea what it means."

I want to say, Humor her. I want to say, My boys and my husband are with me too, more than ever. I look in the old man's eyes and I can read his stubborn, peasant's message: *I have protected this woman as best I can. She is the only person I have left. Give to me or take from me what you will, but I will not sign for it. I will not pretend that I accept.*

In the car, Judith says, "You see what I'm up against? I'm sure they're lovely people, but their stubbornness and ignorance are driving me crazy. They think signing a paper is signing their sons' death warrants, don't they?"

I am looking out the window. I want to say, *In our culture, it is a parent's duty to hope.*

"Now Shaila, this next woman is a real mess. She cries day and night, and she refuses all medical help. We may have to—"

"—Let me out at the subway," I say.

"I beg your pardon?" I can feel those blue eyes staring at me.

It would not be like her to disobey. She merely disapproves, and slows at a corner to let me out. Her voice is plaintive. "Is there anything I said? Anything I did?"

I could answer her suddenly in a dozen ways, but I choose not to. "Shaila? Let's talk about it," I hear, then slam the door.

A wife and mother begins her new life in a new country, and that life is cut short. Yet her husband tells her: Complete what we have started. We who stayed out of politics and came halfway around the world to avoid religious and political feuding have been the first in the New World to die from it. I no longer know what we started, nor how to complete it. I write letters to the editors of local papers and to members of Parliament. Now at least they admit it was a bomb. One MP answers back, with sympathy, but with a challenge. You want to make a difference? Work on a campaign. Work on mine. Politicize the Indian voter.

My husband's old lawyer helps me set up a trust. Vikram was a saver and a careful investor. He had saved the boys' boarding school and college fees. I sell the pink house at four times what we paid for it and take a small apartment downtown. I am looking for a charity to support.

We are deep in the Toronto winter, gray skies, icy pavements. I stay indoors, watching television. I have tried to assess my situation, how best to live my life, to complete what we began so many years ago. Kusum has written me from

Hardwar that her life is now serene. She has seen Satish and has heard her daughter sing again. Kusum was on a pilgrimage, passing through a village when she heard a young girl's voice, singing one of her daughter's favorite *bhajans*. She followed the music through the squalor of a Himalayan village, to a hut where a young girl, an exact replica of her daughter, was fanning coals under the kitchen fire. When she appeared, the girl cried out, "Ma!" and ran away. What did I think of that?

I think I can only envy her.

Pam didn't make it to California, but writes me from Vancouver. She works in a department store, giving make-up hints to Indian and Oriental girls. Dr. Ranganathan has given up his commute, given up his house and job, and accepted an academic position in Texas where no one knows his story and he has vowed not to tell it. He calls me now once a week.

I wait, I listen, and I pray, but Vikram has not returned to me. The voices and the shapes and the nights filled with visions ended abruptly several weeks ago.

I take it as a sign.

One rare, beautiful, sunny day last week, returning from a small errand on Yonge Street, I was walking through the park from the subway to my apartment. I live equidistant from the Ontario Houses of Parliament and the University of Toronto. The day was not cold, but something in the bare trees caught my attention. I looked up from the gravel, into the branches and the clear blue sky beyond. I thought I heard the rustling of larger forms, and I waited a moment for voices. Nothing.

"What?" I asked.

Then as I stood in the path looking north to Queen's Park and west to the university, I heard the voices of my family one last time. *Your time has come,* they said. *Go, be brave.*

I do not know where this voyage I have begun will end. I do not know which direction I will take. I dropped the package on a park bench and started walking.

Pattiann Rogers 1940–

Born in Joplin, Missouri, Pattiann Rogers's career began in her home state as a high-school English teacher in 1961. She switched to kindergarten the following year and from 1963–67 taught in Sugar Land, Texas, at the School for Little Children. Her first book of poetry, *The Expectations of Light* (1981), garnered a Voertmann Poetry Award from the Texas Institute of Letters. Peter Stitt of the *Georgia Review* calls this work "an unusually original first book, surprising for its sophisticated incorporation of modern scientific thinking into poetry. Every poem manages somehow to present accurate knowledge of the physical universe, often in a multifaceted plethora of detail." He later adds, "That

Rogers is able to achieve lyrical beauty through this material is truly a testament to the century in which we live." Rogers has subsequently published seven books of poetry, including *Firekeeper: New and Selected Poems* (1994), which was a finalist for the Lenore Marshall Poetry Prize. Other prizes include the Theodore Roethke Prize from *Poetry Northwest;* the Tietjens Prize and the Hokin Prize, both from *Poetry;* two Strousse Awards from *Prairie Schooner;* four Pushcart Prizes; grants from the National Endowment for the Arts; and Guggenheim and Lannan poetry fellowships. Rogers lives in Colorado with her husband, a geophysicist.

NEARING AUTOBIOGRAPHY

Those are my bones rifted
and curled, knees to chin,
among the rocks on the beach,
my hands splayed beneath my skull
in the mud. Those are my rib   5
bones resting like white sticks
wracked on the bank, laid down,
delivered, rubbed clean
by river and snow.

Ethereal as seedless weeds   10
in dim sun and frost, I see
my own bones translucent as locust
husks, light as spider bones,
as filled with light as lantern
bones when the candle flames.   15
And I see my bones, facile,
willing, rolling and clacking,
reveling like broken shells
among themselves in a tumbling surf.

I recognize them, no other's,   20
raggedly patterned and wrought,
peeled as a skeleton of sycamore
against gray skies, stiff as a fallen
spruce. I watch them floating
at night, identical lake slivers   25
flush against the same star bones
drifting in scattered pieces above.

Everything I assemble, all
the constructions I have rendered
are the metal and dust of my locked   30
and storied bones. My bald cranium
shines blind as the moon.

COUNTING WHAT THE CACTUS CONTAINS

Elf owl, cactus wren, fruit flies incubating
In the only womb they'll ever recognize.
Shadow for the sand rat, spines
And barbary ribs clenched with green wax.
Seven thousand thorns, each a water slide,   5
A wooden tongue licking the air dry.

Inside, early morning mist captured intact,
The taste of drizzle sucked
And sunsplit. Whistle
Of the red-tailed hawk at midnight, rush   10
Of the leaf-nosed bat, the soft slip
Of fog easing through sand held in tandem.

Counting, the vertigo of its attitudes
Across the evening; in the wood of its latticed bones—
The eye sockets of every saint of thirst;   15
In the gullet of each night-blooming flower—the crucifix
Of the arid.

In its core, a monastery of cells, a brotherhood
Of electrons, a column of expanding darkness
Where matter migrates and sparks whorl,   20
And travel has no direction, where distance
Bends backward over itself and the ascension
Of Venus, the stability of Polaris, are crucial.

The cactus, containing
Whatever can be said to be there,   25
Plus the measurable tremble of its association
With all those who have been counting.

Irena Klepfisz 1941–

Born in Warsaw, Poland, in 1941, Irena Klepfisz is a survivor of the Holocaust, whose father perished in the Warsaw Ghetto uprising. With her mother, her only living relative, Klepfisz came to New York City in 1949. She attended the public schools and Yiddish schools sponsored by the Workmen's Circle. Poet, essayist, and playwright, Klepfisz's social and political commitments stem from her dual identities, ones often in conflict: being Jewish and being lesbian. But her sense of identity begins primarily with her escape from genocide and her sense, as Michelle Kwintner puts it, "that she could easily have died with the rest of her family." Klepfisz's writing confronts universal concerns—among them, connection, loss, and social intolerance.

DEDICATION FROM *BASHERT**

These words are dedicated to those who died
These words are dedicated to those who died
because they had no love and felt alone in the world
because they were afraid to be alone and tried to stick it out
because they could not ask   5
because they were shunned
because they were sick and their bodies could not resist the
disease
because they played it safe
because they had no connections   10
because they had no faith
because they felt they did not belong and wanted to die

These words are dedicated to those who died
because they were loners and liked it
because they acquired friends and drew others to them   15
because they took risks
because they were stubborn and refused to give up
because they asked for too much

These words are dedicated to those who died
because a card was lost and a number was skipped   20
because a bed was denied
because a place was filled and no other place was left

---

* *ba-shert* (Yiddish): inevitable, (pre)destined.

These words are dedicated to those who died
because someone did not follow through
because someone was overworked and forgot   25
because someone left everything to God
because someone was late
because someone did not arrive at all
because someone told them to wait and they just couldn't any
longer   30

These words are dedicated to those who died
because death is a punishment
because death is a reward
because death is the final rest
because death is eternal rage   35

These words are dedicated to those who died

Bashert

These words are dedicated to those who survived
These words are dedicated to those who survived
because their second grade teacher gave them books   40
because they did not draw attention to themselves and got lost
in the shuffle
because they knew someone who knew someone else who could
help them and bumped into them on a corner on a Thursday
afternoon   45
because they played it safe
because they were lucky

These words are dedicated to those who survived
because they knew how to cut corners
because they drew attention to themselves and always got picked   50
because they took risks
because they had no principles and were hard

These words are dedicated to those who survived
because they refused to give up and defied statistics
because they had faith and trusted in God   55
because they expected the worst and were always prepared
because they were angry
because they could ask
because they mooched off others and saved their strength
because they endured humiliation   60
because they turned the other cheek
because they looked the other way

These words are dedicated to those who survived
because life is a wilderness and they were savage
because life is an awakening and they were alert   65
because life is a flowering and they blossomed
because life is a struggle and they struggled
because life is a gift and they were free to accept it

These words are dedicated to those who survived

Bashert   70

ETLEKHE VERTER OYF MAME-LOSHN/
A FEW WORDS IN THE MOTHER TONGUE

lemoshl: for example

di kurve   the whore
a woman who acknowledges her passions

di yidene   the Jewess   the Jewish woman
ignorant   overbearing   5
let's face it: every woman is one

di yente   the gossip   the busybody
who knows what's what
and is never caught off guard

di lezbianke   the one with   10
a roommate   though we never used
the word

dos vaybl   the wife
or the little woman

          *   *   *

in der heym   at home   15
where she does everything to keep
yidishkayt alive

yidishkayt   a way of being
Jewish   always arguable

in mark   where she buys   20
di kartofl un khalah
(yes, potatoes and challah)

di kartofl the physical counter-
part of *yidishkayt*

mit tsibeles   with onions   25
that bring *trern tsu di oygn*
tears to her eyes   when she sees
how little it all is
veyniker un veyniker
less and less   30

di khalah   braided
vi irh hor far der khasene
like her hair before the wedding
when she was *aza sheyn meydl*
such a pretty girl   35

di lange shvartse hor
the long black hair
di lange shvartse hor

            *   *   *

a froy kholmt   a woman
dreams   *ihr ort oyf der velt*   40
her place in this world
un zi hot moyre   and she is afraid
so afraid of the words
kurve
yidene   45
yente
lezbianke
vaybl

zi kholmt   she dreams
un zi hot moyre   and she is afraid   50
ihr ort
di velt
di heym
der mark

a meydl kholmt   55
a kurve kholmt
a yidene kholmt
a yente kholmt
a lezbianke kholmt

a vaybl kholmt   60
di kartofl
di khalah

yidishkayt

zi kholmt
di hor   65
di lange shvartse hor

zi kholmt
zi kholmt
zi kholmt

Royal Pearl

Where do new varieties come from?
General Eisenhower is a red tulip which was first recognized in 1951. In 1957 a lemon
yellow mutation appeared in a field of red General Eisenhower tulips. This yellow
mutation proved to be a stable sport which was called—Royal Pearl.

                                         —Brooklyn Botanic Gardens

In dead of winter   imprisoned within
the imprisoned earth   it was a leap
defiant   of all eternal laws   and patterns.
Beneath the frozen earth   it came to be
like a splitting of an inner will   5
a wrenching from a designated path
a sudden burst   from a cause unknown
And then in spring   it opened: a lemon yellow
in a pure red field.

Our words deny the simple beauty   10
the wild energy of the event. *Anomaly*
deviant   mutant   we're always taught
as though this world   were a finished place
and we the dull guardians   of its perfected forms.
Our lives are rooted in such words.   15

Yet each winter   there are some
who watch   the gardens   emptied
only white   as the snow presses
on the fenced-in grounds   just
as on an unclaimed field.   20

And each winter   there are some
who dream   of a splitting of an inner will
a wrenching from the designated path
who dream a purple flower   standing solitary
in a yellow field.   25

Isabel Allende 1942–

Before establishing herself as one of Latin America's most distinguished writers, Isabel Allende worked as a secretary for the United Nations Food and Agricultural Organization, a television commentator, and a journalist. The daughter of a Chilean diplomat and niece of Chile's former President Salvador Allende, she was born in Lima, Peru. A 1973 military coup against Chile's ruling socialist government and the subsequent assassination of her uncle made a critical impact on Allende, dividing her life into "before that day and after that day." As Allende told interviewer Amanda Smith, "In that moment, I realized that everything was possible—that violence was a dimension that was always around you." For safety reasons, she and her family were forced to flee to Venezuela. The impending death of her nearly one-hundred-year-old grandfather inspired Allende to write her first novel, *House of Spirits* (1982), as a way of preserving the memories of her family and her country that, as she told *Mother Jones*, "were being blown by the wind, by the wind of exile." Allende has taught creative writing at a variety of universities, including the University of Virginia, Barnard College, and the University of California. She has published numerous novels, plays, children's stories, and essays.

From THE STORIES OF EVA LUNA

If You Touched My Heart

Amadeo Peralta was raised in the midst of his father's gang and, like all the men of his family, grew up to be a ruffian. His father believed that school was for sissies, you don't need books to get ahead in life, he always said, just balls and quick wits, and that was why he trained his boys to be rough and ready. With time, nevertheless, he realized that the world was changing very rapidly and that his business affairs needed to be more firmly anchored. The era of undisguised plunder had been replaced by one of corruption and bribery; it was time to administer his wealth by using modern criteria, and to improve his image. He called his sons together and assigned them the task of establishing friendships with influential persons and of learning the legal tricks that would allow them to continue to prosper without danger of losing their impunity. He also encouraged them to find sweethearts among the old-line families and in this way see whether they could cleanse the Peralta name of all its stains of mud and blood. By then Amadeo was thirty-two years old; the habit of seducing girls and then abandoning them was deeply ingrained; the idea of marriage was not at all to his liking but he did not dare disobey his father. He began to court the daughter of a wealthy landowner whose family had lived in the same place for six generations. Despite her suitor's murky reputation, the girl accepted, for she was not very attractive and was afraid of ending up an old maid. Then began one of those tedious provincial engagements. Wretched in a white linen suit and polished boots, Amadeo came every day to visit his fiancée beneath the hawklike eye of his future mother-in-law or some aunt, and while the young lady served coffee and guava sweets he would peek at his watch, calculating the earliest moment to make his departure.

A few weeks before the wedding, Amadeo Peralta had to make a business trip through the provinces and found himself in Agua Santa, one of those towns where nobody stays and whose name travelers rarely recall. He was walking down a narrow street at the hour of the siesta, cursing the heat and the oppressive, cloying odor of mango marmalade in the air, when he heard a crystalline sound like water purling between stones; it was coming from a modest house with paint flaked by the sun and rain like most of the houses in that town. Through the ornamental iron grille he glimpsed an entryway of dark paving stones and whitewashed walls, then a patio and, beyond, the surprising vision of a young girl sitting cross-legged on the ground and cradling a blond wood psaltery on her knees. For a while he stood and watched her.

"Come here, sweet thing," he called finally. She looked up, and despite the distance he could see the startled eyes and uncertain smile in a still childish face. "Come with me," Amadeo asked—implored—in a hoarse voice.

She hesitated. The last notes lingered like a question in the air of the patio. Peralta called again. The girl stood up and walked toward him; he slipped his hand through the iron grille, shot the bolt, opened the gate, and seized her hand, all the while reciting his entire repertoire of seduction: he swore that he had seen her in his dreams, that he had been looking for her all his life, that he could not let her go, and that she was the woman fate had meant for him—all of which he could have omitted because the girl was simple and even though she may have been enchanted by the tone of his voice she did not understand the meaning of his words. Hortensia was her name, and she had just turned fifteen; her body was tuned for its first embrace, though she was unable to put a name to the restlessness and temblors that shook it. It was so easy for Peralta to lead her to his car and drive to a nearby clearing that an hour later he had completely forgotten her. He did not recognize her even when a week later she suddenly appeared at his house, one hundred and forty kilometers away, wearing a simple yellow cotton dress and canvas espadrilles, her psaltery under her arm, and inflamed with the fever of love.

Forty-seven years later, when Hortensia was rescued from the pit in which she had been entombed, and newspapermen traveled from every corner of the nation to photograph her, not even she could remember her name or how she had got there.

The reporters accosted Amadeo Peralta: "Why did you keep her locked up like a miserable beast?"

"Because I felt like it," he replied calmly. By then he was eighty, and as lucid as ever; he could not understand this belated outcry over something that had happened so long ago.

He was not inclined to offer explanations. He was a man of authority, a patriarch, a great-grandfather; no one dared look him in the eye; even priests greeted him with bowed head. During the course of his long life he had multiplied the fortune he inherited from his father; he had become owner of all the land from the ruins of the Spanish fort to the state line, and then had launched himself on a political career that made him the most powerful cacique in the territory. He had married the landowner's ugly daughter and sired nine legitimate descendants with her and an indefinite number of bastards with other women, none of whom he remembered since he had a heart hardened to love. The only woman he could not entirely discard was Hortensia; she stuck in his consciousness like a persistent nightmare. After the brief encounter in the tall grass of an empty lot, he had returned to his home, his work, and his insipid, well-bred fiancée. It was Hortensia who had searched until she found *him*; it was she who had planted herself before him and clung to his shirt with the terrifying submission of a slave. This is a fine kettle of fish, he had thought; here I am about to get married with all this hoopla and to-do, and now this idiot girl turns up on my doorstep. He wanted to be rid of her, and yet when he saw her in her yellow dress, with those entreating eyes, it seemed a waste not to take advantage of the opportunity, and he decided to hide her while he found a solution.

And so, by carelessness, really, Hortensia ended up in the cellar of an old sugar mill that belonged to the Peraltas, where she was to remain for a lifetime. It was a large room, dank and dark, suffocating in summer and in the dry season often cold at night, furnished with a few sticks of furniture and a straw pallet. Amadeo Peralta never took time to make her more comfortable, despite his occasionally feeding a fantasy of making the girl a concubine from an Oriental tale, clad in gauzy robes and surrounded with peacock feathers, brocade tented ceilings, stained-glass lamps, gilded furniture with spiral feet, and thick rugs where he could walk barefoot. He might actually have done it had Hortensia reminded him of his promises, but she was like a wild bird, one of those blind guacharos that live in the depths of caves: all she needed was a little food and water. The yellow dress rotted away and she was left naked.

"He loves me; he has always loved me," she declared when she was rescued by neighbors. After being locked up for so many years she had lost the use of words and her voice came out in spurts like the croak of a woman on her deathbed.

For a few weeks Amadeo had spent a lot of time in the cellar with her, satisfying an appetite he thought insatiable. Fearing that she would be discovered, and jealous even of his own eyes, he did not want to expose her to daylight and allowed only a pale ray to enter through the tiny hole that provided ventilation. In the darkness, they coupled frenziedly, their skin burning and their hearts impatient as carnivorous crabs. In that cavern all odors and tastes were heightened to the extreme. When they touched, each entered the other's being and sank into the other's most secret desires. There, voices resounded in repeated echoes; the walls returned amplified murmurs and kisses. The cellar became a sealed flask in which they wallowed like playful twins swimming in amniotic fluid, two swollen, stupefied fetuses. For days they were lost in an absolute intimacy they confused with love.

When Hortensia fell asleep, her lover went out to look for food and before she awakened returned with renewed energy to resume the cycle of caresses. They should have made love to each other until they died of desire; they should have devoured one another or flamed like mirrored torches, but that was not to be. What happened instead was more predictable and ordinary, much less grandiose. Before a month had passed, Amadeo Peralta tired of the games, which they were beginning to repeat; he sensed the dampness eating into his joints, and he began to feel the attraction of things outside the walls of that grotto. It was time to return to the world of the living and to pick up the reins of his destiny.

"You wait for me here. I'm going out and get very rich. I'll bring you gifts and dresses and jewels fit for a queen," he told her as he said goodbye.

"I want children," said Hortensia.

"Children, no; but you shall have dolls."

In the months that followed, Peralta forgot about the dresses, the jewels, and the dolls. He visited Hortensia when he thought of her, not always to make love, sometimes merely to hear her play some old melody on her psaltery; he liked to watch her bent over the instrument, strumming chords. Sometimes he was in such a rush that he did not even speak; he filled her water jugs, left her a sack filled with provisions, and departed. Once he forgot about her for nine days, and found her on the verge of death; he realized then the need to find someone to help care for his prisoner, because his family, his travels, his business, and his social engagements occupied all his time. He chose a tight-mouthed Indian woman to fill that role. She kept the key to the padlock, and regularly came to clean the cell and scrape away the lichens growing on Hortensia's body like pale delicate flowers almost invisible to the naked eye and redolent of tilled soil and neglected things.

"Weren't you ever sorry for that poor woman?" they asked when they arrested her as well, charging her with complicity in the kidnapping. She refused to answer but stared straight ahead with expressionless eyes and spat a black stream of tobacco.

No, she had felt no pity for her; she believed the woman had a calling to be a slave and was happy being one, or else had been born an idiot and like others in her situation was better locked up than exposed to the jeers and perils of the street. Hortensia had done nothing to change her jailer's opinion; she never exhibited any curiosity about the world, she made no attempt to go outside for fresh air, and she complained about nothing. She never seemed bored; her mind had stopped at some moment in her childhood, and solitude in no way disturbed her. She was, in fact, turning into a subterranean creature. There in her tomb her senses grew sharp and she learned to see the invisible; she was surrounded by hallucinatory spirits who led her by the hand to other universes. She left behind a body huddled in a corner and traveled through starry space like a messenger particle, living in a dark land beyond reason. Had she had a mirror, she would have been terrified by her appearance; as she could not see herself, however, she was not witness to her deterioration: she was unaware of the scales sprouting from her skin, or the silkworms that had spun a nest in her long, tangled hair, or the lead-colored clouds covering eyes already dead from peering into shadows. She did not feel her ears growing to capture external sounds, even the faintest and most distant, like the laughter of children at school recess, the ice-cream vendor's bell, birds in flight, or the murmuring river. Nor did she realize that her legs, once graceful and firm, were growing twisted as they adjusted to moving in that confined space, to crawling, nor that her toenails were thickening like an animal's hooves, her bones changing into tubes of glass, her belly caving in, and a hump forming on her back. Only her hands, forever occupied with the psaltery, maintained their shape and size, although her fingers had forgotten the melodies they had once known and now extracted from the instrument the unvoiced sob trapped in her breast. From a distance, Hortensia resembled a tragic circus monkey; on closer view, she inspired infinite pity. She was totally ignorant of the malignant transformations taking place; in her mind she held intact the image of herself as the young girl she had last seen reflected in the window of Amadeo Peralta's automobile the day he had driven her to this lair. She believed she was as pretty as ever, and continued to act as if she were; the memory of beauty crouched deep inside her and only if someone approached very close would he have glimpsed it beneath the external façade of a prehistoric dwarf.

All the while, Amadeo Peralta, rich and feared, cast the net of his power across the region. Every Sunday he sat at the head of a long table occupied by his sons and nephews, cronies and accomplices, and special guests such as politicians and generals whom he treated with a hearty cordiality tinged with sufficient arrogance to remind everyone who was master here. Behind his back, people whispered about his victims, about how many he had ruined or caused to disappear, about bribes to authorities; there was talk that he had made half his fortune from smuggling, but no one was disposed to seek the proof of his transgressions. It was also rumored that Peralta kept a woman prisoner in a cellar. That aspect of his black deeds was repeated with more conviction even than stories of his crooked dealings; in fact, many people knew about it, and with time it became an open secret.

One afternoon on a very hot day, three young boys played hooky from school to swim in the river. They spent a couple of hours splashing around on the muddy bank and then wandered off toward the old Peralta sugar mill that had been closed two generations earlier when cane ceased to be a profitable crop. The mill had the reputation of being haunted; people said you could hear sounds of devils, and many had seen a disheveled old witch invoking the spirits of dead slaves. Excited by their adventure, the boys crept onto the property and approached the mill. Soon they were daring enough to enter the ruins; they ran through large rooms with thick adobe walls and termite-riddled beams; they picked their way through weeds growing from the floor, mounds of rubbish and dog shit, rotted roof tiles, and snake nests. Making jokes to work up their courage, egging each other on, they came to the huge roofless room that contained the ruined sugar presses; here rain and sun had created an impossible garden, and the boys thought they could detect a lingering scent of sugar and sweat. Just as they were growing bolder they heard, clear as a bell, the notes of a monstrous song. Trembling, they almost retreated, but the lure of horror was stronger than their fear, and they huddled there, listening, as the last note drilled into their foreheads. Gradually, they were released from their paralysis; their fear evaporated and they began looking for the source of those weird sounds so different from any music they had ever known. They discovered a small trapdoor in the floor, closed with a lock they could not open. They rattled the wood planks that sealed the entrance and were struck in the face by an indescribable odor that reminded them of a caged beast. They called but no one answered; they heard only a hoarse panting on the other side. Finally they ran home to shout the news that they had discovered the door to hell.

The children's uproar could not be stilled, and thus the neighbors finally proved what they had suspected for decades. First the boys' mothers came to peer through the cracks in the trapdoor; they, too, heard the terrible notes of the psaltery, so different from the banal melody that had attracted Amadeo Peralta the day he had paused in a small alley in Agua Santa to dry the sweat from his forehead. The mothers were followed by throngs of curious and, last of all, after a crowd had already gathered, came the police and firemen, who chopped open the door and descended into the hole with their lamps and equipment. In the cave they found a naked creature with flaccid skin hanging in pallid folds; this apparition had tangled gray hair that dragged the floor, and moaned in terror of the noise and light. It was Hortensia, glowing with a mother-of-pearl phosphorescence under the steady beams of the fire fighters' lanterns; she was nearly blind, her teeth had rotted away, and her legs were so weak she could barely stand. The only sign of her human origins was the ancient psaltery clasped to her breast.

The news stirred indignation throughout the country. Television screens and newspapers displayed pictures of the woman rescued from the hole where she had spent her life, now, at least, half clothed in a cloak someone had tossed around her shoulders. In only a few hours, the indifference that had surrounded the prisoner for almost half a century was converted into a passion to avenge and succor her. Neighbors improvised lynch parties for Amadeo Peralta; they stormed his house, dragged him out, and had the *guardia* not arrived in time, would have torn him limb from limb in the plaza. To assuage their guilt for having ignored Hortensia for so many years, everyone wanted to do something for her. They collected money to provide her a pension, they gathered tons of clothing and medicine she did not need, and several welfare organizations were given the task of scraping the filth from her body, cutting her hair, and outfitting her from head to toe, so she looked like an ordinary old lady. The nuns offered her a bed in a shelter for indigents, and for several months kept her tied up to prevent her from running back to her cellar, until finally she grew accustomed to daylight and resigned to living with other human beings.

Taking advantage of the public furor fanned by the press, Amadeo Peralta's numerous enemies finally gathered courage to launch an attack against him. Authorities who for years had overlooked his abuses fell upon him with the full fury of the law. The story occupied everyone's attention long enough to see the former caudillo in prison, and then faded and died away. Rejected by family and friends, a symbol of all that is abominable and abject, harassed by both jailers and companions-in-misfortune, Peralta spent the rest of his days in prison. He remained in his cell, never venturing into the courtyard with the other inmates. From there, he could hear the sounds from the street.

Every day at ten in the morning, Hortensia, with the faltering step of a madwoman, tottered down to the prison where she handed the guard at the gate a warm saucepan for the prisoner.

"He almost never left me hungry," she would tell the guard in a apologetic tone. Then she would sit in the street to play her psaltery, wresting from it moans of agony impossible to bear. In the hope of distracting her or silencing her, some passersby gave her money.

Crouched on the other side of the wall, Amadeo Peralta heard those sounds that seemed to issue from the depths of the earth and course through every nerve in his body. This daily castigation must mean something, but he could not remember what. From time to time he felt something like a stab of guilt, but immediately his memory failed and images of the past evaporated in a dense mist. He did not know why he was in that tomb, and gradually he forgot the world of light and lost himself in his misfortune.

Rayna Green 1942–

A writer of fiction, folklore, and poetry, as well as a traditional scholar in groundbreaking scholarly areas, Rayna Green has said, "I will write about anything that interests me, regardless of the subject—Indians, women, food, science. . . . As a native American (Oklahoma Cherokee), I feel a great responsibility getting the record straight about Indians, but I feel a similar responsibility towards the truth wherever it's found." Green's important scholarly work began with her doctoral thesis (1973), published as *The Image of the Indian in Vernacular American Culture: The Only Good Indian.* Her work on Native-Indian traditional science and women appears in a range of scholarly journals; her poetry and fiction evoke heroines like Cherokee Nanye'hi, who is "plotting the power of the women . . . dancing the stories / that made us dream over her / shattered breath." Green has also compiled bibliographies on Native-American women and Native-American traditional science (1983) and has edited collections of poetry and fiction by Native-American women.

WHEN I CUT MY HAIR

when I cut my hair
at thirty-five
Grandma said she'd forgive me
for cutting it
without her permission   5

but I cried out everytime
I touched my head

years from then
and Grandma dead
it came back to me last night when   10
you said you wanted it all

your rich body grounding me safe
the touch of your hair
took me out
I saw pigeon feathers   15
red wool
and fur

and it wrapped me
with the startled past
so sudden   20
your hair falling all around us

I touched center
and forgave myself

COOSAPONAKEESA (MARY MATHEWS MUSGROVE BOSOMSWORTH), LEADER OF THE CREEKS, 1700–1783

FOR JOY HARJO

what kind of lovers could they have been
these colonists

good enough to marry them everyone
or was it something else that made her take them on

all woman   5
part swamp rat
half horse
she rode through Georgia
It was hers and the Creeks'
and Oglethorpe wanted it all   10

But she rolled with him too
and kept them at bay
for too long
til they said
she'd sold out for the goods   15

the money and velvet was what she loved
sure enough
but Ossabaw and Sapelo and Savannah more
so she fought them with sex and war
and anything that worked   20
until they rolled over her

The Creeks say Mary came back as Sherman
just to see what they'd taken away
burned to the ground
and returned to her once more   25

The Creek girls in Oklahoma
laugh like Mary now
wild and good
they'll fight you for it
and make you want everything all over again   30

no deals this time though
it's all
or nothing

Sharon Olds 1942–

It is Sharon Olds who is credited with giving legitimacy to certain subjects
for poetry: These include parental abuse, fathers and daughters, parenting,
women's bodies, women's desire. Indeed, it has been written that Olds has "given
authority to personal experience." Her poetry is powerful, often shocking, and
explicit in its explorations of family and other aspects of private life. Born in
San Francisco, holding a B.A. from Stanford University and a Ph.D from Columbia
University, Olds is the recipient of numerous awards and honors. Her first book
of poems, *Satan Says* (1980), won the San Francisco Poetry Center Award; *The
Dead and the Living* (1984) as the Lamont Poetry Selection for 1983 and the
winner of the National Book Critics' Circle Award. Other collections include *The
Gold Cell* (1987) and *The Father* (1992). She teaches at New York University.

THE KNOWING

Afterwards, when we have slept, paradise-
comaed, and woken, we lie a long time
looking at each other.
I do not know what he sees, but I see
eyes of surpassing tenderness   5
and calm, a calm like the dignity
of matter. I love the open ocean
blue-gray-green of his iris, I love
the curve of it against the white,
that curve the sight of what has caused me   10
to come, when he's quite still, deep
inside me. I have never seen a curve

like that, except the earth from outer
space. I don't know where he got
his kindness without self-regard,   15
almost without self, and yet
he chose one woman, instead of the others.
By knowing him, I get to know
the purity of the animal
which mates for life. Sometimes he is slightly   20
smiling, but mostly he just gazes at me gazing,
his entire face lit. I love
to see it change if I cry—there is no worry,
no pity, a graver radiance. If we
are on our backs, side by side,   25
with our faces turned fully to face each other,
I can hear a tear from my lower eye
hit the sheet, as if it is an early day on earth,
and then the upper eye's tears
braid and sluice down through the lower eyebrow   30
like the invention of farming, irrigation, a non-nomadic people.
I am so lucky that I can know him.
This is the only way to know him.
I am the only one who knows him.
When I wake again, he is still looking at me,   35
as if he is eternal. For an hour
we wake and doze, and slowly I know
that though we are sated, though we are hardly
touching, this is the coming the other
brought us to the edge of—we are entering.   40
deeper and deeper, gaze by gaze,
this place beyond the other places,
beyond the body itself, we are making
love.

WHY MY MOTHER MADE ME

Maybe I am what she always wanted,
my father as a woman,
maybe I am what she wanted to be
when she first saw him, tall and smart,
standing there in the college yard with the   5
hard male light of 1937
shining on his black hair. She wanted that

power. She wanted that size. She pulled and
pulled through him as if he were dark
bourbon taffy, she pulled and pulled and   10
pulled through his body until she drew me out,
amber and gleaming, her life after her life.
Maybe I am the way I am
because she wanted exactly that,
wanted there to be a woman   15
a lot like her, but who would not hold back, so she
pressed herself hard against him,
pressed and pressed the clear soft
ball of herself like a stick of beaten cream
against his stained sour steel grater   20
until I came out on the other side of his body,
a big woman, stained, sour, sharp,
but with that milk at the center of my nature.
I lie here now as I once lay
in the crook of her arm, her creature,   25
and I feel her looking down into me the way the
maker of a sword gazes at his face in the
steel of the blade.

MY MOTHER'S COLLEGE

I am going to be there where her body was when it was
perfect—young, sealed, soft,
no passage had been torn in it yet for my
hard head to enter this world, she was
sweet and whole as my daughter's body,   5
she walked on those lawns. Small and curled as a
fox she sat in a warm window-seat,
it makes me sick with desire to think of her,
my first love—when I lay stunned and
tiny in her arms I thought she was the whole world,   10
a world of heat, silky flesh and milk
and that huge heart-beat. But there she had no
children, no one was weaker than she,
she had all her beauty and none of her power, she
moved slowly under the arches   15
literally singing. Half of me was
deep in her body like an Easter egg

with my name on it, gold with red script—
maybe the happiest time of my life as I
glided above the gravel paths   20
deep in the center of the dark universe.
I want to thank the stones she touched,
I want to visit the chapel with its stained and
glassy God, the pews rubbed with the
stolen homes of bees, I want to   25
love her when she had not hurt anyone yet,
she had never lifted a finger to me—
all that had been done to her she
held, still, in her delicate fresh
strong body, where her will rose up like   30
fire and her fear banked it with sand as she
lay on her stomach, still a child, really,
studying for finals, and before the dance she
washed her hair and rinsed it with lemon and then
shook her head so the whole inside of her   35
tiny room was flecked with sour bright citrus.

I Cannot Forget the Woman
in the Mirror

Backwards and upside down in the twilight, that
woman on all fours, her head
dangling and suffused, her lean
haunches, the area of darkness, the flanks and
ass narrow and pale as a deer's and those   5
breasts hanging down toward the center of the earth like
    plummets, when I
swayed from side to side they swayed, it was
so dark I couldn't tell if they were gold or
plum or rose. I cannot get over her   10
moving toward him upside down in the mirror like a
fly on the ceiling, her head hanging down and her
tongue long and dark as an anteater's
going toward his body, she was so clearly an
animal, she was an Iroquois scout creeping   15
naked and noiseless, and when I looked at her
she looked at me so directly, her eyes so

dark, her stare said to me
I belong here, this is mine, I am living out my
true life on this earth.   20

Gail Galloway Adams 1943–

Although she didn't begin to write seriously until age forty-three, Gail Galloway Adams quickly made a name for herself. In 1987, she won the Flannery O'Connor Award in Short Fiction for *The Purchase of Order* and a short-story award from the Texas Institute of Letters for "Inside Dope," which was included in that year's edition of *Best American Short Stories*. Born in the small west Texas town of Graham, Adams spent much of her childhood as an Army "brat" in France, Germany, and the United States. As a child and young woman, she dreamed of being a professional dancer, enrolled in prestigious dance academies, and even began a choreography masters degree at New York University. Although her career in dance did not reach fruition, the creative energies that fueled her love of dance reemerged later in the form of writing. Adams revealed to *Contemporary Authors* that her stories, so often dealing with the theme of loss, "fall into two voices." The first is humorous, "with an element of exaggeration inherent in family oral story-telling." The characters tend to be honest and courageous "blue-collar" types who "work hard to maintain their livelihoods and their dignity." The second category of stories is more poetic. "I use a longer flowing line in the prose, and sometimes during their composition I shift into an almost 'automatic' writing." Adams is currently a professor of English and creative writing at West Virginia University.

THE PURCHASE OF ORDER

Lou Maxey is hanging over the top of the seat, her behind a likely target. She's slipped her pink plastic shoes half off and they dangle like loose skin. There are rustling sounds from the back.

"What in the hell are you doing?" Marlon asks, pushing in the cigarette lighter, which he has to lean around her in order to do.

"I'm looking for that package of Cheese Nuggets I packed in here. I'm hungry."

"We just had breakfast less than an hour ago," he says around his light-up. "You had the Trencherman. You couldn't be hungry."

She looks back over the shoulder, tries to lift her foot up and sideways to jog his knee; it's impossible, so she bumps his shoulder with her rear. "How do you know? You're not me. And I'm hungry."

Lou is one of those little women who never look any older than about sixteen until you're close up. Her hair is crisp and close and dark and her eyes are the brown of spaniels'. She's had five kids, four in the first six years of marriage, and then a decade's wait before her baby Jason, now in the Navy on a ship anchored off Greece. Lou likes to think of her baby in the Mediterranean, near the place and the myth he was named for, and how apt the name she chose. Although there are lots of Jasons now, there weren't many then, and her boy, with his curly golden hair, thick and spongy as sheep wool on his arms and chest, was like a fleecy thing. "It looks like Santa's beard's on his legs," a little cousin said once at the beach.

You could never imagine your own children making love, Lou thought. She could never imagine anyone making love, but she could picture a dark Grecian girl with red ribbons in her hair cradling against Jason's chest. Marlon's body hair was different. It was rusty and tufty with a strange patch on the left chest. He had smooth upper arms that were furred like pelts from elbow to wrist. Everything about the men amazed her, and they'd been married almost thirty years.

Last night at the motel while she watched *The Sting* on TV, Marlon, feet crossed precisely one on top of the other in a wedge, read the local paper, which he always did wherever they stopped. "Guess who this sounds like," he said, reading a letter to the editor from a man who complained about the sewer lines, the garbage pick-up, and the planting of iris bulbs in front of City Hall. "'And in conclusion . . .'" Marlon pulled the sentence out. "'City Council should get going or get out.'"

Lou, who'd only half-listened from the second tirade on, said, "That's your mamma all over, Marlon."

He smiled, shook the paper back into creases, and settled in to reading the classifieds while she got up, one eye on the TV show, and wandered over to the window, which was oddly high, partly blocked by an air-conditioning unit.

"'Two bedroom house for $195,'" Marlon read. "That's not bad." She mmmed that she heard, but mainly was looking for something, anything previous guests might have left behind. Once she'd found a bookmark, navy leather stamped with gold designs, tucked into the Gideon. Another time a little girl's hairbow, fashioned into a rose with a frill of plastic lace. Lou collected such things as souvenirs. She liked to own matchbooks that she found under beds in which she and many others had slept.

Marlon had finished reading, was watching the movie with a bemused expression.

"What part's that?" She bent over him and without a word he flipped her over on her back and splattered his mouth against her stomach. She pushed at his head, saying. "Don't, no, stop, don't you dare," and then Marlon went from splatting to pink belly, and while she giggled and shoved him away, shouting for Robert Redford to save her, she was excited by the sound of his hands patting her stomach, moving fast up and down her flesh.

This summer's trip is following a pattern set ten years ago. The Maxeys hop into their van aiming to just go. That first day when Marlon drove it home, Lou walked around and around it, thinking it was as big as a bus. Marlon scraped off the manufacturer's name KING OF THE ROAD, saying, "That makes me sick. I'll choose my own name." Then he left the space bare, tacky with a residue of stickiness that collects insects and dust. A decade later KI and RD still show like lines in the wax of a magic slate.

This summer, like all before, they'll travel anywhere and everywhere they want, not a plan in their heads, except to follow their own feelings. "What will be, will be" is the Maxeys' motto on these trips, but truth to tell, Lou does worry and marks the maps and schedules the stops so they can visit with all their kids and grandchildren. After Labor Day, when families leave the road to see to purchases of new notebooks and underwear, they turn back too, clean up their van, and park it to the side of the bungalow near Austin where they've decided to spend the rest of their lives.

Lou calls her friends, goes to the YWCA for her Jane Fonda exercise class, and twice weekly puts on her crinolines and she and Marlon go to the Square Dance Club. "No ties, not even string ones" was the deal before he'd go. She loves the way he looks standing across from her in the square, wearing his plaid blue shirt with pearl buttons, open at the collar, jeans turned up in a pale roll, and boots, cut-under heels marking up the gym floor. When the caller does his do-si-do, Marlon moves his nose sideways, lets his eyelids droop in a criminal manner, and swings circle-box-circle until she's his, caught at the waist. Even when these evenings make her ache and soak her feet, see them peel in a pan of Epsom salts, she loves it. She feels exactly as she did when she first met Marlon, then married him, against everybody's will.

Early in their marriage, when he'd lost his job, the one he quit high school for, a restlessness set in in him. She'd be at work, a half-day job her daddy got her at a plate glass company doing bills, and in the afternoons stuffing burgers into bags, when she'd look up to catch Marlon whisking out of sight. Sometimes, later in the day, he'd come to get a roast beef that had got cold. "Can't stick around," he'd say. "Got to see a man."

Sometimes he'd borrow a dollar, or pat her on the belly where the baby now was. They didn't talk much about the baby; somehow she knew it made Marlon too sad. Only at night in bed in the trailer, where the neighbors slammed their glass louvered doors so hard the foundation shook, Lou'd scoot up against him, feeling the swell of their baby between, and she knew how Marlon felt. "Wasn't supposed to be this way," he whispered, turning to embrace her. The baby's bulk pushed him to the wall as she felt the corners of her mouth tingling at the touch of his lips.

Near when the baby was due Lou began to worry about what would happen, how they'd work things out. She'd catch herself sitting at her desk at Mitchell's Glass having stapled the same bill twice. She found it harder and harder to force a smile for customers. The smell of onion and grease at her afternoon job seemed never to leave her. She was constantly figuring out schedules, adding sums in her head even as she sprinkled grated cheese on the taco special.

"I've got a job," Marlon told her when he popped up at the Burger 52 one day right after lunch and was persuaded to sit down and have a cherry coke and onion rings. Everyone liked Marlon. He was even-tempered, told good stories, and he worked hard: it's just there had to be work to do.

"Where is this job?" asked the other hop, whose boyfriend had got the boot a few weeks before Marlon. "In Alaska?"

Marlon looked up, winked, held an onion like a ring over his finger and said, "Yes." Everyone laughed but Lou; she knew Marlon never kidded about change. He ate that ring, finished his coke, and, pointing his finger at her like a gun, said, "Later."

That's how they ended up in a van with a three-week-old baby girl and some household goods, driving to this promised land where Marlon worked construction and Lou watched babies, her own among them, and all they made went for food and rent. The sunsets hung red for hours, it seemed, teasing them with the thought of dark, and Marlon wasn't happy. Evenings he'd sit in front of the television after the baby was in bed and hold his knees, shoving the heel of his hand like gunning a car, fast, faster, staring straight ahead and clenching his jaws.

One night when he came home Lou was nursing the baby, both curled up in a corner of the couch. He sat down on the coffee table facing her, clasping his hands like being good at school; then he leaned his chin against his steepled thumbs.

"Do you want me to rub your neck?" she asked.

He raised his head and his eyes looked swimmy, even though he was smiling. "I've got another job, babe. On the coast, doing something. Don't know what, but I'll guarantee you it'll be dirty and dangerous." He tapped Lou's chin with his fist, gently pulled the baby's hair. Lou was pregnant again, bigger this time, with things going strange. Her ankles swelled straight to her knees, turning white and crackly like old china plates. Marlon would pop her toes at night, rub warmth into her feet with his hands, which were small for a man's.

They never stopped making love, even when it seemed that everything they did or didn't do led to babies. Their second was born in Louisiana, then another boy in Tampa, then a baby girl born on their way from Arizona to Alabama, and Lou's chief memory of those years is of trying to keep her babies clean, keep them up off floors where who-knew-what had gone on. They lived on a live-in ship, in a one-room kitchenette on the third floor of a beach hotel, and once—she doesn't like to think of it—in the back part of a converted van. Some rainy days during that bad time she would gather her children around to sleep huddled like puppies. They saw a lot of places, and Marlon's excitement about them kept her going.

"Living in a place is not the same as visiting it, "he'd said, "because while you get to know the towns better, you know them less." Lou thought that was true. Places were like relatives: somehow the longer you knew one, the less you valued it. Moving off and then coming back for visits let you see all the sweetnesses. She'd picked up Marlon's rhythm by this time and wondered as she wrapped her cups in the Sunday comics, readying for another move, if she could ever go back to one place. She'd met a woman who'd shopped at the same Piggly Wiggly all her life, and Lou marveled at that.

Sometimes the places where they had lived blended into each other, all seeming a dream that held these constants: a laundromat, a convenience store, and a drive-in on the edge of town where she and Marlon would get out to sit on a blanket spread in front of the grille while the children slept on in the back seat, the speakers turned low for their ears. Then sometimes Lou would be struck with a recall of a place so vivid that she thought, If I went back there now, I could find my way around. Sometimes at night, when she couldn't sleep, she played a game with herself. She picked a town they'd lived in and drove around in it in her head. When Marlon heard her muttering, "Turn left for the Dixie Pig," he'd sleepily ask, "Where are you?"

Getting used to change is easy for her now, but it wasn't always. She's happy to think she can adjust, move from place to place, seek out the stores, the banks and the schools. She liked to get the family settled in and clear a place on the refrigerator for the kids' school work while Marlon went off to all the different jobs that he had.

Whenever she went back to the town Marlon came from she saw the same people walking down the same streets. They'd die in the same frame houses they lived in, she thought. Then she wanted to get in the car and go, drive away with Marlon and the kids to somewhere they'd never lived before.

Each year when they start their trip they have a purpose. It is one that has never been taken out and examined, one that is rarely discussed except in memories that come up—a purpose neither of them really knows how to explain. What moves these summers for the Maxeys is a search that has shaped their lives for the last decade: they are looking for a family they once knew, without whose presence everything in life has been more pale, a family they've continued to think about and talk about. Lamont and Jean Dillon and their kids—when they met them twenty-two years ago in Arkansas, it was one of those meetings between two families where everything hits right and it is forever and always. But in this case, the Maxeys don't know how, it fell away through not keeping in touch, both of them moving on too many times.

When Lou wants to make an event memorable, she ransacks her brain for recollections of the Dillons, especially Lamont in his boneless height. "How he keeps his pants up is a mystery, and I'm married to the man," Jean said, rolling her eyes, always in a laugh putting her left hand up to cover where a tooth was gone, another gone gray. Lamont's back seam fell flat between his thighs.

At various times over the years when Lou has helped her children learn to cut meat, do a chain stitch in crochet, or print between the lines, she's seen Lamont's hands as they shaped a little figure with his knife. Concentrating as solemnly as the child who stood waiting to see what would emerge from between the wood and the blade, he'd roll the scrap of pine in his fingers and seem surprised himself to see it become a donkey or a tiny dancing man. He'd lift up his head and his thick eyebrows, under which his eyes, so light a blue they were almost white, were innocent, and smile a fool's smile, the corners of his mouth pulling up into his cheeks.

"Now lookee here," he'd murmur, balancing the figure in the well of his outstretched hand. "Let me take my payment." The knife blade quickly cut the thinnest lock from the edge of the child's hair; the blade tip near their ears made the older ones shiver, the little ones giggle. "This here's magic hair," he'd say. "Have to add it to my pile."

"If he'd ever get money for those carvings we'd have a dozen pillows stuffed with duck fuzz down, if we wanted them," Jean would complain, then light a Tareyton, pulling in smoke, the cigarette moving from the center of her lip like a dowser's rod in the strength of her inhale. When she wanted to be funny she'd cross her eyes before blowing out the match.

That day in the laundromat Lou couldn't have known that Jean would be any other than the kind of friend you usually make there who helps you fold. Even though Marlon was good with the kids, Lou always took her brood with her; too many things can happen in a trailer court on an off-day when men, in work or out, are drinking beer and fixing cars. One guy with a saucer scar on his shoulder scared the kids by popping out his top three teeth and clanking them up and down. At the laundromat Lou would sit her four down, give them Chocolate Soldiers and Nabs, and buy each of them a comic book. Later, during Dry, Marlon would come to help fold. Sometimes he'd wrap himself like an Arab in a sheet, dancing a mummy's dance, and make everybody in the long linoleumed room laugh.

That's how they first met, Jean with her pile of threadbare towels and striped Handi-Wipes she used for washrags—that's what she called them instead of washcloths—and all her kids, who made Lou's crazy. But she was such a good-natured lanky girl, so quick to smile at Marlon's silliness, so willing to let the children be lively in their romping around with peanut shell earrings clamped to their lobes, that Lou liked her right away.

Lou was folding diapers when all of a sudden this woman with hair yanked straight back and features looking forward began to help. "These sure are white," she said. "Why don't you use disposables?"

"Can't afford to," Lou answered, wanting to laugh and not knowing why, but knowing right then that this friendship, based from the beginning on knowing everything bad about each other's underwear, would last.

"Where ya'll staying?" she'd questioned Lou, having said she was Jean Dillon and with a wave of a hand, diaper flapping like a sailor's flag, pointed out her husband Lamont, who was loading a commercial machine with a jumble of goods from towels to blue jeans. Marlon was outside walking all the kids in formation on the parking lot, yelling made-up orders: "Walk on tippy-toes. Now stick out your tongues." The children collapsed on hot tar in giggling heaps.

"My bunch," Jean said, shooing them off, the other hand shaking out a

Tareyton. "Maisie, Jasper, Gordon, Ceil, and Autumn Ann. Where'd you say?" she asked again.

Lou had no choice but to tell her. "We're out at Doakes." She didn't like to be there. It was a rough place. Too many people slept in during the day, and they weren't on the night shifts either.

"Not so good for kids." Jean tongued her cigarette to the side of her mouth, squinted her eyes, and began to fold. "No place to let them run their spirits out."

"I try to get over to the park each day," Lou said.

"Come live by us," Jean offered. "Looks funny from the street—Clark's Courts—but inside it's just the place for kids. I manage there. It's not free, but no more than you're paying at Doakes."

Lou didn't know what to say, looked up at Jean, her lank brown hair wreathed with smoke, her bright blue eyes eager and hopeful. "I'll have to talk to my husband," she said, and right then Marlon burst through the door crying, "Save me. Save me! Please!" holding the plate glass shut against the force of all the sweaty screeching children, pushing and laughing and shoving and shouting out the different sweet treats they wanted. "Stay still!" He mashed a frog face on the glass. "Sit down like sombrero men with your knees drawed up and each and every one of you will get a Fudgsicle." Then he came and stood by Lou and asked, "Who's taking over my diaper duty?"

Jean laughed, then hailed Lamont, who'd been resting, back against the porthole of the big machine, head down, dreaming. "Lamont, come meet these people. I'm getting them to come and live by us."

When Lamont Dillon looked up and smiled. Lou's heart fled out of her and she, who'd never given love to any man but Marlon, knew she loved him; not in the way of Marlon, nor that of her brother who'd died in the war, and for whom she cried for years, waking sometimes in the night, face wet with tears from a dream that he was showing her how to hit a pitch, sock the tetherball and knock it back to him. No, somehow it was as though Lamont Dillon was her, or as if, had she been a man, she'd have been exactly like him. He sauntered toward them, tall, skinny with thick black hair and an eerie half-breed Indian look of dark skin and blue eyes, all of him moving bonelessly and gracefully as he slid his shower shoes along. Lou looked over at Marlon, standing even with Jean's height: both of them looked like lean alley cats, rusty and triangular, emitting energy as they stood. She felt a burning, as if had they joined hands in a ring they'd explode into flames.

"You're at the turpentine camp?" Lamont drawled. His voice was rumbling, deep, almost phony in its bass level.

Marlon was jazzed up; he was joking already as he answered yes.

They moved into Clark's Courts and Lou began to watch Jean Dillon closely for clues on how she lived; usually she let her kids go as wild as her house and the yard. Her kitchen was the kind where a brush filled with her hair sits right next to a stick of melted butter; Lou always washed her own cups there. Once when Lou'd spilled a can of corn, Jean said, "Here, let me help you," then proceeded to kick the kernels under the shelf's overhang. She was always saying her kids were up to no good, even as she passed their school pictures around, and they loved her the same way, interrupting as she read her *True Romance*. "What do you want, you dirty bum?" With a long arm she'd grab a boy and kiss him as he squirmed, protested, "Mamma, no." They asked for Nutty Buddy money or a dime for the picture show. Jean always gave it.

They couldn't scare her either. "See here—spiders," said Ceil, a bony-chested ten-year-old with harlequin glasses that were pearl-tipped. "Bet you'd be afraid to touch them," she challenged Jean, who pulled her face all to the center and said, "Oh yeah?" then mounted them on her fingers and displayed them like rings. "Here, kids, Popsicles," she'd shout, or "Root beer floats, everyone." Her children had cavities and scabbed elbows and greasy hair and grayed knees and were totally secure in their parents' love.

Autumn Ann was a foster baby who'd been given them by a cousin to keep for a weekend, then left for a lifetime. Jean lugged her three-year-old weight around, fat diaper perched on a hip, Autumn sagging back like a Siamese twin joined at the waist. "Autumn Ann's like an extra pair of hands, aren't you, honey?" she said, and the little girl reached out for the bananas that were collecting flies in the fruit bowl. That year they'd taken in a little boy named Traveling Apple, born and raised in a veggie commune; he'd turned orange from being fed too many carrots. "Look at this sweet Seville," Jean said, kissing his apricot face.

"He's got a suntan all right," Lamont said and cradled the baby on his chest, the man's neck showing red in a V, the rest of his torso wiry with each muscle as defined as a drawing under his skivvy shirt. "Sleep, little fellow, sleep," he crooned in that deep voice that hummed the air.

One night they danced out on the cracked concrete patio of the courts. Jean tucked her hands into Lamont's back pocket and he wrapped both arms around her shoulders and all the children came running up to hang from their waists and trouble them; they looked like a whirligig that spins, ribbons floating in a circle. Wedged between was Autumn Ann, fat face pressed against their thighs, baby foot on each of their insteps, making them stiff-legged as they box-stepped to "In the Still of the Night." "Sho do, sha debe do," Lamont sang, and Lou, holding her littlest on her lap, legs dangling into the pool, felt the baby's feet kick splashes on her shins. She felt like crying as she watched them dance to Lamont's music. All the kids were giggling. Lou's and Marlon's trying to get in. They insinuated their arms into the circling couple, dragging their feet, acting like flour sacks instead of kids. Lamont and Jean pretended not to notice, kept their eyes closed and looked extra gooey as they staggered this hoopskirt of children around. Marlon sat down beside Lou, put his arm around her, and rubbed the baby's foot. "Why is it," he said, "life makes people so good and treats them so bad?" Lou buried her head in his neck, smelling chlorine on him, loving him as she felt the baby squirm and wiggle to get free.

So on this trip, like all the others since they began their quest, Lou and Marlon followed the fairs and flea markets and asked in each town where it was that people might raise goats or lots of kids, and always got a laugh. They'd gone to each town in a Louisiana parish Lamont once mentioned he lived in, asking if anyone knew them, knew a fine mechanic, a wood-carver named Dillon, and got no answer but no.

On the third week out they decided to lift their spirits by looking for barbecue. Here on the edge of a Louisiana town they saw a place that was exactly what you looked for when you were hungry for good barbecue: a wood shack, discolored by smoke and redolence rising out of the wood, the sky perfumed with the odor of wood chips and vinegar and crisp roasting, and in the yard off to the side, a lean-to with tables and little children climbing on them.

"Let's stop here," Marlon said, pulling in. When they got out, Lou looked down the slight hill and saw a small frame house with a square dirt yard. A woman about her age in a faded blue housedress and slippers down at the back, a coffee-colored woman with fried hair tucked under at the ends, was sweeping down the yard. On the porch sat a tin watering can and at the side a rake.

"I want a chipped pork," Lou said. Then, "I'm going down there." As she half slid down the slope she could see the other woman looking at her. "I'm Lou Maxey, and excuse me, do. It's only I saw this dirt yard and I simply could not go past it, don't you know?" Lou was talking fast to cover up her nervousness and embarrassment, but she knew she couldn't go back. The woman was husky but her face was kind, with a long, full mouth. "I haven't seen a dirt yard in I don't know how long."

"I'm Lacey," the woman said, nodding toward Lou. Her voice was warm.

"Would you? I mean, this is probably going to sound crazy to you—but would you let me rake a little bit with you? I had a friend once. . . ." She found herself unable to stop. "Jean Dillon—her Granny in Greensboro, North Carolina, had to have a dirt yard or go crazy."

The woman listened. A smile crimpled her cheeks; she held out the broom, walked back to get the rake.

"It's the oddest thing. Here we are—we're looking for them— the Dillons, trying to figure out where in the world they went to. And I saw this yard. How do folks lose track of things?" Lou's scratching the earth now; it is mostly weeded out and very dry. Lacey sprinkles it to keep dust down and even, to try and set the pattern.

"Are you putting the arches here?" Lou asks, then feels compelled to explain, "One time—one time we lived together when we were young in this old crummy motel with kitchenettes and cabins," the woman nods, "with all our kids. You notice now how no one has lots of kids anymore? I had four and that was nothing to my grandma. My fifth was too far apart—like an only baby."

"I had six," says Lacey. "Six and one boy killed in the war, four girls."

"Any of them around here?"

"My youngest girl—up there. She runs the barbecue. A good girl. A fine husband. Three grandkids."

"That's nice," Lou says. "So nice to have the kids near. This time I'm telling you about—the time we made us a dirt yard. We made it from scratch. That sounds funny, doesn't it?"

"It does. It does. Usually you just clears them away."

The two women are moving shoulder to shoulder now, walking backward. Lou sweeps the dirt clear and then Lacey pulls in the design, slightly wavy lines that curve around the cement stepping-stones.

One late August day Lou and Jean sat in plastic strap chairs, fannies hitting the ground, watching the kids run dirty circles around the motel compound. Clark's Courts was marked by a line of soot-covered plaster ducks advancing on a three-legged concrete deer; his left antler was a single metal spike. Rocks, painted alternately blue and white, rimmed the swimming pool, which was choked with leaves and olive algae etched on its sides and circular stairs.

"What you need, Lou, to calm your nerves," Jean said, "is a dirt yard." Lou had had a crying jag that morning as a result of the heat and the baby pressing on her spine and peepee sheets and a three-year-old who bit. "My granny in Greensboro once told me she'd have gone crazy if she hadn't had her dirt yard to rake. Kids love them too." Then she yelled, "Hey kids!" They stopped their wild running to stand sweating as dirt puffed over their feet, then turned to face Jean in a band—Lou's in sunsuits and clean pinafores and roman sandals, Jean's in torn shorts and aprons tied like capes. One wore a nylon bridesmaid's hat.

"I've got a game!" Jean called. They leaped into the air, all in a bunch, mud daubers rising to cluster near the two women. Lou's timid son, tagging at the rear of the group, rested his hand on her bare shoulder. Ceil and Maisie pushed up to the front, Ceil's eyeglass frames balanced on the end of her nose, Maisie's braids fuzzy and coming undone. Autumn Ann clambered up into Jean's lap.

"Get down. It's too hot. And listen to this." Autumn Ann curled closer. Jean huddled them and Lou saw how Gordon and Jasper bent over just like Lamont, as though they had no bones but were willows being arched. "We're going to make us a dirt yard—no more mowing the lawn for us." And all those little children, some not over two years old, never having heard the words "dirt yard" before, knew exactly what she meant. You could see it in their shiny eyes as they looked around the compound to size up the destruction that could be wrought. Autumn Ann picked up a handful of pebbles and licked them. Lou was getting tickled and the baby inside her kicked out—hard. "Ouch!"

"What, Mamma? Mamma, what?" all of hers shrilled, even as their hands ached to pull up clumps of grass.

"Nothing," Lou laughed. "I guess we better start pulling."

"From here . . ." Jean stood up, unfolding her long arm like a measuring rod. "From here to that deer's broke foot, I want down to the dirt by suppertime. Now run get some things to dig with," she said.

"Can we use combs?" Gordon asked.

"Why not?" she shrugged. "Combs, spoons, sticks, anything that'll dig'll do. We need to lay this lawn bare, get it back down to the basics. Now go on and get."

Now, on this day twenty-two years later, as Lou sweats next to Lacey, using a borrowed broom, waiting for her turn at the rake, she tries to tell the story and why, whenever she is feeling low, she'll bring up that afternoon.

"There we were," she says, gesturing with the broom, bringing it down to make half-circles in the dust. "Jean in Lamont's skivvy shirt knotted at the shoulders, cut-offs, and her stringy hair plastered to her head—it must have been 95 degrees—and me, p.g. with a summer top and shorts with that hole cut in the middle for space, feeling air cool against my belly and the sweat running right across my navel, both of us hunkering in the grass, pulling weeds and clover and everything that grew. All those kids—Jean's five, my four, who knows how many others and where they came from, and everybody with a spoon, a stick, a pointed thing. Autumn Ann used the prong of her barrette to scratch the dirt back."

And every one of them, she can't explain, with a purpose, as they unearthed old bottle caps, rusty nails, cigarette butts, a pile of treasure put to one side for when the digging was done. Lou can still see clearly her son squatting, both hands dug deep into the grass, tugging at a clump, straining back on his heels to lift it by its tufted roots, pulling hard to break the sod away; can see him fall back, clod against stomach to cry out triumph just as a grasshopper leaped free, the movement of its wings no more than the shimmer of heat.

"We did it too," she says to Lacey. "We did. By six o'clock that evening, before Marlon and Lamont got home, we had a perfect circle of dirt, so sweet smelling. Too thick to really rake, but the children went and stuck the edges with forks as if it was a big patty pie."

"Lord, Lord." Lacey shakes her head and smiles. She's stopped raking in order to hear this story and she leans on the end of her rake, using it like a cane. How can Lou tell her of the great grass hummock to the side of the yard that got thrown and sat and climbed upon? Jasper mounted to the top of it, put a dirt clod on his head, shouted, "Lookee here! See my false hair?" then blew back dribbles of dirt that peppered his cheeks. All felt the taste of mud melting in their mouths, gritting their teeth, and the thickness of soil caking under their fingernails. As the day deepened into night the sky paled and shadowed the trees while the streetlights outside the Courts sneaked light over the wall. Then the children lay down in that cool damp dirt to push roly-poly bugs around and swim their arms and legs in those dark elements.

"Later," Lou says, "I later lost the baby I carried then, but I've never lost a second of that day." She can still feel life turning inside her as she dug her fingers knuckle-deep into the earth.

Lacey reaches out her hand and lays it on Lou's arm, and as Lou slows her sweeping, her tears spatter the dirt. "Thank you," she says. "Thank you for letting me help you with this yard." Then Lou is confused. She is standing on the edge of the intricate design and she doesn't want to spoil it. Lacey takes her arm and leads her up to the porch and over to the side. "Right here," she motions. There are three steps down to the grass. Lou sees the clothes flapping on the line and up on the hill sees Marlon leaning against a car talking to a man who must be Lacey's son-in-law. Children and a dog circle the car in a running game. Lou realizes she is still holding the broom in her hand and turns back. "Here."

"Wait," the woman says, going quickly through her belled-out screen door; it slams behind. Lou stares at the smooth dirt yard, so different from the one she remembers—this one dry and designed but still powerful enough to move her. The screen door opens again; Lacey is at the steps. "Here." She holds out a navel orange—deep russet and glowing. Lou can already taste the sweet tang of its flesh. They smile at each other, each old enough to remember when an orange was a gift you hoped for, hoped to get tucked into the toe of a stocking, or icy cold from lying on a block of ice when you were sick, sweet pulp sipped over ice chips. The color of carrots, or persimmons, of the baby Lamont cradled on his chest.

"Here's for your traveling," Lacey says and puts the orange into Lou's hand.

"Thank you. Thank you again." Lou, holding the orange tight to her chest, climbs the hill.

Sometimes on these trips, when she's tired, Lou despairs and wonders aloud to Marlon if they will ever find the Dillons. If maybe they should quit, break down and take out ads before it's too late. Maybe Jean and Lamont are dead. He always pats her on the hip, leans close to kiss between the point where her shoulder meets her neck, and says, "You know we'll find them. Now, don't give up. But we'll take out an ad if you want to. Hell, let's buy a banner. Buy a blimp. I can afford it."

She is cheered holding him and being held by him, her face mashed sideways against his shirt buttons, an errant wire of hair pushing from his neck-V. She feels his heart thrumming through her hands as she fits her palm around his shoulder blades. "I love you, honey," she mouths against his buttons. He murmurs back, rocking her in a silent dance.

Two days later Lou can still feel the broom in her hands, the scritch of the dirt, the powder of it as it moved away in patterns, and how it puffed up when Lacey sprinkled it. She fancies that if she holds her right hand cupped over her nose she can still smell the yard, smell again the end of the broomstick stuck into stiff straw, the wood split with paint flecks filling the creases in her hands. She's happy to recall that Lacey leaned on her rake, tucking the end under her breast to stand like a tripod and listen, shake her head, and smile at Lou's telling. The orange she gave her is in the cooler case at this very minute.

When she'd joined Marlon at the hill, looking back to wave, grinning until she thought her face would split, Lou felt mixed up. Once in the van, she turned to Marlon. He was looking straight ahead, left leg bent at the knee and propped up on the seat in a way that was dangerous and drove her crazy. She didn't even know how to begin to tell him what she'd done, and said, or why. She wanted him to already know it.

"That reminded me of Mamma," he said, shifting his position, making the van speed up, slow down.

I could kill you, she thought. She was nothing like that. Marlon's mother was not a thing like that. Never was.

"Reminded me too of the time ya'll dug that whole yard up," he added. Then, alarmed, "Lou, what's the matter? Lou? Why are you bawling?"

She could only shake her head. Then she lowered her face into her hands and cried while Marlon kept changing the stations, swiveling the dial to find some music to comfort her.

That night in bed at the Promo Motel, where everything was harvest gold or green shag and scarred with cigarettes, she tried to tell him what had happened to her in Lacey's yard. He held her, patting, saying, "Hmmm," or "Yeah," or "Oh, honey," gentle interruptions. "It'll be all right, sweetheart." Then he stroked her thigh in a way she always remembered. She moved to him, marveling at the wonder of knowing Marlon all these years, and so long ago, that other Marlon who'd first pulled her away from her safe home and life. She almost thought she could feel that young Marlon, so skinny, so eager, so crazy to get up and go, as he moved in her now.

A few mornings later they are driving along when Lou is alerted by the blue van ahead of them. "Catch up with them," she says. "Hurry, Marlon. That's exactly like the kind of thing they'd drive. Look at all the stickers on it."

The van is plastered with *Knotts Berry Farm* and *Save the Whales* and *Luray Caverns* and *Disneyworld* and the whole back window is covered twice, once with drawn-down green shades that filter light, then with stickers of mountain ranges and other natural wonders in this hemisphere. *Wash me! Quick!* is fingered out in the bumper dust.

Marlon, revved up by Lou's excitement, guns the motor, catches up to cruise side by side with the van. It is muraled on the side with great tongues of flame pointing to the headlights, a map of the United States with stars in every state and a tribute to the Baltimore Orioles. All the side windows are shaded in green too, and the rushing sunlight makes it seem to be traveling underwater.

"That mother's going fast," Marlon says, lowering and twisting his head to see the van off which Lou is reading signs.

"*White Sands Proving Grounds*? They never would go there, would they?"

"Hell, I don't know," Marlon says. "People change."

Lou looks at him. "This seems too new a van for them."

"Look at us, damnit," he says. "We've got a Saab at home. You think Lamont and Jean ever expected to see us in anything but an old Pontiac?" He speeds up even with the driver as Lou pokes her head up and out. The front window of the van is copper glazed with a reflective sheen.

"Speed up some more, Marlon, so I can get the angle." Then she sees, as though through fire, a young man, bearded and bespectacled, singing at the top of his lungs. Marlon pulls ahead, blinkers right, and pulls in front.

"Not them?"

"No." Lou falls back in the seat and adjusts her seat belt. "But it looks like the kind of van they'd be driving." Marlon is looking out the rearview mirror at the van: its great coppery windshield glints, shooting silvery lights off its convexity.

"That guy was singing with his head thrown back—singing at the top of his lungs—just like you do," Lou says, and she puts her hand on Marlon's knee.

He breaks into a tuneless but buoyant "Home, home on the range" as Lou says, "I'm gonna wave anyway. I bet there's little kids in there." She scrambles up and over to the back, undoing her seat belt and standing bent-kneed in the back seat, leans until her upper body is wedged into the back window. She begins to wag her head and wave back and forth, looking like one of those bobbing backview beagles that are so popular. In the rushing of the light made by the two vehicles, Lou's face looks back at her from the other van's copper windshield. In this strange trick of light for a moment it seems that she is sitting beside the young singing driver. She sees herself bronze, smiling, waving back at herself.

"Hold on, honey, I'm pulling out," Marlon says as he steps on the gas and moves them away.

Nikki Giovanni 1943–

Nikki Giovanni was born in Knoxville, Tennessee, and raised in Cincinnati, Ohio. While attending Fisk University, she edited the campus literary magazine, established a campus civil rights organization and, in 1967, graduated magna cum laude with a degree in history. During the Black Arts movement, Nikki Giovanni catapulted to fame with three volumes of poetry ardently read by black audiences: *Black Feeling* (1967), *Black Judgment* (1968), and *Re: Creation* (1970). Receiving honorary degrees and trumpeting her agenda on talk shows, Giovanni became a household name with her militant advocacy of a black revolution to destroy white America for its perpetuation of oppression. By the early 1970s, the market for her message exhausted, Giovanni turned to more personal and introspective poetry with *My House* (1972), a collection of love poems. In some ways her mellowing was due to the 1969 birth of her son, Thomas, which appeared to change her priorities about life: "I just cannot imagine living without [Tommy]. But I can live without the revolution," she told *Harper's Bazaar*. Giovanni has subsequently authored over twenty-five publications, including numerous books of children's verse and acclaimed critical essays with James Baldwin and Margaret Walker. She currently teaches English at Virginia Polytechnic.

NIKKI-ROSA

Nikki Giovanni
childhood remembrances are always a drag
if you're Black
you always remember things like living in Woodlawn
with no inside toilet   5
and if you become famous or something
they never talk about how happy you were to have your mother
all to yourself and
how good the water felt when you got your bath from one of those
big tubs that folk in chicago barbecue in   10
and somehow when you talk about home
it never gets across how much you
understood their feelings
as the whole family attended meetings about Hollydale
and even though you remember   15
your biographers never understand
your father's pain as he sells his stock
and another dream goes
and though you're poor it isn't poverty that
concerns you   20
and though they fought a lot
it isn't your father's drinking that makes any difference
but only that everybody is together and you
and your sister have happy birthdays and very good christ-
masses and I really hope no white person ever has cause to   25
write about me because they never understand Black life
is Black wealth and they'll probably talk about my hard
childhood and never understand that all the while I was
quite happy

WOMAN

she wanted to be a blade
of grass amid the fields
but he wouldn't agree
to be the dandelion

she wanted to be a robin singing   5
through the leaves

but he refused to be
her tree

she spun herself into a web
　　　and looking for a place to rest   10
turned to him
but he stood straight
declining to be her corner

she tried to be a book
but he wouldn't read   15
she turned herself into a bulb
but he wouldn't let her grow

she decided to become
a woman
and though he still refused   20
to be a man
she decided it was all
right

FOR SAUNDRA

i wanted to write
a poem
that rhymes
but revolution doesn't lend
itself to be-bopping   5

then my neighbor
who thinks i hate
asked — do you ever write
tree poems — i like trees
so i thought   10
i'll write a beautiful green tree poem
peeked from my window
to check the image
noticed the school yard was covered
with asphalt   15
no green — no trees grow
in manhattan

then, well, i thought the sky
i'll do a big blue sky poem

but all the clouds have winged   20
low since no-Dick[1] was elected

so i thought again
and it occurred to me
maybe i shouldn't write
at all   25
but clean my gun
and check my kerosene supply
perhaps these are not poetic
times
at all   30

Louise Glück 1943–

Internationally renowned for her precision, economy, and straightforward elegance, Louise Glück is a poet with an uncanny ability to engage the reader. With diction compelling and easy to relate to, she chooses universal themes such as family, relationships, love, death, disappointment, and isolation. States Anna Wooten in the *American Poetry Review*, "Glück's ear never fails her; she manages to be conversational and lyrical at the same time, a considerable achievement when so much contemporary poetry is lamentably prosaic." Born in New York City, Glück attended Sarah Lawrence College and Columbia University. Her collections of poetry include *Ararat* (1990), *The Wild Iris* (1992), which won the Pulitzer Prize, *The First Four Books* (1995), and *Meadowlands* (1996). In 1994, she produced *Proofs and Theories: Essays on Poetry*, a volume of criticism. A recipient of Rockefeller and Guggenheim fellowships and the National Book Critics Circle Award for Poetry, Glück is currently a professor at Williams College.

ILLUMINATIONS[2]

1

My son squats in the snow in his blue snowsuit.
All around him stubble, the brown
degraded bushes. In the morning air

[1] I.e., Richard M. Nixon (1913–1994), thirty-seventh president of the United States.
[2] The title of a sequence of visionary prose poems by the French Symbolist poet Arthur Rimbaud (1854–1891).

they seem to stiffen into words.
And, between, the white steady silence.   5
A wren hops on the airstrip
under the sill, drills
for sustenance, then spreads
its short wings, shadows
dropping from them.   10

2

Last winter he could barely speak.
I moved his crib to face the window:
in the dark mornings
he would stand and grip the bars
until the walls appeared,   15
calling *light*, *light*,
that one syllable, in
demand or recognition.

3

He sits at the kitchen window
with his cup of apple juice.   20
Each tree forms where he left it,
leafless, trapped in his breath.
How clear their edges are
no limb obscured by motion,
as the sun rises   25
cold and single over the map of language.

Nancy Mairs 1943–

A self-described "radical feminist, pacifist, and cripple," Nancy Mairs is the author of six collections of personal essays that candidly and provocatively scrutinize her life. "I am most interested in theoretical bases of issues of social justice, and in particular in the power of language to privilege certain kinds of human perception and experience and to efface other kinds," Mairs told *Contemporary Authors*. "In my writing I aim to speak the 'unspeakable,' in defiance of polite discourse, so as to expose ways in which my personal experiences inscribe cultural values dangerous to women and others creatures worth preserving." Raised in New Hampshire and Massachusetts, Mairs worked as a technical editor at the Smithsonian Astrophysical Observatory, the MIT Press, and the Harvard Law School. In 1972, Mairs moved with her husband and two children to Tuscon, Arizona, where she pursued an M.F.A. in creative writing and a Ph.D. in English literature. During this time, she was diagnosed with multiple sclerosis. Mairs's first book, *In All the Rooms of the Yellow House* (1984), garnered first prize in the Western States Art Foundation book awards competition. Mairs's essay collections include *Plaintext: Deciphering a Woman's Life* (1986); *Remembering the Bone House: An Erotics of Place and Space* (1989); *Carnal Acts* (1990); *Ordinary Time: Cycles in Marriage, Faith and Renewal* (1993); *Voice Lessons: On Becoming a (Woman Writer)* (1994); and *Waist-High in the World: A Life Among the Nondisabled* (1997).

CARNAL ACTS

Inviting me to speak at her small liberal-arts college during Women's Week, a young woman set me a task: "We would be pleased," she wrote, "if you could talk on how you cope with your MS disability, and also how you discovered your voice as a writer." Oh, Lord, I thought in dismay, how am I going to pull this one off? How can I yoke two such disparate subjects into a coherent presentation, without doing violence to one, or the other, or both, or myself? This is going to take some fancy footwork, and my feet scarcely carry out the basic steps, let alone anything elaborate.

To make matters worse, the assumption underlying each of her questions struck me as suspect. To ask *how* I cope with multiple sclerosis suggests that I *do* cope. Now, "to cope," *Webster's Third* tells me, is "to face or encounter and to find necessary expedients to overcome problems and difficulties." In these terms, I have to confess, I don't feel like much of a coper. I'm likely to deal with my problems and difficulties by squawking and flapping around like that hysterical chicken who was convinced the sky was falling. Never mind that in my case the sky really *is* falling. In response to a clonk on the head, regardless of its origin, one might comport oneself with a grace and courtesy I generally lack.

As for "finding" my voice, the implication is that it was at one time lost or missing. But I don't think it ever was. Ask my mother, who will tell you a little wearily that I was speaking full sentences by the time I was a year old and could never be silenced again. As for its being a writer's voice, it seems to have become one early on. Ask Mother again. At the age of eight I rewrote the Trojan War, she will say, and what Nestor was about to do to Helen at the end doesn't bear discussion in polite company.

Faced with these uncertainties, I took my own teacherly advice, something, I must confess, I don't always do. "If an idea is giving you trouble," I tell my writing students, "put it on the back burner and let it simmer while you do something else. Go to the movies. Reread a stack of old love letters. Sit in your history class and take detailed notes on the Teapot Dome scandal. If you've got your idea in mind, it will go on cooking at some level no matter what else you're doing." "I've had an idea for my documented essay on the back burner," one of my students once scribbled in her journal, "and I think it's just boiled over!"

I can't claim to have reached such a flash point. But in the weeks I've had the themes "disability" and "voice" sitting around in my head, they seem to have converged on their own, without my having to wrench them together and bind them with hoops of tough rhetoric. They *are* related, indeed interdependent, with an intimacy that has for some reason remained, until now, submerged below the surface of my attention. Forced to juxtapose them, I yank them out of the depths, a little startled to discover how they were intertwined down there out of sight. This kind of discovery can unnerve you at first. You feel like a giant hand that, pulling two swimmers out of the water, two separate heads bobbling on the iridescent swells, finds the two bodies below, legs coiled around each other, in an ecstasy of copulation. You don't quite know where to turn your eyes.

Perhaps the place to start illuminating this erotic connection between who I am and how I speak lies in history. I have known that I have multiple sclerosis for about seventeen years now, though the disease probably started long before. The hypothesis is that the disease process, in which the protective covering of the nerves in the brain and spinal cord is eaten away and replaced by scar tissue, "hard patches," is caused by an autoimmune reaction to a slow-acting virus. Research suggests that I was infected by this virus, which no one has ever seen and which therefore, technically, doesn't even "exist," between the ages of four and fifteen. In effect, living with this mysterious mechanism feels like having your present self, and the past selves it embodies, haunted by a capricious and meanspirited ghost, unseen except for its footprints, which trips you even when you're watching where you're going, knocks glassware out of your hand, squeezes the urine out of your bladder before you reach the bathroom, and weights your whole body with a weariness no amount of rest can relieve. An alien invader must be at work. But of course it's not. It's your own body. That is, it's you.

This, for me, has been the most difficult aspect of adjusting to a chronic incurable degenerative disease: the fact that it has rammed my "self" straight back into the body I had been trained to believe it could, through high-minded acts and aspirations, rise above. The Western tradition of distinguishing the body from the mind and/or the soul is so ancient as to have become part of our collective unconscious, if one is inclined to believe in such a noumenon, or at least to have become an unquestioned element in the social instruction we impose upon infants from birth, in much the same way we inculcate, without reflection, the gender distinctions "female" and "male." I *have* a body, you are likely to say if you talk about embodiment at all; you don't say, I *am* a body. A body is a separate entity possessable by the "I"; the "I" and the body aren't, as the copula would make them, grammatically indistinguishable.

To widen the rift between the self and the body, we treat our bodies as subordinates, inferior in moral status. Open association with them shames us. In fact, we treat our bodies with very much the same distance and ambivalence women have traditionally received from men in our culture. Sometimes this treatment is benevolent, even respectful, but all too often it is tainted by outright sadism. I think of the bodybuilding regimens that have become popular in the last decade or so, with the complicated vacillations they reflect between self-worship and self-degradation: joggers and aerobic dancers and weightlifters all beating their bodies into shape. "No pain, no gain," the saying goes. "Feel the burn." Bodies get treated like wayward women who have to be shown who's boss, even if it means slapping them around a little. I'm not for a moment opposing rugged exercise here. I'm simply questioning the spirit in which it is often undertaken.

Since as Hélène Cixous points out in her essay on women and writing, "Sorties,"[1] thought has always worked "through dual, hierarchical oppositions" (p. 64), the mind/body split cannot possibly be innocent. The utterance of an "I" immediately calls into being its opposite, the "not-I," Western discourse being unequipped to conceive "that which is neither 'I' nor 'not-I,'" "that which is both 'I' and 'not-I,'" or some other permutation which language doesn't permit me to speak. The "not-I" is, by definition, other. And we've never been too fond of the other. We prefer the same. We tend to ascribe to the other those qualities we prefer not to associate with our selves: It is the hidden, the dark, the secret, the shameful. Thus, when the "I" takes possession of the body, it makes the body into an other, direct object of a transitive verb, with all the other's repudiated and potentially dangerous qualities.

At the least, then, the body had best be viewed with suspicion. And a woman's body is particularly suspect, since so much of it is in fact hidden, dark, secret, carried about on the inside where, even with the aid of a speculum, one can never perceive all of it in the plain light of day, a graspable whole. I, for one, have never understood why anyone would want to carry all that delicate stuff around on the outside. It would make you awfully anxious, I should think, put you constantly on the defensive, create a kind of siege mentality that viewed all other beings, even your own kind, as threats to be warded off with spears and guns and atomic missiles. And you'd never get to experience that inward dreaming that comes when your flesh surrounds all your treasures, holding them close, like a sturdy shuttered house. Be my personal skepticism as it may, however, as a cultural woman I bear just as much shame as any woman for my dark, enfolded secrets. Let the word for my external genitals tell the tale: my pudendum, from the Latin infinitive meaning "to be ashamed."

It's bad enough to carry your genitals like a sealed envelope bearing the cipher that, once unlocked, might loose the chaotic flood of female pleasure—*jouissance*, the French call it—upon the world-of-the-same. But I have an addi-

---

[1] In *The Newly Born Woman*, translated by Betsy Wing (Minneapolis: University of Minnesota Press, 1986). [Mairs's note.]

tional reason to feel shame for my body, less explicitly connected with its sexuality: It is a crippled body. Thus it is doubly other, not merely by the homo-sexual standards of patriarchal culture but by the standards of physical desirability erected for every body in our world. Men, who are by definition exonerated from shame in sexual terms (this doesn't mean that an individual man might not experience sexual shame, of course; remember that I'm talking in general about discourse, not folks), may—more likely must—experience bodily shame if they are crippled. I won't presume to speak about the details of their experience, however. I don't know enough. I'll just go on telling what it's like to be a crippled woman, trusting that, since we're fellow creatures who've been living together for some thousands of years now, much of my experience will resonate with theirs.

I was never a beautiful woman, and for that reason I've spent most of my life (together with probably at least 95 percent of the female population of the United States) suffering from the shame of falling short of an unattainable standard. The ideal woman of my generation was . . . perky, I think you'd say, rather than gorgeous. Blond hair pulled into a bouncing ponytail. Wide blue eyes, a turned-up nose with maybe a scattering of golden freckles across it, a small mouth with full lips over straight white teeth. Her breasts were large but well harnessed high on her chest; her tiny waist flared to hips just wide enough to give the crinolines under her circle skirt a starting outward push. In terms of personality, she was outgoing, even bubbly, not pensive or mysterious. Her milieu was the front fender of a white Corvette convertible, surrounded by teasing crewcuts, dressed in black flats, a sissy blouse, and the letter sweater of the Corvette owner. Needless to say, she never missed a prom.

Ten years or so later, when I first noticed the symptoms that would be diagnosed as MS, I was probably looking my best. Not beautiful still, but the ideal had shifted enough so that my flat chest and narrow hips gave me an elegantly attenuated shape, set off by a thick mass of long, straight, shining hair. I had terrific legs, long and shapely, revealed nearly to the pudendum by the fashionable miniskirts and hot pants I adopted with more enthusiasm than delicacy of taste. Not surprisingly, I suppose, during this time I involved myself in several pretty torrid love affairs.

The beginning of MS wasn't too bad. The first symptom, besides the pernicious fatigue that had begun to devour me, was "foot drop," the inability to raise my left foot at the ankle. As a consequence, I'd started to limp, but I could still wear high heels, and a bit of a limp might seem more intriguing than repulsive. After a few months, when the doctor suggested a cane, a crippled friend gave me quite an elegant wood-and-silver one, which I carried with a fair amount of panache. The real blow to my self-image came when I had to get a brace. As braces go, it's not bad: lightweight plastic molded to my foot and leg, fitting down into an ordinary shoe and secured around my calf by a Velcro strap. It reduces my limp and, more important the danger of tripping and falling. But it meant the end of high heels. And it's ugly. Not as ugly as I think it is, I gather, but still pretty ugly. It signified for me, and perhaps still does, the permanence and irreversibility of my condition. The brace makes my MS concrete and forces me to wear it on the outside. As soon as I strapped the brace on, I climbed into trousers and stayed there (though not in the same trousers, of course). The idea of going around with my bare brace hanging out seemed almost as indecent as exposing my breasts. Not until 1984, soon after I won the Western States Book Award for poetry, did I put on a skirt short enough to reveal my plasticized leg. The connection between winning a writing award and baring my brace is not merely fortuitous; being affirmed as a writer really did embolden me. Since then, I've grown so accustomed to wearing skirts that I don't think about my brace any more than I think about my cane. I've incorporated them, I suppose: made them, in their necessity, insensate but fundamental parts of my body.

Meanwhile, I had to adjust to the most outward and visible sign of all, a three-wheeled electric scooter called an Amigo. This lessens my fatigue and increases my range terrifically, but it also shouts out to the world, "Here is a woman who can't stand on her own two feet." At the same time, paradoxically, it renders me invisible, reducing me to the height of a seven-year-old, with a child's attendant low status. "Would she like smoking or nonsmoking?" the gate agent assigning me a seat asks the friend traveling with me. In crowds I see nothing but buttocks. I can tell you the names of every type of designer jeans ever sold. The wearers, eyes front, trip over me and fall across my handlebars into my lap. "Hey!" I want to shout to the lofty world. "Down here! There's a person down here!" But I'm not, by their standards, quite a person anymore.

My self-esteem diminishes further as age and illness strip away from me the features that made me, for a brief while anyway, a good-looking, even sexy, young woman. No more long, bounding strides: I shuffle along with the timid gait I remember observing, with pity and impatience, in the little old ladies at Boston's Symphony Hall on Friday afternoons. No more lithe, girlish figure: My belly sags from the loss of muscle tone, which also creates all kinds of intestinal disruptions, hopelessly humiliating in a society in which excretory functions remain strictly unspeakable. No more sex, either, if society had its way. The sexuality of the disabled so repulses most people that you can hardly get a doctor, let alone a member of the general population, to consider the issues it raises. Cripples simply aren't supposed to Want It, much less Do It. Fortunately, I've got a husband with a strong libido and a weak sense of social propriety, or else I'd find myself perforce practicing a vow of chastity I never cared to take.

Afflicted by the general shame of having a body at all, and the specific shame of having one weakened and misshapen by disease, I ought not to be able to hold my head up in public. And yet I've gotten into the habit of holding my head up in public, sometimes under excruciating circumstances. Recently, for instance, I had to give a reading at the University of Arizona. Having smashed three of my front teeth in a fall onto the concrete floor of my screened porch, I was in the process of getting them crowned, and the temporary crowns flew out during dinner right before the reading. What to do? I wanted, of course, to rush home and hide till the dental office opened the next morning. But I couldn't very well break my word at this last moment. So, looking like Hansel and Gretel's witch, and lisping worse than the Wife of Bath, I got up on stage and read. Somehow, over the years, I've learned how to set shame aside and do what I have to do.

Here, I think, is where my "voice" comes in. Because, in spite of my demurral at the beginning, I do in fact cope with my disability at least some of the time. And I do so, I think, by speaking about it, and about the whole experience of being a body, specifically a female body, out loud, in a clear, level tone that drowns out the frantic whispers of my mother, my grandmothers, all the other trainers of wayward childish tongues: "Sssh! Sssh! Nice girls don't talk like that. Don't mention sweat. Don't mention menstrual blood. Don't ask what your grandfather does on his business trips. Don't laugh so loud. You sound like a loon. Keep your voice down. Don't tell. Don't tell. Don't tell." Speaking out loud is an antidote to shame. I want to distinguish clearly here between "shame," as I'm using the word, and "guilt" and "embarrassment," which, though equally painful, are not similarly poisonous. Guilt arises from performing a forbidden act or failing to perform a required one. In either case, the guilty person can, through reparation, erase the offense and start fresh. Embarrassment, less opprobrious though not necessarily less distressing, is generally caused by acting in a socially stupid or awkward way. When I trip and sprawl in public, when I wet myself, when my front teeth fly out, I feel horribly embarrassed, but, like the pain of childbirth, the sensation blurs and dissolves in time. If it didn't, every child would be an only child, and no one would set foot in public after the onset of puberty, when embarrassment erupts like a geyser and bathes one's whole life in its bitter stream. Shame may attach itself to guilt or embarrassment, complicating their resolution, but it is not the same emotion. I feel guilt or embarrassment for something I've done; shame, for who I am. I may stop doing bad or stupid things, but I can't stop being. How then can I help but be ashamed? Of the three conditions, this is the one that cracks and stifles my voice.

I can subvert its power, I've found, by acknowledging who I am, shame and all, and, in doing so, raising what was hidden, dark, secret about my life into the plain light of shared human experience. What we aren't permitted to utter holds us, each isolated from every other, in a kind of solipsistic thrall. Without any way to check our reality against anyone else's, we assume that our fears and shortcomings are ours alone. One of the strangest consequences of publishing a collection of personal essays called *Plaintext* has been the steady trickle of letters and telephone calls saying essentially, in a tone of unmistakable relief, "Oh, me too! Me too!" It's as though the part I thought was solo has turned out to be a chorus. But none of us was singing loud enough for the others to hear.

Singing loud enough demands a particular kind of voice, I think. And I was wrong to suggest, at the beginning, that I've always had my voice. I have indeed always had *a* voice, but it wasn't *this* voice, the one with which I could call up and transform my hidden self from a naughty girl into a woman talking directly to others like herself. Recently, in the process of writting a new book, a memoir entitled *Remembering the Bone House*, I've had occasion to read some of my early writing, from college, high school, even junior high. It's not an experience I recommend to anyone susceptible to shame. Not that the writing was all that bad. I was surprised at how competent a lot of it was. Here was a writer who already knew precisely how the language worked. But the voice . . . oh, the voice was all wrong: maudlin, rhapsodic, breaking here and there into little shrieks, almost, you might say, hysterical. It was a voice that had shucked off its own body, its own homely life of Cheerios for breakfast and seventy pages of Chaucer to read before the exam on Tuesday and a planter's wart growing painfully on the ball of its foot, and reeled now wraithlike through the air, seeking incarnation only as the heroine who enacts her doomed love for the tall, dark, mysterious stranger. If it didn't get that part, it wouldn't play at all.

Among all these overheated and vaporous imaginings, I must have retained some shred of sense, because I stopped writing prose entirely, except for scholarly papers, for nearly twenty years. I even forgot, not exactly that I had written prose, but at least what kind of prose it was. So when I needed to take up the process again, I could start almost fresh, using the vocal range I'd gotten used to in years of asking the waiter in the Greek restaurant for an extra anchovy on my salad, congratulating the puppy on making a puddle outside rather than inside the patio door, pondering with my daughter the vagaries of female orgasm, saying good-bye to my husband, and hello, and good-bye, and hello. This new voice—thoughtful, affectionate, often amused—was essential because what I needed to write about when I returned to prose was an attempt I'd made not long before to kill myself, and suicide simply refuses to be spoken of authentically in high-flown romantic language. It's too ugly. Too shameful. Too strictly a bodily event. And, yes, too funny as well, though people are sometimes shocked to find humor shoved up against suicide. They don't like the incongruity. But let's face it, life (real life, I mean, not the edited-for-television version) is a cacophonous affair from start to finish. I might have wanted to portray my suicidal self as a languishing maiden, too exquisitely sensitive to sustain life's wounding pressures on her soul. (I didn't want to, as a matter of fact, but I might have.) The truth remained, regardless of my desires, that when my husband lugged me into the emergency room, my hair matted, my face swollen and gray, my nightgown streaked with blood and urine, I was no frail and tender spirit. I was a body, and one in a hell of a mess.

I "should" have kept quiet about that experience. I know the rules of polite discourse. I should have kept my shame, and the nearly lethal sense of isolation and alienation it brought, to myself. And I might have, except for something the psychiatrist in the emergency room had told my husband. "You might as well take her home," he said. "If she wants to kill herself, she'll do it no matter how many precautions we take. They always do." *They* always do. I was one of "them," whoever they were. I was, in this context anyway, not singular, not aberrant, but typical. I think it was this sense of commonality with others I didn't even know, a sense of being returned somehow, in spite of my appalling act, to the human family, that urged me to write that first essay, not merely speaking out but calling out, perhaps. "Here's the way I am," it said. "How about you?" And the answer came, as I've said: "Me too! Me too!"

This has been the kind of work I've continued to do: to scrutinize the details of my own experience and to report what I see, and what I think about what I see, as lucidly and accurately as possible. But because feminine experience has been immemorially devalued and repressed, I continue to find this task terrifying. "Every woman has known the torture of beginning to speak aloud," Cixous writes, "heart beating as if to break, occasionally falling into loss of language, ground and language slipping out from under her, because for woman speaking—even just opening her mouth—in public is something rash, a transgression" (p. 92).

The voice I summon up wants to crack, to whisper, to trail back into silence. "I'm sorry to have nothing more than this to say," it wants to apologize. "I shouldn't be taking up your time. I've never fought in a war, or even in a schoolyard free-for-all. I've never tried to see who could piss farthest up the barn wall. I've never even been to a whorehouse. All the important formative experiences have passed me by. I was raped once. I've borne two children. Milk trickling out of my breasts, blood trickling from between my legs. You don't want to hear about it. Sometimes I'm too scared to leave my house. Not scared *of* anything, just scared: mouth dry, bowels writhing. When the fear got really bad, they locked me up for six months, but that was years ago. I'm getting old now. Misshapen, too. I don't blame you if you can't get it up. No one could possibly desire a body like this. It's not your fault. It's mine. Forgive me. I didn't mean to start crying. I'm sorry . . . sorry . . . sorry. . . ."

An easy solace to the anxiety of speaking aloud: this slow subsidence beneath the waves of shame, back into what Cixous calls "this body that has been worse than confiscated, a body replaced with a disturbing stranger, sick or dead, who so often is a bad influence, the cause and place of inhibitions. By censuring the body," she goes on, "breath and speech are censored at the same time" (p. 97). But I am not going back, not going under one more time. To do so would demonstrate a failure of nerve far worse than the depredations of MS have caused. Paradoxically, losing one sort of nerve has given me another. No one is going to take my breath away. No one is going to leave me speechless. To be silent is to comply with the standard of feminine grace. But my crippled body already violates all notions of feminine grace. What more have I got to lose? I've gone beyond shame. I'm shameless, you might say. You know, as in "shameless hussy"? A woman with her bare brace and her tongue hanging out.

I've "found" my voice, then, just where it ought to have been, in the body-warmed breath escaping my lungs and throat. Forced by the exigencies of physical disease to embrace my self in the flesh, I couldn't write bodiless prose. The voice is the creature of the body that produces it. I speak as a crippled woman. At the same time, in the utterance I redeem both "cripple" and "woman" from the shameful silences by which I have often felt surrounded, contained, set apart; I give myself permission to live openly among others, to reach out for them, stroke them with fingers and sighs. No body, no voice; no voice, no body. That's what I know in my bones.

Kathryn Stripling Byer 1944–

Author of three books of poetry, *Black Shawl* (1998), *Wildwood Flower* (the 1992 Lamont Poetry Selection), and *The Girl in the Midst of the Harvest* (1986), Kathryn Stripling Byer was born a farmer's daughter in Camilla, Georgia. Byer, whose poems and essays have been widely published in anthologies and periodicals, described her poetry to *Contemporary Authors* as "rooted in the earth of two poetic landscapes, each with its own particular voice and rhythm. One is the flatlands of south Georgia, where I was born and grew up. The other is the mountains of western North Carolina and Tennessee. As far back as I can remember, I heard stories of rugged kinsmen who tilled the land and adventurous kinswomen who took to the Black Hills or the Blue Ridge to find their destiny, to strike it rich digging for the mother lode. I began to see the southern mountains as my destination, and throughout the years I have lived in them, they have provided haven and solitude in which to write about both the southernmost reaches of my memory and the windy places of a solitary woman's imagination." A recipient of a National Endowment for the Arts fellowship, Byer is currently poet-in-residence and English instructor at Western Carolina University in Cullowhee, North Carolina.

DIAMONDS

This, he said, giving the hickory leaf
to me. *Because I am poor.*
And he lifted my hand to his lips,
kissed the fingers that might have worn
gold rings if he had inherited   5

bottomland, not this
impossible rock where the eagles soared
after the long rains were over. He stood
in the wet grass, his open hands empty,
his pockets turned inside out.   10

Queen of the Meadow, he teased me
and bowed like a gentleman.
I licked the diamonds off the green
tongue of the leaf, wanting only
that he fill his hands with my hair.   15

Alice Walker 1944–

B orn the daughter of sharecroppers in Eatonton, Georgia, Alice Walker has overcome obstacles thought impossible by critics. Their assertions that a "shack with only a dozen or so books" was "an unlikely place to discover a young Keats" made Walker wonder why Keats would be "the only kind of poet one would want to grow up to be." Walker subsequently went on to take advantage of college scholarships to Spelman and Sarah Lawrence and published her first volume of verse while teaching at Jackson State University in Mississippi. Entitled *Once: Poems* (1968), the verse draws upon her travels in Africa as well as her civil rights involvement with voter registration in Georgia and the welfare rights movement in Mississippi and New York. Her works in the following prolific thirteen-year period include two novels, a collection of poetry and short stories, and *I Love Myself When I'm Laughing* (1979), her anthology of Zora Neale Hurston's writings. The controversial novel, *The Color Purple* (1982), raised her already formidable profile to a new level of prominence, becoming the first novel by an African-American woman to win the Pulitzer Prize. Like the themes in preceding works, *The Color Purple* examines racism's effects on the relationships of black men and women and the importance of a female support network. With her 1983 collection of essays *In Search of Our Mothers' Gardens: Womanist Prose,* Walker coined the term "womanism." Meant to distance itself from any narrow interpretations of the European-sounding "feminist," Walker's new word was derived from the black folk expression "womanish" and signifies a call to mature, responsible, and courageous behavior. Her creativity continuing unabated, Walker published numerous works in the next fifteen years, including the novels *The Temple of My Familiar* (1989), *Possessing the Secret of Joy* (a 1992 polemic against the practice of female circumcision in Africa), and *By the Light of My Father's Smile* (1998). By giving "voice to centuries not only of silent bitterness and hate but also of neighborly kindness and sustaining love," Walker has transcended the perceived obstacles of her past.

THE FLOWERS

It seemed to Myop as she skipped lightly from hen house to pigpen to smoke-house that the days had never been as beautiful as these. The air held a keenness that made her nose twitch. The harvesting of the corn and cotton, peanuts and squash, made each day a golden surprise that caused excited little tremors to run up her jaws.

Myop carried a short, knobby stick. She struck out at random at chickens she liked, and worked out the beat of a song on the fence around the pigpen. She felt light and good in the warm sun. She was ten, and nothing existed for her but her song, the stick clutched in her dark brown hand, and the tat-de-ta-ta-ta of accompaniment.

Turning her back on the rusty boards of her family's sharecropper cabin, Myop walked along the fence till it ran into the stream made by the spring. Around the spring, where the family got drinking water, silver ferns and wild-flowers grew. Along the shallow banks pigs rooted. Myop watched the tiny white bubbles disrupt the thin black scale of soil and the water that silently rose and slid away down the stream.

She had explored the woods behind the house many times. Often, in late autumn, her mother took her to gather nuts among the fallen leaves. Today she made her own path, bouncing this way and that way, vaguely keeping an eye out for snakes. She found, in addition to various common but pretty ferns and leaves, an armful of strange blue flowers with velvety ridges and a sweetsuds bush full of the brown, fragrant buds.

By twelve o'clock, her arms laden with sprigs of her findings, she was a mile or more from home. She had often been as far before, but the strangeness of the land made it not as pleasant as her usual haunts. It seemed gloomy in the little cove in which she found herself. The air was damp, the silence close and deep.

Myop began to circle back to the house, back to the peacefulness of the morning. It was then she stepped smack into his eyes. Her heel became lodged in the broken ridge between brow and nose, and she reached down quickly, unafraid, to free herself. It was only when she saw his naked grin that she gave a little yelp of surprise.

He had been a tall man. From feet to neck covered a long space. His head lay beside him. When she pushed back the leaves and layers of earth and debris Myop saw that he'd had large white teeth, all of them cracked or broken, long fingers, and very big bones. All his clothes had rotted away except some threads of blue denim from his overalls. The buckles of the overalls had turned green.

Myop gazed around the spot with interest. Very near where she'd stepped into the head was a wild pink rose. As she picked it to add to her bundle she no-ticed a raised mound, a ring, around the rose's root. It was the rotted remains of a noose, a bit of shredding plowline, now blending benignly into the soil. Around an overhanging limb of a great spreading oak clung another piece.

Frayed, rotted, bleached, and frazzled—barely there—but spinning restlessly in the breeze. Myop laid down her flowers.

And the summer was over.

IN SEARCH OF OUR MOTHERS' GARDENS

> I described her own nature and temperament. Told how they needed a larger life for their expression. . . . I pointed out that in lieu of proper channels, her emotions had overflowed into paths that dissipated them. I talked, beautifully I thought, about an art that would be born, an art that would open the way for women the likes of her. I asked her to hope, and build up an inner life against the coming of that day. . . . I sang, with a strange quiver in my voice, a promise song.
>
> —Jean Toomer, "Avey," Cane[1]

> The poet speaking to a prostitute who falls asleep while he's talking—

When the poet Jean Toomer walked through the South in the early twenties, he discovered a curious thing: black women whose spirituality was so intense, so deep, so *unconscious*, that they were themselves unaware of the richness they held. They stumbled blindly through their lives: creatures so abused and mutilated in body, so dimmed and confused by pain, that they considered themselves unworthy even of hope. In the selfless abstractions their bodies became to the men who used them, they became more than "sexual objects," more even than mere women: they became "Saints." Instead of being perceived as whole persons, their bodies became shrines: what was thought to be their minds became temples suitable for worship. These crazy Saints stared out at the world, wildly, like lunatics—or quietly, like suicides; and the "God" that was in their gaze was as mute as a great stone.

Who were these Saints? These crazy, loony, pitiful women?

Some of them, without a doubt, were our mothers and grandmothers.

In the still heat of the post-Reconstruction South[2] this is how they seemed to Jean Toomer: exquisite butterflies trapped in an evil honey, toiling away their lives in an era, a century, that did not acknowledge them, except as "the *mule* of the world."[3] They dreamed dreams that no one knew—not even themselves, in any coherent fashion—and saw visions no one could understand. They

---

[1] The major work of Jean Toomer (1894–1967), one of the writers of the Harlem Renaissance; the book is a mixture of narrative prose and lyric poetry.

[2] I.e., the South after home rule (and thus white supremacy) was restored following the Confederacy's social and political "reconstruction" (1865–77).

[3] An allusion to a statement in Zora Neale Hurston's (1891–1960) *Their Eyes Were Watching God* (1937): "De nigger woman is de mule uh de world."

wandered or sat about the countryside crooning lullabies to ghosts, and drawing the mother of Christ in charcoal on courthouse walls.

They forced their minds to desert their bodies and their striving spirits sought to rise, like frail whirlwinds from the hard red clay. And when those frail whirlwinds fell, in scattered particles, upon the ground, no one mourned. Instead, men lit candles to celebrate the emptiness that remained, as people do who enter a beautiful but vacant space to resurrect a God.

Our mothers and grandmothers, some of them: moving to music not yet written. And they waited.

They waited for a day when the unknown thing that was in them would be made known; but guessed, somehow in their darkness, that on the day of their revelation they would be long dead. Therefore to Toomer they walked, and even ran, in slow motion. For they were going nowhere immediate, and the future was not yet within their grasp. And men took our mothers and grandmothers, "but got no pleasure from it." So complex was their passion and their calm.

To Toomer, they lay vacant and fallow as autumn fields, with harvest time never in sight: and he saw them enter loveless marriages, without joy; and become prostitutes, without resistance; and become mothers of children, without fulfillment.

For these grandmothers and mothers of ours were not Saints, but Artists; driven to a numb and bleeding madness by the springs of creativity in them for which there was no release. They were Creators, who lived lives of spiritual waste, because they were so rich in spirituality—which is the basis of Art—that the strain of enduring their unused and unwanted talent drove them insane. Throwing away this spirituality was their pathetic attempt to lighten the soul to a weight their work-worn, sexually abused bodies could bear.

What did it mean for a black woman to be an artist in our grandmother's time? In our great-grandmothers' day? It is a question with an answer cruel enough to stop the blood.

Did you have a genius of a great-great-grandmother who died under some ignorant and depraved white overseer's lash? Or was she required to bake biscuits for a lazy backwater tramp, when she cried out in her soul to paint watercolors of sunsets, or the rain falling on the green and peaceful pasturelands? Or was her body broken and forced to bear children (who were more often than not sold away from her)—eight, ten, fifteen, twenty children—when her one joy was the thought of modeling heroic figures of rebellion, in stone or clay?

How was the creativity of the black woman kept alive, year after year and century after century, when for most of the years black people have been in America, it was a punishable crime for a black person to read or write? And the freedom to paint, to sculpt, to expand the mind with action did not exist. Consider, if you can bear to imagine it, what might have been the result if singing, too, had been forbidden by law. Listen to the voices of Bessie Smith, Billie

Holiday, Nina Simone, Roberta Flack, and Aretha Franklin[4] among others, and imagine those voices muzzled for life. Then you may begin to comprehend the lives of our "crazy," "Sainted" mothers and grandmothers. The agony of the lives of women who might have been Poets, Novelists, Essayists, and Short-Story Writers (over a period of centuries), who died with their real gifts stifled within them.

And, if this were the end of the story, we would have cause to cry out in my paraphrase of Okot p'Bitek's great poem:[5]

> O, my clanswomen
> Let us all cry together!
> Come,
> Let us mourn the death of our mother,
> The death of a Queen
> The ash that was produced
> By a great fire!
> O, this homestead is utterly dead
> Close the gates
> With *lacari* thorns,
> For our mother
> The creator of the Stool is lost!
> And all the young women
> Have perished in the wilderness!

But this is not the end of the story, for all the young women—our mothers and grandmothers, *ourselves*—have not perished in the wilderness. And if we ask ourselves why, and search for and find the answer, we will know beyond all efforts to erase it from our minds, just exactly who, and of what, we black American women are.

One example, perhaps the most pathetic, most misunderstood one, can provide a backdrop for our mothers' work: Phillis Wheatley,[6] a slave in the 1700s.

Virginia Woolf,[7] in her book *A Room of One's Own*, wrote that in order for a woman to write fiction she must have two things, certainly: a room of her own (with key and lock) and enough money to support herself.

What then are we to make of Phillis Wheatley, a slave, who owned not even herself? This sickly, frail black girl who required a servant of her own at times—her health was so precarious—and who, had she been white, would have been easily considered the intellectual superior of all the women and most of the men in the society of her day.

---

[4] All female black American singers from the 1920s to the present.

[5] The African poet's (b. 1931) *Song of Lawino* (1966). Walker has changed the original's masculine nouns to feminine equivalents.

[6] Highly educated black slave (1753–1784), who wrote formal, neoclassical poems.

[7] British novelist and essayist (1882–1941): *A Room* was published in 1929.

Virginia Woolf wrote further, speaking of course not of our Phillis, that "any woman born with a great gift in the sixteenth century [insert "eighteenth century," insert "black woman," insert "born or made a slave"] would certainly have gone crazed, shot herself, or ended her days in some lonely cottage outside the village, half witch, half wizard [insert "Saint"], feared and mocked at. For it needs little skill and psychology to be sure that a highly gifted girl who had tried to use her gift for poetry would have been so thwarted and hindered by contrary instincts [add "chains, guns, the lash, the ownership of one's body by someone else, submission to an alien religion"], that she must have lost her health and sanity to a certainty."

The key words, as they relate to Phillis, are "contrary instincts." For when we read the poetry of Phillis Wheatley—as when we read the novels of Nella Larsen[8] or the oddly false-sounding autobiography of that freest of all black women writers, Zora Hurston—evidence of "contrary instincts" is everywhere. Her loyalties were completely divided, as was, without question, her mind.

But how could this be otherwise? Captured at seven, a slave of wealthy, doting whites who instilled in her the "savagery" of the Africa they "rescued" her from . . . one wonders if she was even able to remember her homeland as she had known it, or as it really was.

Yes, because she did try to use her gift for poetry in a world that made her a slave, she was "so thwarted and hindered by . . . contrary instincts, that she . . . lost her health. . . ." In the last years of her brief life, burdened not only with the need to express her gift but also with a penniless, friendless "freedom" and several small children for whom she was forced to do strenuous work to feed, she lost her health, certainly. Suffering from malnutrition and neglect and who knows what mental agonies, Phillis Wheatley died.

So torn by "contrary instincts" was black, kidnapped, enslaved Phillis that her description of "the Goddess"—as she poetically called the Liberty she did not have—is ironically, cruelly humorous. And, in fact, has held Phillis up to ridicule for more than a century. It is usually read prior to hanging Phillis's memory as that of a fool. She wrote:

> The Goddess comes, she moves divinely fair,
> Olive and laurel binds her *golden* hair.
> Wherever shines this native of the skies,
> Unnumber'd charms and recent graces rise. [My italics][9]

It is obvious that Phillis, the slave, combed the "Goddess's" hair every morning; prior, perhaps, to bringing in the milk, or fixing her mistress's lunch. She took her imagery from the one thing she saw elevated above all others.

With the benefit of hindsight we ask, "How could she?"

[8] Black woman novelist of the Harlem Renaissance (1893–1964).
[9] From *To His Excellency General Washington* (1775).

But at last, Phillis, we understand. No more snickering when your stiff, struggling, ambivalent lines are forced on us. We know now that you were not an idiot or a traitor; only a sickly little black girl, snatched from your home and country and made a slave; a woman who still struggled to sing the song that was your gift, although in a land of barbarians who praised you for your bewildered tongue. It is not so much what you sang, as that you kept alive, in so many of our ancestors, *the notion of song.*

Black women are called, in the folklore that so aptly identifies one's status in society, "the *mule* of the world," because we have been handed the burdens that everyone else—*everyone* else—refused to carry. We have also been called "Matriarchs," "Superwomen," and "Mean and Evil Bitches." Not to mention "Castraters" and "Sapphire's[10] Mama." When we have pleaded for understanding, our character has been distorted; when we have asked for simple caring, we have been handed empty inspirational appellations, then stuck in the farthest corner. When we have asked for love, we have been given children. In short, even our plainer gifts, our labors of fidelity and love, have been knocked down our throats. To be an artist and a black woman, even today, lowers our status in many respects, rather than raises it: and yet, artists we will be.

Therefore we must fearlessly pull out of ourselves and look at and identify with our lives the living creativity some of our great-grandmothers were not allowed to know. I stress *some* of them because it is well known that the majority of our great-grandmothers knew, even without "knowing" it, the reality of their spirituality, even if they didn't recognize it beyond what happened in the singing at church—and they never had any intention of giving it up.

How they did it—those millions of black women who were not Phillis Wheatley, or Lucy Terry or Frances Harper or Zora Hurston or Nella Larsen or Bessie Smith; or Elizabeth Catlett, or Katherine Dunham,[11] either—brings me to the title of this essay, "In Search of Our Mothers' Gardens," which is a personal account that is yet shared, in its theme and its meaning, by all of us. I found, while thinking about the far-reaching world of the creative black woman, that often the truest answer to a question that really matters can be found very close.

In the late 1920s my mother ran away from home to marry my father. Marriage, if not running away, was expected of seventeen-year-old girls. By the time she was twenty, she had two children and was pregnant with a third. Five children later, I was born. And this is how I came to know my mother: she seemed a large, soft, loving-eyed woman who was rarely impatient in our home. Her

---

[10] Wife of "the Kingfish" in *Amos and Andy*, a popular early radio and television show.

[11] Black American dancer and choreographer (b. 1910). Lucy Terry (1730–1821), black poet and fictionist. Frances E. W. Harper (1825–1911), black woman poet. Elizabeth Catlett (b. 1915?), black educator and sculptor.

quick, violent temper was on view only a few times a year, when she battled with the white landlord who had the misfortune to suggest to her that her children did not need to go to school.

She made all the clothes we wore, even my brothers' overalls. She made all the towels and sheets we used. She spent the summers canning vegetables and fruits. She spent the winter evenings making quilts enough to cover all our beds.

During the "working" day, she labored beside—not behind—my father in the fields. Her day began before sunup, and did not end until late at night. There was never a moment for her to sit down, undisturbed, to unravel her own private thoughts; never a time free from interruption—by work or the noisy inquiries of her many children. And yet, it is to my mother—and all our mothers who were not famous—that I went in search of the secret of what has fed that muzzled and often mutilated, but vibrant, creative spirit that the black woman has inherited, and that pops out in wild and unlikely places to this day.

But when, you will ask, did my overworked mother have time to know or care about feeding the creative spirit?

The answer is so simple that many of us have spent years discovering it. We have constantly looked high, when we should have looked high—and low.

For example: in the Smithsonian Institution in Washington, D.C., there hangs a quilt unlike any other in the world. In fanciful, inspired, and yet simple and identifiable figures, it portrays the story of the Crucifixion. It is considered rare, beyond price. Though it follows no known pattern of quilt-making, and though it is made of bits and pieces of worthless rags, it is obviously the work of a person of powerful imagination and deep spiritual feeling. Below this quilt I saw a note that says it was made by "an anonymous Black woman in Alabama, a hundred years ago."

If we could locate this "anonymous" black woman from Alabama, she would turn out to be one of our grandmothers—an artist who left her mark in the only materials she could afford, and in the only medium her position in society allowed her to use.

As Virginia Woolf wrote further, in *A Room of One's Own:*

> Yet genius of a sort must have existed among women as it must have existed among the working class. [Change this to "slaves" and "the wives and daughters of sharecroppers."] Now and again an Emily Brontë or a Robert Burns [change this to "a Zora Hurston or a Richard Wright" [12]] blazes out and proves its presence. But certainly it never got itself on to paper. When, however, one reads of a witch being ducked, of a woman possessed by devils [or "Sainthood"], of a wise woman selling herbs [our root workers], or even a very remarkable man who had a mother, then I think we are on the track of a lost novelist, a suppressed poet, of some mute and

[12] Black American novelist (1908–1960). Emily Brontë (1819–1848), English novelist and poet. Robert Burns (1759–1796), Scottish poet.

inglorious Jane Austen. . . . Indeed, I would venture to guess that Anon, who wrote so many poems without signing them, was often a woman. . . .

And so our mothers and grandmothers have, more often than not anonymously, handed on the creative spark, the seed of the flower they themselves never hoped to see: or like a sealed letter they could not plainly read.

And so it is, certainly, with my own mother. Unlike "Ma" Rainey's[13] songs, which retained their creator's name even while blasting forth from Bessie Smith's mouth, no song or poem will bear my mother's name. Yet so many of the stories that I write, that we all write, are my mother's stories. Only recently did I fully realize this: that through years of listening to my mother's stories of her life, I have absorbed not only the stories themselves, but something of the manner in which she spoke, something of the urgency that involves the knowledge that her stories—like her life—must be recorded. It is probably for this reason that so much of what I have written is about characters whose counterparts in real life are so much older than I am.

But the telling of these stories, which came from my mother's lips as naturally as breathing, was not the only way my mother showed herself as an artist. For stories, too, were subject to being distracted, to dying without conclusion. Dinners must be started, and cotton must be gathered before the big rains. The artist that was and is my mother showed itself to me only after many years. This is what I finally noticed:

Like Mem, a character in *The Third Life of Grange Copeland*,[14] my mother adorned with flowers whatever shabby house we were forced to live in. And not just your typical straggly country stand of zinnias, either. She planted ambitious gardens—and still does—with over fifty different varieties of plants that bloom profusely from early March until late November. Before she left home for the fields, she watered her flowers, chopped up the grass, and laid out new beds. When she returned from the fields she might divide clumps of bulbs, dig a cold pit, uproot and replant roses, or prune branches from her taller bushes or trees—until night came and it was too dark to see.

Whatever she planted grew as if by magic, and her fame as a grower of flowers spread over three counties. Because of her creativity with her flowers, even my memories of poverty are seen through a screen of blooms—sunflowers, petunias, roses, dahlias, forsythia, spirea, delphiniums, verbena . . . and on and on.

And I remember people coming to my mother's yard to be given cuttings from her flowers; I hear again the praise showered on her because whatever rocky soil she landed on, she turned into a garden. A garden so brilliant with colors, so original in its design, so magnificent with life and creativity, that to this day people drive by our house in Georgia—perfect strangers and imperfect strangers—and ask to stand or walk among my mother's art.

[13] Gertrude Pridgett Rainey (1886–1939), black blues singer and songwriter.
[14] Walker's first novel.

I notice that it is only when my mother is working in her flowers that she is radiant, almost to the point of being invisible—except as Creator: hand and eye. She is involved in work her soul must have. Ordering the universe in the image of her personal conception of Beauty.

Her face, as she prepared the Art that is her gift, is a legacy of respect she leaves to me, for all that illuminates and cherishes life. She has handed down respect for the possibilities—and the will to grasp them.

For her, so hindered and intruded upon in so many ways, being an artist has still been a daily part of her life. This ability to hold on, even in very simple ways, is work black women have done for a very long time.

This poem is not enough, but it is something, for the woman who literally covered the holes in our walls with sunflowers:

> They were women then
> My mama's generation
> Husky of voice—Stout of
> Step
> With fists as well as
> Hands
> How they battered down
> Doors
> And ironed
> Starched white
> Shirts
> How they led
> Armies
> Headragged Generals
> Across mined
> Fields
> Booby-trapped
> Kitchens
> To discover books
> Desks
> A place for us
> How they knew what we
> *Must* know
> Without knowing a page
> Of it
> Themselves.

Guided by my heritage of a love of beauty and a respect for strength—in search of my mother's garden, I found my own.

And perhaps in Africa over two hundred years ago, there was just such a mother; perhaps she painted vivid and daring decorations in oranges and yellows and greens on the walls of her hut; perhaps she sang—in a voice like Roberta Flack's—*sweetly* over the compounds of her village; perhaps she wove the most stunning mats or told the most ingenious stories of all the village storytellers. Perhaps she was herself a poet—though only her daughter's name is signed to the poems that we know.

Perhaps Phillis Wheatley's mother was also an artist.

Perhaps in more than Phillis Wheatley's biological life is her mother's signature made clear.

Ann Beattie 1947–

A prolific writer with four novels and four collections of short stories to her credit, Ann Beattie has established herself as a chronicler of the upper-middle class, particularly as she observes the deluded imperfections of an idealistic "Woodstock generation." Although she has received criticism for her loyalty to the genre, her craftsmanship is well respected. Born in Washington, D.C., she received her B.A. from American University in 1969 and an M.A. a year later from the University of Connecticut. Following a Guggenheim Fellowship in 1978, Beattie became a guest lecturer and writer at Harvard and the University of Virginia. She elects to use chaos as the platform for her oblique narratives and flat, declarative prose, maintaining that chaos is reinforced by her use of non sequiturs. John Updike noted that Beattie's style possesses "a maze of familiar truths that nevertheless has something airy, eerie, and in the end lovely about it." A frequent contributor to *The New Yorker*, Beattie has been described by one critic as an author who mixes black humor, wit, and social realism with an eye for the grotesque.

WHAT WAS MINE

I don't remember my father. I have only two photographs of him—one of two soldiers standing with their arms around each other's shoulder, their faces even paler than their caps, so that it's difficult to make out their features; the other of my father in profile, peering down at me in my crib. In that photograph, he has no discernible expression, though he does have a rather noble Roman nose and thick hair that would have been very impressive if it hadn't been clipped so short. On the back of the picture in profile is written, unaccountably, "Guam," while the back of the picture of the soldiers say, "Happy with baby: 5/28/49."

Until I was five or six I had no reason to believe that Herb was not my uncle. I might have believed it much longer if my mother had not blurted out the truth one night when I opened her bedroom door and saw Herb, naked from the waist down crouched at the foot of the bed, holding out a bouquet of roses much the way teasing people shake a biscuit in front of a sleeping dog's nose. They had been to a wedding earlier that day, and my mother had caught the nosegay. Herb was tipsy, but I had no sense of that then. Because I was a clumsy boy, I didn't wonder about his occasionally knocking into a wall or stepping off a curb a bit too hard. He was not allowed to drive me anywhere, but I thought only that my mother was full of arbitrary rules she imposed on everyone: no more than one hour of TV a day; put Bosco in the glass first, then the milk.

One of the most distinct memories of my early years is of that night I opened my mother's door and saw Herb lose his balance and fall forward on the bouquet like a thief clutching bread under his shirt.

"Ethan," my mother said, "I don't know what you are doing in here at a time when you are supposed to be in bed—and without the manners to knock—but I think the time has come to tell you that Herbert and I are very close, but not close in the way family members such as a brother and sister are. Herbert is not your uncle, but you must go on as if he were. Other people should not know this."

Herb had rolled onto his side. As he listened, he began laughing. He threw the crushed bouquet free, and I caught it by taking one step forward and waiting for it to land in my outstretched hand. It was the way Herb had taught me to catch a ball, because I had a tendency to overreact and rush too far forward, too fast. By the time I had caught the bouquet, exactly what my mother said had become a blur: manners, Herbert, not family, don't say anything.

Herb rolled off the bed, stood, and pulled on his pants. I had the clear impression that he was in worse trouble than I was. I think that what he said to me was that his affection for me was just what it always had been, even though he wasn't actually my uncle. I know that my mother threw a pillow at him and told him not to confuse me. Then she looked at me and said, emphatically, that Herb was not a part of our family. After saying that, she became quite flustered and got up and stomped out of the bedroom, slamming the door behind her. Herb gave the door a dismissive wave of the hand. Alone with him, I felt much better. I suppose I had thought that he might vanish—if he was not my uncle, he might suddenly disappear—so that his continued presence was very reassuring.

"Don't worry about it," he said. "The divorce rate is climbing, people are itching to change jobs every five minutes. You wait: Dwight Eisenhower is going to be reevaluated. He won't have the same position in history that he has today." He looked at me. He sat on the side of the bed. "I'm your mother's boyfriend," he said. "She doesn't want to marry me. It doesn't matter. I'm not going anywhere. Just keep it between us that I'm not Uncle Herb."

My mother was tall and blond, the oldest child of a German family that had immigrated to America in the 1920s. Herb was dark-haired, the only child of a Lebanese father and his much younger English bride, who had considered even on the eve of her wedding leaving the Church of England to convert to Catholicism and become a nun. In retrospect, I realize that my mother's shyness about her height and her having been indoctrinated to believe that the hope of the future lay in her accomplishing great things, and Herb's self-consciousness about his kinky hair, along with his attempt as a child to negotiate peace between his mother and father, resulted in an odd bond between Herb and my mother: she was drawn to his conciliatory nature, and he was drawn to her no-nonsense attitude. Or perhaps she was drawn to his unusual amber eyes, and he was taken in by her inadvertently, sexy, self-conscious girlishness. Maybe he took great pleasure in shocking her, in playing to her secret, more sophisticated desires, and she was secretly amused and gratified that he took it as a given that she was highly competent and did not have to prove herself to him in any way whatsoever.

She worked in a bank. He worked in the automotive section at Sears, Roebuck, and on the weekend he played piano, harmonica, and sometimes tenor sax at a bar off Pennsylvania Avenue called the Merry Mariner. On Saturday nights my mother and I would sit side by side, dressed in our good clothes, in a booth upholstered in blue Naugahyde, behind which dangled nets that were nailed to the wall, studded with starfish, conch shells, sea horses, and clamshells with small painted scenes or decals inside them. I would have to turn sideways and look above my mother to see them. I had to work out a way of seeming to be looking in front of me and listening appreciatively to Uncle Herb while at the very same time rolling my eyes upward to take in those tiny depictions of sunsets, rainbows, and ships sailing through the moonlight. Uncle Herb played a slowish version of "Let Me Call You Sweetheart" on the harmonica as I sipped my cherry Coke with real cherries in it: three, because the waitress liked me. He played "As Time Goes By" on the piano, singing so quietly it seemed he was humming. My mother and I always split the fisherman's platter: four shrimp, one crab cake, and a lobster tail, or sometimes two if the owner wasn't in the kitchen, though my mother often wrapped up the lobster tails and saved them for our Sunday dinner. She would slice them and dish them up over rice, along with the tomato-and lettuce salad she served almost every night.

Some of Uncle Herb's songs would go out to couples celebrating an anniversary, or to birthday boys, or to women being courted by men who preferred to let Uncle Herb sing the romantic thoughts they hesitated to speak. Once during the evening Herb would dedicate a song to my mother, always referring to her as "my own special someone" and nodding—but never looking directly—toward our booth.

My mother kept the beat to faster tunes by tapping her fingers on the shiny varnished tabletop. During the slow numbers she would slide one finger back and forth against the edge of the table, moving her hand so delicately she might have been testing the blade of a knife. Above her blond curls I would see miniature versions of what I thought must be the most exotic places on earth—so exotic that any small reference to them would quicken the heart of anyone familiar with the mountains of Hawaii or the seas of Bora-Bora. My mother smoked cigarettes, so that sometimes I would see these places through fog. When the over-head lights were turned from blue to pink as Uncle Herb played the last set, they would be transformed to the most ideal possible versions of paradise. I was hyp-notized by what seemed to me their romantic clarity, as Herb sang a bemused version of "Stormy Weather," then picked up the saxophone for "Green Eyes," and finished, always with a Billie Holiday song he would play very simply on the piano, without singing. Then the lights went to a dusky red and gradually brightened to a golden light that seemed as stupefying to me as the cloud rising at Los Alamos must have seemed to the observers of Trinity. It allowed people enough light to judge their sobriety, pay the bill, or decide to postpone func-tioning until later and vanish into the darker reaches of the bar at the back. Un-cle Herb never patted me on the shoulder or tousled my cowlick. He usually sank down next to my mother—still bowing slightly to acknowledge the ap-plause—then reached over with the same automatic motion my mother used when she withdrew a cigarette from the pack to run his thumb quickly over my knuckles, as if he were testing a keyboard. If a thunderbolt had left his finger-tips, it could not have been more clear: he wanted me to be a piano player.

That plan had to be abandoned when I was thirteen. Or perhaps it did not really have to be abandoned, but at the time I found a convenient excuse to let go of the idea. One day, as my mother rounded a curve in the rain, the car skid-ded into a telephone pole. As the windshield splattered into cubes of glass, my wrist was broken and my shoulder dislocated. My mother was not hurt at all, al-though when she called Herb at work she became so hysterical that she had to be given an injection in the emergency room before he arrived to take us both away.

I don't think she was ever really the same after the accident. Looking back, I realize that was when everything started to change—though there is every chance that my adolescence and her growing hatred of her job might have changed things anyway. My mother began to seem irrationally angry at Herb and so solicitous of me I felt smothered. I held her responsible, suddenly, for everything, and I had a maniac's ability to transform good things into some-thing awful. The five cherries I began to get in my Cokes seemed an unwanted pollution, and I was sure that my mother had told the waitress to be extra kind. Her cigarette smoke made me cough. Long before the surgeon general warned against the dangers of smoking, I was sure that she meant to poison me. When she drove me to physical therapy, I misconstrued her positive attitude and was sure that she took secret delight in having me tortured. My wrist set wrong, and had to be put in a cast a second time. My mother cried constantly. I turned to Herb to help me with my homework. She relented, and he became the one who drove me everywhere.

When I started being skeptical of my mother, she began to be skeptical of Herb. I heard arguments about the way he arranged his sets. She said that he should end on a more upbeat note. She thought the lighting was too stagy. He began to play—and end—in a nondescript silver glow. I looked at the shells on the netting, not caring that she knew I wasn't concentrating on Herb's playing. She sank lower in the booth, and her attention also drifted: no puffs of smoke carefully exhaled in the pauses between sung phrases; no testing the edge of the table with her fingertip. One Saturday night we just stopped going.

By that time, she had become a loan officer at Riggs Bank. Herb had moved from Sears to Montgomery Ward, where he was in charge of the lawn and leisure-activities section—everything from picnic tables to electric hedge clippers. She served TV dinners. She complained that there wasn't enough money, though she bought expensive high heels that she wore to work. On Wednesday nights Herb played handball with friends who used to be musicians but who were suddenly working white-collar jobs to support growing families. He would come home and say, either with disbelief or with disorientation, that Sal, who used to play in a Latino band, had just had twins, or that Earl had sold his drums and bought an expensive barbecue grill. She read Perry Mason. He read magazine articles about the Second World War: articles, he said, shaking his head, that were clearly paving the way for a reassessment of the times in which we lived.

I didn't have a friend—a real friend—until I was fourteen. That year my soul mate was a boy named Ryuji Anderson, who shared my passion for soccer and introduced me to *Playboy.* He told me to buy Keds one size too large and stuff a sock in that toe so that I could kick hard and the ball would really fly. We both suffered because we sensed that you had to *look* like John F. Kennedy in order to *be* John F. Kennedy. Ryuji's mother had been a war bride, and my mother had lost her husband six years after the war in a freak accident: a painter on scaffolding had lost his footing high up and tumbled backward to the ground, releasing, as he fell, the can of paint that struck my father on the head and killed him. The painter faithfully sent my mother a Christmas card every year, informing her about his own slow recovery and apologizing for my father's death. Uncle Herb met my mother when his mother, dead of leukemia, lay in the room adjacent to my father's room in the funeral home. They had coffee together one time when they both were exiled to the streets, late at night.

It was not until a year later, when he looked her up in the phone book (the number was still listed under my father's name), that he saw her again. That time I went along, and was bought a paper cone filled with french fries. I played cowboy, circling with an imaginary lasso the bench on which they sat. We had stumbled on a carnival. Since it was downtown Washington, it wasn't really a carnival but a small area of the mall, taken over by dogs who would jump through burning hoops and clowns on roller skates. It became a standing refrain between my mother and Herb that some deliberate merriment had been orchestrated just for them, like the play put on in *A Midsummer Night's Dream.*

I, of course, had no idea what to make of the world on any given day. My constants were that I lived with my mother, who cried every night; that I could watch only two shows each day on TV; and that I would be put to bed earlier than I wanted, with a nightlight left burning. That day my mother and Herb sat on the bench, I'm sure I sensed that things were going to be different, as I inscribed two people destined to be together in an imaginary lassoed magic circle. From then on, we were a threesome.

He moved in as a boarder. He lived in the room that used to be the dining room, which my mother and I had never used, since we ate off TV trays. I remember his hanging a drapery rod over the arch — nailing the brackets in, then lifting up the bar, pushing onto it the brocade curtain my mother had sewn, then lowering the bar into place. They giggled behind it. Then they slid the curtain back and forth, as if testing to see that it would really work. It was like one of the games I had had as a baby: a board with a piece of wood that slid back and forth, exposing first the sun, then the moon.

Of course, late a night they cheated. He would simply push the curtain aside and go to her bed. Since I would have accepted anything, it's a wonder they didn't just tell me. A father, an uncle, a saint, Howdy Doody, Lassie — I didn't have a very clear idea of how any of them truly behaved. I believed whatever I saw. Looking back, I can only assume that they were afraid not so much of what I would think as of what others might think, and that they were unwilling to draw me into their deception. Until I wandered into their bedroom, they simply were not going to blow their cover. They were just going to wait for me. Eventually, I was sure to stumble into their world.

"The secret about Uncle Herb doesn't go any farther than this house," my mother said that night after I found them together. She was quite ashen. We stood in the kitchen. I had followed her — not because I loved her so much, or because I trusted her, but because I was already sure of Herb. Sure because even if he had winked at me, he could not have been clearer about the silliness of the slammed door. She had on a beige nightgown and was backlit by the counter light. She cast a pondlike shadow on the floor. I would like to say that I asked her why she had lied to me, but I'm sure I wouldn't have dared. Imagine my surprise when she told me anyway: "You don't know what it's like to lose something forever," she said. "It will make you do anything — even lie to people you love — if you think you can reclaim even a fraction of that thing. You don't know what *fraction* means. It means a little bit. It means a thing that's been broken into pieces."

I knew she was talking about loss. All week, I had been worried that the bird at school, with its broken wing, might never fly again and would hop forever in the cardboard box. What my mother was thinking of, though, was that can of paint — a can of paint that she wished had missed my father's head and sailed into infinity.

We looked down at the sepia shadow. It was there in front of her, and in front of me. Of course it was behind us, too.

Many years later, the day Herb took me out for a "talk," we drove aimlessly for quite a while. I could almost feel Herb's moment of inspiration when it finally came, and he went around a traffic circle and headed down Pennsylvania

Avenue. It was a Saturday, and on Saturdays the Merry Mariner was open only for dinner, but he had a key, so we parked and went inside and turned on a light. It was not one of those lights that glowed when he played, but a strong, fluorescent light. Herb went to the bar and poured himself a drink. He opened a can of Coke and handed it to me. Then he told me that he was leaving us. He said that he himself found it unbelievable. Then, suddenly, he began to urge me to listen to Billie Holiday's original recordings, to pay close attention to the paintings of Vermeer, to look around me and to listen. To believe that what to some people might seem the silliest sort of place might be, to those truly observant, a temporary substitute for heaven.

I was a teenager, and I was too embarrassed to cry. I sat on a bar stool and simply looked at him. That day, neither of us knew how my life would turn out. Possibly he thought that so many unhappy moments would have damaged me forever. For all either of us knew, he had been the father figure to a potential hoodlum, or even to a drifter—that was what the game of pretense he and my mother had been involved in might have produced. He shook his head sadly when he poured another drink. Later, I found out that my mother had asked him to go, but that day I didn't even think to ask why I was being abandoned.

Before we left the restaurant he told me—as he had the night I found him naked in my mother's room—how much he cared for me. He also gave me practical advice about how to assemble a world.

He had been the one who suggested that the owner string netting on the walls. First he and the owner had painted the ocean: pale blue, more shine than paint at the bottom, everything larger than it appeared on land. Then gradually the color of the paint changed, rays of light streamed in, and things took on a truer size. Herb had added, on one of the walls, phosphorescence. He had touched the paintbrush to the wall delicately, repeatedly, meticulously. He was a very good amateur painter. Those who sat below it would never see it, though. Those who sat adjacent to it might see the glow in their peripheral vision. From across the room, where my mother and I sat, the highlights were too delicate, and too far away to see. The phosphorescence had never caught my eye when my thoughts drifted from the piano music, or when I blinked my eyes to clear them of the smoke.

The starfish had been bought in lots of a dozen from a store in Chinatown. The clamshells had been painted by a woman who lived in Arlington, in the suburbs, who had once strung them together as necklaces for church bazaars, until the demand dried up and macramé was all the rage. Then she sold them to the owner of the restaurant, who carried them away from her yard sale in two aluminum buckets years before he ever imagined he would open a restaurant. Before Herb and I left the Merry Mariner that day, there wasn't anything about how the place had been assembled that I didn't know.

Fifteen years after that I drove with my fiancée to Herb's cousin's house to get some things he left with her for safekeeping in case anything happened to him. His cousin was a short, unattractive woman who lifted weights. She had converted what had been her dining room into a training room, complete with Nautilus, rowing machine, and barbells. She lived alone, so there was no one to slide a curtain back for. There was no child, so she was not obliged to play at anything.

She served us iced tea with big slices of lemon. She brought out guacamole and a bowl of tortilla chips. She had called me several days before to say that Herb had had a heart attack and died. Though I would not find out formally until some time later, she also told me that Herb had left me money in his will. He also asked that she pass on to me a large manila envelope. She handed it to me, and I was so curious that I opened it immediately, on the back porch of some muscle-bound woman named Frances in Cold Spring Harbor, New York.

There was sheet music inside: six Billie Holiday songs that I recognized immediately as Herb's favorites for ending the last set of the evening. There were several notes, which I suppose you could call love notes, from my mother. There was a tracing, on a food-stained Merry Mariner place mat, of a cherry, complete with stem, and a fancy pencil-drawn frame around it that I vaguely remembered Herb having drawn one night. There was also a white envelope that contained the two pictures: one of the soldiers in Guam; one of a handsome young man looking impassively at a sleeping young baby. I knew the second I saw it that he was my father.

I was fascinated, but the more I looked at it—the more remote and expressionless the man seemed—the more it began to dawn on me that Herb wanted me to see the picture of my father because he wanted me to see how different he had been from him. When I turned over the picture of my father in profile and read "Guam," I almost smiled. It certainly wasn't my mother's handwriting. It was Herb's, though he had tried to slope the letters so that it would resemble hers. What sweet revenge, he must have thought—to leave me with the impression that my mother had been such a preoccupied, scatterbrained woman that she could not even label two important pictures correctly.

My mother had died years before, of pneumonia. The girl I had been dating at the time had said to me, not unkindly, that although I was very sad about my mother's death, one of the advantages of time passing was sure to be that the past would truly become the past. Words would become suspect. People would seem to be only poor souls struggling to do their best. Images would fade.

Not the image of the wall painted to look like the ocean, though. She was wrong about that. Herb had painted it exactly the way it really looks. I found this out later when I went snorkeling and saw the world underwater for the first time, with all its spooky spots of overexposure and its shimmering irregularities. But how tempting—how reassuring—to offer people the possibility of climbing from deep water to the surface by moving upward on lovely white nets, gigantic ladders from which no one need ever topple.

On Frances's porch, as I stared at the photographs of my father, I saw him as a young man standing on a hot island, his closest friend a tall broomstick of a man whom he would probably never see again once the war was over. He was a hero. He had served his country. When he got off Guam, he would have a life. Things didn't turn out the way he expected, though. The child he left behind was raised by another man, though it is true that his wife missed him forever and remained faithful in her own strange way by never remarrying. As I continued to look at the photograph, though, it was not possible to keep thinking of him as a hero. He was an ordinary man, romantic in context—a sad young soldier on a tropical island what would soon become a forgotten land. When the war was over he would have a life, but a life that was much too brief, and the living would never really recover from that tragedy.

Herb must also have believed that he was not a hero. That must have been what he was thinking when he wrote, in wispy letters, brief, transposed captions for two pictures that did not truly constitute any legacy at all.

In Cold Spring Harbor, as I put the pictures back in the envelope, I realized that no one had spoken for quite some time. Frances tilted her glass, shaking the ice cubes. She hardly knew us. Soon we would be gone. It was just a quick drive to the city, and she would see us off, knowing that she had discharged her responsibility by passing on to me what Herb had said was mine.

Laura Cunningham 1947–

N ative New Yorker Laura Cunningham is an award-winning novelist, playwright, and journalist. A 1966 graduate of New York University, she won a journalism award for best profile for a cover story in *Newsday* (1984) and has contributed articles, short stories, and reviews to publications such as *Atlantic, Vogue, The New Yorker,* and *The New York Times.* She has won National Endowment for the Arts grants for playwriting and creative nonfiction and a fellowship from the New York Foundation of the Arts. In a *Wall Street Journal* review of her memoir, *Sleeping Arrangements* (1989), Cunningham was playfully described as "a memorialist a bit like Truman Capote, if he had been Jewish and female and less bitchy." In this autobiographical novel, Cunningham depicts the awkward vicissitudes of prepubescence with sharp-witted and poignant insight.

From SLEEPING ARRANGEMENTS

I began my life waiting for him. When other children asked, "Where's your father?" I had my mother's answer: "He's fighting in the war."

For the first four years of my childhood, I grew into the anticipation: my father would come home when the war ended. Until that time, my mother and I moved in a holding pattern from one relative's apartment to another. Sleeping on sofas and collapsible cots, we squeezed into odd slices of space. I awakened looking up at the undersides of a dining table, with my mother wedged beside me between chair legs. In the dark of different living rooms, we traded questions and answers that were always the same:

"Did he see me before he left?"

"Once. You were in your crib sleeping."

"Why didn't you wake me?"

"You were fast asleep."

How could I sleep through my single chance to see him? Something's amiss. From the shadow of the dining table I demanded more details.

"What did you wear to the wedding?"

"A beige suit."

"Not a white wedding dress?"

"There wasn't time. He had to fly overseas."

His legend grew, as legends do, in his absence, on the strength of repetition. He could fly a plane, fire a machine gun. He won more medals than anyone. And—this was my favorite detail—he had his own fighting dog, a boxer named Butch, who was a gentle pet when he wasn't ripping apart the enemy.

Who was the enemy? My mother was vague as to the exact identity of the opposition, but specific in attending to our patriotic duties. On national holidays, we hung a dime-store flag from the window. At parades, we sang on the sidelines. In was a red-white-and-blue story, told to the accompaniment of bugles. There was only one flaw: while we waited for my hero father to return from battle, this country was not at war.

No war. I heard the news and rushed to tell my mother, who, in 1950, assured me that World War II was still underway. "Most of the soldiers have come home," she conceded, "but there are still a few outposts that have to be captured."

While my father fought at his faraway front, my mother and I lived in limbo. The interrogations continued—I collected information.

His name was Larry. He was from Alabama. His hair was blond, his eyes were blue. My mother stressed superlatives: he was the handsomest man she'd ever seen; the best dancer. His hair was "so blond it looked white in the sun."

Pressed for evidence, my mother produced a snapshot of Larry, which she showed to me only when we were alone, only at night. The photograph was as transient as we were—my mother rotated its hiding place. As often happens with an irreplaceable item, we concentrated so hard on its safekeeping that it was often misplaced, usually disappearing between the pages of books. We wept when the picture was missing, but never considered having a duplicate made— the risk of entrusting "him" to a photo-processing store was too high. As soon as I could write, I penciled on the reverse side:

The only picture of my father. Big Reward.

Not only was this snapshot elusive, it was overexposed. Technically black-and-white, the photograph, taken in an Army office, seemed to have acquired the khaki color scheme of its setting. My mother and Larry appear in shades of beige, divided by a cone of light so bright it threatened to disintegrate them. By the mysterious method of film, this snapshot seized its own truth: the dissolving dazzle of the soldier at its center. So radiant was he, he might have been the light that blanched the negative.

Beside his brilliance my mother appears blurred—a dark woman whose expression can't be caught by the camera. Her blurriness is profound, as if, at that time, she was so unsure of herself that she could not be clearly photographed. There are such times, when the camera can only record confusion or evasion, the mind turned inward. In person, my mother had a physical habit of ducking sudden, unpleasant truths. Did the camera catch this characteristic dip of her head? Whatever the cause, she is forever out of focus.

My father sits at his desk. Surely, it's his desk. A cigarette burns in the glass ashtray beside his hand. He looks up, a dent of irritation between his pale eyebrows. Interrupted at work?

My mother stands beside him, and because of her blurriness, she projects an impression of movement, of having just stepped into frame. She is flanked by a second woman and another officer, a pair of "strangers" whom my mother and I would have loved to scissor out of the photograph.

The strangers didn't belong in the picture. My mother and I never said so, but we felt that the unknown couple spoiled what we could otherwise regard as an informal wedding portrait.

There was a great deal of precedent for excising unwanted figures from family photos. Our album exhibited a heavily revisionist approach. On almost every page cousins had been cropped from group portraits. Sometimes the entire bodies had been removed, but more often only the offending heads, which gave our family photograph collection an odd, mutilated look. Here and there, couples could be seen in an embrace, but one had been beheaded, leaving a mate with his arms around a well-dressed torso. More women than men had been scissored out of the record, suggesting that the cut-and-pasteup of family history had been executed by a third party. Eventually, I came to know the woman responsible: my grandmother. Years later, I caught her in the act, bent over a group picnic scene with scissors and a razor blade. Her photo-editing sessions were the closest she ever came to domestic endeavor.

My mother and I had none of her malevolent zest. Instead, we collaborated on an alibi for the unknown couple and incorporated them in the scenario: No longer "strangers," they could be "witnesses" at the wedding.

Whenever we stared at the snapshot, my mother recited her tale of rushed romance: the lunch-hour wedding, a goodbye kiss on the tarmac. As she spoke, I envisioned my mother and Larry dashing from the khaki world of the war office into an exterior that was also overexposed. I saw my mother and father race across the bleached streets of noontime Miami Beach, toward a whiteout of a wedding.

Soon, I noticed that my mother colored when anyone asked questions about Larry. Her voice rose high—she almost could not aspirate; "husband" became a gasp for breath. I, too, felt a squeeze on my windpipe when my father was mentioned. It was hard to lie, even if I didn't know the truth.

The fabric of my mother's cover story frayed fast. We were stranded in an awkward interval between wars. My stories of a father "fighting overseas" incited serious interrogation. Other children, teachers, neighbors wanted to know "Where?" Soon, I became the prisoner of war: I didn't want to answer anymore. Sometimes I said, "The Pacific"; other times I whispered, "Europe," which I pictured as a continent-sized Oriental carpet laid out across the sea.

At last: Korea. What a relief. My mother and I could relax on the home front. At least no one looked at us askance and asked, "What war?" anymore.

But even the Korean action came to an end, and with it the first installment of life without father. One afternoon as I demonstrated mock machine-gun fire—"This is how my father kills them"—my mother tapped me on the shoulder and led me a discreet distance from the other girls. As we talked, she said I shouldn't tell that story anymore. I guessed the reason.

"The war's over?"

"In a way it is." Larry would not be flying home after all. His body was already buried overseas. I asked about the medals, the ribbons, perhaps his uniform?

With a vividness of detail I can appreciate in retrospect, my mother explained why there was nothing left to be sent to us. "He was blown up in tiny pieces." His uniform burned, his medals melted, the ribbons charred and lost forever.

Butch? Was Butch riding in the tank? No, he was not. He was on guard duty that day. "The Army needs dogs like Butch." Butch had been reassigned. And so, it appeared, were my mother and I.

No longer transient, we moved to our own efficiency apartment. We were no longer ladies-in-waiting; we were in mourning. On the first night in our new home, my mother lit a memorial candle, and set it in the corner of the bathtub, there to flicker in remembrance without becoming a fire hazard for twenty-four hours to mark my father's death.

Our move had the effect of a magic trick. We changed households in minutes. Our belongings were as portable as we were: everything we owned folded. We moved by subway; my mother with a cot under one arm and a card table under the other.

We left behind our previous accommodation in the narrow living room of an elderly aunt, a crevasse of an apartment set in a medieval-style building itself constricted between two look-alikes. This Gothic housing complex, modeled emotionally as well as architecturally upon feudal times, managed to capture the hopelessness of the era that inspired it. Designed around a sunless courtyard with a defunct fountain, this development appeared inhabited by a nation of Old World munchkins, whose growth was distorted, like bonsai trees, by the ropes and bundles attached to them. A horsedrawn cart seemed to rattle over from Europe, driven by a man of medieval appearance (no teeth, grizzled beard) who cried out in a caw that was unintelligible but had something to do with "old clothes."

My mother and I fled these shadowed parts for what she called the "wide-open spaces." Wide-open they were. Our train tore from the subway tunnel, as if escaping the dark past, and skidded to a halt at our stop, the first outdoor station on the line.

We stood at the edge of the Bronx, on a crest that overlooked the river and Manhattan. Between us and Manhattan lay an infamous whirlpool, which was known to have sucked boats and barges into its spiraling depths, then spit them up as splinters.

There was no mistaking the whooshing uptide in my mother's spirits. She sang as we walked through the dark streets to our new home. Our past had been a string of sequential Sundays, looking, always looking for a place of our own. We'd toured so many model apartments that our dream wafted this specific scent: new pine and shellac.

We arrived at our first apartment: a fresh white studio, with an el, its floor still tacky with resin. We entered on tiptoe, walked the borders, careful to inhabit the place gradually—or it might disappear. My mother lit the memorial candle, and so, serviceable as well as sentimental, this beacon to Larry's memory illuminated our new home. My mother cast a magnified shadow on the walls.

With only a single cot, my mother and I had to initiate new sleeping arrangements. I couldn't quite believe that we were alone, that we could choose where we would sleep. (Although, never having known a bed or a bedroom, I didn't mind sleeping under tables. There was a coziness to claustrophobia, even an accidental elegance; when the tablecloth was left on, my mother and I luxuriated in the canopied effect.) All I ever needed to drift off, feeling snug, was to see her familiar silhouette—the curlicues of her hair, the deep curve of her hip. She was the single constant in my changing nights, my campsite mate in the carved forest.

While I'd always been near her, I had never slept touching her. Now, for the first time, we tried to share. Together we moved the single cot against the wall, for the sense of fortification. I climbed onto the sway-backed military cot (a last link to Larry, who was said to have lugged his Army bed from Europe to Korea).

My mother slid in beside me. It was summer, and her skin scorched. We lay there, our minds ticking, aware almost audibly of each other's thoughts.

I inched toward the abyss of the empty studio, my effort to create distance as palpable as a complaint. Tense as a troubled marriage bed, our cot sagged under the double weight and the realization: this arrangement could not last the night.

My mother volunteered to lie on the floor. She stretched out on top of her dress. Stricken—had I hurt her feelings?—I reached down and touched her hand.

In the morning we showered together. By day, our studio was bright, somehow Scandinavian, divided into geometric patterns of light. And in this bare room, empty as modern art, our romance began.

As happy as newlyweds—alone at last—my mother and I danced with fruit in our hands and celebrated the morning. We were free to be together in ways that had been impossible with screaming cousins and irritated aunts yelling in the cramped corridors. Wearing towel turbans and terry-cloth sarongs, we exulted in our new privacy: ecstasy in 3M.

3M, I saw by hard daylight, was set into a building of schizoid design. While the exterior was blandly modern white brick, the interior was decorated in a style that might be called Babylonian Bronx. In the lobby, murals depicted scenes of Dionysian excess, and mosaic maidens walked a deluded diagonal along the walls toward the mailboxes. The mood and the maidens came to a dead halt at the elevator door. From there, it was a short ride from Babylonia-in-the-Bronx to seven stories of "worker" housing cubicles that could easily fit into Stalingrad. The housewives of AnaMor Towers pushed their wire grocery carts across marble lobby floors, rode the "Ionic" elevator up to "junior fours."

The dual nature of AnaMor Towers (named for the owners, Anna and Morris Snezak) was conducive to the secret life I would lead here: outwardly ordinary, inwardly ornate, owing all inspiration to heathen cultures. I suspected the other tenants felt a tug, too. Who could be immune to the libidinous lobby? I soon discovered the other little girls in AnaMor Towers were deeply indebted to pagan ritual for routine play. How could we avoid it? Every AnaMorite had to pass a frieze of Pompeii on the way to the incinerator.

AnaMor Towers did not stand alone. The entire neighborhood was a cross-section of ersatz bygone cultures. In the park, marble mermaids lounged, with rust running down their navels. Public buildings were supported by semi-nude figures, wearing New Deal chitons. Many of the apartment buildings were modern Towers of Babel, mixing details from Ancient Rome, Syria, Greece. (In retrospect, one wonders if the Jews who designed these edifices were paying some delayed tribute to ancient enemies.)

On my way to kindergarten, I saw that the neighborhood became increasingly extraordinary. There was something inhuman in the scale of the streets. The avenues seemed overly wide, suitable only for mass invasion. The main thoroughfare, Grand Concourse, was a reproduction of the Champs Élysées, with the substitution of Yankee Stadium for the Arc de Triomphe.

The old stadium dominated the area in more than a merely physical way. Built for ritual on a major scale, the arena cast a spiritual net that extended at least ten blocks. (My mother and I soon discovered that AnaMor Towers, a few streets from the stadium, stood on a baseball fault zone. The building reverberated with collective roars of victory or groans of defeat. Twi-night doubleheaders cast an insomniac glow into our efficiency, and night after night my mother and I would lie sleepless, bathed in violet light, listening to megaphoned moans of "It's a homer! It's a homer!")

Golden, softly rounded, the old stadium had a Biblical look. I assumed it had been standing on 161st Street since before Christ. (Years later, when I saw the actual Roman Coliseum, I couldn't suppress an inner gasp of recognition: "Ahhh, it's like Yankee Stadium.")

My mother and I passed the stadium on our way to our separate destinations: she went to work, and I to nursery school. We breakfasted at a diner intended for baseball fans. Even off-season, hot dogs rotated on racks of anticipation. We were ravenous as lovers after a long night.

We had to say goodbye at the nursery schoolyard. She kissed me through the cyclone fence. The other girls lined up too, as their mothers filed past. The children competed: Whose mother was the prettiest? Cries of "Mine" echoed down the line. We ran along the fence to the last possible point of contact, then pursed our lips through the chainlink for "a last one." The mothers planted their kisses, then ran for the subway that took them to "jobs" in the great unknown of "downtown."

Uptown, caged into our reservation, the secret day began. Divided into age groups, threes, fours, and fives, we played at tribal rites, primitive as aborigines. The leader girls forced their followers into scatological ceremonies—to "make" in a carton, kept beyond the teachers' sightlines.

Elaborate scenarios were enacted. I assumed a second self, Deer Girl, a Sioux Indian maiden. As Deer Girl, I led hunting parties across the asphalt. There were enemy tribes afoot—even the noble Sioux were on the warpath.

During my first week in the nursery school, I staged an escape: With two other fives behind me, I scaled the fence, only to be recaptured by a guard. When my mother was told I led the insurrection, she said, "Lily always had leadership traits."

She gave me a costume, a Deer Girl dress: fringed and embroidered with the symbols of the rising sun and a crescent moon. In full regalia, I played Indians for hours at a stretch. There was nothing innocent in the game. (Why do adults talk about the "innocence of childhood"? All I remember is the intuitive guilt.) Without official knowledge of sex or death, we flirted with both. When we found a dying rat in the play yard, I saw a ribbon of excrement unfurling from its rear end, and announced that all living things left the world that way. (It may be true but how could I know?)

The boys were warriors, loved enemies, to be feared if no teacher was looking. It was understood that an unguarded moment was an opportunity for assault. We girls knew that if we encountered a boy in a secluded place he would either hit or kiss us, or perhaps want to watch us "make." In turn we tantalized them: swinging upside-down on the monkey bars, knowing our panties were "showing."

In all our Indian games, the girls fled from capture. I didn't understand the details of what would happen post-capture, but I knew enough to keep running. To be carried off would fulfill my wildest fears. I must fight, scratch, kick, then perhaps give into a frenzy that could not even be imagined.

We all feared being stripped. Threes and fours were stripped on a regular basis by more powerful, savvy fives. In the playground, the enemy was omnipresent, ready to pounce, tug down your panties, and "see."

As one of the faster girls in the nursery, I escaped being "seen," but protecting my "privates" was an almost full-time job. The school sanctioned more nudity than I would have allowed. The coed toilet—the BOYS commode beside the GIRLS—offended my sensibilities, and I conspired not to join the urinary lineups. Couldn't they put up a partition? In a similar spirit, in hot weather, we were expected to "change" into swimsuits "in front" of each other. Squirming on the linoleum floor, I wriggled off to a discreet corner, faced away from the crowd. I peed in a secret "club" carton (only a few select fives were allowed to use it) behind the schoolyard's lone bush, took to wearing my bathing suit "underneath."

Curiously, I was also modest at home. I asked my mother if I could wear my underpants in the bathtub. "Of course," she replied.

At kindergarten, I suffered a single, serious setback. One winter afternoon, I couldn't pull my pants back up, and had to hobble, bound by underwear at the ankle, into the public room. I was immediately taunted—as I knew I would be: "Look, she's wearing two pair." (Well, it was cold.)

I went to kindergarten as if into daily battle. There was only one respite: nap time, when we stretched out in rows of cots, like Civil War wounded.

After school, I often returned alone to the apartment, dense in its atmosphere of solitude. On many an afternoon I spent this time gazing into a terrarium on the windowsill. In this miniature glade, a china figurine—a girl—appeared to be pursued by a youth with a bow and arrow. I invented scenarios, with alternating plots. Sometimes she was fleeing the boy; at other times she was leading him to a secret forest. As this situation evolved, I rubbed the tiny vitreous china figures. Stories seemed to require gesture. As the chase accelerated, so did the massage. After a time, I wore the paint from their porcelain tunics, exposed the coarse white bas-relief. In a similar fashion, I often held a doll, and, without awareness of my actions, worked her plastic eyelids up and down. I owned a dozen "dollar" dolls, whose eyelids and limbs I dislocated: Cinderella developed a permanent astigmatism, and Snow White's arms were twisted round in their plastic sockets. I was hard on their costumes, too. During my agitated imaginings, I rubbed off the nap, leaving them threadbare across the breasts.

Apart from these small gestures, I sat quite still at the window sill, waiting for my mother to return from work. I peered into the terrarium "forest" or stared, unseeing, out onto the street. If darkness descended and my mother had not yet appeared, I became more alert. My heart hammered alarms, until I would see her at last—her wraparound coat flying open, as she ran down the street.

Sometimes, she caught me unawares, glassy-eyed in the twilight of the windowsill. I might gasp and blink: iridescent bubbles dotted the air. These bubbles were linked, like atoms, and it took a moment to clear the air and re-enter the spirit of our studio.

These temporary departures were my lone journeys to another place. Apart from the joy of being with my mother, these secret soarings were my most pleasant moments. A buzz in the blood, a reprieve from the dull tick-tock of real time—transports of delight.

I could not tell time. The symbols on the clock at school puzzled me. At home, the moving wands on our Emerson clock radio had a reverse effect: mesmerized, I lost more time than I found—hours could pass while I watched. But I did have some sense that the hands were intended to keep track. I knew the design for "three"—that was when school let out—and the straight line of "six" meant my mother should be home soon.

When not hypnotized in a sun-soaked stupor, I ran free in the neighborhood. Sometimes, I roamed alone, but more often I played with either Diana or Susan.

Diana and Susan were the only other girls on the loose in this part of town. All the other little girls were supervised, chaperoned to ballet or piano lessons.

Pleased to be victims of benign neglect ("We're so lucky no one watches us"), Diana, Susan, and I exceeded our mothers' wildest fears. We jumped from rooftop to rooftop, balanced on ledges, and swung from fire escapes. Daily we courted death and sexual disaster.

In those lost afternoons and early evenings, it was sometimes hard to choose between the radiance of daydreams and the equivalent adventure on the street. In each, there were impassioned pursuits, magical escapes. . . .

My mother didn't know the life I led in the interval from three to six. "You're careful, aren't you?" she asked.

And I always answered, innocent on a technicality: "I look both ways."

Every baseball season, Diana and I look forward to the annual visitation of the godlike Yankees, who march across Grand Concourse. The Yankees encamp in the area's only luxury hotel, the Concourse Plaza, which is a sports-oriented Ritz, covered in glitz. Everything that can be gilded has been. I can't imagine a more momentous event than the arrival of the Yankees at the Concourse Plaza. The Yankees—sturdy, handsome—seem to arrive to save us from some fate (as indeed they do—the economy of our neighborhood depends on the season).

Am I the only one who thinks Mickey Mantle may be more than mortal? His alliterative name, his batting average, the very word "Mantle"—all seem to imply he may be more than human. I regard Mickey Mantle as enjoying some in-between status—part human, part deity, all Yankee. (Is this wishful memory or did they really wash the street before he crossed it? I know they set down an actual red carpet. And why not?)

To an extent, I lead a baseball-dominated life. Not only does the stadium emit strange lights and sounds—my mother and I soon become accustomed to the twi-nights, accept them as naturally as Norsemen must have tolerated their endless days in the land of the midnight sun—but the entire neighborhood is designed around the sport. Bronze statuettes of baseball heroes pose at the intersections like signposts. I pass "Babe Ruth" on my way to school, meet Diana at Yogi Berra Plaza. Every day, I walk through an outdoor baseball hall of fame.

In season, the streets are clogged with fans; the entire neighborhood is redolent of frankfurter. Off-season, the area's exaggerated scale becomes a problem. The width of the avenues diminishes the residents, turning their ordinary outings to buy groceries into marathon treks. There's no doubt our area is designed for more dramatic events—a stage set for the multitudes.

It's disquieting to see the empty stadium. It too soon takes on the look of a ruin, evoking those ancient arenas of Greece and Rome, while seeming to presage a science-fiction forum of the future. Perhaps sensing this spiritual aura, the stadium owners take to leasing the arena, off season, to Evangelists and Jehovah's Witnesses. Sometimes a fundamentalist preacher can be heard blaring a call to Christ, which probably goes unheeded in this predominantly Jewish neighborhood.

Diana and I routinely invade any stadium event. We even sneak in when the arena stands empty to sniff up the atmosphere. There are rumors that Jehovah's Witnesses leave a "smell." There is a smell, not unpleasant but distinct. Tropical, like banana. "It's their hair oil," says Diana, an authority on these matters.

Beyond the stadium stands another building almost as magical: the Bronx County Courthouse. This mammoth structure squats, like a granite cake box, on the shelf of the Concourse. It features steep stone steps, for climbing, and larger-than-life bas-reliefs. We walk, sidewise, a hundred feet above the ground, pressed against stone figures, and cling to their carved coiffures for dear life.

There are two parks for Diana and me to explore. The first park is a flat cemented place, with a single attraction: the "Lorelei" fountain, a group of marble mermaids, whose bare breasts are a source of scandal in the area. All the children climb onto these mermaids' laps and rub their cold, bitten nipples. Diana and I often sit in a central seashell and finger the cracks.

The other park is known as the "dark park," for it is heavily wooded, and offers the only true shade in the area. The shade casts a psychic shadow as well.

We hear occasional screams from the foliage, and there are tales of people disappearing in there. Also: many accounts of sexual deviants, who possibly pop in and out of the park between arraignments at the courthouse across the street.

Nice people do not go inside the dark park. They sit, sentry-like, on benches at its exposed borders, too frightened to go in.

Diana is the only girl who ventures into the dark park. She dares me to go with her. I never go in without feeling a chill, never leave without experiencing the exhilaration of escape.

Diana shows me the footpaths, natural tunnels, and near caves. We enter the forest as an outdoor theatre: for a few hours of intense entertainment.

There is soon a price to pay for these tense pleasures. One afternoon we are deep in the trance of play. I am the Squaw, storing pods under a heavy-rooted tree. Diana has been scouting the woods for war parties. She creeps back to camp with whispered news: she has spotted a man with "it" out, wandering in agitated circles.

Always high-strung, Diana, on this day, is almost febrile. She has spoken to him, and reports that he will pay us a quarter "*just* to lower our underpants and show him."

I don't want to "show" him. Diana and I are not entirely innocent. We have, in fact, hung upside-down at a grate next to the Concourse Plaza, to peer into the men's room. We have also paid a fat five-year-old boy to pee. (He did, for a dime, in the privacy of a bus shelter.) But we've never been involved directly with an adult male.

Too soon, Diana is back with this sad-sack fellow in tow. Young, pale, wearing rimless glasses. He carries his penis in his hand as an injured part. Red as a frankfurter (which is what we call it: there's no choice in this neighborhood), his organ appears inflamed from constant friction. He has a tortured, tired expression. He's been out for hours, unable to find relief.

"A dollar," Diana insists, breathless as she states the overcharge. I look at her—we half-expect the man to refuse.

He agrees, in exhaustion, and Diana leads him to the darkest corner of our forest; a primordial place shadowed by evergreen and hemmed in by high boulders. Once in this natural crevice, our pervert drives his own bargain: we have to touch it.

A lesson follows. He demonstrates how to move the foreskin up and down. We do. He throws his head back, in agonized ecstasy, but sporadically turns petulant and delivers critiques in an objective tone: Slower. No. Not that way.

He says I don't do the job as well as Diana. He also expresses bitterness at my refusal to "show."

"Little bitch," he says, in a low, almost inaudible voice. He mutters, as if he were alone. (Maybe this is why grown men molest small girls—for privacy to be themselves without adult witness.)

He becomes increasingly in control of the situation. Diana ducks behind a tree and drops her drawers—for one second—then yanks them up again, demanding the dollar.

Not yet. He has her work on him, while I turn spectator. I watch what we call the "cream" splatter, lacquering his pants and a nearby boulder. This rock becomes our instant sexual landmark. For years afterward, Diana and I return to study the stone for signs of the event that has taken place.

"A dollar," Diana gloats. We can do anything, go anywhere, buy anything we want. The man slides back into the shadows, and Diana and I race for home. Then I remember a favorite red hat I was wearing (I picture it hanging on a twig) but decide, without knowing why, that it's not worth going back to retrieve.

Diana and I revise our stories, offer each other expurgated versions of what has just taken place. Even though we know the truth, we pretend to accept our respective explanations, which get increasingly elaborate the closer we get to home. "I didn't really feel his skin," I tell Diana, who had watched me touch him. "I had a leaf hidden in my hand." The leaf, I explain, separated my palm from his skin. Diana's story is even more elaborate and incorporates tree sap that she used to cover her palm, like varnish that sealed her flesh against his.

We spend the dollar on a French luxury ice cream, cherry vanilla, which we eat with the scrutiny of scientists, taking clinical care to excise the cherries and examine them. When my mother finds us bent over the gallon container, she wants to know how we paid for it. We tell tales of finding quarters on the street, exchanging soda bottles for deposits—then admit what happened.

"It's so ugly," I express *de facto* distaste.

"Not always," my mother says in a tone that gives me pause for thought. "When you love a man, it can be the most beautiful thing in the world."

She calls the police, and warns us away from the dark park. We go back anyway, but do not see "our" pervert again. We glimpse others. They seem to come out at dusk, opening their pants like night-blooming hibiscuses to reveal their pistils. Whenever I see that distant wrist motion, or a pale bobble in the shadows, I run the other way.

Diana takes off in the opposite direction. She works the territory for a profit. Soon she knows the local child molesters, and has regular "arrangements." She knows who's interested: At the corner cigar store, she disappears into a back room, and emerges with a pocketful of silver dollars. One afternoon, after she leaves, the proprietor takes a gun and blows off his head.

Diana does not editorialize. After all, she is five years old.

We find other ways to make money, some not too savory, but still an improvement. On Halloween, we stand in a cardboard carton that had contained a refrigerator, and use it as a fortunetelling booth. For a dime I tell any woman customer that she will fall in love and marry. If the woman already wears a wedding band, I predict my ultimate blessing: she will have babies.

On St. Patrick's Day, we fold green toilet paper into carnations, and sell them as corsages. Occasionally, we have honest enterprises, but more often we lead exciting lives of crime. Diana can sweep through the five-and-dime and emerge with half the jewelry counter. I have a more white-collar approach: I switch the price markers, go up to a sales clerk, and pay—at great discount. At the soda fountain, we slide other customers' change to our place. More elaborately, we wear fake Red Cross outfits, and rattle a can to collect for "charity." We spend everything on cherry vanilla ice cream or *Pez*.

Diana takes me to the "in" watering spot: Cascades, a swimming pool tucked directly under the Jerome Avenue El, the elevated train that roars to a distant graveyard that is the literal end of the line. At Cascades we lie on imported sand, beside turquoise water, and converse between trains. Our entire beach trembles, and we watch the incoming and outgoing subway cars, in lieu of surf. Still, Cascades is glamorous, with Turkish-tiled changing rooms and a sinus-clearing scent of chlorine. The poolside conversations sound as if they take place at the Cap d' Antibes: "Yes, we come every summer. It's so invigorating."

Diana teaches me to play hooky. We skip as many school days as we attend. Most often we appear in the morning, but duck out at lunchtime. Two five-year-olds on the street during school hours are as obvious as fleeing felons. We are always picked up, often within minutes, sometimes after movie-style chases.

One afternoon we head down to the river, to the Terminal Market, where we play hide-and-seek among the fruit crates. This is a desolate stretch of the city, a cement groin tucked under the bridge, where men slam hardballs. Diana and I are conspicuous—among the hardball set and the longshoremen. A police car appears, and two officers alight. Diana gives the neighborhood war cry: "Chickie shows!" and runs for her life. I run hard, but the first policeman catches me—a literal collar. Diana turns to see, and is seized. I always remember that if not for me she would have escaped. We are driven, in the back of the patrol car, and remanded to the custody of our kindergarten teacher. I could not feel more a felon.

It seems I am forever guilty. At school, I am routinely summoned to the principal's office, not to answer for my crimes but for my background: "Why is your name different from your father's?"

I feel scalded. I don't know. I say so, but feel as if I'm lying. I begin to invent more interesting answers, including one version in which my father is an Indian chief.

After school, on stoops or sitting on the neighborhood statuary, I keep up a running serial, invented for Diana. Diana listens, taking in my tale with licks of ice cream. As the story quickens, so does her ice-cream licking: we synchronize in our excitement.

I confide to Diana of my other life as Deer Girl, and my involvement with the brave, White Eagle. In most episodes, White Eagle is wounded and I must hide him from his enemies, and nurse him back to health. I usually hide him in a romantic spot—behind a waterfall. And in that damp declivity, mysteriously curtained off from the real world, White Eagle and I draw closer. Later, there are trips to the moon, where we are forced to dance naked in a crater, aboil with lava.

"Go on." Diana likes the idea of trips to the moon. She suggests I sell the story to a comic book.

We move from story to stage-acting. In the somnambulance of summer afternoons, Diana and I often retire to the privacy of 3M, there to sway and whisper of a near-erotic life we live, somewhere, as slaves. . . .

Linda Hogan 1947–

A prolific poet, novelist, playwright, essayist, and screenwriter, Linda Hogan was born of Chickasaw descent in Denver, Colorado. As a child growing up in Oklahoma, her father and grandparents imparted an appreciation for Native-American legends and the art of storytelling. Consequently, her writing uniquely combines the spiritual with the political, addressing feminist, environmental, antinuclear, and Native-American issues in a lyrical style that recognizes the sacred, mystical connection of the natural world and all its inhabitants. Hogan states, "I am interested in the deepest questions, those of spirit, of shelter, of growth and movement toward peace and liberation, inner and outer." She has authored numerous books of poetry, including *Seeing Through the Sun*, winner of the 1986 American Book Award and *Book of Medicines* (1993), which won the Colorado Book Award. Her first novel, *Mean Spirit* (1990), which depicts the U.S. government's illegal reclamation of oil-rich Osage reservation land, won three awards, as well as being a finalist for the Pulitzer Prize and the National Book Critics' Circle Award. Hogan is currently a professor in the English department at the University of Colorado.

LEAVING

Good-bye, divisions of people:
   those hickory-chopping,
   the hump hunters,
   skunk people
   dung people   5
   people who live under trees
   who live in broken houses
   and parts of houses.
   Their house worn out people
   are the meanest of all.   10

My house-cut-off people, I'm saying good-bye
to that person behind me.
She's the one
who tried to please her father,
the one an uncle loved for her dark hair.   15

White coyote behind me
light up your eyes, your white shadows,
your white round mouth

in its cage of black trees, a moon
running from branch to branch.   20
Moon that lives in the water,
snapping turtle that crawled out
at me.

Good-bye shooting horse
      above a dead man's grave.   25
Let that blessed rain
where fish descended from the sky
                              evaporate.

Silver lures, minnows
in that river who is the moon   30
living in a broken house,
who is the coyote
dwelling among the blackjack broken off
people, the turtle
who lives in its round white shell,   35
      I can tell you good-bye.

Good-bye to the carved bone beads
I found by the river. They can grow back
their flesh,
      their small beating hearts,   40
      air in the bones
      and gray wings they fly
      away from me.

Good-bye to the milky way
      who lives in his old worn out place,   45
      dog white
      his trail.

All my people are weeping
when I step out of my old skin
like a locust singing good-bye,   50
feet still clinging
to the black walnut tree.
They say I've burned all my brown sticks
for telling time
and still it passes away.   55

SONG FOR MY NAME

Before sunrise
think of brushing out an old woman's
dark braids.
Think of your hands,
fingertips on the soft hair.   5

If you have this name,
your grandfather's dark hands
lead horses toward the wagon
and a cloud of dust follows,
ghost of silence.   10

That name is full of women
with black hair
and men with eyes like night.
It means no money
tomorrow.   15

Such a name my mother loves
while she works gently
in the small house.
She is a white dove
and in her own land   20
the mornings are pale,
birds sing into the white curtains
and show off their soft breasts.

If you have a name like this,
there's never enough water.   25
There is too much heat.
When lightning strikes, rain
refuses to follow.
It's my name,
that of a woman living   30
between the white moon
and the red sun, waiting to leave.
It's the name that goes with me
back to earth
no one else can touch.   35

THE HANDS

The poor hands, overworked and dry,
dressing the body like maids
who button the lady's silk shirt
and fan her with their palms.

The poor palms   5
with their geography of lines.
One is broken,
another tells us, short life.

It is just like the hands
to tell their stories without shame.   10
Even held down, the white knucklebones
assert themselves through the skin.

Melissa Pritchard 1948–

Known primarily as a writer of short stories, Melissa Pritchard was born in
California and attended the University of California, Santa Barbara, as an
undergraduate and the University of New Mexico and Western Washington
University for graduate study. She has received numerous awards, including a
fellowship from the National Endowment for the Arts and the Flannery O'Connor
Award in Short Fiction. About her work, Pritchard has said, "I am fascinated by
mythology and science, by things of the physical world, by things of the spirit.
Writing fiction has become my center as well as my path outward."

THE INSTINCT FOR BLISS

Frances Waythorn, her face soured and ghastly as a mime's from a cosmetic
paste of yogurt, scrubs walls and wainscoting, praying for bleach, polish, order,
something, to check her daughter's latest slide from innocence. Pockets the Bic
lighter, so Athena can't smoke. Weasels under the bed, dredging out a feculent
nest of candy wrappers, cigarette butts, lewd notes, blood-soiled underwear, so
Athena won't get fat or have sex or die. Frances's motions are selfless and efficient, her behavior a worship extending into grief. She refuses to acknowledge
the poster of Jim Morrison. If she follows her own heat, stripping his deviant's

baby face off the wall above her daughter's bed, who knows what might happen. Mothers like Frances are no longer immune from the retaliation of their daughters. Her face beginning to itch under the dried yogurt, Frances swivels a plush bunny into the center of the eyelet-edged pillow. Her child's room is pulled back, once again, into an immaculate relief of white, except for the poster, unexpungeable as a stain.

Athena, legally halved, is batted lightly between her parents. On alternate weeks she is not at her father's, she resides with Frances, her white room declining into a dank, fetid emporium of sloth. Those Sunday afternoons when Athena arrives, a canny refugee, on her mother's doorstep, a soiled, lumpy pillowcase of belongings over one shoulder, declaring she is an atheist who has drunk the blood of stray cats, Frances's labor, much like that of Sisyphus, begins anew, no hope for reprieve, only the diligent loosening of familiar, defiant knots.

Frances is, in fact, uncrumpling and reading, rereading Athena's smutty notes before packing for her drive to a Navajo wool workshop, when the doorbell rings. Hollering "Wait", then "Sorry," unlocking the door, her face dripping water and patchy, as if with plaster, she sees he has a lovely, surprisingly tender face, this Officer Ruiz, telling her Athena is at the police station with another girl, arrested for shoplifting. He has been busy, attempting to notify the girls' parents. (Guiltily, Frances remembers three distinct times the phone rang as she scavenged under Athena's bed.)

"Where in God's name is her father? She's staying with him this week."

"Ma'am, from what your daughter claims, Mr. Waythorn is in Albuquerque until tomorrow.

He then informs Frances she can come get Athena or agree to her being held overnight in juvenile detention.

"Of course I'll get her, though I am about to leave for Arizona. What about the other girl?" Frances asks, not really caring, angry that once again, and predictably, Athena's father has left her in the dark, told her nothing of his plans, neglected his daughter and spoiled her own small hope for independence.

"Her parents have requested she be held overnight."

"In the Taos jail? Good lord. At their age I was in a convent. Reciting Shakespeare. Doing as I was told. Though Athena's father was a delinquent, a truant, he's boasted that often enough."

Frances's tone is bitter as if she had known him even then, as if she had been harmed, even then, by her husband's arrant boyhood.

So far, Frances decides, this driving across the hammered-flat desert is largely a matter of virulent silence.

Athena catches at a shifting avalanche of cassettes falling from her lap.

"May I play the Red Hot Chili Peppers? Their lyrics are banned." With Frances, almost any "Mother May I?" works.

"Banned?" Frances attends carefully, thinks she identifies the phrase *donkey juice* shouted over and over.

"I can't clearly make them out, honey. The words."

Pleased, Athena spritzes her face and arms with water from the plastic spray bottle she's brought, fogging herself like some fragile, costly plant.

"Want some?"

Tepid mist hits Frances, wetting her face. She has a pale rash from the yogurt.

Right now she would rather feed than punish Athena, pad her with double cheeseburgers, damp fries, chocolate shakes. If she's fat, no boy will want to have sex with her. If she's fat, she might not steal. Possibly no one but her mother will want her. She casts a look at Athena, the combat boots, unpolished and heavy looking as bricks, shredded jeans, black tank top, the front of her hair in two taffetalike maroon flaps, the back of her head a shaved greenish stubble. The starlike design inked onto her upper arm, Frances is afraid to ask if it is a satanic emblem or simply the declaration of an atheist. What if Athena belongs to a cult, a gang? Frances remembers the heavyset woman in a purple tunic on Oprah Winfrey, sobbing, saying you never, ever, know what your children do once they leave the house, you think you do, but you don't. Her son had been machine-gunned outside the front door. Actually, it is Frances whose stomach is bloating, whose thighs have widened.

"Ma-Maah." Athena says it like a doll. "Where are you heisting me?"

"To a workshop on dyeing wool. I signed up for it at an arts fair last month, a freak impulse because I've never woven or dyed a thing in my life. But, Athena, at my age, let me tell you, inventing a new life is no zip-i-dee-doo-dah flick of the wrist."

"May I drive?"

"No."

"Pleeze, Ma-Mah? Dad lets me drive his truck sometimes."

"Absolutely not. You're supposed to be in jail. And your father's decisions, as you well know, are never mine. Look how he's abandoned you."

"He lets me do what I want, that's different. It is grotesque out here, Ma-Maaah."

"Really? I think it has its own beauty. Deserts are spiritual places. Points of transcendence."

This observation rebounds, stilted. And why is Athena talking to her like a rubber doll?

"A couple of things we're to remember when we get there. Can you lower that a bit?"

Athena blunts, reluctantly, her music.

"When you're introduced, you're not to look any of the Navajos directly in the eye."

"Why not?"

"They consider it overly intimate."

"Cool."

Frances glances over. She never knows what will be cool or why.

"A simple enough thing for you."

"What?"

"You never look me in the eye, Athena. Not anymore."

"Not." She pins her mother with a look startlingly lethal.

"Is that genuine? That's frightening."

Athena shrugs. "What was the other thing? You said there were two."

"Fish. You can't eat fish around them. Navajos believe fish are embryonic, unformed humans, something like that. I can't remember. It's in here"— Frances pats the guidebook on Navajo culture she has brought, largely unread.

"Fish sticks make me puke anyways."

"Anyway."

"Any-waaaays. . . ."

With the toe of her boot, Athena turns up the banned, incoherent lyrics.

What finally wakes her, after the others are up, is a sullen drone of flies along the heat-warped window ledge. In a white plastic bucket, blacking the surface of their drinking water, is an uneven rug of drowned flies. A single fly still walks, if walking, she wonders, is how to describe it, along the battered lip of a tin cup. Frances rolls her sleeping bag next to Athena's, against one of the eight cinder-block walls of the hogan. She hasn't the least idea how to function in a Native American environment, but neatness is never an error. Manners are the same the world over, to quote her mother, and politeness, not sex, the true mortar of civilization. Frances's resolve, now that she is divorced against her will, is to "follow her bliss," a phrase she'd recently heard at a Wild Women of the West seminar, where one of the most astonishing things she had participated in was humping the earth to release pent-up male energy. This is why she has driven all the way out here, to a Navajo reservation. On instinct for bliss. She hasn't the least experience with dyeing wool or weaving anything. She can't even sew. What attracted her was being told this would be a place where, temporarily, no men were allowed.

Scraping open the wood door, Frances sees her red car parked under the yard light, haughtily disassociated from the three trucks, two of which have I ♥ SHEEP stickers on their bumpers while her car has a blue sticker, stuck there by Athena, an upside-down cow on it saying MEAT IS DEAD. Athena had left the window on her side down, and with the car so close to the hogan, Frances sees a ratty-tailed, saffron rooster patrolling the front seat, back and forth, back and forth, its flat eye proprietary and arrogant.

"Hey Ma-mah, coffee."

Athena holds out a green, chipped mug; she's wearing yesterday's clothes, her mouth smeared a pinkish mahogany, a beauty dot penciled above the bow of her top lip. Over Athena's bare shoulder, if she squinches up her eyes, Frances can make out a half circle of Navajo women bent over an animal of some sort, trussed and quivering on its back.

"Ma-Mah, poke on your glasses. You need to see this. They're going to kill a sheep."

Before leaving the hogan, neatly dressed in ironed jeans and a white-fringed, turquoise sweatshirt, Frances, her eyeglasses on, hesitates before a Navajo loom, its cotton warp a pale and tranquil lyre rising up from the muted, traditional design. Cocoons of wrapped yarn hang neatly along the rug's perfect edge, where the weaver stopped. Reluctant to go outside, Frances traces the design's black fretwork with one slowed finger, out to its edge.

She drinks her coffee, sitting on the ground beside a small cedar fire that burns with tallowy, weak effect in the morning sunlight. The grandmother squats behind the animal's throat, in a wide, pink-fanning skirt, red argyle socks and tennis shoes, her skirt the same medicinal pink as the outhouse, angled downhill as if it might tumble any time, exposing whoever sits, misfortunate, inside. Athena stands near the workshop instructor, a young Navajo woman named Valencia, who brushes a cedar branch, in blessing, over the animal. The grandmother, a white kerchief splashed with red roses concealing most of her face, pulls hard on its head, twists it, breaking the neck, then saws her long knife like a resined bow so blood sprays then spills with a green rushing of spring into a low white bowl, and the animal's bowels loose a sheen of dung onto the flat, colorless ground.

The fleece is split into a kind of jacket, its creamy lining veined with rich coral. The carcass still cinched within its parchment membrane, legs splayed four airy directions, suggests to Frances, except for the knob of breast, an upside-down table, fit to work on. The head, facing Frances, is set down in the fire. One eye swells, a black, glazed plum, the other sears and spits shut. The yellow wool blackens, crisps, stinks. Now the spirit of the animal is released from all boundaries everywhere.

This placid slaughter consoles Frances. A useful dismemberment, ritualized and strangely clean. The carcass squarely hung by hind feet from a cedar pole near the outdoor kitchen, the parchment membrane flensed back, the pursy insides unlocked, emptied out. The wine brown brooch of liver, for Frances goes to touch it, like warm sea glass. The taupe-gray skeins of intestine are pulled and stretched, the Navajo women pour hot water through the lengthened guts from an old tin coffeepot, squeezing and dribbling out the dung colored stuff. A ripe jewelling of ruby and pewter, pearled matter, a supple kingdom falling over the plain hard canvas of dirt, the dull, droughted, troubled-seeming earth spotted with blood like vital specklings of rain. The stomach with its sallow chenille lining, the drying gloss of lungs, liver, kidneys, draped over a narrow pole. And rising under the callus of blood in the milky flat-faced dish, like a mineral pool, strings of bubbles, a languorous spitting of bubbles, as if something deep under its weight still breathed.

Frances studies these women, the practical details of their butchering, their reverent pulling apart of a life and making it into other, smaller, useful things.

Two emergency room nurses from Lubbock are the only other participants in this workshop, and Frances has made no effort to talk to either one of them.

A Married Rule, that pretense of sociability. The nurses, both skinny, both earnest and, for some reason, wan looking, stick close to the Navajo women, speak in enthusiastic twangings. Frances prays she doesn't resemble them, though she has signed up and paid for this experience, is conscious of being that evil necessity, a tourist with money to purchase a 3-D postcard, Navajo Women at Work on the Reservation. She wants to tell these Indian women she understands, but what is it she understands, and does she?

"Maa, Maaah. . . ."

Bleating, Athena shuffles outside the tilting outhouse, her nose pinched shut.

"You realize there are no males here. None. Except the sheep, and we've just killed him. When we eat him, he'll be gone, too."

"Oh, there are men." Frances's voice is muffled, weary. "Always and eternally there are men." She steps out of the terrible-smelling pink box. "My intent, Athena, was to go somewhere where, for once, there weren't any. And where the Navajo men who usually live here have gone. I can't imagine. I'm sure it's rude to ask."

They walk back down the slope, Frances whacking at her dusty pants. White pants. What had she been thinking?

"I need some smokes. I have to go into town."

"Town. For heaven's sake, Athena. Look where we are."

"Well, a trading post then. Plus I gotta wash my hair, it's getting completely gross. There's a bathroom in their house, I went in and found it, but no water. You turn the faucets and air spits out. There's not even water in the toilet."

"There's a bad drought. I heard Valencia saying it's got something to do with the strip mining, with slurry water the mines use. All month they've been hauling water from town."

"These people should move to where there's more trees, more water. God." Athena narrows her eyes over the arid, hopeless, scrabbly landscape, blowing mournful smoke from her last cigarette. "Look. That dumb chicken's still on your front seat."

Athena runs, arms flapping, cigarette dangling, to swat the rooster out of the car. The Navajo women stop what they're doing to look, and Frances cannot interpret their faces. She jogs to catch up. She had looked forward to this trip by herself. She had hoped to learn something, or at least stop thinking about what exhausts and obsesses her. Now, looking into Athena's bright, provocative face, Frances sees how precisely, like a scissor cut, it matches her own at that age.

"Athena. You have to behave yourself. When you're the guest of another culture, you blend in, you ask intelligent questions."

"I am. I'm going to ask where the nearest store is and where the men are stashed."

"Athena."

"What."

"Please."

"What."

"You could be in prison right now. I could have left you there until your father decided to come and get you."

"Yada yada yada."

"What were you stealing?"

"Undies."

"Underwear? I just bought you plenty of" —

"Sexy underwear, Ma. You've never bought me that."

"May I ask you a simple question? What makes you so sure you are Jim Morrison's wife reincarnated?"

"You're the one who told me about reincarnation."

"Yes, but you can't just make up who you wish you had been. Oh, wouldn't I love to think I was once Thomas Jefferson or Sarah Bernhardt or even Beatrix Potter."

"Thomas Jefferson?"

"I've always wanted to be Thomas Jefferson. Do you know who I was in love with at your age?"

"Dad?"

Frances pauses dramatically. "Carl Sandburg."

"Who's that?"

"He's dead now, but he was a famous poet. I wrote Carl Sandburg several passionate letters. He was in his seventies."

"Cool. Mom in love with an old dude."

"I never mailed them. I knew he had a wife and a goat farm in North Carolina and probably he was happy."

"What about Dad? Oh, never mind. You'll just say something nasty. You're in that stage now."

"Stage?"

"Of divorce. Denial, rage, stuff like that."

"Where'd you pick up that idea?"

"Dad. He has books on divorce. Just like you."

"The same books?"

"Yup. Exactly. You guys are exactly alike."

Right, Frances thinks. Except he's chosen someone else. He's betrayed me.

Doing as she is asked, Athena drags the charred head from the fire by one gristled ear, sets it on a wood block, scrapes off filings of ash with a stick so the head can be wrapped and baked. And when she is certain her mother sees, for isn't her mother always watching, spying, jealous, easy to fool, a cinch to scare, so give her something to really be wigged about, Athena swoops one finger across the bowl of dulling blood and drives it deep into her own mouth. Not long after that, Frances will stand in the parrot yellow kitchen, stuffing gray, salted mutton into her mouth until the women, laughing, caution her to stop, until they stop laughing and take the plate away, saying this will make her sick. Mutton hunger is what they will say she has.

After lunch, they ride in the nurses' truck to the base of a sort of mountain. Everybody gets a plastic grocery sack. They are to follow the grandmother, collect twigs, leaves, roots and mosses, plants Valencia names for them, mullein, lichen, sumac, mountain mahogany, chamiso.

Athena lags behind with the more tired looking nurse, while Frances tracks the grandmother, what she can of her, two red argyled ankles flashing up a rigorous incline. Frances slows from the midday heat, the altitude, the enervating whiteness of the sun. In every direction, sealike troughs of land push up clumps of piñon and cedar, like rich, bronze-green kelp. A hawk skates the air above her in fluid, mahogany curls.

Frances nearly trips over the grandmother, crouched by a blunt formation of black rock, on her knees with a table knife, chipping chrome yellow powder from the rock and dusting it off her hands into a plastic bag.

Valencia looks up kindly. "We use this to get our black, mixing it with piñon pitch and cedar ash. It's pretty hard to find, but Grandmother is amazing, she goes right to where it is."

The taller nurse stands like a sentinel, a lank poplar, behind Frances.

"That stuff looks like uranium. Exactly."

Frances takes her turn scraping, grazing her knuckles; the uranium idea has unnerved her.

"You could hike up here once a year, get a gigantic load of this stuff to last you."

Frances thinks no one has heard, though the nurse's voice is tactless enough. The grandmother is resting in the compressed, thick shade of a piñon tree, while Valencia, wiping sweat from her forehead, answers, a perceptible teacher's edge to her voice.

"We take only what is needed each time. And Grandmother has taught us to leave an offering, a gift, before separating anything from where it is found."

"Halllooooo!" Athena, her arms making rapid pinwheeling motions, appears to be urging them up to the next highest ledge. Frances is busy, spit-washing a smudge of uranium off her turquoise shirt.

When the three white women attain the highest ledge, they hold their plastic bags of roots and twigs, panting, confounded by what they see. Inches deep across the ground lay thousands of pottery shards. The women, winded, hot-faced, are told they are standing on a trash dump, where Anasazi Indians, centuries ago, had thrown their broken pots and garbage.

The Navajo women sit and rest, observe the three white women stooping and bobbing, pecking about for bits of clay, their arms blooming with what they cannot seem to gather up fast enough. At first, the women call back and forth excitedly, then lapse into quiet, the weight of anthropology, the burden of choosing among priceless relics falling almost gloomily upon them. Like children, their greed eventually tires them, and they become aware of the Navajo women, quietly watching. They stop, arms and pockets and bags loaded down, their small congress embarrassed, bits of pottery dropping off them like leaves.

"Perhaps just two or three," says one nurse.

"Those that mean the most," suggests the other.

As Frances sets down her cumbersome pile, Athena, who had wandered off, returns. Between her hands, rests a large, perfect potshard, a black lightning streak down its reddish, curved flank. Exclaiming over its size and near-perfect condition, Frances begins to thank Athena, grateful for the largeness of gesture, the love implied.

"It's for Dad," Athena says softly. "I wanted to bring him something."

"Oh." Frances drops to her knees, shuffling through her little clay bits, as if to choose.

"Did you leave an offering?"

"Yuppers. My last cigarette, one I copped from the nurse."

On the ride back, they stop beside a faded sprawl of prickly pear to pick its mushy, red fruits for pink dye. The driving nurse, feeling unwell, decides to drive to the trading post for stomach medicine. Both nurses drop the women back at the hogan except for Athena, who's begged a ride.

Frances labors alongside her instructor, hefting enamelware kettles and a halved oil drum filled with hauled water, onto different fires. She sorts through gathered plant materials, carries bags and baskets of hand-spun wool skeins out from the hogan, admires Valencia's long, black hair, twisted in a shining bundle at the nape of her neck, noting its resemblance to the skeins of wool, to the little bundles of yarn dangling from the edge of the rug inside the hogan. She wonders how Valencia would raise a daughter, how do the women raise teenagers out here, how, in her own case, could things get much worse.

Swirling the stained waters with an ashy stick, made sleepy by the steam of plants, bitter or sweet smelling, or dense as soured earth, Frances begins to hope Athena might not return until much, much later.

At once she hears the truck, observes it dipping and rising over the rutted gullies, with Athena, cross-legged in the bed of the truck, in a somber corona of dust, brandishing a cigarette. As her daughter trips unsteadily past her, blowing smoke out both nostrils, her maroon hair tangled and shreddy-looking, Frances studies the shaven back of her head so disturbingly infantlike; watches her wobble around a cast-iron pot of chamiso dye, right herself, then pitch behind one side of the hogan and begin, audibly, to vomit.

One of the nurses comes up to Frances.

"I found this in the truck bed."

Frances stares at the half-empty bottle.

The bottle lodged under her arm, Frances uses a peeled stick to raise out of the water one of the skeins of yarn. It hangs from the end of the willow stick, a twist, an eight, of deep, ardent gold.

Worse than finding Athena on the ground, is seeing the rooster, pecking with cold disregard, at her daughter's vomit. Frances is about to kick the rooster, when suddenly, admitting nature's genius, she leaves it to clean the mess Athena has once again made of things.

"G'way." Athena's tattooed arm takes a sodden, backwards sweep at the air. "G'way, stupid."

Her profile, smooshed into the ground, is a mask of vomit and dirt.

"All right. I will go away. I will go get something to wash your filthy face with. You disappoint me, Athena."

Athena's visible eye stays blearily fixed on the rooster.

Inside the dim, stifling hogan, Frances finds the one available cloth, her pink western bandanna. The only water she knows of is in the white plastic bucket. Biting her bottom lip, plunging her arm deep to wet the bandanna, she has to shake off the burred sleeve of flies. She stands quiet before the loom, an object of great dignity, a pursuit, elusive to Frances, of stillness and purpose. Hadn't she tried to make their marriage like that, into fine cloth, enduring design?

Balling up the tepid pink bandanna, wringing it hard, she squats behind Athena, turning her head and wiping her soiled face. As she scrubs under her daughter's chin, a muddy backwash of rage hits.

"There." She throws down the stained rag. "You find something to do with that. I'm taking our things to the car. We're going home, not that either of us has much of a home anymore."

As she finishes stuffing the trunk with their few things, Frances hears the nurse, the one who had shown her the half-empty whiskey bottle, behind her.

"Mrs. Waythorn, your daughter took off running that way. If you take the car, you'll catch up to her. It won't be dark for another fifteen minutes."

The woman's voice is nurse-like, so merciful, so professionally equipped for trauma, Frances wants to collapse against her ordinary sweatshirt, her calm and practical shoulder. She wants to say oh you take care of this, somebody else manage this, I only want to rest.

Even in the drought-smeared violet light, Frances easily makes out the skinny speck of her daughter shambling along the gravel and dirt road. In the middle of nowhere. Going nowhere.

As her car creeps closer, Frances, seeing Athena's set, miserable profile, does a most unexpected thing. She pumps hard on the accelerator and shoots past her daughter, steering with great angry lurches and radical swerves, up over the crest of a small hill and down.

She stops, exhilarated, considering what she has done. Abandoned her daughter. Gone beyond her. Swooped by. Yes.

The top of her foot has a dark wetted gash across it. Athena's potshard, the gift for her father, has rolled off the seat and smashed into pieces around her foot. Frances rests her forehead on the steering wheel. After a long while, she becomes aware of darkness. My god. She switches on the light overhead, lifts up to see the top third of her face in the little mirror. Smeared with dirt, tears, old mascara. Her pants, too, ruined. Her shirt, poisoned with uranium.

Wildly, she feels for the ignition, in a panic, shoves into reverse, backs up the car, coasts down the little hill she'd concealed herself behind.

Frances gets out of the car, sees blurrily, a mile or so away, the mercury yard light she had aimed for the night before. Hears, as if it isn't hers anymore, the sound of weeping.

The car light switched on, Frances is on her knees, searching under the seats, trying to gather back pieces of the clay pot. On the day she had been scrubbing down her child's room, on the day of her daughter's arrest, she had found, while on her belly under Athena's bed, a green cardboard shoe box. Inside were the souvenirs Frances had kept hidden from everyone. The dry, yellowish triangle of Athena's umbilical cord, a wavy, black shank of her ex-husband's hair, the auburn braid of her mother's hair, cut six months before she'd died, and like twin, eerie rattles, two tiny boxes of Frances's own ivoried baby teeth. Athena, searching through her mother's secret things, had taken, out of instinct or curiosity, all she needed.

"Ma-Mah? What is it? What are you doing?"

"My foot's cut."

"Poorest Mommy. You can't drive, bleeding and crying like that. Shh, shh, okay, shh. I'll help you. Shh."

Stripping off, wrapping the black tank top around her mother's foot, Athena, not bothering to ask, gets her old wish to drive. And as the desert night covers, uncovers her white, scarcely touched breasts, as her mother guards, unyielding, the broken potshards. Athena will piece together a stubborn, defiantly remembered, child's way home.

Leslie Marmon Silko   1948–

Considered one of the premier American writers of her generation, Leslie Marmon Silko weaves the real and the mythic into tales that reflect traditional Native-American concepts of nature, spirituality, and time and their relevance in a modern setting. Born in Albuquerque, New Mexico, of Laguna Pueblo, Mexican, and Anglo-American heritage, Silko's fiction concentrates on mixbloods' struggles to define their identity while caught in between two cultures: one that virtually no longer exists and one that does not yet offer full access. In 1981, she was one of twenty-one "exceptionally talented individuals" to be recognized by the MacArthur Foundation as "geniuses"; she subsequently received a five-year award of support. In novels, short stories, poetry, legendary tales, and screenwriting (Silko wrote the screenplay for Marlon Brando's *Black Elks*), she both celebrates and defines her Laguna community. Some of her many works include *Ceremony* (1978), *Storyteller* (1981), and her most recent, *Gardens in the Dunes: A Novel* (1998). Silko has been writer-in-residence at Vassar College as well as an English professor at the University of Arizona and at her alma mater, the University of New Mexico.

LULLABY

The sun had gone down but the snow in the wind gave off its own light. It came in thick tufts like new wool—washed before the weaver spins it. Ayah reached out for it like her own babies had, and she smiled when she remembered how she had laughed at them. She was an old woman now, and her life had become memories. She sat down with her back against the wide cottonwood tree, feeling the rough bark on her back bones; she faced east and listened to the wind and snow sing a high-pitched Yeibechei song. Out of the wind she felt warmer, and she could watch the wide fluffy snow fill in her tracks, steadily, until the direction she had come from was gone. By the light of the snow she could see the dark outline of the big arroyo a few feet away. She was sitting on the edge of Cebolleta Creek, where in the springtime the thin cows would graze on a grass already chewed flat to the ground. In the wide deep creek bed where only a trickle of water flowed in the summer, the skinny cows would wander, looking for new grass along winding paths splashed with manure.

Ayah pulled the old Army blanket over her head like a shawl. Jimmie's blanket—the one he had sent to her. That was a long time ago and the green wool was faded, and it was unraveling on the edges. She did not want to think about Jimmie. So she thought about the weaving and the way her mother had done it. On the tall wooden loom set into the sand under a tamarack tree for shade. She could see it clearly. She had been only a little girl when her grandma gave her the wooden combs to pull the twigs and burrs from the raw, freshly washed wool. And while she combed the wool, her grandma sat beside her, spinning a silvery strand of yarn around the smooth cedar spindle. Her mother worked at the loom with yarns dyed bright yellow and red and gold. She watched them dye the yarn in boiling black pots full of beeweed petals, juniper berries, and sage. The blankets her mother made were soft and woven so tight that rain rolled off them like birds' feathers. Ayah remembered sleeping warm on cold windy nights, wrapped in her mother's blankets on the hogan's sandy floor.

The snow drifted now, with the northwest wind hurling it in gusts. It drifted up around her black overshoes—old ones with little metal buckles. She smiled at the snow which was trying to cover her little by little. She could remember when they had no black rubber overshoes; only the high buckskin leggings that they wrapped over their elkhide moccasins. If the snow was dry or frozen, a person could walk all day and not get wet; and in the evenings the beams of the ceiling would hang with lengths of pale buckskin leggings, drying out slowly.

She felt peaceful remembering. She didn't feel cold any more. Jimmie's blanket seemed warmer than it had ever been. And she could remember the morning he was born. She could remember whispering to her mother, who was sleeping on the other side of the hogan, to tell her it was time now. She did not want to wake the others. The second time she called to her, her mother stood up and pulled on her shoes; she knew. They walked to the old stone hogan together, Ayah walking a step behind her mother. She waited alone, learning the rhythms of the pains while her mother went to call the old woman to help them. The morning was already warm even before dawn and Ayah smelled the bee flowers blooming and the young willow growing at the springs. She could remember that so clearly, but his birth merged into the births of the other children and to her it became all the same birth. They named him for the summer morning and in English they called him Jimmie.

It wasn't like Jimmie died. He just never came back, and one day a dark blue sedan with white writing on its doors pulled up in front of the boxcar shack where the rancher let the Indians live. A man in a khaki uniform trimmed in gold gave them a yellow piece of paper and told them that Jimmie was dead. He said the Army would try to get the body back and then it would be shipped to them; but it wasn't likely because the helicopter had burned after it crashed. All of this was told to Chato because he could understand English. She stood inside the doorway holding the baby while Chato listened. Chato spoke English like a white man and he spoke Spanish too. He was taller than the white man and he stood straighter too. Chato didn't explain why; he just told the military man they could keep the body if they found it. The white man looked bewildered; he nodded his head and he left. Then Chato looked at her and shook his head, and then he told her, "Jimmie isn't coming home any more," and when he spoke, he used the words to speak of the dead. She didn't cry then, but she hurt inside with anger. And she mourned him as the years passed, when a horse fell with Chato and broke his leg, and the white rancher told them he wouldn't pay Chato until he could work again. She mourned Jimmie because he would have worked for his father then; he would have saddled the big bay horse and ridden the fence lines each day, with wire cutters and heavy gloves, fixing the breaks in the barbed wire and putting the stray cattle back inside again.

She mourned him after the white doctors came to take Danny and Ella away. She was at the shack alone that day they came. It was back in the days before they hired Navajo women to go with them as interpreters. She recognized one of the doctors. She had seen him at the children's clinic at Cañoncito about a month ago. They were wearing khaki uniforms and they waved papers at her and a black ball-point pen, trying to make her understand their English words. She was frightened by the way they looked at the children, like the lizard watches the fly. Danny was swinging on the tire swing on the elm tree behind the rancher's house, and Ella was toddling around the front door, dragging the broomstick horse Chato made for her. Ayah could see they wanted her to sign the papers, and Chato had taught her to sign her name. It was something she was proud of. She only wanted them to go, and to take their eyes away from her children.

She took the pen from the man without looking at his face and she signed the papers in three different places he pointed to. She stared at the ground by their feet and waited for them to leave. But they stood there and began to point and gesture at the children. Danny stopped swinging. Ayah could see his fear. She moved suddenly and grabbed Ella into her arms; the child squirmed, trying to get back to her toys. Ayah ran with the baby toward Danny; she screamed for him to run and then she grabbed him around his chest and carried him too. She ran south into the foothills of juniper trees and black lava rock. Behind her she heard the doctors running, but they had been taken by surprise, and as the hills became steeper and the cholla cactus were thicker, they stopped. When she reached the top of the hill, she stopped to listen in case they were circling around her. But in a few minutes she heard a car engine start and they drove away. The children had been too surprised to cry while she ran with them. Danny was shaking and Ella's little fingers were gripping Ayah's blouse.

She stayed up in the hills for the rest of the day, sitting on a black lava boulder in the sunshine where she could see for miles all around her. The sky was light blue and cloudless, and it was warm for late April. The sun warmth relaxed her and took the fear and anger away. She lay back on the rock and watched the sky. It seemed to her that she could walk into the sky, stepping through clouds endlessly. Danny played with little pebbles and stones, pretending they were birds eggs and then little rabbits. Ella sat at her feet and dropped fistfuls of dirt into the breeze, watching the dust and particles of sand intently. Ayah watched a hawk soar high above them, dark wings gliding; hunting or only watching, she did not know. The hawk was patient and he circled all afternoon before he disappeared around the high volcanic peak the Mexicans called Guadalupe.

Late in the afternoon, Ayah looked down at the gray boxcar shack with the paint all peeled from the wood; the stove pipe on the roof was rusted and crooked. The fire she had built that morning in the oil drum stove had burned out. Ella was asleep in her lap now and Danny sat close to her, complaining that he was hungry; he asked when they would go to the house. "We will stay up here until your father comes," she told him, "because those white men were chasing us." The boy remembered then and he nodded at her silently.

If Jimmie had been there he could have read those papers and explained to her what they said. Ayah would have known then, never to sign them. The doctors came back the next day and they brought a BIA policeman with them. They told Chato they had her signature and that was all they needed. Except for the kids. She listened to Chato sullenly; she hated him when he told her it was the old woman who died in the winter, spitting blood; it was her old grandma who had given the children this disease. "They don't spit blood," she said coldly.

"The whites lie." She held Ella and Danny close to her, ready to run to the hills again. "I want a medicine man first," she said to Chato, not looking at him. He shook his head. "It's too late now. The policeman is with them. You signed the paper." His voice was gentle.

It was worse than if they had died: to lose the children and to know that somewhere, in a place called Colorado, in a place full of sick and dying strangers, her children were without her. There had been babies that died soon after they were born, and one that died before he could walk. She had carried them herself, up to the boulders and great pieces of the cliff that long ago crashed down from Long Mesa; she laid them in the crevices of sandstone and buried them in fine brown sand with round quartz pebbles that washed down the hills in the rain. She had endured it because they had been with her. But she could not bear this pain. She did not sleep for a long time after they took her children. She stayed on the hill where they had fled the first time, and she slept rolled up in the blanket Jimmie had sent her. She carried the pain in her belly and it was fed by everything she saw: the blue sky of their last day together and the dust and pebbles they played with; the swing in the elm tree and broomstick horse choked life from her. The pain filled her stomach and there was no room for food or for her lungs to fill with air. The air and the food would have been theirs.

She hated Chato, not because he let the policeman and doctors put the screaming children in the government car, but because he had taught her to sign her name. Because it was like the old ones always told her about learning their language or any of their ways: it endangered you. She slept alone on the hill until the middle of November when the first snows came. Then she made a bed for herself where the children had slept. She did not lie down beside Chato again until many years later, when he was sick and shivering and only her body could keep him warm. The illness came after the white rancher told Chato he was too old to work for him anymore, and Chato and his old woman should be out of the shack by the next afternoon because the rancher had hired new people to work there. That had satisfied her. To see how the white man repaid Chato's years of loyalty and work. All of Chato's fine-sounding English talk didn't change things.

It snowed steadily and the luminous light from the snow gradually diminished into the darkness. Somewhere in Cebolleta a dog barked and other village dogs joined with it. Ayah looked in the direction she had come, from the bar where Chato was buying the wine. Sometimes he told her to go on ahead and wait; and then he never came. And when she finally went back looking for him, she would find him passed out at the bottom of the wooden steps at Azzie's Bar. All the wine would be gone and most of the money too, from the pale blue check that came to them once a month in a government envelope. It was then that she would look at his face and his hands, scarred by ropes and the barbed wire of all those years, and she would think, this man is a stranger; for forty years she had smiled at him and cooked his food, but he remained a stranger. She stood up again, with the snow almost to her knees, and she walked back to find Chato.

It was hard to walk in the deep snow and she felt the air burn in her lungs. She stopped a short distance from the bar to rest and readjust the blanket. But this time he wasn't waiting for her on the bottom step with his old Stetson hat pulled down and his shoulders hunched up in his long wool overcoat.

She was careful not to slip on the wooden steps. When she pushed the door open, warm air and cigarette smoke hit her face. She looked around slowly and deliberately, in every corner, in every dark place that the old man might find to sleep. The bar owner didn't like Indians in there, especially Navajos, but he let Chato come in because he could talk Spanish like he was one of them. The men at the bar stared at her, and the bartender saw that she left the door open wide. Snowflakes were flying inside like moths and melting into a puddle on the oiled wood floor. He motioned to her to close the door, but she did not see him. She held herself straight and walked across the room slowly, searching the room with every step. The snow in her hair melted and she could feel it on her forehead. At the far corner of the room, she saw red flames at the mica window of the old stove door; she looked behind the stove just to make sure. The bar got quiet except for the Spanish polka music playing on the jukebox. She stood by the stove and shook the snow from the her blanket and held it near the stove to dry. The wet wool smell reminded her of new-born goats in early March, brought inside to warm near the fire. She felt calm.

In past years they would have told her to get out. But her hair was white now and her faced was wrinkled. They looked at her like she was a spider crawling slowly across the room. They were afraid; she could feel the fear. She looked at their faces steadily. They reminded her of the first time the white people brought her children back to her that winter. Danny had been shy and hid behind the thin white woman who brought them. And the baby had not known her until Ayah took her into her arms, and then Ella had nuzzled close to her as she had when she was nursing. The blonde woman was nervous and kept looking at a dainty gold watch on her wrist. She sat on the bench near the small window and watched the dark snow clouds gather around the mountains; she was worrying about the unpaved road. She was frightened by what she saw inside too: the strips of venison drying on a rope across the ceiling and the children jabbering excitedly in a language she did not know. So they stayed for only a few hours. Ayah watched the government car disappear down the road and she knew they were already being weaned from these lava hills and from this sky. The last time they came was in early June, and Ella stared at her the way the men in the bar were now staring. Ayah did not try to pick her up; she smiled at her instead and spoke cheerfully to Danny. When he tried to answer her, he could not seem to remember and he spoke English words with the Navajo. But he gave her a scrap of paper that he had found somewhere and carried in his pocket; it was folded in half, and he shyly looked up at her and said it was a bird. She asked Chato if they were home for good this time. He spoke to the white woman and she shook her head. "How much longer?" he asked, and she said she didn't know; but Chato saw how she stared at the boxcar shack. Ayah turned away then. She did not say good-bye.

She felt satisfied that the men in the bar feared her. Maybe it was her face and the way she held her mouth with teeth clenched tight, like there was nothing anyone could do to her now. She walked north down the road, searching for the old man. She did this because she had the blanket, and there would be no place for him except with her and the blanket in the old abode barn near the arroyo. They always slept there when they came to Cebolleta. If the money and the wine were gone, she would be relieved because then they could go home again; back to the old hogan with a dirt roof and rock walls where she herself had been born. And the next day the old man could go back to the few sheep they still had, to follow along behind them, guiding them, into dry sandy arroyos where sparse grass grew. She knew he did not like walking behind old ewes when for so many years he rode big quarter horses and worked with cattle. But she wasn't sorry for him; he should have known all along what would happen.

There had not been enough rain for their garden in five years; and that was when Chato finally hitched a ride into the town and brought back brown boxes of rice and sugar and big tin cans of welfare peaches. After that, at the first of the month they went to Cebolleta to ask the postmaster for the check; and then Chato would go to the bar and cash it. They did this as they planted the garden every May, not because anything would survive the summer dust, but because it was time to do this. The journey passed the days that smelled silent and dry like the caves above the canyon with yellow painted buffaloes on their walls.

He was walking along the pavement when she found him. He did not stop or turn around when he heard her behind him. She walked beside him and she noticed how slowly he moved now. He smelled strong of woodsmoke and urine. Lately he had been forgetting. Sometimes he called her by his sister's name and she had been gone for a long time. Once she had found him wandering on the road to the white man's ranch, and she asked him why he was going that way; he laughed at her and said, "You know they can't run that ranch without me," and he walked on determined, limping on the leg that had been crushed many years before. Now he looked at her curiously, as if for the first time, but he kept shuffling along, moving slowly along the side of the highway. His gray hair had grown long and spread out on the shoulders of the long overcoat. He wore the old felt hat pulled down over his ears. His boots were worn out at the toes and he had stuffed pieces of an old red shirt in the holes. The rags made his feet look like little animals up to their ears in snow. She laughed at his feet; the snow muffled the sound of her laugh. He stopped and looked at her again. The wind had quit blowing and the snow was falling straight down; the southeast sky was beginning to clear and Ayah could see a star.

"Let's rest awhile," she said to him. They walked away from the road and up the slope to the giant boulders that had tumbled down from the red sandrock mesa throughout the centuries of rainstorms and earth tremors. In a place where the boulders shut out the wind, they sat down with their backs against the rock. She offered half of the blanket to him and they sat wrapped together.

The storm passed swiftly. The clouds moved east. They were massive and full, crowding together across the sky. She watched them with the feeling of horses—steely blue-gray horses startled across the sky. The powerful haunches pushed into the distance and the tail hairs streamed white mist behind them. The sky cleared. Ayah saw that there was nothing between her and the stars. The light was crystalline. There was no shimmer, no distortion through earth haze. She breathed the clarity of the night sky; she smelled the purity of the half moon and the stars. He was lying on his side with his knees pulled up near his belly for warmth. His eyes were closed now, and in the light from the stars and the moon, he looked young again.

She could see it descend out of the night sky: an icy stillness from the edge of the thin moon. She recognized the freezing. It came gradually, sinking snowflake by snowflake until the crust was heavy and deep. It had the strength of the stars in Orion, and its journey was endless. Ayah knew that with the wine he would sleep. He would not feel it. She tucked the blanket around him, remembering how it was when Ella had been with her; and she felt the rush so big inside her heart for the babies. And she sang the only song she knew to sing for babies. She could not remember if she had ever sung it to her children, but she knew that her grandmother had sung it and her mother had sung it:

> The earth is your mother,
>   she holds you.
> The sky is your father,
>   he protects you.
> Sleep,
> sleep.
> Rainbow is your sister,
>   she loves you.
> The winds are your brothers,
>   they sing to you.
> Sleep,
> sleep.
> We are together always
> We are together always
> There never was a time
> when this
> was not so.

STORYTELLER

Every day the sun came up a little lower on the horizon, moving more slowly until one day she got excited and started calling the jailer. She realized she had been sitting there for many hours, yet the sun had not moved from the center of the sky. The color of the sky had not been good lately; it had been pale blue, almost white, even when there were no clouds. She told herself it wasn't a good sign for the sky to be indistinguishable from the river ice, frozen solid and white against the earth. The tundra rose up behind the river but all the boundaries between the river and hills and sky were lost in the density of the pale ice.

She yelled again, this time some English words which came randomly into her mouth, probably swear words she'd heard from the oil drilling crews last winter. The jailer was an Eskimo, but he would not speak Yupik[1] to her. She had watched people in other cells, when they spoke to him in Yupik he ignored them until they spoke English.

He came and stared at her. She didn't know if he understood what she was telling him until he glanced behind her at the small high window. He looked at the sun, and turned and walked away. She could hear the buckles on his heavy snowmobile boots jingle as he walked to the front of the building.

It was like the other buildings that white people, the Gussucks,[2] brought with them: BIA[3] and school buildings, portable buildings that arrived sliced in halves, on barges coming up the river. Squares of metal panelling bulged out with the layers of insulation stuffed inside. She had asked once what it was and someone told her it was to keep out the cold. She had not laughed then, but she did now. She walked over to the small double-pane window and she laughed out loud. They thought they could keep out the cold with stringy yellow wadding. Look at the sun. It wasn't moving; it was frozen, caught in the middle of the sky. Look at the sky, solid as the river with ice which has trapped the sun. It had not moved for a long time; in a few more hours it would be weak, and heavy frost would begin to appear on the edges and spread across the face of the sun like a mask. Its light was pale yellow, worn thin by the winter.

She could see people walking down the snow-packed roads, their breath steaming out from their parka hoods, faces hidden and protected by deep ruffs of fur. There were no cars or snowmobiles that day; the cold had silenced their machines. The metal froze; it split and shattered. Oil hardened and moving parts jammed solidly. She had seen it happen to their big yellow machines and the giant drill last winter when they came to drill their test holes. The cold stopped them, and they were helpless against it.

---

[1] Eskimo-Aleut language spoken across arctic America from western Alska to Greenland.

[2] Presumably the Yupik term for "white people."

[3] Bureau of Indian Affairs.

Her village was many miles upriver from this town, but in her mind she could see it clearly. Their house was not near the village houses. It stood alone on the bank upriver from the village. Snow had drifted to the eaves of the roof on the north side, but on the west side, by the door, the path was almost clear: She had nailed scraps of red tin over the logs last summer. She had done it for the bright red color, not for added warmth the way the village people had done. This final winter had been coming even then; there had been signs of its approach for many years.

She went because she was curious about the big school where the Government sent all the other girls and boys. She had not played much with the village children while she was growing up because they were afraid of the old man, and they ran when her grandmother came. She went because she was tired of being alone with the old woman whose body had been stiffening for as long as the girl could remember. Her knees and knuckles were swollen grotesquely, and the pain had squeezed the brown skin of her face tight against the bones; it left her eyes hard like river stone. The girl asked once what it was that did this to her body, and the old woman had raised up from sewing a sealskin boot, and stared at her.

"The joints," the old woman said in a low voice, whispering like wind across the roof. "The joints are swollen with anger."

Sometimes she did not answer and only stared at the girl. Each year she spoke less and less, but the old man talked more—all night sometimes, not to anyone but himself; in a soft deliberate voice, he told stories, moving his smooth brown hands above the blankets. He had not fished or hunted with the other men for many years, although he was not crippled or sick. He stayed in his bed, smelling like dry fish and urine, telling stories all winter, and when warm weather came, he went to his place on the river bank. He sat with a long willow stick, poking at the smoldering moss he burned against the insects while he continued with the stories.

The trouble was that she had not recognized the warnings in time. She did not see what the Gussuck school would do to her until she walked into the dormitory and realized that the old man had not been lying about the place. She thought he had been trying to scare her as he used to when she was very small and her grandmother was outside cutting up fish. She hadn't believed what he told her about the school because she knew he wanted to keep her there in the log house with him. She knew what he wanted.

The dormitory matron pulled down her underpants and whipped her with a leather belt because she refused to speak English.

"Those backwards village people," the matron said, because she was an Eskimo who had worked for the BIA a long time, "they kept this one until she was too big to learn." The other girls whispered in English. They knew how to work the showers, and they washed and curled their hair at night. They ate Gussuck food. She lay on her bed and imagined what her grandmother might be sewing, and what the old man was eating in his bed. When summer came, they sent her home.

The way her grandmother had hugged her before she left for school had been a warning too, because the old woman had not hugged or touched her for many years. Not like the old man, whose hands were always hunting, like ravens circling lazily in the sky, ready to touch her. She was not surprised when the priest and the old man met her at the landing strip, to say that the old lady was gone. The priest asked her where she would like to stay. He referred to the old man as her grandfather, but she did not bother to correct him. She had already been thinking about it; if she went with the priest, he would send her away to a school. But the old man was different. She knew he wouldn't send her back to school. She knew he wanted to keep her.

He told her one time, that she would get too old for him faster than he got too old for her; but again she had not believed him because sometimes he lied. He had lied about what he would do with her if she came into his bed. But as the years passed, she realized what he said was true. She was restless and strong. She had no patience with the old man who had never changed his slow smooth motions under the blankets.

The old man was in his bed for the winter; he did not leave it except to use the slop bucket in the corner. He was dozing with his mouth open slightly; his lips quivered and sometimes they moved like he was telling a story even while he dreamed. She pulled on the sealskin boots, the mukluks with the bright red flannel linings her grandmother had sewn for her, and she tied the braided red yarn tassels around her ankles over the gray wool pants. She zipped the wolfskin parka. Her grandmother had worn it for many years, but the old man said that before she died, she instructed him to bury her in an old black sweater, and to give the parka to the girl. The wolf pelts were creamy colored and silver, almost white in some places, and when the old lady had walked across the tundra in the winter, she was invisible in the snow.

She walked toward the village, breaking her own path through the deep snow. A team of sled dogs tied outside a house at the edge of the village leaped against their chains to bark at her. She kept walking, watching the dusky sky for the first evening stars. It was warm and the dogs were alert. When it got cold again, the dogs would lie curled and still, too drowsy from the cold to bark or pull at the chains. She laughed loudly because it made them howl and snarl. Once the old man had seen her tease the dogs and he shook his head. "So that's the kind of woman you are," he said, "in the wintertime the two of us are no different from those dogs. We wait in the cold for someone to bring us a few dry fish."

She laughed out loud again, and kept walking. She was thinking about the Gussuck oil drillers. They were strange; they watched her when she walked near their machines. She wondered what they looked like underneath their quilted goose-down trousers; she wanted to know how they moved. They would be something different from the old man.

The old man screamed at her. He shook her shoulder so violently that her head bumped against the log wall. "I smelled it!" he yelled, "as soon as I woke up! I am sure of it now. You can't fool me!" His thin legs were shaking inside the baggy wool trousers; he stumbled over her boots in his bare feet. His toenails were long and yellow like bird claws; she had seen a gray crane last summer fighting another in the shallow water on the edge of the river. She laughed out loud and pulled her shoulder out of his grip. He stood in front of her. He was breathing hard and shaking; he looked weak. He would probably die next winter.

"I'm warning you," he said, "I'm warning you." He crawled back into his bunk then, and reached under the old soiled feather pillow for a piece of dry fish. He lay back on the pillow, staring at the ceiling and chewed dry strips of salmon. "I don't know what the old woman told you," he said, "but there will be trouble." He looked over to see if she was listening. His face suddenly relaxed into a smile, his dark slanty eyes were lost in wrinkles of brown skin. "I could tell you, but you are too good for warning now. I can smell what you did all night with the Gussucks."

She did not understand why they came there, because the village was small and so far upriver that even some Eskimos who had been away to school did not want to come back. They stayed downriver in the town. They said the village was too quiet. They were used to the town where the boarding school was located, with electric lights and running water. After all those years away at school, they had forgotten how to set nets in the river and where to hunt seals in the fall. When she asked the old man why the Gussucks bothered to come to the village, his narrow eyes got bright with excitement.

"They only come when there is something to steal. The fur animals are too difficult for them to get now, and the seals and fish are hard to find. Now they come for oil deep in the earth. But this is the last time for them." His breathing was wheezy and fast; his hands gestured at the sky. "It is approaching. As it comes, ice will push across the sky." His eyes were open wide and he stared at the low ceiling rafters for hours without blinking. She remembered all this clearly because he began the story that day, the story he told from that time on. It began with a giant bear which he described muscle by muscle, from the curve of the ivory claws to the whorls of hair at the top of the massive skull. And for eight days he did not sleep, but talked continuously of the giant bear whose color was pale blue glacier ice.

The snow was dirty and worn down in a path to the door. On either side of the path, the snow was higher than her head. In front of the door there were jagged yellow stains melted into the snow where men had urinated. She stopped in the entry way and kicked the snow off her boots. The room was dim; a kerosene lantern by the cash register was burning low. The long wooden shelves were jammed with cans of beans and potted meats. On the bottom shelf a jar of mayonnaise was broken open, leaking oily white clots on the floor. There was no one in the room except the yellowish dog sleeping in the front of the long glass display case. A reflection made it appear to be lying on the knives and ammunition inside the case. Gussucks kept dogs inside their houses with them; they did not seem to mind the odors which seeped out of the dogs. "They tell us we are dirty for the food we eat—raw fish and fermented meat. But we do not live with dogs," the old man once said. She heard voices in the back room, and the sound of bottles set down hard on tables.

They were always confident. The first year they waited for the ice to break up on the river, and then they brought their big yellow machines up river on barges. They planned to drill their test holes during the summer to avoid the freezing. But the imprints and graves of their machines were still there, on the edge of the tundra above the river, where the summer mud had swallowed them before they ever left sight of the river. The village people had gathered to watch the white men, and to laugh as they drove the giant machines, one by one, off the steel ramp into the bogs; as if sheer numbers of vehicles would somehow make the tundra solid. But the old man said they behaved like desperate people, and they would come back again. When the tundra was frozen solid, they returned.

Village women did not even look through the door to the back room. The priest had warned them. The storeman was watching her because he didn't let Eskimos or Indians sit down at the tables in the back room. But she knew he couldn't throw her out if one of his Gussuck customers invited her to sit with him. She walked across the room. They stared at her, but she had the feeling she was walking for someone else, not herself, so their eyes did not matter. The red-haired man pulled out a chair and motioned for her to sit down. She looked back at the storeman while the red-haired man poured her a glass of red sweet wine. She wanted to laugh at the storeman the way she laughed at the dogs, straining against the chains, howling at her.

The red-haired man kept talking to the other Gussucks sitting around the table, but he slid one hand off the top of the table to her thigh. She looked over at the storeman to see if he was still watching her. She laughed out loud at him and the red-haired man stopped talking and turned to her. He asked if she wanted to go. She nodded and stood up.

Someone in the village had been telling him things about her, he said as they walked down the road to his trailer. She understood that much of what he was saying, but the rest she did not hear. The whine of the big generators at the construction camp sucked away the sound of his words. But English was of no concern to her anymore, and neither was anything the Christians in the village might say about her or the old man. She smiled at the effect of the subzero air on the electric lights around the trailers; they did not shine. They left only flat yellow holes in the darkness.

It took him a long time to get ready, even after she had undressed for him. She waited in the bed with the blankets pulled close, watching him. He adjusted the thermostat and lit candles in the room, turning out the electric lights. He searched through a stack of record albums until he found the right one. She was not sure about the last thing he did: he taped something on the wall behind the bed where he could see it while he lay on top of her. He was shriveled and white from the cold; he pushed against her body for warmth. He guided her hands to his thigh; he was shivering.

She had returned a last time because she wanted to know what it was he stuck on the wall above the bed. After he finished each time, he reached up and pulled it loose, folding it carefully so that she could not see it. But this time she was ready; she waited for his fast breathing and sudden collapse on top of her. She slid out from under him and stood up beside the bed. She looked at the picture while she got dressed. He did not raise his face from the pillow, and she thought she heard teeth rattling together as she left the room.

She heard the old man move when she came in. After the Gussuck's trailer, the log house felt cool. It smelled like dry fish and cured meat. The room was dark except for the blinking yellow flame in the mica window of the oil stove. She squatted in front of the stove and watched the flames for a long time before she walked to the bed where her grandmother had slept. The bed was covered with a mound of rags and fur scraps the old woman had saved. She reached into the mound until she felt something cold and solid wrapped in a wool blanket. She pushed her fingers around it until she felt smooth stone. Long ago, before the Gussucks came, they had burned whale oil in the big stone lamp which made light and heat as well. The old woman had saved everything they would need when the time came.

In the morning, the old man pulled a piece of dry caribou meat from under the blankets and offered it to her. While she was gone, men from the village had brought a bundle of dry meat. She chewed it slowly, thinking about the way they still came from the village to take care of the old man and his stories. But she had a story now, about the red-haired Gussuck. The old man knew what she was thinking, and his smile made his face seem more round than it was.

"Well," he said, "what was it?"

"A woman with a big dog on top of her."

He laughed softly to himself and walked over to the water barrel. He dipped the tin cup into the water.

"It doesn't surprise me," he said.

"Grandma," she said, "there was something red in the grass that morning. I remember." She had not asked about her parents before. The old woman stopped splitting the fish bellies open for the willow drying racks. Her jaw muscles pulled so tightly against her skull, the girl thought the old woman would not be able to speak.

"They bought a tin can full of it from the storeman. Late at night. He told them it was alcohol safe to drink. They traded a rifle for it." The old woman's voice sounded like each word stole strength from her. "It made no difference about the rifle. That year the Gussuck boats had come, firing big guns at the walrus and seals. There was nothing left to hunt after that anyway. So," the old lady said, in a low soft voice the girl had not heard for a long time, "I didn't say anything to them when they left that night."

"Right over there," she said, pointing at the fallen poles, half buried in the river sand and tall grass, "in the summer shelter. The sun was high half the night then. Early in the morning when it was still low, the policeman came around. I told the interpreter to tell him that the storeman had poisoned them." She made outlines in the air in front of her, showing how their bodies lay twisted on the sand; telling the story was like laboring to walk through deep snow; sweat shone in the white hair around her forehead. "I told the priest too, after he came. I told him the storeman lied." She turned away from the girl. She held her mouth even tighter, set solidly, not in sorrow or anger, but against the pain, which was all that remained. "I never believed," she said, "not much anyway. I wasn't surprised when the priest did nothing."

The wind came off the river and folded the tall grass into itself like river waves. She could feel the silence the story left, and she wanted to have the old woman go on.

"I heard sounds that night, grandma. Sounds like someone was singing. It was light outside. I could see something red on the ground." The old woman did not answer her; she moved to the tub full of fish on the ground beside the workbench. She stabbed her knife into the belly of a whitefish and lifted it onto the bench. "The Gussuck storeman left the village right after that," the old woman said as she pulled the entrails from the fish, "otherwise, I could tell you more." The old woman's voice flowed with the wind blowing off the river; they never spoke of it again.

When the willows got their leaves and the grass grew tall along the river banks and around the sloughs, she walked early in the morning. While the sun was still low on the horizon, she listened to the wind off the river; its sound was like the voice that day long ago. In the distance, she could hear the engines of the machinery the oil drillers had left the winter before, but she did not go near the village or the store. The sun never left the sky and the summer became the same long day, with only the winds to fan the sun into brightness or allow it to slip into twilight.

She sat beside the old man at his place on the river bank. She poked the smoky fire for him and felt herself growing wide and thin in the sun as if she had been split from belly to throat and strung on the willow pole in preparation for the winter to come. The old man did not speak anymore. When men from the village brought him fresh fish he hid them deep in the river grass where it was cool. After he went inside, she split the fish open and spread them to dry on the willow frame the way the old woman had done. Inside, he dozed and talked to himself. He had talked all winter, softly and incessantly, about the giant polar bear stalking a lone hunter across Bering Sea ice. After all the months the old man had been telling the story, the bear was within a hundred feet of the man; but the ice fog had closed in on them now and the man could only smell the sharp ammonia odor of the bear, and hear the edge of the snow crust crack under the giant paws.

One night she listened to the old man tell the story all night in his sleep, describing each crystal of ice and the slightly different sounds they made under each paw; first the left and then the right paw, then the hind feet. Her grandmother was there suddenly, a shadow around the stove. She spoke in her low wind voice and the girl was afraid to sit up to hear more clearly. Maybe what she said had been to the old man because he stopped telling the story and began to snore softly the way he had long ago when the old woman had scolded him for telling his stories while others in the house were trying to sleep. But the last words she heard clearly: "It will take a long time, but the story must be told. There must not be any lies." She pulled the blankets up around her chin, slowly, so that her movements would not be seen. She thought her grandmother was talking about the old man's bear story; she did not know about the other story then.

She left the old man wheezing and snoring in his bed. She walked through river grass glistening with frost; the bright green summer color was already fading. She watched the sun move across the sky, already lower on the horizon, already moving away from the village. She stopped by the fallen poles of the summer shelter where her parents had died. Frost glittered on the river sand too; in a few more weeks there would be snow. The predawn light would be the color of an old woman. An old woman sky full of snow. There had been something red lying on the ground the morning they died. She looked for it again, pushing aside the grass with her foot. She knelt in the sand and looked under the fallen structure for some trace of it. When she found it, she would know what the old woman had never told her. She squatted down close to the gray poles and leaned her back against them. The wind made her shiver.

The summer rain had washed the mud from between the logs; the sod blocks stacked as high as her belly next to the log walls had lost their square-cut shape and had grown into soft mounds of tundra moss and stiff-bladed grass bending with clusters of seed bristles. She looked at the northwest, in the direction of the Bering Sea. The cold would come down from there to find narrow slits in the mud, rainwater holes in the outer layer of sod which protected the log house. The dark green tundra stretched away flat and continuous. Somewhere the sea and the land met; she knew by their dark green colors there were no boundaries between them. That was how the cold would come: when the boundaries were gone the polar ice would range across the land into the sky. She watched the horizon for a long time. She would stand in that place on the north side of the house and she would keep watch on the northwest horizon, and eventually she would see it come. She would watch for its approach in the stars, and hear it come with the wind. These preparations were unfamiliar, but gradually she recognized them as she did her own footprints in the snow.

She emptied the slop jar beside his bed twice a day and kept the barrel full of water melted from river ice. He did not recognize her anymore, and when he spoke to her, he called her by her grandmother's name and talked about people and events from long ago, before he went back to telling the story. The giant bear was creeping across the new snow on its belly, close enough now that the man could hear the rasp of its breathing. On and on in a soft singing voice, the old man caressed the story, repeating the words again and again like gentle strokes.

The sky was gray like a river crane's egg; its density curved into the thin crust of frost already covering the land. She looked at the bright red color of the tin against the ground and the sky and she told the village men to bring the pieces for the old man and her. To drill the test holes in the tundra, the Gussucks had used hundreds of barrels of fuel. The village people split open the empty barrels that were abandoned on the river bank, and pounded the red tin into flat sheets. The village people were using the strips of tin to mend walls and roofs for winter. But she nailed it on the log walls for its color. When she finished, she walked away with the hammer in her hand, not turning around until she was far away, on the ridge above the river banks, and then she looked back. She felt a chill when she saw how the sky and the land were already losing their boundaries, already becoming lost in each other. But the red tin penetrated the thick white color of earth and sky; it defined the boundaries like a wound revealing the ribs and heart of a great caribou about to bolt and be lost to the hunter forever. That night the wind howled and when she scratched a hole through the heavy frost on the inside of the window, she could see nothing but the impenetrable white; whether it was blowing snow or snow that had drifted as high as the house, she did not know.

It had come down suddenly, and she stood with her back to the wind looking at the river, its smoky water clotted with ice. The wind had blown the snow over the frozen river, hiding thin blue streaks where fast water ran under ice translucent and fragile as memory. But she could see shadows of boundaries, outlines of paths which were slender branches of solidity reaching out from the earth. She spent days walking on the river, watching the colors of ice that would safely hold her, kicking the heel of her boot into the snow crust, listening for a solid sound. When she could feel the paths through the soles of her feet, she went to the middle of the river where the fast gray water churned under a thin pane of ice. She looked back. On the river bank in the distance she could see the red tin nailed to the log house, something not swallowed up by the heavy white belly of the sky or caught in the folds of the frozen earth. It was time.

The wolverine fur around the hood of her parka was white with the frost from her breathing. The warmth inside the store melted it, and she felt tiny drops of water on her face. The storeman came in from the back room. She unzipped the parka and stood by the oil stove. She didn't look at him, but stared instead at the yellowish dog, covered with scabs of matted hair, sleeping in front of the stove. She thought of the Gussuck's picture, taped on the wall above the bed and she laughed out loud. The sound of her laughter was piercing; the yellow dog jumped to its feet and the hair bristled down its back. The storeman was watching her. She wanted to laugh again because he didn't know about the ice. He did not know that it was prowling the earth, or that it had already pushed its way into the sky to seize the sun. She sat down in the chair by the stove and shook her long hair loose. He was like a dog tied up all winter, watching while the others got fed. He remembered how she had gone with the oil drillers, and his blue eyes moved like flies crawling over her body. He held his thin pale lips like he wanted to spit on her. He hated the people because they had something of value, the old man said, something which the Gussucks could never have. They thought they could take it, suck it out of the earth or cut it from the mountains; but they were fools.

There was a matted hunk of dog hair on the floor by her foot. She thought of the yellow insulation coming unstuffed: their defense against the freezing going to pieces as it advanced on them. The ice was crouching on the northwest horizon like the old man's bear. She laughed out loud again. The sun would be down now; it was time.

The first time he spoke to her, she did not hear what he said, so she did not answer or even look up at him. He spoke to her again but his words were only noises coming from his pale mouth, trembling now as his anger began to unravel. He jerked her up and the chair fell over behind her. His arms were shaking and she could feel his hands tense up, pulling the edges of the parka tighter. He raised his fist to hit her, his thin body quivering with rage; but the fist collapsed with the desire he had for the valuable things, which, the old man had rightly said, was the only reason they came. She could hear his heart pounding as he held her close and arched his hips against her, groaning and breathing in spasms. She twisted away from him and ducked under his arms.

She ran with a mitten over her mouth, breathing through the fur to protect her lungs from the freezing air. She could hear him running behind her, his heavy breathing, the occasional sound of metal jingling against metal. But he ran without his parka or mittens, breathing the frozen air; its fire squeezed the lungs against the ribs and it was enough that he could not catch her near his store. On the river bank he realized how far he was from his stove, and the wads of yellow stuffing that held off the cold. But the girl was not able to run very fast through the deep drifts at the edge of the river. The twilight was luminous and he could still see clearly for a long distance; he knew he could catch her so he kept running.

When she neared the middle of the river she looked over her shoulder. He was not following her tracks; he went straight across the ice, running the shortest distance to reach her. He was close then; his face was twisted and scarlet from the exertion and the cold. There was satisfaction in his eyes; he was sure he could outrun her.

She was familiar with the river, down to the instant ice flexed into hairline fractures, and the cracking bone-sliver sounds gathered momentum with the opening ice until the churning gray water was set free. She stopped and turned to the sound of the river and the rattle of swirling ice fragments where he fell through. She pulled off a mitten and zipped the parka to her throat. She was conscious then of her own rapid breathing.

She moved slowly, kicking the ice ahead with the heel of her boot, feeling for sinews of ice to hold her. She looked ahead and all around herself; in the twilight, the dense white sky had merged into the flat snow-covered tundra. In the frantic running she had lost her place on the river. She stood still. The east bank of the river was lost in the sky; the boundaries had been swallowed by the freezing white. But then, in the distance, she saw something red, and suddenly it was as she had remembered it all those years.

She sat on her bed and while she waited, she listened to the old man. The hunter had found a small jagged knoll on the ice. He pulled his beaver fur cap off his head; the fur inside it steamed with his body heat and sweat. He left it upside down on the ice for the great bear to stalk, and he waited downwind on top of the ice knoll; he was holding the jade knife.

She thought she could see the end of his story in the way he wheezed out the words, but still he reached into his cache of dry fish and dribbled water into his mouth from the tin cup. All night she listened to him describe each breath the man took, each motion of the bear's head as it tried to catch the sound of the man's breathing, and tested the wind for his scent.

The state trooper asked her questions, and the woman who cleaned house for the priest translated them into Yupik. They wanted to know what happened to the storeman, the Gussuck who had been seen running after her down the road onto the river late last evening. He had not come back, and the Gussuck boss in Anchorage was concerned about him. She did not answer for a long time because the old man suddenly sat up in his bed and began to talk excitedly, looking at all of them—the trooper in his dark glasses and the housekeeper in her corduroy parka. He kept saying, "The story! The story! Eh-ya! The great bear! The hunter!"

They asked her again, what happened to the man from the Northern Commercial store. "He lied to them. He told them it was safe to drink. But I will not lie." She stood up and put on the gray wolfskin parka. "I killed him," she said, "but I don't lie."

The attorney came back again, and the jailer slid open the steel doors and opened the cell to let him in. He motioned for the jailer to stay to translate for him. She laughed when she saw how the jailer would be forced by this Gussuck to speak Yupik to her. She liked the Gussuck attorney for that, and for the thinning hair on his head. He was very tall, and she liked to think about the exposure of his head to the freezing; she wondered if he would feel the ice descending from the sky before the others did. He wanted to know why she told the state trooper she had killed the storeman. Some village children had seen it happen, he said, and it was an accident. "That's all you have to say to the judge: it was an accident." He kept repeating it over and over again to her, slowly in a loud but gentle voice: "It was an accident. He was running after you and he fell through the ice. That's all you have to say in court. That's all. And they will let you go home. Back to your village." The jailer translated the words sullenly, staring down at the floor. She shook her head. "I will not change the story, not even to escape this place and go home. I intended that he die. The story must be told as it is." The attorney exhaled loudly; his eyes looked tired. "Tell her that she could not have killed him that way. He was a white man. He ran after her without a parka or mittens. She could not have planned that." He paused and turned toward the cell door. "Tell her I will do all I can for her. I will explain to the judge that her mind is confused." She laughed out loud when the jailer translated what the attorney said. The Gussucks did not understand the story; they could not see the way it must be told, year after year as the old man had done, without lapse or silence.

She looked out the window at the frozen white sky. The sun had finally broken loose from the ice but it moved like a wounded caribou running on strength which only dying animals find, leaping and running on bullet-shattered lungs. Its light was weak and pale; it pushed dimly through the clouds. She turned and faced the Gussuck attorney.

"It began a long time ago," she intoned steadily, "in the summertime. Early in the morning, I remember, something red in the tall river grass. . . ."

The day after the old man died, men from the village came. She was sitting on the edge of her bed, across from the woman the trooper hired to watch her. They came into the room slowly and listened to her. At the foot of her bed they left a king salmon that had been slit open wide and dried last summer. But she did not pause or hesitate; she went on with the story, and she never stopped, not even when the woman got up to close the door behind the village men.

The old man would not change the story even when he knew the end was approaching. Lies could not stop what was coming. He thrashed around on the bed, pulling the blankets loose, knocking bundles of dried fish and meat on the floor. The hunter had been on the ice for many hours. The freezing winds on the ice knoll had numbed his hands in the mittens, and the cold had exhausted him. He felt a single muscle tremor in his hand that he could not stop, and the jade knife fell; it shattered on the ice, and the blue glacier bear turned slowly to face him.

Lynn Emanuel 1949–

Lynn Emanuel was born in 1949 in Mount Kisco, New York. Currently a profes-sor of English at the University of Pittsburgh, she is the author of two books of poetry: *Hotel Fiesta* (1984) and *The Dig*, which was selected for the 1992 National Poetry Series. In conjunction with David St. John, she co-edited the 1994–95 edition of *The Pushcart Prize Anthology*, and her work was show-cased in *Best American Poetry 1995*. Emanuel has received two fellowships from the National Endowment for the Arts and two Pushcart Prizes.

INVENTING FATHER IN LAS VEGAS

If I could see nothing but the smoke
From the tip of his cigar, I would know everything
About the years before the war.
If his face were halved by shadow I would know
This was a street where an EATS sign trembled   5
And a Greek served coffee black as a dog's eye.
If I could see nothing but his wrist I would know
About the slot machine and I could reconstruct
The weak chin and ruin of his youth, the summer
My father was a gypsy with oiled hair sleeping   10
In a Murphy bed and practicing clairvoyance.
I could fill his vast Packard with showgirls
And keep him forever among the difficult buttons
Of the bodice, among the rustling of their names,
Miss Christina, Miss Lorraine.   15
I could put his money in my pocket
and wearing memory's black fedora
With the condoms hidden in the hatband
The damp cigar between my teeth,
I could become the young man who always got sentimental 20
About London especially in Las Vegas with its single bridge—
So ridiculously tender—leaning across the river
To watch the starlight's soft explosions.
If I could trace the two veins that crossed
His temple, I would know what drove him   25
To this godforsaken place, I would keep him forever
Remote from war—like the come-hither tip of his lit cigar
Or the harvest moon, that gold planet, remote and pure
    American.

Jamaica Kincaid 1949–

Jamaica Kincaid, originally named Elaine Potter Richardson, was born in 1949 in Antigua, a West Indian island formerly colonized by the British. Longing to leave her provincial lifestyle, she came to the United States at the age of sixteen where she worked as an au pair in New York City. Later, Kincaid studied photography at Franconia College in New Hampshire, but would eventually quit school, calling her college experience a "dismal failure." A voracious reader and largely self-educated, she was given an opportunity to write for *The New Yorker* magazine in the early 1970s and hired as a staff writer in 1976.

Two main elements prevail in much of Kincaid's writing: an acute exploration of the mother-daughter relationship in a third-world and immigrant context and the sense of dislocation that she felt growing up as a colonized West Indian. Her first collection of stories, *At the Bottom of the River* (1983), won the prestigious Morton Dauwen Zabel Award from the American Academy and Institute of Arts and Letters. Her subsequent work includes four critically acclaimed novels and an embittered polemic against colonialism, *A Small Place* (1988). Currently, Kincaid lives with her family in Vermont and teaches at Harvard.

ALIEN SOIL

FROM *THE NEW YORKER*

Whatever it is in the character of the English people that leads them to obsessively order and shape their landscape to such a degree that it looks like a painting (tamed, framed, captured, kind, decent, good, pretty), while a painting never looks like the English landscape, unless it is a bad painting—this quality of character is blissfully lacking in the Antiguan people. I make this unfair comparison (unfair to the Antiguan people? unfair to the English people? I cannot tell, but there is an unfairness here somewhere) only because so much of the character of the Antiguan people is influenced by and inherited, through conquest, from the English people. The tendency to shower pity and cruelty on the weak is among the traits the Antiguans inherited, and so is a love of gossip. (The latter, I think, is responsible for the fact that England has produced such great novelists, but it has not yet worked to the literary advantage of the Antiguan people.) When the English were a presence in Antigua—they first came to the island as slaveowners, when a man named Thomas Warner established a settlement there in 1632—the places where they lived were surrounded

951

by severely trimmed hedges of plumbago, topiaries of willow (casuarina), and frangipani and hibiscus; their grass was green (odd, because water was scarce; the proper word for the climate is not "sunny" but "drought-ridden") and freshly cut; they kept trellises covered with roses, and beds of marigolds and cannas and chrysanthemums.

Ordinary Antiguans (and by "ordinary Antiguans" I mean the Antiguan people, who are descended from the African slaves brought to this island by Europeans; this turns out to be a not uncommon way to become ordinary), the ones who had some money and could live in houses of more than one room, had gardens in which only flowers were grown. This made it even more apparent that they had some money, in that all their outside space was devoted not to feeding their families but to the sheer beauty of things. I can remember in particular one such family, who lived in a house with many rooms (four, to be exact). They had an indoor kitchen and a place for bathing (no indoor toilet, though); they had a lawn, always neatly cut, and they had beds of flowers, but I can now remember only roses and marigolds. I can remember those because once I was sent there to get a bouquet of roses for my godmother on her birthday. The family also had, in the middle of their small lawn, a willow tree, pruned so that it had the shape of a pine tree — a conical shape — and at Christmastime this tree was decorated with colored lights (which was so unusual and seemed so luxurious to me that when I passed by this house I would beg to be allowed to stop and stare at it for a while). At Christmas, all willow trees would suddenly be called Christmas trees, and for a time, when my family must have had a small amount of money, I, too, had a Christmas tree — a lonely, spindly branch of willow sitting in a bucket of water in our very small house. No one in my family and, I am almost certain, no one in the family of the people with the lighted-up willow tree had any idea of the origins of the Christmas tree and the traditions associated with it. When these people (the Antiguans) lived under the influence of these other people (the English), there was naturally an attempt among some of them to imitate their rulers in this particular way — by rearranging the landscape — and they did it without question. They can't be faulted for not asking what it was they were doing; that is the way these things work. The English left, and most of their landscaping influence went with them. The Americans came, but Americans (I am one now) are not interested in influencing people directly; we instinctively understand the childish principle of monkey see, monkey do. And at the same time we are divided about how we ought to behave in the world. Half of us believe in and support strongly a bad thing our government is doing, while the other half do not believe in and protest strongly against the bad thing. The bad thing succeeds, and everyone, protester and supporter alike, enjoys immensely the results of the bad thing. This ambiguous approach in the many is always startling to observe in the individual. Just look at Thomas Jefferson, a great American gardener and our country's third president, who owned slaves and strongly supported the idea of an expanded American border, which meant the extinction of the people who already lived on the land to be taken, while at the same time he was passionately devoted to ideas about freedom—ideas that the descendants of the slave and the people who were defeated and robbed of their land would have to use in defense of themselves. Jefferson, as president, commissioned the formidable trek his former secretary, the adventurer and botany thief Meriwether Lewis, made through the West, sending plant specimens back to the president along the way. The *Lewisia rediviva*, state flower of Montana, which Lewis found in the Bitterroot River valley, is named after him; the clarkia, not a flower of any state as far as I can tell, is named for his co-adventurer and botany thief, William Clark.

What did the botanical life of Antigua consist of at the time another famous adventurer—Christopher Columbus—first saw it? To see a garden in Antigua now will not supply a clue. I made a visit to Antigua this spring, and most of the plants I saw there came from somewhere else. The bougainvillea (named for another restless European, the sea adventurer Louis-Antoine de Bougainville, first Frenchman to cross the Pacific) is native to tropical South America; the plumbago is from southern Africa; the croton (genus *Codiaeum*) is from Malay Peninsula; the *Hibiscus rosa-sinensis* is from Asia and the *Hibiscus schizopetalus* is from East Africa; the allamanda is from Brazil; the poinsettia (named for an American ambassador, Joel Poinsett) is from Mexico; the bird of paradise flower is from southern Africa; the Bermuda lily is from Japan; the flamboyant tree is from Madagascar; the casuarina is from Australia; the Norfolk pine is from Norfolk Island; the tamarind tree is from Africa; the mango is from Asia. The breadfruit, the most Antiguan (to me) and starchy food, the bane of every Antiguan child's palate, is from the East Indies. This food has been the cause of more disagreement between parents and their children than anything else I can think of. No child has ever liked it. It was sent to the West Indies by Joseph Banks, the English naturalist and world traveler and the head of Kew Gardens, which was then a clearinghouse for all the plants stolen from the various parts of the world where the English had been. (One of the climbing roses, *Rosa banksiae*, from China, was named for Banks's wife.) Banks sent tea to India; to the West Indies he sent the breadfruit. It was meant to be a cheap food for feeding slaves. It was the cargo that Captain Bligh was carrying to the West Indies on the ship *Bounty* when his crew so rightly mutinied. It's as though the Antiguan child senses intuitively the part this food has played in the history of injustice and so will not eat it. But, unfortunately for her, it grows readily, bears fruit abundantly, and is impervious to drought. Soon after the English settled in Antigua, they cleared the land of its hardwood forests to make room for the growing of tobacco, sugar, and cotton, and it is this that makes the island drought-ridden to this day. Antigua is also empty of much wildlife natural to it. When snakes proved a problem for the planter, they imported the mongoose from India. As a result there are no snakes at all on the island—nor other reptiles, other than lizards—though I don't know what damage the absence of snakes causes, if any.

What herb of beauty grew in this place then? What tree? And did the people who lived there grow anything beautiful for its own sake? I do not know; I can only make a straightforward deduction: the frangipani, the mahogany tree, and the cedar tree are all native to the West Indies, so these trees are probably indigenous. And some of the botany of Antigua can be learned from medicinal folklore. My mother and I were sitting on the steps in front of her house one day during my recent visit, and I suddenly focused on a beautiful bush (beautiful to me now; when I was a child I thought it ugly) whose fruit I remembered playing with when I was little. It is an herbaceous plant that has a red stem covered with red thorns, and emerald-green, simple leaves, with the same red thorns running down the leaf from the leafstalk. I cannot remember what its flowers looked like, and it was not in flower when I saw it while I saw there with my mother, but its fruit is a small, almost transparent red berry, and it is this I used to play with. We children sometimes called it "china berry," because of its transparent, glassy look—it reminded us of china dinnerware, though we were only vaguely familiar with such a thing as china, having seen it no more than once or twice— and sometimes "baby tomato," because of its size, and to signify that it was not real; a baby thing was not a real thing. When I pointed the bush out to my mother, she called it something else; she called it cancanberry bush, and said that in the old days, when people could not afford to see doctors, if a child had thrush they would make a paste of this fruit and rub it inside the child's mouth, and this would make the thrush go away. But, she said, people rarely bother with this remedy anymore. The day before, a friend of hers had come to pay a visit, and when my mother offered her something to eat and drink the friend declined, because, she said, she had some six-sixty-six and maiden-blush tea waiting at home for her. This tea is taken on an empty stomach, and it is used for all sorts of ailments, including to help bring on abortions. I have never seen six-sixty-six in flower, but its leaves are a beautiful ovoid shape and a deep green—qualities that are of value in a garden devoted to shape and color of leaf.

People who do not like the idea that there is a relationship between garden-ing and wealth are quick to remind me of the cottage gardener, that grim-faced English person. Living on land that is not his own, he has put bits and pieces of things, together, things from here and there, and it is a beautiful jumble—but just try duplicating it; it isn't cheap to do. And I have never read a book praising the cottage garden written by a cottage gardener. This person—the cottage gardener—does not exist in a place like Antigua. Or do casual botanical conver-sation, knowledge of the Latin names for plants, and discussions of the binomial system. If an atmosphere where these things could flourish exists in this place, I am not aware of it. I can remember very well the cruel Englishwoman who was my botany teacher, and that, in spite of her cruelty, botany was one of my two favorite subjects in school. (History was the other.) With this in mind I visited a bookstore (the only bookstore I know of in Antigua) to see what texts are now being used in the schools and to see how their content compares with what was taught to me back then; the botany I had studied was a catalogue of the plants of the British Empire, the very same plants that are now widely cultivated in Antigua and are probably assumed by ordinary Antiguans to be native to their landscape—the mango, for example. But it turns out that botany as a subject is no longer taught in Antiguan schools; the study of plants is now called agriculture. Perhaps that is more realistic, since the awe and poetry of botany cannot be eaten, and the mystery and pleasure in the knowledge of botany cannot be taken to market and sold.

And yet the people of Antigua have a relationship to agriculture that does not please them at all. Their very arrival on this island had to do with the forces of agriculture. When they (we) were brought to this island from Africa a few hundred years ago, it was not for their pottery-making skills or for their way with a loom; it was for the free labor they could provide in the fields. Mary Prince, a nineteenth-century African woman who was born in Bermuda and spent part of her life as a slave in Antigua, writes about this in an autobiographical account, which I found in *The Classic Slave Narratives*, edited by Henry Louis Gates, Jr. She says:

> My master and mistress went on one occasion into the country, to Date Hill, for change of air, and carried me with them to take charge of the children, and to do the work of the house. While I was in the country, I saw how the field negroes are worked in Antigua. They are worked very hard and fed but scantily. They are called out to work before daybreak, and come home after dark; and then each has to heave his bundle of grass for the cattle in the pen. Then, on Sunday morning, each slave has to go out and gather a large bundle of grass; and, when they bring it home, they have all to sit at the manager's door and wait till he come out: often they have to wait there till past eleven o'clock, without any breakfast. After that, those that have yams or potatoes, or fire-wood to sell, hasten to market to buy . . . salt fish, or pork, which is a great treat for them.

Perhaps it makes sense that a group of people with such a wretched historical relationship to growing things would need to describe their current relationship to it as dignified and masterly (agriculture), and would not find it poetic (botany) or pleasurable (gardening).

In a book I am looking at (to read it is to look at it: the type is as tall as a doll's teacup), *The Tropical Garden*, by William Warren, with photographs by Luca Invernizzi Tettoni, I find statements like "the concept of a private garden planted purely for aesthetic purposes was generally alien to tropical countries" and "there was no such tradition of ornamental horticulture among the inhabitants of most hot-weather places. Around the average home there might be a few specimens chosen especially because of their scented flowers or because they were believed to bring good fortune. . . . Nor would much, if any, attention be paid to attractive landscape design in such gardens: early accounts by travellers in the tropics abound in enthusiastic descriptions of jungle scenery, but a reader will search in vain for one praising the tasteful arrangement of massed ornamental beds and contrasting lawns of well-trimmed grass around the homes of natives." What can I say to that? No doubt it is true. And no doubt contrasting lawns and massed ornamental beds are a sign of something, and that is that someone—someone other than the owner of the lawns—has been humbled. To give just one example: on page 62 of this book is a photograph of eight men, natives of India, pulling a heavy piece of machinery used in the upkeep of lawns. They are without shoes. They are wearing the clothing of schoolboys—khaki shorts and khaki short-sleeved shirts. There is no look of bliss on their faces. The caption for the photograph reads, "Shortage of labour was never a problem in the maintenance of European features in large colonial gardens; here a team of workers is shown rolling a lawn at the Gymkhana Club in Bombay."

And here are a few questions that occur to me: what if the people living in the tropics, the ones whose history isn't tied up with and contaminated by slavery and indenturedness, are contented with their surroundings, are happy to observe an invisible hand at work and from time to time laugh at some of the ugly choices this hand makes; what if they have more important things to do than make a small tree large, a large tree small, or a tree whose blooms are usually yellow bear black blooms; what if these people are not spiritually feverish, restless, and fully of envy?

When I was looking at the book of tropical gardens, I realized that the flowers and the trees so familiar to me from my childhood do not now have a hold on me. I do not long to plant and be surrounded by the bougainvillea; I do not like the tropical hibiscus; the corallita (from Mexico), so beautiful when tended, so ugly when left to itself, which makes everything around it look rusty and shabby, is not a plant I like at all. I returned from my visit to Antigua, the place where I was born, to a small village in Vermont, the place where I choose to live. Spring had arrived. The tulips I had planted last autumn were in bloom, and I liked to sit and caress their petals, which felt disgustingly delicious, like scraps of peau de soie. The dizzy-making yellow of dandelions and cowslips was in the fields and riverbanks and marshes. I like these things. (I do not like daffodils, but that's a legacy of the English approach: I was forced to memorize the poem by William Wordsworth when I was a child.) I transplanted to the edge of a grove of pine trees some foxgloves that I grew from seed in late winter. I found some Virginia bluebells in a spot in the woods where I had not expected to find them, and some larches growing grouped together, also in a place I had not expected. On my calendar I marked the day I would go and dig up all the mulleins I could find and replant them in a very sunny spot across from the grove of pine trees. This is to be my forest of mulleins, though in truth it will appear a forest only to an ant. I marked the day I would plant the nasturtiums under the fruit trees. I discovered a clump of Dutchman's-breeches in the wildflower bed that I inherited from the man who built and used to own the house in which I now live, Robert Woodworth, the botanist who invented time-lapse photography. I waited for the things I had ordered in the deep cold of winter to come. They started to come. Mr. Pembroke, who represents our village in the Vermont legislature, came and helped me dig some of the holes where some of the things I wanted to put in were to be planted. Mr. Pembroke is a very nice man. He is never dressed in the clothing of schoolboys. There is not a look of misery on his face; on his face is the complicated look of an ordinary human being. When he works in my garden, we agree on a price; he sends me bill, and I pay it. The days are growing longer and longer, and then they'll get shorter again. I am now used to that ordered progression, and I love it. But there is not order in my garden. I live in America now. Americans are impatient with memory, which is one of the things order thrives on.

Diane Burns 1950–

Born Anishinabe (Ojibwa) and Chemehuevi Indian in Milwaukee, Wisconsin, Diane Burns is a uniquely eclectic person. Besides being a writer of plays, songs, poetry, essays, and short stories, her résumé also includes painter, illustrator, elementary-school teacher, girls' volleyball and gymnastics coach, and U.S. Forest Service fire tower lookout. Awarded the Congressional Medal of Merit for academic and artistic excellence while attending the Institute of American Indian Art in Santa Fe, New Mexico, Burns went on to study at Columbia University's Barnard College in New York City. She was nominated for the William Carlos Williams Award for her first collection of poetry, *Riding the One-Eyed Ford* (1981), and has contributed articles, poems, and short stories to a variety of magazines and journals for children and adults. She has written book reviews for the Council on Interracial Books for Children and has won numerous awards in children's literature, including *Highlights for Children's* annual fiction prize for "Dancing Puppets Mystery" (1986) and the Elizabeth Burr Award for outstanding children's literature for *Cranberries: Fruit of the Bogs*. Burns's joke books have been featured on PBS-TV's *Reading Rainbow*.

BIG FUN

I don't care if you're married I still love you
I don't care if you're married
After the party's over
I will take you home in my One-Eyed Ford
Way   yah hi yo,   Way yah hi yo!

5

Modene!
the roller derby queen!
She's Anishinabe,
    that means Human Being!
That's H for hungry!   10
and B for frijoles!
            frybread!
            Tortillas!
            Watermelon!
            Pomona!   15
Take a sip of this
and a drag of that!
At the rancheria fiesta
It's tit for tat!
Low riders and Levis   20
go fist in glove!
Give it a little pat
a push or a shove
Move it or lose it!
Talk straight or bruise it!   25
Everyone
has her fun
when the sun
is all done
We're all one   30
make a run
hide your gun
Hey!
I'm no nun!
'49 in the hills above   35
            Ventura
Them Okies gotta drum

I'm from Oklahoma
I got no one to call my own
if you will be my honey   40
I will be your sugar pie, way hi yah,
Way yah hey way yah hi yah!

We're gonna sing all night
bring your blanket
or   45
be that way then!

GADOSHKIBOS

Gadoshkibos
the warrior
He would sign no treaties
"Foolish" he called them
The whites are crazy   5
The whites are crazy
they sang around the fires at night
when the Anishinabe knew the trappers were gone.

Gadoshkibos
great grandfather   10
dies in ecstacy
Nakota arrow in his throat, cries
The whites are crazy
Why fight among each other when we know?
The real enemy rushes us like buffaloes into a trap.   15

Gadoshkibos
son of the same
lays at night with his wives.
They ran, hid, but now
they stay put year round.   20
The whites are crazy.
The children starve on commodity food
and he wonders where the Anishinabe warriors have gone.

Gadoshkibos
wife, the second,   25
struggles with her garden
ground is good with blood
spilled there and she knows
the whites are crazy
and she handles her hoe like a rifle.   30
Her sisters in the nations watch the children and know they must wait.

Gadoshkibos
the latest one
reads sociology
at Pomona State   35
and studies just why
the whites are crazy.
Summertimes he goes back to the blanket
and he wanders the woods and wonders where the warriors have gone.

Carolyn Forche 1950–

In 1981, Carolyn Forche forged her reputation as a political poet with *The Country Between Us*. A graphic rendering of the Salvadorans' horrific plight, which she witnessed while working as a human rights activist during the late 1970s civil war, this collection of poems won numerous awards, including the Lamont award from the Academy of American Poets. Raised in the suburbs of Detroit, Michigan, Forche began writing at the age of nine when her mother gave her an anthology of poetry and suggested that she, too, try composing. Fifteen years later, she completed *Gathering the Tribes*, a largely autobiographical initial work and winner of the 1975 Yale Series of Younger Poets Award. She has worked as a foreign correspondent in Beirut, Lebanon, as human rights liaison in South Africa, and has translated the poetry of Salvadorian-exiled poet Claribel Alegria and French Resistance poet Robert Desnos. She has held three fellowships from the National Endowment for the Arts. Her poetry, articles, book reviews, and essays have appeared in a wide variety of distinguished periodicals. Later works include *Against Forgetting* (1993), her anthologized collection of twentieth-century poetry of witness by poets who braved extreme social, political, and historical conditions during this time, and *The Angel of History* (1994), which received the *Los Angeles Times* Book Award.

THE COLONEL

What you have heard is true. I was in his house. His wife carried a tray of coffee and sugar. His daughter filed her nails, his son went out for the night. There were daily papers, pet dogs, a pistol on the cushion beside him. The moon swung bare on its black cord over the house. On the television was a cop show. It was in English. Broken bottles were embedded in the walls around the house to scoop the kneecaps from a man's legs or cut his hands to lace. On the windows there were gratings like those in liquor stores. We had dinner, rack of lamb, good wine, a gold bell was on the table for calling the maid. The maid brought green mangoes, salt, a type of bread. I was asked how I enjoyed the country. There was a brief commercial in Spanish. His wife took everything away. There was some talk then of how difficult it had become to govern. The parrot said hello on the terrace. The colonel told it to shut up, and pushed himself from the table. My friend said to me with his eyes: say nothing. The colonel returned with a sack used to bring groceries home. He spilled many human ears on the table. They were like dried peach halves. There is no other way to say this. He took one of them in his hands, shook it in our faces, dropped it into a water glass. It came alive there. I am tired of fooling around he said.

As for the rights of anyone, tell your people they can go fuck themselves. He swept the ears to the floor with his arm and held the last of his wine in the air. Something for your poetry, no? he said. Some of the ears on the floor caught this scrap of his voice. Some of the ears on the floor were pressed to the ground.

May 1978

Gloria Naylor 1950–

G loria Naylor graduated from Brooklyn College (B.A.) in 1981 and from Yale University (M.A.) in 1983. She began writing her most well-known novel, *The Women of Brewster Place* (1982), while she was an undergraduate; at the time, she also worked as a telephone operator. An African-American writer who has studied both her African forebears and what is usually called the "European tradition," Naylor draws on Western and African-American sources to explore the complexities of life in the United States for African Americans. In addition to *Brewster Place*, her novels include *Bailey's Cafe* (1982), *Linden Hills* (1985), and *Mama Day* (1988). Gloria Naylor has received a number of prestigious honors, including a National Endowment for the Arts Fellowship and a Guggenheim Fellowship. She has taught at a number of colleges and universities and also serves as the president of her film company, One Way Productions. The firm enacts one of Naylor's goals: to develop quality children's programming. Regarding Gloria Naylor's writing, critics note that her fiction ". . . avoids stereotypes and didacticism," suggesting that her work "manages to make the reader understand how the economic and social situation of black lives becomes one with personal lives . . . without diminishing the humanity of the individuals involved."

From THE WOMEN OF BREWSTER PLACE

ETTA MAE JOHNSON

The unpainted walls of the long rectangular room were soaked with the smell of greasy chicken and warm, headless beer. The brown and pink faces floated above the trails of used cigarette smoke like bodiless carnival balloons. The plump yellow woman with white gardenias pinned to the side of her head stood with her back pressed against the peeling sides of the baby grand and tried to pierce the bloated hum in the room with her thin scratchy voice. Undisturbed that she remained for the most part ignored, she motioned for the piano player to begin.

It wasn't the music or the words or the woman that took that room by its throat until it gasped for air—it was the pain. There was a young southern girl, Etta Johnson, pushed up in a corner table, and she never forgot. The music, the woman, the words.

> I love my man
> I'm a lie if I say I don't
> I love my man
> I'm a lie if I say I don't
> But I'll quit my man
> I'm a lie if I say I won't

> My man wouldn't give me no breakfast
> Wouldn't give me no dinner
> Squawked about my supper
> Then he put me out of doors
> Had the nerve to lay
> A matchbox to my clothes
> I didn't have so many
> But I had a long, long, way to go

Children bloomed on Brewster Place during July and August with their colorful shorts and tops plastered against gold, ebony, and nut-brown legs and arms; they decorated the street, rivaling the geraniums and ivy found on the manicured boulevard downtown. The summer heat seemed to draw the people from their cramped apartments onto the stoops, as it drew the tiny drops of perspiration from their foreheads and backs.

The apple-green Cadillac with the white vinyl roof and Florida plates turned into Brewster like a greased cobra. Since Etta had stopped at a Mobil station three blocks away to wash off the evidence of a hot, dusty 1200-mile odyssey home, the chrome caught the rays of the high afternoon sun and flung them back into its face. She had chosen her time well.

The children, free from the conditioned restraints of their older counterparts, ran along the sidewalks flanking this curious, slow-moving addition to their world. Every eye on the block, either openly or covertly, was on the door of the car when it opened. They were rewarded by the appearance of a pair of white leather sandals attached to narrow ankles and slightly bowed, shapely legs. The willow-green sundress, only ten minutes old on the short chestnut woman, clung to a body that had finished a close second in its race with time. Large two-toned sunglasses hid the weariness that had defied the freshly applied mascara and burnt-ivory shadow. After taking twice the time needed to stretch herself, she reached into the back seat of the car and pulled out her plastic clothes bag and Billie Holiday albums.

The children's curiosity reached the end of its short life span, and they drifted back to their various games. The adults sucked their teeth in disappointment, and the more envious felt self-righteousness twist the corners of their mouths. It was only Etta. Looked like she'd done all right by herself—this time around.

Slowly she carried herself across the street—head high and eyes fixed unwaveringly on her destination. The half-dozen albums were clutched in front of her chest like cardboard armor.

> There ain't nothing I ever do
> Or nothing I ever say
> That folks don't criticize me
> But I'm going to do
> Just what I want to, anyway
> And don't care just what people say
> If I should take a notion
> To jump into the ocean
> Ain't nobody's business if I do . . .

Any who bothered to greet her never used her first name. No one called Etta Mae "Etta," except in their minds; and when they spoke to each other about her, it was Etta Johnson; but when they addressed her directly, it was always Miss Johnson. This baffled her because she knew what they thought about her, and she'd always call them by their first names and invited them to do the same with her. But after a few awkward attempts, they'd fall back into the pattern they were somehow comfortable with. Etta didn't know if this was to keep the distance on her side or theirs, but it was there. And she had learned to tread through these alien undercurrents so well that to a casual observer she had mastered the ancient secret of walking on water.

Mattie sat in her frayed brocade armchair, pushed up to the front window, and watched her friend's brave approach through the dusty screen. Still toting around them oversized records, she thought. That woman is a puzzlement.

Mattie rose to open the door so Etta wouldn't have to struggle to knock with her arms full. "Lord, child, thank you," she gushed, out of breath. "The younger I get, the higher those steps seem to stretch."

She dumped her load on the sofa and swept off her sunglasses. She breathed deeply of the freedom she found in Mattie's presence. Here she had no choice but to be herself. The carefully erected decoys she was constantly shuffling and changing to fit the situation were of no use here. Etta and Mattie went way back, a singular term that claimed coknowledge of all the important events in their lives and almost all of the unimportant ones. And by rights of this possession, it tolerated no secrets.

"Sit on down and take a breather. Must have been a hard trip. When you first said you were coming, I didn't expect you to be driving."

"To tell the truth, I didn't expect it myself, Mattie. But Simeon got very ornery when I said I was heading home, and he refused to give me the money he'd promised for my plane fare. So I said, just give me half and I'll take the train. Well, he wasn't gonna even do that. And Mattie, you know I'll be damned if I was coming into this city on a raggedy old Greyhound. So one night he was by my place all drunk up and snoring, and as kindly as you please, I took the car keys and registration and so here I am."

"My God, woman! You stole the man's car?"

"Stole—nothing. He owes me that and then some."

"Yeah, but the police don't wanna hear that. It's a wonder the highway patrol ain't stopped you before now."

"They ain't stopped me because Simeon didn't report it."

"How you know that?"

"His wife's daddy is the sheriff of that county." Laughter hung dangerously on the edge of the two women's eyes and lips.

"Yeah, but he could say you picked his pockets."

Etta went to her clothes bag and pulled out a pair of pink and red mono-grammed shorts. "I'd have to be a damned good pickpocket to get away with all this." The laughter lost its weak hold on their mouths and went bouncing crazily against the walls of the living room.

> Them that's got, shall get
> Them that's not, shall lose
> So the Bible says
> And it still is news

Each time the laughter would try to lie still, the two women would look at each other and send it hurling between them, once again.

> Mamma may have
> Papa may have
> But God bless the child
> That's got his own
> That's got his own

"Lord, Tut, you're a caution." Mattie wiped the tears off her cheeks with the back of a huge dark hand.

Etta was unable to count the years that had passed since she had heard someone call her that. Look a' that baby gal strutting around here like a bantam. You think she'd be the wife of King Tut. The name had stayed because she never lost the walk. The washed-out grime and red mud of backwoods Rock Vale, Tennessee, might wrap itself around her bare feet and coat the back of her strong fleshy legs, but Etta always had her shoulders flung behind her collarbone and her chin thrust toward the horizon that came to mean everything Rock Vale did not.

Etta spent her teenage years in constant trouble. Rock Vale had no place for a black woman who was not only unwilling to play by the rules, but whose spirit challenged the very right of the game to exist. The whites in Rock Vale were painfully reminded of this rebellion when she looked them straight in the face while putting in her father's order at the dry goods store, when she reserved her sirs and mams for those she thought deserving, and when she smiled only if pleased, regardless of whose presence she was in. That Johnson gal wasn't being an uppity nigger, as talk had it; she was just being herself.

> Southern trees bear strange fruit
> Blood on the leaves and blood at the root
> Black bodies swinging
> In the southern breeze
> Strange fruit hanging
> From the poplar trees

But Rutherford County wasn't ready for Etta's blooming independence, and so she left one rainy summer night about three hours ahead of dawn and Johnny Brick's furious pursuing relatives. Mattie wrote and told her they had waited in ambush for two days on the county line, and then had returned and burned down her father's barn. The sheriff told Mr. Johnson that he had gotten off mighty light—considering. Mr. Johnson thought so, too. After reading Mattie's letter, Etta was sorry she hadn't killed the horny white bastard when she had the chance.

Rock Vale had followed her to Memphis, Detroit, Chicago, and even to New York. Etta soon found out that America wasn't ready for her yet—not in 1937. And so along with the countless other disillusioned, restless children of Ham with so much to give and nowhere to give it, she took her talents to the street. And she learned to get over, to hook herself to any promising rising black star, and when he burnt out, she found another.

Her youth had ebbed away quickly under the steady pressure of the changing times, but she was existing as she always had. Even if someone had bothered to stop and tell her that the universe had expanded for her, just an inch, she wouldn't have known how to shine alone.

Etta and Mattie had taken totally different roads that with all of their deceptive winding had both ended up on Brewster Place. Their laughter now drew them into a conspiratorial circle against all the Simeons outside of that dead-end street, and it didn't stop until they were both weak from the tears that flowed down their faces.

"So," Mattie said, blowing her nose on a large cotton handkerchief, "trusting you stay out of jail, what you plan on doing now?"

"Child, I couldn't tell you." Etta dropped back down on the couch. "I should be able to get a coupla thousand for the car to tide me over till another business opportunity comes along."

Mattie raised one eyebrow just a whisper of an inch. "Ain't it time you got yourself a regular job? These last few years them *business opportunities* been fewer and farther between."

Etta sucked her small white teeth. "A job doing what? Come on, Mattie, what kind of experience I got? Six months here, three there. I oughta find me a good man and settle down to live quiet in my old age." She combed her fingers confidently through the thick sandy hair that only needed slight tinting at the roots and mentally gave herself another fifteen years before she had to worry about this ultimate fate.

Mattie, watching the creeping tiredness in her eyes, gave her five. "You done met a few promising ones along the way, Etta."

"No, honey, it just seemed so. Lets' face it, Mattie. All the good men are either dead or waiting to be born."

"Why don't you come to meeting with me tonight. There's a few settle-minded men in our church, some widowers and such. And a little prayer wouldn't hurt your soul one bit."

"I'll thank you to leave my soul well alone, Mattie Michael. And if your church is so full of upright Christian men, why you ain't snagged one yet?"

"Etta, I done banked them fires a long time ago, but seeing that you still keeping up steam . . ." Her eyes were full of playful kindness.

"Just barely, Mattie, just barely."

And laughter rolled inside of 2E, once again.

"Etta, Etta Mae!" Mattie banged on the bathroom door. "Come on out now. You making me late for the meeting."

"Just another second, Mattie. The church ain't gonna walk away."

"Lord," Mattie grumbled, "she ain't bigger than a minute, so it shouldn't take more than that to get ready."

Etta came out of the bathroom in an exaggerated rush. "My, my, you the most impatient Christian I know."

"Probably, the only Christian you know." Mattie refused to be humored as she bent to gather up her sweater and purse. She turned and was stunned with a barrage of colors. A huge white straw hat reigned over layers of gold and pearl beads draped over too much bosom and too little dress. "You plan on dazzling the Lord, Etta?"

"Well, honey," Etta said, looking down the back of her stocking leg to double-check for runs, "last I heard, He wasn't available. You got more recent news?"

"Um, um, um." Mattie pressed her lips together and shook her head slowly to swallow down the laughter she felt crawling up her throat. Realizing she wasn't going to succeed, she quickly turned her face from Etta and headed toward the door. "Just bring your blasphemin' self on downstairs. I done already missed morning services waiting on you today."

Canaan Baptist Church, a brooding, ashen giant, sat in the middle of a block of rundown private homes. Its multi-colored, dome-shaped eyes glowered into the darkness. Fierce clapping and thunderous organ chords came barreling out of its mouth. Evening services had begun.

Canaan's congregation, the poor who lived in a thirty-block area around Brewster Place, still worshiped God loudly. They could not afford the refined, muted benediction of the more prosperous blacks who went to Sinai Baptist on the northern end of the city, and because each of their requests for comfort was so pressing, they took no chances that He did not hear them.

When Israel was in Egypts's land
Let my people go
Oppressed so hard, they could not stand
Let my people go

The words were as ancient as the origin of their misery, but the tempo had picked up threefold in its evolution from the cotton fields. They were now sung with the frantic determination of a people who realized that the world was swiftly changing but for some mystic, complex reason their burden had not.

God said to go down
Go down
Brother Moses
Brother Moses
To the shore of the great Nile River

The choir clapped and stomped each syllable into a devastating reality, and just as it did, the congregation reached up, grabbed the phrase, and tried to clap and stomp it back into oblivion.

Go to Egypt
Go to Egypt
Tell Pharaoh
Tell Pharaoh
Let my people go

Etta entered the back of the church like a reluctant prodigal, prepared at best to be amused. The alien pounding and the heat and the dark glistening bodies dragged her back, back past the cold ashes of her innocence to a time when pain could be castrated on the sharp edges of iron-studded faith. The blood rushed to her temples and began to throb in unison with the musical pleas around her.

Yes, my God is a mighty God
Lord, deliver
And he set old Israel free
Swallowed that Egyptian army
Lord, deliver
With the waves of the great Red Sea

Etta glanced at Mattie, who was swaying and humming, and she saw that the lines in her face had almost totally vanished. She had left Etta in just that moment for a place where she was free. Sadly, Etta looked at her, at them all, and was very envious. Unaccustomed to the irritating texture of doubt, she felt tears as its abrasiveness grated over the fragile skin of her life. Could there have been another way?

The song ended with a huge expulsion of air, and the congregation sat down as one body.

"Come on, let's get us a seat." Mattie tugged her by the arm.

The grizzled church deacon with his suit hanging loosely off his stooped shoulders went up to the pulpit to read the church business.

"That's one of the widowers I was telling you about," Mattie whispered, and poked Etta.

"Unmm." The pressure on her arm brought Etta back onto the uncomfortable wooden pew. But she didn't want to stay there, so she climbed back out the window, through the glass eyes of the seven-foot Good Shepherd, and started again the futile weaving of invisible ifs and slippery mights into an equally unattainable past.

The scenes of her life reeled out before her with the same aging script; but now hindsight sat as the omniscient director and had the young star of her epic recite different brilliant lines and make the sort of stunning decisions that propelled her into the cushioned front pews on the right of the minister's podium. There she sat with the deacons' wives, officers of the Ladies' Auxiliary, and head usherettes. And like them, she would wear on her back a hundred pairs of respectful eyes earned the hard way, and not the way she had earned the red sundress, which she now self-consciously tugged up in the front. Was it too late?

The official business completed, the treasurer pulled at his frayed lapels, cleared his throat, and announced the guest speaker for the night.

The man was magnificent.

He glided to the podium with the effortlessness of a well-oiled machine and stood still for an interminable long moment. He eyed the congregation confidently. He only needed their attention for that split second because once he got it, he was going to wrap his voice around their souls and squeeze until they screamed to be relieved. They knew it was coming and waited expectantly, breathing in unison as one body. First he played with them and threw out fine silken threads that stroked their heart muscles ever so gently. They trembled ecstatically at the touch and invited more. The threads multiplied and entwined themselves solidly around the one pulsating organ they had become and tightened slightly, testing them for a reaction.

The "Amen, brothers" and "Yes, Jesus" were his permission to take that short hop from the heart to the soul and lay all pretense of gentleness aside. Now he would have to push and pound with clenched fists in order to be felt, and he dared not stop the fierce rhythm of his voice until their replies had reached that fevered pitch of satisfaction. Yes, Lord—grind out the unheated tenements! Merciful Jesus—shove aside the low-paying boss man. Perfect Father—fill me, fill me till there's no room, no room for nothing else, not even that great big world out there that exacts such a strange penalty for my being born black.

It was hard work. There was so much in them that had to be replaced. The minister's chest was heaving in long spasms, and the sweat was pouring down his gray temples and rolling under his chin. His rich voice was now hoarse, and his legs and raised arms trembled on the edge of collapse. And as always they were satisfied a half-breath before he reached the end of his endurance. They sat back, limp and spent, but momentarily at peace. There was no price too high for this service. At that instant they would have followed him to do battle with the emperor of the world, and all he was going to ask of them was money for the "Lord's work." And they would willingly give over half of their little to keep this man in comfort.

Etta had not been listening to the message; she was watching the man. His body moved with the air of one who had not known recent deprivation. The tone of his skin and the fullness around his jawline told her that he was well-off, even before she got close enough to see the manicured hands and diamond pinkie ring.

The techniques he had used to brand himself on the minds of the congregation were not new to her. She'd encountered talent like that in poolrooms, nightclubs, grimy second-floor insurance offices, numbers dens, and on a dozen street corners. But here was a different sort of power. The jungle-sharpened instincts of a man like that could move her up to the front of the church, ahead of the deacons' wives and Ladies' Auxiliary, off of Brewster Place for good. She would find not only luxury but a place that complemented the type of woman she had fought all these years to become.

"Mattie, is that your regular minister?" she whispered.

"Who, Reverend Woods? No, he just visits on occasion, but he sure can preach, can't he?"

"What you know about him, he married?"

Mattie cut her eyes at Etta. "I should have figured it wasn't the sermon that moved you. At least wait till after the prayer before you jump all into the man's business."

During the closing song and prayer Etta was planning how she was going to maneuver Mattie to the front of the church and into introducing her to Reverend Woods. It wasn't going to be as difficult as she thought. Moreland T. Woods had noticed Etta from the moment she'd entered the church. She stood out like a bright red bird among the drab morality that dried up the breasts and formed rolls round the stomachs of the other church sisters. This woman was still dripping with the juices of a full-fleshed life—the kind of life he was soon to get up and damn into hell for the rest of the congregation—but how it fitted her well. He had to swallow to remove the excess fluid from his mouth before he got up to preach.

Now the problem was to make his way to the back of the church before she left without seeming to be in a particular hurry. A half-dozen back slaps, handshakes, and thank-you sisters only found him about ten feet up the aisle, and he was growing impatient. However, he didn't dare to turn his neck and look in the direction where he'd last seen her. He felt a hand on his upper arm and turned to see a grim-faced Mattie flanked by the woman in the scarlet dress.

"Reverend Woods, I really enjoyed your sermon," Mattie said.

"Why, thank you, sister—sister?"

"Sister Michael, Mattie Michael." While he was addressing his words to her, the smile he sent over her shoulder to Etta was undeniable.

"Especially the part," Mattie raised her voice a little, "About throwing away temptation to preserve the soul. That was a mighty fine point."

"The Lord moves me and I speak, Sister Michael. I'm just a humble instrument for his voice."

The direction and intent of his smile was not lost to Etta. She inched her way in front of Mattie. "I enjoyed it, too, Reverend Woods. It's been a long time since I heard preaching like that." She increased the pressure of her fingers on Mattie's arm.

"Oh, excuse my manners. Reverend Woods, this is an old friend of mine, Etta Mae Johnson. Etta Mae, Reverend Woods." She intoned the words as if she were reciting a eulogy.

"Please to meet you, Sister Johnson." He beamed down on the small woman and purposely held her hand a fraction longer than usual. "You must be a new member—I don't recall seeing you the times I've been here before."

"Well, no, Reverend, I'm not a member of the congregation, but I was raised up in the church. You know how it is, as you get older sometimes you stray away. But after your sermon, I'm truly thinking of coming back."

Mattie tensed, hoping that the lightning that God was surely going to strike Etta with wouldn't hit her by mistake.

"Well, you know what the Bible says, sister. The angels rejoice more over one sinner who turns around than over ninety-nine righteous ones."

"Yes, indeed, and I'm sure a shepherd like you has helped to turn many back to the fold." She looked up and gave him the full benefit of her round dark eyes, grateful she hadn't put on that third coat of mascara.

"I try, Sister Johnson, I try."

"It's a shame Mrs. Woods wasn't here tonight to hear you. I'm sure she must be mighty proud of your work."

"My wife has gone to her glory, Sister Johnson. I think of myself now as a man alone—rest her soul."

"Yes, rest her soul," Etta sighed.

"Please, Lord, yes," Mattie muttered, giving out the only sincere request among the three. The intensity of her appeal startled them, and they turned to look at her. "Only knows how hard this life is, she's better in the arms of Jesus."

"Yes"—Etta narrowed her eyes at Mattie and then turned back to the minister—"I can testify to that. Being a woman alone, it seems all the more hard. Sometimes you don't know where to turn."

Moreland Woods knew Etta was the type of woman who not only knew which way to turn, but, more often than not, had built her own roads when nothing else was accessible. But he was enjoying this game immensely—almost as much as the growing heat creeping into his groin.

"Well, if I can be of any assistance, Sister Johnson, don't hesitate to ask. I couldn't sleep knowing one of the Lord's sheep is troubled. As a matter of fact, if you have anything you would like to discuss with me this evening, I'd be glad to escort you home."

"I don't have my own place. You see, I'm just up from out of state and staying with my friend Mattie here."

"Well, perhaps we could all go out for coffee."

"Thank you, but I'll have to decline, Reverend," Mattie volunteered before Etta did it for her. "The services have me all tired out, but if Etta wants to, she's welcome."

"That'll be just fine," Etta said.

"Good, good." And now it was his turn to give her the benefit of a mouth full of strong gold-capped teeth. "Just let me say good-bye to a few folks here, and I'll meet you outside."

"Girl, you oughta patent that speed and sell it to the airplane companies," Mattie said outside. "'After that sermon, Reverend, I'm thinking of coming back'—indeed!"

"Aw, hush your fussing."

"I declare if you had batted them lashes just a little faster, we'd of had a dust storm in there."

"You said you wanted me to meet some nice men. Well, I met one."

"Etta, I meant a man who'd be serious about settling down with you." Mattie was exasperated. "Why, you're going on like a schoolgirl. Can't you see what he's got in mind?"

Etta turned an indignant face toward Mattie. "The only thing I see is that you're telling me I'm not good enough for a man like that. Oh, no, not Etta Johnson. No upstanding decent man could ever see anything in her but a quick good time. Well, I'll tell you something, Mattie Michael. I've always traveled first class, maybe not in the way you'd approve with all your fine Christian principles, but it's done all right by me. And I'm gonna keep going top drawer till I leave this earth. Don't you think I got a mirror? Each year there's a new line to cover. I lay down with this body and get up with it every morning, and each morning it cries for just a little more rest than it did the day before. Well, I'm finally gonna get that rest, and it's going to be with a man like Reverend Woods. And you and the rest of those slack-mouthed gossips on Brewster be damned!" Tears frosted the edges of her last words. "They'll be humming a different tune when I show up there the wife of a big preacher. I've always known what they say about me behind my back, but I never thought you were right in there with them."

Mattie was stunned by Etta's tirade. How could Etta have so totally misunderstood her words? What had happened back there to stuff up her senses to the point that she had missed the obvious? Surely she could not believe that the vibrations coming from that unholy game of charades in the church aisle would lead to something as permanent as marriage? Why, it had been nothing but the opening gestures to a mating dance. Mattie had gone through the same motions at least once in her life, and Etta must have known a dozen variations to it that were a mystery to her. And yet, somehow, back there it had been played to a music that had totally distorted the steps for her friend. Mattie suddenly felt the helplessness of a person who is forced to explain that for which there are no words.

She quietly turned her back and started down the steps. There was no need to defend herself against Etta's accusations. They shared at least a hundred memories that could belie those cruel words. Let them speak for her.

Sometimes being a friend means mastering that art of timing. There is a time for silence. A time to let go and allow people to hurl themselves into their own destiny. And a time to prepare to pick up the pieces when it's all over. Mattie realized that this moment called for all three.

"I'll see ya when you get home, Etta," she threw gently over her shoulder.

Etta watched the bulky figure become slowly enveloped by the shadows. Her angry words had formed a thick mucus in her throat, and she couldn't swallow them down. She started to run into the darkness where she'd seen Mattie disappear, but at that instant Moreland Woods came out of the lighted church, beaming.

He took her arm and helped her into the front seat of his car. Her back sank into the deep upholstered leather, and the smell of the freshly vacuumed carpet was mellow in her nostrils. All of the natural night sounds of the city were blocked by the thick tinted windows and the hum of the air conditioner, but they trailed persistently behind the polished back of the vehicle as it turned and headed down the long gray boulevard.

> Smooth road
> Clear day
> But why am I the only one
> Traveling this way
> How strange the road to love
> Can be so easy
> Can there be a detour ahead?

Moreland Woods was captivated by the beautiful woman at his side. Her firm brown flesh and bright eyes carried the essence of nectar from some untamed exotic flower, and the fragrance was causing a pleasant disturbance at the pit of his stomach. He marveled at how excellently she played the game. A less alert observer might have been taken in, but his survival depended upon knowing people, knowing exactly how much to give and how little to take. It was this razor-thin instinct that had catapulted him to the head of his profession and that would keep him there.

And although she cut her cards with a reckless confidence, pushed her chips into the middle of the table as though the supply was unlimited, and could sit out the game until dawn, he knew. Oh, yes. Let her win a few, and then he would win just a few more, and she would be bankrupt long before the sun was up.

And then there would be only one thing left to place on the table—and she would, because the stakes they were playing for were very high. But she was going to lose that last deal. She would lose because when she first sat down in that car she had everything riding on the fact that he didn't know the game existed.

And so it went. All evening Etta had been in another world, weaving his tailored suit and the smell of his expensive cologne into a custom-made future for herself. It took his last floundering thrusts into her body to bring her back to reality. She arrived in enough time to feel him beating against her like a dying walrus, until he shuddered and was still.

She kept her eyes closed because she knew when she opened them there would be the old familiar sights around her. To her right would be the plastic-coated nightstand that matched the cheaply carved headboard of the bed she lay in. She felt the bleached coarseness of the sheet under her sweaty back and predicted the roughness of the worn carpet path that led from the bed to the white-tiled bathroom with bright fluorescent light, sterilized towels, and tissue-wrapped water glasses. There would be two or three small thin rectangles of soap wrapped in bright waxy covers that bore the name of the hotel.

She didn't try to visualize what the name would be. It didn't matter. They were all the same, all meshed together into one lump that rested like an iron ball on her chest. And the expression on the face of this breathing mass to her left would be the same as all the others. She could turn now and go through the rituals that would tie up the evening for them both, but she wanted just one more second of this smoothing darkness before she had to face the echoes of the locking doors she knew would be in his eyes.

Etta got out of the car unassisted and didn't bother to turn and watch the tail-lights as it pulled off down the deserted avenue adjacent to Brewster Place. She had asked him to leave her at the corner because there was no point in his having to make a U-turn in the dead-end street, and it was less than a hundred yards to her door. Moreland was relieved that she had made it easy for him, because it had been a long day and he was anxious to get home and go to sleep. But then, the whole business had gone pretty smoothly after they left the hotel. He hadn't even been called upon to use any of the excuses he had prepared for why it would be a while before he'd see her again. A slight frown crossed his forehead as he realized that she had seemed as eager to get away from him as he had been to leave. Well, he shrugged his shoulders and placated his dented ego, that's the nice part about these worldly women. They understand the temporary weakness of the flesh and don't make it out to be something bigger than it is. They can have a good time without pawing and hanging all onto a man. Maybe I should drop around sometime. He glanced into his rearview mirror and saw that Etta was still standing on the corner, looking straight ahead into Brewster. There was something about the slumped profile of her body, silhouetted against the dim street light, that caused him to press down on the accelerator.

Etta stood looking at the wall that closed off Brewster from the avenues farther north and found it hard to believe that it had been just this afternoon when she had seen it. It had looked so different then, with the August sun highlighting the browns and reds of the bricks and the young children bouncing their rubber balls against its side. Now it crouched there in the thin predawn light, like a pulsating mouth awaiting her arrival. She shook her head sharply to rid herself of the illusion, but an uncanny fear gripped her, and her legs felt like lead. If I walk into this street, she thought, I'll never come back. I'll never get out. Oh, dear God, I am so tired—so very tired.

Etta removed her hat and massaged her tight forehead. Then, giving a resigned sigh, she started slowly down the street. Had her neighbors been out on their front stoops, she could have passed through their milling clusters as anonymously as the night wind. They had seen her come down that street once in a broken Chevy that had about five hundred dollars' worth of contraband liquor in its trunk, and there was even the time she'd come home with a broken nose she'd gotten in some hair-raising escapade in St. Louis, but never had she walked among them with a broken spirit. This middle-aged woman in the wrinkled dress and wilted straw hat would have been a stranger to them.

When Etta got to the stoop, she noticed there was a light under the shade at Mattie's window, and she strained to hear what actually sounded like music coming from behind the screen. Mattie was playing her records! Etta stood very still, trying to decipher the broken air waves into intelligible sound, but she couldn't make out the words. She stopped straining when it suddenly came to her that it wasn't important what song it was—someone was waiting up for her. Someone who would deny fiercely that there had been any concern—just a little indigestion from them fried onions that kept me from sleeping. Thought I'd pass the time by figuring out what you seen in all this loose-life music.

Etta laughed softly to herself as she climbed the steps toward the light and the love and the comfort that awaited her.

Joy Harjo 1951–

Born in Tulsa, Oklahoma, to a Creek father and Cherokee-French mother, Joy Harjo is an enrolled member of the Muskogee tribe. Although her poetic landscape is steeped in Indian history, mythology, and symbols, she relies primarily on contemporary cultural and ethical conflicts in her stories. As Harjo states in *Contemporary Literary Criticism*, "I feel strongly that I have a responsibility to all the sources that I am: to all the past and future ancestors, to my home country, to all the places that I touch down on and that are myself, to all voices, all women, all of my tribe, all people, all earth, and beyond that to all beginnings and endings." She is a graduate of the Institute of American Indian

Arts and the University of New Mexico. In 1978, she received her M.F.A. in creative writing from the University of Iowa Writers' Workshop. Harjo has published five books of poetry, including *In Mad Love and War*, which won the William Carlos Williams Award for the best poetry book of 1991. In addition, she edited *Reinventing the Enemy's Language* (1997), an anthology of Native-American women writers. A recipient of numerous awards and fellowships, she is currently a professor at the University of New Mexico. Harjo also plays saxophone in Poetic Justice, a band that incorporates her spoken lyrics over a "tribal-jazz-reggae" backdrop with additional elements of rock, blues, and prophesy. *Letter from the End of the 20th Century* is the band's critically acclaimed CD.

SHE HAD SOME HORSES

She had some horses.

She had horses who were bodies of sand.
She had horses who were maps drawn of blood.
She had horses who were skins of ocean water.
She had horses who were the blue air of sky.   5
She had horses who were fur and teeth.
She had horses who were clay and would break.
She had horses who were splintered red cliff.

She had some horses.

She had horses with long, pointed breasts.   10
She had horses with full, brown thighs.
She had horses who laughed too much.
She had horses who threw rocks at glass houses.
She had horses who licked razor blades.

She had some horses.   15

She had horses who danced in their mothers' arms.
She had horses who thought they were the sun and their
bodies shone and burned like stars.
She had horses who waltzed nightly on the moon.
She had horses who were much too shy, and kept quiet   20
in stalls of their own making.

She had some horses.

She had horses who liked Creek Stomp Dance songs.
She had horses who cried in their beer.

She had horses who spit at male queens who made   25
them afraid of themselves.
She had horses who said they weren't afraid.
She had horses who lied.
She had horses who told the truth, who were stripped
bare of their tongues.   30

She had some horses.

She had horses who called themselves, "horse."
She had horses who called themselves, "spirit," and kept
their voices secret and to themselves.
She had horses who had no names.   35
She had horses who had books of names.

She had some horses.

She had horses who whispered in the dark, who were afraid to speak.
She had horses who screamed out of fear of the silence, who
carried knives to protect themselves from ghosts.   40
She had horses who waited for destruction.
She had horses who waited for resurrection.

She had some horses.

She had horses who got down on their knees for any saviour.
She had horses who thought their high price had saved them.   45
She had horses who tried to save her, who climbed in her
bed at night and prayed as they raped her.

She had some horses.

She had some horses she loved.
She had some horses she hated.   50

These were the same horses.

REMEMBER

Remember the sky that you were born under,
know each of the star's stories.
Remember the moon, know who she is. I met her
in a bar once in Iowa City.
Remember the sun's birth at dawn, that is the   5
strongest point of time. Remember sundown
and the giving away to night.

Remember your birth, how your mother struggled
to give you form and breath. You are evidence of
her life, and her mother's, and hers.   10
Remember your father. He is your life, also.
Remember the earth whose skin you are:
red earth, black earth, yellow earth, white earth
brown earth, we are earth.
Remember the plants, trees, animal life who all have their   15
tribes, their families, their histories, too. Talk to them,
listen to them. They are alive poems.
Remember the wind. Remember her voice. She knows the
origin of this universe. I heard her singing Kiowa war
dance songs at the corner of Fourth and Central once.   20
Remember that you are all people and that all people
are you.
Remember that you are this universe and that this
universe is you.
Remember that all is in motion, is growing, is you.   25
Remember that language comes from this.
Remember the dance that language is, that life is.
Remember.

YOUR PHONE CALL AT 8 A.M.

Your phone call at eight a.m. could
have been a deadly rope.
All the colors of your voice
were shifted out. The barest part flew
through the wires. Then tight-roped   5
into the comfort of my own home,
where I surrounded myself with smoke
of piñon, with cedar and sage.
Protected the most dangerous places,
for more than survival, I always   10
meant. But what you wanted, this morning
you said, was a few words
and not my heart. What you wanted . . .
But the skeleton of your voice
clicked barely perceptible,   15
didn't you hear it?
And what you said you wanted

was easy enough, a few books
some pages, anything, to cancel
what your heart ever saw in me that you didn't.   20
But you forgot to say that part.
Didn't even recognize it when it
came winging out of you—
the skeleton's meat and blood,
all that you didn't want to remember   25
when you called at eight a.m. . . .
But that's alright because
this poem isn't for you
but for me
　　　after all.   30

Angela Jackson 1951–

Born in Greenville, Mississippi, Angela Jackson is the author of five collections of poetry. She was raised on Chicago's South Side, receiving her B.A. from Northwestern University and her M.A. from University of Chicago. Her collection, *Dark Legs and Silk Kisses: The Beatitudes of the Spinners* (1993), garnered a Carl Sandburg Literary Arts Award, which is given annually to Chicago-area residents. Other collections include *And All These Roads Be Luminous: Poems Selected and New* (1998); *The Man with the White Liver* (1987); *Solo in the Boxcar Third Floor E* (1985); and *Voo Doo Love Magic* (1974). *Booklist* reviewer Donna Seaman describes Jackson's writing as "sinuous and inexhaustible exhalations, complex riffs rich in sensuous detail and resonant with psychological insight. Jackson reanimates myth and history, scrutinizes life from unexpected perspectives, and shares her keen irony, seasoned humor, and hard-won wisdom in poems that conjure diverse times and places, and tell many stories." Currently, Jackson teaches English at Howard University in Washington, D.C.

CAESURA

A highschool girl high over the city
riding the el-train (a whip in midair
flung in tempered steel on long black legs)
on the afterschool second wind of adolescence.

The newspaper on a platform,   5
lines through a window:
Nat King Cole
dead of cancer.
Whatever remark to throw back
at whomever hangs   10
on the windowed air
like a scribble on sweating glass.
Who, girl, are you to know the sudden fall
of voice to whispers in the vestibule
of the funeral home, the steady fan of dreams   15
in the old women's hands,
the broken promise of seductive solace
in the sail of song across the dark waters
of the heart's imagination?
O, Imagination, quick slow schoolgirl   20
riding the flung-out steel
in your promissory sleep,
who are you now to study windows?

The day is punctuated with caesuras,
pauses in the voice, not usually   25
written down.

SONG OF THE WRITER WOMAN

Husband
These poems are your rival.
 They undress me.
 They keep me up nights.
  Turn my eyes to soft fruits   5
  ripe and realized.

Husband
These poems are my best friend.
 They listen to my monotony,
 my unceasing repeating.   10
 Against their patience I
 can never sin.

Husband
These poems are my passionate suitor.
 They go down on one knee.   15

They beg me, "Marry me. Marry me."
I find
I give them my hand.

Husband
This could be exciting: poems&me, you&me,   20
Ménage à trois. Permanently,
Happily.

Husband
Is a woman poet permitted bigamy?
Husband   25
Answer me!

ANGEL

FOR JERRY WARD

I am the only one here.

I stand in my one place
and I can see a good piece
down the road. I am yonder,
further than the chunk of your stone.   5
Right now, directly,
I am persimmon falling free
and the prisoner opening up
in me.
Don't come through my door and   10
want to run my house. I am
the angel who sweep air in and out my own
dancing body. I got good eyes. I can see.
A good piece down the road. Clear to
God murmuring in me. My head is the burning   15
bush. What I hold in my hand is the promised
land. I set my people free in me.
And we walk without wandering like people named
after mere plants,
because we are tree   20
and high-stepping roots
cake-walking
in this promised place.

Where I go is where I am now.
Don't mess with me: you hurt yourself.   25
In the middle of my stride now. I am walking
yes indeed I am walking through my own house.
I am walking yes indeed on my own piece of road.
Toting my own load
and yours and mine.   30
I tell you
I feel fine and clear this morning even
when it's night and a full moon with my thumbprint
on it.
Everything is clamorous and quiet.   35
    I am the only One here.
    And we don't break. No indeed.
    Come hell and high water.
    We don't break
    for nothing.   40

Judith Ortiz Cofer 1952–

Judith Ortiz Cofer's work often explores the challenges of one who must cross cultures, having spent part of her childhood with her mother's family in Puerto Rico and the other in Paterson, New Jersey, near her father's commission in the U.S. Navy. In addition to several books of poetry, including *The Native Dancer* (1981) and *Peregrina* (1986), Cofer has written a three-act play, *Latin Women Pray* (first produced in 1984), and personal essays. Her novel, *The Line of the Sun* (1989), was praised by critic Roberto Marquez, who noted that Cofer is a "writer of authentic gifts, with a genuine and important story to tell." Concerned with the experiences of immigrants and the temptations of assimilation, Cofer notes that her "place of birth itself becomes a metaphor for the things we all must leave behind; the assimilation of a new culture is . . . accepting the terms necessary for survival. My poetry is a study of this process of change, assimilation, and transformation."

PRIMARY LESSONS

My mother walked me to my first day at school at La Escuela Segundo Ruiz Belvis, named after the Puerto Rican patriot born in our town. I remember yellow cement with green trim. All the classrooms had been painted these colors to identify them as government property. This was true all over the Island. Everything was color-coded, including the children, who wore uniforms from first through twelfth grade. We were a midget army in white and brown, led by the hand to our battleground. From practically every house in our barrio emerged a crisply ironed uniform inhabited by the savage creatures we had become over a summer of running wild in the sun.

At my grandmother's house where we were staying until my father returned to Brooklyn Yard in New York and sent for us, it had been complete chaos, with several children to get ready for school. My mother had pulled my hair harder than usual while braiding it, and I had dissolved into a pool of total self-pity. I wanted to stay home with her and Mamá, to continue listening to stories in the late afternoon, at drink *café con leche* with them, and to play rough games with my many cousins. I wanted to continue living the dream of summer afternoons in Puerto Rico, and if I could not have it, then I wanted to go back to Paterson, New Jersey, back to where I imagined our apartment waited, peaceful and cool for the three of us to return to our former lives. Our gypsy lifestyle had convinced me, at age six, that one part of life stops and waits for you while you live another for a while—and if you don't like the present, you can always return to the past. Buttoning me into my stiff blouse while I tried to squirm away from her, my mother attempted to explain to me that I was a big girl now and should try to understand that, like all the other children my age, I had to go to school.

"What about him?" I yelled pointing at my brother who was lounging on the tile floor of our bedroom in his pajamas, playing quietly with a toy car.

"He's too young to go to school, you know that. Now stay still." My mother pinned me between her thighs to button my skirt, as she had learned to do from Mamá, from whose grip it was impossible to escape.

"It's not fair, it's not fair. I can't go to school here. I don't speak Spanish." It was my final argument, and it failed miserably because I was shouting my defiance in the language I claimed not to speak. Only I knew what I meant by saying in Spanish that I did not speak Spanish. I had spent my early childhood in the United States, where I lived in a bubble created by my Puerto Rican parents in a home where two cultures and languages became one. I learned to listen to the English from the television with one ear while I heard my mother and father speaking in Spanish with the other. I thought I was an ordinary American kid—like the children on the shows I watched—and that everyone's parents spoke a secret second language at home. When we came to Puerto Rico right before I started first grade, I switched easily to Spanish. It was the language of fun, of summertime games. But school—that was a different matter.

I made one last desperate attempt to make my mother see reason: "Father will be very angry. You know that he wants us to speak good English." My mother, of course, ignored me as she dressed my little brother in his playclothes. I could not believe her indifference to my father's wishes. She was usually so careful about our safety and the many other areas that he was forever reminding her about in his letters. But I was right, and she knew it. Our father spoke to us in English as much as possible, and he corrected my pronunciation constantly—not "jes" but "y-es." Y-es, sir. How could she send me to school to learn Spanish when we would be returning to Paterson in just a few months?

But, of course, what I feared was not language, but loss of freedom. At school there would be no playing, no stories, only lessons. I would not matter if I did not understand a word, and I would not be allowed to make up my own definitions. I would have to learn silence. I would have to keep my wild imagination in check. Feeling locked into my stiffly starched uniform, I only sensed all this. I guess most children can intuit their loss of childhood's freedom on that first day of school. It is separation anxiety too, but mother is just the guardian of the "playground" or our early childhood.

The sight of my cousins in similar straits comforted me. We were marched down the hill of our barrio where Mamá's robin-egg-blue house stood at the top. I must have glanced back at it with yearning. Mamá's house—a place built for children—where anything that could be broken had already been broken by my grandmother's early batch of offspring (they ranged in age from my mother's oldest sisters to my uncle who was six months older than me.) Her house had long since been made childproof. It had been a perfect summer place. And now it was September—the cruelest month for a child.

La Mrs., as all the teachers were called, waited for her class of first-graders at the door of the yellow and green classroom. She too wore a uniform: It was a blue skirt and a white blouse. This teacher wore black high heels with her "standard issue." I remember this detail because when we were all seated in rows she called on one little girl and pointed to the back of the room where there were shelves. She told the girl to bring her a shoebox from the bottom shelf. Then, when the box had been placed in her hands, she did something unusual. She had the little girl kneel at her feet and take the pointy high heels off her feet and replace them with a pair of satin slippers from the shoe box. She told the group that every one of us would have a chance to do this if we behaved in her class. Though confused about the prize, I soon felt caught up in the competition to bring *La Mrs.* her slippers in the morning. Children fought over the privilege.

Our first lesson was English. In Puerto Rico, every child has to take twelve years of English to graduate from school. It is the law. In my parents' school days, all subjects were taught in English. The U.S. Department of Education had specified that as a U.S. territory, the Island had to be "Americanized," and to accomplish this task, it was necessary for the Spanish language to be replaced in one generation through the teaching of English in all schools. My father began his school day by saluting the flag of the United States and singing "America" and "The Star-Spangled Banner" by rote, without understanding a word of what he was saying. The logic behind this system was that, though the children did not understand the English words, they would remember the rhythms. Even the games the teacher's manuals required them to play became absurd adaptations. "Here We Go Round the Mulberry Bush" became "Here We Go Round the Mango Tree." I have heard about the confusion caused by the use of a primer in which the sounds of animals were featured. The children were forced to accept that a rooster says *cockadoodledoo*, when they knew perfectly well from hearing their own roosters each morning that in Puerto Rico a rooster says *cocorocó*. Even the vocabulary of their pets was changed; there are still family stories circulating about the bewilderment of a first-grader coming home to try to teach his dog to speak in English. The policy of assimilation by immersion failed on the Island. Teachers adhered to it on paper, substituting their own materials for the texts, but no one took their English home. In due time, the program was minimized to the one class in English per day that I encountered when I took my seat in *La Mrs.*'s first grade class.

Catching us all by surprise, she stood very straight and tall in front of us and began to sing in English:

Pollito   — Chicken
Gallina   — Hen
Lápiz   — Pencil
Y Pluma   — Pen.

"Repeat after me, children: Pollito—Chicken," she commanded in her heavily accented English that only I understood, being the only child in the room who had ever been exposed to the language. But I too remained silent. No use making waves or showing off. Patiently *La Mrs.* sang her song and gestured for us to join in. At some point it must have dawned on the class that this silly routine was likely to go on all day if we did not "repeat after her." It was not her fault that she had to follow the rule in her teacher's manual stating that she must teach English *in* English, and that she must not translate, but merely repeat her lesson in English until the children "begin to respond" more or less "unconsciously." This was one of the vestiges of the regimen followed by her predecessors in the last generation. To this day I can recite "Pollito—Chicken" mindlessly, never once pausing to visualize chicks, hens, pencils, or pens.

I soon found myself crowned "teacher's pet" without much effort on my part. I was a privileged child in her eyes simply because I lived in "Nueva York," and because my father was in the navy. His name was an old one in our pueblo, associated with once-upon-a-time landed people and long-gone money. Status is judged by unique standards in a culture where, by definition, everyone is a second-class citizen. Remembrance of past glory is as good as titles and money. Old families living in decrepit old houses rank over factory workers living in modern comfort in cement boxes—all the same. The professions raise a person out of the dreaded "sameness" into a niche of status, so that teachers, nurses, and everyone who went to school for a job were given the honorifics of *El Míster* or *La Mrs.* by the common folks, people who were likely to be making more money in American factories than the poorly paid educators and government workers.

My first impressions of the hierarchy began with my teacher's shoe-changing ceremony and the exaggerated respect she received from our parents. *La Mrs.* was always right, and adults scrambled to meet her requirements. She wanted all our schoolbooks covered in the brown paper now used for paper bags (used at that time by the grocer to wrap meats and other foods). That first week of school the grocer was swamped with requests for paper which he gave away to the women. That week and the next, he wrapped produce in newspapers. All school projects became family projects. It was considered disrespectful at Mamá's house to do homework in privacy. Between the hours when we came home from school and dinner time, the table was shared by all of us working together with the women hovering in the background. The teachers communicated directly with the mothers, and it was a matriarchy of far-reaching power and influence.

There was a black boy in my first-grade classroom who was also the teacher's pet but for a different reason than I: I did not have to do anything to win her favor; he would do anything to win a smile. He was as black as the cauldron that Mamá used for cooking stew and his hair was curled into tight little balls on his head—*pasitas*, like little raisins glued to his skull, my mother had said. There had been some talk at Mamá's house about this boy; Lorenzo was his name. I later gathered that he was the grandson of my father's nanny. Lorenzo lived with Teresa, his grandmother, having been left in her care when his mother took off for "Los Nueva Yores" shortly after his birth. And they were poor. Everyone could see that his pants were too big for him—hand-me-downs—and his shoe soles were as thin as paper. Lorenzo seemed unmindful of the giggles he caused when he jumped up to erase the board for *La Mrs.* and his baggy pants rode down to his thin hips as he strained up to get every stray mark. He seemed to relish playing the little clown when she asked him to come to the front of the room and sing his phonetic version of "o-bootifool, forpashios-keeis," leading the class in our incomprehensible tribute to the American flag. He was a bright, loving child, with a talent for song and mimicry that everyone commented on. He should have been chosen to host the PTA show that year instead of me.

At recess one day, I came back to the empty classroom to get something. My cup? My nickel for a drink from the kiosk man? I don't remember. But I remember the conversation my teacher was having with another teacher. I remember because it concerned me, and because I memorized it so that I could ask my mother to explain what it meant.

"He is a funny *negrito*, and, like a parrot, he can repeat anything you teach him. But his Mamá must not have the money to buy him a suit."

"I kept Rafaelito's First Communion suit; I bet Lorenzo could fit in it. It's white with a bow-tie," the other teacher said.

"But, Marisa," laughed my teacher, "in that suit, Lorenzo would look like a fly drowned in a glass of milk."

Both women laughed. They had not seen me crouched at the back of the room, digging into my schoolbag. My name came up then.

"What about the Ortiz girl? They have money."

"I'll talk to her mother today. The superintendent, *El Americano* from San Juan, is coming down for the show. How about if we have her say her lines in both Spanish and English?"

The conversation ends there for me. My mother took me to Mayagüez and bought me a frilly pink dress and two crinoline petticoats to wear underneath so that I looked like a pink and white parachute with toothpick legs sticking out. I learned my lines, "Padres, maestros, Mr. Leonard, bienvenidos/Parents, teachers, Mr. Leonard, welcome. . . ." My first public appearance. I took no pleasure in it. The words were formal and empty. I had simply memorized them. My dress pinched me at the neck and arms, and made me itch all over.

I had asked my mother what it meant to be a "mosca en un vaso de leche," a fly in a glass of milk. She had laughed at the image, explaining that it meant being "different," but that it wasn't something I needed to worry about.

Rita Dove 1952–

R ita Dove is the first African American since Gwendolyn Brooks to be awarded the Pulitzer Prize for poetry as well as the first African American to be named Poet Laureate of the United States, a post she held from 1993 to 1995. Born in Akron, Ohio, Dove was raised in a middle-class family. Displaying considerable intellectual gifts at an early age, she traveled to the White House in 1970 as a Presidential Scholar, an award given to the top one hundred high-school seniors in the nation. After her graduation from Miami University of Ohio, Dove received a Fulbright scholarship and studied Modern English literature at Tübingen University in West Germany. In 1977, she received a master of fine arts from the University of Iowa Writers' Workshop. Dove's first two collections of poetry, *The Yellow House on the Corner* (1980) and *Museum* (1983), garnered much critical acclaim. The Pulitzer Prize–winning *Thomas and Beulah* (1986), a collection of lyrical narratives loosely based on her maternal grandparents' experiences in the industrial North between 1900 and 1960, established her as a poet of unique subjectivity who can convincingly become that which she is not. Her most recent collection, *Mother Love*, was published in 1995.

CANARY

FOR MICHAEL S. HARPER

Billie Holiday's burned voice
had as many shadows as lights,
a mournful candelabra against a sleek piano,
the gardenia her signature under that ruined face.

(Now you're cooking, drummer to bass,   5
magic spoon, magic needle.
Take all day if you have to
with your mirror and your bracelet of song.)

Fact is, the invention of women under siege
has been to sharpen love in the service of myth.   10

If you can't be free, be a mystery.

AFTER READING *MICKEY IN THE NIGHT KITCHEN* FOR THE THIRD TIME BEFORE BED

"I'm in the milk and
the milk's in me! . . . I'm Mickey!"

My daughter spread her legs
to find her vagina:
hairless, this mistaken   5
bit of nomenclature
is what a stranger cannot touch
without her yelling. She demands
to see mine and momentarily
we're a lopsided star   10
among the spilled toys,
my prodigious scallops
exposed to her neat cameo.

And yet the same glazed
tunnel, layered sequences.   15
She is three; that makes this
innocent. *We're pink!*
she shrieks, and bounds off.

Every month she wants
to know where it hurts and   20
what the wrinkled string means
between my legs. *This is good blood*
I say, but that's wrong, too.
How to tell her that it's what makes us—
black mother, cream child.   25
That we're in the pink
and the pink's in us.

Naomi Shihab Nye 1952–

Naomi Shihab Nye has written six books of poetry, including *Different Ways to Pray* (1980), *Hugging the Jukebox* (1982), *Mint* (1991), and *Fuel* (1998). Shihab Nye believes that for her, ". . . the primary source of poetry has always been local life, random characters met on the streets, our own ancestry sifting down to us through small, essential daily tasks." Born to a Palestinian father and an American mother of German background, Nye spent part of her childhood in St. Louis before she and her family moved to Jerusalem and then back to the United States—to San Antonio, Texas, where she still lives. Shihab Nye also writes essays and short fiction, has edited several anthologies, and also writes books for children. In her work, Shihab Nye frequently investigates the differences and shared experiences of varied cultures and sees the arts as a medium toward international goodwill.

NEWCOMERS IN A TROUBLED LAND

Our four-year-old son is printing his name on a piece of yellow construction paper. I bend to see which name it is today. For awhile he wanted to be *called* Paper. Today he's gone back to the real one. Each blocky letter a house, a mountain, a caboose . . . then he prints my name underneath his. He draws squiggly lines from the letters in my name to the same letters in his own. "Naomi, look, we're inside one another, did you know that? Your name is here, inside mine!"

Every letter of *Naomi* contained in his name *Madison*—we pause together mouths open. I did not know that. Although we have been mouthing one another's names for years, and already as mother and son we contain one another in so many ways it would be hard to name them all.

For a long time he sits staring, smiling at the paper, turning it around on the table. "Do I have any friends," he asks, "who have *their* mother's names inside their names?" We try a few—none does. And the soft afternoon light falling into the kitchen where we sit says, *this is a gift.*

When I was small, the name *Naomi*, which means *pleasant*, seemed hard to live up to. And *Shihab*, shooting star or meteor in Arabic, harder yet. I never met another of either in those days. My mother, whose name meant *bitter*, said I didn't know how lucky I was.

Hiking the tree-lined streets of our St. Louis borough en route to school, I felt common names spring up inside my mouth, waving their leafy syllables. I'd tongue them for blocks, trying them on. Susie. Karen. Debbie. Who would I be if I'd had a different name? I turned right on a street called Louise. Did all Karens have some region of being in which they were related? I called my brother *Alan* for a week without letting our parents hear. He was really Adlai, for Adlai Stevenson, a name that also means *justice* in Arabic, if pronounced with enough flourish.

Neither of us had middle names.

I admired our parents for that. They hadn't tried to pad us or glue us together with any little wad of name stuck in the middle.

Not until I was sixteen, riding slouched and sleepy in the back seat of my best friend's sister's car, did I fall in love with my own name. It had something to do with neon on a shopping center sign, that steady color holding firm as the nervous December traffic swarmed past. Holding my eyes to the radiant green bars of light as the engine idled, I felt the soft glow of my own name stretch warmly awake inside me. It balanced on my tongue. It seemed pleasurable, at long last, to feel recognizable to oneself. Was this a secret everyone knew?

Names of old countries and towns had always seemed exquisitely arbitrary, odd. The tags in the backs of garments, the plump bodies of words. We had moved from the city of one saint to the city of another, San Antonio, whose oldest inner-city streets had names like *Eager* and *Riddle*. We had left the river of many syllables, with a name long enough to be used as a timing device, Mississippi, for a river so small you could call it Creek or Stream and not be too far off. We ate *kousa, tabooleh, baba ghannouj*—Arabic food—on a street called Arroya Vista.

Earlier, I'd stood with my St. Louis schoolmates as the last gleaming silver segment of the Gateway Arch was swung into place by a giant crane. We held our breaths, imagining a crash as the parts clanged together, or a terrible disaster if the piece were to slip loose. Worse yet, what if the section didn't fit? Each of us had been keeping close watch on the massive legs as they grew and grew in what used to be a weedy skid-row riverfront lot, a few blocks from the licorice factory. Each of us had our own ideas about whether we'd really trust the elevator inside that thing. But I doubt if anybody questioned the slogan accompanying its name—Gateway to the West. In those days we probably accepted winning the West as something that had really happened.

Studying history in grade school, we learned that everything our country had ever done was good, good, good. Nothing smoldered with dubious implications. Occasionally my father offered different views on foreign policies, but no one ever suggested a pilgrim or pioneer might have been less than honorable. I recall preferring Indian headdresses to Pilgrim hats. The Indians had a more powerful mystique. I recall feeling profound indignation over missionaries. Somehow they seemed so insulting—like coming into someone else's neighborhood and telling them how to do things. My father, sent to Kansas as an immigrant student because he wanted to go "to the middle" of the country, left his first university town because local evangelists wouldn't leave him alone.

Long later, I'd read the Chilean poet Pablo Neruda, who wrote, "Why wasn't Christopher Columbus able to discover Spain?"

Long later, after our country was able to "celebrate victory" in a war that massacred scores of people no more criminal than you or I, our son sat quietly reading a book called *Stanley*, in which cavemen come out of their caves and build houses for the first time. The animals speak in human tongues. They say, "Don't eat my grass and I'll let you live by me." The cavemen plant flowers around their doorways. They learn how to be nice to one another. They put down their clubs. "Isn't it strange," my son said, "that a caveman would be called Stanley?" He had an older man friend named Stanley. It just didn't seem like a caveman kind of name.

I passed under the Gateway to the West into the land of many questions. On a Christmas Eve as far west as we could go in "our own country," we sat in downtown Honolulu in the back pew of the historic Kawaiho Church, the "Westminster Abbey of the Pacific." We each held a candle wearing a little white collar as short-sleeved men and women filed into the pews, wearing leis, wearing Christmas-patterned Aloha shirts. I grew quietly aware that a group of people had entered and were now sitting in the carved wooden box behind us, the space once reserved for royalty, still set aside by a velvet rope. The matriarch of the group wore black, and a distinguished hat, unusual for Honolulu. She stared straight ahead with handsome queenly elegance. The rest of her family, while attractive, could have blended easily into the crowd.

I don't know why I grew so obsessed with her presence behind us, as we rose for "Joy to the World!" or took seats again for the handbell choir. Maybe it was that row of royal portraits on the second-floor balcony visible over the rail, or my growing curiosity over the ways our fiftieth state had been acquired. I just kept wondering what she thought about it all. Once her family had ruled this little land most remote from all other lands on the globe—a favorite Hawaiian statistic. And now? She was served her wafer and tiny cup of grape juice first, before the rest of the packed congregation. And she walked out into the warm streets, this daughter of Hawaii's last king, on her own two feet when it was over.

My husband first appeared to me in a now-vanished downtown San Antonio eatery with a pleasantly understated name, Quinney's Just Good Food. Businessmen in white shirts and ties swarmed around us, woven together by

steaming plates of fried fish and mashed potatoes. I knew, from the first moment of our chance encounter, that he was "the one"—it felt like a concussion
to know this.

Walking up South Presa Street later with my friend Sue, who'd introduced
us, I asked dizzily, "What *was* his last name?" She said, "Nye, like eye," and the
rhymes began popping into my head. They matched our steps. Like *hi*, like *why*,
like *bye*—suddenly like every word that seemed to matter. She waved good-bye
at her corner and I stood there a long time, staring as the cross-signal changed
back and forth from a red raised hand to a little man walking. And I knew that
every street I crossed from that moment on would be a different street.

Because I am merely a tenant of this name Nye—it is not the house I always occupied—it inspires a traveler's warm affection to me. I appreciate its brevity.
Reading about the thirteenth-century Swedes who fled internal uprisings in
their own country to resettle in Denmark in settlements prefixed by *Ny*—
meaning new, or newcomer—deserves a border-crosser's nod.

Hundreds of families listed in the *Nye Family of America Association*
volumes gather regularly at Sandwich, Massachusetts, to shake hands and share
each other's lives. I would like to join them, which surprises me. They started
their tradition of gathering in 1903. R. Glen Nye writes, "How can we reach you
to tell you how important it is for you to know your origins. . . . Those who read
this are the oldsters of tomorrow . . . a hundred years hence, we will be the very
ones someone will yearn to know about. Who will they turn to then, if we do
not help them now?"

Because my own father came to New York on the boat from his old country
of Palestine in 1950, I am curious about these Nyes who came on the boat just
following the *Mayflower*, who stayed and stayed and stayed, who built the Nye
Homestead on Cape Cod, now a museum pictured on postcards and stationery
notes. They have kept such good track of one another. Thick volumes list them,
family by family, birthdates, children, occupations.

On a driving trip east, my husband and I paused one blustery day to walk
around the cemetery at Sandwich. It felt eerie to sidestep so many imposing
granite markers engraved with our own name. Oh Benjamin, oh Katherine and
Reuben, you who had no burglar alarms, what did you see that we will never
see? And the rest of you Nyes, wandering out across America even as far as
Alaska where cars and trucks and jeeps all have their license plates set into little
metal frames proclaiming NYE in honor of some enterprising car dealer who
claimed the Land of the Midnight Sun as his territory, where did you get your
energy? What told you to go?

Once my husband and I invited every "Nye" in the San Antonio telephone book
to dinner. Such reckless festivity would have been more difficult had our name
been Sanchez or Smith; as it stood, the eleven entries for "Nye" seemed too
provocative to pass up. Eleven groups of people sharing a name within one
city—and we didn't know any of them.

Handwritten invitation—"If you're named Nye, you're invited." Would they *get it?* I was brazen enough to style it a "potluck"—a gathering where the parties themselves would be a potluck—and asked all to RSVP. A week later each family had responded positively, with glinting curiosity, except one humorless fireman, whom I telephoned at the last minute. He was too busy for such frivolous pursuit.

They came in a wild assortment of vehicles, a pickup truck and a white Cadillac pulled sleekly into the driveway. They came, all thirty-two of them, children and wives, in overalls and neckties. One gracious couple, both ninety-two years old, amazed us with their spunk, traveling out in the evening to some inner-city house they didn't even know. Only three groups of the ten present were related or acquainted.

Later I would remember how the picnic table in our backyard spilled a rich offering of pies and green beans and potato salads, how the talk seemed infinite in its variety, how the laughter—"What a wacky idea, Babe!"—some Nye slapping me on the back with sudden gusto—rolled and rolled.

The experience I'd had at a Women's Writing Weekend in Austin where a visiting poet singled me out with displeasure—"What are these three names of yours? So, you've compromised yourself to marriage? I suppose you'd let a *man* publish your work?"—seemed nullified, erased. I'd walked out of that place, throat burning. It probably wouldn't have made any difference had I told her that I happened to *like* the name, or that sometimes it's a pleasure to become someone else midstream in your life. Had the name in question been Smithers or Lumpkin, I might have passed. But this little syllable, this glittering eye, held mine. I could almost have made it up.

No one encouraged us much when we set out one July to drive across the wide western expanse of the United States with a two-year-old. I had a job lined up through rural libraries of the state of Oregon, to be a visiting writer town-to-town for three months. It sounded delicious. It bore the aroma of blackberry jam and grilled salmon. For years I'd said I hoped to live in Oregon someday, if I was lucky enough to get old.

"You'll get old all right, before your time," said our dubious friends. "A two-year-old? Strapped in a car seat for hours on end? You'll be pulling your hair out. *He'll* be pulling your hair out. How will he stand it? How will he be able to sleep in so many strange places?"

One friend asked if we were going to haul his crib on the roof of the car.

I lay awake nights and worried. I rolled his socks into tight balls. Our son, on the other hand, seemed anxious to depart. He'd been throwing things into his little suitcase for weeks. I'd find the salt box in there. Or a wad of dried clay. "I'm ready for Oregon," he kept repeating. "When do we go? I won't stand up in my car seat!"

The moment we rolled onto the highway, exhausted by the tedium of departure, a familiar flood of relief washed over us. We found ourselves driving slowly, casually, absorbing the countryside. Home again! Hadn't Americans become too destination-oriented, leaving toward places when we barely had time enough to get there, driving fast all the way? We didn't want to do that. We wanted to fall back into waltz rhythm. To pull into the long driveway that said FRESH CORN MEAL GROUND TODAY even though we didn't know when we'd have an oven again.

It worked out. We stopped at every playground between San Antonio and Portland. (The best one, for anyone following our circuitous route, is at Baker, Oregon—an old-fashioned paradise of high slides and well-oiled merry-go-rounds.) We ate Japanese food in Santa Fe. We unrolled our moldy-smelling tent on a spot of ground in Utah and by morning it was encircled by clamoring chipmunks, who had found a wealthy source of cracker crumbs. They were calling for more.

We camped high up in Idaho's Sawtooth Forest near the Sublette junction, where pioneers on the Oregon Trail split off south toward California or continued west toward the Columbia River. Some legends say the signs toward Oregon were written in fancy handwriting (Oregon favored literate settlers) while the signs toward California bore only a painted gold chunk. We had been reading aloud in a series of *National Geographics* about these early vagabonds, how the trail was littered with furniture they pitched from their wagons. How many people died, how many got all the way there, paused awhile, and turned back? What was it they didn't find? Some places in Wyoming, Idaho, Oregon, the deep ruts of their wheels are still engraved in the earth.

Inside our zippered tent I finished reading the essays about the Oregon Trail by flashlight, one of those fancy flashlights that do three different things. I felt scared to walk to the car for something I had forgotten. It was so *big* out there. Where had everyone gone? That night I would dream a bear grabbed my toe through the tent's opening and shook it, hard. Long wild voices pulled at us out of the air.

To consider our evolution into good-gas-mileage sedans, with well-fingered atlases tucked between the seats, seemed critical. Long trip? You call this a long trip?

On one of those Idaho back roads, I contemplated deeply the sweet emblem of a stranger's hand raised in passing, a car or truck traveling the other way whose driver wanted somehow to say, "Good journey, I've been where you're going, travel well." I wanted to tell my friends back home who were teaching their children not to talk to strangers that they had it all wrong. Do talk to strangers. Raise your hand to them in strange places, on back roads where leaning fields of tasseled grass have more identity than you do. Ask strangers anything you want. Maybe they'll have an answer. Don't go home with them, don't take your pants off with them, but talk, talk, talk. Anyway, in this mobile twentieth century, who among us is *not* strange?

I remember thinking, that night, that talking to strangers has been the most important thing I do in my life. It seemed doubtful two wagons on the Oregon Trail would have overtaken one another without a word or message being exchanged.

How much have we lost in this cornucopia land?

When my eye picked out a town name Nye on the map near Pendleton, the town famous for woolens in eastern Oregon, it became suddenly imperative to visit it. Only twenty-eight miles off the interstate—I didn't care how far it was. At our stop for lunch I wrote quick, wild messages to every Nye I could think of, planning to mail them there. Like Thoreau, New Mexico, or Valentine, Texas—a luminous postmark. This would be better than the tucked-away alley called Nye in El Paso, which no house even faces. Better than the old schoolhouse called Nye in Laredo, named for a beloved teacher.

The road south from Pendleton loomed rolling and golden as the road to Oz. It held its breath—no signs, structures, other cars. The men slept in the back seat.

I couldn't stop imagining it. Maybe there would be a Nye Café. We could swivel on stools at the gleaming counter, ordering cocoa in thick white cups, or vanilla milkshakes. When people looked at us curiously—you here to visit someone?—we'd say the best thing possible to a little lost place in America: "No, we just came here to see the town." Maybe they'd take us around.

The first thing my husband and I ever did together, after that initial meeting at Quinney's, was stare at a map of Texas and pick out a little village called Sweet Home. We drove there in the first excited flush of our togetherness, simply to see what could *be* at a place called that. All day we sat in a pool hall with the regulars, at a metal-topped table inscribed with the name of some beer. An older woman with a gravelly voice showed us her gold wedding band. "Lemme tell ya, I waited," she proclaimed. Waited?

"Met Randolph back high school days, but wasn't no way he was going to stick around this little old place after we was through. He took off, *off*, and I stayed here ta Sweet Home, with my mama and daddy, all my relatives was here, did farming, my daddy fixed those old kinda tractors nobody uses anymore. I was just a small-town girl, ya know? But I don't marry no one else, no matter who comes along, I keep thinkin' a Randolph and I say to myself, Randolph's the one for me. Well he marry somebody else, up some bigger town by Houston, and they stay married all her life but God bless her she died. And one day last year Randolph come through here just to see how we all turned into nothin'."

She grinned.

"Nothin'"?

"Sure. Like small-town people do. They happy just to stay home and turn into nothin' else than what they started out to be. Yeah? It's not a bad nothin'. So he come through and here I am, not married yet, age sixty-nine and still waitin'!

He sweep me off my feet." Her face grew rosy. "I'm here to say some things can happen good. Ain't it pretty?" She turned the shiny band over and over in the soft afternoon light.

Where was Randolph today? "Up ta Shiner buyin' seed." Had Sweet Home changed much in fifty years? "Oh yeah. Went downhill completely. But we still love it."

After dark we drove back to San Antonio on one of those old two-lanes without much shoulder on either side. I grew sleepy and curled up on the front seat with my head in my husband-to-be's lap. And dreamed, and dreamed. Some things can happen good.

At the junction where Nye, Oregon, was supposed to be, a single ragged spoke spun on a crooked windmill over a leaning, empty shack of a barn. Purely desolate. No human, no house, nothing to indicate this was the place.

We drove one leg of the junction, looking. Fields of lush range grass. The long, lonely land. We tried the other leg—emptier yet. Back at the battered windmill, I turned off the engine. Our boy chanted for juice. While he sucked at the tiny straw and the wind blew through our open doors, a deer bolted, bright-eyed, from a ditch.

It approached our car instead of heading the other way. The deer stared and stared and did not run, examining us with no evident sense of danger. More petite than Texas deer, it sidestepped gracefully around our car, then tiptoed into the brush.

"I think we're here," my husband said, looking down at the map and up again at the small black number that indicated the junction. There was no other sign.

I felt suddenly panicky, my voice shrill in the giant silence. "But where is it? We must be turned around! Wouldn't there be some indication?"

We compared the size of the Nye on the map with a few Oregon towns we'd already been through. "Look, this Nye is bigger than the name of that town we passed through that had a thousand people. This is the size of a three-thousand-person town. Weird! It's got to be here!"

My husband gazed. "I've seen ghost towns better looking than this."

Heaving my stiff legs out the door, I walked around. A tumbled chimney whistled *Home*. Wishing for some scrap of women, or love—lace, a wad of pinned hair—I caught instead the wisp of a woman's gaze staring far off, the sweet hinges of cloud that held it. That long look that said *something else*.

If this were indeed it, where had the toughened settlers gone? Perhaps they wished neighbors to lay down wheels, saying, "I'll build here too"—the slim-sided seed of a town, awakening. Perhaps they wished, and everybody passed them by. Among thistles, broken trough, I poked for a sign. And the ache in the throat of that long wind kept hurting.

Finally a red pickup truck appeared on the highway, and we flagged it. A blonde woman squinted at us, scratched her head. "Yep, that's Nye. Not much to look at, is there? When I was little, someone still lived in that beat-up house, but we never knew him. I have a memory of an old guy bending down in the weeds. It didn't look much better then, that's for sure. Actually, none of us around here ever thought of Nye as anything more than a turnoff, you know? I mean, it seems strange that the map makes it look like a town."

Before she drove off, she apologized. We stood around a while longer, as you would at a grave, before driving off toward Portland quietly. I don't think anyone spoke for a hundred miles.

Later the *Oregon Directory of Geographical Names* would say this point on the highway once boasted a post office named Nye, service discontinued 1917. It had probably been named for A. W. Nye, a well-known early resident, though why he was well known, or anything else about him, had filtered into the wind above Umatilla County and disappeared, perhaps toward the town of Echo, relatively nearby on the road back toward men.

"Go to Newport," people in Portland told us later. "There's a street called Nye in Newport. There's a beach called Nye, and an art center." We saved it for another time.

Sometimes the calls come late at night. "I'm looking for a Nye who was a well-known country-and-western singer in the 1950s. He wore these pants printed with rainbow-colored spurs. That wouldn't happen to be your husband, would it?"

Or, "I'm looking for my great-aunt's friends named Nye—she had a real bad dream, few nights ago, that they drove off a cliff, and she keeps begging us to call them. She can't remember the man's first name. Do you happen to know Celia Withers of Weatherford?"

One evening a rich, musical voice phones in from small-town east Texas. She's seen my husband's name in the Corsicana newspaper, and says she's been looking for him for seventeen years. Her name is Peachy Gardner. "Honey! I took care of babies all my life and no baby ever got into my heart like that little Nye did. He'd tweak my ear and kiss me. HONEY! I loved him so much. I just want to see what he grew into. When his parents moved away I nearly died. They sent me Christmas cards for a while but then—you know what happens. People just get lost."

Then she says they lived in Dallas. My husband never did. And when was the loving baby born? Four years after my husband. I hate to tell her this.

"Are you positive? Are you sure his daddy's name isn't James?"

We talk a while longer. She wrote to the place they had moved and her letter came back. America, she says, eats people up. They get too busy. I promise to start looking for the man with my husband's name, taking her number, in case he appears. We talk about the trees in her part of Texas; she lives in a thicket so dense the light barely shines through. She says, "I guess it's strange to want to see someone so bad this long after. I mean, he wouldn't look twice at me now. I know that. But I can't forget how he said—Peachy. I can't forget—his little hand."

MAKING A FIST

For the first time, on the road north of Tampico,
I felt the life sliding out of me,
a drum in the desert, harder and harder to hear.
I was seven, I lay in the car
watching palm trees swirl a sickening pattern past the glass.   5
My stomach was a melon split wide inside my skin.

"How do you know if you are going to die?"
I begged my mother.
We had been traveling for days.
With strange confidence she answered,   10
"When you can no longer make a fist."

Years later I smile to think of that journey,
the borders we must cross separately,
stamped with our unanswerable woes.
I who did not die, who am still living,   15
still lying in the backseat behind all my questions,
clenching and opening one small hand.

Kitty Tsui 1952–

One critic writes that "The themes that have been central to Kitty Tsui's life are those central to her poems and short prose: her love and admiration of women/self, . . . oppression experienced by Chinese immigrants in the United States, and aspects of her Chinese and American heritage that inform . . . her lesbianism." Born in Hong Kong, she moved with her family to Liverpool, England, and then to San Francisco, California. Tsui left home at sixteen and worked while she attended San Francisco State University, graduating in 1975. Part of Tsui's work has been to record the stories told by her grandmother—her role model. This project has led to her political activism and the writing in which she recreates myths from Asian sources. Her works include *The Words of a Woman Who Breathes Fire* (1983) and the autobiographical essay, "Breaking Silence, Making Waves, and Loving Ourselves." Tsui ". . . shows how we can all empower ourselves to resist or to change conditions that create our poverty, our oppression, our silence."

DON'T CALL ME SIR CALL ME STRONG

i get called sir
all the time.
by women, by men,
waitresses in restaurants,
salesclerks behind counters,   5
stewards on board planes.

it's the short hair
that sets them off.
or maybe it's because
i stand tall,   10
have a wide stance,
broad shoulders
and thick forearms.

or perhaps it's
my wristwatch   15
made for a man.

i get called sir
all the time.
i even get cruised
by men in the castro   20
out looking for fresh meat.

i suppose it's because
i have small breasts,
big fists,
walk with hands in pockets,   25
stand tall
with a wide stance,
broad shoulders
and thick forearms,
i'm taken for a man.   30

it's time to talk back.
hey, don't call me sir
call me strong
call me sassy
call me spirited   35
call me sure-of-myself
call me competent
call me confident
call me powerful

call me proud.   40
don't call me sir
call me strong.

call me
woman who walks
with a long stride,   45
woman with small breasts,
big fists,
hands in pockets,
standing tall
with a wide stance,   50
broad shoulders,
thick forearms
and wears a man's watch.

don't call me sir
call me strong.   55
call me shooting star
call me sea
call me wave upon wave
call me womb
call me woman.   60

a strong woman sighing
a sassy woman loving
a spirited woman working
a sure woman singing
a competent woman rejoicing   65
a confident woman crying
a powerful woman chanting
a proud woman coming.

a proud woman
coming into herself.   70

CHINATOWN TALKING STORY

the gold mountain men said
there were two pairs of eyes
so beautiful
they had the power
to strike you dead,   5

the eyes of
kwan ying lin
and mao dan so.

kwan ying lin, my grandmother,
and mao dan so   10
were stars of the
cantonese opera
and women
rare
in a bachelor society.   15

when my grandmother first came
to gold mountain in 1922
she was interned on angel island
for weeks, a young chinese girl,
prisoner in a strang land.   20

when mao dan so
first arrived
she came on an entertainer's visa
and made $10,000 a year.

it cost $1.25 to see a show,   25
a quarter after nine.
pork chop rice was 15¢.

when theater work was slow
or closed down
other work was found: 30
washing dishes,
waiting tables,
ironing shirts.

in china
families with sons   35
saved and borrowed
the $3,000
to buy a bright boy
promise in a new land.

in china   40
girls born into poverty
were killed or sold.
girls born into
prosperity
had their feet bound,   45
their marriages arranged.

on angel island
paper sons and blood sons
waited
to enter *gum san*   50
eating peanut butter on crackers
for lunch and
bean sprouts at night.

the china men who passed
the interrogations   55
were finally set free.
the ones who failed
were denied entry and deported
or died by their own hands.

in 1940, the year   60
angel island detention center
was closed
a job at macys
paid $27 a week.
only chinese girls   65
without accents please apply.

my grandfather had four wives
and pursued many women
during his life.
the chinese press loved   70
to write of his affairs.

my grandmother,
a woman with three daughters,
left her husband
to survive on her own.   75
she lived with another actress,
a companion and a friend.

the gold mountain men said
mao dan so was as graceful
as a peach blossom in wind.   80
she has worked since
she was eight.
she is seventy two.
she sits in her apartment
in new york chinatown   85
playing solitaire.
her hair is thin and white.
her eyes, sunken in hollows,
are fire bright when she speaks.

the gold mountain men said   90
when kwan ying lin
went on stage
even the electric fans stopped.

today
at the grave   95
of my grandmother
with fresh spring flowers,
iris, daffodil,

i felt her spirit in the wind.
i heard her voice saying: 100

born into the
skin of yellow women
we are born
into the armor of warriors.

Ana Castillo 1953–

Born of Aztec heritage in Chicago, Ana Castillo is a celebrated and prolific Chicana writer. Poet, novelist, short-story writer, and essayist, Castillo's writing often deals with carnal politics, offering sociopolitical commentary while exploring the adversities of womanhood. Marisa Cantù of *The Third Woman* asserts, "Heretofore pretensions to and of virtue have presumed the nonexistence of woman's sexual desires and have generally silenced most poets on the subject. Among Chicanas, I believe [Castillo] is the first effort to break with that silence." According to contributor Patricia De La Fuente, Castillo's 1984 collection of poems, *Women Are Not Roses*, speak "for all women who have at one time or another felt the unfairness of female existence in a world designed by men primarily for men." After receiving her B.A. from Northeastern Illinois University in 1975, Castillo earned an M.A. from the University of Chicago in Latin American and Caribbean Studies in 1979. She received a Ph.D. in 1991 from the University of Bremen, Germany, and has taught fiction writing, women's studies, and Latina literature at many colleges and universities.

AND ALL OCTOBERS BECOME ONE

It's October again
with its usual rain
silver pins/flickering pain
and the loneliness begins.

An occasional friend   5
comes to talk for awhile
we wear Autumn smiles
tired/drawn/feigning
warmth.

When the friend has left   10
there are rum and cigarettes
that burn long into the night
outside the wind warns
of Winter's approach.

And all Octobers become one   15
to form a faded string
of nostalgic blues around
an ancient moon/down
Chicago's neon action strip:

when strangers replace   20
lovers who deserted the front
at Summer's end
and everyone can pretend
indifference.

It's October   25
and if we listen for just
a moment we can hear
the dry leaves break off
and fall from the trees.

Fall   30
fall
with dignity fall
and let be what must be
in October.

THE ANTIHERO

the antihero
always gets the woman
not in the end
an anticlimax instead
in the end   5
spits on her
stretched out body
a spasmodic carpet
yearning still
washes himself   10

doesn't know why
it is that way searching
not finding finding
not wanting wanting more
or nothing   15
in the end the key is
to leave her yearning lest
she discover that is all

Sara Suleri Goodyear 1953–

Sara Suleri Goodyear was born in Karachi, Pakistan, a daughter whose father was a political journalist and mother a Welsh-born professor of English. Goodyear is best known for *Meatless Days* (1989), a book that has been categorized as an autobiography but which she calls an "alternative history" of Pakistan. Detailing her life in Pakistan as well as her immigration to England and the United States, Goodyear's narrative consciously avoids being too "explanatory," a practice that she dislikes in most Third World histories. Goodyear told *Interview* that she attempted to create "a new kind of historical writing, whereby I give no introductions whatsoever. I use the names, the places, but I won't stop to describe them, [thereby making] them register as immediately to the reader as it would to me." She has also published *The Rhetoric of English India* (1992), described by The University of Chicago Press as "a powerful challenge to the obsession with otherness that marks the current study of colonial discourse. Where other scholars tend to observe a strict separation between works by Western and non-Western writers, and between ruling and subject races, [Goodyear] reconstructs a diverse Anglo-India narrative in which English and Indian idioms inevitably collude." Goodyear is founding editor of the *Yale Journal of Criticism* and an English professor at Yale University.

EXCELLENT THINGS IN WOMEN

Leaving Pakistan was, of course, tantamount to giving up the company of women. I can tell this only to someone like Anita, in all the faith that she will understand, as we go perambulating through the grimness of New Haven and feed on the pleasures of our conversational way. Dale, who lives in Boston, would also understand. She will one day write a book about the stern and secretive life of breastfeeding and is partial to fantasies that culminate in an abundance of resolution. And Fawzi, with a grimace of recognition, knows because she knows the impulse to forget.

To a stranger or an acquaintance, however, some vestigial remoteness obliges me to explain that my reference is to a place where the concept of woman was not really part of an available vocabulary: we were too busy for that, just living, and conducting precise negotiations with what it meant to be a sister or a child or a wife or a mother or a servant. By this point admittedly I am damned by my own discourse, and doubly damned when I add yes, once in a while, we naturally thought of ourselves as women, but only in some perfunctory biological way that we happened on perchance. Or else it was a hugely practical joke, we thought, hidden somewhere among our clothes. But formulating that definition is about as impossible as attempting to locate the luminous qualities of an Islamic landscape, which can on occasion generate such aesthetically pleasing moments of life. My audience is lost, and angry to be lost, and both of us must find some token of exchange for this failed conversation. I try to lay the subject down and change its clothes, but before I know it, it has sprinted off evilly in the direction of ocular evidence. It goads me into saying, with the defiance of a plea, "You did not deal with Dadi."

Dadi, my father's mother, was born in Meerut toward the end of the last century. She was married at sixteen and widowed in her thirties, and by her latter decades could never exactly recall how many children she had borne. When India was partitioned, in August of 1947, she moved her thin pure Urdu into the Punjab of Pakistan and waited for the return of her eldest son, my father. He had gone careening off to a place called Inglestan, or England, fired by one of the several enthusiasms made available by the proliferating talk of independence. Dadi was peeved. She had long since dispensed with any loyalties larger than the pitiless give-and-take of people who are forced to live together in the same place, and she resented independence for the distances it made. She was not among those who, on the fourteenth of August, unfurled flags and festivities against the backdrop of people running and cities burning. About that era she would only say, looking up sour and cryptic over the edge of her Quran, "And I was also burned." She was, but that came years later.

By the time I knew her, Dadi with her flair for drama had allowed life to sit so heavily upon her back that her spine wilted and froze into a perfect curve, and so it was in the posture of a shrimp that she went scuttling through the day. She either scuttled or did not: it all depended on the nature of her fight with the Devil. There were days when she so hated him that all she could do was stretch herself out straight and tiny on her bed, uttering most awful imprecation. Sometimes, to my mother's great distress, Dadi could berate Satan in full eloquence only after she had clambered on top of the dining-room table and lain there like a little molding centerpiece. Satan was to blame: he had after all made her older son linger long enough in Inglestan to give up his rightful wife, a cousin, and take up instead with a white-legged woman. Satan had stolen away her only daughter Ayesha when Ayesha lay in childbirth. And he'd sent her youngest son to Swaziland, or Switzerland; her thin hand waved away such sophistries of name.

God she loved, and she understood him better than anyone. Her favorite days were those when she could circumnavigate both the gardener and my father, all in the solemn service of her God. With a pilfered knife, she'd wheedle her way to the nearest sapling in the garden, some sprightly poplar or a newly planted eucalyptus. She'd squat, she'd hack it down, and then she'd peel its bark away until she had a walking stick, all white and virgin and her own. It drove my father into tears of rage. He must have bought her a dozen walking sticks, one for each of our trips to the mountains, but it was like assembling a row of briar pipes for one who will not smoke: Dadi had different aims. Armed with implements of her own creation, she would creep down the driveway unperceived to stop cars and people on the street and give them all the gossip that she had on God.

Food, too, could move her to intensities. Her eyesight always took a sharp turn for the worse over meals—she could point hazily at a perfectly ordinary potato and murmur with Adamic reverence "What *is* it, what *is* it called?" With some shortness of manner one of us would describe and catalog the items on the table. "*Alu ka bhartha*," Dadi repeated with wonderment and joy; "Yes, Saira Begum, you can put some here." "Not too much," she'd add pleadingly. For ritual had it that the more she demurred, the more she expected her plate to be piled with an amplitude her own politeness would never allow. The ritual happened three times a day.

We pondered it but never quite determined whether food or God constituted her most profound delight. Obvious problems, however, occurred whenever the two converged. One such occasion was the Muslim festival called Eid—not the one that ends the month of fasting, but the second Eid, which celebrates the seductions of the Abraham story in a remarkably literal way. In Pakistan, at least, people buy sheep or goats beforehand and fatten them up for weeks with delectables. Then, on the appointed day, the animals are chopped, in place of sons, and neighbors graciously exchange silver trays heaped with raw and quivering meat. Following Eid prayers the men come home, and the animal is killed, and shortly thereafter rush out of the kitchen steaming plates of grilled lung and liver, of a freshness quite superlative.

It was a freshness to which my Welsh mother did not immediately take. She observed the custom but discerned in it a conundrum that allowed no ready solution. Liberal to an extravagant degree on thoughts abstract, she found herself to be remarkably squeamish about particular things. Chopping up animals for God was one. She could not locate the metaphor and was uneasy when obeisance played such a truant to the metaphoric realm. My father the writer quite agreed: he was so civilized in those days.

Dadi didn't agree. She pined for choppable things. Once she made the mistake of buying a baby goat and bringing him home months in advance of Eid. She wanted to guarantee the texture of his festive flesh by a daily feeding of tender peas and clarified butter. Ifat, Shahid, and I greeted a goat into the family with boisterous rapture, and soon after he ravished us completely when we found him at the washingline nonchalantly eating Shahid's pajamas. Of course there was no argument: the little goat was our delight, and even Dadi knew there was no killing him. He became my brother's and my sister's and my first pet, and he grew huge, a big and grinning thing.

Years after, Dadi had her will. We were old enough, she must have thought, to set the house sprawling, abstracted, into a multitude of secrets. This was true, but still we all noticed one another's secretive ways. When, the day before Eid, our Dadi disappeared, my brothers and sisters and I just shook our heads. We hid the fact from my father, who at this time of life had begun to equate petulance with extreme vociferation. So we went about our jobs and tried to be Islamic for a day. We waited to sight moons on the wrong occasion, and watched the food come into lavishment. Dried dates change shape when they are soaked in milk, and carrots rich and strange turn magically sweet when deftly covered with green nutty shavings and smatterings of silver. Dusk was sweet as we sat out, the day's work done, in an evening garden. Lahore spread like peace around us. My father spoke, and when Papa talked, it was of Pakistan. But we were glad, then, at being audience to that familiar conversation, till his voice looked up, and failed. There was Dadi making her return, and she was prodigal. Like a question mark interested only in its own conclusions, her body crawled through the gates. Our guests were spellbound, then they looked away. Dadi, moving in her eerie crab formations, ignored the hangman's rope she firmly held as behind her in the gloaming minced, hugely affable, a goat.

That goat was still smiling the following day when Dadi's victory brought the butcher, who came and went just as he should on Eid. The goat was killed and cooked: a scrawny beast that required much cooking and never melted into succulence, he winked and glistened on our plates as we sat eating him on Eid. Dadi ate, that is: Papa had taken his mortification to some distant corner of the house; Ifat refused to chew on hemp; Tillat and Irfan gulped their baby sobs over such a slaughter. "Honestly," said Mamma, "honestly." For Dadi had successfully cut through tissues of festivity just as the butcher slit the goat, but there was something else that she was eating with that meat. I saw it in her concentration; I know that she was making God talk to her as to Abraham and was showing him what she could do—for him—to sons. God didn't dare, and she ate on alone.

Of those middle years it is hard to say whether Dadi was literally left alone or whether her bodily presence always emanated a quality of being apart and absorbed. In the winter I see her alone, painstakingly dragging her straw mat out to the courtyard at the back of the house and following the rich course of the afternoon sun. With her would go her Quran, a metal basin in which she could wash her hands, and her ridiculously heavy spouted waterpot, that was made of brass. None of us, according to Dadi, were quite pure enough to transport these particular items, but the rest of her paraphernalia we were allowed to carry out. These were baskets of her writing and sewing materials and her bottle of pungent and Dadi-like bitter oils, with which she'd coat the papery skin that held her brittle bones. And in the summer, when the night created an illusion of possible coolness and everyone held their breath while waiting for a thin and intermittent breeze, Dadi would be on the roof, alone. Her summer bed was a wooden frame latticed with a sweet-smelling rope, much aerated at its foot. She'd lie there all night until the wild monsoons would wake the lightest and the soundest sleeper into a rapturous welcome of rain.

In Pakistan, of course, there is no spring but only a rapid elision from winter into summer, which is analogous to the absence of a recognizable loneliness from the behavior of that climate. In a similar fashion it was hard to distinguish between Dadi with people and Dadi alone: she was merely impossibly unable to remain unnoticed. In the winter, when she was not writing or reading, she would sew for her delight tiny and magical reticules out of old silks and fragments she had saved, palm-sized cloth bags that would unravel into the precision of secret and more secret pockets. But none such pockets did she ever need to hide, since something of Dadi always remained intact, however much we sought to open her. Her discourse, for example, was impervious to penetration, so that when one or two of us remonstrated with her in a single hour, she never bothered to distinguish her replies. Instead she would pronounce generically and prophetically, "The world takes on a single face." "Must you, Dadi . . . ," I'd begin, to be halted then by her great complaint: "The world takes on a single face."

It did. And often it was a countenance of some delight, for Dadi also loved the accidental jostle with things belligerent. As she went perambulating through the house, suddenly she'd hear Shahid, her first grandson, telling me or one of my sisters we were vile, we were disgusting women. And Dadi, who never addressed any one of us girls without first conferring the title of lady—so we were "Teellat Begum," "Nuzhat Begum," "Iffatt Begum," "Saira Begum"—would halt in reprimand and tell her grandson never to call her granddaughters women.

"What else shall I call them, men?" Shahid yelled. "Men!" said Dadi, "Men! There is more goodness in a woman's little finger than in the benighted mind of man." "Hear, hear, Dadi! *Hanh, hanh,* Dadi!" my sisters cried. "For men," said Dadi, shaking the name off her fingertips like some unwanted water, "live as though they were unsuckled things." "And heaven," she grimly added, "is the thing Muhammad says (peace be upon him) lies beneath the feet of women!" "But he was a man," Shahid still would rage, if he weren't laughing, as all of us were laughing, while Dadi sat among us as a belle or a May queen.

Toward the end of the middle years my father stopped speaking to his mother, and the atmosphere at home appreciably improved. They secretly hit upon a novel histrionics that took the place of their daily battle. They chose the curious way of silent things: twice a day Dadi would leave her room and walk the long length of the corridor to my father's room. There she merely peered round the door, as though to see if he were real. Each time she peered, my father would interrupt whatever adult thing he might be doing in order to enact a silent paroxysm, an elaborate facial pantomime of revulsion and affront. At teatime in particular, when Papa would want the world to congregate in his room, Dadi came to peer her ghostly peer. Shortly thereafter conversation was bound to fracture, for we could not drown the fact that Dadi, invigorated by an outcast's strength, was sitting alone in the dining room, chanting an appeal: "God give me tea, God give me tea."

At about this time Dadi stopped smelling old and smelled instead of something equivalent to death. It would have been easy to notice if she had been dying, but instead she conducted the change as a refinement, a subtle gradation, just as her annoying little stove could shift its hanging odors away from smoke and into ash. During the middle years there had been something more defined about her being, which sat in the world as solely its own context. But Pakistan increasingly complicated the question of context, as though history, like a pestilence, forbid any definition outside relations to its fevered sleep. So it was simple for my father to ignore the letters that Dadi had begun to write to him every other day in her fine wavering script, letters of advice about the house or the children or the servants. Or she transcribed her complaint: "Oh my son, Zia. Do you think your son, Shahid, upon whom God bestow a thousand blessing, should be permitted to lift up his grandmother's chair and carry it into the courtyard when his grandmother is seated in it?" She had cackled in a combination of delight and virgin joy when Shahid had so transported her, but that little crackling sound she omitted from her letter. She ended it, and all her notes, with her single endearment. It was a phrase to halt and arrest when Dadi actually uttered it: her solitary piece of tenderness was an injunction, really, to her world—"Keep on living," she would say.

Between that phrase and the great Dadi conflagration comes the era of the trying times. They began in the winter war of 1971, when East Pakistan became Bangladesh and Indira Gandhi hailed the demise of the two-nation theory. Ifat's husband was off fighting, and we spent the war together with her father-in-law, the brigadier, in the pink house on the hill. It was an ideal location for antiaircraft guns, so there was a bevy of soldiers and weaponry installed upon our roof. During each air raid the brigadier would stride purposefully into the garden and bark commands at them, as though the crux of the war rested upon his stiff upper lip. Then Dacca fell, and General Yahya came on television to resign the presidency and concede defeat. "Drunk, by God!" barked the brigadier as we sat watching, "Drunk!"

The following morning General Yahya's mistress came to mourn with us over breakfast, lumbering in draped with swathes of overscented silk. The brigadier lit an English cigarette—he was frequently known to avow that Pakistani cigarettes gave him a cuff—and bit on his moustache. "Yes," he barked, "these are trying times." "Oh yes, Gul," Yahya's mistress wailed, "these are such trying times." She gulped on her own eloquence, her breakfast bosom quaked, and then resumed authority over that dangling sentence. "It is so trying," she continued, "I find it so trying, it is trying to us all, to live in these trying, trying times." Ifat's eyes met mine in complete accord: mistress transmogrified to muse; Bhutto returned from the UN to put Yahya under house arrest and become the first elected president of Pakistan; Ifat's husband went to India as a prisoner of war for two years; my father lost his newspaper. We had entered the era of the trying times.

Dadi didn't notice the war, just as she didn't really notice the proliferation of her great-grandchildren, for Ifat and Nuzzi conceived at the drop of a hat and kept popping babies out for our delight. Tillat and I felt favored at this vicarious taste of motherhood: we learned to become that enviable personage, a *khala*, mother's sister, and when our married sisters came to visit with their entourage, we reveled in the exercise of *khala*-love. I once asked Dadi how many sisters she had had. She looked up through the oceanic grey of her cataracted eyes and answered, "I forget."

The children helped, because we needed distraction, there being then in Pakistan a musty taste of defeat to all our activities. The children gave us something, but they also took something away—they initiated a slight displacement of my mother. Because her grandchildren would not speak any English, she could not read stories as of old. Urdu always remained a shyness on her tongue, and as the babies came and went she let something of her influence imperceptibly recede, as though she occupied an increasingly private space. Her eldest son was in England by then, so Mamma found herself assuming the classic posture of an Indian woman who sends away her sons and runs the risk of seeing them succumb to the great alternatives represented by the West. It was a position that preoccupied her; and without my really noticing what was happening, she quietly handed over many of her wifely duties to her two remaining daughters—to Tillat and to me. In the summer, once the ferocity of the afternoon sun had died down, it was her pleasure to go out into the garden on her own. There she would stand, absorbed and abstracted, watering the driveway and breathing in the heady smell of water on hot dust. I'd watch her often, from my room upstairs. She looked like a girl.

We were aware of something, of a reconfiguration in the air, but could not exactly tell where it would lead us. Dadi now spoke mainly to herself; even the audience provided by the deity had dropped away. Somehow there wasn't proper balance between the way things came and the way they went, as Halima the cleaning woman knew full well when she looked at me intently, asking a question that had no question in it: "Do I grieve, or do I celebrate?" Halima had given birth to her latest son the night her older child died in screams of meningitis; once heard, never to be forgotten. She came back to work a week later, and we were talking as we put away the family's winter clothes into vast metal trunks. For in England, they would call it spring.

We felt a quickening urgency of change drown our sense of regular direction, as though something were bound to happen soon but not knowing what it would be was making history nervous. And so we were not really that surprised, then, to find ourselves living through the summer of the trials by fire. It climaxed when Dadi went up in a little ball of flames, but somehow sequentially related were my mother's trip to England to tend her dying mother, and the night I beat up Tillat, and the evening I nearly castrated my little brother, runt of the litter, serious-eyed Irfan.

It was an accident on both our parts. I was in the kitchen, so it must have been a Sunday, when Allah Ditta the cook took the evenings off. He was a mean-spirited man with an incongruously delicate touch when it came to making food. On Sunday at midday he would bluster one of us into the kitchen and show us what he had prepared for the evening meal, leaving strict and belligerent instructions about what would happen if we overheated this or dared brown that. So I was in the kitchen heating up some food when Farni came back from playing hockey, an ominous asthmatic rattle in his throat. He, the youngest, had been my parent's gravest infant: in adolescence he remained a gentle invalid. Of course he pretended otherwise, and was loud and raucous, but it never worked.

Tillat and I immediately turned on him with the bullying litany that actually can be quite soothing, the invariable female reproach to the returning male. He was to do what he hated—stave off his disease by sitting over a bowl of camphor and boiling water and inhaling its acrid fumes. I insisted that he sit on the cook's little stool in the kitchen, holding the bowl of medicated water on his lap, so that I could cook, and Farni could not cheat, and I could time each minute he should sit there thus confined. We seated him and flounced a towel on his reluctant head. The kitchen reeked jointly of cumin and camphor, and he sat skinny and penitent and swathed for half a minute, and then was begging to be done. I slammed down the carving knife and screamed "Irfan!" with such ferocity that he jumped, figuratively and literally, right out of his skin. The bowl of water emptied onto him, and with a gurgling cry Irfan leapt up, tearing at his steaming clothes. He clutched at his groin, and everywhere he touched, the skin slid off, so that between his fingers his penis easily unsheathed, a blanched and fiery grape. "What's happening?" screamed Papa from his room; "What's happening?" echoed Dadi's wail from the opposite end of the house. What was happening was that I was holding Farni's shoulders, trying to stop him from jumping up and down, but I was jumping too, while Tillat just stood there frozen, frowning at his poor ravaged grapes.

This was June, and the white heat of summer. We spent the next few days laying ice on Farni's wounds: half the time I was allowed to stay with him, until the doctors suddenly remembered I was a woman and hurried me out when his body made crazy spastic reactions to its burns. Once things grew calmer and we were alone, Irfan looked away and said, "I hope I didn't shock you, Sara." I was so taken by tenderness for his bony convalescent body that it took me years to realize yes, something female in me had been deeply shocked.

Mamma knew nothing of this, of course. We kept it from her so she could concentrate on what had taken her back to the rocky coastline of Wales, to places she had not really revisited since she was a girl. She sat waiting with her mother, who was blind now and of a fine translucency, and both of them knew that they were waiting for her death. It was a peculiar posture for Mamma to maintain, but her quiet letters spoke mainly of the sharp astringent light that made the sea wind feel so brisk in Wales and so many worlds away from the deadly omnipresent weight of summer in Lahore. There in Wales one afternoon, walking childless among the brambles and the furze, Mamma realized that her childhood was distinctly lost. "It was not that I wanted to feel more familiar," she later told me, "or that I was more used to feeling unfamiliar in Lahore. It's just that familiarity isn't important, really," she murmured absently, "it really doesn't matter at all."

When Mamma was ready to return, she wired us her plans, and my father read the cable, kissed it, then put it in his pocket. I watched him and felt startled, as we all did on the occasions when our parents' lives seemed to drop away before our eyes, leaving them youthfully engrossed in the illusion of knowledge conferred by love. We were so used to conceiving of them as parents moving in and out of hectic days that it always amused us, and touched us secretly, when they made quaint and punctilious returns to the amorous bond that had initiated their unlikely life together.

That summer while my mother was away, Tillat and I experienced a new bond of powerlessness, the white and shaking rage of sexual jealousy in parenthood. I had always behaved toward her as a contentious surrogate parent, but she had been growing beyond that scope and in her girlhood asking me for a formal acknowledgment of equality that I was loath to give. My reluctance was rooted in a helpless fear of what the world might do to her, for I was young and ignorant enough not to see that what I might do was worse. She went out one evening when my father was off on one of his many trips. The house was gaping emptily, and Tillat was very late. Allah Ditta had gone home, and Dadi and Irfan were sleeping; I read, and thought, and walked up and down the garden, and Tillat was very, very late. When she came back she wore that strange sheath of complacency and guilt which pleasure puts on faces very young. It smote an outrage in my heart until despite all resolutions to the contrary I heard myself hiss. "And where were you?" Her returning look was fearful and preening at the same time, and the next thing to be smitten was her face. "Don't, Sara," Tillat said in her superior way, "physical violence is so degrading." "To you, maybe," I answered, and hit her once again.

It set a sorrowful bond between us, for we both felt complicit in the shamefulness that had made me seem righteous whereas I had felt simply jealous, which we tacitly agreed was a more legitimate thing to be. But we had lost something, a certain protective aura, some unspoken myth asserting that love between sisters at least was sexually innocent. Now we had to fold that vain belief away and stand in more naked relation to our affection. Till then we had associated such violence with all that was outside us, as though somehow the more history fractured, the more whole we would be. But we began to lose that sense of the differentiated identities of history and ourselves and become guilty aware that we had known it all along, our part in the construction of unreality.

By this time, Dadi's burns were slowly learning how to heal. It was she who had given the summer its strange pace by nearly burning herself alive at its inception. On an early April night Dadi awoke, seized by a desperate need for tea. It was three in the morning, the household was asleep, so she was free to do the great forbidden thing of creeping into Allah Ditta's kitchen and taking charge, like a pixie in the night. As all of us had grown bored of predicting, one of her many cotton garments took to fire that truant night. Dadi, however, deserves credit for her resourceful voice, which wavered out for witness to her burning death. By the time Tillat awoke and found her, she was a little flaming ball: "Dadi!" cried Tillat in the reproach of sleep, and beat her quiet with a blanket. In the morning we discovered that Dadi's torso had been almost consumed and little recognizable remained from collarbone to groin. The doctors bade us to some decent mourning.

But Dadi had different plans. She lived through her sojourn at the hospital; she weathered her return. Then, after six weeks at home, she angrily refused to be lugged like a chunk of meat to the doctor's for her daily change of dressing: "Saira Begum will do it," she announced. Thus developed my great intimacy with the fluid properties of human flesh. By the time Mamma left for England, Dadi's left breast was still coagulate and raw. Later, when Irfan got his burns, Dadi was growing pink and livid tightropes, strung from hip to hip in a flaming advertisement of life. And in the days when Tillat and I were wrestling, Dadi's vanished nipples started to congeal and convex their cavities into triumphant little love knots.

I learned about the specialization of beauty through that body. There were times, as with love, when I felt only disappointment, carefully easing off the dressings and finding again a piece of flesh that would not knit, happier in the texture of stubborn glue. But then on more exhilarating days I'd peel like an onion all her bandages away and suddenly discover I was looking down at some literal tenacity and was bemused at all the freshly withered shapes she could create. Each new striation was a victory to itself, and when Dadi's hairless groin solidified again and sent firm signals that her abdomen must do the same, I could have wept with glee.

After her immolation, Dadi's diet underwent some curious changes. At first her consciousness teetered too much for her to pray, but then as she grew stronger it took us a while to notice what was missing: she had forgotten prayer. It left her life as firmly as tobacco can leave the lives of only the most passionate smokers, and I don't know if she ever prayed again. At about this time, however, with the heavy-handed inevitability that characterized his relation to his mother, my father took to prayer. I came home one afternoon and looked for him in all the usual places, but he wasn't to be found. Finally I came across Tillat and asked her where Papa was. "Praying," she said. "*Praying?*" I said. "Praying," she said, and I felt most embarrassed. For us it was rather as though we had come upon the children playing some forbidden titillating game and decided it was wisest to ignore it calmly. In an unspoken way, though, I think we dimly knew we were about to witness Islam's departure from the land of Pakistan. The men would take it to the streets and make it vociferate, but the great romance between religion and the populace, the embrace that engendered Pakistan, was done. So Papa prayed, with the desperate ardor of a lover trying to converse life back into a finished love.

That was a change, when Dadi patched herself together again and forgot to put prayer back into its proper pocket, for God could now leave the home and soon would join the government. Papa prayed and fasted and went on pilgrimage and read the Quran aloud with most peculiar locutions. Occasionally we also caught him in nocturnal altercations that made him sound suspiciously like Dadi: we looked askance, but didn't say a thing. My mother was altogether admirable: she behaved as though she'd always known that she'd wed a swaying, chanting thing and that to register surprise now would be an impoliteness to existence. Her expression reminded me somewhat of the time when Ifat was eight and Mamma was urging her recalcitrance into some goodly task. Ifat postponed, and Mamma, always nifty with appropriate fables, quoted meaningfully: "'I'll do it myself,' said the little red hen." Ifat looked up with bright affection. "Good little red hen," she murmured. Then a glance crossed my mother's face, a look between a slight smile and a quick rejection of the eloquent response, like a woman looking down and then away.

She looked like that at my father's sudden hungering for God, which was added to the growing number of subjects about which we, my mother and her daughters, silently decided we had no conversation. We knew there was something other than trying times ahead and would far rather hold our breath than speculate about other surprises the era held up its capacious sleeve. Tillat and I decided to quash our dread of waiting around for change by changing for ourselves, before destiny took the time to come our way. I would move to America, and Tillat to Kuwait and marriage. To both declarations of intention my mother said "I see," and helped us in our preparations: she knew by then her elder son would not return, and was prepared to extend the courtesy of change to her daughters, too. We left, and Islam predictably took to the streets, shaking Bhutto's empire. Mamma and Dadi remained the only women in the house, the one untalking, the other unpraying.

Dadi behaved abysmally at my mother's funeral, they told me, and made them all annoyed. She set up loud and unnecessary lamentations in the dining room, somewhat like an heir apparent, as though this death had reinstated her as mother of the house. While Ifat and Nuzzi and Tillat wandered frozen-eyed, dealing with the roses and the ice, Dadi demanded an irritating amount of attention, stretching out supine and crying out, "Your mother has betrayed your father; she has left him; she has gone." Food from respectful mourners poured in, caldron after caldron, and Dadi relocated a voracious appetite.

Years later, I was somewhat sorry that I had heard this tale, because it made me take affront. When I returned to Pakistan, I was too peeved with Dadi to find out how she was. Instead I listened to Ifat tell me about standing there in the hospital, watching the doctors suddenly pump upon my mother's heart— "I'd seen it on television," she gravely said, "I knew it was the end." Mamma's students from the university had tracked down the rickshaw driver who had knocked her down: they'd pummeled him nearly to death and then camped out in our garden, sobbing wildly, all in hordes.

By this time Bhutto was in prison and awaiting trial, and General Zulu was presiding over the Islamization of Pakistan. But we had no time to notice. My mother was buried at the nerve center of Lahore, an unruly and dusty place, and my father immediately made arrangements to buy the plot of land next to her grave: "We're ready when you are," Shahid sang. Her tombstone bore some pretty Urdu poetry and a completely ficititious place of birth, because some details my father tended to forget. "Honestly," it would have moved his wife to say.

So I was angry with Dadi at that time and didn't stop to see her. I saw my mother's grave and then came back to America, hardly noticing when, six months later, my father called from London and mentioned Dadi was now dead. It happened in the same week that Bhutto finally was hanged, and our imaginations were consumed by that public and historical dying. Pakistan made rapid provisions not to talk about the thing that had been done, and somehow, accidently, Dadi must have been mislaid into that larger decision, because she too ceased being a mentioned thing. My father tried to get back in time for the funeral, but he was so busy talking Bhutto-talk in England that he missed his flight and thus did not return. Luckily, Irfani was at home and he saw Dadi to her grave.

Bhutto's hanging had the effect of making Pakistan feel unreliable, particularly to itself. Its landscape learned a new secretiveness, unusual for a formerly loquacious people. This may account for the fact that I have never seen my grandmother's grave and neither have my sisters. I think we would have tried, had we been together, despite the free-floating anarchy in the air that—like the heroin trade—made the world suspicious and afraid. There was no longer any need to wait for change, because change was all there was, and we had quite forgotten the flavor of an era that stayed in place long enough to gain a name. One morning I awoke to find that, during the course of the night, my mind had completely ejected the names of all the streets in Pakistan, as though to assure that I could not return, or that if I did, it would be returning to a loss. Overnight the country had grown absentminded, and patches of amnesia hung over the hollows of the land like fog.

I think we would have mourned Dadi in our belated way, but the coming year saw Ifat killed in the consuming rush of change and disbanded the company of women for all time. It was a curious day in March, two years after my mother died, when the weight of that anniversary made us all disconsolate for her quietude. "I'll speak to Ifat, though," I thought to myself in America. But in Pakistan someone had different ideas for that sister of mine and thwarted all my plans. When she went walking out that warm March night, a car came by and trampled her into the ground, and then it vanished strangely. By the time I reached Lahore, a tall and slender mound had usurped the grave-space where my father had hoped to lie, next to the more moderate shape that was his wife. Children take over everything.

So, worn by repetition, we stood by Ifat's grave, and took note of the narcissi, still alive, that she must have placed upon my mother on the day that she was killed. It made us impatient, in a way, as though we had to decide that there was nothing so farcical as grief and that it had to be eliminated from our diets for good. It cut away, of course, our intimacy with Pakistan, where history is synonymous with grief and always most at home in the attitudes of grieving. Our congregation in Lahore was brief, and then we swiftly returned to a more geographic reality. "We are lost, Sara," Shahid said to me on the phone from England. "Yes, Shahid," I firmly said, "We're lost."

Today, I'd be less emphatic. Ifat and Mamma must have honeycombed and crumbled now, in the comfortable way that overtakes bedfellows. And somehow it seems apt and heartening that Dadi, being what she was, never suffered the pomposities that enter the most well-meaning of farewells and seeped instead into the nooks and crannies of our forgetfulness. She fell between two stools of grief, which is appropriate, since she was greatest when her life was at its most unreal. Anyway she was always outside our ken, an anecdotal thing, neither more nor less. So some sweet reassurance of reality accompanies my discourse when I claim that when Dadi died, we all forgot to grieve.

For to be lost is just a minute's respite, after all, like a train that cannot help but stop between the stations of its proper destination in order to stage a pretend version of the end. Dying, we saw, was simply change taken to points of mocking extremity, and wasn't a thing to lose us but to find us out, to catch us where we least wanted to be caught. In Pakistan, Bhutto rapidly became obsolete after a succession of bumper harvests, and none of us can fight the ways that the names Mamma and Ifat have become archaisms, quaintnesses on our lips.

Now I live in New Haven and feel quite happy with my life. I miss, of course, the absence of women and grow increasingly nostalgic for a world where the modulations of age are as recognized and welcomed as the shift from season into season. But that's a hazard that has to come along, since I have made myself inhabitant of a population which democratically insists that everyone from twenty-nine to fifty-six occupies roughly the same space of age. When I teach topics in third world literature, much time is lost in trying to explain that the third world is locatable only as a discourse of convenience. Trying to find it is like pretending that history or home is real and not located precisely where you're sitting, I hear my voice quite idiotically say. And then it happens. A face, puzzled and attentive and belonging to my gender, raises its intelligence to question why, since I am teaching third world writing, I haven't given equal space to women writers on my syllabus. I look up, the horse's mouth, a foolish thing to be. Unequal images battle in my mind for precedence—there's imperial Ifat, there's Mamma in the garden, and Halima the cleaning woman is there too, there's uncanny Dadi with her goat. Against all my own odds I know what I must say. Because, I'll answer slowly, there are no women in the third world.

Luci Tapahonso 1953–

Born and raised on the Navajo Nation in Shiprock, New Mexico, Luci Tapahonso grew up in a family of eleven children. Fluent in both her original Navajo tongue and English, she combines the languages in writings such as *Saanii Dahataal: The Women Are Singing: Poems and Stories* (1993), which won a Southwest Book Award. While attending the University of New Mexico, Tapahonso was mentored by renowned Native-American writer Leslie Marmon Silko whose encouragement inspired her first book of poems, *One More Shiprock Night* (1981). Other works include *Blue Horses Rush In: Poems and Stories* (1997); *A Breeze Swept Through* (1987); *Seasonal Woman* (1982); and a children's book, *Navajo ABC: A Dine Alphabet Book* (1995) with illustrator Eleanor Schick. A much sought-after speaker, she is the recipient of many honors and awards including a 1998 Regional Book Award from the Mountains & Plains Booksellers Association, a Southwestern Association for Indian Affairs Literature fellowship, a New Mexico Eminent Scholar Award from the New Mexico Commission of Higher Education, and an Excellent Instructor Award from the University of New Mexico. Currently, Tapahonso is an associate professor of English at the University of Kansas.

SHEEPHERDER BLUES

For Betty Holyan

         "went to NCC for a year,"
         she said,
         "was alright.
         there was some drinking, fights
         i just kept low.   5
         it was alright."

         this friend
         haven't see for a year or two.
         it was a good surprise.
         took her downtown   10
         to catch the next bus
         to Gallup.

         "i went to Oklahoma City,"
         she said,
         "to vacation, visit friends,   15
         have a good time.
         but i got the sheepherder blues
         in Oklahoma City."

         "i kept worrying about my sheep
         if they were okay   20
         really missed them,
         the long days in the sun.
         so after 4 days
         I had to leave Oklahoma City."

         so she went back,   25
         first bus to Gallup,
         then a 2-hour drive
         to her sheep.

BLUE HORSES RUSH IN

For Chamisa Bah Edmo,
who was born March 6, 1991

Before the birth, she moved and pushed inside her mother.
Her heart pounded quickly and we recognized the sound of horses running:

> the thundering of hooves on the desert floor.

Her mother clenched her fists and gasped.
She moans ageless pain and pushes: This is it!   5

Chamisa slips out, glistening wet and takes her first breath.
> The wind outside swirls small leaves
> and branches in the dark.

Her father's eyes are wet with gratitude.
He prays and watches both mother and baby—stunned.   10

This baby arrived amid a herd of horses,
> horses of different colors.

White horses ride in on the breath of the wind.
White horses from the west
where plants of golden chamisa shimmer in the moonlight.   15

She arrived amid a herd of horses.
Yellow horses enter from the east
bringing the scent of prairie grasses from the small hills outside.

She arrived amid a herd of horses.

Blue horses rush in, snorting from the desert in the south. 20
It is possible to see across the entire valley to Niist'áá from Tó.
Bah, from here your grandmothers went to war long ago.

She arrived amid a herd of horses.

Black horses came from the north.
They are the lush summers of Montana and still white winters of Idaho. 25

Chamisa, Chamisa Bah. It is all this that you are.
You will grow: laughing, crying,
and we will celebrate each change you live.

You will grow strong like the horses of your past.
You will grow strong like the horses of your birth.   30

Sandra Cisneros 1954–

Poet, fiction writer, educator, and feminist, Sandra Cisneros emerged in the 1980s as one of the most influential Chicana writers. Born and raised in Chicago's Mexican-American community by a Mexican father, Chicana mother, and six brothers, Cisneros began writing at the age of ten. Although she earned a graduate degree in creative writing from the University of Iowa Writers' Workshop, she claims that she learned "how I didn't want to write." Observing that she did not possess the same type of "communal knowledge" as her classmates, she returned home and immersed herself in the rhythms of language and life in the barrio. She began to write about conflicts that she confronted in her childhood: alienation, poverty, degradation, and divided cultural loyalties. She often addresses sex as something that is oppressive and destructive to women who, by romanticizing it, cooperate with the male point of view. Her works include *The House on Mango Street* (1984), a unique volume of interrelated vignettes that combines short stories with prose poetry; the poetry collection *My Wicked, Wicked Ways* (1987); and *Woman Hollering Creek and Other Stories* (1991).

SIX BROTHERS

In Grimm's tale *The Six Swans* a sister keeps
a six-year silence and weaves six thistle shirts
to break the spell that has changed her brothers
into swans. She weaves all but the left
sleeve of the final shirt, and when the brothers   5
are changed back into men, the youngest lacks
only his left arm and has in its place a swan's
wing.

In Spanish our name means swan.
A great past—castles maybe   10
or a Sahara city,
but more likely
a name that stuck
to a barefoot boy
herding the dusty flock   15
down the bright road.

We'll never know.
Great-grandparents might
but family likes to keep to silence—
perhaps with reason   20
though we don't need far back to go.
On our father's side we have a cousin,
second, but cousin nonetheless,
who shot someone, his wife I think.
And on the other hand, there's   25
mother's brother who shot himself.

Then there's us—
seven ways to make the name or break it.
Our father has it planned:
oldest, you're doctor,   30
second, administration,
me, he shrugs, you should've been reporting weather,
next, musician,
athlete,
genius,   35
and youngest—well,
you'll take the business over.

You six a team
keeping to the master plan,
the lovely motion of tradition.   40
Appearances are everything.
We live for each other's expectations.
Brothers, it is so hard to keep up with you.
I've got the bad blood in me I think,
the mad uncle, the bit of the bullet.   45

Ask me anything.
Six thistle shirts. Keep a vow of silence.
I'll do it. But I'm earthbound
always in my admiration.
My six brothers, graceful, strong.   50
Except for you, little one-winged,
finding it as difficult as me
to keep the good name clean.

MY WICKED WICKED WAYS

This is my father.
See? He is young.
He looks like Errol Flynn.
He is wearing a hat
that tips over one eye,   5
a suit that fits him good,
and baggy pants.
He is also wearing
those awful shoes,
the two-toned ones   10
my mother hates.

Here is my mother.
She is not crying.
She cannot look into the lens
because the sun is bright.   15
The woman,
the one my father knows,
is not here.
She does not come till later.

My mother will get very mad.   20
Her face will turn red
and she will throw one shoe.
My father will say nothing.
After a while everyone
will forget it.   25
Years and years will pass.
My mother will stop mentioning it.

This is me she is carrying.
I am a baby.
She does not know   30
I will turn out bad.

Louise Erdrich 1954–

The daughter of a Chippewa Indian mother and German-American father,
Louise Erdrich grew up in Wahpeton, North Dakota, near the Turtle Mountain
Chippewa Reservation where her parents worked for the Bureau of Indian Affairs
boarding school. At a very young age, Erdrich was encouraged by her parents

to write. "My father used to give me a nickel for every story I wrote," she told *Contemporary Authors,* "and my mother wove strips of construction paper together and stapled them into book covers. So at an early age, I felt myself to be a published author earning substantial royalties." She began to truly publish stories and poems while at Dartmouth College and then received her M.A. in creative writing from Johns Hopkins University in 1979. A collaborative story with chair of Dartmouth's Native American Studies Department and future husband, Michael Dorris, won $5,000 and eventually led to her first novel, *Love Medicine* (1984). This award-winning and unique, seven-narrator novel traces two Native-American families from 1934 to 1984. Subsequent works, such as *The Beet Queen* (1986), *Tracks* (1988), and *The Bingo Palace* (1994), continue her fictional portraits of three interrelated families living in North Dakota between 1912 and 1980. Told nonchronologically, the novels' intricate details are slowly revealed in seemingly random order until finally, a three-dimensional character—with a past and a future—appears.

SKUNK DREAMS

WHEN I WAS FOURTEEN, I slept alone on a North Dakota football field under the cold stars on an early spring night. May is unpredictable in the Red River Valley, and I happened to hit a night when frost formed in the grass. A skunk trailed a plume of steam across the forty-yard line near moonrise. I tucked the top of my sleeping bag over my head and was just dozing off when the skunk walked onto me with simple authority.

Its ripe odor must have dissipated in the frozen earth of its winterlong hibernation, because it didn't smell all that bad, or perhaps it was just that I took shallow breaths in numb surprise. I felt him—her, whatever—pause on the side of my hip and turn around twice before evidently deciding I was a good place to sleep. At the back of my knees, on the quilting of my sleeping bag, it trod out a spot for itself and then, with a serene little groan, curled up and lay perfectly still. That made two of us. I was wildly awake, trying to forget the sharpness and number of skunk teeth, trying not to think of the high percentage of skunks with rabies, or the reason that on camping trips my father always kept a hatchet underneath his pillow.

Inside the bag, I felt as if I might smother. Carefully, making only the slightest of rustles, I drew the bag away from my face and took a deep breath of the night air, enriched with skunk, but clear and watery and cold. It wasn't so bad, and the skunk didn't stir at all, so I watched the moon—caught that night in an envelope of silk, a mist—pass over my sleeping field of teenage guts and glory. The grass in spring that has lain beneath the snow harbors a sere dust both old and fresh. I smelled that newness beneath the rank tone of my bag-mate—the stiff fragrance of damp earth and the thick pungency of newly manured field a mile or two away—along with my sleeping bag's smell, slightly mildewed, forever smoky. The skunk settled even closer and began to breathe rapidly; its feet jerked a little like a dog's. I sank against the earth, and fell asleep too.

Of what easily tipped cans, what molten sludge, what dogs in yards on chains, what leftover macaroni casseroles, what cellar holes, crawl spaces, burrows taken from meek woodchucks, of what miracles of garbage did my skunk dream? Or did it, since we can't be sure, dream the plot of *Moby-Dick*, how to properly age Parmesan, or how to restore the brick-walled, tumbledown creamery that was its home? We don't know about the dreams of any other biota, and even much about our own. If dreams are an actual dimension, as some assert, then the usual rules of life by which we abide do not apply. In that place, skunks may certainly dream themselves into the vests of stockbrokers. Perhaps that night the skunk and I dreamed each other's thoughts or are still dreaming them. To paraphrase the problem of the Chinese sage, I may be a woman who has dreamed herself a skunk, or a skunk still dreaming that she is a woman.

In a book called *Death and Consciousness*, David H. Lund—who wants very much to believe in life after death—describes human dream-life as a possible model for a disembodied existence:

> Many of one's dreams are such that they involve the activities of an apparently embodied person whom one takes to be oneself as long as one dreams.... Whatever is the source of the imagery ... apparently has the capacity to bring about images of a human body and to impart the feeling that the body is mine. It is, of course, just an image body, but it serves as a perfectly good body for the dream experience. I regard it as mine, I act on the dream environment by means of it, and it constitutes the center of the perceptual world of my dream.

Over the years I have acquired and reshuffled my beliefs and doubts about whether we live on after death—in any shape or form, that is, besides the molecular level at which I am to be absorbed by the taproots of cemetery elms or pines and the tangled mats of fearfully poisoned, too-green lawn grass. I want something of the self on whom I have worked so hard to survive the loss of the body (which, incidentally, the self has done a fairly decent job of looking after, excepting spells of too much cabernet and a few idiotic years of rolling my own cigarettes out of Virginia Blond tobacco). I am put out with the marvelous discoveries of the intricate biochemical configuration of our brains, though I realize that the processes themselves are quite miraculous. I understand that I should be self-proud, content to gee-whiz at the fact that I am the world's only mechanism that can admire itself. I should be grateful that life is here today, though gone tomorrow, but I can't help it. I want more.

Skunks don't mind each other's vile perfume. Obviously, they find each other more than tolerable. And even I, who have been in the presence of a direct skunk hit, wouldn't classify their weapon as mere smell. It is more on the order

---

of a reality-enhancing experience. It's not so pleasant as standing in a grove of old-growth red cedars, or on a lyrical moonshed plain, or watching trout rise to the shadow of your hand on the placid surface of an Alpine lake. When the skunk lets go, you're surrounded by skunk presence: inhabited, owned, involved with something you can only describe as powerfully *there.*

I woke at dawn, stunned into that sprayed state of being. The dog that had approached me was rolling in the grass, half-addled, sprayed too. The skunk was gone. I abandoned my sleeping bag and started home. Up Eighth Street, past the tiny blue and pink houses, past my grade school, past all the addresses where I had baby-sat, I walked in my own strange wind. The streets were wide and empty; I met no one—not a dog, not a squirrel, not even an early robin. Perhaps they had all scattered before me, blocks away. I had gone out to sleep on the football field because I was afflicted with a sadness I had to dramatize. Mood swings had begun, hormones, feverish and brutal. They were nothing to me now. My emotions had seemed vast, dark, and sickeningly private. But they were minor, mere wisps, compared to skunk.

I have found that my best dreams come to me in cheap motels. One such dream about an especially haunting place occurred in a rattling room in Valley City, North Dakota. There, in the home of the Winter Show, in the old Rudolph Hotel, I was to spend a weeklong residency as a poet-in-the-schools. I was supporting myself, at the time, by teaching poetry to children, convicts, rehabilitation patients, high-school hoods, and recovering alcoholics. What a marvelous job it was, and what opportunities I had to dream, since I paid my own lodging and lived low, sometimes taking rooms for less than ten dollars a night in motels that had already been closed by local health departments.

The images that assailed me in Valley City came about because the bedspread was so thin and worn—a mere brown tissuey curtain—that I had to sleep beneath my faux fur Salvation Army coat, wearing all of my clothing, even a scarf. Cold often brings on the most spectacular of my dreams, as if my brain has been incited to fevered activity. On that particular frigid night, the cold somehow seemed to snap boundaries, shift my time continuum, and perhaps even allow me to visit my own life in a future moment. After waking once, transferring the contents of my entire suitcase onto my person, and shivering to sleep again, I dreamed of a vast, dark, fenced place. The fencing was chain-link in places, chicken wire, sagging X wire, barbed wire on top, jerry-built with tipped-out poles and uncertain corners nailed to log posts and growing trees. And yet it was quite impermeable and solid, as time-tested, broken-looking things so often are.

Behind it, trees ran for miles—large trees, grown trees, big pines the likes of which do not exist on the Great Plains. In my dream I walked up to the fence, looked within, and saw tawny, humpbacked elk move among the great trunks and slashing green arms. Suave, imponderable, magnificently dumb, they lurched and floated through the dim-complexioned air. One turned, however, before they all vanished, and from either side of that flimsy-looking barrier there passed between us a look, a communion, a long and measureless regard that left me, on waking, with a sensation of penetrating sorrow.

I didn't think about my dream for many years, until after I moved to New Hampshire. I had become urbanized and sedentary since the days when I slept with skunks, and I had turned inward. For several years I spent my days leaning above a strange desk, a green door on stilts, which was so high that to sit at it I bought a barstool upholstered in brown leatherette. Besides, the entire North-east seemed like the inside of a house to me, the sky small and oddly lit, as if by an electric bulb. The sun did not pop over the great trees for hours—and then went down so soon. I was suspicious of Eastern land: the undramatic loveliness, the small scale, the lack of sky to watch, the way the weather sneaked up without enough warning.

The woods themselves seemed bogus at first—every inch of the ground turned over more than once, and even in the second growth of old pines so much human evidence. Rock walls ran everywhere, grown through and tumbled, as if the dead still had claims they imposed. The unkillable and fiercely contorted trees of old orchards, those revenants, spooked me when I walked in the woods. The blasted limbs spread a white lace cold as fire in the spring, and the odor of the blossoms was furiously spectral, sweet. When I stood beneath the canopies that hummed and shook with bees, I heard voices, other voices, and I did not understand what they were saying, where they had come from, what drove them into this earth.

Then, as often happens to sparring adversaries in 1940s movies, I fell in love.

After a few years of living in the country, the impulse to simply *get outside* hit me, strengthened, and became again a habit of thought, a reason for story-telling, an uneasy impatience with walls and roads. At first, when I had that urge, I had to get into a car and drive fifteen hundred miles before I was back in a place that I defined as *out*. The West, or the edge of it anyway, the great level patchwork of chemically treated fields and tortured grazing land, was the outside I had internalized. In the rich Red River Valley, where the valuable cropland is practically measured in inches, environmental areas are defined and proudly pointed out as stretches of roadway where the ditches are not mowed. Deer and pheasants survive in shelter belts—rows of Russian olive, plum, sometimes evergreen—planted at the edges of fields. The former tall-grass prairie has now become a collection of mechanized gardens tended by an array of air-conditioned farm implements and bearing an increasing amount of pesticide and herbicide in each black teaspoon of dirt. Nevertheless, no amount of reality changed the fact that I still *thought* of eastern North Dakota as wild.

In time, though, *out* became outside my door in New England. By walking across the road and sitting in my little writing house—a place surrounded by trees, thick plumes of grass, jets of ferns, and banks of touch-me-not—or just by looking out a screen door or window, I started to notice what there was to see. In time, the smothering woods that had always seemed part of Northeastern civilization—more an inside than an outside, more like a friendly garden—revealed themselves as forceful and complex. The growth of plants, the lush celebratory springs made a grasslands person drunk. The world turned dazzling green, the hills rode like comfortable and flowing animals. Everywhere there was the sound of water moving.

And yet, even though I finally grew closer to these woods, on some days I still wanted to tear them from before my eyes.

I wanted to *see*. Where I grew up, our house looked out on the western horizon. I could see horizon when I played. I could see it when I walked to school. It was always there, a line beyond everything, a simple line of changing shades and colors that ringed the town, a vast place. That was it. Down at the end of every grid of streets; vastness. Out the windows of the high school: vastness. From the drive-in theater where I went parking in a purple Duster: vast distance. That is why, on lovely New England days when everything should have been all right—a fall day, for instance, when the earth had risen through the air in patches and the sky lowered, dim and warm—I feel sick with longing for the horizon. I wanted the clean line, the simple line, the clouds marching over it in feathered masses. I suffered from horizon sickness. But it sounds crazy for a grown woman to throw herself at the sky, and the thing is, I wanted to get well. And so to compensate for horizon sickness, for the great longing that seemed both romantically German and pragmatically Chippewa in origin, I found solace in trees.

Trees are a changing landscape of sound—and the sound I grew attached to, possible only near large deciduous forests, was the great hushed roar of thousands and millions of leaves brushing and touching one another. Windy days were like sitting just out of sight of an ocean, the great magnetic ocean of wind. All around me, I watched the trees tossing, their heads bending. At times the movement seemed passionate, as though they were flung together in an eager embrace, caressing each other, branch to branch. If there is a vegetative soul, an animating power that all things share, there must be great rejoicing out there on windy days, ecstasy, for trees move so slowly on calm days. At least it seems that way to us. On days of high wind they move so freely it must give them a cellular pleasure close to terror.

Unused to walking in the woods, I did not realize that trees dropped branches—often large ones—or that there was any possible danger in going out on windy days, drawn by the natural drama. There was a white pine I loved, a tree of the size foresters call *overgrown*, a waste, a thing made of long-since harvestable material. The tree was so big that three people couldn't reach around it. Standing at the bottom, craning back, fingers clenched in grooves of bark, I held on as the crown of the tree roared and beat the air a hundred feet above. The movement was frantic, the soft-needled branches long and supple. I thought of a woman tossing, anchored in passion: calm one instant, full-throated the next, hair vast and dark, shedding the piercing, fresh oil of broken needles. I went to visit her often, and walked onward, farther, though it was not so far at all, and then one day I reached the fence.

Chain-link in places, chicken wire, sagging X wire, barbed wire on top, jerry-built with tipped-out poles and uncertain corners nailed to log posts and growing trees, still it seemed impermeable and solid. Behind it, there were trees for miles: large trees, grown trees, big pines. I walked up to the fence, looked within, and could see elk moving. Suave, imponderable, magnificently dumb, they lurched and floated through the dim air.

I was on the edge of a game park, a rich man's huge wilderness, probably the largest parcel of protected land in western New Hampshire, certainly the largest privately owned piece I knew about. At forty square miles—25,000 acres—it was bigger than my mother's home reservation. And it had the oddest fence around it that I'd ever seen, the longest and the tackiest. Though partially electrified, the side closest to our house was so piddling that an elk could easily have tossed it apart. Certainly a half-ton wild boar, the condensed and living version of a tank, could have strolled right through. But then animals, much like most humans, don't charge through fences unless they have sound reasons. As I soon found out, because I naturally grew fascinated with the place, there were many more animals trying to get into the park than out, and they couldn't have cared less about ending up in a hunter's stew pot.

These were not wild animals, the elk—since they were grained at feeding stations, how could they be? They were not domesticated either, however, for beyond the no-hunt boundaries they fled and vanished. They were game. Since there is no sport in shooting feedlot steers, these animals—still harboring wild traits and therefore more challenging to kill—were maintained to provide blood pleasure for the members of the Blue Mountain Forest Association.

As I walked away from the fence that day, I was of two minds about the place—and I am still. Shooting animals inside fences, no matter how big the area they have to hide in, seems abominable and silly. And yet, I was glad for that wilderness. Though secretly managed and off limits to me, it was the source of flocks of evening grosbeaks and pine siskins, of wild turkey, ravens, and grouse, of Eastern coyote, oxygen-rich air, foxes, goldfinches, skunk, and bears that tunneled in and out.

I had dreamed of this place in Valley City, or it had dreamed me. There was affinity here, beyond any explanation I could offer, so I didn't try. I continued to visit the tracts of big trees, and on deep nights—windy nights, especially when it stormed—I liked to fall asleep imagining details. I saw the great crowns touching, heard the raving sound of wind and thriving, knocking cries as the blackest of ravens flung themselves across acres upon indifferent acres of tossing, old-growth pine. I could fall asleep picturing how, below that dark air, taproots thrust into a deeper blankness, drinking the powerful rain.

Or was it so only in my dreams? The park, known locally as Corbin's Park, after its founder, Austin Corbin, is knit together of land and farmsteads he bought in the late nineteenth century from 275 individuals. Among the first animals released there, before the place became a hunting club, were thirty buffalo, remnants of the vast Western herds. Their presence piqued the interest of Ernest Harold Bayne, a conservation-minded local journalist, who attempted to break a pair of buffalo calves to the yoke. He exhibited them at country fairs and even knit mittens out of buffalo wool, hoping to convince the skeptical of their usefulness. His work inspired sympathy, if not a trend for buffalo yarn, and collective zeal for the salvation of the buffalo grew until by 1915 the American Bison Society, of which Bayne was secretary, helped form government reserves that eventually more than doubled the herds that remained.

The buffalo dream seems to have been the park's most noble hour. Since that time it has been the haunt of wealthy hunting enthusiasts. The owner of Ruger Arms currently inhabits the stunning, butter-yellow original Corbin mansion and would like to buy the whole park for his exclusive use, or so local gossip has it.

For some months I walked the boundary admiring the tangled landscape, at least all that I could see. After my first apprehension, I ignored the fence. I walked along it as if it simply did not exist, as if I really were part of that place which lay just beyond my reach. The British psychotherapist Adam Phillips has examined obstacles from several different angles, attempting to define their emotional use. "It is impossible to imagine desire without obstacles," he writes, "and wherever we find something to be an obstacle we are at the same time desiring something. It is part of the fascination of the Oedipus story in particular, and perhaps narrative in general, that we and the heroes and heroines of our fictions never know whether obstacles create desire or desire creates obstacles." He goes on to characterize the Unconscious, our dream world, as a place without obstacles: "A good question to ask of a dream is: What are the obstacles that have been removed to make this extraordinary scene possible?"

My dream, however, was about obstacles still in place. The fence was the main component, the defining characteristic of the forbidden territory that I watched but could not enter or experience. The obstacles that we overcome define us. We are composed of hurdles we set up to pace our headlong needs, to control our desires, or against which to measure our growth. "Without obtacles," Phillips writes, "the notion of development is inconceivable. There would be nothing to master."

Walking along the boundary of the park no longer satisfied me. The preciousness and deceptive stability of that fence began to rankle. Longing filled me. I wanted to brush against the old pine bark and pass beyond the ridge, to see specifically what was there: what Blue Mountain, what empty views, what lavender hillside, what old cellar holes, what unlikely animals. I was filled with poacher's lust, except I wanted only to smell the air. The linked web restraining me began to grate, and I started to look for weak spots, holes, places where the rough wire sagged. From the moment I began to see the fence as permeable, it became something to overcome. I returned time after time—partly to see if I could spot anyone on the other side, partly because I knew I must trespass.

Then, one clear, midwinter morning, in the middle of a half-hearted thaw, I walked along the fence until I came to a place that looked shaky—and was. I went through. There were no trails that I could see, and I knew I needed to stay away from any perimeter roads or snowmobile paths, as well as from the feeding stations where the animals congregated. I wanted to see the animals, but only from a distance. Of course, as I walked on, leaving a trail easily backtracked, I encountered no animals at all. Still, the terrain was beautiful, the columns of pine tall and satisfyingly heavy, the patches of oak and elderly maple from an occasional farmstead knotted and patient. I was satisfied, and sometime in the early afternoon, I decided to turn back and head toward the fence again. Skirting a low, boggy area that teemed with wild turkey tracks, heading toward the edge of a deadfall of trashed dead branches and brush, I stared too hard into the sun, and stumbled.

In a half crouch, I looked straight into the face of a boar, massive as a boulder. Cornfed, razor-tusked, alert, sensitive ears pricked, it edged slightly backward into the convening shadows. Two ice picks of light gleamed from its shrouded, tiny eyes, impossible to read. Beyond the rock of its shoulder, I saw more: a sow and three cinnamon-brown farrows crossing a small field of glare snow, lit by dazzling sun. The young skittered along, lumps of muscled fat on tiny hooves. They reminded me of snowsuited toddlers on new skates. When they were out of sight the boar melted through the brush after them, leaving not a snapped twig or crushed leaf in his wake.

I almost didn't breathe in the silence, letting the fact of that presence settle before I retraced my own tracks.

Since then, I've been to the game park via front gates, driven down the avenues of tough old trees, and seen herds of wild pigs and elk meandering past the residence of the gamekeeper. A no-hunting zone exists around the house, where the animals are almost tame. But I've been told by privileged hunters that just beyond that invisible boundary they vanish, becoming suddenly and preternaturally elusive.

There is something in me that resists the notion of fair use of this land if the only alternative is to have it cut up, sold off in lots, condominiumized. Yet the dumb fervor of the place depresses me—the wilderness locked up and managed but not for its sake; the animals imported and cultivated to give pleasure through their deaths. All animals, that is, except for skunks.

Not worth hunting, inedible except to old trappers like my uncle Ben Gourneau, who boiled his skunk with onions in three changes of water, skunks pass in and out of Corbin's Park without hindrance, without concern. They live off the corn in the feeding cribs (or the mice it draws), off the garbage of my rural neighbors, off bugs and frogs and grubs. They nudge their way onto our back porch for catfood, and even when disturbed they do not, ever, hurry. It's easy to get near a skunk, even to capture one. When skunks become a nuisance, people either shoot them or catch them in crates, cardboard boxes, Havahart traps, plastic garbage barrels.

Natives of the upper Connecticut River valley have neatly solved the problem of what to do with such catches. They hoist their trapped mustelid into the back of a pickup truck and cart the animal across the river to the neighboring state—New Hampshire to Vermont, Vermont to New Hampshire—before releasing it. The skunk population is estimated as about even on both sides.

We should take comfort from the skunk, an arrogant creature so pleased with its own devices that it never runs from harm, just turns its back in total confidence. If I were an animal, I'd choose to be a skunk: live fearlessly, eat anything, gestate my young in just two months, and fall into a state of dreaming torpor when the cold bit hard. Wherever I went, I'd leave my sloppy tracks. I wouldn't walk so much as putter, destinationless, in a serene belligerence—past hunters, past death overhead, past death all around.

Marilyn Chin 1955–

A first-generation Chinese American born in Hong Kong and raised in Portland, Oregon, Marilyn Chin has experienced the difficulties of being part of two cultures. Praised for addressing the patriarchal subjugation of Asian women, Chin states: "I believe I have a mission, and that I have many stories to tell on personal . . . familial . . . and historical-social level." Conditions of assimilation and loss are common topics in Chin's writing. In the poem "How I Got That Name," she angrily condemns her parents for selling-out their culture in order to assimilate. She sardonically describes how her father "obsessed with a bombshell blond / transliterated 'Mei Ling' to 'Marilyn.' / And there I was . . . named after some tragic white woman swollen with gin and Nembutal." Chin's books include *The Phoenix Gone, The Terrace Empty* (1994), and *Dwarf Bamboo* (1987). She has received two National Endowment for the Arts writing fellowships, the Mary Roberts Rinehart Award, and a Stegner fellowship from Stanford University. She teaches at San Diego State University.

How I Got That Name

AN ESSAY ON ASSIMILATION

I am Marilyn Mei Ling Chin
Oh, how I love the resoluteness
of that first person singular
followed by that stalwart indicative
of "be," without the uncertain i-n-g   5
of "becoming." Of course,
the name had been changed
somewhere between Angel Island and the sea,
when my father the paperson
in the late 1950s   10
obsessed with a bombshell blond
transliterated "Mei Ling" to "Marilyn."
And nobody dared question
his initial impulse — for we all know
lust drove men to greatness,   15
not goodness, not decency.
And there I was, a wayward pink baby,
named after some tragic white woman
swollen with gin and Nembutal.
My mother couldn't pronounce the "r."   20
She dubbed me "Numba one female offshoot"
for brevity: henceforth, she will live and die
in sublime ignorance, flanked
by loving children and the "kitchen deity."
While my father dithers,   25
a tomcat in Hong Kong trash —
a gambler, a petty thug,
who bought a chain of chopsuey joints
in Piss River, Oregon,
with bootlegged Gucci cash.   30
Nobody dared question his integrity given
his nice, devout daughters
and his bright, industrious sons
as if filial piety were the standard
by which all earthly men are measured.   35

*

Oh, how trustworthy our daughters,
how thrifty our sons!
How we've managed to fool the experts

in education, statistic and demography—
We're not very creative but not adverse to rote-learning.   40
Indeed, they can use us.
But the "Model Minority" is a tease.
We know you are watching now,
so we refuse to give you any!
Oh, bamboo shoots, bamboo shoots!   45
The further west we go, we'll hit east;
the deeper down we dig, we'll find China.
History has turned its stomach
on a black polluted beach—
where life doesn't hinge   50
on that red, red wheelbarrow,
but whether or not our new lover
in the final episode of "Santa Barbara"
will lean over a scented candle
and call us a "bitch."   55
Oh God, where have we gone wrong?
We have no inner resources!

*

Then, one redolent spring morning
the Great Patriarch Chin
peered down from his kiosk in heaven   60
and saw that his descendants were ugly.
One had a squarish head and a nose without a bridge
Another's profile—long and knobbed as a gourd.
A third, the sad, brutish one
may never, never marry.   65
And I, his least favorite—
"not quite boiled, not quite cooked,"
a plump pomfret simmering in my juices—
too listless to fight for my people's destiny.
"To kill without resistance is not slaughter"   70
says the proverb. So, I wait for imminent death.
The fact that this death is also metaphorical
is testament to my lethargy.

*

So here lies Marilyn Mei Ling Chin,
married once, twice to so-and-so, a Lee and a Wong,   75
granddaughter of Jack "the patriarch"
and the brooding Suilin Fong,
daughter of the virtuous Yuet Kuen Wong

and G. G. Chin the infamous,
sister of a dozen, cousin of a million,   80
survived by everybody and forgotten by all.
She was neither black nor white,
neither cherished nor vanquished,
just another squatter in her own bamboo grove
minding her poetry—   85
when one day heaven was unmerciful,
and a chasm opened where she stood.
Like the jowls of a mighty white whale,
or the jaws of a metaphysical Godzilla,
it swallowed her whole.   90
She did not flinch nor writhe,
nor fret about the afterlife,
but stayed! Solid as wood, happily
a little gnawed, tattered, mesmerized
by all that was lavished upon her   95
and all that was taken away!

Rebecca Brown 1956–

Born in San Diego, California, Rebecca Brown has established herself as one of the 1990s most influential lesbian writers. A former teacher, freelance journalist, carpenter, and rock music critic, Brown received her B.A. from George Washington University and her M.F.A. from the University of Virginia. A full-time writer of numerous fictions, she has spent much of her composing time in England. *The Gifts of the Body* (1994), the story of a home-care worker who assists AIDS patients, won several awards, including the Lambda Literary Award for lesbian fiction. Lucy Jane Bledsoe of *Harvard Gay and Lesbian Review* states that Brown "strip[s] the process of death down to its most naked face, relating each tear, each drop of sweat, each fluttering eyelash, each breath drawn, each pill swallowed." Brown's 1996 short-story collection, *What Keeps Me Here*, uses similar attention to detail, achieving its success by intensely concentrating on simple deeds. Brown remarked that she did not write, "so that some deconstructivist will say what an interesting book I've written. I want to excite readers emotionally, intellectually, and artistically."

From THE GIFTS OF THE BODY

The Gift of Hunger

Everyone tried to fatten her up. People brought her casseroles and baked goods and takeout. I could see who'd been there by what was in the fridge. A casserole with pasta and tomatoes and ricotta meant Joe and Tony. A giant paper plate of ribs or a box of Kentucky Fried or a big waxy cup with a plastic lid and two-thirds of a chocolate shake meant some of the kids from the Literacy Program. Homemade chocolate chip cookies meant Ingrid and the twins.

I used to try to be gone when the nurse came at noon, but after we'd over-lapped enough times so that Connie couldn't pretend she wasn't getting home care and nurse visits all the time, I stayed till the nurse got there. It became important to stay so I could talk with the nurse a little before I left.

It was morning rush hour when I got off the bus near her house. I saw her neighbors going to work and they got to know me and ask, "So how's Mrs. Lindstrom?" and I'd say, "She's had a good couple days." Or," Oh, you know . . ."

I checked her mail on the way in. Her little barn mailbox had a weather vane for when there was something for the postal person to pick up. This day there was a package neatly wrapped in a brown paper bag and postmarked Vermont. Plus one of her newsletters and the usual junk mail. She looked at all of it. She said the junk mail kept her up on what was really going on out in the world. Sometimes we looked at the catalogs together because she wanted my opinion on things for her kids.

I knocked on her door and shouted, "Hello!" and let myself in with my set of her keys. The TV was on to the *Today* show. She thought Bryant Gumbel was such a nice young man, and the only one who could ever hold a candle to Barbara Walters.

Connie was lying on the couch. Sometimes, because the couch was beige and the blankets were beige too, and because she was so small, you almost couldn't see her lying there until you saw her face.

"Morning, Connie," I said. I dropped my pack and jacket on the table.

She shouted good morning over the TV and pulled her hand out from the blanket to wave. The light coming in the window behind her caught on her diamond wedding ring. Sometimes I worried it would slide off, but she didn't want to put it anywhere for safekeeping because she didn't want to take it off.

I took the mail over to the couch and asked her how she was doing.

"Fine," she said. She always said she was fine.

"Well, you're gonna feel great when you see your mail." I helped her sit up a little and handed her the package. She looked through the bottom of her bifo-cals. Her eyes widened.

"Oh!" She sounded really happy. "It's from Diane!"

Diane was her daughter in Vermont. She was married to Bob. They had two kids, Robert and Maria, and were expecting a third.

"Can you get me the scissor?"

The sewing box was on the footstool next to the couch. She didn't do the sewing or knitting she used to, but she kept her things close for when Tony came over for his bootie-knitting lessons. He was thrilled about Diane and Bob's new kid. Connie also kept the knitting close in case she felt like it. I got the scissors out of the box. They were in an old leather safety cover. I handed them to her handle first.

She snipped the string and tape on the box. I watched the joints of her finger work. She was still pretty deft. She folded the flaps back and reached down through the foam peanuts.

"Oh, isn't this darling," she said.

It was a can of Vermont maple syrup shaped like a house with a triangular roof. The lid sticking up was supposed to be the chimney. The can was painted with a house, a guy in overalls and a red cap, trees and buckets. There was also an envelope: "For Grandmommy." She slipped a scissor blade under the flap and opened it. She put the scissors down on the couch and started to take the card out but stopped and picked up the scissors and said, "Can you put these away?"

I put them back in their leather case, then back in the box. Connie kept all these habits from having children in her house.

When the scissors were safe she pulled out the card. It had a pencil drawing of maple leaves colored outside the lines with red and orange and yellow crayons. She opened the card. There was a photo inside.

"Oh, don't they look precious!" she said.

I looked over her shoulder. I recognized them all from the photos she'd shown me before. She had pictures everywhere of all the kids at different ages and a few of her and John. She used to be fat.

"So Diane's letting her hair grow," she said. Then she held the picture at arm's length and squinted above and below her bifocal line. "Do you think she's showing yet?"

I looked. "Nah, not yet." It was only a few weeks since Diane had called to tell her mom she was expecting. I didn't know exactly when she was due.

"Well, Bob certainly looks nice with a beard, don't you think?" I nodded but she was still looking at the picture. "Look how Maria is shooting up! Maybe Maria really will be Bob's basketball star . . . and sweet little Robert."

In the picture Maria's arm was around her little brother. They were all in red caps and boots and plaid jackets like the guy on the can of syrup.

"Oh, how absolutely darling," she said again. Then she started to read the card. I gathered up the wrapping paper and foam peanuts. I was about to wad them up and toss them when she said, "You want to save that box and packing material?"

"Oh, sure," I said. Connie saved everything.

"Wrapping things go in the hall closet on the shelf behind the vacuum."

"OK," I said. I folded the paper and put it and the peanuts back in the box and went to the closet.

When I came back to the living room she told me the family news from the letter. I felt like I knew these people.

She picked up the can and held it close then arm's length away and started to read the label: "One hundred percent pure Vermont maple syrup. Great on pancakes—" She stopped.

I sat next to her and finished reading. "—French toast, and waffles. Try it on ice cream."

"Oh, Miss Kitty would love that," she laughed. Miss Kitty, her old cat, had a terrible sweet tooth.

Then she got this look on her face. She picked up the photo again. "You know why they sent me this?"

I didn't tell her what I was thinking.

"Well, I'll tell you," she said. She leaned back on the couch. I fluffed a pillow behind her. She closed her eyes and took a deep breath. I grabbed the TV remote and muted the volume. She was holding the can and the picture tight in her hands. Her skin had brown age spots. Her veins were thick and blue.

"Joe took this trip in junior high," she started. "With the Glee Club. He loved the Glee Club. You know, he still has a beautiful voice."

She told me how the Glee Club went to a ski lodge and gave a concert. It was the first time most of the kids had ever been on a trip like that and they were crazy with excitement. The morning they were to come home they had a huge pancake breakfast. Joe always had an appetite, she said. Then, when Joe got home, he kept going on and on about the trip and the breakfast and how great the pancakes were. All the Lindstroms got tired of Joe going on so much and they said their mom, meaning Connie, could make pancakes just as good, so she made pancakes and Joe said they were good but not *as* good. Everyone else thought the pancakes were great so John—she used to refer to him as her late husband, but now she just called him her husband, or John—so John pulled out a different bottle of syrup from the cupboard and tried that, but Joe said they *still* weren't as good. So the next time Connie went to the store she got another kind of syrup and Joe still said they weren't as good. It was already a joke. No one ever expected Joe to say his mom's pancakes were as good as they were on the trip. But after that everyone in the family would give Joe, then everyone in the family including Joe, would give everyone else in the family, for Christmas or birthdays or their anniversary or even when there wasn't an occasion but just for a present, syrup. Connie said they knew, even the kids when they were young, that it wasn't the pancakes or even the syrup that mattered, but that their family had this special present they gave one another.

"So that's why Diane sent me the syrup," Connie said.

"That's great," I said. "It's a wonderful story."

I gave her a second, then I said, "So. You wanna try some syrup?"

"Of course! I'd love to!" she said with forced enthusiasm. "But I'm not hungry right now."

"OK," I said. "I'll get you your juice and maybe you'll feel like something in a bit."

"All right," she said.

I brought her juice in a big glass without a straw. She liked it when she could drink without a straw. Her new med tray was on her couchside table. She put the syrup and card and picture on the table and I handed her the med tray. She put it on her lap and opened the morning section. She took the meds out one by one. She needed to take them with lots of fluids and she also needed to take them slowly, so this took time. She liked me to sit and talk with her while she took her meds. So I sat next to her and told her about what I'd done the last couple of nights and what I was going to do that weekend. She used to say she liked hearing what young people were up to these days and she passed on to her kids what I told her. I never talked with her about other people I worked with.

Occasionally she said things between her meds but not often because she had to concentrate. She had to be very slow. Sometimes if she was taking an especially long time I tried to encourage her a little, but not too much, because I didn't want her to feel worse like she was also a failure because she was so slow.

After the last med, she drank down all the rest of the juice in the glass. That was good.

"Well," I said, "you ready for some of that syrup and pancakes?"

She hmmmed and clicked the TV back up. "Not just yet. . . . I'll let this settle for a while."

"That's a good idea," I said, as if she'd just come up with that excuse for the first time. "How about if I go tidy up the bathroom?"

I called it "tidying up" rather than "cleaning" so it didn't sound so big or necessary. I went to the bathroom and got out the cleaning stuff. I started with the tub.

Joe usually called her every morning during his break. They talked about what was on the *Today* show and how he was doing and if there was anything he could bring her when he came over. I ran into Joe a few times out and about. He was a sweet guy and so was his boyfriend, Tony. Once Joe told me he felt guilty, like he was the one who should be sick, not his mom. Both he and Tony tested negative. Joe said he knew he shouldn't feel guilty but he did. He said his mother had never done anything wrong and didn't deserve it. I told him he'd never done anything wrong either and that nobody deserved it. It sounded preachy as soon as I said it and I wished I hadn't but Joe just looked at me. He knew his mom didn't blame him. She didn't blame gay guys. She didn't even blame the blood banks, and she could have. But Joe didn't hold what I said against me. He always told me thanks for helping his mom and how glad they all were that she had someone she liked so much and that she finally let someone help her. She never let her kids help her with some things.

When I finished tidying up the bathroom and came out she told me that Joe called and she told him about Diane sending the syrup.

"Hey, you ready for some of that?" I said as if I hadn't asked before.

She hesitated. "Not quite," she said. "But how about a cup of tea? And fix yourself some coffee and we can sit and visit."

"Great idea," I said. I went to the kitchen and put the water on. I spooned some of my French roast I'd brought to keep at her place into a filter and got out a packet of mint tea. I straightened up the kitchen while the water boiled. There was a new casserole in the fridge—looked like a Tony job, macaroni and ham and cream. There was one spoonful out of it.

I watched Connie through the window between the kitchen and the living room. The TV was on but she was looking at the can of syrup.

After the water boiled I took her cup of tea in. I left my coffee in the kitchen. I put the tea down on her table. She leaned over it, blew on it, lifted it to her mouth, and took a little slurp. She held the tea in her mouth a few seconds before she swallowed it.

She sat a while, then exhaled and said, "Oh, that tastes good."

"Good," I said. I stood there.

"OK," she said firmly. "Let's try some pancakes and syrup."

"You got it," I said.

"It was so nice of Diane to send it," she said. "I'm really going to enjoy it." She nodded like it was a done deal. Then she said, "And fix some for yourself."

I put my hand out for the can of syrup to heat up. She hung on to it a few seconds more then gave it to me.

"Thanks," I said, "but I ate before I came."

We had tried lots of different ways. For a while I used to eat with her because it's easier for them sometimes if someone else is eating too. As if you're dining, not just eating to stay alive. But I'd stopped eating with her.

She reached over for her knitting stuff. She dropped the basket. A ball of yarn and a square fell on the floor. I picked them up and handed them to her.

"Thank you," she said.

I went to the kitchen to start the pancakes. I watched her in the living room. She was straightening the knitting stuff in the basket. A couple of times when I first came I'd asked her not to get her knitting all set up while I was fixing something for her to eat because it would only take a minute. But then I realized she did it to calm herself.

I poured pancake mix in a bowl. I added milk and egg and Ensure. There was a case of it in the fridge. You were supposed to try and put it in everything. I cooked the pancakes in lots of butter and threw in a huge handful of blueberries. I poured the syrup into a little pitcher and heated it up in a pan of water. I drank my coffee while I flipped the pancakes. When they were almost done she said, "You know, I think I could eat an egg too. Can you do me an egg on the side?"

"Coming up, ma'am!" I shouted in my short-order-cook voice. She got a kick out of this. Then I sort of sang, "Ooh-vereasy!" which was how she liked them. It was great that she wanted an egg.

I looked at her. She was clicking away at the knitting. That was truly great.

I put two pancakes and the egg on a plate and the syrup and butter and silverware and my coffee on a tray. I took it all to her couchside table and put it down in front of her. She packed up her knitting and tucked it beside her. I moved her tea to the corner of her table to make room for the food. The cup was still full.

"Anything else?" I asked.

"No thanks." She looked at the food a few seconds. "This looks great," she said. "Maybe even Joe would approve of these!"

"Maybe," I laughed with her. But I stood there.

She took a deep breath. "All right, Connie," she said to herself, "dig in."

She started to cut the pancakes. The tendons in her hands were white.

I had stopped eating with her after a while because it didn't help. She'd talk while I ate. The most she would do was stir her food around. So then we changed to where I'd fix her breakfast but I wouldn't sit with her while she ate because she didn't want me to see so I'd go clean some other room.

But she ate hardly anything when I wasn't there so we talked again and finally she said she was embarrassed. She said she didn't want anyone to see her like that—this was before it got so bad all the time—and we came up with this agreement that I could sit with her while she ate but only if I promised to not try to help or ask her if I could help afterward unless she specifically asked me to help. She never asked.

She didn't want anybody around because she didn't want anyone to see. Also, it was one of the few things she still did alone, that she thought she still could do alone.

She poured warm syrup over part of the pancakes. She was careful not to waste the syrup. She put the pitcher down and picked up her fork and got a little bit of pancake. She chewed it a long time before she swallowed. I swigged a gulp of coffee and looked at the TV.

A few seconds after she swallowed she said, "These are terrific! These are really delicious!"

"All right!" I said. I hoped I didn't sound too relieved. "You think they'd pass the Joe test?" I joked.

"They might," she nodded. "They just might." She looked down at the plate. She took a deep breath, let it out, took another bite, chewed, swallowed. For the third bite she tried some egg. I was still looking toward the TV, but I could hear what she was doing.

On the fourth bite I heard her hold it in her mouth. After a few seconds she swallowed some but not all of it. Then after a few more seconds she swallowed the rest of it. I took another gulp of coffee. She asked quietly, as politely and normally as she could, "Could you please take this away?"

"Sure," I said. I tried to sound normal too. I loaded the plate and everything on the tray.

"They're really delicious," she said. "You're a terrific cook." She didn't want to hurt my feelings.

"Hey, Connie," I said, "it's OK. Really."

As I was taking the tray back to the kitchen she said, "I wonder if maybe in a little bit I could try some oatmeal."

"Great!" I said. I wondered if that would be better. Sometimes oatmeal worked when nothing else did.

In the kitchen I put the dishes by the right sink and started the water boiling. I put away the syrup and butter. When the water boiled I stirred in the oatmeal. I got out the milk and brown sugar. When the oatmeal was done I fixed a bowl and took it out to her.

"Thanks," she said. She sounded apologetic.

"Hey, my pleasure," I said, like I was upbeat.

She stuck her spoon into the oatmeal and pulled out a big dollop. She pulled it toward her mouth. I tried to drink my coffee and watch TV but I was really watching her from the corner of my eye. She got the spoon about an inch from her mouth and held it there. Her mouth opened but closed before she put the spoon in. She tipped the spoon over the bowl and shook out most of the oatmeal. There was a little bit of oatmeal stuck to the spoon. She put that little bit in her mouth and closed her mouth and closed her eyes and swallowed. After a while she exhaled. She opened her eyes and said, "Could I have some more milk on this?"

"Sure," I said. "Coming up." I'd already put in the amount she always liked, so this was not a good sign.

I went to the kitchen and got the milk and brought it out. I held it over the bowl and poured till she said "when." She put the spoon back in and stirred. She stirred for a long time.

After a while I put the milk down and said, "Connie."

Very slowly, she lifted a spoonful to her mouth. I heard her trying to swallow. I took a huge gulp of coffee. I looked at the TV. *Swallow. Swallow. Swallow*, I was thinking. I felt my coffee go down inside me. *Stay. Stay. Stay*, I thought.

She put the spoon down carefully. She sat back against the couch. I could hear her taking deep, even breaths.

I started to count. I got to three.

She said, "Excuse me."

"OK," I said. I wanted her to ask me to help, but she didn't.

I put the oatmeal and everything on the tray and carried it back to the kitchen. I turned the hot water on in the left sink and squirted in some soap. I didn't look into the living room to see her get her cane and stumble up, because she didn't want me to see. I didn't ask her if I could help because she'd made me promise I wouldn't.

I stood over the sink, my back to the hall that went to the bathroom and bedroom. I had the water running loud, but I could hear exactly what was happening because it happened the same way every time: the shuffle of her feet and the thump of her cane down the hall. Then the sound of her opening the bathroom door and the sound of her clicking on the light and fan, and then the sound of the fan and her closing the door. Then there was the sound, behind the door, of her sobbing. I turned the water from hot to cold and the faucet from the soapy sink to the other. And then, because she wanted me to, I turned on the disposal. I scraped the pancakes and egg off the plate. I scooped the oatmeal and milk and sugar from the bowl and pushed them down the disposal.

The water was running and the disposal was loud but not so loud it could cover the sound of her being sick.

This was the food she could not eat. None of this could ease her terrible hunger.

It didn't last long and it wasn't much because it was only what she had. Her body kept trying to get rid of it. Her body was emptied out till there was nothing.

Then there was the sound of her breathing hard and the sound of the toilet flushing and then, in a few more seconds, the door being opened, the light switching off. Then she walked down the hall to her bedroom, to the bed where she'd had her babies. She walked with a hand against the wall and a hand around her cane and she pulled herself onto the bed and lay down.

I poured a glass of water from the bottle on the counter. I waited, as she'd asked me to, until I heard her calling. I took the water in to her. In her room I heard her breathing hard. I heard, although she said it so quietly you wouldn't understand unless you'd heard it many times before and knew exactly what to listen for, what she was trying to say. What she was trying to say was this: "I'm thirsty."

I held the glass with the straw in my hands. I knelt beside the bed and slipped my arm around her neck. I lifted her head and she opened her mouth. I held the water to her mouth and hoped that she could drink.

Elizabeth Alexander 1962–

In 1990, Elizabeth Alexander delighted the literary world with her first collection of poems, *The Venus Hottentot*. A regular contributor to such prestigious journals as *Callaloo, Obsidian, American Poetry Review,* and *Southern Review,* Alexander's poetry combines the social with the solitary, using a lyrical and intellectual private voice to address public issues. Notes E. Ethelbert Miller, director of Howard University's African-America Resource Center, "The poetry of Elizabeth Alexander embraces ancestry, innocence, love, music, art, heroes, and history. . . . There is enough intellectual magic in this collection to keep a 'civilization' of critics talking for years." Alexander was born in New York City and raised in Washington, D.C. She received her B.A. from Yale University, her M.A. from Boston University, and her Ph.D. from the University of Pennsylvania. Currently, she is assistant professor of English at the University of Chicago.

LADDERS

Filene's department store
near nineteen-fifty-three:
An Aunt Jemima floor
display. Red bandanna,

apron holding white rolls   5
of black fat fast against
the bubbling pancakes, bowls
and bowls of pale batter.

This is what Donna sees
across the "Cookwares" floor,   10
and hears "Donessa?" *Please,
this can not be my aunt.*

Father's long-gone sister,
nineteen-fifty-three. "Girl?"
Had they lost her, missed her?   15
This is not the question.

This must not be my aunt.
Jemima? Pays the rent.
Family mirrors haunt
their own reflections.   20

Ladders. Sisters. Nieces.
As soon a live Jemima
as a buck-eyed rhesus
monkey. Girl? Answer me.

HOUSE PARTY SONNET: '66

Small, still. Fit through the bannister slit.
Where did our love go? Where did our love go?
Scattered high heels and the carpet rolled back.
Where did our love go? Where did our love go?
My brother and I, tipping down from upstairs   5
Under the cover of "Where Did Our Love Go?"
Cat-eyed Supremes wearing siren-green gowns.
Pink curls of laughter and hips when they shake
Shake a tambourine *where did our love go?*
Where did our love go? Where did our love go?   10

Stale chips next morning, shoes under the couch,
Smoke-smelling draperies, water-paled Scotch.
Matches, stray earrings to find and to keep—
Hum of invisible dancers asleep.

NINETEEN

That summer in Culpeper, all there was to eat was white:
cauliflower, flounder, white sauce, white ice-cream.
I snuck around with an older man who didn't tell me
he was married. I was the baby, drinking rum and Coke
while the men smoked reefer they'd stolen from the campers.   5
I tiptoed with my lover to poison-ivied fields, camp vans.
I never slept. Each fornight I returned to the city,
black and dusty, with a garbage bag of dirty clothes.

At nineteen it was my first summer away from home.
His beard smelled musty. His eyes were black. "The ladies love my   10
    hair,"
he'd say, and like a fool I'd smile. He knew everything
about marijuana, how dry it had to be to burn,
how to crush it, sniff it, how to pick the seeds out. He said
he learned it all in Vietnam. He brought his son to visit   15
after one of his days off. I never imagined a mother.
"Can I steal a kiss?" he said, the first thick night in the field.

I asked and asked about Vietnam, how each scar felt,
what combat was like, how the jungle smelled. He listened
to a lot of Marvin Gaye, was all he said, and grabbed   20
between my legs. I'd creep to my cot before morning.
I'd eat that white food. This was before I understood
that nothing could be ruined in one stroke. A sudden
storm came hard one night; he bolted up inside the van.
"The rain sounded just like that," he said, "on the roofs there."   25

BOSTON YEAR

My first week in Cambridge a car full of white boys
tried to run me off the road, and spit through the window,
open to ask directions. I was always asking directions
and always driving: to an Armenian market
in Watertown to buy figs and string cheese, apricots,   5

dark spices and olives from barrels, tubes of paste
with unreadable Arabic labels. I ate
stuffed grape leaves and watched my lips swell in the mirror.
The floors of my apartment would never come clean.
Whenever I saw other colored people   10
in bookshops, or museums, or cafeterias, I'd gasp,
smile shyly, but they'd disappear before I spoke.
What would I have said to them? Come with me? Take
me home? Are you my mother? No. I sat alone
in countless Chinese restaurants eating almond   15
cookies, sipping tea with spoons and spoons of sugar.
Popcorn and coffee was dinner. When I fainted
from migraine in the grocery store, a Portuguese
man above me mouthed: "No breakfast." He gave me
orange juice and chocolate bars. The color red   20
sprang into relief singing Wagner's *Walküre*.
Entire tribes gyrated and drummed in my head.
I learned the samba from a Brazilian man
so tiny, so festooned with glitter I was certain
that he slept inside a filigreed, Fabergé egg.   25
No one at the door: no salesmen, Mormons, meter
readers, exterminators, no Harriet Tubman,
no one. Red notes sounding in a grey trolley town.

"Radio Days"

In the movie a Latin bandleader
as a nineteen-forty-four bandleader
cradling a chihuahua. His chanteuse wriggles,
snake-hips in orange and white lily hands.

After the movie, my friends says, "Cugat,"   5
and I think, "Charo," on a cheap talk show,
her cuchi-cuchi Spanish. Her fingers vanish
into a blue riot of frantic guitar.

The real bandleader is Tito Puente.
The pussy-willow mutt is tired, and mewls.   10
The frayed orange costume flares out at the bottom;
orange waves break into spume at her feet.

The man sitting behind me, indignant:
"I got radio memories better than that."
"Remember Pearl Harbor?" another friend says.   15
"I saw Jackie Robinson hit that ball."

Jill Bialosky

Born in Cleveland, Ohio, Jill Bialosky is the author of the collections of poems, *The End of Desire: Poems* (1997) and *Wanting a Child* (1998). After earning a bachelor's degree from Ohio University, she received her master of arts at John Hopkins University and a master of fine arts from the Iowa Writers' Workshop. "Fathers in the Snow," anthologized here, is also featured in Eavan Bolands's "Daughters" Web page, part of the Academy of American Poets Web site. Referring to Bialosky's poem as "strong and eloquent," Boland further states, "[t]he daughter is not just spoken to or about here. She speaks. This is a subversive piece. There are no legends allowed to intrude on the dark, unswerving tone of pain and disruption." A recipient of the Elliot Coleman Award in Poetry, Bialosky is currently a book editor residing in New York City.

From FATHERS IN THE SNOW

IN MEMORY OF MILTON ABRAHAM BIALOSKY

1.

The game is called *father*.

My sister lies in the grass.
I take handfuls of leaves
we raked from the lawn   5
spilling them over her body

until she's buried—

her red jacket lost, completely.
Then it's my turn.

Afterwards, we pick the brittle pieces   10
from each other's hair.

2.

After father died
the love was all through the house
untamed and sometimes violent.
When the dates came we went up to our rooms   5
and mother entertained.
Frank Sinatra's "Strangers in the Night,"
the smell of Chanel No. 5 in her hair and the laughter.

We sat crouched at the top of the stairs.
In the morning we found mother asleep on the couch   10
her hair messed, and the smell
of stale liquor in the room.
We knelt on the floor before her,
one by one touched our fingers
over the red flush in her face.   15
The chipped sunlight through the shutters.
It was a dark continent
we and mother shared;
it was sweet and lonesome,
the wake men left in our house.   20

7.

Once there was a game the sisters liked to play
remembering mother at the vanity,
at five o'clock before the sun went down:
she dabbed perfume behind her ears,   5
in the crevice of her breasts.
The mirror lights illuminated her made-up face.
We even imitated the kiss she gave to father.

Then one day her ruby red lips,
mascara lashes, powdered cheeks   10
were veiled underneath black lace,
and on mother's pale face
we saw the color, like a dead light, go out.

Allegra Goodman 1967–

Allegra Goodman is best known for her interrelated cycle of stories, *The Family Markowitz* (1996). Originally written in 1989 as a one-act play, Goodman transformed this successfully produced drama into what would later become her second book. "I just sat down to write different stories," she told *Harvard Magazine*. "I thought about the patterns in them and put them together." The result, according to *Harvard*'s Miriam Lambert, is "a series of subtly shifting vantage points, so that the reader encounters a given character through many pairs of eyes." Goodman claims that the book's changing viewpoints help to debunk "personal subjective mythologies," and show "the difference between people's own perceptions of their life stories and other people's." Her works include *Total Immersion: Stories* (1989) and *Kaaterskill Falls: A Novel* (1998). Goodman received her Ph.D. in English Literature from Stanford

University. She now lives in Cambridge, Massachusetts, with her two children and husband, a "theoretical computer scientist who walks around in circles mumbling to himself and [inventing] algorithms."

VARIANT TEXT

Dear Aunt Ida,

Attalia is screaming under the piano. She has taken it into her head that she needs a pair of skates. Having explained that her mother and I are perfectly willing to provide our children with necessary items but unable to supply their ceaseless demand for toys, clothes, and every extravagance, the vital necessity of which is impressed on them by seven-year-old peers, I have resolved to let her scream herself to sleep. I'd say she's good for at least half an hour.

Beatrix has been exhausting herself. She is in London for the topology conference. As soon as she comes back Sunday, she will have to prepare her paper for Majorca. These conferences are always a strain and raise numerous logistical problems. Beatrix's parents, living upstairs, would seem the logical choice for baby-sitting, but they are really no longer able to control the kids—especially now that Adam can walk. Aunt Clare is out of the question.

Cecil looks fondly at the smooth black surface of his Olivetti electronic and with a grim smile flicks off the switch. If only Beatrix were home to manage the kids. She goes to a three-day conference, and they become unreasonable. Parents over forty-five should use the buddy system. He and Beatrix had made a pact to that effect when Adam was born. If either of them ran away, he or she would take the other along.

They had both thought the baby-sitting situation would be better in Oxford than it had been in Brooklyn. When Beatrix taught math at Hunter and Cecil had a class at Brooklyn College, their schedule had been much more hectic, but there was always Aunt Ida to take care of the kids. Then Beatrix got her chair at St. Ann's, and Cecil had to give up the part-time position in English at Brooklyn. He enjoyed that—the resignation letter, the packing. He feels he has made a small but significant political statement by leaving America, voting with his feet. American culture is dying. Apart from the museums and the ballet, there isn't much left of the city. It was also a relief to leave the Brooklyn shul, which rejected the books of biblical criticism he had donated in his father's memory. But above all, Cecil was making a feminist statement by following his wife to Oxford. And besides, he hadn't got along with his department.

The great domestic advantage of moving was that Beatrix's parents, the

Cahens, owned this enormous Norham Gardens house right here in Oxford, and glad of the company and the cooking, they had given over the first floor to Beatrix and Cecil. It seemed ideal: two live-in baby-sitters upstairs. But naturally there were complications. The Cahens are in their late seventies; last winter Mrs. Cahen slipped on the ice and broke her arm; the cavernous house is un-heatable; and as Beatrix is exhausting herself teaching her seminar and writing papers, it is Cecil who is stuck with the kids. He doesn't really mind baby-sitting within certain limits, and he enjoys replastering the ceilings and shopping for pipe fittings. But keeping up with his research is difficult. Last year, Cecil was invited to apply for a position at Leeds, but nothing came of it. Meanwhile the house and the kids are time-consuming but usually tolerable, except when Beat-rix is away and Attalia decides to scream herself sick. And except for Beatrix's older sister, Clare, who has lived in the Norham Gardens house all her life. Suddenly inspired, Cecil flicks on the Olivetti and continues:

> Attalia is becoming more and more like her aunt Clare—ruining her voice with screaming, and abandoning herself to increasingly frequent rages. Unfortunately, she follows Clare in her slovenliness. Even more unfortunate, Attalia shares her aunt's lack of artistic talent.
>
> In the three years since we moved from New York, Clare has insisted in making life in this house intolerable. She is sullen and angry, a bad influence on both children. But perhaps we will be spared the pleasure of living en famille in this battleship with Victorian plumbing if the sale on the Brooklyn house goes through. Or at least we'll have the cash to fix up this place. It will take at least two years to rewire the house. I don't see why Mr. Cahen won't subdivide it. Most of the other Norham Gardens castles are now quite nice 20th century. . . .

Cecil gives up on the letter to his aunt in New York. He leafs through the new spring issue of *Shavian Studies*. Finally he walks to the piano, and the screams and whimpers stop. He bends down heavily under the keyboard. "Come on to bed now."

Attalia glares at her father through the strands of her slippery brown hair. She screams rather loudly for her size. Fine pair of lungs. Pity she doesn't have an ear for music. Cecil had tested both of his children early on for any signs of musical aptitude. When Attalia was two, he set her on the piano bench. She struck out at the Steinway with her fists, banging the ivory keys. Cecil had waited a few minutes and then given up.

"I'll read to you in bed," he concedes. The tired children scramble up and pad to their room. Cecil glances about for something readable. A stack of *TLS*'s balances on the sofa; the dining room table is weighted with Beatrix's mathematics, Adam's crayons, Attalia's homework (probably not done), a bunch of bananas (probably soft). "This puts me to sleep within minutes," he tells the kids. He opens *Shavian Studies*, spreading it out onto Adam's bed. "Well, well—Lewis has found a variant text of *Major Barbara*." Now both children begin to cry.

The next morning, Cecil rushes to put on his tefillin before the children wake up and the Cahens and Clare come down to be served breakfast. For a moment the house is quiet. The sun glistens on Cecil's black-framed glasses and glows red through his ears. He wraps the leather tefillin straps tightly on his arm and forehead. He knows the prayers by heart, but he reads from a pocket siddur anyway. It's more precise to read than to mumble from memory.

The kitchen stairs begin to creak as the old couple make their way down in the dark, and little shrieks escape from the children's room, where Adam is trying to comb Attalia's hair.

"Molly," Saul Cahen calls out hoarsely, "turn on the lights."

"I can't see the switch."

"Above your head."

"He's going to start a fire with this naked light bulb."

At the bottom step, a wooden door blocks the way to the kitchen. Cecil can hear the two of them pulling and twisting at the knob until the door is jammed.

"Cecil, you've locked us out!"

He shuts his eyes tightly, finishes davening, and runs down the central stairs to let them in. Saul shakes his head at his son-in-law as he helps Molly into the kitchen. She takes a seat, fanning herself with *Advances in Mathematics*, while Cecil pours the coffee. They drink only instant decaffeinated.

Attalia runs in. "Daddy, I can't go to school."

"Oh, yes you can." Cecil lifts her up and seats her at the table. Adam toddles in, with nothing on. "Pot," he says plaintively. "Pot."

After cleaning the living-room rug, Cecil makes an enormous quantity of porridge. Attalia watches morosely as her father dishes it out. She is dressed in dark green corduroy overalls and a brown and blue striped jersey. Cecil and Beatrix are nonsexist, so they dress their children in unisex clothing. Attalia's hair has never been cut. All ballerinas have long hair. Cecil takes her to ballet class every week. Even though she is the smallest girl there, Attalia is the most meticulous about the steps. She always watches her feet to make sure they are in the right places. Cecil pours each of the kids a glass of milk and a glass of orange juice. Adam drills a hole in his oatmeal with the back of his spoon and pours the juice and the milk into it together. Quite a chemist for a three-year-old, Cecil thinks. Delightful fellow.

"Cecil, why do you dress your daughter like that?" Molly's voice gathers strength at the end of her question.

"Daddy, I can't go to school," Attalia whimpers.

"She's afraid to go to school like that! You see that, Cecil? How can you send her in those work clothes?"

"It's a shame," growls Saul. "The way you send them to that school. Why do you send Adam already with the four-year-olds? He's only three years old. You're forcing them to grow up too fast. I won't say it in front of Beatrix and upset her, but now she's gone I think we should talk about this so-called gan. . . ."

The phone rings. "Adam, don't throw food!" Cecil orders as he answers it.

"Bad boy," he says, frowning; then, back into the receiver: "No, I was talking to my son. Sixty thousand dollars! That's below appraisal. I know it's in Brooklyn. The neighborhood was fine when I was there last. Just some perfectly respectable Puerto Rican fellows. Let them drink their beer on the front steps; they'll keep away the crazies. No, not the fridge. I'm shipping it. Why? Do you realize how much a new refrigerator costs? Of course, but it's too small. Frankly"—he lowers his voice—"this thing here is a piece of junk. We want the old one from New York. What do you mean, irrational? They don't make that model anymore. It would cost as much to buy a new fridge here as it would for me to ship the fridge from Brooklyn. Ben? Look, I can't explain the whole thing over long distance; this is costing you a fortune. No, I told you the house doesn't come with the fridge. Talk to you Monday. Well, I'll try a transformer. Either that or I'll rewire it."

Aunt Clare appears and prods the oatmeal with her spoon. "Burnt," she states flatly, and drops the whole pot into the sink.

"Well, we do our best," Cecil answers. But Clare is already deep in the hall closet, pulling on a black trench coat.

"Where are you going?" asks Molly. But her daughter doesn't answer. In the summers, Clare likes to work outside. She spends days in the park with her stack of Hebrew manuscripts. Cecil can't blame her; the house is a mess on the top floors, crammed with odd sunless rooms, dusty with ancient copies of the *Guardian*, old furniture, antique clothes. The Cahens don't throw things out, and they don't dust, either. Molly was never a housewife; she was a Socialist. "Clare, it's seventy degrees outside!" Molly admonishes, standing in the hallway, hands on her hips. "There are going to be patches of sun—you don't need the umbrella."

But Clare slides the thin steel point through her belt loop, and she is gone.

The gan is housed in an annex to the Oxford shul. All the money for it was given anonymously by Marv Pollack, the father of children's vitamins. The playground reminds Cecil of a hamster habitat he once saw displayed in a pet-store window. The sandbox is filled with cedar chips. Sand becomes dirty and stale and collects germs. There is no jungle gym or slide or swing set. Instead, an enormous complex of smooth wood has been built in the shape of an amino acid chain. All the classroom furniture is made out of natural woods and fibers. There are seven computer terminals, with full color capability and joysticks. The art center is decorated with laminated Chagall posters. It is here Adam finger paints, listens to Bible stories, plants pumpkin seeds, and during naptime learns deep relaxation on the futon rolled up in his cubbyhole. In the junior school, Attalia will soon be sitting in a circle of tiny chairs for Good/Bad Talk. On the blackboard, Ms. Nemirov has printed today's question:

HASHEM OR DARWIN?
YOU
DECIDE

"I can't go to school," Attalia wails. She clings to the foam seat of the Mini. Cecil pries her loose, grasping her arms and hair. "Daddy," Attalia howls, "I don't have any teeth!"

"Well, of course you don't. It's part of the human life cycle," Cecil reassures her. "If you could compose yourself, no one would notice. Right now, you're crying and looking ugly as the very devil," he tells her, quoting Higgins, "but when you're all right and quite yourself, you're what I should call attractive." Not having read *Pygmalion*, Attalia sniffles off to class.

Another father passes by, with his little girl and fat wife. Cecil looks at the heavy woman and whispers, "There but for the grace of God . . ." thinking of all the similar types his mother and her anxious friends had introduced to him. He used to call them the girls with the three D's: they were dumpy, dowdy, and devout. Beatrix is none of these things. She is lean and brilliant—and though not devout, she agreed to keep a kosher kitchen and let the kids attend the gan. Cecil does not expect more.

He himself had been brought up in a house of strict observance, exquisite baking, and strenuous but fond academic expectations. Though he does not believe in God, he remains observant. His friends find this contradictory and even hypocritical. His strict religious practice has never matched his agnostic intellectualism, his early fascination with Derrida and Paul De Man. He insists on the immutability of sacred law and at the same time savors the fluidity of secular texts. He loves one as explicit and complete, the other as open and ambiguous. And yet he refuses to smooth away this discontinuity by allowing a divine authorship of sacred work. Cecil has always enjoyed his contradictions, and still nurtures them. He finds spiritual sustenance in academic discipline and intellectual structure in the rituals of his childhood.

He was thirty-five when he married. His parents hadn't lived to see it. His friends, of course, were flabbergasted. They remembered Cecil from his Columbia days, when he refused to go to parties or talk to women. It was against his principles to attend weddings—he went to his own sister's wedding under protest, only after his mother had threatened to disinherit him. He swore he hated children, traveled to the Middle East, and enjoyed Swedish pornographic films.

He met Beatrix on a bus in Israel, and in fact had written to his father in the hospital about "the ugly woman." "She's nothing to write home about," he had written. He showed Beatrix the letter soon after their marriage, and she loved it. Cecil's father had died just before the wedding and left him the Brooklyn house. And so they spent the first years of their marriage there with the old letters and dusty furniture, the faded Schumacher drapes and the framed pictures of Cecil that had been propped up on all the tables by his mother. Cecil as a brown-eyed boy of four, Cecil on his tricycle, Cecil staring hollow-eyed through horn-rimmed glasses in his graduation picture. Cecil and Beatrix never changed anything in the house; they only added books and stacks of papers. In the evenings, Beatrix would tell Cecil about the mathematical problem she was working on. In college he had been a math major before he switched to English, and he remembered just enough to see how beautiful the schemes were. He loved the way the physicists came to Beatrix's seminars to see if they could apply her ideas to their work. But it made him strangely happy when it seemed there wasn't any real-world application for her ideas. The formal structure of Beatrix's mathematics had to be appreciated for its own sake. He's often said the same is true of halakhah.

In the schoolyard, Adam is already rolling in the cedar chips and rubbing dirt in his face and hair. The only clean thing about him is his eyes. Yes, he is a charming fellow, Cecil tells himself as he maneuvers out of the parking lot. There seems to be a bottleneck at the exit, where Margo Bettleheim is standing. Cecil reaches for the flier stuck on the windshield and peers at the bleeding purple Ditto.

TO WHOM IT MAY CONCERN:

As a specialist in Jewish early childhood education with a masters in the subject from the Hebrew University, and as a parent, I am compelled to speak out against a situation which I feel threatens the learning environment of the entire gan.

I will state flatly and unequivocally that I am appalled at the deception and irresponsibility of certain parents who have falsified official gan records and have registered their child under false pretenses. In short, by misrepresenting the age and stage of development attained by this child. Thus endangering the learning process of all involved.

It has been shown by Piaget that perceptual development and physical hand-eye-mouth coordination as well as other behavioral processes require a definite time period to develop. I am not convinced that this child has developed these skills, or that this child is ready to interact at the level of food and toy sharing interpersonal interplay required at a more mature level.

We know the preschool years to be the most significant formative experience in the educational process (Golding and Simon, 1978). Join me in protecting the future of the next generation: fill out the coupon below.

Margo Bettleheim

_____ Yes, I want to focus on the issue of an ordered educational process—and allow each child to develop as an organically centered and responsible member of the community.

_____ No, I am unconcerned with the process of development which is uniquely important to the success of the prescholastic learning environment. I am unconcerned about the interplay of persons of the same age.

Signature _____

Inching toward the exit in the line of cars, Cecil reads the letter and checks the space marked Yes. He signs on the dotted line: *Cecil Eugene Birnbaum*, and he hands the form to Margo, who stands firm at her post with a mass of blond curls and two hard lines of lipstick.

He needs to go to the Bodleian, but he has to buy groceries for Shabbes first, and he can't leave them sitting in the car to melt. It's a brilliant day, a once-in-a-year summer day. Student lie out on the lawns, cadaver white, soaking up the sun. Exams are over, and a bunch of them dash across the street, chanting "Annie! Annie!" They catch her and squirt her with champagne. It makes Cecil feel old. He doesn't mind the feeling in itself, but he'd dearly love a donnish platform, an academic gown to robe his forty-seven years. All of which is trite and self-indulgent, but nonetheless true. He feels he's always watching Oxford. And it's not the punts or waltzes, the processionals, those tourist things—it's the work he misses. The place to work, the time to work, and—he doesn't complain—the notice for it. He had to apply to use the Bodleian. The registrar, with his peculiar, thin librarian's fingers, stamped his card *Unaffiliated*.

He is appalled by the prices in the Covered Market. He buys eggs, Greek olives, currants, even some frozen cranberries from America, but he rejects the outrageously expensive sole just as it is about to be rung up. "I'm not made of money," he tells the old woman behind him in line. She tisks sympathetically. New carts of vegetables are being unloaded. The market is full of exotic produce, and the prices are being driven up. They are even selling kiwifruits and orange-brown mangoes. Next thing you know, they'll put in a cappuccino bar, and gentrify this too. Grasping his carrier bag and his *Times*, Cecil makes his way to the car. A violinist is playing on the sidewalk, and Cecil drops his change in the musician's open violin case.

In the street, Ursula Quince—absurd name—and her mother thumb by without seeing him. Ursula was one of Cecil's pupils during a short tenure at the Dragon School, just after he and Beatrix arrived in England. He taught English and American poetry to the third form, which title belonged to a mass of heavy, plodding little girls with thick hair parted around their faces. They looked strikingly like their own Shetland ponies. Ursula was not the brightest in her English class. Cecil remembers particularly that just before he left, he called on her to explicate some Emily Dickinson: "I love to watch it lap the miles."

"Well, what is it *about*, Miss Quince?"

She looked up at him, affronted, then glanced around at the class, but they were busy looking invisible, so that he wouldn't interrogate them next. It was always amusing to watch these very solid girls try to disappear. They did it by opening their eyes until they looked quite empty; then they would stare ahead silently, mouths slightly ajar.

"I see," said Cecil after Ursula's eloquent silence. "I think then I'll suggest my own interpretation." And he read out again. "'I love to watch it lap the miles.' Clearly this poem is about a cat," he said, and they all nodded. "It's about a cat lapping up miles of milk." They believed this; one girl looked puzzled, but she didn't say anything. He is sure Ursula believes it to this day—if she remembers the poem.

The Cahens sit in the kitchen where he left them, and as he unpacks the groceries they start up again about the kids. This is a talent of theirs, the ability to continue nagging as if no time has passed.

"Why do you send them to that frumnik school?" Saul demands. "You want them to grow up Israelis?"

Molly stands between Cecil and the old fridge, as if to protect it. "I won't have it, Cecil," she declares. "I won't have them sent to that school with the fanatics. Beatrix won't say anything, but I will. Where my grandchildren are concerned, I'm a tiger!"

Cecil swings open the freezer box above her head and deposits the bag of cranberries. She follows him into the pantry, and Saul takes a post in the doorway. "You're taking the grandchildren away from us," he says. "You know very well that Molly and I oppose parochial education. That we've worked all our lives for the Labour party." Hand in one pocket, he stands like an orator in his gray summer suit.

"I'll tell you what they did just yesterday," says Molly. "They threw away the buns I bought Adam for his lunch. You don't know how he cried, he was so hungry."

"They were absolutely right," Cecil says. "I've told you many, many times not to buy those. They aren't kosher; don't do it again."

"They're starving him."

"Nonsense. He eats like a little pig."

"Saul," gasps Molly. "Pawns is what they are. Innocent children just sent adrift."

"Hello. Yes, this is he." Cecil speaks loudly into the telephone receiver. "Oh, Mrs. Greenberg. No. Which policy do you refer to? Yes, he is at a mature stage of development. Well, very nearly trained." He stretches the phone cord into the hall, away from the Cahens. "Listen, I'm off to the Bodleian in just a minute. We can talk after school. Concerned parents? Well, of course. In fact, I signed a statement on a related issue just this morning. Have you seen a copy? You have. Excuse me, this lies outside my field. The prereading center? Ah, Margo Bettleheim. Yes, this morning. But Adam wasn't mentioned on the form. It was a very general sort of statement. What you are saying, in layman's terms, is that my son has peed in the prereading center. And I have petitioned for his removal from the school! I see, the verb to pee is no longer used by educators. What word do you use? No, I do understand. I'm afraid I really can't. I'll talk to you this afternoon. Oh, he's extremely well adjusted. I really—Well, smack him one. Psychological scars? You don't encourage this kind of behavior, do you?"

In the cool, dim rooms of the Bodleian, Cecil muses on the hysteria of adults involved with small children. Taken in the proper perspective, one's children are really rather amusing, actually. Spread before him are his notes on Shaw's music reviews. He may have found a connection between the theory of sound that can be extrapolated from Shaw's music criticism and the form of Shaw's language theory suggested in Higgins's phonetic experiments. A subdued joy fills Cecil as he checks the originality of his idea by searching the bibliographic citations of *Shavian Studies* Sound Theory. Nothing under that heading. Music Criticism. Nothing there. Confidence rising, Cecil checks under Phonetics. He winces. There, in the column of papers on Shaw's phonetic system, is the listing: "'Musical Intonation in Higgins' Phonetic Theory,' *Shav. Qt.* Apr. '59."

Cecil doesn't bother looking up the article. Of course, he could use it; he could write his anyway. But he's so tired of sharing topics, tunneling in the critical anthill. He wants to work on something new. The problem is, Shaw's plays themselves are old for him. He told Beatrix once, "The more I read these things, the less I see in them." Now he smiles, remembering how she laughed at this. "Absurd old thing," she laughed. "What *could* anyone do in that awful field of yours where no one knows what one's about?" She sat curled up in the enormous balding velvet chair she works in at home. "I *always* hated literature," she said. "Write and write, say what you like; there are no right answers." And she settled back among her yellow papers and the pencils that roll under the cushions of her chair. She is contented, like all good mathematicians, unconcerned with how to finish errands or what to buy for dinner. She has the comfort of being consistently disorganized. For example, she always loses things in the same place. When she thinks of it, she collects her pencils from underneath her chair, where they end up among the springs trailing out the bottom.

Junior School Principal Kineret Greenberg wears a daisy-print dress and covers her hair with matching material. "Dr. Birnbaum, as secular principal for the students four through ten, I have been delegated to ask you to withdraw your child from the gan. I think it is clear from our discussion on the phone this morning that Adam's presence at this time could disturb, or even traumatize, the classroom environment."

"My good woman," Cecil begins, but he has to stop to keep a straight face.

"It may seem a trivial matter to you," Kineret says sternly, "but an important principle is involved. The gan is an extremely selective school, and there are many children on the preschool waiting list. Margo Bettleheim, for one, is particularly anxious about her son, Moshe. Her open letter voices a legitimate concern that younger children not yet ready for the gan have been given places, while Moshe has been made to wait and thus fall behind his age group. I'm sure you agree it's only fair for Adam to wait his turn."

"Well," says Cecil, "I was not aware that the school is controlled by propaganda campaigns."

Kineret stiffens. "This school is governed by the standards of Kohlberg, Piaget, the Rav Soloveichik—"

Cecil bursts out laughing. "This is absurd! I see no reason—halakhic, psychological, or otherwise—to withdraw Adam. In fact, I see this decision as entirely his choice."

She nods earnestly. "That is just the reply I had hoped you would make. Yes, do discuss it with your son. The discussion could play a part in your parental bonding. You know, whenever I have to speak as a teacher to a child, I try to think of the experience less as an evaluative encounter and more as an opportunity to nurture growth and understanding."

Cecil raises his eyebrows.

"One other thing," Kineret adds. "Attalia's clothes. Rabbi Rothenberg is concerned about these dungarees she wear to school. I'm sure you are familiar with the whole issue of beged ish."

"Oh, come now," Cecil says. "I really haven't time for this." He glances out the office window. The kids are waiting outside.

"No, hear me out," says Kineret. "The gan is working to teach Yiddishkeit, and that's a complete world picture which includes tsniustic clothes. Attalia has to wear dresses and skirts now if she is to have a healthy sexual and social identity later. Psychologically this is crucial; if she dresses like a boy, she'll never find her place within the peer group and interact normally. That's what we're working for here. We want every child at Kohlberg stage three by the end of the term. And we need help from home to achieve this. We're trying to develop a Torah life-style. . . ."

"I've been extremely patient with you," replies Cecil after this remarkable speech. "But I find myself overcome just now by your particular combination of self-righteousness, ignorance, and sexism." He nods as if to punctuate this and then walks out the door.

The Cahens always sit at the kitchen table and watch while Cecil prepares Shabbes dinner. He can't decide which is worse, Attalia and Adam underfoot, or their grandparents, who ask plaintively "Could I trouble you for a little something in a tiny glass—very sweet?"

He lifts Adam onto the kitchen counter and says briskly, "I hear you made a fool of yourself in school today." Adam giggles and crawls into the sink, where he stands unevenly, with one foot in the drain.

"My God, he's going to maim himself," gasps Molly.

Cecil pulls Adam out of the sink and places him on the floor where he begins to scream.

Attalia runs in from the living room. "Daddy, I have a new tooth," she shrieks. She opens her mouth and points to it.

"Congratulations," says Cecil. "I can't see anything, but I'll take your word for it."

He has to buy a new vegetable peeler. The blade on this one keeps twisting around as he peels. He holds it straight and skids it over a bent carrot. It's such an annoying situation at the gan. There would be some satisfaction in withdrawing the kids, of course. Cecil does enjoy leaving institutions. It's so cathartic. To resign, to withdraw, to speak the unspeakable, pack up, and go. And just now he's itching to tell them off, write up in detail their gross halakhic misconstruals. Beged ish! A perversion of a statute against transvestite dressing into a dictum about skirts for little girls! He piles the carrots on the cutting board and hunts up a pareve knife. Beatrix would be delighted if he yanked the kids out; she's been patient, but if they left she'd be awfully pleased. Unfortunately, so would the Cahens. And it's extremely unpleasant to contemplate living in this house, with the Cahens thinking they've won some kind of independent moral triumph. Even worse to allow a victory to Margo Bettleheim. The problem, he concludes, washing the lettuce, is that he can't seem to do anything without giving in to somebody. The Cahens or Greenberg or Bettleheim. As yet, he see no uncompromising way to act.

He sets out the dinner on the dining-room sideboard: challot choucroute garni (with corned beef, of course), couscous with baked egg and onions, kosher wine, and currant cake with a double measure of currants. Aunt Clare wanders in, with her sheaf of papers. She looks as if she's had too much sun. "How was the park?" Cecil asks. She looks at him reproachfully and climbs the stairs to her room. She knows some extremely strange men and women in the Oxford Parks. Every once in a while she tries to bring in homeless people for the night. Cecil drives them back to their shelters—located surprisingly far away. He has them read the *Times* to him in the car. Seated at the table, Molly looks at the dinner with a veteran eye. The egg in the couscous is overbaked, the kosher wine is like vinegar, the currant cake is burned on the bottom. She looks at Cecil and says sweetly, "Could I trouble you for a piece of bread?"

The next morning, Cecil and the kids walk to shul. Attalia loves shul because she is allowed to wear the pink dress that her American aunt gave her. Beatrix is against pink. But out of courtesy to the relatives, Attalia wears it once in a while. Cecil sports an ABORTION RIGHTS button pinned to the lapel of the suit he bought after his wedding. Beatrix wants him to get a new one, but it's a perfectly good suit, and he sees no reason to buy another until this one falls apart or doesn't fit anymore. He would only buy the identical kind anyway.

They walk through the Indian quarter, past Dildunia Restaurant: "We serve not too spicy food with a smile." Adam runs ahead, and Cecil and Attalia follow, picking up his brown leather kipah. Cecil never liked the crocheted kind, and he particularly hates the ones with names and flowers worked into the borders. He's always felt it was a patriarchal custom for girls to make kippot for their boyfriends. As a young man, he would never have accepted such a gift and often wished for the chance to refuse.

"This is very bad," he says when they reach the shul. Someone is pushing strollers on Shabbat. It's shocking, really, and isn't any different than driving a vehicle or carrying, when you think about it. In fact, there are two strollers on the steps of the building. One of them is cross-stitched along the awning, *M. Bettleheim.*

Attalia stays in the cloakroom to play with the Goldman girls, while Adam follows his father into the men's section. The shul was originally designed for an egalitarian congregation that never made a go of it. Now the sanctuary is rearranged for separate seating, and there are red velvet curtains in front of the ark. But the walls are still covered with cork bulletin boards. One of the notices pinned up is Margo Bettleheim's open letter to the gan parents. Next to it is an advertisement for a cantor:

> YOUNG, VIBRANT JEWISH GROUP IN HONOLULU SEEKS LIKE-MINDED LAY LEADER TO ENERGIZE HOLIDAY SERVICES.
>
> WILL PROVIDE PLANE FARE.
>
> WRITE TO THE BET KNESSET CONNECTION, UNITARIAN CHURCH, OLD PALI RD., HONOLULU, HAWAII, USA.
>
> REF. REQUIRED.
>
> MUST KNOW HEBREW!

"Good God," mutters the man standing next to Cecil.

"Oh, I quite agree—announcements like that in the sanctuary," says Cecil in sympathy. He recognizes the speaker as dark, broad-shouldered George Lewis, the very man who found the variant text of *Major Barbara* and was written up in *Shavian Studies*.

"I was not referring to the notice on the wall," Lewis replies coldly. "I was speaking of the obscene statement you are making by wearing that button on your lapel. I find it extremely offensive."

"Do you now?" Cecil glances down at his large black-and-red button. "Well, if we are to be perfectly candid, I found your little book rather offensive. I can imagine that twenty years ago, a book like yours could accrue some kind reviews and perhaps earn you a lectureship at York. But at this time, at a point when the whole question of the variant text has ceased to be an issue, when it is acknowledged—universally acknowledged, as far as I'm concerned—that every variant is equally valid, when the very concept of a normative, authoritative text has been discarded, I am simply at a loss to understand how your book could contribute anything to the field."

"I do not talk about these things on Shabbes," Lewis replies scornfully. "You know, I am always amazed at your lack of tact. This congregation is not a place for statements, political or otherwise. This is a holy place. A place for family. And I will say this: If you utter a word in *Shavian Studies* challenging my work, I am prepared to write a letter such as the pages of that review have never seen."

Today is Ezra Ben-Zion's Bar Mitzvah. Cecil walks to the back of the shul to congratulate Jonathan Collins, the wiry-bearded anthropology lecturer and shul gabbai who taught Ezra. "He did a fine job with Shacharit. It's nice to hear the proper consonantal values for a change, and not those twisted Hungarian and Rumanian vowels from the old-timers. I compliment you on your teaching."

"Oh, it was nothing, really," Jonathan demurs. "He's Israeli."

"Jonathan, before the Torah reading starts, I'd like to have a word with you." Cecil's compliments were merely a preamble. They duck out of the sanctuary and stand in the atrium.

"We have discussed this many times," Cecil continues, "but nothing has been done about it. You still allow Jack Bettleheim to come up to the Torah. Now, you know as well as I that he isn't shomer Shabbes. And as if that isn't enough, he flaunts it by pushing a stroller to shul."

"Well, if we must be technical, Cecil, Margo Bettleheim pushed the stroller."

Cecil is not amused: "I am not talking about technicalities."

"Why, Cecil!" Jonathan whispers, fascinated. "Do you mean to say you are talking about the principles of Jewish law as they are connected to *God?*"

"God has nothing to do with the problem at hand."

Jonathan looks closely at Cecil's stern face. "Oh, I see," he says slowly. "You've heard about Margo Bettleheim's open letter about Adam."

"Don't try to trivialize this," Cecil snaps impatiently. "What I am saying is that I cannot and shall not participate in a service in which men who are not shomer Shabbes receive aliyot. I thought I made my position perfectly clear when I was forced to resign from the religious practices committee and withdraw my services as baal koreh. If the situation can't be changed, I'll have to leave the service."

"But, Cecil, Jack was the Ben-Zions' choice; they chose all the aliyot for the Bar Mitzvah."

"Where is it written," Cecil says sarcastically, "that the parents of the Bar Mitzvah boy are allowed to choose a man who is not shomer Shabbes? Halakhah is halakhah."

"And God has nothing to do with this?" Jonathan chuckles. "You know, Cecil, you're what Mary Douglas used to call a primitive ritualist—the term 'primitive' meaning nothing derogatory, of course. It's quite the best thing to be, in anthropological circles. I'm sure you've read the book: *Natural Symbols*—developing character through ritual and all that. . . ."

"I found it rather diffuse, as a whole," Cecil replies witheringly. He presses on, with quiet restraint: "Now, I think it's adolescent to make a scene for its own sake. But I cannot and will not suffer a violation of Shabbat. I come here to daven and find Bettleheim's stroller at the door; I go into the sanctuary, and George Lewis threatens me and impugns my freedom of expression on reproductive rights."

"Oh, Cecil, they've got in under your shell and found your soft spots. You're a true Shavian—cool and crustacean on the surface but, underneath, seething with passion for linguistic reform and halakhic order."

Cecil turns away.

"—though I always have felt Lewis was a complete loss," Jonathan adds sympathetically. "I mean, there he is, filling up an academic post, at Wolfson, no less, with an office, a telephone, and half a secretary."

"I don't complain," Cecil says stiffly. "And please try to understand, I am not speaking out of personal or professional ambivalence. This is a matter of principle."

Jonathan coughs politely into his beard. "Dear Cecil, a matter of principle—

you sound just like Margo Bettleheim." He jumps nimbly into the service, and Cecil follows more slowly. As Jonathan calls Jack Bettleheim to the Torah, Cecil folds his tallis deliberately and kneels down on his hands and knees to search under the seats for Adam.

Attalia puts on a full-scale show as they leave the social hall. Walking home, Cecil plans an addition to his letter to Aunt Ida:

> Attalia became violently attached to a certain white cake on the table and refused to leave the shul voluntarily. I explained to her that the cake was really most hideously bourgeois: It was a sticky replica of a Torah scroll formed with two jelly rolls and opened to a quite fictional passage that read:
>
> Best Wishes on Your Bar Mitzvah
> Ezra Ben-Zion
>
> Attalia is uninterested in our efforts to provide nutritional desserts like currant cake. Adam, however, continues to devour his dinners with gusto.

At home, Saul and Molly Cahen are waiting for Shabbes lunch in the kitchen. Cecil puts out a plate of herring, a basket of challah, and for Adam a bowl of mashed salmon. "*Pink!*" Adam screams. Carefully, he pats the salmon into his ears.

"In the mail today, Cecil, I found this." Molly waves an envelope at him. "The gan sends a list of approved and not approved summer camps for the children."

"That's fine," says Cecil. "I don't approve of any of them. They're all far too expensive. And please"—he tosses the letter back onto the pile of unopened mail—"don't talk to me about that school on Shabbes." He looks at Adam and suddenly feels quite ill. "I'm going to lie down," he tells the Cahens. "Do something with the children. Take a walk."

He must have slept for an hour by the time Clare taps on his door. She opens it a crack. "There is a strange man downstairs," she says.

"What kind of strange man?" Cecil mumbles, face crumpled against his pillow.

"He has a high-pitched laugh. Long hair. Manic eyes." This description of Jonathan from Clare—the friend of the homeless, confidante of runaways.

Jonathan jumps up from Beatrix's chair in his nimble, politic way. "Cecil, I thought I'd stop by because I feel frightful about the service. I didn't mean to make light of your problem."

"Oh, that's quite all right," says Cecil. "I don't blame you. If I'm forced to leave the shul, it will be for halakhic and not personal reasons. Have some cake."

"Well, it won't come to that, will it? You won't leave." Jonathan takes the plate, wobbling, on one hand.

"I'll have to see," says Cecil deliberately. "I've been extremely disappointed with the community here."

"But where else could you go?"

"I'll daven by myself if I have to."

"I couldn't keep it up," says Jonathan. "And I'll bet you a hundred pounds you couldn't, either. I firmly believe the religious service is a social experience. And that's not just my personal belief, it's my considered professional opinion—it's my anthropological privilege, you see, to confuse the two. Even in Albania, those last few—you never did read my book about Albania, admit it, I won't be miffed—but believe me, I watched the old dodderers for two years. The youngest was seventy-two, but they came to shul every week, the last survivors of the community, and they came out of spite. Pure ill will and competition, to show the others they'd survived another week. They were lovely; they had such appetites for life, for scandal."

Cecil looks at him sternly. "I would never go to services to gossip."

"Then why *do* you go?" Jonathan reddens a little as he asks this, but he persists. "I don't understand you, Cecil."

"Why should I have an external reason for going?" Cecil protests. "I don't go to minyan because God appears to me every morning and propels me out the door. I don't go because I long to pick up some gauntlet flung down by enemies on my doorstep with the *Times*. I go to go. I uphold halakhic principles for their own sake. I really don't see what is so hard to understand. God is for poets, as far as I'm concerned. Spiritual fulfillment and people needing people is for American daytime television, group therapy. It's for baal tshuvahs who decide to become emotionally involved with Judaism. Who come home, give their parents Art Scroll Haggadahs, and then refuse to eat anything. Now, I'm not a poet, or a baal tshuvah—"

"Oh, you can't be such a Kantian, Cecil. You can't pretend you don't need either God or gossip to keep you going. Perhaps you can do without one, but both! And I must say your doubt of God is the harder bit to believe. You simply can't think you're upholding any sort of commandments if you say you don't believe in Him. I am the Lord your God—that's the first one!"

"When you read a book," says Cecil, "do you have to know the author to enjoy it?"

"Well, what a question from you!" exclaims Jonathan. "If we didn't need to know the author, you wouldn't be in business. Isn't that your job—haggling about who wrote what and which version is the proper one to force down little children's throats in school?"

"No," says Cecil, "that's Lewis's business, not mine, as I'm sure he would tell you."

"Ah, here we are, just as I thought—back gossiping about the men from shul!"

"Jonathan, George Lewis was the example that came to mind, and nothing more. The point is that unlike Lewis, I haven't any interest in comparing the orthographical changes and the single-word excisions in two versions of a play. All the little signals these critics publish pointing to a date or an authorship— the whole question is intensely trivial. Irrelevant to the real value of the words.

Why should the question of authorship suddenly become profound when applied to sacred texts?"

This last sounds flippant and sarcastic, but that is the way Cecil speaks when he is moved. What he wants to tell Jonathan is that when he studies sacred texts, he feels even more powerfully that the words themselves are enough for him; that they need no author or new interpreter. The strict beauty of the law is complete in itself, needing no stalk for support or external scaffold for restoration. How false and ill-founded the apologies for ritual are—the tracings to ancient river valley customs, the explanations of dietary and sexual laws as codes for social hygiene. And equally absurd to think each mitzvah is merely a step toward God, when so clearly the law demands obedience for itself. It is not to be used as a bargaining chip; it is no vehicle for further exaltation. But though Cecil wants to say this fully, he cannot. He can state his position, but he can't describe how passionately he holds it. It would be like telling a stranger about Beatrix and exactly how they fell in love.

The children and the Cahens were tramping about in the hall, back from their walk. Jonathan picks up Adam with the unique benignity of a man without children. "Oh, I do hope you don't pull them from the gan," he says. "You know, Cecil"—he shakes his finger—"if you really act from principle, you shouldn't let the Bettleheims and Lewis and all that ruffle you. And," he adds with mock gravity, "I for one would feel terribly let down if you left off fighting. It's a terrific show, you know, when you're in form."

That night, Cecil sits down at his Olivetti. The letter to Aunt Ida is still in the typewriter. "Most of the other Norham Gardens castles are now quite nice 20th century. . . ." Suddenly he is stricken by a terrible thought: Where will he put the refrigerator when it arrives from Brooklyn? The only clear kitchen space is in front of the door. Never mind. When Beatrix returns, she will work out the math. He will have to shop in London for that transformer on Monday. So much to do. Tickets for the Royal Ballet. The paper for Helsinki still to write. Run down for milk. The Bodleian closed. That ass Lewis.

He unrolls the letter to Aunt Ida and inserts a new piece of paper. "As an active member of the Society for Shavian Studies, I was surprised and not a little disappointed to see . . ."

"Daddy," Attalia stands sleepily in the lighted hallway. "Can I say she-hechiyanu for a new tooth?"

"And while Lewis claims . . ." Cecil types.

"Daddy?"

He looks up. "I'm not really qualified to posk on that question. You'll have to ask a rabbi."

Attalia shuffles back to bed, and Cecil feels a twinge of sadness. He flicks off the typewriter and turns out the lights. He does feel bruised by Bettleheim and Greenberg at the school; he knows they want to humiliate him. And of course with Lewis it's clearly war. Never mind, he tells himself. Beatrix will be home tomorrow. It occurs to him he's been feeling sorry for himself since she left. How weak and defeated, Cecil thinks. Of course he can't resign and withdraw the kids without a fight; he can't give in on such trivial issues. Jonathan is right in that. If one cares enough for principles, one can't feel wounded by colleagues, in-laws, or even the likes of Kineret Greenberg.

He walks down the dark hall and looks in on the sleeping children. The little beasts are lovely when they're sleeping. "Attalia," he whispers, "I think it might be all right to say shehechiyanu." His words surprise him. She rolls over in her sleep, and he adds. "Or some sort of brocha. I'll look it up first thing in the morning."

Nan Cohen 1968–

Nan Cohen was born in Chicago and raised in Reisterstown, Maryland. A Wallace Stegner Fellow in Poetry at Stanford University, Cohen holds degrees in English from Yale University and UCLA. She has taught creative writing and literature at the high-school, community college, and university levels, as well as at Stanford Medical School. Cohen's poetry and prose have appeared in a wide variety of publications, including *Prairie Schooner, Western Humanities Review, The San Francisco Review, Nimrod, Hayden's Ferry Review,* and *Response: A Contemporary Jewish Review.*

A NEWBORN GIRL AT PASSOVER

FOR YAEL

Consider one apricot in a basket of them.
It is very much like all the other apricots—
an individual already, skin and seed.

Now think of this day. One you will probably forget.
The next breath you take, a long drink of air.
Holiday or not, it doesn't matter.

A child is born and doesn't know what day it is.
The particular joy in my heart she cannot imagine.
The taste of apricots is in store for her.

5

Ann Cummins 1954–

Born in the southern Rocky Mountain town of Durango, Colorado during the uranium boom period of the 1950s. Ann Cummins writes frequently about working class people. Her family migrated to Colorado from County Galway, Ireland where her family worked as miners during the early part of the 20th century. When Cummins was nine, her father—a uranium mill worker—moved the family to Shiprock, New Mexico in the northern part of the Navajo Indian Reservation, where Cummins graduated from high school. Although her work extends beyond her ties to the southwest, she is, in her words, "often drawn by landscape and custom to write about the region of [my] birth."

Cummins's short stories have appeared in *The New Yorker, Antioch Review, Cutbank,* and other literary periodicals, with other work anthologized in collections that include *The Best American Short Stories.* Educated at Johns Hopkins University and the University of Arizona, Cummins presently teaches creative writing at Northern Arizona University.

WHERE I WORK

From Room of One's Own

It's piecework that brings in the money. You get four bucks an hour or ten cents a pocket. The old-timers can sew two pockets a minute and make eighteen an hour. They're a whiz. Most get between ten and fifteen. Me, I get four, today maybe five. I'm on my way. You don't worry if you're no good at first. You catch on. You're guaranteed the four bucks no matter if you can't get one pocket on in an hour. This is my third day.

Sam Hunt with the measuring tape comes up to my machine and measures the straightness of my stitching. He wears the tan vest, tan creased pants, brown polished shoes, white shirt. He has a perfectly formed nose, neither upturning nor downturning, and when he stands in front of my machine, I can smell a mysterious cologne coming from him. When he comes this close, I can see that the white shirt does not stick to any part of his skin, because he does not sweat.

But the fat women from Galveston sweat like pigs. Turn up the air conditioning! they'll yell. Today at lunch, I sat with the fat women from Galveston, Texas. You can hear them all over the lunchroom talking about the Texas heat, complaining about this rain. They say, My bones never ached like this in Texas. In Galveston, the fat women plopped their rumps on the beach and watched the hurricanes come in. I have never seen a hurricane. When I sit with the Texans, they tell me all about it.

And they say: How's your love life, darling? These women mull things over.

It is my duty to make them laugh. This is a social skill my brother, Michael, taught me. Make them laugh, he said, and you won't get fired.

Make them laugh or compliment them. Don't tell lies. Don't say things like, "I'd like to tear her little twat out"; if you have to say something like this, say it approximately, not exactly, or you'll scare people. He told me I scare people, and that's one reason why I can't hold a job, and because I tell lies. If you have to tell lies, tell little ones, he says. Try not to talk out loud when you're not talking to anybody.

At lunch yesterday, when they asked me about my lover, I said, He has a waterbed on his roof.

A waterbed on his roof? they said. In this rain?

Some laughed, some didn't. It's difficult to say what will make the women around here laugh.

But I admire their industry. They hardly make mistakes. Sam Hunt docks you a pocket for every mistake, and these add up.

Sam Hunt drives a scooter to work, a very little one. I have seen him from the bus window. He drives on the edge of the road, on the white line, and the Sandy Street bus could squash him like a penny. Then who would see to the time cards? It takes a certain kind of man. Serious. Not a drinker, I'd say. Nice fitting suit, gleaming face.

My brother says my face is better than what you usually see. I would marry my brother in an instant, though he's sinister and disrespectful.

My brother drives a taxi and knows the timing of the streetlights by heart. He drives two-fingered with his foot both on and off the gas pedal, never speeding up, never slowing down, through the city neighborhoods. Some nights I sit on the passenger's side, and the customers sit in the back. My brother's taxi smells like fire. Cinder and ash. In the ashtrays, fat men have stuffed cigars.

I wouldn't mind a fat man. A fat man would be somebody you could wrap yourself around and never meet yourself coming or going. If I married a fat man, I'd draw stars on his back every night. I'd say, How many points does this star have? Now pay attention, termite, I'd say. How many points does this star have?

In his taxi, my brother totes around the downtown whores. Some have the names of the months. June, July, and August. Ask them how much they make a night. Depends on how fast your brother drives, they say. Hurry up, baby; time's money, they like to say. And they spend it in Washington Park, just junkies in Washington Park.

Washington Park smells like garbage, those houses around there. In the Washington Park housing project, don't go up to a black woman's door. They don't want you. Don't go up to the men on the steps. Keep your hands at your sides. Walk fast or run. Don't look in the windows of a car slowing down. Walk slow if there're dogs or they'll chase you. Keep your hand on your purse. If somebody approaches you, if he gets within ten feet, say, "I am fully proficient in the use of semi-automatic weapons."

My brother bought me a gun when I moved out on my own, because a woman living alone in this city should be able to defend herself. You go for the knees. We put cardboard circles on a fence post in the country. I can hit them the majority of the time. If you go for the heart or head and murder a person, you could be held liable by the dead man's family, even if he broke into your apartment. This is the justice system in our country, my brother says, and he's right. The justice system in this country treats us like a bunch of stinking fish.

There. A perfect pocket. This is a keeper, so that's one. These are my practice days. They give you a couple of practice days to start out, and after the third day or so, you begin to develop a system. Like one thing is not to stop when you're coming to a corner—not to slow down or speed up, and keep your hands going with your foot on the pedal and just turn the corner without thinking. If you ruin one, put it in your purse—if it's really bad.

Next week, we're moving to a new line. Sam Hunt said when he oriented me that we're moving out of the blue and into the white. We'll have enough blue by the end of the week. How's your eyes? he says. The white stitches on the white material can blind you, so remember to blink often.

There's something wrong with my eyes. I can't cry. I'm just a happy idiot, my brother says, but I say there's something wrong with my eyes. They are deteriorating in my head. I have that condition—you read about it—where the eyes dry out unnaturally. I don't cry.

All of the women at this table wear glasses. And smoke. The lunchroom's like a chimney. And they say, How's your love life, darling?

The reason I'm not married yet is because I haven't found the right man. I don't know who he is, but I'll know him when I see him, and he'll look like something, and he won't whore around. Which, I'd shoot him, any man who whored around on me. Like that man in the laundry room. He was married, because I saw the ring. And he says, How thin are your wrists? Look at how thin your wrists are. See, he says, I can put my fingers around you and not touch any part, a married man said this.

A lot of the good ones are married. He had green eyes and a friendly manner, and he asked me which was my apartment. He lives right above me—him and his wife. Says, come up and watch TV sometime. I may just do that. I would like to see their home and their furnishings.

I will ask him to help me move furniture in. When I get my first check I'm going to buy a lamp, a nice brass one, and when I save enough I'm going to buy a brass bed, too, and one of those checkerboard coffee tables, the kind with different colors of wood in squares, and some rugs, throw rugs, and ask them to dinner, the man and his wife, which, you could never ask anybody to dinner at Michael's house because nobody ever does the dishes, and there's nothing in that house but Bob Marley posters and dirt and screaming fits.

My brother has paid my rent for the last time. If he's got to have such a screaming fit about it.

Outside the window in my new apartment on the east side is a mystery tree. We don't know what it is. I've asked around but nobody knows. On a muggy night, if you don't turn the light on, you can see animals in the tree. Opossum. Eight, nine, ten of them, gliding along the mystery tree and the tree's branches all in a panic. Black like tar, the branches gleam in the moonlight, all the little opossum claws scratching where you can't see or hear. Shall I open the window? my brother said when he came over. Want some pets? Hold on to your hair. They could get into your hair. He says they're rats, but I have seen them up close. On this, he's wrong. He says this because he's jealous.

Who pays your rent? he says. He says, Who the fuck pays your rent?

My brother has paid my rent for the last time if it's such a big deal.

"My brother had a fire in his taxi."

"What?"

"My brother drives a taxi and somebody started a fire in the back seat."

"Ain't that something." She's the nice one. She says, Sit with us, honey, and tells me about the Texas hurricanes. She's someone you can talk to. "Did he have insurance?"

"What's the difference between a tornado and a hurricane?" The woman has bitten her fingernails to the quick. You can see it from here.

"A tornado? You know, I never considered it. Hey, Lynn. What's the difference between a hurricane and a tornado?"

"One's by sea, one's by land."

"One thing I do know. They can both come up on you in a minute."

"Same with a fire. My brother had a fire in his taxi."

"Ain't that something."

"Somebody left a cigar or cigarette burning in the back. It went, just like that."

"Anybody hurt?"

"They're made of straw. That's why the seats can go just like that."

Then you're walking.

So let him walk. See how that feels.

In the Projects a man came up to me. He says, Woman? Woman? He says, Where can I find a pepper grinder? He says for fish, that he was cooking fish and he wanted some fresh ground pepper, and then started laughing and laughed his fool head off.

In the Projects, a person can get shot and nobody's going to look for you. In the Projects, someone has busted out every streetlight, and there's glass in the street, and children playing in it. In the Projects, you can walk down one street, up another, a street without lights so you don't see the dirty yellow walls all alike, street after street, with dogs that'll chase you and black women who don't want you, and it smells like garbage in the Projects. Those people are filthy.

I don't care if it is cheaper there. He says, You don't have to worry. I'm not going to let anything happen to you. Don't make me cry, Michael. Joyce, I'm not going to let anything happen to you, he says. I told him I'd cry, but there's something wrong with my eyes.

Damn! Now that thread's broken. Where's Sam Hunt? Where's that weasel? Run the flag. Got a problem, he says. Pull this little string. I'll see your flag and respond. They can't be having girls run up and down the aisles looking for the weasel. That way if anything's missing or disturbed anyplace in the vicinity, we'll blame it on Betsy Ross's ghost, he says to me, and has equipped every sewing machine in the place with a little flag. If you have to go to the bathroom, raise the flag, take your purse, don't put it on the floor in the stall, because the weasel is not responsible for stolen or lost property.

Somebody should burn that man up.

There are instances where fires occur by spontaneous combustion, and instances where water will not put a fire out. There are oil slicks on the ocean. In dreams, too—there are people burning on the ocean or in impossible places, instances where burning oil floats on water and your clothes are on fire, and your hair is on fire, and in the water the fire goes inward. If it's dirty with oil and muck. Sometimes there's no way to put the fire out.

In such a dream, go into a well. Make it from rocks. The bottom of the well is very smooth, and the rocks are cool. Close your eyes. Put your cheek against a rock. If you're dizzy, reach your arm out. Touch the other side. Twirl in a circle. Put yourself in a blue well, and keep your eyes closed. Turn around and around until the fire stops.

"Joyce? What is it?"

"My thread broke."

"Your thread broke? Do you remember how I showed you to reload your thread? Did you try that? Here. Show me. Remember? here now, you hook it around this wire first. Remember. Okay, good. That's right. Yes. Down the pole, into the needle. You pull that back or it's going to know when you begin to sew. Good. Very good. See? That wasn't so hard. Was it?"

"How you doing? You getting along okay? You getting to know people?"

"Yes."

"Let's see what you've done today. No, now you're holding your material too tightly. That's what'll give you the tangled stitches. Remember how I told you to roll it under the foot—just like it's a rolling pin and you're making pie crusts. Remember? You bake, Joyce? Just roll it under the foot with a nice, steady movement."

"Yes, I bake."

"No, now this one's not going to work. See, you've got the X in the corner. You can't overshoot the pattern or you'll have a little X. See? And here's another one.

"Joyce, where are the rest of them? I counted sixty pockets out for you this morning. Now I count—let's see—where're the rest of them?"

"That's all you gave me."

"No. This morning I counted out sixty, and now there are—they can't just disappear. Let's see. Forty-eight . . .

"This is your third day? You're not picking this up, are you? Maybe we should transfer you to pant legs. There aren't as many angles. Come and talk with me when your shift's over."

"I can't. I'll miss my bus."

"Catch the next bus. Come and talk to me. We'll take a look at your file. See what we can do."

I can do this.

This is a cinch. Go forward and backward to lock in the stitch. Be careful not to overshoot the pattern—be careful not to overshoot the pattern because that's when the X occurs. You can't rip it out because the buying customer will see where the ripping occurred. Now that's ruined. Put it in your purse.

Here's the rest of them. These are ruined. I forgot about these in my purse. Forgetting is not lying, I'll say. I didn't lie. I forgot, and that's the truth.

What's she smiling at? What's so funny about that pocket? That's a hilarious pocket. These women will laugh behind your back. They listen in on every conversation and then they laugh behind your back. Well, fuck them.

I can do this. So let them laugh. You go forward and backward. Every system has its routine. In a house when you live alone, you check the rock by the front door when you come home to see if it's been moved in your absence. If it's been moved, someone has gone into your house. This is just real funny. I'd like to squash her pea brain. Now that's ruined.

Check the rock and you check for broken windows before you unlock the door, and you keep your gun in the drawer by your bed. I'm going to tell him to give me another chance. This wasn't so good today, but tomorrow's a different story. My brain's ruined for this day. That's a sad thing how a woman will just laugh in your face like that. They think they're so hot.

You keep your gun in the drawer by your bed. If, at three in the morning, some person breaks in your house, you take the phone off the hook, dial 0. You don't have time to dial 911. You've got your gun and you're kneeling in bed or on the floor, and you say, I'm fully proficient in the use of semi-automatic weapons. I live at One One-Three Four East Holly. You're saying this to the operator who will call the cops.

Say, "I am proficient in the use of semi-automatic weapons—"

"What?"

"What are you looking at?"

"What did you say?"

"I didn't say anything."

"Yes, you did."

"What are you looking at?"

"Hey, don't worry about it. Don't sweat it. Sam's okay. Gets a bee in his lugudimous maximus every now and again, but he's O.K."

"They're going to fire me from this job."

"Nah, they ain't going to fire you."

"He's going to look at my file."

"Listen—"

"They look at your file, and then they look at you."

"You've got to—"

"Don't look at me."

"Now, honey—"

"Don't look at me! Don't look at my face."

Don't look anywhere.

They open your files and then they fire you. Everything is ruined now. So who cares.

These are ruined. I ruined these. Meaning to or not, doesn't count. Did you or didn't you? Did you or didn't you? he'll say. He'll call me on the phone. Did you or did you not? Michael will say. I'll say—

When Michael calls—

I'll say, I didn't get to these yet. These were misplaced. I'll say. I'll say, I forgot about these in my purse.

This place is filthy. Somebody ought to clean this place up.

You just do your work. You just pay attention.

I'll leave my coat in the locker. I'll sneak out the back way, and I'll leave my coat in the locker.

I'll say. These are my practice days, Mr. Hunt. I can do this.

I'll sneak out the back way.

I'll catch the Sandy Street bus. If I miss the Sandy Street, I'll catch the Burnside. I won't look at the bums sleeping there. When I walk across the bridge, across the Burnside Bridge—if they ask me for money, I'll look straight ahead.

When Michael calls to ask me how it went—If my brother calls—

I'll say. Not too bad. That's what I'll say.

He'll say, Way to go, Joyce. That's money in the bank.

For dinner, I'll make mashed potatoes or I'll make rice. I'll sit at the table by the kitchen window. I'll watch the sun go down.

I will set my alarm for six so I can catch the Sandy Street bus at seven, because the Burnside bus will get me here too late. Sam Hunt sees to the time cards. Don't be late or you're docked pockets, and these add up.

I will set the alarm for six and I'll go to bed at ten. If I wake up in the night—if a dream or nightmare wakes me, I must not wake up in the night. A working girl needs her sleep.

Credits

Adams, Gail Galloway, "The Purchase of Order" from *The Purchase of Order.* Copyright © 1988 by Gail Galloway Adams. Reprinted with the permission of The University of Georgia Press.

Akhmatova, Anna, "In Memory of M.B." from *Poems of Akhmatova,* translated by Stanley Kunitz with Max Hayward (Boston: Atlantic Monthly Press, 1973). Copyright © 1967, 1968, 1972, 1973 by Stanley Kunitz and Max Hayward. Reprinted with the permission of Darhansoff & Verrill Literary Agency.

Akhmatova, Anna, "Redwinged Birds" and "The Guest," translated by Michael Cuanach (Online. Poems from the Planet Earth: AA. Internet. 7 July 1998). Reprinted with the permission of the translator.

Alexander, Elizabeth, "Ladders"; "House Party Sonnet: '66"; "Nineteen"; "1. Overture" "Boston Year"; "'Radio Days'"; from *The Venus Hottentot.* Copyright © 1990 by the Rector and Visitors of the University of Virginia.

Allende, Isabel, "If You Touched My Heart" from *The Stories of Eva Luna.* Copyright © 1989 by Isabel Allende. English translation copyright © 1991 by Macmillan Publishing Company. Reprinted with the permission of Scribner, a division of Simon & Schuster, Inc.

Angelou, Maya, excerpt from *I Know Why the Caged Bird Sings.* Copyright © 1969 by Maya Angelou. Reprinted with the permission of Random House, Inc.

Angelou, Maya, "A Good Woman Feeling Bad" and "A Georgia Song" from *The Complete Collected Poems of Maya Angelou.* Copyright © 1994 by Maya Angelou. Reprinted with the permission of Random House, Inc.

Atwood, Margaret, "Rape Fantasies" from *Dancing Girls and Other Stories.* Copyright © 1977 by Margaret Atwood. Reprinted with the permission of McClelland & Stewart, Ltd. and the author.

Bambara, Toni Cade, "The Lesson" from *Gorilla, My Love.* Copyright © 1972 by Toni Cade Bambara. Reprinted with the permission of Random House, Inc.

Beattie, Ann, "What Was Mine" from Park City: *New and Selected Stories.* Copyright © 1998 by Ann Beattie. Reprinted with the permission of Alfred A. Knopf, Inc.

Berger, Lili, "On Saint Katerine's Day," translated by Frieda Forman and Ethel Raicus, from Frieda Forman, Ethel Raicus, Sarah Silberstein Swartz and Margie Wolfe (eds.), *Found Treasures: Stories by Yiddish Women Writers.* Copyright © 1994 by Frieda Forman, Ethel Raicus, Sarah Silberstein Swartz and Margie Wolfe. Reprinted with the permission of Second Story Press.

Bialosky, Jill, 1, 2 and 7 from "Fathers in the Snow" from *The End of Desire: Poems.* Copyright © 1997 by Jill Bialosky. Reprinted with the permission of Alfred A. Knopf, Inc.

Bonner, Marita, "On Being Young—a Woman—and Colored" from *Frye Street and Environs.* Copyright © 1987 by Joyce Flynn and Joyce Occomy Stricklin. Reprinted with the permission of Beacon Press, Boston.

Brooks, Gwendolyn, "Five Men Against the Theme 'My Name is Red Hot. Yo Name Ain Doodley Squat'" and "Friend" from *Beckonings.* Copyright © 1975 by Gwendolyn Brooks Blakeley. Reprinted with the permission of Broadside Press.

Brooks, Gwendolyn, "the mother" from *Blacks* (Chicago: Third World Press, 1991). Copyright © 1987 by Gwendolyn Brooks Blakeley. Reprinted with the permission of the author.

Brown, Rebecca, "The Gift of Hunger" from *The Gifts of the Body.* Copyright © 1994 by Rebecca Brown. Reprinted with the permission of HarperCollins Publishers, Inc.

Naylor, Gloria, "Etta Mae Johnson" from *The Women of Brewster Place.* Copyright © 1980, 1982 by Gloria Naylor. Reprinted with the permission of Viking Penguin, a division of Penguin Putnam Inc.

Nye, Naomi Shihab, "Newcomers in a Troubled Land" from *Never in a Hurry: Essays on People and Places* (Columbia: University of South Carolina Press, 1996). Copyright © 1996 by Naomi Shihab Nye. Reprinted with the permission of the author.

Nye, Naomi Shihab, "Making a Fist" from *Words Under the Words: Selected Poems* (Portland, Oregon: Far Corner Books, 1995). Copyright © 1995 by Naomi Shihab Nye. Reprinted with the permission of the author.

Oates, Joyce Carol, "Unmailed, Unwritten Letters" from *The Wheel of Love and Other Stories.* Originally published in *The Hudson Review* (Spring 1969). Copyright © 1970, 1969, 1968, 1967, 1966, 1965 by Joyce Carol Oates. Reprinted with the permission of John Hawkins Associates, Inc.

O'Brien, Edna, "Number Ten" from *A Fanatic Heart.* Copyright © 1978 by Edna O'Brien. Reprinted with the permission of Farrar, Straus & Giroux, LLC.

O'Connor, Flannery, "Good Country People" from *A Good Man Is Hard to Find and Other Stories.* Copyright 1953 by Flannery O'Connor, renewed © 1981 by Mrs. Regina O'Connor. Reprinted with the permission of Harcourt Brace and Company.

Olds, Sharon, "The Knowing" from *American Poetry Review.* Reprinted with the permission of Sharon Olds.

Olds, Sharon, "Why My Mother Made Me" from *The Gold Cell.* Copyright © 1987 by Sharon Olds. Reprinted with the permission of Alfred A. Knopf, Inc.

Olsen, Tillie, "I Stand Here Ironing" from *Tell Me a Riddle.* Copyright © 1956, 1957, 1960, 1961 by Tillie Olsen. Reprinted with the permission of Doubleday, a division of Random House, Inc.

Ozick, Cynthia, "The Shawl" from *The Shawl.* Copyright © 1980, 1983 by Cynthia Ozick. Reprinted with the permission of Alfred A. Knopf, Inc.

Paley, Grace, "Enormous Changes at the Last Minute" from *Enormous Changes at the Last Minute.* Copyright © 1971, 1972, 1974 by Grace Paley. Reprinted with the permission of Farrar, Straus & Giroux, LLC.

Parker, Dorothy, "Indian Summer" and "The Little Old Lady in Lavender Silk" from *Collected Poems.* Copyright 1926, 1928 by Horace Liveright, Inc., renewed 1954, © 1956 by Dorothy Parker. Reprinted with the permission of Viking Penguin, a division of Penguin Putnam Inc.

Piercy, Marge, "Barbie Doll" and "The Woman in the Ordinary" from *Circles on the Water.* Copyright © 1982 by Marge Piercy. Reprinted with the permission of Alfred A. Knopf, Inc.

Plath, Sylvia, "Conversation Among the Ruins" and "Channel Crossing" from *The Collected Poems,* edited by Ted Hughes. Copyright © 1960, 1965, 1971, 1981 by the Estate of Sylvia Plath. Reprinted with the permission of HarperCollins Publishers, Inc. and Faber and Faber, Ltd.

Plath, Sylvia, "Lady Lazarus" from *Ariel.* Copyright © 1963 by Ted Hughes. Reprinted with the permission of HarperCollins Publishers, Inc. and Faber and Faber, Ltd.

Plath, Sylvia, "Daddy" from *Ariel.* Copyright © 1963 by Ted Hughes. Reprinted with the permission of HarperCollins Publishers, Inc. and Faber and Faber, Ltd.

Pritchard, Melissa, "The Instinct for Bliss" from *The Instinct for Bliss.* Copyright © 1995 by Melissa Pritchard. Reprinted with the permission of Zoland Books, Cambridge, Mass.

Raskin, Miriam, "At a Picnic," translated by Henia Reinhartz, from Frieda Forman, Ethel Raicus, Sarah Silberstein Swartz and Margie Wolfe (eds.), *Found Treasures: Stories by Yiddish Women Writers.* Copyright © 1994 by Frieda Forman, Ethel Raicus, Sarah Silberstein Swartz and Margie Wolfe. Reprinted with the permission of Second Story Press.

Regan, Sylvia, Morning Star. Copyright 1950 by Sylvia Regan (Revised); copyright 1939 by Sylvia Regan (under the title *Spangled Banner*). Copyrights renewed © 1966, 1977. CAUTION: The reprinting of *Morning Star* included in this volume is reprinted with the permission of the author and Dramatists Play Service, Inc. The non-professional performance rights in this play are controlled exclusively by Dramatists Play Service, Inc., 440 Park Avenue South, New York, NY 10016. No nonprofessional production of the play may be given without obtaining, in advance, the written permission of Dramatists Play Service, Inc., and paying the requisite fee. Inquiries regarding all other rights should be addressed to Dramatists Play Service, Inc., 440 Park Avenue South, New York, NY 10016.

Rhys, Jean, excerpt from *The Wide Sargasso Sea.* Copyright © 1966 by Jean Rhys. Reprinted with the permission of W. W. Norton & Company, Inc. and the Wallace Literary Agency.

Rich, Adrienne, "When We Dead Awaken: Writing as Re-Vision" from *On Lies, Secrets and Silence: Selected*

Index